RUSSIA

PUBLIC
~A
~ARY
~ANIA
~INE
~OSLAVIA

GEORGIA
ARMENIA
AZERBAIJAN

KAZAKHSTAN

MONGOLIA

NORTH
KOREA

UZBEKI-
STAN

TURK-
MENISTAN

KYHGYZSTAN
TAJIKISTAN
AFGHANISTAN

CHINA

JAPAN

IRAN

UNITED
ARAB
EMIRATES

PAKISTAN

NEPAL

BHUTAN

LAOS
THAILAND
KAMPUCHEA

SOUTH
KOREA

~DAN
KUWAIT
SAUDI
ARABIA

QATAR

TAIWAN

INDIA

HONG KONG

OMAN

YEMEN
ERITREA

VIETNAM

PHILIPPINES

~PIA

DJIBOUTI

BANGLADESH

MYANMAR

BRUNEI

SOMALIA

MALAYSIA

SRI LANKA

UGANDA
~RWANDA
BURUNDI
MALAWI
COMOROS

SEYCHELLES

MALDIVES

PAPUA NEW GUINEA

SINGAPORE

MAYOTTE

INDONESIA

SOLOMON ISLANDS

FIJI

MADAGASCAR

REUNION

AUSTRALIA

NEW CALEDONIA

~OZAMBIQUE
~ABWE

~ND

NEW ZEALAND

Developing nations

Developed nations

Former USSR and Eastern Europe

ECONOMIC DEVELOPMENT

SIXTH EDITION

ECONOMIC DEVELOPMENT

Michael P. Todaro
New York University

Addison–Wesley Publishing Company

Reading, Massachusetts   Menlo Park, California   New York   Don Mills, Ontario
Harlow, United Kingdom   Amsterdam   Bonn   Sydney   Singapore   Tokyo
Madrid   San Juan   Milan   Paris

Senior Sponsoring Editor: Denise J. Clinton
Project Editor: Lena Buonanno
Editorial Assistant: Thomas Park
Associate Production Supervisor: Kathleen A. Manley
Marketing Manager: Mark Childs
Senior Marketing Coordinator: Theresa D. Riley
Text Designer: Sandra Rigney
Associate Cover Design Supervisor: Barbara T. Atkinson
Copy Editor: Bruce Emmer
Prepress Services Buyer: Caroline Fell
Technical Artist: Cracom Corporation
Compositor: Innodata Corporation
Manufacturing Supervisor: Hugh Crawford
Senior Manufacturing Manager: Roy E. Logan

Cover image of two Black African Herero women by Ted Wood,
Black Star Publishing Company.
All other cover images © 1996 Photo Disc, Inc.

Todaro, Michael P.
  Economic development / Michael P. Todaro.—6th ed.
    p.   cm.
  Includes index.
  ISBN 0-201-42187-9
  1. Economic development.   2. Developing countries—Economic
policy.   I. Title.
  HD82.T552   1996
  338.9´009172´4—dc20   96-12710
                                                          CIP

Reprinted with corrections December, 1996.

Published by Addison-Wesley Publishing Company, Inc.

1 2 3 4 5 6 7 8 9 10—MA—0099989796

For Donna Renée

Preface

Audience

This book is designed for use in courses that focus on the economics of development in Africa, Asia, and Latin America, regions often collectively referred to as the Third World. It is structured and written both for students who have had some basic training in economics and for those with little or no formal economics background. For both groups, essential principles and concepts of economics that are particularly relevant for understanding development problems are highlighted in boldface and explained at appropriate points throughout the text. They are also defined in a detailed and extensive glossary which includes other terms and concepts that may be unfamiliar to non-economics majors. Thus the book should be of special value in undergraduate development courses that attract students from a variety of disciplines. Yet the material is sufficiently broad in scope and rigorous in coverage to satisfy any undergraduate and some graduate economics requirements in the field of development.

Approach

Economic Development resulted from five years of living and teaching in Africa as well as two decades of extensive travel throughout Latin America and Asia, first as a director of the Rockefeller Foundation and then as a professor of economics at New York University. These experiences have helped shape and refine a book that is unique among development texts in approach, organization, and pedagogy. Among its most significant innovations are the following:

1. It teaches economic development within the context of a *major set of problems*, such as poverty, inequality, unemployment, population growth, environmental decay, and rural stagnation. Formal, abstract models and concepts are used

to elucidate real-world development problems rather than being presented in isolation from case study illustrations.

2. It adopts a *problem- and policy-oriented approach* to the teaching of development economics on the assumption that a central objective of any development economics course should be the fostering of a student's ability to understand contemporary Third World economic problems and to reach independent and informed judgments and policy conclusions about their possible resolution.

3. It approaches development problems systematically by following a *standard pedogogic procedure* with regard to their analysis and exposition. Each chapter begins by stating the general nature of a problem, its principal issues, and how it is manifested empirically in various developing countries. The chapter then presents main goals and possible objectives, the role of economic analysis in illuminating the problem, and some possible policy alternatives and their likely consequences. This approach not only helps students think systematically about major current development issues but, even more important, provides them with a methodology and an operating procedure for analyzing and reaching policy conclusions about other contemporary and future development problems.

4. It starts from the premise that it is possible to design and structure a broadly based development economics textbook that simultaneously uses the *best available cross-sectional data* from Africa, Asia, and Latin America and *appropriate theoretical tools* to illuminate common Third World problems. Although these problems will of course differ in both scope and magnitude when we deal with such diverse countries as India, Bangladesh, Kenya, Egypt, Nigeria, Brazil, Mexico, and Guatemala, the fact remains that most face similar development problems: widespread poverty and growing income and asset inequalities, rapid population growth, low levels of literacy and nutritional intake, rising levels of urban unemployment and underemployment, and chronic balance of payments and foreign-debt burdens, to name just a few.

5. It focuses on a wide range of developing countries not only as *independent nation-states* but also in relation to one another and in their *interactions with rich nations in a global economy*.

6. It recognizes the necessity of treating the problems of development and underdevelopment from an *institutional* and *structural* (noneconomic) as well as an economic perspective, with appropriate modifications of received general economic principles, theories, and policies. It thus attempts to combine relevant theory with realistic institutional analyses.

7. It views development and underdevelopment in both domestic and international contexts, stressing the *increasing interdependence of the world economy* in areas such as food, energy, natural resources, technology, information, and financial flows.

8. It considers the many economic, social, and institutional problems of underdevelopment as closely interrelated and requiring *simultaneous and coordinated approaches* to their solution at both the national and international levels.

Organization and Orientation

The book is organized into four parts. Part One focuses on the nature and meaning of underdevelopment and its various manifestations in Third World nations. After critically reviewing five alternative theories of economic development, it proceeds to examine the historical growth experience of the now developed countries and ascertains the degree to which this experience is relevant to contemporary developing nations.

Parts Two and Three form the core of the book, focusing on major development problems and policies, both domestic and international. Topics of analysis and review include economic growth, poverty and income distribution, population, unemployment, migration, urbanization, technology, agricultural and rural development, the environment, education, international trade and finance, foreign aid, private foreign investment, and the debt crisis. Finally, Part Four reviews the possibilities and prospects for Third World development. After discussing the theory, practice, and failures of development planning and the role and limitations of financial and fiscal policy in the development process, it analyzes the rapid spread of market economies in the 1990s and the place of less developed nations in an increasingly interdependent but highly unequal global system.

All four parts of the book ask fundamental questions: What kind of development is most desirable? And how can Third World nations best achieve these economic and social objectives either individually or, better, in cooperation with one another and, it is to be hoped, with appropriate and meaningful assistance from the more developed countries of the world?

Case Studies

In order to provide students with up-to-date case study materials, there are 20 *country case studies*, which appear at the ends of chapters, as well as four *comparative case studies*, one at the conclusion of each of the four parts. Each country case study provides a two- to three-page descriptive analysis of the major economic features and critical problems faced by a leading Third World nation. Featured are such countries as Brazil, India, Cuba, Nigeria, Mexico, China, South Africa, the Philippines, and South Korea. The purpose of each country profile is to familiarize students with the basic economic features of important developing economies and thus provide them with the kind of applied material that is often absent from development texts. Furthermore, each country case study is chosen to reflect and illustrate the specific problem analyzed in the chapter to which it is appended—for example, China for population, India for poverty, Ghana for agriculture, Venezuela for foreign debt, South Korea for international trade.

Each comparative case study contrasts two developing countries, one relatively successful and the other less so in dealing with one or more of the critical issues or problem areas discussed in the preceding chapters. For example, at the end of Part One, "Principles and Concepts," is a comparison of Argentina and South Korea intended to illustrate how the five different development approaches discussed in

Chapter 3, "Theories of Development," have been successfully or otherwise pursued in these two countries. At the end of Part Two is a comparison of the relative effectiveness of poverty policies in Bangladesh and Nigeria. And so on for Parts Three and Four, where trade policies in Thailand and the Philippines and privatization strategies in Chile and Poland, respectively, are compared and evaluated.

Changes for the Sixth Edition

In the three years since publication of the fifth edition, many developing countries have undergone rapid, sometimes wrenching economic and political changes. The ideology of market economics and privatization, the emergence of new regional trading blocs, and the increasing globalization of trade, technology, information, and finance have all combined to alter fundamentally the workings of the world economy and the place of the Third World nations within that global system. Accordingly, in addition to an extensive updating of all statistical tables and figures as well as the inclusion of many new ones, this edition incorporates a wide range of new and expanded topics. Here are some examples organized by chapter.

New Concepts, Analytic Frameworks, and Problem-focused Topics

Chapter 2
- The role of ethnicity and religion as significant factors in the development process
- The importance of imperfect markets, incomplete information, and high transaction costs as a characteristic of developing nations
- Recent theoretical and methodological refinements of the United Nations Development Program's *Human Development Index* to account for gender, race, and ethnic disparities as well as income inequality and regional differences in development performance

Chapter 3
- The distinction among the free-market, "market-friendly," public-choice, and new institutional approaches to development theory and policy
- The importance of human capital, externalities, and returns to scale for new endogenous growth theories and the theoretical contrasts between these and traditional neoclassical growth theories for developing countries

Chapter 4
- New evidence on the importance of political stability for economic growth
- The role of skilled human resources, ideas, and ingenuity in the historical growth record

- The recent surge in illegal LDC immigration into North America and Europe and the concomitant increase in restrictive policies in host countries

Chapter 5

- The disproportionate experience of poverty among indigenous populations, especially indigenous women and girls
- Some results of the recent United Nations conferences on poverty (Copenhagen) and women (Beijing)

Chapter 6

- New empirical research on the consequences of population growth
- A brief review of the 1994 U.N. Conference on Population and Development (Cairo)

Chapter 7

- Four dimensions of the LDC employment problem, with special emphasis on women's employment issues
- The problem of jobless growth in many developing countries

Chapter 9

- Linkages among rural credit markets, risk sharing, and informal finance for small farmers

Chapter 10

- Theory and methodology of environmental accounting for sustainable development

Chapter 11

- Recent evidence on the returns to education
- The impact of imperfect capital markets and limited information on the ability of poor students to obtain private financing for their education

Chapter 12

- The changing pattern and composition of Third World exports
- Recent evidence on the terms of trade and export earnings instability
- New "strategic" trade theories under imperfect international competition
- The significance of the increasing globalization of trade and finance
- The role of industrial policy in the export expansion experience of Pacific Rim countries

Chapter 13

- The nature and potential impact of the Uruguay Round of the GATT, the World Trade Organization (WTO), and the North American Free Trade Agreement (NAFTA).

- The potential impact of newly expanded regional trading blocs in Asia and the Pacific and in Latin America

Chapter 14

- Recent trends in the balance of payments of LDCs
- The current status of the Third World debt problem from the perspective of both developed and developing countries
- The differential economic impact of International Monetary Fund and World Bank stabilization and structural adjustment programs

Chapter 15

- The recent growth in private portfolio investment and the expansion of equity and debt markets as sources of finance in middle-income developing countries
- The increasing role of nongovernmental organizations (NGOs) in the field of development assistance

Chapter 16

- Markets versus the state and the relevance of the "East Asian miracle" for other LDCs
- The growing debate about authoritarianism versus democracy in promoting growth and development

Chapter 17

- New views about financial policy and the role and limitations of the state in orchestrating financial reform
- Recent experiences of privatization in LDCS and Eastern Europe

Chapter 18

- The growing importance of Third World countries as major export markets for developed nations
- The continuing and worsening economic crisis in sub-Saharan Africa
- The current status and prospects for economic transition in the former Soviet Union and Eastern Europe
- Some proposals for improving the global economy and international institutions so as better to serve the needs of developing countries in the twenty-first century

New Organizational Arrangement

Chapters 13 and 14 from previous editions have been reversed to show more clearly the transition from trade theory and policy to the balance of payments and international finance.

New Case Studies

In addition to revising and updating all 18 original end-of-chapter Country Case Studies and the four Comparative Case Studies at the end of each part of the text, two new Country Case Studies—on Cuba and South Africa—have been added.

Revised Supplements

Both the *Instructor's Manual* and monograph *Case Studies in Economic Development*—designed to supplement the text and prepared by Professor Stephen C. Smith of the George Washington University—have been revised, updated, and, in the latter case, largely rewritten so as more closely to coordinate with the chapter outline of the main text.

The foregoing highlights of the new edition should indicate how extensively the text has been revised and updated to meet the current needs of undergraduate economic development courses in the late 1990s. I am extremely gratified by the widespread success of previous editions, which have now been translated into ten languages, and by the enthusiastic response and encouragement that I have received from professors and students in both the developed and developing world.

Acknowledgments

My indebtedness and gratitude to the many individuals who have helped shape this new edition cannot adequately be conveyed in a few sentences. However, I must once again record my immense indebtedness to the hundreds of former students and contemporary colleagues who took the time and trouble during the past three years to write or speak to me about the ways in which this text could be further improved. I am indebted to a great number of friends (far too many to mention individually) in both the developing world and the developed world who have directly and indirectly helped shape my ideas about development economics and how an economic development text should be structured. To my former students in Africa and the United States and to my colleagues in Latin America and Asia, I owe a particular debt of gratitude for their probing and challenging questions. Two good friends and colleagues, Edgar O. Edwards and Lloyd G. Reynolds, were particularly helpful at an earlier stage. Kenneth W. Thompson, a close friend and in many ways my mentor in the field of international relations, indirectly provided much of the inspiration for this book.

Extremely useful and detailed suggestions for improving the fifth and sixth editions were received from Stephen C. Smith (who also prepared the four comparative case studies, the excellent *Instructor's Manual,* and the *Case Studies Book* to accompany the sixth edition), Habib Ahmed, Hassein Akhavi-Pour, Valerie Bencivenga, James Boyce, James Cobbe, William Cole, Michael Conroy, Fred Curtis, William Darity, John Davies, Smile Dube, Hadi Salehi Esfahani, Joseph Fosu, S. M. Ghazanfar, Mitchell Harwitz, Allen Heston, John Isbister, Richard Kalish, Kwan Kim, Darryl McLeod, J. Mohan Roa, Amin U. Saplear, Andreas

Savvides, Emilson Silva, Janet Tanski, Frank Thompson, Kenneth Thompson, J. S. Uppal, Wim Vijverberg, Donald Wells, and many anonymous respondents to a questionnaire sent out to users of the book in over 300 universities by my publishers. I should also like to express my gratitude to the Compton Foundation and its chairman, James Compton, for support of my ongoing research in the area of human resources, population, and development. The staff at Addison Wesley Longman, particularly Denise Clinton, Lena Buonanno, Kathy Manley, Bruce Emmer, Thomas Park, Jim Rigney, Theresa Riley, Mark Childs, Beth Toland, and Christopher Harrison, provided ideas, encouragement, and timely assistance to bring a complicated manuscript once again to completion with minimal delays and maximum efficiency.

We gratefully acknowledge the efforts of our reviewers in offering detailed and insightful comments. These individuals include

Habib Ahmed, University of Connecticut
Hassein Akhavi-Pour, Hamline University
Valerie Bencivenga, Cornell University
James Boyce, University of Massachusetts, Amherst
James Cobbe, Florida State University
William Cole, University of Tennessee
Michael Conroy, University of Texas, Austin
Fred Curtis, Drew University
William Darity Jr., University of North Carolina, Chapel Hill
Smile Dube, California State University, Sacramento
Hadi Salehi Esfahani, University of Illinois
Joseph Fosu, Western Illinois University
S. M. Ghazanfar, University of Idaho
Mitchell Harwitz, State University of New York, Buffalo
Allen Heston, University of Pennsylvania
John Isbister, University of California, Santa Cruz
Richard Kalish, State University of New York, Albany
Kwan S. Kim, University of Notre Dame
Darryl McLeod, Fordham University
J. Mohan Rao, University of Massachusetts, Amherst
Amin U. Sarkar, State University of New York, Fredonia
Andreas Savvides, Oklahoma State University
Emilson C. D. Silva, University of Oregon
Stephen C. Smith, George Washington University
Janet Tanski, New Mexico State University
Frank Thompson, University of Michigan
Kenneth W. Thompson, University of Virginia
J. S. Uppal, State University of New York, Albany
Wim Vijverberg, University of Texas, Dallas
Donald A. Wells, University of Arizona

Their input has strengthened the book in many ways and has been much appreciated.

Finally, to my lovely wife, Donna Renée, who typed the entire first-edition manuscript and provided me with the spiritual and intellectual inspiration to persevere under difficult circumstances, I can do no more than reaffirm my eternal devotion. She has always been there to help me maintain a proper perspective on life and living and, through her own creative and artistic talents, to inspire me to think in original and sometimes unconventional ways about the global problems of human development.

Michael P. Todaro
New York, New York

Contents

**4. Historic Growth and Contemporary Development: Lessons
and Controversies**   **104**

10. The Environment and Development

~~~~

Case Studies

Figures

Tables

PART ONE

PRINCIPLES AND CONCEPTS

CHAPTER 1

Economics, Institutions, and Development: A Global Perspective

Development is the most important challenge facing the human race.
—World Bank, *World Development Report*, 1991

While humanity shares one planet, it is a planet on which there are two worlds, the world of the rich and the world of the poor.
—Raanan Weitz, 1986

More than three-fourths of the world's people live in developing countries, but they enjoy only 16% of the world's income—while the richest 20% have 85% of global income.
—United Nations Development Program, *Human Development Report*, 1995

How the Other Three-Quarters Live

As people throughout the world awake each morning to face a new day, they do so under very different circumstances. Some live in comfortable homes with many rooms. They have more than enough to eat, are well clothed and healthy, and have a reasonable degree of financial security. Others, and these constitute more than three-fourths of the earth's 5.8 billion people, are much less fortunate. They may have little or no shelter and an inadequate food supply. Their health is poor, they cannot read or write, they are unemployed, and their prospects for a better life are bleak or uncertain at best. An examination of these global differences in living standards is revealing.

If, for example, we looked first at an average family in North America, we would probably find a "nuclear" family of four with an annual income of approximately $30,000 to $40,000. They would live in a reasonably comfortable city apartment or a suburban house with a small garden. The dwelling would have many comfortable features including a separate bedroom for each of the two children. It would be filled with numerous consumer goods and electrical appliances, many of which were manufactured outside North America in countries as far away as South Korea, Argentina, and Taiwan. Examples might include computer hard disks made in

3

Malaysia, videocassette recorders manufactured in Thailand, garments assembled in Guatemala, and mountain bikes made in China. There would always be three meals a day, and many of the food products would also be imported from overseas: coffee from Brazil, Kenya, or Colombia; canned fish and fruit from Peru, Japan, and Australia; and bananas and other tropical fruits from Central America. Both children would be healthy and attending school. They could expect to complete their secondary education and probably go to a university, choose from a variety of careers to which they are attracted, and live to an average age of 72 to 76 years.

On the surface, this family, which is typical of families in many rich nations, appears to have a reasonably good life. The parents have the opportunity and the necessary education or training to secure regular employment; to shelter, clothe, feed, and educate their children; and to save some money for later life. But against these "economic" benefits, there are always "noneconomic" costs. The competitive pressures to "succeed" financially are very strong, and during inflationary or recessionary times, the mental strain and physical pressure of trying to provide for a family at levels that the community regards as desirable can take its toll on the health of both parents. Their ability to relax, to enjoy the simple pleasures of a country stroll, to breathe clean air and drink pure water, and to see a crimson sunset is rapidly disappearing with the onslaught of economic progress and environmental decay. But on the whole, theirs is an economic status and lifestyle toward which many millions of other less fortunate people throughout the world seem to be aspiring.

Now let us examine a typical "extended" family in rural Asia. The Asian household is likely to comprise 10 or more people, including parents, five to seven children, two grandparents, and some aunts and uncles. They have a combined annual income, in money and in "kind" (i.e., they consume a share of the food they grow), of $250 to $300. Together they live in a poorly constructed one-room house as tenant farmers on a large agricultural estate owned by an absentee landlord who lives in the nearby city. The father, mother, uncle, and older children must work all day on the land. None of the adults can read or write; of the five school-age children, only one attends school regularly, and he cannot expect to proceed beyond three or four years of primary education. There is only one meal a day; it rarely changes, and it is rarely sufficient to alleviate the children's constant hunger pains. The house has no electricity, sanitation, or fresh water supply. There is much sickness, but qualified doctors and medical practitioners are far away in the cities, attending to the needs of wealthier families. The work is hard, the sun is hot, and aspirations for a better life are continually being snuffed out. In this part of the world, the only relief from the daily struggle for physical survival lies in the spiritual traditions of the people.

Shifting to another part of the world, suppose that we were now to visit a large and beautiful city situated along the coast of South America. We would immediately be struck by the sharp contrasts in living conditions from one section of this sprawling metropolis to another. There is a modern stretch of tall buildings and wide, tree-lined boulevards along the edge of a gleaming white beach; just a few hundred meters back and up the side of a steep hill, squalid shanties are pressed together in precarious balance.

If we were to examine two representative families—one a wealthy family from the local ruling class and the other of peasant background—we would no doubt also be struck by the wide disparities in their individual living conditions. The wealthy family lives in a multiroom complex on the top floor of a modern building overlooking the sea, while the peasant family is cramped tightly into a small makeshift shack in a *favela*, or squatters' slum, on the hill behind that seafront building.

For illustrative purposes, let us assume that it is a typical Saturday evening at an hour when the families should be preparing for dinner. In the penthouse apartment of the wealthy family, a servant is setting the table with expensive imported china, high-quality silverware, and fine linen. Russian caviar, French hors d'oeuvre, and Italian wine will constitute the first of several courses. The family's eldest son is home from his university in North America, and the other two children are on vacation from their boarding schools in France and Switzerland. The father is a prominent surgeon trained in the United States. His clientele consists of wealthy local and foreign dignitaries and businesspeople. In addition to his practice, he owns a considerable amount of land in the countryside. Annual vacations abroad, imported luxury automobiles, and the finest food and clothing are commonplace amenities for this fortunate family in the penthouse apartment.

And what about the poor family living in the dirt-floored shack on the side of the hill? They too can view the sea, but somehow it seems neither scenic nor relaxing. The stench of open sewers makes such enjoyment rather remote. There is no dinner table being set; in fact, there is no dinner—only a few scraps of stale bread. Most of the seven illiterate children spend their time out on the streets begging for money, shining shoes, or occasionally even trying to steal purses from unsuspecting people who stroll along the boulevard. The father migrated to the city from the rural hinterland a few years ago, and the rest of the family recently followed. He has had part-time jobs over the years, but nothing permanent. The family income is less than $200 per year. The children have been in and out of school many times, as they have to help out financially in any way they can. Occasionally the eldest teenage daughter, who lives with friends across town, seems to have some extra money—but no one ever asks where it comes from or how it is obtained.

One could easily be disturbed by the sharp contrast between these two ways of life. However, had we looked at almost any other major city in Latin America, Asia, and Africa, we would have seen much the same contrast (although the extent of inequality might have been less pronounced).

As a final aspect of this brief view of living conditions around the world, imagine that you are in the eastern part of Africa, where many small clusters of tiny huts dot a dry and barren land. Each cluster contains a group of extended families, all participating in and sharing the work. There is no money income here because all food, clothing, shelter, and worldly goods are made and consumed by the people themselves—theirs is a **subsistence economy**. There are no roads, schools, hospitals, electric wires, or water supplies, and life here seems to be much as it must have been thousands of years ago. In many respects it is as stark and difficult an existence as that of the people in that Latin American *favela* across the ocean. Yet perhaps it is not as psychologically troubling because there is no luxurious penthouse by the sea to emphasize the relative deprivation of the very poor. Life here seems to be eternal and unchanging—but not for much longer.

One hundred kilometers away, a road is being built that will pass near this village. No doubt it will bring with it the means for prolonging life through improved medical care. But it will also bring information about the world outside, along with the gadgets of modern civilization. The possibilities of a "better" life will be promoted, and the opportunities for such a life will become feasible. Aspirations will be raised, but so will frustrations. In short, the development process will have been set in motion.

Before long, exportable tropical fruits and vegetables will probably be grown in this now sparsely settled region. They may even end up on the dinner table of the rich South American family in the seaside penthouse. Meanwhile, transistor radios made in Southeast Asia and playing music recorded in northern Europe will become prized possessions in this African village. Throughout the world, remote subsistence villages such as this one are gradually but inexorably being linked up with modern civilization. The process is now well under way and will become even more intensified in the coming years.

This first fleeting glimpse at life in different parts of our planet is sufficient to raise various questions. Why does such obvious affluence coexist with such dire poverty not only across different continents but also within the same country or even the same city? How can traditional, low-productivity, subsistence societies be transformed into modern, high-productivity, high-income nations? To what extent are the development aspirations of poor nations helped or hindered by the economic activities of rich nations? By what process and under what conditions do rural subsistence farmers in the remote regions of Nigeria, Brazil, or the Philippines evolve into successful commercial farmers? These and many other questions concerning international and national differences in standards of living, in areas including health and nutrition, education, employment, population growth, and life expectancies, might be posed on the basis of even this very superficial look at life around the world.

This book is designed to help students obtain a better understanding of the major problems and prospects for economic development by focusing specifically on the plight of the three-quarters of the world's population for whom poverty and low levels of living are a fact of life. However, as we shall soon discover, the development process in **Third World** nations cannot be analyzed realistically without also considering the role of economically developed nations in directly or indirectly promoting or retarding that development.[1] Perhaps even more important to students in the developed nations is a fact that we noted in the preface, namely, that as our earth shrinks with the spread of modern transport and communications, the futures of *all* peoples on this small planet are becoming increasingly interdependent. What happens to the health and economic welfare of the poor rural family and many others in Southeast Asia, Africa, the Middle East, or Latin America will in one way or another, directly or indirectly, affect the health and economic welfare of families in Europe and North America, and vice versa. The hows and whys of this growing economic interdependence will unfold in the remaining chapters. But it is within this context of a common future for all humankind in the rapidly shrinking world of the end of the twentieth century that we now commence our study of economic development.

Economics and Development Studies

The study of economic development is one of the newest, most exciting, and most challenging branches of the broader disciplines of economics and political economy. Although one could claim that Adam Smith was the first "development economist" and that his *Wealth of Nations*, published in 1776, was the first treatise on economic development, the systematic study of the problems and processes of economic development in Africa, Asia, and Latin America has emerged only over the past four decades. Yet there are some people who would still claim that development economics is not really a distinct branch of economics in the same sense as, say, macroeconomics, labor economics, public finance, or monetary economics. Rather, they would assert, it is simply an amalgamation and basically an unaltered application of all these traditional fields, but with a specific focus on the individual economies of Africa, Asia, and Latin America.[2]

I disagree with this viewpoint. Although development economics often draws on relevant principles and concepts from other branches of economics in either a standard or modified form, for the most part it is a field of study that is rapidly evolving its own distinctive analytic and methodological identity. Development economics is not the same as the economics of advanced capitalist nations (modern "neoclassical" economics). Nor is it similar to the economics of centralized socialist societies ("Marxist" or "command" economics). It is nothing more or less than the economics of contemporary poor, underdeveloped, Third World nations with varying ideological orientations, diverse cultural backgrounds, and very complex yet similar economic problems that usually demand new ideas and novel approaches. The awarding of the 1979 Nobel Prize in economics to two eminent development economists, W. Arthur Lewis of Princeton University and Theodore Schultz of the University of Chicago for their pioneering studies of the development process, provided dramatic confirmation of the status of economic development as a separate field within the economics discipline. We begin, therefore, by contrasting modern development economics with "traditional" neoclassical economics. We then devote the bulk of this initial chapter to an analysis of the meaning of development. In Chapter 2 we will look at the diverse structure and common characteristics of developing countries.

The Nature of Development Economics

Traditional economics is concerned primarily with the efficient, least-cost allocation of scarce productive resources and with the optimal growth of these resources over time so as to produce an ever-expanding range of goods and services. By traditional economics we simply mean the classical and neoclassical economics taught in mostly American and British introductory textbooks. Traditional neoclassical economics deals with an advanced capitalist world of perfect markets; consumer sovereignty; automatic price adjustments; decisions made on the basis of marginal, private-profit, and utility calculations; and equilibrium outcomes in all product and resource markets. It assumes economic "rationality" and a purely materialistic, individualistic, self-interested orientation toward economic decision making.

Political economy goes beyond traditional economics to study, among other things, the social and institutional processes through which certain groups of economic and political elites influence the allocation of scarce productive resources now and in the future, either exclusively for their own benefit or for that of the larger population as well. Political economy is therefore concerned with the relationship between politics and economics, with a special emphasis on the role of power in economic decision making.

Development economics has an even greater scope. In addition to being concerned with the efficient allocation of existing scarce (or idle) productive resources and with their sustained growth over time, it must also deal with the *economic, social, political*, and *institutional* mechanisms, both public and private, necessary to bring about *rapid* (at least by historical standards) and *large-scale improvements* in levels of living for the masses of poverty-stricken, malnourished, and illiterate peoples of Africa, Asia, and Latin America. Unlike the **more developed countries (MDCs)**, in the **less developed countries (LDCs)**, most commodity and resource markets are highly imperfect, consumers and producers have limited information, major structural changes are taking place in both the society and the economy, and disequilibrium situations often prevail (prices do not equate supply and demand). In many cases, economic calculations are dominated by political and social priorities such as building a new nation in Africa, replacing foreign advisers with local decision makers, resolving tribal or ethnic conflicts, or preserving religious and cultural traditions. At the individual level, family, clan, religious, or tribal considerations may take precedence over private, self-interested utility or profit-maximizing calculations.

Thus development economics, to a greater extent than traditional neoclassical economics or even political economy, must be concerned with the economic, cultural, and political requirements for effecting rapid structural and institutional transformations of entire societies in a manner that will most efficiently bring the fruits of economic progress to the broadest segments of their populations. As such, a larger government role and some degree of coordinated economic decision making directed toward transforming the economy are usually viewed as essential components of development economics.

We who study or practice development economics must therefore be sensitive to the uniqueness and diversity of Third World societies. We must also recognize that there are few, if any, truly universal principles or "laws" of economics governing economic relationships that are immutable at all times and in all places. There are at best only tendencies. For example, increased consumer demand *tends* to elicit a greater quantity supplied. But as we shall discover later, conditions exist in many developing countries under which this positive supply response may not operate.

Because of the heterogeneity of the Third World, there can also be no single development economics, no universal Third World economics applicable to any or all LDCs. Rather, development economics must be eclectic, attempting to combine relevant concepts and theories from traditional economic analysis along with new models and broader multidisciplinary approaches derived from studying the historical and contemporary development experience of Africa, Asia, and Latin

America. Today development economics is a field on the crest of a breaking wave, with new theories and new data continuously emerging. These theories and statistics sometimes confirm and sometimes challenge traditional ways of viewing the world. The ultimate purpose of development economics, however, remains constant: to help us better understand Third World economies in order to help improve the material lives of three-quarters of the global population.

Why Study Development Economics? Some Critical Questions

An introductory course in development economics should help students gain a better understanding of a number of critical questions about the economies of Third World nations. The following is a sample list of 20 such questions followed by the chapters (in parentheses) in which they are discussed. They illustrate the kinds of issues faced by almost every developing nation and, indeed, every development economist.

1. What is the real meaning of *development*, and how can different economic concepts and theories contribute to a better understanding of the development process? (Chapters 1 and 3)

2. What are the sources of national and international economic growth? Who benefits from such growth and why? Why do a few poor countries make rapid progress toward development while the majority remain abjectly poor? (Chapters 2, 4, and 5)

3. Which are the most influential theories of development and are they compatible? Is underdevelopment an internally (domestically) or externally (internationally) induced phenomenon? (Chapter 3)

4. What can be learned from the historical record of economic progress in the now developed world? Are the initial conditions similar or different for contemporary LDCs from what the developed countries faced on the eve of their industrialization? (Chapter 4)

5. How can improvement in the role and status of women have an especially beneficial impact on development prospects? (Chapters 5, 6, 8, 9, and 11)

6. Is rapid population growth threatening the economic progress of developing nations? Do large families make economic sense in an environment of widespread poverty and financial insecurity? (Chapter 6)

7. Why is there so much unemployment in the Third World, especially in the cities, and why do people continue to migrate to the cities from rural areas even though their chances of finding a job are very slim? (Chapters 7 and 8)

8. As 70% to 80% of many LDC populations still reside in rural areas, how can agricultural and rural development best be promoted? Are higher agricultural prices sufficient to stimulate food production, or are rural institutional changes (land redistribution, roads, transport, education, credit, etc.) also needed? (Chapter 9)

9. What do we mean by "environmentally sustainable development"? Are there serious economic costs of pursuing sustainable development as opposed to

simple output growth, and who bears the major responsibility for global environmental damage—the rich North or the poor South? (Chapters 10 and 18)

10. Do Third World educational systems really promote economic development, or are they simply a mechanism to enable certain select groups or classes of people to maintain positions of wealth, power, and influence? (Chapter 11)

11. Is expanded international trade desirable from the point of view of the development of poor nations? Who really gains from trade, and how are the advantages distributed among nations? (Chapter 12)

12. Should exports of primary products such as agricultural commodities be promoted, or should all LDCs attempt to industrialize by developing their own heavy manufacturing industries as rapidly as possible? (Chapter 13)

13. How did Third World nations get into such serious foreign-debt problems, and what are the implications of this debt for the economies of both less developed and more developed nations? (Chapter 14)

14. When and under what conditions should Third World governments adopt a policy of foreign-exchange control, raise tariffs, or set quotas on the importation of certain "nonessential" goods in order to promote their own industrialization or to ameliorate chronic balance of payments problems? What has been the impact of International Monetary Fund "stabilization programs" and World Bank "structural adjustment" lending on the balance of payments and growth prospects of heavily indebted LDCs? (Chapters 13 and 14)

15. Should large and powerful multinational corporations be encouraged to invest in the economies of poor nations, and if so, under what conditions? How have the emergence of the "global factory" and the **globalization** of trade and finance influenced international economic relations? (Chapters 15 and 18)

16. What is the impact of foreign economic aid from rich countries? Should developing countries continue to seek such aid, and if so, under what conditions and for what purposes? Should developed countries continue to offer such aid, and if so, under what conditions and for what purposes? (Chapter 15)

17. Are free markets and economic privatization the answer to development problems, or do Third World governments still have major roles to play in their economies? (Chapters 16 and 18)

18. What is the role of financial and fiscal policy in promoting development? Do large military expenditures stimulate or retard economic growth? (Chapter 17)

19. How will the economic transition from communism to capitalism in the former Soviet Union and Eastern Europe affect international private investment and foreign aid to the Third World? (Chapter 18)

20. What are the most significant issues facing the developing world as we approach the twenty-first century? Will greater global interdependence between First and Third World nations help or hinder development prospects? (Chapter 18)

These and many similar questions are analyzed and explored in the following chapters. The answers are often more complex than one might think. Remember that the ultimate purpose of any course in economics, including development economics, is to help students think *systematically* about economic problems and issues and formulate judgments and conclusions on the basis of relevant analytic principles and reliable statistical information. Because the problems of Third World development are in many cases unique in the modern world and not often easily understood through the use of traditional economic theories, we may often need unconventional approaches to what may appear to be conventional economic problems. Traditional economic principles can play a useful role in enabling us to improve our understanding of development problems, but they should not blind us to the realities of local conditions in less developed countries.

The Important Role of Values in Development Economics

Economics is a social science. It is concerned with human beings and the social systems by which they organize their activities to satisfy basic material needs (e.g., food, shelter, clothing) and nonmaterial wants (e.g., education, knowledge, spiritual fulfillment). Because they are social scientists, economists face the somewhat unusual situation in which the objects of their studies—human beings in the ordinary business of life—and their own activities are rooted in the same social context. Unlike the physical sciences, the social science of economics can claim neither scientific laws nor universal truths. As mentioned earlier, in economics there can only be tendencies, and even these are subject to great variations in different countries and cultures and at different times. Many so-called general economic models are in fact based on a set of implicit assumptions about human behavior and economic relationships that may have little or no connection with the realities of developing economies. To this extent, their generality and objectivity may be more assumed than real. Economic investigations and analyses cannot simply be lifted out of their institutional, social, and political context, especially when one must deal with the human dilemmas of hunger, poverty and ill health that plague so much of the world's population.

It is necessary, therefore, to recognize from the outset that ethical or normative **value premises** about what is or is not desirable are central features of the economic discipline in general and of development economics in particular. The very concepts of economic development and modernization represent implicit as well as explicit value premises about desirable goals for achieving what Mahatma Gandhi once called the "realization of the human potential." Concepts or goals such as economic and social equality, the elimination of poverty, universal education, rising levels of living, national independence, modernization of institutions, political and economic participation, grassroots democracy, self-reliance, and personal fulfillment all derive from subjective value judgments about what is good and desirable and what is not. So too, for that matter, do opposite values—for example, the sanctity of private property, however acquired, and the right of individuals to accumulate unlimited personal wealth; the preservation of traditional hierarchical social institutions and rigid, inegalitarian class structures; and the supposed "natural right" of some to lead while others follow.

When we deal in Parts Two and Three with such major issues of development as poverty, inequality, unemployment, population growth, rural stagnation, and environmental decay, the mere identification of these topics as problems conveys the value judgment that their improvement or elimination is desirable and therefore good. That there is widespread agreement among many different groups of people—politicans, academics, and ordinary citizens—that these are desirable goals does not alter the fact that they arise not only out of a reaction to an objective empirical or positive analysis of what is but also ultimately from a subjective or normative value judgment about what should be.

It follows that value premises, however carefully disguised, are an integral component both of economic analysis and economic policy. Economics cannot be value-free in the same sense as, say, physics or chemistry. Thus the validity of economic analysis and the correctness of economic prescriptions should always be evaluated in light of the underlying assumptions or value premises. Once these subjective values have been agreed on by a nation or, more specifically, by those who are responsible for national decision making, specific development goals (e.g., greater income equality) and corresponding public policies (e.g., taxing higher incomes at higher rates) based on "objective" theoretical and quantitative analyses can be pursued. However, where serious value conflicts and disagreements exist among decision makers, the possibility of a consensus about desirable goals or appropriate policies is considerably diminished. In either case, it is essential that one's value premises, especially in the field of development economics, always be made clear.[3]

Economies as Social Systems: The Need to Go Beyond Simple Economics

Economics and economic systems, especially in the Third World, must be viewed in a broader perspective than that postulated by traditional economics. They must be analyzed within the context of the overall **social system** of a country and, indeed, within an international, global context as well. By social system we mean the interdependent relationships between so-called economic and noneconomic factors. The latter include attitudes toward life, work, and authority; public and private bureaucratic and administrative structures; patterns of kinship and religion; cultural traditions; systems of land tenure; the authority and integrity of government agencies; the degree of popular participation in development decisions and activities; and the flexibility or rigidity of economic and social classes. Clearly, these factors vary widely from one region of the world to another and from one culture and social setting to another. At the international level, we must also consider the organization and rules of conduct of the global economy—how they were formulated, who controls them, and who benefits most from them. This is especially true today with the spread of market economies and the rapid globalization of trade, finance, technology, and labor migration.

Throughout this book we shall discover that resolving problems to achieve development is a much more complicated task than some economists would lead us to believe. Increasing national production, raising levels of living, and promoting widespread employment opportunities are all as much a function of the values, incentives, attitudes and beliefs, and institutional and power structure of both the domestic and the global society as they are the direct outcomes of the manipulation of strategic economic variables such as savings, investment, product and factor prices, and foreign-exchange rates. As Indonesian intellectual Soedjatmoko, former rector of the United Nations University in Tokyo, has so aptly put it:

> Looking back over these years, it is now clear that, in their preoccupation with growth and its stages and with the provision of capital and skills, development theorists have paid insufficient attention to institutional and structural problems and to the power of historical, cultural, and religious forces in the development process.[4]

Just as some economists occasionally make the mistake of confusing their theories with universal truths, so they also sometimes mistakenly dismiss these noneconomic variables as "nonquantifiable" and therefore of dubious importance. Yet they often play a critical role in the success or failure of the development effort.

As we shall see in Parts Two, Three, and Four, many of the failures of development policies in Third World nations have occurred precisely because these **noneconomic variables** (e.g., the role of traditional property rights in allocating resources and distributing income or the influence of religion on attitudes toward modernization and family planning) were intentionally or unintentionally excluded from the analysis. Although the main focus of this book is on development economics and its usefulness in understanding problems of economic and social progress in poor nations, we will try always to be mindful of the crucial roles that **values**, **attitudes**, and **institutions**, both domestic and international, play in the overall development process.

What Do We Mean by Development?

Because the term *development* may mean different things to different people, it is important at the outset that we have some working definition or core perspective on its meaning. Without such a perspective and some agreed-on measurement criteria, we would be unable to determine which country was actually developing and which was not. This will be our task for the remainder of the chapter.

Traditional Economic Measures

In strictly economic terms, **development** has traditionally meant the capacity of a national economy, whose initial economic condition has been more or less static for a long time, to generate and sustain an annual increase in its **gross national product (GNP)** at rates of perhaps 5% to 7% or more. (A measure similar to GNP, known as the *gross domestic product*, or *GDP*, is also used. The difference between GNP and GDP will be explained in Chapter 2.) A common alternative economic index of development has been the use of rates of growth of **income per capita** or **per capita GNP** to take into account the ability of a nation to expand its output at a rate faster than the growth rate of its population. Levels and rates of growth of "real" per capita GNP (monetary growth of GNP per capita minus the rate of inflation) are normally used to measure the overall economic well-being of a population—how much of real goods and services is available to the average citizen for consumption and investment.

Economic development in the past has also been typically seen in terms of the planned alteration of the structure of production and employment so that agriculture's share of both declines and that of the manufacturing and service industries increases. Development strategies have therefore usually focused on rapid industrialization, often at the expense of agriculture and rural development. Finally, these principal economic measures of development have often been supplemented by casual reference to noneconomic **social indicators**: gains in literacy, schooling, health conditions and services, and provision of housing, for instance. A description of various attempts to generate these social indicators of development to supplement per capita GNP—in particular, the United Nations' Human Development Index—is presented in Appendix 2.1 at the end of Chapter 2.

On the whole, therefore, prior to the 1970s, development was nearly always seen as an economic phenomenon in which rapid gains in overall and per capita GNP growth would either "trickle down" to the masses in the form of jobs and other economic opportunities or create the necessary conditions for the wider distribution of the economic and social benefits of growth. Problems of poverty, unemployment, and income distribution were of secondary importance to "getting the growth job done."

The New Economic View of Development

The experience of the 1950s and 1960s, when many Third World nations did realize their economic growth targets but the levels of living of the masses of people remained for the most part unchanged, signaled that something was very wrong with this narrow definition of development. An increasing number of economists and policymakers now clamored for the "dethronement of GNP" and the elevation of direct attacks on widespread absolute poverty, increasingly inequitable income distributions, and rising unemployment. In short, during the 1970s, economic development came to be redefined in terms of the reduction or elimination of poverty, inequality, and unemployment within the context of a growing economy. "Redistribution from growth" became a common slogan. Dudley Seers posed the basic question about the meaning of development succinctly when he asserted:

> The questions to ask about a country's development are therefore: What has been happening to poverty? What has been happening to unemployment? What has been happening to inequality? If all three of these have declined from high levels, then beyond doubt this has been a period of development for the country concerned. If one or two of these central problems have been growing worse, especially if all three have, it would be strange to call the result "development" even if per capita income doubled.[5]

This assertion was neither idle speculation nor the description of a hypothetical situation. A number of developing countries experienced relatively high rates of growth of per capita income during the 1960s and 1970s but showed little or no improvement or even an actual decline in employment, equality, and the real incomes of the bottom 40% of their populations. By the earlier growth definition, these countries were developing; by the newer poverty, equality, and employment criteria, they were not. The situation in the 1980s worsened further as GNP growth rates turned negative for many LDCs and governments, facing mounting foreign-debt problems, were forced to cut back on their already limited social and economic programs.

But the phenomenon of development or the existence of a chronic state of underdevelopment is not merely a question of economics or even one of quantitative measurement of incomes, employment, and inequality. Underdevelopment is a real fact of life for more than 3 billion people in the world—a state of mind as much as a state of national poverty. As Denis Goulet has so forcefully portrayed it:

> Underdevelopment is shocking: the squalor, disease, unnecessary deaths, and hopelessness of it all! No man understands if underdevelopment remains for him a mere statistic reflecting low income, poor housing, premature mortality or underemployment. The most empathetic observer can speak objectively about underdevelopment only after undergoing, personally or vicariously, the "shock of underdevelopment." This unique culture shock comes to one as he is initiated to the emotions which prevail in the "culture of poverty." The reverse shock is felt by those living in destitution when a new self-understanding reveals to them that their life is neither human nor inevitable. . . . The prevalent emotion of underdevelopment is a sense of personal and societal impotence in the face of disease and death, of confusion and ignorance as one gropes to understand change, of servility toward men whose decisions govern the course of events, of hopelessness before hunger and natural catastrophe. Chronic poverty is a cruel kind of hell, and one cannot understand how cruel that hell is merely by gazing upon poverty as an object.[6]

In a 1987 book, Edgar Owens advanced a similar argument:

> Development has been treated by economists as if it were nothing more than an exercise in applied economics, unrelated to political ideas, forms of government, and the role of people in society. It is high time we combine political and economic theory to consider not just ways in which societies can become more productive but the quality of the societies which are supposed to become more productive—the development of people rather than the development of things.[7]

Even the World Bank, which during the 1980s championed economic growth as the goal of development, joined the chorus of observers taking a broader perspective when, in its 1991 *World Development Report*, it asserted:

> The challenge of development . . . is to improve the quality of life. Especially in the world's poor countries, a better quality of life generally calls for higher incomes—but it involves much more. It encompasses as ends in themselves better education, higher standards of health and nutrition, less poverty, a cleaner environment, more equality of opportunity, greater individual freedom, and a richer cultural life.[8]

Development must therefore be conceived of as a multidimensional process involving major changes in social structures, popular attitudes, and national institutions, as well as the acceleration of economic growth, the reduction of inequality, and the eradication of poverty. Development, in its essence, must represent the whole gamut of change by which an entire social system, tuned to the diverse basic needs and desires of individuals and social groups within that system, moves away from a condition of life widely perceived as unsatisfactory toward a situation or condition of life regarded as materially and spiritually better.

Three Core Values of Development

Is it possible to define or broadly conceptualize what we mean when we talk about development as the sustained elevation of an entire society and social system toward a "better" or "more humane" life? What constitutes the good life is a question as old as philosophy and humankind, one that must be periodically re-evaluated and answered afresh in the changing environment of world society. The appropriate answer for Third World nations in the last decade of the twentieth century is not necessarily the same as it would have been in previous decades. But we agree with Goulet and others that at least three basic components or core values should serve as a conceptual basis and practical guideline for understanding the inner meaning of development. These core values—**sustenance, self-esteem**, and **freedom**—represent common goals sought by all individuals and societies.[9] They relate to fundamental human needs that find their expression in almost all societies and cultures at all times. Let us therefore examine each in turn.

Sustenance: The Ability to Meet Basic Needs

All people have certain basic needs without which life would be impossible. These life-sustaining basic human needs include food, shelter, health, and protection.[10] When any of these is absent or in critically short supply, a condition of "absolute underdevelopment" exists. A basic function of all economic activity, therefore, is to provide as many people as possible with the means of overcoming the helplessness and misery arising from a lack of food, shelter, health, and protection. To this extent, we may claim that economic development is a necessary condition for the improvement in the quality of life that is development. Without sustained and continuous economic progress at the individual as well as the societal level, the realization of the human potential would not be possible. One clearly has to "have enough in order to be more."[11] Rising per capita incomes, the elimination of absolute poverty, greater employment opportunities, and lessening income inequalities therefore constitute the *necessary* but not the *sufficient* conditions for development.[12]

An alternative way of saying much the same thing was put forth in the United Nation's 1994 *Human Development Report*. In the opening chapter the report asserts:

> Human beings are born with certain potential capabilities. The purpose of development is to create an environment in which all people can expand their capabilities, and opportunities can be enlarged for both present and future generations. The real foundation of human development is universalism in acknowledging the life claims of everyone. . . . Wealth is impor-

tant for human life. But to concentrate on it exclusively is wrong for two reasons. First, accumulating wealth is not necessary for the fulfillment of some important human choices. . . . Second, human choices extend far beyond economic well-being.[13]

Self-esteem: To Be a Person

A second universal component of the good life is self-esteem—a sense of worth and self-respect, of not being used as a tool by others for their own ends. All peoples and societies seek some basic form of self-esteem, although they may call it authenticity, identity, dignity, respect, honor, or recognition. The nature and form of this self-esteem may vary from society to society and from culture to culture. However, with the proliferation of the "modernizing values" of developed nations, many societies in Third World countries that have had a profound sense of their own worth suffer from serious cultural confusion when they come in contact with economically and technologically advanced societies. This is because national prosperity has become an almost universal measure of worth. Due to the significance attached to material values in developed nations, worthiness and esteem are nowadays increasingly conferred only on countries that possess economic wealth and technological power—those that have "developed." Again, we quote Goulet:

> The relevant point is that underdevelopment is the lot of the majority of the world's population. As long as esteem or respect was dispensed on grounds other than material achievement, it was possible to resign oneself to poverty without feeling disdained. Conversely, once the prevailing image of the better life includes material welfare as one of its essential ingredients it becomes difficult for the materially "underdeveloped" to feel respected or esteemed. . . . Nowadays the Third World seeks development in order to gain the esteem which is denied to societies living in a state of disgraceful "underdevelopment." . . . Development is legitimized as a goal because it is an important, perhaps even an indispensable, way of gaining esteem.[14]

Freedom from Servitude: To Be Able to Choose

A third and final universal value that we suggest should constitute the meaning of development is the concept of human freedom. Freedom here is to be understood in the sense of emancipation from alienating material conditions of life and from social servitude to nature, ignorance, other people, misery, institutions, and dogmatic beliefs. Freedom involves an expanded range of choices for societies and their members together with a minimization of external constraints in the pursuit of some social goal we call development. W. Arthur Lewis stressed the relationship between economic growth and freedom from servitude when he concluded that "the advantage of economic growth is not that wealth increases happiness, but that it increases the range of human choice."[15] Wealth can enable people to gain greater control over nature and the physical environment (e.g., through the production of food, clothing, and shelter) than they would have if they remained poor. It also gives them the freedom to choose greater leisure, to have more goods and services, or to deny the importance of these material wants and live a life of spiritual contemplation. The concept of human freedom should also encompass various components of political freedom including, but not limited to, personal security, the rule of law, freedom of expression, political participation, and equality of opportunity.[16] Some of the most notable economic success stories of the 1970s and 1980s (Saudi Arabia, Chile, South Korea, Singapore, Malaysia, Thailand, Indonesia, Turkey, and China, among others) did not score high on the 1991 Human Freedom Index compiled by the United Nations Development Program (UNDP).[17]

The Three Objectives of Development

We may conclude that development is both a physical reality and a state of mind in which society has, through some combination of social, economic, and institutional processes, secured the means for obtaining a better life. Whatever the specific components of this better life, development in all societies must have at least the following three objectives:

1. *To increase the availability and widen the distribution of basic life-sustaining goods* such as food, shelter, health, and protection

2. *To raise levels of living* including, in addition to higher incomes, the provision of more jobs, better education, and greater attention to cultural and humanistic values, all of which will serve not only to enhance material well-being but also to generate greater individual and national self-esteem

3. *To expand the range of economic and social choices* available to individuals and nations by freeing them from servitude and dependence not only in relation to other people and nation-states but also to the forces of ignorance and human misery

Summary and Conclusions

Development economics is a distinct yet very important extension of both traditional economics and political economy. While necessarily also concerned with efficient resource allocation and the steady growth of aggregate output over time, development economics focuses primarily on the economic, social, and institutional mechanisms needed to bring about rapid and large-scale improvements in levels of living for the masses of poor people in Third World nations. As such, development economics must be concerned with the formulation of appropriate public policies designed to effect major economic, institutional, and social transformations of entire societies in the shortest possible time. Otherwise, the gap between aspiration and reality will continue to widen with each passing year. It is for this reason that the public sector has assumed a much broader and more determining role in development economics than it has in traditional neoclassical economic analysis.

As a social science, economics is concerned with people and how best to provide them with the material means to help them realize their full human potential. But what constitutes the good life is a perennial question, and hence economics necessarily involves values and value judgments. Our very concern with promoting development represents an implicit value judgment about good (development) and evil (underdevelopment). But development may mean different things to different people. Therefore, the nature and character of development and the meaning we attach to it must be carefully spelled out. We did this at the end of the chapter and will continue to explore these definitions throughout the book.

The central economic problems of all societies include traditional questions such as what, where, how, how much, and for whom goods and services should be produced. But they should also include the fundamental question at the national level about who actually makes or influences economic decisions and for whose principal benefit these decisions are made. Finally, at the international level, it is necessary to consider the question of which nations and which powerful groups within nations exert the most influence with regard to the control, transmission, and use of technology, information, and finance. Moreover, for whom do they exercise this power?

Any realistic analysis of development problems necessitates the supplementation of strictly economic variables such as incomes, prices, and savings rates with equally relevant noneconomic institutional factors, including the nature of land tenure arrangements; the influence of social and class stratifications; the structure of credit, education, and health systems; the organization and motivation of government bureaucracies; the machinery of public administration; the nature of popular attitudes toward work, leisure, and self-improvement; and the values, roles, and attitudes of political and economic elites. Economic development strategies that seek to raise agricultural output, create employment, and eradicate poverty have often failed in the past because economists and other policy advisers neglected to view the economy as an interdependent social system in which economic and noneconomic forces are continually interacting in ways that are at times self-reinforcing and at other times contradictory.

Despite the great diversity of developing nations—some large, others small; some resource-rich, others resource-barren; some subsistence economies, others modern manufactured-good exporters; some private-sector-oriented, others run by the government—most share common problems that define their underdevelopment. We will discuss these diverse structures and common characteristics of LDCs in Chapter 2.

The oil price shocks of the 1970s, the foreign-debt crisis of the 1980s, and the globalization and environmental concerns of the 1990s have underlined the increasing dependence of rich nations on poor ones and thus the growing interdependence of all nations and peoples within the international social system. What happens to life in Caracas, Cairo, and Calcutta will in one way or another have important implications for life in New York, London, and Moscow. It was once said that "when the United States sneezes, the world catches pneumonia." A more fitting expression for the 1990s would perhaps be "The world is like the human body: If one part aches, the rest will feel it; if many parts hurt, the whole will suffer."

Third World nations constitute these "many parts" of the global organism. The nature and character of their future development should therefore be a major concern of *all* nations irrespective of political, ideological, or economic orientation. As we look toward the twenty-first century, there can no longer be two futures, one for the few rich and the other for the very many poor. In the words of a poet, "There will be only one future, or none at all."

CASE STUDY

The Economy of Brazil*

GEOGRAPHIC, SOCIAL, AND ECONOMIC INDICATORS

Capital Brasília

Area 8,511,965 km²

Population 157.8 million (1995)

Population (average annual growth rate) 1.9% (1985–1993)

GNP per capita U.S. $3,370 (1994)

GNP per capita (average annual growth rate) –0.4% (1985–1994)

Agriculture as share of GDP 11% (1994)

Exports as share of GDP 7% (1994)

Infant mortality rate (per 1,000 live births) 58% (1995)

Child malnutrition (underweight) 7% (1993)

Females as share of labor force 28% (1994)

Illiteracy rate (age 15+) 19% (1990)

Human Development Index 0.76 (medium)† (1992)

Brazil occupies nearly half the total area of South America. To the north, west, and south it borders every South American country except Chile and Ecuador. To the east it has 13,490 kilometers of South Atlantic coastline.

---

*The single-country case studies in this book are based on a number of sources, principally U.S. Department of State, Bureau of Public Affairs, *Background Notes* (Washington, D.C.: Government Printing Office, various years). Data are from World Bank, *Trends in Developing Countries, 1994* (Washington, D.C.: World Bank, 1994); World Bank, *World Development Report, 1995* (New York: Oxford University Press, 1995); World Bank, *The World Bank Atlas, 1996* (Washington, D.C.: World Bank, 1996); United Nations Development Program, *Human Development Report, 1994* (New York: Oxford University Press, 1994); and Population Reference Bureau, *1995 World Population Data Sheet* (Washington, D.C.: Population Reference Bureau, 1995).

†The Human Development Index (HDI) is a composite indicator of socioeconomic development giving a relative ranking of all LDCs on a scale of 0.0 (lowest) to 1.0 (highest) based on a methodology calculated by the United Nations Development Program (UNDP); see Appendix 2.1 at the end of Chapter 2 for a discussion of the index. In each case study, we give the country's HDI rating and its relative rank (high, medium, or low) on the HDI scale.

With an area of 8.5 million square kilometers, it is the largest country in Latin America and the fifth largest in the world.

About one-half of Brazil is covered by forests. This includes the largest rain forest in the world. Brazil's terrain includes these dense forests, semiarid scrubland, rugged hills and mountains, plains, and a large coastal strip. Its climate is basically tropical or semitropical. Unfortunately, its soil has little agricultural value (only 17% of the land is arable) and is often exhausted after only a few years of farming. Its grasslands are also not very fertile and are better suited to pasture than cultivation.

Brazil is the most populated country in Latin America, with more than 157 million people in 1995. It has a growth rate of 1.9%, which means that the annual population increase is 3.1 million. It ranks as the sixth most populated country in the world. More than 65% of the population lives in urban areas where growth has been very rapid. Undoubtedly, this urbanization has aided the country's economic development, but along with it has come the growth of huge slums and shantytowns. The *favelas* of Rio de Janeiro are a good example of such communities. Most of these communities lack sewage systems, electricity, and clean water. These settlements often account for more than 60% of the total urban population. In addition, as in most other developing countries, the cities in Brazil are unable to create enough jobs to absorb such a large population. Consequently, unemployment is high, and many people resort to activities such as street vending, drug peddling, and prostitution. If we take the city of São Paulo as an example, we find that 43% of its urban labor force is in this "informal" sector of the economy (see Chapter 8). Informal-sector activities include such self-employed jobs as hawking and junk collecting, as well as jobs as mechanics, barbers, and personal servants. Incomes are much lower in this sector, and there is no job or old-age security. Most people try to obtain just enough income for daily survival.

There is a high degree of income inequality in Brazil. At times Brazil has had a booming economy. Yet during these years of prosperity, most Brazilians have benefited very little. Some people make huge profits thanks to the low industrial wages, while urban workers are left on the margin of poverty. This inequality is evident from data on income distribution. For example, the poorest 20% of the Brazilian population receives only 2% of the nation's income, while the highest 10% receives 50.6% of the income and the top 20% accounts for fully 66.6%.

Brazil is one of the **newly industrializing countries (NICs)**. Its industrial development has been largely located in the southeastern states of Rio de Janeiro, São Paulo, Paraná, and Rio Grande do Sul, but it is now expanding to the northeast and the far west. Industry has been the greatest contributor to Brazil's economic growth for at least a decade; today it accounts for nearly 35% of GNP and 60% of exports. Transportation, power, and communications systems such as television and radio have greatly improved within the past few years. The country has a large and increasingly sophisticated industrial base, ranging from basic industries such as steel, chemicals, and petrochemicals to finished consumer goods and extensive military hardware. It is also one of the world's largest producers of hydroelectric power and has begun working with nuclear reactors.

The agricultural sector incorporates 26% of Brazil's population, accounting for 11% of its GDP and almost 40% of its exports. In 1953 coffee made up 80% of total exports; 20 years later it accounted for only 20%, with other products such as cocoa, soy, iron ore, and various industrialized goods becoming dominant. Today Brazil remains the world's largest exporter of coffee and the second largest exporter of cocoa and soybeans. It exports sugar, meat, and cotton and is also the largest exporter of orange juice concentrate. Brazil has tried to widen its agricultural exports and has expanded the cultivation of sugarcane, which is the raw material used in making the ethyl alcohol fuel that now powers more than half of the country's automobiles. This new focus on alcohol fuel was a result of Brazil's effort to reduce its dependence on imported oil. As a result, Brazil's oil imports have fallen by 50%.

Brazil is also fortunate to be well endowed with mineral resources such as iron ore, manganese, nickel, tin, chromite, bauxite, beryllium, copper, lead, tungsten, zinc, and gold. These resources serve as raw materials for local industries as well as export earnings. But even though Brazil is endowed with such abundant natural resources, a huge territory, and a sophisticated industrial sector, it is perhaps best known today for the challenges it faces. Between 1985 and 1994 its growth rate of real per capita income was –0.4%, one of the lowest in Latin America.

Brazil faces major economic problems. The following are just a few of the issues it must contend with:

Inflation Inflation was over 2,700% in 1993 and averaged 913% between 1985 and 1994. The basic causes have been large public deficits at the federal and state levels and deficits incurred by state-owned companies.

Foreign debt As a result of foreign borrowing, including borrowing from private commercial banks and the World Bank, the country's foreign debt in 1993 stood at $119 billion, the highest in the Third World.

Declining real incomes Real incomes have been declining among Brazil's middle and lower classes. Fully 65% of Brazilians earn a minimum salary of less than $40 per month. During the 1980s, the economy stagnated, with no real growth, while real wages fell by 30%.

Fluctuating foreign investment Foreign investment has declined from an average of $2 billion in the 1970s to $500 million per year in 1988. In fact, in the late 1980s, Brazilians were sending more money abroad as interest payments on foreign debt and in capital flight than they were receiving as foreign investment and foreign aid. Foreign direct and "portfolio" (stock and bond) investment did accelerate in the early 1990s only to dry up once again in 1995 after the collapse of the Mexican peso, which scared many investors away from Latin America equity markets (see Chapter 15).

Increasing capital flight It has been estimated that during the 1980s between $6 and $10 billion flowed out of Brazil each year. At least $30 billion is believed to be held outside the country, although by 1994 some of this money began to be repatriated.

Declining exports In 1984, Brazil had a record trade surplus of $13 billion, which was down to $9 billion in 1994. This surplus turned into a $3.5 billion deficit in the first half of 1995.

A dominant state-owned sector The state continues to play a dominant role in the economy. State-owned companies account for 45% of Brazil's GNP and more than half the budget deficit. The state also runs private businesses with extensive regulations such as price controls and wage policies.

Stringent import barriers Until recently, no product could be imported if it was also produced domestically, even if the domestic price was higher. A stubborn refusal to recognize patents had until recently discouraged foreign investors.

Environmental damage Brazil's pursuit of rapid growth at any cost has inflicted severe environmental damage, especially in the Amazon basin, the world's largest remaining tropical rain forest and a critical preserve of global biological diversity. Yet Brazil served as the host country to the United Nations Conference on Environment and Development (UNCED), also known as the Earth Summit, in June 1992 (see Chapter 18).

Some analysts argue that Brazil's enormous resources will help it rectify some of its most pressing problems, such as its huge foreign debt. It has mineral reserves, a large labor force, and a solid industrial base. It therefore has the potential to be one of the world's largest markets. But without the proper economic policies, there will be little improvement. In 1991 a new government instituted numerous policy changes, including administrative and financial reforms, designed to allow the economy to resume steady growth. The severe crisis in the public sector led officials to sell off a number of state companies to private investors. To attract foreign investment, Brazil lowered tariffs on imports so that the number of imports that were banned on the basis that similar items were produced locally was cut from 4,000 to 600.

Finally, in July 1994 the government instituted a new and more severe austerity program known as the *Real* Plan, after the name of the new currency that it introduced. The plan was designed to attack the basic cause of inflation, the large budget deficit, by increasing tax revenues, cutting back on government spending, and maintaining a stable currency. The *Real* Plan was successful in reducing inflation from 50% to 2% per month between July 1994 and May 1995. But along with the liberalization and privatization programs of previous years, it caused the economy to weaken considerably and the formal industrial sector to eliminate about one-third of all jobs—a total of 2.2 million workers were let go. Nevertheless, the government remained confident that in the long run, economic growth and employment would once again accelerate. Whether this actually happens and how it affects the lives of the poor and lower middle classes, who have been the principal victims of the recent austerity measures, remain to be seen.

Concepts for Review*

Attitudes	Noneconomic variables
Development	Per capita GNP
Development economics	Political economy
Freedom	Self-esteem
Globalization	Social indicators
Gross national product (GNP)	Social system
Income per capita	Subsistence economy
Institutions	Sustenance
Less developed countries	Third World
(LDCs)	Traditional economics
More developed countries	Value premises
(MDCs)	Values
Newly industrializing countries	
(NICs)	

*All boldfaced terms that appear in the text are listed in Concepts for Review. The Glossary provides quick reference definitions for these and other more general economics concepts.

Questions for Discussion

1. Why is economics central to an understanding of the problems of Third World development?

2. Is the concept of the Third World a useful one? Why or why not?

3. What do you hope to gain from this course on development economics (besides a passing grade)?

4. Briefly describe the various definitions of the meaning of *development* encountered in the text. What are the strengths and weaknesses of each approach? Do you think that there are other dimensions of development not mentioned in the text? If so, describe them. If not, explain why you believe that the textual description of the meaning of development is adequate.

5. Why is a strictly economic definition of development inadequate? What do you understand *economic development* to mean? Can you give hypothetical or real examples of situations in which a country may be developing economically but still be underdeveloped?

6. Why is an understanding of the meaning of development crucial to policy formulation in Third World nations? Do you think it is possible for a nation to agree on a rough definition of development and orient its strategies accordingly?

Notes

1. The 145 African, Asian, and Latin American member countries of the United Nations often collectively refer to themselves as the *Third World*. They do this primarily to distinguish themselves from the economically advanced capitalist (*First World*) and the formerly socialist (*Second World*) countries of Eastern Europe and the Soviet Union—some of which could now justifiably be considered part of the Third World. It is unfortunate that the terms first, second, and third may sometimes connote superiority and inferiority when in fact they are intended to reflect a historical sequence of industrialization.

2. For a recent example of this argument, see Paul Krugman, "Toward a counter-counter-revolution in development theory," *Proceedings of the World Bank Annual Conference on Development Economics, 1992* (Washington, D.C.: World Bank, 1993), p. 15.

3. For a provocative dissection of the role of values in development economics, see Gunnar Myrdal, *The Challenge of World Poverty* (New York: Pantheon, 1970), chap. 1. A more general critique of the idea that economics can be "value-free" is to be found in Robert Heilbroner's "Economics as a 'value-free' science," *Social Research* 40 (Spring 1973): 129–143, and his *Behind the Veil of Economics* (New York: Norton, 1988). See also Dwight Perkins, "Economic development: The role of values," in Robert J. Myers (ed.), *International Ethics in the Nuclear Age* (Baton Rouge: Louisiana State University Press, 1987), chap. 8; Barbara Ingham, "The meaning of development: Interactions between 'new' and 'old' ideas," *World Development* 21 (November 1993): 1816–1818; Paul P. Streeten, *Strategies for Human Development* (Copenhagen: Handelshøjskolens Forlag, 1994), pt. 1; and Selo Soemardjan and Kenneth W. Thompson (eds.), *Culture, Development, and Democracy* (New York: United Nations University Press, 1994).

4. Soedjatmoko, *The Primacy of Freedom in Development* (Lanham, Md.: University Press of America, 1985), p. 11.

5. Dudley Seers, "The meaning of development," paper presented at the Eleventh World Conference of the Society for International Development, New Delhi (1969), p. 3. See also Richard Brinkman, "Economic growth versus economic development: Toward a conceptual clarification," *Journal of Economic Issues*, 29 (December 1995): 1171–1188.

6. Denis Goulet, *The Cruel Choice: A New Concept in the Theory of Development* (New York: Atheneum, 1971), p. 23. Reprinted with permission of the author.

7. Edgar Owens, *The Future of Freedom in the Developing World: Economic Development as Political Reform* (New York: Pergamon Press, 1987), p. xv.

8. World Bank, *World Development Report, 1991* (New York: Oxford University Press, 1991), p. 4.

9. Goulet, *Cruel Choice*, pp. 87–94. Reprinted with permission of the author.

10. For a description of the "basic needs" approach, see Pradip K. Ghosh (ed.), *Third World Development: A Basic Needs Approach* (Westport, Conn.: Greenwood Press, 1984).

11. Goulet, *Cruel Choice*, p. 124.

12. For an attempt to specify and quantify the concept of basic needs, see International Labor Organization, *Employment, Growth, and Basic Needs* (Geneva: ILO, 1976). A similar view

with a focus on the notion of entitlements and capabilities can be found in Amartya Sen, "Development: Which way now?" *Economic Journal* 93 (December 1983): 754–757.

13. United Nations Development Program, *Human Development Report, 1994* (New York: Oxford University Press, 1994), pp. 13, 15.

14. Goulet, *Cruel Choice*, pp. 89–90. For an even more provocative discussion of the meaning of individual self-esteem and respect in the context of Latin American development, see Paulo Freire, *Pedagogy of the Oppressed* (Harmondsworth, England: Penguin, 1972).

15. W. Arthur Lewis, "Is economic growth desirable?" in *The Theory of Economic Growth* (London: Allen & Unwin, 1963), p. 420. For an outstanding and thoughtful analysis of the importance of freedom in development by a leading Third World intellectual, see Soedjatmoko, *Primacy of Freedom in Development*. See also Owens, *Future of Freedom*.

16. For an interesting attempt to measure political freedom quantitatively and to rank groups of nations according to a "political freedom index," see United Nations Development Program, *Human Development Report, 1992* (New York: Oxford University Press, 1992), pp. 26–33.

17. *Ibid.*, p. 20.

Further Reading

On the complex question of the meaning of development and underdevelopment, see Barbara Ingham, "The meaning of development: Interactions between 'new' and 'old' ideas," *World Development* 21 (November 1993): 1803–1821; Dudley Seers, "The meaning of development," in Nancy Baster (ed.), *Measuring Development: The Role and Adequacy of Development Indicators* (London: Cass, 1972); Denis Goulet, *The Cruel Choice: A New Concept in the Theory of Development* (New York: Atheneum, 1971), chap. 2; Norman L. Hicks and Paul P. Streeten, "Indicators of development: The search for a basic needs yardstick," *World Development* 7 (June 1979); Howard J. Wiarda, "Towards a nonethnocentric theory of development: Alternative conceptions from the Third World," *Journal of Developing Areas* 17 (July 1983); United Nations Development Program, *Human Development Report, 1994* (New York: Oxford University Press, 1994), chaps. 1 and 2; and Syed Nawab Haider Naqvi, "The nature of economic development," *World Development* 23 (April 1995): 543–556. Two very useful introductions to the economies and societies of the Third World can be found in Paul Harrison, *Inside the Third World* (New York: Penguin, 1982), and John P. Cole, *Development and Underdevelopment: A Profile of the Third World* (London: Routledge, 1987).

Students are especially encouraged to read Chapter 1 of Stephen C. Smith, *Case Studies in Economic Development*, 2nd ed. (Reading, Mass.: Addison-Wesley, 1997). Professor Smith's companion book follows the chapter order of this text. It is designed to provide a more detailed application of the concepts and issues discussed in each chapter to the particular experience of a specific developing country. In the Further Reading section of the following chapters, it will be referred to as *Case Studies*.

CHAPTER 2

Diverse Structures and Common Characteristics of Developing Nations

Of course there must be differences between developing countries . . . [but] to maintain that no common ground exists is to make any discussion outside or across the frontiers of a single country meaningless.

—Julian West, Oxford University

The Third World is important because of the massiveness of its poverty.

—Padma Desai, Columbia University

It is hazardous to try to generalize too much about the 145 member countries of the United Nations (U.N.) that constitute the Third World. While almost all are poor in money terms, they are diverse in culture, economic conditions, and social and political structures. Thus, for example, low-income countries include India, with over 931 million people and 25 states, as well as Grenada, with less than 92,000 people, fewer than most large towns in the United States. Large size entails complex problems of national cohesion and administration while offering the benefits of relatively large markets, a wide range of resources, and the potential for self-sufficiency and economic diversity. In contrast, for many small countries the situation is reversed, with problems including limited markets, shortages of skills, scarce physical resources, weak bargaining power, and little prospect of significant economic self-reliance.

In this chapter, we attempt to provide an overview of the great diversity of developing countries. Despite these variations, however, Third World nations share a common set of problems, both domestic and international—problems that in fact define their state of underdevelopment. But before analyzing this diversity and commonality, let's look briefly at various attempts to classify this broad group of nations that we call the Third World.

Some Classifications of Developing Countries

In attempting to classify countries, some analysts, using the U.N. classification system, prefer to distinguish among three major groups within the Third World: the 44 poorest countries designated by the United Nations as "least developed,"[1] the 88 non-oil-exporting "developing nations,"[2] and the 13 petroleum-rich members of the Organization of Petroleum Exporting Countries (OPEC), whose national incomes increased dramatically during the 1970s. Others follow the classification system established by the International Bank for Reconstruction and Development (IBRD), more commonly known as the **World Bank**. It divides 132 countries (both developing and developed) with populations in excess of 1 million into four categories according to their per capita income levels: low-income, middle-income, upper-middle-income, and high-income economies. The first three groups comprise 108 mostly developing countries, while the last group, the high-income economies, consists of 24 countries, 19 of which are typically included in the **First World** and the other five (Hong Kong, Israel, Kuwait, Singapore, and the United Arab Emirates) classified as developing.

The most recent and most ambitious attempt at classification comes from the United Nations Development Program (UNDP). It focuses on aspects of "human development" that go beyond income to include such noneconomic variables as life expectancy at birth and educational attainment along with real per capita income. It then constructs a **Human Development Index (HDI)** in which all countries are ranked into three human development aggregates—"high" (53 nations including several LDCs), "medium" (65 countries), and "low" (55 countries). See Appendix 2.1 for a discussion and analysis of this effort.

Finally, there is the classification system designed by the Organization for Economic Cooperation and Development (OECD) in Paris. It divides the Third World (including countries and territories not in the U.N. system) into 61 **low-income countries (LICs)** (those with a 1993 per capita income of less than $650, including 29 **least developed countries**, or **LLDCs**), 73 **middle-income countries (MICs)**, 11 **newly industrializing countries (NICs)**, and the 13 members of OPEC. Table 2.1 provides a complete listing of the 158 countries included in the OECD classification scheme. Figure 2.1 shows the geographic location of most of the less developed and developed nations. The former Soviet Union and Eastern Europe are represented by neutral shading to reflect their current transitional and uncertain economic status[3] (see Chapter 18). You can locate a particular LDC from Table 2.1 on the map by noting the region indicated in parentheses (see the note to Table 2.1).

Despite the obvious diversity of countries and classification schemes, however, most Third World nations share a set of common and well-defined goals. These include a reduction in poverty, inequality, and unemployment; the provision of minimum levels of education, health, housing, and food to every citizen; the broadening of economic and social opportunities; and the forging of a cohesive nation-state. Related to these economic, social, and political goals are the common problems shared in varying degrees by most developing countries: widespread and chronic absolute poverty, high and rising levels of unemployment and underemployment,

TABLE 2.1 Developing Countries and Territories by Income Group: Classification System of the Organization for Economic Cooperation and Development

LICs: 61 Low-Income Countries	MICs: 73 Middle-Income Countries
*Afghanistan (AS)	Bahamas (LA)
Angola (AF)	Bahrain (ME)
*Bangladesh (AS)	Barbados (LA)
*Benin (AF)	Belize (LA)
*Bhutan (AS)	Bermuda (LA)
Bolivia (LA)	Botswana (AF)
*Burkina Faso (AF)	Brunei (AS)
*Burundi (AF)	Chile (LA)
*Cape Verde (LA)	Colombia (LA)
*Central African Republic (AF)	Congo (AF)
*Chad (AF)	Cook Islands (AS)
China (AS)	Costa Rica (LA)
*Comoros (AF)	Cuba (LA)
Djibouti (AF)	Cyprus (ME)
Egypt (AF/ME)	Dominican Republic (LA)
El Salvador (LA)	Falkland Islands (LA)
Equatorial Guinea (AF)	Fiji (AS)
*Ethiopia (AF)	French Guiana (LA)
*Gambia (AF)	French Polynesia (AS)
Ghana (AF)	Gibraltar (E)
*Guinea (AF)	Guadeloupe (LA)
*Guinea-Bissau (AF)	Guatemala (LA)
*Haiti (LA)	Guyana (LA)
Honduras (LA)	Israel (ME)
India (AS)	Ivory Coast (AF)
Kampuchea (AS)	Jamaica (LA)
Kenya (AF)	Jordan (ME)
*Laos (AS)	Kiribati (AS)
*Lesotho (AF)	Lebanon (ME)
Liberia (AF)	Macao (AS)
Madagascar (AF)	Malaysia (AS)
*Malawi (AF)	Malta (E)
*Maldives (AS)	Martinique (LA)
*Mali (AF)	Mauritius (AF)
Mauritania (AF)	Morocco (AF)
Mayotte (AF)	Nauru (AS)
Mozambique (AF)	Netherlands Antilles (AS)
Myanmar (AS)	New Caledonia (AS)
*Nepal (AS)	Nicaragua (LA)
*Niger (AF)	Niue (AS)
Pakistan (AS)	Oman (ME)
*Rwanda (AF)	Pacific Islands (U.S.) (AS)
Saint Helena (LA)	Panama (LA)
São Tomé and Principe (AF)	Papua New Guinea (AS)

(continued)

TABLE 2.1 *(continued)*	
LICs: 61 Low-Income Countries	**MICs: 73 Middle-Income Countries**
Senegal (AF)	Paraguay (LA)
Sierra Leone (AF)	Peru (LA)
Solomon Islands (Br.) (AS)	Philippines (AS)
*Somalia (AF)	Reunion (AF)
Sri Lanka (AS)	Saint-Pierre and Miquelon (LA)
*Sudan (AF)	Seychelles (AF)
*Tanzania (AF)	Surinam (LA)
Togo (AF)	Swaziland (AF)
Tokelau Islands (AS)	Syria (ME)
Tonga (AS)	Thailand (AS)
Tuvalu (AS)	Trinidad and Tobago (LA)
*Uganda (AF)	Tunisia (AF)
Vanuatu (AS)	Turkey (E)
Vietnam (AS)	Uruguay (LA)
*Yemen (ME)	Wallis and Futuna Islands (AS)
Zaire (AF)	Western Samoa (AS)
Zambia (AF)	West Indies (LA)
	Zimbabwe (AF)
NICs: 11 Newly Industrializing Countries	**OPEC: 13 Organization of Petroleum Exporting Countries**
Argentina (LA)	Algeria (AF)
Brazil (LA)	Ecuador (LA)
Greece (E)	Gabon (AF)
Hong Kong (AS)	Indonesia (AS)
Mexico (LA)	Iran (ME)
Portugal (E)	Iraq (ME)
Singapore (AS)	Kuwait (ME)
South Korea (AS)	Libya (AF)
Spain (E)	Nigeria (AF)
Taiwan (AS)	Qatar (ME)
Yugoslavia (E)	Saudi Arabia (ME)
	United Arab Emirates (ME)
	Venezuela (LA)

*LLDCs (29 least-developed countries).
NOTE: AF = Africa (and offshore islands); AS = Asia (including the Pacific); LA = Latin America (including the Caribbean); ME = Middle East; E = Europe. Refer to Figure 2.1 for the specific geographic location of these countries (not all territories are shown).

wide and growing disparities in the distribution of income, low and stagnating levels of agricultural productivity, sizable and growing imbalances between urban and rural levels of living and economic opportunities, serious and worsening environmental decay, antiquated and inappropriate educational and health systems, severe balance of payments and international debt problems, and substantial and

FIGURE 2.1 The Developed and Developing World, 1996.

RUSSIA

KAZAKHSTAN

MONGOLIA

NORTH
KOREA

JAPAN

KYRGYZSTAN
TAJIKISTAN
AFGHANISTAN

CHINA

SOUTH
KOREA

PAKISTAN

NEPAL BHUTAN

LAOS
THAILAND
KAMPUCHEA

TAIWAN

INDIA

HONG KONG

VIETNAM

PHILIPPINES

BANGLADESH
MYANMAR

BRUNEI

SRI LANKA

MALAYSIA

MALDIVES

SINGAPORE

PAPUA NEW GUINEA

INDONESIA

SOLOMON ISLANDS

FIJI

NEW CALEDONIA

AUSTRALIA

NEW ZEALAND

Developing nations

Developed nations

Former USSR and Eastern Europe

31

increasing dependence on foreign and often inappropriate technologies, institutions, and value systems. It is therefore possible and useful to talk about the similarities of critical development problems and to analyze these problems in a broad Third World perspective. This will be our task in Parts Two and Three.

For the present, we will attempt to identify some of the most important structural *differences* among developing countries and then provide relevant data to delineate some of their most common characteristic features. In spite of obvious physical, demographic, historical, cultural, and structural differences, most Third World nations face very similar economic and social dilemmas.

The Structure of Third World Economies

Any portrayal of the structural diversity of developing nations requires an examination of eight critical components:

1. The size of the country (geographic area, population, and income)
2. Its historical and colonial background
3. Its endowments of physical and human resources
4. Its ethnic and religious composition
5. The relative importance of its public and private sectors
6. The nature of its industrial structure
7. Its degree of dependence on external economic and political forces
8. The distribution of power and the institutional and political structure within the nation

Let us briefly consider each component, focusing on some similarities and differences among countries in Africa, Asia, and Latin America.

Size and Income Level

Obviously, the sheer physical size of a country, the size of its population, and its level of national income per capita are important determinants of its economic potential and major factors differentiating one Third World nation from another. Of the 145 developing countries that were full members of the United Nations in 1992, 90 had fewer than 15 million people, 83 fewer than 5 million. Large and populated nations like Brazil, India, Egypt, and Nigeria exist side by side with small countries like Paraguay, Nepal, Jordan, and Chad. Large size usually presents advantages of diverse resource endowment, large potential markets, and a lesser dependence on foreign sources of materials and products. But it also creates problems of administrative control, national cohesion, and regional imbalances. As we shall see in Chapter 5, there is no necessary relationship between a country's size, its level of per capita national income, and the degree of equality or inequality in its distribution of that income. For example, India, with a 1996 population of over 950 million, had a 1994 per capita income level of $310, while nearby Singapore, with fewer than 3 million people, had a 1994 per capita income of $23,360.

Historical Background

Most African and Asian nations were at one time or another colonies of Western European countries, primarily Britain and France but also Belgium, the Netherlands, Germany, Portugal, and Spain. The economic structures of these nations, as well as their educational and social institutions, have typically been modeled on those of their former colonial rulers. Countries like those in Africa that only recently gained their independence are therefore likely to be more concerned with consolidating and evolving their own national economic and political structures than with simply promoting rapid economic development. Their policies (e.g., the rapid Africanization of former colonial-held civil service jobs) may consequently reflect a greater interest in these immediate political issues.

Perhaps more important, the European colonial powers had a dramatic and long-lasting impact on the economies and political and institutional structures of their African and Asian colonies by their introduction of three powerful and tradition-shattering ideas: private property, personal taxation, and the requirement that taxes be paid in money rather than in kind. As we will discover later, these ideas combined to erode the autonomy of local communities and to expose their people to many new forms of potential exploitation.

In Latin America, a longer history of political independence plus a more shared colonial heritage (Spanish and Portuguese) has meant that in spite of geographic and demographic diversity, the countries possess relatively similar economic, social, and cultural institutions and face similar problems. In Asia, different colonial heritages and the diverse cultural traditions of the indigenous peoples have combined to create different institutional and social patterns in countries such as India (British), the Philippines (Spanish and American), Vietnam (French), and Indonesia (Dutch).

Physical and Human Resources

A country's potential for economic growth is greatly influenced by its endowments of **physical resources** (its land, minerals, and other raw materials) and **human resources** (both numbers of people and their level of skills). The extreme case of favorable physical **resource endowment** is the Persian Gulf oil states. At the other extreme are countries like Chad, Yemen, Haiti, and Bangladesh, where endowments of raw materials and minerals and even fertile land are relatively minimal.

In the realm of human resource endowments, not only are sheer numbers of people and their skill levels important, but so also are their cultural outlooks, attitudes toward work, access to information, willingness to innovate, and desire for self-improvement. Moreover, the level of administrative skills will often determine the ability of the public sector to alter the structure of production and the time it takes for such structural alteration to occur. This involves the whole complex of interrelationships between culture, tradition, religion, and ethnic and tribal fragmentation or cohesion. Thus the nature and character of a country's human resources are important determinants of its economic structure (see Chapter 11), and these clearly differ from one region to the next.

Ethnic and Religous Composition

One of the direct benefits of the end of the 45-year cold war between the United States and the Soviet Union has been a substantial decline in foreign military and political presence in the Third World. An indirect cost of this withdrawal, however, has been the acceleration of ethnic, tribal, and religious conflict. Although ethnic and religious tensions and occasional violence have always existed in LDCs, the waning of superpower influence triggered a revival of these internal conflicts and may even have accelerated the incidence of political and economic discrimination. Ethnicity and religion often play a major role in the success or failure of development efforts. Clearly, the greater the ethnic and religious diversity of a country, the more likely it is that there will be internal strife and political instability. It is not surprising, therefore, that some of the most successful recent development experiences—South Korea, Taiwan, Singapore, and Hong Kong—have occurred in culturally homogenious societies.

Today, more than 40% of the world's nations have more than five significant ethnic populations. In most cases, one or more of these groups face serious problems of discrimination. Over half of the world's LDCs have recently experienced some form of interethnic conflict. Just in the first half of the 1990s, ethnic and religious conflicts leading to widespread death and destruction took place in Afghanistan, Rwanda, Mozambique, Sri Lanka, Iraq, India, Somalia, Ethiopia, Liberia, Angola, Myanmar, Sudan, Yugoslavia, Haiti, and Zaire.[4]

But neither overt physical conflict nor widespread violence is necessary to disrupt an economy or cause political instability. If development is about improving human lives and providing a widening range of choice to all peoples, racial, ethnic, or religious discrimination can be equally pernicious. For example, throughout Latin America, indigenous populations have significantly lagged behind other groups on almost every measure of economic and social progress. Whether in Bolivia, Brazil, Peru, Mexico, Guatemala, or Venezuela, indigenous groups have benefited little from overall economic growth. To give just one illustration, almost 90% of Guatemala's native population is poor, compared to 50% of the rest of the population. Being indigenous makes it much more likely that an individual will be less educated, in poorer health, and in a lower socioeconomic stratum than a nonindigenous citizen.[5] This is particularly true for indigenous women.

Ethnic and religous diversity need not, however, necessarily lead to inequality, turmoil, or instability. There have been numerous instances of successful economic and social integration of minority or indigenous ethnic populations in countries as diverse as Malaysia, Mauritius, and Zimbabwe. The point is that the ethnic and religious composition of a developing nation and whether or not that diversity leads to conflict or cooperation can be important determinants of the success or failure of development efforts. Too often economists neglect to recognize this fundamental fact.

Relative Importance of the Public and Private Sectors

Most Third World countries have **mixed economic systems**, featuring both public and private ownership and use of resources. The division between the two and their relative importance are mostly a function of historical and political circumstances.

Thus, in general, Latin American and Southeast Asian nations have larger private sectors than South Asian and African nations. The degree of foreign ownership in the private sector is another important variable to consider when differentiating among LDCs. A large foreign-owned private sector usually creates economic and political opportunities as well as problems not found in countries where foreign investors are less prevalent. Often countries like those in Africa with severe shortages of skilled human resources have tended to put greater emphasis on public-sector activities and state-run enterprises on the assumption that limited skilled manpower can be best used by coordinating rather than fragmenting administrative and enterpreneurial activities. The widespread economic failures and financial difficulties of many of these public concerns in countries such as Ghana, Senegal, Kenya, and Tanzania raise questions, however, about the validity of this assumption. As a result, these and other African nations have moved in recent years toward less public and more private enterprise.

Economic policies, such as those designed to promote more employment, will naturally be different for countries with large public sectors and ones with sizable private sectors. In economies dominated by the public sector, direct government investment projects and large rural works programs will take precedence, whereas in private-oriented economies, special tax allowances designed to induce private businesses to employ more workers might be more common. Although the problem of widespread unemployment may be similar, the solution can differ in countries with significant differences in the relative importance of the public and private sectors.

Industrial Structure

The vast majority of developing countries are agrarian in economic, social, and cultural outlook. Agriculture, both subsistence and commercial, is the principal economic activity in terms of the occupational distribution of the labor force, if not in terms of proportionate contributions to the gross national product. As we shall see in Chapter 9, farming is not merely an occupation but a way of life for most people in Asia, Africa, and Latin America. Nevertheless, there are great differences between the structure of agrarian systems and patterns of land ownership in Latin America and Africa. Asian agrarian systems are somewhat closer to those of Latin America in terms of patterns of land ownership, but the similarities are lessened by substantial cultural differences.

It is in the relative importance of both the manufacturing and service sectors that we find the widest variation among developing nations. Most Latin American countries, having a longer history of independence and generally higher levels of national income than African or Asian nations, possess more advanced industrial sectors. But in the 1970s and 1980s, countries like Taiwan, South Korea, Hong Kong, and Singapore greatly accelerated the growth of their manufacturing output and are rapidly becoming industrialized states. In terms of sheer size, India has one of the largest manufacturing sectors in the Third World, but this sector is nevertheless small in relation to the nation's enormous rural population. Table 2.2 provides information on the distribution of labor force and gross domestic product (GDP) between agriculture and industry in 17 developing countries, the United States,

TABLE 2.2 Industrial Structure in Seventeen Developing Countries, United States, and the United Kingdom, 1993

Country	Percentage of Labor Force		Percentage of Gross Domestic Product	
	Agriculture	Industry	Agriculture	Industry
Africa				
Kenya	81	7	29	19
Nigeria	54	5	36	38
Tanzania	90	5	61	12
Uganda	86	4	56	11
Zaire	75	12	30	32
Asia				
Bangladesh	64	14	33	17
India	65	13	31	27
Indonesia	55	10	19	40
Philippines	46	16	22	33
South Korea	21	27	7	45
Sri Lanka	46	13	25	25
Latin America				
Brazil	31	27	11	37
Colombia	30	24	16	35
Guatemala	60	12	25	20
Mexico	28	19	8	28
Peru	37	19	8	30
Venezuela	16	28	5	41
All developing countries	70	12	17	36
United States	2	25	2	29
United Kingdom	1	24	2	37

SOURCES: United Nations Development Program, *Human Development Report, 1994* (New York: Oxford University Press, 1994), tab. 26; World Bank, *The World Bank Atlas, 1995* (Washington, D.C.: World Bank, 1995), pp. 18–19; Central Intelligence Agency, *The World Factbook, 1994* (Washington, D.C.: Central Intelligence Agency, 1994).

and the United Kingdom. The contrasts among the industrial structures of these countries is striking, especially in terms of the relative importance of agriculture.

In spite of common problems, therefore, Third World development strategies may vary from one country to the next, depending on the nature, structure, and degree of interdependence among its **primary**, **secondary**, and **tertiary industrial sectors**. The primary sector consists of agriculture, forestry, and fishing; the secondary, mostly of manufacturing; and the tertiary, of commerce, finance, transport, and services.

External Dependence: Economic, Political, and Cultural

The degree to which a country is dependent on foreign economic, social, and political forces is related to its size, resource endowment, and political history. For most Third World countries, this dependence is substantial. In some cases, it touches almost every facet of life. Most small nations are highly dependent on foreign trade with the developed world (see Chapter 12). Almost all small nations are dependent on the importation of foreign and often inappropriate technologies of production (Chapter 8). This fact alone exerts an extrordinary influence on the character of the growth process in these dependent nations.

But even beyond the strictly economic manifestations of dependence in the form of the international transfer of goods and technologies is the international transmission of institutions (most notably systems of education and governance), values, patterns of consumption, and attitudes toward life, work, and self. Later chapters show that this transmission phenomenon brings mixed blessings to most LDCs, especially to those with the greatest potential for self-reliance. A country's ability to chart its own economic and social destiny is significantly affected by its degree of dependence on these and other external forces.

Political Structure, Power, and Interest Groups

In the final analysis, it is often not the correctness of economic policies alone that determines the outcome of national approaches to critical development problems. The political structure and the vested interests and allegiances of ruling elites (e.g., large landowners, urban industrialists, bankers, foreign manufacturers, the military, trade unionists) will typically determine what strategies are possible and where the main roadblocks to effective economic and social change may lie.

The constellation of interests and power among different segments of the populations of most developing countries is itself the result of their economic, social, and political histories and is likely to differ from one country to the next. Nevertheless—whatever the specific distribution of power among the military, the industrialists, and the large landowners of Latin America; the politicians and high-level civil servants in Africa; the oil sheiks and financial moguls of the Middle East; or the landlords, moneylenders, and wealthy industrialists of Asia—most developing countries are ruled directly or indirectly by small and powerful elites to a greater extent than the developed nations are.

Effective social and economic change thus requires either that the support of elite groups be enlisted or that the power of the elites be offset by more powerful democratic forces. Either way, and this point will be repeated often throughout this book, economic and social development will often be impossible without corresponding changes in the social, political, and economic institutions of a nation (e.g., land tenure systems, forms of governance, educational structures, labor market relationships, property rights, the distribution and control of physical and financial assets, laws of taxation and inheritance, and provision of credit).

Common Characteristics of Developing Nations

The foregoing discussion should have demonstrated why it it is sometimes risky to generalize too much about such a diverse set of nations as those in Africa, Asia, and Latin America. Nevertheless, common economic features of developing countries permit us to view them in a broadly similar framework. We will attempt to identify these similarities and provide illustrative data to demonstrate their importance. For convenience, we can classify these common characteristics into seven broad categories:

1. Low levels of living, characterized by low incomes, high inequality, poor health, and inadequate education
2. Low levels of productivity
3. High rates of population growth and dependency burdens
4. High and rising levels of unemployment and underemployment
5. Substantial dependence on agricultural production and primary-product exports
6. Prevalence of imperfect markets and limited information
7. Dominance, dependence, and vulnerability in international relations

Low Levels of Living

In developing nations, general **levels of living** tend to be very low for the vast majority of people. This is true not only in relation to their counterparts in rich nations but often also in relation to small elite groups within their own societies. These low levels of living are manifested quantitatively and qualitatively in the form of low incomes (poverty), inadequate housing, poor health, limited or no education, high infant mortality, low life and work expectancies, and in many cases a general sense of malaise and hopelessness. Let us look at some recent statistics comparing certain aspects of life in the underdeveloped countries and in the more economically advanced nations. Although these statistics are national aggregates, often incorporate substantial errors of measurement, and in some cases are not strictly comparable due to exchange-rate variations, they do provide at least a summary indication of relative levels of living in different nations.

Per Capita National Income

The **gross national product (GNP)** per capita is often used as a summary index of the relative economic well-being of people in different nations. The GNP itself is the most commonly used measure of the overall level of economic activity. It is calculated as the total domestic and foreign value added claimed by a country's residents without making deductions for depreciation of the domestic capital stock. The **gross domestic product (GDP)** measures the total value for final use of output produced by an economy, by both residents and nonresidents. Thus GNP comprises GDP plus the difference between the income residents receive from abroad for factor services (labor and capital) less payments made to nonresidents who contribute to the domestic economy. Where there is a large nonresident population playing a major role in the domestic economy (such as foreign corporations), these differences can be significant (see Chapter 12). In 1992, the total national product of all the nations of the world was valued at more than U.S. $23 trillion, of which more than $18.3 trillion originated in the economically developed regions and less than $4.8 trillion was generated in the less developed nations. When one takes account of the distribution of world population, this means that approximately 80% of the world's total income is produced in the economically developed regions by 20% of the world's people. Thus four-fifths of the world's population is producing only one-fifth of total world output. More important, on the income side, the Third World, with almost 80% of the world's population, subsists on less than 20% of the world's income. The collective per capita incomes of the underdeveloped countries average less than one-twentieth the per capita incomes of rich nations.

As an illustration of the per capita income gap between rich and poor nations, look at Figure 2.2. Notice that in 1994, the country with the highest per capita income, Switzerland, had 286 times the per capita income of one of the world's poorest countries, Ethiopia, and 120 times that of one of the world's largest nations, India.

Per capita GNP comparisons between developed and less developed countries like those shown in Figure 2.2 are, however, sometimes exaggerated by the use of official foreign-exchange rates to convert the LDC national currency figures into U.S. dollars. This conversion does not measure the relative domestic purchasing power of different currencies. In an attempt to rectify this problem, researchers have tried to compare relative GNPs and GDPs by using **purchasing power parities (PPPs)** instead of exchange rates as conversion factors. PPPs use a common set of international prices for all goods and services produced. More precisely, purchasing power parity is defined as the number of units of a foreign country's currency required to purchase the identical quantity of goods and services in the local (LDC) market as $1 would buy in the United States. Clearly, if LDC domestic prices are lower, PPP measures of GNP per capita will be higher than estimates using foreign-exchange rates as the conversion factor. Income gaps between rich and poor nations thus tend to be less when PPPs are used.

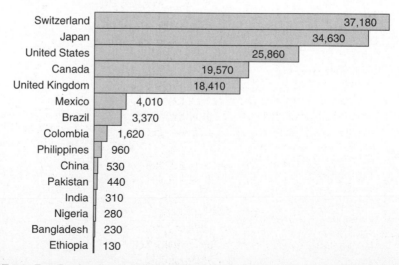

FIGURE 2.2 **Per Capita Gross National Product in Selected Countries, 1994 (in U.S. dollars at official exchange rates).** *Source*: World Bank, *The World Bank Atlas, 1996* (Washington, D.C.: World Bank, 1996), pp. 18–19.

In terms of Figure 2.2, the 1994 GNP per capita calculations measured in PPP international dollars would be as follows: United States, 25,860; Switzerland, 24,390; Japan, 21,350; Canada, 21,320; United Kingdom, 18,170; Mexico, 7,050; Colombia, 5,970; Brazil, 5,630; Philippines, 2,800; China, 2,510; Pakistan, 2,210; Nigeria, 1,430; Bangladesh, 1,350; India, 1,290; and Ethiopia, 410. (Table 2.3 provides a comparison of exchange rate and PPP GNP per capitas for 20 developing countries.) Measured in PPP dollars, the gap between the highest-income country (the United States) and the lowest-income country (Ethiopia) would be 63 to 1 instead of the 286 to 1 gap using official foreign-exchange rates. The truth is probably somewhere in between.[6]

Relative Growth Rates of National and Per Capita Income

In addition to having much lower levels of per capita income, many Third World countries have experienced slower GNP growth than the developed nations. Among all developing countries, for example, growth slowed considerably during the 1980s and, as shown in Figure 2.3, real per capita GDP actually declined by 0.2% in 1990 and again in 1991. Although Asian countries continued to grow at a slow pace during the 1980s, between 1980 and 1992 economic growth in Latin America and the Caribbean averaged –0.2% and in Africa –0.8%. Table 2.4 provides figures on recent

TABLE 2.3 A Comparison of Per Capita GNPs Using Official Exchange Rate and Purchasing Power Parity Conversions, 1994: Twenty Developing Countries

Country	GNP per capita	
	Exchange Rate	Purchasing Power Parity
Argentina	$ 8,060	$ 8,920
Bolivia	770	2,520
Botswana	2,800	5,320
Cameroon	680	1,970
Chile	3,560	9,060
Costa Rica	2,380	5,760
Ghana	430	2,020
Guatemala	1,190	3,490
Indonesia	880	3,690
Kenya	260	1,350
Malawi	140	600
Malaysia	3,520	8,610
Nicaragua	330	1,850
Sierra Leone	150	770
Sri Lanka	640	3,150
Thailand	2,210	6,870
Uganda	200	940
Venezuela	2,760	7,890
Zambia	350	1,000
Zimbabwe	490	2,040

SOURCE: World Bank, *The World Bank Atlas, 1996* (Washington, D.C.: World Bank, 1996), pp. 18–19.

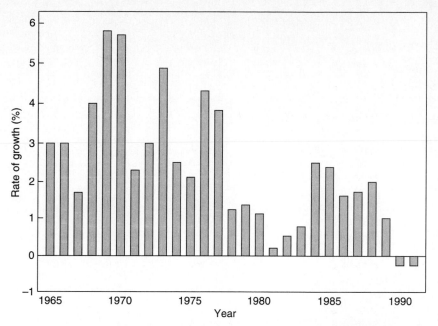

FIGURE 2.3 Growth Rate of Real Per Capita Gross Domestic Product in All Developing Countries, 1965–1991. *Source: The New York Times,* April 16, 1992, p. D-2. Copyright © 1991 by The New York Times Company. Reprinted with permission.

growth rates of real GNP per capita for some representative countries. For them, the 1980s was a lost decade for development. In fact, during the 1980s and early 1990s, the **income gap** between rich and poor nations widened at the fastest pace in more than three decades. The impact of this widening gap is striking. If, for example, we look at the income levels of the richest 20% of the world's population in comparison with the poorest 20%, we find that whereas in 1960 the income ratio was 30 to 1, at the end of 1991 the rich were receiving 61 times the income of the poor![7] Table 2.4 provides recent data on comparative trends in the growth of real GNP per capita between 1980 and 1990 and 1985 and 1994 for the same group of 17 developing countries as Table 2.2. Table 2.5 gives the details of the ever-growing income disparity between the richest and poorest 20% of the world's population.

Distribution of National Income

The growing gap between per capita incomes in rich and poor nations is not the only manifestation of the widening economic disparity between the world's rich and poor. To appreciate the breadth and depth of Third World poverty, it is also necessary to look at the growing gap between rich and poor *within* individual LDCs. We discuss the question of income distribution and equity more fully in Chapter 5, but a few remarks at this point seem appropriate.

First, all nations of the world show some degree of *income inequality*. There are large disparities between incomes of the rich and poor in both developed and underdeveloped countries. Nevertheless, the gap between rich and poor is generally

TABLE 2.4 Growth Rates of Real Gross National Product Per Capita, Percentage Average Annual Growth, 1980–1990 and 1985–1994

Country	1980–1990	1985–1994
Africa		
Kenya	0.3	0.0
Nigeria	–3.0	1.2
Tanzania	–0.7	1.1
Uganda	0.8	3.0
Zaire	1.5	–0.8
Asia		
Bangladesh	1.0	2.1
India	3.2	2.9
Indonesia	4.1	6.0
Philippines	–1.5	1.8
South Korea	8.9	7.8
Sri Lanka	2.4	2.8
Latin America		
Brazil	0.6	–0.4
Colombia	1.1	1.9
Guatemala	–2.1	0.9
Mexico	–0.9	0.6
Peru	–2.0	–2.5
Venezuela	–2.0	0.6

SOURCES: World Bank, *The World Bank Atlas, 1991* (Washington, D.C.: World Bank, 1991), pp. 6–9; World Bank, *The World Bank Atlas, 1996* (Washington, D.C.: World Bank, 1996), pp. 18–19.

greater in less developed nations than in developed nations. For example, if we compare the share of national income that accrues to the poorest 40% of a country's population with that of the richest 20% as an arbitrary measure of the degree of inequality, we discover that countries like Brazil, Ecuador, Colombia, Jamaica, Mexico, Venezuela, Kenya, Sierra Leone, South Africa, and Guatemala have sub-

TABLE 2.5 Global Income Disparity between the Richest and Poorest 20 Percent of the World's Population, 1960–1991

Year	Percentage of Global Income		Ratio of Income Shares
	Poorest 20%	Richest 20%	Richest to Poorest
1960	2.3	70.2	30 to 1
1970	2.3	73.9	32 to 1
1980	1.7	76.3	45 to 1
1991	1.4	85.0	61 to 1

SOURCES: United Nations Development Program, *Human Development Report, 1992* (New York: Oxford University Press, 1992), p. 36; United Nations Development Program, *Human Development Report, 1994* (New York: Oxford University Press, 1994), p. 35.

stantial income inequality; others like India, Tanzania, Chile, Malaysia, Costa Rica, and Libya have moderate inequality; and others like Taiwan, Hong Kong, Indonesia, Canada, Japan, Sweden, and South Korea have relatively lesser inequalities in overall income distribution. Moreover, there is no obvious relationship or correlation between levels of per capita income and degree of income inequality. Kenya, with the same low per capita income as India, has a much wider income disparity between the top 20% and bottom 40% of the population. Similarly, Kuwait, with almost the same high per capita income as Belgium, has a much lower percentage of its income distributed to the bottom 40% of its population. This phenomenon underlines the important point that economic development cannot be measured solely in terms of the level and growth of overall income or income per capita; one must also look at how that income is distributed among the population—at who benefits from development.

Extent of Poverty

The magnitude and extent of poverty in any country depend on two factors: the average level of national income and the degree of inequality in its distribution. Clearly, for any given level of national per capita income, the more unequal the distribution, the greater the incidence of poverty. Similarly, for any given distribution, the lower the average income level, the greater the incidence of poverty. But how is one to measure poverty in any meaningful quantitative sense?

During the 1970s, as interest in problems of poverty increased, development economists took the first step in measuring its magnitude within and across countries by attempting to establish a common poverty line. They went even further and devised the now widely used concept of **absolute poverty**. It is meant to represent a specific minimum level of income needed to satisfy the basic physical needs of food, clothing, and shelter in order to ensure continued survival. A problem, however, arises when one recognizes that these minimum subsistence levels will vary from country to country and region to region, reflecting different physiological as well as social and economic requirements. Economists have therefore tended to make conservative estimates of world poverty in order to avoid unsubstantiated exaggerations of the problem. One common methodology has been to establish an **international poverty line** at, say, a constant U.S. $370 (based, for example, on the value of the 1985 dollar) and then attempt to estimate the **purchasing power equivalent** of that sum of money in terms of a developing country's own currency.

Figure 2.4 provides a picture of both the extent of absolute poverty (the proportion of a country's population with real incomes below the international poverty line) and its numeric magnitude (the actual number of people who can be classified as "absolutely poor"). We see that as the 1990s began, almost 1.25 billion people, or 23% of the world population, were living in absolute poverty. In terms of the proportion of Third World populations, the absolute poor comprised almost one out of every three persons. Looking at individual regions, we find the highest poverty rate (62%) in sub-Saharan Africa and the greatest number of extremely poor in Asia (675 million). With the continuing deterioration of many of the LDC economies in the early 1990s—recall Figure 2.3—and the continued rapid increase in world population, it is safe to conclude that these numbers are still rising rapidly (we will look into this matter in greater detail in Chapter 5).

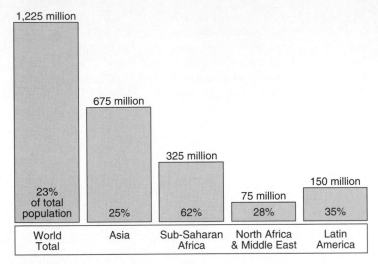

FIGURE 2.4 People Living in Absolute Poverty, 1989 (estimated). *Source:* United Nations Population Fund, *Population, Resources, and the Environment: The Critical Challenge* (New York: United Nations Population Fund, 1991), p. 16. Copyright © United Nations. All United Nations rights reserved.

Health

In addition to struggling on low income, many people in Third World nations fight a constant battle against malnutrition, disease, and ill health. Although there have been some significant improvements since the 1960s, in the least developed countries of the world, life expectancy in 1992 still averaged only 52 years, compared to 61 years among other Third World countries and 75 years in developed nations. **Infant mortality rates** (the number of children who die before their first birthday out of every 1,000 live births) average about 90 in the least developed countries, compared with approximately 72 in other less developed countries and 10 in developed countries. The rates for some specific countries are shown in Figure 2.5.

Tables 2.6 and 2.7 are even more revealing. In the mid-1970s, more than 1 billion people, almost half the population of the developing world (excluding China), were living on diets deficient in essential calories. One-third of them were children under 2 years of age. These people were concentrated in the poorest countries and, within these poor countries, in the lowest income groups. In the 1980s and early 1990s, the situation continued to deteriorate in sub-Saharan Africa, with deep declines in food consumption and widespread famine. In both Asia and Africa, over 60% of the population barely met minimum caloric requirements necessary to maintain adequate health. Moreover, it has been estimated that this caloric deficit amounted to less than 2% of the world cereal production. This contradicts the widely held view that malnutrition is the inevitable result of an imbalance between world population and world food supplies. The more likely explanation can be found in the enormous imbalance in world income distribution. Thus **malnutrition** and poor health in the developing world are perhaps even more a matter of poverty than of food production, even though the two factors are indirectly interrelated. Table 2.7 provides

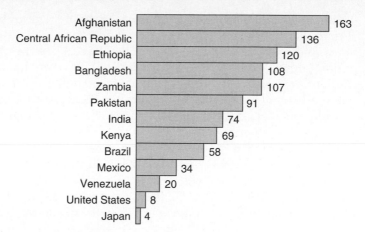

FIGURE 2.5 Infant Mortality Rates in Selected Countries, 1995 (per 1,000 live births).
Source: Population Reference Bureau, *1995 World Population Data Sheet* (Washington, D.C.:
Population Reference Bureau, 1995).

TABLE 2.6 Population with Consumption below Caloric Requirements

Region	People (millions)	Percentage of Population
Latin America	112	36
Asia	707	63
Middle East	61	33
Africa	193	61
Total	1,073	55

SOURCE: S. Reutlinger and M. Selowsky, *Malnutrition and Poverty: Magnitude and Policy Options*
(Baltimore: Johns Hopkins University Press, 1976). Published for the World Bank by the Johns
Hopkins University Press. Reprinted with permission.

TABLE 2.7   Human Health Deprivation in the Third World, 1992

Nature of Health Deprivation	Numbers Deprived
Without access to health services	1.0 billion
Without access to safe water	1.3 billion
Without access to sanitation	1.9 billion
Children dying before age 5	12.2 million
Malnourished children under age 5	192 million

SOURCE: United Nations Development Program, *Human Development Report, 1994* (New York:
Oxford University Press, 1994), pp. 134–135.

1992 estimates of the extent of human deprivation in terms of some key health indicators. We see, for example, that 1 billion people in poor countries are without access to health services, 1.3 billion do not have access to safe drinking water, 1.9 billion (almost half the population) live without sanitation facilities, and 192 million children under age 5 (those who managed to live that long) are malnourished. Another often-used measure of child malnutrition is the percentage of children who are underweight. In the early 1990s, statistics revealed that 67% of the children in Bangladesh were underweight, 63% in India, 43% in South Africa, 42% in Vietnam, 38% in Ethiopia, and 36% in Ghana and Nigeria.[8]

The importance of access to clean drinking water, which is one of the most important measures of sanitation, cannot be overemphasized. Waterborne diseases such as typhoid fever, cholera, and a wide array of serious or fatal diarrheal illnesses are responsible for more than 35% of the deaths of young children in Africa, Asia, and Latin America. Most of these diseases and resulting deaths would be quickly eliminated with safe water supplies.

Finally, medical care is an extremely scarce social service in many parts of the developing world. Recent data reveal that in 1990, the number of doctors per 100,000 people averaged only 4.8 in the least developed countries, compared with 210 in the developed countries. The ratio of hospital beds to population is similarly divergent between these two sets of nations. Moreover, when one realizes that most of the medical facilities in developing nations are concentrated in urban areas where only 25% of the population resides, the woefully inadequate provision of health care to the masses of poor people becomes strikingly clear. For example, in India, 80% of the doctors practice in urban areas where only 20% of the population resides. In Bolivia, only one-third of the population lives in cities, but 90% of the health facilities are found there. In Kenya, the population-to-physician ratio is 672 to 1 for the capital city of Nairobi and 20,000 to 1 in the rural countryside where 87% of the Kenyan population lives. In terms of health expenditures, more than 75% of LDC government outlays are devoted to urban hospitals that provide expensive, Western-style curative care to a minority of the population. Reducing this amount to 50% and using the difference to train 1 million health workers could, according to a United Nations Children's Fund (UNICEF) study, provide much-needed health services to the poorest billion people in the Third World.[9]

Education

As a final illustration of the very low levels of living that are pervasive in Third World nations, consider the spread of educational opportunities. The attempt to provide primary school educational opportunities has probably been the most significant of all LDC development efforts. In most countries, education takes the largest share of the government budget. Yet in spite of some impressive quantitative advances in school enrollments, literacy levels remain strikingly low compared with the developed nations. For example, among the least developed countries, literacy rates average only 45% of the population. The corresponding rates for other Third World nations and the developed countries are approximately 64% and 99%, respectively. Currently, it is estimated that more than 300 million children have dropped out of primary and secondary school, and of the estimated 1 billion illiterate adults, more than 60% are women. The education of children who do attend school regularly is often inappropriate and irrelevant to the development needs of the nation.

Summarizing our discussion so far, we can list the following common characteristics of developing countries:

1. Low relative levels and, in many countries, slow growth rates of national income

2. Low levels and, in many countries, stagnating rates of real income per capita growth

3. Highly skewed patterns of income distribution, with the top 20% of the population receiving 5 to 10 times as much income as the bottom 40%

4. Consequently, great masses of Third World populations suffering from absolute poverty, with up to 1.3 billion people living on subsistence incomes of less than $370 per year

5. Large segments of the populations suffering from ill health, malnutrition, and debilitating diseases, with infant mortality rates running as high as 10 times those in developed nations

6. In education, low levels of literacy, significant school dropout rates, and inadequate and often irrelevant educational curricula and facilities

Most important is the interaction of all six characteristics, which tends to reinforce and perpetuate the pervasive problems of "poverty, ignorance, and disease" that restrict the lives of so many people in the Third World.

Low Levels of Productivity

In addition to low levels of living, developing countries are characterized by relatively low levels of **labor productivity**. The concept of a **production function** systematically relating outputs to different combinations of factor inputs for a given technology is often used to describe the way in which societies go about providing for their material needs. But the technical engineering concept of a production function must be supplemented by a broader conceptualization that includes among its other inputs managerial competence, access to information, worker motivation, and institutional flexibility. Throughout the developing world, levels of labor productivity (output per worker) are extremely low compared with those in developed countries. This can be explained by a number of basic economic concepts.

For example, the principle of diminishing marginal productivity states that if increasing amounts of a variable factor (labor) are applied to fixed amounts of other factors (e.g., capital, land, materials), the extra or marginal product of the variable factor declines beyond a certain number. Low levels of labor productivity can therefore be explained by the absence or severe lack of "complementary" factor inputs such as physical capital or experienced management.

To raise productivity, according to this argument, domestic *savings* and foreign *finance* must be mobilized to generate new investment in physical capital goods and build up the stock of human capital (e.g., managerial skills) through investment in education and training. Institutional changes are also necessary to maximize the potential of this new physical and human investment. These changes might include such diverse activities as the reform of land tenure, corporate tax, credit, and banking structures; the creation or strengthening of an independent, honest, and efficient administrative service; and the restructuring of educational and training programs to make them more appropriate to the needs of the developing societies. These and other noneconomic inputs into the social production function must be taken into account if strategies to raise productivity are to succeed. An old proverb says that "you can lead a horse to water, but you can't make it drink." In underdeveloped nations, it is equally true that you can create the economic opportunities for self-improvement, but without the proper institutional and structural arrangements you cannot succeed.

One must also take into account the impact of worker and management *attitudes* toward self-improvement; people's degree of alertness, adaptability, ambition, and general willingness to innovate and experiment; and their attitudes toward manual work, discipline, authority, and exploitation. Added to all these must be the physical and mental capacity of the individual to do the job satisfactorily. The economic success stories of the four "Asian tigers"—South Korea, Singapore, Hong Kong, and Taiwan—are often attributed to the quality of their human resources, the organization of their production systems, and the institutional arrangements undertaken to accelerate their productivity growth.

The area of physical health most clearly reveals the close linkage that exists between low levels of income and low levels of productivity in developing nations. It is well known, for example, that poor nutrition in childhood can severely restrict the mental and the physical growth of individuals.[10] Poor dietary habits, inadequate food, and low standards of personal hygiene in later years can cause further deterioration in a worker's health and can therefore adversely influence attitudes toward the job and the other people at work. The worker's low productivity may be due in large part to physical lethargy and the inability, both physical and emotional, to withstand the daily pressures of competitive work.

We may conclude, therefore, that low levels of living and low productivity are self-reinforcing social and economic phenomena in Third World countries and, as such, are the principal manifestations of and contributors to their underdevelopment. Myrdal's well-known theory of "circular and cumulative causation" in underdeveloped countries is based on these mutually reinforcing interactions between low living levels and low productivity.[11]

High Rates of Population Growth and Dependency Burdens

Of the world's population of approximately 5.8 billion people in 1995, more than three-fourths live in Third World countries and less than one-fourth in the more developed nations. Both birth and death rates are strikingly different between the two groups of countries. Birthrates in less developed countries are generally very high, on the order of 30 to 40 per 1,000, whereas those in the developed countries are less than half that figure. Indeed, as shown in Table 2.8, the **crude birthrate** (the

TABLE 2.8 Crude Birthrates throughout the World, 1995	
Crude Birthrate	Countries
50	Niger, Mali, Yemen, Uganda, Ivory Coast, Somalia, Gaza, Oman, Afghanistan
45	Zaire, Sierra Leone, Cambodia, Kenya, Ethiopia, Tanzania, Iraq, Angola, Zambia, Malawi, Liberia, Gambia
40	Lesotho, Saudi Arabia, Botswana, Cameroon, Chad, Pakistan, Laos, Iran, Nepal, Sudan, Syria, Guatemala, Zimbabwe
35	Honduras, Paraguay, Bolivia, Haiti, Jordan, Bangladesh, Gabon, Nepal, Namibia
30	Peru, Malaysia, Myanmar, Philippines, Botswana, South Africa, Algeria, Egypt, Morocco, Venezuela, India, Vietnam
25	Brazil, Colombia, Panama, Indonesia, Costa Rica, Mexico, Kuwait, Turkey, Jamaica
20	China, Sri Lanka, Chile, Argentina, Thailand
15	United States, Canada, Australia, Ireland, Cuba, South Korea, Taiwan, Singapore
10	Switzerland, Austria, Germany, Hong Kong, Japan, Russia

SOURCE: Population Reference Bureau, *1995 World Population Data Sheet* (Washington, D.C.: Population Reference Bureau, 1995).
NOTE: Crude birthrate = yearly number of live births per 1,000 population.

yearly number of live births per 1,000 population) is probably one of the most efficient ways of distinguishing the less developed from the more developed countries. There are few less developed countries with a birthrate below 25 per 1,000 and no developed nations with a birthrate above it.

Death rates (the yearly number of deaths per 1,000 population) in Third World countries are also high relative to the more developed nations, but thanks to improved health conditions and the control of major infectious diseases, the differences are substantially smaller than the corresponding differences in birthrates. As a result, the average rate of population growth is now about 2.0% per year in Third World countries (2.3% excluding China), compared to population growth of 0.5% per year in the industrialized world.

A major implication of high LDC birthrates is that children under age 15 make up almost 40% of the total population in these countries, as opposed to less than 21% of the total population in the developed countries. Thus in most developing countries, the active labor force has to support proportionally almost twice as many children as it does in richer countries. By contrast, the proportion of people over the age of 65 is much greater in the developed nations. Older people as well as children are often referred to as an economic **dependency burden** in the sense that they are nonproductive members of society and therefore must be supported financially by a country's labor force (usually defined as citizens between the ages of 15 and 64). The overall dependency burden (i.e., both young and old) represents only about one-third of the populations of developed countries but almost 45% of the populations of the less developed nations. Moreover, in the latter countries, almost 90% of the dependents are children, whereas only 66% are children in the richer nations.

We may conclude, therefore, that not only are Third World countries characterized by higher rates of population growth, but they must also contend with greater dependency burdens than rich nations. The circumstances and conditions under which population growth becomes a deterrent to economic development is a critical issue and will be examined in Chapter 6.

High and Rising Levels of Unemployment and Underemployment

One of the principal manifestations of and factors contributing to the low levels of living in developing nations is their relatively inadequate or inefficient utilization of labor in comparison with the developed nations. Underutilization of labor is manifested in two forms. First, it occurs as **underemployment**—people, both rural and urban, who are working less than they could (daily, weekly, or seasonally). Underemployment also includes those who are normally working full time but whose productivity is so low that a reduction in hours would have a negligible impact on total output. The second form is **open unemployment**—people who are able and often eager to work but for whom no suitable jobs are available.

Current rates of open unemployment in the Third World average 10% to 15% of the labor force. But this is only part of the story. Unemployment among young people aged 15 to 24, many of whom have a substantial education, is typically almost twice as high as the overall average. Table 2.9 provides some estimates of open unemployment during the 1980s for 13 selected Third World countries. However, the data shown in the table represent only the tip of the iceberg of LDC labor underutilization. The problem is much more serious. When the underemployed are added

TABLE 2.9 Open Unemployment Rates in Thirteen Less Developed Countries, 1980s

Country	Area	Year	Average Percentage Unemployed
Bangladesh	Total country	1986	12
Botswana	Urban areas	1984–1985	31
Brazil	Urban areas	1984	8
Chile	Urban areas	1985	18
Colombia	Urban areas	1986	14
Ecuador	Urban areas	1986	13
Kenya	Urban areas	1986	16
Liberia	Total country	1984	13
Malaysia	Total country	1987	9
Philippines	Total country	1986	7
Sri Lanka	Total country	1981	18
Tanzania	Dar es Salaam	1984	22

SOURCE: International Labor Organization, *World Labor Report, 1989* (Geneva: International Labor Organization, 1989), tabs. 1.7 and 1.12, fig. 1.7.

to the openly unemployed and when "discouraged workers"—those who have given up looking for a job—are added in, almost 35% of the combined urban and rural labor forces in Third World nations is unutilized.

Given recent and current birthrates in most LDCs, their labor supply will be expanding rapidly for some time to come. This means that jobs will have to be created at equivalent rates simply to keep pace. Moreover, in urban areas where rural-to-urban migration is causing the labor force to grow at explosive annual rates of 5% to 7% in many countries (especially in Africa), the prospects for coping effectively with rising levels of unemployment and underemployment and for dealing with the frustrations and anxieties of an increasingly vocal and educated but unemployed youth are frighteningly poor. We will examine the dimensions and implications of the unemployment and migration problem further in Chapters 7 and 8.

Substantial Dependence on Agricultural Production and Primary-Product Exports

The vast majority of people in Third World nations live and work in rural areas. Over 65% are rurally based, compared to less than 27% in economically developed countries. Similarly, 62% of the labor force is engaged in agriculture, compared to only 7% in developed nations. Agriculture contributes about 20% of the GNP of developing nations but only 3% of the GNP of developed nations.

Small-Scale Agriculture

Table 2.10 provides a breakdown of population, labor force, and agricultural production by regions of the developed and the less developed world. Note in particular the striking difference between the proportionate size of the agricultural population in Africa (75%) and South Asia (63%) versus North America (5%). In terms of actual numbers, there were almost 685 million agricultural labor force members in Asia and Africa producing an annual volume of output valued at U.S. $195 million in the late 1980s.[12] By contrast, in North America, less than 1% of this total number of agricultural workers (4.5 million) produced almost one-third as much total output ($60 million). This means that the average productivity of agricultural labor expressed in U.S. dollars is almost 35 times greater in North America than in Asia and Africa combined. Although international comparative figures such as these are often of dubious quality regarding both precision and methods of measurements, they nevertheless give us rough orders of magnitude. Even adjusting them for, say, undervaluing Third World nonmarketed agricultural output, the differences in agricultural labor productivity would still be very sizable.

The basic reason for the concentration of people and production in agricultural and other primary production activities in developing countries is the simple fact that at low income levels, the first priorities of any person are food, clothing, and shelter. Agricultural productivity is low not only because of the large numbers of people in relation to available land but also because LDC agriculture is often characterized by primitive technologies, poor organization, and limited physical and human capital inputs. Technological backwardness persists because Third World agriculture is predominantly noncommercial peasant farming. In many parts of the

TABLE 2.10 Population, Labor Force, and Production in Developed and Less Developed Regions, 1992

Region	Population (millions)	Urban (%)	Rural (%)	Labor Force in Agriculture (%)	Agricultural Share of GNP (%)
World	5,420	43	57	45	—
Developed countries	1,224	73	27	7	3
Europe	511	75	25	9	7
Former USSR	284	66	34	20	N.A.
North America	283	75	25	5	2
Japan	124	77	23	11	3
Less developed countries	4,196	34	66	62	17
Africa	654	30	70	75	32
South Asia	1,682	28	72	63	33
East Asia	1,386	34	66	51	21
Latin America	453	70	30	32	10

SOURCES: Population Reference Bureau, *1992 World Population Data Sheet* (Washington, D.C.: Population Reference Bureau, 1992); World Bank, *World Development Report, 1988* (New York: Oxford University Press, 1988), annex tabs. 3 and 31; World Bank, *World Development Report, 1992: Development and the Environment* (New York: Oxford University Press, 1992), tab. 3.

world, especially in Asia and Latin America, it is characterized further by land tenure arrangements in which peasants rent rather than own their small plots of land. As we shall see in Chapter 9, such land tenure arrangements take away much of the economic incentive for output expansion and productivity improvement. Even where land is abundant, primitive techniques and the use of hand plows, drag harrows, and animal (oxen, buffalo, donkey) or raw human power necessitate that typical family holdings be not more than 5 to 8 hectares (12 to 20 acres). In fact, in many countries, average holdings can be as low as 1 to 3 hectares. The number of people that this land must support both directly (through on-the-farm consumption) and indirectly (through production for urban and nonfarm rural food consumption) often runs as high as 10 to 15 people per hectare. It is no wonder that efforts to improve the efficiency of agricultural production and increase the average yields of rice, wheat, maize (corn), soybeans, and millet are now and will continue to be top-priority development objectives.

Dependence on Primary Exports

Most economies of less developed countries are oriented toward the production of primary products (agriculture, fuel, forestry, and raw materials) as opposed to secondary (manufacturing) and tertiary (service) activities. These primary commodities form their main exports to other nations (both developed and less developed). For example, as Figure 2.6 shows, in 1990, for all non-Asian Third World countries, these primary products accounted for over 70% of exports. Except in those countries blessed with abundant supplies of petroleum and other valuable mineral resources and a few leading Asian exporters of manufactured goods, most LDC exports

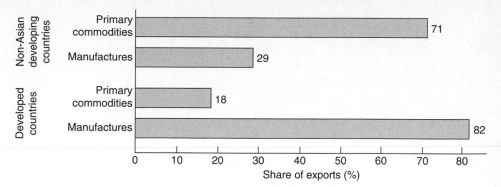

FIGURE 2.6 Composition of World Exports, 1992 (percentages of primary and manufactured products). *Source*: World Bank, *World Bank Development Report, 1994* (New York: Oxford University Press, 1994), tab. 15.

consist of basic foodstuffs, nonfood cash crops, and raw materials. In sub-Saharan Africa, for example, primary products account for over 88% of total export earnings.

As we shall see in Chapter 15, most poor countries need to obtain **foreign exchange** in addition to domestic savings in order to finance priority development projects. Although private foreign investment and foreign aid are a significant but rapidly declining source of foreign exchange, exports of primary products typically account for 60% to 70% of the annual flow of foreign currency into the developing world. Unfortunately for many debt-ridden LDCs, much of the foreign exchange earned through exports in the 1980s went to pay the interest on earlier borrowing. In fact, during recent years, these countries have witnessed a negative international flow of capital, with more foreign currency flowing out of the LDCs than they actually received!

Even though exports are so important to many developing nations, Third World export growth (excluding oil exports) has barely kept pace with that of developed countries. Consequently, even in their best years, most non-oil-exporting developing nations have been losing ground in terms of their share of total world trade to the more developed countries. In 1950, for example, their share was nearly 33%. It has fallen in almost every year since and by 1991 had reached 22%. Countries with the poorest 20% of the world's population did even worse: By 1991, their share of world trade had fallen to 1.4%, while countries with the richest 20% had captured 85% of world trade.[13] Most of the success in export promotion since 1970 has been captured by a few OPEC countries in the 1970s and the four Asian tigers, along with a few other NICs in the 1980s and early 1990s. The majority of LDCs have experienced a continuing decline in their share of world trade (see Chapter 12).

Prevalence of Imperfect Markets and Incomplete Information

In the 1980s and 1990s, almost every developing country was moving at varying speeds toward the establishment of market economies. Many did so at the behest of the World Bank, which kept advocating "market-friendly" economic policies as preconditions for loans. There seemed to be a growing consensus that there had been too much government intervention in the workings of Third World economies and that free markets and unfettered competition held the key to rapid economic growth. But as we shall discover in greater detail in later chapters, the presumed benefits of market economies and market-friendly policies depend heavily on the existence of institutional, cultural, and legal prerequisites that most of us in industrial societies take for granted.

In many LDCs, these legal and institutional foundations are either absent or extremely weak. They include, for example, the existence of a legal system that enforces contracts and validates property rights, a stable and trustworthy currency, an infrastructure of roads and utilities that results in low transport and communication costs so as to facilitate interregional trade, a well-developed system of banking and credit allocation that selects projects on the basis of relative economic profitability and enforces rules of repayment, and substantial market information for consumers and producers about prices, quantities, and qualities of products and resources as well as the creditworthiness of potential borrowers. These five factors, along with the existence of economies of scale in major sectors of the economy (e.g., the extractive industries), thin markets for many products due to limited demand and few sellers, widespread externalities (costs or benefits that accrue to companies or individuals not doing the producing or consuming) in production and consumption, and the prevalence of common property resources (e.g., grazing lands, waterholes) mean that markets are often highly imperfect. Moreover, information is limited and costly to obtain, thereby often causing goods, finances, and resources to be misallocated. Whether or not these **imperfect markets** and **incomplete information** systems justify a more active role for government (which is also subject to similar problems of incomplete and imperfect information) is an issue that we will be dealing with in later chapters. But their existence remains a common characteristic of developing nations.

Dominance, Dependence, and Vulnerability in International Relations

For many less developed countries, a final significant factor contributing to the persistence of low levels of living, rising unemployment, and growing income inequality is the highly unequal distribution of economic and political power between rich and poor nations. As we shall see later, these unequal strengths are manifested not only in the dominant power of rich nations to control the pattern of international trade but also in their ability often to dictate the terms whereby technology, foreign aid, and private capital are transferred to developing countries.

Other equally important aspects of the international transfer process can serve to inhibit the development of poor nations. One subtle but nonetheless significant factor has been the transfer of First World values, attitudes, institutions, and standards of behavior to Third World nations. Examples include the colonial transfer of often inappropriate educational structures, curricula, and school systems; the formation of Western-style trade unions; the organization and orientation of health services in accordance with the Western curative rather than preventive model; and the importation of inappropriate structures and procedures for public bureaucratic and administrative systems. Of even greater potential significance may be the influence of rich-country social and economic standards on developing-country salary scales, elite lifestyles, and general attitudes toward the private accumulation of wealth. Whether there are market-friendly policies or extensive government intervention, such attitudes can often lead to corruption and economic plunder by a privileged minority. Finally, the penetration of rich-country attitudes, values, and standards also contributes to a problem widely recognized and referred to as the international **brain drain**—the migration of professional and skilled personnel, who were often educated in the developing country at great expense, to the various developed nations. Examples include doctors, nurses, scientists, engineers, computer programmers and even economists.

The net effect of all these factors is to create a situation of vulnerability among Third World nations in which forces largely outside their control can have decisive and dominating influences on their economic and social well-being. Many countries—most of the 42 least developed certainly—are small, and their economies are dependent, with very little prospect for self-reliance. Their withdrawal from the world economy is virtually impossible. But as we shall see in Chapter 13, hope can be found in their joining forces economically to promote some form of collective self-reliance. Such cooperation can also strengthen the joint bargaining power of small nations and enable them to scrutinize more carefully and be more selective about foreign investment and technical assistance.

For Third World nations that possess greater assets and relatively more bargaining power, the phenomenon of dominance becomes manifested more in the general tendency of the rich to get richer, often at the expense of the poor. But as mentioned, this is not simply a matter of rich nations growing at a faster pace than poor nations. It is also a matter of rich and dominating sectors or groups *within* the LDC economy (e.g., the modern industrial or agricultural sector; landlords, trade union leaders, industrialists, politicians, bureaucrats, and civil servants in positions of power) growing richer, often at the expense of the much larger but politically and economically less powerful masses of poor people. This dual process of rich nations and powerful groups within poor nations prospering while others stagnate is by no means an isolated phenomenon. We shall see that it is a rather common characteristic of international economic relations.

Conclusion

The phenomenon of underdevelopment must be viewed in both a national and an international context. Problems of poverty, low productivity, population growth, unemployment, primary-product export dependence, and international vulnerability have both domestic and global origins and potential solutions. Economic and social forces, both internal and external, are therefore responsible for the poverty, inequality, and low productivity that characterize most Third World nations. The successful pursuit of economic and social development will require not only the formulation of appropriate strategies within the Third World but also a modification of the present international economic order to make it more responsive to the development needs of poor nations.

Although the picture of life in much of the Third World painted throughout our review may seem bleak, it should be remembered that many countries have succeeded in raising incomes, lowering infant mortality, improving educational access, and increasing life expectancy.[14] By pursuing appropriate economic and social policies both at home and abroad and with effective assistance from developed nations, poor countries do indeed have the means to realize their development aspirations. Parts Two, Three, and Four will discuss the ways in which these hopes and objectives can be attained.

CASE STUDY

The Economy of Nigeria

GEOGRAPHIC, SOCIAL, AND ECONOMIC INDICATORS

Capital Abuja

Area 923,768 km^2

Population 111.2 million (1995)

Population (average annual growth rate) 2.9% (1985–1993)

GNP per capita U.S. $280 (1994)

GNP per capita (average annual growth rate) 1.2% (1985–1994)

Agriculture as share of GDP 43% (1994)

Exports as share of GDP 22% (1994)

Infant mortality rate (per 1,000 live births) 84 (1992)

Child malnutrition (underweight) 43% (1993)

Females as share of labor force 34% (1994)

Illiteracy rate (age 15+) 49% (1990)

Human Development Index 0.35 (low) (1992)

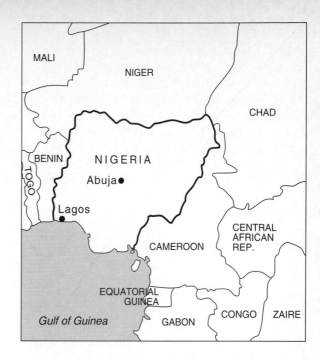

Located on the west coast of the African continent, Nigeria is bounded on the south by the Gulf of Guinea, on the east by Cameroon and Chad, on the north by Niger, and on the west by Benin. The most populous country in Africa, Nigeria accounts for one in five of sub-Saharan Africa's people. Although fewer than 25% of Nigerians are urban dwellers, at least 24 cities have populations of more than 100,000. The varieties of customs, languages, and traditions among Nigeria's 250 ethnic groups gives the country a rich diversity.

The dominant ethnic group in the northern two-thirds of the country is the Hausa-Fulani, most of whom are Muslims. Other major ethnic groups of the north are the Nupe, Tiv, and Kanuri. The Yoruba people are predominant in the southwest. About half of the Yorubas are Christian and half Muslim. The Ibos, primarily Catholic, are the largest ethnic group in the southeast. Persons of different language backgrounds ordinarily communicate in English, although knowledge of two or more Nigerian languages is common. Hausa, Yoruba, and Ibo are the most widely used.

Nigeria was granted full independence from Britain on October 1, 1960, as a federation of three regions (Northern, Western, and Eastern) and 30 states under a constitution that provided for a parliamentary form of government. From the outset, Nigeria experienced ethnic, regional, and religious tensions, magnified by the significant disparities in economic and educational development between the south and the north.

The Nigerian economy underwent profound changes during the 1970s and 1980s. Once an agriculturally based economy and a major exporter of cocoa, peanuts, and palm products, Nigeria now relies on oil for more than 90% of its export earnings, 30% of its GDP, and 70% of its federal budget resources. However, a combination of declining oil prices, overly ambitious industrialization programs, neglect of the agricultural sector, excessive foreign borrowing, and widespread economic corruption and mismanagement during those decades caused the Nigerian

57

economy to experience a prolonged period of economic stagnation and decline.

Prior to the oil boom of the 1970s, Nigeria was one of the world's poorest and least economically developed countries. It had a per capita GNP of only $90 in 1968. But with the oil boom of the 1970s and the discovery of large new deposits, Nigeria embarked on a decade of rapid economic expansion and major structural transformation. Between 1968 and 1980, per capita GNP grew by more than 1,000%, to $1,020. But this growth process was reversed in the 1980s, so that by 1994, GNP per capita had *declined* by more than 70% to $280, the same level as in 1973.

With by far the largest population in Africa (over 114 million in 1996) and a current growth rate of almost 3% per annum, Nigeria adds 3.3 million people every year. If population growth is not reduced, Nigeria will have a population in excess of 150 million by the year 2010 and 300 million by 2035.

Significantly, the oil boom and the consequent neglect of agriculture in the 1970s and early 1980s caused a massive movement of people from rural to urban centers and a major problem of high urban unemployment. Moreover, regional income disparities are among the worst in the world. For example, the gap in per capita income between a rich state, Bendel, and a poor one, Kaduna, is five to one. Adult literacy in Borno is 12%, less than one-quarter the national average.

If Nigeria is to turn the tide of its economic misfortunes and mismanagement, it will have to take steps to raise domestic food production and labor productivity; use oil revenues more rationally to diversify economic activity and reduce the burden of its foreign debt; lower population growth through a combination of effective family planning programs, improved rural health and education, and a reduction in absolute poverty; seek increased foreign aid and investment, including significant debt relief; make greater use of market price incentives to allocate resources while endeavoring to improve public and private decision making; and maintain political stability between rural ethnic and religious groups. Only then will Nigeria begin to achieve its potential as the major economic force on the African continent and a leader of Third World nations.

Concepts for Review

Absolute poverty	Incomplete information
Brain drain	Infant mortality rate
Crude birthrate	International poverty line
Death rate	Labor productivity
Dependency burden	Least developed countries (LLDCs)
First World	Levels of living
Foreign exchange	Low income counties (LICs)
Gross domestic product (GDP)	Malnutrition
Gross national product (GNP)	Middle-income countries (MICs)
Human Development Index (HDI)*	Mixed economic systems
Human resources	Newly industrializing countries (NICs)
Imperfect markets	Open unemployment
Income gap	Physical Quality of Life Index (PQLI)*
Income inequality	Physical resources

*Introduced in Appendix 2.1

Primary industrial sector	Secondary industrial sector
Production function	Tertiary industrial sector
Purchasing power equivalent	Underemployment
Purchasing power parity (PPP)	World Bank
Resource endowment	

Questions for Discussion

1. For all of their diversity, less developed countries are linked by a range of common problems. What are these problems? Which do you think are the most important? Why?

2. Explain the distinction between low levels of living and low per capita incomes. Can low levels of living exist simultaneously with high levels of per capita income? Explain and give some examples.

3. Can you think of other common characteristics of less developed countries not mentioned in the text? List four or five.

4. What are the advantages and disadvantages of using a concept such as an international poverty line? Do you think that a real annual income of $370 in, say, Mexico has the same meaning as in, say, Nigeria or Thailand? Explain your answer.

5. Do you think that there is a strong relationship between health, labor productivity, and income levels? Explain.

6. What is meant by the statement that many Third World nations are subject to "dominance, dependence, and vulnerability" in their relations with rich nations? Can you give some examples?

7. Explain the many ways in which Third World countries may differ in their economic, social, and political structures.

Notes

1. These countries are sometimes even referred to as the Fourth World to underline their situation as the "poorest of the poor" Third World countries and their special need for international assistance. For a description and analysis, see Harold C. Low and John W. Howe, "Focus on the Fourth World," in *World Development: Agenda for Action, 1975* (New York: Praeger, 1974), pp. 35–54.

2. Whether most of these countries are actually developing is an open question. It all depends on one's definition of development (see Chapter 1). However, for expository convenience and to avoid semantic confusion, we will use the adjectives *developing, less developed*, and *underdeveloped* interchangeably throughout the text when referring to Third World countries. To do otherwise would unnecessarily complicate the discussion.

3. The breakup of the Soviet Union into 12 independent republics and the economic and political realignment of Eastern Europe have created a whole new group of nations out of what was formerly referred to as the Second World. Some of these countries should

be classified as underdeveloped, but for our purposes we will limit discussion of LDCs to the traditionally poor countries in Africa, Asia, the Middle East, and Latin America.

4. For a more detailed account of these conflicts, with data on casualties and refugee results see United Nations Development Program, *Human Development Report, 1994* (New York: Oxford University Press, 1994), pp. 32–46, and United Nations, *World Social Situation in the 1990s* (New York: United Nations, 1994), chap. 13.

5. For a discussion of these issues, see H. Lee, *The Ethnic Dimension of Poverty and Income Distribution in Latin America* (Washington, D.C.: World Bank, 1993).

6. For a description of the use of PPPs for international GNP comparisons, see Robert Summers and Alan Heston, "A new set of international comparisons of real product and price level estimates for 130 countries, 1950–1985," *Review of Income and Wealth* 34 (March 1988): 1–24, and "The Penn world table (Mark 5): An expanded set of international comparisons, 1950–88," *Quarterly Journal of Economics* 56 (May 1991): 327–368. Clearly, where exchange rates are highly unstable and currencies are weak, PPP estimates of GDP and GNP will be much higher than exchange-rate conversion estimates. Unfortunately, the reliability of PPP estimates for Third World GNPs is much lower than for OECD countries because the former are typically only rough approximations, whereas the latter are quite reliable.

There are also many other limitations of GNP (or, for that matter, PPP) calculations as measures of economic performance and welfare. For example, GNP does not take account of the depletion or degradation of natural resources. It assigns positive values to natural disasters (e.g., earthquakes, hurricanes, floods), to polluting activities, and to the costs of environmental cleanups (see Chapter 10). It ignores nonmonetary transactions, household unpaid labor, and subsistence consumption, each significant activities in LDCs (see Chapter 9). Finally, GNP figures take no account of income distribution (Chapter 5) or unemployment (Chapter 7).

7. United Nations Development Program, *Human Development Report, 1994* (New York: Oxford University Press, 1994), p. 35.

8. World Bank, *The World Bank Atlas, 1995* (Washington, D.C.: World Bank, 1994), pp. 8–9.

9. United Nations Children's Fund, *The State of the World's Children, 1990* (New York: Oxford University Press, 1990), pp. 42–44.

10. See, for example, Alan Berg, Nevin S. Scrimshaw, and David L. Call (eds.), *Nutrition, National Development, and Planning* (Cambridge, Mass.: MIT Press, 1973), pts. 1 and 2.

11. See Gunnar Myrdal, *Asian Drama* (New York: Pantheon, 1968), app. 2.

12. The total value of actual agricultural output was probably somewhat higher than this figure, for much of the food output in LDCs is consumed directly by farm families and is therefore not always estimated in aggregate production figures.

13. United Nations Development Program, *Human Development Report, 1994*, p. 35.

14. For an elaboration of this point, see Lawrence H. Summers and Vinod Thomas, "Recent lessons of development," *World Bank Research Observer* 8 (July 1993): 241–254, and Pam Woodall, "The global economy," *Economist* (October 1, 1994): 3–38.

Further Reading

For a very informative survey of the diverse structures of Third World nations, see John P. Cole, *Development and Underdevelopment: A Profile of the Third World* (London: Routledge, 1987), and Paul Harrison, *Inside the Third World* (New York: Penguin, 1982). For regional surveys, see, for Asia, Gunnar Myrdal, *Asian Drama* (New York: Pantheon, 1968), and David Drakakis-Smith, *Pacific Asia* (London: Routledge, 1991); for Africa, Peter Robson and Dennis Lury (eds.), *The Economies of Africa* (London: Allen & Unwin, 1969), and Robert J. Berg and Jennifer Seymour Whitaker (eds.), *Strategies for African Development* (Berkeley: University of California Press, 1986); and for Latin America, Celso Furtado, *Economic Development in Latin America* (London: Cambridge University Press, 1970); John Sheahan, *Patterns of Development in Latin America* (Princeton, N.J.: Princeton University Press, 1987); and Alan Gilbert, *Latin America* (London: Routledge, 1990). Additional material can be found in three volumes of readings and statistics edited by Pradip K. Ghosh, *Developing South Asia, Developing Africa,* and *Developing Latin America* (Westport, Conn.: Greenwood Press, 1984).

Information on current economic, social, and demographic trends within individual Third World countries and regions can best be obtained from the annual *World Development Report* published by the World Bank, the annual *World Economic Outlook* published by the International Monetary Fund, and various United Nations publications including the annual *Statistical Yearbook,* the UNDP's annual *Human Development Report,* and the regular publications of the U.N.'s Economic Commission for Latin America (ECLA), Economic Commission for Africa (ECA), and Economic and Social Commission for Asia and the Pacific (ESCAP). Concise statistical summaries can also be obtained from the annual *World Bank Atlas.* The World Bank and International Monetary Fund also do studies of individual countries; see their current publications list for the most recent titles.

For a contrasting perspective on two African countries—Zaire and Botswana—see Stephen C. Smith, *Case Studies,* Chapter 2.

APPENDIX 2.1

Social Indicators as Alternative Measures of Development: The Physical Quality of Life and Human Development Indexes

Rationale and Initial Measurement Attempts

The problems associated with using per capita GNP as a measure of development are well known. Among the major objections to this measure are its failure to include nonmarketed (and therefore nonpriced) subsistence production, including much of women's work, and to incorporate welfare and income distribution considerations. As a result, there have been numerous efforts both to remedy its defects and to create other composite indicators that could serve as complements or alternatives to this traditional measure.[1] Basically, such indicators fall into two groups—those that seek to measure development in terms of a "normal" or "optimal" pattern of interaction among social, economic, and political factors and those that measure development in terms of the quality of life.

One of the early major studies on the first group of composite indicators was carried out by the United Nations Research Institute on Social Development (UNRISD) in 1970.[2] The study was concerned with the selection of the most appropriate indicators of development and an analysis of the relationship between these indicators at different levels of development. The result was the construction of a composite social development index. Originally, 73 indicators were examined. However, only 16 core indicators (9 social indicators and 7 economic indicators) were ultimately chosen (see Table A2.1). These indicators were selected on the basis of their high intercorrelation to form a development index using weights derived from their various degrees of correlation. The development index was found to correlate more highly with individual social and economic indicators than per capita GNP correlated with the same indicators. Rankings of some countries under the development

---

TABLE A2.1 United Nations Research Institute on Social Development (UNRISD) List of Core Indicators of Socioeconomic Development

Expectation of life at birth
Percentage of population in localities of 20,000 and over
Consumption of animal protein per capita per day
Combined primary and secondary enrollment
Vocational enrollment ratio
Average number of persons per room
Newspaper circulation per 1,000 population
Percentage of economically active population with electricity, gas, water, etc.
Agricultural production per male agricultural worker
Percentage of adult male labor in agriculture
Electricity consumption, kw per capita
Steel consumption, kg per capita
Energy consumption, kg of coal equivalent per capita
Percentage GDP derived from manufacturing
Foreign trade per capita, in 1960 U.S. dollars
Percentage of salaried and wage earners to total economically active population

SOURCE: United Nations Research Institute on Social Development, *Contents and Measurements of Socioeconomic Development* (Geneva: UNRISD, 1970), p. 63. Copyright © United Nations. All United Nations rights reserved.

index differed from per capita GNP rankings. It was also found that the development index was more highly correlated with per capita GNP for developed countries than for developing ones. The study concluded that social development occurred at a more rapid pace than economic development up to a level of $500 per capita (1960 prices).

Another study that sought to measure development in terms of a pattern of interaction among social, economic, and political factors was conducted by Irma Adelman and Cynthia Morris, who classified 74 developing countries according to the 40 variables listed in Table A2.2.[3] Factor analysis was used to examine the interdependence between social and political variables and the level of economic development. The researchers found numerous correlations between certain key variables and economic development.

The major criticism of these studies is that they seek to measure development in terms of structural change rather than in terms of human welfare. There is also the implicit assumption that developing countries must develop along the lines of the developed countries, as illustrated by researchers' use of indicators such as animal protein consumption or energy consumption per capita. Furthermore, there is usually an emphasis on measuring inputs, such as the number of doctors or hospital beds per 1,000 population or enrollment rates in schools to measure health and education, when outputs, such as life expectancy and literacy, are the actual objectives of development. In response to these criticisms, several studies have sought to develop composite indicators that measure development in terms of meeting the basic needs of the majority of the population or in terms of the quality of life.

The Physical Quality of Life Index (PQLI)

One well-known endeavor in this area was Morris D. Morris's development of the **Physical Quality of Life Index (PQLI)**.[4] Three indicators—life expectancy at age 1, infant mortality, and literacy—were used to form a simple composite index. For each indicator, the performance of individual countries is rated on a scale of 1 to 100, where 1 represents the worst performance by any country and 100 the best performance. For life expectancy, the upper limit of 100 was assigned to 77 years (achieved by Sweden in 1973) and the lower limit of 1 was assigned to 28 years (the life expectancy of Guinea-Bissau in 1950). Within these limits, each country's life expectancy figure is ranked from 1 to 100. For example, a life expectancy of 52, midway between the upper and lower limits of 77 and 28, would be assigned a rating of 50. Similarly, for infant mortality, the upper limit was set at 9 per 1,000 (achieved by Sweden in 1973) and the lower limit at 229 per 1,000 (Gabon, 1950). Literacy rates, measured as percentages from 1 to 100, provide their own direct scale. Once a country's performance in life expectancy, infant mortality, and literacy has been rated on the scale of 1 to 100, the composite index for the country is calculated by averaging the three ratings, giving equal weight to each.

Although the study found that countries with low per capita GNP tended to have low PQLIs and countries with high per capita GNP tended to have high PQLIs, the correlations between GNP and PQLI were not substantially close. Some countries with high per capita GNP had very low PQLIs—even below the average of the poorest countries. Other countries with very low per capita GNP had PQLIs that were higher than the average for the upper-middle-income countries. Table A2.3 provides a sample of Third World countries ranked both by per capita incomes and by PQLIs in the early 1980s. The data seem to indicate that significant improvements in the basic quality of life can be achieved before there is any great rise in per capita GNP or, conversely, that a higher level of per capita GNP is not a guarantee of a better quality of life. Note in particular the wide PQLI variations for countries with similar levels of per capita income such as Angola and Zimbabwe, China and India, Tanzania and Gambia, Taiwan and Iraq, and Costa Rica and Brazil. A particularly striking contrast is that between Saudi Arabia and Sri Lanka.

TABLE A2.2 Social, Political, and Economic Variables Used by Adelman and Morris

Size of the traditional agricultural sector
Extent of dualism
Extent of urbanization
Character of basic social organization
Importance of the indigenous middle class
Extent of social mobility
Extent of literacy
Extent of mass communication
Degree of cultural and ethnic homogeneity
Degree of social tension
Crude fertility rate
Degree of modernization of outlook
Degree of national integration and sense of national unity
Extent of centralization of political power
Strength of democratic institutions
Degree of freedom of political opposition and press
Degree of competitiveness of political parties
Predominant basis of the political party system
Strength of the labor movement
Political strength of the traditional elite
Political strength of the military
Degree of administrative efficiency
Extent of leadership commitment to economic development
Extent of political stability
Per capita GNP in 1961
Rate of growth of real per capita GNP between 1950–1951 and 1963–1964
Abundance of natural resources
Gross investment rate
Level of modernization of industry
Change in degree of industrialization since 1950
Character of agricultural organization
Level of modernization of techniques in agriculture
Degree of improvement in agricultural productivity since 1950
Level of adequacy of physical overhead capital
Degree of improvement in physical overhead capital since 1950
Level of effectiveness of the tax system
Degree of improvement in the tax system since 1950
Level of effectiveness of financial institutions
Degree of improvement in human resources
Structure of foreign trade

SOURCE: Irma Adelman and Cynthia Taft Morris, *Society, Politics, and Economic Development* (Baltimore: Johns Hopkins University Press, 1967). Reprinted with permission.

TABLE A2.3 Per Capita Gross National Product (GNP) and Physical Quality of Life Index (PQLI) for Selected Less Developed Countries, 1981

Country	Per Capita GNP (U.S. $)	PQLI
Gambia	348	20
Angola	790	21
Sudan	380	34
Pakistan	349	40
Saudi Arabia	12,720	40
India	253	42
Iraq	3,020	48
Qatar	27,790	56
Tanzania	299	58
Zimbabwe	815	63
Brazil	2,214	72
China	304	75
Sri Lanka	302	82
Singapore	5,220	86
Taiwan	2,503	87
Costa Rica	1,476	89

SOURCE: John P. Lewis and Valeriana Kallab (eds.), *U.S. Foreign Policy and the Third World, Agenda 1983* (New York: Praeger, 1983), tab. C-3. Reprinted with permission.

The Human Development Index (HDI)

The latest and most ambitious attempt to analyze the comparative status of socioeconomic development in both developing and developed nations systematically and comprehensively has been undertaken by the United Nations Development Program (UNDP) in its annual series of *Human Development Reports.*[5] The centerpiece of these reports, which were initiated in 1990, is the construction and refinement of the **Human Development Index (HDI)**. Like the PQLI, the HDI attempts to rank all countries on a scale of 0 (lowest human development) to 1 (highest human development) based on three goals or end products of development: *longevity* as measured by life expectancy at birth, *knowledge* as measured by a weighted average of adult literacy (two-thirds) and mean years of schooling (one-third), and *standard of living* as measured by real per capita income adjusted for the differing purchasing power parity (PPP) of each country's currency to reflect cost of living and for the assumption of rapidly diminishing marginal utility of income above average world income levels. Using these three measures of development and applying a complex formula to 1992 data for 173 countries, the HDI ranks all countries into three groups: low human development (0.0 to 0.50), medium human development (0.51 to 0.79), and high human development (0.80 to 1.0). It should be noted that for any given year, HDI measures *relative*, not absolute, levels of human development and that its focus is on the *ends* of development (longevity, knowledge, material choice) rather than the means (as with per capita GNP alone).

Table A2.4 shows the 1992 Human Development Index for a sample of 20 developed and developing nations ranked from low to high human development (column 3) along with their respective GNP per capita (column 4) and a measure of the differential between the GNP per capita rank and the HDI rank (column 5). A positive number shows by how much a country's relative ranking rises when HDI is used instead of GNP per capita, and a

TABLE A2.4 Human Development Index for Twenty Selected Countries, 1992

Country	Relative Ranking (lowest to highest)	Human Development Index (HDI)	GNP per Capita (U.S. $)	GNP Rank minus HDI Rank
Low human development				
Guinea	173	0.191	500	−44
Ethiopia	161	0.249	410	10
Bangladesh	146	0.309	220	13
Nigeria	139	0.348	350	6
India	135	0.382	330	12
Kenya	125	0.434	340	21
Medium human development				
Egypt	110	0.551	610	12
Indonesia	105	0.586	610	16
China	94	0.644	370	49
South Africa	93	0.650	2,540	−33
Sri Lanka	90	0.665	500	38
Brazil	63	0.756	2,920	−11
Thailand	54	0.798	1,650	28
High human development				
Mexico	52	0.804	3,080	−1
Costa Rica	39	0.848	1,870	36
South Korea	32	0.859	6,350	4
United Kingdom	10	0.919	16,600	9
United States	8	0.925	22,340	1
Japan	3	0.929	26,840	0
Canada	1	0.932	20,510	10

SOURCE: United Nations Development Program, *Human Development Report, 1994* (New York: Oxford University Press, 1994), pp. 129–131. Reprinted with permission.

negative number shows the opposite. Clearly, this is the critical issue for the HDI as well as any other composite social indicator such as the PQLI. If country rankings did not vary much when the HDI is used instead of GNP per capita, the latter would (as some economists claim) serve as a reliable proxy for socioeconomic development, and there would be no need to worry about such things as health and education indicators.

We see from Table A2.4 that the country with the lowest HDI (0.191) in 1992 was Guinea and the one with the highest (0.932) was Canada. What is more interesting for our purposes is that even though countries with high HDIs tend to have higher per capita incomes, within and across the three subgroups we find some countries whose HDI is considerably higher than others even though the latter have substantially higher per capita incomes. Thus, for example, we see that Kenya's HDI is more than twice that of Guinea, even though Guinea's GNP per capita is almost 50% higher than Kenya's. Similarly, Sri Lanka, with less than 20% of the income of South Africa, has an HDI that is higher, while Brazil, with a 56% higher GNP per capita than Costa Rica, has an 11% lower HDI. Although far less significant, the United States, with a higher income, has a lower HDI than Canada.

To emphasize the point that countries at similar levels of GNP per capita can have significantly different human development indicators, depending on how that income is used, let's look briefly at Table A2.5. We see, for example, that Nicaragua and Pakistan had identical per capita incomes in 1992, but the former's HDI was almost 50% higher than the latter's. Similar results are shown for, say, Jordan and El Salvador or Chile and Iraq.

One of the major innovations of the Human Development Index over the past few years has occurred through the disaggregation of a country's overall HDI into separate components to distinguish between men and women, different social classes reflecting skewed income distributions, and different regions and ethnic groups.[6] The results show, not surprisingly, that men generally fare far better than women for almost every socioeconomic indicator. For example, in the 43 countries for which gender-based income data were available, women's income averaged less than 40% of men's in 14 countries (mostly developing countries, although the figure was 35% in Japan and 33% in Ireland) and above 60% in only 11, all of which were developed nations like Sweden and Norway.

When the aggregate HDI for various countries was adjusted for income distribution, the relative rankings of many developing nations also changed significantly. For example, Brazil and Botswana have highly unequal distributions so that their rankings slip by seven and eight places respectively, while China and Sri Lanka see their HDI rankings rise by a similar factor due to their more egalitarian distributions. When HDIs were then adjusted for race, region, and ethnicity, we find, for example, that even though South Africa's overall HDI is 0.650 (medium), the HDI for whites is 0.876 (high), while for blacks it is 0.462 (low); even though Brazil's HDI is 0.756, its wealthy southern regions (Rio de Janeiro and São Paulo) have an HDI of 0.838, while its poor northeast regions have an HDI of 0.549; and even though Nigeria has an HDI of 0.348, its richest state, Bendel, has an HDI of 0.666, while the poorest, Borno, has a value of only 0.156 (lower even than lowest-ranked Guinea).

The United Nations Human Development Index has thus made a major contribution to improving our understanding of what constitutes development, which countries are

TABLE A2.5 Human Development Index Variations for Similar Incomes, 1992

Country	GNP Per Capita (U.S. $)	HDI	HDI rank	Life Expectancy (years)	Adult Literacy (%)	Infant Mortality (per 1,000 live births)
GNP per capita around $400 to $500						
Sri Lanka	500	0.665	90	71.2	89	24
Nicaragua	400	0.583	106	65.4	78	53
Pakistan	400	0.393	132	58.3	36	99
Guinea	500	0.191	173	43.9	27	135
GNP per capita around $1,000 to $1,100						
Ecuador	1,010	0.718	74	66.2	87	58
Jordan	1,060	0.628	98	67.3	82	37
El Salvador	1,090	0.543	112	65.2	75	46
Congo	1,040	0.461	123	51.7	59	83
GNP per capita around $2,300 to $2,600						
Chile	2,360	0.848	38	71.9	94	17
Malaysia	2,520	0.794	57	70.4	80	14
South Africa	2,540	0.650	93	62.2	80	53
Iraq	2,550	0.614	100	65.7	63	59

SOURCE: United Nations Development Program, *Human Development Report, 1994* (New York: Oxford University Press, 1994), p. 15. Reprinted with permission.

succeeding (as reflected by rises in their HDIs over time), and how different groups and regions within countries are faring. By combining social and economic data, the HDI allows nations to take a broader measure of their development performance, both relatively and absolutely, and thus to focus their economic and social policies more directly on those areas in need of improvement.

The HDI, like the per capita GNP measure, is, however, not without its limitations and its critics. Some academic economists argue that its assumption of the rapidly diminishing marginal value of money income above the world average threshold of $5,120 real GDP per capita distorts some HDI estimates and limits its applicability. They also claim that its basic statistical methodology is compromised by insufficient or inaccurate data so that cross-country comparisons and measures of development over time are highly suspect.[7]

Although these are somewhat valid criticisms, the fact remains that the HDI, when used *in conjunction* with traditional economic measures of development, greatly increases our understanding of which countries are really experiencing development and which are not. More important, by examining each of the three major components of the HDI-adjusted real per capita income, life expectancy, and literacy and schooling measures and by disaggregating a country's overall HDI to reflect income distribution, gender, regional, and ethnic differentials, we are now able to identify not only whether a country is developing but also whether various significant groups within that country are participating in that development.

Notes to Appendix 2.1

1. Two excellent early surveys of social indicators are Nancy Bastor, "Development indicators: An introduction," in Nancy Bastor (ed.), *Measuring Development: The Role and Adequacy of Development Indicators* (London: Cass, 1972), and Norman L. Hicks and Paul P. Streeten, "Indicators of development: The search for a basic needs yardstick," *World Development* 7 (June 1979): 567–580.

2. United Nations Research Institute on Social Development, *Contents and Measurements of Socioeconomic Development* (Geneva: UNRISD, 1970).

3. Irma Adelman and Cynthia Taft Morris, *Society, Politics, and Economic Development* (Baltimore: Johns Hopkins University Press, 1967).

4. Morris D. Morris, *Measuring the Condition of the World's Poor: The Physical Quality of Life Index* (London: Cass, 1979). An alternative and more controversial attempt to measure the quality of life in LDCs was undertaken in 1987 when the Population Crisis Committee of Washington, D.C., published the International Human Suffering Index. This index was created to measure, in a single figure, differences in living conditions among countries. Each country index was compiled by adding 10 measures of human welfare related to economics, demography, health, and governance. The index of suffering incorporates income, inflation, demand for new jobs, urban population pressures, infant mortality, nutrition, clean water, energy use, adult literacy, and personal freedom. The greatest suffering was found to exist in Mozambique, Angola, and Afghanistan, while the best living conditions existed in Switzerland, western Germany, and Luxembourg.

5. United Nations Development Program, *Human Development Report, 1994* (New York: Oxford University Press, 1994).

6. *Ibid.*, pp. 96–101.

7. See, for example, T. N. Srinivasan, "Human development: A new paradigm or reinvention of the wheel?" *American Economic Review* 84 (May 1994): 238–243.

CHAPTER 3

Theories of Development: A Comparative Analysis

It matters little how much information we possess about development if we have not grasped its inner meaning.

—Denis Goulet, *The Cruel Choice*

Development must be redefined as an attack on the chief evils of the world today: malnutrition, disease, illiteracy, slums, unemployment and inequality. Measured in terms of aggregate growth rates, development has been a great success. But measured in terms of jobs, justice and the elimination of poverty, it has been a failure or only a partial success.

Paul P. Streeten, Director, World Development Institute

Development theory by itself has little value unless it is applied, unless it translates into results, and unless it improves people's lives.

—Lewis T. Preston, Former President, World Bank

Every nation strives after development. Economic progress is an essential component, but it is not the only component. As we discovered in Chapter 1, development is not purely an economic phenomenon. In an ultimate sense, it must encompass more than the material and financial side of people's lives. Development should therefore be perceived as a multidimensional process involving the reorganization and reorientation of entire economic and social systems. In addition to improvements in incomes and output, it typically involves radical changes in institutional, social, and administrative structures as well as in popular attitudes and, in many cases, even customs and beliefs. Finally, although development is usually defined in a national context, its widespread realization may necessitate fundamental modification of the international economic and social system as well.

In this chapter, we explore the recent historical and intellectual evolution in scholarly thinking about how and why development does or does not take place. We do this by examining five major and often competing development theories. In addition to presenting these differing approaches, we will discover how each offers valuable insight and a useful perspective on the nature of the development process.

69

Leading Theories of Economic Development: Five Approaches

The post–World War II literature on economic development has been dominated by four major and sometimes competing strands of thought: (1) the linear-stages-of-growth model, (2) theories and patterns of structural change, (3) the international dependence revolution, and (4) the neoclassical, free-market counterrevolution. In addition, the past few years have witnessed the emergence of a fifth approach that has been called the new or endogenous theory of economic growth.

Theorists of the 1950s and early 1960s viewed the process of development as a series of successive stages of economic growth through which all countries must pass. It was primarily an economic theory of development in which the right quantity and mixture of saving, investment, and foreign aid were all that was necessary to enable Third World nations to proceed along an economic growth path that historically had been followed by the more developed countries. Development thus became synonymous with rapid, aggregate economic growth.

This linear-stages approach was largely replaced in the 1970s by two competing economic (and indeed ideological) schools of thought. The first, which focused on theories and patterns of structural change, used modern economic theory and statistical analysis in an attempt to portray the internal process of structural change that a "typical" developing country must undergo if it is to succeed in generating and sustaining a process of rapid economic growth. The second, the international dependence revolution, was more radical and political in orientation. It viewed underdevelopment in terms of international and domestic power relationships, institutional and structural economic rigidities, and the resulting proliferation of dual economies and dual societies both within and among the nations of the world. Dependence theories tended to emphasize external and internal institutional and political constraints on economic development. Emphasis was placed on the need for major new policies to eradicate poverty, to provide more diversified employment opportunities, and to reduce income inequalities. These and other egalitarian objectives were to be achieved within the context of a growing economy, but economic growth per se was not given the exalted status accorded to it by the linear-stages and the structural-change models.

Throughout much of the 1980s, a fourth approach prevailed. This neoclassical counterrevolution in economic thought emphasized the beneficial role of free markets, open economies, and the privatization of inefficient and wasteful public enterprises. Failure to develop, according to this theory, is not due to exploitive external and internal forces as expounded by dependence theorists. Rather, it is primarily the result of too much government intervention and regulation of the economy.

Finally, in the late 1980s and early 1990s, a few neoclassical and institutional economists began to develop the new growth theory. It attempts to modify and extend traditional growth theory in a way that helps explain why some countries develop rapidly while others stagnate and why, even in a neoclassical world of private markets, governments may still have an important role to play in the development process.

We now look at each of these alternative approaches in greater detail.

The Linear–Stages Theory

When interest in the poor nations of the world really began to materialize following the Second World War, economists in the industrialized nations were caught off guard. They had no readily available conceptual apparatus with which to analyze the process of economic growth in largely peasant, agrarian societies characterized by the virtual absence of modern economic structures. But they did have the recent experience of the Marshall Plan, under which massive amounts of U.S. financial and technical assistance enabled the war-torn countries of Europe to rebuild and modernize their economies in a matter of a few years. Moreover, was it not true that all modern industrial nations were once undeveloped agrarian societies? Surely their historical experience in transforming their economies from poor agricultural subsistence societies to modern industrial giants had important lessons for the "backward" countries of Asia, Africa, and Latin America. The logic and simplicity of these two strands of thought—the utility of massive injections of capital and the historical pattern of the now developed countries—was too irresistible to be refuted by scholars, politicans, and administrators in rich countries to whom people and ways of life in the Third World were often no more real than U.N. statistics or scattered chapters in anthropology books.

Rostow's Stages of Growth

Out of this somewhat sterile intellectual environment, fueled by the cold war politics of the 1950s and 1960s and the resulting competition for the allegiance of newly independent nations, came the **stages-of-growth model of development**. Its most influential and outspoken advocate was the American economic historian Walt W. Rostow. According to the Rostow doctrine, the transition from underdevelopment to development can be described in terms of a series of steps or stages through which all countries must proceed. As Rostow wrote in the opening chapter of his *Stages of Economic Growth*:

> This book presents an economic historian's way of generalizing the sweep of modern history. . . . It is possible to identify all societies, in their economic dimensions, as lying within one of five categories: the traditional society, the pre-conditions for take-off into self-sustaining growth, the take-off, the drive to maturity, and the age of high mass consumption. . . . These stages are not merely descriptive. They are not merely a way of generalizing certain factual observations about the sequence of development of modern societies. They have an inner logic and continuity. . . . They constitute, in the end, both a theory about economic growth and a more general, if still highly partial, theory about modern history as a whole.[1]

The advanced countries, it was argued, had all passed the stage of "take-off into self-sustaining growth," and the underdeveloped countries that were still in either the traditional society or the "preconditions" stage had only to follow a certain set of rules of development to take off in their turn into self-sustaining economic growth.

One of the principal tricks of development necessary for any takeoff was the mobilization of domestic and foreign saving in order to generate sufficient investment to accelerate economic growth. The economic mechanism by which more investment leads to more growth can be described in terms of the **Harrod-Domar growth model**.

The Harrod–Domar Growth Model

Every economy must save a certain proportion of its national income, if only to replace worn-out or impaired capital goods (buildings, equipment, and materials). However, in order to grow, new investments representing net additions to the **capital stock** are necessary. If we assume that there is some direct economic relationship between the size of the total capital stock, K, and total GNP, Y—for example, if $3 of capital is always necessary to produce a $1 stream of GNP—it follows that any net additions to the capital stock in the form of new investment will bring about corresponding increases in the flow of national output, GNP.

Suppose that this relationship, known in economics as the **capital-output ratio**, is roughly 3 to 1. If we define the capital-output ratio as k and assume further that the national **savings ratio**, s, is a fixed proportion of national output (e.g., 6%) and that total new investment is determined by the level of total savings, we can construct the following simple model of economic growth:

1. Saving (S) is some proportion, s, of national income (Y) such that we have the simple equation

$$S = sY. \tag{3.1}$$

2. Investment (I) is defined as the change in the capital stock, K, and can be represented by ΔK such that

$$I = \Delta K. \tag{3.2}$$

But because the total capital stock, K, bears a direct relationship to total national income or output, Y, as expressed by the capital-output ratio, k, it follows that

$$\frac{K}{Y} = k$$

or

$$\frac{\Delta K}{\Delta Y} = k$$

or, finally,

$$\Delta K = k\Delta Y. \tag{3.3}$$

3. Finally, because total national savings, S, must equal total investment, I, we can write this equality as

$$S = I. \tag{3.4}$$

But from Equation 3.1 we know that $S = sY$ and from Equations 3.2 and 3.3 we know that

$$I = \Delta K = k\Delta Y.$$

It therefore follows that we can write the "identity" of saving equaling investment shown by Equation 3.4 as

$$S = sY = k\Delta Y = \Delta K = I \tag{3.5}$$

or simply as

$$sY = k\Delta Y. \tag{3.6}$$

Dividing both sides of Equation 3.6 first by Y and then by k, we obtain the following expression:

$$\frac{\Delta Y}{Y} = \frac{s}{k}. \tag{3.7}$$

Note that the left-hand side of Equation 3.7, $\Delta Y / Y$, represents the rate of change or rate of growth of GNP (i.e., it is the percentage change in GNP).

Equation 3.7, which is a simplified version of the famous Harrod-Domar equation in their theory of economic growth,[2] states simply that the rate of growth of GNP ($\Delta Y / Y$) is determined jointly by the national savings ratio, s, and the national capital-output ratio, k. More specifically, it says that in the absence of government, the growth rate of national income will be directly or positively related to the savings ratio (i.e., the more an economy is able to save—and invest—out of a given GNP, the greater will be the growth of that GNP) and inversely or negatively related to the economy's capital-output ratio (i.e., the higher k is, the lower will be the rate of GNP growth).

The economic logic of Equation 3.7 is very simple. In order to grow, economies must save and invest a certain proportion of their GNP. The more they can save and invest, the faster they can grow. But the actual rate at which they can grow for any level of saving and investment—how much additional output can be had from an additional unit of investment—can be measured by the inverse of the capital-output ratio, k, because this inverse, $1/k$, is simply the output-capital or output-investment ratio. It follows that multiplying the rate of new investment, $s = I/Y$, by its productivity, $1/k$, will give the rate by which national income or GNP will increase.

Obstacles and Constraints

Returning to the stages-of-growth theories and using Equation 3.7 of our simple Harrod-Domar growth model, we learn that one of the most fundamental "tricks" of economic growth is simply to increase the proportion of national income saved (i.e., not consumed). If we can raise s in Equation 3.7, we can increase $\Delta Y / Y$, the rate of GNP growth. For example, if we assume that the national capital-output ratio in some less developed country is, say, 3 and the aggregate saving ratio is 6% of GNP, it follows from Equation 3.7 that this country can grow at a rate of 2% per year because

$$\frac{\Delta Y}{Y} = \frac{s}{k} = \frac{6\%}{3} = 2\% . \tag{3.8}$$

Now if the national savings rate can somehow be increased from 6% to, say, 15%—through increased taxes, foreign aid, and/or general consumption sacrifices—GNP growth can be increased from 2% to 5% because now

$$\frac{\Delta Y}{Y} = \frac{s}{k} = \frac{15\%}{3} = 5\% . \tag{3.9}$$

In fact, Rostow and others defined the takeoff stage in precisely this way. Countries that were able to save 15% to 20% of GNP could grow ("develop") at a much faster rate than those that saved less. Moreover, this growth would then be self-sustaining. The tricks of economic growth and development, therefore, are simply a matter of increasing national savings and investment.

The main obstacle to or constraint on development, according to this theory, was the relatively low level of new capital formation in most poor countries. But if a country wanted to grow at, say, a rate of 7% per year and if it could not generate savings and investment at a rate of 21% of national income (assuming that k, the final aggregate capital-output ratio, is 3) but could only manage to save 15%, it could seek to fill this "savings gap" of 6% through either foreign aid or private foreign investment.

Thus the "capital constraint" stages approach to growth and development became a rationale and (in terms of cold war politics) an opportunistic tool for justifying massive transfers of capital and technical assistance from the developed to the less developed nations. It was to be the Marshall Plan all over again, but this time for the underdeveloped nations of the Third World!

Necessary versus Sufficient Conditions: Some Criticisms of the Stages Model

Unfortunately, the tricks of development embodied in the theory of stages of growth did not always work. And the basic reason they didn't work was not because more saving and investment isn't a **necessary condition** for accelerated rates of economic growth—it is—but rather because it is not a **sufficient condition**. Once again we have an example of what we discussed in Chapter 1: the inappropriateness of some of the implicit assumptions of Western economic theory for the actual conditions in Third World nations. The Marshall Plan worked for Europe because the European countries receiving aid possessed the necessary structural, institutional, and attitudinal conditions (e.g., well-integrated commodity and money markets, highly developed transport facilities, a well-trained and educated workforce, the motivation to succeed, an efficient government bureaucracy) to convert new capital effectively into higher levels of output. The Rostow and Harrod-Domar models implicitly assume the existence of these same attitudes and arrangements in underdeveloped nations. Yet in many cases they are lacking, as are complementary factors such as managerial competence, skilled labor, and the ability to plan and administer a wide assortment of development projects.

But at an even more fundamental level, the stages theory failed to take into account the crucial fact that contemporary Third World nations are part of a highly integrated and complex international system in which even the best and most intelligent development strategies can be nullified by external forces beyond the countries' control. One simply cannot claim, as many economists did in the 1950s and 1960s, that development is merely a matter of removing obstacles and supplying various missing components like capital, foreign-exchange, skills, and management—tasks in which the developed countries could theoretically play a major role. It was because of numerous failures and growing disenchantment with this strictly economic theory of development that a radially different approach was championed primarily by Third World intellectuals, one that attempted to combine economic and institutional factors into a social systems model of international development and underdevelopment. This is the international dependence paradigm, which we will review shortly. But first we examine two prominent examples of what emerged as mainstream Western theories of development during the 1970s: the theoretical and empirical models of structural change.

Structural–Change Models

Structural-change theory focuses on the mechanism by which underdeveloped economies transform their domestic economic structures from a heavy emphasis on traditional subsistence agriculture to a more modern, more urbanized, and more industrially diverse manufacturing and service economy. It employs the tools of neoclassical price and resource allocation theory and modern econometrics to describe how this transformation process takes place. Two well-known representative examples of the structural-change approach are the "two-sector surplus labor" theoretical model of W. Arthur Lewis and the "patterns of development" empirical analysis of Hollis B. Chenery.

The Lewis Theory of Development

Basic Model

One of the best-known early theoretical models of development that focused on the **structural transformation** of a primarily subsistence economy was that formulated by Nobel laureate W. Arthur Lewis in the mid-1950s and later modified, formalized, and extended by John Fei and Gustav Ranis.[3] The **Lewis two-sector model** became the general theory of the development process in surplus-labor Third World nations during most of the 1960s and early 1970s. It still has many adherents today, especially among American development economists.

In the Lewis model, the underdeveloped economy consists of two sectors: a traditional, overpopulated rural subsistence sector characterized by zero marginal labor productivity—a situation that permits Lewis to classify this as **surplus labor** in the sense that it can be withdrawn from the agricultural sector without any loss of output—and a high-productivity modern urban industrial sector into which labor from the subsistence sector is gradually transferred. The primary focus of the model is on both the process of labor transfer and the growth of output and employment in the modern sector. Both labor transfer and modern-sector employment growth are brought about by output expansion in that sector. The speed with which this expansion occurs is determined by the rate of industrial investment and capital accumulation in the modern sector. Such investment is made possible by the excess of modern-sector profits over wages on the assumption that capitalists reinvest all their profits. Finally, the level of wages in the urban industrial sector is assumed to be constant and determined as a given premium over a fixed average subsistence level of wages in the traditional agricultural sector. (Lewis assumed that urban wages would have to be at least 30% higher than average rural income to induce workers to migrate from their home areas.) At the constant urban wage, the supply curve of rural labor to the modern sector is considered to be perfectly elastic.

We can illustrate the Lewis model of modern-sector growth in a two-sector economy by using Figure 3.1. Consider first the traditional agricultural sector portrayed in the two right-side diagrams of Figure 3.1b. The upper diagram shows how subsistence food production varies with increases in labor inputs. It is a typical agricultural **production function** where the total output or product (TP_A) of food is determined by changes in the amount of the only variable input, labor (L_A), given a fixed quantity of capital, $\bar{K}_A$, and unchanging traditional technology, $\bar{t}_A$. In the lower right diagram, we have the **average** and **marginal product** of labor curves, AP_{LA} and MP_{LA}, which are derived from the total product curve shown immediately above. The quantity of agricultural labor (Q_{LA}) available is the same on both horizontal axes and is expressed in millions of workers, as Lewis is describing an underdeveloped economy where 80% to 90% of the population lives and works in rural areas.

Lewis makes two assumptions about the traditional sector. First, there is surplus labor in the sense that MP_{LA} is zero, and second, all rural workers share *equally* in the output so that the rural real wage is determined by the *average* and not the marginal product of labor (as will be the case in the modern sector). Assume that there are L_A agricultural workers producing TP_A food, which is shared equally as W_A food per person (this is the average product, which is equal to TP_A/L_A). The marginal product of these L_A workers is zero, as shown in the bottom diagram of Figure 3.1b; hence the surplus-labor assumption.

The upper-left diagram of Figure 3.1a portrays the total product (production function) curves for the modern, industrial sector. Once again, output of, say,

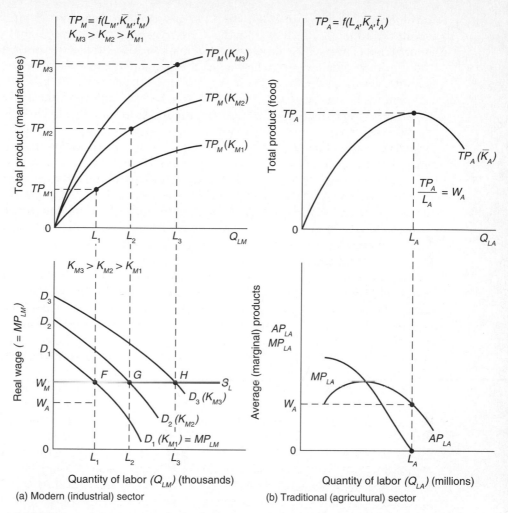

FIGURE 3.1 The Lewis Model of Modern-Sector Growth in a Two-Sector Surplus-Labor Economy.

manufactured goods (TP_M) is a function of a variable labor input, L_M, for a given capital stock $\bar{K}_M$ and technology $\bar{t}_M$. On the horizontal axes, the quantity of labor employed to produce an output of, say, TP_{M1}, with capital stock K_{M1} is expressed in thousands of urban workers, L_1. In the Lewis model, the modern-sector capital stock is allowed to increase from K_{M1} to K_{M2} to K_{M3} as a result of the reinvestment of profits by capitalist industrialists. This will cause the total product curves in Figure 3.1a to shift upward from $TP_M(K_{M1})$ to $TP_M(K_{M2})$ to $TP_M(K_{M3})$. The process that will generate these capitalist profits for reinvestment and growth is illustrated in the lower-left diagram of Figure 3.1a. Here we have modern-sector marginal labor product curves derived from the TP_M curves of the upper diagram. Under the assumption of perfectly competitive labor markets in the modern sector, these marginal product of labor curves are in fact the actual demand curves for labor. Here is how the system works.

W_A in the lower diagrams of Figures 3.1a and 3.1b represents the average level of real subsistence income in the traditional rural sector. W_M in Figure 3.1a is therefore the real wage in the modern capitalist sector. At this wage, the supply of rural labor is assumed to be unlimited or perfectly elastic, as shown by the horizontal labor supply curve $W_M S_L$. In other words, Lewis assumes that at urban wage W_M above rural average income W_A, modern-sector employers can hire as many surplus rural workers as they want without fear of rising wages. (Note again that the quantity of labor in the rural sector, Figure 3.1b, is expressed in millions whereas in the modern urban sector, Figure 3.1a, units of labor are expressed in thousands.) Given a fixed supply of capital K_{M1} in the initial stage of modern-sector growth, the demand curve for labor is determined by labor's declining marginal product and is shown by the negatively sloped curve $D_1(K_{M1})$ in the lower-left diagram. Because profit-maximizing modern-sector employers are assumed to hire laborers to the point where their marginal physical product is equal to the real wage (i.e., the point F of intersection between the labor demand and supply curves), total modern-sector employment will be equal to L_1. Total modern-sector output, TP_{M1}, would be given by the area bounded by points OD_1FL_1. The share of this total output paid to workers in the form of wages would be equal, therefore, to the area of the rectangle OW_MFL_1. The balance of the output shown by the area W_MD_1F would be the total profits that accrue to the capitalists. Because Lewis assumes that all of these profits are reinvested, the total capital stock in the modern sector will rise from K_{M1} to K_{M2}. This larger capital stock causes the total product curve of the modern sector to rise to $TP_M(K_{M2})$, which in turn induces a rise in the marginal product demand curve for labor. This outward shift in the labor demand curve is shown by line $D_2(K_{M2})$ in the bottom half of Figure 3.1a. A new equilibrium modern-sector employment level will be established at point G with L_2 workers now employed. Total output rises to TP_{M2} or OD_2GL_2 while total wages and profits increase to OW_MGL_2 and W_MD_2G, respectively. Once again, these larger (W_MD_2G) profits are reinvested, increasing the total capital stock to K_{M3}, shifting the total product and labor demand curves to $TP_M(K_{M3})$ and to $D_3(K_{M3})$, respectively, and raising the level of modern-sector employment to L_3.

This process of modern-sector **self-sustaining growth** and employment expansion is assumed to continue until all surplus rural labor is absorbed in the new industrial sector. Thereafter, additional workers can be withdrawn from the agricultural sector only at a higher cost of lost food production because the declining labor-to-land ratio means that the marginal product of rural labor is no longer zero. Thus the labor supply curve becomes positively sloped as modern-sector wages and employment continue to grow. The structural transformation of the economy will have taken place, with the balance of economic activity shifting from traditional rural agriculture to modern urban industry.

Criticisms of the Lewis Model

Although the Lewis two-sector development model is both simple and roughly in conformity with the historical experience of economic growth in the West, three of its key assumptions do not fit the institutional and economic realities of most contemporary Third World countries.

First, the model implicitly assumes that the rate of labor transfer and employment creation in the modern sector is proportional to the rate of modern-sector capital accumulation. The faster the rate of capital accumulation, the higher the growth rate of the modern sector and the faster the rate of new job creation. But what if capitalist profits are reinvested in more sophisticated laborsaving capital equipment rather than just duplicating the existing capital as is implicitly assumed in the Lewis model? (We are, of course, here accepting the debatable assumption that capitalist profits are in fact reinvested in the local economy and not sent abroad as a form of "capital flight" to be added to the deposits of Western banks!) Figure 3.2 reproduces the lower, modern-sector diagram of Figure 3.1a, only this time the labor demand curves do not shift uniformly outward but in fact cross. Demand curve $D_2(K_{M2})$ has a greater negative slope than $D_1(K_{M1})$ to reflect the fact that additions to the capital stock embody laborsaving technical progress—that is, K_{M2} technology requires much less labor per unit of output than K_{M1} technology does.

We see that even though total output has grown substantially (i.e., OD_2EL_1 is significantly greater than OD_1EL_1), total wages (OW_MEL_1) and employment (L_1) remain unchanged. All of the extra output accrues to capitalists in the form of excess profits. Figure 3.2 therefore provides an illustration of what some might call "antidevelopmental" economic growth—*all* the extra income and output growth are distributed to the few owners of capital, while income and employment levels for the masses of workers remain largely unchanged. Although total GNP would rise, there would be little or no improvement in aggregate social welfare measured, say, in terms of more widely distributed gains in income and employment.

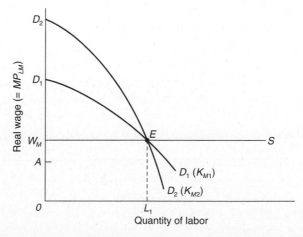

FIGURE 3.2 The Lewis Model Modified by Laborsaving Capital Accumulation: Employment Implications.

The second questionable assumption of the Lewis model is the notion that surplus labor exists in rural areas while there is full employment in the urban areas. As we will discover in Chapters 7 and 8, most contemporary research indicates that the reverse is more likely true in many Third World countries—there is substantial unemployment in urban areas but little general surplus labor in rural locations. True, there are both seasonal and geographic exceptions to this rule (e.g., parts of the Asian subcontinent and isolated regions of Latin America where land ownership is very unequal), but by and large, development economists today agree that the assumption of urban surplus labor is empirically more valid than Lewis's assumption of rural surplus labor.

The third unreal assumption is the notion of a competitive modern-sector labor market that guarantees the continued existence of constant real urban wages up to the point where the supply of rural surplus labor is exhausted. It will be demonstrated in Chapter 8 that prior to the 1980s, a striking feature of urban labor markets and wage determination in almost all developing countries was the tendency for these wages to rise substantially over time, both in absolute terms and relative to average rural incomes, even in the presence of rising levels of open modern-sector unemployment and low or zero marginal productivity in agriculture. Institutional factors such as union bargaining power, civil service wage scales, and multinational corporations' hiring practices tend to negate whatever competitive forces might exist in Third World modern-sector labor markets.

We conclude, therefore, that when one takes into account the laborsaving bias of most modern technological transfer, the existence of substantial capital flight, the widespread nonexistence of rural surplus labor, the growing prevalence of urban surplus labor, and the tendency for modern-sector wages to rise rapidly even where substantial open unemployment exists, the Lewis two-sector model—though extremely valuable as an early conceptual portrayal of the development process of sectoral interaction and structural change—requires considerable modification in assumptions and analysis to fit the reality of contemporary Third World nations.

Structural Change and Patterns of Development

Like the earlier Lewis model, the **patterns-of-development analysis** of structural change focuses on the sequential process through which the economic, industrial, and institutional structure of an underdeveloped economy is transformed over time to permit new industries to replace traditional agriculture as the engine of economic growth. However, in contrast to the Lewis model and the original stages view of development, increased savings and investment are perceived by patterns-of-development analysts as necessary but not sufficient conditions for economic growth. In addition to the accumulation of capital, both physical and human, a set of interrelated changes in the economic structure of a country are required for the transition from a traditional economic system to a modern one. These structural changes involve virtually all economic functions, including the transformation of production and changes in the composition of consumer demand, international trade, and resource use as well as changes in socioeconomic factors such as urbanization and the growth and distribution of a country's population.

Empirical structural-change analysts emphasize both domestic and international constraints on development. The domestic ones include economic constraints such as a country's resource endowment and its physical and population size as well as institutional constraints such as government policies and objectives. International constraints on development include access to external capital, technology, and international trade. Differences in development level among developing countries are largely ascribed to these domestic and international constraints. However, it is the international constraints that make the transition of currently developing countries differ from that of now industrialized countries. To the extent that developing countries have access to the opportunities presented by the industrial countries as sources of capital, technology, and manufactured imports as well as markets for exports, they can make the transition at an even faster rate than that achieved by the industrial countries during the early periods of their economic development. Thus, unlike the earlier stages model, the structural-change model recognizes the fact that developing countries are part of a highly integrated international system that can promote (as well as hinder) their development.

The best-known model of structural change is the one based largely on the empirical work of Harvard economist Hollis B. Chenery, who examined patterns of development for numerous Third World countries during the postwar period.[4] His empirical studies, both cross-sectional (among countries at a given point in time) and time-series (over long periods of time), of countries at different levels of per capita income led to the identification of several characteristic features of the development process. These included the shift from agricultural to industrial production, the steady accumulation of physical and human capital, the change in consumer demands from emphasis on food and basic necessities to desires for diverse manufactured goods and services, the growth of cities and urban industries as people migrate from farms and small towns, and the decline in family size and overall population growth as children lose their economic value and parents substitute child quality (education) for quantity (see Chapter 6).

Conclusions and Implications

The structural changes that we have described are the "average" patterns of development Chenery and colleagues observed among countries in time-series and cross-sectional analyses. The major hypothesis of the structural-change model is that development is an identifiable process of growth and change whose main features are similar in all countries. However, as mentioned earlier, the model does recognize that differences can arise among countries in pace and pattern of development, depending on their particular set of circumstances. Factors influencing the development process include a country's resource endowment and size, its government's policies and objectives, the availability of external capital and technology, and the international trade environment.

In short, empirical studies on the process of structural change lead to the conclusion that the pace and pattern of development can vary according to both domestic and international factors, many of which lie beyond the control of an individual developing nation. Yet despite this variation, structural-change economists argue that one can identify certain patterns occurring in almost all countries during the development process. And these patterns, they argue, may be affected by the choice of development policies pursued by LDC governments as well as the international trade and foreign-assistance policies of developed nations. Hence structural-change analysts are basically optimistic that the "correct" mix of economic policies will generate beneficial patterns of self-sustaining growth. The international-dependence school, in contrast, is much less sanguine and is in many cases downright pessimistic. Proponents argue that not only are the statistical averages that structural-change economists calculate from a diverse range of rich and poor countries of limited practical value in identifying the critical factors in a particular nation's development process, but more important, they divert attention from the real factors in the global economy that maintain and perpetuate the poverty of Third World nations. Let's now see what this dependence theory is all about.

The International–Dependence Revolution

During the 1970s, international-dependence models gained increasing support, especially among Third World intellectuals, as a result of growing disenchantment with both the stages and structural-change models. Essentially, international-dependence models view Third World countries as beset by institutional, political, and economic rigidities, both domestic and international, and caught up in a **dependence** and **dominance** relationship with rich countries. Within this general approach are three major streams of thought: the neocolonial dependence model, the false-paradigm model, and the dualistic-development thesis.

The Neocolonial Dependence Model

The first major stream, which we call the **neocolonial dependence model**, is an indirect outgrowth of Marxist thinking. It attributes the existence and continuance of Third World underdevelopment primarily to the historical evolution of a highly unequal international capitalist system of rich country-poor country relationships. Whether because rich nations are intentionally exploitative or unintentionally neglectful, the coexistence of rich and poor nations in an international system dominated by such unequal power relationships between the **center** (the developed countries) and the **periphery** (the LDCs) renders attempts by poor nations to be self-reliant and independent difficult and sometimes even impossible.[5] Certain groups in the developing countries (including landlords, entrepreneurs, military rulers, merchants, salaried public officials, and trade union leaders) who enjoy high incomes, social status, and political power constitute a small elite ruling class whose principal interest, knowingly or not, is in the perpetuation of the international capitalist system of inequality and conformity by which they are rewarded. Directly and indirectly, they serve (are dominated by) and are rewarded by (are dependent on) international special-interest power groups including multinational corporations, national bilateral-aid agencies, and multilateral assistance organizations like the World Bank or the International Monetary Fund (IMF), which are tied by allegiance or funding to the wealthy capitalist countries. The elites' activities and viewpoints often serve to inhibit any genuine reform efforts that might benefit the wider population and in some cases actually lead to even lower levels of living and to the perpetuation of **underdevelopment**. In short, the neo-Marxist, neocolonial view of underdevelopment attributes a large part of the Third World's continuing and worsening poverty to the existence and policies of the industrial capitalist countries of the Northern Hemisphere and their extensions in the form of small but powerful elite or *comprador* **groups** in the less developed countries.[6] Underdevelopment is thus seen as an *externally* induced phenomenon, in contrast to the linear-stages and structural-change theories' stress on *internal* constraints such as insufficient savings and investment or lack of education and skills. Revolutionary struggles or at least major restructurings of the world capitalist system are therefore required to free dependent Third World nations from the direct and indirect economic control of their First World and domestic oppressors.

One of the most forceful statements of the international-dependence school of thought was made by Theotonio Dos Santos:

> Underdevelopment, far from constituting a state of backwardness prior to capitalism, is rather a consequence and a particular form of capitalist development known as dependent capitalism.... Dependence is a conditioning situation in which the economies of one group of countries are conditioned by the development and expansion of others. A relationship of interdependence between two or more economies or between such economies and the world trading system becomes a dependent relationship when some countries can expand through self-impulsion while others, being in a dependent position, can only expand as a reflection of the expansion of the dominant countries, which may have positive or negative effects on their immediate development. In either case, the basic situation of dependence causes these countries to be both backward and exploited. Dominant countries are endowed with technological, commercial, capital and socio-political predominance over dependent countries—the form of this predominance varying according to the particular historical moment— and can therefore exploit them, and extract part of the locally produced surplus. Dependence, then, is based upon an international division of labor which allows industrial development to take place in some countries while restricting it in others, whose growth is conditioned by and subjected to the power centers of the world.[7]

Curiously, a very similar but obviously non-Marxist perspective was expounded by Pope John Paul II in his widely quoted 1988 encyclical letter (a formal, elaborate expression of papal teaching) *Sollicitude rei socialis* (The Social Concerns of the Church), in which he declared:

> One must denounce the existence of economic, financial, and social mechanisms which, although they are manipulated by people, often function almost automatically, thus accentuating the situation of wealth for some and

poverty for the rest. These mechanisms, which are manuevered directly or indirectly by the more developed countries, by their very functioning, favor the interests of the people manipulating them. But in the end they suffocate or condition the economies of the less developed countries.

Various components of the neocolonial dependence argument will be explored in greater detail when we discuss problems of poverty, income distribution, unemployment, international trade, and foreign assistance in Parts Two and Three.

The False–Paradigm Model

A second and a less radical international-dependence approach to development, which we might call the **false-paradigm model**, attributes Third World underdevelopment to faulty and inappropriate advice provided by well-meaning but often uninformed, biased, and ethnocentric international "expert" advisers from developed-country assistance agencies and multinational donor organizations. These experts offer sophisticated concepts, elegant theoretical structures, and complex econometric models of development that often lead to inappropriate or incorrect policies. Because of institutional factors such as the central and remarkably resilient role of traditional social structures (tribe, caste, class, etc.), the highly unequal ownership of land and other property rights, the disproportionate control by local elites over domestic and international financial assets, and the very unequal access to credit, these policies, based as they often are on mainstream, Lewis-type surplus-labor or Chenery-type structural-change models, in many cases merely serve the vested interests of existing power groups, both domestic and international.

In addition, according to this argument, leading university intellectuals, trade unionists, future high-level government economists, and other civil servants all get their training in developed-country institutions where they are unwittingly served an unhealthy dose of alien concepts and elegant but inapplicable theoretical models. Having little or no really useful knowledge to enable them to come to grips in an effective way with real development problems, they often tend to become unknowing or reluctant apologists for the existing system of elitist policies and institutional structures. In university economics courses, for example, this typically entails the perpetuation of the teaching of many irrelevant Western concepts and models, while in government policy discussions too much emphasis is placed on attempts to measure capital-output ratios, to increase savings and investment ratios, or to maximize GNP growth rates. As a result, desirable institutional and structural reforms, many of which we have discussed, are neglected or given only cursory attention.

The Dualistic–Development Thesis

Implicit in structural-change theories and explicit in international-dependence theories is the notion of a world of dual societies, of rich nations and poor nations and, in the developing countries, pockets of wealth within broad areas of poverty. **Dualism** is a concept widely discussed in development economics. It represents the existence and persistence of increasing divergences between rich and poor nations and rich and poor peoples on various levels. Specifically, the concept of dualism embraces four key elements:[8]

1. Different sets of conditions, of which some are "superior" and others "inferior," can coexist in a given space. Examples of this element of dualism include Lewis's notion of the coexistence of modern and traditional methods of production in urban and rural sectors; the coexistence of wealthy, highly educated elites with masses of illiterate poor people; and the dependence notion of the coexistence of powerful and wealthy industrialized nations with weak, impoverished peasant societies in the international economy.

2. This coexistence is chronic and not merely transitional. It is not due to a temporary phenomenon, in which case time could eliminate the discrepancy between superior and inferior elements. In other words, the international coexistence of wealth and poverty is not simply a historical phenomenon that will be rectified in time. Although both the stages-of-growth theory and the structural-change models implicity make such an assumption, the facts of growing international inequalities seem to refute it.

3. Not only do the degrees of superiority or inferiority fail to show any signs of diminishing, but they even have an inherent tendency to increase. For example, the productivity gap between workers in developed countries and their counterparts in most LDCs seems to widen with each passing year.

4. The interrelations between the superior and inferior elements are such that the existence of the superior elements does little or nothing to pull up the inferior element, let alone "trickle down" to it. In fact, it may actually serve to push it down—to "develop its underdevelopment."

Conclusions and Implications

Whatever their ideological differences, the advocates of the neocolonial-dependence, false-paradigm, and dualism models reject the exclusive emphasis on traditional Western economic theories designed to accelerate the growth of GNP as the principal index of development. They question the validity of Lewis-type two-sector models of modernization and industrialization in light of their questionable assumptions and recent Third World history. They further reject the claims made by Chenery and others that there exist well-defined empirical patterns of development that should be pursued by most poor countries on the periphery of the world economy. Instead, dependence, false-paradigm, and dualism theorists place more emphasis on international power imbalances and on needed fundamental economic, political, and institutional reforms, both domestic and worldwide. In extreme cases, they call for the outright expropriation of privately owned assets in the expectation that public asset ownership and control will be a more effective means to help eradicate absolute poverty, provide expanded employment opportunities, lessen income inequalities, and raise the levels of living (including health, education, and cultural enrichment) of the masses. Although a few radical neo-Marxists would even go so far as to say that economic growth and structural change do not matter, the majority of thoughtful observers recognize that the most effective way to deal with these diverse social problems is to accelerate the pace of economic growth through domestic and international reforms accompanied by a judicious mixture of both public and private economic activity.

Dependence theories have two major weaknesses. First, although they offer an appealing explanation of why many Third World countries remain underdeveloped, they offer little formal or informal explanation of how countries initiate and sustain development. Second, and perhaps more important, the actual economic experience of LDCs that have pursued revolutionary campaigns of industrial nationalization and state-run production has been mostly negative. As we shall discover in later chapters, governments can fail as well as markets; the key to successful development performance is achieving a careful balance among what government can successfully accomplish, what the private market system can do, and what both can best do together.

At the same time in the 1970s that the international dependence revolution in development theory was capturing the imagination of many Western and Third World scholars, a neoclassical free-market counterrevolution was beginning to emerge, ultimately to dominate Western (and, to a lesser extent, Third World) development writings during the 1980s and 1990s.

The Neoclassical Counterrevolution

Challenging the Statist Model: Free Markets, Public Choice, and Market-friendly Approaches

In the 1980s, the political ascendancy of conservative governments in the United States, Canada, Britain, and West Germany brought with it a **neoclassical counterrevolution** in economic theory and policy. In more developed nations, this counterrevolution favored supply-side macroeconomic policies, rational expectations theories, and the privatization of public corporations. In developing countries it called for freer markets and the dismantling of public ownership, statist planning, and government regulation of economic activities. Neoclassicists obtained controlling votes on the boards of the world's two most powerful international financial agencies—the World Bank and the International Monetary Fund. In conjunction and with the simultaneous erosion of influence of organizations such as the International Labor Organization (ILO), the United Nations Development Program (UNDP), and the United Nations Conference on Trade and Development (UNCTAD), which more fully represent the views of Third World delegates, it was inevitable that the neoconservative, free-market challenge to the interventionist arguments of dependence theorists would gather momentum.

The central argument of the neoclassical counterrevolution is that underdevelopment results from poor resource allocation due to incorrect pricing policies and too much state intervention by overly active Third World governments. Rather, the leading writers of the counterrevolution school, including Lord Peter Bauer, Deepak Lal, Ian Little, Harry Johnson, Bela Balassa, Julian Simon, Jagdish Bhagwati, and Anne Krueger, argue that it is this very state intervention in economic activity that slows the pace of economic growth. The neoconservatives argue that by permitting competitive **free markets** to flourish, privatizing state-owned enterprises, promoting free trade and export expansion, welcoming investors from developed countries, and eliminating the plethora of government regulations and price distortions in factor, product, and financial markets, both economic efficiency and economic growth will be stimulated. Contrary to the claims of the dependence theorists, the neoclassical counterrevolutionaries argue that the Third World (many don't even accept this terminology) is underdeveloped not because of the predatory activities of the First World and the international agencies that it controls but rather because of the heavy hand of the state and the corruption, inefficiency, and lack of economic incentives that permeate the economies of developing nations. What is needed, therefore, is not a reform of the international economic system, a restructuring of dualistic developing economies, an increase in foreign aid, attempts to control population growth, or a more effective central planning system. Rather, it is simply a matter of promoting free markets and laissez-faire economics within the context of permissive governments that allow the "magic of the marketplace" and the "invisible hand" of market prices to guide resource allocation and stimulate economic development. They point both to the success of countries like South Korea, Taiwan, Hong Kong, and Singapore as "free market" examples (although, as we shall see later, these Asian tigers are far from the laissez-faire prototype ascribed to them by neoconservatives) and to the failures of the public-interventionist economies of Africa and Latin America.[9]

The neoclassical challenge to the prevailing development orthodoxy can be divided into three component approaches: the free-market approach, the public-choice (or "new political economy") approach, and the "market-friendly" approach. **Free-market analysis** argues that markets alone are efficient—product markets provide the best signals for investments in new activities; labor markets respond to these new industries in appropriate ways; producers know best what to produce and how to produce it efficiently; and product and factor prices reflect accurate scarcity values of goods and resources now and in the future. Competition is effective, if not perfect; technology is freely available and costless to absorb; information is also perfect and costless to obtain. Under these circumstances, any government intervention in the economy is by definition distortionary and counterproductive. Free-market development economists have tended to assume that Third World markets are efficient and that whatever imperfections exist are of little consequence.

Public-choice theory, also known as the **new political economy approach**, goes even further to argue that governments can do nothing right. This is because public-choice theory assumes that politicians, bureaucrats, citizens, and states act solely from a self-interested perspective, using their power and the authority of government for their own selfish ends. Citizens use political influence to obtain special benefits (called "rents") from government policies (e.g., import licenses or rationed foreign exchange) that restrict access to important resources. Politicians use government resources to consolidate and maintain positions of power and authority. Bureaucrats and public officials use their positions to extract bribes from rent-seeking citizens and to operate protected businesses on the side. Finally, states use their power to confiscate private property from individuals. The net result is not only a misallocation of resources but also a general reduction in individual freedoms. The conclusion, therefore, is that minimal government is the best government.[10]

The **market-friendly approach** is the most recent variant on the neoclassical counterrevolution. It is associated principally with the writings of the World Bank and its economists, many of whom were more in the free-market and public-choice camps during the 1980s.[11] This approach recognizes that there are many imperfections in Third World product and factor markets and that governments do have a key role to play in facilitating the operation of markets through "nonselective" (market-friendly) interventions—for example, by investing in physical and social infrastructure, health care facilities, and educational institutions and by providing a suitable climate for private enterprise. The market-friendly approach also differs from the free-market and public-choice schools of thought by accepting the notion that market failures are more widespread in developing countries in areas such as investment coordination and environmental outcomes. Moreover, phenomena such as missing and incomplete information, externalities in skill creation and learning, and economies of scale in production are also endemic to LDC markets. In fact it is the recognition of these last three phenomena that gives rise to the newest school of development theory, the *new* or *endogenous growth* school of thought, to which we turn shortly.

Traditional ("Old") Neoclassical Growth Theory

Another cornerstone of the neoclassical free-market argument is the assertion that liberalization (opening up) of national markets draws additional domestic and foreign investment and thus increases the rate of capital accumulation. In terms of GNP growth, this is equivalent to raising domestic savings rates, which enhances **capital-labor ratios** and per capita incomes in capital-poor developing countries. Traditional neoclassical models of growth are a direct outgrowth of the Harrod-Domar and Solow[12] models, which both stress the importance of savings.

The **Solow neoclassical growth model** in particular represented the seminal contribution to the neoclassical theory of growth and later earned Solow the Nobel Prize in economics. It expanded on the Harrod-Domar formulation by adding a second factor, labor, and introducing a third independent variable, technology, to the growth equation. Unlike the fixed-coefficient, constant-returns-to-scale assumption of the Harrod-Domar model, Solow's neoclassical growth model exhibited diminishing returns to labor and capital separately and constant returns to both factors jointly. Technological progress became the residual factor explaining long-term growth, and its level was assumed by Solow and other growth theorists to be determined exogenously, that is, independently of all other factors.

More formally, the Solow neoclassical growth model used the standard aggregate production function (similar to the Lewis modern-sector equation) in which $Y = Ae^{\mu t} K^{\alpha} L^{1-\alpha}$, where Y is gross domestic product, K is the stock of human and physical capital, L is unskilled labor, A is a constant that reflects the base level of technology, and $e^{\mu t}$ reflects the constant exogenous rate at which technology grows. Thus α represents the elasticity of output with respect to capital (the percentage increase in GDP resulting from a 1% increase in human and physical capital). It is usually measured statistically as the share of capital in a country's national income accounts. Since α is assumed to be less than 1 and private capital is assumed to be paid its marginal product so that there are no external economies, this formulation of neoclassical growth theory yields diminishing returns to capital and labor.

According to **traditional (old) neoclassical growth theory**, output growth results from one or more of three factors: increases in labor quantity and quality (through population growth and education), increases in capital (through saving and investment), and improvements in technology (see Chapter 4). **Closed economies** (those with no external activities) with lower savings rates (other things being equal) grow more slowly in the short run than those with high savings rates and tend to converge to lower per capita income levels. **Open economies** (those with trade, foreign investment, etc.), however, experience income convergence at higher levels as capital flows from rich countries to poor countries where capital-labor ratios are lower and thus returns on investments are higher. Consequently, by impeding the inflow of foreign investment, the heavy-handedness of LDC governments, according to neoclassical growth theory, will retard growth in the economies of the Third World.

Conclusions and Implications

Like the dependence revolution of the 1970s, the neoclassical counterrevolution of the 1980s had its origin in an economics cum ideological view of the Third World and its problems. Whereas dependence theorists (many, but certainly not all, of whom were Third World economists) saw underdevelopment as an externally induced phenomenon, neoclassical revisionists (most, but certainly not all, of whom were Western economists) saw the problem as an internally induced LDC phenomenon, one of too much government intervention and bad economic policies. Such finger-pointing on both sides is not uncommon in issues so contentious as those that divide rich and poor nations.

But what of the neoclassical counterrevolution's contention that free markets and less government provide the basic ingredients for Third World development? On strictly efficiency (as opposed to equity) criteria, there can be little doubt that market price allocation usually does a better job than state intervention. The problem is that many Third World economies are so different in structure and organization from their Western counterparts that the behavioral assumptions and policy precepts of traditional neoclassical theory are sometimes questionable and often incorrect. Competitive markets simply do not exist, nor, given the institutional, cultural, and historical context of many LDCs, would they necessarily be desirable from a long-term economic and social perspective (see Chapter 16). Consumers as a whole are rarely sovereign about anything, let alone about what goods and services are to be produced, in what quantities, and for whom. Information is limited, markets are fragmented, and much of the economy is still nonmonetized.[13] There are widespread externalities of both production and consumption as well as discontinuities in production and indivisibilities (i.e., economies of scale) in technology. Producers, private or public, have great power in determining market prices and quantities sold. The ideal of competition is typically just that—an ideal with little relation to reality. Instead of the equilibrium, automatic-adjustment framework of neoclassical theory, many LDC markets are better analyzed through disequilibrium, structural-adjustment models in which responses to price and wage movements can be "perverse" (not in the direction predicted by traditional free-market models; see Chapters 8, 9, and 13). Although monopolies of resource purchase and product sale are a pervasive Third World phenomenon, the traditional neoclassical theory of monopoly also offers little insight into the day-to-day activities of public and private corporations. Decision rules can vary widely with the social setting, so that profit maximization may be a low-priority objective in comparison with, say, the creation of jobs or the replacement of foreign managers with local personnel (see Chapter 17). Finally, the invisible hand often acts not to promote the general welfare but rather to lift up those who are already well-off while pushing down the vast majority.

Much can be learned from neoclassical theory with regard to the importance of elementary supply-and-demand analysis in arriving at "correct" product, factor, and foreign-exchange prices for efficient production and resource allocation. However, do not confuse free markets with price allocation. Enlightened governments can also make effective use of prices as signals and incentives for influencing socially optimal resource allocations. Indeed, we will often demonstrate the usefulness of various tools of neoclassical theory in our later analysis of problems such as population growth, agricultural stagnation, unemployment and underemployment, the environment, educational demands, export promotion versus import substitution, devaluation, project planning, monetary policy, and economic privatization. Nevertheless, the reality of the institutional and political structure of many Third World economies—not to mention their differing value systems and ideologies—often makes the attainment of appropriate economic policies based either on markets or enlightened public intervention an exceedingly difficult endeavor. In an environment of widespread institutional rigidity and severe socioeconomic inequality, *both* markets and governments will typically fail. It is not simply an either-or question based on ideological leaning; rather it is a matter of assessing each individual country's situation on a case-by-case basis. Development economists must therefore be able to distinguish between textbook neoclassical theory and the institutional and political reality of contemporary LDCs.[14] They can then choose the neoclassical concepts and models that can best illuminate issues and dilemmas of Third World development and discard those that cannot. This will be our task in Parts Two, Three, and Four.

Let us now turn to our final topic in this chapter, the recent emergence of a fifth approach to analyzing development.

The New Growth Theory

Motivation for the New Growth Theory

The poor performance of neoclassical theories in illuminating the sources of long-term economic growth has led to a general dissatisfaction with traditional theory. In fact, according to traditional theory, there is no intrinsic characteristic of economies that causes them to grow over extended periods of time. The literature is instead concerned with the dynamic process through which capital-labor ratios approach long-run equilibrium levels. In the absence of external "shocks" or technological change, all economies will converge to zero growth. Hence rising per capita GNP is considered a temporary phenomenon resulting from a change in technology or a short-term equilibrating process in which an economy approaches its long-run equilibrium. Unsurprisingly, this body of theory fails to provide a satisfactory explanation for the remarkably consistent pace of historical growth in economies around the globe (see Chapter 4).

Any increases in GNP that cannot be attributed to short-term adjustments in stocks of either labor or capital are ascribed to a third category, commonly referred to as the **Solow residual**. This residual, despite its name, is responsible for roughly 50% of historical growth in the industrialized nations.[15] In a rather ad hoc manner, neoclassical theory credits the bulk of economic growth to an exogenous or completely independent process of technological progress. Though intuitively plausible, this approach has at least two insurmountable drawbacks. First, using the neoclassical framework, it is impossible to analyze the determinants of technological advance because it is completely independent of the decisions of economic agents. And second, the theory fails to explain large differences in residuals across countries with similar technologies. In other words, a great deal of faith has been placed in a poorly understood external process for which there is little theoretical or empirical support.

Disenchantment with traditional neoclassical models of economic growth intensified during the late 1980s and early 1990s as the Third World debt crisis escalated and it became increasingly clear that traditional theory was at a loss to explain the dramatic disparities in economic performance across countries. According to neoclassical theory, the low capital-labor ratios of Third World countries promise exceptionally high rates of return on investment. The free-market reforms imposed on highly indebted countries by the World Bank and the International Monetary Fund should thus have prompted higher investment, rising productivity, and improved standards of living. Yet even after the prescribed liberalization of trade and domestic markets, many LDCs experienced little or no growth and failed to attract new foreign investment or to halt the flight of domestic capital. The anomalous behavior of Third World capital flows (from poor to rich nations) helped provide the impetus for the development of the newest approach to the economics of growth and development: the concept of **endogenous growth** or, more simply, the **new growth theory**. Though still eclectic and not quite as fully developed as the four earlier approaches, the new growth theory represents a key component of the emerging development theory.[16]

Endogenous Growth

The new growth theory provides a theoretical framework for analyzing endogenous growth, persistent GNP growth that is determined by the system governing the production process rather than by forces outside that system. In contrast to traditional neoclassical theory, these models hold GNP growth to be a natural consequence of long-run equilibrium. The principal motivations of the new growth theory are to explain both growth rate differentials across countries and a greater proportion of the growth observed. More succinctly, endogenous growth theorists seek to explain the factors that determine the size of μ, the rate of growth of GDP that is left unexplained and exogenously determined in the Solow neoclassical growth equation (i.e., the Solow residual).

Models of endogenous growth bear some structural resemblance to their neoclassical counterparts, but they differ considerably in their underlying assumptions and the conclusions drawn. The most significant theoretical differences stem from three factors: Models of endogenous growth discard the neoclassical assumption of diminishing marginal returns to capital investments, permit increasing returns to scale in aggregate production, and frequently focus on the role of externalities in determining the rate of return on capital investments.[17] By assuming that public and private investments in human capital generate external economies and productivity improvements that offset the natural tendency for diminishing returns, endogenous growth theory seeks to explain the existence of increasing returns to scale and the divergent long-term growth patterns among countries. And whereas technology still plays an important role in these models, it is no longer necessary to explain long-run growth.

A useful way to contrast the new (endogenous) growth theory with traditional (old) neoclassical theory is to recognize that many endogenous growth theories can be expressed by the simple equation $Y = AK$. In this formulation, A is intended to represent any factor that affects technology, and K again includes both physical and human capital. But notice that there are no diminishing returns to capital in this formula; so the possibility exists that investments in physical and human capital can generate external economies and productivity improvements that exceed private gains by an amount sufficient to offset diminishing returns. This in turn creates the further possibility that investments that generate these external economies cause α in the Solow equation to equal unity so that the neoclassical growth equation $Y = Ae^{\mu t}K^{\alpha}L^{1-\alpha}$ reduces to the endogenous growth equation $Y = Ae^{\mu t}K$. The net result is sustained long-term growth resulting from increasing returns to scale—an outcome prohibited by traditional neoclassical growth theory. Thus even though the new growth theory reemphasizes the importance of savings and human capital investments for achieving rapid growth in the Third World, it also leads to several implications for growth that are in direct conflict with traditional theory. First, there is no force leading to the equilibration of growth rates across closed economies; national growth rates remain constant and differ across countries depending on national savings rates and technology levels. Furthermore, there is no tendency for per capita income levels in capital-poor countries to catch up with those in rich countries with similar savings rates. A serious consequence of these facts is that a temporary or prolonged recession in one country leads to a permanent increase in the income gap between itself and wealthier countries.

But perhaps the most interesting aspect of endogenous growth models is that they help explain anomalous international flows of capital that exacerbate wealth disparities between the First World and Third World. The potentially high rates of return on investment offered by developing economies with low capital-labor ratios are greatly eroded by lower levels of **complementary investments** in human capital (education), infrastructure, or research and development (R&D).[18] In turn, poor countries benefit less from the broader social gains associated with each of these alternative forms of capital expenditure.[19] Because individuals receive no personal gain from the positive externalities created by their own investments, the free market leads to the accumulation of less than the optimal level of complementary capital.

Where complementary investments produce social as well as private benefits, governments may improve the efficiency of resource allocation. They can do this by providing public goods (infrastructure) or encouraging private investment in knowledge-intensive industries where human capital can be accumulated and subsequent increasing returns to scale generated. Unlike the Solow model, new growth theory models explain technological change as an endogenous outcome of public and private investments in human capital and knowledge-intensive industries. Thus in contrast to neoclassical counterrevolution theories, models of endogenous growth suggest an active role for public policy in promoting economic development through direct and indirect investments in human capital formation and the encouragement of foreign private investment in knowledge-intensive industries such as computer software and telecommunications. Though in many ways endogenous growth theory remains strongly rooted in the neoclassical tradition, it represents a departure from strict adherence to the dogma of free markets and passive governments.

Criticisms of the New Growth Theory

An important shortcoming of the new growth theory is that it remains dependent on a number of traditional neoclassical assumptions that are often inappropriate for Third World economies. Economic growth in developing countries is frequently impeded by inefficiencies arising from poor infrastructure, inadequate institutional structures, and imperfect capital and goods markets. Because endogenous growth theory overlooks these very influential factors, its applicability for the study of economic development is limited, especially when country-to-country comparisons are involved. For example, existing theory fails to explain low rates of factory capacity utilization in low-income countries where capital is scarce. In fact, poor incentive structures may be as responsible for sluggish GNP growth as low rates of saving and human capital accumulation. Allocational inefficiencies are common in economies undergoing the transition from traditional to commercialized markets. However, their impact on short- and medium-term growth has been neglected due to the new theory's overemphasis on the determinants of long-term growth rates. Finally, empirical studies of the predictive value of endogenous growth theories have to date offered only limited support.[20]

Theories of Development: Reconciling the Differences

In this chapter we have reviewed a range of competing theories and approaches to the study of economic development. Each approach has its strengths and weaknesses.

The fact that there exists such controversy—be it ideological, theoretical, or empirical—is what makes the study of economic development both challenging and exciting. Even more than other fields of economics, development economics has no universally accepted doctrine or paradigm. Instead, we have a continually evolving pattern of insights and understandings that together provide the basis for examining the possibilities of contemporary development of the diverse nations of Africa, Asia, and Latin America.

You may wonder how consensus could emerge from so much disagreement. Although it is not implied here that such a consensus exists today or can indeed ever exist when such sharply conflicting values and ideologies prevail, we do suggest that something of significance can be gleaned from each of the five approaches that we have described. For example, the linear-stages model emphasizes the crucial role that saving and investment plays in promoting sustainable long-run growth. The Lewis two-sector model of structural change underlines the importance of attempting to analyze the many linkages between traditional agriculture and modern industry, and the empirical research of Chenery and his associates attempts to document precisely how economies undergo structural change while identifying the numeric values of key economic parameters involved in that process. The thoughts of international-dependence theorists alert us to the importance of the structure and workings of the world economy and the many ways in which decisions made in the developed world can affect the lives of millions of people in the developing world. Whether or not these activities are deliberately designed to maintain the Third World in a state of dependence is often beside the point. The fact of their very dependence and their vulnerability to key economic decisions made in the capitals of North America, Western Europe, or Japan (not to mention those made by the IMF and the World Bank) forces us to recognize the validity of many of the propositions of the international-dependence school. The same applies to arguments regarding the dualistic structures and the role of ruling elites in the domestic economies of the Third World.

Although a good deal of conventional neoclassical economic theory needs to be modified to fit the unique social, institutional, and structural circumstances of Third World nations, there is no doubt that promoting efficient production and distribution through a proper, functioning price system is an integral part of any successful development process. Many of the arguments of the neoclassical counterrevolutionaries, especially those related to the inefficiency of state-owned enterprises and the failures of development planning (see Chapter 16) and the harmful effects of government-induced domestic and international price distortions (see Chapter 8, 13, and 15) are as well taken as those of the dependence and structuralist schools. By contrast, the unquestioning exaltation of free markets and open economies along with the universal disparagement of public-sector leadership in promoting growth with equity in the Third World is open to serious challenge. As we shall discover all too often in Parts Two, Three, and Four, successful development requires a skillful and judicious balancing of market pricing and promotion where markets can indeed exist and operate efficiently, along with intelligent and equity-oriented government intervention in areas where unfettered market forces would lead to undesirable economic and social outcomes.

Finally, although still in its formative stage, the new growth theory is contributing to a better theoretical understanding of the divergent long-run growth experiences of the developed and developing worlds by focusing on the principal sources of endogenous economic growth. Though steeped in the neoclassical tradition, these new models modify and expand the assumptions of traditional growth theory to help explain the observed patterns of growth among nations. Perhaps most important, they restore a significant role for government policy in promoting long-run growth and development. We will examine the many lessons of this historical growth experience in Chapter 4.

In summary, each of these approaches to understanding development has something to offer. Their respective contributions will become clearer later in the book when we explore in detail both the origins of and possible solutions to a wide range of problems such as poverty, population growth, unemployment, rural development, international trade, and the environment.

CASE STUDY

The Economy of Cuba*

GEOGRAPHIC, SOCIAL, AND ECONOMIC
INDICATORS

Area 114,524 km^2

Population 10.9 million (1994)

Population (average annual growth rate)
0.9% (1985–1994)

GNP per capita $1250 (1993)

**GNP per capita (average annual growth
rate)** –8.1% (1989–1993)

Agriculture as share of GDP 11% (1993)

Exports as share of GDP 11% (1993)

**Infant mortality rate (per 1,000 live
births)** 10 (1992)

Child malnutrition (underweight)
5% (1992)

Females as share of labor force
32% (1994)

Illiteracy rate (age 15+) 6% (1990)

Human Development Index 0.769
(medium) 1992

Cuba, larger than the other Caribbean islands combined (about the same size as
England), separates the Gulf of Mexico from
the Caribbean Sea.

From its discovery by Columbus in 1492
until gaining nominal political independence in 1902, Cuba was the center of the
Spanish colonial system in the Western
Hemisphere. The Spanish eradicated the
aboriginal population and imported slaves
from Africa to work in the burgeoning
sugar industry. The contemporary Cuban
ethnic mixture is a complex and seamless
continuum from Spanish to African with
recognizable additional components including Chinese descendants of laborers
imported in the nineteenth century. In the
two Cuban wars for independence from

*Prepared by Professor Frank Thompson, an economist at the
University of Michigan, at the author's invitation. Reprinted
with permission.

Spain (1868–1878, 1895–1898), both the leadership and the body of the insurgent forces
included former slaves as well as creoles
(Cuban-born Spaniards).

In the long decline of Spanish power in
Latin America, ownership and control of
much of the Cuban economy went over to U.S.
firms during the nineteenth century. As
Cuban insurgents approached victory over
colonial rule in 1898, the Americans invaded
Cuba, and the peace treaty between Spain and
the United States later that year transferred
sovereignty to the latter. Annexation was considered, but instead Cuban formal independence was declared in 1902 after an elected
Cuban government reluctantly accepted an
amendment to the first Cuban constitution
granting the United States unlimited powers
of intervention. (The last remaining U.S. military installation in Cuba, at Guantánamo,
dates from 1902.)

American-based firms dominated every
major sector of the Cuban economy until the
island's 1959 revolution. The largest industries were sugar and tourism, but other significant ones included utilities (the Cuban

Telephone Company did not even have a Spanish name), railways, petroleum, cement, and mining. Regulations modeled on southern U.S. Jim Crow laws were imposed, and Havana, the Cuban capital, became known as "the Bordello" for U.S. vacationers seeking pleasures forbidden at home. Cuban governments in this period, notoriously corrupt and compliant to U.S. interests, culminated in the brutal dictatorship of Fulgencio Batista.

On January 1, 1959, after an improbably successful six-year struggle, a revolutionary movement with middle-class leadership, but initially based in the destitute peasantry of eastern Cuba, overthrew the Batista dictatorship. Its most prominent leader was Fidel Castro, a 1951 Havana University law graduate. The new government immediately instituted dramatic economic changes beginning with nationalization of agricultural land in excess of 400 hectares (largely foreign-owned sugar plantations). In a quick succession of tit-for-tat measures, the United States reduced Cuba's sugar import quota, Cuba nationalized other U.S.-owned assets (including petroleum and telephones), and the United States imposed a punitive embargo. In February 1960, Cuba negotiated a sugar-for-oil exchange arrangement with the Soviet Union that began an extraordinarily rapid transformation of the Cuban economy from a *de facto* component of the U.S. economy to, two years later, an anomalous Western Hemisphere nation conducting 85% of its foreign trade with the Soviet bloc.

The extent of Cuba's political subservience to Soviet policy demands over the ensuing three decades is disputed, but that Cuba became economically dependent on the Soviet bloc is clear. Cuba exported agricultural products, mostly sugar, in exchange for oil and manufactured goods with an implicit subsidy (estimated relative to world market prices) for Cuba in the range of $5 billion per year. Except for an economically significant sector of private farms, the Cuban economy became almost entirely state-owned and state-managed.

After the U.S.-sponsored invasion by Cuban counterrevolutionaries was defeated at the Bay of Pigs in 1961 and the diffusal of the Cuban Missile Crisis of 1962, in which Soviet missiles were withdrawn and the United States pledged not to invade the island, Cuba then proceeded on a path of economic development unique in the Third World.

The major consequences of this development course were a substantial increase in national income per capita and, even more strikingly, an egalitarian shift in the distribution of national income. By 1986, the nation's income unequality index had become the lowest in the developing world. Especially notable was the transformation in health and education. Despite the emigration of most professionals, largely to the United States, in the early 1960s the health and education systems were dramatically expanded until by the early 1980s, Cuba's life expectancy, infant mortality, literacy, and scientific and technical education statistics resembled those of First World countries, even though per capita income, though substantially increased since the revolution, remained in the Third World range.

In the early 1960s, Cuba had suffered an enormous economic shock. Abruptly severed from its traditional markets by the U.S. embargo, the country unsteadily reoriented its production and trade to the possibilities and demands of the Soviet bloc. The resulting system differed importantly from Soviet models but was not significantly more efficient. Nevertheless, substantial economic development took place. But with the collapse of Eastern European communism in the early 1990s, Cuba suffered an even more traumatic economic shock than it did after the U.S. embargo was imposed. The advantageous Cuban sugar–for–Soviet oil national development strategy evaporated. Essential inputs and spare parts for the whole of Cuban industry became unobtainable. Aggregate output plummeted by at least one-third and perhaps by as much as one-half.

The reaction of Cuban economic authorities to this fundamental crisis has been to undertake a thorough restructuring of national economic policy. One element of this restructuring has been a dramatic liberalization of domestic economic policy. State-owned resources, beginning in agriculture, have been turned over to worker-managed cooperatives or even private holders at a rapid rate. Free markets now allocate a substantial portion of consumption even while a meager ration system from state resources remains in place. A sector comprised of small enterprises has been allowed to flourish, turning what had previously been illicit economic activities into legally regulated private production.

Perhaps most important in the long run, Cuba has been dramatically opened to foreign investment. In spite of intense U.S. opposition, billions of investment dollars have flowed into Cuba since 1990, primarily from Mexican, Canadian, and European multinationals. The most noticeable investments have occurred in tourism, which was almost entirely dormant in Cuba for the preceding three decades. Substantial sums have also been committed to petroleum and mineral (especially nickel) extraction and refining, telecommunications, and other areas. In a startling reversal, Cuba has become "open for business" and is competing with substantial advantages in unexploited opportunities and offering, for a developing country, an unusually healthy and well-educated labor force. The one foreign party left out of this investment boom remains the United States, although a number of U.S. firms have been gingerly probing opportunities in Cuba in surreptitious defiance of the official U.S. embargo.

Even with accelerating foreign investment, the overwhelming bulk of the Cuban economy remains in native Cuban hands. Almost all joint venture agreements limit foreign investors to a minority stake, and some relatively dynamic sectors, including pharmaceuticals for Third World markets, are entirely state-owned. But a large portion of the state sector remains astonishingly inefficient, and dramatic further changes in economic policy are widely expected.

The transformation of the Cuban economy in the 1990s has been wrenching for Cuban society. A dramatic fall in per capita income has been accompanied by visible unemployment for the first time since the earliest 1960s, and an "inversion of the social pyramid" has occurred—not only has income inequality increased, but the beneficiaries of this increase have been almost entirely those involved, licitly or illicitly, in the sectors of the economy being transformed by foreign investment, especially tourism. The U.S. dollar denominates a portion of the Cuban economy from which most Cubans, especially those who have most supported and benefited from the revolution of 1959, are largely excluded.

The future of the political economy of Cuba is not predictable with any confidence. Much depends on U.S. policy, which has been the fundamental determinant of Cuba's fortunes for two centuries. (Emigration fiascoes since the revolution are a well publicized example. Until August 1994, Cubans who succeeded in setting foot on U.S. soil were legally entitled to nearly automatic status providing benefits starkly denied other economic refugees from the region, a politically motivated emigration system which dramatically shaped Cuban domestic and foreign policy.) An end to the embargo, when it comes, is expected to unleash a wave of catch-up U.S. investment that could conceivably return Cuba once again to the status of a *de facto* U.S. economic subsidiary. But U.S. investors are bound to suffer from the late start, and, even more importantly, the popular Cuban perception of having achieved national political and economic independence since the revolution is potent. This nationalist sentiment is the bedrock of popular support for the regime still headed by Fidel Castro, which, though by no means the most authoritarian or repressive in Latin America since 1959, remains unwilling to risk domestic political competition.

For three and a half decades, Cuba has been a unique example of relative Third World success in providing adequate fundamental resources for successful human functioning on an egalitarian basis. But for most of this period, Cuba's wagon was hitched to a now fallen star. Nevertheless, Cuba remains unique in combining a high level of development of its human capital with a generally low level of development of the rest of its political economy.

Concepts for Review

Average product	Neocolonial dependence model
Capital-labor ratio	New growth theory
Capital-output ratio	New institutionalism
Capital stock	New political economy approach
Center	Open economy
Closed economy	Patterns-of-development analysis
Complementary investments	Periphery
Comprador groups	Production function
Dependence	Public-choice theory
Dominance	Savings ratio
Dualism	Self-sustaining growth
Endogenous growth	Solow neoclassical growth model
False-paradigm model	Solow residual
Free market	Stages-of-growth model of development
Free-market analysis	Structural-change theory
Harrod-Domar growth model	Structural transformation
Lewis two-sector model	Sufficient condition
Marginal product	Surplus labor
Market-friendly approach	Traditional (old) neoclassical growth theory
Necessary condition	Underdevelopment
Neoclassical counterrevolution	

Questions for Discussion

1. Explain the essential distinctions among the stages-of-growth theory of development, the structural-change models of Lewis and Chenery, and the theory of international dependence in both its neo-Marxist and false-paradigm conceptualizations. Which model do you think provides the best explanation of the situation in most Third World nations? Explain.

2. Explain the meaning of *dualism* and *dual societies*. Do you think that the concept of dualism adequately portrays the development picture in most Third World countries? Explain.

3. Some people claim that international dualism and domestic dualism are merely different manifestations of the same phenomenon. What do you think they mean by this, and is it a valid conceptualization? Explain.

4. What is meant by the term *neoclassical counterrevolution*? What are its principal arguments, and how valid do you think they are? Explain.

5. Given the diversity of developing countries, do you think that there could ever be a single, unified theory of development? Explain.

6. Is the neoclassical, free-market theory necessarily incompatible with dependence theory? How might these two approaches work together?

7. Distinguish between the old (traditional) and new theories of growth. What are the implications, if any, for public policy in each approach?

Notes

1. Walt W. Rostow, *The Stages of Economic Growth: A Non-Communist Manifesto* (London: Cambridge University Press, 1960), pp. 1, 3, 4, and 12. For an extensive and critical review of the Rostow stages doctrine from a Marxist perspective, see Paul Baran and Edward Hobsbawm, "The stages of economic growth," *Kyklos* 14 (1961): 234–242.

2. This model is named after two economists, Sir Roy Harrod of England and Professor Evesey Domar of the United States, who separately but concurrently developed a variant of it in the early 1950s.

3. W. Arthur Lewis, "Economic development with unlimited supplies of labour," *Manchester School* 22 (May 1954): 139–191; John C. H. Fei and Gustav Ranis, *Development of the Labor Surplus Economy: Theory and Policy* (Homewood, Ill: Irwin, 1964). In fact, many of the basic ideas of the Lewis and Fei-Ranis model were originally expounded by Ragnar Nurkse in his famous little book *Problems of Capital Formation in Underdeveloped Countries* (New York: Oxford University Press, 1953). I am indebted to Professor Harold Votey for reminding me of this often forgotten fact.

4. See Hollis B. Chenery, *Structural Change and Development Policy* (Baltimore: Johns Hopkins University Press, 1979); Hollis B. Chenery and Moshe Syrquin, *Patterns of Development, 1950–70* (London: Oxford University Press, 1975); and Moshe Syrquin, "Patterns of structural change," in Hollis B. Chenery and T. N. Srinivasan (eds.), *Handbook of Development Economics* (Amsterdam: North Holland, 1989), vol. 1, pp. 205–273.

5. For one of the most comprehensive introductions to the neo-Marxist view of international development and underdevelopment, see Paul Baran, *The Political Economy of Neo-Colonialism* (London: Heinemann, 1975). An outstanding literature review is contained in Keith Griffin and John Gurley, "Radical analysis of imperialism, the Third World, and the transition to socialism: A survey article," *Journal of Economic Literature* 23 (September 1985): 1089–1143. See also Ted C. Lewellen, *Dependency and Development: An Introduction to the Third World* (Westport, Conn.: Bergin and Garvey, 1995).

6. A provocative and well-documented application of this argument to the case of Kenya can be found in Colin Leys, *Underdevelopment in Kenya: The Political Economy of Neo-Colonialism* (London: Heinemann, 1975).

7. Theotonio Dos Santos, "The crisis of development theory and the problem of dependence in Latin America," *Siglo* 21 (1969). See also Benjamin J. Cohen, *The Question of Imperialism: The Political Economy of Dominance and Dependence* (New York: Basic Books, 1973).

8. Hans Singer, "Dualism revisited: A new approach to the problems of dual societies in developing countries," *Journal of Development Studies* 7 (1970): 60–61.

9. For examples of the literature of neoclassical counterrevolutionaries, see, among others, Peter T. Bauer, *Reality and Rhetoric: Studies in the Economics of Development* (London: Weidenfield & Nicolson, 1984); Deepak Lal, *The Poverty of Development Economics* (Cambridge, Mass.: Harvard University Press, 1985); Harry Johnson, "A word to the Third World: A Western economist's frank advice," *Encounter* 37 (1971); Ian Little, *Economic Development: Theories, Policies, and International Relations* (New York: Basic Books, 1982); and any mid-1980s issue of the World Bank's *World Development Report* (New York: Oxford University Press) and the International Monetary Fund's *Annual World Economic Outlook*. An outstanding critique of this literature can be found in John Toye, *Dilemmas of Development: Reflections on the Counter-revolution in Development Theory and Policy* (Oxford: Blackwell, 1987). See also Frances Stewart, "The fragile foundations of the neoclassical approach to development," *Journal of Development Studies* 21 (January 1985); Hla Myint, "The neoclassical resurgence in development economics: Its strength and limitations," in Gerald M. Meier (ed.), *Pioneers in Development: Second Series* (New York: Oxford University Press, 1987); Paul Krugman, "Toward a counter-counterrevolution in development theory," *World Bank Annual Conference on Development Economics, 1992* (Washington, D.C.: World Bank, 1993); Charles Maechling, Jr., "The next century: Can the free market panacea survive?" *Virginia Quarterly Review* 71 (Winter 1994): 1–18; and Ziya Onis, "The limits of neoliberalism: Toward a reformulation of development theory," *Journal of Economic Issues* 29 (March 1995): 97–119.

10. For a good explication of the tenets of the public-choice theory, see Merilee S. Grindle and John W. Thomas, *Public Choices and Public Policy Change: The Political Economy of Reform in Developing Countries* (Baltimore: Johns Hopkins University Press, 1991). The classic article in the field is by Nobel laureate James M. Buchanan, "Social choice, democracy and free markets," *Journal of Political Economy* 62 (April 1954): 114–123. For a critique see Paul P. Streeten, "Markets and states: Against minimalism," *World Development* 21 (August 1993): 1281–1298, and Amartya Sen, "Rationality and social choice," *American Economic Review* 85 (March 1995): 1–24.

11. See any of the 1990s *World Development Reports* and also World Bank, *The East Asian Miracle* (New York: Oxford University Press, 1993). For a critique of this approach, see A. Singh, "State intervention and 'market-friendly' approach to development: A critical analysis of the World Bank theses," in Amitava K. Dutt, Kwan S. Kim, and Ajit Singh (eds.), *The States, Markets and Development* (London: Elgar, 1994).

12. Robert Solow, "A contribution to the theory of economic growth," *Quarterly Journal of Economics* 70 (February 1956): 65–94.

13. For a discussion of these and related issues, see H. W. Arndt, " 'Market failure' and underdevelopment," *World Development* 16 (February 1988).

14. A possible fourth component of the neoclassical counterrevolution—one that goes to the essence of development issues—has been called the *new institutionalism*. The institutions include property rights, prices and market structures, money and financial institutions, firms and industrial organization, and relationships between government and markets. The basic message of the new institutionalism is that even in a neoclassical world, the success or failure of development efforts will depend on the nature, existence, and proper functioning of a country's fundamental institutions. The origins of the new institutionalism can be found in the theory of institutions pioneered by the work of Nobel laureate Ronald Coase. See Ronald Coase, "The institutional structure of production,"

American Economic Review 82 (December 1992); Howard Stein, "Theories of institutions and economic reform in Africa," *World Development* 22 (December 1994); and Oliver E. Williamson, "The institutions and governance of economic development and reform," *Proceedings of the World Bank Annual Conference on Development Economics 1994* (Washington, D.C.: World Bank, 1995): 171–197.

15. Oliver J. Blanchard and Stanley Fischer, *Lectures on Macroeconomics* (Cambridge, Mass.: MIT Press, 1989).

16. Actually, the new growth theory represents only one (although perhaps the most widely discussed) component of the new, broader-based, and more eclectic and pragmatic fifth approach to understanding development. Other key components of this emerging new paradigm include the new dynamic theories of North-South trade with imperfect competition (Chapter 12), the rediscovery of human resource analysis (Chapter 11), and the new economics of the environment and sustainable development (Chapter 10). The two common themes linking these disparate topics are the limitations of free markets and the important complementary role that enlightened governments can play. New growth theory and its counterparts therefore reflect a growing dissatisfaction with some of the basic tenets of the neoclassical counterrevolution.

17. For a short history of the evolution of theoretical models of growth, see Nicholas Stern, "The determinants of growth," *Economic Journal* 101 (January 1991). For a more detailed but technical discussion of endogenous growth models, see Xavier Sala-i-Martin, "Lecture notes on economic growth," I and II, National Bureau for Economic Research Working Papers 3563 and 3564 (December 1990); and Elhanan Helpman, "Endogenous macroeconomic growth theory," *European Economic Review* 36 (April 1992).

18. *Ibid.* See also Paul M. Romer, "Increasing returns and long-run growth," *Journal of Political Economy* 94 (1986): 1002–1037; Robert B. Lucas, "On the mechanics of economic development," *Journal of Monetary Economics* 22 (June 1988): 3–42; and Robert Barro, "Government spending in a simple model of endogenous growth," *Journal of Political Economy* 98 (October 1990).

19. For a concise technical discussion of the importance of human capital as a complementary input, see Robert B. Lucas, "Why doesn't capital flow from rich to poor countries?" *AEA Papers and Proceedings* 80 (May 1990): 92–96.

20. For an excellent review and empirical critique of the new growth theory, see Howard Pack, "Endogenous growth theory: Intellectual appeal and empirical shortcomings," *Journal of Economic Perspectives* 8 (Winter 1994): 55–72. See also articles by Paul M. Romer and Robert Solow in the same issue. A similar critique from a historical perspective can be found in Marvin Goodfriend and John McDermott, "Early development," *American Economic Review* 85 (March 1995): 116–133. For an argument that endogenous theory performs well in explaining differences in growth rates among countries, see Robert Barro and Xavier Sala-i-Martin, *Economic Growth* (New York: McGraw-Hill, 1994).

Further Reading

Thoughtful and provocative analyses can be found in Amartya Sen, "Development: Which way now?" *Economic Journal* 93 (December 1983): 745–762; H. W. Arndt, *Economic Development: The History of an Idea* (Chicago: University of Chicago Press, 1987); Diana Hunt, *Economic Theories of Development* (Totawa, N.J.: Rowman & Littlefield, 1987); Nicholas Stern, "The economics of development: A survey," *Economic Journal* 99 (September 1989):

597–685; Robert Dorfman, "Economic development from the beginning to Rostow," *Journal of Economic Literature* 29 (June 1991): 573–591; Hollis B. Chenery and T. N. Srinivasan (eds.), *Handbook of Development Economics* (Amsterdam: North Holland, 1989), vol. 1, pt. 1 articles by Sen, Lewis, Bardhan, and Ranis; and World Bank, *World Development Report, 1991* (New York: Oxford University Press, 1991), chap. 2.

For an excellent summary statement of the concept of dualism and dual societies, see Hans Singer, "Dualism revisited: A new approach to the problems of dual society in developing countries," *Journal of Development Studies* 7 (January 1970): 60–61.

Among a number of recent surveys of the dependence literature as applied to problems of underdevelopment, the following are perhaps the best: Keith Griffin and John Gurley, "Radical analysis of imperialism, the Third World, and the transition to socialism: A survey article," *Journal of Economic Literature* 23 (September 1985): 1089–1143; Samir Amin, *Imperialism and Unequal Development* (New York: Monthly Review Press, 1977); F. H. Cardoso, "Dependence and development in Latin America," *New Left Review*, July–August 1972, pp. 83–95; Patrick O'Brien, "A critique of Latin American theories of dependency," in Iver Oxaal *et al.* (eds.), *Beyond the Sociology of Development* (London: Routledge, 1975); Sanjaya Lall, "Is 'dependence' a useful concept in analysing underdevelopment?" *World Development* 3 (1975): 799–810; G. Kay, *Development and Underdevelopment: A Marxist Analysis* (London: Macmillan, 1975); Gabriel Palma, "Dependency: A formal theory of underdevelopment or a methodology for the analysis of concrete situations of underdevelopment," *World Development* 6 (1978); Celso Furtado, "Underdevelopment: To conform or reform?" in Gerald M. Meier (ed.), *Pioneers in Development: Second Series* (New York: Oxford University Press, 1987), pp. 203–207; and Ted C. Lewellen, *Dependency and Development: An Introduction to the Third World* (Westport, Conn.: Bergin and Garvey, 1995).

Readings on the neoclassical counterrevolution, in addition to those cited in note 9, include Peter T. Bauer, *Dissent on Development* (London: Weidenfeld & Nicolson, 1972); Julian Simon, *The Ultimate Resource* (Princeton, N.J.: Princeton University Press, 1981); Ian Little, "An economic renaissance," in W. Galenson (ed.), *Economic Growth and Structural Change in Taiwan* (Ithaca, N.Y.: Cornell University Press, 1979); and World Bank, *World Development Report, 1982* and *1983* (New York: Oxford University Press, 1982, 1983). See also Tony Killick, "Twenty-five years of development: The rise and impending decline of market solutions," *Development Policy Review* 4 (June 1986).

A concise history of the evolution of growth theory is offered in Nicholas Stern, "The determinants of growth," *Economic Journal* 101 (January 1991), and an informative survey and evaluation of the new growth theory can be found in the symposium "New growth theory," *Journal of Economic Perspectives* 8 (Winter 1994): 3–72, especially the articles by Paul M. Romer and Howard Pack. See also Pranab Bardhan, "The contributions of endogenous growth theory to the analysis of development problems: An assessment," in J. Behrman and T. N. Srinivasan (eds.), *Handbook of Development Economics* (Amsterdam: North Holland, 1995), vol. 3.

CHAPTER 4

Historic Growth and Contemporary Development: Lessons and Controversies

The growth position of the less developed countries today is significantly different in many respects from that of the presently developed countries on the eve of their entry into modern economic growth.

—Simon Kuznets, Nobel Laureate, Economics

What is the meaning of growth if it is not translated into the lives of people?
—United Nations, *Human Development Report, 1995*

The Growth Game

For the past three decades, a primary focus of world economic attention has been on ways to accelerate the growth rate of national incomes. Economists and politicians from all nations, rich and poor, capitalist, socialist, and mixed, have worshiped at the shrine of economic growth. At the end of every year, statistics are compiled for all countries of the world showing their relative rates of GNP growth. "Growthmanship" has become a way of life. Governments can rise or fall if their economic growth performance ranks high or low on this global scorecard. As we have seen, Third World development programs are often assessed by the degree to which their national outputs and incomes are growing. In fact, for many years the conventional wisdom equated development almost exclusively with the rapidity of national output growth.

In view of the central role that this concept has assumed in worldwide assessment of relative national economic performance, it is important to understand the nature and causes of economic growth. In this chapter, therefore, we start by examining some of the basic concepts of the theory of economic growth, using the simple production possibility framework to portray the level, composition, and growth of national output. After looking briefly at the historical record of economic growth in contemporary rich nations, we then isolate six economic, structural, and institutional components that appear to have characterized all growing economies.

We conclude by asking the question, Of what relevance is the historical growth experience of contemporary developed countries to the plans and strategies of present-day Third World nations?

The Economics of Growth: Capital, Labor, and Technology

Three factors or components of economic growth are of prime importance in any society:

1. Capital accumulation, including all new investments in land, physical equipment, and human resources
2. Growth in population and hence eventual growth in the labor force
3. Technological progress

Let us look briefly at each.

Capital Accumulation

Capital accumulation results when some proportion of present income is saved and invested in order to augment future output and income. New factories, machinery, equipment, and materials increase the physical **capital stock** of a nation (the total net real value of all physically productive capital goods) and make it possible for expanded output levels to be achieved. These directly productive investments are supplemented by investments in what is known as social and economic **infrastructure**—roads, electricity, water and sanitation, communications, and the like—which facilitates and integrates economic activities. For example, investment by a farmer in a new tractor may increase the total output of the vegetables he can produce, but without adequate transport facilities to get this extra product to local commercial markets, his investment may not add anything to national food production.

There are other, less direct ways to invest in a nation's resources. The installation of irrigation facilities may improve the quality of a nation's agricultural land by raising productivity per hectare. If 100 hectares of irrigated land can produce the same output as 200 hectares of nonirrigated land using the same other inputs, the installation of such irrigation is the equivalent of doubling the quantity of nonirrigated land. Use of chemical fertilizers and the control of insects with pesticides may have equally beneficial effects in raising the productivity of existing farmland. All these forms of investment are ways of improving the quality of existing land resources. Their effect in raising the total stock of productive land is, for all practical purposes, indistinguishable from the simple clearing of hitherto unused arable land.

Similarly, investment in human resources can improve its quality and thereby have the same or even a more powerful effect on production as an increase in human numbers. Formal schooling, vocational and on-the-job training programs, and adult and other types of informal education may all be made more effective in augmenting human skills and resources as a result of direct investments in buildings, equipment, and materials (e.g., books, film projectors, personal computers, science equipment, vocational tools, and machinery such as lathes and grinders). The advanced and relevant training of teachers, as well as good textbooks in economics, may make an enormous difference in the quality, leadership, and productivity of a given labor force. The concept of investment in human resources and the creation of **human capital** is therefore analogous to that of improving the quality and thus the productivity of existing land resources through strategic investments.[1]

All of these phenomena and many others are forms of investment that lead to capital accumulation. Capital accumulation may add new resources (e.g., the clearing of unused land) or upgrade the quality of existing resources (e.g., irrigation, fertilizer, pesticides), but its essential feature is that it involves a trade-off between present and future consumption—giving up a little now so that more can be had later.

Population and Labor Force Growth

Population growth, and the associated eventual increase in the labor force, has traditionally been considered a positive factor in stimulating economic growth. A larger labor force means more productive workers, and a large overall population increases the potential size of domestic markets. However, it is questionable whether rapidly growing supplies of workers in surplus-labor developing countries exert a positive or a negative influence on economic progress (see Chapter 6 for a lengthy discussion of the pros and cons of population growth for economic development). Obviously, it will depend on the ability of the economic system to absorb and productively employ these added workers—an ability largely associated with the rate and kind of capital accumulation and the availability of related factors, such as managerial and administrative skills.

Given an initial understanding of these first two fundamental components of economic growth and disregarding for a moment the third (technology), let us see how they interact via the **production possibility curve** to expand society's potential total output of all goods. For a given technology and a given amount of physical and human resources, the production possibility curve portrays the *maximum* attainable output combinations of any two commodities, say, rice and radios, when all resources are fully and efficiently employed. Figure 4.1 shows two production possibility curves for rice and radios.

Suppose now that with unchanged technology, the quantity of physical and human resources were to double as a result of either investments that improved the quality of the existing resources or investment in new resources—land, capital, and, in the case of larger families, labor. Figure 4.1 shows that this doubling of total resources will cause the entire production possibility curve to shift uniformly outward from P–P to P'–P'. More radios and more rice can now be produced.

Because these are assumed to be the only two goods produced by this economy, it follows that the gross national product (the total value of all goods and services produced) will be higher than before. In other words, the process of economic growth is under way.

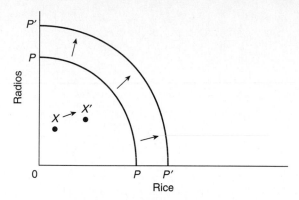

FIGURE 4.1 **Effect of Increases in Physical and Human Resources on the Production Possibility Frontier.**

Note that even if the country in question is operating with underutilized physical and human resources as at point X in Figure 4.1, a growth of productive resources can result in a higher total output combination as at point X', even though there may still be widespread unemployment and underutilized or idle capital and land. But note also that there is nothing deterministic about resource growth leading to higher output growth. This is not an economic law, as attested by the poor growth record of many contemporary developing countries. Nor is resource growth even a necessary condition for *short run* economic growth because the better utilization of idle existing resources can raise output levels substantially, as portrayed in the movement from X to X' in Figure 4.1. Nevertheless, in the *long run*, the improvement and upgrading of the quality of existing resources and new investments designed to expand the quantity of these resources are principal means of accelerating the growth of national output.

Now, instead of assuming the proportionate growth of *all* factors of production, let us assume that, say, only capital or only land is increased in quality and quantity. Figure 4.2 shows that if radio manufacturing is a relatively large user of capital equipment and rice production is a relatively land-intensive process, the shifts in society's production possibility curve will be more pronounced for radios when capital grows rapidly (Figure 4.2a) and for rice when the growth is in land quantity or quality (Figure 4.2b). However, because under normal conditions both products will require the use of both factors as productive inputs, albeit in different combinations, the production possibility curve still shifts slightly outward along the rice axis in Figure 4.2a when only capital is increased and along the radio axis in Figure 4.2b when only the quantity or quality of land resources is expanded.

Technological Progress

It is now time to consider the third, and to many economists the most important, source of economic growth, **technological progress**. In its simplest form, technological progress results from new and improved ways of accomplishing traditional tasks

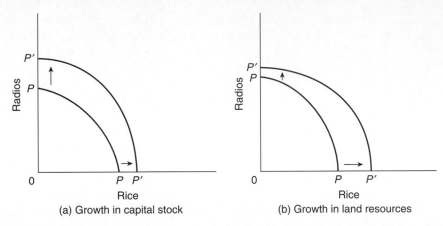

FIGURE 4.2 Effect of Growth of Capital Stock and Land on the Production Possibility Frontier.

such as growing crops, making clothing, or building a house. There are three basic classifications of technological progress: neutral, laborsaving, and capital-saving.

Neutral technological progress occurs when higher output levels are achieved with the same quantity and combinations of factor inputs. Simple innovations like those that arise from the division of labor can result in higher total output levels and greater consumption for all individuals. In terms of production possibility analysis, a neutral technological change that, say, doubles total output is conceptually equivalent to a doubling of all productive inputs. The outward-shifting production possibility curve of Figure 4.1 could therefore also be a diagrammatic representation of neutral technological progress.

By contrast, progress may either be laborsaving or capital-saving technological progress (i.e., higher levels of output can be achieved with the same quantity of labor or capital inputs). Electronic computers, automated looms, high-speed electric drills, tractors, and mechanical ploughs—these and many other kinds of modern machinery and equipment can be classified as products of **laborsaving technological progress**. As we will discover in Chapter 8, technological progress in the twentieth century has consisted largely of rapid advances in laborsaving technologies for producing everything from beans to bicycles to bridges.

Capital-saving technological progress is a much rarer phenomenon. But this is primarily because almost all of the world's scientific and technological research is conducted in developed countries, where the mandate is to save labor, not capital. In the labor-abundant (capital-scarce) countries of the Third World, however, capital-saving technological progress is what is needed most. Such progress results in more efficient (lower-cost) labor-intensive methods of production—for example, hand- or rotary-powered weeders and threshers, foot-operated bellows pumps, and back-mounted mechanical sprayers for small-scale agriculture. As we will see in Chapter 8, the indigenous LDC development of low-cost, efficient, labor-intensive (capital-saving) techniques of production is one of the essential ingredients in any long-run employment-oriented development strategy.

Technological progress may also be labor- or capital-augmenting. **Labor-augmenting technological progress** occurs when the quality or skills of the labor force are upgraded—for example, by the use of videotapes, televisions, and other electronic communications media for classroom instruction. Similarly, **capital-augmenting technological progress** results in the more productive use of existing capital goods as, for example, the substitution of steel for wooden plows in agricultural production.

We can use our production possibility curve for rice and radios to examine two very specific examples of technological progress as it relates to output growth in developing countries. In the 1960s, agricultural scientists at the International Rice Research Institute in the Philippines developed a new and highly productive hybrid rice seed, known as IR-8, or "miracle rice." These new seeds, along with later further scientific improvements, enabled some rice farmers in parts of South and Southeast Asia to double and triple their yields in a matter of a few years. In effect, this technological progress was "embodied" in the new rice seeds (one could also say it was "land-augmenting"), which permitted higher output levels to be achieved with essentially the same complementary inputs (although more fertilizer and pesticides were recommended). In terms of our production possibility analysis, the higher-yielding varieties of hybrid rice could be depicted, as in Figure 4.3, by an outward shift of the curve along the rice axis with the intercept on the radio axis remaining essentially unchanged (i.e., the new rice seeds could not be directly used to increase radio production).

In terms of the technology of radio production, the invention of transistors probably has had as significant an impact on communications as the discovery of the steam engine had on transportation. Even in the remotest parts of Africa, Asia, and Latin America, the transistor radio has become a prized possession. The introduction of the transistor, by obviating the need for complicated, unwieldy, and fragile tubes, led to an enormous growth of radio production. The production process became less complicated, and workers were able to increase their total productivity significantly. Figure 4.4 shows that, as in the case of higher-yielding rice seeds, the technology of

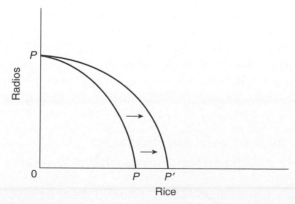

FIGURE 4.3 Effect of Technological Change in the Agricultural Sector on the Production Possibility Frontier.

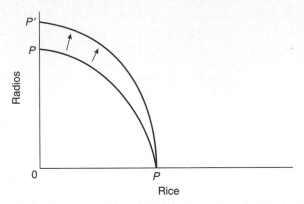

FIGURE 4.4 Effect of Technological Change in the Industrial Sector on the Production Possibility Frontier.

the transistor can be said to have caused the production possibility curve to rotate outward along the vertical axis. For the most part, the rice axis intercept remains unchanged (although perhaps the ability of rice paddy workers to listen to music on their transistor radio while working may have made them more productive!).

Conclusion

We can summarize the discussion so far by saying that the sources of economic progress can be traced to a variety of factors, but by and large, investments that improve the quality of existing physical and human resources, that increase the quantity of these same productive resources, and that raise the productivity of all or specific resources through invention, innovation, and technological progress have been and will continue to be primary factors in stimulating economic growth in any society. The production possibility framework conveniently allows us to analyze the production choices open to an economy, to understand the output and opportunity cost implications of idle or underutilized resources, and to portray the effects on economic growth of increased resource supplies and improved technologies of production.

Having provided this introduction to the simple economics of growth, we can now look more carefully at the historical experience of contemporary developed nations in order to analyze in detail the nature of the economic and noneconomic factors that were basic to their long-term growth. We will then see what relevance all this has for the growth prospects of developing countries.

The Historical Record: Kuznets's Six Characteristics of Modern Economic Growth

Professor Simon Kuznets, who received the Nobel Prize in economics in 1971 for his pioneering work in the measurement and analysis of the historical growth of national incomes in developed nations, has defined a country's **economic growth** as "a long-term rise in capacity to supply increasingly diverse economic goods to its population, this growing capacity based on advancing technology and the institutional and ideological adjustments that it demands."[2] All three principal components of this definition are of great importance.

1. The sustained rise in national output is a manifestation of economic growth, and the ability to provide a wide range of goods is a sign of economic maturity.
2. Advancing technology provides the basis or preconditions for continuous economic growth—a necessary but not sufficient condition.
3. To realize the potential for growth inherent in new technology, institutional, attitudinal, and ideological adjustments must be made. Technological innovation without concomitant social innovation is like a light bulb without electricity—the potential exists, but without the complementary input, nothing will happen.

In his exhaustive analysis, Kuznets has isolated six characteristic features manifested in the growth process of almost every developed nation:

1. High rates of growth of per capita output and population
2. High rates of increase in total factor productivity
3. High rates of structural transformation of the economy
4. High rates of social and ideological transformation
5. The propensity of economically developed countries to reach out to the rest of the world for markets and raw materials
6. The limited spread of this economic growth to only a third of the world's population.

The first two are aggregate economic variables, 3 and 4 are structural-transformation variables, and 5 and 6 affect the international spread of growth. Let us briefly examine each of these six characteristics.

High Rates of Per Capita Output and Population Growth

In the case of both per capita output and population growth, all contemporary developed countries have experienced large multiples of their previous historical rates during the epoch of modern economic growth, roughly from around 1770 to the present. For the now industrialized countries, annual growth rates over the past 200 years averaged almost 2% for per capita output and 1% for population, or 3% for total output (real GNP). These rates, which imply a doubling time of roughly 36 years for per capita output, 72 years for population, and 24 years for real GNP, were far greater than those experienced during the entire era before the industrial revolution began in the late eighteenth century. For example, per capita output during the past two centuries has been estimated at almost 10 times that of the premodern era; population has grown at a multiple of 4 or 5 times its rate in the earlier period; and the acceleration in the growth rate of total output or GNP is therefore estimated to have been some 40 or 50 times as large as that experienced before the nineteenth century!

High Rates of Total Factor Productivity Increase

The second aggregate economic characteristic of modern growth is the relatively high rate of rise in **total factor productivity (TFP)**, the output per unit of all inputs. Recent World Bank studies have confirmed Kuznets's finding that total factor productivity growth is what determines the rate of growth in developing countries.[3] Because TFP shows the efficiency with which all inputs are used in a production function, economists often measure its growth separately from the growth of factor inputs. Diagrammatically, an increase in TFP causes the production function of Figure 3.1a (the Lewis modern sector) to shift upward without an increase in the capital stock. Similarly, in Figure 4.1, an increase in TFP would cause the production possibility frontier to shift outward from $P–P$ to $P'–P'$ without any increase in labor or capital. Kuznets found substantial rises in TFP during the modern growth era.

Other studies show that rates of total productivity increase account for anywhere from 50% to 75% of the historical growth of per capita output in developed countries. In other words, technological progress, including the upgrading of existing physical and human resources, accounts for most of the measured historical increase in per capita GNP. We will discuss shortly the crucial role that technological advance has played in generating and sustaining this economic growth.

High Rates of Economic Structural Transformation

The historical growth record of contemporary developed nations reveals a third important characteristic: a high rate of structural and sectoral change inherent in the growth process. Some of the major components of this structural change include the gradual shift away from agricultural to nonagricultural activities and, more recently, away from industry to services; a significant change in the scale or average size of productive units (away from small family and personal enterprises to the impersonal organization of huge national and multinational corporations); and finally, a corresponding shift in the spatial location and occupational status of the labor force away from rural, agricultural, and related nonagricultural activities toward urban-oriented manufacturing and service pursuits. For example, in the United States, the proportion of the total labor force engaged in agricultural activities was 53.5% in 1870. By 1960, this figure had declined to less than 7%. Similarly, in a European country like Belgium, the agricultural labor force dropped from 51% of the total in 1846 to 12.5% in 1947 and less than 7% in 1970. In view of the fact that it took many centuries for agricultural labor forces to drop to even half of the total labor supply prior to the nineteenth century, a drop of 40 to 50 points in the past 100 years in countries such as the United States, Japan, Germany, Belgium, and Great Britain underlines the rapidity of this structural change.

High Rates of Social, Political, and Ideological Transformation

For significant economic structural change to take place in any society, concomitant transformations in attitudes, institutions, and ideologies are often necessary. Obvious examples of these social transformations are the general urbanization process and the adoption of the ideals, attitudes, and institutions of what has come to be known as "modernization." Gunnar Myrdal has provided a lengthy list of these **modernization ideals** in his seminal treatise on underdevelopment in Asia.[4] They include the following:

1. *Rationality*—the substitution of modern methods of thinking, acting, producing, distributing, and consuming for age-old, traditional practices. According to India's first prime minister, Jawaharlal Nehru, what underdeveloped nations need is "a scientific and technological society. It employs new techniques whether it is in the farm, in the factory or in transport. Modern technique is not a matter of just getting a tool and using it. Modern technique follows modern thinking. You can't get hold of a modern tool and have an ancient mind. It won't work."[5] The quest for rationality implies that opinions about economic strategies and policies should be logically valid inferences rooted as deeply as possible in knowledge of relevant facts.

2. *Economic planning*—the search for a rationally coordinated system of policy measures that can bring about and accelerate economic growth and development (see Chapter 16).

3. *Social and economic equalization*—the promotion of more equality in status, opportunities, wealth, incomes, and levels of living.

4. *Improved institutions and attitudes*—necessary to increase labor efficiency and diligence; promote effective competition, social and economic mobility, and individual enterprise; permit greater equality of opportunities; make possible higher productivity; raise levels of living; and promote development. Among the social institutions needing change are outmoded land tenure systems, social and economic monopolies, educational and religious structures, and systems of administration and planning. In the area of attitudes, the concept of "modern humanity" embodies such ideals as efficiency, diligence, orderliness, punctuality, frugality, honesty, rationality, change orientation, integrity and self-reliance, cooperation, and willingness to take the long view.

In Part Two, we will look more carefully at some of these characteristics of modernization as they relate to contemporary Third World countries to see how they fit into a development-oriented economic strategy.

International Economic Outreach

The last two characteristics of modern economic growth deal with the role of developed countries in the international arena. The first of these relates to the historical and ongoing propensity of rich countries to reach out to the rest of the world for primary products and raw materials, cheap labor, and lucrative markets for their manufactured products. Such outreach activities are made feasible by the increased power of modern technology, particularly in transport and communication. These had the effect of unifying the globe in ways that were not possible before the nineteenth century. They also opened the possibilities for political and economic dominance of poor nations by their more powerful neighbors. In the nineteenth and early twentieth centuries, the establishment of colonies and the opening up or partitioning of previously inaccessible areas such as sub-Saharan Africa and parts of Asia and Latin America provided the expanding economies of the Northern Hemisphere with cheap raw materials and with export markets for their growing manufacturing industries.

Limited International Spread of Economic Growth

In spite of the enormous increases in world output over the past two centuries, the spread of modern economic growth is still largely limited to less than one-fourth of the world's population. As we discovered in Chapter 2, this minority of the world's population enjoys almost 80% of the world's income. Moreover, as we saw later in that chapter, unequal international power relationships between developed and underdeveloped countries have a tendency to exacerbate the gap between rich and poor. The further economic growth of the former is often achieved at the expense of the growth of the latter.

Conclusions: The Interdependence of Growth Characteristics

The six characteristics of modern growth reviewed here are interrelated and mutually reinforcing. High rates of per capita output result from rapidly rising levels of factor productivity. High per capita incomes in turn generate high levels of per capita consumption, thus providing the incentives for changes in the structure of production (because as incomes rise, the demand for manufactured goods and services rises at a much faster rate than the demand for agricultural products). Advanced technology needed to achieve these output and structural changes causes the scale of production and the characteristics of economic enterprise units to change in both organization and location. This in turn necessitates rapid changes in the location and structure of the labor force and in status relationships among occupational groups (e.g., the income shares of landlords and farmers tend to decline, while those of manufacturers and industrialists tend to rise). It also means changes in other aspects of society, including family size, urbanization, and the material determinants of self-esteem and dignity. Finally, the inherent dynamism of modern economic growth, coupled with the revolution in the technology of transportation and communication, necessitates an international outreach on the part of the countries that developed first. But the poor countries affected by this international outreach may for institutional, ideological, or political reasons either not be in a position to benefit from the process or simply be weak victims of the policies of rich countries designed to exploit them economically.

If the common ingredient and linkage in all these interrelated growth characteristics is, as Kuznets suggests, the "mass application of technological innovations," then the rapid growth that makes possible the economic surplus to finance further progress in scientific research has a built-in tendency to be self-generating. In other words, rapid economic growth makes possible basic scientific research, which in turn leads to technological inventions and innovations, which propel economic growth even further.[6]

We have an important hint here why the growth process often seems to benefit the already rich nations disproportionately in relation to many poor ones: Over 90%

of all scientific research is undertaken in rich countries, on their problems. This research and the resulting technological progress can be of little direct benefit to poor nations whose resource and institutional conditions differ greatly from those of the developed nations. Wealthy nations can afford basic scientific research; poor ones cannot. Developed countries can therefore provide a continuous mechanism for self-sustaining technological and economic advance that is beyond the financial and technical capabilities of most developing countries. Although Third World nations have the potential advantage of importing this advanced technology either directly through international trade or indirectly through the vehicle of the multinational corporation (see Chapter 15), many do not possess the complementary resources (human capital), the required access to information, and the requisite institutional structures to adapt the technology to meet their own unique domestic needs. This is one of the reasons why some poor nations, especially those in sub-Saharan Africa, have such difficulty in generating a high level of self-sustaining economic growth.

The Limited Value of the Historical Growth Experience: Differing Initial Conditions

One of the principal failures of development economics of the 1950s and 1960s was its inability to recognize and take into account the limited value of the historical experience of economic growth in the West for charting the development path of contemporary Third World nations. Stages-of-growth economic theories and related models of rapid industrialization gave too little emphasis to the very different and less favorable initial economic, social, and political conditions of developing countries in the postwar era. The fact is that the growth position of these countries today is in many important ways significantly different from that of the currently developed countries when they embarked on their era of modern economic growth. We can identify at least eight significant differences in initial conditions—differences that require a much amended analysis of the growth prospects and requirements of modern economic development:

1. Physical and human resource endowments
2. Per capita incomes and levels of GNP in relation to the rest of the world
3. Climate
4. Population size, distribution, and growth
5. Historical role of international migration
6. International trade benefits
7. Basic scientific and technological research and development capabilities
8. Stability and flexibility of political institutions

We will discuss each of these conditions with a view to formulating a more realistic set of requirements and priorities for generating and sustaining economic growth as we approach the twenty-first century.

Physical and Human Resource Endowments

Contemporary Third World countries are often less well endowed with natural resources than the currently developed nations were at the time when the latter nations began their modern growth. A few Third World nations are blessed with abundant supplies of petroleum, other minerals, and raw materials for which world demand is growing; most less developed countries, however—especially in Asia, where almost one-third of the world's population resides—are poorly endowed with natural resources. Moreover, in parts of Latin America and Africa, where natural resources are more plentiful, heavy investments of capital are needed to exploit them. Such financing is not easy to come by without sacrificing substantial autonomy and control to the powerful developed-country multinational corporations that alone are currently capable of large-scale, efficient resource exploitation.

The difference in skilled human resource endowments is even more pronounced. The ability of a country to exploit its natural resources and to initiate and sustain long-term economic growth is dependent on, among other things, the ingenuity and the managerial and technical skills of its people and its access to critical market and product information at minimal cost.[7] The populations of today's Third World nations are generally less educated, less informed, less experienced, and less skilled than their counterparts were in the early days of economic growth in the West. According to economist Paul Romer, today's developing nations "are poor because their citizens do not have access to the ideas that are used in industrial nations to generate economic value."[8] For Romer, the technology gap between rich and poor nations can be divided into two components, a physical **object gap**, involving factories, roads, and modern machinery, and an **idea gap**, including knowledge about marketing, distribution, inventory control, transactions processing, and worker motivation. It is this idea gap, or what Thomas Homer-Dixon calls the **ingenuity gap** (the ability to apply innovative ideas to solve practical social and technical problems), between rich and poor nations that lies at the core of the development divide. No such human resource gaps existed for the now developed countries on the eve of their industrialization.

Relative Levels of Per Capita Income and GNP

The three-fourths of the world's population at present living in developing countries have on the average a much lower level of real per capita income than their counterparts had in the nineteenth century. First of all, as we discovered in Chapter 2, well over 70% of the population of Third World countries is attempting to subsist at bare minimum levels. Obviously, the average standard of living in, say, early-nineteenth-century England was nothing to envy or boast about, but it was not as economically debilitating or precarious as it is today for most people in the Third World, especially those in the 40 or so least developed countries.

Second, at the beginning of their modern growth era, today's developed nations were economically in advance of the rest of the world. They could therefore take advantage of their relatively strong financial position to widen the income gaps between themselves and less fortunate countries. By contrast, today's LDCs begin their growth process at the low end of the international per capita income scale.

Their relatively weak position in the world economy is analogous to that of a 1,500-meter race between a young athlete and an old man in which the former is given a 1,000-meter head start. Not only is such backwardness economically difficult to overcome or even reduce, but psychologically it creates a sense of frustration and a desire to grow at any cost. This can in fact inhibit the long-run improvement in national levels of living.

Climatic Differences

Almost all Third World countries are situated in tropical or subtropical climatic zones. It has been observed that the economically most successful countries are located in the temperate zone.[9] The dichotomy cannot simply be attributed to coincidence; it must bear some relation to the special difficulties caused directly or indirectly by differing climatic conditions.

It is undeniable that the extremes of heat and humidity in most poor countries contribute to deteriorating soil quality and the rapid depreciation of many natural goods. They also contribute to the low productivity of certain crops, the weakened regenerative growth of forests, and the poor health of animals. Finally, and perhaps most important, extremes of heat and humidity not only cause discomfort to workers but can also weaken their health, reduce their desire to engage in strenuous physical work, and generally lower their levels of productivity and efficiency. Whether or not these factors are major influences on the success or failure of development efforts, however, has never been carefully examined.

Population Size, Distribution, and Growth

In Chapter 6, we will examine in detail some of the development problems and issues associated with rapid population growth. At this point, it is sufficient to note that Third World population size, density, and growth constitute another important difference between less developed and developed countries. Before and during their early growth years, Western nations experienced a very slow rise in population growth. As industrialization proceeded, population growth rates increased primarily as a result of falling death rates but also because of slowly rising birthrates. However, at no time during their modern growth epoch did European and North American countries have natural population growth rates in excess of 2% per annum.

By contrast, the populations of many Third World countries have been increasing at annual rates in excess of 2.5% over the past few decades, and some are rising even faster today. Moreover, the concentration of these large and growing populations in a few areas means that most LDCs today start with considerably higher person-to-land ratios than the European countries did in their early growth years. Finally, in terms of comparative absolute size, it is a fact that with the exception of the former Soviet Union, no country that embarked on a long-term period of economic growth approached the present-day population size of India, Egypt, Pakistan, Indonesia, Nigeria, or Brazil. Nor, as we have just seen, were their rates of natural increase anything like that of present-day Mexico, Kenya, the Philippines, Bangladesh, Zaire, or Guatemala. In fact, many observers doubt whether the industrial revolution and the high long-term growth rates of contemporary developed countries could have been achieved or proceeded so fast and with so few setbacks and disturbances, especially for the very poor, had their populations been expanding so rapidly.

The Historical Role of International Migration

Of perhaps equal historical importance to the differing rates of natural population increase is the fact that in the nineteenth and early twentieth centuries, there was a major outlet for excess rural populations in international migration, which was both widespread and large-scale. In countries such as Italy, Germany, and Ireland, periods of severe famine or pressure on the land often combined with limited economic opportunities in urban industry to push unskilled rural workers toward the labor-scarce nations of North America and Australia. Thus, as Brinley Thomas argues, the "three outstanding contributions of European labor to the American economy—1,187,000 Irish and 919,000 Germans between 1847 and 1855, 418,000 Scandinavians and 1,045,000 Germans between 1880 and 1885, and 1,754,000 Italians between 1898 and 1907—had the character of evacuations."[10]

Whereas the main thrust of international emigration up to the First World War was both distant and permanent, the period since the Second World War has witnessed a resurgence of international migration within Europe itself, which is essentially over short distances and to a large degree temporary. However, the economic forces giving rise to this migration are basically the same; that is, during the 1950s and especially the 1960s, surplus rural workers from southern Italy, Greece, and Turkey flocked into areas of labor shortages, most notably West Germany and Switzerland. The fact that this more contemporary migration from regions of surplus labor in southern and southeastern Europe was initially of both a permanent and a nonpermanent nature provided a valuable dual benefit to the relatively poor areas from which these unskilled workers migrated. The home governments were relieved of the costs of providing for people who in all probability would remain unemployed, and because a large percentage of the workers' earnings were sent home, these governments received a valuable and not insignificant source of foreign exchange.[11]

In view of the foregoing discussion, you might reasonably ask why the large numbers of impoverished peoples in Africa, Asia, and Latin America do not follow the example of workers from southeastern Europe and seek temporary or permanent jobs in areas of labor shortage. Historically, at least in the case of Africa, migrant labor both within and between countries was rather common and did provide some relief for locally depressed areas. Even today, considerable benefits accrue and numerous potential problems are avoided by the fact that thousands of unskilled laborers in Burkina Faso (formerly Upper Volta) are able to find temporary work in neighboring Ivory Coast. The same is true for Egyptians, Pakistanis, and Indians in Kuwait and Saudi Arabia; Tunisians, Moroccans, and Algerians in southern Europe; Colombians in Venezuela; and Haitians in the Dominican Republic. The fact remains, however, that there is very little scope for reducing the pressures of overpopulation in Third World countries today through massive international emigration. The reasons for this relate not so much to a lack of local knowledge about opportunities in other countries as to the combined effects of geographic (and thus economic) distance and, more important, the very restrictive nature of immigration laws in modern developed countries.

Despite these restrictions, at least 35 million people from the Third World have managed to migrate to the developed world since 1960. Six million of these are undocumented or illegal migrants, whose numbers increased dramatically between 1980 and 1995. From the point of view of recipient industrialized nations, the problem of illegal Third World migrants has become so serious that drastic action is being called for. These migrants are perceived as taking jobs away from poor, unskilled citizen workers. Moreover, illegal migrants and their families are believed to be taking unfair advantage of free local health, educational, and social services, causing upward pressure on local taxes to support these services. As a result, major debates are now under way in both the United States and Europe regarding the treatment of illegal migrants. Many citizens want severe restrictions, even total bans, on the number of immigrants that are permitted to enter or reside in developed countries. Others call for legislation to bar illegal workers and their families from the generous benefits that states and localities offer to their citizens. In the United States, the backlash against illegal migrants was most vividly evident in 1994, when voters in the state of California overwhelmingly passed Proposition 187, denying economic and social benefits to all illegal workers and their families. It is likely, therefore, that in the coming years, we will witness an ever-increasing clash between the forces driving unskilled, unemployed Third World workers to seek jobs in developed country markets and pressures in recipient countries to stop the flow of illegal migrants.[12] Whatever the outcome, few people expect the historical safety valve of international migration to be as open as it has historically been for the vast numbers of contemporary unskilled Third World workers.

The irony of international migration today, however, is not merely that this traditional outlet for surplus people has effectively been closed off but that many of the people who migrate *legally* from poor to richer lands are the very ones that Third World countries can least afford to lose: the highly educated and skilled. Since the great majority of these migrants move on a permanent basis, this perverse **brain drain** not only represents a loss of valuable human resources but could prove to be a serious constraint on the future economic progress of Third World nations. For example, between 1960 and 1990, more than a million high-level professional and technical workers from the developing countries migrated to the United States, Canada, and the United Kingdom alone. By the late 1980s, Africa had lost nearly one-third of its skilled workers, with up to 60,000 middle and high-level managers migrating to Europe and North America between 1985 and 1990. Sudan, for example, lost 17% of its doctors and dentists, 20% of its university teachers, 30% of its engineers, and 45% of its surveyors. The Philippines lost 12% of its professional workers to the United States, and 60% of Ghanaian doctors now practice abroad.[13] The fundamental point remains, however, that the possibility of *legal* international migration of unskilled workers on a scale resembling that of the nineteenth and early twentieth centuries no longer exists to provide an effective safety valve for the contemporary surplus populations of Africa, Asia, and Latin America.

The Growth Stimulus of International Trade

International **free trade** has often been referred to as the "engine of growth" that propelled the development of today's economically advanced nations during the nineteenth and early twentieth centuries. Rapidly expanding export markets provided an additional stimulus to growing local demands that led to the establishment of large-scale manufacturing industries. Together with a relatively stable political structure and flexible social institutions, these increased export earnings enabled the developing country of the nineteenth century to borrow funds in the international capital market at very low interest rates. This capital accumulation in turn stimulated further production, made possible increased imports, and led to a more diversified industrial structure. In the nineteenth century, European and North American countries were able to participate in this dynamic growth of international exchange largely on the basis of relatively free trade, free capital movements, and the unfettered international migration of unskilled surplus labor.

Today, the situation for many LDCs is very different. With the exception of a few very successful East Asian and Latin American countries, the non-oil-exporting (and, indeed, some oil-exporting) developing countries face formidable difficulties in trying to generate rapid economic growth on the basis of world trade. Ever since the First World War, many developing countries have experienced a deteriorating trade position. Their exports have expanded, but usually not as fast as the exports of developed nations. Their **terms of trade** (the price they receive for their exports relative to the price they have to pay for imports) have declined steadily. Export volume has therefore had to grow faster just to earn the same amount of foreign currencies as in previous years. Moreover, the developed countries are so far ahead of the LDCs economically that they can afford through their advanced science and technology to remain more competitive, develop more new products (often synthetic substitutes for traditional LDC primary commodity exports), and obtain international financing on much better terms. Finally, where developing countries are successful at becoming lower-cost producers of competitive products with the developed countries (e.g., textiles, clothing, shoes, some light manufactures), the latter have typically resorted to various forms of tariff and nontariff barriers to trade, including import quotas, sanitary requirements, and special licensing arrangements.

We will discuss the economics of international trade and finance in detail in Part Three. For now, it is sufficient to point out that the so-called international engine of growth that roared across the Northern Hemisphere in the nineteenth century has for the most part, for lack of sufficient fuel and need of repairs, struggled and crawled for most newcomers to the growth game in the twentieth century.

Basic Scientific and Technological Research and Development Capabilities

A recurrent theme throughout this chapter has been the crucial role played by basic scientific research and technological development in the modern economic growth experience of contemporary developed countries. Their high rates of growth have been sustained by the interplay between mass applications of many new technological innovations based on a rapid advancement in the stock of scientific knowledge and further additions to that stock of knowledge made possible by growing surplus wealth. And even today, the process of scientific and technological advance in all its stages, from basic research to product development, is heavily concentrated in the rich nations. We saw earlier that over 90% of all world **research and development (R&D)** expenditures originate in these countries. Moreover, as we also saw, research funds are spent on solving the economic and technological problems of concern to rich countries in accordance with their own economic priorities and resource endowments. Rich countries are interested mainly in the development of sophisticated products, large markets, and technologically advanced production methods using large inputs of capital and high levels of skills and management while economizing on their relatively scarce supplies of labor and raw materials. The poor countries, by contrast, are much more interested in simple products, simple designs, saving of capital, use of abundant labor, and production for smaller markets. But they have neither the financial resources nor the scientific and the technological know-how at present to undertake the kind of research and development that would be in their best long-term economic interests. Their dependence on "inappropriate" foreign technologies can create and perpetuate the internal economic dualism that we discussed in Chapter 3.

We may conclude, therefore, that in the important area of scientific and technological research, contemporary Third World nations are in an extremely disadvantageous competitive position vis-à-vis the developed nations. In contrast, when the latter countries were embarking on their early growth process, they were scientifically and technologically greatly in advance of the rest of the world. They could consequently focus on staying ahead by designing and developing new technology at a pace dictated by their long-term economic growth requirements.

Stability and Flexibility of Political and Social Institutions

The final distinction between the historical experience of developed countries and the situation faced by contemporary Third World nations relates to the nature of social and political institutions. One very obvious difference between the now developed and the underdeveloped nations is that well before their industrial revolutions, the former were independent consolidated nation-states able to pursue national policies on the basis of consensus toward modernization. As Gunnar Myrdal has correctly pointed out, the now developed countries

> formed a small world of broadly similar cultures, within which people and ideas circulated rather freely. . . . Modern scientific thought developed in these countries (long before their industrial revolutions) and a modernized technology began early to be introduced in their agriculture and their industries, which at that time were all small-scale.[14]

In contrast to those preindustrial, culturally homogeneous, materially oriented, and politically unified societies, with their emphasis on rationalism and modern scientific thought, many Third World countries of today have only recently gained political independence and have yet to become consolidated nation-states with an effective ability to formulate and pursue national development strategies. Moreover, the modernization ideals embodied in the notions of rationalism, scientific thought, individualism, social and economic mobility, the work ethic, and dedication to national material and cultural values are concepts largely alien to many contemporary Third World societies, except perhaps among their educated ruling elites. Until stable and flexible political institutions can be consolidated with broad public support, the present social and cultural fragmentation of many developing countries is likely to inhibit their ability to accelerate national economic progress.[15]

With the end of the cold war and the rapid globalization of trade, finance, and technology, social and political stability has assumed even greater importance for economic development. For example, given modern technology and the ability to move money around the world in a matter of seconds, international financial flows can respond quickly to changes in the political and economic climate of LDCs. The advent of these "hot money" flows was never more evident than after the surprise devaluation of the Mexican peso in December 1994. Huge sums of money were withdrawn by foreign investors not only from Mexico but throughout Latin America and even from emerging markets in Asia. This turned a serious foreign-exchange situation into a crisis for many countries. We will return to this theme in Part Three.

The critical importance of political stability for economic growth is further underlined by a number of recent quantitative studies.[16] Researchers have found that growth is more influenced by the stability of the political regime than by its type (democracy or dictatorship). They also found that in the transition from dictatorship to democracy, the tremendous pressures from competing interest groups tend to slow down economic growth, but in the longer run, stable democracies experience higher growth than dictatorships.[17]

Conclusions

We may conclude that due to very different initial conditions, the historical experience of Western economic growth is of only limited relevance for contemporary Third World nations. Nevertheless, one of the most significant and relevant lessons to be learned from this historical experience is the critical importance of concomitant and complementary technological, social, and institutional changes, which must take place if long-term economic growth is to be realized. Such transformations must occur not only within individual developing countries but, perhaps more important, in the international economy as well. In other words, unless there is some major structural, attitudinal, and institutional reform in the world economy, one that accommodates the rising aspirations and rewards the outstanding performances of individual developing nations, internal economic and social transformation within the Third World may be insufficient.

CASE STUDY

The Economy of Kenya

GEOGRAPHIC, SOCIAL, AND ECONOMIC INDICATORS

Capital Nairobi

Area 582,646 km^2

Population 28.3 million (1995)

Population (average annual growth rate) 2.9% (1985–1994)

GNP per capita U.S. $260 (1994)

GNP per capita (average annual growth rate) –0.0% (1985–1994)

Agriculture as share of GDP 29% (1994)

Exports as share of GDP 38% (1994)

Infant mortality rate (per 1,000 live births) 69 (1995)

Child malnutrition (underweight) 22% (1993)

Females as share of labor force 39% (1994)

Illiteracy rate (age 15+) 31% (1990)

Human Development Index 0.43 (low) (1992)

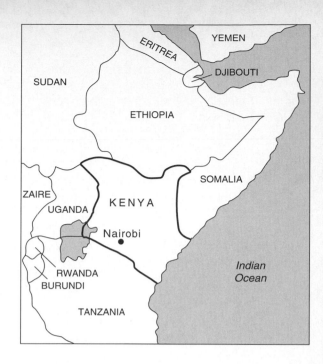

Kenya is a country of diverse geographic and climatic endowment located in eastern Africa. Three-fifths of the nation is semiarid desert (mostly in the north), and the resulting infertility of this land has dictated the location of 85% of the population and almost all economic activity in the southern two-fifths of the country. Kenya's rapidly growing population is composed of many tribes and is extremely heterogeneous (including traditional herders, subsistence and commercial farmers, Arab Muslims, and cosmopolitan residents of Nairobi). The standard of living, at least in the major cities, is relatively high compared to the average of other sub-Saharan African countries. However, widespread poverty, high unemployment, and growing income inequality make Kenya a country of economic as well as geographic diversity. Agriculture is the most important economic activity. Fully 88% of the population still lives in rural areas, and about 7 million workers are employed in agriculture, accounting for three-quarters of the total workforce.

Despite many changes in the democratic system, including the switch from a federal to a republican government, the conversion of the prime ministerial system into a presidential one, the transition to a unicameral legislature, and the creation of a one-party state, Kenya has displayed relatively high political stability (by African standards) since gaining independence from Britain in 1963. Since independence, there have been only two presidents. However, this once stable and prosperous capitalist nation witnessed widespread ethnic violence and political upheavals in 1992 as a deteriorating economy, unpopular one-party rule, and charges of government corruption created a tense situation.

An expansionary economic policy characterized by large public investments, support of small agricultural production units, and incentives for private (domestic and foreign) industrial investment played an important role in the early 7% rate of GDP growth in the first decade after independence. In the following seven years (1973–1980), the oil crisis helped lower GDP growth to an annual 5% rate. Along with the oil price shock, a lack of adequate domestic saving and investment slowed the growth of the economy. Various economic policies designed to promote industrial growth led to a neglect of agriculture and a consequent decline in farm prices, farm production, and farmer incomes. As peasant farmers became poorer, more of them migrated to Nairobi, swelling an already overcrowded city and pushing up an existing high rate of urban unemployment. Very high birthrates along with a steady decline in death rates (mainly through lower infant mortality) led Kenya's population growth to become the highest in the world (4.1% per year) in 1988.

The slowdown in GDP growth persisted in the following five years (1980–1985), when the annual average was 2.6%. It was a period of stabilization in which the political shakiness of 1982 and the severe drought in 1984 contributed to brake industrial growth. Interest rates rose and wages fell in the public and private sectors. An improvement in the budget deficit and in the current account trade deficit obtained through cuts in development expenditures and recessive policies aimed at reducing imports contributed to lower economic growth. By 1990, Kenya's per capita income was 9% *lower* than it was in 1980: $370 compared to $410. It continued to decline in the early 1990s, falling to $340 in 1991, $310 in 1992, and $260 in 1993 and 1994. At the same time, the urban unemployment rate rose to 30%.

Comprising 29% of GDP and 65% of exports, agricultural production is the backbone of the Kenyan economy. Because of its importance, the Kenyan government has implemented several policies to nourish the agricultural sector. Two such policies include setting attractive producer prices and making available increasing amounts of fertilizer. Kenya's chief agricultural exports are coffee, tea, sisal, cashew nuts, pyrethrum, and horticultural products. Traditionally, coffee has been Kenya's chief earner of foreign exchange. Yet in 1987, due to depressed international prices, coffee lost its leading position to tourism.

Although Kenya is chiefly agrarian, it is still the most industrialized country in eastern Africa. Public and private industry accounted for 13.7% of GNP in 1990. Kenya's chief manufacturing activities are food processing and the production of beverages, tobacco, footwear, textiles, cement, metal products, paper, and chemicals.

Kenya currently faces a multitude of problems. These include a stagnating economy, growing political unrest, a huge budget deficit, high unemployment, and a substantial balance of payments problem. Kenya's fundamental problem, however, is its high population growth rate. With a significant rise in fertility and a sharp decline in death rates during the past two decades, one-half of Kenya's population is now under 15 years of age. This dependency burden places a great economic strain on the members of the workforce, who must care for these mostly unproductive people.

With an unemployment rate already at 30% and its growing population, Kenya faces the major task of employing its burgeoning labor force. Yet only 10% of seekers land jobs in the modern industrial sector. The remainder must find jobs in the self-employed sector; work in the agricultural sector, where wages are low and opportunities are scarce; or join the masses of the unemployed.

In addition to the employment problem, Kenya must always be concerned with how to feed its growing population. An increasing population means an increasing demand for food. Yet only 20% of Kenya's land is arable. This implies that the land must become increasingly productive. Unfortunately, several factors work to constrain Kenya's food output, among them fragmented land holdings, increasing environmental degradation, the high cost of agricultural inputs, and burdensome governmental involvement in the purchase, sale, and pricing of agricultural output.

For the fiscal year 1993 the Kenyan budget deficit was $260 million, well above the government's target rate. Dealing with a high budget deficit is a second problem Kenya currently faces. Following the collapse of the East African Common Market, Kenya's industrial growth rate has declined; as a result, the government's tax base has diminished. To supplement domestic savings, Kenya has had to turn to external sources of finance, including foreign aid grants from Western governments. Its highly protected public enterprises have been turning in a poor performance, thus absorbing a large chunk of the government budget. To pay for its expenses, Kenya has had to borrow from international banks on top of receiving foreign aid. In recent years, government borrowing from the international banking system rose dramatically and contributed to a rapid growth in the money supply. This translated into high inflation and pinched availability of credit.

Kenya has also had a chronic international balance of payments problem. Decreasing prices for its exports, combined with increasing prices for its imports, left Kenya with a trade deficit of almost $500 million in 1993. World demand for coffee, Kenya's predominant export, remains below supply. Hence Kenya cannot make use of its comparative advantage in coffee production, and its stock of coffee has been increasing. Tea, another main export, has also had difficulties. In 1987, Pakistan, the second largest importer of Kenyan tea, slashed its purchases. Combined with a general oversupply on the world market, this fall in demand drove the price of tea downward. Hence Kenya experienced both a lowered dollar value and quantity demanded for one of its principal exports.

Although it faces major challenges, the Kenyan government is attempting to undertake a structural adjustment program aimed at raising the GNP growth rate. In response to a suspension of U.S. $600 million in foreign aid by Western nations, the government agreed in 1992 to limit its participation in the private sector, put up for sale its stake in 207 companies, revitalize the agricultural sector through more responsive producer prices, and limit the public-sector deficit. Kenya is one of the few African nations where the benefits of privatization can be substantial. Its capital market is relatively competitive, so privatizing state enterprises would probably improve their efficiency. But political fears of foreign takeovers of local assets have slowed down the overall privatization process.

Unfortunately, structural adjustment usually takes a long time. Whether the Kenyan political and economic system can withstand any further deterioration in living conditions is a major question. Public protests for greater democracy and a growing incidence of ethnic violence may be harbingers of things to come.

Concepts for Review

Brain drain
Capital accumulation
Capital-augmenting technological progress
Capital-saving technological progress
Capital stock
Economic growth
Economic planning
Equalization (economic and social)
Free trade
Human capital
Idea gap
Infrastructure
Ingenuity gap
Labor-augmenting technological progress

Laborsaving technological
     progress
Modernization ideals
Neutral technological progress
Object gap
Production possibility curve

Rationality
Research and development (R&D)
Technological progress
Terms of trade
Total factor productivity (TFP)

Questions for Discussion

1. How would you describe the economic growth process in terms of production possibility analysis? What are the principal sources of economic growth, and how can they be illustrated using *P–P* frontier diagrams?

2. What does the historical record reveal about the nature of the growth process in the now developed nations? What were its principal ingredients?

3. Of what relevance is the historical record of modern economic growth for contemporary Third World nations? How important are differences in "initial conditions"? Give some examples of the initial conditions in a Third World country with which you are familiar that make it different from most contemporary developed nations at the beginning of their modern growth experience.

4. "Social and institutional innovations are as important for economic growth as technological and scientific inventions and innovations." What is meant by this statement? Explain your answer.

5. What do you think were the principal reasons why economic growth spread rapidly among the now developed nations during the nineteenth and early twentieth centuries but has failed to spread to an equal extent to contemporary LDCs?

Notes

1. Recall from our discussion of the new growth theory in Chapter 3 how central a role human capital investment plays in generating positive externalities, increasing returns to scale in production, and sustained long-term growth in output.

2. Simon Kuznets, "Modern economic growth: Findings and reflections," Nobel lecture delivered in Stockholm, Sweden, December 1971, and published in the *American Economic Review* 63 (September 1973): 247–258. Much of the information and analysis in this section is based on Kuznet's trailblazing work.

3. See World Bank, *The East Asian Miracle* (New York: Oxford University Press, 1993).

4. Gunnar Myrdal, *Asian Drama* (New York: Pantheon, 1968), pp. 57–69.

5. Jawaharlal Nehru, "Strategy of the Third Plan," in *Problems in the Third Plan: A Critical Miscellany* (New Delhi: Ministry of Information and Broadcasting, 1961), p. 46.

6. A recent and more theoretical contribution to the literature on historical growth and its relevance to contemporary developing countries can be found in Marvin Goodfriend and John McDermott, "Early development," *American Economic Review* 85 (March 1995): 116–133. Goodfriend and McDermott argue that long-term economic development

involves four fundamental processes: the exploitation of increasing returns to specialization, the transition from household to market production, knowledge and human capital accumulation, and industrialization. With regard to LDCs they argue that "the continuing widespread use of primitive production processes alongside relatively modern techniques is the most striking feature of less-developed countries" (p. 129).

7. For an interesting and provocative analysis of the critical role of "ideas" and "ingenuity" in long-term economic growth, see Paul M. Romer, "Idea gaps and object gaps in economic development," *Journal of Monetary Economics* 32 (December 1993): 543–573, and Thomas Homer-Dixon, "The ingenuity gap: Can poor countries adapt to resource scarcity?" *Population and Development Review* 21 (September 1995): 587–612.

8. Romer, "Idea gaps," 543.

9. See, for example, Andrew M. Kamarck, *The Tropics and Economic Development: A Provocative Inquiry into the Poverty of Nations* (Baltimore: Johns Hopkins University Press, 1976). For a different view, though with a focus on global warming unrelated to other climate conditions in the tropics, see William D. Nordhaus, "Climate and economic development: Climates past and climate change future," *Proceedings of the World Bank Annual Conference on Development Economics 1993* (Washington, D.C.: World Bank, 1994): 355–376. The title of Nordhaus's article is a misnomer as he doesn't deal at all with the kinds of issues briefly mentioned in this text and treated extensively in the Kamarck book, other than to dismiss them as inaccurate or irrelevant.

10. Brinley Thomas, *Migration and Economic Growth* (London: Cambridge University Press, 1954), p. viii.

11. For a description and analysis of the economic implications of international migration from the Mediterranean area to Western Europe, see W. R. Böhnung, "Some thoughts on emigration from the Mediterranean area," *International Labour Review* 14 (1975).

12. For an analysis of this issue, see Douglas Massey, "The new immigration and ethnicity in the United States," *Population and Development Review* 21 (September 1995): 631–652. A frightening scenario of the clash of interests can be found in Matthew Connally and Paul Kennedy, "Must it be the rest against the West?" *Atlantic Monthly*, December 1994, pp. 61–91.

13. United Nations Development Program, *Human Development Report, 1992* (New York: Oxford University Press, 1992), p. 57.

14. Gunnar Myrdal, *The Challenge of World Poverty* (New York: Pantheon, 1970), pp. 30–31.

15. For evidence, see Tony Killick, "Flexibility and economic progress," *World Development* 23 (May 1995): 721–734.

16. For a review of these studies, see Alberto Alesina and Roberto Perotti, "The political economy of growth: A critical survey of the recent literature," *World Bank Economic Review* 8 (September 1994): 351–371.

17. See, for example, Manuel Pastor, Jr. and Joe Ho Sung, "Private investment and democracy in the developing world," *Journal of Economic Issues* 29 (March 1995): 223–243.

Further Reading

On the historical record of economic growth, the classic study is that of the Nobel Prize–winning Harvard economist Simon Kuznets, whose lifetime work is best revealed in two volumes: *Modern Economic Growth: Rate, Structure, and Spread* (New Haven, Conn.: Yale

University Press, 1966) and *Economic Growth of Nations: Total Output and Production Structure* (Cambridge, Mass.: Harvard University Press, 1971). A concise summary of his findings is given in Simon Kuznets, "Modern economic growth: Findings and reflections," *American Economic Review* 63 (September 1973): 247–258. See also Barry E. Supple (ed.), *The Experience of Economic Growth* (New York: Random House, 1963), especially pt. 2, for a comparison of the growth experience in a number of contemporary developed countries. For the most comprehensive general statement on the nature of economic growth as applied to less developed countries, see W. Arthur Lewis's classic work, *Theory of Economic Growth* (London: Unwin, 1955).

An extensive critique of the historical growth record of developed nations as applied to Third World countries can be found in Gunnar Myrdal, *The Challenge of World Poverty* (New York: Pantheon, 1970), chap. 2, and in his *Asian Drama* (New York: Pantheon, 1968), chap. 14. See also Louis Lefeber, "On the paradigm for economic development," *World Development* 2 (January 1974), and Keith Griffin, "Underdevelopment in history," in Charles Wilber (ed.), *The Political Economy of Development and Underdevelopment* (New York: Random House, 1979), chap. 6. A somewhat different view, stressing what can be learned from the historical growth experience and applied to contemporary developing nations, can be found in Andrew J. Youngson (ed.), *Economic Development in the Long Run* (New York: St. Martin's Press, 1973), and especially in Lloyd G. Reynolds, "The spread of economic growth to the Third World," *Journal of Economic Literature* 21 (September 1983): 956–958. An attempt to model long-term economic growth focusing on the new growth theory ideas of increasing returns and human capital accumulations can be obtained from Marvin Goodfriend and John McDermott, "Early development," *American Economic Review* 85 (March 1995): 116–133.

Finally, in Chapter 4 of *Case Studies*, Stephen C. Smith tells the story of Guangdong province, China which has recorded the fastest growth in economic history.

Contributions of Alternative Approaches to Development

Contributed by Stephen C. Smith

A closer examination of two countries confirms the conclusion in the text that each of the first four broad approaches to development—stages of growth, structural patterns of development, dependence, and neoclassical—provides important insights about development processes and policy.* South Korea and Argentina are reasonably well matched for such a comparison; for example, both are mid-size in population (34 million in Argentina and 44 million in South Korea), and both are classified as middle-income countries (although today South Korea has more than double the per capita income of Argentina, whereas 25 years earlier the reverse was true).

South Korea

Stages of growth

South Korea confirms some linear-stages views, albeit in a limited way. In recent years, its share of investment in national income has been among the highest in the world, and this is a critical part of the explanation of the nation's rapid ascent. To remind us of just how rapid this ascent has been, we should consider that the country did not even rate a mention in Rostow's *Stages of Economic Growth*, and in 1960, when the book was published, few of the "pre-conditions for take-off" were in place. Gross domestic investment has grown at a rate of over 14% over the past three decades. But as a share of GNP, the investment ratio, at 15%, was still below takeoff levels in 1965.

*The fifth approach, endogenous growth theory, is not treated here, although the importance of human capital development, externalities, and economies of scale have obvious relevance to South Korea's growth experience, and, to date, little relevance for Argentina.

Yet it rose dramatically to 37% of GNP in 1990. Still, South Korea today does seem well characterized by Rostow's notion of an economy in the midst of a "drive to maturity," well on its way toward mastering the range of currently available technologies.

Rostow claimed that maturity is attained some 60 years after takeoff begins, but he never denied unique experiences for each country, and it may well be that the gap between traditional and advanced technology can actually be crossed more quickly at later stages of development. The larger the productivity gap between countries, the quicker that income can grow once takeoff has been achieved. For example, whereas Britain doubled its output per person in the first 60 years of its industrial revolution and America did so in 45 years, Korea accomplished this in the decade from 1966 to 1977; incredibly, Guangdong province in China (adjacent to Hong Kong) recently performed this feat in less than half that time. South Korea certainly meets the "maturity" criterion of becoming integrated with the world economy through new types of exports and imports. Although the fact that India, rather than South Korea, was picked by Rostow for takeoff shows the limits of the predictive powers of the stages theory, the case of Korea nonetheless offers some confirmation of their value.

Structural patterns

South Korea also confirms some patterns-of-development structural-change models. In particular, South Korea's rise over the past generation has been characterized by rapidly increasing agricultural productivity, shifts of labor from agriculture to industry, the steady growth of the capital stock and of education and skills, and the demographic transition from high to low fertility. These changes occurred while South Korea's per capita income grew by more than 7% annually for the whole 1965–1990 period. In the late 1940s and 1950s, South Korea carried out very thoroughgoing land reform, so agriculture was not neglected; but otherwise its growth through rapid expansion of the percentage of the labor force in industry has broadly conformed with the Lewis model of development. After about 1970, productivity growth in agriculture also increased rapidly, owing in part to a successful integrated rural development program.

Dependence revolution

But South Korea poses a serious challenge to the dependence revolution models. Here is a poor country that became tied in with the international economy: It was strongly dependent in international relations (it was a Japanese colony until 1945) and wholly dependent on maintaining the goodwill of the United States for defense against invasion by North Korea. It received a large part of its national budget in the form of U.S. aid in the 1950s and both exported and imported a great deal from developed countries, especially the United States and Japan. The shape of the nation's development was thus "conditioned" in large part by export opportunities to developed countries, and dependence theory would predict that retarded development opportunities should result. Yet South Korea today is widely considered a candidate for developed-country status (its income is now greater than to that of Greece and over half that of New Zealand). Of course, dependence theorists could and do claim that South Korea is an exception because of the magnitude of aid it received and the self-interests of the advanced countries in seeing its full successful development because of its role as a bulwark against communism. And the Korean government pursued some particular policies

that the dependence school would by and large applaud, including carrying out an extremely active industrial upgrading policy, sharply limiting the role of multinational corporations and deliberately establishing indigenous industries as an alternative, and using debt rather than direct foreign equity investment to finance extraordinary levels of investment. South Korea also implemented one of the most thoroughgoing land reform programs in the developing world and placed strong emphasis on primary rather than university education, two policies of exceptional importance. But this does not explain how South Korea was able to adopt such policies to break out of dependence in the first place. And when too many exceptions start to be made in any theory, it usually indicates that the theory doesn't reflect the whole truth.

Neoclassical counterrevolution

South Korea likewise poses a strong challenge to the neoclassical counterrevolution models. Although some members of this school have tried to claim South Korea as their own, by now an overwhelmingly large body of scholarship makes it clear that the nation was highly interventionist at home and in international trade, with the government making extensive use of development planning, using a wide range of tax breaks and incentives to induce firms to follow government directives and interventions, setting individual company export targets, orchestrating efforts in various industries to upgrade the average technological level, coordinating foreign technology licensing agreements, using monopoly power to get the best deal from competing multinationals, and generally inducing firms to move rapidly up the ladder of (dynamic) comparative advantage. These policies addressed real technology and skill-raising market failure problems of development, and very few cases of glaring government failure can be pointed to in this experience. Of course, it does confirm that firms respond to economic incentives.

Argentina

In contrast, for the case of Argentina, stages and patterns theories give relatively little understanding of economic history, whereas the dependence revolution and neoclassical counterrevolution theories together offer important insights.

Stages of growth

The history of Argentina poses a strong challenge to the linear-stages approach. Rostow defined takeoff as "the interval when the old blocks and resistances to steady growth are finally overcome. . . . Growth becomes its normal condition." In 1870, Argentina ranked eleventh in the world in per capita income (ahead of Germany); today, it is not even in the top 50. Although Rostow said that in determining a country's stage, technology absorption, not income per inhabitant, is what matters, he dated Argentina's preconditions for takeoff as an extended period before 1914 and concluded that takeoff "in some sense" began in the First World War, but "in the mid-1930s . . . a sustained take-off was inaugurated, which by and large can now [1960] be judged to have been successful," concluding that "in Latin America the take-off has been completed in two major cases (Mexico and Argentina)." Rostow attributes the fact that preconditions were there for some time before takeoff to excessive import of foreign capital over too long a period without increasing domestic savings. (But South Korea was also a heavy foreign borrower until very recently.) Argentina certainly satisfied Rostow's criterion of developing manufacturing sectors at a rapid rate.

But now let's look at what happened in Argentina since Rostow put the country forward as an example. According to World Bank data, Argentina had a *negative* growth rate throughout the 1965–1990 period, and in the 1980s, domestic investment shrank at a −8.3% rate, falling back well below Rostow's threshold takeoff investment levels. Argentina, like many other Latin American and African countries in the 1970s and 1980s, demonstrated that development progress is not irreversible and that seemingly sustained growth can come to an end.

Structural patterns

Argentina did exhibit many of the usual structural patterns of development, as agricultural productivity rose, industrial employment grew (albeit slowly), urbanization took place, fertility fell, and so on. But the fact that many structural regularities of development were observed even as living standards in the country stagnated illustrates some of the shortcomings of relying too much on selected pieces of data without the assistance of guiding theory on how the parts fit together.

Dependence revolution

In contrast to South Korea, the case of Argentina offers some vindication for dependence theories in that the country relied to a large extent on exporting primary goods, and the real prices of these goods fell compared to imports. Multinational corporations played a large role, and Argentina was unable to create its own viable manufacturing *export* industries, ultimately having to submit to stringent structural-adjustment programs, sell state industries to foreign companies, and other constraints. Dependence theorists can claim with some justification that Argentina's conditioned development fell victim to developed-country economic interests, especially those of British and American corporations.

Neoclassical counterrevolution

But Argentina also offers some vindication for neoclassical counterrevolution theory in that faulty interventionist restrictions, inefficient state enterprise, bias against production for exports, and unnecessary red tape ended up hurting industry and entrepreneurship. Government policy consistently seemed to support privileged interests rather than broad goals of development, and government failure was usually worse than market failure in the country. In the mid-1990s, however, there were signs that a liberalization and privatization program was beginning to reinvigorate growth in Argentina.

Summary

It is interesting that as South Korea provides a challenge to both dependence and neoclassical theory, the starkest opposites in many ways, Argentina can be viewed more as a vindication for these two theories; and South Korea serves more to confirm linear stages of growth and conclusions about structural patterns of development, whereas Argentina poses challenges to their universal importance. Yet each of these four approaches has added something vital to our understanding of development experiences and prospects in just these two countries.

Sources: Walt W. Rostow, *The Stages of Economic Growth: A Non-Communist Manifesto* (London: Cambridge University Press, 1960); *Financial Times* and *Washington Post*, various issues; World Bank, *Korea: Managing the Industrial Transition* (Washington, D.C.: World Bank, 1987); various other World Bank documents; Michael Porter, *Competitive Advantage of Nations* (New York: Free Press, 1990); Lester Thurow, *Head to Head* (New York: Morrow, 1992).

PART TWO

PROBLEMS AND POLICIES: DOMESTIC

A Note to the Student

A note to the student on the organizational structure and operating procedure for analyzing development problems in Parts Two and Three

I N PART ONE, we examined the major characteristics of Third World nations, reviewed some basic models and theories of development, and explored the nature and meaning of economic growth. In Parts Two and Three, we focus on specific problems that are priority issues in almost all developing countries. Our task here is not only to describe the nature of these problems but also to demonstrate how economic analysis can contribute to their ultimate resolution. It is of little value to understand basic economic concepts and principles if one is not able to apply them to real-world development problems.

Accordingly, the problem-focused chapters in Parts Two and Three are generally organized around a common five-stage operating procedure. This procedure, I would argue, provides a convenient methodology for analyzing and solving any problem, in economics or any other field. The five stages of problem analysis are these:

1. *Statement of the problem and main issues*
2. *Relative importance of the problem in various developing countries*
3. *Possible goals and objectives*
4. *Role of economics and economic principles*
5. *Policy alternatives and consequences*

1. Statement of Problem and Main Issues

Each discussion begins with an analysis of what we are trying to understand (e.g., population growth, unemployment, poverty). Basically, four questions are asked:

a. *What is the problem all about?*
b. *Why is it a problem?*
c. *How important is it?*
d. *What are the principal issues?*

The purpose of this first step is to clarify the nature and importance of the problem so that you can recognize why it receives so much attention in newspapers, political speeches, and the writings of scholars and journalists.

2. Relative Importance of Problems in Various Developing Countries

Using the most recent available data, we attempt here to provide a capsule statistical summary of the relative importance of the particular problem under review in diverse developing nations. How does it vary from one country to the next, and what, if any, are the qualitative and quantitative differences in Africa, Asia, and Latin America? It is clear, for example, that although rising unemployment is a common phenomenon in developing nations, the nature, extent, and significance of the problem may be quite different in sub-Saharan Africa, in Latin America, than in South Asia. Our purpose is not to overload you with comparative statistics. Rather, it is to give you a feel for the ubiquitous nature of certain development problems while advising that the significance and principal manifestations of the problem may vary from country to country and region to region. As a result, policy approaches designed to cope with the problem can and often do differ in scope and content.

3. Possible Goals and Objectives

Next we set out the likely development goals and objectives as they relate to each particular issue. Here we must unavoidably deal with value judgments and priorities. For example, if greater equality is an overall objective of government policy, factors such as the distribution of income, the spread of educational opportunities, and the role of labor-intensive rural development projects become significant. If, however, the objective is maximum growth of GNP irrespective of its distribution, these factors may be less important. The point is that any attempt to deal with real-world development problems must be based on explicit economic and social-value premises about what is desirable and what the priorities are among different desirable goals. In fact, the very selection of specific problems to be discussed and analyzed in Parts Two and Three (e.g., poverty, inequality, unemployment, population growth, the environment, education, rural development, trade, debt, aid, technology) reflects a value judgment on the part of the author, albeit one that is rooted in the consensus of the majority of people who study or act on Third World development problems.

4. Role of Economics and Economic Principles

It is important for comprehensive understanding that we ask the following pertinent questions:

a. *What are the economic components of the problem?*

b. *How can economic concepts and principles help us understand the problem better and possibly solve it?*

c. *Do the economic components dominate the problem, and in any event, how might they be related to the noneconomic components?*

5. Policy Alternatives and Consequences

The final step in our problem-solving procedure is to set forth alternative economic policy approaches and their possible consequences for the problem under review.

Policy options expounded at the end of each chapter are intended primarily to stimulate group discussion and individual analysis. You are encouraged, therefore, to formulate your own conclusions and to feel free to disagree with those put forward in the book. The policy options available to governments depend on the economic aspects of the overall problem. Each policy alternative must be evaluated in light of development priorities. As a result, the possibility of trade-offs between goals must always be considered. For example, the goal of rapid GNP growth may or may not be compatible with the elimination of unemployment or the eradication of rural poverty. Similarly, the encouragement of private foreign investment may not be compatible with the desire to be more self-reliant. In any case, when such a conflict of goals becomes apparent, choices have to be made on the basis of priorities and the socioeconomic consequences of giving up or curtailing one objective in favor of another. It is at this final stage of evaluating the *indirect* ways in which a policy designed to eliminate one problem might exacerbate other problems that the wisdom of the broad-gauged development economist can be most important.

By following the five-step problem-solving procedure, not only will you secure a more comprehensive understanding of critical development issues, but more important, you will also be better able to approach and reach independent judgments about other contemporary or future development problems. In the long run, the possible "costs" of trying to analyze all problems within a somewhat rigid five-stage framework rather than following a less tightly organized discussion will be greatly outweighed by the benefits.

CHAPTER 5

Growth, Poverty, and Income Distribution

No society can surely be flourishing and happy, of which by far the greater part of the numbers are poor and miserable.

—Adam Smith, 1776

A society that is not socially just and does not intend to be puts its own future in danger.

—Pope John Paul II, Brazil, 1980

The unfinished business of the 21st century is the eradication of poverty.
—Juan Somavia, United Nations World Summit for Social Development, 1995

The Growth Controversy

The 1970s witnessed a remarkable change in public and private perceptions about the ultimate nature of economic activity. In both rich and poor countries, there was a growing disillusionment with the idea that the relentless pursuit of growth was the principal economic objective of society. In the developed countries, the major emphasis seemed to shift toward more concern for the quality of life, a concern manifested mainly in the environmental movement. There was an outcry against the concomitants of industrial growth: the pollution of air and water, the depletion of natural resources, and the destruction of many scenic wonders. An influential book, *The Limits to Growth*, published under the auspices of the Club of Rome, appeared in 1972 and purported to document the fact, first expounded in the early nineteenth century by David Ricardo and especially by the Reverend Thomas Malthus, that the earth's finite resources could not sustain a continuation of high growth rates without major economic and social catastrophes. It is a testimony to the mood of the times that in spite of obvious flaws in logic and many dubious assumptions, this book became widely publicized and acclaimed.

In the poor countries, the main concern focused on the question of growth versus income distribution. That development required a higher GNP and a faster growth rate was obvious. The basic issue, however, was (and is) not only how to make GNP grow but also who would make it grow, the few or the many. If it were the rich, it would most likely be appropriated by them, and poverty and inequality would continue to worsen. But if it were generated by the many, they would be its principal beneficiaries, and the fruits of economic growth would be shared more evenly. Thus many Third World countries that had experienced relatively high rates of economic growth by historical standards began to realize that such growth had brought little in the way of significant benefits to their poor. For those hundreds of millions of people in Africa, Asia, and Latin America, levels of living seemed to stagnate and in some countries even to decline in real terms. Rates of rural and urban unemployment and underemployment were on the rise. The distribution of incomes seemed to become less equitable with each passing year. Many people felt that rapid economic growth had failed to eliminate or even reduce widespread absolute poverty.

In both the developing and developed worlds, the call for the dethronement of GNP as the major objective of economic activity was widely heard. In its place, concern for the problems of poverty and equality became the major theme of the 1970s. Although the revival of neoclassical economics and the new growth theories in the 1980s and 1990s once again put growth at the forefront, the poverty problem not only persisted but continued to worsen as Third World economies, particularly those in Latin America and sub-Saharan Africa, began to crumble under staggering debt burdens (see Chapter 14), widespread famine, and government austerity programs that seemed to fall most heavily on the poor. In September 1994, the Program of Action at the Cairo International Conference on Population and Development asserted that "despite decades of development efforts, both the gap between rich and poor nations and inequalities within nations have widened. . . . Widespread poverty remains the major challenge to development efforts."[1] This view was echoed again and again at the United Nations World Summit for Social Development held in Copenhagen in March 1995 and attended by more than 134 heads of state.

Because the elimination of widespread poverty and growing income inequality are at the core of all development problems and, in fact, define for many people the principal objective of development policy, we begin Part Two by focusing on the nature of the poverty and inequality problem in Third World countries. Although our main focus is on economic inequalities in the distribution of incomes and assets, it is important to keep in mind that this is only a small part of the broader inequality problem in the developing world. Of parallel or even greater importance are inequalities of power, prestige, status, gender, job satisfaction, conditions of work, degree of participation, freedom of choice, and many other dimensions of the problem that relate more to our second and third components of the meaning of development, self-esteem and freedom to choose. But as in most social relationships, we cannot really separate the economic from the noneconomic manifestations of inequality. Each reinforces the other in a complex and often interrelated process of cause and effect.

Our basic problem-solving approach will be as outlined. First, we define the nature of the poverty and income distribution problem and consider its quantitative significance in various Third World nations. We then set forth possible goals and objectives, examine in what ways economic analyses can shed light on the problem, and finally explore alternative possible policy approaches directed at the elimination of poverty and the reduction of excessively wide disparities in Third World distributions of income. A thorough understanding of these two fundamental economic manifestations of underdevelopment provides the basis for analysis in subsequent chapters of more specific development issues including population growth, unemployment, rural development, education, international trade, and foreign assistance.

In this chapter, therefore, we will examine the following five critical questions about the relationship between economic growth, income distribution, and poverty:

1. What is the extent of relative inequality in Third World countries, and how is this related to the extent of absolute poverty?

2. Who are the poor, and what are their economic characteristics?

3. What determines the nature of economic growth—that is, who benefits?

4. Are rapid economic growth and more equitable distributions of income compatible or conflicting objectives for low-income countries? To put it another way, is rapid growth achievable only at the cost of greater inequalities in the distribution of income, or can a lessening of income disparities contribute to higher growth rates?

5. What kinds of policies are required to reduce the magnitude and extent of absolute poverty?

Some Basic Concepts: Size and Functional Distributions of Income

We can get some idea of the answers to questions 1 and 2 relating to the extent and character of inequality and poverty in developing countries by pulling together some recent evidence from a variety of sources. In this section, we define the dimensions of the income distribution and poverty problems and identify some similar elements that characterize the problem in many Third World nations. But first we should be clear about what we are measuring when we speak about the distribution of income.

Economists usually like to distinguish between two principal measures of income distribution for both analytic and quantitative purposes: the personal or size distribution of income and the functional or distributive factor share distribution of income.

Size Distributions

The **personal** or **size distribution of income** is the measure most commonly used by economists. It simply deals with individual persons or households and the total incomes they receive. The way in which that income was received is not considered. What matters is how much each earns irrespective of whether the income was derived solely from employment or came also from other sources such as interest, profits, rents, gifts, or inheritance. Moreover, the locational (urban or rural) and occupational sources of the income (e.g., agriculture, manufacturing, commerce, services) are neglected. If Ms. X and Mr. Y both receive the same personal income, they are classified together irrespective of the fact that Ms. X may work 15 hours a day as a doctor while Mr. Y doesn't work at all but simply collects interest on his inheritance.

Economists and statisticians therefore like to arrange all individuals by ascending personal incomes and then divide the total population into distinct groups, or sizes. A common method is to divide the population into successive **quintiles** (fifths) or **deciles** (tenths) according to ascending income levels and then determine what proportion of the total national income is received by each income group. For example, Table 5.1 shows a hypothetical but fairly typical distribution of income for a developing country. In this table, 20 individuals (or more commonly, households), representing the entire population of the country, are arranged in order of ascending annual personal income, ranging from the individual with the lowest income (0.8 units) to the one with the highest (15.0 units). The total or national income of all individuals amounts to 100 units and is the sum of all entries in column 2. In column 3, the population is grouped into quintiles of four individuals each. The first quintile represents the bottom 20% of the population on the income scale. This group receives only 5%

TABLE 5.1 Hypothetical (but Typical) Size Distribution of Personal Income in a Developing Country by Income Shares—Quintiles and Deciles

Individuals	Personal Income (money units)	Percentage Share in Total Income	
		Quintiles	Deciles
1	0.8		
2	1.0		1.8
3	1.4		
4	1.8	5	3.2
5	1.9		
6	2.0		3.9
7	2.4		
8	2.7	9	5.1
9	2.8		
10	3.0		5.8
11	3.4		
12	3.8	13	7.2
13	4.2		
14	4.8		9.0
15	5.9		
16	7.1	22	13.0
17	10.5		
18	12.0		22.5
19	13.5		
20	15.0	51	28.5
Total (national income)	100.0	100	100.0

NOTE: Measure of inequality – ratio of bottom 40% to top 20% = 14/51 = 0.28.

(i.e., a total of 5 money units) of the total national income. The second quintile (individuals 5–8) receives 9% of the total income. Alternatively, the bottom 40% of the population (quintiles 1 plus 2) is receiving only 14% of the income, while the top 20% (the fifth quintile) of the population receives 51% of the total income.

A common measure of income inequality that can be derived from column 3 is the ratio of the incomes received by the bottom 40% and top 20% of the population. This ratio is often used as a measure of the degree of inequality between the two extremes of very poor and very rich in a country. In our example, this inequality ratio is equal to 14 divided by 51, or approximately 1 to 3.7, or 0.28.

To provide a more detailed breakdown of the size distribution of income, decile (10%) shares are listed in column 4. We see, for example, that the bottom 10% of the population (the two poorest individuals) is receiving only 1.8% of the total income, while the top 10% (the two richest individuals) receives 28.5%. Finally, if we wanted to know what the top 5% receives, we would divide the total population into 20 equal groups of individuals (in our example, this would simply be each of the 20 individuals) and calculate the percentage of total income received by the top group. In Table 5.1, we see that the top 5% of the population (the twentieth individual) receives 15% of the income, a higher share than the combined shares of the lowest 40%.

Lorenz Curves

Another common way to analyze personal income statistics is to construct what is known as a **Lorenz curve**.[2] Figure 5.1 shows how it is done. The numbers of income recipients are plotted on the horizontal axis, not in absolute terms but in *cumulative percentages*. For example, at point 20 we have the lowest (poorest) 20% of the population, at point 60 we have the bottom 60%, and at the end of the axis all 100%

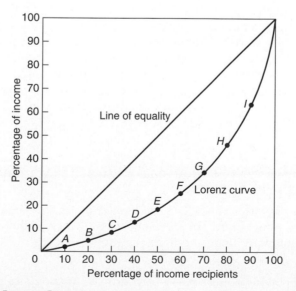

FIGURE 5.1 The Lorenz Curve.

of the population has been accounted for. The vertical axis shows the share of total income received by each percentage of population. It also is cumulative up to 100%, meaning that both axes are equally long. The entire figure is enclosed in a square, and a diagonal line is drawn from the lower left corner (the origin) of the square to the upper right corner. At every point on that diagonal, the percentage of income received is *exactly equal* to the percentage of income recipients—for example, the point halfway along the length of the diagonal represents 50% of the income being distributed to exactly 50% of the population. At the three-quarter point on the diagonal, 75% of the income would be distributed to 75% of the population. In other words, the diagonal line in Figure 5.1 is representative of "perfect equality" in size distribution of income. Each percentage group of income recipients is receiving that same percentage of the total income; for example, the bottom 40% receives 40% of the income, while the top 5% receives only 5% of the total income.[3]

The Lorenz curve shows the *actual* quantitative relationship between the percentage of income recipients and the percentage of the total income they did in fact receive during, say, a given year. In Figure 5.1, we have plotted this Lorenz curve using the decile data contained in Table 5.1. In other words, we have divided both the horizontal and vertical axes into 10 equal segments corresponding to each of the 10 decile groups. Point *A* shows that the bottom 10% of the population receives only 1.8% of the total income, point *B* shows that the bottom 20% is receiving 5% of the total income, and so on for each of the other eight cumulative decile groups. Note that at the halfway point, 50% of the population is in fact receiving only 19.8% of the total income.

The more the Lorenz line curves away from the diagonal (perfect equality), the greater the degree of inequality represented. The extreme case of perfect inequality (i.e., a situation in which one person receives all of the national income while everybody else receives nothing) would be represented by the congruence of the Lorenz curve with the bottom horizontal and right-hand vertical axes. Because no country exhibits either perfect equality or perfect inequality in its distribution of income, the Lorenz curves for different countries will lie somewhere to the right of the diagonal in Figure 5.1. The greater the degree of inequality, the greater the bend and the closer to the bottom horizontal axis the Lorenz curve will be. Two representative distributions are shown in Figure 5.2, one for a relatively equal distribution (Figure 5.2a) and the other for a more unequal distribution (Figure 5.2b). (Can you explain why the Lorenz curve could not lie above or to the left of the diagonal at any point?)

Dualistic Development and Shifting Lorenz Curves: Some Stylized Typologies

In his important book *Poverty, Inequality and Development*, Gary S. Fields demonstrates how Lorenz curves can be used to analyze three limiting cases of dualistic development along the lines suggested by the Lewis model.[4] He distinguishes among three stylized development typologies:

1. The *modern-sector enlargement* growth typology, in which the two-sector economy develops by enlarging the size of its modern sector while maintaining con-

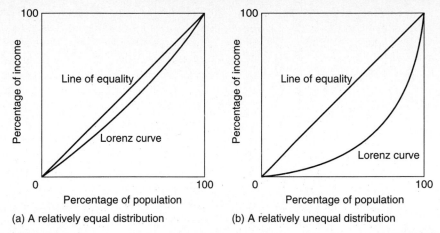

FIGURE 5.2 The Greater the Curvature of the Lorenz Line, the Greater the Relative Degree of Inequality.

stant wages in both sectors. This is the case depicted by the Lewis model in Chapter 3. It corresponds roughly to the historical growth pattern of Western developed nations and, to a lesser extent, the pattern in countries like Japan, South Korea, and Taiwan.

2. The *modern-sector enrichment* growth typology, in which the economy grows but such growth is limited to a fixed number of people in the modern sector, with both the numbers of workers and their wages held constant in the traditional sector. This has been the experience of many Latin American and African economies.

3. The *traditional-sector enrichment* growth typology, in which all of the benefits of growth are equally divided among traditional-sector workers, with little or no growth occurring in the modern sector. This was the case in Maoist China and a few other revolutionary, socialist economies.

Using these three special cases and Lorenz curves, Fields is able to demonstrate the validity of the following propositions (reversing the order just presented):

1. In the *traditional-sector enrichment* typology, growth results in higher income, a *more equal* relative distribution of income, and less poverty. Traditional-sector enrichment growth causes the Lorenz curve to shift uniformly upward and closer toward the line of equality, as portrayed in Figure 5.3.

2. In the *modern-sector enrichment* growth typology, growth results in higher incomes, a *less equal* relative distribution of income, and no change in poverty. Modern-sector enrichment growth causes the Lorenz curve to shift downward and farther from the line of equality, as shown in Figure 5.4.

3. Finally, in the case of Lewis-type *modern-sector enlargement* growth, absolute incomes rise and absolute poverty is reduced, but the Lorenz curves will always cross so that we cannot make any unambiguous statement about changes in relative inequality. It may improve or worsen. Fields shows that in fact it is likely

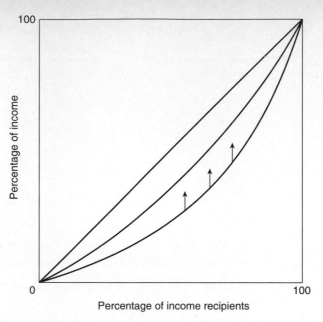

FIGURE 5.3 Improved Income Distribution under the Traditional-Sector Enrichment Growth Typology.

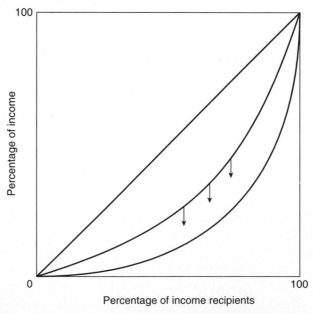

FIGURE 5.4 Worsened Income Distribution under the Modern-Sector Enrichment Growth Typology.

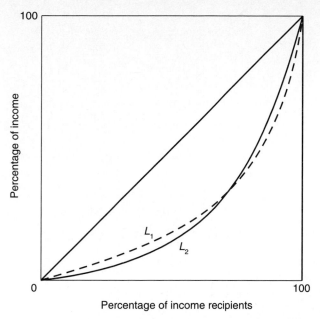

FIGURE 5.5   Crossing Lorenz Curves in the Modern-Sector Enlargement Growth Typology.

first to worsen in the early stages of development and then to improve. The crossing of the Lorenz curves is demonstrated in Figure 5.5.

The explanation for the crossing in Figure 5.5 is as follows: The poor who remain in the traditional sector have their incomes unchanged, but these incomes are now a smaller fraction of the larger total, so that the new Lorenz curve, L_2, lies *below* the old Lorenz curve, L_1, at the lower end of the income distribution scale. Each modern-sector worker receives the same absolute income as before, but now the share received by the richest income group is smaller, so that the new Lorenz curve lies *above* the old one at the higher end of the income distribution scale. Therefore, somewhere in the middle of the distribution, the old and new Lorenz curves must cross, with the result that no unambiguous welfare judgment based on changes in relative inequality can be made. Each country has to be analyzed on a case-by-case basis.[5]

Gini Coefficients and Aggregate Measures of Inequality

A final and very convenient shorthand summary measure of the relative degree of income inequality in a country can be obtained by calculating the ratio of the area between the diagonal and the Lorenz curve divided by the total area of the half-square in which the curve lies. In Figure 5.6, this is the ratio of the shaded area A to the total area of the triangle BCD. This ratio is known as the *Gini concentration ratio* or more simply as the **Gini coefficient**, named after the Italian statistician who first formulated it in 1912.

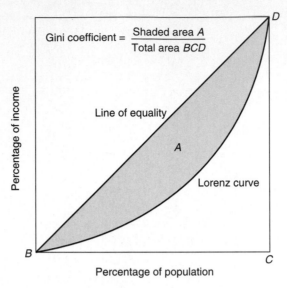

FIGURE 5.6 **Estimating the Gini Coefficient.**

Gini coefficients are aggregate inequality measures and can vary anywhere from 0 (perfect equality) to 1 (perfect inequality). In actual fact, as we shall soon discover, the Gini coefficient for countries with highly unequal income distributions typically lies between 0.50 and 0.70, while for countries with relatively equitable distributions, it is on the order of 0.20 to 0.35. The coefficient for our hypothetical distribution of Table 5.1 and Figure 5.1 is approximately 0.61—a relatively unequal distribution. However, although Gini coefficients provide useful information on levels and changes in relative income inequality based on past and present shapes of the Lorenz curve, a problem arises when Lorenz curves cross, as in the case of the dualistic development modern-sector enlargement typology portrayed in Figure 5.5. Curves L_1 and L_2 may indeed yield different Gini coefficients, but it is problematic whether we can in this special case claim that a higher coefficient means a more unequal distribution. More careful analysis is required.

Functional Distributions

The second common measure of income distribution used by economists, the **functional** or **factor share distribution of income**, attempts to explain the share of total national income that each of the **factors of production** (land, labor, and capital) receives. Instead of looking at individuals as separate entities, the theory of functional income distribution inquiries into the percentage that labor receives as a whole and compares this with the percentages of total income distributed in the form of rent, interest, and profit (i.e., the returns to land and financial and physical capital). Although specific individuals may receive income from all these sources, that is not a matter of concern for the functional approach.

A sizable body of theoretical literature has been built up around the concept of functional income distribution. It attempts to explain the income of a factor of production by the contribution that this factor makes to production. Supply and demand curves are assumed to determine the unit prices of each productive factor. When these unit prices are multiplied by quantities employed on the assumption of efficient (minimum-cost) factor utilization, we get a measure of the total payment to each factor. For example, the supply of and demand for labor are assumed to determine its market wage. When this wage is then multiplied by the total level of employment, we get a measure of total wage payments, also sometimes called the *total wage bill*.

Figure 5.7 provides a simple diagrammatic illustration of the traditional theory of functional income distribution. We assume that there are only two factors of production: capital, which is a fixed (given) factor, and labor, which is the only variable factor. Under competitive market assumptions, the demand for labor will be determined by labor's marginal product (i.e., additional workers will be hired up to the point where the value of their marginal product equals their real wage). But in accordance with the principle of diminishing marginal products, this demand for labor will be a declining function of the numbers employed. Such a negatively sloped labor demand curve is shown by line D_L in Figure 5.7. With a traditional neoclassical upward-sloping labor supply curve S_L, the equilibrium wage will be equal to W_E and the equilibrium level of employment will be L_E. Total national output (which equals total national income) will be represented by the area $OREL_E$.[6] This national income will be distributed in two shares: OW_EEL_E going to workers in the form of wages and W_ERE remaining as capitalist profits (the return to owners of capital). Hence in a competitive market economy with constant-returns-to-scale production functions (a doubling of all inputs doubles output), factor prices are determined by factor supply and demand curves, and factor shares always combine to exhaust the total national product. Income is distributed by function—

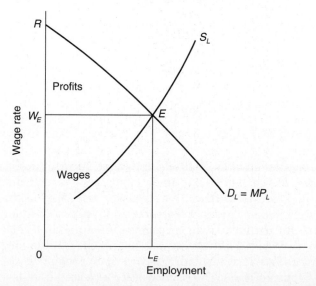

FIGURE 5.7   **Functional Income Distribution in a Market Economy: An Illustration.**

laborers receive wages, owners of land receive rents, and capitalists obtain profits. It is a neat and logical theory in that each and every factor gets paid only in accordance with what it contributes to national output—no more, no less. In fact, as you may recall from Chapter 3, this model of income distribution is at the core of the Lewis theory of modern-sector growth based on the reinvestment of rising capitalist profits.

Unfortunately, the relevance of the functional theory is greatly diminished by its failure to take into account the important role and influence of nonmarket forces such as power in determining these factor prices—for example, the role of collective bargaining between employers and trade unions in the setting of modern-sector wage rates and the power of monopolists and wealthy landowners to manipulate prices on capital, land, and output to their own personal advantage. Later in this chapter we will have more to say about the relative strengths and weaknesses of the size and functional approaches to analyzing income distribution. But first let us review some empirical data to get a better idea of the magnitude of the problems of inequality and poverty in a wide range of developing nations.

A Review of Evidence: Inequality and Absolute Poverty in Third World Countries

Inequality: Variations among Countries

As a first step in determining the significance of the income distribution and poverty problems in Third World countries, let us look at data collected from 15 countries on the percentage shares in total national income going to different percentile groups (see Table 5.2). Though methods of collection, degree of coverage, and specific definitions of personal income may vary from country to country, the figures recorded in Table 5.2 give a first approximation of the magnitude of **income inequality** in these developing countries.[7] For example, we see from the last row that by averaging income shares for different percentile groups among all 15 countries, on average the poorest 20% of the population receives only 5.7% of the income while the highest 10% and 20% receive 33.8% and 49.5%, respectively. By contrast, in a more developed country like Japan, the poorest 20% receives a much higher 8.7% of the income while the richest 10% and 20% get only 22.4% and 37.5%, respectively.

Consider now the relationship, if any, between levels of per capita income and degree of inequality. Are higher incomes associated with greater or lesser inequality, or can no definitive statement be made? Table 5.3 provides recent data on income distribution in relation to per capita GNP for a sample of 10 developing countries. Income distribution is measured in three ways: as the total share of income received by the poorest 40% of the population, as the ratio of the share going to the richest 20% divided by that of the poorest 20%, and as measured by the Gini coefficient. The countries are arranged from lowest to highest in terms of per capita income.

TABLE 5.2 Some Income Distribution Estimates

	Quintile						
Country	1st	2nd	3rd	4th	5th	Highest 10%	Year
Bangladesh	9.5	13.4	17.0	21.6	38.6	24.6	1989
Botswana	3.6	6.9	11.4	19.2	58.9	42.9	1986
Brazil	2.1	4.9	8.9	16.8	67.5	51.3	1989
Colombia	3.6	7.6	12.6	20.4	55.8	39.5	1991
Costa Rica	4.0	9.1	14.3	21.9	50.8	34.1	1989
Ghana	7.0	11.3	15.8	21.8	44.1	25.2	1989
Guatemala	2.1	5.8	10.5	18.6	63.0	46.6	1989
Hong Kong	5.4	10.8	15.2	21.6	47.0	31.3	1980
India	8.8	12.5	16.2	21.3	41.3	27.1	1990
Jamaica	6.0	9.9	14.5	21.3	48.4	32.6	1990
Pakistan	8.4	12.9	16.9	22.2	39.7	25.2	1991
Peru	4.9	9.2	13.7	21.0	51.4	35.4	1986
Philippines	6.5	10.1	14.4	21.2	47.8	32.1	1988
Sri Lanka	8.9	13.1	16.9	21.7	39.3	25.2	1990
Venezuela	4.8	9.5	14.4	21.9	49.5	33.2	1989
Averages	5.7	9.8	14.2	20.8	49.5	33.8	

SOURCE: World Bank, *World Development Report, 1995: Workers in an Integrating World* (New York: Oxford University Press, 1995), annex tab. 30.

What clearly emerges from Table 5.3 is that per capita incomes are not highly correlated with any of our three measures of inequality. For example, we see that Sri Lanka has only one-fifth the income of Brazil, but its three inequality measures are

TABLE 5.3 Per Capita Income and Inequality in Developing Countries

Country	GNP Per Capita, 1993 (U.S. $)	Income Share of Lowest 40% of Households, 1980–1991	Ratio of Highest 20% to Lowest 20%, 1980–1991	Gini Coefficient, 1980s
Bangladesh	220	22.9	4.1	0.34
Kenya	270	9.1	22.6	0.55
Sri Lanka	600	13.3	11.5	0.45
Indonesia	730	20.8	4.9	0.31
Philippines	830	16.6	7.4	0.45
Jamaica	1,390	15.9	8.1	0.46
Peru	1,490	14.1	10.5	0.31
Costa Rica	2,160	13.1	12.7	0.42
Brazil	3,020	7.0	32.1	0.57
Malaysia	3,160	12.9	11.7	0.48

SOURCES: United Nations Development Program, *Human Development Report, 1992* and *1994* (New York: Oxford University Press, 1992, 1994), tabs. 17 and 18, respectively; World Bank, *World Bank Atlas 1995* (Washington, D.C.: World Bank), pp. 18–19.

much less pronounced than Brazil's. Its Gini coefficient is 0.45, compared to Brazil's 0.57—a large difference in terms of the normal range of Gini coefficients. Similarly, Kenya, with income almost 22% higher than that of Bangladesh, shows much greater inequality. Conversely, Malaysia, with five times the income of Sri Lanka and more than three times the income of the Philippines, shows inequality measures that are not much different from these two lower-income nations. We can conclude, therefore, that there is no apparent relationship between levels of per capita income and the degree of income concentration over a relevant range of LDC incomes.

Finally, let's look at changes in inequality from 1960 to 1980 as reported by Irma Adelman.[8] Table 5.4 presents a summary of changes in income distribution in groups of non-Communist developing countries in the form of changing Gini coefficients. We see that between 1960 and 1980, income inequality increased substantially for the entire noncommunist Third World—that is, the Gini coefficient grew from 0.544 to 0.602. However, within these countries, income distribution improved in middle-income, non-oil-producing nations but worsened in both low-income and oil-exporting countries. Furthermore, the higher Gini coefficients of the last two groups reflect a worsening income distribution both between different countries and within individual LDCs. Adelman concludes that "reductions in *either* source of inequality (both within and between countries) can make important contributions to poverty reduction." Inequality has continued to grow for the majority of developing countries, particularly those in sub-Saharan Africa and Latin America.

We might note in passing that since the 1970s, inequality has increased in many of the industrialized countries as well. For example, the free-market philosophy of privatization, reduced taxation for the rich, and curtailed government activity helped the richest 1% in the United States capture 60% of the growth in after-tax income between 1977 and 1992. Conversely, the bottom 40% experienced little or no improvement, and their income shares actually declined.

Absolute Poverty: Extent and Magnitude

Now let's switch our attention from relative income shares of various percentile groups within a given population to the more significant question of the extent and magnitude of **absolute poverty** in developing countries. In Chapter 2, we de-

---

TABLE 5.4 Trends in Income Distribution, 1960–1980

Group of Countries	Income Distribution Gini Coefficient	
	1960	1980
All noncommunist developing countries	0.544	0.602
Low-income countries	0.407	0.450
Middle-income, non-oil-exporting countries	0.603	0.569
Oil-exporting countries	0.575	0.612

SOURCE: Irma Adelman, "A poverty-focused approach to development policy," in John P. Lewis and Valeriana Kallab (eds.), *Development Strategies Reconsidered* (Washington, D.C.: Overseas Development Council, 1986), p. 53. Reprinted with permission.

fined the extent of absolute poverty as the number of people who are unable to command sufficient resources to satisfy basic needs. They are counted as the total number living below a specified minimum level of real income—an imaginary international poverty line. That line knows no national boundaries and is independent of the level of national per capita income. Absolute poverty can and does exist, therefore, as readily in New York City as it does in Calcutta, Cairo, Lagos, or Bogotá, although its magnitude is likely to be much lower in terms of percentages of the total population. In the most comprehensive and widest-ranging study to date, the World Bank in its 1990 *World Development Report* attempted to estimate the magnitude of Third World poverty.[9] To permit cross-country comparisons and aggregation, it established two global poverty lines for 1985. Any household with an income in 1985 purchasing power parity dollars below $275 was categorized as "extremely poor," and those below $370 were classified as "poor." Table 5.5 presents the results of this exercise for various regions and for all developing countries for 1985 with updated figures for 1990 from the World Bank's 1992 *World Development Report*.

We see that in 1985, some 1.051 billion people lived below the poverty line, with an overall poverty rate of 30.5%. "Extremely poor" were 633 million people, or 18% of the population of the developing world. For all practical purposes, the distinction between extremely poor (below $275) and poor (below $370) is rather tenuous; it is appropriate to classify the entire 1.051 billion as "absolutely poor." The rightmost columns of Table 5.5 show the World Bank estimates for 1990. Instead of declining as the World Bank predicted in its 1990 report, poverty claimed an additional 72 million Third World people, rising from 1.051 to 1.133 billion between 1985 and 1990. We see that in 1990, the highest poverty rate is found in sub-Saharan Africa (49.7%), followed by South Asia (49.0%) and the Middle East and North Africa (33%), with by far the greatest number of absolute poor in South Asia (562 million). Finally, recent evidence indicates that by 1994, the number of absolute poor had risen to 1.3 billion and that the overall poverty rate remained constant despite some impressive GNP growth rates. Regionally, the incidence of poverty continued to rise in Africa and Latin America while falling in Asia.[10]

To estimate poverty levels for individual countries rather than regional aggregates, we have constructed Table 5.6. It presents our calculations of both the extent of absolute poverty and its numeric magnitude in 1995 for 35 developing nations in Latin America, Africa, and Asia using 1995 population figures and 1980–1990 poverty estimates. Using conservative methodologies, these studies reveal an overall 31% incidence of absolute poverty. The proportions, however, are much higher in a number of heavily populated low-income countries like Bangladesh (78%), India (40%), and Nigeria (40%). But note that the very low poverty figure for heavily populated China (some would question the accuracy of this particular number given by the Chinese government) lowers the overall poverty rate for Asia. In terms of total numbers, we see that 765 million Asians, 188 million Latin Americans, and 389 million Africans are barely achieving minimum subsistence incomes. If we then multiply the last figure in column 3, representing the average proportion of Third World populations below the poverty line (31%), by the total population of the developing world in 1995 (4.533 billion), we

TABLE 5.5 Poverty in the Third World, 1985 and 1990 (World Bank estimates)

| Region | 1985 | | | | | 1990 | |
| | Extremely Poor | | Poor (Including Extremely Poor) | | | | |
	Number (millions)	Percentage of Population	Number (millions)	Percentage of Population		Number (millions)	Percentage of Population
Sub-Saharan Africa	120	30.0	184	47.6		216	49.7
East Asia	120	9.0	182	13.2		169	11.3
South Asia	300	29.0	532	51.8		562	49.0
Middle East and North Africa	40	21.0	60	30.6		73	33.1
Latin America and the Caribbean	50	12.0	87	22.4		108	25.5
All developing countries	633	18.0	1,051	30.5		1,133	25.5

SOURCES: World Bank, *World Development Report, 1990: Poverty* (New York: Oxford University Press, 1990), tab. 2.1; World Bank, *World Development Report, 1992: Development and the Environment* (New York: Oxford University Press, 1992), tab. 1.1.

TABLE 5.6 Population below the Poverty Line in Thirty-five Developing Countries, 1995

Region and Country	Per Capita Gross National Product, 1994 (U.S. $)	Population, 1995 (millions)	Percentage of Population in Poverty[a]	People in Poverty (millions)
Latin America (all countries)	2,690	481.0	39	187.6
Argentina	8,060	34.6	16	5.5
Brazil	3,370	157.8	47	74.2
Chile	3,560	14.3	16	2.3
Colombia	1,620	37.7	42	15.8
Costa Rica	2,380	3.3	29	1.0
Guatemala	1,190	10.6	71	7.5
Honduras	580	5.5	37	2.0
Mexico	4,010	93.7	30	28.1
Panama	2,670	2.6	42	1.1
Peru	1,890	24.0	32	7.7
Venezuela	2,760	21.8	31	6.8
Asia (all countries except Japan)	560	3,326.0	23	765.0
Bangladesh	230	119.2	78	93.0
China	530	1,218.8	9	109.7
India	310	930.6	40	372.2
Indonesia	880	198.4	25	49.6
Malaysia	3,520	19.9	16	3.2
Nepal	200	22.6	60	13.6
Pakistan	440	129.7	28	36.3
Philippines	960	68.4	54	36.9
South Korea	8,220	44.9	5	2.2
Thailand	2,210	60.2	30	18.0
Africa (all countries)	530	720.0	54	388.8
Burkina Faso	300	10.4	35	3.6
Egypt	710	61.9	23	14.2
Ethiopia (including Eritrea)	130	56.0	64	35.8
Ghana	430	17.5	42	7.4
Kenya	260	28.3	52	14.7
Malawi	140	9.7	82	8.0
Morocco	1,150	29.2	37	10.8
Nigeria	280	101.2	40	40.5
Senegal	610	8.3	29	2.4
Sudan	260	28.1	85	23.9
Tanzania	90	28.5	58	16.5
Tunisia	1,800	8.9	18	1.6
Uganda	200	21.3	45	9.6
Zambia	350	9.1	64	5.8
All developing countries	1,040	4,533.0	31	1,405.2

SOURCES: World Bank, *The World Bank Atlas 1996* (Washington, D.C.: World Bank, 1996). Population Reference Bureau, *1995 World Population Data Sheet* (Washington, D.C.: Population Reference Bureau, 1995); United Nations Development Program, *Human Development Report, 1994* (New York: Oxford University Press, 1994), pp. 164–165, World Bank, *World Bank Development Report, 1990: Poverty* (New York: Oxford University Press, 1990), chap. 2; Eliana Cardoso and Ann Helwege, "Below the line: Poverty in Latin America," *World Development 20* (January 1992), tabs. 6 and 8.

[a]Poverty percentages are for various years between 1980 and 1990; these were applied to the 1995 population figures in column 2 to calculate the 1995 poverty estimates in column 4.

arrive at a contemporary total of 1.405 billion people who face a precarious and uncertain struggle for survival.

Finally, we can note again from Table 5.6 that high per capita incomes do not necessarily preclude the existence of substantial absolute poverty. Because the degree of inequality of income distribution varies widely among countries, poverty can be equally serious in countries with very different per capita income levels. For example, if we compare Panama with Costa Rica, we discover that even though Panama had a 12% higher per capita GNP in 1994, it had a greater percentage of its population below the poverty line than Costa Rica (42% versus 29%). Ghana, with approximately the same income level as Pakistan, nevertheless had 50% more of its population below the poverty line (42% versus 28%). Guatemala and Morocco had similar income levels, yet the former's poverty rate was almost twice that of the latter. Even adjusting for measurement errors, these results are striking.

In many respects, however, simply counting the number of people below an agreed-on poverty line can have its limitations. For example, if the poverty line is set at U.S. $300, it makes a big difference whether most of the absolute poor earn $280 or $200 per year. Both are accorded the same weight when calculating the proportion of the population that lies below the poverty line; clearly, however, the poverty problem is much more serious in the latter instance. Some economists therefore attempt to calculate a **poverty gap** that measures the total amount of income necessary to raise everyone who is below the poverty line up to that line. Figure 5.8 illustrates how we could measure the poverty gap as the shaded area between poverty line, *PV*, and the annual income profile of the population.

Even though in both country A and country B, 50% of the population falls below the same poverty line, the poverty gap in country A is greater than in country B. Therefore, it will take more of an effort to eliminate absolute poverty in country A. Given our limited information, however, the best that we can do with current cross-country statistical comparisons is try to measure absolute poverty in percentages of a total LDC population.

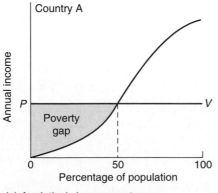
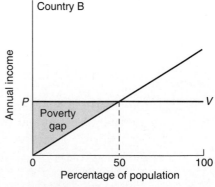

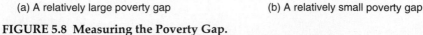

FIGURE 5.8 Measuring the Poverty Gap.

We should make one final point, analogous to our earlier observation regarding the apparent absence of any necessary relationship between levels of per capita income and the distribution of that income: High per capita incomes per se do not guarantee the absence of significant numbers of absolute poor. Because the share of income accruing to the lowest percentile of a population can vary widely from one country to another, it is possible for a country with a high per capita income to have a larger percentage of its population below an international poverty line and a larger poverty gap than a country with a lower per capita income. Therefore, problems of poverty and highly unequal distributions of income are not just the result of natural economic growth processes. Rather, they depend on the type of economic growth and the political and institutional arrangements according to which rising national incomes are distributed among the broad segments of a population.

Economic Characteristics of Poverty Groups

So far we have painted a broad picture of the income distribution and poverty problem in developing countries. We argued that the magnitude of absolute poverty results from a combination of low per capita incomes and highly unequal distributions of that income. Clearly, for any given distribution of income, the higher the level of per capita income, the lower the numbers of the absolutely poor. But as we have seen, higher levels of per capita income are no guarantee of lower levels of poverty. An understanding of the nature of the size distribution of income, therefore, is central to any analysis of the poverty problem in low-income countries.

But painting a broad picture of Third World poverty is not enough. Before we can formulate effective policies and programs to attack poverty at its source, we need some specific knowledge of these poverty groups and their economic characteristics. As we will show later, it is not sufficient simply to focus on raising growth rates of GNP in the expectation or hope that this national income growth will "trickle down" to improve levels of living for the very poor. On the contrary, many observers argue that direct attacks on poverty by means of poverty-focused policies and plans can be more effective in both the short and long runs. And we cannot attack poverty directly without detailed knowledge of its location, extent, and characteristics.[11]

Rural Poverty

Perhaps the most valid generalizations about the poor are that they are disproportionately located in rural areas, that they are primarily engaged in agricultural and associated activities, that they are more likely to be women and children than adult males, and that they are often concentrated among minority ethnic groups and indigenous peoples. Data from a broad cross section of Third World nations support these generalizations. We find, for example, that about two-thirds of the very poor scratch out their livelihood from subsistence agriculture either as small farmers or as low-paid farm workers. Some of the remaining one-third are also located in rural areas but engaged in petty services, and others are located on the fringes and in marginal areas of urban centers where they engage in various forms of self-employment such as street-hawking, trading, petty services, and small-scale commerce. On the average, we may conclude that in Africa and Asia, about 80% to 90% of all target poverty groups are located in the rural areas, as are about 50% in Latin America. Some data for specific countries are provided in Table 5.7.

It is interesting to note in the light of the rural concentration of absolute poverty that the largest share of most LDC government expenditures over the past quarter century has been directed toward the urban area and, within that area, toward the relatively affluent modern manufacturing and commercial sectors. Whether in the realm of directly productive economic investments or in the fields of education, health, housing, and other social services, this urban modern-sector bias in government expenditures is at the core of many of the development problems that will be discussed in succeeding chapters. We need only point out here that in view of the disproportionate numbers of the very poor who reside in rural areas, any policy designed to alleviate poverty must necessarily be directed to a large extent toward rural development in general and the agricultural sector in particular (we will discuss this matter in detail in Chapter 9).

Women and Poverty

More than 70% of the world's poorest people are women. If we compared the lives of the inhabitants of the poorest communities across the Third World, we would discover that virtually everywhere, women and children experience the harshest

TABLE 5.7 Rural Poverty as a Percentage of Total Poverty

Region and Country	Rural Population as a Percentage of the Total	Rural Poor as a Percentage of the Total
Sub-Saharan Africa		
Ghana	65	80
Ivory Coast	57	86
Kenya	80	96
Asia		
India	77	79
Indonesia	73	91
Malaysia	62	80
Philippines	60	67
Thailand	70	80
Latin America		
Guatemala	59	66
Mexico	31	37
Panama	50	59
Peru	44	52
Venezuela	15	20

SOURCE: World Bank, *World Development Report, 1990: Poverty* (New York: Oxford University Press, 1990), tab. 2.2.

deprivation. Women and children are more likely to be poor and malnourished and less likely to receive medical services, clean water, sanitation, or other benefits.[12] The prevalence of female-headed households, the lower earning capacity of women, and their limited control over their spouses' income all contribute to this disturbing phenomenon. In addition, women have less access to education, formal-sector employment, social security, and government employment programs. These facts combine to ensure that poor women's financial resources are meager and unstable relative to men's.

The poorest segments of Third World populations live in households headed by women, in which there are generally no male wage earners. Women head roughly 20% of households in India, 17% in Costa Rica, and 40% in rural Kenya, and the proportion is rising throughout most of the Third World. Because the earning potential of women is considerably below that of their male counterparts, women are more likely to be among the very poor. In general, women in female-headed households have less education, lower incomes, and higher fertility. In addition to placing a greater strain on the single parent, larger household size is associated with lower per capita food expenditure.

A portion of the income disparity between male- and female-headed households can be explained by the large earnings differentials between men and women. In addition to the fact that women are often paid less for performing similar tasks, they are essentially barred from higher-paying occupations. In urban areas, women are much less likely to obtain formal employment in private companies or public agencies and are frequently restricted to illegal, low-productivity jobs. The illegality of piecework, as in the garment industry, prevents it from being regulated and renders it exempt from minimum-wage laws or social security benefits. Similarly, rural women have less access to the resources necessary to generate stable incomes and are frequently subject to laws that further compromise earning potential. Legislation often prohibits women from owning property or signing financial contracts without a husband's signature, and women are typically ineligible for institutionally provided resources such as credit and training. With a few notable exceptions, government employment or income-enhancing programs are accessible exclusively to men, exacerbating existing income disparities between men and women.

But household income alone fails to describe the severity of women's relative deprivation. Because a higher proportion of female-headed households are situated in the poorest areas, which have little or no access to government-sponsored services such as piped water, sanitation, and health care, household members are more likely to fall ill and are less likely to receive medical attention. In addition, children in female-headed households are less likely to be enrolled in school and more likely to be working in order to provide additional income.

The degree of economic hardship may also vary widely within a household. We have already discussed the fact that GNP per capita is an inadequate measure of development because it fails to reflect the extent of absolute poverty. Likewise, household income is a poor measure of individual welfare because the distribution of income within the household may be quite unequal. In fact, among the poor, the economic status of women provides a better indication of their own welfare, as well as that of their children. Existing studies of intrahousehold resource allocation clearly indicate that in many regions of the world, there exists a strong bias against females in areas such as nutrition, medical care, education, and inheritance. For example, it is estimated that in India, girls are four times as likely to suffer from acute malnutrition and boys are 40 times more likely to be taken to a hospital when ill. Moreover, empirical research has shown that these gender biases in household resource allocation significantly reduce the rate of survival among female infants. As a result, recorded female-male sex ratios in countries like China are so much below their expected values that 200 million girls are said to be "missing."[13] The favor shown toward boys reflects the fact that men have a greater potential for contributing financially to family survival.

The extent of these internal biases is strongly influenced by the economic status of women. Studies have found that where women's share of income within the home is relatively high, there is less discrimination against girls, and women are better able to meet their own needs as well as those of their children. When household income is marginal, virtually 100% of women's income is contributed toward household nutritional intake. Since this fraction is considerably smaller for men, a rise in male earnings leads to a less than proportionate increase in the funds available for the provision of daily needs. It is thus unsurprising that programs designed to increase nutrition and family health are more effective when targeting women than when targeting men. In fact, significant increases in total household income do not necessarily translate into improved nutritional status. The persistence of low levels of living among women and children is common where the economic status of women remains low.

Women's control over household income and resources is limited for a number of reasons. Of primary importance is the fact that a relatively large proportion of the work performed by women is unremunerated—for example, collecting firewood and cooking—and may even be intangible, as with mothering. Women's control over household resources may also be constrained by the fact that many women from poor households are not paid for the work they perform in family agriculture or business. For example, in Mexico, 22.5% of women in the agricultural sector and 7.63% of women in the nonagricultural sectors work full time without pay. These figures are greatly understated in that they do not include women who work part time in family production. It is common for the male head of household to control all funds from cash crops or the family business, even though a significant portion of the labor input is provided by his spouse. In addition, in many cultures, it is considered socially unacceptable for women to contribute significantly to household income, and hence women's work may remain concealed or unrecognized. These combined factors perpetuate the low economic status of women and can lead to strict limitations on their control over household resources.

Development policies that increase the productivity differentials between men and women are likely to worsen earnings disparities as well as further erode women's economic status within the household. Since government programs to alleviate poverty work almost exclusively with men, they tend to exacerbate these inequalities. In urban areas, training programs to increase earning potential and formal-sector employment are generally limited to men, while agricultural extension programs promote male-dominated crops, frequently at the expense of women's vegetable plots. Studies have shown that development efforts can actually increase women's workload while at the same time reduce the share of household resources over which they exercise control. Consequently, women and their dependents remain the most economically vulnerable group in developing countries.

The fact that the welfare of women and children is strongly influenced by the design of development policy underscores the importance of integrating women into development programs. To improve living conditions for the poorest individuals, women must be drawn into the economic mainstream. This would entail increasing female participation rates in educational and training programs, formal-sector employment, and agricultural extension programs. It is also of primary importance that precautions be taken to ensure that women have equal access to government resources provided through schooling, services, employment, and social security programs. Legalizing informal sector employment where the majority of the female labor force is employed would also improve the economic status of women.

The consequences of declines in women's relative or absolute economic status has both ethical and long-term economic implications. Any process of growth that fails to improve the welfare of the people experiencing the greatest hardship, broadly recognized to be women and children, has failed to accomplish one of the principal goals of development. In the long run, the low status of women is likely to translate into slower rates of economic growth. This is true because the educational attainment and future financial status of children are much more likely to reflect those of the mother than those of the father. Thus the benefits of current investments in human capital are more likely to be passed on to future generations if women are successfully integrated into the growth process. And considering that human capital is perhaps the most important prerequisite for growth, education and enhanced economic status for women are critical to meeting long-term development objectives. This was one of the major themes of the 1995 United Nations International Conference on Women, held in Beijing, China.

Ethnic Minorities, Indigenous Populations, and Poverty

A final generalization about the incidence of Third World poverty is that it falls especially heavily on minority ethnic groups and indigenous populations. We pointed out in Chapter 2 that some 40% of the world's nation-states have more than five sizable ethnic populations, one or more of which faces serious economic, political, and social discrimination. In recent years, domestic conflicts and even civil wars have arisen out of ethnic groups' perceptions that they are losing out in the competition for limited resources and dwindling job opportunities. The poverty problem is even more serious for indigenous peoples, whose numbers exceed 300 million in 70 countries. Their plight was highlighted when the United Nations declared 1993 the Year of Indigenous People.

Although detailed data on the relative poverty of minority ethnic and indigenous peoples is difficult to obtain (for political reasons, few countries wish to highlight these problems), researchers have recently compiled data on the poverty of indigenous people in Latin America.[14] The results clearly demonstrate that most indigenous groups live in extreme poverty and that being indigenous greatly increases

TABLE 5.8 Indigenous Poverty in Latin America

	Percentage of Population below the Poverty Line	
Country	Indigenous	Nonindigenous
Bolivia	64.3	48.1
Guatemala	86.6	53.9
Mexico	80.6	17.9
Peru	79.0	49.7

SOURCE: George Psacharopoulos and Harry A. Patrinos, "Indigenous people and poverty in Latin America," *Finance and Development* 31 (March 1994): 41. Reprinted with permission.

the chances that an individual will be malnourished, illiterate, in poor health, and unemployed. For example, the research showed that in Mexico, over 80% of the indigenous population is poor, compared to 18% of the nonindigenous population. Table 5.8 shows that similar situations exist in countries such as Bolivia, Guatemala, and Peru (not to mention Native American Indian populations in the United States and Canada). Whether we speak of Kurds in Iraq, Tamils in Sri Lanka, Karens in Myanmar, Muslims in India, or Tibetans in China, the poverty plight of ethnic minorities in the Third World is as serious as that of indigenous peoples. Clearly, being an indigenous, rural woman is the worst-case poverty scenario of all.

Income Levels, Growth, and the Extent of Poverty: The Kuznets Hypothesis and Other Tests

We have already discussed the fact that exclusive reliance on the natural forces of economic growth to reduce the extent of absolute poverty in most developing countries would probably be insufficient. This issue is so central to development theory and policy that it warrants further examination. The basic question is the following: Does the pursuit of economic growth along traditional GNP-maximizing lines tend to improve, worsen, or have no necessary effect on the distribution of income and the extent of poverty in developing countries? Unfortunately, economists do not at present possess any definitive knowledge of the specific factors that affect changes in the distribution of income over time for individual countries. Simon Kuznets, to whom we owe so much for his pioneering analysis of the historical growth patterns of contemporary developed countries, has suggested that in the early stages of economic growth, the distribution of income will tend to *worsen*, whereas at later stages it will improve.[15] This observation came to be characterized by the "inverted U" **Kuznets curve** because a longitudinal (time-series) plot of changes in the distribution of income—as measured, for example, by the Gini coefficient—seemed, when per capita GNP expanded, to trace out an inverted U-shaped curve, as shown in Figure 5.9.

Explanations as to why inequality seemed first to worsen during the early stages of economic growth before eventually improving are numerous. They almost al-

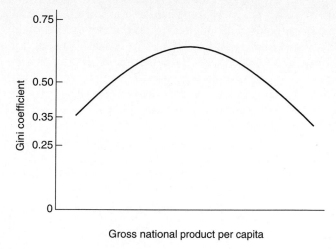

FIGURE 5.9 The "Inverted U" Kuznets Curve.

ways relate to the nature of structural change. Early growth may, in accordance with the Lewis model, be concentrated in the modern industrial sector, where employment is limited but wages and productivity are high. The income gap between the modern and traditional sectors may widen quickly at first before beginning to converge. Inequality in the expanding modern sector may be much greater than inequality in the stagnant traditional sector. Income transfers from the rich to the poor and poverty-reducing public expenditures are more difficult to undertake by governments in very low income countries.

Whatever the theoretical explanation for the Kuznets curve, the empirical validity of the phenomenon remains open to question. Although long-run data for Western nations do seem to support this proposition, studies of the phenomenon in Third World nations have produced conflicting results. Part of the problem is methodological. Because of the absence of time-series information for most LDCs, researchers have to test a *longitudinal* phenomenon with *cross-sectional* data (that is, they examine many different countries at one point in time rather than one country over a long period of time). Drawing conclusions from cross-sectional data for a time-series phenomenon is fraught with hazards. Moreover, some critics have noted that studies in support of the Kuznets curve can sometimes be reversed simply by eliminating one or two countries (the outliers) from the statistical sample.[16]

Disregarding the merits of the methodological debate, few development economists would argue that the Kuznets sequence of increasing and then declining inequality is inevitable. There are now enough case studies and specific examples of countries such as Taiwan, South Korea, China, Costa Rica, Sri Lanka, and Hong Kong to demonstrate that higher income levels can be accompanied by falling and not rising inequality. It all depends, as we shall see, on the nature of the development process. Theorists who argue for the inevitability of the Kuznets process—especially political leaders in countries with large and growing inequalities—more often than not are simply searching for a convenient conceptual smokescreen behind which to mask their goals of economic aggrandizement or to cover policy failures.

Having examined the relationship between inequality and levels of per capita income, let us look now at the relationship, if any, between economic growth and the extent of poverty. In Figure 5.10, we have plotted rates of growth of GNP for 13 developing countries on the horizontal axis and the growth rate of income of the lowest 40% of their population along the vertical axis. The data are for the time span shown in parentheses after each country, and the scatter is intended to reveal any obvious relationships between GNP growth rates and improvements in income levels for the very poor. Each country's data, therefore, are plotted in the figure at a point reflecting its combination of GNP growth and the income growth of the lowest 40% of its population. Countries above the 45° line are those where the distribution of income has improved—that is, the incomes of the bottom 40% grew faster than the overall GNP growth rate—whereas countries below the 45° line have experienced a worsening of their income distributions over the indicated period.

The scatter of points in Figure 5.10 does not reveal any strong or obvious relationship between GNP growth and the distribution of income.[17] High growth rates do not necessarily worsen the distribution of income, as some observers have suggested. Indeed, countries like Taiwan, Iran, and South Korea have experienced relatively high rates of GNP growth and have shown improved or at least unchanged distributions of income. Nevertheless, countries like Mexico and Panama have

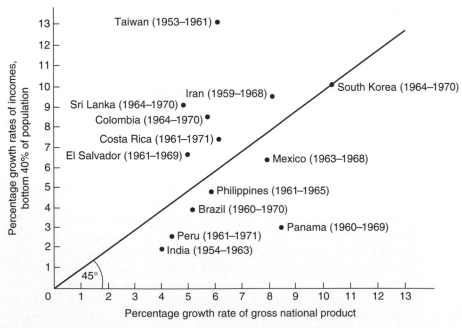

FIGURE 5.10 Comparison of Gross National Product Growth Rates and Income Growth Rates of the Bottom 40 Percent of the Population in Selected Less Developed Countries.

grown just as fast but have experienced a deterioration of their income distribution. However, there does not seem to be a necessary relationship between low GNP growth and improved income distribution. In developing countries like India, Peru, and the Philippines, low rates of GNP growth appear to have been accompanied by a deterioration of the relative income shares of the bottom 40%. And yet Sri Lanka, Colombia, Costa Rica, and El Salvador, with similarly low GNP growth rates, managed to improve the relative economic well-being of their low-income populations.

Although admittedly sketchy and limited to a short period of time, these data suggest once again that it is the **character of economic growth** (how it is achieved, who participates, which sectors are given priority, what institutional arrangements are designed and emphasized, etc.) that determines the degree to which that growth is or is not reflected in improved living standards for the very poor. It is not the mere fact of rapid growth per se that determines the nature of its distributional benefits.

This character-of-growth argument is further reinforced by an extensive empirical study of 43 developing nations that analyzed the relationship between the shares of income accruing to the poorest 60% of the population and a country's aggregate economic performance.[18] It was found that the primary impact of economic development on income distribution has generally been to decrease both the absolute and the relative incomes of the poor. There was no evidence of any automatic trickle-down of the benefits of economic growth to the very poor. On the contrary, the growth process experienced by these 43 LDCs has typically led to a "trickle-up" in favor of the small middle class and especially the very rich. The authors conclude that "economic structure, not level or rate of economic growth, is the basic determinant of patterns of income distribution."[19]

Redefining Development Goals: Growth with Improved Income Distribution

The necessity of reorienting development priorities away from an exclusive preoccupation with maximizing rates of GNP growth and toward broader social objectives such as the eradication of poverty and the reduction of excessive income disparities is now widely recognized throughout the Third World. The gap between problem redefinition and specific action can, however, be quite enormous. There are, of course, serious political, institutional, and power structure problems involved in any reorientation of development strategy toward greater concern for the very poor. Moreover, economics itself has very little in the way of a received theory of how developing economies grow or what investment strategies can maximize economic growth rates. There is relatively little consensus among economists on what strategies should be followed and whether any strictly economic strategy can eliminate or greatly reduce the incidence of poverty. Quite simply, the theoretical determinants of income distribution are poorly understood with respect to the developed countries toward which the bulk of existing theory has been directed—let alone with respect to the underdeveloped countries, where much of this theory is even less relevant.

Although rapid economic growth does not automatically provide the answer, it nevertheless remains an essential ingredient in any realistic poverty-focused program of development. Moreover, rapid economic growth and more equitable distributions of income are not necessarily incompatible as development objectives. The choice is not between more growth and more equality but about the type of economic growth that Third World countries wish to pursue—one that principally benefits the very rich or one in which the benefits are more widely distributed. In the next section, we will look at some of the economic arguments why growth and equality are not in conflict. For our present purposes, however, we may conclude that development strategy requires not only a concern with accelerating economic growth but also a direct concern with improving the material standards of living for the very sizable segments of Third World populations who have been largely bypassed by the economic growth of the past three decades.

A principal development objective, therefore, should be to generate a desired pattern of overall and broad-based income growth with special emphasis on accelerating the growth of incomes of "target" poverty groups. Such an aim requires a very different strategy from one that is simply oriented toward maximizing the growth rate of GNP, irrespective of the distributional consequences.

The Role of Economic Analysis: Redistribution from Growth

Growth versus Income Distribution

The Traditional Argument: Factor Shares, Savings, and Economic Growth

Although much of economic analysis has been strangely silent on the relationship between economic growth and the resulting distribution of income, a large body of theory in essence asserts that highly *unequal* distributions are *necessary* conditions for generating rapid growth.[20] In fact, in the 1960s and early 1970s and then again to a more limited extent in the 1980s with the neoclassical counterrevolution, the explicit and implicit acceptance of this proposition by economists from both developed and underdeveloped countries tended to turn their collective and individual attentions away from problems of poverty and income distribution. If wide inequalities are a necessary condition of maximum growth and if, in the long run, maximum growth is a necessary condition of rising standards of living for all, through the natural trickle-down processes of competitive and mixed economic systems, it follows that direct concern with the alleviation of poverty would be self-defeating. Needless to say, such a viewpoint, correct or not, provided a psychological, if not conscious, rationalization for the accumulation of wealth by powerful elite groups.

The basic economic argument to justify large income inequalities was that high personal and corporate incomes were necessary conditions of *saving*, which made possible investment and economic growth through a mechanism such as the Harrod-Domar model described in Chapter 3. If the rich save and invest significant proportions of their incomes while the poor spend all their income on consumption goods, and if GNP growth rates are directly related to the proportion of national income saved, then apparently an economy characterized by highly unequal distributions of income would save more and grow faster than one with a more equitable distribution of income. Eventually, it was assumed, national and per capita incomes would be high enough to make sizable redistributions of income possible through tax and subsidy programs. But until such a time is reached, any attempt to redistribute incomes significantly would serve only to lower growth rates and delay the time when a larger income pie could be cut up into bigger slices for all population groups.

A Counterargument

There are four general reasons why many development economists believe the foregoing argument to be incorrect and why greater equality in developing countries may in fact be a condition for self-sustaining economic growth.[21]

First, common sense, supported by a wealth of recent empirical data, bears witness to the fact that unlike the historical experience of the now developed countries, the rich in contemporary Third World countries are *not* noted for their frugality or for their desire to save and invest substantial proportions of their incomes in the local economy. Instead, landlords, business leaders, politicans, and other rich elites are known to squander much of their incomes on imported luxury goods, gold, jewelry, expensive houses, and foreign travel or to seek safe havens abroad for their savings in the form of capital flight.[22] Such savings and investments do not add to the nation's productive resources; in fact, they represent substantial drains on these resources in that the income so derived is extracted from the sweat and toil of common, uneducated, and unskilled laborers. In short, the rich do not necessarily save and invest significantly larger proportions of their incomes (in the real economic sense of productive domestic saving and investment) than the poor.[23] Therefore, a growth strategy based on sizable and growing income inequalities may in reality be nothing more than an opportunistic myth designed to perpetuate the vested interests and maintain the status quo of the economic and political elites of Third World nations, often at the expense of the great majority of the general population. Such strategies might better be called "antidevelopmental."[24]

Second, the low incomes and low levels of living for the poor, which are manifested in poor health, nutrition, and education, can lower their economic productivity and thereby lead directly and indirectly to a slower-growing economy. Strategies to raise the incomes and levels of living of, say, the bottom 40% would therefore contribute not only to their material well-being but also to the productivity and income of the economy as a whole.[25]

Third, raising the income levels of the poor will stimulate an overall increase in the demand for locally produced necessity products like food and clothing, whereas the rich tend to spend more of their additional incomes on imported luxury goods. Rising demand for local goods provides a greater stimulus to local production, local employment, and local investment. Such demand thus creates the conditions for rapid economic growth and a broader popular participation in that growth.[26]

Fourth and finally, a more equitable distribution of income achieved through the reduction of mass poverty can stimulate healthy economic expansion by acting as a powerful material and psychological incentive to widespread public participation in the development process. By contrast, wide income disparities and substantial absolute poverty can act as powerful material and psychological disincentives to economic progress. They may even create the conditions for an ultimate rejection of progress by the masses of frustrated and politically explosive people, especially those with considerable education.[27]

We can conclude, therefore, that promoting rapid economic growth and reducing poverty and inequality are not mutually conflicting objectives. The World Bank reached a similar conclusion in its 1990 report on poverty when it declared:

> Discussions of policy toward the poor usually focus on the trade-off between growth and poverty. But the review of country experience suggests that this is not a critical trade-off. With appropriate policies, the poor can participate in growth and contribute to it, and when they do, rapid declines in poverty are consistent with sustained growth.[28]

GNP as a Biased Index of National Development and Welfare

We have already criticized reliance on GNP and its growth rate as the principal indicator of development and economic well-being. Figures for GNP per capita give no indication of how national income is actually distributed and who is benefiting most from the growth of production. We have seen, for example, that a rising level of absolute and per capita GNP can camouflage the fact that the poor are no better off than before.

Although many people (including some economists) are unaware of this fact, the calculation of the rate of GNP growth is largely a calculation of the rate of growth of the incomes of the upper 40% of the population, who receive a disproportionately large share of the national product. Therefore, the GNP growth rates can be a very misleading index of improved welfare. To give an extreme example, suppose that an economy consisted of only 10 people and that 9 of them had no income at all and the tenth received 100 units of income. The GNP for this economy would therefore be 100 and per capita GNP would be 10. Now suppose that everyone's income increases by 20% so that GNP rises to 120 while per capita income grows to 12. For the 9 individuals with no income before and still no income now (i.e., 1.20 × 0 = 0), such a rise in per capita income provides no cause for rejoicing. The one rich individual still has all the income. And GNP, instead of being a welfare index of society as a whole, is merely measuring the welfare of a single individual!

The same line of reasoning applies to the more realistic situation where incomes are very unequally distributed, although not perfectly unequal as in our example. Taking the figures from Table 5.1, where we divided the population into quintiles that received 5%, 9%, 13%, 22%, and 51% income shares, respectively, we found that these income shares are a measure of the relative economic welfare of each income class and that the rate of income growth in each quintile is a measure of the economic welfare growth of that class. We can approximate the growth in the total welfare of society as the simple weighted sum of the growth of income in each class. This is in fact what the rate of GNP growth measures—the weights applied to each income class are their respective shares of national income. To be specific, in the case of a population divided into quintiles according to rising income levels, we would have

$$G = w_1 g_1 + w_2 g_2 + w_3 g_3 + w_4 g_4 + w_5 g_5, \tag{5.1}$$

where G = a weighted index of growth of social welfare, g_i = the growth rate of income of the ith quintile (where the i quintiles are ordered 1, 2, 3, 4, and 5 in our example), and w_i = the "welfare weight" of the ith quintile (in our example, $w_1 = 0.05$, $w_2 = 0.09$, $w_3 = 0.13$, $w_4 = 0.22$, and $w_5 = 0.51$). As long as the weights add up to unity and are nonnegative, our overall measure of the growth of social welfare, G, must fall somewhere between the maximum and minimum income growth rates in the various quintiles. In the extreme case of all income accruing to one individual or one group of individuals in the highest quintile and where the welfare weights are the income shares (as they are with GNP growth calculations), Equation 5.1 would be written as

$$G = 0g_1 + 0g_2 + 0g_3 + 0g_4 + 1.0g_5 = 1.0g_5. \tag{5.2}$$

The growth of social welfare would therefore be associated exclusively with the growth of incomes of the top quintile of the population!

In the example derived from Table 5.1, the GNP income share weighted index of social welfare would be written as

$$G = 0.05g_1 + 0.09g_2 + 0.13g_3 + 0.22g_4 + 0.51g_5. \tag{5.3}$$

Now suppose that the income growth rate of the bottom 60% of the population is zero (i.e., $g_1 = g_2 = g_3 = 0$) while that of the top 40% is 10% (i.e., $g_4 = g_5 = 0.10$). Equation 5.3 could therefore be written as

$$G = 0.05(0) + 0.09(0) + 0.13(0) + 0.22(0.10) + 0.51(0.10) = 0.073, \tag{5.4}$$

and the social welfare index would rise by more than 7%, which is the rate of growth of GNP (i.e., GNP would rise from 100 in Table 5.1 to 107.3 if the incomes of the 4th and 5th quintiles grew by 10%). Thus we have an illustration of a case where GNP rises by 7.3%, implying that social well-being has increased by this same proportionate amount even though 60% of the population is no better off than before. This bottom 60% still has only 5, 13, and 22 units of income, respectively. Clearly, the distribution of income would be worsened (the relative shares of the bottom 60% would fall) by such a respectable growth rate of GNP.

The numeric example given by Equation 5.4 illustrates our basic point. The use of the growth rate of GNP as an index of social welfare and as a method of comparing the development performance of different countries can be misleading, especially where countries have markedly different distributions of income. The welfare weights attached to the growth rates of different income groups are unequal, with a heavy social premium being placed on the income growth of the highest-quintile groups. In the example of Equation 5.3, a 1% growth in the income of the top quintile carries more than 10 times the weight of a 1% growth in the lowest quintile (0.51 compared with 0.05) because it implies an absolute increment that is 10 times larger. In other words, using the measure of GNP growth as an index of improvements in social welfare and development accords to each income group a welfare valuation that corresponds to its respective income share (i.e., a 1% increase in the income of the richest 20% of the population is implicitly assumed to be more than 10 times as important to society as a 1% increase in the income of the bottom 20%). It follows that the best way to maximize social welfare growth is to maximize the rate of growth of the incomes of the rich while neglecting the poor! If ever there was a case for *not* equating GNP growth with development, this example should provide a persuasive illustration.

Constructing a Poverty-weighted Index of Social Welfare

An alternative to using a simple **GNP growth rate** or **distributive share index** of social welfare would be to construct an equal-weights or even a poverty-weighted index. The latter two indexes might be especially relevant for countries concerned with the elimination of poverty as a major development objective. As its name indicates, an **equal-weights index** weights the growth of income in each income class not by the proportion of total income in that class but rather by the proportion of the total population—that is, all people are treated ("weighted") equally. In an economy divided into quintiles, such an index would give a weight of 0.2 to the growth of income in each quintile. So a 10% increase in the income of the lowest 20% of the population would have the same bearing on the overall measure of social welfare improvements as a 10% increase in the top 20% group or in any other quintile group, even though the absolute increase in income for the bottom group will be much smaller than for the upper groups.

Using an equal-weights index in our example of a 10% income growth of the top two quintiles with the bottom three remaining static, we would have

$$G = 0.20g_1 + 0.20g_2 + 0.20g_3 + 0.20g_4 + 0.20g_5 \tag{5.5}$$

or, inserting growth rates for g_1 through g_5,

$$G = 0.20(0) + 0.20(0) + 0.20(0) + 0.20(0.10) + 0.20(0.10) = 0.04. \tag{5.6}$$

Social welfare will have increased by only 4%, compared to the 7.3% increase recorded by using the distributive shares or GNP growth rate index. Even though recorded GNP still grows by 7.3%, this alternative welfare index of development shows only a 4% rise.

Finally, consider a developing country that is genuinely and solely concerned with improving the material well-being of, say, the poorest 40% of its population. Such a country might wish to construct a **poverty-weighted index** of development, which places "subjective" social values on the income growth rates of only the bottom 40%. In other words, it might arbitrarily place a welfare weight on w_1 of 0.60 and on w_2 of 0.40 while giving w_3, w_4, and w_5 zero weights. Using our same numeric example, the social welfare growth index for this country would be given by the expression

$$G = 0.60g_1 + 0.40g_2 + 0g_3 + 0g_4 + 0g_5, \tag{5.7}$$

which, when substituting $g_1 = g_2 = g_3 = 0$ and $g_4 = g_5 = 0.10$, becomes

$$G = 0.60(0) + 0.40(0) + 0(0) + 0(0.10) + 0(0.10) = 0. \tag{5.8}$$

The poverty-weighted index therefore records *no* improvement in social welfare (no development), even though recorded GNP has grown by 7.3%!

Although the choice of welfare weights in any index of development is purely arbitrary, it does represent and reflect important social value judgments about goals and objectives for a given society. It would certainly be interesting to know, if this were possible, the real implicit welfare weights of the various development strategies of different Third World countries. Our main point, however, is that as long as the growth rate of GNP is explicitly or implicitly used to compare development performances, we know that a "wealthy weights" index is actually being employed.

To put some real-world flavor into the discussion of alternative indexes of improvements in economic welfare and to illustrate the usefulness of different weighted growth indexes in evaluating the economic performance of various countries, consider the data in Table 5.9. The table shows the growth of income in 17 countries as measured first by the rate of growth of GNP, second by an equal-weights index, and third by a poverty-weighted index where the actual weights assigned to income growth rates of the lowest 40%, the middle 40%, and the top 20% of the population are 0.6, 0.4, and 0.0, respectively. Some interesting conclusions emerge from a review of the last three columns of Table 5.9.

1. Economic performance as measured by equal-weights and poverty-weighted indexes is notably worse in some otherwise high-GNP-growth countries like Brazil, Mexico, and Panama. Because these countries all experienced a deterioration in income distribution and a growing concentration of income growth in the upper groups over this period, the equal-weights and poverty-weighted indexes naturally show a less impressive development performance than the simple GNP measure.

2. In five countries (Colombia, Costa Rica, El Salvador, Sri Lanka, and Taiwan), the weighted indexes show a better performance than GNP growth because the relative income growth of lower-income groups proceeded more rapidly over the period in question in those five countries than that of the higher-income groups.

TABLE 5.9 Income Distribution and Growth in Seventeen Selected Countries

Country	Income Growth			Annual Increase in Welfare		
	Upper 20%	Middle 40%	Lowest 40%	GNP Weights	Equal Weights	Poverty Weights
Brazil	6.7	3.1	3.7	5.2	4.1	3.5
Canada	7.0	5.3	6.5	6.2	6.1	6.1
Colombia	5.2	7.9	7.8	6.2	7.3	7.8
Costa Rica	4.5	9.3	7.0	6.3	7.4	7.8
El Salvador	3.5	9.5	6.4	5.7	7.1	7.4
Finland	6.0	5.0	2.1	5.1	4.0	3.1
France	5.6	4.5	1.4	4.8	3.5	2.4
India	5.3	3.5	2.0	4.2	3.3	2.5
Mexico	8.8	5.8	6.0	7.8	6.5	5.9
Panama	8.8	9.2	3.2	8.2	6.7	5.2
Peru	3.9	6.7	2.4	4.6	4.4	3.8
Philippines	5.0	6.7	4.4	5.5	5.4	5.2
South Korea	12.4	9.5	11.0	11.0	10.7	10.5
Sri Lanka	3.1	6.3	8.3	5.0	6.5	7.6
Taiwan	4.5	9.1	12.1	6.8	9.4	11.1
United States	5.6	5.2	4.1	5.2	4.8	4.5
Yugoslavia	5.0	5.0	4.3	4.9	4.7	4.5

SOURCE: Montek S. Ahluwalia and Hollis B. Chenery, "A conceptual framework for economic analysis," in Hollis B. Chenery, John Duloy, and Richard Jolly, *Redistribution with Growth: An Approach to Policy* (Washington, D.C.: World Bank, 1973), p. 5. Reprinted by permission.

3. In four countries (Peru, the Philippines, South Korea, and the former Yugoslavia), little change in income distribution during the period in question results in little variation between the GNP measure and the two alternative weighted indexes of social welfare.

We may conclude, therefore, that a useful summary measure of the degree to which economic growth is biased toward the relative improvement of high-income or low-income groups is the positive or negative divergence between a weighted social welfare index and the actual growth rate of GNP.

Finally, our analysis leads us to conclude that the presumed trade-off between rapid economic growth and a more equitable distribution of income is in reality better expressed as a trade-off between income growth rates among different income groups. If a weighted welfare index is used to measure economic development, it not only is possible but may even be desirable for a lower growth rate of GNP to be associated with a higher rate of economic development, at least in terms of the value judgments of an egalitarian society.

Combining the Economics of Growth and Distribution

The reformulation of indexes of development to take account of alternative social premiums for different income groups takes us a long way toward a better understanding of the relationship between economic growth and income distribution. For one thing, the use of such indexes underlines the importance of focusing on the *direct* improvement in living standards for the lowest-income groups rather than worrying about presumed conflicts between growth and distribution or about the overall pattern of income distribution in Third World countries. However, the recognition that real development entails direct attacks on the sources of poverty within a country is useless without a better understanding of the factors that determine income shares and the relative rates of growth within different income groups. Unfortunately, economic theory offers little guidance, for it has always been concerned not with the size distribution of income (who gets what) but rather with the determinants of the functional distribution of income (how much of the total GNP is attributable to the total productivity of labor, capital, land, etc.). Even if the traditional theory of the determinants of functional income distribution had relevance for understanding the economic processes of contemporary developing nations (which, as we saw, it does not, because of unreal assumptions about factor pricing, competitive markets, and the influence of power), knowledge of how incomes are functionally distributed would not help us understand how and why incomes tend to be concentrated in certain population groups. For this we need to know how income-earning factors of production are distributed among different groups of people. We know, for example, that personal income consists not only of income derived from the supply of an individual's labor but also, and primarily for upper-income groups, from an individual's control over other income-earning assets such as land and capital (both physical and financial).

When we analyze the real determinants of unequal distributions of income, it is the very unequal distribution of the ownership of productive assets such as land and capital within different segments of Third World populations that largely accounts for the wide income divergence between rich and poor. The concentration of physical and financial capital as well as land in the hands of small economic and political elites enables them to expand their stock of human capital through education and thereby to control even greater shares of the national product. As in the international sphere, it is another case of the rich getting richer while the poor stagnate. Any attempt to improve significantly the living standards of the poor must therefore focus not only on increasing the economic returns to the limited factors they possess (i.e., raising the returns to their labor through more employment) but also on progressively altering the existing pattern of concentration of both physical and human capital toward low-income groups. Such redistribution can probably best be achieved in a growing economy. This leads us directly to our concluding sections on alternative policy approaches.

The Range of Policy Options: Some Basic Considerations

Developing countries that aim to reduce poverty and excessive inequalities in their distribution of income need to know how best to achieve their aim. What kinds of economic and other policies might LDC governments adopt to reduce poverty and inequality while maintaining or even accelerating economic growth rates? As we are concerned here with moderating the size distribution of incomes in general and raising the income levels of, say, the bottom 40% of the population in particular, it is important to understand the various determinants of the distribution of income in an economy and see in what ways government intervention can alter or modify their effect.

Areas of Intervention

We can identify four broad areas of possible government policy intervention, which correspond to the following four major elements in the determination of a developing economy's distribution of income:

1. *Functional distribution*—the returns to labor, land, and capital as determined by factor prices, utilization levels, and the consequent shares of national income that accrue to the owners of each factor.

2. *Size distribution*—the functional income distribution of an economy translated into a size distribution by knowledge of how ownership and control over productive assets and labor skills are concentrated and distributed throughout the population. The distribution of these asset holdings and skill endowments ultimately determines the distribution of personal income.

3. *Moderating (reducing) the size distribution at the upper levels* through progressive taxation of personal income and wealth. Such taxation increases government revenues and converts a market- and asset-determined level of personal income into a fiscally corrected "disposable" personal income. An individual or family's **disposable income** is the actual amount available for expenditure on goods and services and for saving.

4. *Moderating (increasing) the size distribution at the lower levels* through public expenditures of tax revenues to raise the incomes of the poor either directly (e.g., by outright money transfers) or indirectly (e.g., through public employment creation or the provision of free or subsidized primary education). Such public policies raise the real income levels of the poor above their market-determined personal income levels.

Policy Options

Third World governments have many options and alternative possible policies to operate in the four broad areas of intervention just outlined. Let us briefly identify the nature of some of them.

Altering the Functional Distribution of Income through Policies Designed to Change Relative Factor Prices

Altering the functional distribution represents the traditional economic approach. It is argued that as a result of institutional constraints and faulty government policies, the relative price of labor (basically, the wage rate) is higher than what would be determined by the free interplay of the forces of supply and demand. For example, the power of trade unions to raise minimum wages to artificially high levels (higher than those that would result from supply and demand) even in the face of widespread unemployment is often cited as an example of the "distorted" price of labor. From this it is argued that measures designed to reduce the price of labor relative to capital (e.g., through market-determined wages in the public sector or public wage subsidies to employers) will cause employers to substitute labor for capital in their production activities. Such factor substitution increases the overall level of employment and ultimately raises the incomes of the poor, who typically possess only their labor services.

However, it is often also correctly pointed out that the price of capital equipment is "institutionally" set at artificially low levels (below what supply and demand would dictate) through various public policies such as investment incentives, tax allowances, subsidized interest rates, overvalued exchange rates, and low tariffs on capital goods imports such as tractors and automated equipment. If these special privileges and capital subsidies were removed so that the price of capital would rise to its true "scarcity" level, producers would have a further incentive to increase their utilization of the abundant supply of labor and lower their uses of scarce capital. Moreover, owners of capital (both physical and financial) would not receive the artificially high economic returns they now enjoy. Their personal incomes would thereby be reduced.

Because factor prices are assumed to function as the ultimate signals and incentives in any economy, correcting these prices (i.e., lowering the relative price of labor and raising the relative price of capital) would not only increase productivity and efficiency but would also reduce inequality by providing more wage-paying jobs for currently unemployed or underemployed unskilled and semiskilled workers. It would also lower the artificially high incomes of owners of capital. Removal of such **factor-price distortions** would therefore go a long way toward combining more growth, efficiently generated, with higher employment, less poverty, and greater equality.

We deal more extensively with the important question of factor-price distortions, employment generation, and choice of appropriate production techniques in Chapter 7. For the present, we may conclude that there is much merit to the traditional factor-price distortion argument and that correcting prices should contribute to a reduction in poverty and an improved distribution of income. How much it actually contributes will depend on the degree to which firms and farms switch to more labor-intensive production methods as the relative price of labor falls and the relative price of capital rises. This is an important empirical question, the answer to which will vary from country to country. But some improvement can be expected.

Modifying the Size Distribution through Progressive Redistribution of Asset Ownership

Given correct resource prices and utilization levels for each type of productive factor (labor, land, and capital), we can arrive at estimates for the total earnings of each asset. But to translate this functional income into personal income, we need to know the distribution and ownership concentration of these assets among and within various segments of the population. Here we come to what is probably the most important fact about the determination of income distribution within an economy: The ultimate cause of the unequal distribution of personal incomes in most Third World countries is the unequal and highly concentrated patterns of **asset ownership** in these countries. The principal reasons why less than 20% of their population receives over 50% of the national income is that this 20% probably owns and controls well over 80% of the productive resources, especially physical capital and land but also human capital in the form of better education. Correcting factor prices is certainly not sufficient to reduce income inequalities substantially or to eliminate widespread poverty where physical asset ownership and education are highly concentrated.

It follows that the second and perhaps more important line of policy to reduce poverty and inequality is to focus directly on reducing the concentrated control of assets, the unequal distribution of power, and the unequal access to educational and income-earning opportunities that characterize many developing countries. A classic case of such **redistribution policies** as they relate to the rural poor, who comprise 70% to 80% of the target poverty group, is **land reform**. The basic purpose of land reform is to transform tenant cultivators into smallholders who will then have an incentive to raise production and improve their incomes. But as we shall see in Chapter 9, land reform may be a weak instrument of income redistribution if other institutional and price distortions in the economic system prevent small farm holders from securing access to much needed critical inputs such as credit, fertilizers, seeds, marketing facilities, and agricultural education. Similar reforms in urban areas could include the provision of commercial credit at market rates (rather than through exploitive moneylenders) to small entrepreneurs (so-called microloans—see Chapter 17) so that they can expand their business and provide more jobs to local workers.

In addition to the redistribution of existing productive assets, dynamic redistribution policies could be gradually pursued. For example, Third World governments could transfer a certain proportion of annual savings and investments to low-income groups so as to bring about a more gradual and perhaps politically more acceptable redistribution of additional assets as they accumulate over time. This is what is often meant by the expression "redistribution from growth." Whether such a gradual redistribution from growth is any more possible than a redistribution of existing assets is a moot point, especially in the context of very unequal power structures. But some form of asset redistribution, whether static or dynamic, seems to be a necessary condition for any significant reduction of poverty and inequality in most Third World countries.

Human capital in the form of education and skills is another example of the unequal distribution of productive asset ownership. Public policy should therefore promote wider access to educational opportunities as a means of increasing income-earning potential for more people. But as in the case of land reform, the mere provision of greater access to education is no guarantee that the poor will be any better off, unless complementary policies—for example, the provision of more productive employment opportunities for the educated—are adopted to capitalize on this increased human capital. The relationship among education, employment, and development is discussed further in Chapter 11.

Reducing the Size Distribution at the Upper Levels through Progressive Income and Wealth Taxes

Any national policy attempting to improve the living standards of the bottom 40% must secure sufficient financial resources to transform paper plans into program realities. The major source of such development finance is the direct and progressive taxation of both income and wealth. Direct **progressive income taxes** focus on personal and corporate incomes, with the rich required to pay a progressively larger percentage of their total income in taxes than the poor. Taxation on wealth (the stock of accumulated assets and income) typically involves personal and corporate property taxes but may also include progressive inheritance taxes. In either case, the burden of the tax is designed to fall most heavily on the upper-income groups.

Unfortunately, in many developing countries (and developed countries as well), the gap between what is supposed to be a progressive tax structure and what different income groups actually pay can be substantial. Progressive tax structures on paper often turn out to be **regressive taxes** in practice, in that the lower- and middle-income groups pay a proportionately larger share of their incomes in taxes than the upper-income groups. The reasons for this are simple. The poor are often taxed at the source of their incomes or expenditures (by withholding taxes from wages, general poll taxes, or **indirect taxes** levied on the retail purchase of goods such as cigarettes and beer). By contrast, the rich derive by far the largest part of their incomes from the return on physical and financial assets, which often go unreported. They often also have the power and ability to avoid paying taxes without fear of government reprisal. Policies to enforce progressive rates of direct taxation on income and wealth, especially at the highest levels, are what are most needed in this area of redistribution activity (see Chapter 17 for a further discussion of taxation for development).

Increasing the Size Distribution at the Lower Levels through Direct Transfer Payments and the Public Provision of Goods and Services

The direct provision of tax-financed **public consumption** goods and services to the very poor is another potentially important instrument of a comprehensive policy designed to eradicate poverty. Examples include public health projects in rural villages and urban fringe areas, school lunches and preschool nutritional supplementation programs, and the provision of clean water and electrification to remote rural areas. Direct money transfers and subsidized food programs for the urban and rural poor, as well as direct government policies to keep the price of essential foodstuffs low, represent additional forms of public consumption **subsidies**. All these policies have the effect of raising the real personal income levels of the very poor beyond their actual market-derived monetary incomes. Unfortunately, in the 1980s and early 1990s, with the Third World debt crisis and the implementation of World Bank- and IMF-induced structural adjustment programs, the first victims of mandated public expenditure retrenchments were the rural and urban poor—especially women.

Summary and Conclusions: The Need for a Package of Policies

To summarize our discussion of alternative policy approaches to the problem of growth, poverty, and inequality in Third World countries, the need is not for one or two isolated policies but for a "package" of complementary and supportive policies, including the following three basic elements:[29]

1. A policy or set of policies designed to correct factor-price distortions so as to ensure that market or institutionally established prices provide accurate (i.e., socially correct) signals and incentives to both producers and resource suppliers. Correcting distorted prices should contribute to greater productive efficiency, more employment, and less poverty. Equally important may be the promotion of indigenous technological research and development of efficient, labor-intensive methods of production (see Chapter 7).

2. A policy or set of policies designed to bring about far-reaching structural changes in the distribution of assets, power, and access to education and associated income-earning (employment) opportunities. Such policies go beyond the narrow realm of economics and touch on the whole social, institutional, cultural, and political fabric of the developing world. But without such radical structural changes and asset redistributions, whether immediately achieved (e.g., through public-sector interventions) or gradually introduced over time (through redistribution from growth), the chances of improving significantly the living conditions of the masses of rural and urban poor will be highly improbable, perhaps even impossible.

3. A policy or set of policies designed to modify the size distribution of income at the upper levels through the enforcement of legislated progressive taxation on incomes and wealth and at the lower levels through direct transfer payments and the expanded provision of publicly provided consumption goods and services. The net effect is to create a social "safety net" for people who may be bypassed by the development process.

CASE STUDY

The Economy of India

GEOGRAPHIC, SOCIAL, AND ECONOMIC INDICATORS

Capital New Delhi

Area 3,287,263 km^2

Population 930.6 million (1995)

Population (average annual growth rate)
2.0% (1985–1994)

GNP per capita U.S. $310 (1994)

GNP per capita (average annual growth rate) 2.9% (1985–1994)

Agriculture as share of GDP 30% (1994)

Exports as share of GDP 12% (1994)

Infant mortality rate (per 1,000 live births) 74 (1995)

Child malnutrition (underweight)
63% (1993)

Females as share of labor force
25% (1994)

Illiteracy rate (age 15+) 52% (1990)

Human Development Index
0.38 (low) (1992)

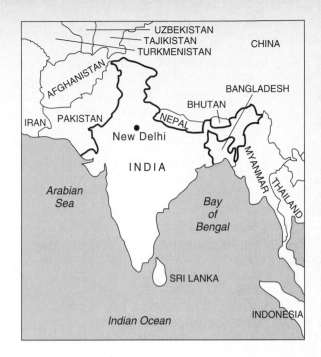

India is the largest country in South Asia and the seventh largest in the world. It can be divided into three geographic areas: the Himalaya Mountains, the Gangetic plane (the most populated), and the peninsula.

India has the world's second largest population with over 930 million people in 1995 and a rate of growth that averaged 2.0% during the past decade. Its 1994 per capita income of $310 is still one of the lowest in the world outside of Africa. Its rapidly expanding population has not only retarded economic progress but also put increasing pressure on natural resources, contributed to severe environmental deterioration, and produced a labor force whose growth and size continue to exceed the economy's absorptive capacity. Absolute poverty remains widespread, illiteracy exceeds 50%, and the infant mortality rate remains close to 75 per 1,000. Over 40% of the world's poor—those who live on less than $1 a day—reside in India. Poverty claims over one-third of India's rural population and one-fifth of its urban residents. Its population is projected to exceed 1 billion by the year 2000, and it should surpass China as the world's most populous country soon thereafter.

India was granted independence in 1947 after a long struggle against British rule. Both contemporary India and Pakistan were created at that time as Britain divided its Indian colony to satisfy Hindu (India) and Muslim (Pakistan) interests. India was for many years a socialist democratic republic with a federal government inspired by the British parliamentary system. However, in the late 1980s and early 1990s, India moved away from its socialist economic and political orientation and aggressively adopted aspects of market capitalism.

Agriculture is the most important economic activity, occupying three-quarters of the labor force and accounting for 30% of GDP. After the "green revolution" of the late 1960s and early 1970s, agricultural production started increasing at an annual rate of 3%. This was due largely to improvements in

177

agricultural technologies and irrigation systems. As a result, India became self-sufficient in grain production. It was able to increase its wheat production from 10 million tons in 1964 to over 45 million tons in 1985, while total food grain production rose to 150 million tons in 1984. Production kept up with rapid population growth. By the year 2000, however, it is estimated that India will need 280 million tons of food grain each year to feed a population that is projected to expand by another 50 million. This will be a very difficult task, particularly because Indian farmlands have suffered severe ecological damage through deforestation, soil erosion, and other degradation, which have affected over 2 million square kilometers of land.

Although GNP grew at an average rate of 5.3% in the 1980s, the parallel growth of population led to smaller gains in per capita income. Cotton and jute textile production is still the most important industrial activity, although large publicly owned and operated manufacturing companies producing steel, machine tools, electric and transport machinery, and chemicals have existed since 1960. In the early 1990s, many of these state-owned enterprises were being transferred into private hands through the process of privatization. Important new initiatives that the Indian government has undertaken in the 1990s include the gradual deregulation of industry and trade favored by a system of incentives and a set of policies aimed at encouraging the transfer of advanced technology. Specifically, the privatization of the telecommunications equipment sector, the liberalization of exports for the electronics and computer industries, the introduction of more flexible production processes in automotive and machine tool industries, and the adoption of several measures to facilitate imports of capital goods represent the bulk of the new development initiatives followed by the Indian authorities. Economic growth has allowed India to achieve some success in the battle against poverty, despite the still high population growth rate.

Three major policy directions contained in the seventh five-year plan (1985–1990) emphasized the importance of an export-oriented growth program designed to generate foreign exchange, the need to expand antipoverty efforts and human resource development, and the desire to slow the rate of population growth. In 1991, a new government initiated a fresh set of economic reforms, including currency devaluation designed to promote exports and curtail imports; a reduction of production subsidies, import duties on capital goods, and quantitative import restrictions; a progressive liberalization of interest rates to promote saving and investment; a revision of the personal income tax system; and a speedup of the privatization process with further encouragement to foreign investors.

As the Indian economy rapidly turns away from the socialist model that has traditionally guided its economic development and moves toward greater reliance on free markets and a more open economy, there are increasing concerns that any improvements in economic efficiency and economic growth may be achieved at the expense of greater income inequality, higher unemployment, continued environmental damage, and declining real income for the poor and middle classes. Thus the major challenge facing the Indian government as we approach the twenty-first century will be how to balance growth with equity, efficiency with employment, food production with distribution, and free markets with poverty alleviation—all while dealing with rapid population growth and mounting ethnic violence between Hindu and Muslim fundamentalists. It will be a daunting task.

CASE STUDY

The Economy of South Africa

GEOGRAPHIC, SOCIAL, AND ECONOMIC INDICTORS

Capital Pretoria (administrative), Cape Town (legislative)

Area 1,200,000 km^2

Population 43.5 million (1995)

Population (average annual growth rate) 2.4% (1985–1993)

GNP per capita U.S. $3,010 (1994)

GNP per capita (average real annual growth rate) –1.4% (1985–1994)

Agriculture as share of GDP 5% (1994)

Exports as share of GDP 24% (1994)

Infant mortality rate (per 1,000 live births) 46 (1995)

Child malnutrition (underweight) 43% (1992)

Females as share of labor force 36% (1993)

Illiteracy rate (age 15+) 36% (1994)

Human Development Index 0.65 (medium); whites 0.88 (high), blacks 0.46 (low) (1992)

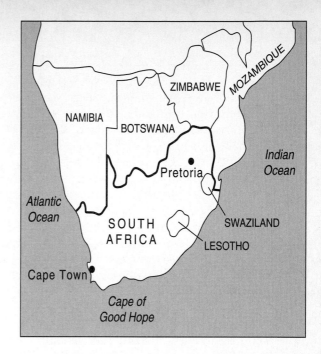

South Africa is in the midst of monumental and unprecedented change. After many years of white rule and black segregation in the context of two countries—one rich and the other poor—within a common border, contemporary South Africa is undergoing a delicate transition. If successful, it could turn out to be the most unexpected peaceful transition from white to black rule in the whole of sub-Saharan Africa.

Some historical background of how South Africa reached its present situation is in order. People have inhabited southern Africa for thousands of years. Members of the Khoisan language groups are the oldest surviving inhabitants of the land; however, only a few are left in South Africa today, in the western sections. Most of today's black South Africans belong to the Bantu language group, which migrated south from central Africa, settling in the Transvaal region sometime before A.D. 100. The Nguni, ancestors of the Zulu and Xhosa, occupied most of the eastern coast by 1500.

The Portuguese were the first Europeans to reach the Cape of Good Hope, arriving in 1488. However, permanent white settlement did not begin until 1652, when the Dutch East India Company established a provisioning station on the Cape. In subsequent decades, French Huguenot refugees, Dutch, and Germans began to settle in the Cape Colony. They form the Afrikaner segment of today's population.

The establishment of these settlements had far-reaching social and political effects on the groups already settled in the area, leading to upheaval in their societies and the subjugation of their people. By 1779, European settlements extended throughout the southern part of the Cape and east toward the Great Fish River. It was here that Dutch authorities and the Xhosa fought the first frontier war.

The British gained control of the Cape of Good Hope at the end of the eighteenth century. Subsequent British settlement and rule marked the beginning of a long conflict between the Afrikaners and the English. The discovery of diamonds at Kimberley in 1870 and of large gold deposits in the Witwatersrand region of the Transvaal in 1886 caused an influx of European (mainly British) immigration and investment. Many blacks also moved into the area to work in the mines. The construction by mine owners of hostels to house and control their workers set patterns that later extended throughout the region. The reactions of white farmers (Boers) to this influx, along with British political intrigues, led to the Anglo-Boer Wars of 1880–1881 and 1899–1902. British forces prevailed in the conflict, and the lands were incorporated into the British Empire. In May 1910, the various republics and colonies formed the Union of South Africa, a self-governing dominion of the British Empire. The Union's constitution kept all political power in the hands of whites.

In 1912, the South Africa Native National Congress was formed in Bloemfontein and eventually became known as the African National Congress (ANC). Its goals were the elimination of restrictions based on color and enfranchisement and parliamentary representation for blacks. Despite these efforts, the government continued to pass laws limiting the rights and freedoms of blacks. In 1948, the National Party (NP) won the all-white elections and began passing legislation codifying and enforcing an even stricter policy of white domination and racial separation known as *apartheid* ("separateness").

In 1984, a new constitution came into effect in which whites allowed coloreds (persons of mixed heritage) and Asians a limited role in the national government and control over their own affairs in certain areas. Ultimately, however, all power remained in white hands. Blacks remained effectively disenfranchised. Popular uprisings in black and colored townships in 1976 and 1985 helped convince some NP members of the need for change. Secret discussions between those members and imprisoned ANC leader Nelson Mandela began in 1986. In February 1990, President F. W. de

Klerk, who had come to power in September 1989, announced the unbanning of the ANC and all other antiapartheid groups. Two weeks later, Mandela was released from prison. In 1991, the Group Areas Act, Land Acts, and the Population Registration Act—the last of the so-called pillars of apartheid—were abolished. A long series of negotiations ensued, resulting in a new constitution promulgated into law in December 1993. The country's first nonracial elections were held April 26–29, 1994, resulting in the installation of Nelson Mandela as president on May 10, 1994.

Until 1991, South African law divided the population into four major racial categories: Africans (black), whites, coloreds, and Asians. Although this law has been abolished, many South Africans still view themselves and each other according to these categories. Africans comprise about 75% of the population and are divided into a number of different ethnic groups. Whites comprise about 14% of the population. The coloreds trace their lineage to the earliest settlers, who married indigenous peoples. They comprise about 9% of the total population. Asians descend from Indian workers brought to South Africa in the mid-nineteenth century to work on the sugar estates in Natal Province. They constitute about 2% of the population and are concentrated in that area.

Education is in a state of flux. Under the apartheid system, schools were segregated, and the quantity and quality of education varied significantly across racial groups. Although the laws governing this segregation have been abolished, the long and arduous process of restructuring the country's educational system is just beginning. The challenge is to create a single nondiscriminatory, nonracial system that offers the same standards of education to all people.

South Africa has a broad-based, industrialized economy that, paradoxically, exhibits most of the characteristics associated with developing economies: a division of labor between formal and informal sectors, a highly uneven distribution of wealth and income, a dependence on commodity exports, and a legacy of government intervention.

The formal sector, based on mining and manufacturing, is well developed. Smaller but important agricultural and service sectors exist. Despite a strong private sector, there has been substantial governmental intervention in the economy. There also are a number of large government-owned corporations.

Economic policy has concentrated on the formal sector, but since the mid-1980s, the policy has sought to develop the informal sector, focusing on education and training, job creation, and small-business assistance. The transition to a democratic, nonracial government, begun in early 1990, stimulated debate on future economic policies to achieve sustained economic growth, redress the socioeconomic disparities created by apartheid, and improve the standard of living for the majority of the population.

The government is pursuing market-based policies, with the private sector as generator of wealth and the government trying to address inequities in health, education, housing, and social services. It has embarked on a five-year, $10.5 billion reconstruction and development program intended to reduce unemployment, provide free medical care to pregnant mothers and children under age 6, electrify houses in African-populated townships, and build 1 million new homes. To accomplish its goals without undermining business confidence, the government's first-year budget called for continued fiscal discipline and strict monetary controls. South Africa aims to establish and maintain a pro-business environment and is encouraging both foreign and domestic investment.

South Africa has rich mineral resources; the only major mineral products it lacks are petroleum and bauxite. It is the world's largest producer and exporter of gold and also exports a significant amount of coal. The value-added processing of minerals to produce ferroalloys, stainless steels, and similar products is a major industry and an important potential growth area. The country's diverse manufacturing leads the world in several specialized sectors, including railway rolling stock, synththic fuels, and mining equipment and machinery.

Agriculture accounts for about 5% of the gross domestic product, focusing on citrus fruits, corn, dairy products, sugarcane, tobacco, wine, and wool. However, because of inadequate and erratic rainfall, only about 15% of the land is suitable for farming. South Africa has many developed irrigation schemes and is a net exporter of food.

The transportation infrastructure is well developed, supporting both domestic and regional needs. The telecommunications and electrical infrastructure provide First World service to white urban areas.

The economy is recovering from a five-year recession, thanks primarily to significant gains in the agricultural sector. South Africa's economic future looks hopeful, with GDP expected to increase and its currency, the rand, expected to depreciate against the dollar. However, several factors could alter these forecasts, including future commodity prices and the duration of the rebound in the global economy.

Exports and imports account for more than 24% of the GDP. With the lifting of sanctions (imposed to protest apartheid) in 1993, the United States regained its position as South Africa's principal trading partner. South Africa is the largest export market for U.S. goods and services in sub-Saharan Africa. In 1993, U.S. exports to South Africa totaled $2.4 billion, representing about 14% of South Africa's total imports. Other major trading partners are Germany, Japan, and the United Kingdom. Trade with other sub-Saharan African countries, which represents a considerable portion of South Africa's trade, has continued to increase substantially.

Although South Africa has abolished apartheid, the country's native black Africans live in an entirely different world from the whites. South African whites, who now constitute about 14% of the population, own 88% of the country's private property and, along with foreign investors, over 90% of commerce and industry. Over half of the black population lives below the poverty line, and 40% of rural black children are stunted by malnutrition. With a black illiteracy rate of 33% and over three-quarters of black teachers unqualified for their jobs, the educational system continues to perpetuate a vicious cycle of deprivation and discrimination. The distribution of income between whites and blacks is among the most unequal in the world. The United Nations Development Program's 1994 *Human Development Report* notes that the disparity between whites and blacks in South Africa is four times larger than in the United States, with average white income per capita almost 10 times average black income. Moreover, the report states, "If white South Africa were a separate country, it would rank 24th in the world (just after Spain). Black South Africa would rank 123rd in the world (just above Congo). Not just two different peoples, these are almost two different worlds."*

In March 1995, Nelson Mandela unveiled a new economic plan. It discontinued the long-standing dual currency system to promote foreign investment, and it allocated $1.5 billion for housing, education, and employment creation directed to the poor. With a 3% growth in GNP in 1995, over $2.5 billion of U.S. investment in 1994, and a 26% rise in the local stock market, the new South African government has high hopes that past and existing inequities will soon be diminished and eventually eliminated. It will be a fascinating process to watch.

*United Nations Development Program, *Human Development Report, 1994* (New York: Oxford University Press, 1994), p. 98.

Concepts for Review

Absolute poverty	Indirect taxes
Asset ownership	Kuznets curve
Character of economic growth	Land reform
Deciles	Lorenz curve
Disposable income	Personal distribution of income
Distributive share index	Poverty gap
Equal-weights index	Poverty-weighted index
Factor-price distortions	Progressive income tax
Factor share distribution of income	Public consumption
Factors of production	Quintiles
Functional distribution of income	Redistribution policies
Gini coefficient	Regressive tax
GNP growth rate index	Size distribution of income
Income inequality	Subsidy

Questions for Discussion

1. Most development economists now seem to agree that the level and rate of growth of GNP and per capita income do not provide sufficient or even accurate measures of a country's development. What is the essence of their argument? Give some examples.

2. Distinguish between size and functional distributions of income in a nation. Which do you feel is the more appropriate concept? Explain.

3. What is meant by *absolute poverty* and the *poverty gap*? Why should we be concerned with the measurement of absolute poverty in Third World nations?

4. What are the principal economic characteristics of poverty groups? What do these characteristics tell us about the possible nature of a poverty-focused development strategy?

5. Describe the Kuznets hypothesis. Discuss the conceptual merits and limitations of this hypothesis for contemporary developing countries.

6. In the text, when we examined statistics from a wide range of Third World countries, we found no direct relationship (positive or negative) between a country's level of GNP, GNP per capita, and rate of economic growth and its extent of absolute poverty or the degree of equality in its distribution of income. Assuming that these data are indeed correct, what do they tell us about the importance of the character of a nation's growth process and about its institutional structure?

7. What is the relationship between a Lorenz curve and a Gini coefficient? Give some examples of how Lorenz curves and Gini coefficients can be used as summary measures of equality and inequality in a nation's distribution of income.

8. It is asserted in the text that the major determinant of a country's income distribution is its distribution of productive and income-earning assets. Explain the meaning of this statement, giving examples of different kinds of productive and income-earning assets.

9. Are rapid economic growth (as measured by either GNP or per capita GNP) and a more equitable distribution of personal income necessarily conflicting objectives? Summarize the arguments both for and against the presumed conflict of objectives, and state and explain your own view.

10. GNP growth is called a biased index of national development and economic welfare. Explain the meaning of this statement, giving a specific hypothetical or real example of such bias.

11. What is the value of constructing an equal-weights or a poverty-weighted index of social welfare? Under what conditions will these welfare indexes differ from GNP? Explain your answer.

12. Economic growth is said to be a "necessary but not sufficient condition" to eradicate absolute poverty and reduce inequality. What is the reasoning behind this argument?

13. Outline the range of major policy options available to LDC governments to alter and modify the size distribution of their national incomes. Which policy or policies do you believe are absolutely essential, and which are important but not crucial? Explain your answer.

Notes

1. United Nations, *International Conference on Population and Development, Program of Action* (New York: United Nations, 1994), pp. 3.11, 3.13.

2. The Lorenz curve is named after Conrad Lorenz, an American statistician who in 1905 devised this convenient and widely used diagram to show the relationship between population groups and their respective income shares.

3. A more precise definition of perfect equality would take into account the age structure of a population and expected income variations over the "life cycle" of all households within that population. See Morton Paglin, "The measurement and trend of inequality: A basic revision," *American Economic Review* 65 (September 1975).

4. Gary S. Fields, *Poverty, Inequality and Development* (Cambridge: Cambridge University Press, 1980), pp. 46–56.

5. *Ibid.*, p. 52.

6. The sum of all workers' marginal product must equal total national product (GNP), which will be distributed as the national income. For the mathematically inclined, total product is simply the integral of the marginal product curve between 0 and L_E. This is because the marginal product function is the derivative of the total product curve: $TP = f(L, \bar{K})$; $MP_L = f'(L)$.

7. For an excellent review of methods of measuring poverty and inequality in developing countries along with data requirements, see Gary S. Fields, "Data for measuring poverty and inequality changes in developing countries," *Journal of Development Economics* 44 (1994): 87–102. See also D. L. Blackwood and R. G. Lynch, "The measurement of inequality and poverty: A policy maker's guide to the literature," *World Development* 22 (April 1994): 567–578.

8. Irma Adelman, "A poverty-focused approach to development policy," in John P. Lewis and Valeriana Kallab (eds.), *Development Strategies Reconsidered* (Washington, D.C.: Overseas Development Council, 1986), pp. 49–65.

9. World Bank, *World Development Report, 1990: Poverty* (New York: Oxford University Press, 1990), pp. 27–34.

10. Shaohua Chen, Gaurav Datt, and Martin Ravallion, *Is Poverty Increasing in the Developing World?* Policy Research Working Paper No. 1146 (Washington, D.C.: World Bank, 1994).

11. For an excellent overview of the nature, magnitude, and incidence of poverty in the developing world, see World Bank, *World Development Report, 1990,* chap. 2.

12. For a comprehensive analysis of how poverty directly affects women's lives in developing countries, see Mayra Buvinic, Margaret A. Lycette, and William P. McGreevey

(eds.), *Women and Poverty in the Third World* (Baltimore: Johns Hopkins University Press, 1983); Judith Bruce and Daisy Dwyer (eds.), *A Home Divided: Women and Income in the Third World* (Stanford, Calif.: Stanford University Press, 1988); Janet Momsen, *Women and Development in the Third World* (New York: Routledge, 1991); and Diane Elson, "Gender-aware analysis and economic development," *Journal of International Development* 5 (1993). An excellent statistical survey can be found in United Nations, *The World's Women, 1995; Trends and Statistics* (New York: United Nations, 1995).

13. Amartya Sen, "Missing women," *British Medical Journal* 304 (1992): 587–588.

14. See, for example, Haeduck Lee, *The Ethnic Dimension of Poverty and Income Distribution in Latin America* (Washington, D.C.: World Bank, 1993), and George Psacharopoulos and Harry A. Patrinos, "Indigenous people and poverty in Latin America," *Finance and Development* 31 (March 1994): 41–43.

15. Simon Kuznets, "Economic growth and income inequality," *American Economic Review* 45 (March 1955): 1–28; and "Quantitative aspects of the economic growth of nations," *Economic Development and Cultural Change* 11 (March 1963): 1–80.

16. Cross-sectional studies supporting the Kuznets hypothesis include Harry Oshima, "The international comparison of size distribution of family incomes with special reference to Asia," *Review of Economics and Statistics* (November 1962): 439–445; Felix Paukert, "Income distribution at different levels of development: A survey of evidence," *International Labor Review* 108 (August–September 1973): 97–125; and Montek S. Ahluwalia, Nicholas G. Carter, and Hollis B. Chenery, "Growth and poverty in developing countries," *Journal of Development Economics* 16 (September 1979): 298–323. Studies arguing against the hypothesis include Ashwani Saith, "Development and distribution: A critique of the cross country U-hypothesis," *Journal of Development Economics* 13 (1983): 367–382; and S. Anand and S. M. R. Kanbur, "The Kuznets process and the inequality-development relationship," *Journal of Development Economics* 23 (February 1993). See also Gustav Papanek and Oldrich Kyn, "Flattening the Kuznets curve: The consequences for income distribution of development strategy, government intervention, income and the rate of growth," *Pakistan Development Review* 26 (Spring 1987): 1–54; and World Bank, *World Development Report, 1990*, pp. 46–47.

17. This finding is strongly supported by a much more rigorous empirical study of both cross-sectional and time-series data for 83 countries. See Gustav Papanek and Oldrich Kyn, "The effect on income distribution of development, the growth rate and economic strategy," *Journal of Development Economics* 23 (1986): 55–65. For evidence that higher growth is more often associated with *lower* inequality, see World Bank, *World Development Report, 1991* (New York: Oxford University Press, 1991), fig. 7.2.

18. Irma Adelman and Cynthia Taft Morris, *Economic Growth and Social Equality in Developing Countries* (Stanford, Calif.: Stanford University Press, 1973).

19. *Ibid.*, p. 186. More recent evidence to support this claim can be found in Irma Adelman, "What is the evidence on income inequality and development?" in Donald Savoie and Irving Brecker (eds.), *Equity and Efficiency in Economic Development* (Toronto: University of Toronto Press, 1993). Some contrary evidence, however, in the case of Brazil is presented in an article by Gary S. Fields, "Who benefits from economic development? A reexamination of Brazilian growth in the 1960s," *American Economic Review* 67 (September 1977). For a review of other empirical studies, see Arne Bigsten, "Poverty, inequality and development," in Norman Gemmell (ed.), *Surveys in Development Economics* (Oxford: Blackwell, 1987), pp. 146–157.

20. One of the earliest and best-known articles on the subject is Walter Galenson and Harvey Leibenstein, "Investment criteria, productivity, and economic development," *Quarterly Journal of Economics* (August 1955): 343–370.

21. For an additional argument, drawn from the experiences of Taiwan and South Korea, against the notion that growth and equity are necessarily in conflict, see Gustav Ranis, "Development and the distribution of income: Some counter-evidence," *Challenge*, September–October 1977.

22. For a recent study and documentation of the substantial magnitude of capital flight, see Donald R. Lessard and John Williamson, *Capital Flight: The Problem and Policy Responses* (Washington, D.C.: Institute for International Economics, 1987). We discuss capital flight in greater detail in Chapter 14.

23. Various U.N. studies on sources of savings in Third World nations show that small farmers and individuals seem to be among the highest savers. Also see Gustav Ranis, "Investment criteria, productivity and economic development: An empirical comment," *Quarterly Journal of Economics* (May 1962); K. L. Gupta, "Personal saving in developing countries: Further evidence," *Economic Record* (June 1970); and Andrew Mason, "Savings, economic growth and demographic change," *Population and Development Review* 14 (March 1988): 113–144.

24. For empirical support of this argument with regard to rural saving and investment, see Keith Griffin, "Rural development: The policy options," in Edgar O. Edwards (ed.), *Employment in Developing Nations* (New York: Columbia University Press, 1974), pp. 190–191.

25. For a theoretical proof that greater equality in income distribution leads to improved nutrition, more employment, and greater output growth, see Partha Dasgupta and Debraj Ray, "Inequality as a determinant of malnutrition and unemployment policy," *Economic Journal* 97 (March 1987): 177–188.

26. An empirical study of variables explaining LDC growth during the 1960–1973 period provides strong econometric confirmation of our argument that policies designed to promote better distribution and reduce poverty are, on balance, growth-stimulating rather than growth-retarding. See Norman L. Hicks, "Growth vs. basic needs: Is there a trade-off?" *World Development* (1979): 985–994; and Adriana Marshall, "Income distribution, the domestic market and growth in Argentina," *Labour and Society* 13 (January 1988): 79–103.

27. For robust empirical evidence on how improved distribution can increase domestic demand, promote political stability, and generate higher growth rates, see Alberto Alesina and Roberto Perotti, "The political economy of growth: A critical survey of the recent literature," *World Bank Economic Review* 8 (September 1994): 351–371, and Alberto Alesina and Dani Rodrik, "Distributive policies and economic growth," *Quarterly Journal of Economics* 109 (May 1994): 465–490.

28. World Bank, *World Development Report, 1990*, pp. 51–52. See also Albert Fishlow, "Inequality, poverty and growth: Where do we stand?" in Michael Bruno and Boris Pleskovic (eds.), *Proceedings of the World Bank Annual Conference on Development Economics, 1995* (Washington, D.C.: World Bank, 1996); Nancy Budsall, David Ross, and Richard Sabot, "Inequality and growth reconsidered:. Lessons from East Asia," *World Bank Economic Review* 9 (September 1995): 477–508; and George R. G. Clarke, "More evidence on income distribution and growth," *Journal of Development Economics* 47 (August 1995).

29. For other discussions of poverty policies, see Bigsten, "Poverty, inequality and development," pp. 157–163; Adelman and Morris, *Economic Growth and Social Equality*, pp. 54–65; Jagdish N. Bhagwati, "Poverty and public policy," *World Development* 16 (May 1988):

539–555; World Bank, *World Development Report, 1990*, chaps. 7 and 8; Irma Adelman and Sherman Robinson, "Income distribution and development" in Hollis B. Chenery and T. N. Srinivasan (eds.), *Handbook of Development Economics*, vol. 2 (Amsterdam: North Holland, 1989), pp. 982–996; and especially Paul P. Streeten, *Strategies for Human Development: Global Poverty and Unemployment* (Copenhagen: Handelshøjskolens Forlag, 1994).

Further Reading

A comprehensive description of the various meanings and measurements of income distribution can be found in Jan Pen, *Income Distribution* (Harmondsworth, England: Penguin, 1971), chaps. 1–3. See also Anthony B. Atkinson, *The Economics of Inequality* (New York: Oxford University Press, 1975). The best overall surveys are found in Irma Adelman and Sherman Robinson "Income distribution and development," in Hollis B. Chenery and T. N. Srinivasan (eds.), *Handbook of Development Economics*, vol. 2 (Amsterdam: North Holland, 1989), pp. 950–1008, and Gary S. Fields, "Data for measuring poverty and inequality changes in developing countries," *Journal of Development Economics* 44 (1994): 87–102.

For summaries of the poverty and income distribution problem in LDCs using cross-country data with appropriate analysis and alternative policy strategies, see especially World Bank, *World Development Report, 1990: Poverty* (New York: Oxford University Press, 1990); Eliana Cardoso and Ann Helwege, "Below the line: Poverty in Latin America," *World Development* 20 (January 1992): 19–37; and R. M. Sundrum, *Income Distribution in Less Developed Countries* (London: Routledge, 1992). See also Hollis B. Chenery, John Duloy, and Richard Jolly, *Redistribution with Growth* (Washington, D.C.: World Bank, 1974); Mahbub ul-Haq, *The Assault on World Poverty* (Baltimore: Johns Hopkins University Press, 1975); Montek S. Ahluwalia, Nicholas G. Carter, and Hollis B. Chenery, "Growth and poverty in developing countries," *Journal of Development Economics* (September 1979); Hollis B. Chenery, *Structural Change and Development Policy* (London: Oxford University Press, 1980); Gary S. Fields, *Poverty, Inequality and Development* (Cambridge: Cambridge University Press, 1980); Arne Bigsten, "Poverty, inequality and development," in Norman Gemmell (ed.), *Surveys in Development Economics* (Oxford: Blackwell, 1987), chap. 4; "Poverty and Well-Being in Developing Countries" (Symposium), *American Economic Review* 84 (May 1994): 211–231; and Albert Fishlow "Inequality, poverty and growth: Where do we stand?" and Pranab Bardhan, "Research on poverty and development twenty years after *Redistribution with Growth*," in Michael Bruno and Boris Pleskovic (eds.), *Proceedings of the World Bank Annual Conference on Development Economics, 1995* (Washington, D.C.: World Bank, 1996).

Other useful works include William R. Cline, *Income Distribution and Economic Development: A Survey and Tests for Selected Latin American Cities* (Washington, D.C.: Brookings Institution, 1973); Gunnar Myrdal, "Equity and growth," *World Development* 1 (November 1973); Felix Paukert, "Income distribution at different levels of development: A survey of evidence," *International Labor Review* 108 (August–September 1973); A. B. Atkinson, "On the measurement of inequality," *Journal of Economic Theory* (September 1970); Irma Adelman and Cynthia Taft Morris, "An anatomy of income distribution patterns in developing nations," *Development Digest*, October 1971; Arun Shourie, "Growth, poverty and inequalities," *Foreign Affairs* 51 (February 1973); Roger D. Hansen, "The emerging challenge: Global distribution of income and economic opportunity," in Overseas Development Council, *Agenda for Action, 1975* (New York: Praeger, 1975); Arne Bigsten, *Income Distribution and Development Theory, Evidence and Policy* (London: Heinemann, 1983); Gary S. Fields, "Employment, income distribution and economic growth in seven small economies," *Economic Journal* 94 (1984): 74–83;

Emanuel De Kant, "Of markets, might and mullaks: A case for equity, pluralism and tolerance in development," *World Development* 13 (1985): 549–556. Gustav Papanek and Oldrich Kyn, "The effect on income distribution of development, the growth rate and economic strategy," *Journal of Development Economics* 23 (1986): 55–65; Irma Adelman, "A poverty-focused approach to development policy," in John P. Lewis and Valeriana Kaleb (eds.), *Development Strategies Reconsidered* (Washington, D.C.: Overseas Development Council, 1986), pp. 49–65; Jagdish N. Bhagwati, "Poverty and public policy," *World Development* 16 (May 1988): 539–555; and Partha Dasgupta, *An Inquiry into Well-Being and Destitution* (New York: Oxford University Press, 1993).

Two valuable recent surveys of women and poverty in the Third World are World Resources Institute, *World Resources 1994–1995* (New York: Oxford University Press, 1994), chap. 3; and especially United Nations Development Program, *Human Development Report, 1995* (New York: Oxford University Press, 1995).

Compelling discussions of the special circumstances faced by poor women and children are presented in Judith Bruce and Daisy Dwyer (eds.), *A Home Divided: Women and Income in the Third World* (Stanford, Calif.: Stanford University Press, 1988); and Mayra Buvinic, Margaret A. Lycette, William P. McGreevey (eds.), *Women and Poverty in the Third World* (Baltimore: Johns Hopkins University Press, 1983). For more detailed analysis of discrimination in intrahousehold resource allocation, see Meera Chatterjee, *Indian Women, Health and Productivity*, Women in Development Working Paper No. 442 (Washington, D.C.: World Bank, 1990); Angus Deaton, *The Allocation of Goods within the Household: Adults, Children and Gender*, Living Standards Measurement Study Working Paper No. 39 (Washington, D.C.: World Bank, 1987); Duncan Thomas, *Gender Differences in Household Resource Allocations*, Living Standards Measurement Study Working Paper No. 79 (Washington, D.C.: World Bank, 1991); and Lawrence Haddad, *Gender and Poverty in Ghana: A Descriptive Analysis* (Washington, D.C.: World Bank, 1991).

See also Stephen C. Smith, *Case Studies*, Chapters 5 and 6 on women in Bangladesh and Kenya.

CHAPTER 6

Population Growth and Economic Development: Causes, Consequences, and Controversies

The central issue of our time may well turn out to be how the world addresses the problem of ever-expanding human numbers.

—James Grant, Former Director General, UNICEF

What governments and their people do today to influence our demographic future will set the terms for development strategy well into the next century.

—A. W. Clausen, Former President, World Bank

Population-related goals and policies are integral parts of cultural, economic and social development.

—Program of Action, 1994 United Nations International Conference on Population and Development

As 1995 came to an end, the world's population was estimated to be almost 5.8 billion people. Projections by the United Nations placed the figure at more than 6.3 billion by the end of the twentieth century, 8.5 billion by the year 2025, and almost 10 billion by 2050. Over five-sixths of that population will inhabit the developing world. What will be the economic and social implications for levels of living, national and personal esteem, and freedom of choice—in short, for development—if such quantitative projections are realized? Are such projections inevitable, or will they depend on the success or failure of Third World development efforts? Finally, even more significant, is rapid population growth per se as serious a problem as many people believe, or is it a manifestation of more fundamental problems of underdevelopment and the unequal utilization of global resources between rich and poor nations, as others argue?

In this chapter, we examine many of the issues relating population growth to economic development. We begin, however, by looking at historical and recent population trends and the changing geographic distribution of the world's people. After explaining basic demographic concepts, we present some well-known

189

economic models and hypotheses regarding the causes and consequences of rapid population growth in contemporary LDCs. Controversies surrounding the significance of the population factor in general and these models and hypotheses in particular are then explored. Finally, we evaluate a range of alternative policy options that Third World countries may wish to adopt to influence the size and growth of their populations, as well as ways in which industrialized countries can contribute to a more manageable global population and resource environment.

The Basic Issue: Population Growth and the Quality of Life

Every year, more than 87 million people are being added to the world's population. More than 78 million of these additional people each year will be born in Third World countries. These increases are unprecedented in history. But the problem of population growth is not simply a problem of numbers. It is a problem of human welfare and of development as defined in Chapter 1. Rapid population growth can have serious consequences for the well-being of all of humanity. If development entails the improvement in people's levels of living—their incomes, health, education, and general well-being—and if it also encompasses their self-esteem, respect, dignity, and freedom to choose, then the really important question about population growth is this: How does the contemporary population situation in many Third World countries contribute to or detract from their chances of realizing the goals of development, not only for the current generation but also for future generations? Conversely, how does development affect population growth?

Among the major issues relating to this basic question are the following:

1. Will Third World countries be capable of improving the levels of living for their people with the current and anticipated levels of population growth? To what extent does rapid population increase make it more difficult to provide essential social services, including housing, transport, sanitation, and security?

2. How will the developing countries be able to cope with the vast increases in their labor forces over the coming decades? Will employment opportunities be plentiful, or will it be a major achievement just to keep unemployment levels from rising?

3. What are the implications of higher population growth rates among the world's poor for their chances of overcoming the human misery of absolute poverty? Will world food supply and its distribution be sufficient not only to meet the anticipated population increase in the coming decades but also to improve nutritional levels to the point where all humans can have an adequate diet?

4. Given the anticipated population growth, will developing countries be able to extend the coverage and improve the quality of their health and educational systems so that everyone can at least have the chance to secure adequate health care and a basic education?

5. To what extent are low levels of living an important factor in limiting the freedom of parents to choose a desired family size? Is there a relationship between poverty and family size?

6. To what extent is the growing affluence among the economically more developed nations an important factor preventing poor nations from accommodating their growing populations? And is the inexorable pursuit of increasing affluence among the rich more detrimental to the global environment and to rising living standards among the poor than the absolute increase in their numbers?

A Review of Numbers: Population Growth—Past, Present, and Future

World Population Growth through History

Throughout most of the more than 2 million years of human existence on earth, humanity's numbers have been few. When people first started to cultivate food through agriculture some 12,000 years ago, the estimated world population was no more than 5 million, less than the number of people living today in Mexico City, Lagos, Buenos Aires, or Bangkok (see Table 6.1). At the beginning of the Christian era 2,000 years ago, world population had grown to nearly 250 million, less than a quarter of the population of China today. From A.D. 1 to the beginning of the

TABLE 6.1 Estimated World Population Growth through History

Year	Estimated Population (in millions)	Estimated Annual Percentage Increase in the Intervening Period
10,000 B.C.	5	
A.D. 1	250	0.04
1650	545	0.04
1750	728	0.29
1800	906	0.45
1850	1,171	0.53
1900	1,608	0.65
1950	2,576	0.91
1970	3,698	2.09
1980	4,448	1.76
1990	5,292	1.73
2000 (projected)	6,260	1.70

SOURCES: Warren S. Thompson and David T. Lewis, *Population Problems,* 5th ed. (New York: McGraw-Hill, 1965), p. 384; United Nations, *Demographic Yearbook for 1971* (New York: United Nations, 1971); Population Reference Bureau, *1990 World Population Data Sheet* (Washington, D.C.: Population Reference Bureau, 1990); United Nations Population Fund, *Populations, Resources and the Environment: The Critical Challenges* (New York: United Nations, 1991), p. 9.

industrial revolution around 1750, it tripled to 728 million people, less than the total number living in India today. During the next 200 years (1750–1950), an additional 1.7 billion people were added to the earth's numbers. But in just four decades thereafter (1950–1990), world population more than doubled again, bringing the total figure to around 5.3 billion. If this trend continues, the world will enter the twenty-first century with 6.3 billion people. Figure 6.1 shows how rapidly total population grew in the four decades after 1950 in comparison with the two centuries before that. It vividly portrays the magnitude of population growth in the less developed regions of the world since 1950, both as a percentage of the total (Figure 6.1a) and in terms of absolute increases (Figure 6.1b). Finally, it provides projections to the year 2100, when world population is expected to stabilize at around 11 billion.

Turning from absolute numbers to percentage growth rates, we can see from Table 6.2 that for almost the whole of humankind's existence on earth until approximately 300 years ago, population grew at an annual rate not much greater than zero (0.002%, or 20 per million). Naturally, this overall rate was not steady; there were many ups and downs as a result of natural catastrophes and variations in growth rates among regions. By 1750, the population growth rate had accelerated by 150 times, from 0.002% to 0.3% per year. By the 1950s, the rate had again accelerated, tripling to about 1.0% per year. It continued to accelerate into the 1970s, when it peaked at 2.3%.[1] Today the world's population growth rate remains at a historically very high rate of 1.5% per year.

The relationship between annual percentage increases and the time it takes for a population to double in size is shown in the rightmost column of Table 6.2. We see that before 1650, it took nearly 36,000 years, or about 1,400 generations, for the world population to double. Today, in less than 47 years, little more than one generation, world population will double.[2] Moreover, whereas it took almost 1,750 years to add 480 million people to the world's population between A.D. 1 and the onset of the industrial revolution, at current growth rates this same number of people is being added to the earth's population every six years!

The reason for the sudden change in overall population trends is that for almost all of recorded history, the rate of population change, whether up or down, had been strongly influenced by the combined effects of famine, disease, malnutrition, plague, and war—conditions that resulted in high and fluctuating death rates. In the twentieth century, such conditions came increasingly under technological and economic control. As a result, human mortality (the death rate) is now lower than at any other point in human existence. It is this decline in mortality resulting from rapid technological advances in modern medicine and the spread of modern sanitation measures throughout the world, particularly within the past 50 years, that has resulted in the unprecedented increases in world population growth, especially in Third World countries. For example, death rates in Africa, Asia, and Latin America have fallen by as much as 50% during the past 30 to 40 years, whereas birthrates have only recently begun to decline.

In short, population growth today is primarily the result of a rapid transition from a long historical era characterized by high birthrates and death rates to one in which death rates have fallen sharply but birthrates, especially in developing countries, are only just beginning to fall from their historic high levels.

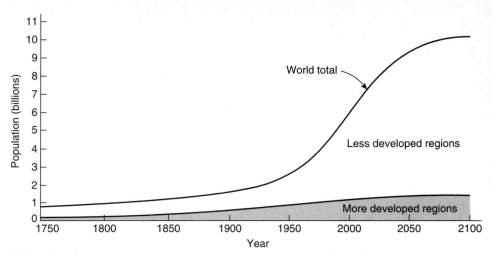

(a) Absolute size

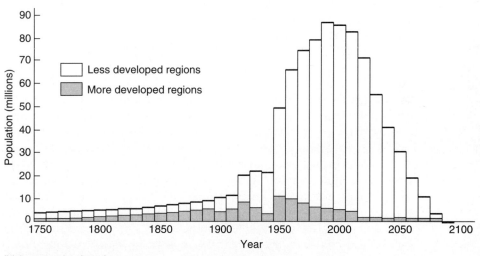

(b) Increase by decade

FIGURE 6.1 Population Growth, 1750–2100: World, Less Developed Regions, and More Developed Regions. *Source*: Thomas W. Merrick, "World population in transition," *Population Bulletin* 41 (April 1986): 4. Reprinted with permission.

NOTE: The less developed regions are Africa, Asia (minus Japan), and Latin America; the more developed regions are Europe, the former USSR, Japan, Oceania (including Australia and New Zealand), and North America (Canada and the United States).

TABLE 6.2 World Population Growth Rates and Doubling
Times: A Historical Review

Period	Approximate Growth Rate (percent)	Doubling Time (years)
Appearance of humans to early historical times	0.002	36,000
1650–1750	0.3	240
1850–1900	0.6	115
1930–1950	1.0	72
1960–1980	2.3	31
Present (1995)	1.5	47

SOURCES: Warren S. Thompson and David T. Lewis, *Population Problems*, 5th ed.
(New York: McGraw-Hill, 1965), p. 384; Population Reference Bureau, *1995 World
Population Data Sheet* (Washington, D.C.: Population Reference Bureau, 1995).

Structure of the World's Population

Geographic Region

The world's population is very unevenly distributed by geographic region, by fertility and mortality levels, and by age structures. Of the world's total population in 1995, more than three-quarters lived in developing countries and less than one-quarter in the economically developed nations. Figure 6.2 shows the regional distribution of the world's population as it existed in 1990 and as it is projected for 2020.

Given current population growth rates in different parts of the world (significantly higher in the LDCs), the regional distribution of the world's population will inevitably change by 2020. By that time, it is likely that there will be almost 6 billion more people on the earth than in 1950 and more than 2.5 billion more than in 1990. However, it is estimated that over 60% of the added people will be in Asia, where overall population size will have increased by 400% since 1950. The corresponding increases in Africa and Latin America are estimated at almost 500%, with an addition of almost 1.3 billion people. Together these three Third World continents will probably hold over 85% of the world's population by 2020, as contrasted with 70% in 1950 and 78% in 1990. Correspondingly, the proportion of the world's population living in Europe, the former Soviet Union, and North America will have fallen from 30% to less than 15% of the total.

Consider, finally, the distribution of national populations. Table 6.3 lists the 15 largest countries in the world in 1995. Together they account for over 70% of the world's population. Although these countries are on all the continents and in both developed and underdeveloped regions, it is instructive to note that in terms of annual increases in world population, countries such as India, Indonesia, Brazil, Bangladesh, Pakistan, and Nigeria all add more to the world's annual population increase than most of the economically more developed countries do. For example, Pakistan, ranked eighth in size, adds almost twice as many people to the absolute

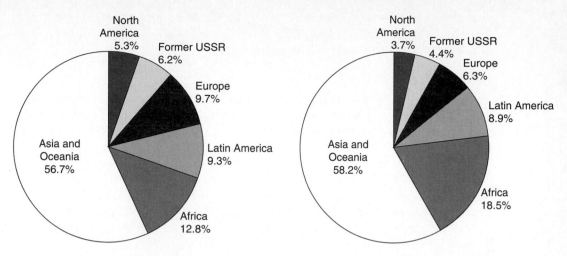

1990: Total population 5.286 billion

2020: Projected population 7.992 billion

FIGURE 6.2 World Population Distribution by Region, 1990 and 2020. *Source*: Data from Population Reference Bureau, *1990 World Population Data Sheet* (Washington, D.C.: Population Reference Bureau, 1990).

TABLE 6.3 The Fifteen Largest Countries and Their Annual Population Increases, 1995

Country	Rank	Total Population, 1995 (millions)	Rate of Natural Increase, 1995 (percent)	Annual Increase (millions)
China	1	1,218.8	1.1	13.41
India	2	930.6	1.9	17.68
United States	3	263.2	0.7	1.84
Indonesia	4	198.4	1.6	3.17
Brazil	5	157.8	1.7	2.68
Russia	6	147.5	−0.6	−0.87
Pakistan	7	129.7	2.9	3.76
Japan	8	125.2	0.3	0.38
Bangladesh	9	119.2	2.4	2.86
Nigeria	10	101.2	3.1	3.14
Mexico	11	93.7	2.2	2.06
Germany	12	81.7	−0.1	−0.08
Vietnam	13	75.0	2.3	1.73
Philippines	14	68.4	2.1	1.44
Turkey	15	61.4	1.6	0.98

SOURCE: Population Reference Bureau, *1995 World Population Data Sheet* (Washington, D.C.: Population Reference Bureau, 1995).

growth of the world's population than the United States, which ranks third. Similarly, Mexico, ranked eleventh, adds more people annually than either Russia or Japan, ranked sixth and seventh, respectively.

Fertility and Mortality Trends

The **rate of population increase** is quantitatively measured as the percentage yearly net relative increase (or decrease, in which case it is negative) in population size due to **natural increase** and **net international migration**. Natural increase simply measures the excess of births over deaths or, in more technical terms, the difference between **fertility** and **mortality**. Net international migration is of negligible, though growing, importance today (although in the nineteenth and early twentieth centuries it was an extremely important source of population increase in North America, Australia, and New Zealand and corresponding decrease in Western Europe). Population increases in Third World countries therefore depend almost entirely on the difference between their birth and death rates.

The difference between developing and developed nations in terms of rates of population growth can be explained simply by the fact that **birthrates** (fertility) in developing countries are generally much higher than in the rich nations. Third World **death rates** (mortality) are also higher. However, these death rate differences are substantially smaller than the differences in birthrates. As a result, the average rate of population growth in the developing countries is now about 2.0% per year (2.3% excluding China), whereas most of the economically developed countries have annual growth rates of only 0.4% to 0.7%. Figure 6.3 shows recent and projected trends in population growth for both developed and less developed nations. Note that the overall population growth rate in developing countries appears to have peaked at an annual rate of 2.35% in the late 1960s and early 1970s and is now slowly declining.

As just noted, the major source of difference in population growth rates between the less developed and the more developed countries is the sizable difference in their birthrates. Recall from Chapter 2 that most Third World nations have birthrates ranging from 30 to 40 per 1,000. By contrast, in almost all developed countries, the rate is less than 15 per 1,000. Moreover, LDC birthrates today are substantially higher than they were in preindustrial Western Europe. This is largely because of early and almost universal marriage in contemporary Third World countries. But there has been a substantial decline in LDC fertility over the past two decades, not only in countries like Taiwan, South Korea, Singapore, and Hong Kong, where rapid economic and social development have taken place, but also in nations where growth has been less rapid, including Mexico and Zimbabwe, and in some where growth has stagnated, such as Bangladesh. Table 6.4 lists seven countries that experienced significant fertility declines between 1970 and 1992.

While fertility has been declining in LDCs, there has been a rapid narrowing of the gap in mortality rates between developed and less developed countries. The primary reason is undoubtedly the improvement in health conditions throughout the Third World. Modern vaccination campaigns against malaria, smallpox, yellow fever, and cholera as well as the proliferation of public-health facilities, clean water supplies, improved nutrition, and public education have all worked together

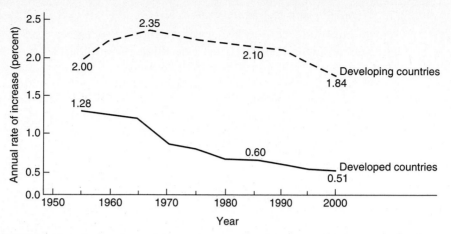

FIGURE 6.3 Population Growth Rates in Developed and Developing Countries, 1950–2000.

over the past 25 or 30 years to lower death rates by as much as 50% in parts of Asia and Latin America and by over 30% in much of Africa and the Middle East. Nevertheless, the average life span remains almost 16 years greater in the developed countries. But even this gap has been sharply reduced over the past 25 years. For example, in 1950, **life expectancy at birth** for people in Third World countries averaged 35 to 40 years, compared with 62 to 65 years in the developed world. By 1980, the difference had fallen to 16 years as life expectancy in the LDCs increased to 56 years (a gain of 42%) while in the industrial nations it had risen to 72 years (an increase of 13%). Today, because of still relatively high **infant mortality rates**, Africa has the lowest life expectancy, 55 years, while the most favorable region is Western Europe, where life expectancy at birth now averages about 77 years.

TABLE 6.4 Fertility Rate for Selected Countries, 1970 and 1992		
	Total Fertility Rate	
Country	1970	1992
Bangladesh	7.0	4.0
Colombia	5.3	2.7
Indonesia	5.5	2.9
Jamaica	5.3	2.7
Mexico	4.9	3.2
Thailand	5.5	2.2
Zimbabwe	7.7	4.6

SOURCE: World Bank, *World Development Report 1994* (New York: Oxford University Press, 1994), tab. 26.
NOTE: The *total fertility rate (TFR)* is the average number of children born to women surviving the reproductive period.

Age Structure and Dependency Burdens

World population today is very youthful, particularly in the Third World. Children under the age of 15 constitute almost 40% of the total population of Third World countries but only 20% of the population of developed nations. For example, 45% of Nigeria's population and 49% of Kenya's was under 15 in 1990; for Mexico, the comparable figure was 38%, and for Syria, Pakistan, and India it was 49%, 44%, and 36%, respectively. In countries with such an age structure, the **youth dependency ratio**—the proportion of youths (under age 15) to economically active adults (ages 15 to 64)—is very high. Thus the workforce in developing countries must support almost twice as many children as it does in the wealthier countries. For example, in Sweden and the United Kingdom, the workforce age group (15 to 64) amounts to almost 65% of the total population. This workforce has to support only 18% and 19%, respectively, of the population as youthful dependents. Their main problems relate more to their low population growth and old-age dependents (over age 65), who represent 16% to 18% of their populations. By contrast, in countries like Nigeria, Bangladesh, and Ghana, the economically active workforces and the child dependents each make up about 50% of the total population. In general, the more rapid the population growth rate, the greater the proportion of dependent children in the total population and the more difficult it is for people who are working to support those who are not. This phenomenon of youth dependency also leads to an important concept, the **hidden momentum of population growth**.

The Hidden Momentum of Population Growth

Perhaps the least understood aspect of population growth is its tendency to continue even after birthrates have declined substantially. Population growth has a built-in tendency to continue, a powerful momentum that, like a speeding automobile when the brakes are applied, tends to keep going for some time before coming to a stop. In the case of population growth, this momentum can persist for decades after birthrates drop.

There are two basic reasons for this. First, high birthrates cannot be altered substantially overnight. The social, economic, and institutional forces that have influenced fertility rates over the course of centuries do not simply evaporate at the urging of national leaders. We know from the experience of European nations that such reductions in birthrates can take many decades. Consequently, even if developing countries assign top priority to the limitation of population growth, it will still take many years to lower national fertility to desired levels.

The second and less obvious reason for the hidden momentum of population growth relates to the age structure of LDC populations. We saw that nations with high birthrates have large proportions of children and adolescents in their population, sometimes as high as 50%. In such a high-fertility population, young people greatly outnumber their parents, and when their generation reaches adulthood, the number of potential parents will inevitably be much larger than at present. It follows that even if these new parents have only enough children to replace themselves (two per couple as compared with their parents, who may have had four children), the fact that the total number of couples having two children is much greater than the number of couples who previously had four children means that the total population will still increase substantially before leveling off.

Some examples of the hidden momentum process are illustrated in Figure 6.4. The first bar for each of the four countries listed gives the 1990 population. The second bar portrays the population size that will be reached when replacement-level fertility (two children per family) is finally achieved according to World Bank estimates. The final bar shows the ultimate projected level of population stability. We see, for example, that if Bangladesh reaches replacement fertility in 2025 at a population of slightly over 200 million, its population will not ultimately stabilize until 2150, when it will have grown by another 100 million people! Nigeria, with its very youthful population and rapid growth rate, can expect an almost fourfold increase in its population before stability is finally attained. Iran can expect a quadrupling of its population, and Brazil's will more than double from present levels. Globally, estimates by demographer John Bongaarts indicate that population momentum alone would increase the number of people in the developing world from 4.5 billion in 1995 to 7.3 billion in 2100 before stabilization would occur.[3] In other words, if LDC replacement fertility were achieved today, the population of the Third World would grow by an additional 2.8 billion, or 62%, before leveling off.

These illustrations vividly demonstrate the extent to which most Third World countries are *already* virtually assured of substantial population increases, whatever happens to fertility levels. As they set goals for desirable future population sizes, they may as well accept the fact that increases on the order of 60% to 125% are coming regardless of the policy strategies they adopt. But this should not be a cause for despair or a diminished commitment on the part of countries that genuinely believe that slowing population growth is in their best national interest. The

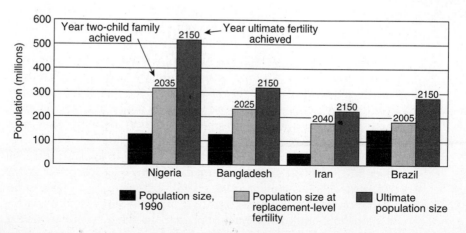

FIGURE 6.4 The Hidden Momentum of Population Growth: Some Illustrations. *Source*: Population Reference Bureau, *World Population: Fundamentals of Growth* (Washington, D.C.: Population Reference Bureau, 1990), p. 14. Reprinted with permission.

important message of population momentum is that every year that passes without a reduction in fertility means a larger multiple of the present total population size before it can eventually level off.

The Demographic Transition

The process by which fertility rates eventually decline to replacement levels has been portrayed by a famous concept in economic demography called the **demographic transition**. The demographic transition attempts to explain why all contemporary developed nations have more or less passed through the same three stages of modern population history. Before their economic modernization, these countries for centuries had stable or very slow growing populations as a result of a combination of high birthrates and almost equally high death rates. This was stage I. Stage II began to occur when modernization, associated with better public-health methods, healthier diets, higher incomes, and other improvements led to a marked reduction in mortality that gradually raised life expectancy from under 40 years to over 60 years. However, the decline in death rates was not immediately accompanied by a decline in fertility. As a result, the growing divergence between high birthrates and falling death rates led to sharp increases in population growth compared to past centuries. Stage II thus marks the beginning of the demographic transition (the transition from stable or slow-growing populations first to rapidly increasing numbers and then to declining rates). Finally, stage III was entered when the forces and influences of modernization and development caused the beginning of a decline in fertility; eventually, falling birthrates converged with lower death rates, leaving little or no population growth.

Figure 6.5 roughly depicts the three historical stages of the demographic transition in Western Europe. Before the early nineteenth century, birthrates hovered around 35 per 1,000 while death rates fluctuated around 30 per 1,000. This resulted in population growth rates of around 5 per 1,000, or less than 0.5% per year. Stage II, the beginning of Western Europe's demographic transition, was initiated around the first quarter of the nineteenth century by slowly falling death rates as a result of improving economic conditions and the gradual development of disease and death control through modern medical and public health technologies. The decline in birthrates (stage III) did not really begin until late in the nineteenth century, with most of the reduction many decades after modern economic growth had begun and long after death rates began their descent. But since the initial level of birthrates was generally low in Western Europe as a result of either late marriage or celibacy, overall rates of population growth seldom exceeded the 1% level, even at their peak. By the end of Western Europe's demographic transition in the second half of the twentieth century, the relationship between birth and death rates that marked the early 1800s had reversed, with birthrates fluctuating and death rates remaining fairly stable or rising slightly. This latter phenomenon is simply due to the older age distributions of contemporary European populations.

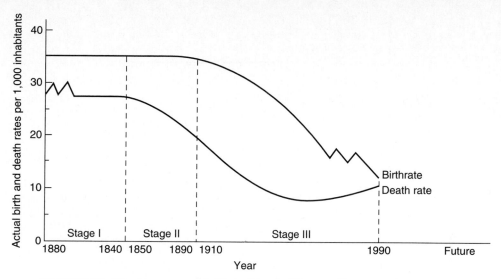

FIGURE 6.5   The Demographic Transition in Western Europe.

Figure 6.6 shows the population histories of contemporary Third World countries, which contrast with those of Western Europe and fall into two patterns.

Birthrates in many underdeveloped countries today are considerably higher than they were in preindustrial Western Europe. This is because women tend to marry at an earlier age. As a result, there are both more families for a given population size and more years in which to have children. Beginning in the 1940s and especially in the 1950s and 1960s, stage II of the demographic transition occurred throughout most of the Third World. The application of highly effective imported modern medical and public health technologies caused LDC death rates to fall much more rapidly than in nineteenth-century Europe. Given their historically high birthrates (over 40 per 1,000 in many countries), this has meant that stage II of the LDC demographic transition has been characterized by population growth rates well in excess of 2.0% to 2.5% per annum.

With regard to stage III, we can distinguish between two broad classes of developing countries. In case A in Figure 6.6, modern methods of death control combined with rapid and widely distributed rises in levels of living have resulted in death rates falling as low as 10 per 1,000 and birthrates also falling rapidly, to levels between 20 and 30 per 1,000. These countries, most notably Taiwan, South Korea, Costa Rica, China, Cuba, Chile, and Sri Lanka, have thus entered stage III of their demographic transition and have experienced rapidly falling rates of overall population growth. In the 1980s, several other countries, including Colombia, Indonesia, the Dominican Republic, Thailand, Malaysia, Mexico, and Brazil, appeared to be entering a period of sustained fertility decline consistent with case A.

But the majority of Third World countries fall into case B of Figure 6.6. After an initial period of rapid decline, death rates have failed to drop further, largely because of the persistence of widespread absolute poverty and low levels of living. Moreover, the continuance of high birthrates as a result of these low levels of

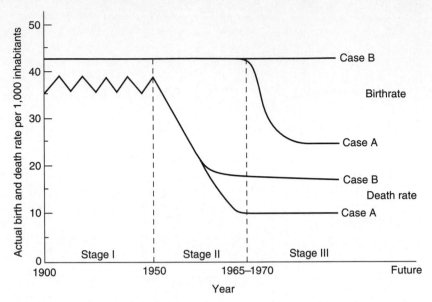

FIGURE 6.6 The Beginning of a Demographic Transition in Third World Countries.
Source: Based on National Academy of Sciences, *The Growth of World Population*
(Washington, D.C.: National Academy of Sciences, 1963), p. 15.

living causes overall population growth rates to remain relatively high. These countries, including most of those in sub-Saharan Africa and the Middle East, are still in stage II of their demographic transition.

The important question, therefore, is this: When and under what conditions are Third World nations likely to experience falling birthrates and a slower expansion of population? To answer this question, we need to ask a prior one. What are the principal determinants or causes of high fertility rates in developing countries, and can these determinants of the "demand" for children be influenced by government policy? To try to answer this critical question, we turn to a very old and famous classical macroeconomic and demographic model, the Malthusian "population trap," and a contemporary and highly influential neoclassical microeconomic model, the household theory of fertility.

The Causes of High Fertility in Developing Countries: The Malthusian and Household Models

The Malthusian Population Trap

Two centuries ago, the Reverend Thomas Malthus put forward a theory of the relationship between population growth and economic development that still survives today. Writing in 1798 in his *Essay on the Principle of Population* and drawing on the concept of diminishing returns, Malthus postulated a universal tendency for the population of a country, unless checked by dwindling food supplies, to grow at a geometric rate, doubling every 30 to 40 years.[4] At the same time, because of diminishing returns to the fixed factor, land, food supplies could expand only at a roughly arithmetic rate. In fact, as each member of the population would have less land to work, his or her marginal contribution to food production would actually start to decline. Because the growth in food supplies could not keep pace with the burgeoning population, per capita incomes (defined in an agrarian society simply as per capita food production) would have a tendency to fall so low as to lead to a stable population existing barely at or slightly above the subsistence level. Malthus therefore contended that the only way to avoid this condition of chronic low levels of living or absolute poverty was for people to engage in "moral restraint" and limit the number of their progeny. Hence we might regard Malthus, indirectly and inadvertently, as the father of the modern birth control movement.

Modern economists have given a name to the Malthusian idea of a population inexorably forced to live at subsistence levels of income. They have called it the *low-level equilibrium population trap* or, more simply, the **Malthusian population trap**. Diagrammatically, the basic Malthusian model can be illustrated by comparing the shape and position of curves representing population growth rates and aggregate income growth rates when these two curves are each plotted against levels of per capita income. This is done in Figure 6.7.

On the vertical axis, we plot numeric percentage changes, both positive and negative, in the two principal variables under consideration (total population and aggregate income). On the horizontal axis are levels of per capita income. Look first at the dashed curve portraying the assumed relationship between rates of population growth $\Delta P/P$ (measured vertically) and levels of per capita income, Y/P (measured horizontally). At a very low level of per capita income, Y_0, the rate of population change will be nil, and a stable population will exist.[5] Thus Y_0 might represent our concept of absolute poverty. Birth and death rates are equal, and the population is barely holding its own absolute level. The situation is analogous to stage I of the demographic transition theory. At per capita income levels beyond (to the right of) Y_0, it is assumed that population size will begin to increase under the pressure of falling death rates. Higher incomes means less starvation and disease. And with birthrates always assumed to be at the biological maximum, falling death rates provide the impetus for an expanding population (i.e., stage II).

In Figure 6.7, population growth achieves its maximum rate, roughly 3.3%, at a per capita income level of Y_2. It is assumed to remain at that level until much higher per capita income levels are realized. Thereafter (beyond Y_5), in accordance with stage III of the demographic transition, birthrates will begin to decline, and the population growth rate curve becomes negatively sloped and once again approaches the horizontal axis.

The other part of the Malthusian theory requires us to plot a relationship between the growth rate of aggregate income (in the absence of population growth) and levels of per capita income. We can then compare the two rates (aggregate income and total population). If aggregate income (total product) is rising faster,

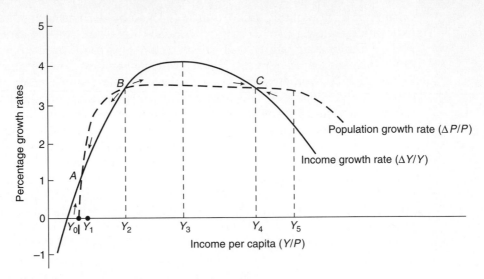

FIGURE 6.7   The Malthusian Population Trap.

per capita income by definition must be increasing; if total population is growing faster than total income, per capita income must be falling. In Figure 6.7, the rate of aggregate income growth (also measured vertically) is assumed at first to be positively related to levels of per capita income; that is, the higher the level of per capita income, the higher the rate of increase in aggregate income. The economic reason for this positive relationship is the assumption that savings vary positively with income per capita. Countries with higher per capita incomes are assumed to be capable of generating higher savings rates and thus more investment. Given a Harrod-Domar–type model of economic growth (see Chapter 3), higher savings rates mean higher rates of aggregate income growth. Beyond a certain per capita income point (Y_3), however, the income growth rate curve is assumed to level off and then begin to decline as new investments and more people are required to work with fixed quantities of land and natural resources. This is the point of diminishing returns in the Malthusian model (note that the possibility of technological progress is not considered). The aggregate income growth curve is therefore conceptually analogous to the total product curve in the basic theory of production.

Observe that in Figure 6.7, the curves are drawn so that they intersect at three points, A, B, and C. Point A represents the point at which the Malthusian population trap level of per capita income (Y_1) is attained. It is a stable equilibrium point—any small movement to the left or right of point A will cause the per capita income equilibrium point to return to Y_1. For example, as per capita income rises from Y_1 toward Y_2, the rate of population increase will exceed the rate of aggregate income growth (the $\Delta P/P$ curve is vertically higher than the $\Delta Y/Y$ curve). We know that whenever population is growing faster than income, per capita income must fall. The arrow pointing in the direction of A from the right therefore shows that per capita income must fall back to its very low level at Y_1 for all points between Y_1 and

Y_2. Similarly, to the left of point A, incomes grow faster than population, causing the equilibrium per capita income level to rise to Y_1.

According to the neo-Malthusians, poor nations will never be able to rise much above their subsistence levels of per capita income unless they initiate **preventive checks** (birth control) on their population growth. In the absence of such preventive checks, Malthusian **positive checks** (starvation, disease, wars) on population growth will inevitably provide the restraining force.

Completing our description of the population trap portrayed in Figure 6.7, we see that point B is an "unstable" equilibrium point. If per capita income can somehow jump rapidly from Y_1 to Y_2 (e.g., as a result of "big push" investment and industrialization programs) before Malthusian positive checks take their toll, it will continue to grow until the other stable equilibrium point C at per capita income level Y_4 is reached. Point B is an unstable equilibrium point in the sense that any movement to the left or right will continue until either A or C is reached.

Criticisms of the Malthusian Model

The Malthusian population trap provides a simple and in many ways appealing theory of the relationship between population growth and economic development. Unfortunately, it is based on a number of simplistic assumptions and hypotheses that do not stand the test of empirical verification. We can criticize the population trap on two major grounds.

First, and most important, the model (and, indeed, Malthus) assumes away or ignores the enormous impact of technological progress in offsetting the growth-inhibiting forces of rapid population increases. As we discovered in Chapter 4, the history of modern economic growth has been closely associated with rapid technological progress in the form of a continuous series of scientific, technological, and social inventions and innovations. Increasing rather than decreasing returns to scale have been a distinguishing feature of the modern growth epoch. While Malthus was basically correct in assuming a limited supply of land, he did not—and in fairness could not at that time—anticipate the manner in which technological progress could augment the availability of land by raising its quality (its productivity) even though its quantity might remain roughly the same.

In terms of the population trap, rapid and continuing technological progress can be represented by an upward shift of the income growth (total product) curve so that at *all* levels of per capita income it is vertically higher than the population growth curve. This is shown in Figure 6.8. As a result, per capita income will grow steadily over time. All countries therefore have the potential of escaping the Malthusian population trap.

The second basic criticism of the trap focuses on its assumption that national rates of population increase are directly (positively) related to the level of national per capita income. According to this assumption, at relatively low levels of per capita income, we should expect to find population growth rates increasing with increasing per capita income. But research on LDCs indicates that there appears to be no clear correlation between population growth rates and levels of per capita income in Third World nations. As a result of modern medicine and public health

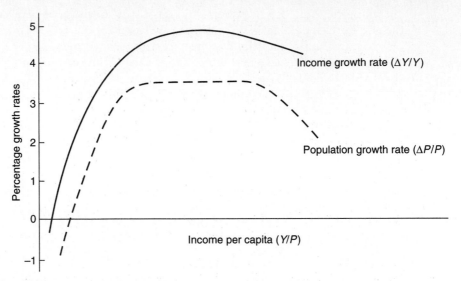

FIGURE 6.8 How Technological and Social Progress Allows Nations to Avoid the Population Trap.

programs, death rates have fallen rapidly and have become less dependent on the level of per capita income. Moreover, as we can readily observe from Figure 6.9, birthrates seem to show no definable relationship with per capita income levels. Note how widely fertility rates vary for countries with the same per capita income, especially in the relevant range of incomes below $1,000. Our conclusion, therefore, is that it is not so much the aggregate level of per capita income that matters for population growth but rather how that income is distributed. It is the level of household income, not the level of per capita income, that seems to matter most. The social and economic institutions of a nation and its philosophy of development are probably greater determinants of population growth rates than aggregate economic variables and simple models of macroeconomic growth.

We can thus largely reject the Malthusian and neo-Malthusian theories as applied to contemporary Third World nations on the following grounds:

1. They do not take adequate account of the role and impact of technological progress.

2. They are based on a hypothesis about a macro relationship between population growth and levels of per capita income that does not stand up to empirical testing.

3. They focus on the wrong variable, per capita income, as the principal determinant of population growth rates. A much better and more valid approach to the question of population and development centers on the microeconomics of family-size decision making in which individual, and not aggregate, levels of living become the principal determinant of a family's decision to have more or fewer children.

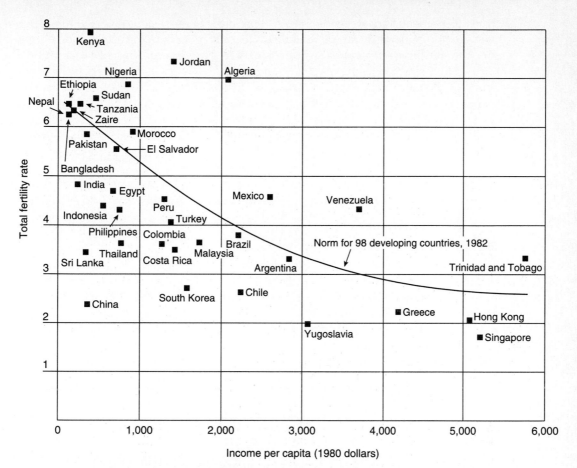

FIGURE 6.9 Fertility in Relation to Income in Developing Countries. *Source*: Nancy Birdsall, "Economic approaches to population growth," in Hollis B. Chenery and T. N. Srinivasan (eds.), *Handbook of Development Economics*, vol. 1 (Amsterdam: North Holland, 1988), p. 482. Reprinted with permission.

NOTE: Total fertility rate and birthrate, though not conceptually the same, are nevertheless highly correlated.

The Microeconomic Household Theory of Fertility

In recent years, economists have begun to look more closely at the microeconomic determinants of family fertility in an attempt to provide a better theoretical and empirical explanation for the observed falling birthrates associated with stage III of the demographic transition. In doing this, they have drawn on the traditional neoclassical theory of household and consumer behavior for their basic analytical model and have used the principles of economy and optimization to explain family size decisions.

The conventional theory of consumer behavior assumes that an individual with a given set of tastes or preferences for a range of goods (a "utility function") tries to maximize the satisfaction derived from consuming these goods subject to his or her own income constraint and the relative prices of all goods. In the application of this theory to fertility analysis, children are considered as a special kind of consumption (and in LDCs, investment) good so that fertility becomes a rational economic response to the consumer's (family's) demand for children relative to other goods. The usual income and substitution effects are assumed to apply. That is, if other factors are held constant, the desired number of children can be expected to vary directly with household income (this direct relationship may not hold for poor societies; it depends on the strength of demand for children relative to other consumer goods and to the sources of increased income, such as female employment), inversely with the price (cost) of children, and inversely with the strength of tastes for other goods relative to children. Mathematically, these relationships can be expressed as follows:

$$C_d = f(Y, P_c, P_x, t_x), \quad x = 1, \ldots, n, \tag{6.1}$$

where C_d, the demand for surviving children (an important consideration in low-income societies where infant mortality rates are high), is a function of the given level of household income (Y), the "net" price of children (the difference between anticipated costs, mostly the opportunity cost of a mother's time, and benefits, potential child income and old-age support, P_c), the prices of all other goods (P_x), and the tastes for goods relative to children (t_x). Under normal (neoclassical) conditions, we would expect the following:

$\delta C_d / \delta Y > 0$ The higher the household income, the greater the demand for children.

$\delta C_d / \delta P_c < 0$ The higher the net price of children, the lower the quantity demanded.

$\delta C_d / \delta P_x > 0$ The higher the prices of all other goods relative to children, the greater the quantity of children demanded.

$\delta C_d / \delta t_x < 0$ The greater the strength of tastes for goods relative to children, the fewer children demanded.

Figure 6.10 provides a simplified diagrammatic presentation of the **microeconomic theory of fertility**. The number of desired (surviving) children, C_d, is measured along the horizontal axis, and the total quantity of goods consumed by the parents, G_p, is measured on the vertical axis.

Household desires for children are expressed in terms of an indifference map representing the subjective degree of satisfaction derived by the parents for all possible combinations of commodities and children. Each individual indifference curve portrays a locus of commodity-children combinations that yield the same amount of satisfaction. Any point (or combination of goods and children) on a "higher" indifference curve—that is, on a curve farther out from the origin—represents a higher level of satisfaction than any point on a lower indifference curve. But each indifference curve is a "constant satisfaction" locus.

In Figure 6.10, only four indifference curves, I_1 to I_4, are shown; in theory, there is an infinite set of such curves, filling the whole quadrant and covering all possi-

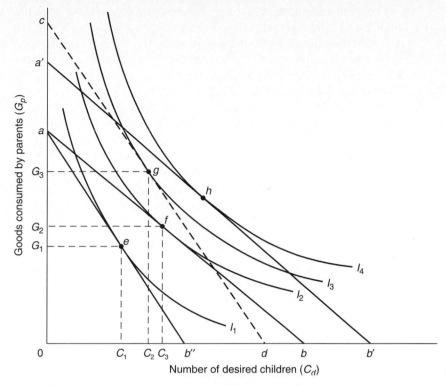

FIGURE 6.10 Microeconomic Theory of Fertility: An Illustration.

ble commodity-children combinations. The household's ability to "purchase" alternative combinations of goods and children is shown by the budget constraint line, *ab*. Thus all combinations on or below line *ab* (within the triangular area 0*ab*) are financially attainable by the household on the basis of its perceived income prospects and the relative prices of children and goods, as represented by the slope of the *ab* budget constraint. The steeper the slope of the budget line, the higher the price of children relative to goods.

According to the demand-based theory of fertility, the household chooses from among all attainable combinations the one combination of goods and children that maximizes family satisfaction on the basis of its subjectively determined preferences. Diagrammatically, this optimal combination is represented by point *f*, the tangency point between the budget constraint, *ab*, and indifference curve I_2. Therefore, C_3 children and G_2 goods will be demanded.

A rise in family income, represented in Figure 6.10 by the parallel outward shift of the budget line from *ab* to *a'b'*, enables the household to attain a higher level of satisfaction (point *h* on curve I_4) by consuming more of *both* commodities and children—that is, if children, like most commodities, are assumed to be normal goods (demand for them rises with income), an important if in low-income countries where children are often demanded primarily as a source of future financial security.

Similarly, an increase in the price (opportunity cost) of children relative to other goods will cause households to substitute commodities for children. Other factors (namely, income and tastes) being constant, a rise in the relative price of children causes the household utility-maximizing consumption combination to occur on a lower indifference curve, as shown by the movement of the equilibrium point from f to e when the budget line rotates around point a to ab''.

Note, finally, that if there is a simultaneous increase in household income and net child price as a result of, say, expanding female employment opportunities and a rise in wages coupled with a tax on children beyond a certain number per family, there will be *both* an outward shift and downward rotation of the budget constraint line of Figure 6.10 to, say, dashed line cd. The result is a new utility-maximizing combination that includes fewer children per family (point g compared with point f). In other words, higher levels of living for low-income families in combination with a relative increase in the price of children (whether brought about directly by fiscal measures or indirectly by expanded female employment opportunities) will motivate households to have fewer children while still improving their welfare. This is just one example of how the economic theory of fertility can shed light on the relationship between economic development and population growth as well as suggest possible lines of policy.

The Demand for Children in Developing Countries

As we have seen, the economic theory of fertility assumes that the household demand for children is determined by family preferences for a certain number of surviving (usually male) children (i.e., in regions of high mortality, parents may produce more children than they actually desire in the expectation that some will not survive), by the price or "opportunity cost" of rearing these children, and by levels of family income. Children in poor societies are seen partly as economic investment goods in that there is an expected return in the form of both child labor and the provision of financial support for parents in old age. As Simon Kuznets has noted in an exhaustive empirical study, the LDCs

> are prolific because under their economic and social conditions large proportions of the population see their economic and social interests in more children as a supply of family labor, as a pool for a genetic lottery, and as a matter of economic and social security in a wealthy organized, non-protecting society.[6]

However, in many developing countries, there is a strong intrinsic psychological and cultural determinant of family size, so that the first two or three children should be viewed as "consumer" goods for which demand may not be very responsive to relative price changes.

The choice mechanism in the economic theory of fertility as applied to LDCs is assumed, therefore, to exist primarily with regard to the additional or marginal children who are considered as investments. In deciding whether or not to have *additional* children, parents are assumed to weigh private economic benefits against private costs, where the principal benefits are, as we have seen, the expected income from child labor, usually on the farm, and financial support for elderly parents. Balanced against these benefits are the two principal elements of cost: the opportunity cost of the mother's time (the income she could earn if she were not at home caring for her children) and the opportunity and actual cost of educating children—the financial trade-off between having fewer "high-quality," high-cost, educated children with high-income-earning potentials versus more "low-quality," low-cost, uneducated children with much lower earnings prospects.

Using the same thought processes as in the traditional theory of consumer behavior, the theory of family fertility as applied to LDCs concludes that when the price or cost of children rises as a result of, say, increased educational and employment opportunities for women or a rise in school fees or the establishment of minimum-age child labor laws or the provision of publicly financed old-age social security schemes, parents will demand fewer additional children, substituting, perhaps, quality for quantity or a mother's employment income for her child-rearing activities. It follows that one way to induce families to desire fewer children is to raise the price of child rearing by, say, providing greater educational opportunities and a wider range of higher-paying jobs for young women.

Some Empirical Evidence

Statistical studies in a broad spectrum of developing countries have provided strong support for the economic theory of fertility.[7] For example, it has been found that high female employment opportunities outside the home and greater female school attendance, especially at the primary and secondary levels, are associated with significantly lower levels of fertility. As women become better educated, they tend to earn a larger share of household income and to produce fewer children. Moreover, these studies have confirmed the strong association between declines in child mortality and the subsequent decline in fertility. Assuming that households desire a target number of surviving children, increased female education and higher levels of income can decrease child mortality and therefore increase the chances that the firstborn will survive. As a result, fewer births may be necessary to attain the same number of surviving children. This fact alone underlines the importance of educating women and improving public-health and child nutrition programs in reducing Third World fertility levels.

Implications for Development and Fertility

All of the foregoing can be summarized by saying that the effect of social and economic progress in lowering fertility in developing countries will be the greatest when the majority of the population and especially the very poor share in its benefits. Specifically, birthrates among the very poor are likely to fall where there is

1. An increase in the education of women and a consequent change in their role and status

2. An increase in female nonagricultural wage employment opportunities, which raises the price or cost of their traditional child-rearing activities

3. A rise in family income levels through the increased direct employment and earnings of a husband and wife or through the redistribution of income and assets from rich to poor

4. A reduction in infant mortality through expanded public-health programs and better nutritional status for both mother and child

5. The development of old-age and other social security systems outside the extended family network to lessen the economic dependence of parents, especially women, on their offspring

In short, expanded efforts to make jobs, education, and health more broadly available to poverty groups in general and women in particular will not only contribute to their economic and psychic well-being (i.e., to their development) but can also contribute substantially to their motivation for smaller families (i.e., their freedom to choose), which is vital to reducing population growth rates. Where such motivation exists, well-executed **family-planning programs** can then be an effective tool.[8] But before discussing policy issues and what government might or might not do, we should point out that while there seems to be considerable agreement regarding the determinants or causes of population growth, substantial disagreement and controversy remain regarding its consequences.

The Consequences of High Fertility: Some Conflicting Opinions

For many years, development economists and other social scientists have debated the seriousness of the consequences of rapid population growth. Nowhere was this debate more vocal than at the first World Population Conference held in Bucharest in 1974.[9] On the one hand, we must recognize that population growth is not the only, or even the primary, source of low levels of living, eroding self-esteem, and limited freedom in Third World nations. On the other hand, it would be equally naive to think that rapid population growth in many countries and regions is not a serious intensifier and multiplier of those integral components of underdevelopment, especially the first and third. The following summarizes some of the main arguments for and against the idea that the consequences of rapid population growth lead to serious development problems. It then forms the basis for considering whether some consensus can be reached so that specific policy goals and objectives can be postulated.[10]

Population Growth Is Not a Real Problem

We can identify three general lines of argument on the part of people who assert that population growth is not a cause for concern:

1. The problem is not population growth but other issues.

2. Population growth is a false issue deliberately created by dominant rich-country agencies and institutions to keep LDCs in their underdeveloped, dependent condition.

3. For many developing countries and regions, population growth is in fact desirable.

Other Issues

Many knowledgeable people from both rich and poor nations argue that the real problem is not population growth per se but one or all of the following four issues.

Underdevelopment If correct strategies are pursued and lead to higher levels of living, greater esteem, and expanded freedom, population will take care of itself. Eventually, it will disappear as a problem, as it has in all of the present economically advanced nations. According to this argument, underdevelopment is the real problem, and development should be the only goal. With it will come economic progress and social mechanisms that will more or less automatically regulate population growth and distribution. As long as the vast majority of people in Third World countries remain impoverished, uneducated, and physically and psychologically weak, the large family will constitute the only real source of social security (i.e., parents will continue to be denied the freedom to choose a small family if they so desire). Proponents of the underdevelopment argument then conclude that birth control programs will surely fail, as they have in the past, when there is no motivation on the part of poor families to limit their size.

World Resource Depletion and Environmental Destruction Population can only be an economic problem in relation to the availability and utilization of scarce natural and material resources. The fact is that developed countries, with less than one-quarter of the world's population, consume almost 80% of the world's resources (see Table 6.5). For example, the average North American or European consumer uses up, directly and indirectly, almost 16 times as much of the world's food, energy, and material resources as his or her counterpart in Third World countries. In terms of the depletion of the world's limited resources, therefore, the addition of another child in the developed countries is as significant as the birth of 16 additional children in the underdeveloped countries. According to this argument, developed nations should curtail their excessively high consumption standards instead of asking less developed nations to restrict their population growth. The latter's high fertility is really due to their low levels of living, which are in turn largely the result of the "overconsumption" of the world's scarce resources by rich nations. This combination of rising affluence and extravagant consumption habits in rich countries and among rich people in poor countries, and not population growth, should be the major world concern. We will analyze issues of the environment and development in Chapters 10 and 18.

Population Distribution According to this third argument, it is not the number of people per se that is causing population problems but their distribution in space. Many regions of the world (e.g., parts of sub-Saharan Africa) and many regions within countries (e.g., the northeastern and Amazon regions of Brazil) are in fact underpopulated in terms of available or potential resources. Others simply have too many people concentrated in too small an area (e.g., central Java or most urban

TABLE 6.5 Consumption of Major Resource Commodities by Region, 1984

Population and Resource	Developing Countries	Developed Countries	Former USSR and Eastern Europe
Population (millions)	3,592	792	388
Percent of total	75.3	16.6	8.1
Commercial fuels (metric tons of coal equivalent, thousands)	1,953,187	4,603,777	2,241,617
Percent of total	22.2	52.3	25.5
Per capita (kilograms)	543.8	5,816.0	5,777.4
Steel (metric tons, thousands)	200,656	313,799	193,87
Percent of total	28.6	44.3	27.4
Per capita (kilograms)	55.9	396.2	499.7
Cereals (production) (metric tons, thousands)	929,000	595,704	276,980
Percent of total	51.6	33.1	15.4
Per capita (kilograms)	250.3	752.2	713.9
Wood (cubic meters, thousands)	91,400	363,000	178,600
Percent of total	14.4	57.3	28.2
Per capita (kilograms)	24.6	458.3	460.3

SOURCE: Robert Repetto, "Population, resources, environment: An uncertain future," *Population Bulletin* 42 (July 1987), tab. 4. Reprinted with permission.

concentrations in LDCs). Governments should therefore strive not to moderate the rate of population growth but rather to reduce rural-urban migration and to bring about a more natural spatial distribution of the population in terms of available land and other productive resources.

Subordination of Women As we have seen in Chapter 5 and will discover again later, women often bear the disproportionate burdens of poverty, poor education, lack of jobs, and limited social mobility. In many cases, their inferior roles, low status, and restricted access to birth control is manifested in their high fertility. According to this argument, population growth is a natural outcome of women's lack of economic opportunity. If women's health, education, and economic well-being are improved along with their role and status in both the family and the community, this **empowerment of women** will inevitably lead to smaller families and lower population growth. This was the principal message of the United Nations International Conference on Population and Development held in Cairo in 1994.[11]

A Deliberately Contrived False Issue

The second main line of argument denying the significance of population growth as a major development problem is closely allied to the neocolonial dependence theory of underdevelopment discussed in Chapter 3. Basically, it is argued that the frenetic overconcern in the rich nations with the population growth of poor nations is really an attempt by the former to hold down the development of the latter in order to maintain an international status quo that is favorable to their self-interests. Rich nations are pressuring poor nations to adopt aggressive population control programs even though they themselves went through a period of sizable population increase that accelerated their own development processes.

A radical neo-Marxist version of this argument views population control efforts by rich countries and their allied international agencies as racist or genocidal attempts to reduce the relative or absolute size of the poor, largely nonwhite populations of the world who may someday pose a serious threat to the welfare of the rich, predominantly white societies. Worldwide birth control campaigns are seen as manifestations of the fears of the developed world in the face of a possible radical challenge to the international order by the people who are its first victims.

A Desirable Phenomenon

A more conventional economic argument is that of population growth as an essential ingredient to stimulate economic development. Larger populations provide the needed consumer demand to generate favorable economies of scale in production, to lower production costs, and to provide a sufficient and low-cost labor supply to achieve higher output levels. Population "revisionist" economists of the neoclassical counterrevolution school argue, for example, that free markets will always adjust to any scarcities created by population pressures.[12] Such scarcities will drive up prices and signal the need for new cost-saving production technologies. In the end, free markets and human ingenuity (Julian Simon's "genius" as the "ultimate resource") will solve any and all problems arising from population growth. This revisionist viewpoint was clearly in contrast with the traditional "orthodox" argument of the 1950s to 1970s that rapid population growth had serious economic consequences that, if left uncorrected, would slow economic development.

At the other end of the political spectrum, it has been argued by some Third World neo-Marxist pronatalists that many rural regions in developing countries are in reality underpopulated in the sense that much unused but arable land could yield large increases in agricultural output if only more people were available to cultivate it. Many regions of tropical Africa and Latin America and even parts of Asia are said to be in this situation. With respect to Africa, for example, some observers have noted that many regions had larger populations in the remote past than exist today.[13] Their rural depopulation resulted not only from the slave trade but also from compulsory military service, confinement to reservations, and the forced-labor policies of former colonial governments. For example, the sixteenth-century Congo kingdom is said to have had a population of approximately 2 million. But by the time of the colonial conquest, which followed 300 years of slave trade, the population of the region had fallen to less than one-third of that figure. Today parts of Zaire have barely caught up to the sixteenth-century numbers.[14] Other regions of western and eastern Africa provide similar examples—at least in the eyes of advocates of rapid population growth in Africa.

In terms of ratios of population to arable land (land under cultivation, fallow land, pastures, and forests), Africa south of the Sahara is said by these supporters of population expansion to have a total of 1.4 billion arable hectares. Land actually being cultivated amounts to only 170 million hectares, or about 1 hectare per rural inhabitant. Thus only 12% of all potential arable land is under cultivation, and this very low rural population density is viewed as a serious drawback to raising agricultural output.[15] Similar arguments have been expounded with regard to such Latin American countries as Brazil and Argentina.

Three other noneconomic arguments, each found to some degree in a wide range of developing countries, complete the "population growth is desirable" viewpoint. First, many countries claim a need for population growth to protect currently underpopulated border regions against the expansionist intentions of neighboring nations. Second, there are many ethnic, racial, and religious groups within less developed countries whose attitudes favoring large family size have to be protected for both moral and political reasons. Finally, military and political power are often seen as dependent on a large and youthful population.

Many of these arguments have a certain realism about them—if not in fact, then at least in the perceptions of vocal and influential individuals in both the developed and the developing worlds. Clearly, some of the arguments have greater validity for some Third World countries than others. The important point is that they represent a considerable range of opinions and viewpoints and therefore need to be seriously weighed against the counterarguments of theorists who believe that rapid population growth is indeed a real and important problem for underdeveloped countries. Let us now look at some of these counterarguments.

Population Growth Is a Real Problem

Positions supporting the need to curtail population growth because of the negative economic, social, and environmental consequences are typically based on one of the following three arguments.

The Extremist Argument: Population and the Global Crisis

The extreme version of the population-as-problem position attempts to attribute almost all of the world's economic and social evils to excessive population growth. Unrestrained population increase is seen as the major crisis facing humankind today. It is regarded as the principal cause of poverty, low levels of living, malnutrition, ill health, environmental degradation, and a wide array of other social problems. Value-laden and incendiary terms such as "population bomb" or "population explosion" are tossed around at will. Indeed, dire predictions of world food catastrophes and ecological disaster are attributed almost entirely to the growth in world numbers.[16] Such an extreme position leads some of its advocates to assert that "world" (i.e., LDC) population stabilization or even decline is the most urgent contemporary task even if it requires severe and coercive measures such as compulsory sterilization to control family size in some of the most populated Third World countries like India and Bangladesh.

The Theoretical Argument: Population–Poverty Cycles and the Need for Family Planning Programs

The **population-poverty cycle** theory is the main argument advanced by economists who hold that too rapid population growth yields negative economic consequences and thus should be a real concern of Third World countries. Advocates start from the basic proposition that population growth intensifies and exacerbates the economic, social, and psychological problems associated with the condition of underdevelopment. Population growth is believed to retard the prospects for a better life for the already born by reducing savings rates at the household and national levels. It also severely draws down limited government revenues simply to provide the most rudimentary economic, health, and social services to the additional people. This in turn further reduces the prospects for any improvement in the levels of living of the existing generation and helps transmit poverty to future generations of low-income families.

The basic model that economists use to demonstrate these adverse consequences of rapid population growth is a simplification of the standard Solow-type neoclassical growth equation.[17] Using the standard production function, $Y = f(K, L, R, T)$, that is, output is a function of capital, labor, resources, and technology, and holding the resource base fixed, we can derive the result that

$$y - l = \alpha\,(k - l) + t \tag{6.2}$$

where y = rate of GNP growth, l = rate of labor force (population) growth, k = rate of growth of the capital stock, α = capital elasticity of output (usually found to be constant), and t = the effect of technological change (the Solow residual in empirical studies of sources of economic growth in MDCs—see Chapter 3).

Assuming constant returns to scale, Equation 6.2 simply states that the rate of per capita income growth ($y - l$) is directly proportional to the rate of growth of the capital-labor ratio ($k - l$) plus the residual effects of technological progress (including improved human and physical capital). Therefore, in the absence of technological change, the higher the rate of population growth (l), the more rapid the rate of capital stock growth (k) must be and thus the greater the concomitant savings and investment rate just to maintain constant levels of per capita income (note the similarity to the Harrod-Domar model in Chapter 3). Moreover, because k may not be independent of l as is traditionally assumed in neoclassical growth models but may in fact be inversely related due to the reduced savings impact implied by the higher dependency burden effects of rapid population growth, it follows that the negative economic impact of population growth may even be greater than these models imply. Finally, if low incomes induce poor families to have more children as a source of cheap labor and old-age security, then we have another vicious cycle in progress—poor people have large families partly to compensate for their poverty, but large families mean greater population growth, higher dependency burdens, lower savings, less investment, slower economic growth, and ultimately greater poverty. Population growth is thus seen as both a cause and a consequence of underdevelopment!

Because widespread absolute poverty and low levels of living are thus seen as a major cause of large family size, and large families retard economic growth, it follows that more egalitarian economic and social development is a necessary condition for bringing about an eventual slowing or cessation of population growth at low levels of fertility and mortality. But according to this argument, it is not a sufficient condition—that is, development provides people with the incentives and motivations to limit their family size, but family-planning programs are needed to provide them with the technological means to avoid unwanted pregnancies. Even though countries like France, Japan, the United States, Great Britain, and, more recently, Taiwan and South Korea were able to reduce their population growth rates without widespread family-planning clinics, it is argued that the provision of these services will enable other countries desiring to control excessive population growth to do so more rapidly than if these family-planning services were not available.

The Empirical Argument: Seven Negative Consequences of Population Growth

According to the latest empirical research, the potential negative consequences of population growth for economic development can be divided into seven categories: its impact on economic growth, poverty and inequality, education, health, food, the environment, and international migration.[18]

Economic Growth   Evidence shows that rapid population growth lowers per capita income growth in most LDCs, especially those that are already poor, dependent on agriculture, and experiencing pressures on land and natural resources.

Poverty and Inequality   Even though aggregate statistical correlations between measures of poverty and population growth at the national level are often inconclusive, at the household level the evidence is strong and compelling. The negative consequences of rapid population growth fall most heavily on the poor because they are the ones who are made landless, suffer first from cuts in government health and education programs, bear the brunt of environmental damage, and are the main victims of job cuts due to the slower growth of the economy. Poor women once again bear the greatest burden of government austerity programs, and another vicious cycle is set in motion. To the extent that large families perpetuate poverty, they also exacerbate inequality.

Education   Although the data are sometimes ambiguous on this point, it is generally agreed that large family size and low incomes restrict the opportunities of parents to educate all their children. At the national level, rapid population growth causes given educational expenditures to be spread more thinly, lowering quality for the sake of quantity. This in turn feeds back on economic growth because the stock of human capital is reduced by rapid population growth.

Health   High fertility harms the health of mothers and children. It increases the health risks of pregnancy, and closely spaced births have been shown to reduce birth weight and increase child mortality rates.

Food   Feeding the world's population is made more difficult by rapid population growth—over 90% of additional LDC food requirements are caused by population increases. New technologies of production must be introduced more rapidly, as the best lands have already been cultivated. International food relief programs become more widespread.

Environment   Rapid population growth contributes to environmental degradation in the form of forest encroachment, deforestation, fuel-wood depletion, soil erosion, declining fish and animal stocks, inadequate and unsafe water, air pollution, and urban congestion (See Chapter 10).

International Migration   Many observers consider the rapid increase in international migration, both legal and illegal, to be one of the major consequences of Third World population growth. Though many factors cause migration (see Chapter 8), an excess of job seekers (caused by rapid population growth) over job opportunities in the LDC economy is surely one of them. However, unlike the first six consequences listed here, some of the economic and social costs of international migration falls on recepient countries—increasingly in the developed world. It is not surprising, therefore, that this issue has recently taken on political importance in North America and Europe (see Chapters 4 and 18).

Goals and Objectives: Toward a Consensus

In spite of what may appear to be seriously conflicting arguments about the positive and negative consequences of population growth, during the past decade there emerged a common ground on which many people on both sides of the debate could agree. This position is best characterized by Robert Cassen in his recent book, *Population Policy: A New Consensus*:

> After decades of controversy over the issue of population policy, there is a new international consensus among and between industrial and developing countries that individuals, countries, and the world at large would be better off if population were to grow more slowly. The consequences of rapid population growth should be neither exaggerated nor minimized. Some past expressions of alarm have been counterproductive, alienating the very audiences they were intended to persuade; at the same time, claims that population growth was not all that important have had the effect of diminishing a proper concern for the subject.[19]

The following four propositions constitute the essential components of this intermediate or consensus opinion.

1. Population growth is not the primary cause of low levels of living, gross inequalities, or the limited freedom of choice that characterize much of the Third World. The fundamental causes of these problems must be sought, rather, in the

"dualistic" nature of the domestic and international economic and social order, as well as in the failures of many development plans to create jobs and incomes for poor families, especially women.

2. The problem of population is not simply one of numbers but involves the quality of life and material well-being. Thus LDC population size must be viewed in conjunction with developed-country affluence in relation to the quantity, distribution, and utilization of world resources, not just in relation to indigenous resources of the LDCs.

3. But rapid population growth does serve to intensify problems of underdevelopment and make prospects for development that much more remote. As we have seen, the momentum of growth means that barring catastrophe, the population of developing countries will increase dramatically over the coming decades, no matter what fertility control measures are adopted now. It follows that high population growth rates, though not the principal cause of underdevelopment, are nevertheless important contributing factors in specific countries and regions of the world.

4. Many of the real problems of population arise not from its overall size but from its concentration, especially in urban areas as a result of accelerated rural-urban migration (see Chapter 8). A more rational and more efficient spatial distribution of national populations thus becomes an alternative, in some countries, to the slowdown of overall population growth.

In view of these four propositions, we may conclude that the following three policy goals and objectives might be included in any realistic approach to the issue of population growth in developing countries.

1. In countries or regions where population size, distribution, and growth are viewed as an existing or potential problem, the primary objective of any strategy to limit further growth must deal not only with the population variable per se but also with the underlying social and economic conditions of underdevelopment. Problems such as absolute poverty, gross inequality, widespread unemployment (especially among women), limited female access to education, malnutrition, and poor health facilities must be given high priority. Their amelioration is both a necessary concomitant of development and a fundamental motivational basis for the expanded freedom of the individual to choose an optimal—and, in many cases, smaller—family size.

2. To bring about smaller families through development-induced motivations, family-planning programs providing both the education and the technological means to regulate fertility for people who wish to regulate it should be established.

3. Developed countries should assist developing countries to achieve their lowered fertility and mortality objectives not only by providing contraceptives and funding family-planning clinics but, more important, by curtailing their own excessive depletion of nonrenewable world resources through programs designed to cut back on the unnecessary consumption of products that intensively use

such resources; by making genuine commitments to eradicating poverty, illiteracy, disease, and malnutrition in Third World countries as well as their own; and by recognizing in both their rhetoric and their international economic and social dealings that development is the real issue, not simply population control.

Some Policy Approaches

In view of these broad goals and objectives, what kinds of economic and social policies might LDC and developed-country governments and international assistance agencies consider to bring about long-term reductions in the overall rate of world population growth? Three areas of policy can have important direct and indirect influences on the well-being of present and future world populations:

1. General and specific policies that LDC governments can initiate to influence and perhaps even control their population growth and distribution

2. General and specific policies that developed-country governments can initiate in their own countries to lessen their disproportionate consumption of limited world resources and promote a more equitable distribution of the benefits of global economic progress

3. General and specific policies that developed-country governments and international assistance agencies can initiate to help developing countries achieve their population objectives.

Let us deal with each of these areas in turn.

What Developing Countries Can Do

Earlier discussions have led to the conclusion that the principal variables influencing the demand for children at the family level are the ones most closely associated with the concept of development as we have defined it in Part One of this book. Thus certain development policies are particularly crucial in the transition from a high-growth to a low-growth population. These policies aim at eliminating absolute poverty; lessening income inequalities; expanding educational opportunities, especially for women; providing increased job opportunities for both men and women; bringing the benefits of modern preventive medicine and public health programs, especially the provision of clean water and sanitation, to the rural and urban poor; improving maternal and child health through more food, better diets, and improved nutrition so as to lower infant mortality; and creating a more equitable provision of other social services to wide segments of the population. Again, it is not numbers per se or parental irrationality that is at the root of the LDC "population problem." Rather, it is the pervasiveness of absolute poverty and low levels of living that provides the economic rationale for large families and burgeoning populations. And it is the spillover effects or negative social externalities of these private parental decisions (e.g., for education, health care, food supplies, resource degradation, job creation, and income distribution) that provide the strictly economic justification (in terms of "market failure" arguments) for government intervention in population matters. Clearly, there are noneconomic justifications as well.

Although long-run development policies of the kind just outlined are essential to ultimate population stabilization, there are some more specific policies that LDC governments might try to adopt to lower birthrates in the short run.[20] Governments can attempt to control fertility in six ways.

First, they can try to *persuade people* to have smaller families through the media and the educational process, both formal (school system) and informal (adult education).

Second, they can *establish family-planning programs* to provide health and contraceptive services to encourage the desired behavior. Such publicly sponsored or officially supported programs now exist in 47 Third World Countries (see Table 6.6). Today only a few large countries, such as Myanmar, Ethiopia, Nigeria, and Zaire, do not have such publicly sponsored or officially endorsed family-planning programs.

TABLE 6.6 Countries Adopting Family-planning Programs to Reduce Rates of Population Growth, 1960–1990

| Region | Before 1960 | Date of Adoption of National Family-planning Program | | | | |
		1960–1964	1965–1969	1970–1974	1975–1979	1980–1990
Asia	India	China Fiji South Korea Pakistan	Indonesia Iran Malaysia Nepal Singapore Sri Lanka Taiwan Turkey	Bangladesh Hong Kong Philippines Thailand	Vietnam	Yemen
Latin America			Barbados Dominican Republic Jamaica Trinidad and Tobago	Colombia El Salvador Mexico Puerto Rico	Guatemala	Haiti Honduras Peru Brazil
Africa			Egypt Ghana Kenya Mauritius Morocco Tunisia	Botswana		Algeria Burundi Gambia Lesotho Rwanda Senegal Uganda Zimbabwe
Total	1	4	18	9	2	13

SOURCE: Population Council, *Data Bank, 1992* (Washington, D.C.: Population Council, 1992).

Third, they can deliberately *manipulate economic incentives and disincentives* for having children—for example, through the elimination or reduction of maternity leaves and benefits, the reduction or elimination of financial incentives, or the imposition of financial penalties for having children beyond a certain number; the establishment of old-age social security provisions and minimum-age child labor laws; the raising of school fees and the elimination of heavy public subsidies for secondary and higher education; and the subsidization of smaller families through direct money payments. Although some form of population-related incentive or disincentive schemes now exist in over 30 LDCs, Singapore, India, Taiwan, South Korea, and China are especially prominent in experimenting with policies to reduce family size. For example, Singapore allocates scarce public housing without giving consideration to family size. It is also limiting paid maternity leave to a maximum of two children, scaling the delivery fee according to number of children, and reducing income tax relief from five to three children. In 1984, it even went so far as to give special priority in school admission to all children born to women with university degrees while penalizing non-degree-holding women with more than two children. The presumed but dubious rationale was that educated women have brighter children whose births should be encouraged while discouraging the less educated (and presumably less intelligent) women from bearing more children.

In India, a tea estate in the mid-1970s experimented with making deposits into savings accounts for individual female workers during their periods of nonpregnancy. The deposits were scaled according to the number of children, and the whole account could be canceled if a woman bore too many children. These accumulated savings were then paid out when the woman reached the age of 45, as a form of social security in the place of children. Today, in northern India, women (or, more usually, their husbands) are provided with cash incentives for sterilization. In Taiwan, there is an experiment in a rural township in which the local government is depositing funds into bank accounts for young couples to cover the costs of educating their first two children. However, if the couple has a third child, part of this money is forfeited. *All* of it is forfeited at the birth of a fourth child. The program is expressly designed to encourage families to have fewer but better-educated children. South Korea has also initiated a national system of rewards and penalties to encourage small family size. It offers educational allowances and free medical care to all two-child families provided that one of the parents has been sterilized.

China has by far the most comprehensive set of state-enforced incentives and disincentives. In 1980, it initiated a tough new drive on births with a goal of lowering the annual birthrate to 1% during the decade. Stringent and often draconian measures to achieve that goal were introduced in 1982–1983 as the Chinese government adopted a policy of one child per family. Social and political pressures to limit family size to one child have included requiring women to appeal to the neighborhood committee or council for formal permission to become pregnant. Although first births are routinely approved, second births are usually approved only if the first child has a serious birth defect or if the woman has remarried. Economic pressures include giving priority to one-child families in housing, medical care, and education. Mothers of two or more children are often denied promotions, and steep fines, sometimes in excess of 10 times China's per capita income, are levied for second and third children. Given such rigid national policies and a strong preference for male children, there have been reports of an alarming increase in female infanticide, with estimates that, based on the normal ratio of women to men of 1.022, there are 44 million "missing women" in China.[21]

Early results seem to indicate that some of these economic and social experiments are achieving their goals. Others have been counter-productive. For example, in the mid-1970s, India conducted a major vasectomy program, in which thousands of men were either pressured on the job or given direct cash payments, transistor radios, or even free tickets to championship soccer matches if they agreed to undergo "voluntary" sterilization. Not surprisingly, the program had a negative political effect that set back government family-planning efforts for a number of years. The impact of the recent Chinese population control programs is also uncertain. Only time will tell whether the benefits of reduced population growth achieved through severe social and economic pressures for one-child families will be worth the cost of a harsh break with traditional family norms and perceptions regarding the value of children. Resistance in rural areas, where 80% of the population still resides, was apparently so widespread that in August 1988, when the Chinese government discovered to its surprise that the population had already passed the 1.1 billion mark, it decided to increase its enforcement of the one-child norm in rural as well as urban areas. However, popular opposition has once again caused it to relax its stringent controls and to focus more on elevating the status of women and providing greater old-age security.

As a fourth tactic, countries can attempt to *redirect their populations* away from the rapidly growing urban areas by eliminating the current imbalance in economic and social opportunities in urban versus rural areas. As we shall see in Chapter 8, rural development programs are being increasingly emphasized in contemporary Third World development strategies, in part to stem the rising tide of rural-urban population movements and thus to promote a more geographically balanced distribution of the population.

Fifth, governments can attempt to *coerce people* into having smaller families through the power of state legislation and penalties. For obvious reasons, few governments would attempt to engage in such coercion; not only is it often morally repugnant and politically unacceptable, but it is also almost always extremely difficult to administer. The defeat of Indian Prime Minister Indira Gandhi's government in 1977 was largely due to the popular backlash against the government's forced-sterilization program. Her return to power in 1980–1984 was accompanied by a commitment not to reintroduce coercive birth control policies. China's current policy borders on overt coercion and continues to meet with widespread resistance.

Finally, no policy measures will be successful in controlling fertility unless efforts are made to *raise the social and economic status of women* and hence create conditions favorable to delayed marriage and lower marital fertility. A crucial ingredient in any program designed to lower fertility rates is the increased education of women, followed by the creation of employment for them outside the home. The availability of income-earning opportunities can lead young women to delay marriage by enabling them to become economically self-sufficient and therefore in a better position to exercise control over the choice of partner and the timing of marriage. It can also reduce family pressures for early marriage by allowing women to make a contribution to parental household income. An independent source of income also secures a stronger position for married women in the household, reducing their dependence on other family members, particularly male offspring, for economic security. Furthermore, it enables women to consider the opportunity costs of additional children when childbearing competes with income-generating activities. In general, the availability of outside sources of income offers women genuine alternatives to early marriage and frequent childbearing, which are often motivated by their lack of resources. An additional benefit of employment outside the home is that it reduces women's isolation, which is often an impediment to the provision of family-planning services.

The importance of these policies to improve the role and status of women was underlined at the 1994 Cairo Internation Conference on Population and Development, where, unlike the first two conferences, held in Bucharest in 1974 and in Mexico City in 1984, less emphasis was placed on the provision of family-planning services and more on the general "empowerment" of women, especially in the area of **reproductive choice**. The Cairo Program of Action summarized this position in the following manner:

> The empowerment and autonomy of women and the improvement of their political, social, economic and health status . . . [are] essential for the achievement of sustainable development and . . . for the long-term success of population programs. Experience shows that population and development programs are most effective when steps have simultaneously been taken to improve the status of women.[22]

What the Developed Countries Can Do: Resources, Population, and the Global Environment

When we view the problems of population from the perspective of global resources and the environment, as we should, the question of the relationship between population size and distribution and the depletion of many nonrenewable resources in developed and underdeveloped countries assumes major importance. In a world where 6% of the population, located in one country, the United States, accounts for 40% of annual world resource use and where slightly over 20% of the world's population accounts for 80% of annual resource use, we are clearly not dealing only or even primarily with a problem of numbers. We must also be concerned with the impact of rising affluence and the very unequal worldwide distribution of incomes on the depletion of many nonrenewable resources such as petroleum, certain basic metals, and other raw materials essential for economic growth.

In terms of food consumption, basic grains like wheat, corn, and rice are by far the most important source of humanity's direct food energy supply (52%). Consumed indirectly (e.g., grain is fed to livestock, which is then consumed as beef, poultry, pork, and lamb or indirectly as milk, cheese, and eggs), they make up a significant share of the remainder. In resource terms, more than 70% of the world's cropland goes into grain production. Yet the average North American directly and indirectly consumes five times as much grain and the corresponding agricultural resources—land, fertilizer, water—as his or her counterpart in India, Nigeria, or Colombia. With regard to energy, probably the second most essential resource to modern society, the average American's consumption of energy fuels (fossil oil and coal, nuclear, and hydroelectric) in 1990 was 25 times the average Brazilian's, 60 times the average Indian's, 191 times the average Nigerian's, and 351 times the average Ethiopian's consumption level! This use of fossil fuel energy to power private automobiles, operate home and office air conditioners, and acti-vate electric toothbrushes in the developed nations is by far the major contributor of carbon dioxide (CO_2) gases into the atmosphere and to the phenomenon of ozone depletion and greenhouse global warming.[23] It also means that there is potentially that much less to fertilize small family farms in the less developed nations. Alternatively, it means that poor families will have to pay more to obtain these valuable resource inputs.

Many similar examples could be given of the gross inequalities in global resource use. Perhaps more important, one could cite innumerable instances of the unnec-essary and costly waste of many scarce and nonrenewable resources by the afflu-ent developed nations. The point, therefore, is that any worldwide program designed to engender a better balance between resources and people by limiting Third World population growth through social intervention and family planning must also include the responsibility of rich nations systematically to simplify their own consumption demands and lifestyles. Such changes would free resources that could then be used by poor nations to generate the social and economic develop-ment essential to slow population growth.

In addition to simplifying lifestyles and consumption habits, one other positive but unlikely internal policy that rich nations could adopt to mitigate current world population problems would be to liberalize the legal conditions for the international immigration of poor, unskilled workers and their families from Africa, Asia, and Latin America to North America, Europe, Japan, and Australia. The international migration of peasants from Europe to North America, Australia, and New Zealand in the nineteenth and early twentieth centuries was a major factor in moderating the problems of underdevelopment and population pressure in European countries. No such safety valve or outlet exists today for Third World countries. In fact, what few outlets existed have over the past two decades been progressively closed. Yet clearly, many underpopulated regions of the world and many labor-scarce societies could benefit economically from international migration, and the benefits to developing countries would be enormous. For example, the United Nations has estimated that current legal barriers to international migration from the Third World to the First World cost developing nations at least $250 billion a year.[24]

How Developed Countries Can Assist Developing Countries with Their Population Programs

There are also a number of ways in which the governments of rich countries and multilateral donor agencies can assist the governments of developing countries achieve their population policy objectives in shorter periods of time. The most important of these concerns the willingness of rich countries to be of genuine assistance to poor countries in their development efforts. Such genuine support would consist not only of expanded public and private financial assistance but also of improved trade relations, more appropriate technology transfers, assistance in developing indigenous scientific research capacities, better international commodity-pricing policies, and a more equitable sharing of the world's scarce natural resources. (These and other areas of international economic relations between rich and poor countries will be examined in Parts Three and Four.)

There are two other activities more directly related to fertility moderation where rich-country governments, international donor agencies, and private nongovernmental organizations (NGOs) can play an important assisting role. The first of these is the whole area of research into the technology of fertility control, the contraceptive pill, modern intrauterine devices (IUDs), voluntary sterilization procedures, and, particularly for Africa in the age of AIDS, effective barrier contraception. Research has been going on in this area for a number of years, almost all of it financed by international donor organizations, private foundations, and aid agencies of developed countries. Further efforts to improve the effectiveness of this contraceptive technology while minimizing the health risks should be encouraged.

The second area includes financial assistance from developed countries for family-planning programs, public education, and national population policy research activities in the developing countries. This has traditionally been the primary area of developed-country assistance in the field of population. Total resources devoted to these activities have risen dramatically from around $2 million in 1960 to almost $3 billion by the 1990s. It remains an open question, however, whether such resources (especially those allocated to premature family-planning programs) might not have been more effectively used to achieve their fertility goals had they instead been devoted directly to assisting LDCs to raise the levels of living of their poorest people. As we have seen, it is of little value to have sophisticated family-planning programs when people are not motivated to reduce family size.

CASE STUDY

The Economy of China

GEOGRAPHIC, SOCIAL, AND ECONOMIC INDICATORS

Capital Beijing

Area 9,600,000 km^2

Population 1.22 billion (1995)

Population (average annual growth rate) 1.4% (1985–1994)

GNP per capita U.S. $530 (1994)

GNP per capita (average annual growth rate) 6.9% (1985–1994)

Agriculture as share of GDP 19% (1994)

Exports as share of GDP 26% (1994)

Infant mortality rate (per 1,000 live births) 44 (1995)

Child malnutrition (underweight) 24% (1993)

Females as share of labor force 43% (1994)

Illiteracy rate (age 15+) 27% (1990)

Human Development Index 0.64 (medium) (1992)

The People's Republic of China, located in eastern Asia, is the third largest country in the world in terms of total area (after Russia and Canada). However, two-thirds of China's area is mountainous or semidesert; only about one-tenth is cultivated. Ninety percent of the people live on 16% of the land. China's population is by far the largest in the world. In 1995, it was estimated at 1.2 billion people and growing at a rate of 17 million per year. Overall annual population growth dropped by nearly 40%, from 2.3% in 1973 to 1.2% in 1988, but has recently been climbing again; if current fertility rates remain unchanged, China's population will reach 2 billion by 2050. The Chinese government is calling for a target family size of three and has introduced incentives to limit the number of children per family to one or two. The one-child family would bring about zero population growth by the year 2000, when total population will be around 1.3 billion.

When the People's Republic was established in 1949, China's economy was characterized by severe dislocations from decades of war and inflation. The new government's immediate concerns were consolidation of power, restoration of public order, and elimination of widespread unemployment and starvation.

Most of these problems were resolved by 1952. In the following year, the Chinese decided to remold the economy, using Soviet central planning as a model. They reduced state investment in agriculture and centered their first five-year plan on the rapid buildup of heavy industry, especially that relating to national defense. A large number of facilities were imported from the Soviet Union and installed with the aid of Soviet technicians.

China's economic growth since 1957 (5.7% per annum) has been considerable, but political turmoil, poor planning, and natural disasters have prevented it from achieving higher levels of development. The experiments of the so-called Great Leap Forward (1958–1960)—rural collectivization, elimination of wage incentives, backyard steel plants, and great leeway for local

228

initiatives—plunged China into a depression in the early 1960s. Compounding these domestic difficulties was the withdrawal of Soviet assistance and technicians in August 1960 as the Sino-Soviet dispute worsened. Beijing responded by emphasizing "self-reliance," and a greater share of its investment was redirected toward agriculture. After a brief period of growth, politics—this time the Cultural Revolution and its aftermath (1966–1976)—again wreaked havoc with the economy, injecting ideology into economic planning, disrupting foreign trade, and virtually shutting down educational and training facilities.

In 1975, Premier Zhou Enlai outlined a new set of economic goals designed to elevate China to the status of a front-rank economic power by the year 2000. This multistaged effort, known now as the Four Modernizations program, was aimed at rapidly accelerating production in agriculture, industry, science and technology, and national defense. In 1976, the death of Chairman Mao Zedong, the arrest of the Gang of Four, and the gradual establishment of a new government under Deng Xiaoping and Hua Guofeng sharply reduced the role of ideology in Chinese policy. The stage was set for a more pragmatic look at the political and economic problems the country faced.

China's commitment to the Four Modernizations was reaffirmed in 1978 at the Fifth National People's Congress, where a 10-year plan assigned a major role to massive imports of complete plants and technology from the West. By the end of 1978, China had signed contracts committing itself to foreign purchases totaling $7 billion.

Since 1978, the fundamental premise of China's economic policy has been that consumer welfare, economic productivity, and political stability are indivisible. Emphasis has been on raising personal income and consumption and introducing new productivity, incentive, and management systems.

A controversial reform package aimed at reducing the role of central management in favor of a mixed, planned-market economy was introduced at the third session of the Fifth National People's Congress in August 1980 and endorsed in the sixth five-year plan. Key elements were promulgation of agricultural reforms (including long-term leases on land and permission for farmers to specialize in cash crops and to engage in nonagricultural activities), self-management rights, introduction of greater competition in the marketplace, easing of the tax burden on nongovernment enterprises, and facilitation of direct contact between Chinese and foreign trading companies.

The reforms produced great successes. National income and agricultural and industrial output all grew at 10% compound rates during the 1980s and reached nearly 13% in 1994. Peasants per capita real income doubled; urban dwellers' per capita real income increased by half. China became self-sufficient in grain production; rural industries boomed and accounted for 23% of agricultural output, helping absorb surplus labor in rural areas. Industrial reforms increased the variety of light industrial and consumer goods available. The leadership demonstrated its ability to adjust to economic pressures by adopting a variety of fiscal and administrative measures. The result of these policy changes and mixtures of central direction and local initiative was the creation of a hybrid economy, which the Chinese call a socialist commodity system influenced by market mechanisms. Much of the success represented a recovery from the economically disastrous Cultural Revolution period.

But economic reform and the introduction of a more market-oriented economy also brought with it rising inflation (which reached 21.7% in 1994, the highest since Communist rule began in 1949), increased crime and corruption, declining agricultural output, greater unemployment, and widening income and regional disparities. There are estimates that up to 100 million rural peasants are without jobs and that by 2000 there may be as many as 300 million idle rural workers scouring towns and cities in search of employment. On the political front, the economic reforms of the 1980s occurred without concomitant political reform as cries for greater democratic participation began to be sounded. Unfortunately for both the Chinese people and their economy, the harsh repression that culminated in June 1989 in the Tiananmen Square massacre set back the pace of political reform and social progress. Much will depend on how the issue of political democracy and economic reform is resolved. If it is resolved successfully, China will resume its inexorable march toward the top of the world's economic powers. If not, China will likely remain a country of enormous potential but limited progress. Recall from our discussion of Simon Kuznets's reading of economic history in Chapter 4 how crucial the resolution of political conflict is for long-term economic growth. The eyes of the world will be on China to see what lessons can be learned for other market-oriented developing nations governed by authoritarian regimes.

Concepts for Review

Birthrate
Death rate
Demographic transition
Doubling time
Empowerment of women
Family-planning programs
Fertility
Hidden momentum of population growth
Infant mortality rate
Life expectancy at birth

Malthusian population trap
Microeconomic theory of fertility
Mortality
Natural increase
Net international migration
Population-poverty cycle
Positive checks
Preventive checks
Rate of population increase
Reproductive choice
Youth dependency ratio

Questions for Discussion

1. Population growth in Third World nations has proceeded at unprecedented rates over the past few decades. Compare and contrast the present rate of population growth in less developed countries with that of the modern developed nations during their early growth years. What has been the major factor contributing to rapid Third World population growth since the Second World War? Explain.

2. What is the relationship between the age structure of a population and its dependency burden? Is the dependency burden higher or lower in Third World countries? Why?

3. Explain the meaning of the notion of the hidden momentum of population growth. Why is this an important concept for projecting future population trends in different Third World nations?

4. Describe briefly the theory of the demographic transition. At what stage in this transition do most developing countries seem to be? Explain.

5. How does the microeconomic theory of fertility relate to the theory of consumer choice? Do you think that economic incentives and disincentives influence family size decisions? Explain your answer, giving some specific examples of such incentives and disincentives.

6. "The world population problem is not just a matter of expanding numbers but also one of rising affluence and limited resources. It is as much a problem caused by developed nations as it is one deriving from Third World countries." Comment on this statement.

7. List and briefly describe the principal causes of high population growth in LDCs and the major consequences.

8. Outline and comment briefly on some of the arguments *against* the idea that population growth is a serious problem in Third World nations.

9. Outline and comment briefly on some of the arguments *in favor of* the idea that population growth is a serious problem in Third World nations.

10. Outline and comment briefly on the various policy options available to Third World governments in their attempt to modify or limit the rate of population growth.

Notes

1. The decade of the 1970s represented a watershed in the history of world population growth. By the end of the decade, it became clear that rates had begun to decline in a growing number of developing countries and that world population growth had finally peaked. For some evidence of this turning point, see Bernard Berelson, W. Parker Mauldin, and Sheldon Segal, "Population: Current status and policy options," *Social Science and Medicine* (May 1980), and, especially, World Bank, *World Development Report, 1984* (New York: Oxford University Press, 1984), pt. 2, chap. 4.

2. A convenient shorthand method of calculating **doubling time** is simply to divide any growth rate into the number 72. For example, something (an asset, population, GNP, etc.) growing at 2% per year will double its value in approximately 36 years.

3. John Bongaarts, "Population policy options in the developing world," *Science* 263 (February 11, 1994).

4. A geometric progression is simply a doubling (or some other multiple) of each previous number, as in 1, 2, 4, 8, 16, 32, 64, 128, 256, 512, 1,024, and so on. Like compound interest, geometric progressions have a way of reaching large numbers very rapidly.

5. Actually, between Y_0 and Y_1, population would be growing ever so slightly as a result of positive income growth. See the discussion of equilibrium points A, B, and C in the figure in the text.

6. Simon Kuznets, *Fertility Differentials between Less Developed and Developed Regions: Components and Implications,* Discussion Paper No. 217 (New Haven, Conn.: Economic Growth Center, Yale University, 1974), pp. 87–88.

7. See, for example, T. Paul Schultz, *Fertility Determinants: A Theory, Evidence, and Application to Policy Evaluation* (Santa Monica, Calif.: Rand Corp., 1974); Nancy Birdsall, "Economic approaches to population growth," in Hollis B. Chenery and T. N. Srinwasan (eds.),

Handbook of Development Economics, vol. 1 (Amsterdam: North Holland, 1988), pp. 478–542; Jean Drèze, Mamta Murthi, and Anne-Catherine Guio, "Mortality, fertility and gender bias in India: A district level analysis," *Population and Development Review* 21 (December 1995): 745–782; and Partha Dasgupta, "The population problem: Theory and evidence," *Journal of Economic Literature*, 33 (December 1995): 1879–1902.

8. For strong empirical evidence that low fertility results mostly from economic, social, cultural, and educational improvements in a population and only slightly from the availability of family planning programs, see Lant H. Pritchett, "Desired fertility and the impact of population policies," *Population and Development Review* 20 (March 1994): 1–55.

9. For an analysis of this conflict, see Jason L. Finkle and Barbara Crane, "The politics of Bucharest: Population, development and the new international economic order," *Population and Development Review* 1 (1975): 87–114. Although this conflict was less visible in the Second World Population Conference held in Mexico City in August 1984 and was a minor issue beneath that of reproductive choice and the empowerment of women at the Third Conference held in Cairo in 1994, it remained prominent in the thoughts and discussions of many Third World delegates.

10. For a more detailed discussion of these divergent opinions, see Michael S. Teitelbaum, "Population and development: Is a consensus possible?" *Foreign Affairs* (July 1974): 749–757. See also Timothy King and Allen Kelley, *The New Population Debate: Two Views on Population Growth and Economic Development*, Population Trends and Public Policy Paper No. 7 (Washington, D.C.: Population Reference Bureau, 1985), and Robert H. Cassen, *Population Policy: A New Concensus* (Washington, D.C.: Overseas Development Council, 1994).

11. See United Nations, *International Conference on Population and Development: Program of Action* (New York: United Nations, 1994). The full text of this declaration is reprinted in *Population and Development Review* 21 (March and June 1995). For an analysis of the politics of the Cairo Conference, see C. Alison McIntosh and Jason L. Finkle, "The Cairo Conference on population and development: A new paradigm?" *Population and Development Review* 21 (June 1995): 223–260.

12. See, for example, Colin Clark, "The 'population explosion' myth," *Bulletin of the Institute of Development Studies* (May 1969); Julian Simon, *The Ultimate Resource* (Princeton, N.J.: Princeton University Press, 1981); Nick Eberstadt, "Population and economic growth," *Wilson Quarterly* (Winter 1986): 95–129; and National Research Council, *Population Growth and Economic Development: Policy Questions* (Washington, D.C.: National Academy Press, 1986).

13. Samir Amin, "Underpopulated Africa," paper presented at the African Population Conference, Accra, December 1971.

14. *Ibid.*, fn. 2.

15. *Ibid.*, p. 3.

16. For example, see Paul R. Ehrlich and Anne H. Ehrlich, *Population, Resources, and Environment: Issues in Human Ecology*, 2d ed. (San Francisco: Freeman, 1972); Lester R. Brown, *In the Human Interest: A Strategy to Stabilize World Population* (New York: Norton, 1974); and Paul R. Ehrlich and Anne H. Erlich, *The Population Explosion* (New York: Simon & Schuster, 1990).

17. I am grateful to Professor Harold Votey for suggesting this illustration.

18. For a detailed review of this evidence, see Cassen, *Population Policy*, pp. 14–22; Dennis A. Ahlburg *et al.*, *Population and Economic Development: A Report to the Government of the*

Commonwealth of Australia (April 1994); and Geoffrey McNicoll, "Effects of population growth: Visions and revisions," *Population and Development Review* 21 (June 1995): 307–340. As the Ahlberg report demonstrates, not all of these consequences are unambiguously negative. Much depends on the particular country and its demographic situation.

19. Cassen, *Population Policy*, p. 12.

20. See Birdsall, "Economic approaches to population growth," pp. 523–529.

21. Amartya Sen, "Missing women," *British Medical Journal* 304 (1992): 587–588.

22. United Nations, *International Conference*, para. 4.1. See also Nancy Folbre, "Engendering economics: New perspectives on women, work and demographic change," in Michael Bruno and Boris Pleskovic (eds.), *Proceedings of the World Bank Annual Conference on Development Economics, 1995* (Washington, D.C.: World Bank, 1996).

23. For a highly informative analysis of the relative responsibilities of developed and less developed countries as well as the role of population growth in contributing to global environmental damage, see John Bongaarts, "Population growth and global warming," *Population and Development Review* 18 (June 1992): 299–319.

24. United Nations Development Program, *Human Development Report, 1992* (New York: Oxford University Press, 1992), p. 58.

Further Reading

For an introduction to the study of population, including basic concepts, analysis, and recent statistical trends, see Helen Daugherty and Kenneth Kammeyer, *An Introduction to Population* (New York: Guilford, 1995). See also Thomas W. Merrick, "World population in transition," *Population Bulletin* 41 (April 1986): 1–51; Paul Demeny, "The world demographic situation," in Jane Menken (ed.), *World Population and U.S. Policy* (New York: Norton, 1986), pp. 27–66; and United Nations Population Fund, *The State of World Population, 1995* (New York: United Nations Population Fund, 1995). A handy statistical summary is found in the annual *World Population Data Sheet* (Washington, D.C.: Population Reference Bureau).

An excellent early survey article on the various interrelationships between population and economic development is Robert H. Cassen, "Population and development: A survey," *World Development* 4 (October 1976). Two additional volumes of readings on the subject are Ronald Ridker (ed.), *Population and Development: The Search for Selective Interventions* (Baltimore: Johns Hopkins University Press, 1976), and Richard Easterlin (ed.), *Population and Economic Change in Developing Countries* (Chicago: University of Chicago Press/National Bureau of Economic Research, 1980). The best overall recent reviews are Nancy Birdsall, "Economic approaches to population growth," in Hollis B. Chenery and T. N. Srinivasan (eds.), *Handbook of Development Economics*, vol. 1. (Amsterdam: North Holland, 1988), pp. 478–542, and Dennis A. Ahlburg *et al.*, *Population and Economic Development: A Report to the Government of the Commonwealth of Australia* (April 1994), and Partha Dasgupta, "The population problem: Theory and evidence," *Journal of Economic Literature*, 33 (December 1995): 1879–1902.

On the new microeconomics of fertility, see Harvey Leibenstein, "An interpretation of the economic theory of fertility: Promising path or blind alley?" *Journal of Economic Literature* 12 (1974); T. Paul Schultz, *Fertility Determinants: A Theory, Evidence, and Application to Policy Evaluation* (Santa Monica, Calif.: Rand Corp., 1974); Richard A. Easterlin, "An economic framework for fertility analysis," *Studies in Family Planning* (March 1975); Marc Nerlove,

"Household and economy: Toward a new theory of population and economic growth," *Journal of Political Economy* 82 (June 1974); and Susan H. Cochrane, "A review of some microeconomic models of fertility," *Population Studies* 29 (1975).

For a survey of how population relates to resources and the environment, see United Nations Population Fund, *Population, Resources and the Environment: The Critical Challenges* (New York: United Nations, 1991); John Bongaarts, "Population growth and global warming," *Population and Development Review* 18 (June 1992): 299–319; and World Resources Institute, *World Resources, 1994–95* (New York: Oxford University Press, 1994), chap. 2.

For a concise and informative summary of the debate on population and development, see Michael S. Teitelbaum, "Population and development: Is a consensus possible?" *Foreign Affairs* (July 1974): 749–757, Timothy King and Allen Kelley, *The New Population Debate: Two Views on Population Growth and Economic Development*, Population Trends and Public Policy Paper No. 7 (Washington, D.C.: Population Reference Bureau, 1985); and Robert H. Cassen, *Population Policy: A New Consensus* (Washington, D.C.: Overseas Development Council, 1994).

Two informative analyses of the fertility impact of family-planning programs are John Bongaarts, W. Parker Mauldin, and James Phillips, *The Demographic Impact of Family Planning Programs* (Washington, D.C.: Population Council, 1990), and W. Parker Mauldin and John A. Ross, *Family Planning Programs: Efforts and Results, 1982–89* (Washington, D.C.: Population Council, 1991). For an economic critique of the effectiveness of family planning in developing countries, see Lant H. Pritchett, "Desired fertility and the impact of population policies," *Population and Development Review* 20 (March 1994): 1–55. For a feminist critique, see Betsy Hartmann, *Reproductive Rights and Wrongs: The Global Politics of Population Control and Contraceptive Choice* (New York: Harper & Row, 1987), and Gita Sen, Adrienne Germain, and Lincoln Chen (eds.), *Population Policies Reconsidered* (New York: International Women's Health Coalition, 1994).

See also Stephen C. Smith, *Case Studies*, Chapters 7 and 8 for an analysis of population, famine, and entitlement theory as applied to Somalia, and the impact of AIDS in Uganda.

CHAPTER 7

Unemployment: Issues, Dimensions, and Analyses

Many parts of the world are witnessing a new phenomenon—jobless growth.
Even when output increases, increase in employment lags way behind.
—United Nations Development Program, *Human Development Report, 1993*

The current employment situation represents an enormous waste of resources
and an unacceptable level of human suffering. It has led to growing social
exclusion, rising inequality, . . . and a host of social ills.
—International Labor Organization, *World Employment Report, 1995*

The Employment Problem: Some Basic Issues

Historically, the economic development of Western Europe and North America has often been described in terms of the continuous transfer of economic activity and people from rural to urban areas, both within and between countries. As urban industries expanded, new employment opportunities were created; and over the same period, laborsaving technological progress in agriculture reduced rural labor needs. Although urban slums and unemployment were evident in nineteenth-century England, the combination of urban industrialization and agricultural mechanization made it possible for Western nations to undergo a systematic rural-to-urban transfer of their human resources.

On the basis of this shared experience, many economists concluded that economic development in the Third World, too, necessitated a concentrated effort to promote rapid urban industrial growth. They therefore tended to view cities as growth centers, the focal points of an expanding economy. Unfortunately, this strategy of rapid industrialization has in many instances failed to bring about the desired results predicted by historical experience.

Today many developing countries are plagued by a historically unique combination of massive rural-to-urban population movements, stagnating agricultural productivity, and growing urban and rural unemployment and underemployment. Substantial unemployment in LDC economies is probably one of the most striking symptoms of their inadequate development. In a wide spectrum of poor countries, **open unemployment**, especially in urban areas, now affects 10% to 20% of the labor force.[1] The incidence of unemployment is much higher among the young and increasingly more educated in the 15–24 age bracket. Even larger fractions of both urban and rural labor forces suffer from **underemployment**. They have neither the complementary resources (if they are working full time) nor the opportunities (if they work only part time) for increasing their very low incomes to levels comparable with those in modern manufacturing, commerce, and the service sector. Because of its relationship to the problem of Third World poverty, the employment issue occupies a central place in the study of underdevelopment.

But the dimensions of the employment problem go beyond the simple shortage of work opportunities or the underutilization and low productivity of people who work long hours. The unemployment crisis of the 1980s and 1990s is both more serious and quite different in origin and solution from the problem in the 1960s and 1970s. In earlier decades, the dilemma was linked to the failure of domestic job creation to keep pace with rapid industrial output growth. But the macroeconomic environment of LDCs changed dramatically in the 1980s. Unemployment grew rapidly, largely due to economies being "demand-constrained" by external factors such as a worsening balance of payments, rising debt problems, and IMF-induced austerity programs (see Chapter 14), all of which caused a marked deceleration of industrial growth, a rapid decline in real wages, and falling urban and rural employment.

The employment problem in Third World countries therefore has a number of facets that make it historically unique and thus subject to a variety of unconventional economic analyses. There are three major reasons for this:

1. Unemployment and underemployment regularly and chronically affect much larger proportions of LDC labor forces than unemployment did in the industrialized countries, even during the worst years of the Great Depression.

2. Third World employment problems have much more complex causes than employment problems in the developed countries. They therefore require a variety of policy approaches that go far beyond simple Keynesian-type policies to expand aggregate demand.

3. Whatever the dimensions and causes of unemployment in Third World nations, it is associated with human circumstances of abject poverty and low levels of living such as have rarely been experienced in the now developed countries. There is an urgent need for concerted policy action by both the less developed and the more developed nations. As we shall see, the LDCs need to readjust domestic policies to include employment creation as a major social and economic objective, while the developed countries need to review and readjust their traditional economic policies via-à-vis the Third World, especially in the areas of trade, aid, and technology transfer.

As it is impossible to do justice to the many complexities and nuances of employment problems in diverse Third World countries, our focus in this chapter and the next will be on two major questions that almost all LDCs face:

1. Why did rapid industrial growth in many developing countries fail to generate substantial new employment opportunities in the 1960s and 1970s, and what does the changed global economic environment of the 1990s augur for LDC employment creation in the future?

2. Why do great numbers of people continue to migrate from rural areas into the crowded and congested cities despite high and rising levels of urban unemployment?

In investigating these two issues, we will see why the **urbanization** process in less developed countries has differed so markedly from the historical experience of the now developed countries and why growing unemployment and underemployment are not, as many economists believed, merely self-correcting, transitory phenomena present in the early stages of economic growth. We will see why they are, instead, symptoms of more far-reaching economic and social disturbances both within LDCs and in their relationship with developed countries.

Our purpose in this chapter is to examine the dimensions as well as the analytics of the employment problem in developing nations. The chapter begins with a quantitative profile of current and anticipated trends in Third World unemployment. It then focuses on the nature and characteristics of the employment problem and the linkages among unemployment, poverty, and income distribution. Unemployment in its simplest dimension results from a relatively slow growth of labor demand in both the modern, industrial sector and in traditional agriculture combined with a rapidly growing labor supply, especially as a result of accelerated population growth and high levels of rural-urban migration. Demand factors are examined in this chapter in the form of both traditional and contemporary models of employment determination, and the supply factors are analyzed in Chapter 8, where we look at the problem of urban population growth and the economics of rural-urban migration. Chapter 8 then concludes with an analysis of alternative policy approaches to cope with diverse LDC employment problems.

Dimensions of Third World Unemployment: Evidence and Concepts

First let us look at some of the quantitative and qualitative dimensions of the unemployment problem in developing nations.[2]

Employment and Unemployment: Trends and Projections

During the 1970s, increased interest in the widespread and growing problem of Third World unemployment and underemployment on the part of individual development economists, national planning authorities, and international assistance agencies led to a much broader and more precise picture of the quantitative dimensions of the problem. In particular, at the beginning of the decade, the International Labor Organization (ILO) launched its ambitious World Employment Program with a series of detailed case studies of the employment problem in such diverse countries as Colombia, Kenya, Sri Lanka, Iran, and the Philippines. These and similar studies in other countries documented the seriousness of the existing problem and the likelihood that it would worsen over the coming years.

Table 7.1 provides a summary picture of employment and unemployment trends from 1960 to 1990, both for developing countries as a whole and for Africa, Asia, and Latin America. Before reciting these statistics, however, it is important to point out that data on open unemployment in LDCs are especially ambiguous and often misleading. This is because of the enormous numbers of **discouraged workers** who have dropped out of the **labor force** (are no longer seeking formal-sector work) and are not counted in employment surveys. Third World unemployment rates therefore invariably understate the magnitude of the problem. Looking at Table 7.1, we see first that recorded unemployment grew from approximately 36.5 million in 1960 to over 54 million workers in 1973, an increase of 46%. This averages out to an annual rate of increase of 3%, which is higher than the annual rate of employment growth during this same period. In the developing world as a whole, unemployment was growing faster than employment.

TABLE 7.1 Employment and Unemployment in Developing Countries, 1960–1990 (in thousands)

Indicator	1960	1970	1973	1980	1990
All Developing Countries[a]					
Employment[b]	507,416	617,244	658,000	773,110	991,600
Unemployment	36,466	48,798	54,130	65,620	88,693
Unemployment rate (percent)	6.7	7.4	7.6	7.8	8.2
Combined unemployment and					
underemployment rate (percent)[c]	25	27	29		
Africa	31	39	38		
Asia	24	26	28		
Latin America	18	20	25		
All Africa					
Employment[b]	100,412	119,633	127,490	149,390	191,180
Unemployment	8,416	12,831	13,890	15,973	21,105
Unemployment rate (percent)	7.7	9.6	9.8	9.8	9.9
All Asia					
Employment[b]	340,211	413,991	441,330	516,800	660,300
Unemployment	24,792	31,440	34,420	43,029	59,485
Unemployment rate (percent)	6.8	7.1	7.2	7.7	8.3
All Latin America					
Employment[b]	66,793	83,620	89,180	106,920	140,120
Unemployment	3,258	4,527	5,820	6,618	8,103
Unemployment rate (percent)	4.7	5.1	6.1	5.8	5.5

SOURCE: Yves Sabolo, "Employment and unemployment, 1960–1990," *International Labor Review* 112 (June 1975), tab. 3 and app. Reprinted with permission.
[a]Excluding China.
[b]Including underemployment.
[c]Not calculated for 1980 and 1990.

When we also consider that the underemployed in 1973 comprised approximately an additional 250 million people, the combined unemployment and underemployment rate reaches a staggering 29% for all developing countries, with Africa experiencing a labor underutilization rate of 38%. Moreover, with rapid labor force growth, the marginal unemployment rate (the proportion of new labor force entrants unable to find regular jobs) is likely to be even higher than the average figures shown in Table 7.1. Although the extent of labor underutilization is lower in Asia and Latin America than in Africa, the quantitative and qualitative dimensions of the problem are just as serious. For example, even though Asia may have a lower rate of unemployment than Africa, the absolute numbers involved are many times larger (34.4 million in 1973, compared with 13.9 million for Africa).

Projections to 1990 made in this 1975 study (Table 7.1) indicated that the rate of Third World unemployment would rise steadily and that the total numbers unemployed would reach almost 90 million. In fact, these projections were overly optimistic. The 1990 projection for each and every region of the Third World was considerably below current estimates. Because of the debt problem and the slowdown in world economic growth during the 1980s, total LDC unemployment is at least twice as large as the 90 million estimate. This is evident when we compare actual 1980s open unemployment rates as reported in Table 7.2 with those projected in Table 7.1. In particular, note how much higher the actual rates are in Africa and Latin America. Adding projections for the underemployed could give a figure as high as 700 million workers in the 1990s who are unemployed or employed part time or whose productivity is very low. Although these figures are only estimates, they strikingly underline the seriousness of the problem.

Four Dimensions of the Employment Problem

The unique nature of the employment problem in developing countries is most vividly revealed in four areas: the educated unemployed, self-employment, women's work, and youth unemployment.

The Educated Unemployed

We will examine the relationship between education and development in Chapter 11. For the present, we note the existence of an unexpected positive relationship between levels of education and rates of unemployment in developing countries—the opposite of the situation in developed countries and contrary to what one might expect. Table 7.3 shows that for many Third World nations, unemployment rates rise with higher levels of schooling. For example, in India in 1989, the unemployment rate was 2% for people with no education, but it was 9% for those with a secondary education and 12% for university graduates. One reason for this puzzling phenomenon is that the least educated cannot afford to be openly unemployed and must seek any kind of work in the urban informal sector (see Chapter 8). Even though they may be grossly underemployed—working, say, only one day a week—these people are not counted as being unemployed. Secondary school and university graduates can usually afford to search for higher-paying jobs and are thus more likely to be counted among the openly unemployed. In Bangladesh, 40% of

TABLE 7.2 Open Unemployment Rates in Developing Countries, 1980s and 1990s

Country	Unemployment Rate (percent)	
	Urban	Total
Sub-Saharan Africa		
Botswana	31	25
Kenya	23	24
Nigeria	10	28
Tanzania	22	N.A.
Zambia	31	N.A.
Latin America		
Argentina	6	10
Brazil	8	5
Chile	17	5
Colombia	14	8
Ecuador	12	8
Venezuela	13	9
Asia		
Bangladesh	12	N.A.
Malaysia	9	3
Philippines	7	9
South Korea	4	3

SOURCES: International Labor Organization, *World Labor Report, 1989* (Geneva: International Labor Organization, 1989), tabs. 1.7 and 1.12, fig. 1.8; Central Intelligence Agency, *The World Factbook, 1994* (Washington, D.C.: Central Intelligence Agency, 1994).

TABLE 7.3 Unemployment by Educational Level in Selected Developing Countries (percent)

Country	Year	No Education	Primary	Secondary	Postsecondary
Algeria	1989	9.2	24.2	28.9	5.8
Tunisia	1989	11.2	20.4	17.4	5.2
Ghana	1988	3.4	7.6	13.5	14.7
Kenya	1986	13.5	15.6	22.2	5.4
Zimbabwe	1987	1.6	6.8	11.6	N.A.
Malaysia	1985	4.7	22.9	30.6	3.9
India	1989	2.0	3.0	9.0	12.0
Indonesia	1985	0.6	1.5	7.5	5.3
Sri Lanka	1981	4.5	14.5	15.1	4.2
Ivory Coast	1985	1.0	5.2	21.7	13.7

SOURCE: United Nations Development Program, *Human Development Report, 1993* (New York: Oxford University Press, 1993), p. 38. Reprinted with permission.

people with a master's degree are believed to be unemployed, and in Thailand, unemployment rates among university graduates in the 1970s and early 1980s ranged from 20% to 35%. The problem is becoming particularly acute in Africa, where the educational system continues to turn out many more graduates than there are jobs to accommodate. We see, for example, from Table 7.3 that unemployment rates among Kenyan secondary school graduates in 1986 exceeded 22%. We return to this issue in Chapter 11.

Self-employment

As a second example of how the employment problems of Third World nations differ from those of the more developed countries, consider Table 7.4. In many developing countries, the inability of people to find salaried employment in the modern (formal-sector) economy forces them to pursue self-employment in the traditional or "informal" economy, in both urban and rural areas. Table 7.4 shows that much larger percentages of LDC labor forces are engaged in self-employment activities than workers in developed countries. Moreover, while almost all of the self-employed in developed countries are involved in small businesses as either sole proprietors, limited partners, or professionals (lawyers, doctors, accountants, etc.), in developing countries the majority of the self-employed are street vendors, hawkers, small shop owners, prostitutes, rickshaw drivers, and artisans. Their objective is day-to-day survival, and they constitute most of the underemployed.

Women and Employment

Although women's participation in Third World labor forces had increased dramatically by 1990, rising to 43% in East Asia, 32% in Latin America, and 13% in the Arab world, most women were employed in a very limited range of low-

TABLE 7.4 **Self-employment in Selected Countries**

Country	Self-employed in Total Labor Force (percent)	Year
Ghana	68	1984
Pakistan	56	1984
Nigeria	56	1983
Mexico	48	1981
Philippines	36	1987
India	31	1981
France	11[a]	1987
Germany	8[a]	1987
United States	8[a]	1987
Canada	7[a]	1987

SOURCE: United Nations Development Program, *Human Development Report, 1993* (New York: Oxford University Press, 1993), tab. 3.2.
[a]Percentage of self-employed in nonagricultural labor force.

productivity jobs where hours worked were long and pay was low. Most economically active women work either in agriculture (78% in Africa and 80% in Asia) or in the urban informal sector (25% to 40% in Latin America). Their nonagricultural jobs tend to be in low-status production-line work, often for export (as in Southeast Asia, where they comprise 80% of the workforce in such industries as food processing, electronics, textiles, footwear, toys, and sporting goods). Women are routinely discriminated against in terms of pay scales, job advancement, and job security. They are also more likely to be unemployed than men. Table 7.5 provides some data on male-female differentials in unemployment rates, earnings, and hours worked for five developing countries in 1990.

Youth Unemployment and Child Labor

The most conspicuous dimension of the unemployment problem in Third World countries is its prevalence among people between the ages of 15 and 24 years. Youth unemployment affects both educated and uneducated, women as well as men. David Turnham has estimated the youth unemployment rate to be in excess of 30% in a large number of developing countries.[3] And as we shall discover in Chapter 8 and as depicted in Table 7.6, unemployed young people tend to be concentrated in urban areas. Many have recently migrated from the rural countryside, and their expectations of finding well-paid work are often unrealistically high. With rapid population growth rates, a sizable youth dependency ratio, and a burgeoning labor force of young new entrants, youth unemployment poses a serious threat to future development in many less developed countries.

There is however another, darker, side to the question of jobs for young people. This is the problem of *child labor*. The International Labor Office has estimated that almost 60 million LDC children under the age of 14 work long hours for pitiable low wages under horrible (some say satanic) working conditions. The situation is particularly grim in Pakistan where in 1994 the Human Rights Commission of Pakistan estimated that 11 to 12 million children, half of whom were under the age of 10, were working in effect, if not in fact, as indentured servants. They earned less than half the adult wage and often worked in excess of 80 hours per week. Most

---

TABLE 7.5 Unemployment, Earnings, and Hours Worked for Women in Selected Countries, 1990

Country	Unemployment Rate (percent)		Women's Nonagricultural Earnings as a Percentage of Men's	Hours Worked per Week (including housework)	
	Men	Women		Men	Women
Kenya	15.6	18.6	80.5	40.1	47.2
Sri Lanka	10.8	24.3	78.5	52.4	56.7
Costa Rica	4.2	5.9	65.9	45.7	48.3
South Korea	2.9	1.8	53.5	48.2	53.3
Colombia	8.1	13.2	N.A.	N.A.	N.A.

SOURCE: United Nations Development Program, *Human Development Report, 1993* (New York: Oxford University Press, 1993), p. 45, box 3.5.

TABLE 7.6 Age-specific Urban Unemployment Rates (percent)

Country	Overall Rate	Age 15–24	Age 25+	Year
Kenya	14.1	38.1	8.2	1986
India	7.1	19.4	3.4	1988
Indonesia	7.3	23.4	2.6	1986
Sri Lanka	19.5	40.2	11.5	1986
Philippines	9.0	18.6	5.6	1983
Bolivia	11.5	15.2	N.A.	1988
Colombia	9.3	14.2	5.1	1988
Venezuela	9.1	17.6	6.5	1987

SOURCE: David Turnham, *Employment and Development: A New Review of Evidence* (Paris: Organization for Economic Cooperation and Development, 1993), tab. 2.3. Reprinted with permission.

worked in carpet- and brick-making factories although they could be found in almost every industrial site.

Labor Force: Present and Projected

The number of people searching for work in a less developed country depends primarily on the size and age composition of its population. Among the numerous processes relating trends in overall population growth to the growth of indigenous labor forces, two are of particular interest. First, whatever the overall magnitude of the population growth rate, its fertility and mortality components have a separate significance. A 3% (30 per 1,000) natural growth rate has different labor force implications when crude birth and death rates are, say, 50 and 20 per 1,000 as opposed to 40 and 10. This is because the **age structure of the population** will be different for a high-birth-and-death-rate economy than for a low-birth-and-death-rate one, even though the natural rate of increase is the same for both. Because birthrates obviously affect only the numbers of newly born, whereas death rates affect all age groups (although unevenly), a high-birth-and-death-rate economy will have a greater percentage of the total population in the dependent age group (0–15 years) than a low-birth-and-death-rate economy will. The rapid reductions in death rates recently experienced by most LDCs have therefore expanded the size of their present labor forces, while continuous high birth rates create high current dependency ratios and rapidly expanding future labor forces.[4]

Second, the impact of fertility decline on labor force size and age structure operates only with very long lags, even when the decline is rapid. The reason is the phenomenon of population momentum described in Chapter 6. For example, a 50% fall in LDC fertility rates by 2000 will reduce the male labor force by only 13% by the year 2015, a reduction from about 1.39 to 1.21 billion workers. This is certainly not a trivial reduction, and its long-run impact would clearly be substantial. Nevertheless, the essential fact remains that everyone who will enter the labor force over the next 15 years has already been born, and the size of the labor force two decades hence is largely determined by current fertility rates.

Present labor force statistics reveal annual increases on the order of 2.2% for all less developed regions during the 1980s and approximately 2.1% for the 1990s. But in terms of actual numbers, which demonstrate the prospective magnitude of the LDC employment problem more dramatically, the total developing-world work-force of around 1.8 billion people in 1990 is expected to grow by 300 million by 2000 and by an additional 1 billion during the first quarter of the twenty-first century. Every year during the 1990s, Third World countries will have to create more than 30 million new jobs just to prevent the present extraordinary total of 500 million unemployed or underemployed LDC workers from growing even more.[5] Unfortunately, present projections by the International Labor Organization (ILO) indicate that while the labor force in Latin America will grow by 27%, employment will grow by only 14%. The figures for sub-Saharan Africa and South Asia are similar.

Labor Underutilization: Some Definitional Distinctions

To get a full understanding of the significance of the employment problem, we must take into account, in addition to the openly unemployed, the larger numbers of workers who may be visibly active but in an economic sense are grossly underutilized. As Edgar O. Edwards pointed out in his comprehensive survey of employment problems in developing countries:

> In addition to the numbers of people unemployed, many of whom may receive minimal incomes through the extended family system, it is also necessary to consider the dimensions of (1) time (many of those employed would like to work more hours per day, per week or per year), (2) intensity of work (which brings in considerations of health and nutrition), and (3) productivity (lack of which can often be attributed to inadequate **complementary resources** with which to work). Even these are only the most obvious dimensions of effective work, and factors such as motivation, attitudes, and cultural inhibitions (as against women, for example) must also be considered.[6]

Edwards distinguishes among the following five forms of **underutilization of labor**:

1. *Open unemployment*—both voluntary (on the part of people who exclude from consideration some jobs for which they could qualify, implying some means of support other than employment) and involuntary. Although voluntary unemployment (e.g., among the educated) was more prevalent in the growth decades of the 1960s and 1970s, in the slow-growth and demand-constrained 1980s and 1990s, most unemployment has been of the involuntary variety.

2. *Underemployment*—people working less (daily, weekly, or seasonally) than they would like to work. This, along with category 3, is the predominant form of contemporary labor underutilization. For example, while Peru reported an open unemployment rate of 15% in 1992, its underemployment rate was estimated at 70%.[7]

3. *The visibly active but underutilized*—people who would not normally be classified as either unemployed or underemployed by the definitions just given but who in fact have found alternative means of "marking time," including these:

   a. *Disguised underemployment*. Many people seem occupied on farms or employed in government on a full-time basis even though the services they render may actually require much less than full time. Social pressures on public and private industry may also result in substantial amounts of disguised underemployment. If available work is openly shared among the employed, the disguise disappears and underemployment becomes explicit.

   b. *Hidden unemployment*. Many people are engaged in second-choice nonemployment activities, such as education or housekeeping, primarily because job opportunities are not available either at the levels of education already attained or, for women, due to social mores. Educational institutions and households become employers of last resort. Moreover, many people enrolled for further education may be among the less able as indicated by their inability to compete successfully for jobs before pursuing further education.

   c. *Premature retirement*. This phenomenon is especially evident, and apparently growing, in the civil service. In many countries, retirement ages are falling at the same time that longevity is increasing, primarily as a means of creating promotion opportunities for some of the large numbers pressing up from below.

4. *The impaired*—people who may work full time but whose intensity of effort is seriously impaired through malnutrition or lack of common preventive medicine.

5. *The unproductive*—people who can provide the human resources necessary for productive work but who struggle long hours with inadequate complementary resources to make their inputs yield even the essentials of life.

Although all these manifestations of the underutilization of labor in LDCs are highly interrelated and each in its own way is of considerable significance, we shall for convenience limit our discussion throughout the remainder of this chapter to the specific problems of unemployment and underemployment.

Linkages among Unemployment, Poverty, and Income Distribution

A close relationship exists between high levels of unemployment and underemployment, widespread poverty, and unequal distributions of income. Table 7.7 clearly reveals this linkage in five Latin American countries. We see that 47% to 65% of the unemployed are concentrated in the bottom two quintiles of the income distribution scale, while unemployment rates among the bottom 40% are three to four times the amount of those of the top 40%.

For the most part, people without regular employment or with only scattered part-time employment are also among the very poor. Those with regular paid employment in the public and private sectors are typically among the middle- and upper-income groups. But it would be wrong to assume that everyone who does

TABLE 7.7 Unemployment and Income Distribution in Latin America						
	Income quintile					
Country	First	Second	Third	Fourth	Fifth	Total
Distribution of the unemployed by income quintile (percent)						
Brazil	40.4	24.5	16.7	13.2	5.2	100
Colombia	31.2	25.7	19.7	14.7	8.4	100
Costa Rica	31.1	21.9	25.6	14.4	6.8	100
Panama	33.6	29.9	22.0	12.9	1.4	100
Venezuela	21.9	25.6	25.6	17.2	11.3	100
Unemployment rates per income quintile (percent)						
Brazil	9.3	4.8	3.3	2.7	1.1	
Colombia	22.1	18.3	12.9	9.0	5.3	
Costa Rica	10.0	7.3	6.0	3.9	1.8	
Panama	19.1	12.3	8.8	4.9	0.6	
Venezuela	13.2	12.4	10.6	8.0	5.5	

SOURCE: David Turnham, *Employment and Development: A New Review of Evidence* (Paris: Organization for Economic Cooperation and Development, 1993), tab. 2.8. Reprinted with permission.

not have a job is necessarily poor or that all who work full time are relatively well-off. There may be unemployed urban workers who are voluntarily unemployed in the sense that they are searching for a very specific kind of job, perhaps because of high expectations based on their presumed educational or skill qualifications (see Table 7.3). They refuse to accept jobs they feel to be inferior and are able to do this because they have outside sources of financial support (relatives, friends, local moneylenders). Such people are unemployed by definition, but they may not be poor. By the same token, many individuals may work full time in terms of hours per day but may nevertheless earn very little income. Many self-employed workers in the urban **informal sector** (e.g., traders, hawkers, petty service providers, workers in repair shops) may be so classified (see Chapter 8). Such people are by definition fully employed, but often they are still very poor.

In spite of these reservations about a too literal linkage between unemployment and poverty, it still remains true that one of the major mechanisms for reducing poverty and inequality in less developed nations is the provision of adequate-paying, productive employment opportunities for the very poor. As we saw in Chapter 5, the creation of more employment opportunities should not be regarded as the sole solution to the poverty problem. More far-reaching economic and social measures are needed. But the provision of more work and the wider sharing of the work that is available would certainly go a long way toward solving the problem. Employment must therefore be an essential ingredient in any poverty-focused development strategy.

The Phenomenon of Jobless Growth and the Output–Employment Lag

During the 1960s, one of the major doctrines of the development literature was that successful economic development could be realized only through the twin forces of substantial capital accumulation and rapid industrial growth. By concentrating on the development of a modern industrial sector to serve the domestic market and to facilitate the absorption of "redundant" or "surplus" rural laborers in the urban economy, less developed countries, it was argued, could proceed most rapidly toward the achievement of considerable economic self-sufficiency. As we will discover in Chapter 8, an inevitable consequence of this emphasis has been the extraordinary growth of urban centers resulting from an accelerated influx of rural, unskilled workers in search of urban jobs.

Unfortunately, optimistic predictions regarding the ability of the modern industrial sector to absorb these migrants have not always been realized. In fact, the failure of modern urban industries to generate a significant number of employment opportunities is one of the most obvious failures of the development process over the past few decades. For example, as Table 7.8 shows, for many developing countries, the growth of manufacturing output, even during the rapid-growth years of the 1960s, exceeded the growth of employment by a factor of 3 or 4 to 1. For the majority of LDCs, this phenomenon of **jobless growth** or what has more formally been called the **output-employment lag** continued into the 1980s, when output growth slowed and real wages declined, particularly in Africa and Latin America. And it is projected to continue further to the year 2000 as shown in Table 7.9.

Too much emphasis, however, cannot be placed on the expansion of the modern industrial sector to solve the unemployment problem. The reason is that in most Third World countries, it employs only 10% to 20% of the total labor force. For example, if the manufacturing sector employs, say, 20% of the country's labor force, it would need to increase employment by 15% per year just to absorb the increase in a total workforce growing at 3% per year ($0.2 \times 0.15 = 0.03$). None of the countries in Table 7.8 has yet been able to achieve such a high rate of employment growth in its manufacturing sector. In fact, such industrial employment growth is virtually impossible to achieve in any economy.

Again the contrast between the present urban situation in LDCs and the historical situation in the now more developed countries is worth noting. In nineteenth-century Western Europe, the pace of **industrialization** was much faster than that of urbanization. The percentage of the workforce in industry was always higher than that of the population living in cities. For example, in France in 1850, only 10% of the total population lived in cities of 20,000 inhabitants and more, but 20% of the workforce was engaged in manufacturing. In Germany in 1870, the corresponding figures were 12% and 30%, respectively. As the labor forces of both France and Germany were growing at no more than 1% per annum over this period, the manufacturing sector needed to grow at a rate of only 3.3% to absorb the total yearly labor force increases.

By contrast, the pace of industrialization in less developed countries has been much slower than that of urbanization. In almost all Third World countries, the

TABLE 7.8 Industrialization and Employment in Developing Countries, 1963–1969

Country	Manufacturing Annual Output Growth (percent)	Manufacturing Employment Growth (percent)
Africa		
Egypt	11.2	0.7
Ethiopia	12.8	6.4
Kenya	6.4	4.3
Nigeria	14.1	5.3
Asia		
India	5.9	5.3
Pakistan	12.3	2.6
Philippines	6.1	4.8
Thailand	10.7	−12.0
Latin America		
Brazil	6.5	1.1
Colombia	5.9	2.8
Costa Rica	8.9	2.8
Dominican Republic	1.7	−3.3
Ecuador	11.4	6.0
Panama	12.9	7.4

SOURCE: David Morawetz, "Employment implications of industrialization in developing countries," *Economic Journal* 84 (September 1974). Reprinted with permission.

percentage of the population living in cities greatly exceeds the proportion engaged in manufacturing. For example, in 1990, Brazil had over 71% of its population living in urban areas of 500,000 or more, but only 20% of its people were engaged in manufacturing. Colombia had an urbanization rate of almost 68% but only 17% of its population engaged in manufacturing.[8] Given these very different demographic and structural economic circumstances, it would be unrealistic to rely solely on accelerated modern-sector industrial growth to solve the problems

TABLE 7.9 Jobless Growth: GDP and Employment, 1990–2000 (1975 = 100)

Region	1990 (actual)		2000 (projected)	
	GDP	Employment	GDP	Employment
Sub-Saharan Africa	141	121	196	150
Latin America	143	131	191	148
South Asia	198	137	299	154
East Asia	304	183	518	256

SOURCE: Data from United Nations Development Program, *Human Development Report, 1993* (New York: Oxford University Press, 1993), fig. 3.2.

of growing unemployment, even if such growth were to have a substantial labor-using bias, which it usually doesn't, and even if rapid industrial output growth were to reappear.

Economic Models of Employment Determination

Over the years, economists have formulated a number of economic models of employment determination. The majority of these models have focused on or been derived from the social, economic, and institutional circumstances of the developed nations. They have nevertheless often been uncritically and inappropriately applied to the unique circumstances of employment problems in developing countries. In recent years, the use of more relevant and realistic models of employment and development has often led to policy conclusions diametrically opposite to those of the traditional theories.

We will review three economic models of employment determination. The first, the **free-market classical model**, forms the substance of the traditional theory of employment. The second and third models grow out of the more recent neoclassical tradition of economics. The second, the **output-employment macro model**, focuses on the relationship among capital accumulation, industrial output growth, and employment generation. The third, the **price-incentive micro model**, considers the impact of distorted factor prices on resource (especially labor) utilization. Both the output-employment and price-incentive models concentrate exclusively on the demand side of the employment equation; they focus on policies to increase labor demand. A fourth model or group of models, which we designate as *two-sector labor transfer* or **rural-urban migration models**, focus on the determinants of both demand and supply. These will be the subject of Chapter 8. Even more than neoclassical equilibrium models (although still in the same tradition), the *disequilibrium labor-transfer migration models* seek to take purposeful account of the institutional and economic realities of Third World nations.

We conclude this chapter, therefore, by examining the first three of the above four models of employment determination and then devote some considerable space in the next chapter to the fourth.[9]

The Traditional Competitive Free–Market Model

Flexible Wages and Full Employment

In traditional free-market economics—characterized by consumer sovereignty, individual utility and profit maximization, perfect competition, and economic efficiency with many "atomistic" producers and consumers, none of whom is large enough to influence prices or wages—the level of employment and the wage rate are determined simultaneously with all other prices and factor uses in the economy by the forces of demand and supply. Producers demand more workers as long as the value of the marginal product produced by an additional worker (that worker's physical marginal product multiplied by the market price of the product he or she produces) exceeds his or her cost (the going wage rate). As the law of diminishing marginal product is assumed to apply and as product prices are fixed by the market, the value of labor's marginal product and thus the demand curve for labor will be negatively sloped, as shown in Figure 7.1. More workers will be hired only at successively lower wage rates.

On the supply side, individuals are assumed to operate on the principle of utility maximization. They will therefore divide their time between work and leisure in accordance with the relative marginal utility of each. A rise in wage rates is equivalent to an increase in the price (or opportunity cost) of leisure. When the price of any item rises, its quantity demanded will ordinarily decrease, and other items will be substituted. It follows that more labor services will be supplied at successively higher wage rates, so that the aggregate supply curve of labor will be positively sloped. This supply curve is also depicted in Figure 7.1.

We see from Figure 7.1 that only at one point, the **equilibrium wage rate** W_e, will the amount of work that individuals are willing to supply just equal the amount that employers will demand. At any higher wage, like W_2, the supply of labor will exceed its demand, and competitive pressures among workers will force the wage rate down to W_e. At any lower price, like W_1, the labor quantity demanded will exceed the quantity supplied, and competition among producers will drive the wage rate up until it reaches its equilibrium level at W_e. At W_e total employment will be L_e on the horizontal axis. *By definition*, this will be **full employment**—at the equilibrium wage and only at this wage will all people willing to work be able to obtain jobs so that there is no involuntary unemployment. In other words, in the idealized **flexible wages** world of classical free-market economics, there can never be unemployment!

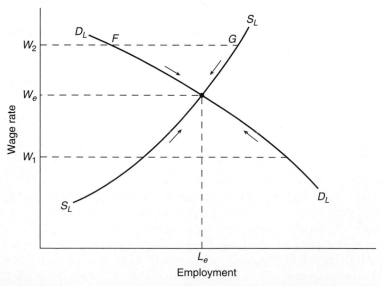

FIGURE 7.1 Wage and Employment Determination by Demand and Supply: The Traditional Free-Market Approach.

Limitations of the Competitive Model
for Developing Countries

The traditional competitive model offers little insight into the realities of wage and employment determination in Third World countries, especially in the modern manufacturing sector and in public-sector employment, where most of the desirable jobs are located.[10] Money wage rates are typically inflexible downward because they are largely determined by institutional forces, such as trade union pressures, legislated government salary scales, and multinational corporation hiring practices. Even though the economic decline of the 1980s in Latin America and Africa, resulting in part from debt-induced government wage repression policies, led in many instances to severe declines in real wages (money wages adjusted for inflation),[11] there were still many more laborers seeking employment at the going wage than there were jobs available. Involuntary unemployment (and, especially, underemployment) is pervasive and inexorably rising. For example, if the wage were institutionally set at W_2 in Figure 7.1, there would be an *excess supply* of labor equal to line FG. The automatic adjustment mechanism of the market would not work to push real wages down to W_e, the equilibrium or "shadow" wage. Even if it did, the assumptions of the competitive model (e.g., that lower real wages result in an increase in the quantity of labor demanded or that all labor and commodity markets clear simultaneously) are rendered empirically suspect by the phenomenon of declining wages, falling employment, and rising unemployment in much of Latin America and Africa in the past decade. Nevertheless, as we will show, this concept of the **shadow price** for a factor of production such as labor, even though it may differ from actual factor prices, still has important analytic meaning for development policy. The classical model, therefore, is useful to the extent that it gives comparative baselines for examining price distortions that can exacerbate unemployment in developing countries.[12]

Output and Employment Growth: Conflict or Congruence?

Growth Models and Employment Levels: The Conflict Argument

A natural extension of the growth models that dominated many theories of development in the 1950s and 1960s (and was evident again in the supply-side environment of the 1980s) focused on policies to increase the levels of national output rapidly through accelerated capital formation. Because these models associated levels of employment uniquely with levels of GNP, it followed that by maximizing the rate of growth of GNP, Third World countries could also maximize their rate of labor absorption. The principal theoretical tool used to describe the growth process was the simple Harrod-Domar model described in Chapter 3. Although many sophisticated variants of this model appeared later, the basic idea remained the same. Economic growth is explained as the combined result of the rate of saving and the resultant physical capital accumulation on the one hand and the capital-output ratio (the physical productivity of new investment) on the other. For a given aggregate capital-output ratio, therefore, the rate of national output and employment growth could be maximized by maximizing the rate of saving and investment. A natural and inevitable outgrowth was the emphasis on generating domestic savings and foreign exchange to make possible heavy capital investments in the growing industrial sector. The "big push" for rapid industrialization thus became the code word for development and growth.[13]

But as we saw in Tables 7.6 and 7.7, in spite of relatively impressive rates of industrial output growth in many less developed countries, the rate of employment growth has lagged significantly behind. In a number of cases it has even stagnated. Why has rapid industrial output growth failed to generate correspondingly rapid rates of employment growth? Why has the **"big push" theory of development** not lived up to its billing?

Basically, the answer lies in the growth in labor productivity. By definition, the rate of growth in output (Y) minus the rate of growth in labor productivity (Y/L) approximately equals the rate of growth of employment (L); that is,

$$\frac{\Delta Y}{Y} - \frac{\Delta(Y/L)}{Y/L} = \frac{\Delta L}{L}.$$

(7.1)

It follows that if output is growing at 8% per year while employment is expanding by only 3%, the difference is due to the rise in labor productivity. The original Harrod-Domar model did not specifically incorporate technological change (although later modifications did). It featured **fixed input coefficients** (it assumed a fixed relationship between changes in output levels and changes in the capital stock). This constant capital-output ratio was then paralleled in early versions of the model by a constant output-labor ratio (a fixed labor coefficient). It follows from this constant labor productivity assumption that a 10% increase in national output (GNP) will always be accompanied by a 10% increase in employment. In reality, if labor productivity is rising, meaning that fewer workers are required to produce any given level of total output, a 10% output growth may only result in, say, a 3% increase in employment.

The phenomenon of rising labor productivity associated with higher capital-labor ratios can be explained better (at least theoretically) with the aid of a variable-proportions neoclassical growth model. Recall that this model of savings, capital accumulation, and economic development—this last term defined simply as maximum output growth—purports to demonstrate that higher capital-labor ratios (more capital-intensive production methods) will generate larger profit shares, higher savings rates, and thus higher rates of growth. The "optimal" savings rate—the one that leads to maximum output growth—can be generated only by relatively capital-intensive methods of production. Maximum output and maximum employment growth are therefore seen as conflicting objectives.

Growth and Employment: The Congruence Argument

In general, increases in labor productivity are desirable. But what is really desirable are increases in total factor productivity: output per unit of all resources. The productivity of labor can increase for a variety of reasons, some good and some not so good. Improved education, better training, and better management are all desirable reasons for increased productivity. But increases as a result of the substitution of capital for labor in production processes or as a result of the importation of sophisticated and expensive laborsaving machinery and equipment (e.g., tractors, power tools, fully automated textile machinery, heavy construction equipment) may be less satisfactory in heavily populated nations. Not only can such capital accumulation waste valuable domestic financial resources and foreign exchange, but it can also curtail the growth of new employment opportunities. Moreover, the importation of inappropriate and expensive laborsaving capital equipment may in fact reduce total factor productivity and thereby increase average costs of production even though it increases labor productivity. In other words, even though average labor costs fall, the average total costs of production may rise because of the underutilized productive capacity that often results when expensive mechanical equipment designed for large-scale production in developed countries is imported into less developed countries where the local market is too small for its efficient use.

Our conclusion, therefore, is that typical Harrod-Domar and neoclassical models of capital accumulation and economic growth, and the kinds of economic policies they imply, can and often do lead to rapid output growth but with lagging employment creation. If the overriding development objective is to maximize the rate of GNP growth, these approaches may be the right ones. But if it is equally or more important to create jobs, different policies (e.g., focusing on the promotion of labor-intensive industries such as small-scale agriculture and manufacturing) may be better.

Moreover, it is far from self-evident that higher levels of employment must necessarily be achieved at the expense of output growth. Just as there is now widespread disagreement with the conventional wisdom of the 1950s and 1960s that assumed that GNP growth and more equitable distributions of income were mutually exclusive objectives, many economists have now come around to the view that an employment-oriented (and therefore, indirectly, a poverty-oriented) development strategy is likely also to be one that *accelerates* rather than retards overall economic progress.[14] This is especially true with regard to the growth and development of the rural and small-scale urban sectors. More employment means more income for the poor, which in turn implies a greater demand for locally produced basic consumption goods. Since these products tend to be more labor-intensive than many of those produced by large-scale industry, both domestic and foreign, it follows that more jobs and higher incomes can become self-reinforcing phenomena. They ultimately lead to higher growth rates of both national output and aggregate employment. But to achieve this dual objective, a complementary policy of removing factor-price distortions and promoting labor-intensive technologies of production may be required. This leads us to the third model of employment determination.

Appropriate Technology and Employment Generation: The Price–Incentive Model

Choice of Techniques: An Illustration

We briefly discussed the question of factor-price distortions and their impact on poverty and employment in Chapter 5 and at other points in earlier chapters. However, because the neoclassical price-incentive school of thought has occupied such a prominent place in the debate about employment problems in developing countries, it is important to reintroduce it here.[15]

The basic proposition of the **neoclassical price-incentive model** is quite simple and in the best tradition of the neoclassical theory of the firm. Following the principle of economy, producers (firms and farms) are assumed to face a given set of relative factor prices (e.g., of capital and labor) and to use the combination of capital and labor that minimizes the cost of producing a desired level of output. They are further assumed to be capable of producing that output with a variety of technological production processes, ranging from highly labor-intensive to highly capital-intensive methods. Thus if the price of capital is very expensive relative to the price of labor, a relatively labor-intensive process will be chosen. Conversely, if labor is relatively expensive, our economizing firm or farm will use a more capital-intensive method of production—it will economize on the use of the expensive factor, which in this case is labor.

The conventional economics of technical choice is portrayed in Figure 7.2. Assume that the firm, farm, industry, or economy in question has only two techniques of production from which to choose: technique or process $0A$, which requires larger inputs of (homogeneous) capital relative to (homogeneous) labor; and technique or process $0B$, which is relatively labor-intensive. Points F and G represent *unit* output levels for each process, and the line Q_1FGQ_1' connecting F and G is therefore a unit-output isoquant. (Note that in the traditional neoclassical model, an infinite number of such techniques or processes are assumed to exist so that the isoquant or equal-product line takes on its typical convex curvature.)

According to this theory, optimum (least-cost) capital-labor combinations (efficient or **appropriate technologies**) are determined by relative factor prices. Assume for the moment that market prices of capital and labor reflect their scarcity or shadow values

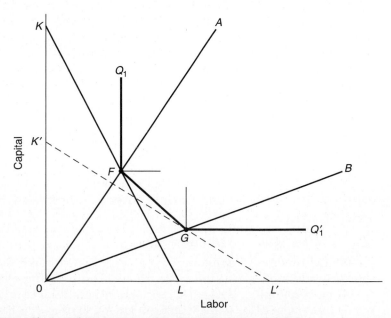

FIGURE 7.2 Choice of Techniques: The Price-Incentive Model.

and that the desired output level is Q_1 in Figure 7.2. If capital is cheap relative to labor (price line *KL*), production will occur at point *F* using capital-intensive process *0A*. Alternatively, if the market prices of labor and capital are such that labor is the relatively cheap (abundant) factor (line *K'L'*), optimal production will occur at point *G*, with the labor-intensive technique, *0B*, chosen. It follows that for any technique of production currently in use, a fall in the relative price of labor, all other things being equal, will lead to a substitution of labor for capital in an optimal production strategy. (Note that if capital-intensive process *0A* "dominates" labor-intensive process *0B*—that is, if technology *0A* requires less labor *and* less capital than *0B* for all levels of output— then for any factor price ratio, the capital-intensive technique will be chosen.)[16]

Factor–Price Distortions and Appropriate Technology

Given that most Third World countries are endowed with abundant supplies of labor but possess very little financial or physical capital, we would naturally expect production methods to be relatively labor-intensive. But in fact we often find production techniques in both agriculture and industry to be heavily mechanized and capital-intensive. Large tractors and combines dot the rural landscape of Asia, Africa, and Latin America while people stand idly by. Gleaming new factories with the most modern and sophisticated automated machinery and equipment are a common feature of urban industries while idle workers congregate outside the factory gates. Surely, this phenomenon could not be the result of a lesser degree of economic rationality on the part of Third World farmers and manufacturers.

The explanation, according to the price-incentive school, is simple. Because of a variety of structural, institutional, and political factors, the actual market price of labor is higher and that of capital is lower than their respective true scarcity, or shadow, values would dictate. In Figure 7.2, the shadow price ratio would be given by line *K'L'*, whereas the actual (distorted) market price ratio is shown by line *KL*. Market wage structures are relatively high because of trade union pressure, politically motivated minimum-wage laws, an increasing range of employee fringe benefits, and the high-wage policies of multinational corporations. In former colonial nations, high-wage structures are often relics of expatriate remuneration scales based on European levels of living and "hardship" premiums. By contrast, the price of (scarce) capital is kept artificially low by a combination of liberal capital depreciation allowances, low or even negative real interest rates, low or negative effective rates of protection on capital goods imports, tax rebates, and overvalued foreign-exchange rates (see Chapter 13).

The net result of these **factor-price distortions** is the encouragement of inappropriate capital-intensive methods of production in both agriculture and manufacturing. Note that from the private-cost-minimizing viewpoint of individual firms and farms, the choice of a capital-intensive technique is correct. It is their rational response to the existing structure of price signals in the market for factors of production. However, from the viewpoint of society as a whole, the social cost of underutilized capital and, especially, labor can be very substantial. Government policies designed to "get the prices right"—that is, to remove factor-price distortions—would contribute not only to more employment but also to a better overall utilization of scarce capital resources through the adoption of more appropriate technologies of production.[17]

The Possibilities of Labor–Capital Substitution

The actual employment impact of removing factor-price distortions will depend on the degree to which labor can be substituted for capital in the production processes of various Third World industries. Economists refer to this as the **elasticity of factor substitution** and define it roughly as the ratio of the percentage change in the proportion of labor used relative to capital (the labor–capital or L/K ratio) compared to a given percentage change in the price of capital relative to labor (P_K/P_L). Algebraically, the elasticity of substitution, η_{LK}, can be defined as follows:

$$\eta_{LK} = \frac{d(L/K)/(L/K)}{d(P_K/P_L)/(P_K/P_L)}. \tag{7.2}$$

For example, if the relative price of capital rises by 1% in the manufacturing sector and the labor-capital ratio rises as a result by, say, 1.5%, the elasticity of substitution in the manufacturing industry will be equal to 1.5. If P_K/P_L falls by, say, 10% while L/K falls by only 6%, the elasticity of substitution for that industry would be 0.6. Relatively high elasticities of substitution (ratios greater than about 0.7) are indicative that factor-price adjustments can have a substantial impact on levels and combinations of factor utilization. In such cases, factor-price modifications may be an important means of generating more employment opportunities.

In general, most empirical studies of the elasticity of substitution for manufacturing industries in less developed countries reveal coefficients in the range 0.5–1.0.[18] These results indicate that a relative reduction in wages (either directly or by holding wages constant while letting the price of capital rise) of, say, 10% will lead to a 5% to 10% increase in employment. But given the fact that the organized wage and manufacturing sector in most LDCs employs only a small proportion of the total labor force, the *total* impact of even a 10% increase in industrial employment will not be sufficient to solve the employment problem. It can, however, make a contribution to the ultimate solution. Policies to eliminate factor-price distortions therefore do have an important role to play in any overall employment-oriented development strategy.

Conclusion

The three economic models of employment reviewed in this chapter provide insights into the complex nature of LDC labor market problems. Taken together, they reveal three things: (1) that factor prices do matter for resource allocation and employment creation; (2) that government policies designed to promote industrialization often at the expense of agricultural growth have typically exacerbated the unemployment and underemployment problems of both urban and rural areas; and (3) that policies intended to stimulate efficient, labor-intensive methods of production need not lead to lower levels of output growth. Finally, the urban bias found in many development strategies has contributed directly and indirectly to both an excessive rate of rural-to-urban migration and a rapid rise in urban unemployment—issues we address in the next chapter.

CASE STUDY

The Economy of Egypt

GEOGRAPHIC, SOCIAL, AND ECONOMIC INDICATORS

Capital Cairo

Area 1,101,258 km^2

Population 61.9 million (1995)

Population (average annual growth rate) 2.0% (1985–1994)

GNP per capita U.S. $710 (1994)

GNP per capita (average annual growth rate) 1.6% (1985–1994)

Agriculture as share of GDP 20% (1994)

Exports as share of GDP 22% (1994)

Infant mortality rate (per 1,000 live births) 62 (1995)

Child malnutrition (underweight) 9% (1993)

Females as share of labor force 11% (1994)

Illiteracy rate (age 15+) 52% (1990)

Human Development Index 0.55 (medium) (1992)

The Arab Republic of Egypt is located in the northeastern corner of the continent of Africa. It is surrounded on the north by the Mediterranean Sea, on the east by Israel and the Red Sea, on the south by Sudan, and on the west by Libya. Egypt encompasses an area of 1.1 million square kilometers. Population figures for 1995 give Egypt's population as 61.9 million, with an annual growth rate of 2.0%. Estimated figures from 1994 give the per capita GNP of Egypt as U.S. $710 with an annual real growth rate of 1.6% between 1985 and 1994.

The terrain in Egypt is mostly desert (96.5%). Cultivated areas take up another 2.8% with inland water making up the difference (0.7%). It is interesting to note that the urban areas are located in the desert. The two major cities are the capital, Cairo, and Alexandria.

The major types of industry in Egypt are food processing, textiles, chemicals, petro-chemicals, construction, light manufacturing, iron and steel, aluminium, cement, and military equipment. Egypt has been endowed with few natural resources. Petroleum and natural gas are the two most important ones. Petroleum is a major export.

The main agricultural products are cotton, rice, onions, beans, citrus fruits, wheat, corn, barley, and sugar. Almost all the farming in Egypt is done in the very fertile Nile Valley. The climate and the ready availability of water in effect double the productivity of each crop. Considering the traditional methods used, productivity is quite high.

Substantial strides have been made in the area of education. But there are problems relating to dropout rates and employment policies. In 1990, the adult literacy rate stood at 48%, despite compulsory schooling from ages 6 to 12. Schooling is free through the university level for students who meet academic standards. An estimated 80% of school-age children enter elementary school, but only half finish the sixth grade. Of those who enter the school system, only 2% graduate from university.

Egypt has a quality health-care system for a country at its general level of economic development. Free medical care is provided through the Ministry of Health's rural units. Egypt's nine state medical schools graduate about 3,500 new physicians each year, fulfilling the need for doctors. The emigration of many doctors to the Arab states, Africa, the United Kingdom, and the United States has contributed to a brain drain. Current life expectancy in Egypt is 61 years. The infant mortality rate is 62 per 1,000 live births.

Although Egypt's private sector is expanding, public-sector enterprises remain predominant in industry and employ about 1.3 million people. Most sizable industries are owned by the state. Only 35% of industrial production and 20% of exports originate in the private sector, but these figures are increasing. The dominant manufacturing activities are food processing and cotton textiles, although the engineering and metallurgical sectors are growing.

The agricultural sector remains mostly private even though it is regulated by the government through price controls, import allocations, and guidelines on production. Egypt relies to a great extent on imports to supply all of its food needs even with the substantial growth of agriculture in recent years. The problem lies in the unavailability of farmland. Only the narrow Nile Valley is suitable for agriculture.

Poverty has not been as pervasive in Egypt as in many other LDCs. However, owing to the 2.0% rate of population growth and the strains of economic transition to a more market-oriented economy, the number of people living in poverty has hovered around the 14 million level for more than two decades. (See Table 5.6.)

Rapid urbanization is a serious problem. Cairo's population will reach 12 million in 2000, more than doubling in a mere 25 years. Some 60% of the population of Cairo lives in slums. Such rapid urbanization is almost certainly to be accompanied by high unemployment.

The current unemployment rate of 20% poses both a social and an economic burden on society. Egypt faces the problems of underemployment of skilled workers and a shortage of skilled artisans and technicians. Most publicly owned factories have been overstaffed in an effort to abolish unemployment. Employment is estimated at 20% to 25% above actual needs in some public-sector jobs. The result has been lower job productivity and exploding government expenditure on public subsidies. In 1993, the government initiated a program to privatize more than 70 state enterprises. But this privatization scheme has resulted in the loss of more than 100,000 jobs, exacerbating an already serious problem of unemployment, especially among young men and women. To combat some of the negative effects of these job losses, the Social Fund for Development was established to protect the most vulnerable groups—unemployed youth, female-headed households, and displaced public-enterprise employees.

The government's policy of guaranteeing a job to all college graduates has also contributed to the surplus-labor problem. This policy has induced students to enter college to secure a high-paying government job. As a result, Egypt has a simultaneous shortage of skilled workers and overstaffing in government jobs.

The problem of a shortage of skilled workers has been made worse by the emigration of skilled personnel to the neighboring oil-rich Arab states. The government is now beginning a concerted effort to develop an independent training program that will increase the supply of skilled workers. Incentives to slow the overseas drain of trained personnel are also needed.

One of the most serious and immediate problems facing Egyptian planners is the shortage of housing units of all types. The urban housing problem has worsened because of the high urban population growth rate. Heavy migration to the cities has played a major role in the crisis. Urban growth is estimated at 4% per year and increasing. In addition, much of the existing housing is of poor quality and lacking in clean water and sanitary facilities.

The problems that Egypt faces will persist. Economic hardships for the nation began in 1986. Falling oil prices and low tourist earnings made it very difficult to service the $38 billion foreign debt that Egypt had accumulated. Fortunately, much of this debt was forgiven following Egypt's active role in the 1991 Persian Gulf War against Iraq. Thereafter, the Egyptian government initiated a major review of economic policy, aimed at promoting a greater role for the private sector. This program enabled Egypt to qualify for additional financial assistance from the International Monetary Fund (IMF). The chronic trade deficit that Egypt has accumulated will be very difficult to deal with. Egypt's major imports are foodstuffs. The desert terrain makes it increasingly difficult to grow the necessary items domestically. As a consequence, Egypt must look to export promotion of manufactured goods as a possible solution. But considering the highly competitive nature of the world market for manufactured exports, it could be in for some difficult times.

The success or failure of the government's Economic Reform and Structural Adjustment Program, however, will hinge not so much on how many public enterprises are privatized or whether the trade deficit and public deficit are reduced. Rather, it will depend on Egypt's ability to control its rising unemployment rates by creating enough jobs to offset its burgeoning labor force. With a population growth rate that adds more than 1.2 million people every year, this will be an enormous task.

Concepts for Review

Age structure of the population	Informal sector
Appropriate technologies	Jobless growth
"Big push" theory of development	Labor force
Complementary resources	Neoclassical price-incentive model
Discouraged workers	Open unemployment
Disguised underemployment	Output-employment lag
Elasticity of factor substitution	Output-employment macro model
Equilibrium wage rate	Premature retirement
Factor-price distortions	Price-incentive micro model
Fixed input coefficients	Rural-urban migration models
Flexible wages	Shadow price
Free-market classical model	Underemployment
Full employment	Underutilization of labor
Hidden unemployment	Urbanization
Industrialization	Voluntary unemployment

Questions for Discussion

1. Discuss the nature of the employment problem in Third World countries. Include in your discussion a review of the various manifestations of the underutilization of labor.

2. Why should we be so concerned with unemployment and underemployment? Why do they constitute a serious development problem?

3. To what extent does traditional economic theory illuminate the employment problems of developing countries? What are some of the limitations? Be specific.

4. What is the relationship, if any, between unemployment (and underemployment) and the problems of poverty and inequality?

5. What are the principal economic reasons for the widespread failure of rapid LDC industrial growth to generate equally rapid employment growth? Is such a large output-employment lag an inevitable result of the process of modern industrial growth? Explain your answer.

Notes

1. It is worth pointing out at this early stage that the same unemployment figures can have different meaning and significance in different parts of the Third World. For example, in Latin America, a 10% measured rate of open unemployment has a somewhat similar significance to that in the United States or Western Europe—people without work and, in the absence of government transfer programs, no visible means of support. By contrast, a 10% rate in Africa or Asia, where extended family ties are much stronger, may be less significant for individuals in the short run. See Vali Jamal and John Weeks, *Africa Misunderstood* (Geneva: International Labor Organization, 1988). I am indebted to Professor John Weeks for his valuable comments on this chapter.

2. For an authoritative and informative annual review of employment and unemployment trends and processes in Third World nations, see International Labor Organization, *World Labor Report* (Geneva: International Labor Organization, various years). The most comprehensive analysis of issues related to employment problems in developing countries can be found in David Turnham, *Employment and Development: A New Review of Evidence* (Paris: Organization for Economic Cooperation and Development, 1993); International Labor Organization, *World Employment Report, 1995* (Geneva: International Labor Organization, 1995); and World Bank, *World Development Report, 1995: Workers in an Integrating World* (New York: Oxford University Press, 1995).

3. Turnham, *Employment and Development*, p. 74.

4. A perceptive discussion of the relationship of population growth, labor supply, and employment can be found in David Bloom and Richard Freeman, "The effects of rapid population growth on labor supply and employment in developing countries," *Population and Development Review* 12 (September 1986): 384–414.

5. United Nations Population Fund, *Population, Resources and the Environment* (New York: United Nations Population Fund, 1991), p. 56.

6. Edgar O. Edwards (ed.), *Employment in Developing Countries* (New York: Columbia University Press, 1974), pp. 10–11.

7. Central Intelligence Agency, *The World Factbook, 1994* (Washington, D.C.: U.S. Government Printing Office, 1994), p. 314.

8. Although it is true that the urbanization ratio exceeds the manufacturing employment ratio for all countries, both developed and developing, in the LDCs this divergence is much greater than in the developed nations. Moreover, in almost all LDCs, the ratio of

the industrial labor force proportion to the urbanization proportion is much lower and is growing more slowly than in the developed countries when they were at a similar stage in their economic evolution.

9. In recent years, there have emerged two new classes of still mostly untested models focusing on the supply side of and wage determination in LDC labor markets, a traditionally weak component of the Keynesian model. A good survey of this new area, including nutrition-based *efficiency-wage* theories and linkages between malnutrition, consumption, and unemployment, can be found in Nicholas Stern, "The economics of development: A survey," *Economic Journal* 99 (September 1989): 657–659.

10. For more detailed arguments in support of this proposition, see Gerry Rodgers, "Labour markets, labour processes and economic development," *Labour and Society* 11 (May 1986): 237–263.

11. For data on the substantial declines in real wages in Latin America, see Eliana Cardoso and Ann Helwege, "Below the line: Poverty in Latin America," *World Development* 20 (January 1992), tab. 4.

12. Many people would also argue that this flexible-wage model provides a useful depiction of LDC labor market interactions in small-scale informal industry and agriculture. Although it is true that wages are more flexible and competitively determined in urban informal and rural traditional industry, the classic concept of full employment is hardly adequate for these purposes.

13. For a modern version of the "big push" theory, see Paul Krugman, "Towards a counter-counterrevolution in development theory," *Proceedings of the World Bank Annual Conference on Development Economics, 1992* (Washington, D.C.: World Bank, 1993): 15–38.

14. For one of the best-known arguments that output growth and employment creation are congruent rather than conflicting development objectives, see Paul P. Streeten and Frances Stewart, "Conflicts between output and employment objectives in developing countries," *Oxford Economic Papers* 11 (July 1979): 145–168. For more recent discussions and evidence, see David Turnham, *Employment and Development*, chap. 6; Alberto Alesina and Roberto Perotti, "The political economy of growth: A critical survey of recent literature," *World Bank Economic Review* 8 (September 1994): 351–371; Louis Emmerij, "The employment problem and the international economy," *International Labour Review* 133 (December 1994): 449–466; and Paul P. Streeten, *Strategies for Human Development: Global Poverty and Unemployment* (Copenhagen: Handelshøjskolens Forlag, 1994).

15. For a literature survey of appropriate technology and factor-price distortions, see Henry Bruton, "Technology choice and factor proportions problems in LDCs," in Norman Gemmell (ed.), *Surveys in Development Economics* (Oxford: Blackwell, 1987), chap. 7.

16. This argument as applied to LDCs was first expounded in Richard S. Eckaus's seminal article "The factor proportions problem in underdeveloped areas," *American Economic Review* 45 (September 1955). The existence of dominant technologies that use both less labor and less capital per unit of output, thus causing productivity to rise and employment to fall, raises major policy problems for LDCs. Also, it should be mentioned in passing that whereas the conclusions of the neoclassical price-incentive model may hold at the firm level, they may not be applicable to the economy as a whole. This is known as the "reswitching debate."

17. For an extensive analysis of this issue from a theoretical, empirical, and policy perspective, see Howard Pack, "Industrialization and trade," in Hollis B. Chenery and T. N. Srinivasan (eds.), *Handbook of Development Economics*, vol. 1 (Amsterdam: North Holland, 1988), pp. 334–380.

18. For a useful summary of evidence on this issue, see David Morawetz, "Employment implications of industrialization in developing countries," *Economic Journal* 84 (September 1974). Additional data are contained in Jere Behrman, "Country and sectoral variations in manufacturing elasticities of substitution between capital and labor," in Anne Krueger (ed.), *Trade and Employment in Developing Countries* (Chicago: University of Chicago Press, 1982), and International Labor Organization, *World Labor Report, 1989* (Geneva: International Labor Organization, 1989), tab. 1. Empirical estimates of labor-capital substitution suffer a host of theoretical and econometric problems, so the elasticity figures quoted here should be viewed as indicative of general orders of magnitude, not as precise statistical coefficients.

Further Reading

The literature on Third World employment problems has grown to voluminous proportions over the past few years. Of many excellent surveys, the following are perhaps the best: David Turnham, *Employment and Development: A New Review of Evidence* (Paris: Organization for Economic Cooperation and Development, 1993); Louis Emmerij, "The employment problem and the international economy," *International Labour Review* 133 (December 1994): 449–466; World Bank, *World Development Report, 1995: Workers in an Integrating World* (New York: Oxford University Press, 1995); Richard Jolly *et al.* (eds.), *Third World Employment: Problems and Strategy* (Harmondsworth, England: Penguin, 1973); International Labor Organization, *Employment in Africa: Some Critical Issues* (Geneva: International Labor Organization, 1974); Paul Bairoch, *Urban Unemployment in Developing Countries* (Geneva: International Labor Organization, 1973); Lyn Squire, *Employment Policy in Developing Countries: A Survey of Issues and Evidence* (New York: Oxford University Press, 1981); Dharam Ghai, *Economic Growth, Structural Change and Labour Absorption in Africa, 1960–85* (Geneva: United Nations Research Institute for Social Development, 1987); Albert Berry, "The labour market and human capital in LDCs," in Norman Gemmell (ed.), *Surveys in Development Economics* (Oxford: Blackwell, 1987), chap. 1; and International Labor Oganization, *World Employment Report, 1995* (Geneva: International Labor Organization, 1995).

For comparative and comprehensive country studies of Colombia, Kenya, Sri Lanka, and the Philippines, see the various ILO expert mission reports available from the International Labor Organization in Geneva and its various U.N. distributional outlets in Africa, Asia, and Latin America.

On the question of technology and employment, see especially Frances Stewart, "Technology and employment in LDCs," in Edgar O. Edwards, *Employment in Developing Countries* (New York: Columbia University Press, 1974), pp. 83–132; Amartya Sen, *Employment, Technology and Development* (London: Oxford University Press, 1975); Pradip K. Ghosh (ed.), *Appropriate Technology in Third World Development* (Westport, Conn.: Greenwood Press, 1984); Henry Bruton, "Technology choice and factor proportions problems in LDCs," in Norman Gemmell (ed.), *Surveys in Development Economics* (Oxford: Blackwell, 1987), chap. 7; Bela Balassa, "The interaction of factor and product market distortions in developing countries," *World Development* 16 (April 1988): 449–464; and Howard Pack, *Productivity, Technology, and Industrial Development* (New York: Oxford University Press, 1987).

See also Stephen C. Smith, *Case Studies*, Chapter 10 which focuses on appropriate technology in Kenya and the Philippines.

CHAPTER 8

Urbanization and Rural-Urban Migration: Theory and Policy

The cities are filling up and urban unemployment steadily grows. . . . The "marginal men," the wretched strugglers for survival on the fringes of farm and city, may already number more than half a billion, by 1990 two billion. Can we imagine any human order surviving with so gross a mass of misery piling up at its base?

—Robert S. McNamara, Former President, World Bank

We are firmly persuaded that the most fundamental and promising attack on employment problems in developing countries is in efforts to redress the present urban bias in development strategies.

—Edgar O. Edwards, *Employment in Developing Countries*

In the early 1990s, approximately half the governments of the world, mostly those of developing countries, considered the patterns of population distribution to be unsatisfactory. A key issue was the rapid growth of urban areas.
—Program of Action, 1994 International Conference on Population and Development

The Migration and Urbanization Dilemma

In this chapter, we focus on one of the most perplexing dilemmas of the development process: the phenomenon of massive and historically unprecedented movements of people from the rural countryside to the burgeoning cities of Africa, Asia, and Latin America. In Chapter 6, we documented the extraordinary increase in world and especially Third World population over the past few decades. By 2000, world population could reach 6.3 billion people, and nowhere will population growth be more dramatic than in the major cities of the developing world.

After reviewing trends and prospects for overall urban population growth, we examine in this chapter the growth of the urban informal economy and try to ascertain its potential role and functions. We then turn to a well-known theoretical model of rural-urban labor transfer in the context of rapid growth and high urban unemployment. In the final section, we evaluate various policy options that LDC governments may wish to pursue in their attempts to curtail the heavy flow of rural-to-urban migration and to ameliorate the serious unemployment problems that continue to plague their crowded cities.

Urbanization: Trends and Projections

One of the most significant of all postwar demographic phenomena and the one that promises to loom even larger in the future is the rapid growth of cities in developing countries. In 1950, some 275 million people were living in Third World cities, 38% of the 724 million total urban population. According to U.N. estimates, the world's urban population had reached 2.3 billion by 1990, with 61% (1.4 billion) living in metropolitan areas of developing countries. The United Nations estimates that in 2000, over 2.1 billion, or 66%, of the urban dwellers of the world will reside in less developed regions. This will represent an overall increase of 166%, or 1.32 billion new urbanites in Africa, Asia, and Latin America. Depending on the nature of development strategies pursued, the final total could be substantially higher or lower than the 2.1 billion estimate. Figure 8.1 provides a three-stage portrayal of the projected growth of urban populations in four Third World regions and China between 1950 and 2000; Table 8.1 presents a more detailed statistical breakdown with projections to 2025.

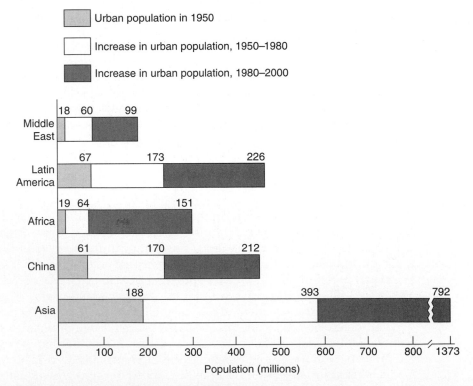

FIGURE 8.1 Urban Population, 1950–2000.

TABLE 8.1 Urban Population in Major World Regions, 1950–2025 (millions)

Region	1950	1960	1970	1980	1990	2000[a]	2025[a]
World	724	1,012	1,352	1,807	2,282	3,208	5,187
More developed regions	449	573	698	834	881	965	1,177
Less developed regions	275	439	654	972	1,401	2,101	4,011
Africa	32	50	83	133	206	331	857
Latin America	68	107	162	241	315	431	592
Asia	218	342	407	596	879	1,291	2,556

SOURCES: United Nations, *Patterns of Urban and Rural Population Growth* (New York: United Nations, 1980); Pii Elina Berghäll, *Habitat II and the Urban Economy: A Review of Recent Developments and Literature* (Helsinki: United Nations University World Institute for Development Economics Research, 1995), tabs. 2 and 4.
[a]Estimate.

With regard to particular cities, current rates of urban population growth range from under 1% per annum in two of the world's largest cities, New York and London, to over 7% per annum in many African cities including Nairobi, Lagos, and Accra. In Asia and Latin America, many cities are growing at rates in excess of 5%. Table 8.2 provides data on the world's 25 largest cities in 1990 with U.N. projections to 2000. Note that only 6 of the 25 are in the developed countries. In 1950, their combined population was 42 million; by 2000, they will have increased in size by 36 million people, a gain of 86%. The remaining 19 cities are located in developing countries and had a combined population of 58 million in 1950. However, in contrast to the moderate growth of developed-nation cities, these 19 urban areas in the Third World are projected to grow by 350%, for an additional 203 million inhabitants. Looking at specific cities, we find that the two largest cities in the year 2000 will be Mexico City and São Paulo, with a projected population of 24.4 and 23.6 million, respectively. Calcutta and Bombay will reach nearly 16 million, Shanghai will approach 15 million, and Tehran, Jakarta, Buenos Aires, Rio de Janeiro, Seoul, Delhi, and Lagos are all expected to surpass 12 million people.

A central question related to the unprecedented size of these urban agglomerations is how these Third World cities will cope—economically, environmentally, and politically—with such acute concentrations of people. While it is true that cities offer the cost-reducing advantages of agglomeration economies and economies of scale and proximity as well as numerous economic and social externalities (e.g., skilled workers, cheap transport, social and cultural amenities), the social costs of a progressive overloading of housing and social services, not to mention increased crime, pollution, and congestion, tend gradually to outweigh these historical urban advantages. Former World Bank president Robert McNamara expressed his skepticism that huge urban agglomerations could be made to work at all:

These sizes are such that any economies of location are dwarfed by costs of congestion. The rapid population growth that has produced them will have far outpaced the growth of human and physical infrastructure needed

TABLE 8.2 Twenty-five Largest Cities, 1990 and 2000		
City	1990 Population (millions)	Projected 2000 Population (millions)
Mexico City, Mexico	19.4	24.4
São Paulo, Brazil	18.4	23.6
Tokyo, Japan	20.5	21.3
New York City, United States	15.7	16.1
Calcutta, India	11.8	15.9
Bombay, India	11.1	15.4
Shanghai, China	12.6	14.7
Tehran, Iran	9.2	13.7
Jakarta, Indonesia	9.4	13.2
Buenos Aires, Argentina	11.6	13.1
Rio de Janeiro, Brazil	11.1	13.0
Seoul, South Korea	11.3	13.0
Delhi, India	8.6	12.8
Lagos, Nigeria	7.6	12.5
Cairo, Egypt	9.1	11.8
Karachi, Pakistan	7.7	11.6
Manila, Philippines	8.4	11.5
Beijing, China	9.7	11.5
Dhaka, Bangladesh	6.4	11.3
Osaka, Japan	10.5	11.2
Los Angeles, United States	10.5	10.9
London, United Kingdom	10.6	10.8
Bangkok, Thailand	7.2	10.3
Moscow, Russia	9.4	10.1
Tianjin, China	8.4	10.0

SOURCE: Population Reference Bureau, *World Population: Fundamentals of Growth* (Washington, D.C.: Population Reference Bureau, 1990). Reprinted with permission.

for even moderately efficient economic life and orderly political and social relationships, let alone amenity for their residents.[1]

Along with the rapid spread of urbanization and the **urban bias** in development strategies, has come the prolific growth of huge slums and shantytowns. From the *favelas* of Rio de Janeiro and the *pueblos jovenes* of Lima to the *bustees* of Calcutta and the *bidonvilles* of Dakar, such makeshift communities have been doubling in size every 5 to 10 years. Today slum settlements represent over one-third of the urban population in all developing countries; in many cases they account for more than 60% of the urban total (see Table 8.3). During the late 1980s, fully 72 out of every 100 new households established in urban areas of developing countries were located in shanties and slums. In Africa, the number was 92 out of every 100. Most of the settlements are without clean water, sewage systems, or electricity. For example, metropolitan Cairo is attempting to cope with a population of 10 million people with a water and sanitation system built to serve 2 million.

TABLE 8.3 Slums and Squatter Settlements as a Percentage of Urban Population

City	Slums as Percentage of City Population
Latin America	
Bogotá, Colombia	60
Mexico City, Mexico	46
Caracas, Venezuela	42
Middle East and Africa	
Addis Ababa, Ethiopia	79
Casablanca, Morocco	70
Ankara, Turkey	60
Cairo, Egypt	60
Kinshasa, Zaire	60
Asia	
Calcutta, India	67
Manila, Philippines	35
Seoul, South Korea	29
Jakarta, Indonesia	26

SOURCE: Population Crisis Committee, *World Population Growth and Global Security,* Report No. 13 (Washington, D.C.: Population Crisis Committee, 1983), p. 2. Reprinted with permission.

Although population growth and accelerated rural-to-urban migration are chiefly responsible for the explosion in urban shantytowns, part of the blame rests with LDC governments. Their misguided policies regarding urban planning and outmoded building codes often means that 80% to 90% of new urban housing is "illegal." For example, colonial-era building codes in Nairobi, Kenya, make it impossible to build an "official" house for less than $3,500. The law also requires every dwelling to be accessible by car. As a result, two-thirds of Nairobi's land is occupied by 10% of the population, while 100,000 slum dwellings cannot legally be improved. Similarly in Manila, Philippines, 88% of the population is too poor to be able to buy or rent an officially "legal" house.[2]

The extent of Third World government concern and even alarm at the trends in urban population growth was vividly revealed in a 1988 United Nations report on population policies in the world.[3] It showed that out of a total of 158 countries, 73, all but five of which were developing nations, considered the geographic distribution of their population "highly unacceptable." Another 66 countries, 42 of them developing, considered their urban population size "unacceptable to a degree." Only six developing countries considered their distribution acceptable. Almost all countries dissatisfied with the size and growth of their urban population believed that internal rural-urban migration was the most prominent factor contributing to city growth. Statistics show that rural migrants constitute anywhere from 35% to 60% of recorded urban population growth (see Table 8.4). Accordingly, 90 out of 116 developing countries responding to the U.N. survey indicated that they had initiated policies to slow down or reverse their accelerating trends in rural-urban migration.

TABLE 8.4 Importance of Rural-Urban Migration as a Source of Urban Population Growth in Selected Developing Countries

Country	Annual Urban Growth (percent)	Share of Growth Due to Migration (percent)
Argentina	2.0	35
Brazil	4.5	36
Colombia	4.9	43
India	3.8	45
Indonesia	4.7	49
Nigeria	7.0	64
Philippines	4.8	42
Sri Lanka	4.3	61
Tanzania	7.5	64
Thailand	5.3	45

SOURCE: K. Newland, *City Limits: Emerging Constraints on Urban Growth*, Worldwatch Paper No. 38 (Washington, D.C.: Worldwatch, 1980), p. 10. Reprinted with permission.

Given the widespread dissatisfaction with rapid urban growth in developing countries, the critical issue that needs to be addressed is the extent to which national governments can formulate development policies that can have a definite impact on trends in urban growth. It is clear that the unquestioning pursuit of the orthodox development strategies of the past few decades, with their emphasis on industrial modernization, technological sophistication, and metropolitan growth, created a substantial geographic imbalance in economic opportunities and contributed significantly to the steadily accelerating influx of rural migrants into urban areas. Is it possible and or even desirable now to attempt to reverse these trends by pursuing a different set of population and development policies? With birthrates beginning to decline in some Third World countries, the serious and worsening problem of rapid urban growth and accelerated rural-urban migration will undoubtedly be one of the most important development and demographic issues of the early twenty-first century. And within urban areas, the growth and development of the informal sector as well as its role and limitations for labor absorption and economic progress will assume increasing importance. A brief look at this unique component of Third World cities is therefore in order.

The Urban Informal Sector

As we learned in Chapter 3, a major focus of development theory has been on the dualistic nature of developing countries' national economies—the existence of a modern urban capitalist sector geared toward capital-intensive, large-scale production and a traditional rural subsistence sector geared toward labor-intensive, small-scale production. In recent years, this dualistic analysis has also been applied specifically to the urban economy, which has been decomposed into a formal and an informal sector.

The existence of an unorganized, unregulated, and mostly legal but unregistered **informal sector** was recognized in the early 1970s following observations in several developing countries that massive additions to the urban labor force failed to show up in formal modern-sector unemployment statistics. The bulk of new entrants to the urban labor force seemed to create their own employment or to work for small-scale family-owned enterprises. The self-employed were engaged in a remarkable array of activities, ranging from hawking, street vending, letter writing, knife sharpening, and junk collecting to selling fireworks, prostitution, drug peddling, and snake charming. Others found jobs as mechanics, carpenters, small artisans, barbers, and personal servants. Still others were highly successful small-scale entrepreneurs with several employees (mostly relatives) and high incomes. Some could even eventually graduate to the formal sector, where they become legally registered, licensed, and subject to government labor regulations. Studies reveal that the share of the urban labor force engaged in informal-sector activities ranges from 20% to 70%, the average being around 50% (see Table 8.5). With the unprecedented rate of growth of the urban population in developing countries expected to continue and with the increasing failure of the rural and urban formal sectors to absorb additions to the labor force, more attention is being devoted to the role of the informal sector in serving as a panacea for the growing unemployment problem.

The informal sector is characterized by a large number of small-scale production and service activities that are individually or family owned and use labor-intensive and simple technology. They tend to operate like monopolistically competitive firms with ease of entry, excess capacity, and competition driving profits (incomes) down to the average supply price of labor of potential new entrants. The usually self-employed workers in this sector have little formal education, are generally unskilled, and lack access to financial capital. As a result, worker productivity and income tend to be lower in the informal sector than in the formal sector. Moreover, workers in the informal sector do not enjoy the measure of protection afforded by the formal modern sector in terms of job security, decent working conditions, and old-age pensions. Most workers entering this sector are recent migrants from rural areas unable to find employment in the formal sector. Their motivation is usually to obtain sufficient income for survival, relying on their own indigenous resources to create work. As many members of the household as possible are involved in income-generating activities, including women and children, and they often work very long hours. Most inhabit shacks that they themselves have built in slums and squatter settlements, which generally lack minimal public services such as electricity, water, drainage, transportation, and educational and health services. Others are even less fortunate. Many millions are homeless, living on the pavements of Calcutta, Manila, Dakar, Nairobi, Rio de Janeiro, and Bogotá—to mention just a few Third World cities. They find sporadic temporary employment in the informal sector as day laborers and hawkers, but their incomes are insufficient to provide even the most rudimentary shelter.

In terms of its relationship with other sectors, the informal sector is linked with the rural sector in that it allows excess labor to escape from rural poverty and underemployment, although under living and working conditions and for incomes that are not much better. It is closely connected with the formal urban sector: The formal sector depends on the informal sector for cheap inputs and wage goods for its workers, and the informal sector in turn depends on the growth of the formal sector for a good portion of its income and clientele. The informal sector also often

TABLE 8.5 Estimated Share of the Urban Labor Force in the Informal Sector in Selected Developing Countries

Area	Share (percent)
Africa	
Abidjan, Ivory Coast	31
Lagos, Nigeria	50
Kumasi, Ghana	60–70
Nairobi, Kenya	44
Urban areas, Senegal	50
Urban areas, Tunisia	34
Asia	
Calcutta, India	40–50
Ahmedabad, India	47
Jakarta, Indonesia	45
Colombo, Sri Lanka	19
Urban areas, western Malaysia	35
Singapore	23
Urban areas, Thailand	26
Urban areas, Pakistan	69
Latin America	
Córdoba, Argentina	38
São Paulo, Brazil	43
Urban areas, Brazil	30
Rio de Janeiro, Brazil	24
Belo Horizonte, Brazil	31
Urban areas, Chile	39
Bogotá, Colombia	43
Santo Domingo, Dominican Republic	50
Guayaquil, Ecuador	48
Quito, Ecuador	48
San Salvador, El Salvador	41
Federal District and State of Mexico	27
Mexico, D.F., Guadalajara, and Monterey	42
Asunción, Paraguay	57
Urban areas, Peru	60
Urban areas, Venezuela	44
Caracas, Venezuela	40
Kingston, Jamaica	33

SOURCE: S. U. Sethuraman, *The Urban Informal Sector in Developing Countries* (Geneva: International Labor Organization, 1981). Copyright © 1981 International Labor Organization, Geneva. Reprinted with permission.

subsidizes the formal sector by providing raw materials and basic commodities for its workers at artificially low prices maintained through the formal sector's economic power and legitimacy granted by the government.

The important role that the informal sector plays in providing income opportunities for the poor is no longer open to debate. There is some question, however, as to whether the informal sector is merely a holding ground for people awaiting entry into the formal sector and, as such, is a transitional phase that must be made as comfortable as possible without perpetuating its existence until it is itself absorbed by the formal sector or whether it is here to stay and should in fact be promoted as a major source of employment and income for the urban labor force.[4]

There seems to be a good argument in support of the latter view. The formal sector in developing countries has a small base in terms of output and employment. In order to absorb future additions to the urban labor force, the formal sector must be able to generate employment at a very high rate of at least 10% per annum, according to estimates made by the International Labor Organization (ILO). This means that output must grow at an even faster rate, since employment in this sector increases less than proportionately in relation to output. This sort of growth seems highly unlikely in view of current trends. Thus the burden on the informal sector to absorb more labor will continue to grow unless other solutions to the urban unemployment problem are provided.

Moreover, the informal sector has demonstrated its ability to generate employment and income for the urban labor force. As pointed out earlier, it is already absorbing an average of 50% of the urban labor force. Some studies have shown the informal sector generating almost one-third of urban income.

Several other arguments can be made in favor of promoting the informal sector. First, scattered evidence indicates that the informal sector generates surplus even under the currently hostile policy environment, which denies it access to the advantages offered to the formal sector such as the availability of credit, foreign exchange, and tax concessions. Thus the informal sector's surplus could provide an impetus to growth in the urban economy. Second, as a result of its low capital intensity, only a fraction of the capital needed in the formal sector is required to employ a worker in the informal sector, offering considerable savings to developing countries so often plagued with capital shortages. Third, by providing access to training and apprenticeships at substantially lower costs than that provided by formal institutions and the formal sector, the informal sector can play an important role in the formation of human capital. Fourth, the informal sector generates demand for semiskilled and unskilled labor whose supply is increasing in both relative and absolute terms and is unlikely to be absorbed by the formal sector with its increasing demands for a skilled labor force. Fifth, the informal sector is more likely to adopt appropriate technologies and make use of local resources, allowing for a more efficient allocation of resources. Sixth, the informal sector plays an important role in recycling waste materials, engaging in the collection of goods ranging from scrap metals to cigarette butts, many of which find their way to the industrial sector or provide basic commodities for the poor. Finally, promotion of the informal sector would ensure an increased distribution of the benefits of development to the poor, many of whom are concentrated in the informal sector.

Promotion of the informal sector is not, however, without its disadvantages. One of the major disadvantages in promoting the informal sector lies in the strong relationship between rural-urban migration and labor absorption in the informal sector. Migrants from the rural sector have both a lower unemployment rate and a shorter waiting period before obtaining a job in the informal sector. Promoting income and employment opportunities in the informal sector could therefore aggravate the urban unemployment problem by attracting more labor than either the informal or the formal sector could absorb. Furthermore, there is concern over the environmental consequences of a highly concentrated informal sector in the urban areas. Many informal-sector activities cause pollution and congestion (e.g., pedicabs) or inconvenience to pedestrians (e.g., hawkers and vendors). Moreover, increased densities in slums and low-income neighborhoods, coupled with poor urban services, could cause enormous problems for urban areas. Any policy measures designed to promote the informal sector must be able to cope with these various problems.

There has been little discussion in the literature as to what sorts of measures might be adopted to promote the informal sector. The ILO has made some general suggestions. To begin with, governments will have to dispense with the currently hostile attitude toward the informal sector and maintain a more positive and sympathetic posture. For example, in Latin America, bureaucratic red tape and an inordinate number of administrative procedures needed to register a new business typically result in delays up to 240 days in Ecuador, 310 days in Venezuela, and 525 days in Guatemala. Brazil, Mexico, and Chile all require more than 20 applications before a company can be approved for business. These procedures not only cause excessive delays but can also inflate the costs of doing business by up to 70% annually. So informal-sector businesses simply skirt the law.

Because access to skills plays an important role in determining the structure of the informal sector, governments should facilitate training in the areas that are most beneficial to the urban economy. In this way, the government can play a role in shaping the informal sector so that it contains production and service activities that provide the most value to society. Specifically, such measures might promote legal activities, and discourage illegal ones, by providing proper skills and other incentives. It could also generate taxes that now go unpaid.

The lack of capital is a major constraint on activities in the informal sector. The provision of credit would therefore permit these enterprises to expand, produce more profit, and hence generate more income and employment. Access to improved technology would have similar effects. Providing infrastructure and suitable locations for work (e.g., designating specific areas for stalls) could help alleviate some of the environmental consequences of an expanded informal sector. Most important, better living conditions must be provided, if not directly, then by promoting growth of the sector on the fringes of urban areas or in smaller towns where the population will settle close to its new area of work, away from the urban density. Promotion of the informal sector outside the urban areas may also help redirect the flow of rural-urban migration, especially if carried out in conjunction with the policies discussed at the end of this chapter.

Women in the Informal Sector

In some regions of the world, women predominate among rural-urban migrants and may even comprise the majority of the urban population. Though historically many of these women were simply accompanying their spouses, a growing number of unattached women in Latin America, Asia, and Africa migrate to seek economic opportunity. Few of these migrants are able to find employment in the formal sector, which is generally dominated by men. As a consequence, women often represent the bulk of the informal-sector labor supply, working for low wages at unstable jobs with no employee or social security benefits. The increase in the number of single female migrants has also contributed to the rising proportion of urban households headed by women, which tend to be poorer, experience tighter resource constraints, and retain high fertility rates. The changing composition of migration flows has important economic and demographic implications for many urban areas of the Third World.

Because members of female-headed households are generally restricted to low-productivity informal-sector employment and experience higher dependency burdens, they are more likely to be poor and malnourished and less likely to obtain formal education, health care, or clean water and sanitation. Among the Brazilian poor, for example, male-headed households are four times as likely as female-headed households to have access to government-sponsored health services. Dropout rates among children from households headed by women are much higher because they are more likely to be working so as to contribute to household income.

Many women run small business ventures, called *microenterprises*, which require little or no start-up capital and usually involve the marketing of homemade foodstuffs and handicrafts. Though women's restricted access to capital leads to high rates of return on their tiny investments, the extremely low capital-labor ratios confine women to low-productivity undertakings. Studies in Latin America and Asia have found that where credit is available to women with informal-sector microenterprises, repayment rates have been as high as or higher than those for men. And because women are able to make more productive use of capital, their rates of return on investments often exceed those for men.

Despite the impressive record of these credit programs, they remain few in number. The vast majority of institutional credit is channeled through formal-sector agencies, and as a result, women generally find themselves ineligible for small loans. Government programs to enhance income in poor households will inevitably neglect the neediest households so long as governments continue to focus on formal-sector employment of men and allocation of resources through formal-sector institutions. To solve the plight of poor urban women and their children, it is imperative that efforts be made to integrate women into the economic mainstream. Ensuring that women benefit from development programs will require that women's special circumstances be considered in policy design.

The legalization and economic promotion of informal-sector activities, where the majority of the urban female labor force is employed, could greatly improve women's financial flexibility and the productivity of their ventures. However, to enable women to reap these benefits, governments must repeal laws that restrict women's rights to own property, conduct financial transactions, or limit their fertility. Likewise, barriers to women's direct involvement in technical training programs and extension services must be eradicated. And finally, the provision of affordable child-care and family-planning services would lighten the burden of women's reproductive roles and permit them a greater degree of economic participation.

Urban Unemployment

As we have seen, one of the major consequences of the rapid urbanization process has been the burgeoning supply of job seekers into both the modern (formal) and informal sectors of the urban economy. In many developing countries, the supply of workers far exceeds the demand, the result being extremely high rates of unemployment and underemployment in urban areas. Table 8.6 provides some detailed data on urban and rural unemployment for 36 countries. Note that the table focuses solely on rates of open unemployment. It thus excludes the very many more people who are chronically underemployed in the informal sector. The problem is therefore much more serious than even these data suggest. Also, as these statistics are from the 1960s (unfortunately, more recent detailed data for these countries is nonexistent), they are likely to show unemployment rates considerably below current levels, especially in Latin America and sub-Saharan Africa (see Table 2.9 for some 1980s data), where economic decline during the 1980s substantially increased urban unemployment and underemployment.[5] Nevertheless, Table 8.6 indicates that even in the 1960s, before the labor force explosion of the 1970s and 1980s, developing countries had very high rates of open urban unemployment. Nine out of the 36 countries listed had rates above 15%, and 22 countries had rates in excess of 10%.

With the exception of Iran, recorded unemployment was higher in urban areas than in rural areas. For the vast majority of the countries, the urban rate was at least twice as high as the rural rate, and in 47% of the countries, it was three times as high. This is in marked contrast to the situation in developed countries, where urban unemployment has been much lower and where the general tendency has been for urban rates to be lower than rural rates. If we had included scattered information on the very substantial numbers of the urban labor force who were underemployed in part-time informal-sector service activities, the overall figures for urban surplus labor (both openly unemployed and underemployed) would well exceed 30% in many developing countries. Moreover, had we focused on residents in the 15–24 age bracket (the majority of whom are recent migrants), the rate would typically exceed 50%. Because a major contributing factor to both high rates of urban growth and high rates of unemployment is rural-urban migration, it is essential to investigate this critical issue in some detail.

Migration and Development

Until recently, **rural-urban migration** was viewed favorably in the economic development literature. Internal migration was thought to be a natural process in which surplus labor was gradually withdrawn from the rural sector to provide needed manpower for urban industrial growth. The process was deemed socially beneficial because human resources were being shifted from locations where their social marginal product was often assumed to be zero to places where this marginal product was not only positive but also rapidly growing as a result of capital accumulation and technological progress. This process was formalized in the

TABLE 8.6 Rates of Urban and Rural Unemployment as a Percentage of the Active Population

Country	Year	Area	Unemployment (percent) Urban	Unemployment (percent) Rural
Africa				
Algeria	1966	Urban areas	26.6	—
Benin	1968	Urban areas	13.0[a]	—
Burundi	1963	Capital city	18.7[a]	—
Cameroon	1962	Largest city	13.0[a]	—
	1964	Capital city	17.0[a]	—
Ghana	1960	Large towns	12.0	—
	1970	Two large cities	9.0	—
Ivory Coast	1963	Capital city	15.0[a]	—
Kenya	1968–1969	Capital city	10.0[a]	—
	1968–1969	Second largest city	14.0[a]	—
Morocco	1960	Urban areas	20.5	5.4
Nigeria	1963	Urban areas	12.6	—
Sierra Leone	1967	Capital city	15.0	—
Tanzania	1965	Urban areas	7.0	3.9
	1971	Seven towns	5.0[a]	
Zaire	1967	Capital city	12.9	—
Latin America				
Argentina	1968	Capital city	5.4	—
Bolivia	1966	Urban areas	13.2	—
Chile	1968	Urban areas	6.1	2.0
Colombia	1967	Urban areas	15.5	—
Costa Rica	1966–1967	Capital city	5.6	—
El Salvador	1961	Capital city	6.6	—
Guatemala	1964	Capital city	5.4	—
Guyana	1965	Capital city	20.5	—
Honduras	1961	Capital city	7.8	—
Jamaica	1960	Capital city	19.0	12.4
Panama	1960	Urban areas	15.5	3.6
	1967	Urban areas	9.3	2.8
Peru	1964	Capital city	4.2	—
	1969	Capital city	5.2	—
Uruguay	1963	Urban areas	10.9	2.3
Venezuela	1961	Urban areas	17.5	4.3
	1968	Urban areas	6.5	3.1
Asia				
India	1961–1962	Urban areas	3.2	1.7
Indonesia	1961	Urban areas	9.5	—
Iran	1966	Urban areas	5.5	11.3
Malaysia	1967	Western urban areas	11.6	7.4
Philippines	1967	Urban areas	13.1	6.9
Singapore	1966	Urban areas	9.1	—
South Korea	1963–1964	Urban areas	7.0	1.8

(continued)

TABLE 8.6 (*continued*)

Country	Year	Area	Unemployment (percent) Urban	Rural
Sri Lanka	1959–1960	Urban areas	14.3	10.0
Syria	1967	Urban areas	7.3	—
Thailand	1966	Urban areas	2.8	—

SOURCES: Paul Bairoch, *Urban Unemployment in Developing Countries* (Geneva: International Labor Organization, 1973), p. 49; Josef Gugler, *Internal Migration: The New World and the Third World*, ed. A. Richmond and D. Kubat (Beverly Hills, Calif.: Sage, 1976), p. 185.
[a]Men only.

Lewis theory of development discussed in Chapter 3. As Richard Jolly, former director of the Institute of Development Studies at the University of Sussex, has noted:

> Far from being concerned with measures to stem the flow, the major interest of these economists (i.e., those who stressed the importance of labor transfer) was with policies that would *release* labor to *increase* the flow. Indeed, one of the reasons given for trying to increase productivity in the agricultural sector was to release *sufficient* labor for urban industrialization. How irrelevant most of this concern looks today.[6]

In contrast to this viewpoint, it is now abundantly clear from recent LDC experience that rates of rural-urban migration continue to exceed rates of urban job creation and to surpass greatly the absorption capacity of both industry and urban social services. No longer is migration viewed by economists as a beneficent process necessary to solve problems of growing urban labor demand. On the contrary, migration today must be seen as the major factor contributing to the ubiquitous phenomenon of urban surplus labor, as a force that continues to exacerbate already serious urban unemployment problems caused by economic and structural imbalances between urban and rural areas.

Migration exacerbates these rural-urban structural imbalances in two direct ways. First, on the supply side, internal migration disproportionately increases the growth rate of urban job seekers relative to urban population growth, which itself is at historically unprecedented levels, because of the high proportion of well-educated young people in the migrant system. Their presence tends to swell the urban labor supply while depleting the rural countryside of valuable human capital. Second, on the demand side, urban job creation is generally more difficult and costly to accomplish than rural job creation because of the need for substantial complementary resource inputs for most jobs in the industrial sector. Moreover, the pressures of rising urban wages and compulsory employee fringe benefits in combination with the unavailability of appropriate, more labor-intensive production technologies means that a rising share of modern-sector output growth is accounted for by increases in labor productivity. Together this rapid supply increase and lagging demand growth tend to convert a short-run problem of resource imbalances into a long-run situation of chronic and rising urban surplus labor.

But the impact of migration on the development process is much more pervasive than its obvious exacerbation of urban unemployment and underemployment. In fact, the significance of the migration phenomenon in most developing countries is not necessarily in the process itself or even in its impact on the sectoral allocation of human resources. Rather, its significance lies in its implications for economic growth in general and for the character of that growth, particularly its distributional manifestations.

We must recognize at the outset, therefore, that migration in excess of job opportunities is both a symptom of and a contributor to Third World underdevelopment. Understanding the causes, determinants, and consequences of internal rural-urban labor migration is thus central to understanding the nature and character of the development process and to formulating policies to influence this process in socially desirable ways. A simple yet crucial step in underlining the centrality of the migration phenomenon is to recognize that any economic and social policy that affects rural and urban real incomes will directly or indirectly influence the migration process. This process will in turn itself tend to alter the pattern of sectoral and geographic economic activity, income distribution, and even population growth. Because all economic policies have direct and indirect effects on the level and growth of either urban or rural incomes or of both, they all will have a tendency to influence the nature and magnitude of the migration stream. Although some policies may have a more direct and immediate impact (e.g., wages and income policies and employment promotion programs), there are many others that, though less obvious, may in the long run be no less important. Included among these policies, for example, would be land tenure arrangements; commodity pricing; credit allocation; taxation; export promotion; import substitution; commercial and exchange-rate policies; the geographic distribution of social services; the nature of public investment programs; attitudes toward private foreign investors; the organization of population and family-planning programs; the structure, content, and orientation of the educational system; the functioning of labor markets; and the nature of public policies toward international technology transfer and the location of new industries. There is thus a clear need to recognize the central importance of internal and, for many countries, even international migration and to integrate the two-way relationship between migration and population distribution on the one hand and economic variables on the other into a more comprehensive framework designed to improve development policy formulation.

In addition, we need to understand better not only why people move and what factors are most important in their decision-making process but also what the consequences of migration are for rural and urban economic and social development. If all development policies affect migration and are affected by it, which are the most significant, and why? What are the policy options and trade-offs among different and sometimes competing objectives (e.g., curtailing internal migration and expanding educational opportunities in rural areas)? Part of our task in the following sections will be to seek answers to these and other questions relating to migration, unemployment, and development.

Internal Migration in Developing Nations: Some General Facts

An understanding of the causes and determinants of rural-urban migration and the relationship between migration and relative economic opportunities in urban and rural areas is central to any analysis of Third World employment problems. Because migrants comprise a significant proportion of the urban labor force in many developing nations, the magnitude of rural-urban migration has been and will continue to be a principal determinant of the supply of new job seekers. And if migration is a key determinant of the urban labor supply, the migration process must be understood before the nature and causes of urban unemployment can be properly understood. Government policies to ameliorate the urban unemployment problem must be based, in the first instance, on knowledge of who comes to town and why.

The Migration Process

The factors influencing the decision to migrate are varied and complex. Because migration is a selective process affecting individuals with certain economic, social, educational, and demographic characteristics, the relative influence of economic and noneconomic factors may vary not only between nations and regions but also within defined geographic areas and populations. Much of the early research on migration tended to focus on social, cultural, and psychological factors while recognizing, but not carefully evaluating, the importance of economic variables. Emphasis has variously been placed in five broad areas:

1. Social factors, including the desire of migrants to break away from traditional constraints of social organizations

2. Physical factors, including climate and meteorological disasters like floods and droughts

3. Demographic factors, including the reduction in mortality rates and the concomitant high rates of rural population growth

4. Cultural factors, including the security of urban extended-family relationships and the allure of the "bright city lights"

5. Communication factors, including improved transportation, urban-oriented educational systems, and the modernizing impact of the introduction of radio, television, and the cinema

All these noneconomic factors are, of course, relevant. However, there now seems to be widespread agreement among economists and noneconomists alike that rural-urban migration can be explained primarily by the influence of economic factors. These include not only the standard push from subsistence agriculture and the pull of relatively high urban wages but also the potential push back toward rural areas as a result of high urban unemployment.

Migrant Characteristics

It is convenient to divide the main characteristics of migrants into three broad categories: demographic, educational, and economic.

Demographic Characteristics

Urban migrants in Third World countries tend to be young men and women between the ages of 15 and 24. Various studies in Africa and Asia have provided quantitative evidence of this phenomenon in countries such as Kenya, Tanzania, Ghana, Nigeria, India, Thailand, South Korea, and the Philippines. In recent years, the proportion of migrating women has increased as their educational opportunities have expanded. This increase, substantial in many countries, has been particularly evident in Latin America, Southeast Asia, and West Africa. In fact, women now constitute the majority of the migration stream in Latin America, largely as a result of its relatively advanced state of urbanization compared with other developing regions.[7] Basically, there are two types of female migration: the "associational" migration of wives and daughters accompanying the "primary" male migrant and the migration of unattached females. It is the latter type of migration that is increasing most rapidly.

Educational Characteristics

One of the most consistent findings of rural-urban migration studies is the positive correlation between educational attainment and migration. There seems to be a clear association between the level of completed education and the propensity to migrate—people with more years of schooling, everything else being equal, are more likely to migrate than those with fewer. In a comprehensive study of migration in Tanzania by Barnum and Sabot, for example, the relationship between education and migration was clearly documented, especially in terms of the impact of declining urban employment opportunities on the educational characteristics of migrants.[8] High school dropouts were found to constitute a rising proportion of the migration stream. The explanation that Barnum and Sabot offered was that limited urban employment opportunities were being rationed by educational levels, and only workers with at least some secondary education had a chance of finding a job. Those with only a primary school education were finding it very difficult to secure employment, and hence their proportionate numbers in the migrant stream had begun to decline.

Economic Characteristics

For many years, the largest percentage of urban migrants were poor, landless, and unskilled individuals whose rural opportunities were for the most part nonexistent. In colonial Africa, seasonal migration was predominant, with migrants from various income levels seeking short-term urban jobs. Recently, however, with the emergence of a stabilized, modern industrial sector in most urban areas of the less developed countries, the situation has changed. Migrants, both male and female, seem to come from all socioeconomic strata, with the majority being very poor only because most rural inhabitants are poor.

Toward an Economic Theory of Rural–Urban Migration

As we saw in Chapter 4, the economic development of Western Europe and the United States was closely associated with, and in fact defined in terms of, the movement of labor from rural to urban areas. For the most part, with a rural sector dominated by agricultural activities and an urban sector focusing on industrialization, overall economic development in these countries was characterized by the gradual reallocation of labor out of agriculture and into industry through rural-urban migration, both internal and international. Urbanization and industrialization were in essence synonymous. This historical model served as a blue-print for the development of Third World nations, as evidenced, for example, by the original Lewis theory of labor transfer (see Chapter 3).

But the overwhelming evidence of the 1960s and 1970s, when Third World nations witnessed a massive migration of their rural populations into urban areas despite rising levels of urban unemployment and underemployment, lessens the validity of the Lewis two-sector model of development.[9] An explanation of the phenomenon, as well as policies to address the resulting problems, must be sought elsewhere. In a series of articles, I have attempted to develop a theory of rural-urban migration to explain the apparently paradoxical relationship (at least to economists) of accelerated rural-urban migration in the context of rising urban unemployment.[10] This theory has come to be identified in the literature as the **Todaro migration model**.

A Verbal Description of the Todaro Model

Starting from the assumption that migration is primarily an economic phenomenon, which for the individual migrant can be a quite rational decision despite the existence of urban unemployment, the Todaro model postulates that migration proceeds in response to urban-rural differences in **expected income** rather than actual earnings. The fundamental premise is that migrants consider the various labor market opportunities available to them in the rural and urban sectors and choose the one that maximizes their expected gains from migration. Expected gains are measured by the difference in real incomes between rural and urban work and the probability of a new migrant's obtaining an urban job. A schematic framework showing how the varying factors affecting the migration decision interact is given in Figure 8.2.

In essence, the theory assumes that members of the labor force, both actual and potential, compare their expected incomes for a given time horizon in the urban sector (the difference between returns and costs of migration) with prevailing average rural incomes and migrate if the former exceeds the latter.

Consider the following illustration. Suppose that the average unskilled or semi-skilled rural worker has a choice between being a farm laborer (or working his own land) for an annual average real income of, say, 50 units or migrating to the city, where a worker with his skill or educational background can obtain wage employment yielding an annual real income of 100 units. The more commonly used economic models of migration, which place exclusive emphasis on the income

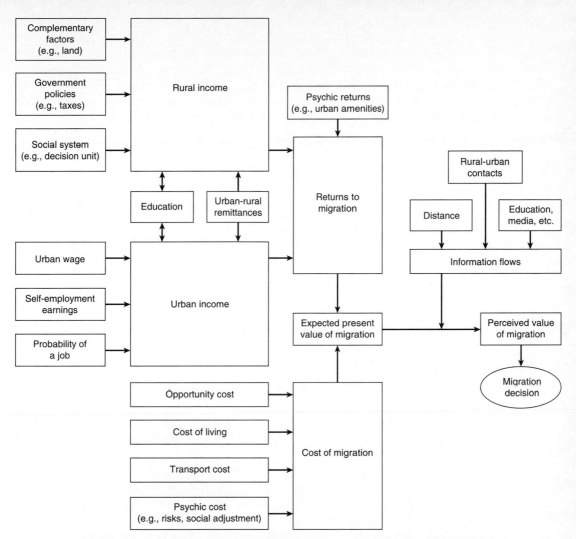

FIGURE 8.2 Schematic Framework for Analyzing the Migration Decision. *Source*: Derek Byerlee, "Rural-urban migration in Africa: Theory, policy, and research implications," *International Migration Review* 3 (Winter 1974): 553. Reprinted with permission.

differential factor as the determinant of the decision to migrate, would indicate a clear choice in this situation. The worker should seek the higher-paying urban job. It is important to recognize, however, that these migration models were developed largely in the context of advanced industrial economies and hence implicitly assume the existence of full or near-full employment. In a full-employment environment, the decision to migrate can be based solely on the desire to secure the highest-paid job wherever it becomes available. Simple economic theory would then indicate that such migration should lead to a reduction in wage differentials through the interaction of the forces of supply and demand, in areas of both emigration and immigration.

Unfortunately, such an analysis is not realistic in the context of the institutional and economic framework of most Third World nations. First, these countries are beset by a chronic unemployment problem so that a typical migrant cannot expect to secure a high-paying urban job immediately. In fact, it is much more likely that on entering the urban labor market, many uneducated, unskilled migrants will either become totally unemployed or will seek casual and part-time employment as vendors, hawkers, repairmen, and itinerant day laborers in the urban traditional or informal sector, where ease of entry, small scale of operation, and relatively competitive price and wage determination prevail. In the case of migrants with considerable human capital in the form of a secondary or university certificate, opportunities are much better, and many will find formal-sector jobs relatively quickly. But they constitute only a small proportion of the total migration stream. Consequently, in deciding to migrate, the individual must balance the probabilities and risks of being unemployed or underemployed for a considerable period of time against the positive urban-rural real income differential. The fact that a typical migrant can expect to earn twice the annual real income in an urban area than in a rural environment may be of little consequence if the actual probability of his securing the higher-paying job within, say, a one-year period is one chance in five. Thus the actual probability of his being successful in securing the higher-paying urban job is 20%, and therefore his expected urban income for the one-year period is in fact 20 units and not the 100 units that an urban worker in a full-employment environment would expect to receive. So with a one-period time horizon and a probability of success of 20%, it would be irrational for this migrant to seek an urban job, even though the differential between urban and rural earnings capacity is 100%. However, if the probability of success were 60% and the expected urban income therefore 60 units, it would be entirely rational for our migrant with his one-period time horizon to try his luck in the urban area, even though urban unemployment may be extremely high.

If we now approach the situation by assuming a considerably longer time horizon—a more realistic assumption, especially in view of the fact that the vast majority of migrants are between the ages of 15 and 24—the decision to migrate should be represented on the basis of a longer-term, more permanent income calculation. If the migrant anticipates a relatively low probability of finding regular wage employment in the initial period but expects this probability to increase over time as he is able to broaden his urban contacts, it would still be rational for him to migrate, even though expected urban income during the initial period or periods might be lower than expected rural income. As long as the **present value** of the net stream of expected urban income over the migrant's planning horizon exceeds that of the expected rural income, the decision to migrate is justifiable. This, in essence, is the process portrayed in Figure 8.2.

Rather than equalizing urban and rural wage rates, as would be the case in a competitive model, we see that rural-urban migration in our model acts as an equilibrating force that equates rural and urban expected incomes. For example, if average rural income is 60 and urban income is 120, a 50% urban unemployment rate would be necessary before further migration would no longer be profitable. Because expected incomes are defined in terms of both wages and employment probabilities, it is possible to have continued migration despite the existence of sizable rates of urban unemployment. In our example, migration would continue even if the urban unemployment rate were 30% to 40%.

A Diagrammatic Presentation

This process of achieving an unemployment equilibrium between urban expected wages and average rural income rather than an equalized rural-urban wage as in the traditional neoclassical free-market model (see Figure 7.1) can also be explained by a diagrammatic portrayal of the basic Todaro model. This is done in Figure 8.3.[11] Assume only two sectors, rural agriculture and urban manufacturing. The demand for labor (the marginal product of labor curve) in agriculture is given by the negatively sloped line AA'. Labor demand in manufacturing is given by MM' (reading from right to left). The total labor force is given by line $O_A O_M$. In a neoclassical, flexible-wage, full-employment market economy, the equilibrium wage would be established at $W_A^* = W_M^*$, with $O_A L_A^*$ workers in agriculture and $O_M L_M^*$ workers employed in urban manufacturing. All available workers are therefore employed.

But what if urban wages are institutionally determined (inflexible downward) as assumed by Todaro at a level $\overline{W}_M$, which is at a considerable distance above W_A^*? If for the moment we continue to assume that there is no unemployment, $O_M L_M$ workers would get urban jobs, and the rest, $O_A L_M$, would have to settle for rural employment at $O_A W_A^{**}$ wages (below the free-market level of $O_A W_A^*$). So now we have an urban-rural real wage gap of $\overline{W}_M - W_A^{**}$, with $\overline{W}_M$ institutionally fixed. If rural workers were free to migrate (as they are almost everywhere except China),

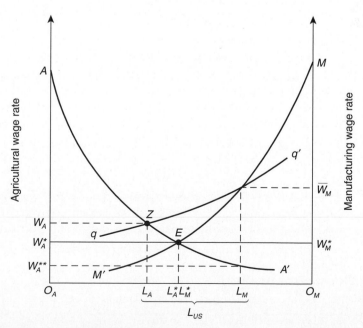

FIGURE 8.3 The Todaro Migration Model.

then despite the availability of only $O_M L_M$ jobs, they are willing to take their chances in the urban job lottery. If their chance (probability) of securing one of these favored jobs is expressed by the ratio of employment in manufacturing, L_M, to the total urban labor pool, L_{US}, then the expression

$$W_A = \frac{L_M}{L_{US}}(\overline{W}_M) \tag{8.1}$$

shows the probability of urban job success necessary to equate agricultural income W_A with urban expected income $(L_M/L_{US})(\overline{W}_M)$ thus cause a potential migrant to be indifferent between job locations. The locus of such points of indifference is given by the qq' curve in Figure 8.3.[13] The new unemployment equilibrium now occurs at point Z, where the urban-rural actual wage gap is $\overline{W}_M - W_A$, $O_A L_A$ workers are still in the agricultural sector, and $O_M L_M$ of these workers have modern (formal)-sector jobs paying $\overline{W}_M$ wages. The rest $L_{US} = O_M L_A - O_M L_M$ are either unemployed or engaged in low-income informal-sector activities. This explains the existence of urban unemployment and the private economic rationality of continued rural-to-urban migration despite this high unemployment. However, although it may be privately rational from a cost-benefit perspective for an individual to migrate to the city despite high unemployment, it can, as we shall soon discover, be socially very costly. Finally, note that if instead of assuming that all urban migrants are the same, we incorporate the reality of different levels of human capital (education), we can understand why a higher proportion of the rural educated migrate than the uneducated—because they have a better chance (a higher probability) of earning even higher urban wages than unskilled migrants.

To sum up, the Todaro migration model has four basic characteristics:

1. Migration is stimulated primarily by rational economic considerations of relative benefits and costs, mostly financial but also psychological.

2. The decision to migrate depends on expected rather than actual urban-rural real wage differentials where the expected differential is determined by the interaction of two variables, the actual urban-rural wage differential and the probability of successfully obtaining employment in the urban sector.

3. The probability of obtaining an urban job is directly related to the urban employment rate and thus inversely related to the urban unemployment rate.

4. Migration rates in excess of urban job opportunity growth rates are not only possible but also rational and even likely in the face of wide urban-rural expected-income differentials. High rates of urban unemployment are therefore inevitable outcomes of the serious imbalance of economic opportunities between urban and rural areas in most underdeveloped countries.

Five Policy Implications

Although the Todaro theory might at first seem to devalue the critical importance of rural-urban migration by portraying it as an adjustment mechanism by which workers allocate themselves between rural and urban labor markets, it does have important policy implications for development strategy with regard to wages and incomes, rural development, and industrialization.

First, imbalances in urban-rural employment opportunities caused by the urban bias of development strategies must be reduced. Because migrants are assumed to respond to differentials in expected incomes, it is vitally important that imbalances between economic opportunities in rural and urban sectors be minimized. Permitting urban wage rates to rise at a greater pace than average rural incomes will stimulate further rural-urban migration in spite of rising levels of urban unemployment. This heavy influx of people into urban areas not only gives rise to socioeconomic problems in the cities but may also eventually create problems of labor shortages in rural areas, especially during the busy seasons. These social costs may exceed the private benefits of migration.

Second, urban job creation is an insufficient solution for the urban unemployment problem. The traditional (Keynesian) economic solution to urban unemployment (the creation of more urban modern-sector jobs without simultaneous attempts to improve rural incomes and employment opportunities) can result in the paradoxical situation where more urban employment leads to higher levels of urban unemployment! Once again, the imbalance in expected income-earning opportunities is the crucial concept. Because migration rates are assumed to respond positively to *both* higher urban wages *and* higher urban employment opportunities (or probabilities), it follows that for any given positive urban-rural wage differential (in most LDCs, urban wages are typically three to four times as large as rural wages), higher urban employment rates will widen the expected differential and induce even higher rates of rural-urban migration. For every new job created, two or three migrants who were productively occupied in rural areas may come to the city. Thus if 100 new jobs are created, there may be as many as 300 new migrants and therefore 200 more urban unemployed. Hence a policy designed to reduce urban unemployment may lead not only to higher levels of urban unemployment but also to lower levels of agricultural output, due to **induced migration**.

Third, indiscriminate educational expansion will lead to further migration and unemployment. The Todaro model also has important policy implications for curtailing investment in excessive educational expansion, especially at the higher levels. The heavy influx of rural migrants into urban areas at rates much in excess of new employment opportunities has necessitated a rationing device in the selection of new employees. Although within each educational group such selection may be largely random, many observers have noted that employers tend to use educational attainment or number of years of completed schooling as the typical rationing device. For the same wage, they will hire people with more education in preference to those with less, even though extra education may not contribute to better job performance. Jobs that could formerly be filled by those with a primary education (sweepers, messengers, filing clerks, etc.) now require secondary training; those formerly requiring a secondary certificate (clerks, typists, bookkeepers, etc.) must now have a university degree. It follows that for any given urban wage, if the probability of success in securing a modern-sector job is higher for people with more education, their expected income differential will also be higher, and they will be more likely to migrate to the cities. The basic Todaro model therefore provides an economic rationale for the observed fact in most LDCs that rural inhabitants with more education are more likely to migrate than those with less.

From the viewpoint of educational policy, it is safe to predict that as job opportunities become scarce in relation to the number of applicants, students will experience increasing pressure to proceed further up the educational ladder. The private demand for education, which in many ways is a derived demand for urban jobs, will continue to exert tremendous pressure on governments to invest in postprimary school facilities. But for many of these students, the specter of joining the ranks of the "educated unemployed" becomes more of a reality with each passing year. Government overinvestment in postprimary educational facilities thus often turns out to be an investment in idle human resources. Chapter 11 will focus on this and other issues related to the economics of education in greater detail.

Fourth, wage subsidies and traditional scarcity factor pricing can be counterproductive. As we have seen in Chapter 7, a standard economic policy prescription for generating urban employment opportunities is to eliminate factor-price distortions by using "correct" prices, perhaps implemented by wage subsidies (fixed government subsidies to employers for each worker employed) or direct government hiring. Because actual urban wages generally exceed the market or "correct" wage as a result of a variety of institutional factors, it is often argued that the elimination of wage distortions through price adjustments or a subsidy system will encourage more labor-intensive modes of production. Although such policies can generate more labor-intensive modes of production, they can also lead to higher levels of unemployment in accordance with our argument about induced migration. The overall welfare impact of a **wage subsidy** policy when both the rural and urban sectors are taken into account is not immediately clear. Much will depend on the level of urban unemployment, the size of the urban-rural expected-income differential, and the magnitude of induced migration as more urban jobs are created.

Finally, programs of integrated rural development should be encouraged. Policies that operate only on the demand side of the urban employment picture, such as wage subsidies, direct government hiring, elimination of factor-price distortions, and employer tax incentives, are probably far less effective in the long run in alleviating the unemployment problem than policies designed directly to regulate the supply of labor to urban areas. Clearly, however, some combination of both kinds of policies is most desirable.

Policies of rural development are crucial to this aim. Many informed observers agree on the central importance of rural and agricultural development if the urban unemployment problem is to be solved. Most proposals call for the restoration of a proper balance between rural and urban incomes and for changes in government policies that currently give development programs a strong bias toward the urban industrial sector (e.g., policies in the provision of health, education, and social services).

Given the prevailing urban bias and thus the political difficulties of reducing urban-rural real-wage differentials, the need continuously to expand urban employment opportunities through judicious investments in small- and medium-scale labor-intensive industries, and the inevitable growth of the urban industrial sector, every effort must be made to broaden the economic base of the rural economy. The present unnecessary economic incentives for rural-urban migration must be minimized through creative and well-designed programs of integrated rural development. These should focus on both farm and nonfarm income generation, employment growth, health-care delivery, educational improvement, infrastructure development (electricity, water, roads, etc.), and the provision of other rural amenities. Successful rural development programs adapted to the socioeconomic and environmental needs of particular countries and regions seem to offer the only viable long-run solution to the problem of excessive rural-urban migration.

To assert, however, that there is an urgent need for policies designed to curb the excessive influx of rural migrants is not to imply an attempt to reverse what some observers have called inevitable historical trends. Rather, the implication of the Todaro migration model is that there is a growing need for a policy package that does not exacerbate these historical trends toward urbanization by artifically creating serious imbalances in economic opportunities between urban and rural areas.

Summary and Conclusions: The Shape of a Comprehensive Migration and Employment Strategy

At various points throughout this chapter and Chapter 7, we have looked at possible policy approaches designed to improve the very serious migration and employment situation in Third World countries. We conclude with a summary of what appears to be the consensus of most economists on the shape of a comprehensive migration and employment strategy.[14] This would appear to have six key elements:

1. *Creating an appropriate rural-urban economic balance.* A more appropriate balance between rural and urban economic opportunities appears to be indispensable to ameliorating both urban and rural unemployment problems and to slowing the pace of rural-urban migration. The main thrust of this activity should be in the integrated development of the rural sector, the spread of small-scale industries throughout the countryside, and the reorientation of economic activity and social investments toward the rural areas.

2. *Expansion of small-scale, labor-intensive industries.* The composition or "product mix" of output has obvious effects on the magnitude (and, in many cases, the location) of employment opportunities because some products (often basic consumer goods) require more labor per unit of output and per unit of capital than others. Expansion of these mostly small-scale and labor-intensive industries in both urban and rural areas can be accomplished in two ways: directly, through government investment and incentives, particularly for activities in the urban informal sector, and indirectly, through income redistribution (either directly or from future growth) to the rural poor, whose structure of consumer demand is both less import-intensive and more labor-intensive than that of the rich.

3. *Elimination of factor-price distortions.* There is ample evidence to demonstrate that correcting factor-price distortions primarily by eliminating various capital subsidies and curtailing the growth of urban wages through market-based pricing would increase employment opportunities and make better use of scarce

capital resources. But by how much or how quickly these policies would work is not clear. Moreover, their migration implications would have to be ascertained. Correct pricing policies by themselves are insufficient to alter significantly the present employment situation for the reasons described in Chapter 7.

4. *Choosing appropriate labor-intensive technologies of production.* One of the principal factors inhibiting the success of any long-run program of employment creation both in urban industry and rural agriculture is the almost complete technological dependence of Third World nations on imported (typically laborsaving) machinery and equipment from the developed countries. Both domestic and international efforts must be made to reduce this dependence by developing technological research and adaptation capacities in the developing countries themselves. Such efforts might first be linked to the development of small-scale, labor-intensive rural and urban enterprises. They could also focus on the development of low-cost, labor-intensive methods of meeting rural infrastructure needs, including roads, irrigation and drainage systems, and essential health and educational services. This is an area where scientific and technological assistance from the developed countries could prove extremely helpful.

5. *Modifying the direct linkage between education and employment.* The emergence of the phenomenon of the educated unemployed is calling into question the appropriateness of the massive quantitative expansion of educational systems, especially at the higher levels. Formal education has become the rationing tunnel through which all prospective jobholders must pass. As modern-sector jobs multiply more slowly than the numbers of persons leaving the educational tunnel, it becomes necessary to extend the length of the tunnel and to narrow its exit. Although a full discussion of educational problems and policies must await Chapter 11, one way to moderate the excessive demand for additional years of schooling (which in reality is a demand for modern-sector jobs) would be for governments, often the largest employers, to base their hiring practices and their wage structures on other criteria. Moreover, the creation of attractive economic opportunities in rural areas would make it easier to redirect educational systems toward the needs of rural development. At present, many Third World educational systems, being transplants of Western systems, are oriented toward preparing students to function in a small modern sector employing at the most 20% to 30% of the labor force. Many of the necessary skills for development remain largely neglected.

6. *Reducing population growth* through reductions in absolute poverty and inequality, particularly for women, along with the expanded provision of family planning and rural health services. Clearly, any long-run solution to Third World employment and urbanization problems must involve a lowering of current high rates of population growth. Even though the labor force size for the next two decades is already determined by today's birthrates, the hidden momentum of population growth applies equally as well to labor force growth. Together with the demand policies identified in points 1 through 5, the population and labor supply reduction policies described in Chapter 6 provide an essential ingredient in any strategy to combat the severe employment problems that developing countries face now and in future years.

CASE STUDY

The Economy of Mexico

GEOGRAPHIC, SOCIAL, AND ECONOMIC INDICATORS

Capital Mexico City

Area 1,973,000 km²

Population 93.7 million (1995)

Population (average annual growth rate 2.2% (1985–1994)

GNP per capita U.S. $4,010 (1994)

GNP per capita (average annual growth rate) 0.6% (1985–1994)

Agriculture as share of GDP 8% (1994)

Exports as share of GDP 13% (1994)

Infant mortality rate (per 1,000 live births) 34 (1995)

Child malnutrition (underweight) 14% (1993)

Females as share of labor force 27% (1994)

Illiteracy rate (age 15+) 13% (1990)

Human Development Index 0.80 (high) (1992)

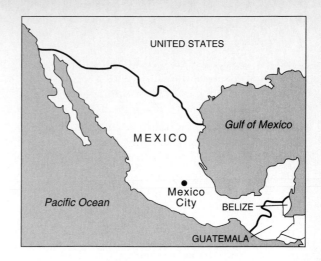

Mexico, with nearly 2 million square kilometers of land, is the third largest nation in Latin America, following Brazil and Argentina. On the north it is bordered by the United States, and on the south, by Guatemala and Belize. The Spanish conquest of the ancient Aztec Empire in 1519 was the beginning of a 300-year history of colonial rule in Mexico. The Spanish heavily influenced the nation's language, religion, economics, and politics. The War of Independence from Spain in the early nineteenth century was followed by further chaos and warfare. During this period, Mexico lost half of its territory to the young expansionist United States. But the spirit of nationalism, which remains strong today, was first implanted in the Mexican people in the early twentieth century by the Mexican Revolution. The leaders of the revolution advocated land reform, nationalization of U.S.-owned companies, and social justice for all Mexicans.

Like Brazil, Mexico is a newly industrializing country (NIC) with abundant resources and great economic potential. It is the fifteenth largest economy in the world and the fourth largest oil exporter. It has a large industrial manufacturing base, fertile and productive agricultural land, and an enormous potential export market to its immediate north in the United States. However, also like Brazil, Mexico still suffers from high population growth, widespread poverty, excessive income inequalities, severe unemployment (especially in the cities), and a massive foreign-debt burden.

Due to strong external demand and severe shortages during World War II and the early postwar period, Mexico's economy experienced tremendous growth in the 1940s. During this period, the manufacturing sector was also stimulated by increased domestic demand created through government policies of import controls and import substitution. The United States was and still is Mexico's biggest trading partner. For the next 30 years, the Mexican economy was propelled mainly by its industrial sector. To finance this expansion, Mexico earned foreign exchange through agricultural exports. By 1974, Mexico had joined the ranks of the NICs, with manufac-

290 PROBLEMS AND POLICIES: DOMESTIC

tured goods representing 50% of total exports and agricultural goods falling back to 39%. In the late 1970s and early 1980s, however, after the discovery of large deposits of oil and natural gas and the second international oil price rise, the Mexican government aggressively promoted industrial growth through oil-financed public expenditure. This expenditure contributed to a large public deficit and rapidly rising inflation. At the same time, the peso was overvalued so as artificially to increase export prices and augment foreign-exchange earnings from petroleum, which faced inelastic demand. But this also had the negative effect of making non-oil exports, which faced elastic demand, less competitive on world markets. By 1980, oil exports represented 75% of Mexico's foreign-exchange earnings.

In 1982, Mexico headed into a severe recession and a liquidity crisis caused by rising government budget deficits, a deteriorating trade balance, a major recession in the industrialized countries, a world oil glut, a mounting foreign debt, and a declining foreign-exchange reserve. Drastic government austerity policies and devaluation of the peso were adopted to correct economic imbalances. The IMF rescheduled Mexico's debt with its 530 creditors. Exacerbating these problems was the massive amount of capital flight (Mexicans sending money abroad) resulting from a loss of public confidence in the peso.

Since 1982, several debt-restructuring programs have been agreed on with foreign banks, resulting in an extension of the repayment schedule and reduced rates of interest (see Chapter 14 for a discussion of trade deficits and the debt crisis). A large proportion of Mexico's foreign exchange earned from exports goes to debt-service payments rather than to capital goods for development.

Despite rapid economic development during the 1950s and 1960s, distribution of income and wealth in Mexico was and still is highly uneven. Working with household data, the World Bank has reported that the wealthiest 10% of the Mexican population receives 40.6% of the national income; the poorest 20% receives only 2.9% of that income.

Mexico also has a serious population problem. Since 1973, when the population growth rate was as high as 3.4% per annum, the Mexican government has been concerned with its rapidly increasing population. Through concerted efforts, the government had succeeded at lowering the population growth rate to about 2% by 1995. Although this campaign has been one of the most successful family-planning programs in the world, the hidden momentum of Mexico's population growth will still strain the economy because there will be an increasing number of young people for whom education, employment, and social services must be provided.

Another major and continuing problem for Mexico is its rapid rate of urbanization. For 25 years, rural migrants have been pouring into cities and towns in search of high wages and modern-sector jobs. Over 70% of the population now lives in urban areas. Mexico City, the most concentrated center, with almost 20 million residents in 1995, is expected soon to become the largest city in the world. The Mexican government has tried to decentralize industry and growth away from the capital toward rural areas. However, these efforts have been unsuccessful, and rural peasants continue to flock into Mexico City seeking elusive jobs. Few succeed, and many decide to continue north and attempt to cross the border to search for jobs in the United States. As a result, the United States has become a major outlet for Mexico's population pressures through illegal international migration.

The Mexican government has taken many steps in recent years to restructure the economy. Monetary and fiscal discipline and a wage and price stabilization program reduced inflation from over 150% in 1987 to 10% in 1991. With the acceleration of market-oriented reforms, Mexico's real GDP growth rate went from 2% in 1987 to 4% in 1990. The Mexican economy has gradually decreased its dependence on petroleum exports, which accounted for 34% of 1990 exports, down from 75% in 1982.

The government also took steps to put public finance on a sound footing through privatization and deregulation of state-owned companies, elimination of subsidies to inefficient industries, a dramatic reduction of tariff rates, and shrinking the overall financial deficit from nearly 17% of GDP in 1987 to 2% of GDP in 1991. In 1982, the Mexican government owned 1,155 enterprises; by late 1990, the number had dropped to 452. Real short-term interest rates were down to about 9% in mid-1991 from 30% a year earlier.

In addition, in 1989, Mexico was the first country to participate in the U.S.-sponsored Brady Plan to help developing countries reduce their debt to foreign commercial banks. This helped reduce Mexico's debt from a high of $107 billion in 1987 to about $97 billion in 1990. This temporarily restored business confidence and sparked a return of expatriated capital. One of the Mexican government's most salient initiatives was its participation in the North American Free Trade Agreement (NAFTA) with the United States and Canada. It thereby hoped to attract high levels of private foreign investment and promote jobs and wealth. Unfortunately, in its desire to at-

tract this private foreign investment, the Mexican government in 1993 and 1994 tried to ignore deep-seated structural problems that were leading to a severe drain on its foreign-exchange reserves. In late 1994 and early 1995, it startled the world financial community by allowing the peso to be devalued by 40% and sending the Mexican economy into an economic tailspin.* Private foreign investors withdrew huge sums of money, the Mexican stock market crashed, workers saw their real income and savings plummet by 30% to 40%, 2 million jobs were lost, and many unskilled workers joined others in illegally migrating across the border to the United States. After a $50 billion emergency rescue package was orchestrated by the U.S. government, Mexico was forced to announce a new austerity program in March 1995. It cut government spending by 9.8% and increased sales taxes by up to 15%. As a result, inflation was expected to rise to 42% in 1995, and GNP was predicted to fall by 2% to 3%. Once again, it was the poor and the middle classes who bore the brunt of the new austerity measures, and it is they who are likely to suffer the greatest financial hardships.

---

*For a review and analysis of the Mexican peso crisis, see *Report of an Independent Task Force, Lessons of the Mexican Peso Crisis* (New York: Council on Foreign Relations, 1996).

Concepts for Review

Efficiency wage	Present value
Expected income	Rural-urban migration
Induced migration	Todaro migration model
Informal sector	Urban bias
Labor turnover	Wage subsidy

Questions for Discussion

1. Why might the problem of rapid urbanization turn out to be a more significant population policy issue than curtailing Third World population growth rates over the next two decades? Explain.

2. Describe briefly the essential assumptions and major features of the Todaro model of rural-urban migration. One of the most significant implications of this model is the paradoxical conclusion that government policies designed to create more urban employment may in fact lead to more urban unemployment. Explain the reasons for such a paradoxical result.

3. "The key to solving the serious problem of excessive rural-urban migration and rising urban unemployment and underemployment in Third World countries is to restore a proper balance between urban and rural economic and social opportunities." Discuss the reasoning behind this statement, and give a few specific examples of government policies that will promote a better balance between urban and rural economic and social opportunities.

4. For many years, the conventional wisdom of development economics assumed an inherent conflict between the objectives of maximizing output growth and promoting rapid industrial employment growth. Why might these two objectives be mutually supportive rather than conflicting? Explain.

5. What is meant by the expression "getting prices right"? Under what conditions will eliminating factor-price distortions generate substantial new employment opportunities? (Be sure to define factor-price distortions.)

6. The informal sector is becoming an ever-larger part of the urban economy. Distinguish between the urban formal and informal sectors, and discuss both the positive and negative aspects of the informal urban labor market.

Notes

1. Robert S. McNamara, "The population problem: Time bomb or myth?" *Foreign Affairs* 62 (1984): 1107–1131. For additional information on the problems of rapid urban population growth, see Bertrand Renaud, *National Urbanization Policy in Developing Countries* (New York: Oxford University Press, 1981). A less concerned viewpoint is expressed in Jeffrey G. Williamson, "Migration and urbanization," in Hollis B. Chenery and T. N. Srinivasan (eds.), *Handbook of Development Economics*, vol. 1 (Amsterdam: North Holland, 1988), pp. 426–465.

2. United Nations Population Fund, *Population, Resources, and the Environment* (New York: United Nations, 1991), p. 61.

3. United Nations Population Division, *World Population Monitoring, 1987* (New York: United Nations, 1988). These results were reiterated in the Program of Action of the 1994 International Conference on Population and Development, para. 9.1.

4. For a concise review of this debate, see Cathy A. Rakowski, "Convergence and divergence in the informal sector debate: A focus on Latin America, 1984–92," *World Development* 22 (April 1994): 501–516.

5. For evidence of the deteriorating urban employment situation in Latin America and sub-Saharan Africa during the 1980s, see the International Labor Organization's *World Labor Reports* for 1988 and 1989; Dharam Ghai, *Economic Growth, Structural Change and Labour Absorption in Africa, 1960–85*, Discussion Paper No. 1 (Geneva: United Nations Research Institute for Social Development, 1987); and especially Charles M. Becker, Andrew M. Hammer, and Andrew R. Morrison, *Beyond Urban Bias in Africa: Urbanization in an Era of Structural Adjustment* (Portsmouth, N.H.: Heinemann, 1994).

6. Richard Jolly, "Rural-urban migration: Dimensions, causes, issues and policies," in *Prospects for Employment Opportunities in the Nineteen Seventies* (Cambridge: Cambridge University Press, 1970), p. 4.

7. Pamela Brigg, *Migration to Urban Areas: A Survey*, World Bank Staff Working Paper, No. 107 (Washington, D.C.: World Bank, 1971), and United Nations, *The Prospects of World Urbanization* (New York: United Nations, 1988).

8. Henry N. Barnum and Richard H. Sabot, *Migration, Education and Urban Surplus Labour*, OECD Development Center Employment Series Monograph, October 1975.

9. Although the *rate* of rural-urban migration slowed during the 1980s, especially in Latin America and sub-Saharan Africa, as a result of declining urban real wages and fewer formal-sector employment opportunities, the actual number of migrants continued to expand.

10. See Michael P. Todaro, "A model of labor migration and urban unemployment in less developed countries," *American Economic Review* 59 (March 1969): 138–148, and John R. Harris and Michael P. Todaro, "Migration, unemployment, and development: A two-sector analysis," *American Economic Review* 60 (March 1970): 126–142.

11. This graph was first introduced in W. Max Corden and Ronald Findlay, "Urban unemployment, intersectoral capital mobility, and development policy," *Economica* 42 (1975): 59–78, and reproduced and described in Williamson, "Migration and urbanization," pp. 443–445.

12. While the Todaro model focuses on the institutional determinants of urban wage rates above the equilibrium wage, several other authors have sought to explain this phenomenon by focusing on the high costs of **labor turnover** in urban areas and the notion of an **efficiency wage**; an above-equilibrium urban wage enables employers to secure a higher-quality workforce and greater productivity on the job. For a review of these various models, see Joseph Stiglitz, "Alternative theories of wage determination and unemployment in LDCs: The labor turnover model," *Quarterly Journal of Economics* 88 (May 1974), and Janet L. Yellen, "Efficiency wage models of unemployment," *American Economic Review* 74 (May 1984).

13. Note that qq' is a rectangular hyperbola, a unitary-elasticity curve showing a constant urban wage bill; that is, $L_M \times W_M$ is fixed.

14. See, for example, Gary S. Fields, "Public policy and the labor market in less developed countries," in David P. Newbery and Nicholas Stern (eds.), *The Theory of Taxation for Developing Countries* (New York: Oxford University Press, 1987); Becker, Hammer, and Morrison, *Beyond Urban Bias in Africa*, chaps. 4–7; David Turnham, *Employment and Development: A New Review of Evidence* (Paris: Organization for Economic Coordination and Development, 1993), pp. 245–253; and Paul P. Streeten, *Strategies for Human Development: Global Poverty and Unemployment* (Copenhagen: Handelshøjskolens Forlag, 1994), pp. 50–64.

Further Reading

Useful surveys of urbanization issues in developing nations are G. S. Tolley and V. Thomas, *The Economics of Urbanization and Urban Policies in Developing Countries* (Washington, D.C.: World Bank, 1987); Alan Gilbert and Josef Gugler, *Cities, Poverty and Development*, 2d ed. (New York: Oxford University Press, 1992); Pradip K. Ghosh (ed.), *Urban Development in the Third World* (Westport, Conn.: Greenwood Press, 1984); Charles M. Becker, Andrew M. Hammer, and Andrew R. Morrison, *Beyond Urban Bias in Africa: Urbanization in an Era of Structural Adjustment* (Portsmouth, N.H.: Heinemann, 1994); and Pii Elina Berghäll, *Habitat II and the Urban Economy: A Review of Recent Development and Literature* (Helsinki: United Nations University, World Institute for Development Economics Research, 1995).

Among the many readings on the critical problem of rural-urban migration in developing countries, the following are perhaps the most comprehensive: Derek Byerlee, "Rural-urban migration in Africa: Theory, policy, and research implications," *International Migration Review* 3 (Winter 1974); John R. Harris and Michael P. Todaro, "Migration, unemployment, and development: A two-sector analysis," *American Economic Review* 60 (March 1970): 126–142; Michael P. Todaro, *Internal Migration in Developing Countries: A Review of Theory, Evidence, Methodology and Research Priorities* (Geneva: International Labor Organization, 1976); Sally Findlay, *Planning for Internal Migration* (Washington, D.C.: U.S. Department of Commerce, 1977); N. Shrestha, "Institutional policies and migration behavior: A selective review," *World Development* 15 (1987); and Oded Stark, *The Migration of Labour* (Oxford: Blackwell, 1991).

For a suggested national and international strategy to combat Third World poverty and unemployment, see International Labor Organization, *Employment, Growth and Basic Needs: A One-World Problem* (Geneva: International Labor Organization, 1976); Lyn Squire, *Employment Policy in Developing Countries: A Survey of Issues and Evidence* (New York: Oxford University Press, 1981); Subbiah Kannappan, *Employment Problems and the Urban Labor Market in Developing Nations* (Ann Arbor: University of Michigan Press, 1983); and Gary S. Fields, "Public policy and the labor market in less developed countries," in David P. Newbery and Nicholas Stern (eds.), *The Theory of Taxation for Developing Countries* (New York: Oxford University Press, 1987).

Readings on the informal sector include S. U. Sethuraman, *The Urban Informal Sector in Developing Countries: Employment, Poverty and Environment* (Geneva: International Labor Organization, 1981); Deepak Mazumdar, "The urban informal sector," *World Development* 4 (1976); Harry W. Richardson, "The role of the informal sector in developing countries: An overview," *Regional Development Dialogue* (Autumn 1984); Alejandro Portes and Richard Schauffler, "Competing perspectives on the Latin American informal sector," *Population and Development Review* 19 (March 1993); and Cathy A. Rakowski, "Convergence and divergence in the informal sector debate: A focus on Latin America, 1984–92," *World Development* 22 (April 1994): 501–516.

See also Stephen C. Smith, *Case Studies*, Chapter 11 on rural-urban migration and urbanization in India and Botswana.

CHAPTER 9

Agricultural Transformation and Rural Development

It is in the agricultural sector that the battle for long-term economic development will be won or lost.

—Gunnar Myrdal, Nobel Laureate in Economics

The main burden of development and employment creation will have to be borne by the part of the economy in which agriculture is the predominant activity, that is, the rural sector.

—Francis Blanchard, Director General, International Labor Organization

The Imperative of Agricultural Progress and Rural Development

If migration to the cities in Africa, Asia, and Latin America is proceeding at historically unprecedented rates, a large part of the explanation can be found in the economic stagnation of the outlying rural areas. This is where the people are. Over 2.3 billion people in the Third World grind out a meager and often inadequate existence in agricultural pursuits. Over 3.1 billion people lived in rural areas in 1995. Estimates indicate that this figure will rise to almost 3.4 billion by the year 2000. In Latin America and Asia, people living in the countryside comprise considerably more than half the population of such diverse nations as Bolivia, Guatemala, India, Indonesia, Myanmar, Ecuador, Sri Lanka, Pakistan, the Philippines, and China. In Africa, the ratios are much higher, with almost every country having rural dwellers in excess of three-quarters of the total population. In spite of the massive migration to the cities, the absolute population increase in rural areas of most Third World nations will continue to be greater than that of urban areas for at least the next decade.

Of greater importance than sheer numbers is the fact that the vast majority (almost 70%) of the world's poorest people are also located in rural areas and engaged primarily in subsistence agriculture. Their basic concern is survival. Many hundreds of millions of people have been bypassed by whatever economic progress has been attained. In their daily struggle to subsist, their behavior may often seem irrational to Western economists who have little comprehension of the precarious nature of subsistence living and the importance of avoiding risks. If development is to take place and become self-sustaining, it will have to start in the rural areas in general and the agricultural sector in particular. The core problems of widespread poverty, growing inequality, rapid population growth, and rising unemployment all find their origins in the stagnation and often retrogression of economic life in rural areas.

Traditionally, the role of agriculture in economic development has been viewed as passive and supportive. Based on the historical experience of Western countries, economic development was seen as requiring a rapid structural transformation of the economy from one predominantly focused on agricultural activities to a more complex modern industrial and service society. As a result, agriculture's primary role was to provide sufficient low-priced food and manpower to the expanding industrial economy, which was thought to be the dynamic "leading sector" in any overall strategy of economic development. Lewis's famous two-sector model discussed in Chapter 3 is an outstanding example of a theory of development that places heavy emphasis on rapid industrial growth with an agricultural sector fueling this industrial expansion by means of its cheap food and surplus labor.

Today, as we have seen, development economists are less sanguine about the desirability of placing such heavy emphasis on rapid industrialization. They have come to realize that far from playing a passive, supporting role in the process of economic development, the agricultural sector in particular and the rural economy in general must be the dynamic and leading elements in any overall strategy, at least for the vast majority of contemporary Third World countries.

An agriculture- and employment-based strategy of economic development requires at a minimum three basic complementary elements: (1) accelerated output growth through technological, institutional, and price incentive changes designed to raise the productivity of small farmers; (2) rising domestic demand for agricultural output derived from an employment-oriented urban development strategy; and (3) diversified, nonagricultural, labor-intensive rural development activities that directly and indirectly support and are supported by the farming community.[1] To a large extent, therefore, the 1970s and 1980s witnessed a remarkable transition in development thinking in which agricultural and rural development came to be seen by many as the *sine qua non* of national development. Without such **integrated rural development**, industrial growth either would be stultified or, if it succeeded, would create such severe internal imbalances in the economy that the problems of widespread poverty, inequality, and unemployment would become even more pronounced.

Five main questions, therefore, need to be asked about Third World agriculture and rural development as these relate to overall national development:

1. How can total agricultural output and productivity per capita be substantially increased in a manner that will directly benefit the average small farmer and the landless rural dweller while providing a sufficient food surplus to support a growing urban, industrial sector?

2. What is the process by which traditional low-productivity peasant farms are transformed into high-productivity commercial enterprises?

3. When traditional family farmers and peasant cultivators resist change, is their behavior stubborn and irrational, or are they acting rationally within the context of their particular economic environment?

4. Are economic and price incentives sufficient to elicit output increases among peasant agriculturalists, or are institutional and structural changes in rural farming systems also required?

5. Is raising agricultural productivity sufficient to improve rural life, or must there be concomitant off-farm employment creation along with improvements in educational, medical, and other social services? In other words, what do we mean by *rural development*, and how can it be achieved?

Our approach in this chapter is to start with a brief factual account of growth and stagnation of the agricultural sector over the past four decades. Next we describe and analyze the basic characteristics of agrarian systems in Latin America, Asia, and Africa to see if we can identify some important similarities and differences. We then look at the economics of peasant subsistence agriculture and discuss the stages of transition from subsistence to commercial farming in Third World nations. Our focus here is not only the economic factors but also the social, institutional, and structural requirements of small-farm modernization. We then explore the meaning of rural development and review alternative policies designed to raise levels of living in Third World rural areas.

Agricultural Stagnation and Growth, 1950–1990

We have seen that many developing countries experienced respectable rates of GNP growth during the past few decades. The greatest proportionate share of this overall growth occurred in the manufacturing and commerce sectors, where recorded rates of annual output growth often exceeded 10%. In contrast, agricultural output growth for most developing regions was much less robust during these decades, and the share of agricultural output in total GNP declined. Table 9.1 reveals that in spite of the fact that the agricultural sector accounts for most of the employment in developing countries, it accounts for a much lower share of the output. In fact, in no Third World region does agricultural production constitute more than 35% of the total national product. This is in marked contrast to the historical experience of advanced countries, where agricultural output in their early stages of growth always contributed at least as much to total output as the share of the labor force engaged in these activities. The fact that contemporary Third World agricultural employment is typically twice as large in proportion to the total as is agricultural output simply reflects the relatively low levels of labor productivity compared with those in manufacturing and commerce.

The data in Table 9.1 and especially in Chapter 5, where we discussed the sectoral location of absolute poverty, strongly suggest that a direct attack on rural poverty through accelerated agricultural development is necessary to raise living

TABLE 9.1 Output and Employment in Third World Agriculture, 1990

Region	Percentage of the Labor Force in Agriculture	Output of Agriculture as a Percentage of Gross Domestic Product
South Asia	64	33
East Asia (including China)	62	26
Latin America	29	12
Africa	68	32

SOURCES: World Bank, *World Development Report, 1992: Development and the Environment* (New York: Oxford University Press, 1992), annex tab. 3; United Nations Development Program, *Human Development Report, 1992* (New York: Oxford University Press, 1992), tab. 16.

standards. Mere concern with maximizing GNP growth may not be enough. Unfortunately, the record of the past four decades offers only limited hope, as can be seen from Table 9.2 and Figure 9.1.

Over the two decades that ended in 1970, **per capita food production** and **per capita agricultural production** (which includes not only food but also nonedible agricultural products like cotton, sisal, wool, and rubber) each increased less than 1% per year in the Third World as a whole. Moreover, as Table 9.2 shows, the rates of growth of both these measures of agricultural performance were much slower in the 1960s than in the 1950s. In fact, the agricultural sector in many developing countries completely stagnated in the 1960s. People on the whole were little or no better off in terms of the per capita availability of food at the end of the decade than they were at the beginning. The situation improved somewhat during the 1970s as developing countries increasingly turned their attention to raising agricultural productivity. As a result, from 1970 to 1980, per capita food production grew at an annual rate of 0.5%, almost matching its 1950s performance. Unfortunately, in the 1980s, per capita production once again slowed down, with the notable exception of the Far East, which includes countries such as India, Indonesia, Pakistan, Thailand, and the Philippines. However, even here, where India looms most important, a devastating and famine-generating drought drastically lowered food production in 1987. In contrast, in the more developed countries, per capita food production continued to rise at a much more rapid annual rate, primarily because of much slower population growth.

From Table 9.2 and Figure 9.1 we can also see that these same broad tendencies were at work within each of the major regions of the Third World. In Latin America, there was some increase in the growth of per capita food production in the 1970s especially and in the 1980s, but agricultural production in the 1960s as a whole showed no such increase. The picture for Africa is more dismal. Per capita food production has declined steadily since the 1970s (see Figure 9.1). Although the data reflect changes in per capita food production, which may differ from food consumption due to foreign trade, it is clear that the average African has suffered a fall in the level of food consumption over the past decades. Because food consumption constitutes by far the largest component in a typical African's standard of living,

TABLE 9.2 Change in Per Capita Food and Agricultural Output in Third World Regions and Developed Countries, 1950–1985

Region	Change in Per Capita Food Production (percent)				Change in Per Capita Agricultural Production (percent)			
	1948/1952–1960	1960–1970	1970–1930	1980–1985	1948/1952–1960	1960–1970	1970–1980	1980–1985
Latin America	0.4	0.6	0.9	0.3	0.2	0.0	0.7	0.4
Far East (excluding Japan)	0.8	0.3	0.7	1.2	0.7	0.3	0.6	1.1
Near East (excluding Israel)	0.7	0.0	0.7	0.2	0.8	0.0	0.4	0.1
Africa (excluding South Africa)	0.0	-0.7	-1.2	-0.4	0.3	-0.5	-1.4	-0.3
All developing countries	0.6	0.1	0.5	0.3	0.6	0.0	0.8	0.5
Developed countries	1.1	0.9	1.3	1.5	1.0	0.6	1.2	1.3

SOURCES: Keith Griffin, "Agrarian policy: The political and economic context," *World Development* 1 (November 1973): 3; United Nations Conference on Trade and Development, *Annual Report*, 1981 suppl., tab. 6.5A; International Institute for Environment and Development, *World Resources, 1987* (New York: Basic Books, 1987), tabs. 4.1–4.3; Population Reference Bureau, *1987 World Population Data Sheet* (Washington, D.C.: Population Reference Bureau, 1987).

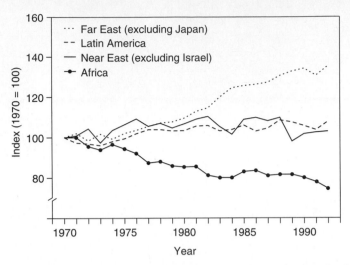

FIGURE 9.1 Index of Per Capita Food Production in Developing Regions, 1970–1992.
Source: World Resources Institute, *World Resources, 1994–95* (New York: Oxford University Press, 1994), p. 108. Reprinted with permission.

the sharp decline in per capita food production and consumption meant that the region as a whole was becoming even more underdeveloped during the period 1970–1992. Some reasons for the disappointing negative growth of African per capita food production include insufficient and inappropriate innovation, cultivation of marginal and sensitive lands, severe deforestation and erosion, sporadic civil wars, and misguided (incentive-reducing) pricing and marketing policies—all of which were exacerbated by the highest rate of population growth in the world. We will examine the crisis in sub-Saharan Africa in greater detail in Chapter 18 when we look at the key development issues for the twenty-first century.

The agricultural performance in Asia was varied. In the Near East, there was a decline in the rate of growth compared to the pre-1960 period. During the 1960s, both per capita food and agricultural production tended to stagnate, whereas in the 1970s, food production rose sufficiently to provide slight increases in per capita output. In the 1980s, however, Near East food production failed to surpass population growth. Only in the Far East region of Asia has per capita production expanded steadily over the past two decades. But, as noted earlier, India's great drought of 1987 demonstrated the still precarious nature of Third World food production.

We may conclude that in spite of some impressive rates of per capita GNP growth recorded in Third World regions during the past 35 or 40 years, per capita growth in the agricultural sector not only showed negligible progress overall but in some regions even declined. Because the vast majority of people in developing countries seek their livelihoods in this sector, the data of Table 9.2 and Figure 9.1 confirm what we discovered in Chapter 5: The magnitude and extent of Third World poverty has improved only marginally in Asia and Latin America and has steadily worsened for Africa. This becomes especially apparent when we realize that per capita aggregates for food production mask the inherently unequal distribution of that production and consumption, just as per capita GNP figures often mask the magnitude of absolute poverty.

As noted earlier, in sub-Saharan Africa, the situation is particularly acute. The United Nations Food and Agriculture Organization (FAO) has repeatedly warned of catastrophic food shortages during the next decade. In a majority of African countries, the average per capita calorie intake has now fallen below minimal nutritional standards. The FAO estimates that of Africa's 720 million people, more than 250 million suffer from some form of malnutrition associated with inadequate food supplies. Whereas the severe famine of 1973–1974 took the lives of hundreds of thousands and left many more with permanent damage from malnutrition, its geographic impact was limited to the Sahelian belt that stretches below the Sahara from Cape Verde, off the coast of Senegal in the west, across the continent to Ethiopia. By contrast, in 1982–1984 and again in 1987–1988, 1991–1992, and 1993–1994, the food crisis became much more widespread, with more than 22 nations threatened by severe famine, including, in addition to the Sahelian nations, Zambia, Tanzania, Malawi, Uganda, Botswana, Mozambique, Zimbabwe, and Angola.[2]

A major reason for the relatively poor performance of Third World agriculture has been the neglect of this sector in the development priorities of their governments. This neglect of agriculture and the accompanying bias toward investment in the urban industrial economy can in turn be traced largely to the misplaced emphasis on rapid industrialization via import substitution and exchange-rate overvaluation (see Chapter 13) that permeated development thinking and strategy during the postwar decades. For example, during the 1950s and throughout most of the 1960s, the share of total national investment allocated toward the agricultural sector in a sample of 18 LDCs was approximately 12%, even though agriculture in these countries accounted for almost 30% of GNP and more than 60% of total employment.[3] As we saw in Chapter 8, one significant manifestation of this rural neglect and the corresponding emphasis on urban growth has been the massive migration of rural peasants into the teeming cities of Third World nations.

As a result of this disappointing experience and the realization that the future of most underdeveloped countries will depend to a large extent on what happens to their agriculture, there has been a marked shift in development thinking and policymaking. This shift, which began in the late 1970s and has continued into the 1990s, has been away from the almost exclusive emphasis on rapid industrialization toward a more realistic appreciation of the overwhelming importance of agricultural and rural development for national development. A first step toward understanding what is needed for agricultural and rural development, however, must be a comprehension of the nature of agricultural systems in diverse Third World regions and, in particular, of the economic aspects of the transition from subsistence to commercial agriculture.

The Structure of Third World Agrarian Systems

Two Kinds of World Agriculture

When we look at the state of contemporary agriculture in most poor countries, we realize the enormity of the task that lies ahead. A brief comparison between agricultural productivity in the developed nations and the underdeveloped nations makes this clear. World agriculture, in fact, comprises two distinct types of farming: (1) the highly efficient agriculture of the developed countries, where substantial productive capacity and high output per worker permit a very small number of farmers to feed entire nations, and (2) the inefficient and low-productivity agriculture of developing countries, where in many instances the agricultural sector can barely sustain the farm population, let alone the burgeoning urban population, even at a minimum level of subsistence.[4]

The gap between the two kinds of agriculture is immense. This is best illustrated by the disparities in labor productivity, shown in Table 9.3. In 1960, the agricultural population of the developed nations totaled about 115 million people. They produced a total output amounting to $78 billion, or about $680 per capita. In contrast, the per capita product of the agricultural population in the underdeveloped countries in 1960 was only $52. In other words, agricultural labor productivity in developed countries was more than 13 times that in the less developed countries. Projections for the end of the century show this **productivity gap** widening to 40 to 1. Another manifestation of the productivity gap relates to land productivity. Table 9.4 shows variations in land productivity (measured as tons of grain harvested per hectare of agricultural land) between Japan and the United States on the one hand and six heavily populated countries in Asia, Africa, and Latin America on the other. We see that Japanese and U.S. land productivity varies from as high as 725% and 600%, respectively, of Nigerian productivity to 263% and 218%, respectively, of productivity in Bangladesh and Mexico.

In the developed countries, there has been a steady growth of agricultural output since the mid-eighteenth century. This growth has been spurred by technological and biological improvements, which have resulted in even higher levels of labor and land productivity. The growth rate accelerated after the First World War and particularly after the Second World War. The end result is that fewer farmers are able to produce more food. This is especially the case in the United States, where in 1994 only 2% of the total workforce was agricultural, compared with more than 70% in the early nineteenth century. For example, in 1820, the American farmer could produce only four times his own consumption. One hun-

TABLE 9.3 Agricultural Population and Production in More Developed Countries (MDCs) and Less Developed Countries (LDCs), 1960–2000

	1960		1980		2000	
	MDCs	LDCs	MDCs	LDCs	MDCs	LDCs
Agricultural population (millions)	115	850	75	1,230	50	1,480
Total agricultural production (billions of dollars)	78	43	125	77	186	135
Per capita agricultural production (dollars)	680	52	1,660	63	3,720	91

SOURCE: Data from Raanan Weitz, *From Peasant to Farmer: A Revolutionary Strategy for Development* (New York: Columbia University Press, 1971). Copyright © 1971 by the Twentieth Century Fund. Used by permission.

	TABLE 9.4 Land Productivity in Developed and Developing Countries, 1985	
Country	Average Grain Yield (tons per hectare)	Population (million)
Japan	5.8	122
United States	4.8	241
Bangladesh	2.2	104
Mexico	2.1	82
Brazil	1.8	143
India	1.6	785
Pakistan	1.6	102
Nigeria	0.8	105

SOURCE: Edward C. Wolf, "Rising agricultural productivity," in Worldwatch Institute, *State of the World, 1987* (New York: Norton, 1987), tab. 8.2. Reprinted with permission.

dred years later, in 1920, his productivity had doubled, and he could provide enough for eight persons. It took only another 32 years for this productivity to double again, and then only 12 more years for it to double once more. By 1987, a single American farmer could provide enough food to feed almost 80 people. Moreover, during the entire period, average farm incomes in North America rose steadily.[5]

The picture is entirely different when we turn to the agricultural production experience of Third World nations. In many poor countries, agricultural production methods have changed relatively slowly over time. Later in this chapter, we will discover that much of this technological stagnation can be traced to the special circumstances of peasant agriculture, with its high risks and uncertain rewards. Rapid rural population growth has compounded the problem by causing great pressure to be exerted on existing resources. Where fertile land is scarce, especially throughout South and Southeast Asia but also in many parts of Latin America and Africa, rapid population growth has led to an increase in the number of people living on each unit of land. Given the same farming technology and the use of traditional nonlabor inputs (e.g., simple tools, animal power, traditional seeds), we know from the principle of diminishing returns that as more and more people are forced to work on a given piece of land, their marginal (and average) productivity will decline. The net result is a continuous deterioration in real living standards for rural peasants.

To avert massive starvation and raise levels of living for the average rural dweller, agricultural production and the productivity of both labor and land must be rapidly increased throughout Asia, Africa, and Latin America. Most Third World nations need to become more self-sufficient in their food production; others can rely on their successful nonagricultural exports to secure the necessary foreign exchange to import their food requirements. But for the majority of debt-ridden, inefficient, and unsuccessful exporters, unless major economic, institutional, and structural changes are made in their farming systems, their food dependence, especially on North American supplies, will increase in the coming years.

Peasant Agriculture in Latin America, Asia, and Africa

In many developing countries, various historical circumstances have led to a concentration of large areas of land in the hands of a small class of powerful landowners. This is especially true in Latin America and parts of the Asian subcontinent. In Africa, both historical circumstances and the availability of relatively more unused land have resulted in a different pattern and structure of agricultural activity; however, in terms of levels of farm productivity, there is little to distinguish among the three regions.

A common characteristic of agriculture in all three regions, and for that matter in many developed countries, is the position of the family farm as the basic unit of production. As Raanan Weitz points out:

> For the vast number of farm families, whose members constitute the main agricultural work force, agriculture is not merely an occupation or a source of income; it is a way of life. This is particularly evident in traditional societies, where farmers are closely attached to their land and devote long, arduous days to its cultivation. Any change in farming methods perforce brings with it changes in the farmer's way of life. The introduction of biological and technical innovations must therefore be adapted not only to the natural and economic conditions, but perhaps even more to the attitudes, values, and abilities of the mass of producers, who must understand the suggested changes, must be willing to accept them, and must be capable of carrying them out.[6]

Thus in spite of the obvious differences between agricultural systems in Asia, Latin America, and Africa and among individual nations within each region, certain broad similarities enable us to make some generalizations and comparisons. In particular, **agrarian systems** in many parts of Asia and Latin America show more structural and institutional similarities than differences, and subsistence farmers in all three regions exhibit many of the same economic behavior patterns. We examine first the major features of agricultural systems in Latin America and Asia.

Latin America and Asia: Similarities and Differences

Although Latin America and Asia have very different heritages and cultures, peasant life in these two regions is in many ways similar. Francis Foland has succinctly described these similar features:

> Both the Latin American and Asian peasant is a rural cultivator whose prime concern is survival. Subsistence defines his concept of life. He may strive to obtain his and his family's minimal needs by tilling an inadequate piece of land which is his own or, more often, which is rented from or pawned to a landlord or moneylender, or by selling his labour for substandard wages to a commercial agricultural enterprise. Profits which might come to him through the fortunes of weather or market are windfalls, not preconceived goals. Debt rather than profit is his normal fate, and therefore, his farming techniques are rationally scaled to his level of dis-

posable capital: human and animal power rather than mechanized equipment; excrement rather than chemical fertilizers; traditional crops and seeds rather than experimental cultivations.

No effective social security, unemployment insurance, or minimum-wage law ease his plight. His every decision and act impinge directly upon his struggle for physical survival. In countries with a high proportion of peasantry, traditional food crops which a rural family can itself convert readily into the daily fare for its grain- or tuber-based diet dominate the agriculture; corn in Mexico, rice in Indonesia, mandioca in Brazil, soybeans in China. India's is typical of peasant agriculture with seventy-five percent of the cropped land devoted to food grains such as rice, wheat, millets, barley and lentils. When these fail, as in Maharashtra in 1972, a peasant is reduced to trading his bullocks for a few bananas.[7]

Although the day-to-day struggle for survival permeates the lives and attitudes of peasants in both Latin America and Asia (and also Africa, although the rural structure and institutions are considerably different), the nature of their agrarian existence differs markedly. In Latin America, the peasant's plight is rooted in the *latifundio-minifundio* system. In Asia, it lies primarily in fragmented and heavily congested dwarf parcels of land.

The Latifundio–Minifundio Pattern and Resource Underutilization in Latin America

In Latin America, as indeed in Asia and Africa, agrarian structures are not only part of the production system but also a basic feature of the entire economic, social, and political organization of rural life. The agrarian structure that has prevailed in Latin America since colonial times and has provided much of the region with its social organization is the pattern of agricultural dualism known as *latifundio-minifundio*.[8] Basically, **latifundios** are very large landholdings. They are defined in Latin America as farms large enough to provide employment for more than 12 people. In contrast, **minifundios** are the smallest farms. They are defined as farms too small to provide employment for a single family (two workers) with the typical incomes, markets, and levels of technology and capital prevailing in each country or region.

According to the FAO, 1.3% of landowners in Latin America hold 71.6% of the entire area of land under cultivation. If we exclude countries that have carried out drastic land reforms during the past 60 years (Mexico, Bolivia, and Cuba), Latin America's agrarian structure seems to follow a uniform pattern. This pattern is basically one in which a small number of *latifundios* control a large proportion of the agricultural land while a vast number of *minifundios* must scratch out a survival existence on a meager fraction of the occupied land.

Table 9.5 provides a dramatic picture of this unequal distribution of landholdings in seven Latin American countries. In no case do *minifundios*, which comprise up to 90% of the total farms, occupy more than 17% of the total agricultural land. In countries with dense indigenous populations like Ecuador, Guatemala and Peru, *minifundios* are particularly widespread. In all countries, the *latifundios* comprise

TABLE 9.5 *Minifundios* and *Latifundios* in the Agrarian Structure of Selected Latin American Countries (percent)

Country	Minifundios		Latifundios	
	Farms	Occupied Land	Farms	Occupied Land
Argentina	43.2	3.4	0.8	36.9
Brazil	22.5	0.5	4.7	59.5
Chile	36.9	0.2	6.9	81.3
Colombia	64.0	4.9	1.3	49.5
Ecuador	89.9	16.6	0.4	45.1
Guatemala	88.4	14.3	0.1	40.8
Peru	88.0	7.4	1.1	82.4

SOURCE: Celso Furtado, *Economic Development in Latin America* (New York: Cambridge University Press, 1970), p. 54. Reprinted with permission.

less than 7% of the total farms. Yet they occupy as much as 82% of the agricultural land. The average size of the *latifundios* in Argentina is 270 times that of the *minifundios* in Guatemala, and the *latifundio* is often as much as 1,732 times the size of the *minifundio*.

But *latifundios* and *minifundios* do not constitute the entire gamut of Latin American agricultural holdings. A considerable amount of production is also earned on what are known as **family farms** and **medium-sized farms**. The former provides work for 2 to 4 people (recall that the *minifundio* could provide work for fewer than 2 people), and the latter, also sometimes known as *multifamily farms*, employ 4 to 12 workers (just below the *latifundio*). We see from Table 9.6 that in Argentina, Brazil, and Colombia, these intermediate forms of farm organization account for over 60% of total agricultural output and employ similar proportions of agricultural labor. Finally, Figure 9.2 uses Lorenz curve methodology to demonstrate how much more unequal the land distribution is in Latin America than in East and South Asia.[9]

The economic and social ramifications of heavy land concentration in the hands of a few large landowners are compounded by the relative inefficiency of *latifundios* in comparison with other Latin American farm organizations. Economists normally assume that large farms (or firms) use productive resources more efficiently than small ones on the grounds that large enterprises can take advantage of economies of large-scale production and thereby lower costs. In terms of agriculture, the efficient utilization of large tractors and combine harvesters requires large tracts of land—otherwise, this capital equipment will be grossly underutilized. Recent evidence from a wide range of Third World countries, however, clearly demonstrates that small farms are more efficient (lower-cost) producers of most agricultural commodities.[10] For example, *minifundios* in Argentina, Brazil, and Chile yield more than twice the value of output per hectare under cultivation than the *latifundios* and more than 10 times the value per hectare of total farmland.[11] This finding does not contradict the theory for most large farms in developed countries are lower-cost producers than small family farms. Rather, the explanation lies in

TABLE 9.6 Agrarian Structure Indicators in Selected Latin American Countries (percent)

Country and Measure	*Minifundios*	Family Farms	Medium-sized Farms	*Latifundios*
Argentina				
Total farmland	3	46	15	36
Value of agricultural product	12	47	26	15
Labor employed	30	49	15	6
Brazil				
Total farmland	—	6	34	60
Value of agricultural product	3	18	43	36
Labor employed	11	26	42	21
Chile				
Total farmland	—	8	13	79
Value of agricultural product	4	16	23	57
Labor employed	13	28	21	38
Colombia				
Total farmland	5	25	25	45
Value of agricultural product	21	45	19	15
Labor employed	58	31	7	4
Guatemala				
Total farmland	14	13	32	41
Value of agricultural product	30	13	36	21
Labor employed	68	13	12	7

SOURCE: Celso Furtado, *Economic Development in Latin America* (New York: Cambridge University Press, 1970), p. 55. Reprinted with permission.

the poor utilization of productive farm resources in developing nations—especially land resources on *latifundios* in Latin America. In terms of **farm yields** per unit of land actually under cultivation, the *latifundios* of Argentina, Brazil, Chile, Colombia, and Guatemala are all below not only the *minifundios* but also the medium-sized family farms.[12] Moreover, in Brazil it has been estimated that the *latifundios*, with an average area 31.6 times larger than that of the family farm, invest only 11 times as much. A considerable portion of the arable *latifundio* land is thus left idle. The net result is that total factor productivity on family farms was twice as high (and, therefore, unit costs twice as low) as on the large *latifundio* tracts of land. It follows from this inverse relation between productivity and farm size that a redistribution of these large unused arable lands to family farms would probably raise national agricultural output and productivity.

A major explanation for the relative economic inefficiency of farming the fertile land on the *latifundios* in comparison with *minifundios* is simply that the wealthy landowners often value these holdings not for their potential contributions to national agricultural output but rather for the considerable power and prestige that they bring. (And as will be seen, this problem is not unique to Latin America.) Much of the land is left idle or farmed less intensively than *minifundios*. Also, *latifundio* **transaction costs**, especially the cost of supervising hired labor, are much higher than the low effective cost of using family labor on peasant farms. It follows that raising

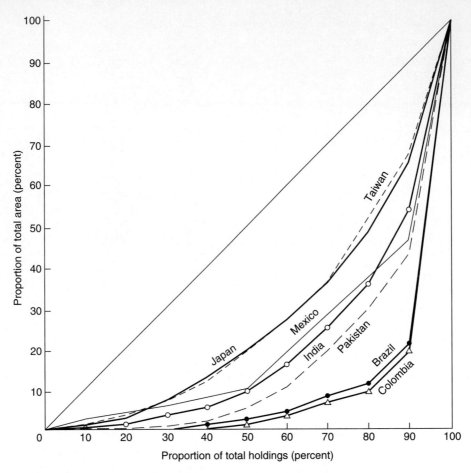

FIGURE 9.2 Lorenz Curves of Agricultural Land Distribution by Operational Holdings.
Source: Bruce F. Johnston and Peter Kilby, *Agriculture and Structural Transformation: Economic Strategies in Late-Developing Countries* (London: Oxford University Press, 1975), tab. 1.2. Used by permission.

agricultural production and improving the efficiency of Latin American agrarian systems in particular will require much more than direct economic policies that lead to the provision of better seeds, more fertilizer, less distorted factor prices, higher output prices, and improved marketing facilities. It will also require a reorganization of rural social and institutional structures to provide Latin American peasants, who now constitute almost 70% of the rural population, a real opportunity to lift themselves out of their present state of economic subsistence and social subservience.[13]

Fragmentation and Subdivision of Peasant Land in Asia

If the major agrarian problem of Latin America can be identified as too much land under the control of too few people, the basic problem in Asia is one of too many people crowded onto too little land. For example, the per capita availability of arable land in India, China, and Japan is 0.29, 0.20, and 0.07 hectares, respectively. Central

Java in Indonesia is an extreme example of the pressure of population on limited land that characterizes the Asian agrarian scene. It has the dubious distinction of possessing the world's record population density—over 1,500 persons per square kilometer.[14]

Throughout much of the twentieth century, rural conditions in Asia deteriorated. Gunnar Myrdal has identified three major interrelated forces that have molded the traditional pattern of land ownership into its present fragmented condition: (1) the intervention of European rule, (2) the progressive introduction of monetized transactions and the rise in power of the moneylender, and (3) the rapid growth of Asian populations.[15]

The traditional Asian agrarian structure before European colonization was organized around the village. Local chiefs and peasant families each provided goods and services—produce and labor from the peasants to the chief in return for protection, rights to use community land, and the provision of public services. Decisions on the allocation, disposition, and use of the village's most valuable resource, land, belonged to the tribe or community, either as a body or through its chief. Land could be redistributed among village members as a result of either population increase or natural calamities such as drought, flood, famine, war, or disease. Within the community, families had a basic right to cultivate land for their own use, and they could be evicted from their land only after a decision by the whole village.

The arrival of the Europeans (mainly the British, French, and Dutch) led to major changes in the traditional agrarian structure, some of which had already begun. As Myrdal points out, "Colonial rule acted as an important catalyst to change, both directly through its effects on property rights and indirectly through its effects on the pace of monetization of the indigenous economy and on the growth of population."[16] In the area of property rights, European land tenure systems of private property ownership were both encouraged and reinforced by law. One of the major social consequences of the imposition of these systems was, as Myrdal explains, the

> breakdown of much of the earlier cohesion of village life with its often elaborate, though informal, structure of rights and obligations. The landlord was given unrestricted rights to dispose of the land and to raise the tribute from its customary level to whatever amount he was able to extract. He was usually relieved of the obligation to supply security and public amenities because these functions were taken over by the government. Thus his status was transformed from that of a tribute receiver with responsibilities to the community to that of an absolute owner unencumbered by obligations toward the peasants and the public, other than the payment of land taxes.[17]

Contemporary **landlords** in India and Pakistan are able to avoid much of the taxation on income derived from their ownership of land. Today the typical landlord in South Asia is an absentee owner who lives in the town and turns over the working of the land to **sharecroppers** and **tenant farmers**. In many respects, therefore, his position of power in the economic, political, and social structure of the rural community is analogous to that of the Latin American **patrón**. There is a difference in that the former is an absentee owner, whereas the latter often lives on his *latifundio*. But the efficiency and productivity implications are the same.

The creation of individual titles to land made possible the rise to power of another dubious agent of change in Asian rural socioeconomic structures, the **money-lender**. Once private property came into effect, land became a negotiable asset that could be offered by peasants as security for loans and, in the case of default, could be forfeited and transferred to the often unscrupulous moneylender. At the same time, Asian agriculture was being transformed from a subsistence to a commercial orientation, both as a result of rising local demand in new towns and, more important, in response to external food demands of colonial European powers. With this transition from subsistence to commercial production, the role of the moneylender changed drastically. In the subsistence economy, his activities had been restricted to supplying the peasant with money to tide him over a crop failure or to cover extraordinary ceremonial expenditures such as family weddings or funerals. Most of these loans were paid in kind (in the form of food) at very high rates of interest. With the development of commercial farming, however, the peasant's cash needs grew significantly. Money was needed for seeds, fertilizer, and other inputs. It was also needed to cover his food requirements if he shifted to the production of cash crops such as tea, rubber, or jute. Often moneylenders were more interested in acquiring peasant lands as a result of loan defaults than they were in extracting high rates of interest. By charging exorbitant interest rates or inducing peasants to secure larger credits than they could manage, moneylenders were often able to drive the peasants off their land. They could then reap the profits of land speculation by selling this farmland to rich and acquisitive landlords. Many became powerful landlords themselves. At any rate, largely as a consequence of the moneylender's influence, Asian peasant cultivators have seen their economic status deteriorate steadily over time.[18]

The final major force altering the traditional agrarian structure in Asia has been the rapid rate of population growth, especially over the past 30 years. Myrdal notes in reference to the population phenomenon that

> when and where expansion in the cultivated area was a feasible alternative—whether for physical, technical, social, economic, or institutional reasons—population growth was reflected, in the first instance, in the cumulative subdivision and fragmentation of the acreages already under cultivation. Later this process, in combination with the emergence of private property and the rise of commercial agriculture and moneylending, often contributed to the rise of large landowners, the demise of small peasant proprietors, and the increase of the landless.[19]

The ultimate impoverishment of the peasantry was the inevitable consequence of this process of fragmentation, economic vulnerability, and loss of land to rich and powerful landlords.

To understand the deterioration of rural conditions in some Asian countries during the twentieth century, consider the cases of India, Indonesia, and the Philippines. In 1901, there were 286 million Indians; now there are three times that number. The Indonesian population grew from 28.4 million in 1900 to its present level of 198 million. The population of central Luzon in the Philippines has increased over 10-fold from its level of 1 million in 1903. In each case, severe fragmentation of landholdings inevitably followed, so that today average peasant holdings in many areas of these countries are less than 1 hectare.

As these holdings shrink even further, production falls below the subsistence level, and chronic poverty becomes a way of life. Peasants are forced to borrow even more from the moneylender at interest rates ranging from 50% to 200%. Most cannot repay these loans. They are then compelled to sell their land and become tenants with large debts. Because land is scarce, they are forced to pay high rents. If they are sharecroppers, they typically have to give the landlord 50% to 80% of their crop. And because labor is abundant, wages are extremely low. Peasants thus get trapped in a vise of chronic poverty from which, in the absence of major rural reconstruction and reform, there is no escape. Like their Latin American counterparts, many rural Asians are gradually being transformed from small proprietors to tenant farmers and sharecroppers, then landless rural laborers, then jobless vagrants, and finally migrant slum dwellers on the fringes of modern urban areas.[20] Not only have their levels of living deteriorated, but their sense of self-esteem and freedom from exploitation, which may previously have been relatively high despite low incomes, has also vanished. These many hundreds of millions of people in Asia and Latin America have therefore been bypassed by whatever economic development and social progress the region has experienced. An excerpt from the diary notes of sociologist Mead Cain, who returned after a two-year absence to a small rural village, Char Gopalpur, in Bangladesh, where he had done earlier research, vividly depicts the precarious existence of a typical peasant farmer's life in South Asia.

> This past year has indeed been a poor one economically for Bangladesh, with a succession of poor harvests. . . . The tranquility of the village setting hides an enduring, harsh existence, and a number of persistent degenerative social processes. The recent drought, bringing with it a series of poor harvests, accelerated the process of economic differentiation; the process by which marginal farmers lose their land and eventually become landless, while at the same time, larger farmers accumulate land. A typical example from the village will illustrate the process of economic differentiation and the kinds of effects generated among marginal farmers by this past year's drought. The case is that of Amir Hossain, a man who is about 50 years old, who owns slightly less than two acres of arable land, and who lives with his wife, one married son, the son's wife, and several unmarried children. In a good year, the produce from the two acres will just about provide for the consumption needs of Amir's family. This past year, because of poor harvests, Amir's son had to work as an agricultural wage laborer for a period. In addition, Amir took a loan from a local bank in order to purchase paddy for consumption; he also used part of the loan to purchase paddy, have his wife husk paddy, and then resell the processed rice for a profit. The distress of Amir and his family was compounded when a bull that he had purchased for 900 taka in January contracted a disease and died in April of this year. The combination of the poor

harvest, the untimely death of the bull, and the inadequacy of the various supplementary sources of income that the family collectively exploited, forced Amir to sell one tenth of an acre of land.

The experience of Amir Hossain and his family is significant because it is not at all unusual among farmers with similar or smaller land holdings. With as little land as they own, small differences in yield can force such families into debt or the distress sale of land. The case also illustrates the importance of luck and the ominous uncertainty of the environment in which the villagers live. The death of the bull was unrelated to the drought. The value of the bull was 900 taka and the value of the land sold was 1,300 taka. It is unlikely that the family would have been forced to sell the land if the bull had not died. Even in a normal or relatively good agricultural year, the individual experience of particular farmers will vary widely. The distribution among farmers of good and bad experiences in a given year is largely random. However, the ability of families to absorb dips in fortune depends very much on the size of a family's land holdings and on the size and composition of the family. Other things [being] equal, those with smaller holdings and with certain demographic characteristics (e.g., few able-bodied males) are less resilient and are more at risk of enduring loss in times of hardship.[21]

Subsistence Agriculture and Extensive Cultivation in Africa

As in Asia and Latin America, **subsistence farming** on small plots of land is the way of life for the vast majority of African people. However, the organization and structure of African agricultural systems differ markedly from those found in contemporary Asia or Latin America. Except in former colonial settlement areas like White Highlands of Kenya and some of the large sugar, cocoa, and coffee plantations of East and West Africa, the great majority of farm families in tropical Africa still plan their output primarily for their own subsistence. Since the basic variable input in African agriculture is farm family and village labor, African agriculture systems are dominated by three major characteristics: (1) the importance of subsistence farming in the village community; (2) the existence of some (though rapidly diminishing) land in excess of immediate requirements, which permits a general practice of shifting cultivation and reduces the value of land ownership as an instrument of economic and political power; and (3) the rights of each family (both nuclear and extended) in a village to have access to land and water in the immediate territorial vicinity, excluding from such access use by families that do not belong to the community even though they may be of the same tribe.

The low-productivity subsistence farming characteristic of most traditional African agriculture results from a combination of three historical forces restricting the growth of output:

1. In spite of the existence of some unused and potentially cultivable land, only small areas can be planted and weeded by the farm family at a time when it uses only traditional tools such as the short-handled hoe, the ax, and the long-han-

dled knife or *panga*. In some countries, use of animals is impossible because of the notorious tsetse fly or a lack of fodder in the long dry seasons, and traditional farming practices must rely primarily on the application of human labor to small parcels of land.

2. Given the limited amount of land that a farm family can cultivate in the context of a traditional technology and the use of primitive tools, these small areas tend to be intensively cultivated. As a result, they are subject to rapidly diminishing returns to increased labor inputs. In such conditions, **shifting cultivation** is the most economic method of using limited supplies of labor on extensive tracts of land. Under shifting cultivation, once the minerals are drawn out of the soil as a result of numerous croppings, new land is cleared, and the process of planting and weeding is repeated. In the meantime, formerly cropped land is allowed to recover fertility until it can be used again. Under such a process, manure and chemical fertilizers are unnecessary, although in most African villages some form of manure (mostly animal waste) is applied to nearby plots that are intensively cultivated in order to extend their period of fertility.

3. Labor is scarce during the busiest part of the growing season, planting and weeding times. At other times, much of the labor is underemployed. Because the time of planting is determined by the onset of the rains and because much of Africa experiences only one extended rainy season, the demand for workers during the early weeks of this rainy season usually exceeds all available rural labor supplies.

The net result of these three forces had been a relatively constant level of agricultural total output and labor productivity throughout much of Africa. As long as population size remained relatively stable, this historical pattern of low productivity and shifting cultivation enabled most African tribes to meet their subsistence food requirements. But the feasibility of shifting cultivation has now broken down as population densities increase. It has largely been replaced by sedentary cultivation on small owner-occupied plots. As a result, the need for other nonhuman productive inputs and new technologies grows, especially in the more densely populated agricultural regions of Kenya, Nigeria, Ghana, and Uganda. Moreover, with the growth of towns, the penetration of the monetary economy, soil erosion and deforestation of marginal lands, and the introduction of land taxes, pure subsistence-agricultural practices are no longer viable. Mixed and modern commercial farming must appear, as indeed they have in parts of sub-Saharan Africa.

As noted in Table 9.2, of all the major regions of the world, Africa has suffered the most from its inability to expand food production at a sufficient pace to keep up with its rapid population growth. As a result of declining production, African per capita food consumption fell dramatically during the 1980s and early 1990s, while dependence on imports—particularly wheat and rice—increased. And World Bank projections to the year 2000 offer little reason to expect a reversal of this trend. Per capita production is expected to continue to decline at an annual rate of 1.2%, with the result that the proportion of Africans living below the poverty line is expected to increase from 60% to 75% (see Chapter 18).

Conclusions

We may conclude our analysis by noting that although traditional African communal social systems differ markedly from agrarian structures prevalent throughout much of Asia and Latin America, the contemporary economic status of the small farmer is not very different among the three regions. Achieving subsistence is still the major objective of Third World peasant agriculture. Even though the small African farmer once had more room in which to maneuver than his typical Asian or Latin American counterpart, the rapid growth of rural populations throughout sub-Saharan Africa has led to a similar fragmentation of smallholder agriculture. Unless low-productivity peasant agriculture can be transformed rapidly into higher-productivity farming in Asia and Latin America (primarily through judicious land reform accompanied by concomitant structural changes in socioeconomic institutions) and Africa (basically through improved farming practices and greater price incentives), the hundreds of millions of impoverished and increasingly landless rural dwellers face an even more precarious existence in the years immediately ahead.

The Important Role of Women

A major and often overlooked feature of Third World agrarian systems, particularly in Africa and Asia, is the crucial role played by women in agricultural production.[22] In Africa, where subsistence farming is predominant and shifting cultivation remains important, nearly all tasks associated with subsistence food production are performed by women. Although men who remain home generally perform the initial task of cutting trees and bushes on a potentially cultivable plot of land, women are responsible for all subsequent operations, including removing and burning felled trees, sowing or planting the plot, weeding, harvesting, and preparing the crop for storage or immediate consumption. In her pioneering work on women and development, Ester Boserup examined many studies on African women's participation in agriculture and found that in nearly all cases recorded, women did most of the agricultural work. In some cases, they were found to do around 70% and in one case nearly 80% of the total. Typically, these tasks are performed only with the most primitive tools and require many days of long, hard labor simply to produce enough output to meet the family's subsistence requirements, while the men often attempt to generate cash income through work on nearby plantations or in the cities.

Women fulfill a wide variety of functions in Third World agricultural sectors. In addition to their reproductive roles, they provide an important source of labor for cash crop production, cultivate food for household consumption, raise and market livestock, generate additional income through cottage industries, collect firewood and water, and perform household chores including the processing and cooking of foods. Due to the time-consuming nature of their diverse responsibilities, women tend to work longer hours than their male counterparts. Studies concerning the allocation of women's time among different activities have greatly increased international recognition of the importance of rural women's economic contribution. It has become clear that since women produce a large share of agricultural output, successful agricultural reform will require raising women's productivity.

The diversity of women's duties makes it difficult to determine their share of agricultural production, much less place an economic value on their work. However, current estimates underscore the importance of women's agricultural labor. It is estimated that in addition to work within the household, women provide 60% to 80% of agricultural labor in Africa and Asia and about 40% in Latin America. Much of this work, however, is statistically "invisible" in that women often receive no payment for the work they perform.

Women make an important contribution to the agricultural economy through the labor they supply in the cultivation of **cash crops**. Though the production and profits from commercial crops are generally controlled by men, women are usually responsible for the strenuous jobs of weeding and transplanting. As population density increases and land becomes more fragmented, the length of time that women must spend walking to and from the fields increases, often in very hot climates that make strenuous work exceedingly difficult. In addition to commercial crops, women frequently cultivate small vegetable gardens that provide food for domestic consumption. Though the cash value of produce from these gardens may be small, it often represents an important component of the total resources available to women.

Women's work in the household involves a range of demanding tasks including processing and pounding raw grains, tending livestock, cooking over primitive stoves, and caring for children. Collecting increasingly scarce firewood and water from distant sources may add several hours to the workday. To raise additional income, it is common for women to engage in household production of goods for sale in village markets. These items are specific to each region, but a few examples are homemade beer, processed foods, handicrafts, and textiles.

Perhaps the most important role of women, though not immediately apparent, is providing food security for the household. This is accomplished through the supplementation of household earnings, diversification of household income sources, and raising of livestock to augment household assets. The production of vegetables for household consumption helps insulate households from dramatic swings in food prices and reduces cash outlays for the purchase of household necessities during periods of slack income. Women's investments in revenue-generating projects and livestock are crucial to stabilizing household income, especially in female-headed households where resource constraints are the most severe.

However, financial investments are inherently risky, and the poorer the household, the more averse its members are to taking any kind of risk. When credit and resources are unavailable, reducing the variability of household earnings generally entails choosing less efficient methods of production and thus lower income. This trade-off occurs most frequently in female-headed households, where resource constraints are greatest. Thus as a consequence of their restricted range of choices, women tend to retain traditional modes of economic activity. The upshot is that their productivity has stagnated while that of men has continued to improve.

Where the structure of agriculture is becoming more commercialized, women's roles and thus their economic status are changing. In many regions of the Third World, women are still unremunerated for the long hours they contribute to the tending of commercial crops. As revenue-generating cash cropping rises in importance, the proportion of resources controlled by women tends to diminish. This is largely due to the fact that household resources, such as land and inputs, are transferred away from women's crops in order to promote the production of cash crops.

Government extension programs that provide resources exclusively to men tend to exacerbate existing disparities between men's and women's access to resources. If credit is provided solely or preferentially to men for the purpose of cash cropping, commercial production will increase at the expense of women's vegetable gardens. Since homegrown vegetables must be replaced by purchased substitutes, significant increases in a male spouse's cash contribution are necessary to offset a woman's losses. If the market price of vegetables increases markedly (there are now fewer producers) and the increase in the husband's contribution is not sufficient to compensate for the increased need for cash, the welfare of the woman and her children will decline.

This fall in the well-being of household members is due to the fact that a considerably higher proportion of women's income than men's is used for nutrition and basic necessities. Thus if men's incomes rise at the expense of women's resources, as many studies have indicated, an increase in household income will not necessarily lead to improvements in health and nutrition. Changes in land use that increase household income but reduce women's economic status can be detrimental to the welfare of both women and children. Consequently, it is important that the design of government extension programs reflect the interests of all household members.

Yet government-sponsored programs continue to exclude women, often because women lack collateral for loans or are barred by law from owning property or conducting financial transactions without their husband's permission. Agricultural inputs and training are rarely provided to female applicants. Even efforts to reduce poverty through land reforms have been found to reduce female income and economic status because they distribute land titles only to male heads of household. Cultural and social barriers to women's integration into agricultural programs remain strong because in many countries, women's income is perceived as a threat to men's authority. While men are taught new agricultural techniques to increase their productivity, women, if involved at all, are trained to perform low-productivity tasks that are considered compatible with their traditional roles, such as sewing, cooking, or basic hygiene. Women's components of development projects are frequently little more than welfare programs that fail to improve economic well-being. Furthermore, these projects tend to depend on the unpaid work of women, while men are remunerated for their efforts.

The few development projects specifically designed to increase the productivity of women have produced impressive results. For example, the Grameen Bank in Bangladesh, which offers small loans to poor rural entrepreneurs (the vast majority of whom are women), has experienced remarkable loan performance. Repayment rates exceed 98% and the rate of return on women's investments is in excess of 150% when the opportunity cost of their time is valued at female wage rates.

Though efforts to increase the income of women by providing direct access to credit and inputs have experienced considerable success, programs that work indirectly with women have frequently fallen short of their stated goals. Studies have found that projects are most likely to elicit the cooperation of women when resources are placed directly under their control. Clearly, projects that depend on the unremunerated labor of women are likely to obtain only minimal support. Adoption of new crops and technologies will be more effective where patterns of production are consistent with the interests of female household members. Because the active participation of women is critical to agricultural prosperity, policy design should ensure that women benefit equally from development efforts.

The Economics of Agricultural Development: Transition from Peasant Subsistence to Specialized Commercial Farming

For expository convenience, we can identify three broad stages in the evolution of agricultural production.[23] The first and most primitive is the pure, low-productivity, mostly subsistence-level, peasant farm. The second stage is what might be called diversified or mixed family agriculture, where part of the produce is grown for consumption and part for sale to the commercial sector. The third stage represents the modern farm, exclusively engaged in high-productivity specialized agriculture geared to the commercial market.

Agricultural modernization in mixed-market developing economies may be described in terms of the gradual but sustained transition from subsistence to diversified and specialized production. But such a transition involves much more than reorganizing the structure of the farm economy or applying new agricultural technologies. We have seen that in most traditional societies, agriculture is not just an economic activity; it is a way of life. Any government attempting to transform its traditional agriculture must recognize that in addition to adapting the farm structure to meet the demand for increased production, profound changes affecting the entire social, political, and institutional structure of rural societies will often be necessary. Without such changes, agricultural development will either never get started or, more likely, simply widen the already sizable gap between the few wealthy large landholders and the masses of impoverished tenant farmers, smallholders, and landless laborers.

Before analyzing the economics of agricultural and rural development, therefore, we need to understand how the agricultural system of a developing nation tends to evolve over time from a predominately subsistence-level and small-scale peasant orientation to more diversified and larger extended family operations and eventually to the dominance in total production of large-scale commercial enterprises.

Subsistence Farming: Risk Aversion, Uncertainty, and Survival

On the classic peasant subsistence farm, most output is produced for family consumption (although some may be sold or traded in local markets), and a few **staple food** crops (usually including wheat, barley, sorghum, rice, or corn) are the chief sources of food intake. Output and productivity are low, and only the simplest traditional methods and tools are used. Captial investment is minimal; land and labor are the principal factors of production. The law of diminishing returns is in operation as more labor is applied to shrinking (or shifting) parcels of land. The failure of the rains, the appropriation of his land, and the appearance of the moneylender to collect outstanding debts are the banes of the peasant's existence and cause him to fear for his survival. Labor is underemployed for most of the year, although workers may be fully occupied at seasonal peak periods such as planting and harvest. The peasant usually cultivates only as much land as his family can manage without the need for hired labor, although many peasant farmers intermittently employ one or two landless laborers. The environment is harsh and static. Technological limitations, rigid social institutions, and fragmented markets and communication networks between rural areas and urban centers tend to discourage higher levels of production. Any cash income that is generated comes mostly from nonfarm wage labor.[24]

Throughout much of the Third World, agriculture is still in this subsistence stage. But in spite of the relative backwardness of production technologies and the misguided convictions of some foreigners who attribute the peasants' resistance to change as a sign of incompetence or irrationality, the fact remains that given the static nature of the peasants' environment, the uncertainties that surround them, the need to meet minimum survival levels of output, and the rigid social institutions into which they are locked, most peasants behave in an economically rational manner when confronted with alternative opportunities. As one informed observer of peasant agricultural systems has noted:

> Despite the almost infinite variety of village-level institutions and processes to be found around the world, they have three common characteristics which are pertinent to change: 1, they have historically proven to be successful, i.e., the members have survived; 2, they are relatively static, at least the general pace of change is below that which is considered desirable today; and 3, attempts at change are frequently resisted, both because these institutions and processes have proven dependable and because the various elements constitute something akin to an ecological unity in the human realm.[25]

The traditional two-factor neoclassical theory of production where land (and perhaps captial) is fixed and labor is the only variable input provides some insight into the economics of subsistence agriculture. Specifically, it provides an economic rationale for the observed low productivity of traditional agriculture in the form of the law of diminishing marginal productivity.

Unfortunately, this theory does not satisfactorily explain why peasant agriculturalists are often resistant to technological innovation in farming techniques or to the introduction of new seeds or different cash crops. According to the standard theory, a rational income or profit-maximizing farm or firm will always choose a method of production that will increase output for a given cost (in this case, the available labor time) or lower costs for a given output level. But the theory is based on the crucial assumption that farmers possess "perfect knowledge" of all technological input-output relationships as well as current information about prevailing factor and product prices. This is the point at which the theory loses a good deal of its validity when applied to the environment of subsistence agriculture in much of Asia, Africa, and Latin America. Furthermore, when access to information is highly imperfect, the transaction costs of obtaining this information are usually high. As a result, peasant farmers often face **price bands** (a wide range) rather than a single input price. Along with limited access to credit and insurance, such an environment is not conducive to the type of behavior posited by neoclassical theory and goes a long way to explain the actual day-to-day behavior of peasant farmers.[26]

Subsistence agriculture is thus a highly risky and uncertain venture. It is made even more so by the fact that human lives are at stake. In regions where farms are extremely small and cultivation is dependent on the uncertainties of variable rainfall, average output will be low, and in poor years the peasant and his family will be exposed to the very real danger of starvation. In such circumstances, the main motivating force in the peasant's life may be the maximization not of income but rather of his family's chances of survival. Accordingly, when risk and uncertainty are high, a small farmer may be very reluctant to shift from a traditional technology and crop pattern that over the years he has come to know and understand to a new one that promises higher yields but may entail greater risks of crop failure. When sheer survival is at stake, it is more important to avoid a bad year (total crop failure) than to maximize the output in better years. In the jargon of economic statistics, risk-avoiding peasant farmers are likely to prefer a technology of food production that combines a low *mean* per-hectare yield with low *variance* (less fluctuations around the average) to alternative technologies and crops that may promise a higher mean yield but also present the risk of a greater variance.

Figure 9.3 provides a simple illustration of how attitudes toward risk among small farmers may militate against apparently economically justified innovations.[27] In the figure, levels of output and consumption are measured on the vertical axis and different points in time on the horizontal axis, and two straight lines are drawn. The lower horizontal line measures the minimum consumption requirements (MCR) necessary for the farm family's physical survival. This may be taken as the starvation minimum fixed by nature. Any output below this level would be catastrophic for the peasant and his family. The upper, positively sloped straight line represents the minimum level of food consumption that would be desirable given the prevailing cultural factors affecting village consumption standards. It is assumed that the minimum desirable consumption level (MDCL) rises over time to reflect rising expectations as traditional societies are opened up to external influences. The producer's attitude toward risk will be largely conditioned by his historical output performance relative to these two standards of reference.

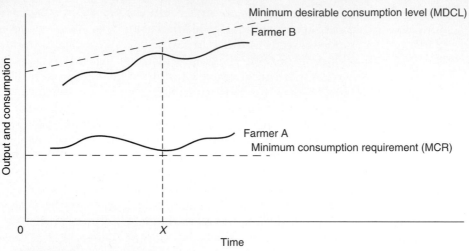

FIGURE 9.3 Small-Farmer Attitudes toward Risk: Why It Is Sometimes Rational to Resist Innovation and Change.

Looking at Figure 9.3, we see that at time X, farmer A's output levels have been very close to MCR. He is barely getting by and cannot take a chance of any crop failure. He will have a greater incentive to minimize risk than farmer B, whose output performance has been well above the minimum subsistence level and is close to the culturally determined MDCL. Farmer B will therefore be more likely to innovate and change than farmer A.

For the more statistically minded, there is an alternative way to look at risk-aversion decisions of peasant farmers. In Figure 9.4, two graphs portraying hypothetical probabilities for crop yields are depicted. The higher graph (technique A) shows a production technology with a lower mean crop yield (10) than that of technique B (12), shown by the lower graph. But it also has a lower variance around that mean yield than technique B. Clearly, the chances of starving are much greater with technique B, so risk-averse peasant farmers would naturally choose technique A, the one with the lower mean yield.[28]

Many programs to raise agricultural productivity among small farmers have suffered because of failure to provide adequate insurance (both financial credit and physical "buffer" stocks) against the risks of crop shortfalls, whether these risks are real or imagined. An understanding of the major role that risk and uncertainty play in the economics of subsistence agriculture would have prevented early and unfortunate characterizations of subsistence or traditional farmers as technologically backward, irrational producers with limited aspirations or just plain "lazy natives" as in the colonial stereotype. Moreover, in many parts of Asia and Latin America, a closer examination of why peasant farmers have apparently not responded to an "obvious" economic opportunity will often reveal that (1) the landlord secured all the gain, (2) the moneylender captured all the profits, (3) the government's "guaranteed" price was never paid, or (4) complementary inputs (fertilizers, pesticides, assured supplies of water, adequate nonusurious credit, etc.) were never made available.

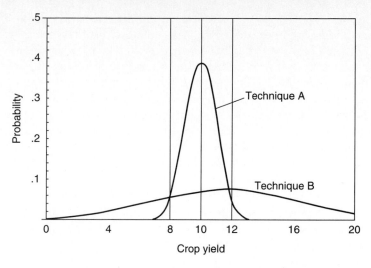

FIGURE 9.4 Crop Yield Probability Densities of Two Different Farming Techniques.

We may conclude that peasant farmers do act rationally and are responsive to economic incentives and opportunities. Where innovation and change fail to occur, we should not assume that peasants are stupid, irrational, or conservative; instead, we should examine carefully the environment in which the small farmer operates to search for the particular institutional or commercial obstacles that may be blocking or frustrating constructive change. As Keith Griffin has pointed out:

> If peasants sometimes appear to be unresponsive or hostile to proposed technical changes, it is probably because the risks are high, the returns to the cultivator are low—for example, because of local custom or land tenure conditions, or because credit facilities and marketing outlets are inadequate and the necessary inputs—including knowledge—are missing.[29]

Efforts to minimize risk and remove commercial and institutional obstacles to small-farmer innovation are therefore essential requirements of agricultural and rural development.

Sharecropping and Interlocking Factor Markets

The phenomenon of risk aversion among peasant farmers also helps explain the prevalence of sharecropping throughout much of Asia and Latin America.[30] Although there are different forms of relationships that may arise between the owners of land and those who work on them (e.g., they could rent or act as wage laborers), in fact we find widespread sharecropping. Sharecropping occurs when a peasant farmer uses the landowner's farmland in exchange for a share of food output, such as half of the rice or wheat that he grows. The landlord's share may vary from less than a third to more than two-thirds of output, depending on local labor availability, and the other inputs (such as seeds and hoes) that the landlord provides, but in the following discussion we will assume that output is split 50–50 between landlord and sharecropper.

Sharecropping was long considered by economists to be economically ineffi- cient. Alfred Marshall observed that the farmer was in effect paid half, rather than all, of his marginal product and would rationally reduce work effort accordingly. But more recent studies suggest that sharecropping is efficient after all, in that it makes the best out of an inherently uncertain and risky situation for both parties.[31] If the landlord pays the tenant a straight wage, which would be efficient if the ten- ant always gave his full effort and it didn't cost the landlord anything to make sure of this, the tenant has every incentive to accept the money and not work hard. If the tenant pays a straight rent for the land, he faces the appalling risk that there will be a particularly lean year, such as a drought, and there will not be enough food left over after the rent is paid up to prevent starvation. Thus sharecropping is now understood to represent a compromise between two types of risk: the risk to the landlord that the tenant will not do much work and the risk to the tenant that a fixed rent will in some years leave him no income. So even though sharecropping would be inefficient in a world of perfect certainty, in the real world it is "as effi- cient as we can get."

But the economic and social framework in which sharecropping takes place is one of extraordinary social inequality and far-reaching market failure. When the peasant faces his landlord, he faces not only the individual whom he must per- suade to rent him productive land but at the same time his prospective employer, his loan officer, and often his ultimate customer for any crops he wishes to sell. These are the conditions known as **interlocking factor markets**, and they pro- vide the rural landlord with abundant sources of monopoly and monopsony power, making traditional rural economic and social organization hardly resis- tant to efforts at reform. The consequences of this have been explored with eco- nomic theory and with case studies of agrarian regions. Suppose, for example, that a well-meaning government puts a cap on the interest rates that the land- lord can charge. The landlord may simply respond by lowering the wage, the tenant's share of the crop, or the price the landlord pays for any crops the tenant seeks to sell or by raising the implicit price of seeds and tools advanced to the tenant. Under very plausible conditions—in particular, the availability of a per- fectly elastic supply of tenants and the ability of the landlord to subdivide his land into as many plots as he chooses—the peasant is forced to the same *reser- vation utility level*, or next-best income opportunity, as before. One key feature of this analysis is that the peasant's effort per hectare increases with decreases in plot size. Interlocked-factor-market sharecropping does have the advantage that it is in the landlord's interest to see to it that his sharecropper receives credit from the lowest-cost source. Attempting to regulate several of these interlocked mar- kets at once in an uncertain economy will generally lead to extreme inefficiency, if not leave most tenants unemployed as landlords switch to entirely different uses for their land. The analysis often concludes that nothing short of land re- form will affect the tenant's welfare. We discuss the pros and cons of land reform later in the chapter.

The Transition to Mixed and Diversified Farming

It is neither realistic nor necessarily desirable to think of instantly transforming a traditional agrarian system that has prevailed for many generations into a highly specialized commercial farming system. Attempts to introduce cash crops indiscriminately in subsistence farms have more often than not resulted in the peasants' loss of land to moneylenders or landlords. Subsistence living is merely substituted for subsistence production. For small farmers, exclusive reliance on cash crops can be even more precarious than pure subsistence agriculture because the risks of price fluctuations are added to the uncertainty of nature.

Diversified or **mixed farming** therefore represents a logical intermediate step in the transition from subsistence to specialized production. In this stage, the staple crop no longer dominates farm output, and new cash crops such as fruits, vegetables, coffee, tea, and pyrethrum are established, together with simple animal husbandry. These new activities can take up the normal slack in farm workloads during times of the year when disguised unemployment is prevalent. This is especially desirable in the vast majority of Third World nations where rural labor is abundantly available for better and more efficient use.

For example, if the staple crop occupies the land during only parts of the year, new crops can be introduced in the slack season to take advantage of both idle land and family labor. And where labor is in short supply during peak planting seasons, as in many parts of Africa, simple laborsaving devices (such as small tractors, mechanical seeders, or animal-operated steel plows) can be introduced to free labor for other farm activities. Finally, the use of better seeds, fertilizers, and simple irrigation to increase the yields of staple crops like wheat, maize, and rice can free part of the land for cash crop cultivation while ensuring an adequate supply of the staple food. The farm operator can thus have a marketable surplus, which he can sell to raise his family's consumption standards or invest in farm improvements. Diversified farming can also minimize the impact of staple crop failure and provide a security of income previously unavailable.

The success or failure of such efforts to transform traditional agriculture will depend not only on the farmer's ability and skill in raising his productivity but, even more important, on the social, commercial, and institutional conditions under which he must function. Specifically, if he can have a reasonable and reliable access to credit, fertilizer, water, crop information, and marketing facilities; if he receives a fair market price for his output; and if he can feel secure that he and his family will be the primary beneficiaries of any improvements, there is no reason to assume that the traditional farmer will not respond to economic incentives and new opportunities to improve his standard of living. Evidence from such diverse countries as Colombia, Mexico, Nigeria, Ghana, Kenya, India, Pakistan, Thailand, and the Philippines shows that under proper conditions, small farmers are responsive to price incentives and economic opportunities and will make radical changes in what they produce and how they produce it.[32] Lack of innovation in agriculture, as we have seen, is usually due not to poor motivation or fear of change per se but to inadequate or unprofitable opportunities.

From Divergence to Specialization: Modern Commercial Farming

The specialized farm represents the final and most advanced stage of individual holding in a mixed market economy. It is the most prevalent type of farming in advanced industrial nations. It has evolved in response to and parallel with development in other areas of the national economy. General rises in living standards, biological and technical progress, and the expansion of national and international markets have provided the main impetus for its emergence and growth.

In **specialized farming**, the provision of food for the family with some marketable surplus is no longer the basic goal. Instead, pure commercial profit becomes the criterion of success, and maximum per-hectare yields derived from synthetic (irrigation, fertilizer, pesticides, hybrid seeds, etc.) and natural resources become the object of farm activity. Production, in short, is entirely for the market. Economic concepts such as fixed and variable costs, saving, investment and rates of return, optimal factor combinations, maximum production possibilities, market prices, and price supports take on quantitative and qualitative significance. The emphasis in resource utilization is no longer on land, water, and labor as in subsistence and often mixed farming. Instead, capital formation, technological progress, and scientific research and development play major roles in stimulating higher levels of output and productivity.

Specialized farms vary in both size and function. They range from intensively cultivated fruit and vegetable farms to the vast wheat and corn fields of North America. In most cases, sophisticated laborsaving mechanical equipment, ranging from huge tractors and combine harvesters to airborne spraying techniques, permits a single family to cultivate many thousands of hectares of land.

The common features of all specialized farms, therefore, are their emphasis on the cultivation of one particular crop; their use of capital-intensive and, in many cases, laborsaving techniques of production; and their reliance on economies of scale to reduce unit costs and maximize profits. For all practical purposes, specialized farming is no different in concept or operation from large industrial enterprises. In fact, some of the largest specialized farming operations in both the developed and especially the less developed nations are owned and managed by large agribusiness multinational corporate enterprises.

Conclusions

Although we can find all three types of farms—subsistence, mixed, and specialized commercial—coexisting in almost all LDCs at any given time, for the majority of countries, contemporary agricultural systems are still dominated by peasant subsistence and small-scale mixed family farms. The further transition to a preponderance of commercial enterprises may be difficult to achieve, depending as it does on the solution to many other short- and intermediate-term problems. We may conclude, therefore, that the improvement of small- and medium-scale mixed farming practices that will not only raise farm incomes and average yields but, if labor-intensive, also effectively absorb underutilized rural labor offers the major immediate avenue toward the achievement of real people-oriented rural development.

Large-scale commercial farms will continue to increase in number, but given the population, poverty, and urban employment problems of Third World nations, they should not form the basis of most agricultural development strategies.

Toward a Strategy of Agricultural and Rural Development: Some Main Requirements

If the major objective of agricultural and rural development in Third World nations is the progressive improvement in rural levels of living achieved primarily through increases in small-farm incomes, output, and productivity, it is important to identify the principal sources of agricultural progress and the basic conditions essential to its achievement. These are necessarily interrelated, but for purposes of description we may separate them and further divide each into three components:

Sources of Small-Scale Agricultural Progress

1. Technological change and innovation
2. Appropriate government economic policies
3. Supportive social institutions

Conditions for General Rural Advancement

1. Modernizing farm structures to meet rising food demands
2. Creating an effective supporting system
3. Changing the rural environment to improve levels of living

Let us look at each of these six interrelated components.

Improving Small–Scale Agriculture

Technology and Innovation

In most developing countries, new agricultural technologies and innovations in farm practices are preconditions for sustained improvements in levels of output and productivity. In many parts of Africa and Latin America, however, increased output in earlier years was achieved without the need for new technology simply by extending cultivation into unused but potentially productive lands. Almost all of these opportunities have by now been exploited, however, and there is not much scope for further significant improvement.

Two major sources of technological innovation can increase farm yields. Unfortunately, both have somewhat problematic implications for Third World agricultural development. The first is the introduction of mechanized agriculture to replace human labor. The introduction of laborsaving machinery can have a dramatic effect on the volume of output per worker, especially where land is extensively cultivated and labor is scarce. For example, one man operating a huge combine harvester can accomplish in a single hour what would require hundreds of workers using traditional methods.

But in the rural areas of most developing nations where land parcels are small, capital is scarce, and labor is abundant, the introduction of heavily mechanized techniques is not only often ill suited to the physical environment but, more important, often has the effect of creating more rural unemployment without necessarily lowering per-unit costs of food production.[33] Importation of such machinery can therefore be antidevelopmental in that its efficient deployment requires large tracts of land (and thus the expropriation of small holdings by landlords and moneylenders) and tends to exacerbate the already serious problems of rural poverty and unemployment. And if mechanized techniques exclude women, the male-female productivity gap could widen further, with serious repercussions.[34]

By contrast, biological (hybrid seeds), water control (irrigation), and chemical (fertilizer, pesticides, insecticides, etc.) innovations—the second major source—are not without their own problems. They are land-augmenting; that is, they improve the quality of existing land by raising yields per hectare. Only indirectly do they increase output per worker. Improved seeds; advanced techniques of irrigation and crop rotation; the increasing use of fertilizers, pesticides, and herbicides; and new developments in veterinary medicine and animal nutrition represent major scientific advances in modern agriculture. These measures are technologically **scale-neutral**; theoretically, they can be applied equally effectively on large and small farms. They do not necessarily require large capital inputs or mechanized equipment. They are therefore particularly well suited for tropical and subtropical regions and offer enormous potential for raising agricultural output in Third World nations.

Institutional and Pricing Policies: Providing the Necessary Economic Incentives

Unfortunately, although the new hybrid "miracle seed" varieties of wheat, corn, and rice, together with needed irrigation and chemicals (often collectively referred to as the **Green Revolution**) are scale-neutral and thus offer the potential for small-farm progress, the social institutions and government economic policies that accompany their introduction into the rural economy often are *not* scale-neutral.[35] On the contrary, they often merely serve the needs and vested interests of the wealthy landowners. Because the new hybrid seeds require access to complementary inputs such as irrigation, fertilizer, insecticides, credit, and agricultural extension services, if these are provided only to a small minority of large landowners, the effective impact of the Green Revolution can be (and has been in parts of South Asia and Mexico) the further impoverishment of the masses of rural peasants. Large landowners, with their disproportionate access to these complementary inputs and support services, are able to gain a competitive advantage over smallholders and eventually drive them out of the market. Large-scale farmers obtain access to low-interest government credit, while smallholders are forced to turn to moneylenders. The inevitable result is the further widening of the gap between rich and poor and the increased consolidation of agricultural land in the hands of a very few so-called progressive farmers. A developmental innovation with great potential for alleviating rural poverty and raising agricultural output can thus turn out to be antidevelopmental if public policies and social institutions militate against the active participation of the small farmer in the evolving agrarian structure.[36]

Another critical area calling for major improvements in government policies relates to the pricing of agricultural commodities, especially food grains and other staples produced for local markets. Many LDC governments, in their headlong pursuit of rapid industrial and urban development, have maintained low agricultural prices in an attempt to provide cheap food for the urban modern sector. Farmers have been paid prices below either world competitive or free-market internal prices. The relative internal price ratio between food and manufactured goods (the domestic terms of trade) thus turned against farmers and in favor of urban manufacturers. With farm prices so low—in some cases below the costs of production—there was no incentive for farmers to expand output or invest in new productivity-raising technology. As a result, local food supplies continually fell short of demand, and many Third World nations, especially in sub-Saharan Africa, that were once self-sufficient in food production had to import the balance of their food needs. This caused further strains on their international balance of payments situation and contributed to the worsening foreign-exchange and international debt crisis of the 1980s (see Chapters 13 and 14 for further analysis of the international trade and debt problems).

Economists therefore argue that if Third World governments are to promote increases in agricultural production through new Green Revolution technologies, they must not only make the appropriate institutional and credit market adjustments but must also provide incentives for small and medium sized farmers by implementing pricing policies that truly reflect internal market conditions.[37] This often means less government intervention (especially in Africa) in the form of public agricultural marketing boards, which monopolize the purchase and distribution of farm output and set producer prices that are typically well below world market prices.[38]

Conditions for Rural Development

Let us now collect what has already been said to formulate three propositions that in essence constitute the necessary conditions for the realization of a people-oriented agricultural and rural development strategy.[39]

Land Reform

> *Proposition 1: Farm structures and land tenure patterns must be adapted to the dual objectives of increasing food production and promoting a wider distribution of the benefits of agrarian progress.*

Agricultural and rural development that benefits the masses of people can succeed only through a joint effort by the government and *all* farmers, not just the large farmers. A first step in any such effort, especially in Latin America and Asia, is the provision of secured tenure rights to the individual farmer. A small farmer's attachment to his land is profound. It is closely bound up with his innermost sense of self-esteem and freedom from coercion. When he is driven off his land or is gradually impoverished through accumulated debts, not only is his material well-being damaged, but more important, his sense of self-worth and his desire for self- and family improvement can be permanently destroyed.

It is for these humane reasons as well as for reasons of higher agricultural output and the simultaneous achievement of both greater efficiency and more equity that **land reform** is often proposed as a necessary first condition for agricultural development in many LDCs. In most countries, the highly unequal structure of land ownership is probably the single most important determinant of the existing highly inequitable distribution of rural income and wealth. It is also the basis for the character of agricultural development. When land is very unevenly distributed, rural peasants can have little hope for economic advancement.

Land reform usually entails a redistribution of the rights of ownership or use of land away from large landowners in favor of cultivators with very limited or no landholdings. It can take many forms: the transfer of ownership to tenants who already work the land to create family farms (Japan, South Korea, Taiwan); transfer of land from large estates to small farms (Mexico), rural cooperatives (Cuba), or state farms (Peru); or the appropriation of large estates for new settlement (Kenya). All go under the heading of land reform and are designed to fulfill one central function: the transfer of land ownership or control directly or indirectly to the people who actually work the land.

There is widespread agreement among economists and other development specialists on the need for land reform. To Myrdal, land reform holds the key to agricultural development in Asia. The Economic Commission for Latin America (ECLA) has repeatedly identified land reform as a necessary precondition for agricultural and rural progress. An FAO report concluded that in many Third World regions, land reform remains a prerequisite for development. The report argued that such reform was more urgent today than ever before, primarily because (1) income inequalities and unemployment in rural areas have worsened, (2) rapid population growth threatens further to worsen existing inequalities, and (3) recent and potential technological breakthroughs in agriculture (the Green Revolution) can be exploited primarily by large and powerful rural landholders and hence can result in an increase in their power, wealth, and capacity to resist future reform. Finally, as noted earlier, from a strict view of economic efficiency and growth, there is ample empirical evidence that land redistribution not only increases rural employment and raises rural incomes but also leads to greater agricultural production and more efficient resource utilization.

If programs of land reform can be legislated and effectively implemented by the government, the basis for improved output levels and higher standards of living for rural peasants will be established. Unfortunately, many land reform efforts have failed because LDC governments (especially those in Latin America) bowed to political pressures from powerful landowning groups and failed to implement the intended reforms.[40] But even an egalitarian land reform program alone is no guarantee of successful agricultural and rural development.[41] This leads to our second proposition.

Supportive Policies

> *Proposition 2: The full benefits of small-scale agricultural development cannot be realized unless government support systems are created that provide the necessary incentives, economic opportunities, and access to needed inputs to enable small cultivators to expand their output and raise their productivity.*

Though land reform is essential in many parts of Asia and Latin America, it is likely to be ineffective and perhaps even counterproductive unless there are corresponding changes in rural institutions that control production (e.g., banks, moneylenders, seed and fertilizer distributors), in supporting government aid services (e.g., technical and educational extension services, public credit agencies, storage and marketing facilities, rural transport and feeder roads), and in government pricing policies with regard to both inputs (e.g., removing factor-price distortions) and outputs (paying market-value prices to farmers). Even where land reform is not necessary but where productivity and incomes are low (as in the whole of Africa and much of Southeast Asia), this broad network of external support services, along with appropriate governmental pricing policies related to both farm inputs and outputs, is an essential condition for sustained agricultural progress.

Integrated Development Objectives

Proposition 3: Rural development, though dependent primarily on small-farmer agricultural progress, implies much more. It encompasses (a) efforts to raise both farm and nonfarm rural real incomes through job creation, rural industrialization, and the increased provision of education, health and nutrition, housing, and a variety of related social and welfare services; (b) a decreasing inequality in the distribution of rural incomes and a lessening of urban-rural imbalances in incomes and economic opportunities; and (c) the capacity of the rural sector to sustain and accelerate the pace of these improvements over time.

This proposition is self-explanatory. We need only add that the achievement of its three objectives is vital to national development. This is not only because the majority of Third World populations are located in rural areas but also because the burgeoning problems of urban unemployment and population congestion must find their ultimate solution in the improvement of the rural environment. By restoring a proper balance between urban and rural economic opportunities and by creating the conditions for broad popular participation in national development efforts and rewards, developing nations will have taken a giant step toward the realization of the true meaning of development.

CASE STUDY

The Economy of Bangladesh

GEOGRAPHIC, SOCIAL, AND ECONOMIC
INDICATORS

Capital Dhaka

Area 143,988 km²

Population 119.2 million (1995)

**Population (average annual growth
rate)** 2.0% (1985–1994)

GNP per capita U.S. $230 (1994)

**GNP per capita (average annual growth
rate)** 2.1% (1985–1994)

Agriculture as share of GDP 30% (1994)

Exports as share of GDP 12% (1994)

**Infant mortality rate (per 1,000 live
births)** 108 (1995)

Child malnutrition (underweight) 68%
(1993)

Females as share of labor force 8% (1994)

Illiteracy rate (age 15+) 65% (1990)

Human Development Index 0.31 (low)
(1992)

Bangladesh is located on the Tropic of Cancer in South Asia. It has the world's highest annual rainfall, which affects the topography of the territory and the location of economic activities. Much of the territory is partly submerged or subject to flooding during the rainy season, and the cultivation of rice and jute employs a very large portion of the workforce.

Bangladesh is the most densely populated agricultural country in the world, with 119 million people in 1995. It is also one of the poorest and least developed countries, with a per capita GNP of only $230, a life expectancy of 55 years, and a literacy rate of only 35%. Its labor force is expanding rapidly as a result of high population growth rates, and unemployment and underemployment currently exceed 30%. Although its income is more evenly distributed than in other LDCs, because of its very low per capita income (fifth lowest in the world), Bangladesh has a very high poverty rate (78%; 86% in rural areas).

Despite the high speed of the urbanization process, approximately 83% of the population still lives in rural areas, most engaged in subsistence farming. In addition to its vulnerability to frequent monsoons and other natural disasters, the Bangladesh economy suffers from structural constraints such as poor transportation and communications facilities, which persist despite attempts by policymakers to remove them.

Agriculture accounts for approximately one-half of both GDP and exports. The heavy dependence on agriculture has not allowed Bangladesh to absorb its rapidly growing labor force or generate a sufficient flow of foreign-exchange earnings. This is the reason why recent plans have emphasized growth in industry (which accounts for only some 17% of GDP) and expansion of labor-intensive exports as primary objectives for achieving growth and development.

Bangladesh's labor force is largely unskilled and uneducated, so despite the large population, human resource development is extremely low. The economy is characterized by a very low domestic savings rate and a large balance of payments deficit. Consequently, external assistance (foreign aid) continues to play an important role in providing budgetary and balance of payments support.

Despite repeated disruptions by natural disasters, Bangladesh made significant progress in many areas in the 1980s. The foreign-trade deficit was reduced through policies designed to promote exports and improve foreign-exchange-rate management. Government deficits were lowered through cutbacks in public investment. Policies were pursued to provide incentive prices to farmers, to deregulate private-investment licensing procedures, and to undertake a major decentralization of public enterprises. These policies enabled Bangladesh to achieve a respected average real rate of per capita GNP growth of 2.1% between 1985 and 1994.

The primary objective of the current government's development effort is to alleviate Bangladesh's ubiquitous poverty through increased production of and access to food and other basics. The achievement of these objectives will require a sustained economic growth rate averaging at least 5.0% to 5.5% per annum over the longer term and a rapid reduction in the rate of population growth. With its heavy dependence on uncertain foreign aid, a sharp decline in overseas worker remittances after the Persian Gulf War, and the need to increase domestic saving and investment by 10% to 15%, the prospect for achieving these objectives in the short-term is not very promising.

CASE STUDY

The Economy of Ghana

GEOGRAPHIC, SOCIAL, AND ECONOMIC INDICATORS

Capital Accra

Area 238,538 km²

Population 17.5 million (1995)

Population (average annual growth rate) 3.1% (1985–1994)

GNP per capita U.S. $430 (1994)

GNP per capita (average annual growth rate) 1.4% (1985–1994)

Agriculture as share of GDP 46% (1994)

Exports as share of GDP 25% (1994)

Infant mortality rate (per 1,000 live births) 81 (1995)

Child malnutrition (underweight) 36% (1993)

Females as share of labor force 39% (1994)

Illiteracy rate (age 15+) 40% (1990)

Human Development Index 0.38 (low) (1992)

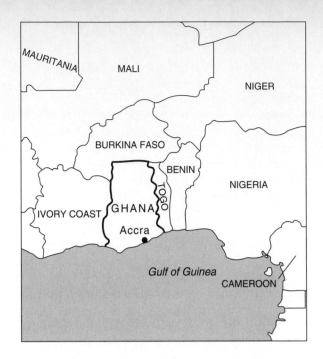

Ghana is situated on West Africa's Gulf of Guinea, a few degrees north of the equator. Many people live on the coast or in the northern areas near the Ivory Coast; the principal cities are Accra and Kumasi, the latter being inland in the Ashanti region. According to tradition, most Ghanaians are descended from migrating tribes that probably came down the Volta River valley at the beginning of the thirteenth century. The history of the Gold Coast region before the last quarter of the fifteen century is derived primarily from traditions preserved in tribal stories and folklore. Many of the traditions refer to migrations from the ancient kingdoms of the western Sudan (the area of Mauritania and Mali).

In May 1956, Prime Minister Kwame Nkrumah's Gold Coast government issued a white paper containing proposals for Gold Coast independence, including a proposal to change the name of the country to Ghana (after one of the ancestral inland kingdoms). The British government stated that it would agree to a firm date for independence if a reasonable majority for such a step were obtained in the Gold Coast legislative assembly after a general election. Ghana became Africa's first postcolonial independent state on March 6, 1957, when the United Kingdom relinquished its control over the colony of the Gold Coast and Ashanti, the Northern Territories protectorate, and British Togoland.

By West African standards, Ghana has a diverse and valuable resource base. The country is mainly agricultural, however, with most of its workers engaged in subsistence farming. Cash crops consist primarily of cacao and cacao products, which provide about two-thirds of export revenues; timber products; coconuts and other palm products; shea nuts (which produce an edible fat); and coffee. Corn, plantains, rice, cassava, and peanuts are the basic foodstuffs. Local fish, poultry, and meat are also important in the Ghanaian diet.

Minerals, primarily gold, diamonds, manganese ore, and bauxite, are produced and exported. Only one commercially exploitable oil field has been discovered and is producing oil. The government hopes that other fields of oil and natural gas will be found.

Ghana's industrial base is relatively advanced, compared to that of many other African countries. Import substitution industries include textiles, steel (using scrap for the raw material), tires, oil refining, simple consumer goods, and car, truck, and bus assembly. However, these industries depend on imports for most of their raw materials and, due to depressed economic conditions, were running far below capacity in the 1980s.

At independence in 1957, Ghana had a substantial physical and social infrastructure and $481 million in foreign reserves. But during the Nkrumah era, investments consisted of public works with little revenue-generating capacity and poorly conceived and badly managed agricultural and industrial schemes. With cacao prices falling and the country's reserves fast disappearing, Nkrumah's government resorted to supplier credits to finance many projects. By the mid-1960s, Ghana's reserves were gone, and it was evident that the country would be unable to repay its suppliers on schedule.

Prime Minister Busia's government (1969–1972) liberalized controls in an effort to attract foreign investment and to encourage domestic entrepreneurship. Investors were cautious, however, and cacao prices began declining in the midst of an import surge, precipitating a serious trade deficit. Although the Busia regime received considerable foreign assistance and benefited from some debt relief, it, too, was unable to overcome the inherited restraints on growth posed by the debt-service burden, balance of payments imbalances, foreign-exchange shortages, and mismanagement.

Although foreign assistance helped prevent economic collapse in the post-Nkrumah era and was responsible for subsequent improvements in many sectors, the economy stagnated in the 10-year period preceding the

National Redemption Council takeover in 1972. Population growth offset the modest increase in gross domestic product, and real earnings declined for many Ghanaians.

In September 1979, the new civilian government of Hilla Limann faced continued economic deterioration. Problems included declining real per capita income during the previous five years; stagnant industrial and agricultural production because of inadequate supplies of imported raw materials, spare parts, and machinery; shortages of imported and locally produced goods; a sizable budget deficit (almost 40% of expenditures in 1979); inflation still at high levels, "moderating" to 54% in 1979; an increasingly overvalued currency; flourishing black-market activities such as smuggling and other trade malpractices; unemployment and underemployment, particularly among urban youth; deterioration in the transportation network; and continued foreign-exchange constraints.

Nearby Nigeria then announced that undocumented aliens were to be expelled, and an estimated 1 million Ghanaian returnees had to be absorbed into the population. An abnormally low rainfall and other problems resulted in shortages of food, fuel, funds, electric power, and water, complicating the implementation of an economic recovery program announced in 1983. An austerity budget included a change in exchange-rate policy and a short-term program designed to boost the export sector by concentrating the recovery on the rehabilitation of that part of the economy.

In 1985, Nigeria expelled almost 100,000 more unregistered Ghanaians in an additional attempt to rid itself of illegal aliens. However, the Ghanaian economy in 1985 began to show signs of slow but steady recovery, and the government announced a medium-term program that stressed recovery in the social sector, especially education.

The economic recovery program initially succeeded in reversing the decline in real per capita incomes that had occurred during the

1970s and early 1980s. Since 1983, the Ghanaian economy has grown at a 4% annual rate. Nevertheless, Ghana, which once had one of the highest standards of living in sub-Saharan Africa, now has more than half its population living in absolute poverty, very high levels of unemployment, and levels of health and literacy not much higher than those of other African nations. Its long-term public debt is one of the highest in the world as a percentage of GDP, and its vulnerability to fluctuations in cacao prices and earnings makes it difficult for Ghana to plan for sustained long-term economic growth. Much will depend on the success or failure of its closely watched free-market reforms and whether or not foreign investors will return to participate in its economy. After early successes in the late 1980s, these reforms began to crumble in the 1990s as a result of sharp declines in economic growth and a return to high inflation (averaging 28.4% in 1985–1994), growing budget deficits, and a steep drop in agricultural and manufacturing output.

Concepts for Review

Agrarian systems
Cash crops
Diversified farming
Family farm
Farm yields
Green Revolution
Integrated rural development
Interlocking factor markets
Landlord
Land reform
Latifundio
Minifundio
Mixed farming

Moneylender
Per capita agricultural production
Per capita food production
Price bands
Productivity gap
Scale-neutral
Sharecropper
Shifting cultivation
Specialized farming
Staple foods
Subsistence farming
Tenant farmer
Transaction costs

Questions for Discussion

1. Why should any analysis of Third World development problems place heavy emphasis on the study of agricultural systems, especially peasant agriculture, and the rural sector?

2. What were the principal reasons for the relative stagnation of Third World agriculture during the so-called development decades of the 1960s and 1970s? How can this disappointing performance be improved on in the future? Explain.

3. It is sometimes said that the world consists of two kinds of agriculture. Explain what is meant by this statement, and indicate how it might be illustrated both between and within countries.

4. Compare and contrast the nature of peasant or small-scale agriculture in Asia, Africa, and Latin America. How do overall agricultural systems differ among these regions? What are the common characteristics?

5. Explain the meaning of Gunnar Myrdal's quote at the beginning of this chapter: "It is in the agricultural sector that the battle for long-term economic development will be won or lost."

6. It is sometimes asserted that small peasant farmers are backward and ignorant because they seem to resist agricultural innovations that could raise farm yields substantially. Does this resistance stem from an inherent irrationality on their part, or might it be attributable to some other factors often overlooked by Western economists? Explain your answer.

7. In the chapter, we described three stages in the transition from subsistence to specialized agriculture. What are the principal characteristics of these stages?

8. There appears to be widespread agreement that in regions where the distribution of land ownership is highly unequal (mainly Latin America but also parts of Asia), land reform is a necessary but not sufficient condition for promoting and improving small-scale agriculture. What is meant by this statement and by the concept of land reform? Give some examples of supportive policy measures that might accompany land reform.

9. What is meant by comprehensive or integrated rural development? What criteria would you use to decide whether or not such integrated rural development was or was not taking place?

Notes

1. John W. Mellor, "Agriculture on the road to industrialization," in John P. Lewis and Valeriana Kallab (eds.), *Development Strategies Reconsidered* (Washington, D.C.: Overseas Development Council, 1986), pp. 67–89; see also Subrata Ghatak, "Agriculture and economic development," in Norman Gemmell (ed.), *Surveys in Economic Development* (Oxford: Blackwell, 1987), chap. 10; and Charles P. Timmer, "The agricultural transformation," in Hollis B. Chenery and T. N. Srinivasan (eds.), *Handbook of Development Economics*, vol. 1 (Amsterdam: North Holland, 1988), pp. 276–331.

2. For a quantitative review of recent trends in food and agricultural production, see World Resources Institute, *World Resources, 1994–95* (New York: Oxford University Press, 1994), chap. 6.

3. E. F. Scepanik, "Agricultural capital formation in selected developing countries," *Agricultural Planning Studies* 11 (1970).

4. See Raanan Weitz, *From Peasant to Farmer: A Revolutionary Strategy for Development* (New York: Columbia University Press, 1971), pp. 6–9. This statement is not meant to imply that no high-productivity farming is done in LDCs or that no low-productivity family farms operate in developed countries. Rather, it is meant to emphasize the enormous productivity differences that exist when we look at the overall distribution of farm structures and aggregate productivity across the entire agricultural sector for both less developed and developed countries.

5. *Ibid.*, pp. 7–8 (U.S. Census Bureau data). Although much of the success of developed-country agriculture is the result of the application of advanced farm technology, such factors as agricultural protectionism, massive price supports, and huge "pork barrel" public investment programs have also contributed to developed-country output expansion.

6. *Ibid.*, p. 9.

7. Reprinted from *World Development* 2, Francis M. Foland, "Agrarian unrest in Asia and Latin America," 56, 1974, with kind permission from Elsevier Science Ltd., The Boulevard, Langford Lane, Kidlington OX5 IGB, UK.

8. Beginning in the early 1960s, many countries in Latin America initiated land reform programs that did not alter the highly unequal distribution of land ownership but did do away with some of the more feudal patron-client social relationships associated with *latifundios* and *minifundios*. For pedagogical purposes, we will continue to use these terms more as a designation of the dualistic agrarian structure that still permeates Latin America than as a description of contemporary rural social relationships.

9. For data showing that land concentration has not changed much in Latin America for 20 years, see Alain de Janvry, E. Sadoulet, and L. Wilcox, *Rural Labor in Latin America*, ILO Working Paper No. 10-6/WP79 (Geneva: International Labor Organization, 1986), tab. 11.

10. For a summary of the empirical evidence on this point, see R. Albert Berry and William Cline, *Agrarian Structure and Productivity in Developing Countries* (Baltimore: Johns Hopkins University Press, 1979), chap. 3 and app. B; G. A. Cornia, "Farm size, land yields and the agricultural production function: An analysis of fifteen developing countries," *World Development* 13 (December 1985): 513–534; and Nancy L. Johnson and Vernon Ruttan, "Why are farms so small?" *World Development* 22 (May 1994): 691–706.

11. Celso Furtado, *Economic Development in Latin America* (Cambridge: Cambridge University Press, 1970), p. 56.

12. *Ibid.*, pp. 57–58.

13. For evidence that land redistribution is likely to lead to greater output and higher productivity levels, see Cornia, "Farm size, land yields."

14. Foland, "Agrarian unrest," 57.

15. Gunnar Myrdal, *Asian Drama* (New York: Pantheon, 1968), pp. 1033–1052.

16. *Ibid.*, p. 1035.

17. *Ibid.*

18. A somewhat more positive view of the efficiency of land leases and access to credit through moneylenders and other informal sources of credit in Asia (and Latin America) has been the focus of the "new agrarian economics" of the late 1970s and 1980s. In general, the position that this school of thought has taken is that land contracting and usurious moneylending are efficient given the existence of other market failures, imperfect information, high transaction costs, moral hazards, and the like. Whether or not they are as efficient as these writers claim is far from clear, but their ultimate exploitive nature is difficult to deny. For an example of this literature, see Pranab Bardhan, *Land, Labor, and Rural Poverty: Essays in Development Economics* (New York: Columbia University Press, 1984); K. Otsuka and Yujiro Hayami, "Theories of shared tenancy: A critical survey," *Economic Development and Cultural Change* (July 1988); Karla Hoff and Joseph E. Stiglitz, "Imperfect information and rural credit markets: Puzzles and policy perspectives," *World Bank Economic Review* 4 (September, 1990): 235–250; and Timothy Besley, "How do market failures justify interventions in rural credit markets?" *World Bank Research Observer* 9 (January 1994): 27–47.

19. Myrdal, *Asian Drama*, p. 1048.

20. For a discussion of the phenomenon of landlessness in Third World countries with a particular emphasis on Asia, see Mahmood H. Khan, "Landlessness and rural poverty in underdeveloped countries," *Pakistan Development Review* 25 (Autumn 1986): 371–394.

21. Mead Cain, "Char Gopalpur revisited," diary notes, Center for Policy Studies, Population Council, October 1979 (mimeograph). Reprinted with permission.

22. An especially informative book on women's role in Third World agriculture is Carolyn Sachs, *The Invisible Farmers: Women in Agriculture* (Totowa, N.J.: Rowman & Littlefield, 1983). The classic and still influential treatment of the subject can be found in Ester Boserup, *Women's Role in Economic Development* (New York: St. Martin's Press, 1970).

23. See Weitz, *From Peasant to Farmer*, pp. 15–28, from which much of the following material is drawn. The three stages of farm evolution outlined in this section should not be interpreted as inevitable periods or sequences of time in which all farms are simultaneously in one of these stages before moving on to the next. In reality, of course, all three types of farms exist in every country at all points in time. Clearly, however, peasant farming predominates in most LDCs, whereas commercial agriculture tends to dominate in most developed countries.

24. See C. D. Deere and Alain de Janvry, "A conceptual framework for the empirical analysis of peasants," *American Journal of Agricultural Economics*, 61 (November 1979), where it is reported in tab. 5 that in Latin America almost 50% of the income generated by smallholders came from their wage labor. See also de Janvry *et al.*, *Rural Labor in Latin America*, tab. 24.

25. Clifton R. Wharton Jr., "Risk, uncertainty, and the subsistence farmer," *Development Digest* 7 (1969): 3.

26. For an analysis of these issues, see Alain de Janvry, M. Fafchamps, and E. Sadoulet, "Peasant household behavior with missing markets: Some paradoxes explained," *Economic Journal* 101 (1991): 1400–1417 and Alain de Janvry and E. Sadoulet, "Structural adjustment under transaction costs," paper presented at the 29th Conference of the European Association of Agricultural Economists, September 1992.

27. See Marvin P. Miracle, "Subsistence agriculture: Analytical problems and alternative concepts," *American Journal of Agricultural Economics*, 50 (May 1968): 292–310.

28. I am grateful to Professor Frank Thompson for this suggestion.

29. Keith Griffin, "Agrarian policy: The political and economic context," *World Development* 1 (November 1973): 6.

30. I am grateful to Professor Stephen Smith for this information.

31. See, for example, N. Singh, "Theories of sharecropping," in Pranab Bardhan (ed.), *Theories of Agricultural Institutions* (Oxford: Oxford University Press, 1992); David M. Newbery, "Risk-sharing, sharecropping, and uncertain labor markets," *Review of Economic Studies* (October 1977); and Joseph E. Stiglitz, "Sharecropping," in John Eatwell *et al.* (eds.), *The New Palgrave: Economic Development* (London: Macmillan, 1989), pp. 308–315.

32. For a detailed analysis of the responsiveness of Third World farmers to price incentives, see World Bank, *World Development Report, 1986* (New York: Oxford University Press, 1986), chaps. 4 and 5.

33. For an extensive analysis of these adverse effects of premature mechanization, see Montague Yudelman *et al.*, *Technological Change in Agriculture and Employment in Developing Countries* (Paris: Organization for Economic Cooperation and Development, 1971), and Yujiro Hayami and Vernon Ruttan, *Agricultural Development: An International Perspective* (Baltimore: Johns Hopkins University Press, 1985).

34. Two informative articles on appropriate mechanization for development are Hans Binswanger, "Agricultural mechanization: A comparative historical perspective," *World*

Bank Research Observer 1 (January 1986), and Hans Binswanger and Prabhu Pingali, "Technological priorities for farming in sub-Saharan Africa," *World Bank Research Observer* 3 (January 1988).

35. An excellent analysis of the role of institutions in rural development can be found in Brian van Arkadie, "The role of institutions in development," *Proceedings of the World Bank Annual Conference on Development Economics, 1989* (Washington, D.C.: World Bank, 1989), pp. 153–192.

36. For an analysis of the impact of the Green Revolution in the developing world, see Keith Griffin, *The Political Economy of Agrarian Change* (London: Macmillan, 1974); Chris Manning, "Rural employment creation in Java: Lessons from the Green Revolution and oil boom," *Population and Development Review* 14 (March 1988): 17–18; and Donald K. Freebairn, "Did the Green Revolution concentrate incomes? A quantitative study of research reports," *World Development* 23 (February 1995): 265–279.

37. An informative discussion of the important role of appropriate pricing policies in stimulating agricultural production can be found in A. Drazen and Z. Eckstein, "On the organization of rural markets and the process of economic development," *American Economic Review* 78 (June 1988). A massive five-volume research report, *The Political Economy of Agrarian Pricing Policy*, published by the World Bank in 1991, found similar results in the 18 developing countries investigated.

38. For an extensive critique of inappropriate government policies hindering agricultural development in sub-Saharan Africa as well as elsewhere in the Third World, see World Bank, *World Development Report, 1986*, chaps. 4 and 5.

39. For a more comprehensive review of integrated programs for rural development, see Alain de Janvry, *The Economics of Investment in Rural Development: Private and Social Accounting Experiences from Latin America*, Working Paper No. 464 (Berkeley: University of California, Department of Agricultural and Resource Economics, 1988).

40. See Alain de Janvry, *The Agrarian Question and Reformism in Latin America* (Baltimore: Johns Hopkins University Press, 1981).

41. For an analysis of the successes and failures of various reform efforts, see World Bank, *World Development Report, 1990: Poverty* (New York: Oxford University Press, 1990), pp. 64–73, and Peter Dorner, *Latin American Land Reforms in Theory and Practice: A Retrospective Analysis* (Madison: University of Wisconsin Press, 1992).

Further Reading

An excellent survey of agrarian systems in developing countries can be found in Dharam Ghai *et al.* (eds.), *Agrarian Systems and Rural Development* (New York: Holmes & Meier, 1979). There are also a number of studies on agriculture and agrarian systems in specific Third World regions. For Africa, see Peter Robson and Dennis A. Lury (eds.), *The Economies of Africa* (London: Allen & Unwin, 1969). For Asia, see Gunnar Myrdal, *Asian Drama* (New York: Pantheon, 1968), chaps. 22, 23, and 26. For Latin America, see Rodolfo Stavenhagen (ed.), *Agrarian Problems and Peasant Movements in Latin America* (New York: Doubleday, 1970); Celso Furtado, *Economic Development in Latin America* (London: Cambridge University Press, 1970), chaps. 7 and 14; Solon Barraclough, *Agrarian Structure in Latin America* (Lexington, Mass.: Lexington Books, 1973), and Alain de Janvry, *The Agrarian Question and Reform in Latin America* (Baltimore: Johns Hopkins University Press, 1981). Comparative analyses of landlessness and rural poverty can be found in Milton J. Esman, *Landlessness and Near-*

Landlessness in Developing Countries (Ithaca, N.Y.: Cornell University Press, 1978); Erick Eckholm, *The Dispossessed of the Earth: Land Reform and Sustainable Development*, Worldwatch Paper No. 13 (Washington, D.C., Worldwatch Institute, 1979); and Mahmood H. Khan, "Landlessness and rural poverty in underdeveloped countries," *Pakistan Development Review* 25 (Autumn 1986).

Three outstanding comparative studies of Third World agrarian systems are Guy Hunter, *Modernizing Peasant Societies: A Comparative Study of Asia and Africa* (London: Oxford University Press, 1969); Keith Griffin, *The Political Economy of Agrarian Change* (London: Macmillan, 1974); and Thomas P. Tomich, Peter Kilby, and Bruce F. Johnston, *Transforming Agrarian Economies: Opportunities Seized, Opportunities Missed* (Ithaca, N.Y.: Cornell University Press, 1995).

For a general introduction to the economics of agricultural and rural development in Third World countries, see Carl Eicher and John Stoatz (eds.), *Agricultural Development in the Third World* (Baltimore: Johns Hopkins University Press, 1984); Erik Thorbecke (ed.), *The Role of Agriculture in Economic Development* (New York: Columbia University Press, 1969): Raanan Weitz, *From Peasant to Farmer: A Revolutionary Strategy for Development* (New York: Columbia University Press, 1971); Bruce F. Johnston, "Agriculture and structural transformation in developing countries: A survey of research," *Journal of Economic Literature* 8 (1970); John W. Mellor, *The Economics of Agricultural Development* (Ithaca, N.Y.: Cornell University Press, 1966); Arthur T. Mosher, *Creating a Progressive Rural Structure* (New York: Agricultural Development Council, 1969); Theodore W. Schultz, *Transforming Traditional Agriculture* (New Haven, Conn.: Yale University Press, 1964); Robert d'A. Shaw, *Jobs and Agricultural Development* (Washington, D.C.: Overseas Development Council, 1970); Nurul Islam (ed.), *Agricultural Policy in Developing Countries* (New York: Halstead Press, 1974): World Bank, *Rural Development: Sector Policy Paper* (Washington, D.C.: World Bank, 1975); World Bank, *World Development Report, 1986* (New York: Oxford University Press, 1986), which contains an examination of trends in Third World agriculture; C. Peter Timmer, Walter Falcon, and Scott Pearson, *Food Policy Analysis* (Baltimore: Johns Hopkins University Press, 1983); and Subrata Ghatak, "Agriculture and economic development," in Norman Gemmell (ed.), *Surveys in Development Economics* (Oxford: Blackwell, 1987), chap. 10.

Descriptions of the policies and problems associated with integrating women into agricultural reforms are provided in Mahabub Hossain, *Credit for Alleviation of Rural Poverty: The Grameen Bank in Bangladesh*, Research Report No. 65 (Washington, D.C.: International Food Policy Research Institute, 1988); Monica Fong and Heli Perrett, *Women and Credit* (Milan: Finafrica, 1991); and Sharon Holt and Helena Ribe, *Developing Financial Institutions for the Poor and Reducing Barriers to Access for Women*, World Bank Discussion Paper No. 117 (Washington, D.C.: World Bank, 1991).

For case studies of rural development and land reform in Mexico, and sharecropping in India, see Stephen C. Smith, *Case Studies*, Chapters 12 and 13.

CHAPTER 10

The Environment and Development

Much of the environmental degradation witnessed today is due primarily to two groups of people—the top billion richest and the bottom billion poorest.
—Nafis Sadik, Executive Director, United Nations Population Fund, 1991

Sustainability must be strengthened as a guiding principle of development.
—Boutros Boutros-Ghali, Secretary General, United Nations, 1994

Environmental degradation poses a major threat to human security.
—United Nations, *Human Development Report, 1995*

Economics and the Environment

During the past decade, economists have become increasingly aware of the important implications of environmental issues for the success of development efforts. We now understand that the interaction between poverty and environmental degradation can lead to a self-perpetuating process in which, as a result of ignorance or economic necessity, communities may inadvertently destroy or exhaust the resources on which they depend for survival. Rising pressures on increasingly taxed environmental resources in developing countries can have severe consequences for Third World self-sufficiency, income distribution, and future growth potential.

Environmental degradation can also detract from the pace of economic development by imposing high costs on developing countries through health-related expenses and the reduced productivity of resources. The poorest 20% of the world's population is the group that will experience the consequences of environmental ills most acutely. Severe environmental degradation, due to population pressures on marginal land, has led to falling farm productivity and per capita food production. Since the cultivation of marginal land is largely the domain of lower-income groups, the losses are suffered by those who can least afford them. Similarly, the inaccessibility of sanitation and clean water mainly affects the poor and is believed to be responsible for 80% of disease worldwide. Because the solutions to these and many other environmental problems involve enhancing the productivity of resources and improving living conditions among the poor, achieving environmentally sustainable growth is synonymous with our definition of economic development.

Though there is considerable dispute concerning the environmental costs associated with various economic activities, consensus is growing among development economists that environmental considerations should form an integral part of policy initiatives.[1] The exclusion of environmental costs from calculations of GNP is largely responsible for the historical absence of environmental considerations from development economics. Damage to soil, water supplies, and forests resulting from unsustainable methods of production can greatly reduce long-term national productivity but will have a positive impact on current GNP figures. It is thus very important that the long-term implications of environmental quality be considered in economic analysis. Rapid population growth and expanding economic activity in the Third World are likely to do extensive environmental damage unless steps are taken to mitigate their negative consequences.

The growing consumption needs of Third World populations may have global implications as well. There is increasing concern in the First World that the destruction of the world's remaining forests, which are concentrated in a number of highly indebted developing countries including Brazil, Mexico, Peru, and the Philippines, will greatly contribute to global warming and the greenhouse effect. In this chapter, we examine the economic causes and consequences of environmental devastation and explore potential solutions to the cycle of poverty and resource degradation. We begin, as in previous chapters, with a survey of basic issues, including discussions of sustainable development and the linkages among population, poverty, economic growth, rural development, urbanization, and the LDC environment. We next look at the applicability of traditional economic models of the environment, depict some typical environmental situations, and provide some relevant data. We then broaden our scope to include issues of global interdependence and conclude by analyzing the prospects for setting an international environmental agenda for achieving worldwide sustainable development.

Environment and Development: The Basic Issues

Seven basic issues define the environment of development. Many grow out of the discussions in the preceding chapters. The seven issues are (1) the concept of sustainable development, and linkages between the environment and (2) population and resources, (3) poverty, (4) economic growth, (5) rural development, (6) urbanization, and (7) the global economy. We briefly discuss each in turn.

Sustainable Development and Environmental Accounting

Environmentalists have used the term *sustainability* in an attempt to clarify the desired balance between economic growth on the one hand and environmental preservation on the other. Although there are many definitions,[2] basically *sustainability* refers to "meeting the needs of the present generation without compromising the needs of future generations."[3] For economists, a development path is sustainable "if and only if the stock of overall capital assets remains constant or rises over time."[4] Implicit in these statements is the fact that future growth and overall quality of life are critically dependent on the quality of the environment. The natural resource base of a country and the quality of its air, water, and land represents a common heritage for all generations. To destroy that endowment indiscriminately in the pursuit of short-term economic goals penalizes both present and, especially, future generations. It is therefore important that development planners incorporate some form of **environmental accounting** into their policy decisions. For example, the preservation or loss of valuable environmental resources should be factored into estimates of economic growth and human well-being. Alternatively, policymakers may set a goal of no net loss of environmental assets. In other words, if an environmental resource is damaged or depleted in one area, a resource of equal or greater value should be regenerated elsewhere.

An example of environmental accounting is offered by Pearce and Warford.[5] Overall capital assets are meant to include not only manufactured capital (machines, factories, roads) but also human capital (knowledge, experience, skills) and **environmental capital** (forests, soil quality, rangeland). By this definition, **sustainable development** requires that these overall capital assets not be decreasing and that the correct measure of **sustainable national income** or *sustainable net national product (NNP*)* is the amount that can be consumed without diminishing the capital stock. Symbolically,

$$NNP^* = GNP - D_m - D_n,$$

where NNP* is sustainable national income, D_m is the depreciation of manufactured capital assets, and D_n is depreciation of environmental capital—the monetary value of environmental decay over the course of a year.

An even better measure, though more difficult to calculate with present data collection methods, would be

$$NNP^* = GNP - D_m - D_n - R - A$$

where D_m and D_n are as before, R is expenditure required to restore environmental capital (forests, fisheries, etc.), and A is expenditure required to avert destruction of environmental capital (air pollution, water and soil quality, etc.)

In light of rising consumption levels worldwide combined with high rates of population growth, the realization of sustainable development will be a major challenge. We must ask ourselves, What are realistic expectations about sustainable standards of living? From present information concerning rapid destruction of many of the world's resources, it is clear that meeting the needs of a world population that is projected to grow by an additional 3.7 billion in the next 30 years will require radical and early changes in consumption and production patterns. We discuss these needed changes later in the chapter.

Population, Resources, and the Environment

Much of the concern over environmental issues stems from the perception that we may reach a limit to the number of people whose needs can be met by the earth's finite resources. This may or may not be true, given the potential for new technological discoveries, but it is clear that continuing on our present path of accelerating environmental degradation would severely compromise the ability of present and future generations to meet their needs. A slowing of population growth rates would help ease the intensification of many environmental problems. However, the rate and timing of fertility declines, and thus the eventual size of world population, will largely depend on the commitment of governments to creating economic and institutional conditions that are conducive to limiting fertility (see Chapter 6).

Rapidly growing Third World populations have led to land, water, and fuelwood shortages in rural areas and to urban health crises stemming from lack of sanitation and clean water.[6] In many of the poorest regions of the globe, it is clear that increasing population density has contributed to severe and accelerating degradation of the very resources that these growing populations depend on for survival. To meet expanding Third World needs, environmental devastation must be halted and the productivity of existing resources stretched further so as to benefit more people. If increases in GNP and food production are slower than population growth, per capita levels of production and food self-sufficiency will fall. Ironically, the resulting persistence of poverty would be likely to perpetuate high fertility rates, given, as we discovered in Chapter 6, that the poor are often dependent on large families for survival.

Poverty and the Environment

Too often, however, high fertility is blamed for problems that are attributable to poverty itself. For example, China's population density per acre of arable land is twice that of India, yet yields are also twice as high. Though it is clear that environmental destruction and high fertility go hand in hand, they are both direct outgrowths of a third factor, absolute poverty. For environmental policies to succeed in Third World countries, they must first address the issues of landlessness, poverty, and lack of access to institutional resources. Insecure land tenure rights, lack of credit and inputs, and absence of information often prevent the poor from making resource-augmenting investments that would help preserve the environmental assets from which they derive their livelihood. Hence preventing environmental degradation is more often a matter of providing institutional support to the poor than fighting an inevitable process of decay. For this reason, many goals on the international environmental agenda are very much in harmony with the three objectives of development articulated in Chapter 1.

Growth versus the Environment

If, in fact, it is possible to reduce environmental destruction by increasing the incomes of the poor, is it then possible to achieve growth without further damage to the environment? Evidence indicates that the worst perpetrators of environmental destruction are the billion richest and billion poorest people on earth. It has even been suggested that the bottom billion are more destructive than all 3.2 billion middle-income people combined. It follows that increasing the economic status of the poorest group would provide an environmental windfall. However, as the income and consumption levels of everyone else in the economy also rise, there is likely to be a net increase in environmental destruction. Meeting increasing consumption demand while keeping environmental degradation at a minimum will be no small task.

Rural Development and the Environment

To meet the expanded food needs of rapidly growing Third World populations, it is estimated that food production in developing countries will have to double by the year 2010. Because land in many areas of the Third World is being heavily overtaxed by existing populations, meeting these output targets will require radical changes in the distribution, use, and quantity of resources available to the agricultural sector. And because women are frequently the caretakers of rural resources such as forests and water supplies and provide much of the agricultural supply of labor, it is of primary importance that they be integrated into environmental programs. In addition, poverty alleviation efforts must target women's economic status in particular to reduce their dependence on unsustainable methods of production.

The increased accessibility of agricultural inputs to small farmers and the introduction (or reintroduction) of sustainable methods of farming will help create attractive alternatives to current environmentally destructive patterns of resource use. Land-augmenting investments can greatly increase the yields from cultivated land and help ensure future food self-sufficiency.

Urban Development and the Environment

Chapter 8 demonstrated that rapid population increase accompanied by heavy rural-urban migration is leading to unprecedented rates of urban population growth, sometimes at twice the rate of national growth. Consequently, few governments are prepared to cope with the vastly increased strain on existing urban water supplies and sanitation facilities. The resulting environmental ills pose extreme health hazards for the growing numbers of people exposed to them. Such conditions threaten to precipitate the collapse of the existing urban infrastructure and create circumstances ripe for epidemics and national health crises. These conditions are exacerbated by the fact that under existing legislation, much urban housing is illegal. This makes private household investments risky and renders large portions of urban populations ineligible for government services.

Congestion, vehicular and industrial emissions, and poorly ventilated household stoves also inflate the tremendously high environmental costs of urban crowding. Lost productivity of ill or diseased workers, contamination of existing water sources, and destruction of infrastructure, in addition to increased fuel expenses incurred by people's having to boil unsafe water, are just a few of the costs associated with poor urban conditions. Research reveals that the urban environment appears to worsen at a faster rate than urban population size increases so that the marginal environmental cost of additional residents rises over time.

The Global Environment

As total world population grows and incomes rise, net global environmental degradation is likely to worsen. Some trade-offs will be necessary to achieve sustainable world development. By using resources more efficiently, a number of environmental changes will actually provide economic savings, and others will be achieved at relatively minor expense. However, because many essential changes will require substantial investments in pollution abatement technology and resource management, significant trade-offs between output and environmental improvements will occasionally become necessary. The poorer the country, the more difficult it will be to absorb these costs. Yet a number of issues, including biodiversity, rain forest destruction, and population growth, will focus international attention on some of the most economically strapped countries in the world. In the absence of substantial assistance to low-income countries, environmental efforts will necessarily have to be funded at the expense of other social programs, such as education, health services, and employment schemes, that themselves have important implications for the preservation of the global environment.

Exactly what sacrifices need to be made and who should make them will continue to be matters of great controversy. Nowhere was this more evident than at the second United Nations Conference on Environment and Development (UNCED)—the so-called Earth Summit—held in Rio de Janeiro in June 1992 (see Chapter 18). Most cumulative environmental destruction to date has been caused by the First World. However, with high fertility rates, rising average incomes, and increasing inequality in the Third World, this pattern is likely to reverse sometime in the next century.[7] It is thus unclear how the costs of global reform should be divided. Apportionment of responsibility for reducing environmental damage essentially hinges on the manner in which the question is framed. For example, if a limit is placed globally on levels of per capita pollution emissions, the approach would clearly favor lower-income countries that have much lower per capita consumption levels. Conversely, if international pressures try to limit the growth rate of per capita emissions or even to impose limits on the growth of national emissions, any movement in that direction would tend to freeze Third World incomes at a small fraction of those of their First World counterparts.

The Scope of Environmental Degradation: A Brief Statistical Review

The most pressing environmental challenges in developing countries in the next few decades will be caused by poverty. These will include health hazards created by lack of access to clean water and sanitation, indoor air pollution from biomass stoves, and deforestation and severe soil degradation—all most common where households lack economic alternatives to unsustainable patterns of living.[8] Table 10.1 summarizes the principal health and productivity consequences of environmental damage in the Third World. It divides this damage into seven categories: water pollution and water scarcity, air pollution, solid and

TABLE 10.1 Principal Health and Productivity Consequences of Environmental Damage		
Environmental Problem	Effect on Health	Effect on Productivity
Water pollution and water scarcity	More than 2 million deaths and billions of illnesses a year attributable to pollution; poor household hygiene and added health risks caused by water scarcity	Declining fisheries; rural household time and municipal costs of providing safe water; aquifer depletion leading to irreversible compaction; constraint on economic activity because of water shortages
Air pollution	Many acute and chronic health impacts: excessive urban particulate matter levels are responsible for 300,000 to 700,000 premature deaths annually and for half of childhood chronic coughing; 400 million to 700 million people, mainly women and children in poor rural areas, affected by smoky indoor air	Restrictions on vehicle and industrial activity during critical episodes; effect of acid rain on forests and water bodies
Solid and hazardous wastes	Diseases spread by rotting garbage and blocked drains; risks from hazardous wastes typically local but often acute	Pollution of groundwater resources
Soil degradation	Reduced nutrition for poor farmers on depleted soils; greater susceptibility to drought	Field productivity losses in range of 0.5% to 1.5% of gross national product (GNP) common on tropical soils; offsite siltation of reservoirs, river-transport channels, and other hydrologic investments
Deforestation	Localized flooding, leading to death and disease	Loss of sustainable logging potential and of erosion prevention, watershed stability, and carbon sequestration provided by forests

(continued)

TABLE 10.1 *(continued)*		
Environmental Problem	Effect on Health	Effect on Productivity
Loss of biodiversity	Potential loss of new drugs	Reduction of ecosystem adaptability and loss of genetic resources
Atmospheric changes	Possible shifts in vector-borne diseases; risks from climatic natural disasters; diseases attributable to ozone depletion (perhaps 300,000 additional cases of skin cancer a year worldwide; 1.7 million cases of cataracts)	Sea-rise damage to coastal investments; regional changes in agricultural productivity; disruption of marine food chain

SOURCE: World Bank, *World Development Report, 1992: Development and the Environment* (New York: Oxford University Press, 1992), tab. 1. Reprinted with permission.

hazardous wastes, soil degradation, deforestation, loss of biodiversity and atmospheric changes.

In the 1980s, per capita levels of arable land fell by 1.9% annually, leading to worsening land shortages, which have forced many of the poorest onto marginal land with extremely limited cultivability. It is estimated that over 60% of the poorest peoples residing in developing countries struggle for survival on agriculturally marginal soils. This trend is greatly worsened in some areas of the Third World by strong inequalities in the distribution of land, which force an ever-growing class of landless workers onto increasingly taxed, ecologically sensitive soils. The growing intensification of cultivation on fragile lands leads to rapid soil degradation and loss of productivity. Roughly 270,000 square kilometers of soil lose virtually all of their productivity each year. An area the size of India and China combined, or about 1.2 billion acres, has been significantly degraded. The resulting annual loss in agricultural productivity is estimated to be between 0.5% and 1.5% of annual worldwide GNP. As a result of rapid population increases and the failure of agricultural production to keep pace, per capita food production declined in 69 countries during the 1980s (see Chapter 9).

An environmental problem shared by both the urban and rural poor is the prevalence of unsanitary conditions created by the lack of clean water and sanitation. This in turn contributes greatly to the spread of infectious diseases. It has been estimated that waterborne pathogens that contribute to typhoid, cholera, amoebic infections, bacillary dysentery, and diarrhea account for 80% of all disease in developing countries and for 90% of the 13 million child deaths each year. Yet the number of people living without clean water and sanitation rose by 135 million during the period 1970–1984, and deteriorating environmental conditions were cited as a contributing factor to the spread of cholera epidemics in a number of countries in Latin America and Africa in 1991 and 1992.

Rapid population growth and heavy rural-urban migration make it difficult to extend urban services to many people who need them. For example, to provide clean water to all urban dwellers in Latin American cities by 2030, the numbers served by public facilities will have to be increased by 250%. Though this figure itself is staggering, it excludes the 1.2 billion rural individuals whose needs must also be met. A comparable aim for the provision of sanitation would require 400% and 900% increases for urban and rural communities, respectively. On average throughout the Third World, 72% of all new urban households are located in shanties or slums. In Africa, the proportion is even greater, at 92%, most of which have no access to public services.

Airborne pollutants also take a high toll on the health of Third World citizens. Dependence on **biomass fuels** such as wood, straw, and manure is closely related to poverty. The burning of biomass fuels for cooking and the boiling of water create dangerously high levels of indoor pollution to which 400 million to 700 million people, mostly women and children, are exposed each year. Smoke and fumes from indoor stoves are believed to contribute significantly to the 4.3 million childhood deaths each year from respiratory diseases and to an ever-larger number of chronic respiratory illnesses (see Table 10.1).

In urban areas, other sources of pollution pose serious threats to physical well-being. According to the World Health Organization, 1.3 billion people live in urban areas with unsafe levels of airborne pollutants. Yet it is projected that by 2030, manufacturing in developing countries will expand to 600% of current levels, vastly increasing potential concentrations of pollutants. Just to maintain current urban air standards until 2030 (which means conceding to conditions much worse than those existing in the urban centers of developed countries), average emissions from LDC industries and electric generators would have to be reduced by 90% to 95% per unit of output.

Rural Development and the Environment: A Tale of Two Villages

To clarify how rural poverty and environmental degradation interact, let's take a brief look at two hypothetical Third World villages, one in Africa and the other in South America.

The population of the African village, located in a semiarid landscape, has been warned by international "experts" that cutting the remaining trees and cultivating marginal land will only worsen the hardships that they already endure. The advice runs counter to each family's first priority, which remains obtaining the basic necessities for survival. Here trees fulfill many different functions, but most important, they provide firewood for cooking. Without wood it would be impossible to prepare many foods, make cornmeal (*posho*), or boil water. As a result of the intensification of land use by a rapidly growing population, the cutting of trees for firewood, and the clearing of marginal land for cultivation, the soil is increasingly exposed to destructive environmental forces. The loss of vegetation, which helps mitigate the destructive impact of heavy winds, rain, and desiccation by the sun, leads to more rapid erosion of precious topsoil needed for cultivation. Good yields are more difficult to obtain and the consequences of drought years are more intense. **Desertification**—encroachment of the desert into areas where erosion has been most severe—threatens to consume even the more productive land.

As a result of the loss of precious topsoil and declining output, there are fewer crops to bring to market to barter for necessities. In many households there is less food for the children. And yet the family must spend longer hours trying to obtain enough income to survive. There is little paid work to be found locally, though some households earn a small amount of additional income by sending family members to work on larger, more prosperous farms.

It is generally the job of women to collect enough firewood for the day's cooking. It may take several hours to walk to and from an area where it is available, adding considerably to the day's work. Though this is a relatively inefficient use of a woman's time, there are no alternative forms of fuel sold in the local market, and even if there were, there would be insufficient household funds with which to purchase them. In fact, many women spend additional time collecting precious firewood to make charcoal, which can then be sold in the cities for the equivalent of a few pennies, which helps buy household necessities. The low opportunity cost of a woman's time perpetuates the wasteful use of forests and worsens local environmental conditions.[9]

Consider now another hypothetical village, this time on the edge of a vast rain forest in South America.

The great majority of farmers here are newcomers, drawn by government promises of land and prosperity. The public resettlement program, which distributes property titles to settlers willing to clear the land, is designed to reduce the overcrowding of cities and stem the flow of rural-urban migrants. In contrast to the African village, this settlement has no shortage of rainfall, wildlife, or trees. In fact, the forest is an obstacle for migrant farmers and is regularly burned to make room for cultivation.

Though burning the forest may temporarily provide the landless with a modest source of income, the land, like 90% of rain forest soil worldwide, is very infertile and can sustain intensive cultivation for only a few years. Complementary inputs and farming know-how that might help improve levels of output are in short supply, and yields begin to drop rapidly after the first few years. Settlers are then forced to burn their way deeper into the forest. Because the settlers are located on marginal soils and must constantly seek new fertile ground, with little prospect of rising above a subsistence existence, the government program may be antidevelopmental in the long run. Household incomes remain low and unstable, there is little or no gain in average productivity, and the migrating population leaves environmental devastation in its wake, further reducing the productivity of all.

Though heavy urbanization is leading to rapid demographic changes, at present the majority of the very poor live in rural areas similar to the two villages we described. Frequently, 70% to 80% of the poor in LDCs reside in the agricultural sector, where economic necessity often forces small farmers to use resources in ways that guarantee short-term survival but reduce the future productivity of environmental assets. Unsustainable patterns of living may be imposed by economic necessity. In periods of prolonged and severe food shortages, desperately hungry farmers have been known to eat the seeds with which they would have planted the next year's crop, knowingly paving the way for future disaster. Because it happens more slowly, the tendency of impoverished peoples to degrade agricultural resources on which they depend for survival is less dramatic, but it is motivated by similar circumstances.

The causes and consequences of rural environmental destruction vary greatly by region. However, persistent poverty is frequently the root cause. The majority of the poor in developing countries survive on the meager yield obtained from cultivation of small plots of land whose soil may be too shallow, too dry, or too sandy to sustain permanent cultivation. If the land is not in some way replenished through either shifting cultivation or the use of manufactured fertilizers, it becomes exhausted, and yields decrease with successive harvests. But the poor generally do not have the wherewithal to increase the productivity of the land by allowing it to lay fallow or by making on-farm investments in irrigation and fertilizer. In addition, where fertility rates are high and children provide a vital economic contribution through wages or on-farm labor, population and the intensity of cultivation are likely to increase over time, speeding the rate at which the soil becomes exhausted.

One immediate result of this type of environmental pressure is **soil erosion**. With little plant cover to protect it from wind and water, precious topsoil may be blown or washed away, further reducing the productivity of the land. This process of environmental degradation leads to persistent declines in local per capita food production and may eventually lead to desertification. This phenomenon is likely to spur increases in rural-to-urban migration and may force the remaining local population onto even less fertile land, where the same process is repeated.

Another factor in the cycle of rural poverty and environmental destruction is **deforestation**. The vast majority of wood cut in the Third World is used as fuel for cooking. Loss of tree cover has two potentially devastating environmental implications for predominantly poor rural populations. Deforestation can lead to a number of environmental maladies that, over a period of time, can greatly lower agricultural yields and increase rural hardships. On a day-to-day basis, however, the increasing scarcity of firewood means that women must spend large portions of the day in search of fuel, diverting time from other important activities such as income generation and child care. In the worst cases, fuel shortages are sufficient to require the burning of biomass or natural fertilizers, such as manure, which are important on-farm inputs for maintaining crop yields.

Environmental degradation that begins on a local scale can quickly escalate into a regional problem. For example, clearing of vegetation at high elevations may increase the exposure of cultivated lands at lower altitudes. Soil that has been carried away by heavy rains may silt rivers and pollute drinking water. Plants help retain rainfall, which percolates down through the soil into underground reserves called *groundwater*. The water is in turn tapped by a variety of plants during dry seasons in arid regions. A loss of vegetation leads to a decrease in the rate at which groundwater is replenished. The subsequent drop in the water level leads to the death of plants with shallow root systems, including young trees. This self-perpetuating process can spread the malady to previously unaffected regions. Not surprisingly, the increase in natural disasters associated with environmental degradation, including floods, droughts, and mudslides, can have a devastating impact on both the local and the regional agricultural economy. India and Bangladesh provide prime examples of this phenomenon.

Traditional Economic Models of the Environment

Privately Owned Resources

We will review some common economic models of the environment in countries with highly developed monetized markets. In each model, the market's failure to account for environmental externalities is the exception rather than the rule, and neoclassical theory is then applied in order to cure or circumvent an inefficiency.[10] Neoclassical theory has been applied to environmental issues to determine what conditions are necessary for the efficient allocation of resources and how market failures lead to inefficiencies and to suggest ways in which these distortions can be corrected.

Figure 10.1 demonstrates how the market determines the optimal consumption of a natural resource. Finding the optimal market outcome involves maximizing the total net benefits to society from a resource, which is the difference between the total benefits derived from a resource and the total costs to producers of providing it. This is equal to the shaded area in Figure 10.1. **Total net benefit** is maximized when the **marginal cost** of producing or extracting one more unit of the resource is equal to its marginal benefit to the consumer. This occurs at Q^*, where the demand and supply curves intersect. In a perfectly competitive market, the "invisible hand" will ensure that Q^* is the quantity produced. The marginal cost curve in Figure 10.1 is upward-sloping because extraction costs increase as a resource

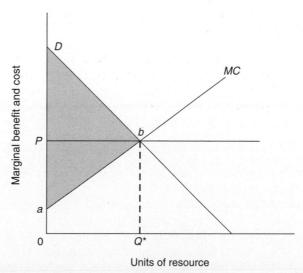

FIGURE 10.1 Static Efficiency in Resource Allocation.

becomes more scarce. The resulting **producer surplus**, or profit, is called a **scarcity rent**. In the diagram, the producer surplus is area *aPb*, and the **consumer surplus** is area *DPb*. Together they yield a maximum net benefit equal to *Dab*.

If resources are scarce and are rationed over time, scarcity rents may arise even when the marginal cost of production is constant, as in Figure 10.2. The owner of a scarce resource has a finite volume of a resource *X* to sell (75 units) and knows that by saving a portion of it for future sales, she can charge a higher price today. The price of a good that is being rationed intertemporally (over time) must equate the **present value** of the **marginal net benefit** of the last unit consumed in each period. That is, the consumer must be indifferent between obtaining the next unit today or tomorrow. In Figure 10.2, assume that a resource owner has 75 units available. If she is willing to offer only 50 units for sale today, the market price for the scarce resource is P_S. The scarcity rent collected by the owner of the resource is equal to P_SabP, the shaded region in the diagram between price and marginal cost. It is the owner's ability to collect these rents that creates the rationing effect and is thus necessary to ensure the efficient allocation of resources over time. In the absence of scarcity, all of the resource will be sold at the extraction cost $P = MC$, 75 units will be consumed at one time, and no rents will be collected.

The proponents of neoclassical free-market theory stress that inefficiencies in the allocation of resources result from impediments to the operation of the free market or imperfections in the property rights system. So long as all resources are privately owned and there are no market distortions, resources will be allocated efficiently. Perfect **property rights** markets are characterized by four conditions:

1. *Universality*—all resources are privately owned.
2. *Exclusivity*—it must be possible to prevent others from benefiting from a privately owned resource.

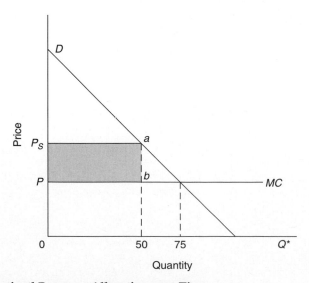

FIGURE 10.2 Optimal Resource Allocation over Time.

3. *Transferability*—the owner of a resource may sell the resource when desired.
4. *Enforceability*—the intended market distribution of the benefits from resources must be enforceable.

Under these conditions, the owner of a scarce resource has an economic incentive to maximize the net benefit from its sale or use. For example, a farmer who owns his land will choose the levels of investment, technology, and output that maximize the net yield from the land. Because the value of the land may be used as collateral, any viable on-farm investment can be financed by obtaining a loan at the prevailing market rate of interest.

If the foregoing conditions are not met simultaneously, inefficiencies are likely to arise. Thus the way to correct the misallocation of resources is generally to remove any market distortions. A number of models have been designed to explain apparent inefficiencies in resource allocation. We will now look at two simple models of inefficiency arising from imperfections in property markets. We will also explore the limitations of these frameworks for addressing Third World environmental issues.

Common Property Resources

If a scarce resource (such as arable land) is publicly owned and thus freely available to all (for, say, farming or grazing animals), as is the case with a **common property resource**, any potential profits or scarcity rents will be competed away. As we have noted, neoclassical theory suggests that in the absence of scarcity rents, inefficiencies will arise. Using a somewhat different framework, we will investigate the misallocation of resources under a common property system. Figure 10.3 describes the relationship between the returns to labor on a given piece of land and the number of laborers cultivating it.

Suppose for the moment that title to this piece of land is privately held. Conventional wisdom tells us that the landowner will hire additional labor to work the land until the marginal product of the last worker is equal to the market wage, W, at point L^*. The workload is shared equally among the employees, each of whom produces the *average* product. However, assuming decreasing returns to labor, each new worker hired reduces the average product of all workers. The *marginal* product of each additional worker is thus equal to his average product minus the decrease in the average product across all other workers. If an additional employee is hired beyond L^*, his cost to the producer, W, will be greater than his marginal product, and the difference will represent a net loss to the landowner. A profit maximizer will thus hire L^* workers, with a total output equal to average product AP^* multiplied by the number of workers, L^*. Scarcity rents collected by the landowner will equal AP^*CDW.

Society's total net benefit from land will be lower under a system of common property. If land is commonly owned, each worker is able to appropriate the entire product of his work, which is equal to the average product of all workers. Worker income will continue to exceed the wage until enough workers are attracted so that the average product falls to the level of the wage, at which point the labor force

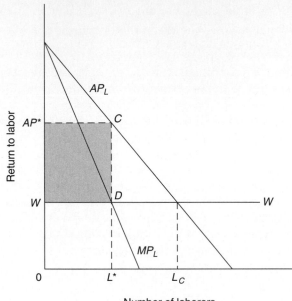

FIGURE 10.3 Common Property Resources and Misallocation.

equals L_C. Though total farm output may either rise or fall (depending on whether MP_L is positive or negative—it is negative as drawn in Figure 10.3), the marginal product of the additional workers is below the wage. Because we are assuming that all workers could be employed elsewhere with productivity equal to or greater than W, it follows that social welfare must fall when marginal product falls below W. No scarcity rent is collected at L_C. The implication of the common property resource model is that where possible, privatization of resources will lead to an increase in aggregate welfare and an efficient allocation of resources.

It should be noted here that these neoclassical models are strictly concerned with efficiency and do not address issues related to equity. Income distribution is not considered to be relevant, and the theory is unconcerned with the distributional issues arising when all scarcity rents from national resources accrue to a few private owners.

Criticisms of the Neoclassical Common Property Framework

The conclusions drawn from this model of common property can be questioned on a number of grounds. The first problem is one shared with the Lewis model discussed in Chapter 3. The common property model assumes that full employment prevails and that every additional worker is drawn away from more productive employment elsewhere, where his marginal productivity is at least as great as the wage. A closer look at Third World economies, where substantial urban unemployment exists alongside widespread rural underemployment, forces us to reject this assumption. If new arrivals were previously on family farms where their marginal product was below the wage but alternative employment was not available, their marginal product might actually rise, pulling up average product and social welfare.

Another unrealistic assumption of the model is that landowners tend to maximize profit and will thus choose the optimal level of production. In fact, as discussed in Chapter 9, large landholders are frequently not the most efficient producers because they may hold land for purposes other than cultivation. A perfect property market is consequently not a sufficient condition for the efficient use of land. The same may hold true for other natural resources regarding which a variety of social, political, and economic factors may militate against the socially optimal allocation. In addition, by forcing small farmers onto marginal land, the consolidation of land into the hands of a few large landholders may intensify existing population pressures in areas already threatened by deforestation or desertification.

But probably the most important criticism of the model from a development perspective is that it fails to address the vital issues of equity and basic needs. Simply put, neoclassical market efficiency can be achieved even in a highly dualistic economy where extreme poverty and extraordinary wealth exist side by side. If the primary goal of development is to raise incomes sufficiently so that households may meet their basic needs, the distribution of the benefits from scarce resources rises to primary importance. And although neoclassical theorists have sometimes suggested that an optimal outcome may be achieved through the taxation and then "lump sum" redistribution of the gains accruing to the owners of scarce natural resources, the historical record for such efforts is not encouraging. This is especially true where the authorities responsible for legislating and coordinating such redistributions are also the owners. Thus the large-scale commercial privatization of resources does not necessarily ensure an improvement in standards of living for the impoverished majority.

Beyond the standard neoclassical arguments, there are a number of alternative reasons why individuals making use of publicly owned resources may make inefficient use of them within the context of Third World farming systems. Family farmers, who, as we saw in Chapter 9, are generally the most efficient cultivators of land, may be reluctant to make land-augmenting investments if they are afraid of losing tenure on the common property plot. They may also have insufficient funds to hire additional labor or purchase complementary resources due to a lack of collateral, a factor that frequently excludes the poor from competitive credit markets (see Chapter 17). It is therefore possible that conferring extended tenancy rights or ownership of land to family farmers would raise productivity. The relevant question for the property rights structure is then, Who should obtain title to the land if privatization is to occur? A simple auction of publicly owned land to the highest bidder is unlikely to be consistent with development objectives.

Public Goods and Bads: Regional Environmental Degradation and the Free-Rider Problem

In the preceding discussion, each additional worker who joined those cultivating commonly held land created a negative **externality** by lowering the returns to all other workers without providing any compensation. An externality occurs when one person's consumption or production behavior affects that of another without any compensation. The benefits and costs of one's actions are said to be *internalized* when one is made to bear them in full. In the previous common property problem, the externalities associated with decreasing average product were easily internalized by reestablishing perfect property markets through the privatization of public property. In many cases, the **internalization** of externalities is not so easily accomplished. This is especially the case where the consequences of an individual's actions constitute a public good or a public bad. A **public good** is anything that provides a benefit to everyone and the availability of which is in no way diminished by its simultaneous enjoyment by others. Common examples include clean air and national defense. A **public bad** is any product or condition that decreases the well-being of others in a nonexhaustive manner. Air pollution and water pollution are examples. Intuitively, it is clear that given human nature and the fact that individuals do not pay the full costs associated with their actions, too much of a public bad will be produced. The result is a socially nonoptimal outcome. We will demonstrate this shortly using a diagrammatic representation.

Let us consider the case of a particular public bad, regional environmental degradation, caused by deforestation. Increased exposure to the forces of erosion, excessive drying of the soil, regional loss of groundwater, silting or pollution of public water supplies, and potential climatic changes are all public bads associated with the clear-cutting or burning of trees. Whether these trees are on private or commonly held property, the clearing of protective ground cover, either for cultivation or for the extraction of timber, may lead to more widespread regional environmental degradation. To simplify our analysis, we will translate this public bad problem into a public good framework. Environmental conservation through the protection of trees provides a benefit to all and is thus a public good.

The most obvious difference between a public good and a purely private good is that aggregate demand for the public resource is determined by summing individual demand curves vertically rather than horizontally, as is the case for private goods. Figure 10.4 demonstrates both types of summation. The difference results from the fact that many individuals may enjoy the same unit of a public good, but only one may benefit from a unit of a normal, private consumption good. Through vertical summation we are sure to capture all benefits accruing to all individuals from each unit of a public good. The marginal cost associated with the preservation of an additional tree is equal to the forestry maintenance cost plus the opportunity cost of the tree, that is, the most valuable alternative use of the tree, such as for firewood, charcoal, animal fodder, or lumber. Figure 10.4 illustrates the problem of pricing public goods.

In Figure 10.4a, the socially optimal number of trees is Q^*. It is determined by the intersection of the (vertically summed) aggregate demand curve with the supply (MC) curve. At Q^*, total net benefits to society from the public good, $P_M Dc$, are maximized. However, due to what we call the **free-rider problem**, the free market will not lead to this optimal quantity. Because individuals are able to enjoy the benefits of trees provided by others, each will contribute less than what he or she would if acting independently. At a price of P_M, the free market will satisfy person B's demand Q_B while not denying person A's requirements of Q_A; that is, A can free ride

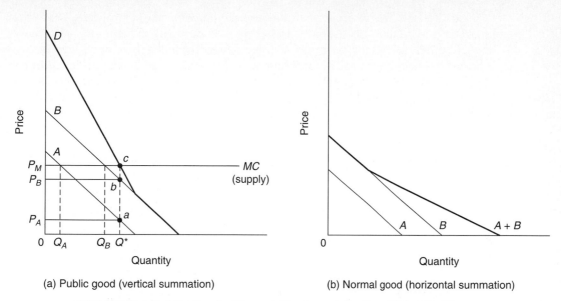

FIGURE 10.4 Public Goods, Normal Goods, and the Free-Rider Problem.

on B's contribution. The market will therefore provide a suboptimal level of forest preservation, Q_B. To restore optimality (Q^* of the public good), some form of government intervention is required. The most effective solution is to charge each consumer just enough per unit, P_A and P_B for individuals A and B, respectively, to entice each of them to demand the preservation of the optimal quantity of trees, Q^*. Their joint payments, $P_A \times Q^*$ for A plus $P_B \times Q^*$ for B, represent a total contribution equal to $P_M \times Q^*$, exactly the sum required to purchase the socially optimal level of preservation.

Criticisms of the Public-Good Framework

The problem with the public-good pricing mechanism is, of course, how to know which prices to charge. People have no incentive to divulge how much they really benefit from a public good because by shirking, they may ride free on the contributions of others and avoid paying their full share. A government may be capable of reducing market inefficiencies, but it is unlikely to be able to produce a perfect allocation of resources due to deficiencies in the information available to it. Hypothetically, collected fees can be used to provide a public good by preserving existing forests or managing a sustainable timber production program that will supply the community's needed timber. Although charging fees to the people benefiting from the preservation of a resource may sound practical, it is exceedingly difficult. In a development context, the problems become even more complicated. When the collection of fees entails taxing deeply impoverished populations with little or no cash income, such a program becomes an impossibility. It would be equally difficult to collect payment from people who are cutting trees to meet subsistence needs.

Neoclassical theory can be useful for explaining why market failures lead to the inefficient allocation of resources in highly commercialized economies and how these inefficiencies may be mitigated. However, these theories have limited applicability to problems arising in nonmarket or mixed-market economies or in regions where individuals are too impoverished to be able to take advantage of alternatives that would maximize the financial rewards from natural resources.

Urban Development and the Environment

The Ecology of Urban Slums

In some ways, life among the poor in urban slums is similar to that of the poor in rural villages; families work long hours, income is uncertain, and difficult trade-offs must be made between expenditures on nutrition, medical care, and education. Though on average, urban dwellers are likely to have higher incomes, the poorest are frequently at greater risk of being exposed to dangerous environmental conditions. Let's contrast our earlier look at environmental conditions in an African and a South American rural community with those of an Asian urban shanty.

In a typical urban slum in an Asian metropolis, health-threatening pollutants are commonplace both inside and outside the home. Women are scarcely aware that the smoke from the fuels they burn in the home to cook and boil water may have severe long-term consequences for the health of their children. However, even if they did, knowledge alone would do little to alter the economic necessity of cooking with relatively dirty but cheap and accessible fuels. Conditions resulting from poor ventilation in the home are equivalent to smoking several packs of cigarettes per day, and women and their children are exposed to these fumes for long portions of each day. Though some children actually avoid much of this exposure by attending school, many are kept out of school to assist their mothers in market work or the production of goods at home. Thus from an early age, chronic and acute bronchitis are a cruel fact of life. Debilitating and ultimately fatal respiratory infections among the poor are commonplace.

But it is not only in the home that individuals are exposed to harmful pollutants. Street vendors and market workers are constantly exposed to high levels of other pollutants. Untreated sewage runs in open drains along the roads, providing a conduit for infectious diseases. Because food and drinking water are frequently contaminated, diarrhea is common, especially among young children. Frequent spells of the illness cause malnourishment, even when food is more plentiful, making the young more susceptible to other diseases. Many of the weakest children die from severe dehydration. Because the fuels used to cook foods and boil water must be purchased in the market and consume a large portion of the daily earnings, there is sometimes insufficient fuel to boil the household's drinking water, increasing the chance of infection. The costs associated with obtaining medical treatment for sick children may be very high, involving the opportunity cost of time spent traveling to and from clinics and long hours in crowded waiting rooms, in addition to medical fees. For many households, the forgone earnings can be ill afforded. In many of the poorest households, only boys receive medical attention because they are expected to contribute more to household income. It is thus not surprising that they are more likely than their sisters to survive to adulthood.

Children playing in the streets and others working outdoors are also exposed to the combined emissions from automobiles and factories. Dangerously high levels of atmospheric lead are common because few cars are equipped with the expensive catalytic converters now mandated in the West. Due both to physical and mental impairments suffered as a result of exposure to environmental factors and to repeated absence from school, children in the poorest neighborhoods will find it difficult to meet basic academic standards. And with many thousands of new migrants locating their families in this urban shanty each year, the conditions are likely to worsen in the future.

The urban centers of the Third World will absorb over 80% of future increases in world population. Much of the intensification of urban congestion, however, will result from heavy rural-urban migration. It is expected that by the year 2010, the rural population of developing countries will stabilize at 2.8 billion, at which point rural-urban migration will be sufficient to counteract any additional population growth. The rapid expansion of the urban centers of the Third World has placed increasing strain on the resources of developing-country governments attempting to provide adequate infrastructure and services to their inhabitants.

Though the health implications of environmental degradation are currently highest in rural areas, due to rapid urbanization the vast bulk of future increases in human exposure to unsafe conditions will occur in the cities. Unsanitary environmental conditions exacerbated by rapidly increasing urban congestion and industrial emissions pose severe health hazards (see Table 10.1). Exposure to high concentrations of toxic pollutants as well as pathogens in contaminated air and water can cause a variety of health problems at tremendous cost to a struggling economy. Left unchecked, environmental hazards tend to grow exponentially as the size of Third World cities increases.

Because the urban poor are much less able than the wealthy to insulate themselves from the negative effects of a tainted environment, they are more likely to suffer serious consequences resulting from environmental degradation. In addition, malnutrition and poor health among people living in urban shantytowns tend to reduce individual resistance to environmental hazards. Though 60% of people residing in the cities of developing countries already live in squatter settlements, this number may rise in the future, because a much higher proportion of new housing each year is located in shantytowns.

The bulk of any increases in mortality and morbidity in urban areas will result from health complications due to chronic exposure to factors that weaken the body's defenses. Thus bronchitis and diarrhea, which afflict large portions of LDC populations, are likely to impose greater burdens on the poor than fatalities resulting from sudden exposure to toxins. It is therefore important to concentrate our analysis on the conditions experienced by urban populations on a day-to-day basis.

Much of the environmental degradation of urban areas and the consequences for economic growth and human health are avoidable. However, to explore viable solutions, it is necessary to have a clear understanding of the sources of problems and the ways in which they interact. The causes of severe urban environmental problems are numerous, but for simplicity of analysis we will divide these factors into two categories—those associated with urbanization and industrial growth and those that must be dealt with in any community but tend to be exacerbated by the congestion of urban settings.

Industrialization and Urban Air Pollution

The early stages of urbanization and industrialization in developing countries are generally accompanied by rising incomes and worsening environmental conditions. Cross-sectional analysis of numerous countries at different levels of income suggest that similar to Gini coefficients, urban pollution tends first to rise with national income levels and then to fall.[11] According to the 1992 *World Development Report*, pollution levels for even the worst quartile of high-income cities are better than for the best quartile of low-income cities. Indeed, at higher incomes it is easier to afford expensive **clean technologies**. However, there is nothing inevitable about the trend. Air (and water) quality is closely related to the extent of government regulation.

The principal sources of air pollution, which pose the greatest health threat associated with modernization, are energy use, vehicular emissions, and industrial production. Industrialization can lead to increases in waste either through direct emissions or indirectly by altering patterns of consumption and boosting demand for manufactured goods. The production of manufactured goods generally entails the creation of by-products that may be detrimental to the environment. The extent to which they degrade the environment will depend on a number of factors, including the type of by-products produced, their quantities, and their means of disposal. Unfortunately, in the absence of regulation, the cheapest way to dispose of unwanted by-products is usually to release them untreated into the air and waterways or to dump them on the ground where runoff is free to sink into groundwater or wash into rivers. Due to the broader transmission of ideas, greater availability of goods, and increased incomes, changes in patterns of consumption and their environmental consequences are likely to appear first in cities. Until technologies and infrastructures capable of coping with environmental consequences are introduced, modernization is likely to lead to high urban environmental costs.

We have already looked briefly at the issue of externalities and the fact that many of the costs of pollutants are borne by someone other than the polluter. This suggests that the price paid for the consumption of a good is below the social cost associated with the good. Figure 10.5 depicts the typical supply and demand curves. In this case, however, we have labeled the supply curve $S = MC_P$ because it represents the marginal **private costs** associated with producing good X. The free-market equilibrium output and price are Q_M and P_M, respectively. If there are externalities associated with the consumption or production of each

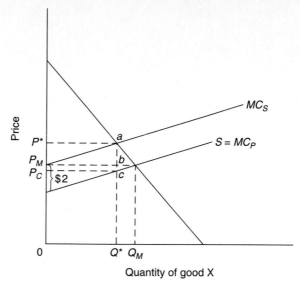

FIGURE 10.5 Pollution Externalities: Private versus Social Costs and the Role of Taxation.

unit of good X, the MC_P curve does not represent the true costs to society of the good. If each unit of good X imposes a cost of $2 on a third party, we can obtain the true marginal social cost curve MC_S by legislating a $2-per-unit sales tax on the output. This **pollution tax** shifts the private cost curve upward by $2 at every point to MC_S in Figure 10.5. At the new intersection between the demand curve and the marginal **social cost** curve, Q^* is the efficient outcome and P^*, the price. Therefore, by incorporating the social costs of pollution into the analysis, the actual output of the polluting product is reduced to the socially optimal level while the price charged to the consumer rises from P_M to P^*, and the price received by the producer falls from P_M to P_C. Depending on the relative elasticities of the demand and supply curves, the burden of the pollution tax is shared by both consumers and producers. In Figure 10.5, the consumer pays ab and the producer bc of the ac tax.

At sufficiently high levels, most emissions will be toxic to humans or otherwise damaging to the environment, whereas at low levels, per-unit costs may be insignificant. This is due to the fact that humans have some tolerance for most toxins, though the ability to tolerate exposure may rapidly decline as concentrations in drinking water and air increase. The environment also has an **absorptive capacity** that enables it to assimilate a quantity of most pollutants. Once this critical quantity has been exceeded, however, concentrations and hence toxicity are likely to rise rapidly. In Figure 10.6, a more realistic marginal social cost curve is drawn. As concentrations of pollutants increase (as total output increases), the gap between the social and private cost curves increases. While aggregate demand remains low, this differential will be small. However, as the demand curve shifts outward from D to D' with rapid urbanization and rising incomes, the importance of externalities

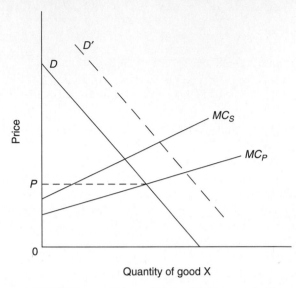

FIGURE 10.6 Increasing Pollution Externalities with Economic Growth.

rises at an increasing rate. This would suggest that the costs associated with curing urban ills caused by congestion will increase faster than the rate of increase of the population.

Health hazards are created by toxic air emissions as well as increasing volumes of waste that contaminate water supplies and land. Though research on the issue has been scanty, there is increasing evidence that in the absence of regulation, current and future increases in LDC manufacturing and transport will have serious consequences for public health. It is estimated that in the latter half of the 1980s, by World Health Organization (WHO) standards, 1.3 billion people lived in cities with unsafe levels of airborne particulate matter and 1 billion were exposed to unacceptably high levels of sulfur dioxide.[12] Other compounds, such as nitrous oxides and organic compounds, rise in importance as industrialization proceeds. By contaminating water supplies, contributing to dangerous levels of air pollution, and damaging public and private property, industrial pollution can exact a high toll in terms of human health and economic prosperity.

A number of case studies indicate the potential severity of industrial pollution. In Bangkok, high levels of airborne lead have led to such severe consequences for the development of small children that the average child's IQ has been lowered by four or more points by the age of 7. Seventy percent of children in Mexico City have abnormally high blood levels of lead by WHO standards. Due to serious air pollution in 1980, the industrial town of Cubatão, Brazil, reported 10,000 medical emergencies involving respiratory ailments in a total population of 80,000. Health complications caused by smog tend to be worse in Third World countries, where poor nutrition and general ill health greatly lower individual tolerance to pollutants. The implications for health are the worst for young children, who inhale roughly twice as many pollutants per unit of body weight as adults do.

Problems of Congestion and the Availability of Clean Water and Sanitation

Though rising levels of industrial emissions of pollution pose a serious threat to the health of urban inhabitants in developing countries, at present the two most important environmental factors affecting the health of the urban poor are the inaccessibility of clean water and the lack of sanitation. It is estimated that 1 billion people worldwide have no access to clean water and an additional 1 billion live in areas with chronic water shortages; 1.7 billion have no access to sanitation. Between 1970 and 1988, the number of urban households in the Third World without adequate sanitation rose by 247% and those without safe water increased by 56%. In 1985, at least 25% of urban communities (and 58% of rural ones) were without clean water for sanitation needs. Because there are no alternative sources, many of the poor collect drinking water from rivers, streams, and canals that are polluted with human excreta and chemicals.

Though the poorest urban dwellers experience many of the same adverse environmental conditions as the rural poor, including heavy indoor pollution and unsanitary conditions, crowding can intensify exposure. Raw sewage runs in the streets, mixing with garbage and contributing to the spread of disease. This is reflected in the fact that death rates in urban shanties are occasionally higher than in rural areas, even though the latter generally have fewer services. Though survival rates in developing countries have been improving for some time, these achievements are now being threatened by rapidly increasing numbers of poor with no access to clean water or sanitation.

The health and economic costs associated with these conditions are enormous and represent formidable obstacles to the improvement of living standards. The prevalence of disease and the potential for epidemics is closely linked to the accessibility of clean water and the success of a community in eliminating exposure to sources of infectious diseases. Some 900 million cases of diarrheal diseases, 200 million cases of schistosomiasis, and 900 million cases of hookworm occur each year. Cholera, typhoid, and paratyphoid also contribute greatly to human suffering. Provision of clean water and sanitation can greatly reduce mortality rates. For example, children in households with adequate facilities are 60% less likely to die from diarrhea than those in households without.

The enormous economic costs resulting from lost productivity and the cost of medical care represent a drag on economic development. Chronic ill health is both a consequence and a cause of poverty. It can contribute to poor nutrition, poor school performance, reduced productivity, and permanent disability and thus give little hope for economic advancement. In addition to averting fatalities, improvements in the supply of water and sanitation reduce the incidence and severity of illnesses, thereby reducing other costs associated with waterborne disease.

Although higher-income households generally have access to either publicly or privately provided services, the poorest are usually without services. This is frequently due to the illegal status of much low-income housing, which renders it ineligible for government services and makes it risky for private individuals to invest in upgrading equipment. It is estimated that as much as 70% of new urban housing in the Third World is in some way illegal. As a result, the majority of the poor must purchase water, which is frequently contaminated, from vendors at an average of 10 times the cost of piped water.

To take a typical example, in Lima, Peru, poor households consume one-sixth as much water as higher-income households, but their water bills are on average three times as high. In addition, this low-quality water must be boiled, leading to expensive fuel bills and adding to indoor pollution. If these households were to boil water for periods of time recommended by the government, the additional fuel costs would consume 29% of household income. In Jakarta, $50 million is spent per year on boiling water. Much of these costs could be avoided, and total expenditures on water could be decreased, if clean water were made widely available.

Postponement of investments in the infrastructure required for provision of urban water and sanitation can lead to much greater costs in the future. Poor access to water has led to widespread systems of private wells, which can overtax existing groundwater supplies. In a number of large cities including Bangkok, Mexico City, and Jakarta, this phenomenon has led to the collapse of existing infrastructure and the destruction of property through subsidence of the land and flooding. In coastal areas, overuse can draw salt water into supplies, leading to their permanent salinization. Where raw sewage is untreated and is improperly disposed of, underground and surface water is frequently contaminated, creating long-term shortages of clean water and threatening public health.

Foreign-exchange earnings also may be severely threatened by contaminated water supplies. Strict First World health standards may prohibit the importation of agricultural goods produced with potentially contaminated water. An outbreak of cholera in Peru in 1991 led to an estimated $1 billion combined loss in export and tourism markets within a few months. In light of these problems, it is not surprising that the costs of preventive measures are much lower than those associated with lost revenues, resources, and infrastructure. Investment in clean water and sanitation can essentially provide economic returns because relatively small initial outlays may be used to avert the much larger costs associated with urban crises. It is imperative, however, that efforts to provide improved urban sanitation and clean water be carried out simultaneously in rural areas. This leads us to consider needed policy reforms and the crucial question of financial feasibility. We do this in the next section and at the conclusion of this chapter.

The Need for Policy Reform

There is a growing recognition that insufficient action has been taken to reduce environmental hazards through primary health care, education, and the provision of services such as clean water and sanitation. According to one estimate, expenditure on these programs will have to double over the next few years just to maintain the current situation. But the structure of some existing programs may actually hinder progress. Currently, few low-budget grassroots services are provided, even though they tend to be more cost-effective, especially when community organizations become involved. Annually, $10 billion, or only about 0.5% of developing-country GDP, is spent on sanitation and water services; 80% is spent on programs costing at least $550 per person, and less than 20% is spent on programs costing less than $30 per person. Similar patterns occur in the health professions. As a consequence, government schemes tend to reach a relatively select group of constituents while falling far short of providing universal access for the poor, who, as we have described, are subject to the worst environmental conditions. Unless governments vastly increase the breadth of the population served by programs, these disparities will tend to worsen with increased urbanization in the future.

To meet their targets in the face of increasing financial shortages, governments will have to radically change the manner in which scarce resources are managed. In the past, many policies designed to cure environmental ills have actually worsened the problems that they were designed to alleviate. Where scarce resources have been provided to recipients at prices far below the cost of provision, artificial scarcities have arisen. For example, on average in developing countries, the price paid for piped water is only 35% of the total cost of supplying it. Due to rationing, such subsidies frequently benefit only people with higher incomes. The poor are thus forced to buy water from vendors at a price 10 times that of piped water. Many governments provide free water service at little or no charge, even in areas with water shortages. The result is the waste of precious resources. In Cairo, Jakarta, Lima, Manila, and Mexico City, among other Third World cities, more than half of urban water supplies remain unaccounted for. Ironically, while chronic water shortages affect 2 billion people annually, overirrigation and waterlogging have contributed to the salinization of roughly 25% of all irrigated land, greatly reducing its productivity.

Similar patterns are repeated for energy and agricultural inputs. The average price paid for electricity in the Third World, which, again, is usually available only to the relatively well-to-do, represents less than half the cost of supplying it, and losses in transmission are three to four times higher than in industrialized countries.

Better pricing policies and efficiency requirements would lead to improvements in the allocation of resources, as well as substantial savings on fuel imports. Fertilizer and pesticide subsidies, which most frequently benefit larger farmers, tend to promote monocultures that deplete soils and to discourage the use of sustainable methods such as integrated pest management. Used excessively, they can lead to the contamination of underground and surface water supplies.[13]

Another factor that needs more careful consideration in the design of environmental policy is the important role of women in the management of resources. Through their roles as managers of fuel and water supplies, agricultural producers, and guardians of household health, women control the fate of many of the world's resources. Yet they are rarely consulted in the design of government services or have access to extension programs. Women in the Third World, who commonly work 60 to 90 hours a week, will have little or no use for resources unless they are made easily accessible. Further investments in the educational attainment of women, which is closely related to the health of their children, can thus greatly enhance environmental efforts.

The Global Environment: Rain Forest Destruction and Greenhouse Gases

Though early Malthusian predictions of environmental calamity proved to be overly pessimistic, recent scientific studies indicate that there is cause for concern with respect to the limited ability of the earth's ecosystem to regenerate itself. Increasing evidence regarding the extent of **ozone depletion** and encroaching **global warming** present alarming implications for the global climate. Concerns range from an increase in the incidence of skin cancer to desertification and rising oceans. The potential costs of climate changes are likely to vary from region to region, with losses being greatest for people already living in semiarid regions. Because the vast majority of Third World countries have predominantly agricultural economies and so many are located in warm semiarid regions of the globe, any increase in temperatures is likely to have harsh implications for LDC incomes and food self-sufficiency.

It is through changes in patterns of land use that the developing countries currently make their largest contribution to global concentrations of **greenhouse gases**. It is estimated that deforestation alone accounts for roughly 25% of all CO_2 emissions worldwide.[14] Also of great significance is the fact that deforestation leads to the destruction of a vital source of atmospheric oxygen. Because trees consume carbon dioxide and release oxygen during the process of photosynthesis, the tropical rain forests represent an important mechanism through which the ecosystem regenerates itself. Clearing the rain forests will reduce the environment's absorptive capacity for CO_2.

The majority of tropical rain forest destroyed, about 60%, is cleared for cultivation by small farmers. Each year, 4.5 million hectares are cleared for this purpose, much of it, like 90% of rain forest land worldwide, so infertile that it will be cultivable for no more than a few years. The land is then frequently sold to large farmers who use it for grazing cattle, often under heavy government subsidy, leading to further desertification. The previous tenants are then forced to clear new forest in a desperate attempt to derive a livelihood for the next few years. In the past, rain forest settlement programs have regularly been encouraged and financed by LDC governments, often with the assistance of international development banks. A review by the World Bank of its own support for settlement programs found that they were exceptionally expensive—on average, $10,000 per household—and could be environmentally destructive. Policymakers in such countries as Brazil, Bolivia, and Peru with large rain forests are therefore experiencing increasing pressure from foreign public and private agencies to implement policies that will reduce the rate of tropical forest destruction. It is argued that the resulting decrease in the growth of concentration of greenhouse gases will be in everyone's interests. Thus rain forest preservation provides a public good.

Because the political and economic costs of preserving the rain forests are often masked or ambiguous, maintaining a forest may appear to be an almost costless venture. In fact, because of the important roles that rain forests play in LDC's domestic economies, the true costs of preserving all remaining forests may be extraordinarily high. The opportunity costs arising from the preservation of rain forests will involve the loss of an important source of domestic fuel, forgone foreign-exchange earnings from timber and beef, and the loss of a temporary solution to the problem of land shortages and population pressures. It is therefore unreasonable to assume that the few highly indebted countries that contain the majority of remaining rain forests should be responsible for single-handedly providing this global public good.

Several steps must be taken to preserve the rain forests. Third World countries could vastly increase the efficiency of their economic use of rain forests by managing them (less than 1% of rain forests have been replanted or cut in a sustainable manner) and by developing alternative markets for other rain forest products such as meats, nuts, fruits, oils, sweeteners, resins, tannin, fibers, construction materials, and natural medicinal compounds. The international community should also assist in the preservation effort (see Chapter 18). By reducing trade barriers to the alternative goods just mentioned, developed countries reduce the dependence of LDCs on unsustainable modes of production. Forgiving debt and debt-for-nature swaps (to be explained shortly) also reduce the need for the rapid exploitation of forests to raise foreign exchange. Finally, funds for the preservation and maintenance of tropical rain forests are necessary to guarantee the success of conservation programs that provide a public good. It is important that such funds not be viewed as aid because the ultimate benefits are to be shared by all.

The heavy indebtedness of many Third World countries may make it exceptionally difficult for governments with large debt burdens to finance the expenses of environmental programs designed to protect natural resources. In total, developing countries owe in excess of $1.3 trillion (see Chapter 14). In 1986, total long-term debt of countries in sub-Saharan Africa (excluding South Africa) was 58% of GNP, and by 1990, the proportion had increased to over 90%. Slowdowns in the downward movement of fertility rates in the Philippines, India, Tunisia, Morocco, Colombia, and Costa Rica have been attributed to cuts in health care and family-planning programs arising from efforts to reduce foreign debt. The result is the persistence of environmentally destructive poverty and population pressures. Ironically, heavy debt servicing can undermine the long-term creditworthiness of borrower nations by diverting domestic funds away from programs designed to maintain the productivity of national resources.

Because they require dramatic cuts in services and programs, the structural adjustment and stabilization policies imposed on highly indebted countries by the World Bank and the International Monetary Fund (policies detailed in Chapter 14) have often intensified poverty and its environmental consequences. In recent years, however, a number of international assistance agencies, including the World Bank, have established environmental divisions to promote more environmentally conscientious patterns of lending. They have also initiated their own programs to address environmental issues directly. Their success in the future may largely depend on the compatibility of such efforts with the economic realities confronting LDC governments.

Policy Options in Developing and Developed Countries

What Less Developed Countries Can Do

A range of policy options is available for LDC governments. Six stand out: (1) proper resource pricing, (2) community involvement, (3) clearer property rights and resource ownership, (4) improving economic alternatives for the poor, (5) raising the economic status of women, and (6) policies to abate industrial emissions. Let's briefly examine each in turn.[15]

Proper Resource Pricing

The most obvious area for reform is probably in government pricing policy, which can exacerbate resource shortages or encourage unsustainable methods of production. Often programs that were ostensibly designed to reduce hardships for the very poor have had little impact on poverty and have worsened existing inequalities. Due to the rationing of resources, high-income households have frequently been the predominant beneficiaries of energy, water, and agricultural subsidies. The results have often included the wasteful and unsustainable use of resources. Even though elimination of misdirected subsidies is a relatively costless (or profitable) way of protecting the environment, the political stakes are high where powerful elites stand to lose lucrative government transfers.

Community Involvement

Programs to improve environmental conditions are likely to be most effective when they work in tandem with community networks, ensuring that program design is consistent with both local and national objectives. The experience of development agencies has demonstrated that grassroots efforts can be more cost-effective because they generally involve the use of low-cost alternatives and provide jobs to local populations. When poor communities truly benefit from public-works programs, residents are often willing and able to contribute much or all of the program costs.

Clearer Property Rights and Resource Ownership

Investments in household sanitation and water and on-farm improvements often represent a large portion of lifetime savings for the poor, the loss of which can impose harsh economic consequences on households. Hence the lack of secure tenure on rural or urban property can greatly hinder investment in environmental upgrading. Legalization of tenure can lead to improved living conditions for the poor and increases in agricultural investments.

In many cases, however, land reform may be necessary (see Chapter 9). It is not uncommon for renters or sharecroppers to lose the economic gains from their on-farm investments because it is relatively easy for landlords to extract higher rents once the productivity of the land has been improved. Transferring title to tenants may be the only means of ensuring that financial rewards from land-augmenting investments accrue to the investor. Land reform may also be required where unequal distribution of land has led to large tracts of uncultivated high-quality land in close proximity to overexploited marginal lands cultivated by large numbers of landless workers.

Programs to Improve the Economic Alternatives of the Poor

Further environmental devastation in rural areas may be avoidable in many cases through on-farm investments in irrigation and sustainable farming techniques, the use of alternative fuels, and the creation of barriers to erosion. However, the economic costs of each of these alternatives is prohibitive for the vast majority of impoverished family producers. Ironically, the greater the environmental devastation, the less likely that a rural population will be able to afford alternative methods of production. It is therefore important that government programs make credit and land-augmenting inputs accessible to small farmers. By providing rural economic opportunities outside the home, governments can also create alternative employment opportunities so that the very poor are not forced to cultivate marginal lands. For example, programs to build rural infrastructure (roads, storage facilities, etc.) create local jobs, alleviate population pressures on ecologically sensitive land, stimulate rural development, and reduce the flow of rural-to-urban migration.

Raising the Economic Status of Women

Improving the educational attainment of women and increasing their range of economic alternatives raise the opportunity cost of their time and may lead to decreases in desired family size (see Chapter 6). Education also tends to increase women's access to information concerning child nutrition and hygiene, a factor that has been linked to rapid declines in child mortality. It is important that community-based environmental programs work closely with women because their own day-to-day activities may largely determine patterns of resource use and their ability to meet the needs of their families is dependent on the sustainable management of water and fuel supplies.

Industrial Emissions Abatement Policies

A range of policy options is available to developing-country governments for the purpose of limiting industrial pollution, including the taxation of emissions, tradable emissions permits, quotas, and standards. There is some evidence to suggest that the first two policies, which are market-based, are more effective because they tend to reward the more efficient producers, allow greater flexibility for firms, and are generally easier to enforce. Regulations should be as simple as possible and must be enforceable. Additional incentives to adopt clean technologies may be provided through tax credits and subsidies specifically tied to the purchase or development of pollution abatement technologies. Ironically, the hardest industries to regulate are those run by governments themselves because the profit motive is often not a consideration and, as a general rule, it is difficult for any group to regulate itself.[16]

How Developed Countries Can Help LDCs

Industrial countries can help Third World nations in their efforts to improve the environment of development in three areas: (1) trade liberalization, (2) debt relief, and (3) financial and technological assistance.

First World Trade Policies

The focus of much current discussion concerning the environment is the desperate need to break the cycle of poverty and environmental destruction in developing countries. However, the increasing protectionism of First World countries during the 1980s caused international markets for Third World products, and thus earning capacity, to shrink dramatically (see Chapters 12 and 13). According to the United Nations' 1992 *Human Development Report*, annual losses of the Third World due to the lack of access to the goods markets of the First World were greater than 150% of the total amount of aid received in 1990. If lack of access to capital and labor markets is also included, annual losses total about $500 billion. Eliminating trade barriers against developing-country exports, by stimulating economic growth in the Third World, creating new jobs, and encouraging rural development, could significantly reduce both the level and growth of absolute poverty.

In addition to trade barriers, the industrialized countries penalize Third World exports by heavily subsidizing their own agricultural sectors. The resulting large surpluses are often dumped on international markets, unfairly undercutting the agricultural exports of Third World countries in markets for which they are presumed to have a comparative advantage. Reducing the estimated $300 billion in annual agricultural subsidies in developed countries could help guarantee the success of rural development efforts in LDCs by reducing poverty and the environmental decay that it causes. Wider access to international markets would not only raise incomes but could also improve the ability of heavily indebted countries to service their debt. They would thereby reduce their dependence on the unsustainable exploitation of rain forests and other resources to raise foreign exchange.

Debt Relief

Heavy debt servicing drastically reduces funds available to Third World governments for domestic social programs, including those designed to alleviate poverty and reduce environmental degradation (see Chapter 14). Debt forgiveness may be required if Third World governments are to be given the flexibility to make the sweeping changes necessary to achieve sustainable development.

Debt-for-nature swaps offer an attractive and mutually beneficial way for the Third World to retire its foreign-denominated debt while guaranteeing the protection of tropical rain forests.[17] In a debt-for-nature swap, a foreign private environmental organization such as the U.S.-based Rainforest Alliance or the Nature Conservancy, working in conjunction with a local environmental organization, purchases Third World debt on financial markets at a fraction, say, 30%, of the face value. The debt is then exchanged for government bonds denominated in the debtor-country currency but worth the full value of the original foreign debt. The environmental organization purchasing the debt is thus able to leverage its funds by 230%. Income from the securities is used to maintain forest or wildlife reserves. In this way the developing country no longer owes debt in scarce hard currencies and is able to set up endowments for the preservation of national resources. The foreign donor is able to make an effective contribution several times larger than the actual outlay of cash and obtains a verbal guarantee that the endowment will be used to protect natural resources. By 1991, debt-for-nature swaps had amounted to

$98 million in face value ($61 million in local-currency equivalents) and had been negotiated in 10 countries, including Costa Rica, Ecuador, the Philippines, Mexico, and Ghana. Though debt-for-nature swaps provide an exciting, albeit partial, solution to Third World tropical deforestation, a number of persistent economic and political obstacles limit the potential scope of such schemes, not the least of which is fear of foreign control over domestic resource decisions.

First World Assistance

The World Bank estimated in its 1992 *World Development Report* that an additional 2% to 3% annual investment is necessary in Third World countries to achieve sustainable development. These investments would be used for a variety of programs to alleviate poverty, provide services, and promote sustainable patterns of production. Additional aid from First World countries earmarked for these purposes could have a positive impact on developing-country environments (see Chapter 15).

However, even greater sums would be necessary to maintain tropical rain forests, which provide benefits to the entire international community through reduced CO_2 emissions. As mentioned earlier, external funds provided for this purpose should not be considered aid because they are in the interests of all living beings.

What Developed Countries Can Do for the Global Environment

Perhaps most important, developed countries, which currently consume over 70% of the earth's resources (see Table 6.4), can directly contribute to global environmental improvement through their own efforts to (1) reduce harmful emissions, (2) develop clean technologies for themselves and for LDCs, and (3) alter their own environmentally harmful patterns of demand.

First World Emissions

Perhaps the greatest contribution of the First World to the global environment will be through a clear demonstration of its own commitment to a cleaner environment. Because it remains the main polluter of air and sea, developed-country demonstration effects leading to global changes in current and future patterns of production can greatly broaden the initial impact of its own steps toward achieving sustainable growth. However, if wealthy nations do not achieve significant and sustained reductions in the production of greenhouse gases and ozone-depleting chemicals, there will be very little reason for the Third World to do so, considering that their per capita emissions levels are far below those in the industrialized countries.

Research and Development

The First World must also take a leadership role in research and development efforts. Growing public support for stricter environmental regulation in the First World is likely to lead to the development of both cheaper emissions abatement technologies and cleaner production processes. Innovations resulting from research and development will enhance Third World efforts to reduce emissions if they are adopted in developing countries. Currently, many clean technologies are prohibitively expensive for Third World industries. It is thus unrealistic to expect low-income countries to attain standards set in high-income countries. However, it is not necessary for developing countries to reproduce environmental debacles endured during the onset of industrialization in the First World, as depicted, for example, in Charles Dickens's *Hard Times*. Making cheaper, cleaner abatement technologies accessible to LDCs can help limit a principal source of global emissions— the rapid industrialization of the Third World.

First World Demand

Through its importation of products that are associated with environmentally unsustainable production, the First World has an indirect but important impact on the global environment. International treaties to limit the destruction of endangered resources will have little effect if wealthy nations continue to provide lucrative markets for the sale of such goods. Import restrictions are an effective way of reducing undesired international trade. Consumer sovereignty expressed through boycotts and other forms of pressure on corporations can be effective. However, they require strong leadership and tend to focus on large firms, which represent only a relatively small portion of the overall problem.

Many of the aforementioned issues and policies were on the agenda at the 1992 Earth Summit in Rio de Janeiro. We will examine the nature and outcome of this historic UNCED conference in Chapter 18, when we focus on the key issues likely to affect economic development into the twenty-first century.

CASE STUDY

The Economy of Pakistan

GEOGRAPHIC, SOCIAL, AND ECONOMIC INDICATORS

Capital Islamabad

Area 803,934 km²

Population 129.7 million (1995)

Population (average annual growth rate) 2.8% (1985–1994)

GNP per capita U.S. $440 (1994)

GNP per capita (average annual growth rate) 1.6% (1985–1994)

Agriculture as share of GDP 25% (1994)

Exports as share of GDP 16% (1994)

Infant mortality rate (per 1,000 live births) 91 (1995)

Child malnutrition (underweight) 40% (1993)

Females as share of labor force 13% (1994)

Illiteracy rate (age 15+) 65% (1990)

Human Development Index 0.39 (low) (1992)

Pakistan extends from the Arabian Sea 1,600 kilometers northward. It borders Iran, Afghanistan, China, and India; parts of its boundaries with India and Afghanistan are disputed.

The idea of establishing Pakistan as a separate Muslim state through the partition of India developed in the 1930s, especially after the popular elections of 1937. At the end of World War II, Great Britain, suffering from the effects of the war, took the final steps to grant India independence. The Congress Party and the Muslim League could not, however, agree on the terms for drafting a constitution or establishing an interim government. In June 1947, the British government declared that it would grant full dominion status to two successor states, India and Pakistan. Pakistan would consist of the contiguous Muslim-majority districts of British India; Bengal and the Punjab would be partitioned; and the various princely states could freely accede to either India or Pakistan. This resulted in a bifurcated Pakistan separated by more than 1,600 kilometers. Pakistan became a self-governing dominion within the British Commonwealth on August 14, 1947.

Massive population movements accompanied the partition of the Indian subcontinent in 1947; communal bloodshed followed, resulting in the loss of uncounted thousands of lives. Some 6 million Muslims fled to Pakistan, and about as many Hindus and Sikhs fled to India—perhaps the largest spontaneous population transfer in history. The eastern portion of Bengal declared its independence as Bangladesh in 1971.

Pakistan's economy has been expanding at a per capita rate of about 1.6% a year during the past decade. Relative to other low-income LDCs, Pakistan's long-term growth rate has been respectable, with real per capita income levels in 1994 about twice as large as in 1950. Excellent harvests and continued good performance by the industrial sector have contributed to this steady growth. Nevertheless, Pakistan bears burdens common to many Third World nations: a large (130 million) and

373

rapidly growing (2.8%) population, a highly stratified and traditional society, inadequate social and health services with military spending in 1994 more than twice as high as spending on health and education combined, high infant mortality (95 per 1,000) and illiteracy (65%) rates, a primary school drop-out rate of 63% compared with a South Asia average of 50%, a sizable proportion of the population living in poverty, an estimated 12 million children (half under the age of 10) working under near slavery conditions, and a rapidly deteriorating urban and rural environment.

Like its neighbor India, Pakistan has experienced considerable environmental damage. Much of its forests has been destroyed for firewood, the soil is rapidly eroding, water supplies are being depleted, and the process of desertification is moving inexorably forward. This declining natural resource base is beginning to lead to agricultural problems, and the natural environment itself must struggle to support the large population. Agriculture currently accounts for about 25% of Pakistan's GDP and occupies almost 55% of its workforce. Cotton is the most important crop, followed by rice and sugar. Even though most small farmers practice traditional methods of cultivation, productivity has risen during the past 20 years.

At independence, Pakistan had little industry. During the 1950s and 1960s, manufacturing developed rapidly, and a broad industrial base now produces a wide range of products. Cotton textile manufacturing is the most important single industry. Other major industries are food processing, chemicals, fertilizers, pharmaceuticals, steel, petroleum re-fining, tires, cement, and transport equipment. After stagnating in the early 1970s, industrial production accelerated in the late 1970s after the government switched from extensive centralized control to greater private initiative in product ownership and control. In the 1980s and early 1990s, the government continued to encourage the private sector, to allow the market greater leeway to regulate price movements, and to emphasize export-led industrial growth. Government expenditure has been directed to three priority areas—energy conservation, educational expansion, and improved public health care. For the most part, the results have been satisfactory.

For the late 1990s, Pakistan will need to focus on four additional priority objectives if it is to succeed in promoting sustained and equitable economic development: (1) a reduction in population growth, (2) a major effort to upgrade human resources through the continued expansion of educational and health services, (3) a reduction in the chronic fiscal and foreign-trade deficits through further policies designed to promote the privatization of state-owned industries and the expansion of export markets, and (4) a reversal or at least a curtailment of the serious environmental stresses currently being placed on the country's natural resource base, particularly in the three key areas of forestland preservation, water supplies for irrigation, and reduction of salinization on agricultural land. It is essential, however, that in the process of achieving these objectives, Pakistan maintain its stated commitment to protect low-income groups from any adverse consequences.

Concepts for Review

Absorptive capacity	Debt-for-nature swap
Biomass fuels	Deforestation
Clean technologies	Desertification
Common property resource	Environmental accounting
Consumer surplus	Environmental capital

Externality	Producer surplus
Free-rider problem	Property rights
Global warming	Public bad
Greenhouse gases	Public good
Internalization	Scarcity rent
Marginal cost	Social costs
Marginal net benefit	Social erosion
Ozone depletion	Sustainable development
Pollution tax	Sustainable national income
Present value	Total net benefit
Private costs	

Questions for Discussion

1. Is sustainable development a practical and feasible goal for Third World nations? What might be some of the difficulties and possible trade-offs? Explain.

2. In what ways does poverty lead to environmental degradation? What types of environmental problems do the rural and urban poor share? What are some differences in the conditions they face?

3. How are population growth, poverty, and land pressures interrelated? Explain how these problems can create a vicious cycle of events.

4. What steps might governments in less developed countries take to reduce over-exploitation of natural resources? What impact do pricing policies have?

5. Why are national environmental concerns in LDCs likely to focus increasingly on urban problems in the future? How are urban conditions related to rural-urban migration?

6. Why are the objectives of economic development and sustainable growth mutually reinforcing?

7. In what ways does neoclassical theory provide a useful framework for analyzing environmental issues? What are some of its limitations?

8. What are some of the costs associated with environmental degradation? How might they detract from economic growth? What are the developmental implications?

9. Why are children more susceptible to health risks posed by their environment?

10. In what ways can First World nations best contribute to the alleviation of global and domestic LDC environmental problems? Be specific.

Notes

1. For a comprehensive view of the range of issues linking the environment to economic development, see World Bank, *World Development Report, 1992: Development and the Environment* (New York: Oxford University Press, 1992); David W. Pearce, Edward

Barbier, and Alvin Markandya, *Sustainable Development: Economics and Environment in in the Third World* (Chaltenham, U.K.: Elgar, 1990); and J. M. Antle and G. Heidebrink, "Environment and development: Theory and international evidence," *Economic Development and Cultural Change* 43 (April 1995).

2. For a comparative analysis of various definitions of sustainable development, see Sharachchandra A. Lele, "Sustainable development: A critical review," *World Development* 19 (January 1991): 607–621.

3. World Commission on Environment and Development, *Our Common Future* (New York: Oxford University Press, 1987), pp. 4, 8.

4. David W. Pearce and Jeremy J. Warford, *World without End: Economics, Environment, and Sustainable Development: A Summary* (Washington, D.C.: World Bank, 1993), p. 2.

5. *Ibid.*, pp. 2–3.

6. See United Nations Population Fund, *Population, Resources and the Environment: The Critical Challenge* (New York: United Nations, 1991), for a review and an analysis of these critical population-environment linkages. See also Maureen L. Cropper and Charles Griffiths, "The interaction of population growth and environmental quality," *American Economic Review* 84 (May 1994): 250–254.

7. A careful description of the factors leading to the production of greenhouse gases in Third World countries is offered in John Bongaarts, "Population growth and global warming," *Population and Development Review* 18 (June 1992): 299–319.

8. For a detailed statistical, descriptive portrait of environmental damage in the Third World, see the most recent edition of World Resources Institute, *World Resources: A Guide to Global Environment* (New York: Oxford University Press, annually). Most of the data quoted in this and succeeding sections of the chapter come from the 1994–1995 edition, as well as from World Bank, *World Development Report, 1992* and United Nations, *Population, Resources and the Environment.*

9. For a provocative look at the issue of gender and the environment, see Cecile Jackson, "Doing what comes naturally: Women and environment in development," *World Development* 21 (December 1993): 1947–1963.

10. For a basic and detailed presentation of models of environmental economics, see Tom Tietenberg, *Environmental and Natural Resources Economics* (Glenview, Ill.: Scott, Foresman, 1990); John M. Hartwick and N. Olewiler, *The Economics of Natural Resource Use* (New York: Harper & Row, 1986); G. Tyler Miller, *Living in the Environment* (Belmont, Calif.: Wadsworth, 1990); and Maureen L. Cropper and Wallace E. Oates, "Environmental economics: A survey," *Journal of Economic Literature* 30 (June 1992): 675–740.

11. World Bank, *World Development Report, 1992*, fig. 4.

12. *Ibid.*, fig. 2.4.

13. A discussion of the dangers of pesticide misuse in developing countries is presented in Ruth Norris (ed.), *Pills, Pesticides and Profits* (Croton-on-Hudson, N.Y.: North River Press, 1982), and Ruth Norris, *Sustainability: The Case for Reducing the Use of Chemical Pesticides* (Rome: Pesticide Action Network, 1987).

14. Two excellent sources of information concerning tropical deforestation are World Resources Institute, *World Resources, 1994–1995*, chap. 7; and World Bank, *World Development Report, 1992*, chap. 7.

15. For an extensive discussion of public environment policies that LDC governments might pursue, see World Bank, *World Development Report, 1992*, chaps. 3 and 7; and World Resources Institute, *World Resources, 1992–1993*. chaps. 3 and 14.

16. An interesting and lucid discussion of government policy options in this area can be found in Stephen W. Salant, "The economics of natural resource extraction: A primer for development economists," *World Bank Research Observer* 10 (February 1995): 93–111.

17. For more information concerning debt-for-nature swaps, see World Resources Institute, *World Resources, 1992–1993*, pp. 122–123 and tab. 20.6; and World Bank, *World Debt Tables, 1991–1992* (Washington, D.C.: World Bank, 1992), box 4.5. See also Chapter 14.

Further Reading

For a lively and easy-to-follow economics-based review of environment and development issues, see David W. Pearce and Jeremy J. Warford, *World without End: Economics, Environment, and Sustainable Development: A Summary* (Washington, D.C.: World Bank, 1993). An advanced and thorough overview of the literature relating to current models of the environment and their policy implications is provided in Maureen L. Cropper and Wallace E. Oates, "Environmental economics: A survey," *Journal of Economic Literature* 30 (June 1992): 675–740.

Comprehensive discussions of Third World environmental problems, including desertification, deforestation, access to clean water and sanitation, and soil degradation, are offered in World Bank, *World Development Report, 1992: Development and the Environment* (New York: Oxford University Press, 1992), and World Resources Institute's annual publication *World Resources* (New York: Oxford University Press).

For more detailed information concerning the causes and consequences of environmental degradation in developing countries, see Scott Barrett, "Optimal soil conservation and the reform of agricultural pricing policies," *Journal of Development Economics* 36 (October 1991): 167–187; Gordon McGranahan, "Fuelwood, subsistence foraging, and the decline of common property," *World Development* 19 (October 1991): 1275–1285; and Steven L. Rhodes, "Rethinking desertification: What do we know and what have we learned?" *World Development* 19 (September 1991): 1137–1143.

Careful descriptions of the socioeconomic causes of deforestation may be found in Nicholas Guppy, "Tropical deforestation: A global view," *Foreign Affairs* (Spring 1984): 928–965, and Robert Repetto, "Deforestation in the tropics," *Scientific American*, April 1990, pp. 36–42.

For a general description of the application of economics to global warming, see Thomas C. Schelling, "Some economics of global warming," *American Economic Review* 82 (1992): 1–14. A variety of suggestions concerning the policy implications of global warming for First World governments are available in Dieter Helm (ed.), *Economic Policy towards the Environment* (Cambridge: Blackwell, 1991). For analysis of the growing contribution of Third World countries to the production of greenhouse gases, see John Bongaarts, "Population growth and global warming," *Population and Development Review* 18 (June 1992): 299–319 and Stephen W. Salant, "The economics of natural resource extraction: A primer for development economists," *World Bank Research Observer* 10 (February 1995): 93–111.

For additional information concerning the impact of population on the environment, see United Nations Population Fund, *Population, Resources and Environment: The Critical Challenges* (New York: United Nations, 1991). See also Kingsley Davis and Mikail S. Bernstam (eds.), *Resources, Environment and Population*, supplement to *Population and Development Review* 16 (1990), and Richard Bilsborrow and M. Geores, *Population, Land Use and the Environment in Developing Countries: What Can We Learn from Cross-national Data?* (Washington, D.C.: National Academy of Sciences, 1991).

See Chapters 14 and 15 of Stephen C. Smith's *Case Studies* for an analysis of deforestation in Brazil and debt-for-nature swaps in Bolivia.

CHAPTER 11

Education and Development

The school in many underdeveloped countries is a reflection and a fruit of the surrounding underdevelopment, from which arises its deficiency, its quantitative and qualitative poverty: But little by little, and there lies the really serious risk, the school in these underdeveloped countries risks becoming in turn a factor of underdevelopment.

—Joseph Kizerbo, Former Minister of Education, Burkina Faso

Virtually every serious commentator agrees that major reform within Third World education is long overdue.

—Richard Jolly, Deputy Director General, UNICEF

Investing in people, if done right, . . . provides the firmest foundation for lasting development.

—World Bank, *World Development Report, 1991*

Education and Human Resources

Most economists argue that it is the **human resources** of a nation, not its physical capital or its natural resources, that ultimately determine the character and pace of its economic and social development. For example, according to the late Professor Frederick Harbison of Princeton University:

> Human resources . . . constitute the ultimate basis for the wealth of nations. Capital and natural resources are passive factors of production; human beings are the active agents who accumulate capital, exploit natural resources, build social, economic and political organizations, and carry forward national development. Clearly, a country which is unable to develop the skills and knowledge of its people and to utilize them effectively in the national economy will be unable to develop anything else.[1]

The principal institutional mechanism for developing human skills and knowledge is the formal educational system. Most Third World nations have been led to believe or have wanted to believe that the rapid *quantitative* expansion of educational opportunities is the key to national development: The more education, the more rapid the development. All countries have committed themselves, therefore, to the goal of universal education in the shortest possible time. This quest has become a politically sensitive, but often economically costly, sacred cow. Until recently, few politicians, statesmen, economists, or educational planners inside or outside of the Third World would have dared publicly to challenge the cult of formal education.

Nevertheless, the challenge is now gathering momentum, and it comes from many sources. It can be found most clearly in the character and results of the development process itself. After more than three decades of rapidly expanding enrollments and hundreds of billions of dollars of educational expenditure, the plight of the average citizen in many parts of Asia, Africa, and Latin America seems little improved. Absolute poverty is chronic and pervasive. Economic disparities between rich and poor widen with each passing year. Unemployment and underemployment have reached staggering proportions, with the "educated" increasingly swelling the ranks of the unemployed.

It would be foolish and naive to blame these problems on the failures of the **formal educational system**. At the same time, we must recognize that many of the early claims made on behalf of the unfettered quantitative expansion of educational opportunities—that it would accelerate economic growth, that it would raise levels of living especially for the poor, that it would generate widespread and equal employment opportunities for all, that it would acculturate diverse ethnic or tribal groups, and that it would encourage "modern" attitudes—have been shown to be greatly exaggerated and, in many instances, simply false.[2]

As a result, there has been a growing awareness in many developing nations that the expansion of formal schooling is not always to be equated with the spread of learning, that the acquisition of school certificates and higher degrees is not necessarily associated with an improved ability to undertake productive work, that education oriented almost entirely toward preparation for work in the modern urban sector can greatly distort student aspirations, and that too much investment in formal schooling, especially at the secondary and higher levels, can divert scarce resources from more socially productive activities (e.g., direct employment creation) and thus be a drag on national development rather than a stimulus.

The educational systems of Third World nations strongly influence and are influenced by the whole nature, magnitude, and character of their development process. The role of formal education is not limited to imparting the knowledge and skills that enable individuals to function as economic change agents in their societies. Formal education also imparts values, ideas, attitudes, and aspirations, which may or may not be in the nation's best developmental interests. Education absorbs the greatest share of LDC recurrent government expenditures, occupies the time and activities of the greatest number of adults and children (almost 30% of Third World populations), and carries the greatest psychological burden of development aspirations. We must therefore examine its fundamental economic basis in developing countries and also its social and institutional ramifications.

The economics of education is a vital yet somewhat amorphous component of the economics of development. It is a young subject, having emerged as a separate branch of economics only in the early 1960s. Yet when we recognize the principal motivation or demand for education in developing countries as a desire for economic improvement by means of access to better-paid jobs, we must understand the economic processes through which such aspirations are either realized or frustrated.

In this chapter, we explore the relationship between development and quantitative and qualitative educational expansion in terms of six basic issues that grow directly out of the discussions of previous chapters:

1. How does education influence the rate, structure, and character of economic growth? Conversely, how do the rate, structure, and character of economic growth influence the nature of the educational system?

2. Does education in general and the structure of Third World educational systems in particular contribute to or retard the growth of domestic inequality and poverty?

3. What is the relationship of education to rural-urban migration and urban unemployment? Are rising levels of the educated unemployed a temporary or chronic phenomenon?

4. Do women lag behind men in educational attainment, and is there a relationship between the education of women and their desired family size?

5. Do contemporary Third World formal educational systems tend to promote or retard agricultural and rural development?

6. What is the relationship, if any, among Third World educational systems, developed-country educational systems, and the international migration of highly educated professional and technical workers from the less developed to the more developed nations?

We begin with a profile of the status of education in a range of developing countries. In this profile, we focus on public expenditure levels, enrollment ratios, literacy levels, dropout rates, educational costs and earnings differentials, and the educational gender gap. Then we will review some basic concepts in the economics of education, including the determinants of the demand for and supply of school places and the distinction between private and social benefits and costs of investment in education. Next we examine in detail the six listed issues to see if we can reach any conclusions about the relationship between education and various key components of the development process. We end with a review of alternative policy options open to Third World governments in their attempts to evolve an educational system that will more efficiently serve the needs and aspirations of all their people.

Education in Developing Regions

Public Educational Expenditure

In many developing countries, formal education is the largest "industry" and the greatest consumer of public revenues.[3] Poor nations have invested huge sums of money in education. The reasons are numerous. Literate farmers with at least a primary education are thought to be more productive and more responsive to new agricultural technologies than illiterate farmers. Specially trained artisans and mechanics who can read and write are assumed to be better able to keep up to date with changing products and materials. Secondary school graduates with some knowledge of elementary computer operations and information retrival processes along with basic clerical skills are needed to perform technical and administrative functions in growing public and private bureaucracies. In former colonial countries, many people with such skills are also needed to replace departing expatriates. University graduates with advanced training are needed to provide the professional and managerial expertise necessary for a modernized public and private sector.

In addition to these obvious human resource needs, the people themselves, both rich and poor, have exerted tremendous political pressure for the expansion of school places in developing countries. Parents have realized that in an era of scarce skilled manpower, the more schooling and the more certificates their children can accumulate, the better will be their chances of getting secure and well-paid jobs. More years of schooling have been perceived as the only avenue of hope for poor children to escape from poverty.

As a result of these forces acting on both demand and supply, there has been a tremendous acceleration in LDC public expenditures on education during the past three decades. The proportion of national income and of national budgets spent on education has increased rapidly. In Asia, total public expenditures tripled during the 1960s and 1970s; in Africa and Latin America, public educational expenditures more than doubled. In fact, the increase in public expenditure on education in the 1960s and 1970s exceeded increases in any other sector of the economy. By the early 1990s, educational budgets in many Third World nations were absorbing 15% to 27% of total government recurrent expenditure. Although this is a sizable expenditure in terms of overall budget, developing nations nevertheless were spending only $229 per capita on public education, compared to $468 per capita spent in the developed world. Moreover, with declining or stagnating economic growth combined with rising debt burdens and pressures to reduce government spending, most Third World governments—primarily the least developed countries of Africa and Asia—were forced in the 1980s and early 1990s to curtail their educational (as well as health and social services) budget.

Enrollments

Between 1960 and 1990, the total number of persons enrolled in the three main levels of education in Africa, Asia, the Middle East, and Latin America rose from 163 million to 440 million—an average annual increase of 5%. Although the largest part of this increase has been in primary education, it is in the secondary and tertiary levels that the greatest proportionate increases have occurred—12.7% and 14.5% per annum, respectively. Nevertheless, primary enrollment still accounts for nearly 78% of the total LDC school enrollments.

In terms of the proportion of children of school age actually attending school at the primary, secondary, and tertiary levels, the differential between the developed and the less developed regions and among Third World regions themselves is substantial. African countries lag behind at all levels, with only 67% of their primary school–aged children actually enrolled. Table 11.1 shows comparative data on **enrollment ratios** at the primary, secondary, and higher education levels for a selected group of low- and middle-income developing countries in 1965 and 1992. The remarkable increases in enrollments at both the primary and secondary levels are strikingly evident from this table.

The statistics of Table 11.1, however, can be very misleading. They tell us the proportion of school-age children and teenagers enrolled in primary, secondary, and higher educational institutions at a single point in time. They do not tell us how many of these students remain in school for the duration. In fact, one of the major educational problems of developing nations is the high percentage of students who drop out before completing a particular cycle. For example, in Latin America, an estimated 60 out of every 100 students who enter primary school drop out before completion. In some Latin American countries, the primary school **dropout rate** is as high as 75%. In Africa and Asia, the median dropout rate is approximately 54% and 20%, respectively. But the variation among countries has been wide, with dropout rates as high as 81% in certain African nations and 64% in certain Asian ones.

At the secondary level, median dropout rates for entering students were 38.7% in Africa and 18% in Latin America and Asia. In Europe, the rate was approximately

TABLE 11.1 Enrollment Ratios in Selected Developing Countries: Primary, Secondary, and Higher Education, 1965 and 1992

| | Numbers Enrolled as a Percentage of Age Group | | | | | |
| | Primary | | Secondary | | Tertiary | |
Country	1965	1992	1965	1992	1965	1992
Low-income LDCs						
Bangladesh	49	77	13	19	1	4
Ethiopia	11	22	2	12	0	1
Haiti	50	56	5	22	0	1
India	74	100	27	44	5	6
Sri Lanka	93	100	35	74	2	6
Tanzania	32	68	2	5	0	1
Middle-income LDCs						
Colombia	84	100	17	55	3	15
Guatemala	50	79	8	28	2	9
Mexico	92	100	17	55	4	14
Philippines	100	100	41	74	19	28
South Korea	100	100	35	90	6	42
Thailand	78	97	14	33	2	19
Developed countries	100	100	61	93	21	51

SOURCE: World Bank, *World Development Report, 1992* and *1995* (New York: Oxford University Press, 1992, 1995), annex tab. 28.

11.4%. One consequence of this phenomenon, particularly for Africa, is the serious and growing problem of the secondary school dropout who joins the ranks of the educated unemployed.

Literacy

Literacy, the ability to read, write, and comprehend information, is obviously a fundamental component of human resource development. The percentage of LDC adults (persons 15 years of age and older) who are illiterate has fallen from 60% in 1960 to 36% in 1990. However, as a result of rapid population growth, the actual number of adult illiterates has risen over this same period by nearly 120 million to an estimated total of over 940 million in 1990. The highest illiteracy rates are found in Africa (50%) and the Arab states (45%), followed by South Asia (45%), East Asia (24%), and Latin America (15%). In North America and Europe, illiteracy rates are a mere 1.0% and 2.5%, respectively.

Costs and Earnings

There has been growing criticism in recent years of the very serious disproportionate per-pupil costs of education at various levels in the LDCs. The imbalance is particularly apparent when we compare secondary and higher educational costs with primary-level costs. Whereas much of the early criticism was based on scattered ad hoc empirical and interpretative information, in the 1970s and 1980s a highly regarded comparative series of studies provided detailed data on the magnitude of these cost divergences.[4]

Table 11.2 compares the ratio of total costs per student year by educational level for a group of developed and less developed countries. Although these data are from the 1960s, similar ratios still prevail today. The data reveal that whereas in the three developed countries shown the ratio of total per-pupil cost of secondary to primary education is 6.6 to 1 and that of higher to primary education is 17.6 to 1, in the seven LDCs shown these relative costs are 11.9 and 87.9 to 1, respectively. In other words, taking the 87.9 figure, for the equivalent cost of educating one university student for a year, 88 primary school children could have received a year of schooling. In many African countries (Sierra Leone, Malawi, Kenya, Tanzania), cost ratios per pupil between higher and primary education range as high as 283 to 1. Since in over half of the world's developing countries the ratio of students in

TABLE 11.2 Ratios of Total Costs by Educational Level per Student Year

	Relative Cost	
Groups of Countries	Secondary versus Primary	Higher versus Primary
United States, Great Britain, New Zealand	6.6	17.6
Malaysia, Ghana, South Korea, Kenya, Uganda, Nigeria, India	11.9	87.9

SOURCE: George Psacharopoulos, *The Returns to Education: An International Comparison* (Amsterdam: Elsevier, 1972), tab. 8.2. Reprinted with permission.

primary schools to students in higher education is above 100 to 1 (compared, for example, with ratios of less than 10 to 1 in the developed countries), it follows that LDCs spend large proportions of their educational budgets on a very small proportion of their students enrolled in universities and professional schools. For example, a 1985 study of the distribution of public educational expenditures revealed that in developing countries as a whole, the 6% of students attaining higher education received almost 40% of the resources. In Africa, less than 2% of the students who go to universities received over 35% of the public expenditures. In Latin America, 12% of students received 42% of the educational resources.[5]

If we then compare the data in Table 11.3, showing the relative average earnings of individuals by educational level, with those on costs, it becomes clear that relative earnings differentials by educational level are much less than unit cost differentials in the developing compared with the developed countries. For example, looking at the figures at the lower right in Tables 11.2 and 11.3, we see that whereas an LDC university student costs 87.9 times as much as a primary pupil to educate for one year, the university student on the average earns only 6.4 times as much as the typical primary pupil—a very high (and often artificial) differential, but not as high as the cost differential. To the extent that average relative earnings reflect average relative productivity, the wide disparity between relative earnings and relative costs of higher versus primary education implies that in the past, LDC governments may have unwisely invested too much in higher education. These funds might have been more productively invested in primary school expansion. This does not necessarily imply that future relative cost-benefit ratios will continue to favor primary school expansion; much depends on the relative employment prospects of the various educational groups. Moreover, although most empirical studies in the 1980s and early 1990s revealed that both the private and the social rates of return to investment in education were the highest at the primary level regardless of the number of students (see Table 11.4),[6] research by Behrman and Birdsall casts considerable doubt on this widely held belief.[7] Their studies indicate that it is the quality of education (the quality of teaching, facilities, and curricula) and not its quantity alone (years of schooling) that best explains differential earnings and productivity. The implication is that governments should spend more to upgrade existing schools and less to expand the number of school places—that is, they should deepen the investment in human capital rather than extend it to more people. Unfortunately, this raises serious equity questions, which we will examine shortly.

TABLE 11.3 Ratios of Average Annual Earnings of Labor by Educational Level

	Relative Earnings	
Groups of Countries	Secondary versus Primary	Higher versus Primary
United States, Canada, Great Britain	1.4	2.4
Malaysia, Ghana, South Korea, Kenya, Uganda, Nigeria, India	2.4	6.4

SOURCE: George Psacharopoulos, *The Returns to Education: An International Comparison* (Amsterdam: Elsevier, 1972), tab. 8.4. Reprinted with permission.

TABLE 11.4 The Rates of Return to Investment in Education by Level of Education, Country Type, and Region (percent)

Country Type and Region	Social Rate of Return[a]			Private Rate of Return[a]		
	Primary	Secondary	Higher	Primary	Secondary	Higher
Developing						
Sub-Saharan Africa	24	18	11	41	27	28
Asia	20	13	12	39	19	20
Latin America	18	13	12	26	17	20
Developed	14	10	9	22	12	12

SOURCE: George Psacharopoulous, "Returns to investment in education: A global update," *World Development* 2 (September 1993): tab. 1.
[a]See note 6 on page 409 for a description of how these rates of return are calculated. Reprinted with permission.

The Gender Gap: Women and Education

Young females receive considerably less education than young males in almost every developing country. In 66 out of 108 countries, women's enrollment in primary and secondary education is lower than that of men by at least 10 percentage points. This **educational gender gap** is the greatest in the poorest countries and regionally in the Middle East and North Africa. Table 11.5 provides data on female-male gaps in literacy, mean years of schooling, and enrollments for 10 Third World countries in 1992. For all developing countries taken together, the female literacy rate was 29% lower than male literacy, women's mean years of schooling were 45% lower than men's, and females' enrollment rates in primary, secondary, and tertiary schools were 9%, 28% and 49% lower, respectively, than the corresponding male rate.

TABLE 11.5 The Educational Gender Gap: Females as a Percentage of Males, 1992

Country	Adult Literacy	Mean Years of Schooling	Primary Enrollment	Secondary Enrollment	Tertiary Enrollment
Afghanistan	32	14	52	50	24
Algeria	66	18	89	79	44
Bangladesh	47	29	86	46	19
Egypt	54	41	79	82	52
India	55	34	97	57	45
Mexico	94	96	97	100	76
Morocco	62	37	68	70	58
Nigeria	65	28	93	74	37
South Korea	95	61	100	96	49
Sudan	28	45	71	87	70
All LDCs	71	55	91	72	51

SOURCE: United Nations Development Program, *Human Development Report, 1994* (New York: Oxford University Press, 1994), tab. 9.
NOTE: All figures are expressed in relation to the male average, which is indexed to equal 100. The smaller the figure, the bigger the gap.

Why is female education important? Is it simply a matter of equity? The answer is that there now exists ample empirical evidence that educational discrimination against women hinders economic development in addition to reinforcing social inequality. Closing the educational gender gap by expanding educational opportunities for women is economically desirable for four reasons:[8]

1. The rate of return on women's education is higher than that on men's in most developing countries.

2. Increasing women's education not only increases their productivity on the farm and in the factory but also results in greater labor force participation, later marriage, lower fertility, and greatly improved child health and nutrition.

3. Improved child health and nutrition and more educated mothers lead to multiplier effects on the quality of a nation's human resources for many generations to come.

4. Because women carry a disproportionate burden of the poverty and landlessness that permeates developing societies, any significant improvements in their role and status via education can have an important impact on breaking the vicious cycle of poverty and inadequate schooling.

The Economics of Education and Employment

Much of the literature and public discussion about education and economic development in general, and education and employment in particular, revolves around two fundamental economic processes: (1) the interaction between economically motivated demands and politically responsive supplies in determining how many school places are provided, who gets access to these places, and what kind of instruction they receive; and (2) the important distinction between social and private benefits and costs of different levels of education and the implications of these differentials for educational investment strategy.

Educational Supply and Demand: The Relationship between Employment Opportunities and Educational Demands

The amount of schooling received by an individual, although affected by many nonmarket factors, can be regarded as largely determined by demand and supply, like any other commodity or service.[9] However, because most education is publicly provided in less developed countries, the determinants of the amount demanded turn out to be much more important than the determinants of supply. On the demand side, the two principal influences on the amount of schooling desired are (1) a more educated student's prospects of earning considerably more income through future modern-sector employment (the family's **private benefits of education**) and (2) the educational costs, both direct and indirect, that a student or family must bear. The amount of education demanded is thus in reality a **derived demand** for high-wage employment opportunities in the modern sector. This is because access to such jobs is largely determined by an individual's education. Most people (especially the poor) in less developed nations do not demand education for its intrinsic noneconomic benefits but simply because it is the only means of securing modern-sector employment. These derived benefits must in turn be weighed against the costs of education.

On the supply side, the quantity of school places at the primary, secondary, and university levels is determined largely by political processes, often unrelated to economic criteria. Given mounting political pressure throughout the Third World for greater numbers of school places, we can for convenience assume that the public supply of these places is fixed by the level of government educational expenditures. These are in turn influenced by the level of aggregate private demand for education.

Because it is the amount of education that is demanded that largely determines the supply (within the limits of government financial feasibility), let us look more closely at the economic (employment-oriented) determinants of this derived demand.

The amount of schooling demanded sufficient to qualify an individual for modern-sector jobs appears to be related to or determined by the combined influence of the following four variables:

1. *The wage or income differential.* This is the wage differential between jobs in the modern sector and those outside it (family farming, rural and urban self-employment, etc.), which for simplicity we can call the traditional sector. Entry into modern-sector jobs depends initially on the level of completed education, whereas income-earning opportunities in the traditional sector have no fixed educational requirements. The greater the income differential between the modern and traditional sectors, the greater the quantity of education demanded. Thus our first relationship states that the quantity of education demanded is positively related to the modern sector–traditional sector wage differential. Since we know from empirical studies that these differentials can be considerable in developing nations, we might expect the quantity demanded to be relatively high.

2. *The probability of success in finding modern-sector employment.* An individual who successfully completes the necessary schooling for entry into the modern-sector labor market has a higher probability of getting that well-paid urban job than someone who does not. Clearly, if urban unemployment rates among the educated are growing or if the supply of secondary school graduates continually exceeds the number of new job openings for which a secondary graduate can qualify, we need to modify the actual wage differential and instead speak once again about an *expected* income differential (see Chapter 8). As the probability of success is inversely related to the unemployment rate, we can argue that the quantity of education demanded through the secondary level will be inversely related to the current unemployment rate among secondary school graduates.[10]

3. *The direct private costs of education.* We refer here to the current out-of-pocket expenses of financing a child's education. These expenses include school fees, books, clothing, and related costs. We would expect that the quantity of education demanded would be inversely related to these direct costs—that is, the higher the school fees and associated costs, the lower the private demand for

education, everything else being equal. For poor people, direct primary school costs often represent a major burden and a real financial constraint. In much of Africa, for example, the average cost of sending a child to primary school (not including opportunity costs) is typically in excess of 20% of per capita income.

4. *The indirect or opportunity costs of education.* An investment in a child's education involves more than just the direct out-of-pocket costs of that education, especially when the child reaches the age at which he can make a productive contribution to family income. At this point, for each year the child continues his education, he in effect forgoes the money income he could expect to earn or the output he could produce for the family farm. This **opportunity cost of education** must also be included as a variable affecting its demand.[11] We would expect the relationship between opportunity cost and quantity demanded to be inverse—that is, the greater the opportunity cost, the lower the quantity demanded.

Although several other important variables, many of them noneconomic (e.g., cultural traditions, social status, education of parents, and size of family), certainly influence the amount of education demanded, concentrating on the four variables just described can give important insights into the relationship between the quantity of education demanded and the supply of employment opportunities.

For example, suppose that we have a situation in an LDC where the following conditions prevail:

1. The modern-traditional or urban-rural wage gap is of the magnitude of, say, 100% for secondary versus primary school graduates.

2. The rate of increase in modern-sector employment opportunities for primary school dropouts is slower than the rate at which such individuals enter the labor force. The same may be true at the secondary level and even the university level in countries such as India, Mexico, Egypt, Pakistan, Ghana, Nigeria, and Kenya.

3. Employers, facing an excess of applicants, tend to select by level of education. They will choose candidates with secondary rather than primary education even though satisfactory job performance may require no more than a primary education.

4. Governments, supported by the political pressure of the educated, tend to bind the going wage to the level of educational attainment of jobholders rather than to the minimum educational qualification required for the job.

5. School fees at the early primary level are often nominal or even nonexistent. They tend to rise sharply at the late primary and secondary level and then decline again at the university level as the state bears a larger proportion of the college student's costs.

Under these conditions, which conform closely to the realities of the employment and education situation in many developing nations, we would expect the quantity of education demanded to be substantial. This is because the anticipated private benefits of more schooling would be large compared to the alternative of little or no schooling, while the direct and indirect private educational costs are relatively low. And the demand spirals upward over time. As job opportunities for the uneducated diminish, individuals must safeguard their position by acquiring a complete primary education. This may suffice for a while, but the internal dynamics of the employment demand-supply process eventually lead to a situation in which job prospects for those with only primary education begin to decline. This in turn increases the demand for secondary education. But the amount of primary education must increase concurrently, as some people who were previously content with no education are now being squeezed out of the labor market.

The irony is that the more unprofitable a given level of education becomes as a terminal point, the greater the demand for it as an intermediate stage or precondition to the next level of education! This puts great pressure on governments to expand educational facilities at *all* levels to meet the growing demand. If they cannot respond fast enough, the people may do so on their own, as evidenced, for example, by the Harambee school self-help movement in Kenya, where community-sponsored secondary schools were built throughout the country with the knowledge that their maintenance would be taken over later by the government.

The upshot of all this is the chronic tendency for developing nations to expand their educational facilities at a rate that is extremely difficult to justify either socially or financially in terms of optimal resource allocations. Supply and amount demanded are equated not by a price-adjusting market mechanism but rather institutionally, largely by the state. The **social benefits of education** (the payoff to society as a whole) for all levels of schooling fall far short of the private benefits (see Table 11.4). Each worsening of the employment situation calls forth an increased amount demanded for (and supply of) more formal education at all levels. At first, it is primarily the uneducated who are found among the ranks of the unemployed. However, over time, there is an inexorable tendency for the average educational level of the unemployed to rise as the supply of school graduates continues to exceed the demand for middle- and high-level workers. The better-educated must, after varying periods of unemployment during which aspirations are scaled downward, take jobs requiring lower levels of education. The diploma and degree thus become basic requirements for employment; they no longer provide entrée into a high-paid job, nor do they provide the education they were intended to signify.

Governments and private employers in many LDCs tend to reinforce this trend by continuously upgrading formal educational entry requirements for jobs previously filled by less educated workers. Excess educational qualification becomes formalized and may resist downward adjustment. Moreover, to the extent that trade unions succeed in binding going wages to the educational attainments of jobholders, the going wage for each job will tend to rise (even though worker productivity in that job does not significantly increase). Existing distortions in wage differentials will be magnified, thus stimulating the amount of education demanded even further.

As a result of this **educational certification** and displacement phenomenon, students who for some reason (primarily poverty) are unable to continue their education will fall by the wayside as unemployed school dropouts. At the same time, the more affluent continue to overqualify themselves through more years of education. In the extreme case, a situation evolves like that of contemporary India,

Pakistan, and Bangladesh, where the higher education system is in effect an "absorber of last resort" for the great numbers of educated unemployed.[12] This is a terribly expensive form of unemployment compensation. Moreover, because people cannot remain students until they retire, these great masses will eventually have to emerge from behind the walls of academia into a world of tight labor markets. The result will be more visible unemployment among people who are both highly educated and highly vocal. For example, a study in Bangladesh revealed that the unemployment rate among university graduates in 1980 was 47%.[13]

Finally, it should be pointed out that many individuals tend to resist what they see as a downgrading of their job qualifications. Consequently, even though on the demand-for-labor side employers will attempt to substitute the more educated for the less educated for a given job, on the supply side there will be many job seekers whose expectations exceed the emerging realities of the labor market. They might prefer to remain unemployed for some time rather than accept a job that they feel is beneath them. It follows that as a result of these frictional effects and lags in adjustment on the supply side, unemployment will exist at all levels of education even though it is concentrated at lower levels and, in general, is inversely related to educational attainment.

Social versus Private Benefits and Costs

The inexorable attraction of ever-higher levels of education is even more costly than this simple picture suggests. Typically in developing countries, the **social costs of education** (the opportunity cost to society as a whole resulting from the need to finance costly educational expansion at higher levels when these limited funds might be more productively used in other sectors of the economy) increase rapidly as students climb the educational ladder. The **private costs of education** (those borne by students themselves) increase more slowly or may even decline.

This widening gap between social and private costs provides an even greater stimulus to the demand for higher education than it does for education at lower levels. Educational demand therefore becomes increasingly exaggerated at the higher (postsecondary) levels. But educational opportunities can be accommodated to these distorted demands only at full social cost. As demands are generated progressively through the system, the social cost of accommodation grows much more rapidly than the places provided. More and more resources may be misallocated to educational expansion in terms of social costs, and the potential for creating new jobs will consequently diminish for lack of public financial resources.

Figure 11.1 provides an illustration of this divergence between private and social benefits and costs. It also demonstrates how this divergence can lead to a misallocation of resources when private interests supersede social investment criteria. In Figure 11.1a, expected private returns and actual private costs are plotted against years of completed schooling. As a student completes more and more years of schooling, her expected private returns grow at a much faster rate than her private costs, for reasons explained earlier. To maximize the difference between expected benefits and costs (and thereby the private rate of return to investment in education), the optimal strategy for a student would be to secure as much schooling as possible.

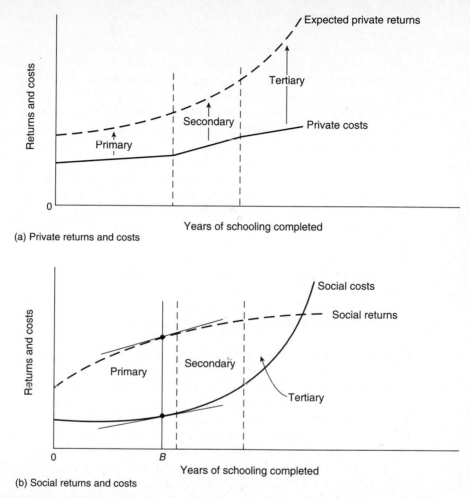

FIGURE 11.1 Private versus Social Benefits and Costs of Education: An Illustration.

Now consider Figure 11.1b, where social returns and social costs are plotted against years of schooling. The social benefits curve rises sharply at first, reflecting the improved levels of productivity of, say, small farmers and the self-employed that result from receipt of a **basic education** and the attainment of literacy, arithmetic skills, and elementary vocational skills. Thereafter, the marginal social benefit of additional years of schooling rises more slowly, and the social returns curve begins to level off. By contrast, the social cost curve shows a slow rate of growth for early years of schooling (basic education) and then a much more rapid growth for higher levels of education. This rapid increase in the marginal social costs of postprimary education is the result both of the much more expensive capital and recurrent costs of higher education (buildings and equipment) and, more important, of the fact that much postprimary education in developing countries is heavily subsidized.[14]

It follows from Figure 11.1b that the optimal strategy from a social viewpoint, the one that maximizes the net social rate of return to educational investment, would be one that focuses on providing all students with at least B years of schooling. Beyond B years, *marginal* social costs exceed *marginal* social benefits, so additional educational investment in new, higher-level school places will yield a *negative* net social rate of return. Moreover, in light of the recent empirical results of the Behrman and Birdsall study, the optimal social investment strategy may be to upgrade the quality of existing primary schools rather than to expand their quantity. This quality-quantity trade-off would be represented in the figure by an upward shift of the social returns curve in Figure 11.1b.

Figure 11.1 therefore illustrates the inherent conflict between optimal private and social investment strategies—a conflict that will continue to exist as long as private and social valuations of investment in education continue to diverge as students climb the educational ladder (see Table 11.4 for evidence of the magnitude of these divergences).

To a large degree, the problem of divergent social versus private benefits and costs has been artificially created by inappropriate public and private policies with regard to wage differentials, educational selectivity, and the pricing of educational services. As a result, private perceptions of the value of education exceed its social value, which must take account of rising unemployment. As long as artificial and nonmarket incentives in the form of disproportionate expected benefits and subsidized costs continue to exist and place a premium on the number of years one spends getting an education, the individual will decide that it is in his best private interests to pursue a lengthy formal education process even though he may be aware that modern-sector jobs are becoming more scarce and unemployment rates are rising. Unless these various price signals are made to conform more closely to social realities, the misallocation of national resources (in this case, too much expenditure on formal education) will persist and possibly increase.

What is needed is a properly functioning reward and cost structure that develops and allocates human resources in accordance with requirements and opportunities in various segments of the economy. Where this is absent (where high wage premiums are paid to workers in the modern urban sector and scarce jobs are allocated on the basis of ever-increasing educational credentials), two obvious misallocations of human resources are likely to occur. First, with the output of the educational system greatly in excess of what the economy can absorb, many students will emerge seeking jobs for which they may be educationally qualified but which have been preempted by others with even more education. They become temporarily unemployed for as long as it takes for their aspirations and status requirements, partly perhaps instilled in them by the educational system itself, to adjust to the stinging realities of unemployment in the modern sector. Second, those who adjust their sights downward and secure modern-sector employment normally have to take jobs for which they are overeducated in terms of the number of years spent in school. Those who fail to get modern-sector jobs at all swell the ranks of the permanently unemployed or become self-employed in the informal sector. They are thus denied the opportunity to contribute productively to the society that invested so heavily in their education. This combination of the overpaid and, in many cases, overeducated employed and the impoverished and unproductive educated unemployed reflects a serious misallocation of scarce national resources. The resources allocated to the expansion of the educational system might alternatively have been spent on needed rural public works projects. Such investment would provide emergency employment opportunities for recent graduates as well as for people with less education.

Having looked at the economics of education and employment, we can now examine some of the broader interrelationships among education, society, and development.

Education, Society, and Development: Some Issues

We cannot discuss the relationship between education and development without explicitly linking the structure of the educational system to the economic and social character of the Third World society in which it is contained. Educational systems more often than not reflect the essential nature of that society. For example, if the society is inegalitarian in economic and social structure, the educational system will probably reflect that bias in terms of who is able to proceed through the system. At the same time, education *can* influence the future shape and direction of society in a number of ways. Thus the link between education and development goes both ways. By reflecting the socioeconomic structures of the societies in which they function (whether egalitarian or not), educational systems tend to perpetuate, reinforce, and reproduce those economic and social structures. Conversely, educational reform, whether introduced from within or outside the system, has the great potential for inducing corresponding social and economic reform in the nation as a whole.

With these general observations in mind, let us look at five specific economic components of the development question—growth, inequality and poverty, population and fertility, migration, and rural development—to see in what way they influence or are influenced by most LDC educational systems. Such an examination will demonstrate the important two-way relationship that exists between education and development. It should also provide us with an even broader understanding of the development problems and issues that have been discussed in previous chapters.

Education and Economic Growth

For many years, the proposition that educational expansion promoted and in some cases even determined the rate of overall GNP growth remained unquestioned. The logic seemed fairly straightforward. Third World nations were deficient in their supply of semiskilled and skilled manpower. Without such manpower, which, it was assumed, could be created only through the formal educational system, development leadership in both the public and private sectors would be woefully lacking.

Impressive statistics and numerous quantitative studies of the sources of economic growth in the West were paraded out to demonstrate that it was not the growth of physical capital but rather of human capital (the *residual* in econometric production function estimates) that was the principal source of economic progress in the developed nations.[15] Clearly, in the newly independent nations of Africa and Asia, there was an immediate need to build up the human as well as physical capital infrastructure in order to provide indigenous leadership for the major tasks of development. Rapid quantitative expansion of enrollments therefore appeared justified in light of the substantial manpower scarcities of the 1950s and 1960s. And although it is often difficult to document statistically, it seems clear that the expansion of educational opportunities at all levels has contributed to aggregate economic growth[16] by (1) creating a more productive labor force and endowing it with increased knowledge and skills; (2) providing widespread employment and income-earning opportunities for teachers, school and construction workers, textbook and paper printers, school uniform manufacturers, and related workers; (3) creating a class of educated leaders to fill vacancies left by departing expatriates or otherwise vacant positions in governmental services, public corporations, private businesses, and professions; and (4) providing the kind of training and education that would promote literacy and basic skills while encouraging "modern" attitudes on the part of diverse segments of the population. Even if alternative investments in the economy could have generated greater growth, this would not detract from the important contributions, noneconomic as well as economic, that education can make and has made to promoting aggregate economic growth. That an educated and skilled labor force is a necessary condition of sustained economic growth cannot be denied.

However, any evaluation of the role of education in the process of economic development should go beyond the analysis of the single statistic of aggregate growth. We must also consider the structure and pattern of that economic growth and its distribution implications—who benefits.

Education, Inequality, and Poverty

Studies on the economics of education in both developed and developing nations formerly focused on the link among education, labor productivity, and output growth. This is not surprising in light of the main objective of development during the 1950s and 1960s, the maximization of aggregate rates of output growth. As a result, the impact of education on the distribution of income and on the elimination of absolute poverty was largely neglected. Recent studies, however, have demonstrated that contrary to what might have been assumed, the educational systems of many developing nations sometimes act to increase rather than to decrease income inequalities.[17]

The basic reason for this perverse effect of formal education on income distribution is the positive correlation between level of education and level of lifetime earnings. This correlation holds especially for workers who are able to complete secondary and university education where income differentials over workers who have completed only part or all of their primary education can be on the order of 300% to 800%. And as levels of earned income are clearly dependent on years of completed schooling, it follows that large income inequalities will be reinforced if students from the middle and upper income brackets are represented disproportionately in secondary and university enrollments. In short, if for financial or other reasons the poor are effectively denied access to secondary and higher educational opportunities, the educational system can actually perpetuate and even increase inequality in developing countries.

Educational economist John Simmons gives the following sketch of how the poor are beginning to regard education:

> Schooling, the poor quickly learn, in most countries, is an escape from poverty for only a few. The poor are the first to drop out because they need to work, the first to be pushed out because they fall asleep in class as one result of malnourishment, and the first to fail their French and English tests because upper income children have had better opportunities at home. The hope brought to village parents by the construction of the primary school soon fades. Enough schooling to secure a steady, even menial job for their son, let alone for their daughter, seems just beyond their grasp. Before . . . any schooling would have done to achieve their aspiration. Now a primary school certificate is needed, and some are saying that even students with some secondary schooling cannot get a steady job; and they could never afford to send their son away to town for secondary schooling.[18]

There are two fundamental economic reasons why one might suspect that many LDC educational systems are inherently inegalitarian, in the sense that poor students have less chance of completing any given educational cycle than more affluent students. First, the private costs of primary education (especially in view of the opportunity cost of a child's labor to poor families) are higher for poor students than for more affluent students. Second, the expected benefits of primary education are lower for poor students. Together, the higher costs and lower expected benefits of education mean that a poor family's rate of return from investment in a child's education is lower than it is for other families. The poor are therefore more likely to drop out during the early years of schooling. Let's examine in slightly more detail the reason why costs might be relatively higher and benefits relatively lower for a poor child.

First, the higher opportunity cost of labor to poor families means that even if the first few years of education are free, they are not without cost to the family. Children of primary school age are typically needed to work on family farms, often at the same times as they are required to be at school. If a child cannot work because he or she is at school, the family will either suffer a loss of valuable subsistence output or be required to hire paid labor to replace the absent child. In either case, there is a real cost to a poor family of having an able-bodied child attend school when there is productive work to be done on the farm—a cost not related to tuition and of much less significance to higher-income families, many of whom may live in urban areas where child work is not needed.

As a result of these higher opportunity costs, school attendance, and therefore school performance, tends to be much lower for children of poor families than for those from higher-income backgrounds. Thus in spite of the existence of free and universal primary education in many LDCs, children of the poor, especially in rural areas, are seldom able to proceed beyond the first few years of schooling. Their relatively poor school performance may have nothing to do with a lack of cognitive abilities; it may merely reflect their disadvantaged economic circumstances.

This financial process of eliminating the relatively poor during their first few years of schooling is often compounded by the substantial tuition charged at the secondary level. In many developing countries, annual tuition (especially at the better private schools) is roughly equivalent to the per capita national income. The cost of education therefore becomes prohibitive to lower-income families. This in effect amounts to a system of educational advancement and selection based not on any criteria of merit but strictly on family income levels. It thus perpetuates concentration of income within certain population groups and means that earned income will accrue primarily to people who already possess the bulk of unearned income and wealth—those whose assets already place them in the upper deciles of the personal income distribution scale.[19]

The inegalitarian nature of many Third World educational systems is compounded even further at the university level, where the government may pay the full cost of tuition and fees and even provide university students with income grants in the form of stipends. Because most university students already come from the upper-income brackets (and were so selected at the secondary level), highly subsidized university education using public funds often amounts to a transfer payment from the poor to the wealthy in the name of "free" higher education![20]

Table 11.6 shows how government educational spending benefits different occupational (and thus income) groups in various Third World regions. The last three columns are the most significant. Each shows the ratio of the percentage of public educational resources received by (1) low-income farmers, (2) middle-income manual workers and traders, and (3) higher-income white collar workers to their percentage representation in the population. A subsidy-benefit ratio of 1.00 would mean, for example, that a group comprising 25% of the working population receives 25% of all government spending on education. The data clearly show that the children of white-collar families receive disproportionate public educational benefits, whereas farm children are undersubsidized. For example, in Francophone, Africa, children from (mostly urban) white-collar families receive more than 10 times as much in state subsidies than children from rural farm families. When we combine this information with data measuring the incidence of direct and indirect taxation, which, as we shall see in Chapter 17, is often regressive in developing countries, it becomes clear that the educational system is not a vehicle for promoting greater equality. It often works in the opposite direction to reinforce or widen inequality.

Education, Internal Migration, and the Brain Drain

Education seems to be an important factor influencing rural-urban migration. Numerous studies of migration in diverse countries have documented the positive relationship between the educational attainment of an individual and his or her propensity to migrate from rural to urban areas. Basically, individuals with higher levels of education face wider urban-rural real-income differentials and higher probabilities of obtaining modern-sector jobs than those with lower levels of

TABLE 11.6 Share of Public Resources for Education Appropriated by Different Socioeconomic Groups, by Region

Region	Percentage in the Population			Percentage of Public School Resources			Ratio between Percentage of Resources and of Population		
	Farmers	Manual Workers and Traders	White-Collar Workers	Farmers	Manual Workers and Traders	White-Collar Workers	Farmers	Manual Workers and Traders	White-Collar Workers
Africa									
Anglophone	76	18	6	56	21	23	0.73	1.19	3.78
Francophone	76	18	6	44	21	36	0.58	1.15	5.93
Asia	58	32	10	34	38	28	0.59	1.19	2.79
Latin America	36	49	15	18	51	31	0.49	1.04	2.03
Middle East and North Africa	42	48	10	25	46	29	0.60	0.35	2.87
Members of the Organization for Economic Cooperation and Development (OECD)	12	53	35	11	46	42	0.95	0.87	1.2

SOURCE: Emmanuel Jimenez, "The public subsidization of education and health in developing countries: A review of equity and efficiency," *World Bank Research Observer* 1 (January 1986): tab. 3. Reprinted with permission.

education (recall from Chapter 8 how income differentials and job probabilities interact to determine migration patterns). The probability variable in particular accounts for the growing proportion of the more educated rural migrants in the face of rising levels of urban unemployment among the less educated.[21]

Education also plays a powerful role in the growing problem of the international migration of high-level educated workers—the so-called **brain drain**—from poor to rich countries. This is particularly true in the case of scientists, engineers, academics, and physicians, many thousands of whom have been trained in home-country institutions at considerable social cost only to reap the benefits from and contribute to the further economic growth of the already affluent nations.

The international brain drain deserves mention not only because of its effects on the rate and structure of LDC economic growth but also because of its impact on the style and approach of Third World educational systems. The brain drain, broadly construed, has not merely reduced the supply of vital professional people available within developing countries (see Chapter 4); perhaps even more serious, it has diverted the attention of the scientists, physicians, architects, engineers, and academics who remain from important local problems and goals. These include the development of appropriate technology: the promotion of low-cost preventive health care; the construction of low-cost housing, hospitals, schools, and other service facilities; the design and building of functional yet inexpensive labor-intensive roads, bridges, and machinery; the development of relevant university teaching materials such as appropriate introductory economics texts; and the promotion of problem-oriented research on vital domestic development issues. Such needs are often neglected as, dominated by rich-country ideas as to what represents true professional excellence, those highly educated and highly skilled Third World professionals who do not physically migrate to the developed nations nevertheless migrate intellectually in terms of the orientation of their activities. This "internal" brain drain is much more serious than the external one.

For example, we constantly find developing nations with numerous physicians specializing in heart diseases while preventive tropical medicine is considered a second-rate specialty. Architects are concerned with the design of national monuments and modern public buildings, while low-cost housing, schools, and clinics remain an area of remote concern. Engineers and scientists concentrate on the newest and most modern electronic equipment while simple machine tools, hand- or animal-operated farm equipment, basic sanitation and water-purifying systems, and labor-intensive mechanical processes are relegated to the attention of "foreign experts." Finally, some academic economists teach and research totally irrelevant, sophisticated mathematical models of nonexistent competitive economies, while problems of poverty, unemployment, rural development, and education are considered less intellectually interesting. In all these diverse professional activities, performance criteria are based not on contributions to national development but rather on praise from the international community (professional mentors in the developed nations). The publication of an LDC scholar's paper in an international professional journal or the receipt of an invitation to attend a professional meeting in London, Paris, New York, or Moscow is often deemed more important than finding a solution to a local technological, agricultural, medical, or economic problem.

Education of Women, Fertility, and Child Health

With regard to the education and fertility relationship, the evidence is also clear.[22] Most studies reveal an inverse relationship between the education of women and their size of family, particularly at the lower levels of education. Assuming that lower levels of urban unemployment (especially among the educated) and lower levels of fertility are important policy objectives for Third World governments, the basic issue is whether the continued rapid quantitative expansion of the formal educational system (and the resource allocation decisions implicit therein) will ameliorate or exacerbate the twin problems of accelerating internal migration and rapid population growth. With respect to this issue, both theory and evidence seem once again to indicate that given limited government resources, the further excessive quantitative expansion of school places beyond perhaps basic education is both undesirable and unwise. There are two main reasons for this conclusion.

First, as we discovered earlier in the chapter, any rapid expansion of the formal primary system creates inexorable pressures on the demand side for the expansion of secondary and tertiary school places. The net result is the widespread phenomenon of excessive expansion of school places from the standpoint of real resource needs and the associated dilemma of rising levels of rural-urban migration and urban unemployment among a cadre of increasingly more educated and more politically vocal migrants.

Second, if, as many observers have argued, the education of women does affect their fertility behavior, primarily through the mechanism of raising the opportunity cost of their time in child-rearing activities (see Chapter 6), then it follows that unless sufficient employment opportunities for women (as well as for men) can be created, the reliance on educational expansion as a policy instrument for lowering fertility will be much less effective. However, reallocating *existing* educational resources to women's education, in combination with an aggressive program of rural and urban female employment creation, could go a long way toward achieving the twin goals of fertility reduction and poverty alleviation.

Finally, as mentioned earlier in the chapter, educating women has been shown to be a critical ingredient in breaking the vicious multigenerational cycle of poor child health, low educational performance, low income, high fertility, and poor child health. Numerous studies have documented that women's education leads to lower infant mortality rates. These studies also point to a delayed fertility reduction that results not only in healthier children but also in children possessing greater human capital as parents substitute child quality (fewer, better-educated children) for child quantity.

Education and Rural Development

In Chapter 9, we argued that if national development is to become a reality in Third World nations, there must be a better balance between rural and urban development. Because most of the priority projects of the past few decades focused on the modernization and development of the urban sector, much more emphasis must be placed in future years on expanding economic and social opportunities in rural areas. Although agricultural development represents the main component of any successful rural development program simply because 70% of Third World rural populations are engaged directly or indirectly in agricultural activities, rural development must nevertheless be viewed in a broader perspective.

First and foremost, it should be viewed in the context of far-reaching transformations of economic and social structures, institutions, relationships, and processes in rural areas. The goals of rural development cannot simply be restricted to agricultural and economic growth. Rather, they must be viewed in terms of a balanced economic and social development with emphasis on the equitable distribution, as well as the rapid generation, of the benefits of higher levels of living. Among these broader goals, therefore, are the creation of more productive employment opportunities both on and off the farm; more equitable access to arable land; more equitable distribution of rural income; more widely distributed improvements in health, nutrition, and housing; and broadened access to both formal (in-school) and **nonformal** (out-of-school) **education**, for adults as well as children, of a sort that will have direct relevance to the needs and aspirations of rural dwellers.

How do present Third World systems of education fit into this holistic view of the meaning of rural development? Basically, not very well. The formal primary school system in most LDCs is, with minor modifications, a direct transplant of the system in developed countries. The overriding goal is to prepare all children to pass standard qualifying examinations for secondary schools; hence the curricula have a very strong urban bias. The priority needs of the greatest proportion of students— those who will live and work in rural areas—are given minimal attention. Major groups with important rural training needs, such as out-of-school children and youth, women, and small subsistence farmers, are largely neglected by organized educational programs, both formal and nonformal. As a result, much of the education in the rural communities of developing nations contributes little toward improving levels of agricultural productivity or assisting students to function more effectively in the rural environment.

What, then, might be the real and lasting educational needs for rural development? Philip H. Coombs and Manzoor Ahmed have provided one very appealing typology. They group these educational needs for both young people and adults, males and females, into four main categories:[23]

1. General or basic education (literacy, arithmetic, an elementary understanding of science and the immediate environment, etc.)—what most primary and secondary schools now seek to achieve

2. Family improvement education—designed primarily to impart knowledge, skills, and attitudes useful for improving the quality of family life and including such subjects as health and nutrition, homemaking and child care, home repairs and improvements, and family planning

3. Community improvement education—designed to strengthen local and national institutions and processes through instruction in such matters as local and national government, cooperatives, and community projects

4. Occupational education—designed to develop particular knowledge and skills associated with various economic activities that are useful in making a living

For the most part, only category 1—general education—has been emphasized in developing countries. But the learning needs of the three principal occupational subgroups of rural areas—farmers and farm workers, persons engaged in nonfarm rural enterprises, and rural general personnel—are likely in each case to fit quite poorly with most formal educational curricula. Table 11.7 shows how these learning needs vary among the three groups. Effective and well-designed educational programs catering to each of these occupational groups are needed if education is to make its essential contribution to rural development.

Summary and Conclusions: Major Educational Policy Options

Developing nations are confronted with two basic alternatives in their policy approaches to problems of education.[24] They can continue automatically to expand formal systems at the fastest possible pace with perhaps some minor modifications in curricula, teaching methods, and examinations, while retaining the same institutional labor market structures and educational costing policies. Or they can attempt to reform the overall educational system by modifying the conditions of demand for and the supply of educational opportunities and by reorienting curricula in accordance with the real resource needs of the nation. Our evidence leads to the conclusion that the first alternative is likely to exacerbate the problems of unemployment, poverty, inequality, rural stagnation, and international intellectual dominance that now define the conditions of underdevelopment in much of Africa, Asia, and Latin America and that the second alternative should therefore be pursued.

Because educational systems largely reflect and reproduce rather than alter the economic and social structures of the societies in which they exist, any program or set of policies designed to make education more relevant for development needs must operate simultaneously on two levels:

1. Modifying the economic and social signals and incentives *outside* the educational system that largely determine the magnitude, structure, and orientation of the aggregate private demand for education and consequently the political response in the form of the public supply of school places.

2. Modifying the *internal* effectiveness and equity of educational systems through appropriate changes in course content (especially for rural areas), structures of public versus private financing, methods of selection and promotion, and procedures for occupational certification by educational level.

Only by policies designed simultaneously to achieve these two objectives can the real positive links between education and development be successfully forged. Let us conclude, therefore, with a brief review of what these external and internal policies might specifically encompass.

TABLE 11.7 Illustrative Rural Occupational Groups and Their Learning Needs

Groups	Types of Learning Needs at Varying Levels of Sophistication and Specialization
A. Persons directly engaged in agriculture	
1. Commercial farmers	Farm planning and management, rational decision making, recordkeeping, cost and revenue computations, use of credit
2. Small subsistence and semisubsistence farm families	
3. Landless farm workers	Application of new inputs, varieties, improved farm practices
	Storage, processing, food preservation
	Supplementary skills for farm maintenance and improvement, and sideline jobs for extra income
	Knowledge of government services, policies, programs, targets
	Knowledge and skills for family improvement (e.g., health, nutrition, home economics, child care, family planning)
	Civic skills (e.g., knowledge of how cooperatives, local government, national government function)
B. Persons engaged in off-farm commercial activities	
1. Retailers and wholesalers of farm supplies and equipment, goods and other items	New and improved technical skills applicable to particular goods and services
2. Suppliers of repair and maintenance services	Quality control
3. Processors, storers, and shippers of agricultural commodities	Technical knowledge of goods handled sufficient to advise customers on their use, maintenance, etc.
4. Suppliers of banking and credit services	Management skills (business planning; recordkeeping and cost accounting; procurement and inventory control; market analysis and sales methods; customer and employee relations; knowledge of government services, regulations, taxes; use of credit)
5. Construction and other artisans	
6. Suppliers of general transport services	
7. Small manufacturers	
C. General services personnel: rural administrators, planners, technical experts	
1. General public administrators, broad-gauged analysts, and planners at subnational levels	General skills for administration, planning, implementation, information flows, promotional activities
2. Managers, planners, technicians, and trainers for specific public services (e.g., agriculture, transport, irrigation, health, small industry, education, family services, local government)	Technical and management skills applying to particular specialties
	Leadership skills for generating community enthusiasm and collective action, staff team work, and support from higher echelons
3. Managers of cooperatives and other farmer associations	
4. Managers and other personnel of credit services	

SOURCE: Philip H. Coombs and Manzoor Ahmed, *Attacking Rural Poverty: How Nonformal Education Can Help* (Baltimore: Johns Hopkins University Press, 1974), p. 17. Reprinted with permission.

Policies Largely External to Educational Systems

Adjusting Imbalances, Signals, and Incentives

Policies that tend to remedy major economic imbalances and incentive distortions (e.g., in income and wage differentials) and alleviate social and political constraints on upward mobility can have the multiple beneficial effect of increasing job opportunities, slowing the rate of rural-urban migration, and facilitating development-related modifications of educational systems.

Modifying Job Rationing by Educational Certification

To break the vicious cycle in which overstated job specifications make **overeducation** necessary for employment, policies are needed that will induce or require public and private employers to seek realistic qualifications even though the task of job rationing may be made somewhat more difficult as a result. Basic to this procedure would be the elimination of school certificates for many jobs, especially in the public sector (janitors, messengers, file clerks, etc.), which tends to set the pattern for the private sector.

Curbing the Brain Drain

Controlling or taxing the international migration of indigenously trained high-level professionals is a very sensitive area. It can potentially infringe on the basic human right and freedom to choose the nature and location of one's work. In a repressive regime, such a restrictive policy can be morally repugnant. However, when a nation invests scarce public financial resources in the education and training of its people only then to forgo the social returns on that investment as a result of international migration, it seems both economically and morally justifiable to seek either temporarily to restrict that movement in the national interest or, better, to tax the overseas earnings of professional migrants and reinvest those revenues in programs of national development. Such a tax on overseas earnings would act as a financial disincentive to migrate. Its implementation, however, would require the cooperation and assistance of the governments of the countries to which these professionals migrate.[25]

Policies Internal to Educational Systems

Educational Budgets

Where politically feasible, educational budgets should grow more slowly than in the past to permit more revenue to be used for the creation of rural and urban employment opportunities. Moreover, a larger share of educational budgets should be allocated to the development of primary as opposed to secondary and higher education in order to promote self-education and rural work-related learning experiences in later life.

Subsidies

Subsidies for the higher levels of education should be reduced as a means of overcoming distortions in the aggregate private demand for education. Policies should be promoted by which the beneficiary of education (as opposed to the student's family or society as a whole) would bear a larger proportion of educational costs as the student proceeds through the system. This should be done either directly, through loan repayments, or by service in rural areas. At the same time, low-income groups should be provided with sufficient subsidies to permit them to overcome the sizable private costs (including opportunity costs) of schooling.[26]

Primary School Curricula in Relation to Rural Needs

To maximize the productivity of rural human resources, primary school curricula and nonformal educational opportunities for school dropouts and adults should be directed more toward the occupational requirements of rural inhabitants, whether in small-farm agriculture, nonfarm artisan and entrepreneurial activities, or public and commercial services. Such curricula and task-related reorientations of rural learning systems, however, will not be effective in eliciting popular support unless rural economic opportunities are created so that small farmers, artisans, and entrepreneurs can make use of their vocational knowledge and training. Without these incentives, people will justifiably view such formal and nonformal occupational training programs with considerable skepticism. They would probably rather pursue the formal school certificate and take their chances in the urban job lottery.

Quotas

To compensate for the inequality effects of most existing formal school systems, some form of **quotas** may be required to ensure that the proportion of low-income students at secondary and higher educational levels at least bears some relationship to their proportion in the overall population. Under present systems, implicit quotas by income status often determine which students proceed through the educational system. Replacing this de facto quota system with an alternative that ensures that capable low-income students will be able to improve their own and their family's well-being by overcoming the financial barriers to educational advancement through loans and subsidies would go a long way toward making educational systems true vehicles of economic and social equality. The nature of such quota systems will obviously vary from country to country. But there is no a priori basis for assuming that such a quota by income level for academically qualified low-income students will not be more efficient and more socially productive for both growth and equity than the present system, which tends to perpetuate poverty and inequality while maintaining growth-inhibiting dualistic economic and social structures.

CASE STUDY

The Economy of Malaysia

GEOGRAPHIC, SOCIAL, AND ECONOMIC INDICATORS

Capital Kuala Lumpur

Area 330,000 km²

Population 19.9 million (1995)

Population (average annual growth rate) 2.5% (1985–1994)

GNP per capita U.S. $3,520 (1994)

GNP per capita (average annual growth rate) 5.7% (1985–1994)

Agriculture as share of GDP 14% (1994)

Exports as share of GDP 90% (1994)

Infant mortality rate (per 1,000 live births) 14 (1992)

Child malnutrition (underweight) 21% (1993)

Females as share of labor force 36% (1994)

Illiteracy rate (age 15+) 22% (1990)

Human Development Index 0.79 (medium) (1992)

Malaysia occupies the southern half of the Malay peninsula and the northern coast of the island of Borneo, some 650 kilometers to the east across the South China Sea. Peninsular Malaysia (known as Malaya) borders Thailand in the north and is separated from Singapore in the south by the narrow Johor Strait.

Malaysia's population of about 20 million people is growing at a rate of 2.5% a year. About 38% of the inhabitants are under 15 years of age. Population distribution is uneven, with three-fourths of the residents concentrated in the Malayian lowlands. Over the past three decades, Malaysia has been one of the top-performing developing nations. It has invested heavily in education. Virtually all Malaysian children attend primary school, and well over 50% attend secondary school. These are substantial accomplishments for a country long beset by civil war, racial tensions, and less than 40 years of political independence. By combining educational investment with health expenditures and employment creation, Malaysia has achieved one of the lowest poverty rates (26%) among all LDCs.

Malaysia's population comprises many ethnic groups; the Malays, the largest, make up 49%. The politically dominant Malays are indigenous and, by constitutional definition, all Muslim. Despite rapid urbanization, they remain largely rural and lag economically behind the large Chinese minority. Nearly one-third of the Malaysians are Chinese, most of whose ancestors immigrated during the nineteenth and early twentieth centuries. The Chinese are mainly urban, and by virtue of their important role in trade, business, and finance, they possess considerable economic power.

About 85% of Malaysia's population speaks Malay, the official language, though with considerable variation in facility. English is used widely in government and business. Literacy rates range from 60% in the Borneo states (Sarawak, Sabah, and Labuan) to 80% in Malaya.

On independence from British rule in 1957, Malaysia inherited an economy dominated by two commodities, rubber and tin. In the ensuing years, Malaysia's economic record has been one of the most successful in Asia. From 1965 to 1984, the economy experienced a period of broad diversification and sustained rapid growth averaging 7% to 8%. Per capita gross national product reached $2,000 in 1984. Palm oil, timber, cacao, and pepper were added to Malaysia's export crops. Malaysia is the world's leading producer of rubber, tin, palm oil, and tropical timber. The petroleum sector expanded rapidly after 1980, making Malaysia a significant exporter of oil and liquefied natural gas.

New foreign and domestic investment in manufacturing, much of it from the United States and Japan, led to increasing exports of electronic components, electric consumer goods, textile products, and other manufactures. Manufacturing grew from 13.4% of gross domestic product in 1970 to an estimated 35% in 1994.

The worldwide recession in 1981–1982 depressed the prices of Malaysia's traditional commodity exports. Growth slackened and investment fell. The government sought to stimulate the economy and speed up the growth of industry through increased spending on a number of heavy-industry and infrastructure projects. Public entities and government-owned companies also spent heavily to acquire majority control of most of the large foreign-owned plantations. Much of the increased public spending was financed by foreign borrowing, pushing Malaysia's foreign debt to $15 billion in 1984.

Malaysia's long period of high growth came to an abrupt halt in 1985–1986. The sharp fall in world commodity prices (oil and palm oil prices were halved) sent Malaysia's economy into recession. Real output was stagnant during 1985–1986, but the worsening of Malaysia's terms of trade (the prices of the country's exports compared to the prices of imports) caused nominal GNP to fall by 11.5% in 1985 and 1986 combined. Per capita GNP fell from $2,000 in 1984 to $1,600 in 1986.

The size of the public-sector deficit and the growth of Malaysia's foreign debt had already led the government to alter its policies. Public spending and foreign borrowing were cut back, although depreciation of the Malaysian currency against the yen and European currencies since 1985 has magnified the size of the debt measured in Malaysian or U.S. dollars. The ambitious growth and spending targets of the Fifth Malaysia Plan (1986–1990) were abandoned. The government has also placed greater emphasis on the role of the private sector in development and is taking steps to privatize a number of government-owned corporations and government agencies. Shares in the national airline and the national shipping company have been sold to investors, and telecommunications has been turned into a corporation (still 100% government-owned) in preparation for an eventual stock market listing.

Malaysia's recovery from recession began in late 1986 and has gained strength since. Improved commodity prices and strong growth in exports of manufactured goods have led the recovery. The government estimates that real per capita GDP grew impressively at an average annual rate of 5.7% between 1985 and 1994. The recovery was led by foreign demand for Malaysia's exports, with net exports accounting for more than three-quarters of this growth.

Malaysia's prospects for continuing growth and prosperity are good. It possesses abundant resources and land, a well-educated workforce, and a stable political environment. Strong domestic savings provide adequate funds for investment, and Malaysia remains attractive to foreign investors. Rising currency values in Taiwan and South Korea have heightened Malaysia's competitive position in the region. The economy, however, remains vulnerable to external shocks. Exports account for 90% of GNP, and a prolonged recession in the industrial economies would have severe repercussions for the country.

Concepts for Review

Basic education	Literacy
Brain drain	Nonformal education
Derived demand	Opportunity cost of education
Dropout rate	Overeducation
Educational certification	Private benefits of education
Educational gender gap	Private costs of education
Enrollment ratios	Quotas
Formal educational system	Social benefits of education
Human resources	Social costs of education

Questions for Discussion

1. What reasons would you give for the rather sizable school dropout rates in Third World countries? What might be done to lower these rates?

2. What are the differences between formal and nonformal education? Give some examples of each.

3. It is often asserted that Third World educational systems, especially in rural areas, are unsuited to the real social and economic needs of development. Do you agree or disagree with this statement? Explain your reasoning.

4. How would you explain the fact that relative costs of and returns to higher education are so much higher in LDCs than in developed countries?

5. What is the supposed rationale for subsidizing higher education in many Third World countries? Do you think that it is a legitimate rationale from an economic viewpoint? Explain.

6. Early childhood environmental factors are said to be important determinants of school performance. What are some of these factors, how important do you think they are, and what might be done to ensure that these factors are not negative?

7. What do we mean by the economics of education? To what extent do you think educational planning and policy decisions ought to be guided by economic considerations? Explain, giving hypothetical or actual examples.

8. What is meant by the statement "The demand for education is a 'derived demand' for high-paying modern-sector job opportunities"? Many educational specialists claim that families and children in LDCs demand education not so much as an investment good but as a consumption good. What do you think this statement means, and what do you think is the relative importance of the consumption demand for education among your student friends?

9. What are the links among educational systems, labor markets, and employment determination in many Third World countries? Describe the process of educational job displacement.

10. Distinguish carefully between private and social benefits and costs of education. What economic factors give rise to the wide divergence between private and social benefit-to-cost valuations in most developing countries? Should governments attempt through their educational and economic policies to narrow the gap between private and social valuations? Explain.

11. Describe and comment on each of the following education-development relationships:

   a. Education and economic growth: Does education promote growth? How?

   b. Education, inequality, and poverty: Do educational systems typical of most LDCs tend to reduce, exacerbate, or have no effect on inequality and poverty? Explain with specific reference to a country with which you are familiar.

   c. Education and migration: Does education stimulate rural-urban migration? Why?

   d. Education and fertility: Does the education of women tend to reduce their fertility? Why and how?

   e. Education and rural development: Do most LDC formal educational systems contribute substantially to the promotion of rural development? Explain.

   f. Education and the brain drain: What factors cause the international migration of high-level educated workers from LDCs to developed countries? What do we mean by the internal brain drain? Explain, giving examples.

12. Governments can influence the character, quality, and content of their educational systems by manipulating important economic and noneconomic factors or variables both outside of and within educational systems. What are some of these external and internal factors, and how can government policies make education more relevant to the real meaning of development?

Notes

1. Frederick H. Harbison, *Human Resources as the Wealth of Nations* (New York: Oxford University Press, 1973), p. 3. See also Theodore W. Schultz, "Investment in human capital," *American Economic Review* 51 (March 1961).

2. For a counterargument stressing the broad economic benefits of a continuous expansion of formal education (though not denying its often antiegalitarian results), see George Psacharopoulos, "Education and development: A review," *World Bank Research Observer* 3 (January 1988): 99–116; also see Wadi D. Haddad *et al., Education and Development: Evidence for New Priorities,* World Bank Discussion Paper No. 95 (Washington, D.C.: World Bank, 1990).

3. For an additional analysis and profile of education, see Psacharopoulos, "Education and development."

4. George Psacharopoulos, *The Returns to Education: An International Comparison* (Amsterdam: Elsevier, 1972), and *ibid.*

5. Alain Mingat and J. P. Tan, "On equity in education again: An international comparison," *Journal of Human Resources* 20 (Spring 1985): 298–308.

6. For a detailed review of the empirical studies of rates of returns to investment in education, see George Psacharopoulos, "Returns to education: An updated international comparison," *Comparative Education* 17 (June 1981); Christopher Colclough, "The impact of primary schooling on economic development: A review of the evidence," *World Development* 10 (April 1982); and George Psacharopoulos, "Returns to investment in education: A global update," *World Development* 22 (September 1994) 1325–1343. According to George Psacharopoulos, "Education as investment," *Finance and Development*: (September 1982), p. 40:

> Estimates of the private rate of return to a given level of education are calculated by comparing the discounted benefits over the lifetime of an educational investment "project" to the costs of such a project. Thus, for a calculation of the private rate of return to four years of university education, benefits are estimated by taking the difference between existing statistics on the mean post-tax earnings of university graduates by age and those of a sample group of secondary school graduates. The earnings of the latter also represent the opportunity costs of staying in school. Direct costs are obtained from statistics on a student's out-of-pocket expenditures that are strictly due to the costs of college attendance. Given these data, the rate of return to investment in a college degree compared with a secondary school qualification is the rate of interest that reduces to zero the net present value of the discounted difference between the costs and benefits. A simple equation for the private rate of return is

$$\text{Private rate of return} = \frac{\left(\begin{array}{c}\text{Mean annual post-tax}\\\text{earnings of university}\\\text{graduates}\end{array}\right) - \left(\begin{array}{c}\text{Mean annual post-tax}\\\text{earnings of secondary}\\\text{school graduates}\end{array}\right)}{\left(\begin{array}{c}\text{Four}\\\text{years}\\\text{of study}\end{array}\right) \times \left(\begin{array}{c}\text{Mean annual post-tax}\\\text{earnings of second}\\\text{school of graduates}\end{array}\right) + \left(\begin{array}{c}\text{Mean annual}\\\text{private direct}\\\text{cost of study}\end{array}\right)}$$

> A social rate of return to college education could be calculated in the same way, although earnings should be pretax (as taxes are a transfer from the point of view of society at large) and the direct cost should include the full amount of resources committed per student for higher education, rather than the usually smaller part of expenditure borne by the student.

7. Jere Behrman and Nancy Birdsall, "The quality of schooling: Quantity alone is misleading," *American Economic Review* 73 (December 1983): 928–946. See also Eric A. Hanushek, "Interpreting recent research on schooling in developing countries," *World Bank Research Observer* 10 (August 1995): 227–246.

8. Haddad *et al., Education and Development*, pp. 12–15.

9. Much of the material in this section is drawn from Michael P. Todaro and Edgar O. Edwards, "Educational demand and supply in the context of growing unemployment in less developed countries," *World Development* 1 (March-April 1973): 107–117.

10. In fact, because most expectations for the future tend to be based on a static picture of the employment situation that currently prevails, we might anticipate that when the

employment situation is worsening, individuals tend to overestimate their expected incomes and demand even more education than is justified in terms of "correct" private calculations of benefits and costs.

11. For an estimate of the private direct and opportunity costs of primary, secondary, and postsecondary education in the 1980s, see Emmanuel Jimenez, "The public subsidization of education and health in developing countries: A review of equity and efficiency," *World Bank Research Observer* 1 (January 1986), tab. 6.

12. For a penetrating analysis of the Indian education and employment problems, see Marc Blaug *et al.*, *Causes of Graduate Unemployment in India* (Harmondsworth, England: Penguin, 1967).

13. R. Islam, "Graduate unemployment in Bangladesh: A preliminary analysis," *Bangladesh Development Studies* (Autumn 1980): 47–74.

14. For evidence of this, see Jimenez, "Public subsidization," 123.

15. See, for example, Edward F. Denison, *The Sources of Economic Growth in the United States* (New York: National Bureau of Economic Research, 1962), and Robert Solow, "Technical change and the aggregate production function," *Review of Economics and Statistics* 39 (August 1957): 312–320.

16. Psacharopoulos, "Education and development," 100–102.

17. See, for example, Jagdish N. Bhagwati, "Education, class structure and income equality," *World Development* 1 (May 1973); Jimenez, "Public subsidization"; and Alberto Alesina and Roberto Perotti, "The political economy of growth: A critical survey of the recent literature," *World Bank Economic Review* 8 (September 1994): 360.

18. John Simmons, *Education, Poverty and Development*, World Bank Staff Working Paper No. 188 (Washington, D.C.: World Bank, 1974), p. 32.

19. Another explanation is that where perfect capital markets exist, all individuals can borrow for their education in anticipation of high future earnings. But in LDCs with very imperfect capital markets, limited information about individual abilities, and poor loan enforcement, it is extremely difficult for the poor to borrow to finance their education. This is not, however, a problem for the rich, who can rely on their own resources to invest in education. So the system of inequality has a built-in tendency to reproduce itself with each generation.

20. For some evidence of the regressive nature of educational subsidies in Latin America, see Jean-Pierre Jallade, *Public Expenditures on Education and Income Distribution in Colombia* (Baltimore: Johns Hopkins University Press, 1974), and *Basic Education and Income Inequality in Brazil: The Long-Term View*, World Bank Staff Working Paper No. 268 (Washington, D.C.: World Bank, 1977).

21. For evidence of this in the case of Tanzania, see Henry N. Barnum and Richard H. Sabot, *Migration, Education and Urban Surplus Labor*, OECD Development Center Employment Series Monograph, October 1975 (mimeograph).

22. See World Bank, *World Development Report, 1991* (New York: Oxford University Press, 1991), box 3.2.

23. Philip H. Coombs and Manzoor Ahmed, *Attacking Rural Poverty: How Nonformal Education Can Help* (Baltimore: Johns Hopkins University Press, 1974), p. 17.

24. As in other chapters, the policies put forward here are designed primarily to stimulate group discussion and individual analysis. Although in our opinion they are sensible policies with a solid economic rationale, they should not be viewed as absolute, immutable, or beyond challenge.

25. For an analysis of the problem, see Jagdish N. Bhagwati and William Dellalfar, "The brain drain and income taxation," *World Development* 1 (January 1973): 94–101; see also the entire September 1975 issue of the *Journal of Development Economics*, which was devoted to the subject of the international brain drain, and the discussion of trends in United Nations Development Program, *Human Development Report, 1992* (New York: Oxford University Press, 1992), pp. 54–58.

26. For an interesting analysis of alternative mechanisms for financing higher education, see Alain Mingat and J. P. Tan, "Financing public higher education in developing countries: The potential role of loan schemes," *Higher Education* 15 (September 1986): 283–297.

Further Reading

For an informative general approach to the study of education and human resource development, see Frederick H. Harbison, *Human Resources as the Wealth of Nations* (New York: Oxford University Press, 1973). For more modern version focusing on the revolution in information and communications technology and the skill requirements to compete globally in the 1990s, see Ajit Singh, "Global economic changes, skills and international competitiveness," *International Labour Review* 133 (June 1994): 167–183.

Excellent surveys of economic issues relating education to development can be found in John Simmons, "Education for development reconsidered," *World Development* 7 (1979): 1005–1016; Marc Blaug, *An Introduction to the Economics of Education* (Harmondsworth, England: Penguin, 1970); George Psacharopoulos and Maureen Woodhall, *Education for Development: An Analysis of Investment Choices* (New York: Oxford University Press, 1987); World Bank, *The Financing of Education in Developing Countries: An Exploration of Policy Options* (Washington, D.C.: World Bank, 1986), and Wadi D. Haddad *et al., Education and Development: Evidence for New Priorities.* World Bank Discussion Paper No. 95 (Washington, D.C.: World Bank, 1990).

A good review of the empirical research on the economic returns to investment (both private and social) in education can be found in George Psacharopoulos. "Returns to investment in education: A global update," *World Development* 22 (September 1994): 1325–1343, and "Education and development: A review," *World Bank Research Observer* 3 (January 1988): 99–116; an alternative view focusing on the quality rather than quantity of education is contained in Jere Behrman and Nancy Birdsall, "The quality of schooling: Quantity alone is misleading," *American Economic Review* 73 (December 1983): 928–946.

For a broad analysis of how education can promote rural development, see Philip H. Coombs and Manzoor Ahmed, *Attacking Rural Poverty: How Nonformal Education Can Help* (Baltimore: Johns Hopkins University Press, 1974).

A challenging and critical view of the role of education in society can be found in Ivan Illich, *Deschooling Society* (New York: Harper & Row, 1970), and also in Ronald Dore, *The Diploma Disease* (Berkeley: University of California Press, 1976).

A good summary of the issues involved in the question of education and inequality can be obtained from Jagdish N. Bhagwati, "Education, class structure and income equality," *World Development* 1 (May 1973); Alain Mingat and J. P. Tan, "On equity in education again: An international comparison," *Journal of Human Resources* 20 (Spring 1985): 298–308, and "Who profits from the public funding of education: A comparison by world regions," *Comparative Education* 22 (June 1986).

For an analysis of the many benefits of educating girls in Pakistan, see Stephen C. Smith, *Case Studies*, Chapter 16.

Poverty Policy

Contributed by Stephen C. Smith

Bangladesh, with a 1994 GNP per capita of just $230, and Nigeria, at $280, are both very low income countries: These figures make Bangladesh the twelfth poorest and Nigeria the twenty-first poorest among countries with at least 1 million population. (At purchasing power parity, these incomes become $1,350 and $1,430, respectively, with a similar ranking.) These countries are the two largest among those poorer than India and China; 119 million people live in Bangladesh, 101 million in Nigeria.

Life expectancy is similar in the two countries, at 55 in Bangladesh and 52 in Nigeria according to World Bank data. (Independent survey estimates suggest that Nigeria's true life expectancy may be even lower.) Illiteracy is worse in Bangladesh, with 78% of adult women and 65% of adult men illiterate; compared with still appalling figures of 61% and 49%, respectively, in Nigeria. Infant mortality is 108 per 1,000 in Bangladesh and 72 per 1,000 in Nigeria. Poverty is severe in Bangladesh, with the government placing more than 50% and the United Nations fully 85% of its population below the poverty line. No accurate figure is available for Nigeria, where the urban-rural disparities are as sharp as anywhere in the world. Malnutrition has been rising in rural Nigeria. Population growth has been rapid—and faster than growth of food production—in both countries.

Both Bangladesh and Nigeria have recently been engaged in extensive "austerity" structural adjustment programs (SAPs), and generally, the poor have suffered. Supporters stress, however, that the SAPs in each country change economic incentives to the benefit of rural producers and are convinced that the poor will be better off over the longer term

and that there was in any case no possibility of continuing as the countries had before. The evidence suggests that Bangladesh has done more to break the fall of the poor and that Nigeria, with more resources, could have done much more than it did. Encouragingly, there is some evidence of recent poverty policy improvements in both countries.

Bangladesh

Bangladesh is struggling to keep its head above water, both figuratively and literally. The Bangladesh government reports that half of its people are absolutely poor, but independent appraisals put the number much higher. About 1 million children under the age of 5 die each year of malnutrition and preventable disease. The problems of the poor in Bangladesh are exacerbated by harsh weather conditions: Famines, floods from excessive monsoons, and an average of 16 cyclones each decade batter the country. Excessive floods and storm tides destroy crops, contaminate wells, spread diseases like cholera, and wash away entire villages. Overall, the land is shrinking due in large part to poor environmental practices, demonstrating the close link between poverty and environmental degradation discussed in Chapter 10.

Ordinary tornadoes, like the one that killed almost 1,000 people in April 1989, are hardly noticed by the outside world. But when an April 1991 cyclone killed at least 100,000 people, perhaps as many as 200,000, more than $200 million in foreign humanitarian aid reached the country. Many people were saved at the storm shelters that have been built; there were reports of refugees packed inside and on the roof, but thousands who were unable to get in were washed away in flood tides. The government did a good job distributing emergency supplies, especially compared with other very low income countries faced with similar disasters. After much discussion, the Coastal Embankments Project for flood control, undertaken with planning and financial assistance from the World Bank, is now under way. The Bank is also financing the Shelter Development Project to greatly expand the lifesaving shelter system. But progress has been slow, and independent observers claim that too little has been done to prevent a recurrence. They question whether the government is up to so sophisticated a task, especially when problems are compounded by widespread corruption.

The country also suffered from a large drop in remittances by the many Bangladeshis who worked in Kuwait before the Iraqi invasion and had to flee. Worse still, the refugees themselves suffered huge losses of savings and possessions while fleeing the war zone. Few have been able to return, and most have joined the ranks of the unemployed.

Modern-sector enlargement growth (see Chapter 5) has been seen in the Bangladesh textile and garment industries, with about half a million jobs created for women. Further growth is threatened, however, as the nation is subjected to developed-country protectionist measures such as the multifiber agreement (see Chapter 14).

World Bank–financed structural-adjustment programs designed to reduce inflation and foreign debt burdens have increased public food distribution system prices, and this also hurt the poor. But the country recently expanded its public agricultural extension and rural credit services. Aid-financed imports, improved storage and distribution infrastructure, and grain price stabilization measures have assisted the absolutely poor, and a number of other efforts at poverty reduction are being implemented.

The Food for Work Program (FFWP), which organizes and pays with food for the construction and maintenance of agriculture-supporting infrastructure, mainly irrigation, drainage, and embankment works, has also been a significant help to the poor. One advantage is that unlike poverty programs in most developing countries, this one really reaches the poor rather than subsidizes everyone or even disproportionately favors the more affluent. The basic reason is that an incentive for self-selection is built into the program: Few nonpoor persons can be expected to choose to work in labor-intensive construction all day for pay in basic foodstuffs, a conjecture strongly supported by the available evidence. Such programs always have opportunity costs for the poor, and most participants must give up some farm or nonfarm self-employment work time to participate. But net gains to the poor remain substantial. The program also benefits rural development, including poor farmers, by producing valuable infrastructure. Moreover, it avoids the reductions in the incentive to work caused by some welfare programs. Finally, the FFWP compares favorably with an irrigation project financed by the World Bank in the 1970s that benefited well-off farmers.

Recognizing the limits of its resources and personnel, Bangladesh has encouraged nongovernmental organizations, of which there are over 400, in addition to more than 12,000 voluntary social welfare agencies, to play a central role in poverty alleviation. Independent development groups, such as the Bangladesh Rural Advancement Committee, have been extremely important. They assist the poor, often focusing on the needs of women, providing basic nutrition, health care, basic education such as literacy training, skill development, family planning, and small-scale credit.

A good example is the Nonformal Primary Education Program (NPEP), begun in 1983. A major reason parents do not send their children to school is that their work at home and on the farm is needed to help the family survive. A second reason is the intimidation and alienation uneducated parents and their children feel in traditional school settings. This program, conducted in nearly 750 centers, arranges the school schedule so as not to interfere with farm work. It operates $2\frac{1}{2}$ hours a day. During peak harvest times, parents decide whether school sessions will be held in early morning or early evening. The three-year schools stress literacy and numeracy, health and hygiene, basic science, and social studies. The teachers are usually village residents trained and supervised by a professional staff. Over 90% of graduates have gained admission to fourth grade in mainstream primary schools; the dropout rate is less than 2%; and most important, girls make up some 60% of the enrollment. These impressive results have encouraged the government to begin a rural "satellite" lower primary school program on the NPEP model.

A separate pilot program is experimenting with paying poor peasant families a small sum for sending their children to elementary school; this makes up for the loss of work the children could perform on the farm and should help keep poverty from being transmitted to the next generation.

Traditional-sector enrichment growth has been aided by the policies of the public-cooperative Grameen Bank, which has enabled close to 1 million poor Bangladeshis, a large majority of them landless women, to start their own businesses. Grameen is incorporated as a publicly supported credit union, with borrowers owning 75% of the bank's stock and the government owning the remainder. It sets its own policy with strong borrower input, independent of government control. Grameen's annualized interest rate on loans is 16%, which can be compared with traditional moneylenders' loansharking rates of 120% to 200%.

To qualify for uncollateralized loans, potential borrowers form five-member groups.

Each member must undergo a two-week training session before any member can secure a loan, and the training sessions are followed up with weekly group meetings with a bank officer. Grameen relies on what could be called the collateral of peer pressure. Once a member of the group receives a loan, no other member may borrow until a regular repayment record has been established, and no repeat loans are approved until all members' accounts are settled. Members know the characters of group members and only join groups with members that they believe are likely to repay their loans. Peer oversight has contributed to an astonishing 98% repayment rate. (The Industrial Bank of Bangladesh, by contrast, is famous for having almost all of its loans to the relatively wealthy in default.) The group structure facilitates the formation of cooperatives or joint ventures among the participants, encouraging ventures too large or too risky for poor individuals to undertake alone. Grameen also works to facilitate saving among its members.

Loans have financed activities from sari weaving to shoe repair, from livestock raising to food processing. The average income of borrowers was about half the national average, and incomes of participants have been found to increase very significantly.

None of this is to say that the government of Bangladesh has created ideal conditions for the rural poor to better their lives. Powerful landlords, with the help of bands of paid thugs, often seize fertile new farmlands formed by frequent changes in the nation's many riverbeds. The warlords then demand "tribute" from the peasants who seek to till the soil. By law, these lands are to be distributed to peasants who lose their farms to other changes in river channels. But the landlords form part of a corrupt political system that prevents enforcement. A government fully committed to poverty alleviation would take greater risks to empower the poor.

Moreover, it could be argued that Bangladesh enjoys special advantages of a population homogeneous in ethnicity, religion, and language; relative lack of civil strife; location in Asia, the world's growth center; and rich soil, in contrast to that in other very poor areas like the Sahel and Haiti. But developing countries with fewer such advantages, including Malaysia, Sri Lanka, and Malawi, have benefited from imitating the Grameen Bank.

Nigeria

Nigeria has been more a case of modern-sector enrichment, with some modern-sector enlargement but relative neglect of the rural sector. The country has special problems, among them the division into 10 main ethnic groups and nearly 200 small tribal groupings, each with its own language and culture, that are often in conflict. It has long stressed university education at the expense of expanded resources for primary, middle, and high schools. Agriculture employs over 70% of the workforce but commands a minuscule part of the public budget. Since independence in 1960, it has mostly been run by a military dictatorship, though there are plans for a transition to civilian rule.

The country has been notorious for its overwhelming corruption. Attitudes toward government and government service have been characterized by Nigerians as "see a piece of the pie and cut your own share." These attitudes, which have their roots in the colonial experience, are in desperate need of reform.

Nigeria squandered a major opportunity to alleviate poverty in the 1970s during the country's oil boom. Nigeria did not use its oil wealth to finance a solution to poverty. Instead, oil exports led to overvalued exchange rates, and activities of the poor were crowded out. Large sums were spent on projects such as the expensive new showcase capital at Abuja. Nigeria used its image as an oil-rich country to borrow a crushing debt that amounted to some $30 billion by the end of 1992. Per capita incomes fell precipitously with the 1980s oil glut. As a result of its mismanagement of its economy, Nigeria was obliged to follow World Bank–IMF advice on structural adjustment. But to date it has been unable to follow the IMF guidelines closely enough for debt relief approval. There have been some gains, but the rigors of adjustment have led to an enormous brain drain among the most educated, as well as the large-scale flight of capital, much of it acquired by dubious means.

Nigeria has a poorly developed infrastructure for the agricultural areas, including a complete lack of roads in many areas and roads unusable in the rainy season in others. There are many very small holdings that are too tiny for tractors, and agricultural practices are rudimentary—typically, slash and burn. Clarification of property rights is needed in many cases. But there is no real shortage of farmland.

The current Nigerian thinking is to have agriculture reabsorb as much labor as possible. The country has highlighted its first lady's project, rural development for bettering the life of women. But problems of poor rural women are overwhelming and have yet to be addressed seriously. The nature of the problems vary across regions and ethnic groups. Generally, a husband controls the allocation of his wife's labor. The wife owes a certain amount of labor to the husband, after which she may grow crops or engage in other income-generating pursuits of her own. The wife is often responsible for providing materially as well as maternally for her children. The switch to labor-intensive cash crops like tobacco has often increased the demands on women's time for crops owned and controlled by husbands, which may have a net adverse effect on the welfare of women and children. In some areas, a rural woman may be one of four wives, responsible for performing almost all the agricultural work on her homesite. She may perceive that her only security lies in bearing large numbers of children, despite her difficulties in providing for them.

There has been some modest recent progress in attitudes and programs in Nigeria, but it has a very long way to go to initiate and maintain policies for genuine development and improvement in the life of the poor. There have been some attempts to soften the impact of structural adjustment on the poor, generally at the urging of international development agencies, but there seem to be no innovative programs worthy of international emulation such as are found in Bangladesh.

Summary

Nigeria is by no means the worst case in lost opportunities for the poor; Zaire, for instance, is far worse. Conditions of rural women are little short of tragic throughout Africa and in many other poor regions such as Bangladesh. These case studies were not selected with the intent of contrasting a perfect case with a uniquely dismal one. Neither Bangladesh nor Nigeria did all that it could. Each country has had authoritarian governments plagued by corruption and inefficiency. But comparing the two countries, Bangladesh must receive higher marks. Despite severe resource constraints, Bangladesh showed a capacity to innovate, an openness to new ideas for the poor, and a creative interchange between nongovernmental groups and governmental agencies. Nigeria, with tremendous oil resources, had far easier circumstances to take steps for the alleviation of poverty and sustainable rural development but accomplished less.

Sources: World Bank, *Reaching the Poor through Rural Public Employment* (Washington, D.C.: World Bank, 1990), and various other World Bank documents; *Washington Post* and *Financial Times,* various issues; Lewis D. Solomon, "Microenterprise: Human reconstruction in America's inner cities," *Harvard Journal of Law and Public Policy* (Winter 1992); Bangladeshi and Nigerian government documents; Frances Stewart, *Basic Needs in Developing Countries* (Baltimore: Johns Hopkins University Press, 1985), which adduces statistical evidence for the better basic needs performance of Bangladesh relative to Nigeria on a resource-adjusted basis (e.g., tab. 4.4); Robin Theobald, *Corruption, Development, and Underdevelopment* (Durham, N.C.: Duke University Press, 1990); Jean Davison (ed.), *Agriculture, Women and Land: The African Experience* (London: Westview Press, 1988); and lectures by Nigerian agriculture expert Aloysius Nwosu.

PART THREE

PROBLEMS AND POLICIES: INTERNATIONAL

CHAPTER 12

Trade Theory
and Development Experience

The opening of a foreign trade . . . sometimes works a sort of industrial revolution in a country whose resources were previously underdeveloped.

—John Stuart Mill, 1846

For unto everyone that hath shall be given, and he shall have abundance; but from him that hath not shall be taken away, even that which he hath.

—Matthew 25:29

The Importance of International Trade and Finance

International trade has often played a crucial though not necessarily benign role in the historical development of the Third World. Throughout Africa, Asia, the Middle East, and Latin America, primary product exports have traditionally accounted for a sizable proportion of individual gross national products. In some of the smaller countries, anywhere from 25% to 40% of the monetary GNP is derived from the overseas sale of agricultural and other **primary products** or commodities such as coffee, cotton, cacao, sugar, palm oil, and copper. In the special circumstances of the oil-producing nations in the Persian Gulf and elsewhere, the sale of unrefined and refined petroleum products to countries throughout the world accounts for over 70% of their national incomes. But unlike the oil-producing states and a few newly industrializing countries like South Korea, Taiwan, and Singapore, most developing countries must depend on nonmineral primary-product exports for the vast majority of their foreign-exchange earnings. Because the markets and prices for these exports are often unstable, primary-product **export dependence** carries with it a degree of risk and uncertainty that few nations desire.

In addition to their export dependence, many developing countries rely, generally to an even greater extent, on the importation of raw materials, machinery, capital goods, intermediate producer goods, and consumer products to fuel their industrial expansion and satisfy the rising consumption aspirations of their

419

people. For most developing nations, import demands have increasingly exceeded their capacity to generate sufficient revenues from the sale of exports. This has led to chronic deficits on their balance of payments position vis-à-vis the rest of the world. Whereas such deficits on the **current account** (an excess of import *payments* over export *receipts* for goods and services) were often more than compensated for by a surplus on the **capital account** of their balance of payments table (a receipt of foreign private and public lending and investment in excess of repayment of principal and interest on former loans and investments), in recent years the debt burden of repaying earlier international loans and investments has become increasingly acute. In a number of LDCs, severe deficits on current and capital accounts have therefore led to a rapid depletion of their international monetary reserves and a slowdown in economic growth.

In the 1980s, this combination of rising trade deficits, growing foreign debts, accelerated capital flight, and diminished international reserves led to the widespread adoption of fiscal and monetary austerity measures (often at the instigation of the International Monetary Fund), which may have further exacerbated the slowdown in economic growth and the worsening of poverty and unemployment problems throughout the developing world. The precise meaning of these various concepts of international economics will be explained later in this chapter and in the next two. Here the point is merely that a chronic excess of foreign expenditures over receipts (which may have nothing to do with an LDC's inability to handle its financial affairs but rather may be related to its vulnerability to global economic disturbances) can significantly retard development efforts. It can also greatly limit a poor nation's ability to determine and pursue its most desirable economic strategies.

But international trade and finance must be understood in a much broader perspective than simply the intercountry flow of commodities and financial resources. By opening their economies and societies to world trade and commerce and by looking outward to the rest of the world, Third World countries invite not only the international transfer of goods, services, and financial resources but also the developmental or antidevelopmental influences of the transfer of production technologies; consumption patterns; institutional and organizational arrangements; educational, health, and social systems; and the more general values, ideals, and lifestyles of the developed nations of the world. The impact of such technological, economic, social, and cultural transfers on the character of the development process can be either benign or malevolent. Much will depend on the nature of the political, social, and institutional structure of the recipient country and its development priorities. Whether it is best for LDCs to look outward and promote more exports, as the free traders and cultural internationalists advocate; to look inward and substitute domestic production for imports, as the protectionists and cultural nationalists propose; or to be simultaneously and strategically outward- and inward-looking in their international economic policies cannot be stated a priori. Individual nations must appraise their present and prospective situations in the world community realistically in the light of their specific development objectives. Only thus can they judge how much to expose themselves to the obvious benefits and the many risks of international commerce.

Unfortunately, many small and very poor countries (and these constitute well over half of all Third World nations) have little choice about whether to opt out or not. They have to trade. As we shall see, however, a potentially promising strategy, especially for these smaller LDCs, may be to look outward but in a different direction (toward trade and cooperation with other LDCs) and inward toward each other as members of a group of nations trying to integrate their economies and coordinate their joint development strategies in an effort to achieve greater collective self-sufficiency.

The study of foreign trade and international finance is among the oldest and most controversial branches of the discipline of economics. It dates back to the sixteenth century and Europe's mercantilist passion for Spanish gold. It flowered in the eighteenth and nineteenth centuries as modern economic growth was fueled and propelled by the engine of international trade. The greatest minds in economics—Adam Smith, David Ricardo, and John Stuart Mill—provided the basic concepts and insights that endure to this day. A deep and abiding concern with global international relations flourishes even more today, not only because of the still bitter controversies between people who advocate more trade and those who advocate less, especially in the context of development, but also because modern transport and communications are rapidly shrinking the world to a "global village." It is for these and the other reasons mentioned that we now turn to this important and still controversial area of economic analyses and policy.

Five Basic Questions about Trade and Development

To give the discussion contemporary relevance, our objective in this chapter is to focus on traditional and more contemporary theories of international trade in the context of five basic themes or questions of particular importance to developing nations.

1. How does international trade affect the rate, structure, and character of LDC economic growth? This is the traditional "trade as an engine of growth" controversy, set in terms of contemporary development aspirations.

2. How does trade alter the distribution of income and wealth within a country and among different countries? Is trade a force for international and domestic equality or inequality? In other words, how are the gains and losses distributed, and who benefits at whose expense (for every winner must there be at least one or, more likely, many losers)?

3. Under what conditions can trade help LDCs achieve their development objectives?

4. Can LDCs by their own actions determine how much they trade?

5. In the light of past experience and prospective judgment, should LDCs adopt an outward-looking policy (freer trade, expanded flows of capital and human resources, ideas and technology, etc.) or an inward-looking one (protectionism in the interest of self-reliance), or should they pursue some combination of both,

for example, in the form of regional economic cooperation? What are the arguments for and against these alternative trade strategies for development?

Clearly, the answers or suggested answers to these five questions will not be uniform throughout the diverse economies of the Third World. The whole economic basis for international trade rests on the fact that countries do differ in their resource endowments, their economic and social institutions, and their capacities for growth and development. Developing countries are no exception to this rule. Some are very populous yet deficient in natural resources and human skills. Others are sparsely populated yet endowed with abundant mineral and raw material resources. Still others—the majority—are small and economically weak, having at present neither the human nor the material resources on which to base a sustained and largely self-sufficient strategy of economic and social development. Yet with the notable exception of the now very wealthy oil nations of the Middle East and a few other countries rich in internationally demanded mineral resources, most developing nations face similar issues and choices in their international relations with the developed countries and with each other. Consequently, though an effort will be made here to place generalizations about LDC trade prospects and policy alternatives in the context of a broad typology of developing nations, the goal of being comprehensive in coverage will necessitate a number of sweeping generalizations, many of which may not hold for a particular country at a particular time. On balance, however, the benefits of this broad Third World perspective outweigh the costs of having to make some analytic and policy generalizations.

Accordingly, we begin with a statistical summary of recent Third World trade performance and patterns. There follows a simplified presentation of the basic neoclassical theory of international trade and its effect on efficiency, equity, stability, and growth (four basic economic concepts related to the central questions outlined here). We then provide a critique of free-trade theories in the light of both historical experience and the contemporary realities of the world economy in the last decade of the twentieth century. Like free markets, **free trade** has many desirable theoretical features, not the least of which is the promotion of static economic efficiency and optimal resource allocation. But also like free markets and perfect competition, free trade exists more in theory than in practice—and today's developing nations have to function in the imperfect and often highly unequal real world of international commerce. Consequently, as part of our critique of the neoclassical theory, we will briefly discuss more recent alternative trade models, including North-South models of exchange that focus on the real world of imperfect competition, unequal trade, and the dynamic effects of differential human resource and technological growth. In Chapters 13 and 14, we will learn something about a country's balance of payments, review some issues in international finance, engage in an in-depth analysis of the Third World debt crisis, and explore the range of commercial policies (tariffs, subsidies, quotas, exchange-rate adjustments, etc.) that LDCs might wish to adopt within the broader context of the ongoing debate about the relative merits of export promotion versus import substitution.

The Importance of Trade for Development: A Statistical Review

Third World Exports: Trends and Patterns

The volume, value, and structure of world trade have undergone considerable change over the past three decades. The world economy expanded rapidly in the 1960s and 1970s, with most countries, rich and poor, participating in that growth. Since 1980, however, the real value of world exports has actually declined by about 10% even though the nominal value has increased (see Table 12.1). Third World countries bore the brunt of most of this decline, with an almost 18% drop in the real value of their exports between 1980 and 1994. The main reasons for this severe contraction include the effects of the two global recessions, one in 1980–1983 and the other in 1991–1993, with a period of relatively slow world economic growth in between; a precipitous 40% decline in Third World commodity export prices; a steady rise in protectionism in the developed countries; and the ongoing debt crisis throughout Latin America, Africa, and Asia. Facing an unhealthy combination of declining export prices, worsening trade balances (import payments exceeding export receipts), and rising debt repayment obligations, most developing countries have had to curtail imports as part of fiscal and monetary austerity measures. This has in turn led many to experience a slowdown in overall economic growth, a rise in unemployment, and a general increase in the incidence of severe poverty. We will be discussing these and related issues in Chapter 14, where we look at the origins and future of the Third World debt crisis.

However, even though Table 12.1 shows that between 1970 and 1990 the Third World's share of total world trade remained roughly constant between 17% and 28%, within the developing world some exporters have prospered—notably the

TABLE 12.1 Trends in World Exports, 1970–1994

	1970	1980	1983	1986	1990	1994
World exports						
Nominal value (billions of dollars)	312	2,002	1,814	2,113	3,187	2,550
Real value (billions of 1980 dollars)	590	2,002	1,620	1,780	1,940	1,781
Share of world exports (%)						
Developed countries	71.9	66.3	64.1	69.0	74.6	70.8
Developing countries	17.6	27.9	24.9	20.8	17.8	25.9
Centrally planned economies and their successors[a]	10.5	8.8	11.0	10.2	7.5	3.3

SOURCES: John Sewell, Stuart Tucker, and contributors, *Growth, Exports and Jobs in a Changing World Economy: Agenda 1988* (New Brunswick, N.J.: Transaction Books, 1988), tab. A.1; World Bank, *World Development Report, 1992: Development and the Environment* (New York: Oxford University Press, 1992), tab. 14; International Monetary Fund, *World Economic Outlook, May 1995* (Washington, D.C.: International Monetary Fund, 1995), tabs. A, B, A22, and A31.

[a]Soviet Union, Eastern Europe, China, and a few Asian LDCs.

Asian newly industrializing countries (NICs) South Korea, Hong Kong, Singapore, and Taiwan. Exports of manufactures from these four successful Asian countries have caused their share of world trade to more than double while their share of total Third World manufactured exports grew by more than 250%, from 30.8% in 1965 to 82.8% in 1990 (see Table 12.2). At the same time, most other LDCs (particularly in sub-Saharan Africa and parts of Latin America) have seen their shares of global trade steadily drop along with their export revenues.

For the vast majority of low- and middle-income developing countries (over 120 nations), the export of primary commodities (food, food products, raw materials, minerals, and fossil fuels) still accounts for more than three-quarters of their total export earnings. During the early 1990s, for example, primary-commodity exports continued to represent over 90% of the total exports of sub-Saharan Africa and over 65% of the exports of most low- and middle-income Asian and Latin American countries. Table 12.3 lists the major primary-product exports of developing countries and the principal LDC suppliers of those exports.

Importance of Exports to Different Developing Nations

Although the overall Third World figures for export volumes and values are important indicators of patterns of trade for the group as a whole, the varying importance of exports to the economic well-being of individual nations is masked by these aggregate statistics. Table 12.4 has been compiled to provide a capsule picture of the relative importance of commodity export earnings to various developing nations of different sizes and in different regions. For purposes of comparison, three key developed countries are included at the bottom of the table.

We see that large countries like Brazil and India tend to be less dependent on foreign trade in terms of national income than relatively small countries like those in tropical Africa and East Asia. As a group, however, less developed nations are more dependent on foreign trade in terms of its share in national income than the very highly developed countries are. This is shown clearly in the cases of the United States and Japan, whose exports amount to roughly 8% of GDP, whereas most developing nations average anywhere from 20% to 35%.

A critical dimension of the Third World's **merchandise trade balance**—the excess or deficit in the value of its exports relative to its imports—relates to the commodity composition of that trade. Although the past quarter century has seen considerable expansion in exports of manufactured goods, this progress has, as noted, been largely concentrated in four East Asian nations, which together account for more than three-fourths of total developing-country manufactured exports. In the rest of the Third World, primary products, the traditional mainstay, remain the predominant export. The last two columns of Table 12.4 show that most LDCs still depend heavily on their exports of primary products, whereas the developed nations export primarily manufactured goods. Between 1981 and 1992, the average annual rate of LDC commodity export growth was 2.1%. Manufactured exports from developed countries grew at an annual rate of 5.1%. In real-value terms, however, Third World commodity exports actually declined while rich-country export values increased over the same period.

TABLE 12.2 Major Developing-Country Exporters of Manufactures, 1965–1990

Country	Manufactured Exports as a Percentage of Total Exports					Total Exports as a Percentage of Gross National Product				Percentage of Total Developing-Country Manufactured Exports				
	1965	1970	1975	1980	1990	1970	1975	1980	1990	1965	1970	1975	1980	1990
Taiwan	46.0	78.6	83.6	90.8	93.0	26.3	34.5	49.4	50.7[a]	4.6	13.8	17.1	23.4	28.5
Korea	52.0	74.9	76.8	80.1	94.1	9.4	24.3	28.5	32.6	2.0	7.4	15.0	18.2	24.6
Hong Kong	92.4	95.3	96.7	95.6	95.8	56.4	49.0	49.6	50.1	17.9	23.1	17.2	17.0	16.7
Singapore	28.9	26.7	39.9	45.6	73.0	81.1	94.5	178.0	132.9	6.3	4.9	8.3	11.5	13.0
Brazil	5.0	9.7	23.3	32.8	53.1	6.5	7.1	8.3	6.7	1.8	3.1	7.8	8.6	6.4
Mexico	14.1	30.0	29.5	11.0	44.2	3.4	3.5	8.5	18.9	3.1	4.3	3.4	2.2	3.2
Argentina	5.2	12.3	23.6	21.4	36.0	8.3	8.4	14.3	15.2	1.7	2.6	2.7	2.2	1.0

SOURCES: United Nations, *Handbook of International Trade and Development Statistics* (New York: United Nations, various years); World Bank, *World Debt Tables* (Washington, D.C.: World Bank, 1985, 1992); Council for Economic Planning and Development, Republic of China, *Taiwan Statistical Data Book, 1984*; International Monetary Fund, *World Economic Outlook, 1992* (Washington, D.C.: International Monetary Fund, 1992).

[a]Estimate.

TABLE 12.3 Major Primary-Commodity Exports of Developing Countries and Principal Suppliers

Commodity	Billions of Dollars	Percentage of World Exports of Commodity	Major Developing-Country Suppliers — Percentage of World Exports of Commodity			
Petroleum	216.5	81.0	Saudi Arabia 26.8	Mexico 5.8	United Arab Emirates 5.7	Iran 5.6
Sugar	8.5	69.1	Cuba 36.6	Brazil 5.9	Philippines 3.5	Thailand 3.5
Coffee	8.3	91.6	Brazil 20.0	Colombia 16.4	Ivory Coast 4.8	El Salvador 4.6
Copper	5.1	63.8	Chile 22.1	Zambia 12.2	Zaire 7.3	Peru 4.8
Timber	4.6	27.8	Malaysia 11.0	Indonesia 3.8	Ivory Coast 1.9	Philippines 1.7
Iron ore	3.2	46.8	Brazil 24.9	India 5.2	Liberia 4.4	Venezuela 3.3
Rubber	3.0	98.3	Malaysia 47.0	Indonesia 24.8	Thailand 15.4	Sri Lanka 4.2
Cotton	2.9	43.4	Egypt 6.5	Pakistan 5.5	Turkey 4.2	Mexico 3.0
Rice	2.5	55.0	Thailand 22.5	Pakistan 9.2	China 5.5	India 5.2
Tobacco	2.3	51.3	Brazil 9.8	Turkey 7.4	China 6.0	India 4.6
Maize	2.0	19.2	Argentina 8.7	Thailand 3.5	Yugoslavia[a] 1.2	Zimbabwe 0.5
Tin	1.9	74.7	Malaysia 28.6	Indonesia 13.4	Thailand 12.7	Bolivia 10.0
Cacao	1.9	92.1	Ivory Coast 26.4	Ghana 16.3	Nigeria 12.2	Brazil 11.8
Tea	1.5	84.6	India 26.6	Sri Lanka 18.2	China 12.8	Kenya 8.9
Palm oil	1.4	81.6	Malaysia 70.1	Indonesia 7.0	Ivory Coast 1.7	Papua New Guinea 0.5
Beef	1.3	16.7	Argentina 5.4	Uruguay 2.5	Brazil 2.2	Yugoslavia[a] 1.3
Bananas	1.2	86.7	Costa Rica 16.7	Honduras 14.2	Ecuador 13.8	Colombia 10.2
Wheat	1.2	6.9	Argentina 5.7	Turkey 0.4	Uruguay 0.1	Yugoslavia[a] 0.1
Phosphate rock	1.1	62.9	Morocco 34.1	Jordan 8.5	Togo 4.8	Senegal 3.0

SOURCE: World Bank, *Commodity Trade and Price Trends* (Washington, D.C.: World Bank, 1986), tabs. 7 and 8.

[a]Prior to breakup.

TABLE 12.4 Export Earnings as a Percentage of Gross Domestic Product (GDP) and Share of Primary and Manufactured Commodities in Total Exports for Selected Countries, 1993

Country	Percentage of GDP	Percentage Share of Primary Commodities	Percentage Share of Manufactures
Developing countries			
Hong Kong	150.3	7	93
Nigeria	37.9	92	8
Saudi Arabia	33.6	91	9
Sri Lanka	30.1	28	72
Kenya	29.3	89	11
Togo	28.4	94	6
Jamaica	27.4	34	66
South Korea	24.9	7	93
Venezuela	22.1	86	14
Philippines	20.1	24	76
India	9.6	25	75
Mexico	8.8	56	44
Brazil	8.7	47	53
Developed countries			
United Kingdom	22.0	19	81
Japan	8.6	3	97
United States	7.4	18	82

SOURCE: World Bank, *World Development Report, 1995: Workers in an Integrating World* (New York: Oxford University Press, 1995), annex tabs. 3, 13, and 15.

Demand Elasticities and Export Earnings Instability

We have an important clue here as to why the export performance of the majority of LDCs has been relatively weak compared with the export performance of rich countries. It relates to the concept of elasticity of demand. Most statistical studies of world demand patterns for different commodity groups reveal that in the case of primary products, the **income elasticity of demand** is relatively low—the percentage increase in quantity of primary products demanded by importers (mostly rich nations) will rise by less than the percentage increase in their GNPs. By contrast, for fuels, certain raw materials, and manufactured goods, income elasticity is relatively high.[1] For example, it has been estimated that a 1% increase in developed-country incomes will normally raise their import of foodstuffs by 0.6%, agricultural raw materials such as rubber and vegetable oils by 0.5%, petroleum products and other fuels by 2.4%, and manufactures by about 1.9%. Consequently, when incomes rise in rich countries, their demand for food, food products, and raw materials from the Third World nations goes up relatively slowly, whereas their own as well as LDC demand for manufactures, the production of which is dominated by the developed countries, goes up very rapidly.

The net result of these low income elasticities of demand is the tendency for the relative price of primary products to decline over time. Moreover, since the **price elasticity of demand** for (and supply of) primary commodities also tends to be quite low (i.e., inelastic), any shifts in demand or supply curves can cause large and volatile price fluctuations. Together these two elasticity phenomena contribute to what has come to be known as **export earnings instability**, which has been shown to lead to lower and less predictable rates of economic growth.

The Terms of Trade and the Prebisch–Singer Thesis

The question of changing relative price levels for different commodities brings us to another important quantitative dimension of the trade problems historically faced by Third World nations. The total value of export earnings depends not only on the volume of these exports sold abroad but also on the price paid for them. If export prices decline, a greater volume of exports will have to be sold merely to keep total earnings constant. Similarly, on the import side, the total foreign exchange expended depends on both the quantity and the price of imports.

Clearly, if the price of a country's exports is falling relative to the prices of the products it imports, it will have to sell that much more of its export product and enlist more of its scarce productive resources merely to secure the same level of imported goods that it purchased in previous years. In other words, the real or social opportunity costs of a unit of imports will rise for a country when its export prices decline relative to its import prices.

Economists have a special name for the relationship or ratio between the price of a typical unit of exports and the price of a typical unit of imports. This relationship is called the **commodity terms of trade**, and it is expressed as P_x/P_m, where P_x and P_m represent the export and import price indexes, respectively, calculated on the same base period (e.g., 1985 = 100). The commodity terms of trade are said to deteriorate for a country if P_x/P_m falls, that is, if export prices decline *relative to* import prices, even though both may rise. Historically, the prices of primary commodities have declined relative to manufactured goods. As a result, the terms of trade have on the average tended to worsen over time for the non-oil-exporting developing countries while showing a relative improvement for the developed countries. For example, recent empirical studies suggest that real primary-product prices have declined at an average annual rate of 0.6% since 1900. In the 15 years between 1977 and 1992, the prices of non-oil commodities relative to those of exported manufactures declined by almost 60% so that by 1992 they had reached their lowest point in 90 years.[2] Figure 12.1 shows the continuous deterioration in the relative real prices of non-oil primary commodities between 1977 and 1992. Because of this precipitous decline in real export prices of their commodities, LDCs had to sell greater quantities of their primary products (the international demand for which, as we have seen, is relatively income- and price-inelastic) in order to purchase a given quantity of manufactured imports. One estimate has placed the extra costs of these deteriorating terms of trade for the LDCs at over $2.5 billion per year during the past decade. As a result, Third World merchandise trade balances steadily worsened during the 1980s and early 1990s, falling from +$55.8 billion in 1981 to –$42.9 billion in 1994.

A good deal of the argument against primary-product export expansion and in favor of diversification into manufactured exports for developing countries

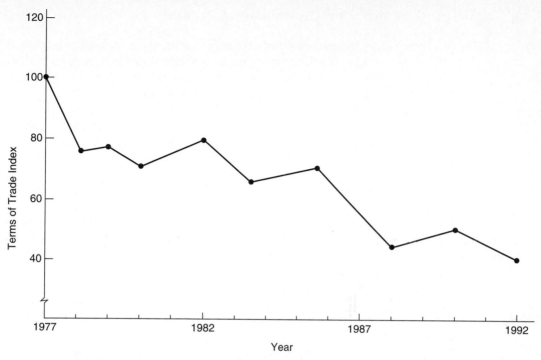

FIGURE 12.1 Real Non-oil Commodity Terms of Trade, 1977–1992. *Source:* International Monetary Fund, *World Economic Outlook, October 1994* (Washington, D.C.: International Monetary Fund, 1994), p. 92.

NOTE: Commodity prices are deflated by the export unit values of manufactured goods.

during the 1950s and 1960s was based on the presumed secular deterioration of the non-oil commodity terms of trade. This terms of trade pessimism has come to be known as the **Prebisch-Singer thesis**, after two famous development economists who explored its implications in the 1950s.[3] They argued that there was and would continue to be a secular decline in the terms of trade of primary-commodity exporters due to a combination of low income and price elasticities of demand. This decline resulted in a long-term transfer of income from poor to rich countries that could be combated only by efforts to protect domestic manufacturing industries through a process that has come to be known as import substitution (see Chapter 13).

But we are getting ahead of ourselves here. Because the international economic vulnerability of developing nations is not solely confined to adverse movements in commodity or income terms of trade, it is important that we first understand both the broader theory and the practice of international economics. We will therefore briefly review the traditional theory of international trade and then look at some alternative models including North-South, structuralist, and vent-for-surplus theories that try to incorporate some of the factors that determine the actual trade patterns and performances of developing nations.

The Traditional Theory of International Trade

The phenomenon of transactions and exchange is a basic component of human activity throughout the world. Even in the most remote villages of Africa, people regularly meet in the village market to exchange goods, sometimes for money but most often for other goods through simple **barter transactions**. A transaction is an exchange of two things—something is given up in return for something else. In an African village, women may barter food such as cassava for cloth or simple jewelry for clay pots. Implicit in all transactions is a price. For example, if 20 cassavas are traded for a meter of bark cloth, the implicit price (or terms of trade) of the bark cloth is 20 cassavas. If 20 cassavas can also be exchanged for one small clay pot, it follows that clay pots and 1-meter pieces of bark cloth can be exchanged on a one-to-one basis. A price system is already in the making.

Why do people trade? Basically, because it is profitable to do so. Different people possess different abilities and resources and may want to consume goods in different proportions. Diverse preferences as well as varied physical and financial endowments open up the possibility of profitable trade. People usually find it profitable to trade the things they possess in large quantities relative to their tastes or needs in return for things they want more urgently. Because it is virtually impossible for individuals or families to provide themselves with all the consumption requirements of even the simplest life, they usually find it profitable to engage in the activities for which they are best suited or have a **comparative advantage** in terms of their natural abilities or resource endowments. They can then exchange any surplus of these home-produced commodities for products that others may be relatively more suited to produce. The phenomenon of **specialization** based on comparative advantage arises, therefore, to some extent in even the most primitive of subsistence economies.

These same principles of specialization and comparative advantage have long been applied by economists to the exchange of goods between individual nations. In answer to the question of what determines which goods are traded and why some countries produce some things while others produce different things, economists since the time of Adam Smith have sought the answer in terms of international differences in costs of production and prices of different products. Countries, like people, specialize in a limited range of production activities because it is to their advantage to do so. They specialize in activities where the gains from specialization are likely to be the largest.

But why, in the case of international trade, should costs differ from country to country? For example, how can Germany produce cameras, electrical appliances, and automobiles cheaper than Kenya and exchange these manufactured goods for Kenya's relatively cheaper agricultural produce (fruits, vegetables, coffee, and tea)? Again, the answer is to be found in international differences in the structure of costs and prices. Some things (basically manufactured goods) are relatively cheaper to produce in Germany and can profitably be exported to other countries like Kenya; other things (agricultural goods) can be produced in Kenya at a lower relative cost and are therefore imported into Germany in exchange for its manufactures.

The concept of *relative* cost and price differences is basic to the theory of international trade. The *principle of comparative advantage*, as it is called, asserts that a country will specialize in the export of the products that it can produce at the lowest *relative cost*. Germany may be able to produce cameras and cars as well as fruits and vegetables at lower *absolute* unit costs than Kenya, but because the commodity cost differences between countries are greater for the manufactured goods than for agricultural products, it will be to Germany's advantage to specialize in the production of manufactured goods and exchange them for Kenya's agricultural produce. So even though Germany may have an **absolute advantage** in the cost of both commodities, its comparative cost advantage lies in manufactured goods. Conversely, Kenya may be at an absolute disadvantage vis-à-vis Germany in both manufacturing and agriculture in that its absolute unit costs of production are higher for both types of products. It can nevertheless still engage in profitable trade because it has a comparative advantage in agricultural specialization (or, alternatively, because its absolute disadvantage is less in agriculture). It is this phenomenon of differences in comparative advantage that gives rise to profitable trade even among the most unequal trading partners.

Relative Factor Endowments and International Specialization: The Neoclassical Model

The classical comparative advantage theory of free trade is a static model based strictly on a one-variable-factor (labor cost), complete-specialization approach to demonstrating the gains from trade. This nineteenth-century free-trade model, primarily associated with David Ricardo and John Stuart Mill, was modified and refined in the twentieth century by two Swedish economists, Eli Hecksher and Bertil Ohlin, to take into account differences in factor supplies (mainly land, labor, and capital) on international specialization. The Hecksher-Ohlin neoclassical (or variable-proportions) **factor endowment trade theory** also enables us to describe analytically the impact of economic growth on trade patterns and the impact of trade on the structure of national economies and on the differential returns or payments to various factors of production.

Unlike the classical labor cost model, however, where trade arises because of fixed but differing labor productivities for different commodities in different countries, the neoclassical factor endowment model assumes away inherent differences in relative labor productivity by postulating that all countries have access to the same technological possibilities for all commodities. If domestic factor prices were the same, all countries would use identical methods of production and would therefore have the same relative domestic product price ratios and factor productivities. The basis for trade arises not because of inherent technological differences in labor productivity for different commodities between different countries but because countries are endowed with different factor supplies. Given different factor supplies, relative factor prices will differ (e.g., labor will be relatively cheap in labor-abundant countries), and so too will domestic commodity price ratios and factor combinations. Countries with cheap labor will have a relative cost and price advantage over countries with relatively expensive labor in commodities that make abundant use of labor (e.g., primary products). They should therefore focus on the production of these labor-intensive products and export the surplus in return for imports of capital-intensive goods.

Conversely, countries well endowed with capital will have a relative cost and price advantage in the production of manufactured goods, which tend to require relatively large inputs of capital compared with labor. They can thus benefit from specialization in and export of capital-intensive manufactures in return for imports of labor-intensive products from labor-abundant countries. Trade therefore serves as a vehicle for a nation to capitalize on its abundant resources through more intensive production and export of commodities that require large inputs of those resources while relieving its factor shortage through the importation of commodities that use large amounts of its relatively scarce resources.

To summarize, the factor endowment theory is based on two crucial propositions:

1. Different products require productive factors in different relative proportions. For example, agricultural products generally require relatively greater proportions of labor per unit of capital than manufactured goods, which require more machine time (capital) per worker than most primary products. The proportions in which factors are actually used to produce different goods will depend on their relative prices. But no matter what factor prices may be, the factor endowment model assumes that certain products will always be relatively more capital-intensive while others will be relatively more labor-intensive. These relative factor intensities will be no different in India than in the United States; primary products will be the relatively labor-intensive commodities compared with secondary manufactured goods in both India and the United States.

2. Countries have different endowments of factors of production. Some countries, like the United States, have large amounts of capital per worker and are thus designated capital-abundant countries. Others, like India, Egypt, or Colombia, have little capital and much labor and are thus designated labor-abundant countries. In general, developed countries are relatively capital-abundant (one could also add that they are well endowed with skilled labor), while most developing countries are labor-abundant.

The factor endowment theory goes on to argue that capital-abundant countries will tend to specialize in such products as automobiles, aircraft, sophisticated electronic communication goods, and computers, which use capital intensively in their technology of production. They will export some of these capital-intensive products in exchange for the labor- or land-intensive products like food, raw materials, and minerals that can best be produced by countries that are relatively well endowed with labor or land.

This theory, which played a predominant role in the early literature on trade and development, encouraged developing countries to focus on their labor- and land-intensive primary-product exports. It was argued that by trading these primary commodities for the manufactured goods that developed countries were theoretically best suited to produce, developing nations could realize the enormous potential benefits to be had from free trade with the richer nations of the world. This free-trade doctrine also served the political interests of colonizing nations searching for raw materials to feed their industrial expansion and for market outlets for their manufactured goods.

The mechanism whereby the benefits of trade are transmitted across national boundaries under the factor endowment approach is analogous to that of the classical labor cost approach. However, in the factor endowment case, with the possibility of differing factor combinations for producing different commodities, nations are assumed to be operating initially at some point on their concave (or increasing opportunity cost) production possibility frontier determined by domestic demand conditions. For example, consider the standard two-country, two-commodity model. Let the two countries be "Third World" and "Rest of World" and the two commodities, agricultural goods and manufactured goods. Figure 12.2 portrays the theoretical benefits of free trade with the Third World's domestic (no-trade) production possibility frontier shown in Figure 12.2a and Rest of World's frontier in Figure 12.2b. Point A on Third World production possibility frontier P-P in Figure 12.2a provides the illustration. With full employment of all resources and under perfectly competitive assumptions, Third World will be producing and consuming at point A, where

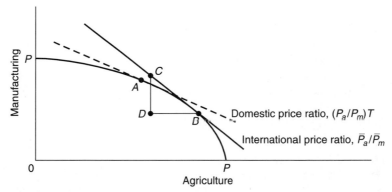

(a) Third World (without trade, production and consumption occur at A; with trade, production is at B, consumption is at C; exports = BD; imports = DC)

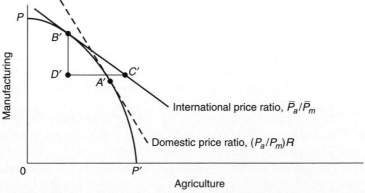

(b) Rest of World (without trade, production and consumption occur at A'; with trade, production is at B', consumption is at C'; exports = $B'D'$; imports = $D'C'$)

FIGURE 12.2 Trade with Variable Factor Proportions and Different Factor Endowments.

the relative price ratio, P_a/P_m, will be given by the slope of the dotted line, $(P_a/P_m)T$, at point A.[4] Similarly, Rest of World may be producing and consuming at point A' in Figure 12.2b, with a domestic price ratio, $(P_a/P_m)R$, that differs (agricultural goods are relatively more costly, or conversely, manufactured goods are relatively cheaper) from that of Third World. Note that with a closed economy, both countries will be producing both commodities. However, Third World, being poorer, will produce a greater proportion of food products in its (smaller) total output.

The relative difference in costs of production and prices at points A and A' (i.e., their different slopes) gives rise once again to the possibilities of profitable trade. As in the classical labor cost model, the international free-trade price ratio, $\bar{P}_a/\bar{P}_m$, will settle somewhere between $(P_a/P_m)T$ and $(P_a/P_m)R$, the domestic price ratios of Third World and Rest of World, respectively. The lines $\bar{P}_a/\bar{P}_m$ in both graphs in Figure 12.2 denote the common world price ratio. For Third World, this steeper slope of $\bar{P}_a/\bar{P}_m$ means that it can get more manufactured goods for a unit of agriculture than in the absence of trade; that is, the world price of agricultural goods in terms of manufacturers is higher than Third World's domestic price ratio. It will therefore reallocate resources away from its costly capital-intensive manufacturing sector and specialize more on labor-intensive agricultural production. Under perfectly competitive assumptions, it will produce at point B on its production frontier, where its relative production (opportunity) costs are just equal to relative world prices. It can then trade along $\bar{P}_a/\bar{P}_m$, the prevailing international price line, exporting BD agricultural products in return for DC manufactured imports and arrive at a final consumption point C with more of *both* goods than before trade. To give a numerical example, suppose that the free-trade international price ratio, $\bar{P}_a/\bar{P}_m$, were 2 to 1. In other words, a unit of agricultural good sells at a price twice that of a unit of manufactured goods. This means that for every unit of agriculture that Third World exports to Rest of World, it can import two units of manufactured goods. The slope of the international price line graphically portrays this trading ratio, these terms of trade. If Third World exports BD agriculture (say, 30 units), it will receive DC manufactures (60 units) in return.

Similarly, for Rest of World, the new international price ratio means more agricultural products in exchange for manufactured goods than at domestic prices. Graphically, the international price ratio has a lesser slope than Rest of World's domestic price ratio (see Figure 12.2b). Rest of World will therefore reallocate its abundant capital resources so as to produce more manufactured goods and less agriculture, as at point B', where its relative domestic production costs are just equal to relative world prices. It can then trade $B'D'$ (= DC) of these manufactures for $D'C'$ (= BD) of Third World's agricultural products. Rest of World can therefore also move outside the confines of its production frontier and end up consuming at a point like C' in Figure 12.2b. Trade is balanced—the value of exports equals the value of imports for both regions. Moreover, it has resulted in increased consumption of *both* goods for both regions, as shown by a comparison between free-trade points C and C' and no-trade points A and A' in Figure 12.2.

The main conclusions of the neoclassical model of free trade are that all countries gain from trade and world output is increased. However, there are several others in addition to these two basic conclusions. First, due to increasing opportunity costs associated with resource shifting among commodities with different factor intensities of production, complete specialization will not occur as in the simple comparative-advantage model. Countries will tend to specialize in products that use their abundant resources intensively. They will compensate for their scarce resources by importing products that use these scarce resources most intensively. But rising domestic costs and therefore prices in excess of world prices will prevent complete specialization from occurring.

Second, given identical technologies of production throughout the world, the equalization of domestic product price ratios with the international free-trade price ratio will tend to equalize factor prices across trading countries. Wage rates, for example, will rise in labor-abundant Third World as a result of the more intensive use of human resources in the production of additional agricultural output. But the price of scarce capital will decline due to the diminished production of manufactured goods, which are heavy users of capital. In Rest of World, the price of its abundant capital will rise relative to its scarce labor as more emphasis is placed on the production of capital-intensive manufactured goods and less on labor-intensive agriculture.

The neoclassical factor endowment theory therefore makes the important prediction that international real wage rates and capital costs will gradually tend toward equalization.[5] In recent years many highly-paid manufacturing workers in the more developed countries were worried that freer trade and greater international competition would drive their wages down to Third World levels (see Chapter 18). However, the reality is that, with the exception of a few Asian NICs, the wage gap between developed and less developed country workers remains as wide as ever.

Third, within countries, the factor endowment theory predicts that the economic return to owners of the abundant resources will rise in relation to owners of scarce resources as the abundant factor is more intensively used; in Third World countries, this would generally mean a rise in the share of national income going to labor. In the absence of trade, labor's share might be smaller. Thus trade tends to promote more equality in domestic income distributions.

Finally, by enabling countries to move outside their production possibility frontiers and secure capital as well as consumption goods from other parts of the world, trade is assumed to stimulate economic growth. It also enables a nation to obtain the domestically expensive raw materials and other products (as well as knowledge, ideas, new technologies, etc.) with which it is relatively less well endowed at lower world market prices. It can thus create the conditions for a more broadly based and self-sustaining growth of its industrial output.

Trade Theory and Development: The Traditional Arguments

We are now in a position to summarize the theoretical answers to our five basic questions about trade and development derived from the neoclassical free-trade model:

1. Trade is an important stimulator of economic growth. It enlarges a country's consumption capacities, increases world output, and provides access to scarce resources and worldwide markets for products without which poor countries would be unable to grow.

2. Trade tends to promote greater international and domestic equality by equalizing factor prices, raising real incomes of trading countries, and making efficient use of each nation's and the world's resource endowments (e.g., raising relative wages in labor-abundant countries and lowering them in labor-scarce countries).

3. Trade helps countries achieve development by promoting and rewarding the sectors of the economy where individual countries possess a comparative advantage, whether in terms of labor efficiency or factor endowments.

4. In a world of free trade, international prices and costs of production determine how much a country should trade in order to maximize its national welfare. Countries should follow the dictates of the principle of comparative advantage and not try to interfere with the free workings of the market.

5. Finally, to promote growth and development, an outward-looking international policy is required. In all cases, self-reliance based on partial or complete isolation is asserted to be economically inferior to participation in a world of unlimited free trade.

Some Criticisms of Traditional Free-Trade Theory in the Context of Third World Experience

The conclusions of traditional international trade theory are derived from a number of explicit and implicit assumptions that in many ways are often contrary to the reality of contemporary international economic relations. This theory therefore often leads to conclusions foreign to both the historical and the contemporary trade experience of many developing nations. This is not to deny the potential benefits of a world of free trade but rather to recognize that free trade exists mostly in the diagrams and models of economists, whereas the real world is beset by all sorts of national protection and international noncompetitive pricing policies.

What are the major and crucial assumptions of the traditional factor endowment theory of trade, and how are these assumptions violated in the real world? What are the implications for the trade and financial prospects of developing nations when a more realistic assessment of the actual mechanism of international economic and political relations is made?

Six basic assumptions of the neoclassical trade model must be scrutinized:

1. All productive resources are fixed in quantity and constant in quality across nations. They are fully employed, and there is no international mobility of productive factors.

2. The technology of production is fixed (classical model) or similar and freely available to all nations (factor endowment model). Moreover, the spread of such technology works to the benefit of all. Consumer tastes are also fixed and independent of the influence of producers (international consumer sovereignty prevails).

3. Within nations, factors of production are perfectly mobile between different production activities, and the economy as a whole is characterized by the existence of perfect competition. There are no risks or uncertainties.

4. The national government plays no role in international economic relations; trade is carried out among many atomistic and anonymous producers seeking to minimize costs and maximize profits. International prices are therefore set by the forces of supply and demand.

5. Trade is balanced for each country at any point in time, and all economies are readily able to adjust to changes in the international prices with a minimum of dislocation.

6. The gains from trade that accrue to any country benefit the nationals of that country.

We can now take a critical look at each of these assumptions in the context of the contemporary position of developing countries in the international economic system. Some of these criticisms form the basis of other, nonneoclassical theories of trade and development, including vent-for-surplus, structuralist, and North-South models.

Fixed Resources, Full Employment, and the International Immobility of Capital and Skilled Labor

Trade and Resource Growth: North-South Models of Unequal Trade

This initial assumption about the static nature of international exchange—that resources are fixed, fully utilized, and internationally immobile with same product production functions everywhere identical—is central to the whole traditional theory of trade and finance. In reality, the world economy is characterized by rapid change, and factors of production are fixed neither in quantity nor in quality. Not only do capital accumulation and human resource development take place all the time, but trade has always been and will continue to be one of the main determinants of the *unequal growth* of productive resources in different nations. This is especially true with respect to resources most crucial to growth and development, such as physical capital, entrepreneurial abilities, scientific capacities, the ability to carry out technological research and development, and the upgrading of technical skills in the labor force.

It follows, therefore, that relative factor endowments and comparative costs are not given but are in a state of constant change. Moreover, they are often determined by, rather than themselves determining, the nature and character of international specialization. In the context of unequal trade between rich and poor nations, this means that any initial state of unequal resource endowments will tend to be reinforced and exacerbated by the very trade that these differing resource endowments were supposed to justify. Specifically, if rich nations (the *North*) as a result of historical forces, are relatively well endowed with the vital resources of capital, entrepreneurial ability, and skilled labor, their continued specialization in products and processes that use these resources intensively will create the necessary conditions and economic incentives for their further growth. By contrast, Third World countries (the *South*), endowed with abundant supplies of unskilled labor, by specializing in products that intensively use unskilled labor and for which world demand prospects and terms of trade may be very unfavorable, often find themselves locked into a stagnant situation that perpetuates their comparative advantage in unskilled, unproductive activities. This will in turn inhibit the domestic growth of needed capital, entrepreneurship, and technical skills. Static efficiency becomes dynamic inefficiency, and a cumulative process is set in motion in which trade exacerbates already unequal trading relationships, distributes the benefits largely to the people who already "have," and perpetuates the physical and human resource underdevelopment that characterizes Third World nations. As one well-known Third World scholar put it, "With few exceptions, the technological distance between the developing and the developed countries is widening. Neoclassical international trade theory, by postulating identical production functions for different products in various countries, assumes this problem away."[6]

In recent years, some economists have therefore challenged the static neoclassical model with alternative dynamic models of trade and growth that emphasize the process of factor accumulation and uneven development along the lines suggested in the preceding paragraphs. These so-called **North-South trade models** focus specifically on trade relations between rich and poor countries, whereas the traditional model was assumed to apply to all nations. The typical North-South model argues, for example, that initial higher endowments of capital in the industrialized North generate external economies in manufacturing output and higher profit rates. This, in combination with the rise in monopoly power, stimulates higher Northern growth rates (in accordance with Harrod-Domar and factor-share growth models discussed earlier) through further capital accumulation. As a result, the rapidly growing North develops a cumulative competitive advantage over the slower-growing South. If we then add differential income elasticities of demand (higher for Northern "capital goods" than for Southern "consumption goods") and capital mobility to the model (in the form of South-to-North capital flight, as occurred in the 1980s), the basis for the Third World trade pessimism is even further enhanced.[7]

No country likes to think of itself as specializing in unskilled labor activities while letting foreigners reap the rewards of higher skills, technology, and capital. By pursuing the theoretical dictates of their endowments, however, less developed countries may lock themselves into a domestic economic structure that reinforces such relatively poor endowments and is inimical to their long-run development aspirations. Some countries, like the Four Asian Tigers (Taiwan, South Korea, Singapore, and Hong Kong), may succeed in transforming their economies through purposeful effort from unskilled-labor to skilled-labor to capital-intensive production. However, for the vast majority of poor nations, the possibilities of trade itself stimulating similar structural economic changes are much more remote.

Another interesting example of the new, postneoclassical genre of international trade models is contained in Michael E. Porter's *Competitive Advantage of Nations*.[8] Porter's fundamental departure from the standard, neoclassical factor endowment theory is to posit a *qualitative* difference between basic factors and advanced factors of production. He argues that standard trade theory applies only to basic factors like undeveloped physical resources and unskilled labor. For the advanced factors, which are more specialized and include highly trained workers with specific skills, and knowledge resources such as government and private research institutes, major universities, and leading industry associations, standard theory does not apply. Porter concludes that

> the central task facing developing countries is to escape from the straitjacket of factor-driven national advantage . . . where natural resources, cheap labor, locational factors and other basic factor advantages provide a fragile and often fleeting ability to export . . . [and are] vulnerable to exchange rate and factor cost swings. Many of these industries are also not growing, as the resource intensity of advanced economies falls and demand becomes more sophisticated. Creation of advanced factors is perhaps the first priority.[9]

Unemployment, Resource Underutilization, and the Vent-for-Surplus Theory of Trade

The assumption of full employment in traditional trade models, like that of the standard perfectly competitive equilibrium model of microeconomic theory, violates the reality of unemployment and underemployment in developing nations. Two conclusions could be drawn from the recognition of widespread unemployment in the Third World. The first is that underutilized human resources create the opportunity to expand productive capacity and GNP at little or no real cost by producing for export markets products that are not demanded locally. This is known as the **vent-for-surplus theory of international trade**. First formulated by Adam Smith, it has been expounded more recently in the context of developing nations by the Burmese economist Hla Myint.

According to this theory, the opening of world markets to remote agrarian societies creates opportunities not to reallocate fully employed resources as in the traditional models but rather to make use of formerly *underemployed* land and labor resources to produce greater output for export to foreign markets. The colonial system of plantation agriculture as well as the commercialization of small-scale subsistence agriculture were made possible, according to this view, by the availability of unemployed and underemployed human resources. In terms of our production possibility analyses, the vent-for-surplus argument can be represented by a shift in production from point V to point B in Figure 12.3, with trade enlarging final domestic consumption from V to C.

We see that before trade, the resources of this closed Third World economy were grossly underutilized. Production was occurring at point V, well within the confines of the production possibility frontier, and $0X$ primary products and $0Y$ manufactures were being produced and consumed. The opening up of the nation to foreign markets (probably as a result of colonization) provides the economic impetus to utilize these idle resources (mostly excess land and labor) and expand primary-product exportable production from $0X$ to $0X'$ at point B on the production frontier. Given the international price ratio $\bar{P}_a/\bar{P}_m$, $X'-X$ (equal to VB) primary products can now be exported in exchange for $Y-Y'$ (equal to VC) manufactures, with the result that the final consumption point, C, is attained with the same primary products (X) being consumed as before but with $Y'-Y$ more imported manufactures now available.

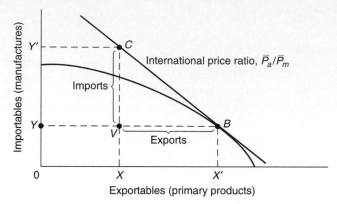

FIGURE 12.3 The Vent-for-Surplus Theory of Trade in LDCs.

The vent-for-surplus argument does provide a more realistic analytical scenario of the historical trading experience of many LDCs than either the classical or neo-classical model. However, in the short run, the beneficiaries of this process were often colonial and expatriate entrepreneurs rather than LDC nationals. And in the long run, the heavy structural orientation of the LDC economy toward primary-product exports in many cases created an export "enclave" situation and thus inhibited needed structural transformation in the direction of a more diversified and self-reliant economy.

The second conclusion that we may draw from the recognition of widespread unemployment in the Third World is that a major way to create substantial local job opportunities is to protect domestic industries (both manufacturing and agriculture) against low-cost foreign competition. This protection is accomplished through the erection of various trade barriers such as tariffs or quotas. We will discuss the pros and cons of commercial policy in Chapter 13; the point here is that LDCs that place priority on employment creation may wish to pursue a short-run protectionist policy in order to build up local rural and urban industries to absorb their surplus labor. This is what South Korea and Taiwan did in the 1960s.

International Factor Mobility and Multinational Corporations

The third component of the crucial first assumption of traditional trade theory—the international immobility of productive factors—is, after the assumption of perfect competition, the most unrealistic of all premises of classical and neoclassical trade theory. Capital and skilled labor have always moved between nations. The nineteenth-century growth experience of Western nations can largely be explained in terms of the impact of international capital movements. Perhaps the most significant development in international economic relations during the past two decades has been the spectacular rise in power and influence of the giant multinational corporations. These international carriers of capital, technology, and skilled labor, with their diverse productive operations throughout the Third World, greatly complicate the simple theory of international trade, especially as regards the distribution of its benefits. Companies like IBM, Ford, Exxon, Philips, Hitachi, British Petroleum, Renault, Volkswagen, and Coca-Cola have so internationalized their production process that calculations of the distribution of the benefits of international production between foreigners and nationals becomes exceedingly difficult. We return to this important issue in Chapter 15, where we examine the pros and cons of private foreign investment.[10] For the present, let us recognize that enormous international movements of capital and skills play a crucial role in international economic relations. To assume away their existence and their impact on the economies and economic structures of developing nations, as in the classical and factor endowment theories of trade, is to blind ourselves to the realities of the contemporary world economy. In fact, one of two ironies of the 1980s was that because of the phenomenon of capital flight, over $250 billion of capital fled the larger Third World countries and added to the stock of capital in the already capital-abundant developed nations! The second irony is that as a result of stagnating economies and limited financial opportunities, skilled labor (the resource most in demand in poor countries—recall Porter's advanced factors) has been moving in great numbers from the South to the North. As pointed out in earlier chapters, this brain drain has severely affected numerous African economies in the 1980s and 1990s.

Fixed, Freely Available Technology and Consumer Sovereignty

Just as capital resources are rapidly growing and being dispersed to maximize the returns of their owners throughout the world, so too is rapid technological change (mostly in the West) profoundly affecting world trading relationships. One of the most obvious examples of the impact of developed-country technological change on Third World export earnings is the development of synthetic substitutes for many traditional primary products. Over the past 35 years, **synthetic substitutes** for such diverse commodities as rubber, wool, cotton, sisal, jute, hides, and skins have been manufactured in increasing quantities. The Third World's market shares of these natural products in all cases has fallen steadily. For example, between 1950 and 1980, the share of the natural rubber in total world rubber consumption fell from 62% to 28%, and cotton's share of total fiber consumption dropped from 41% to 29%. Technological substitution, together with the low income and price elasticities of demand for primary products and the rise of agricultural protection in the markets of developed nations, goes a long way toward explaining why uncritical adherence to the theoretical dictates of comparative advantage can be a risky and often unrewarding venture for many LDCs.

On the other side of the ledger, however, is the argument that the worldwide availability of new technologies developed in the West has provided many newly industrializing countries the opportunity to capitalize on Western research and development expenditures. By first imitating products developed abroad but not on the frontiers of technological research, certain LDCs with sufficient human capital (e.g., the Asian NICs) can follow the **product cycle** of international trade. Using their relatively lower wages, they move from low-tech to high-tech production, filling manufacturing gaps left vacant by the more industrialized nations.

The assumption of fixed worldwide consumer tastes and preferences dictating production patterns to market-responsive atomistic producers is another fiction of trade theory. Not only are capital and production technologies disseminated throughout the world by means of the multinational corporations often aided and abetted by their home governments, but consumption technologies (consumer preferences and tastes) are often created and reinforced by the advertising campaigns of the powerful financial giants who dominate local markets. By creating demands for imported goods, market-dominating international enterprises can create the conditions for their own further aggrandizement. This is particularly significant in LDCs, where limited and imperfect information in both production and consumption creates a situation of highly incomplete markets. For example, it has been estimated that in many developing nations, more than 90% of all advertising is financed by foreign firms selling in the local market. As pointed out earlier, contemporary consumers are rarely sovereign about anything, let alone about what and how much major corporations are going to produce.

Internal Factor Mobility and Perfect Competition: The Structuralist Critique and the Phenomenon of Increasing Returns, Imperfect Competition, and Controlled Markets

The traditional theory of trade assumes that nations are readily able to adjust their economic structures to the changing dictates of world prices and markets. Movements along production possibility frontiers involving the reallocation of resources from one industry to another may be easy to make on paper, but according to structuralist arguments, such reallocations are extremely difficult to achieve in practice. This is especially true in developing nations, where production structures are often very rigid and factor movements are largely restricted. The most obvious example of this is plantation and small-farm commercial agriculture. In economies that have gradually become heavily dependent on a few primary-product exports, the whole economic and social infrastructure (roads, railways, communications, power locations, credit and marketing arrangements, etc.) may be geared to facilitate the movement of goods from production locations to shipping and storage depots for transfer to foreign markets. Over time, cumulative investments of capital may have been sunk into these economic and infrastructure facilities, and they cannot easily be transferred to Third World manufacturing activities located elsewhere. Thus the more dependent nations become on a few primary-product exports, the more inflexible their economic structures become, and the more vulnerable they are to the unpredictabilities of international markets. It may take many years to transform an underdeveloped economy from an almost exclusively primary-product, export-oriented reliance to a more diversified, multisector structure.

More generally, structuralists argue that all kinds of politically and institutionally generated structural rigidities, including product supply inelasticities, lack of intermediate products, fragmented money markets, limited foreign exchange, government licensing, import controls, poor transport and distribution facilities, and scarcities of managerial and skilled labor, often inhibit an LDC's ability to respond in the smooth and frictionless way of the neoclassical trade model to changing international price signals.[11]

Thus the internal processes of adjustment and resource reallocation necessary to capitalize on changing world economic conditions are much more difficult for the less diversified economies of the Third World to realize than for their rich counterparts in the Northern Hemisphere. And yet, curiously enough, the LDCs that can expand their capacities to produce low-cost, labor-intensive manufactured goods for export in industries such as textiles, shoes, sporting goods, handbags, processed foodstuffs, wigs, and rugs often find these exports blocked by tariff and nontariff barriers erected by developed countries to restrict the entry of such low-cost goods into their home markets. The World Bank has estimated that such trade restrictions cost the LDCs $75 billion annually—3% of their GNP. For textiles and clothing alone, phasing out the North's multifiber arrangement could increase the South's exports by $24 billion a year.[12] The reasons usually given by the North are that this low-cost foreign competition will create unemployment among the higher-cost domestic industries of the developed country and that the problems of internal economic adjustment are too serious to permit such unfettered foreign competition! Hence the internal **factor mobility** assumption turns out to have limited applicability—whether because of real or imagined rationales—in even the most diversified economies of the developed nations.

We need not dwell on the limitations of the perfectly competitive model here, as this issue was discussed earlier. Nevertheless, it is essential to point out two major limitations of the application of this model to the theory of international trade. First, by assuming either fixed or diminishing **returns to scale** (fixed or increasing production costs as output is expanded), the labor cost and factor endowment theories of trade neglect one of the most important phenomena in international economic relations. This is the pervasive and income-widening effect of increasing returns to scale and hence decreasing costs of production. Decreasing production costs mean simply that large existing firms are able to underprice smaller or new firms and thus exert monopolistic control over world markets. Far from being a rare exception, as the defenders of free trade would like to suggest, economies of scale are a pervasive factor in determining trade patterns—and not least in the area of agriculture, where huge agribusiness enterprises in developed countries are able to underprice the lower-productivity family farms of developing countries. Economies of large-scale production lead to monopolistic and oligopolistic control of world supply conditions (just as they do in domestic markets) for a wide range of products. Moreover, this process of market domination and control is largely irreversible—poor-country industries, once behind, simply cannot compete with giant corporations.

In addition, **monopolistic** and **oligopolistic market control** of internationally traded commodities along with widespread product differentiation, intraindustry trade, and external economies of production means that large individual corporations are able to manipulate world prices and supplies (and often demands as well) in their own private interest. Instead of competition, we find joint producer activities and oligopolistic bargaining among giant buyers and sellers as the most pervasive price- and quantity-determining force in the international economy.[13] But from the perspective of developing nations trying to diversify their economies and promote industrial exports in particular, the phenomenon of **increasing returns** and **product differentiation** (monopolistic competition) combined with the noneconomic power of large multinational corporations (their political influence with many governments) means that those who were first to industrialize (the rich nations) are able to take advantage of these economies of scale and differentiated products to perpetuate their dominant position in world markets. Recent theoretical attempts to take account of the important role of imperfect competition in international trade have led to a number of conclusions that contradict those of free-trade theory. For example, in static models, we can demonstrate how intraindustry trade in differentiated products can be abetted with selective tariff protection. In the more interesting North-South dynamic models with product differentiation and imperfect competition, these results suggest that in a free-trade environment, the capital-rich North gains a technological leadership that lasts forever, as do its net exports of manufactured differentiated products.[14]

The second major limitation of the perfectly competitive assumption of trade models is its exclusion of **risk** and **uncertainty** in international trading arrangements. Even if we were to accept all the unreal assumptions of the traditional trade model as applied to the LDCs, it may still not be in their long-run interest to invest heavily in primary-product export promotion given the historical instability of world markets for primary commodities in comparison to those for manufactured goods. As was already pointed out, concentration on one or two vital primary exports can play havoc with LDC development plans when foreign-exchange earnings are largely unpredictable from one year to the next. Hence following the dictates of static comparative advantage even in the unreal world of traditional trade theory may not be the best long-run development strategy.

The Absence of National Governments in Trading Relations

In domestic economies, the coexistence of rich and poor regions, of rapidly growing and stagnating industries, and of the persistent disproportionate regional distribution of the benefits of economic growth can all, at least in theory, be counteracted and ameliorated by the intervention of the state. Cumulative processes for inequality within nation-states by which **growth poles** may enrich themselves at the expense of the regions left behind can be modified by government legislation, taxes, transfer payments, subsidies, social services, regional development programs, and so forth. But since there is no effective international government to modify and counter the natural tendency of the rich nations to grow, often at the trading expense of the poor, the highly uneven gains from trade can easily become self-sustaining. This result is then reinforced by the uneven power of national governments to promote and protect the interests of their own countries. The spectacular export successes of Japan and, more recently, South Korea and Taiwan were in no small way aided and abetted by government planning and promotion of favored export industries.[15]

By focusing on the atomistic behavior of competitive firms in the context of different commodities being produced in anonymous countries, standard trade theory has ignored the crucial role governments play in international economic affairs.

They are not impartial bystanders. Rather, governments are often partisan players whose activist interventions in this area of **industrial policy** (guiding the market through strategic coordination of business investments to increase export market shares) are specifically designed to create a comparative advantage where none existed before but where world demand is likely to rise in the future. The history of industrial growth in Japan in the 1950s and 1960s with its famous Ministry of International Trade and Industry (MITI) and more recently in Taiwan and South Korea are outstanding examples of industrial policies. A classic statement explaining the mechanics of an activist industrial policy has been expressed by Japan's Vice-Minister Ojimi of the MITI as follows:

> The MITI decided to establish in Japan industries that require intensive employment of capital and technology, industries that in consideration of comparative cost of production should be the most inappropriate for Japan, industries such as steel, oil-refining, petro-chemicals, automobiles, aircraft, industrial machinery of all sorts, and electronics, including electronic computers. From a short-run, static viewpoint, encouragement of such industries would seem to conflict with economic rationalism. But from a long-range viewpoint, these are precisely the industries where income elasticity of demand is high, technological progress is rapid, and labor productivity rises fast.[16]

Governments also possess many instruments of commercial policy, such as **tariffs**, import **quotas**, and export **subsidies**, and can manipulate commodity prices and thus their trade position vis-à-vis the rest of the world. Moreover, when developed-nation governments pursue restrictive economic policies designed to deal with purely domestic issues like inflation or unemployment, these policies can have profound negative effects on the economies of poor nations.

The reverse, however, is not true. Third World domestic economic policies generally have little impact on the economies of rich nations. Moreover, governments of developed countries often join to promote their shared interests through coordinated trade and other economic ventures. Though these governments may not intend for such activities to promote their own welfare at the expense of that of poor countries, this is often the result.

Our point, therefore, is quite simple. Traditional trade theories neglect the crucial role that national governments can and do play in the international economic arena. Governments often serve to reinforce the unequal distribution of resources and **gains from trade** resulting from differences in size and economic power. Rich-country governments can influence world economic affairs by their domestic and international policies. They can resist countervailing economic pressures from weaker nations and can act in **collusion** and often in conjunction with their powerful multinational corporations to manipulate the terms and conditions of international trade to their own national interests. There is no superagency or world government to protect and promote the interests of the weaker parties (the LDCs) in such international affairs. Trade theory makes no mention of these powerful governmental forces. Its prescriptions are therefore greatly weakened by this neglect.

Balanced Trade and International Price Adjustments

The theory of international trade, like other perfectly competitive general-equilibrium models in economics, is not only a full-employment model but also one in which flexible domestic and international product and resource prices always adjust instantaneously to conditions of supply and demand. In particular, the terms of trade (international commodity price ratios) adjust to equate supply and demand for a country's exportable and importable products so that trade is always balanced; that is, the value of exports (quantity times price) is always equal to the value of imports. With **balanced trade** and no international capital movements, balance of payments problems never arise in the pure theory of trade. But the realities of the world economy in the 1980s, especially in the period following the rapid increase in international oil prices in the 1970s, were such that balance of payments deficits and the consequent depletion of foreign reserves (or the need to borrow foreign funds to cover commodity deficits) were a major cause of concern for all nations, rich and poor.

For the non-oil-producing poor nations in particular, a combination of declining terms of trade and sluggish international demands for their export products has meant chronic merchandise **trade deficits**. The gradual drying up of bilateral and multilateral foreign assistance and the growing concern of LDCs with the social costs of private foreign investment (see Chapter 15) have meant that severe balance of payments problems necessitate further departures from relatively free trade. In addition to coping with chronic balance of payments deficits and rising foreign-debt burdens in the 1980s, developing nations faced a new and even more serious economic threat in the early 1990s—a world recession and then slow growth accompanied by high U.S. interest rates, declining foreign investment, and persistent local inflation. All in all, gross imperfections in the international economy and the prevalence of non-market-determined commodity pricing systems make the automatic-adjustment mechanism of traditional trade theory appear rather farfetched.

Trade Gains Accruing to Nationals

The sixth and final major assumption of traditional trade theory, that trade gains accrue to nationals in the trading countries, is more implicit than the other five. It is rarely spelled out, nor need it be if we accept the assumption that factors are internationally immobile. But given the gross unreality of that assumption, we need to examine the implicit notion, rarely challenged, that if developing countries do benefit from trade, it is the people of these countries who reap the benefits. The issue thus revolves around the question of who owns the land, capital, and skills that are rewarded as a result of trade. Are they nationals or foreigners? If both, in what proportions are the gains distributed?

We know, for example, that in the **enclave economies** in the Third World, such as those with substantial foreign-owned mining and plantation operations, foreigners pay very low rents for the rights to use land, bring in their own foreign capital and skilled labor, hire local unskilled workers at subsistence wages, and have a minimal effect on the rest of the economy even though they may generate significant export revenues. Although mining and plantation enclaves are gradually disappearing in the Third World, they are often being replaced by "manu-facturing export enclaves" (e.g., personal computer assembly) as a result of the economic penetrations of multinational corporations. The distinction, therefore, between gross domestic product (GDP), which is a measure of the value of output generated within defined geographic boundaries, and gross national product (GNP), which measures the income actually earned by nationals of that country, becomes extremely important. To the extent that the export sector, or for that matter any sector of the economy, is foreign owned and operated, GDP will be that much higher than GNP, and few of the benefits of trade will actually accrue to LDC nationals. It is even possible for the value of exports to be greater than GNP—that is, foreign export earnings may exceed the total value of domestically accrued income.

Our point here is an important one. With the proliferation of multinational corporations and the international ownership of the means of production in a wide range of countries, aggregate statistics for LDC export earnings (and, indeed, GDP) may mask the fact that LDC nationals, especially those in lower income brackets, may not benefit at all from these exports. The major gains from trade may instead accrue to nonnationals, who often repatriate large proportions of these earnings. The inter- and intraindustry trade that is being carried out may look like trade between rich and poor nations. But in reality such trade is being conducted between rich nations and *other nationals of rich nations* operating in Third World countries! Until recently, the activities of most mining and plantation operations had this characteristic. More important, much of the recent export enclave manufacturing activities in poor countries may merely be masking the fact that a large proportion of the benefits are still being reaped by foreign enterprises. In short, LDC export performances can be deceptive unless we analyze the character and structure of export earnings by ascertaining who owns or controls the factors of production that are rewarded as a result of export expansion.

Some Conclusions on Trade and Economic Development: The Limits of Theory

We can now attempt to provide some preliminary general answers to the five questions posed at the beginning of the chapter. Again, we must stress that our conclusions are general and set in the context of the diversity of developing nations. Many will not be valid for specific nations at any given point in time. But on the whole these conclusions do appear to represent the consensus of current economic thinking, especially among Third World economists, on the relationship between trade and development, as the latter term has been defined throughout this book.

First, with regard to the rate, structure, and character of economic growth, our conclusion is that trade can be an important stimulus to rapid economic growth. This has been amply demonstrated by the successful experiences of countries like Malaysia, Thailand, Brazil, Chile, Taiwan, Singapore, and South Korea. Access to the markets of developed nations (an important factor for developing nations bent on export promotion) can provide an important stimulus for the greater utilization of idle human and capital resources. Expanded **foreign-exchange earnings** through improved export performance also provide the wherewithal by which LDCs can augment their scarce physical and financial resources. In short, where opportunities for profitable exchange arise, foreign trade can provide an important stimulus to aggregate economic growth along the lines suggested by the traditional theory.[17]

But as we have seen in earlier chapters, rapid growth of national output may have little impact on development. An export-oriented strategy of growth, particularly when a large proportion of export earnings accrue to foreigners, may not only bias the structure of the economy in the wrong directions (by not catering to the real needs of local people) but also reinforce the internal and external dualistic and inegalitarian character of that growth. Therefore, the fact that trade may promote expanded export earnings and even increase output levels does not mean that it is an unambiguously desirable strategy for economic and social development. It all depends on the nature of the export sector, the distribution of its benefits, and its linkages with the rest of the economy.

As for the distributional effects of trade, it is fair to claim that the principal benefits of world trade have accrued disproportionately to rich nations and, within poor nations, disproportionately to foreign residents and wealthy nationals. This should not be construed as an indictment of the inherent nature of trade. Rather, it reflects the highly inegalitarian institutional, social, and economic ordering of the global system, in which a few powerful nations and their multinational corporations control vast amounts of world resources. The conclusion of traditional trade theory that free trade will tend to equalize incomes is no more than a theoretical construct. Trade, like education, tends to reinforce existing inequalities. But it has the added defect of being conducted at the international level, where the absence of a supranational government eliminates the possibility, which at least exists in theory at the national level, of redistributing the gains or investing them to promote development in disadvantaged regions. Factors such as the widespread existence of increasing returns, the highly unequal international distribution of economic assets and power, the growing influence of large multinational corporations, the often blatant collusion among a few powerful governments and their giant corporations, and the combined ability of both government and business to manipulate international prices, levels of production, and patterns of demand—all these factors, assumed not to exist in the traditional theory of trade, are crucial. Together, they lead us to the general conclusion that many developing countries have in the past benefited disproportionately less from their economic dealings with developed nations and, in the long run, many may have in fact even suffered absolutely from this association.

It should be apparent by now that the answer to the third question—the question of the conditions under which trade can help LDCs achieve their development aspirations—is to be found largely in the ability of developing nations (probably as a group) to extract favorable trade concessions from the developed nations, especially in the form of the latter's elimination of barriers to LDC exports of labor-intensive manufactured goods. Here the recently concluded Uruguay Round of the General Agreement on Tariffs and Trade (GATT) negotiations lowering worldwide tariff barriers is a helpful start (see Chapter 13). Also, the extent to which LDC exports can efficiently utilize scarce capital resources while making maximum use of abundant but presently underutilized labor supplies will determine the degree to which export earnings benefit the ordinary citizen. Links between export earnings and other sectors of the economy are crucial. For example, small-farm agricultural export earnings will expand the demand for domestically produced simple household goods, whereas export earnings from capital-intensive manufacturing industries are more likely to find their way back to rich nations in payment for luxury imports. Finally, much will depend on how well LDCs can influence and control the activities of private foreign enterprises. These nations' ability to deal effectively with multinational corporations in guaranteeing a fair share of the benefits to local citizens is extremely important.

The answer to the fourth question—whether LDCs can determine how much they trade—can only be speculative. For most small and poor countries, the option of not trading at all, by closing their borders to the rest of the world, is not realistic. Not only do they lack the resources and market size to be self-sufficient, but their very survival, especially in the area of food production, often depends on their ability to secure foreign goods and resources. Some 32 of the least developed countries face annual threats of severe famine for which international assistance is not a choice but a necessity. Whether to trade or to remain in isolation is not the major issue that developing countries face in the 1990s. All countries trade. As Chichilnisky and Heal note, the real issue is

> whether or not to expand exports, and if so which exports to promote. The question is often the right balance between the domestic sectors and the international sectors of the economy. . . . The neoclassical theory of gains from trade provides little guidance on such policy questions.[18]

These and other issues of trade policy will be discussed in Chapter 13.

And even for the bulk of developing nations, the international economic system, however unequal and biased against their long-run development interests, still offers the only real source of scarce capital and needed technological knowledge. The conditions under which such resources are obtained will greatly influence the character of the development process. As we show in Chapter 13, the long-run benefits from trade among Third World countries themselves through the creation of **regional trading blocs** similar to the original Common Market or the European Union (EU) may offer better prospects for a balanced and diversified development strategy than the current almost exclusive reliance on the very unequal trading relations that they individually engage in with the developed nations. Finally, for the few countries rich in mineral resources and raw materials, especially those that have been able to establish an effective international bargaining stance against the large corporations that purchase their exports (e.g., the members of OPEC), trade has been and continues to be a vital source of development finance.

The fifth question—whether on balance it is best for Third World countries to look outward toward the rest of the world or more inward toward their own capacities for development—turns out not to be an either-or question at all. It is possible to favor both genuinely free world trade among individual countries and mutual cooperation among groups of LDCs in the form of greater **collective self-reliance**.[19] The argument goes like this: Trade in the past has not been "free" despite the elegant propositions of the neoclassical theory. While a few newly industrializing countries prospered under existing trade regimes, most benefited only a little and others were kept in a state of economic dependence. Given the existing imbalance in international power and wealth, pursuit of free-trade policies and a more equitable distribution of the benefits of trade will more than likely continue to be subverted by the wealthy nations to further their own private or national interests. Therefore, LDCs have to be very selective in their economic relations with the developed countries. They should expand exports where possible while guarding against entering into agreements and joint production ventures over which they are likely to relinquish control. While exploring profitable opportunities for trade with the rest of the world, developing countries should seek ways to expand their share of world trade and extend their economic ties with one another. For example, by pooling their resources, small countries can overcome the limits of their small individual markets and their serious resource constraints while retaining an important degree of autonomy in pursuing their individual development aspirations. Though it is impossible for most LDCs to be self-reliant individually, some form of trade and economic cooperation among equals is probably preferable to each country's attempting to go it alone in a world of unequal trade, technological dominance, and widespread market imperfection.

If interregional political rivalries can be transcended and the debt crisis resolved without too much further damage to fragile Third World economies (see Chapter 14), it seems clear that increased regional cooperation among developing nations at roughly equal stages of development offers one viable alternative to their present pursuit of separate and very unequal trade relationships with the rest of the world. Thus it may still be possible for LDCs to capture some of the real potential gains from specialization and trade (among themselves) while minimizing some of the development-inhibiting effects of a contemporary world economy and trading system dominated by a small group of rich nations and their powerful transnational corporations.

CASE STUDY

The Economy of South Korea

GEOGRAPHIC, SOCIAL, AND ECONOMIC
INDICATORS

Capital Seoul

Area 98,500 km²

Population 44.9 million (1995)

**Population (average annual growth
rate)** 1.0% (1985–1994)

GNP per capita U.S. $ 8,220 (1994)

**GNP per capita (average annual growth
rate)** 7.8% (1985–1994)

Agriculture as share of GDP 7% (1994)

Exports as share of GDP 28% (1994)

**Infant mortality rate (per 1,000 live
births)** 11 (1995)

Child malnutrition (underweight)
<1% (1992)

Females as share of labor force
34% (1994)

Illiteracy rate (age 15+) 4% (1990)

Human Development Index 0.86 (high)
(1992)

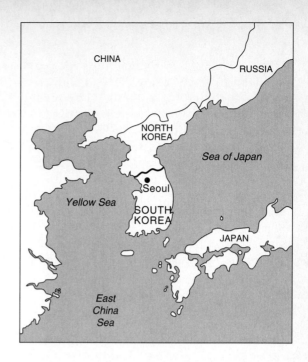

The Republic of Korea (South Korea) occupies the southern portion of a mountainous peninsula projecting southeast from China and separating the Sea of Japan from the Yellow Sea. South Korea's only land boundary is with North Korea, formed by the military demarcation line (MDL) marking the line of separation between the belligerent sides at the close of the Korean War. With nearly 45 million people, South Korea has one of the world's highest population densities—much higher, for example, than India or Japan—while the territorially larger North Korea has about 24 million people.

Over the past 30 years, South Korea's economic growth has been spectacular. The nation has advanced in a single generation from being one of the world's poorest countries to the threshold of full industrialization, despite the need to maintain one of the world's largest military establishments. Lacking natural resources, Korea's greatest asset is its industrious, literate people.

The division of the Korean peninsula in 1945 created two distorted economic units. North Korea inherited most of the mineral and hydroelectric resources and most of the existing heavy industrial base built by the Japanese during their lengthy occupation. South Korea was left with a large, unskilled labor pool and most of the peninsula's limited agricultural resources. Although both the North and South suffered from the widespread destruction caused by the 1950s Korean War, an influx of refugees added to the South's economic woes. For these reasons, South Korea began the postwar period with a per capita gross national product far below that of the North.

South Korea's meager mineral resources include tungsten, anthracite coal, iron ore, limestone, kaolinite, and graphite. There is no oil, and energy is a concern for the nation's economic planners. The country's ambitious program to build nuclear power plants is well under way with several plants in operation in 1994.

South Korea was self-sufficient in rice production in 1977, but rising demand and several disappointing harvests have since made it a net importer. Its economy is rapidly approaching full maturity—a marked change from the 1960s and 1970s, when it was a major recipient of U.S. foreign assistance (direct U.S. aid to South Korea ended in 1980).

The nation's successful industrial growth began in the early 1960s, when the government instituted sweeping economic reforms emphasizing exports and labor-intensive light industries. The government also carried out currency reform, strengthened financial institutions, and introduced flexible economic planning. South Korea's rapid and sustained development can be ascribed to a peculiar combination of social and economic factors: the high level of industriousness and literacy among the people, the introduction in the early 1960s of economic reforms (including land reform) aimed at expanding exports and labor-intensive industries, the gradual removal of import barriers, the extreme flexibility of economic management (always ready to react to signals and incentives coming from the economy), the close cooperation between government and private industry, and the autonomy of the banking system and the development of an efficient financial market.

From 1963 to 1978, real GNP rose at an annual rate of nearly 10%, with average real growth of more than 11% for the years 1973–1978. While South Korea's national production was rising throughout the 1960s and 1970s, the annual population growth rate declined to 1.7%, resulting in a 20-fold increase in per capita GNP in those two decades. Per capita GNP, which reached $100 for the first time in 1963, now exceeds $8,200, far above that of North Korea.

Internal economic distortions, the political and social unrest that followed the 1979 assassination of President Park, and the effect of world economic developments, such as the drastic increase in world oil prices in 1979, triggered a severe recession in South Korea in 1980. The economy recovered somewhat in the following two years, but it was not until the spring of 1983 and the strengthening of economic recovery in the United States that South Korean economic performance began to take on the buoyancy of earlier days. The nation's economic planners have shifted their emphasis from high to stable growth. After registering 5% real GNP growth in 1985, low by traditional standards, the South Korean economy rebounded impressively. The years 1986–1988 were widely viewed as the economy's most successful ever, as booming exports led once again to a double-digit annual growth rate of 15%. South Korea continued to manage its large external debt (about $42 billion in 1992) and had an annual rate of real per capita income growth, second only to Thailand, between 1985 and 1994 (7.8%). Long-term growth prospects remain extremely bright.

South Korea is now the tenth largest trading economy in the world. By many standards, it is no longer a developing country. In fact, in early 1996, its per capita income crossed the $8,356 barrier that separates "high-income" from "middle-income" countries in the World Bank classification system. Between 1965 and 1993, exports grew by more than 20% a year. Heavy investment in education, as well as high savings and capital accumulation, led to a phenomenal 11% annual increase in labor productivity in the 1960s and 1970s. Export growth has shifted from labor-intensive light industry (textiles and footwear) to skill-intensive, high-quality production (electronics, automobiles) as South Korea adapted foreign technologies to its low-wage but increasingly well educated labor force.

As a major new force in the international economy and one of the most economically powerful of the newly industrializing countries of the Third World, South Korea represents the most conspicuous example of suc-cessful long-term economic development. Its economic success has been so spectacular in fact that in 1995 it formally applied to join the Organization for Economic Cooperation and Development in Paris as a fully industrialized aid-giving developed country. However, to move beyond economic development to full social and political development in the twenty-first century, South Korea will have to deal effectively with growing internal politi-cal conflicts and widening popular demands for greater individual freedoms and democ-ratic participation.

Concepts for Review

Absolute advantage
Balanced trade
Barter transactions
Capital account
Collective self-reliance
Collusion
Commodity terms of trade
Comparative advantage
Current account
Enclave economies
Export dependence
Export earnings instability
Factor endowment trade theory
Factor mobility
Factor-price equalization
Foreign-exchange earnings
Free trade
Gains from trade
Growth poles
Income elasticity of demand
Income terms of trade
Increasing returns

Industrial policy
Merchandise trade balance
Monopolistic market control
North-South trade models
Oligopolistic market control
Prebisch-Singer thesis
Price elasticity of demand
Primary products
Product cycle
Product differentiation
Quotas
Regional trading blocs
Returns to scale
Risk
Specialization
Subsidies
Synthetic substitutes
Tariffs
Trade deficits
Uncertainty
Vent-for-surplus theory of
    international trade

Questions for Discussion

1. The effects of international trade on a country's development are often related to four basic economic concepts: efficiency, growth, equity, and stability. Briefly explain what is meant by each of these concepts as they relate to the theory of international trade.

2. Compare and contrast the classical labor cost theory of comparative advantage with the neoclassical factor endowment theory of international trade. Be sure to include an analysis of both assumptions and conclusions.

3. Briefly summarize the major conclusions of the traditional theory of free trade with regard to its theoretical effects on world and domestic efficiency, world and domestic economic growth, world and domestic income distribution, and the pattern of world production and consumption.

4. Proponents of free trade, primarily developed-country economists, argue that the liberalization of trading relationships between rich and poor countries (the removal of tariff and nontariff barriers) would work toward the long-run benefit of *all* countries. Under what conditions might the removal of all tariffs and other impediments to trade work to the best advantage of developing countries? Explain.

5. What factors—economic, political, or historical—do you think will determine whether or not a particular developing nation is more or less dependent on international exchange? Explain your answer, giving a few specific examples of different LDCs.

6. Explain some of the reasons why most non-oil-producing countries of the Third World seem to have benefited relatively less than the developed nations over the past 30 years from their participation in international trade.

7. Traditional free-trade theories are based on six crucial assumptions, which may or may not be valid for Third World nations (or for developed nations for that matter). What are these crucial assumptions, and how might they be violated in the real world of international trade?

8. Traditional free-trade theory is basically a *static* theory of international exchange leading to certain conclusions about the benefits likely to accrue to all participants. What *dynamic* elements in real-world economies will tend to negate the widespread distribution of the benefits of free trade? Explain this dynamic process.

9. Third World critics of international trade sometimes claim that present trading relationships between developed and underdeveloped countries can be a source of "antidevelopment" for the latter and merely serve to perpetuate their weak and dependent status. Explain their argument. Do you tend to agree or disagree? Explain why.

Notes

1. For data on relative income elasticities of demand for selected commodities in relation to manufactures, see World Bank, *1994 Global Economic Prospects and the Developing Countries* (Washington, D.C.: World Bank, 1994), tab. 2.5. A good discussion of primary-product export earnings instability can be found in chap. 2.

2. International Monetary Fund, *World Economic Outlook, October 1994* (Washington, D.C.: International Monetary Fund, 1994), p. 92. An alternative measure of the terms of trade is the **income terms of trade**, which measures the relative purchasing power of a country's exports. Some economists argue that this gives a better picture of the relationship between exports (and export earnings instability) and growth because it abstracts from relative price movements. For example, Matthias Lutz has found that there is a strong

negative relationship between income terms of trade volatility and economic growth rates, confirming earlier studies that found a negative relationship between volatility in commodity terms of trade and economic growth. See Matthias Lutz, "The effects of volatility in the terms of trade on output growth," *World Development* 22 (December 1994): 1959–1975.

3. See Raul Prebisch, *The Economic Development of Latin America and Its Principal Problems* (New York: United Nations, 1950), and Hans W. Singer, "The distribution of gains between borrowing and investing countries," *American Economic Review* 40 (May 1950): 473–485.

4. Recall that the slope of a line tangent to any point on the concave production possibility frontier will show the opportunity or real costs of reducing the output of one commodity in order to produce more of the other. In a world of perfect competition, these relative costs would also equal relative market prices. Therefore, the slope of the dotted line tangent to point *A* also shows relative commodity prices. The steeper the slope, the higher would be the price of *a* relative to *m*. As we move from left to right (e.g., from point *A* to point *B* in Figure 12.2a), the slope of the tangent line becomes progressively steeper, indicating increasing opportunity costs of producing more food. Similarly, a right-to-left movement along the production frontier (from *B* to *A*) would represent increasing opportunity costs of producing more manufactured goods in terms of forgone food output.

5. The classic article on **factor-price equalization** is Paul A. Samuelson, "International trade and equalization of factor prices," *Economic Journal* 48 (June 1948): 163–184.

6. Manmohan Singh, "Development policy research: The task ahead," *Proceedings of the World Bank Annual Conference on Development Economics, 1989* (Washington, D.C.: World Bank, 1990), p. 12. Singh was secretary general of the South Commission, Geneva, at the time of this address.

7. For some representative literature on North-South trade models, as well as other nontraditional theories, see Paul Krugman, "Trade, accumulation and uneven development," *Journal of Development Economics* 8 (April 1981): 149–161; Graciella Chichilnisky, "A general equilibrium theory of North-South trade," in Walter Heller et al. (eds.), *Essays in Honor of Kenneth J. Arrow* (New York: Cambridge University Press, 1986), chaps. 4 and 7; José Antonio Ocampo, "New developments in trade theory and LDCs," *Journal of Development Economics* 22 (June 1986): 129–170; and Amitova K. Dutt, "Monopoly power and uneven development: Baran revisited," *Journal of Development Studies* 24 (January 1988): 161–176.

8. Michael E. Porter, *The Competitive Advantage of Nations* (New York: Free Press, 1990). I am indebted to Professor Stephen C. Smith for this information.

9. *Ibid.*, pp. 675–680.

10. Mention should also be made of the recent enormous growth of speculative private-equity financial flows into and out of the "emerging" stock markets of developing countries, especially those of East Asia and Latin America (see Chapter 15).

11. See H. W. Arndt, "The origins of structuralism," *World Development* 13 (February 1985): 151–159.

12. United Nations Development Program, *Human Development Report, 1992* (New York: Oxford University Press, 1992), p. 6.

13. For a review of how imperfect competition pervades international trading relations, see Elhanan Helpman, "The noncompetitive theory of international trade and trade pol-

icy," *Proceedings of the World Bank Annual Conference on Development Economics, 1989* (Washington, D.C.: World Bank, 1990), pp. 193–216, and David Greenaway, "New trade theories and developing countries," in V. N. Balasubramanyan and Sanjaya Lall (eds.), *Current Issues in Development Economics* (London: Macmillan, 1992), pp. 159–169.

14. Helpman, "Noncompetitive theory," 196.

15. For an excellent analysis of the important role that governments played in the free-market export successes of the four Asian Tigers, see Stephen C. Smith, *Industrial Policy in Developing Countries: Reconsidering the Real Sources of Export-led Growth* (Washington, D.C.: Economic Policy Institute, 1991), and Robert Wade, *Governing the Market: Economic Theory and the Role of Government in East Asian Industrialization* (Princeton, N.J.: Princeton University Press, 1990).

16. Quoted in Ajit Singh, "Openness and the market-friendly approach to development: Learning the right lessons from the development experience," *World Development* 22 (December 1994): 1814.

17. For evidence that trade-oriented developing countries seem to have higher rates of aggregate economic growth (although in many cases it is difficult to isolate the true sources of that growth), see World Bank, *World Development Report, 1992* (New York: Oxford University Press, 1992), and Jagdish N. Bhagwati, "Export-promoting trade strategy: Issues and evidence," *World Bank Research Observer* 3 (January 1988): 27–57.

18. Graciella Chichilnisky and Geoffrey Heal, *The Evolving International Economy* (New York: Cambridge University Press, 1986), p. 44.

19. See, for example, the Santiago Declaration of Third World economists, April 1973, and the Communiqué of the Third World Forum, Karachi, 1975. A more recent presentation of a similar though less radical view can be found in United Nations, *Development and International Economic Cooperation: An Agenda for Development* (New York: United Nations, 1994).

Further Reading

For an explication of the traditional classical and neoclassical theories of free trade, see Peter Kenen, *International Economics*, 2nd ed. (Englewood Cliffs, N.J.: Prentice Hall, 1967); Gerald M. Meier, *The International Economics of Development: Theory and Policy* (New York: Harper & Row, 1968), chap. 2; and David Greenaway (ed.), *Economic Development and International Trade* (London: Macmillan, 1987).

A more comprehensive and slightly advanced survey of trade theory can be found in Jagdish N. Bhagwati, "The pure theory of international trade: A survey," *Economic Journal* 74 (March 1964): 1–84, and an excellent overall review and critique of alternative models of trade and development is provided by Sheila Smith and John Toye, "Three stories about trade and poor economies," *Journal of Development Studies* 15 (1979), and David Greenaway and Chris Milner, "Trade theory and the less developed countries," in Norman Gemmell (ed.), *Surveys in Development Economics* (Oxford: Blackwell, 1987), chap. 1.

For a critique of the traditional theory of trade as applied to underdeveloped nations, see Hla Myint, "The classical theory of international trade and the underdeveloped countries," *Economic Journal* 68 (1958): 317–337; H. Kitamura, "Capital accumulation and the theory of international trade," *Malayan Economic Review* 3 (March 1968); Gunnar Myrdal, *The Challenge of World Poverty* (New York: Pantheon, 1970), chap. 9; Hla Myint, "International trade and the developing countries," in Paul A. Samuelson (ed.), *International Economic Relations*

(London: Macmillan, 1969); Thomas Balogh, "Fact and fancy in international economic relations, part 1," *World Development* 1 (January 1973); special issue on trade and poor economies, *Journal of Development Studies* 15 (April 1979); James Riedel, *Trade as an Engine of Growth in Developing Countries: A Reappraisal*, World Bank Staff Working Papers No. 555 (Washington, D.C.: World Bank, 1983); John Toye, *Dilemmas of Development: Reflections on the Counter-revolution in Development Theory and Policy* (Oxford: Blackwell, 1987), pp. 82–89; and Graciella Chichilnisky and Geoffrey Heal, *The Evolving International Economy* (New York: Cambridge University Press, 1986).

Examples of the recent trend in trade theory to focus on noncompetitive markets and increasing returns include Elhanan Helpman, "The noncompetitive theory of international trade and trade policy," *Proceedings of the World Bank Annual Conference on Development Economics, 1989* (Washington, D.C.: World Bank, 1990), pp. 193–216; Paul Krugman and Elhanan Helpman, *Trade Policy and Market Structure* (Cambridge, Mass.: MIT Press, 1989); David Greenaway, "New trade theories and developing countries," in V. N. Balasubramanyam and S. Lall (eds.), *Current Issues in Development Economics* (London: Macmillan, 1992); and Gene M. Grossman and Elhanan Helpman, "Endogenous innovation in the theory of growth," *Journal of Economic Perspectives* 8 (Winter 1994): 23–44.

CHAPTER 13

The Trade Policy Debate: Export Promotion, Import Substitution, and Economic Integration

[The] nations of the West must recognize and understand to what extent current economic conditions impede our development and condemn us to backwardness. We cannot accept that the South pay for the disequilibrium of the North.

—Raul Alfonsin, President of Argentina, 1987

It is ironic that while national [LDC] markets are opening, global markets remain restricted. Where can developing nations sell their products unless global markets are also freed of protectionist restraints?

—William H. Draper III, United Nations
Development Program Administrator, 1992

The world has become a global financial village. . . . But the poorest 20% of the world's people have benefited little from the increased globalization of economies. In world trade their share is only 1%.

—United Nations, *Human Development Report, 1995*

In this chapter, we move from trade theory to trade policy issues by examining a wide range of LDC commercial policies, including import tariffs, physical quotas, export promotion versus import substitution, exchange-rate adjustments, international commodity agreements, and economic integration. Our objective is to ascertain the conditions under which these policies might help or harm developing countries in their dealings with the industrial world and with one another. We then summarize the various positions in the ongoing debate between the "trade optimists" (free traders) and "trade pessimists" (protectionists), between outward- and inward-looking strategies of development. Finally, we look at the trade policies of developed countries to see in what ways they directly and indirectly affect the economies of the Third World. In Chapters 14 and 15 we will turn to the financial aspects of LDC international exchange. Chapter 14 examines current balance of payments issues and the status of the Third World debt crisis. The growing importance of private foreign physical and portfolio investment and foreign public and private aid in financing economic development programs and projects is the subject of Chapter 15.

Trade Strategies for Development: Export Promotion versus Import Substitution

A convenient and instructive way to approach the complex issues of appropriate trade policies for development is to set these specific policies in the context of a broader LDC strategy of looking outward or looking inward.[1] In the words of Paul P. Streeten, **outward-looking development policies** "encourage not only free trade but also the free movement of capital, workers, enterprises and students . . . , the multinational enterprise, and an open system of communications."[2] By contrast, **inward-looking development policies** stress the need for LDCs to evolve their own styles of development and to control their own destiny. This means policies to encourage indigenous "learning by doing" in manufacturing and the development of indigenous technologies appropriate to a country's resource endowments. According to proponents of inward-looking trade policies, greater self-reliance can be accomplished only if "you restrict trade, the movement of people and communications, and if you keep out the multinational enterprise, with its wrong products and wrong want-stimulation and hence its wrong technology."[3]

Within these two broad philosophical approaches to development, a lively debate has been carried on in the development literature since the early 1950s. This is the debate between the free traders, who advocate outward-looking export promotion strategies of industrialization, and the protectionists, who are proponents of inward-looking import substitution strategies. The balance of the debate has swung back and forth, with the import substitutors predominating in the 1950s and 1960s and the export promoters gaining the upper hand in the late 1970s and, especially among Western and World Bank economists, in the 1980s and 1990s. Among many Third World economists and certain developed-country advocates of the "new" or "strategic" trade theories discussed in Chapter 12, however, the philosophical foundations of import substitution and collective self-reliance remained almost as strong in the 1990s as they were in prior decades.

Basically, the distinction between these two trade-related development strategies is that advocates of **import substitution** (IS) believe that LDCs should initially substitute domestic production of previously imported simple consumer goods (first-stage IS) and then substitute through domestic production for a wider range of more sophisticated manufactured items (second-stage IS)—all behind the protection of high tariffs and quotas on these imports. In the long run, IS advocates cite the benefits of greater domestic industrial diversification ("balanced growth") and the ultimate ability to export previously protected manufactured goods as economies of scale, low labor costs, and the positive externalities of learning by doing cause domestic prices to become more competitive with world prices.

By contrast, advocates of **export promotion** (EP) of both primary and manufactured goods cite the efficiency and growth benefits of free trade and competition, the importance of substituting large world markets for narrow domestic markets, the distorting price and cost effects of protection, and the tremendous successes of the East Asian export-oriented economies of South Korea, Taiwan, Singapore, and Hong Kong.

In practice, the distinction between IS and EP strategies is much less pronounced than many advocates would imply. Most LDCs have employed both strategies with different degrees of emphasis at one time or another. For example, in the 1950s and 1960s, the inward-looking industrialization strategies of the larger Latin American and Asian countries such as Chile, Peru, Argentina, India, Pakistan, the Philippines, and Bangladesh were heavily IS-oriented. By the end of the 1960s, some of the key sub-Saharan African countries like Nigeria, Ethiopia, Ghana, and Zambia began to pursue IS strategies, and some smaller Latin American and Asian countries also joined in.[4] However, since the mid-1970s, the EP strategy has been increasingly adopted by a growing number of countries. The early EP adherents—South Korea, Taiwan, Singapore, and Hong Kong—were thus joined by the likes of Brazil, Chile, Thailand, and Turkey, which switched from an earlier IS strategy. It must be stressed, however, that even the four most successful East Asian export promoters have pursued protectionist IS strategies sequentially and simultaneously in certain industries, so it is inaccurate to call them free traders, although they are definitely outward-oriented.[5]

Against this background, we can now examine the issue of outward-looking export promotion versus inward-looking import substitution in more detail by applying the following fourfold categorization:

1. Primary outward-looking policies (encouragement of agricultural and raw material exports)
2. Secondary outward-looking policies (promotion of manufactured exports)
3. Primary inward-looking policies (mainly agricultural self-sufficiency)
4. Secondary inward-looking policies (manufactured commodity self-sufficiency through import substitution)

Export Promotion: Looking Outward and Seeing Trade Barriers

The promotion of LDC primary or secondary exports has long been considered a major ingredient in any viable long-run development strategy. The colonial territories of Africa and Asia, with their foreign-owned mines and plantations, were classic examples of primary outward-looking regions. It was partly in reaction to this enclave economic structure and partly as a consequence of the industrialization bias of the 1950s and 1960s that newly independent states, as well as older LDCs, put great emphasis on the production of manufactured goods initially for the home market (secondary inward) and then for export (secondary outward). Let us therefore look briefly at the scope and limitations of LDC export expansion, first with respect to primary products and then with respect to manufactured exports.

Primary-Commodity Export Expansion: Limited Demand, Shrinking Markets

As we discovered in Chapter 12, the Third World still relies on primary products for over 70% of its export earnings. With the notable exception of petroleum exports and a few needed minerals, primary-product exports have grown more slowly than total world trade. Moreover, the LDC share of these exports has been falling over the past few decades. Because food, nonfood agricultural products, and raw materials make up almost 40% of all LDC exports and, for the vast majority of Third World nations, constitute their principal source of foreign-exchange earnings (see Table 12.3), we need to examine the factors affecting the demand for and supply of primary-product exports.

On the demand side, there appear to be at least five factors working against the rapid expansion of Third World primary-product and especially agricultural exports to the developed nations (their major markets). First, the income elasticities of demand for agricultural foodstuffs and raw materials are relatively low compared with those for fuels, certain minerals, and manufactures. For example, the income elasticities of demand for sugar, cacao, tea, coffee, and bananas have all been estimated at less than 1, with most in the range of 0.3–0.5.[6] This not only contributes to problems of export earnings instability but also means that only a sustained high rate of per capita income growth in the developed countries can lead to even modest export expansion of these particular commodities from the LDCs. Such high growth rates prevailed in the 1960s but have not been matched since. Second, developed-country population growth rates are now at or near the replacement level, so little expansion can be expected from this source. Third, the price elasticity of demand for most nonfuel primary commodities is relatively low. When relative agricultural prices are falling, as they have been during most of the past three decades, such low elasticities mean less total revenue for exporting nations. For example, between June 1980 and June 1982, the price of sugar fell by 78%, rubber by 37%, and copper by 35%. Between 1989 and 1991, commodity prices fell by about 20%. Tin prices were so low that smelting was no longer profitable, and the real prices of coffee and tea were lower than at any time since 1950. Figure 13.1 shows that with the exception of the mid-1970s, non-oil real commodity prices fell by almost 50% between 1957 and 1995. Such a decline, especially in the 1980s and early 1990s when prices fell by over 40%, has hurt the least developed countries the most.

A device that is widely used to attempt to modify the tendency for primary-product prices to decline relative to other traded goods is that of establishing **international commodity agreements**. Such agreements are intended to set overall output levels, to stabilize world prices, and to assign quota shares to various producing nations for such items as coffee, tea, copper, lead, and sugar. To work effectively, they require cooperation and compromise among participants. Commodity agreements can also provide greater protection to individual exporting nations against excessive competition and the overexpansion of world production. Such overexpansion of supply tends to drive down prices and curtail the growth of earnings for all countries. In short, commodity agreements attempt to guarantee participating nations a relatively fixed share of world export earnings and a more stable world

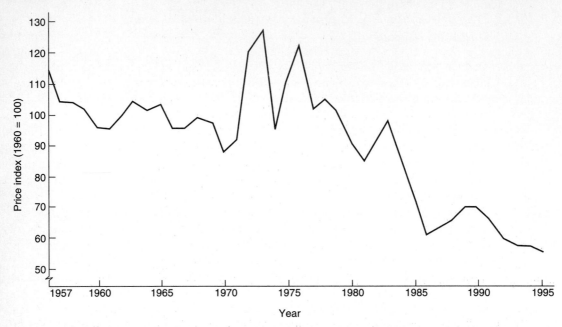

FIGURE 13.1 Real Non-oil Commodity Prices, 1957–1995. *Source*: International Monetary Fund, *World Economic Outlook, 1987* and *1995* (Washington, D.C.: International Monetary Fund, 1987, 1995).

price for their commodity. It is for this reason that at its fourth world conference, held in Nairobi, Kenya, in May 1976, the United Nations Conference on Trade and Development (UNCTAD) advocated the establishment of an $11 billion common fund to finance "buffer stocks" to support the prices of some 19 primary commodities (including sugar, coffee, tea, bauxite, jute, cotton, tin, and vegetable oil) produced by various Third World nations. Unfortunately for LDC exporters, there has been little progress on the UNCTAD proposal, and most existing non-oil commodity agreements have either failed (tin) or been largely ignored by producers (coffee and sugar).

The fourth and fifth factors working against the long-run expansion of LDC primary-product export earnings—the development of synthetic substitutes and the growth of agricultural protection in the developed countries—are perhaps the most important. **Synthetic substitutes** for commodities like cotton, rubber, sisal, jute, hide, skins, and recently even copper (with glass fibers for communication networks) act both as a brake against higher commodity prices and as a direct source of competition in world export markets. As we saw in Chapter 12, the synthetic share of world market export earnings has steadily risen over time while the share of natural products has fallen. In the case of agricultural protection, which usually takes the form of tariffs, quotas, and nontariff barriers such as sanitary laws regulating food and fiber imports, the effects can be devastating to Third World export earnings. The common agricultural policy of the European Union, for example, is much more discriminatory against LDC food exports than the policies that had formerly prevailed in the individual member nations.

On the supply side, a number of factors also work against the rapid expansion of primary-product export earnings. The most important is the structural rigidity of many Third World rural production systems. We discussed rigidities—such as limited resources; poor climate; bad soils; antiquated rural institutional, social, and economic structures; and nonproductive patterns of land tenure—in Chapter 9. Whatever the international demand situation for particular commodities (and these will certainly differ from commodity to commodity), little export expansion can be expected when rural economic and social structures militate against positive supply responses from peasant farmers who are averse to risk. Furthermore, in developing nations with markedly dualistic farming structures (i.e., large corporate capital-intensive farms existing side by side with thousands of fragmented, low-productivity peasant holdings), any growth in export earnings is likely to be distributed very unevenly among the rural population. Small farmers are further disadvantaged in countries (mostly in Africa) in which agricultural marketing boards act as middlemen between the farmers and export markets. Marketing boards often constrain export expansion by forcing cultivators to sell their goods at a fixed price—usually well below world market prices. They thereby remove the incentive to increase output. Finally, we should mention here the pernicious effects of developed-country trade policies (such as the United States' sugar quota) and foreign aid policies that depress agricultural prices in LDCs and discourage production. For example, the European Union's policy of selling subsidized beef to the nations of West Africa in the guise of foreign assistance has devastated cattle prices in those countries.[7]

We may conclude, therefore, that the successful promotion of primary-product exports cannot occur unless there is a reorganization of rural social and economic structures along the lines suggested in Chapter 9 to raise total agricultural productivity and distribute the benefits more widely. The primary objective of any Third World rural development strategy must be to provide sufficient food to feed the indigenous people *first* and only then be concerned about export expansion. But having accomplished this most difficult internal development task, LDCs may be able to realize the potential benefits of their comparative advantage in world primary commodity markets only if they can (1) cooperate with one another, (2) be assisted by developed nations in formulating and carrying out workable international commodity agreements, and (3) secure greater access to developed-country markets. Unfortunately, given the structure of world demands for primary products, the threat of local food shortages and thus the desire for agricultural self-sufficiency, the inevitability of the development of further synthetic substitutes, and the unlikelihood of significantly lower levels of agricultural protection among developed nations, the real scope for primary-product export expansion in individual LDCs seems limited.[8]

Expanding Exports of Manufactured Goods: Some Successes, Many Barriers

The expansion of Third World manufactured exports has been given great stimulus by the spectacular export performances of countries like South Korea, Singapore, Hong Kong, Taiwan, Mexico, and Brazil over the past three decades (see

Table 12.2).[9] For example, Taiwan's total exports grew at an annual rate of over 20%, and exports from South Korea grew even faster. In both cases, this export growth was led by manufactured goods, which contributed over 80% of both nations' foreign-exchange earnings. For the Third World as a whole, manufactured exports grew from 6% of total merchandise exports in 1950 to almost 45% by 1990 (recall, however, from Table 12.2 that in 1990 South Korea, Taiwan, Singapore, and Hong Kong accounted for 82.8% of these exports). Despite this growth, the LDC share of total world trade in manufactures has remained relatively small, even though it did grow from 7% in 1965 to 18% in 1990.

The export successes of recent decades, especially among the four Asian Tigers, have provided the primary impetus for arguments by neoclassical counterrevolutionaries (see Chapter 3)—particularly those at the World Bank and the IMF—that LDC economic growth is best served by allowing market forces, free enterprise, and open economies to prevail while minimizing government intervention. Unfortunately, the reality of the East Asian cases does not support this view of how their export success was achieved. In South Korea, Taiwan, and Singapore (as in Japan earlier), the production and composition of exports was not left to the market but resulted as much from carefully planned intervention by the government.[10]

The demand problems for LDC export expansion of manufactured goods, though different in basic economic content from those for primary products, are nonetheless similar. Although income and price elasticities of international demand for manufactured goods in the aggregate are higher than for primary commodities, they afford little relief to many developing nations bent on expanding their exports. This is largely because of the growing protection in developed nations against the manufactured exports of LDCs—which is in part the direct result of the successful penetration of low-cost labor-intensive manufactures from countries like Taiwan, Hong Kong, and South Korea during the 1960s and 1970s. The Canadian economist Gerald K. Helleiner makes the point well:

> Of fundamental importance to the issue of Third World manufacturing export prospects are the barriers which are erected by the developed countries to restrict entry of these products to their own markets. Tariffs, quotas and other barriers in the markets of the rich constitute a major impediment to large-scale industrial exports. The tariff structures of the rich nations are such as to offer the greatest degree of effective protection to their producers in the very industries in which poor countries are most likely to be competitive—light industries relatively intensive in the use of unskilled labour such as textiles, footwear, rugs, sporting goods, handbags, processed foodstuffs, etc. This is precisely because of these industries' inability freely to compete, unskilled labour-intensity putting them at a comparative disadvantage within the context of their relatively high wage economies.[11]

Industrial-nation trade barriers are pervasive. During the 1980s, for example, 20 of the 24 industrial countries *increased* their protection against LDC manufactured or processed products. Moreover, their rates of protection are considerably higher against LDC exports than against those of other industrial nations. Making matters worse, MDC protection often increases with the level of processing (e.g., the tariff on processed cacao, or cocoa, is twice that of raw cacao, so chocolate imports are discouraged; raw sugar faces tariffs below 2% while processed sugar products are blocked by 20% tariffs). Then there are the nontariff barriers, which now form the main protection against Third World manufactured exports, affecting at least one-third of them. The most significant is the **Multi-Fiber Arrangement (MFA)**, a complex system of mostly bilateral quotas against LDC exports of cotton, wool, and synthetic fiber products. The United Nations Development Program estimates that the MFA costs the Third World $24 billion a year in lost textile and clothing export earnings. All in all, trade restrictions by developed countries cost LDCs at least $40 billion a year in foreign exports and lowers their GNP by more than 3%.[12] If these barriers could be dropped—for example, if the recently concluded Uruguay Round of multilateral GATT negotiations can actually be implemented—developing-country manufactured exports could grow by $30 to $40 billion annually. Whether displaced high-wage workers in developed-country manufactures will permit the unimpeded entry of low-wage LDC products remains to be seen.[13]

As in the case of agricultural and other primary production, the uncertain export outlook should be no cause for curtailing the needed expansion of manufacturing production to serve local LDC markets. There is great scope for mutually beneficial trade in manufactures among developing countries themselves within the context of the gradual economic integration of their national economies. Too much emphasis has been placed on the analysis of trade prospects of individual LDCs with the developed nations (North-South trade) and not enough on the prospects for mutually beneficial trade with one another (South-South trade).

Import Substitution: Looking Inward but Still Paying Outward

During the 1950s and 1960s, developing countries experienced a decline in world markets for their primary products and growing balance of payments deficits on their current accounts. Given a general belief in the magic of industrialization as well as the terms of trade arguments of the Prebisch-Singer hypothesis, they turned to an import substitution strategy of urban industrial development.

Some countries still follow this strategy for both economic and political reasons, although pressure from the IMF and the World Bank lay heavy opportunity costs on such endeavors. As we noted earlier, import substitution entails an attempt to replace commodities that are being imported, usually manufactured consumer goods, with domestic sources of production and supply. The typical strategy is first to erect tariff barriers or quotas on certain imported commodities, then to try to set up a local industry to produce these goods—items such as radios, bicycles, or household electrical appliances. Typically, this involves joint ventures with foreign companies, which are encouraged to set up their plants behind the wall of tariff protection and given all kinds of tax and investment incentives. Although initial costs of production may be higher than former import prices, the economic rationale put forward for the establishment of import-substituting manufacturing operations is either that the industry will eventually be able to reap the benefits of large-scale production and lower costs (the so-called **infant industry** argument for tariff protection) or that the balance of payments will be improved as fewer consumer goods are imported. Often a combination of both arguments is advanced. Eventually, it is hoped, the infant industry will grow up and be able to complete in world markets. It will then be able to generate net foreign-exchange earnings once it has lowered its average costs of production. Let us see how the theory of protection can be used to demonstrate this process.

Tariffs, Infant Industries, and the Theory of Protection

A principal mechanism of the import substitution strategy is the erection of protective **tariffs** (taxes on imports) or **quotas** (limits on the quantity of imports) behind which IS industries are permitted to operate. The basic economic rationale for such protection is the infant industry argument mentioned earlier. Tariff protection against the imported commodity is needed, so the argument goes, in order to allow the now higher-priced domestic producers enough time to learn the business and to achieve the economies of scale in production and the external economies of learning by doing that are necessary to lower unit costs and prices. With enough time and sufficient protection, the infant will eventually grow up, be directly competitive with developed-country producers, and no longer need this protection. Ultimately, as in the case of many formerly protected IS industries in South Korea and Taiwan, domestic LDC producers will be able to produce not only for the domestic market without a tariff wall or government subsidies but also to export their now lower-cost manufactured goods to the rest of the world. Thus for many Third World industries, in theory, an IS strategy becomes the prerequisite for an EP strategy. It is for this reason, among others (including the desire to reduce dependence and attain greater self-reliance, the need to build a domestic industrial base, and the ease of raising substantial tax revenue from tariff collections),[14] that import substitution appealed to so many LDC governments.

The basic theory of protection is an old and controversial issue in the field of international trade. It is relatively simple to demonstrate. Consider Figure 13.2. The top portion of the figure shows standard domestic supply and demand curves for the industry in question (say, shoes) if there were no international trade—that is, in a closed economy. The equilibrium home price and quantity would be P_1 and Q_1. If this LDC then were to open its economy to world trade, its small size in relation to the world market would mean that it would face a horizontal, perfectly elastic demand curve. In other words, it could sell (or buy) all it wanted at a lower world price, P_2. Domestic consumers would benefit from the lower price of imports and the resultant greater quantity purchased, while domestic producers and their employees would clearly suffer as they lose business to lower-cost foreign suppliers. Thus at the lower world price, P_2, quantity demanded rises from Q_1 to Q_3, whereas the quantity supplied by domestic producers falls from Q_1 to Q_2. The difference between what domestic producers are willing to supply at the lower P_2 world price (Q_2) and what consumers want to buy (Q_3) is the amount that will be imported—shown as line *ab* in Figure 13.2.

Facing the potential loss of domestic production and jobs as a result of free trade and desiring to obtain infant industry protection, local LDC producers will seek tariff relief from the government. The effects of a tariff (equal to t_0) are shown in

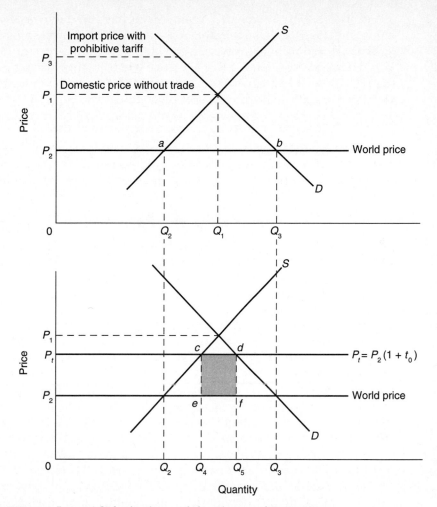

FIGURE 13.2 Import Substitution and the Theory of Protection.

the lower half of Figure 13.2. The tariff causes the domestic price of shoes to rise from P_2 to P_t—that is, $P_t = P_2 (1 + t_0)$. Local consumers now have to pay the higher price and will reduce their quantity demanded from Q_3 to Q_5. Domestic producers can now expand production (and employment) up to quantity Q_4 from Q_2. The rectangular area *cdfe* measures the amount of the tariff revenue collected by the government on imported shoes.

Clearly, the higher the tariff, the closer to the domestic price will be the sum of the world price plus the import tax. In the classic infant-industry IS scenario, the tariff may be so high that it raises the price of the imported produce above P_1 to, say, P_3 in the upper diagram of Figure 13.2, so that imports are effectively prohibited and the local industry is allowed to operate behind a fully protective tariff wall, once again selling Q_1 output at P_1 price. In the short run, it is clear that the impact of such a prohibitive tariff is to penalize consumers, who are in effect subsidizing domestic producers and their employees through higher prices and lower consumption. Alternatively, we can say that a tariff redistributes income from consumers to producers. However, in the longer run, advocates of IS protection for LDC infant industries argue that everyone will benefit as domestic and other shoe manufacturers reap the benefits of economies of scale and learning by doing so that ultimately the domestic price falls below P_2 (the world price). Production will then occur for *both* the domestic and the world market, domestic consumers as well as domestic producers and their employees will benefit, protective tariffs can be removed, and the government will be able to replace any lost tariff revenue with taxes on the now very much higher incomes of domestic manufactures. It all sounds logical and persuasive in theory. But how has it performed in practice?

The IS Industrialization Strategy and Results

Most observers agree that the import-substituting strategy of industrialization has been largely unsuccessful.[15] Specifically, there have been five undesirable outcomes. First, secure behind protective tariff walls and immune from competitive pressures, many IS industries (both publicly and privately owned) remain inefficient and costly to operate. Second, the main beneficiaries of the import substitution process have been the foreign firms that were able to locate behind tariff walls and take advantage of liberal tax and investment incentives. After deducting interest, profits, and royalty and management fees, most of which are remitted abroad, the little that may be left over usually accrues to the wealthy local industrialists with whom foreign manufacturers cooperate and who provide their political and economic cover.

Third, most import substitution has been made possible by the heavy and often government-subsidized importation of capital goods and intermediate products by foreign and domestic companies. In the case of foreign companies, much of this is purchased from parent and sister companies abroad. There are two immediate results. First, capital-intensive industries are set up, usually catering to the consumption habits of the rich while having a minimal employment effect. Second, far from improving the LDCs' balance of payments situation and alleviating the debt problem, indiscriminate import substitution often worsens the situation by increasing a need for imported capital-good inputs and intermediate products while, as we have just seen, a good part of the profits is remitted abroad in the form of private transfer payments.

A fourth detrimental effect of many import substitution strategies has been their impact on traditional primary-product exports. To encourage local manufacturing through the importation of cheap capital and intermediate goods, **exchange rates** (the rate at which the central bank of a nation is prepared to purchase foreign currencies) are often artificially overvalued. This has the effect of raising the price of exports and lowering the price of imports in terms of the local currency. For example, if the free-market exchange rate between Pakistani rupees and U.S. dollars was 20 to 1 but the official exchange rate was 10 to 1, an item that cost $10 in the United States could be imported into Pakistan for 100 rupees (excluding transport costs and other service charges). If the **free-market exchange rate** (the exchange rate determined by the supply and demand for Pakistani rupees in terms of dollars) prevailed, that item would cost 200 rupees. Thus by means of an **overvalued exchange rate**, LDC governments are able effectively to lower the domestic currency price of their imports. At the same time, their export prices are increased— for example, at an exchange rate of 10 to 1, U.S. importers would have to pay 10 cents for every 1-rupee item rather than the 5 cents they would pay if the hypothetical free-market ratio of 20 to 1 were in effect. Table 13.1 provides rough estimates of the extent of currency overvaluation in nine developing countries during the 1980s.

The net effect of overvaluing exchange rates in the context of import substitution policies is to encourage capital-intensive production methods still further (because the price of imported capital goods is artificially lowered) and to penalize the traditional primary-product export sector by artificially raising the price of exports in terms of foreign currencies. This overvaluation, then, causes local farmers to be less competitive in world markets. In terms of its income distribution effects, the outcome of such government policies may be to penalize the small farmer and the self-employed while improving the profits of the owners of capital, both foreign and domestic. Industrial protection thus has the effect of taxing agricultural goods in the home market as well as discouraging agricultural exports. Import substitution policies have in practice often worsened the local distribution of income by favoring the urban sector and higher-income groups while discriminating against the rural sector and lower-income groups.

TABLE 13.1 Degree of Currency Overvaluation in Selected LDCs, 1980–1989 (median values of annual end-of-year premiums)

Country	Overvaluation Premium, 1980–1989[a]	Largest Overvaluation Premium during the Period
Low premium		
Indonesia	3.4	15.5
Mexico	17.7	66.0
Venezuela	75.2	213.0
Moderate premium		
Kenya	15.2	44.9
Brazil	43.1	173.0
Bolivia	17.6	293.1
High premium		
Peru	27.0	278.9
Tanzania	214.3	809.1
Ghana	142.0	4,263.7

SOURCE: Data from Miguel Kiguel and Stephen A. O'Connell, "Parallel exchange rates in developing countries," *World Bank Research Observer* 10 (February 1995): 23.
[a]The overvaluation premium is the difference between the official exchange rate (E) and the free-market exchange rate (F) and is measured as $(F - E)/E \times 100$.

Fifth, and finally, import substitution, which may have been conceived with the idea of stimulating infant industry growth and self-sustained industrialization by creating "forward" and "backward" linkages with the rest of the economy, has often inhibited that industrialization. Many infants never grow up, content to hide behind protective tariffs, and governments loath to force them to be more competitive by lowering tariffs. In fact, LDC governments themselves often operate protected industries as state-owned enterprises. Moreover, by increasing the costs of inputs to potentially forward-linked industries (those that purchase the output of the protected firm as inputs or intermediate products in their own productive process, such as a printer's purchase of paper from a locally protected paper mill) and by purchasing their own inputs from overseas sources of supply rather than through backward linkages to domestic suppliers, inefficient import-substituting firms may in fact block the hoped-for process of self-reliant integrated industrialization.

A consideration of patterns of import substitution leads to conclusions such as those of Gerald Helleiner, whose views seem to reflect a consensus among development economists:

> It is difficult to find any rationale for the pattern of import substituting industrialization which has, whether consciously or not, actually been promoted. It has given undue emphasis to consumer goods in most countries; it has given insufficient attention to potential long-run comparative advantages, i.e., resource endowments and learning possibilities; and it has employed alien and unsuitable, i.e., capital-intensive, technologies to an extraordinary and unnecessary degree. If a selective approach to import substitution is to be pursued at all, and there is a strong case to be made for a more generalized approach, the selection actually employed in recent years has left a great deal to be desired. The consequence has too frequently been the creation of an inefficient industrial sector operating far below capacity, and creating very little employment, very little foreign exchange saving, and little prospect of further productivity growth. The object of policy must now be gradually to bring incentive structures and thus the relative efficiencies of various industrial activities into some sort of balance, thereby encouraging domestic manufacture of intermediate and capital goods at the expense of importable consumer goods and the development eventually of manufacture for export.[16]

Tariff Structures and Effective Protection

Because import substitution programs are based on the protection of local industries against competing imports primarily through the use of tariffs and physical quotas, we need to analyze the role and limitations of these commercial policy instruments in developing nations. As we have already discussed, governments impose tariffs and physical quotas on imports for a variety of reasons. For example, tariff barriers may be erected to raise public revenue. In fact, given the administrative and political difficulties of collecting local income taxes, fixed-percentage taxes on imports collected at a relatively few ports or border posts often constitute one of the cheapest and most efficient ways to raise government revenue. In many

LDCs, these foreign trade taxes are thus a central feature of the overall fiscal system (see note 14). Physical quotas on imports like automobiles and other luxury consumer goods, though more difficult to administer and more subject to delay, inefficiency, and rent-seeking corruption (e.g., with regard to the granting of import licenses), provide an effective means of restricting the entry of particularly troublesome commodities. Tariffs, too, may serve to restrict the importation of nonnecessity products (usually expensive consumer goods). By restricting imports, both quotas and tariffs can improve the balance of payments. And like overvaluing the official rate of foreign exchange, tariffs may be used to improve a nation's terms of trade. However, in a small country unable to influence world prices of its exports or imports (in other words, most LDCs), this argument for tariffs (or devaluation) has little validity. Finally, as we have just seen, tariffs may form an integral component of an import substitution policy of industrialization.

Whatever the means used to restrict imports, such restriction always protects domestic firms from competition with producers from other countries. To measure the degree of protection, we need to ask by how much these restrictions cause the domestic prices of imports to exceed what their prices would be if there were no protection. There are two basic measures of protection: the nominal rate and the effective rate.

The **nominal rate of protection** shows the extent, in percentages, to which the domestic price of imported goods exceeds what their price would be in the absence of protection. Thus the nominal (ad valorem) tariff rate (t) refers to the final prices of commodities and can be defined simply as

$$t = \frac{p' - p}{p} \tag{13.1}$$

where p' and p are the unit prices of industry's output with and without tariffs, respectively.

For example, if the domestic price (p') of an imported automobile is \$5,000 whereas the CIF (cost plus insurance and freight) price (p) when the automobile arrives at the port of entry is \$4,000, the nominal rate of tariff protection (t) would be 25%. This is the kind of tariff depicted as t_0 in Figure 13.2.

By contrast, the **effective rate of protection** shows the percentage by which the **value added** at a particular stage of processing in a domestic industry can exceed what it would be without protection. In other words, it shows by what percentage the sum of wages, interest, profits, and depreciation allowances payable by local firms can, as a result of protection, exceed what this sum would be if these same firms had to face unrestricted competition (no tariff protection) from foreign producers.[17] The effective rate (g) can therefore be defined as the difference between value added (percent of output) in domestic prices and value added in world prices, expressed as a percentage of the latter, so that

$$g = \frac{v' - v}{v} \tag{13.2}$$

where v' and v are the value added per unit of output with and without protection, respectively. The result can be either positive or negative, depending on whether v' is greater or less than v. For most LDCs, it is highly positive (a negative g would imply that domestic production is so inefficient that it is destroying value!). Table 13.2 provides some estimates of effective protection in selected Third World countries. In general, IS countries like Pakistan and Uruguay by definition have much higher rates of protection than EP countries like South Korea and Singapore.

The important difference between nominal and effective rates of protection can be illustrated by means of an example.[18] Consider a nation without tariffs in which automobiles are produced and sold at the international or world price of $10,000. The value added by labor in the final assembly process is assumed to be $2,000, and the total value of the remaining inputs is $8,000. Assume for simplicity that the prices of these nonlabor inputs are equal to their world prices. Suppose that a nominal tariff of 10% is now imposed on imported automobiles, which raises the domestic price of cars to $11,000 but leaves the prices of all the other importable intermediate units unchanged. The domestic process of automobile production can now spend $3,000 per unit of output on labor inputs, as contrasted with $2,000 per unit before the tariff. The theory of effective protection therefore implies that under these conditions, the nominal tariff of 10% on the final product (automobiles) has resulted in an effective rate of protection of 50% for the local assembly process in terms of its value added per unit of output. It follows that for any given nominal tariff rate, the effective rate is greater the smaller the value added of the process; that is, $g = t/1 - a$ where t is the nominal rate on final product and a is the proportionate value of the importable inputs in a free market where these inputs are assumed to enter the country duty-free.

Most economists argue that the effective rate is the more useful concept (even though the nominal or ad valorem rate is simpler to measure) for ascertaining the degree of protection and encouragement afforded to local manufacturers by a given country's tariff structure. This is because effective rates of protection show the net effect on a firm or industry of restrictions on the imports of both its outputs and its inputs. For most countries, developing and developed, the effective

---

TABLE 13.2   Effective Protection Rate in Selected Third World Countries

Country	Average Effective Protection Rate (%)
Uruguay	384
Pakistan	356
India	69
Brazil	63
Ivory Coast	41
Thailand	27
Singapore	22
Colombia	19
South Korea	−1

SOURCE: Data from David Greenaway and Chris Milner, "Trade theory and the less developed countries," in Norman Gemmell (ed.), *Surveys in Development Economics* (Oxford: Blackwell, 1987), tab. 1.5.

rate normally exceeds the nominal rate, sometimes by as much as 200%. For example, Little, Scitovsky, and Scott found that average levels of effective protection during the early 1960s exceeded 200% for India and Pakistan, 100% for Argentina and Brazil, 50% for the Philippines, 33% for Taiwan, and 25% for Mexico.[19]

Among the many implications of analyzing effective versus nominal tariff structures with regard to developing countries, two stand out as particularly noteworthy. First, most developing countries, as we have seen, have pursued import-substituting programs of industrialization with emphasis on the local production of final consumer goods for which a ready market was presumed to exist. Moreover, final goods production is generally less technically sophisticated than intermediate capital-goods production. The expectation was that in time, rising demand and economies of scale in finished-goods production would create strong backward linkages leading to the creation of domestic intermediate-goods industries. The record of performance, as we have also seen, has been disappointing for most developing countries. Part of the reason for this lack of success has been that developing-country tariff structures have afforded exceedingly high rates of effective protection to final-goods industries while intermediate and capital goods have received considerably less effective protection. The net result is an attraction of scarce resources away from intermediate-goods production and toward the often inefficient production of highly protected final consumer goods. Backward linkages do not develop, intermediate-good import costs rise, and, perhaps most important in the long run, the development of an indigenous capital-goods industry focusing on efficient, low-cost, labor-intensive techniques is severely impeded.

Second, even though nominal rates of protection in developed countries on imports from the developing countries may seem relatively low, effective protection rates can be quite substantial. As we saw earlier in the cases of cacao and sugar, raw materials are usually imported duty-free whereas processed products such as roasted and powdered coffee, coconut oil, and cocoa butter appear to have low nominal tariffs. The theory of effective protection suggests that in combination with zero tariffs on imported raw materials, low nominal tariffs on processed products can represent substantially higher effective rates of protection. For example, if a tariff of 10% is levied on processed coconut oil whereas copra (dried coconut) can be imported duty-free, and if the value added in making oil from copra is 5% of the total value of coconut oil, the *process* is actually being protected at 200%! This greatly inhibits the development of food and other raw-material-processing industries in developing nations and ultimately cuts back on their potential earnings of foreign exchange.

Effective rates of protection are considerably higher than nominal rates in the developed countries. For example, the effective rate on thread and yarn, textile fabrics, clothing, wood products, leather, and rubber goods averages more than twice the nominal rate on these same items in the United States and the members of the European Union. In the EU, effective rates on coconut oil are 10 times the nominal rate (150% compared with 15%), and those on processed soybeans are 16 times the nominal rate (160% as opposed to 10%).

To sum up, the standard argument for tariff protection in developing countries has four major components:

1. Duties on trade are the major source of government revenue in most LDCs because they are a relatively easy form of taxation to impose and even easier to collect.

2. Import restrictions represent an obvious response to chronic balance of payments and debt problems.

3. Protection against imports is one of the most appropriate means for fostering economies of scale, positive externalities, and industrial self-reliance as well as overcoming the pervasive state of economic dependence in which most Third World countries find themselves.

4. By pursuing policies of import restriction, developing countries can gain greater control over their economic destinies while encouraging foreign business interests to invest in local import-substituting industries, generating high profits and thus the potential for greater saving and future growth. They can also obtain imported equipment at relatively favorable prices and reserve an already established domestic market for local or locally controlled producers. Eventually, they may even become competitive enough to export to the world market.

Although these arguments can sound convincing and some protective policies have proved highly beneficial to the developing world, as we discovered, many have failed to bring about their desired results. Protection *does* have an important role to play in the development of the Third World, for both economic and noneconomic reasons, but it is a tool of economic policy that must be employed selectively and wisely, not as panacea to be applied indiscriminately and without reference to both short- and long-term ramifications.

Foreign–Exchange Rates, Exchange Controls, and the Devaluation Decision

We have already briefly discussed the question of foreign-exchange rates. Remember that a country's **official exchange rate** is the rate at which its central bank is prepared to transact exchanges of its local currency for other currencies in approved foreign-exchange markets. Official exchange rates are usually quoted in terms of U.S. dollars—so many pesos, reals, pounds, shillings, rupees, bhat, or yen per dollar. For example, the official exchange rate of Egyptian pounds for U.S. dollars in 1995 was approximately 0.30 per dollar, and the Indian rupee was officially valued at approximately 32 rupees per dollar. If an Egyptian manufacturer wished to import fabrics from an Indian textile exporter at a cost of 32,000 rupees, he would need 300 pounds to make the purchase. However, since almost all foreign-exchange transactions are conducted in U.S. dollars, the Egyptian importer would need to purchase $1,000 worth of foreign exchange from the central bank of Egypt for his 300 pounds and then transmit these dollars through official channels to the Indian exporter.

Official foreign-exchange rates are not necessarily set at or near the economic equilibrium price for foreign exchange—that is, the rate at which the domestic demand for a foreign currency such as dollars would just equal its supply in the absence of governmental regulation or intervention. In fact, as we saw in Table 13.1, the currencies of most Third World countries are usually overvalued by the exchange rate. Whenever the official price of foreign exchange is established at a level that, in the absence of any governmental restrictions or controls, would result in an excess of local demand over the available supply of foreign exchange, the domestic currency in question is said to be overvalued.

In situations of excess demand, LDC central banks have three basic policy options to maintain the official rate of exchange. First, they can attempt to accommodate the excess demand by running down their reserves of foreign exchange (as Mexico did from 1991 to 1994) or by borrowing additional foreign exchange abroad and thereby incurring further debts (as many African countries did in the 1980s). Second, they can attempt to curtail the excess demand for foreign exchange by pursuing commercial policies and tax measures designed to lessen the demand for imports (e.g., tariffs, physical quotas, licensing). Third, they can regulate and intervene in the foreign-exchange market by rationing the limited supply of available foreign exchange to "preferred" customers.[20] Such rationing is more commonly known as **exchange control**. The policy is in wide use throughout the Third World and is probably the major financial mechanism for preserving the level of foreign-exchange reserves at the prevailing official exchange rate.

The mechanism and operation of exchange control can be illustrated diagrammatically with the aid of Figure 13.3. Under free-market conditions, the equilibrium price of foreign exchange would be P_e, with a total of M units of foreign exchange demanded and supplied. If, however, the government maintains an artificially low price of foreign exchange (i.e., an overvaluation of its domestic currency) at P_a, the supply of foreign exchange will amount to only M' units because

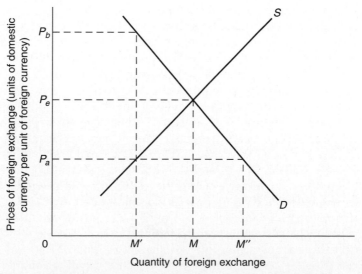

FIGURE 13.3 Free-Market and Controlled Rates of Foreign Exchange.

exports are overpriced. But at price P_a, the demand for foreign exchange will be M'' units, with the result that there is an "excess demand" equal to $M'' - M'$ units. Some mechanism will therefore have to be devised to ration the available supply of M'. If the government were to auction this supply, importers would be willing to pay a price of P_b for the foreign exchange. In such a case, the government would make a profit of $P_b - P_a$ per unit. However, such open auctions are rarely carried out, and limited supplies of foreign exchange are allocated through some administrative quota or licensing device. Opportunities for corruption, evasion, and the emergence of black markets are thus made possible because importers are willing to pay as much as P_b per unit of foreign exchange.

Why have most Third World governments opted for an overvalued official exchange rate? Basically, as we have seen, they have done so as part of widespread programs of rapid industrialization and import substitution. Overvalued exchange rates reduce the domestic currency price of imports below the level that would exist in a free market for foreign exchange (i.e., by the forces of supply and demand). Cheaper imports, especially capital and intermediate producer goods, are needed to fuel the industrialization process. But overvalued exchange rates also lower the domestic currency price of imported consumer goods, especially expensive luxury products. Third World nations wishing to limit such unnecessary and costly imports often need to establish import controls (mostly physical quotas) or to set up a **dual** or **parallel exchange rate** system with one rate, usually highly overvalued and legally fixed, applied to capital and intermediate-good imports and the other, much lower and illegal (or freely floating), for luxury consumption-good imports. Such dual exchange-rate systems make the domestic price of imported luxury goods very high while maintaining the artificially low and thus subsidized price of producer-good imports. Needless to say, dual exchange-rate systems, like exchange controls and import licenses, present serious problems of administration and can promote blackmarkets, corruption, evasion, and **rent seeking** (see note 20).[21]

However, overvalued currencies reduce the return to local exporters and to import-competing industries that are not protected by heavy tariffs or physical quotas. Exporters receive less domestic currency for their products than would be forthcoming if the free-market exchange rate prevailed. Moreover, in the absence of export subsidies to reduce the foreign-currency price of an LDC's exports, exporters, mostly farmers, become less competitive in world markets because the price of their produce has been artificially elevated by the overvalued exchange rate. In the case of import-competing but unprotected local industries, the overvalued rate artificially lowers the domestic currency price of foreign imports of the same product (e.g., radios, tires, bicycles, or household utensils).

Hence in the absence of effective government intervention and regulation of the foreign-exchange dealings of its nationals, overvalued exchange rates have a tendency to exacerbate balance of payments and foreign-debt problems simply because they cheapen imports while making exports more costly. Chronic payments deficits resulting primarily from current account transactions (exports and imports) can possibly be ameliorated by a currency **devaluation**. Simply defined, a country's currency is devalued when the official rate at which its central bank is prepared to exchange the local currency for dollars is abruptly increased. A currency **depreciation**, by contrast, refers to a gradual decrease in the purchasing power of a domestic currency in foreign markets relative to domestic markets; *appreciation* refers to a gradual increase.[22] For example, a devaluation of the Egyptian pound and the Indian rupee would occur if their official exchange rates of approximately 0.30 pound and 32 rupees to the dollar were changed to, say, 2 pounds and 40 rupees per dollar. Following these devaluations, U.S. importers of Egyptian and Indian goods would pay fewer dollars to obtain the same products. But U.S. exports to Egypt and India would become more expensive, requiring more pounds or rupees to purchase than before. In short, by lowering the *foreign*-currency price of its exports (and thereby generating more foreign demand) while raising the *domestic*-currency price of its imports (and thereby lowering domestic demand), Third World nations that devalue their currency hope to improve their trade balance vis-à-vis the rest of the world. This is a principal reason why devaluation is always a key component of IMF stabilization policies.

An alternative to a currency devaluation would be to allow foreign-exchange rates to fluctuate freely in accordance with changing conditions of international demand and supply. Freely fluctuating or flexible exchange rates in the past were not thought to be desirable, especially in developing nations heavily dependent on exports and imports, because they are extremely unpredictable, subject to wide and uncontrollable fluctuations, and susceptible to foreign and domestic currency speculation. Such unpredictable fluctuations can wreak havoc with both short- and long-range development plans. Nevertheless, during the global balance of payments and debt crises of the 1980s, a number of developing countries, including Mexico, Argentina, Chile, and the Philippines, were forced by the IMF to let their exchange rates float freely in order to correct sizable payments imbalances and to prevent continued capital flight.

The present international system of floating exchange rates, formally legalized at the 1976 Jamaica IMF meeting, represents a compromise between a fixed (artificially "pegged") and a fully **flexible exchange rate** system. Under this "managed" floating system, major international currencies are permitted to fluctuate freely, but erratic swings are limited through central bank intervention. Most developing countries, however, have decided to continue to peg their currencies to those of developed countries. Some, like Kenya, have gone further and decided to tie their currencies to the movements of a weighted index of the world's major currencies rather than to tie them to a particular currency, like the U.S. dollar or the pound sterling.

One final point that should be made about Third World currency devaluations, particularly in the light of previous discussions, concerns their probable effect on domestic prices. Devaluation has the immediate effect of raising prices of imported goods in terms of the local currency. Imported shirts, shoes, radios, records, foodstuffs, and bicycles that formerly cost x rupees now cost $(1 + d)x$ rupees, depending on the percentage magnitude of the devaluation, d. If, as a result of these higher prices, domestic workers seek to preserve the real value of their purchasing power, they are likely to initiate increased wage and salary demands. Such increases, if granted, will raise production costs and tend to push local prices up even higher.

A **wage-price spiral** of domestic inflation is thereby set in motion. In fact, a vicious cycle of devaluation—domestic wage and price increases, higher export prices, and worsened balance of trade—could result. Thus the devaluation decision could simply exacerbate the external balance of payments problem while generating galloping inflation domestically. The experience of many Latin American nations, with such chronic and uncontrollable inflation along with the inability of their governments to repress wages, has made them reluctant users of the tool of currency devaluation despite IMF pressures and Western protestations.

As for the distributional effects of a devaluation, it is clear that by altering the domestic price and returns of "tradable" goods (exports and imports) and creating incentives for the production of exports as opposed to domestic goods, devaluation will benefit certain groups at the expense of others. In general, urban wage earners, people with fixed incomes, the unemployed, and the small farmers and rural and urban small-scale producers and suppliers of services who do not participate in the export sector stand to be financially hurt by the domestic inflation that typically follows a devaluation. Conversely, large exporters (usually large landowners and foreign-owned corporations) and medium-sized local businesses engaged in foreign trade stand to benefit the most. Although we cannot categorically assert that devaluation tends to worsen income distribution, we may conclude that the more that ownership of and control over the export sector is concentrated in private rather than public hands, the greater is the likelihood that devaluation will have an adverse effect on income distribution.[23] For this reason, among others, international commercial and financial problems (e.g., chronic balance of payments deficits) cannot be divorced from domestic problems (e.g., poverty and inequality) in Third World nations. Policy responses to alleviate one problem can either improve or worsen others.

Summary and Conclusions: Trade Optimists and Trade Pessimists

We are now in a position to summarize the major issues and arguments in the great ongoing debate between advocates of free-trade, outward-looking development and export promotion policies—the **trade optimists**—and advocates of greater protection, more inward-looking strategies, and greater import substitution—the **trade pessimists**.[24] Let's begin with the latter school of thought.

Trade Pessimist Arguments

Trade pessimists tend to focus on three basic themes: (1) the limited growth of world demand for primary exports, (2) the secular deterioration in the terms of trade for primary producing nations, and (3) the rise of "new protectionism" against the exports of LDC manufactured and processed agricultural goods.

LDC exports grow slowly because of (1) a shift in developed countries from low-technology, material-intensive goods to high-technology, skill-intensive products, which decreases the demand for Third World raw materials; (2) increased efficiency in industrial uses of raw materials; (3) the substitution of synthetics for natural raw materials like rubber, copper, and cotton; (4) the low income elasticity of demand for primary products and light manufactured goods; (5) the rising productivity of agriculture in developed countries; and (6) the rising tide of protectionism for both agriculture and labor-intensive developed-country industries.

The terms of trade deteriorate because of (1) oligopolistic control of factor and commodity markets in developed countries combined with increasing competitive sources of supply of LDC exportables and (2) a generally lower level of the income elasticity of demand for LDC exports.

The rise of **new protectionism** in the developed world results from the very success of a growing number of LDCs in producing a wider range of both primary and secondary products at competitive world market prices, combined with the quite natural fears of workers in higher-cost developed-country industries that their jobs will be lost. They pressure their governments in North America, Europe, and Japan to curtail or prohibit competitive imports from the Third World. The trade pessimists therefore conclude that trade hurts Third World development because (1) the slow growth in demand for their traditional exports means that export expansion results in lower export prices and a transfer of income from poor to rich nations; (2) without import restrictions, the high elasticity of Third World demand for imports combined with the low elasticity for their exports means that developing countries must grow slowly to avoid chronic balance of payments and foreign-exchange crises; and (3) because developing nations have their "static" comparative advantage in primary products, export-promoting free-trade policies tend to inhibit industrialization, which is in turn the major vehicle for the accumulation of technical skills and entrepreneurial talents.

Trade Optimist Arguments

Trade optimists tend to underplay the role of international demand in determining the gains from trade. Instead, they focus on the relationship between LDC trade policy, export performance, and economic growth.[25] They argue that **trade liberalization** (including export promotion, currency devaluation, removal of trade restrictions, and generally "getting prices right") generates rapid export and economic growth because free trade provides a number of benefits:

1. It promotes competition, improved resource allocation, and economies of scale in areas where LDCs have a comparative advantage. Costs of production are consequently lowered.

2. It generates pressures for increased efficiencies, product improvement, and technical change, thus raising factor productivity and further lowering costs of production.

3. It accelerates overall economic growth, which raises profits and promotes greater saving and investment and thus furthers growth.

4. It attracts foreign capital and expertise, which are in scarce supply in LDCs.

5. It generates needed foreign exchange that can be used to import food if the agricultural sector lags behind or suffers droughts or other natural catastrophes.

6. It eliminates costly economic distortions caused by government interventions in both the export and foreign-exchange markets and substitutes market allocation for the corruption and rent-seeking activities that usually result from an over-active government sector.

7. It promotes more equal access to scarce resources, which improves overall resource allocation.

Trade optimists argue, finally, that even though export promotion may at first be difficult with limited gains—especially in comparison with the easy gains of first-stage import substitution—over the longer run the economic benefits tend to build up momentum, whereas import substitution faces rapidly diminishing returns.

Reconciling the Arguments: The Data and the Consensus

We can evaluate the debate on two levels, the empirical and the philosophical. In his study of the experience of developing countries over the past three decades, Rostam M. Kavoussi argues that the empirical evidence demonstrates quite clearly that neither the trade optimists nor the trade pessimists are correct at all times. It all depends on fluctuations in the world economy.[26] Thus when the world economy was expanding rapidly during the period from 1960 to 1973, the more open-economy LDCs clearly outperformed (in terms of aggregate export and economic growth) the more closed-economy nations. The trade optimists' arguments appear validated during this period of rapid world growth. But when the world economy slowed down between 1973 and 1977, the more open economies (with the notable exception of the four Asian NICs) had a more difficult time and the trade pessimists fared better. A follow-up 1988 study by Hans W. Singer and Patricia Gray, which extended Kavoussi's empirical analysis for the period 1977–1983, when world economic conditions were even more unfavorable, supports the finding that high growth rates of export earnings occur only when external demand is strong.[27] Changes in trade policy appear to have little or no effect. Furthermore, low-income countries were found to fare worse across all time periods. Singer and Gray argue that contrary to the position of the World Bank and other trade optimists, an outward-oriented policy is not necessarily valid for all LDCs. To conclude, therefore, that either export promotion or import substitution is always an unambiguously better strategy—even for promoting economic growth narrowly conceived, let alone our broader definition of development—is to miss a key conceptual and empirical insight that a growing number of development economists are beginning to recognize.

In the final analysis, it is not a developing country's inward- or outward-looking stance vis-à-vis the rest of the world that will determine whether or not it develops along the lines described in Chapter 1 and in many other parts of this book. Inward-looking, protectionist policies such as tariffs, quotas, and exchange-rate adjustments do not necessarily guarantee more jobs, higher incomes that are more equitably distributed, adequate nutrition and health, clean water, or relevant education any more than outward-looking, noninterventionist policies do. Even though policies of export promotion appear to have contributed more to GNP growth than import substitution did during the 1960s and 1970s, similar results were not forthcoming in the period from 1979 to 1991. And what will happen in the remainder of the 1990s is beyond anyone's ability to predict. Moreover, in terms of our broadened definition of development, the results of the past three decades are largely ambiguous. Much depends on the structure of both the domestic LDC economy and the world economy. In fact, as Paul P. Streeten skillfully pointed out at a conference on trade and development:

> A curious paradox came out of the discussion [of the effects of trade on LDC inequalities]. It seemed that both inward-looking, import-substituting, protectionist, interventionist policies and outward-looking, market-orientated, noninterventionist policies tend to increase market imperfections and monopolies and reduce the demand for labour-intensive processes, the latter because the market rewards most those factors that are relatively scarce (capital, management, professional skills) and penalizes those in abundant supply and because the market strengthens the ability to accumulate of those who have against those who have not. But though it is paradoxical that both a protectionist "distorted" system of prices, interest rates, wages and exchange rates and a market-determined one should increase inequalities, there is no contradiction. It is plausible that within a certain social and political framework, both export-orientated market policies and import-substitution-orientated, interventionist, "distorting" policies should aggravate inequalities, though one set may do this somewhat more than the other. Perhaps economists have been barking up the wrong tree when disputing which set of price policies contributes more to equality. In an inegalitarian power structure, both make for inequality; in an egalitarian power structure, both may make for equality.[28]

In short, the current consensus leans toward an eclectic view that attempts to fit the relevant arguments of both the free-trade and protectionist models to the specific economic, institutional, and political realities of diverse Third World nations at different stages of development. What works for one may not work for another. For example, the East Asian success stories may have little relevance for other developing nations beyond the important conclusion reached by Colin I. Bradford:

> What seems to distinguish the East Asian development experiences is not the dominance of market forces, free enterprise, and internal liberalization, but effective, highly interactive relationships between the public and private sectors characterized by shared goals and commitments embodied in the development strategy and economic policy of the government. The dichotomy between market forces and government intervention is not only overdrawn: it misconceives the fundamental dynamic at work. It is the *degree of consistency* between the two sectors—rather than the extent of implicit or explicit conflict—that has been important in the successful development cases. A coherent development strategy was not only

formulated but followed by both the government and the private sector in providing an unusual degree of common direction to national energies in these cases.[29]

Finally, all of the foregoing discussion has left out perhaps the most viable long-run trade policy for small and medium-sized developing economies, one that is oriented simultaneously outward *and* inward in an area that has shown slow but steady growth over the past few decades. This is the expansion of trade among the developing countries—South-South rather than North-South trade—and the possibilities of economic integration in Third World regions.

South-South Trade and Economic Integration: Looking Outward and Inward

The Growth of Trade among Developing Countries

Although trade among the LDCs still represents a meager 7% of total world trade, twice its share in 1970, it grew rapidly during the 1980s. By 1990, South-South trade represented almost 33% of all Third World exports (see Figure 13.4). Trade in manufactures has risen from only 5% in 1960 to almost 35% of all exports in the early 1990s. Much of the growth of these inter-LDC exports helped compensate for weak demand and growing protectionism in the developed world.

Many development economists have argued that Third World countries should therefore orient their trade more toward one another.[30] Their arguments usually entail four basic points:

1. There are relative comparative-advantage changes to South-South as opposed to North-South trade.
2. There are greater dynamic gains to be realized from such trade.
3. Export instability resulting from fluctuations in developed-country economic activity can be reduced.
4. Greater collective self-reliance will be fostered.

Let us examine the nature of these arguments.

Economic Integration: Theory and Practice

One strong variant of the South-South trade hypothesis is that LDCs should go beyond greater trade with one another and move in the direction of **economic integration**. Economic integration occurs whenever a group of nations in the same region, ideally of relatively equal size and at equal stages of development, join together to form an **economic union** or **regional trading bloc** by raising a common tariff wall against the products of nonmember countries while freeing internal trade among members. In the terminology of integration literature, nations that levy common external tariffs while freeing internal trade are said to have formed a **customs union**. If external tariffs against outside countries differ among member nations

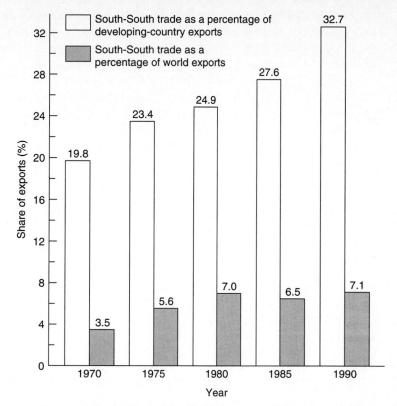

FIGURE 13.4 The Expansion of South-South Trade, 1970–1990. *Sources*: John W. Sewell and Stewart K. Tucker (eds.), *Growth, Exports, and Jobs in a Changing World Economy: Agenda 1988* (New Brunswick, N.J.: Transaction Books, 1988), tab. A-7; United Nations Development Program, *World Development Report, 1991* (New York: Oxford University Press, 1991), chap. 5.

while internal trade is free, the nations are said to have formed a **free-trade area**. Finally, a **common market** possesses all the attributes of a customs union (common external tariffs and free internal trade) plus the free movement of labor and capital among the partner states.

The theory of customs unions and economic integration is associated primarily with the work of Jacob Viner of Princeton University in the 1940s. The traditional core of this theory, which focuses on the static resource and production reallocation effects within highly integrated and flexible industrialized nations, is of limited value to contemporary developing nations intent on building up their industrial base. Yet many concepts of the theory of integration provide valid criteria on which to evaluate the probable short-run success or failure of economic cooperation among Third World countries.

The basic economic rationale for the gradual integration of less developed economies is a long-term dynamic one: Integration provides the opportunity for industries that have not yet been established as well as for those that have to take advantage of economies of large-scale production made possible by expanded markets. Integration therefore needs to be viewed as a mechanism to encourage a rational division of labor among a group of countries, each of which is too small to benefit from such a division by itself. In the absence of integration, each separate country may not provide a sufficiently large domestic market to enable local industries to lower their production costs through economies of scale. In such cases, import-substituting industrialization will typically result, as we have seen, in the establishment of high-cost, inefficient local industries. Moreover, in the absence of integration, the same industry (e.g., textiles or shoes) may be set up in two or more adjoining small nations. Each will be operating at less than optimal capacity but will be protected against the imports of the other by high tariff or quota barriers. Not only does such duplication result in wasted scarce resources, but it also means that consumers are forced to pay a higher price for the product than if the market were large enough for high-volume, low-cost production to take place at a single location.

This leads to a second dynamic rationale for LDC economic integration. By removing barriers to trade among member states, the possibility of coordinated industrial planning is created, especially in industries where economies of scale are likely to exist. Examples include fertilizer and petrochemical plants, heavy industry like iron and steel, capital goods and machine tool industries, and small-farm mechanical equipment. But the coordinated planning of industrial expansion that enables all member states to accelerate their rates of industrial growth by assigning given industries to different members takes the partners that much closer to full economic and eventual political union. Problems of sovereignty and national self-interest impinge at this stage. To date they have overwhelmed the economic logic of a close and coordinated union. However, as Third World nations, especially small ones, continue to experience the futility of either development in isolation (**autarchy**) or full participation in the highly unequal world economy, it is likely that interest will increase in the coming decades in the long-run benefits of some form of economic (and perhaps political) cooperation.

In addition to these two long-term dynamic arguments for integration, there are also the standard static evaluative criteria known as **trade creation** and **trade diversion**. Trade creation is said to occur when common external barriers and internal free trade lead to a shift in production from high- to low-cost member states. For example, before integration, both country A and country B may produce textiles for their respective local markets. Country A may be a lower-cost producer, but its exports to country B are blocked by the latter's high tariffs. If A and B form a customs union by eliminating all barriers to internal trade, country A's more efficient low-cost textile industry will service both markets. Trade will have been created in the sense that the removal of barriers has led to a shift in country B's consumption from its own relatively high cost textiles to the lower-cost textiles of country A.

Similarly, trade diversion is said to occur when the erection of external tariff barriers causes production and consumption of one or more member states to shift from lower-cost nonmember sources of supply (e.g., a developed country) to higher-cost member producers. Trade diversion is normally considered undesirable because both the world and member states are perceived to be worse off as a result of diversion of production from more efficient foreign suppliers to the less efficient domestic industries of member states. But this static argument against economic integration ignores two basic facts. First, because of potential economies of scale, the creation of local jobs, and the circular flow of income within the integrated region, static trade diversion may turn out to be dynamic trade creation. This is simply a variant of the standard infant industry argument for protection, but with the more likely possibility that the infant will grow up as a result of the larger market in which it now operates. Second, if in the absence of integration, each member state were to protect its local import-substituting industry against all lower-cost foreign suppliers, the common external tariff of member states would cause no more trade diversion than would have happened anyway. But as we just saw, if there are scale economies, the possibility of dynamic trade creation can emerge. Hence we conclude that static concepts like trade creation and trade diversion are useful. However, it is important that they be analyzed in the dynamic context of growth and development and based on the realities of current commercial policies of developing nations, rather than in the theoretical vacuum of traditional free-trade models.

Regional Trading Blocs and the Globalization of Trade

We may conclude, therefore, that Third World countries at relatively equal stages of industrial development with similar market sizes and with a strong interest in coordinating and rationalizing their joint industrial growth patterns stand to benefit most from the combined inward- and outward-looking trade policies represented by economic integration.[31] In particular, regional groupings of small nations like those of Central America and southern and western Africa can create the economic conditions (mainly in the form of large internal markets) for accelerating their joint development efforts. Such groupings can also promote long-run development by enabling nations to block certain forms of trade with the more powerful developed nations and perhaps also to restrict or prohibit the deep penetration of multinational corporations into their industrial sectors. In any event, integration is crucial: Without cooperation and integration, the prospects for sustained economic progress by most low- and middle-income LDCs will be greatly diminished.

But even if such an integration strategy may seem economically logical and persuasive on paper (and may in fact be the only long-run solution to the economic problems of small nations), in practice it requires a degree of statesmanship and a regional rather than nationalistic orientation that is often lacking in many countries. The unfortunate demise of both the Central American Common Market and the East African Community in the 1970s demonstrates how political and ideological conflict can more than offset the economic logic of regional cooperation. As Table 13.3 illustrates, the only LDC regional trading blocs to experience rising intraunion trade during the 1980s were those in West Africa. Prior to the 1990s, therefore, intraregional conflict prevented trade liberalization from succeeding.

But prospects for the future are much more positive. As trade becomes increasingly globalized, even the largest industrialized nations now realize that they

TABLE 13.3 Trade within Third World Regional Trading Blocs, 1970–1987 (as a percentage of total exports)

Trading Bloc	1970	1980	1987
Association of Southeast Pacific States	14.7	17.8	17.7
Central African Customs and Economic Union	3.4	4.1	0.9
Central American Common Market	26.8	22.0	11.9
Caribbean Community	7.3	6.4	6.3
Latin America Free Trade Area	10.2	13.5	11.3
Andean Group	2.3	3.5	3.2
West African Economic Community	9.1	6.9	7.7
Economic Community of West African States	2.1	3.9	4.5

SOURCE: World Bank, *World Development Report, 1991* (New York: Oxford University Press, 1991), tab. 5.4.

cannot go it alone. In Europe, a single economic market became a reality at the end of 1992 as all internal trade barriers were removed. By the end of the decade, the European Union may have a single currency, requiring close monetary coordination and in effect creating the largest global economic entity. Similar efforts are under way in North America, where the North American Free Trade Agreement (NAFTA) represents a unique arrangement in that a developing country, Mexico, has joined a developed-country trading bloc, Canada and the United States. (Chile, a NIC, may also seek membership.) Two major trading blocs now exist in Latin America. Argentina, Brazil, Paraguay, and Uruguay in 1994 finalized arrangements for a free-trade area called the Southern Cone Common Market, also known as Mercosur. In the four years after the original treaty was signed in 1990, regional trade in Mercosur more than tripled to $12 billion and Brazil replaced the United States as Argentina's largest trading partner. Once Brazil and Argentina were bitter rivals. Mercosur is taking advantage of sizable economies of scale and a new expanded market of 180 million people and $800 billion of economic activity. The other Latin American bloc, the Andean Group (consisting of Bolivia, Colombia, Ecuador, Peru, and Venezuela), established a full-fledged common market in 1995. In Africa, moves are under way to promote regional economic integration, the most promising hope being the newly formed South African Development Community (SADC). Thanks to well-developed railroad and air links, the 10 members of SADC—Angola, Botswana, Lesotho, Malawi, Mozambique, Nambia, South Africa, Swaziland, Zambia, and Zimbabwe—anticipate new and much greater trading opportunities.

The critical question about all these new regional trading blocs is not whether they will promote greater internal growth (which they likely will) but whether such regional groupings will fragment the world economy and run counter to the recent globalization of trade. Most economists believe that **globalization** is here to stay, particularly as multinational corporations set up subsidiaries throughout the world. For LDCs, effective regional blocs can provide a buffer against the negative effects of globalization while still permitting the dynamic benefits of intraunion specialization and greater equality among members to take place.

Trade Policies of Developed Countries: The Need for Reform

We have seen that a major obstacle to LDC export expansion, whether in the area of primary products or manufactures, has been the various trade barriers erected by developed nations against the principal commodity exports of developing countries. In the absence of economic integration or even in support of that effort, the prospects for future LDC trade and foreign-exchange expansion depend largely on the domestic and international economic policies of developed nations. Although internal structural and economic reform may be essential to economic and social progress, an improvement in the competitive position of industries in which LDCs do have a dynamic comparative advantage will be of little benefit to them or the world as a whole so long as their access to major world markets is restricted by rich-country commercial policies.

Developed countries' economic and commercial policies are most important from the perspective of future Third World foreign-exchange earnings in three major areas:

1. Tariff and nontariff barriers to LDC exports

2. Adjustment assistance for displaced workers in developed-country industries hurt by freer access of labor-intensive, low-cost LDC exports

3. The general impact of rich-country domestic economic policies on developing economies

Rich–Nation Tariff and Nontariff Trade Barriers and the 1995 Uruguay Round GATT Agreement

Until 1995, the new-protectionist tariff and **nontariff trade barriers** (e.g., excise taxes, quotas, sanitary regulations) imposed by rich nations on the commodity exports of poor ones were the most significant obstacle to the expansion of the latter's export-earning capacities. Moreover, as we have seen, many of these tariffs increased with the degree of product processing; that is, they were higher for processed foodstuffs than for basic foodstuffs (e.g., peanut oil compared with peanuts), higher for, say, shirts than for raw cotton. These high effective tariffs inhibited LDCs from developing and diversifying their own secondary-export industries and thus acted to restrain their industrial expansion.

The overall effect of developed-country tariffs, quotas, and nontariff barriers has been to lower the effective price received by LDCs for their exports, reduce the quantity exported, and diminish foreign-exchange earnings. Although the burdens that developed-country tariffs imposed on LDC primary- and secondary-product exports varied from commodity to commodity, it has been estimated that the net impact of trade barriers on all products has reduced Third World foreign-exchange earnings by more than $40 billion per year.

However, the final act of the **Uruguay Round** agreement that was signed in April 1994 and became effective in 1995 after passage by 124 national legislatures substantially reduced tariff and nontariff trade barriers in many sectors. It also established a new **World Trade Organization (WTO)** to replace the 47-year-old **General Agreement on Tariffs and Trade (GATT)**. The Geneva-based WTO is to oversee the trade agreement and settle trade disputes. The three major provisions of the new accord, from the perspective of Third World nations, are the following:[32]

1. Developed countries will cut tariffs on manufactures by an average of 40% in five equal annual reductions. Tariffs will be eliminated in 10 major sectors (beer, construction equipment, distilled spirits, farm machinery, furniture, medical equipment, paper, pharmaceuticals, steel, and toys). Developing countries in turn agreed to not raise tariffs by 'binding' in recent trade reforms.

2. Trade in agricultural products will come under the authority of the WTO and be progressively liberalized. Developed-country nontariff barriers are to be converted into tariffs and reduced to 36% of the 1986–1988 level by the year 2000. Agricultural subsidies will also be reduced.

3. For textiles and apparel, the Multi-Fiber Arrangement (MFA), which has long penalized exports of developing countries, will be phased out by 2005, with most of the reductions taking effect toward the end of the period.

One optimistic study that attempted to assess the quantitative impact of the agreement on developing-country economies concluded that the Third World's real income could grow by as much as $78 billion (in 1992 dollars).[33] But even if correct, these gains would be very unevenly distributed. Many of the poorest LDCs— especially those that are net food importers and will face higher import prices as DC agriculture subsidies are removed—are likely to lose. LDCs in Africa currently enjoying trade preferences may also be harmed. Finally, environmental groups have been critical of the agreement for its exclusive focus on growth and its lack of attention to the preservation of sensitive and threatened environmental resources. In short, while many analysts are optimistic that the new GATT accord represents a major transition to a more liberal world trading system that will inevitable help the majority of developing countries, it remains to be seen whether the least developed countries will in fact benefit or whether the Uruguay Round agreement will further widen the gap between rich and poor nations.

The Problem of Adjustment Assistance

One of the major obstacles to lowering tariff barriers of rich countries against the manufactured exports of poorer nations is the political pressure exerted by traditional light manufacturing industries that find their products underpriced by low-cost, labor-intensive foreign goods. Not only can this cause economic disruption for these higher-cost domestic industries, but it can also lead to a loss of employment for their workers. In classical trade theory, the answer to this dilemma would be simple: Merely shift these rich-country workers with their complementary resources to the other more capital-intensive industries where a comparative advantage still exists. Everybody will be better off as a result.

Unfortunately, even in the most industrialized and economically integrated societies of the world, the process of adjustment is not so simple. More important, the political power of many of these older industries is such that whenever they feel threatened by low-cost foreign imports, they are able to muster enough support effectively to block competition from the LDCs.

Unless some scheme of **adjustment assistance** is established whereby the governments of developed nations assist industries and their workers financially in the transition to alternative and more profitable activities, trade barriers against competitive Third World exports will be difficult to remove. Many such schemes have been proposed. To date, none has been really effective in persuading threatened industries and industrial workers to forgo their private interests in the interest of maximum world welfare. This is not surprising. In fact, the typical response of developed-country governments has been to subsidize new investment in threatened industries to keep them afloat. Nevertheless, continuous efforts must be made to search for an acceptable program of adjustment assistance that will not unduly penalize displaced workers, who themselves often come from the lower income brackets.[34] Without the introduction of such programs in developed nations, the world market for Third World manufactured exports will always remain restricted, both for new entrants and for the growth of existing suppliers.

Domestic Economic Policies

Although it is beyond the scope of this chapter to examine the myriad ways in which the economic welfare of many export-oriented poor nations is tied to the domestic fiscal and monetary macroeconomic policies of rich nations, the importance of this link must not be overlooked. The major factor determining the level and growth of Third World export earnings (and this was clearly confirmed by their relatively good performance in the 1960s and their sharp decline during the recessions of the 1970s and 1980s) has been the ability of rich nations to sustain high rates of economic growth without inflation. Even a low income elasticity of demand for LDC exports can be compensated for by a high rate of income growth in a developed country. It follows that under present international economic relationships, Third World export performance is directly related to the growth and price stability of developed-country economies.

But just as the poor are often said to be the last to be hired and the first to be fired, so too, when international economic disruptions occur, the world's poor nations feel the effects much sooner and more substantially than the rich nations do. The worldwide inflationary spiral of the 1970s caused by a combination of Keynesian-type excess aggregate demand pull and natural resource, especially petroleum, cost push factors provides a classic example of this phenomenon. Facing rampant inflation at home, developed countries were able to call on traditional macroeconomic policies designed to restrict aggregate demand (e.g., lower government expenditure, higher taxes, higher interest rates, a slower-growing money supply) while attempting to control wage and price rises. When rapid inflation is accompanied by growing balance of payments deficits and rising domestic unemployment as in the 1970s, these deflationary domestic fiscal and monetary policies tend to be reinforced by specific government actions to curtail imports and control the outflow of foreign exchange. The nations hit the hardest by these belt-tightening measures are usually the weakest, most vulnerable, and most dependent of the world, the 40 or so poorest LDCs. Although they are not the intended victims of such domestic economic policies, the fact remains that they are the main victims.

Clearly, we cannot blame the developed nations for looking first after their own domestic economic interests. Nevertheless, it would not seem unreasonable to ask them to try to ease the burden of their spending cutbacks on the poorest nations by giving the exports of these nations some form of preferential treatment. But the lesson is clear. As long as developing nations, either individually or as a group, whether willingly or unwillingly, permit their economies to be linked too closely to the economic policies of rich nations, they will remain the chief, albeit innocent, victims in times of stress and but minimally rewarded in times of prosperity. Even more disturbing is the loss of their capacity to control their own economic and social destinies.

The lessons of the past 30 years thus revealed to Third World nations, as no economic model could, their need to make every effort to reduce their individual and joint economic vulnerabilities. One method of achieving this goal is to pursue policies of greater collective self-reliance within the context of mutual economic cooperation. Though not denying their interdependence with developed nations and their need for growing export markets, many developing countries now realize that in the absence of major reforms of the international economic order, a concerted effort at reducing their current economic dependence and vulnerability is essential to any successful development strategy.

CASE STUDY

The Economy of Jamaica

GEOGRAPHIC, SOCIAL, AND ECONOMIC INDICATORS

Capital Kingston

Area 10,991 km^2

Population 2.4 million (1995)

Population (average annual growth rate) 0.9% (1985–1994)

GNP per capita U.S. $1,420 (1994)

GNP per capita (average annual growth rate) 1.7% (1985–1994)

Agriculture as share of GDP 8.0% (1994)

Exports as share of GDP 58% (1994)

Infant mortality rate (per 1,000 live births) 13.2 (1995)

Child malnutrition (underweight) 7% (1994)

Females as share of labor force 46% (1994)

Illiteracy rate (age 15+) 2.0% (1990)

Human Development Index 0.75 (medium) (1992)

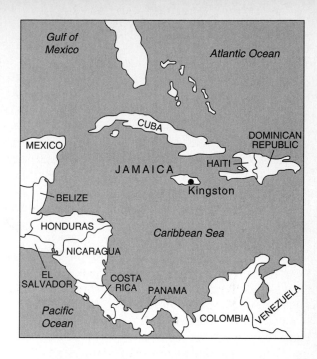

Jamaica, which occupies the third largest island of the Greater Antilles, lies in the Caribbean Sea about 90 miles south of Cuba and 120 miles west of Haiti. It is 220 kilometers long and has a population of 2.4 million people. Population pressure has been relieved by large-scale emigration, mainly to Great Britain, the United States, and Canada. Emigration from Jamaica exceeded 10,000 people per year during the 1980s. Consequently, even though the number of births over deaths was sufficient to increase the population at a rate exceeding 2% per year, Jamaica's population in fact increased at an annual rate of under 1% and in some years actually decreased.

Many Jamaicans have migrated to the cities, especially Kingston, the major urban area, which is also the capital, chief port, and commercial center. Population pressure on the land has promoted rapid urbanization.

Barely two out of five Jamaicans live in rural areas, mainly in the interior uplands. However, the cities do not have enough industries to support the people who inhabit them. As a result, there is massive urban unemployment, as well as severe underemployment in rural areas.

Jamaica's GDP per capita was $1,420 in 1994. However, this figure is understated because it excludes the value of the vast but unreported marijuana crop. In the 1960s and early 1970s, Jamaica's national income grew rapidly at an average annual rate of 4.7%—3.2% on a per capita basis. But from 1973 to 1984, national income per capita fell at an average rate of 3.1% before rising at an anemic 0.9% rate from 1985 to 1994.

Agriculture and the mining industry are the dominant sectors in Jamaica's economy. The agricultural sector employs nearly one-third of the workforce. There are large-scale plantations meant for export production and tiny peasant farms, which produce mainly for subsistence and local markets. The plantations, concentrated in the southern coastal lowlands, grow sugarcane, from which molasses, rum, and refined sugar are made.

491

Peasant farms are mostly located on steep hillsides and raise cattle and grow marijuana, cassava, potatoes, breadfruit, coconuts, and other fruits and vegetables, mainly for local consumption. They also grow some ginger, coffee, cacao, and sugarcane for export. Jamaican farmers suffered tremendous crop damage from Hurricane Gilbert in 1988. However, by 1990 sugar and banana production were back up to the level before the hurricane.

Manufacturing accounts for approximately one-sixth of Jamaica's recorded GDP. The main industrial products are processed foods, beverages, textiles, sugar, paper products, and cigarettes. Other important manufacturing industries, most of which are foreign-owned and dependent on imported materials, produce chemicals, machinery and tools, glass, cement, and metal products and refine bauxite and petroleum. Most manufacturing is for domestic consumption, but there is also significant export of manufactured goods to Jamaica's partners in the Caribbean Common Market. Jamaican manufacturing is expanding at a slow rate, and the high cost of local credit continues to prevent the manufacturing sector from realizing its full potential.

Mining has assumed major importance since 1950. Bauxite, from which aluminum is obtained, is Jamaica's main mineral resource. Bauxite and aluminum contributed to more than half of Jamaica's recorded export income during the 1970s. However, during the 1980s, bauxite production fell sharply in response to steadily declining export prices.

Jamaica pays much more for necessary imports than it can earn through legal exports. In 1992, Jamaica spent $1.5 billion on imports but reported export earnings of only $1.1 billion. Although Jamaica obtained $600 million from tourism, this was offset by heavy payments for imported services, repatriated profits, and interest on its foreign debts. During the past decade, Jamaica's foreign trade deficit has been financed in part by more than $700 million per year of contraband marijuana exports, by financial aid of more than $100 million per year from the U.S. government, and by increases in the country's foreign indebtedness, which soared from less than $800 million in 1980 to more than $4.5 billion in 1992.

Despite Jamaica's chronic and growing merchandise trade deficit, the overall balance of payments recorded a surplus of $117 million in 1992. Jamaica's balance of payments shows export and tourism revenues including outside assistance (loans and grants) offsetting major outflows of debt service and import payments.

Jamaica's economy was seriously hurt by the catastrophic 1988 hurricane. It caused economic growth to drop about 5% in just one year. In addition, Jamaica's high domestic interest rates and rising inflation (30%) pose major problems for growth. It is now attempting market reforms, including the elimination of all import quotas and widespread tariff reductions so that it can continue to obtain World Bank structural adjustment loans. Its fortunes, however, are still tied to movements in the U.S. economy and, in particular, to U.S. and U.K. immigration policies.

Concepts for Review

Adjustment assistance	Devaluation
Autarchy	Dual exchange rate
Common market	Economic integration
Customs union	Economic union
Depreciation	Effective rate of protection

Exchange control

Exchange rate

Export promotion

Flexible exchange rate

Free-market exchange rate

Free-trade area

General Agreement on Tariffs and Trade (GATT)

Globalization

Import substitution

Infant industry

International commodity agreements

Inward-looking development policies

Multi-Fiber Arrangement (MFA)

New protectionism

Nominal rate of protection

Nontariff trade barriers

Official exchange rate

Outward-looking development policies

Overvalued exchange rate

Parallel exchange rate

Quotas

Regional trading bloc

Rent seeking

Synthetic substitutes

Tariffs

Trade creation

Trade diversion

Trade liberalization

Trade optimists

Trade pessimists

Uruguay Round

Value added

Wage-price spiral

World Trade Organization (WTO)

Questions for Discussion

1. Explain the distinction between primary and secondary inward- and outward-looking development policies.

2. Briefly summarize the range of commercial policies available to Third World countries, and explain why some of these policies might be adopted.

3. What are the possibilities, advantages, and disadvantages of export promotion in developing nations with reference to specific types of commodities (e.g., primary food products, raw materials, fuels, minerals, manufactured goods)?

4. Most less developed countries in Latin America, Africa, and Asia have pursued policies of import substitution as major components of their development strategies. Explain the theoretical and practical arguments in support of import substitution policies. What have been some of the weaknesses of these policies in practice, and why have the results often not lived up to expectations?

5. Explain some of the arguments in support of the use of tariffs, quotas, and other trade barriers in developing countries.

6. What issues form the basis of the debate between trade optimists and trade pessimists? Is either side more correct? Explain your answer.

7. What are the basic static and dynamic arguments for economic integration in less developed countries? Briefly describe the various forms that economic integration can take (e.g., customs union, free-trade areas). What are the major obstacles to effective economic integration in Third World regions?

8. How do the trade policies of developed countries affect the ability of less developed countries to benefit from greater participation in the world economy? How do nontrade domestic economic policies of rich nations affect the export earnings of Third World countries? What is meant by adjustment assistance, and why is it so important to the future of Third World manufactured export prospects? Explain.

Notes

1. For an excellent discussion of inward versus outward development policies, see Paul P. Streeten, "Trade strategies for development: Some themes for the seventies," *World Development* 1 (June 1973): 1–10, and Donald B. Keesing, *Trade Policy for Developing Countries*, World Bank Staff Working Paper No. 53 (Washington, D.C.: World Bank, 1979). Among the many more recent reviews, two alternative perspectives are particularly noteworthy: Rudiger Dornbusch, "The case for trade liberalization in developing countries," *Journal of Economic Perspectives* 6 (Winter 1992): 69–85, and Dani Rodrik, "The limits of trade policy reform in developing countries," *Journal of Economic Perspectives* 6 (Winter 1992): 87–105.

2. Streeten, "Trade strategies," 1.

3. *Ibid.*, 2.

4. Colin Kirkpatrick, "Trade policy and industrialization in LDCs," in Norman Gemmell (ed.), *Surveys in Development Economics* (Oxford: Blackwell, 1987), pp. 71–72.

5. See, for example, Colin I. Bradford, Jr., "East Asian 'models': Myths and lessons," in John P. Lewis and Valeriana Kallab (eds.), *Development Strategies Reconsidered* (Washington, D.C.: Overseas Development Council, 1986), chap. 5; Stephen C. Smith, *Industrial Policy in Developing Countries* (Washington, D.C.: Economic Policy Institute, 1991); and Robert Wade, *Governing the Market: Economic Theory and the Role of Government in East Asian Industrialization* (Princeton, N.J.: Princeton University Press, 1990).

6. Alfred Maizels, *Exports and Economic Growth of Developing Countries* (London: Cambridge University Press, 1968).

7. I am indebted to Professor Andreas Savvides for pointing these facts out to me.

8. For a good review of the difficulties that LDCs had with primary exports in the 1980s, see United Nations Development Program, *Human Development Report, 1992* (New York: Oxford University Press, 1992), pp. 59–62; World Bank, *World Development Report, 1991* (Washington, D.C.: World Bank, 1991), pp. 105–110; and World Bank, *Global Economic Prospects and the Developing Countries* (Washington, D.C.: World Bank, 1994), chap. 2.

9. For a comprehensive empirical analysis extolling the growth-inducing benefits of manufactured export promotion based on the 1960s and 1970s experience, see Anne O. Krueger, *Trade and Employment in Developing Countries: Vol. 3. Synthesis and Conclusions* (Chicago: University of Chicago Press / National Bureau of Economics Research, 1983). See also Jagdish N. Bhagwati, "Export-promoting trade strategy: Issues and evidence," *World Bank Research Observer* 3 (January 1988): 27–57, and World Bank, *World Development Report, 1987* (Washington, D.C.: World Bank, 1987). For a recent empirical critique of this research, however, see Sabastian Edwards, "Openness, trade liberalization and growth in developing countries," *Journal of Economic Literature* 31 (September 1993): 1358–1393,

and Behzad Yaghmaian, "An empirical investigation of exports, development and growth in developing countries: Challenging the neoclassical theory of export-led growth," *World Development* 22 (December 1994): 1977–1995.

10. Bradford, "East Asian 'models' "; Smith, *Industrial Policy in Developing Countries*; Jene Kwon, "The East Asian challenge to neoclassical orthodoxy," *World Development* 22 (December 1994): 635–644; Paul Krugman, "The myth of Asia's miracle," *Foreign Affairs* 73 (December 1994): 62–78.

11. Gerald K. Helleiner, *International Trade and Economic Development* (Harmondsworth, England: Penguin, 1972), pp. 69–70.

12. United Nations Development Program, *Human Development Report, 1992*, p. 63. For an interesting and provocative counterargument to the shift in development thinking toward greater emphasis on export promotion in imitation of Taiwan and South Korea, see Paul P. Streeten, "A cool look at 'outward-looking' industrialization and trade strategies," *PIDE Tidings*, November-December 1982; William R. Cline, "Can the East Asian model of development be generalized?" *World Development* 10 (February 1982); Gary Fields, "Employment, income distribution, and economic growth in seven small open economies," *Economic Journal* 94 (March 1984): 74–83; and Kirkpatrick, "Trade policy and industrialization."

13. For an interesting discussion of this issue, see "Working man's dread," *Economist*, October 1, 1994, pp. 14–19.

14. For many LDCs, trade taxes represent a major source of government revenue. For example, Pakistan, Ghana, and Ecuador derive 36%, 41%, and 47% of their income, respectively, from this source.

15. For a comprehensive analysis and critique of import substitution policies in developing countries, see Ian Little, Tibor Scitovsky, and Maurice Scott, *Industry and Trade in Some Developing Countries* (London: Oxford University Press, 1970). See also Kirkpatrick, "Trade policy and industrialization," pp. 71–75; Hubert Schnitz, "Industrialization strategies in less developed countries: Some lessons of historical experience," *Journal of Development Studies* 21 (October 1984): 1–21; and Dornbusch, "Case for trade liberalization."

16. Helleiner, *International Trade and Economic Development*, p. 105. It should be mentioned, however, that in light of some of the new trade theories, with their emphasis on economies of scale, externalities, and human capital investments, the arguments for selective tariff protection are coming back into vogue. See Helleiner's more recent volume, *Trade Policy, Industrialization and Development* (Oxford: Clarendon Press, 1992), chap. 1, for a survey of these issues.

17. Little *et al.*, *Industry and Trade*, p. 39.

18. Herbert G. Grubel, "Effective tariff protection: A non-specialist introduction to the theory, policy implications and controversies," in Herbert G. Grubel and Harry Johnson (eds.), *Effective Tariff Protection* (Geneva: GATT, 1971), p. 2.

19. Little *et al.*, *Industry and Trade*, p. 4. For more recent data, see Table 13.2.

20. Such preferred customers are often identified in the literature as "rent seekers" because they spend a great amount of time and effort engaged in activities, such as bribery, designed to capture the "economic rent" generated by government-induced price distortions like overvalued exchange rates. See Anne O. Krueger, "The political economy of the rent-seeking society," *American Economic Review* 64 (June 1974).

21. For an analysis of multiple exchange rates and their effects on the economy, see Miguel Kiguel and Stephen A. O'Connell, "Parallel exchange rates in developing countries,"

World Bank Research Observer 10 (February 1995): 21–52. Black market premiums in the 1980s ranged from 66% in Mexico and 173% in Brazil to 4,264% in Ghana; see Table 13.3.

22. For example, in December 1994, the Mexican government *devalued* its currency, the peso, by 35% against the dollar. By February 1995, the peso had *depreciated* by another 15% before recovering some of its losses in the foreign-exchange market.

23. For a concise discussion of some issues related to devaluation, see Karim Nashashibi, "Devaluation in developing countries: The difficult choices," *Finance and Development* 20 (March 1983).

24. For an excellent review and analysis of these issues, from which much of the following discussion is drawn, see Rostam M. Kavoussi, "International trade and economic development: The recent experience of developing countries," *Journal of Developing Areas* 19 (April 1985): 379–392. See also Dornbusch, "Case for trade liberalization," and Rodrik, "Limits of trade policy reform."

25. A statement of these views can be found in Deepak Lal and Sarath Rajapatirana, "Foreign trade regimes and economic growth in developing countries," *World Bank Research Observer* 2 (July 1987), and Bhagwati, "Export-promoting trade strategy."

26. Kavoussi, "International trade and economic development," 388–390.

27. Hans W. Singer and Patricia Gray, "Trade policy and growth of developing countries: Some new data," *World Development* 16 (March 1988): 395–403.

28. Streeten, "Trade strategies," 3–4.

29. Bradford, "East Asian 'models'", p. 123.

30. See, for example, W. Arthur Lewis's Nobel Prize lecture, "The slowing down of the engine of growth," *American Economic Review* 70 (September 1980): 555–564, and Frances Stewart, "The direction of international trade: Gains and losses for the Third World," in Gerald K. Helleiner (ed.), *A World Divided* (Cambridge: Cambridge University Press, 1976).

31. For a useful summary of Third World regional integration experiences, see Felipe Pazos, "Regional integration of trade among less developed countries," *World Development* 1 (July 1973): 1–12; David Morawetz, *The Andean Group: A Case Study in Economic Integration among Developing Countries* (Cambridge, Mass.: MIT Press, 1974); and Peter Robson, *Integration, Development and Equity: Economic Integration in West Africa* (London: Allen & Unwin, 1983). For an empirically based argument for expanded trade among developing countries as a stimulant to long-term growth and development, see Yves Sabolo, "Trade between developing countries, technology transfers and employment," *International Labour Review* 122 (September-October 1983), and World Bank, *World Development Report, 1991*, pp. 105–108.

32. International Monetary Fund, *World Economic Outlook, May 1994* (Washington, D.C.: International Monetary Fund, 1994), annex 1.

33. Ian Goldin and Odin Knudson (eds.), *Agricultural Trade Liberalization: Implications for Developing Countries* (Paris: OECD Development Center, 1990). For a more recent analysis, see Will Martin and L. Alan Winters, "The Uruguay Round and the developing economies," *World Bank Discussion Paper No. 307* (October 1995).

34. For a discussion of developed-country blue-collar responses to the new GATT treaty and the NAFTA accord, see "Working man's dread" (note 13) and Adrian Wood, "How trade hurt unskilled workers," *The Journal of Economic Perspectives* 9 (Summer 1995): 57–82.

Further Reading

Five of the best general sources of information on trade policies and strategies for development are Gerald K. Helleiner, *International Trade and Economic Development* (Harmondsworth, England: Penguin, 1972); Donald B. Keesing, *Trade Policy for Developing Countries*, World Bank Staff Working Paper No. 53 (Washington, D.C.: World Bank, 1979); World Bank, *World Development Report, 1987* (New York: Oxford University Press, 1987), chaps. 5–8; Colin Kirkpatrick, "Trade policy and industrialization in LDCs," in Norman Gemmell (ed.), *Surveys in Development Economics* (Oxford: Blackwell, 1987), chap. 2; and Dominick Salvatore and Thomas Hatcher, "Inward-oriented and outward-oriented trade strategies," *Journal of Development Studies* 23 (April 1991): 7–25. See also Pradip K. Ghosh (ed.), *International Trade and Third World Development* (Westport, Conn: Greenwood Press, 1984); Ronald W. Jones and Peter B. Kenen, *Handbook of International Economics* (Amsterdam: North Holland, 1988), chaps. 11, 12, 16, and 19, for a useful collection of readings and statistics; and Gerald K. Helleiner (ed.), *Trade Policy, Industrialization and Development: New Perspectives* (Oxford: Clarendon Press, 1992).

For a lively debate about the relative merits of trade policy, see Rudiger Dornbusch, "The case for trade liberalization in developing countries," *Journal of Economic Perspectives* 6 (Winter 1992): 69–85, and Dani Rodrik, "The limits of trade policy reform in developing countries," *Journal of Economic Perspectives* 6 (Winter 1992): 87–105. In addition to the many outstanding articles and books cited in the notes to this chapter, the following are more specialized readings on the topics covered: R. L. Allen, "Integration in less developed areas, *Kyklos* 14 (1961): 315–336; Bela Balassa, "The impact of industrial countries' tariff structure on their imports of manufactures from less developed areas," *Economica* 34 (1967): 372–383; Bela Balassa, "Trade policies in developing countries," *American Economic Review* 61 (1971): 178–187; Henry Bruton, "The import-substitution strategy of economic development: A survey," *Pakistan Development Review* 10 (1970): 123–146; and Charles Cooper and Benton Massell, "Toward a general theory of customs unions for developing countries," *Journal of Political Economy* 73 (1965): 461–474.

See Stephen C. Smith, *Case Studies*, Chapter 17 for an analysis of the impact of NAFTA on Mexico and Latin America, and Chapter 18 for a review of export and industrial policies in South Korea.

CHAPTER 14

Balance of Payments, Third World Debt, and the Macroeconomic Stabilization Controversy

The problems of many heavily indebted developing countries are a cause of economic and political concern and can be a threat to world stability.

—Declaration of "Group of Seven" Industrialized Countries, 1988

Each of us [is a] witness, in the anguished course of our daily life, to the perverse effects of an international situation which we have not created but which falls on us and has converted us into net exporters of capital. Adjustments are demanded of us [in Latin America] which the developed countries give no signs of being willing to undertake in their own economies.

—José Sarney, President of Brazil, 1987

If I were the president of a Third World nation . . ., I would be far more frightened by a well-dressed gentleman bringing loans from the IMF or Citibank than by a bearded guerrilla muttering threats of revolution.

—Lewis Lapham, *Imperial Masquerade*, 1990

In Chapters 12 and 13, we examined the scope and limitations of traditional trade theory and policy. Our focus was primarily on international commodity trade in theory and practice and its likely effects on Third World growth, efficiency, equity, and stability. In this chapter and the next, we extend this analysis in the following ways. First, in this chapter, after looking at a country's balance of payments accounts and recent trends in LDC trade balances, we dissect the dimensions and ramifications of the Third World debt dilemma. Our focus will be on how the debt crisis emerged during the 1970s and 1980s, what is being done about it, and who is bearing the burden of stabilization and adjustment programs induced by the International Monetary Fund (IMF). Specifically, we ask the question, "Is the 1980s debt crisis a nonissue for the 1990s, or has the problem simply receded from the headlines as developed-country commercial banks write down their bad loans?" In Chapter 15, we extend our analysis of the role of finance in trade to examine the international flow of financial resources consisting of (1) the flow of private foreign direct investments, primarily via the carrier of the modern multinational corporation; (2) the recent resurgence of private financial "portfolio investments" in support of newly organized or refurbished Third World "emerging" stock and bond markets; (3) the flow of public financial and technical resources in the form of bilateral and multilateral foreign aid; and (4) the growing importance of private financial and technical assistance to the poorest LDCs in the form of nongovernmental organization (NGO) foreign aid programs.

The Balance of Payments Account

General Considerations

The extension of our analysis beyond simple mechandise trade into areas related to the international flow of financial resources permits us to examine the **balance of payments** of developing nations. A balance of payments table is designed to summarize a nation's financial transactions with the outside world. It is divided into three components, as shown by the summary in Table 14.1. The **current account** focuses on the export and import of goods and services, investment income, debt-service payments, and private and public net remittances and transfers. Specifically, it subtracts the value of imports from exports (the *merchandise trade balance* of Chapter 12) and then adds flows of the net investment income received from abroad (e.g., the difference between interest and dividend payments on foreign stocks, bonds, and bank deposits owned by LDC nationals and brought into the country, as opposed to being left overseas, and those securities, if any, of the LDC owned by foreigners plus repatriated profits of multinational corporations). Taking this total $(A - B + C$ in Table 14.1), it subtracts item D, debt-service payments, which represents a major and growing component of Third World current account deficits, and

---

TABLE 14.1 A Schematic Balance of Payments Account

Exports of goods and services	A
Imports of goods and services	B
Investment income	C
Debt-service payments	D
Net remittances and transfers	E
Total *current account* balance $(A - B + C - D + E)$	F
Direct private investment	G
Foreign loans (private and public), minus amortization	H
Increase in foreign assets of domestic banking system	I
Resident capital outflow	J
Total *capital account* balance $(G + H - I - J)$	K
Increase (or decrease) in *cash reserve account*	L
Errors and omissions $(L - F - K)$	M

SOURCE: Adapted from John Williamson and Donald R. Lessard, *Capital Flight: The Problem and Policy Responses* (Washington, D.C.: Institute for International Economics, 1987), tab. 1.

adds item E, net private and public remittances and transfers, such as money sent home by LDC nationals working abroad (e.g., Mexicans and Filipinos in the United States, Algerians in France, Pakistanis in Kuwait). The final result ($A - B + C - D + E$ in Table 14.1) yields the current account balance—a positive balance is called a **surplus**, a negative balance a **deficit**. The current account therefore allows us to analyze the impact of various commercial policies, primarily on merchandise trade but also indirectly on investment income, debt-service payments, and private transfers.

The **capital account** records the value of private foreign direct investment (mostly by multinational corporations), foreign loans by private international banks, and loans and grants from foreign governments (as in the form of foreign aid) and multilateral agencies such as the IMF and the World Bank. It then subtracts an extremely important item, especially for the major debtor countries of Latin America such as Mexico, Brazil, Argentina, and Venezuela. This is what is called "resident capital outflow" in Table 14.1, otherwise known as **capital flight**. During the 1980s debt crisis, capital flight by wealthy LDC nationals, who sent vast amounts of money into developed-nation bank accounts, real estate ventures, and stock and bond purchases, is estimated to have contributed up to half the total debt of some Latin debtor nations.[1] It dwarfed the receipt of private and public loans and investments and was a major contributor to the worsening balance of payments of many Third World nations. The balance on capital account is therefore calculated as items $G + H - I - J$ in Table 14.1. Again, a positive balance is a surplus and a negative one a deficit.

Finally, the **cash account**, or **international reserve account** (item L), is the balancing item (along with the "errors and omissions" item M, which reconciles statistical inequalities) that is lowered (shows a net outflow of foreign reserves) whenever total disbursements on the current and capital accounts exceed total receipts. Table 14.2 presents a simple chart of what constitutes positive (credit) and negative (debit) items in a balance of payments table. Nations accumulate international cash reserves in any or all of the following three forms: (1) foreign **hard currency** (primarily U.S. dollars, but increasingly Japanese yen, pounds sterling, or German marks) whenever they sell more abroad than they purchase; (2) gold,

---

TABLE 14.2 Positive and Negative Effects on Balance of Payments Accounts

Positive Effects (Credits)	Negative Effects (Debits)
1. Any sale of goods or services abroad (export)	1. Any purchase of goods and services abroad (import)
2. Any earning on an investment in a foreign country	2. Any investment in a foreign country
3. Any receipt of foreign money	3. Any payment to a foreign country
4. Any gift or aid from a foreign country	4. Any gift or aid given abroad
5. Any foreign sale of stocks or bonds	5. Any purchase of stocks or bonds from abroad

SOURCE: Reprinted by permission of the publisher, from *The ABCs of International Finance* by John Charles Pool and Stephen C. Stamos (Lexington, Mass.: Lexington Books, D.C. Heath & Co., Copyright 1987, D.C. Heath & Co.).

mined domestically or purchased; and (3) deposits with the IMF, which acts as a reserve bank for individual nations' central banks.

A Hypothetical Illustration: Deficits and Debts

A numerical example might prove helpful at this point. In Table 14.3, a hypothetical balance of payments table for a developing country is portrayed. First, under the *current account*, there is a $10 million negative merchandise trade balance made up of $35 million of commodity export receipts (of which over 70%—$25 million—are derived from primary agricultural and raw material products), minus $45 million of mostly manufactured consumer, intermediate, and capital goods import payments. To this total we add $5 million in payments for the services of foreign shipping firms and $1 million of investment income receipts representing net interest transmitted on foreign bond holdings, subtract $15 million of debt-service payments representing this year's interest costs on the accumulated foreign debt of the LDC, and add $2 million of remittance and transfer receipts derived from payments of domestic workers living overseas who send home part of their earnings. Together, all of these items add up to a *deficit* on current account of $27 million.

TABLE 14.3 A Hypothetical Balance of Payments Table for a Developing Nation

Item		Amounts (millions of dollars)
A. Current Account		
Commodity exports		+35
Primary products	+25	
Manufactured goods	+10	
Commodity imports		−45
Primary products	−10	
Manufactured goods	−35	
Services (e.g., shipping costs)		−5
Investment income		+1
Debt-service payments		−15
Net remittances and transfers		+2
Balance on current account	−27	
B. Capital Account		
Private direct foreign investment		+3
Private loans and portfolio investments		+4
Government and multilateral flows (net)		+3
Loans	+8	
Grants	+1	
Debt amortization	−6	
Resident capital outflow		−8
Balance on capital account	+2	
Balance on current and capital accounts	−25	
C. Cash Account		
Net decrease in official monetary reserves		+25
Balance on cash account	+25	

Turning now to the *capital account*, we see that there is a net inflow of $7 million of foreign private investment consisting of $3 million of direct investment from multinational corporations in the form of new local factories and $4 million in private loans (from international commercial banks) and private portfolio (stock and bond) investments by foreign individuals and mutual funds (see Chapter 15). There is also a net positive $3 million inflow of public loans and grants in the form of foreign aid and multilateral agency assistance. Note that the gross *inflow* of $9 million in public loans and grants is partly offset by a $6 million capital *outflow* representing **amortization** (gradual reduction) of the principal on former loans. However, as shown later in Table 14.4, these figures were reversed in the 1980s— the outflow to repay accumulated debts exceeded the inflow of *both* public aid and new refinancing bank loans. As a result, a $35.9 billion net transfer from developed to developing countries in 1981 became a $22.5 billion transfer from poor to rich nations by 1990.

Returning to Table 14.3, we see that a major reason for the perverse flow of financial capital from poor to rich nations is the very high levels of resident capital outflow. This capital flight is estimated to have amounted to almost $100 billion during the first half of the 1980s from just five of the principal countries involved (Argentina, Brazil, Mexico, the Philippines, and Venezuela)[2] and almost $200 billion over the 10-year period 1976–1985. In Table 14.3, it is listed as an outflow of $8 million. The net result is a $2 million positive balance on capital account, bringing the total balance on current and capital accounts to a deficit of $25 million.

TABLE 14.4 **Current Account Balances and Capital Account Net Financial Transfers of Developing Countries, 1978–1990 (billions of dollars)**

Year	Current Account	Capital Account Net Financial Transfers
1978	−32.1	33.2
1979	+10.0	31.2
1980	+30.6	29.5
1981	−48.6	35.9
1982	−86.9	20.1
1983	−64.0	3.7
1984	−31.7	−10.2
1985	−24.9	−20.5
1986	−46.4	−23.6
1987	−4.4	−34.0
1988	−22.4	−35.2
1989	−18.4	−29.6
1990	−3.0	−22.5

SOURCES: International Monetary Fund, *World Economic Outlook, 1988* and *1992* (Washington, D.C.: International Monetary Fund, 1988, 1992), tab. A-33; United Nations Development Program, *Human Development Report, 1992* (New York: Oxford University Press, 1992), tab. 4.3.

Financing and Reducing Payments Deficits: Some Initial Policy Issues

To finance this $25 million negative balance on combined current and capital accounts, our hypothetical country will have to draw down $25 million of its central bank holdings of official monetary reserves. Such reserves consist of gold, a few major foreign currencies, and special drawing rights at the IMF (these will be explained shortly). **International reserves** serve for countries the same purpose that bank accounts serve for individuals. They can be drawn on to pay bills and debts, they are increased with deposits representing net export sales and capital inflows, and they can be used as collateral to borrow additional reserves.

We see, therefore, that the balance on current account *plus* the balance on capital account must be offset by the balance on cash account. This is shown by the net *decrease* of $25 million in official monetary reserves. If the country is very poor, it is likely to have a very limited stock of these reserves. This overall balance of payments deficit of $25 million may therefore place severe strains on the economy and greatly inhibit the country's ability to continue importing needed capital and consumer goods. In the least developed nations of the world, which have to import food to feed a hungry population and possess very limited stocks of monetary reserves, such payments deficits may spell disaster for millions of people.

Facing existing or projected balance of payments deficits on combined current and capital accounts, developing nations have a variety of policy options. First, they can seek to improve the balance on current account by promoting export expansion or limiting imports (or both). In the former case, there is the further choice of concentrating on primary or secondary product export expansion. In the latter case, policies of import substitution (the protection and stimulus of domestic industries to replace previously imported manufactured goods in the local market) and/or selective tariffs and physical quotas or bans on the importation of specific consumer goods may be tried. Alternatively, countries can seek to achieve both objectives simultaneously by altering their official foreign-exchange rates through a currency devaluation that lowers export prices and increases import prices. They can also follow very restrictive fiscal and monetary policies (called *structural adjustment* by the World Bank and *stabilization policies* by the IMF—see Appendix 14.1 for a history and description of these organizations). These policies are designed to reduce domestic demand so as to lower imports and reduce the inflationary pressures that may have contributed to the "overvalued" exchange rate that slowed exports and promoted imports.

A second alternative, often not exclusive of the first, is for developing countries to try to improve the balance on their capital account by encouraging more private foreign direct or portfolio investment, borrowing from international commercial banks, or seeking more public foreign assistance. But neither private foreign investment nor a major proportion of foreign aid comes in the form of gifts (outright grants). The receipt of loan assistance implies the necessity of future repayments of principal and interest. Directly productive foreign investments in, say, building local factories entail the potential repatriation of sizable proportions of the profits of the foreign-owned enterprise. Moreover, as shown in Chapter 15, the encouragement of private foreign investment has broader development implications than the mere transfer of financial or physical capital resources.

Finally, Third World nations can seek to modify the detrimental impact of chronic balance of payments deficits by expanding their stocks of official monetary reserves. One way of doing this is through the acquisition of a greater share of a new international "paper gold" known as **special drawing rights (SDRs)**. Traditionally, under the workings of the international monetary system, countries with deficits in their balance of payments were required to pay for these deficits by drawing down on their official reserves of the two principal international monetary assets, gold and U.S. dollars. But with the phenomenal growth in the volume and value of world trade, a new kind of international asset was needed to supplement the limited stock of gold and dollars. Consequently, in 1970 the IMF was given the authority to create $10 billion of these special drawing rights. These new international assets perform many of the functions of gold and dollars in settling balance of payments accounts. They are valued on the basis of a basket of currencies (a weighted average of the value of five different currencies—the U.S. dollar, the French franc, the German mark, the pound sterling, and the Japanese yen) and constitute claims on the IMF. They may thus be exchanged for convertible currencies to settle international official transactions. By 1988, the total value of SDR holdings was in excess of $28 billion, of which $5 billion, or 17.7%, was designated for the developing countries. In 1995, the approximate dollar value of one SDR was $0.72. Eventually, the IMF would like to see all international financial settlements conducted in SDRs, with gold and dollars dropped as official mediums of exchange.

A major issue of great concern to developing countries, therefore, is the distribution of the benefits of SDRs. The present formula for distributing SDRs gives 75% of the total to the 25 industrial nations. This leaves only 25% to be distributed among the 90 or so Third World countries that participate in the international monetary system. Dissatisfied with this situation, these countries are now, as a group, exerting pressure on the developed nations to agree to the creation of supplementary SDRs that would be allocated in preferential amounts or on preferential terms to developing nations.

Having summarized some basic balance of payments concepts and issues as they relate to both commodity trade and international flows of financial resources, we can now briefly review recent trends in the balance of payments of developing nations and then focus our attention on a detailed analysis of the Third World debt problem.

Recent Trends in LDC Balance of Payments

For most developing countries, the 1980s marked a major transition in their balance of payments accounts with the rest of the world. Prior to 1980, the conventional development strategy had Third World nations operating with sizable current account deficits, for imports of capital and intermediate goods were required to provide the machinery and equipment for rapid industrialization. Export earnings paid for most, but not all, of these imports. The financing of these deficits was therefore made possible by large resource transfers in the capital account in

TABLE 14.5 Developing Countries: Summary of Payments Balances on Current Account, 1980–1996 (billions of dollars)

	1980	1981	1985	1987	1990	1991	1992	1993	1994	1995[a]	1996[a]
All developing countries	30.6	-48.6	-24.9	-4.4	-3.0	-83.6	-73.5	-98.3	-91.0	-85.4	-90.8
By region											
Africa	-2.1	-22.3	-1.2	-4.4	-3.0	-4.3	-9.1	-9.1	-12.6	-14.2	-12.7
Asia	-14.4	-19.0	-13.1	23.4	1.2	1.6	1.2	-14.4	-11.2	-20.4	-28.7
Middle East	92.5	50.0	-7.6	-12.2	0.8	-63.2	-30.6	-29.9	-19.2	-19.6	-18.6
Latin America	-29.8	-42.9	-1.9	-11.1	-2.0	-17.7	-35.1	-44.9	-47.9	-31.2	-30.6
By predominant export											
Fuel exporters	96.4	34.8	-0.8	-12.6	3.4	-76.9	-57.8	-46.8	-43.8	-19.7	-18.2
Non-fuel exporters	65.7	-83.3	-17.5	8.2	-6.4	-6.7	-15.8	-51.5	-47.2	-65.7	-72.6
Primary product exporters	-37.0	-56.0	-10.2	-15.3	-5.7	-8.9	-19.0	-23.7	-24.5	-21.3	-23.6
Agricultural exporters	-35.2	-39.4	-7.9	-11.4	-2.1	-5.2	-13.7	-17.3	-19.5	-15.8	-17.8
Mineral exporters	-1.8	-16.6	-2.3	-3.9	-3.6	-3.8	-5.3	-6.4	-5.0	-5.5	-5.9
Four Asian (NIC) exporters of manufactures	N.A.	N.A.	11.0	32.8	17.0	12.7	12.8	18.0	11.2	12.1	16.0

SOURCE: International Monetary Fund, *World Economic Outlook, 1988 and 1995* (Washington, D.C.: International Monetary Fund, 1988, 1995), tabs. A-33, A-30.
[a]Estimated. N.A. = not available.

the form of country-to-country (bilateral) foreign aid, direct private investment by multinational corporations, private loans by international banks to both LDC governments and local businesses, and multilateral loans from the World Bank and other international development agencies. Capital account surpluses, therefore, typically more than compensated for current account deficits so that international reserves were being accumulated.

However, after 1980 the developing world experienced a substantial deterioration in both current and capital account balances. As Table 14.4 shows, the net financial transfers component of the capital account (which includes everything in Table 14.3 except private direct foreign investment) turned sharply negative beginning in 1984. The overall transition amounted to more than $68 billion, comparing the positive $33.2 billion capital account balance in 1978 with the negative $35.2 billion balance in 1988. Meanwhile, the brief period of large current account surpluses, which reflects entirely OPEC's booming export revenues of 1979–1980, abruptly turned negative in 1981 and stayed negative throughout the decade. The smallest negative balance ($3.0 billion) occurred in 1990, and as Table 14.5 shows, this was entirely due to the $17.0 billion surplus generated by the four Asian manufactured goods exporters (Taiwan, South Korea, Singapore, and Hong Kong).

The reasons for the decline in current account balances in the 1980s and 1990s include (1) a dramatic fall in commodity prices, including oil; (2) global recessions in 1981–1982 and 1991–1993, which caused a general contraction in world trade; and (3) increasing protectionism in the developed world against Third World exports.

The capital account showed its dramatic turn as a combined result of rising Third World debt-service obligations, sharp declines in lending by international banks, and massive capital flight. Together these factors turned what had previously been a positive annual resource flow of $25 billion to $35 billion from developed to less developed countries into a negative annual flow of $25 billion to $35 billion from the Third World to the First World. Behind all these disturbing trends, however, lies the key international problem faced by developing nations during the 1980s and early 1990s: the debilitating dilemma of Third World debt.

The Third World Debt Crisis

Background and Analysis

The accumulation of **external debt** is a common phenomenon of Third World countries at the stage of economic development where the supply of domestic savings is low, current account payments deficits are high, and imports of capital are needed to augment domestic resources. Prior to the early 1970s, the external debt of developing countries was relatively small and primarily an official phenomenon, the majority of creditors being foreign governments and international financial institutions such as the IMF, the World Bank, and regional development banks. Most loans were on concessional (low-interest) terms and were extended for purposes of implementing development projects and expanding imports of capital goods. However, during the late 1970s and early 1980s, commercial banks began playing a large role in international lending by recycling surplus OPEC "petrodollars" and issuing general-purpose loans to LDCs to provide balance of payments support and expansion of export sectors.

Although foreign borrowing can be highly beneficial, providing the resources necessary to promote economic growth and development, it has its costs. In recent years, these costs have greatly outweighed the benefits for many developing nations. The main cost associated with the accumulation of a large external debt is **debt service**. Debt service is the payment of amortization (liquidation of the principal) and accumulated interest; it is a contractually fixed charge on domestic real income and savings. As the size of the debt grows or as interest rates rise, debt-service charges increase. Debt-service payments must be made with foreign exchange. In other words, debt-service obligations can be met only through export earnings, curtailed imports, or further external borrowing. Under normal circumstances, most of a country's debt-service obligations are met by its export earnings. However, should the composition of imports change or should interest rates rise significantly, causing a ballooning of debt-service payments, or should export earnings diminish, debt-servicing difficulties are likely to arise. This has been the experience of most of the heavily indebted Third World nations.

However, before delving into the statistical details and tracing the origins of and prospects for the Third World debt crisis, it is necessary to understand a fundamental concept known as the **basic transfer**.[3] The basic transfer of a country is defined as the net foreign-exchange inflow or outflow related to its international borrowing. It is measured as the difference between the net capital inflow and interest payments on the existing accumulated debt. The net capital inflow in turn is simply the difference between the gross inflow and the amortization on past debt. The basic transfer is an important concept because it represents the amount of foreign exchange that a particular LDC is gaining or losing each year from international capital flows. As we shall soon discover, the basic transfer turned very negative for developing nations during the 1980s, causing a loss of foreign exchange and a net outflow of capital.

The basic transfer equation can be expressed as follows. Let the net capital inflow, F_N, be expressed as the rate of increase of total external debt, and let D represent the total accumulated foreign debt. If d is the percentage rate of increase in that total debt, then

$$F_N = dD. \tag{14.1}$$

Because interest must be paid each year on the accumulated debt, let us let r equal the average rate of interest so that rD measures total annual interest payments. The basic transfer (BT) then is simply the net capital inflow minus interest payments, or

$$BT = dD - rD = (d - r)D. \tag{14.2}$$

BT will be positive if $d > r$, and the country will be gaining foreign exchange. However if $r > d$, the basic transfer turns negative, and the nation loses foreign exchange.

Any analysis of the evolution of and prospects for the Third World debt crisis requires an examination of the various factors that cause d and r to rise and fall.

In the early stages of debt accumulation, when an LDC has a relatively small total debt, D, the rate of increase, d, is likely to be high. Also, because most first-stage debt accumulation comes from official (as opposed to private) sources in the form of bilateral foreign aid and World Bank lending, most of the debt is incurred on concessional terms—that is, at below-market interest rates with lengthy repayment periods. Consequently, r is quite low and in any event less than d. As long as this accumulating debt is being used for productive development projects with rates of return in excess of r, the additional foreign exchange and rising foreign debt represented by the positive basic transfers pose no problems for recipient nations. In fact, as we have seen in earlier chapters, this process of debt accumulation for productive investments in both rural and urban areas represents an essential ingredient in any viable strategy of long-term development.

A serious problem arises, however, when (1) the accumulated debt becomes very large so that its rate of increase, d, naturally begins to decline as amortization rises relative to rates of new gross inflows; (2) the sources of foreign capital switch from long-term "official flows" on fixed, concessional terms to short-term, variable-rate private bank loans at market rates that cause r to rise; (3) the country begins to experience severe balance of payments problems as commodity prices plummet and the terms of trade rapidly deteriorate; (4) a global recession or some other external shock, such as a jump in oil prices, a steep rise in U.S. interest rates on which variable-rate private loans are based, or a sudden change in the value of the dollar, in which most debts are denominated, takes place; (5) a loss in confidence in an LDC's ability to repay resulting from points 2, 3, and 4 occurs, causing private international banks to cut off their flow of new lending; and (6) perhaps most important, a substantial flight of capital is precipitated by local residents who for political or economic reasons (e.g., expectations of currency devaluation) send great sums of money out of the country to be invested in developed-country financial securities, real estate, and bank accounts. All six factors can combine to lower d and raise r in the basic transfer equation, with the net result that the overall basic transfer becomes highly negative, and capital flows from the underdeveloped to the developed world (as shown in Table 14.5). The debt crisis then becomes a self-reinforcing phenomenon, and heavily indebted Third World countries are forced into a downward spiral of negative basic transfers, dwindling foreign reserves, and stalled development prospects. The story of the debt crisis of the 1980s is largely told by the simple analysis of the factors affecting the basic transfer mechanism of Equation 14.2. Against this analytical background, we can now look at the specific details of the Third World debt crisis and the various efforts to deal with it.

Dimensions of the Crisis

In the 26-year period 1970–1995, the external debt of developing nations grew from $68.4 billion to just over $1.7 trillion, an increase of more than 2,300% (see Table 14.6). Debt-service payments increased by 2,118% to exceed $220 billion by the mid-1990s. Although a great deal of the debt was concentrated in four Latin American

TABLE 14.6 Dimensions of the Developing-Country Debt Crisis, 1970–1996

	1970	1975	1980	1985	1990	1991	1992	1993	1994	1995[a]	1996[a]
Total external debt											
(billions of dollars)	68.4	180	635.8	949	1298.7	1371.6	1447.0	1559.2	1623.1	1716.0	1796.7
Of which Africa	—	14.9	55.6	64.7	225.9	235.5	234.2	239.6	245.3	258.7	268.0
Debt-service payments[b]											
(billions of dollars)	11.0	25.8	102.4	128	155.0	178.8	175.1	180.0	216.0	220.2	214.4
Of which Africa	—	1.3	4.1	27.6	26.4	26.4	27.1	22.8	23.6	27.9	22.2
Debt-to-export ratio[c]											
(percent)	99.4	76.4	81.9	154.5	132.6	132.5	127.1	127.8	118.7	111.2	104.4
Of which Africa	—	—	92.5	189.0	227.1	246.3	246.2	258.9	264.5	249.7	240.9
Debt-service ratio[d]											
(percent of exports)	13.5	9.5	13.2	20.9	7.1	7.5	6.3	6.6	6.1	6.5	6.6
Of which Africa	5.7	—	14.4	27.6	10.5	10.4	9.3	8.7	11.3	12.4	8.7
Debt-to-GDP ratio[e]											
(percent)	13.3	15.4	24.4	36.4	34.8	35.2	33.7	33.0	31.3	29.4	27.5
Of which Africa	20.9	—	28.3	46.6	60.7	64.2	60.6	63.5	65.7	61.2	63.2

SOURCES: International Monetary Fund, *World Economic Outlook, 1988* and *1995* (Washington, D.C.: International Monetary Fund, 1988, 1995), tabs. A-38, A-41, and A-42.

[a]Projections.

[b]Actual payments of interest on total debt plus actual amortization payments on long-term debt.

[c]Ratio of external debt to exports of goods and services.

[d]Debt service as a percentage of exports of goods and services. Excludes service payments to the IMF.

[e]Ratio of external debt to gross domestic product (GDP).

nations (Brazil, Mexico, Argentina, and Venezuela), 16 countries have been singled out by the World Bank as *severely indebted* (see Table 14.7). Their debts were deemed most vulnerable to default because of the very large share owed to commercial creditors at variable rates of interest. Although only 3 of the 16 severely indebted countries (SICs) are in sub-Saharan Africa, the debt problems of this region are made more troublesome by declining per capita incomes and stagnating economies. Both their debt-to-export and debt-service ratios are well above the overall LDC average and, in some cases, even above the ratios of other SICs.

The seeds of the 1980s debt crisis were sown in the 1974–1979 period, when there was a virtual explosion in international lending, precipitated by the first major OPEC oil price increase. By 1974, developing countries had begun playing a larger role in the world economy, having averaged growth rates of 6.6% in 1967–1973. The newly industrializing countries, particularly those like Mexico, Brazil, Venezuela, and Argentina in Latin America, had growth rates well above the developing countries' average. To meet their growth needs, many countries had begun importing heavily, especially capital goods, oil, and food. Following outward-looking development strategies, they expanded their exports agressively. In the face of high oil prices and a world recession, in which the growth rates of the industrialized countries fell from an average of 5.2% in 1967–1974 to an average of 2.7% for the rest of the 1970s, many developing countries sought to sustain their high growth rates through increased borrowing. While lending from official sources, particularly nonconcessional lending, increased significantly, it was insufficient to meet the growth needs of the middle-income and newly industrializing developing countries. Furthermore, countries with an excess of imports over lagging exports were reluctant to approach official sources, such as the IMF, that might submit them to painful policy adjustments. So the middle-income and newly industrializing developing countries turned to commercial banks and other private lenders, which began issuing general-purpose loans to provide balance of payments support. Commercial banks, holding the bulk of the OPEC surplus (which had jumped from $7 billion in 1973 to $68 billion in 1974 and ultimately peaked at $115 billion in 1980) and facing a low demand for capital from the slower-growing industrialized countries, aggressively competed in lending to developing countries on comparatively permissive and favorable terms. Figure 14.1 portrays the mechanism by which OPEC petrodollars were recycled, starting with Middle Eastern oil export earnings being deposited in U.S. and European banks, which then lent these dollar balances to Third World public- and private-sector borrowers. Over $350 billion was recycled from OPEC countries between 1976 and 1982.

As a result of all these factors, the total external debt of developing countries more than doubled from $180 billion in 1975 to $406 billion in 1979, increasing over 20% annually. More significant, an increasing portion of the debt was now on nonconcessional terms involving shorter maturities and market rates of interest, often variable rates. In 1971, about 40% of the total external debt was on nonconcessional terms. This increased to 68% by 1975, and by 1979 over 77% of the debt was on harder terms. Although the increase in nonconcessional lending by official institutions was partly responsible for this rising proportion, the more than tripling of lending by private capital markets played the major role.

TABLE 14.7 Debt and Growth in the Severely Indebted Countries, 1990

Country	Debt Outstanding, 1990[a]		Debt Service, 1990[a] (billions of dollars)		Debt Indicators, 1990 (percent)		Average Annual Growth Rate, 1982–1990 (percent per annum)				
	Total (billions of dollars)	Total Private Sources (percent)	Total	Interest	Debt-to-GNP Ratio, 1990	Interest-to-Exports Ratio, 1990	Gross National Product[b]	Exports[c]	Imports[c]	Investment[d]	Per Capita Consumption[d]
Algeria	26.8	71.6	8.3	2.1	52.9	15.1	1.9	-0.7	-2.2	-1.2	-0.6
Argentina	61.1	76.9	5.1	2.8	61.7	18.4	-0.0	5.6	1.2	-8.3	-1.1
Bolivia	4.3	15.3	0.4	0.2	101.0	15.9	1.0	1.0	2.2	-10.5	-1.7
Brazil	116.2	76.3	7.4	2.9	22.8	8.6	2.5	5.3	-0.1	1.3	0.5
Bulgaria	10.9	99.1	1.3	0.5	56.9	6.4	1.0	-1.8	-0.2	3.0	3.8
Congo	5.1	37.2	0.3	0.2	203.6	9.3	1.1	2.3	0.7	-18.9	-0.7
Cote d'Ivoire	18.0	59.5	1.4	0.5	203.9	13.3	-0.4	3.3	2.8	-12.4	-4.7
Ecuador	12.1	64.2	1.1	0.5	120.6	14.5	2.0	2.2	-1.5	-4.1	-0.5
Mexico	96.8	69.8	12.1	7.3	42.1	16.7	1.6	5.3	5.0	-2.6	-1.1
Morocco	23.5	25.1	1.9	0.9	97.1	11.7	4.0	10.0	5.4	1.4	0.9
Nicaragua	10.5	36.8	0.0	0.0	—	3.0	-3.8	-2.1	-0.8	-7.5	-6.5
Peru	21.1	62.7	0.5	0.2	60.1	5.2	-1.4	0.6	-1.8	-9.3	-3.5
Poland	49.4	42.8	1.0	0.3	82.4	1.6	1.8	6.3	2.5	4.8	2.6
Syria	16.4	14.0	1.5	0.2	118.1	3.9	1.8	9.2	-2.6	-9.1	-1.7
Venezuela	33.3	85.1	4.3	3.2	71.0	15.6	1.1	0.5	-7.7	-10.7	-1.2
Nigeria	36.1	47.4	3.0	1.8	117.9	12.1	1.9	1.8	-8.4	-9.6	-2.3

SOURCE: World Bank, *World Debt Tables, 1991–92* (Washington, D.C.: World Bank, 1992), p. 25.

[a]Debt, debt service, and interest include the use of IMF credit. Figures are based on actual payments on all external debt in 1990.
[b]In U.S. dollars.
[c]In current U.S. dollars.
[d]1982–1989.

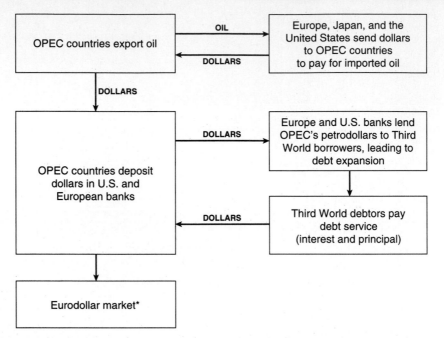

FIGURE 14.1 The Mechanics of Petrodollar Recycling. *Source*: Reprinted with the permission of Lexington Books, an imprint of Macmillan, Inc., from *The ABCs of International Finance* by John Charles Pool, Stephen C. Stamos, and Patrice Franko Jones. Copyright © 1987, 1991 by Lexington Books.

*Eurodollars are dollar deposits in any bank outside of the United States, not necessarily in Europe only. Rather than send their surplus dollars to the United States, foreign banks began in the 1970s to accept direct dollar deposits, pay interest on them, and lend them directly to LDC borrowers.

Together, the large increase in the size of debt and the larger proportion scheduled on harder terms were responsible for the tripling of debt-service payments, which rose from $25 billion in 1975 to $75 billion in 1979. Table 14.6 summarizes the statistical evolution of the debt and debt-service problems of developing nations between 1970 and 1996.

Despite the sizable increases in debt-servicing obligations, the ability of most developing countries to meet their debt-service payments during the late 1970s remained largely unimpaired. This was primarily a function of the international economic climate that prevailed during that period. Specifically, a combination of declining real oil prices as a result of inflation, low or negative real interest rates, and increased export earnings narrowed current account deficits toward the end of the decade and enabled developing countries to sustain relatively high growth rates, averaging 5.2% during 1973–1979, through massive borrowing.

In sum, the surge in international lending following the first oil shock was largely during the period 1974–1979. In a congenial economic atmosphere, it permitted developing countries to maintain relatively high rates of growth with little debt-servicing difficulty. It also facilitated the recycling of a huge surplus from oil exporters to oil importers through the lending activities of private international banks, and it helped dampen the recession in industrialized countries by providing for increased export demand on the part of Third World countries.

Unfortunately, this success was short-lived, and, in fact, the surge in international lending that occurred in 1974–1979 had laid the groundwork for all the problems that were to come. The second oil shock, which occurred in 1979, brought about a complete reversal of the economic conditions conducive to the success of international lending in the previous period. Now developing countries faced an abrupt increase in oil prices that added to oil import bills and affected industrial goods imports. There was also a huge increase in interest rates caused by the industrialized countries' economic stabilization policies and a decrease in Third World export earnings resulting from a combination of slowed growth in the more developed nations and a precipitous decline of over 20% in primary commodity export prices. Moreover, developing countries inherited from the previous period a huge debt and debt-service obligation, which was made even more onerous by burgeoning interest rates and more precarious as a result of the bunching of short-term maturities.

Finally, during the entire period of debt accumulation, one of the most significant and persistent trends was the tremendous increase in private capital flight. It is estimated that between 1976 and 1985, about $200 billion fled the heavily indebted countries.[4] This was the equivalent of 50% of the total borrowings by LDCs over the same period. Fully 62% of Argentina's and 71% of Mexico's debt growth are estimated to have resulted from capital flight. In fact, some researchers have argued that the 1985 level of Mexican debt would have been $12 billion (rather than the actual $96 billion) were it not for the huge private capital flight.[5]

Facing this critical situation, Third World countries had two policy options. They could either curtail imports and impose restrictive fiscal and monetary measures, thus impeding growth and development objectives, or they could finance their widening current account deficits through more external borrowing. Unable, and sometimes unwilling, to adopt the first option as a means of solving the balance of payments crisis, many countries were forced in the 1980s to rely on the second option, borrowing even more heavily. As a result, massive debt-service obligations accumulated, so that by 1990 countries like Bolivia, Nigeria, Argentina, Ecuador, and Peru had experienced negative economic growth in the 1980s and thus faced severe difficulties in paying even the interest on their debts out of export earnings (see Table 14.7). They could no longer borrow funds in the world's private capital markets. In fact, not only did private lending dry up, but by 1984 the developing countries were paying back $10.2 billion *more* to the commercial banks than they were receiving in new loans. When paybacks to international lenders such as the IMF and the World Bank are included, as Figure 14.2 shows, the net financial flows (new lending minus debt service) for all indebted LDCs went from +$35.9 billion in 1981 to –$35.2 billion in 1988 before a resumption of private lending and equity investing caused it to rise again to +$18 billion in 1992. Now SICs had no recourse but to seek IMF assistance and face up to the IMF stabilization program, the conditions of which were tantamount to the first policy option.

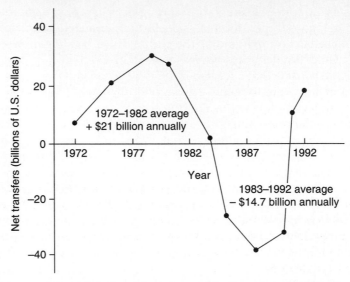

FIGURE 14.2 Net Financial Transfers from Developed to Developing Countries, 1972–1992. *Source*: United Nations Development Program, *Human Development Report, 1994* (New York: Oxford University Press, 1994), fig. 4.4.

Attempts at Alleviation: Macroeconomic Instability, IMF Stabilization Policies, and Their Critics

The IMF Stabilization Program

One course of action that was increasingly but often reluctantly used by countries facing serious **macroeconomic instability** (high inflation and severe government budget and foreign payments deficits) along with growing foreign-debt obligations was to renegotiate loans with private international banks. The basic idea was to stretch out the payment period for principal and interest or to obtain additional financing on more favorable terms. Typically, however, such debtor countries had to deal with the IMF before a consortium of international banks would agree to refinance or defer existing loan schedules. Relying on the IMF to impose its usual "conditionality" medicine of tough **stabilization policies** before it first agreed to lend LDCs funds in excess of their legal IMF quotas, the private banks interpreted successful negotiations with the IMF as a sign that borrowing countries were making serious efforts to reduce payments deficits and earn the foreign exchange needed to repay earlier loans. There are four basic components to the typical IMF stabilization program:[6]

1. Abolition or liberalization of foreign exchange and import controls
2. Devaluation of the official exchange rate

3. A stringent domestic anti-inflation program consisting of (a) control of bank credit to raise interest rates and reserve requirements; (b) control of the government deficit through curbs on spending, especially in the areas of social services for the poor and staple food subsidies, along with increases in taxes and in public enterprise prices; (c) control of wage increases, in particular ensuring that such increases are at rates less than the inflation rate (i.e., abolishing wage indexing); and (d) dismantling of various forms of price controls and promoting freer markets

4. Greater hospitality to foreign investment and a general opening up of the economy to international commerce

In the early 1980s, numerous debtor countries with greatly depleted foreign reserves, including Mexico, Brazil, Argentina, and the Philippines, had to turn to the IMF to secure additional foreign exchange. By 1992, 10 countries had arranged to borrow a total of 37.2 billion special drawing rights (equal to approximately $27 billion) from the IMF. The countries, their loan amounts, and the year of their borrowing are given in Table 14.8. To receive their loans and, more important, to negotiate additional credits from private banks, all were required to adopt some or all of the enumerated stabilization policies. Although such policies may be successful in reducing inflation and improving the LDCs' balance of payments situation,[7] they can be politically very unpopular (as evidenced by anti-IMF riots in Venezuela and Nigeria in the early 1990s) because they strike at the heart of development efforts by disproportionately hurting the lower- and middle-income groups.[8] Alternatively, they have often been viewed by Third World leaders as representing a double standard—harsh adjustment policies for LDC debtors and no adjustment of the huge budget or trade deficits for the world's greatest debtor, the

TABLE 14.8 Countries Borrowing from the International Monetary Fund, 1980–1992

Country	Year	Loans (billions of special drawing rights)[a]
Argentina	1988	5.2
Bangladesh	1985	1.2
Bolivia	1989	0.4
Brazil	1988	6.1
Ghana	1988	1.2
Mexico	1989	10.2
Morocco	1987	1.9
Philippines	1988	2.1
Venezuela	1986	6.0
Yugoslavia	1989	2.9

SOURCE: *New York Times*, April 26, 1992, sec. 3, p. 6.

[a] 1.37 SDRs = $1.

United States. Finally, because IMF policies are being imposed by an international agency that is perceived by many economists, especially those of the dependency school, to be merely an arm of the rich industrial nations, stabilization policies are often viewed as measures designed primarily to maintain the poverty and dependence of Third World nations while preserving the global market structure for the industrialized nations. For example, in an extensive dependence critique of the IMF and its stabilization programs, Cheryl Payer has argued that the IMF functions within a First World–dominated global trading system "as the chosen instrument for imposing imperialist financial discipline upon poor countries" and thus creates a form of "international peonage" or debt slavery in which the balance of payments problems of LDCs are perpetuated rather than resolved. Payer further argues that the IMF encourages LDCs to incur additional debt from international financial institutions while it "blackmails" them (through threats of loan rejection) into antidevelopmental stabilization programs. This added debt burden thus becomes a source of future balance of payments problems, so that a vicious cycle sets in—one in which Third World debtor nations have to run faster merely to stay in place.[9]

Less radical observers view the IMF as neither a developmental nor an antidevelopmental institution but simply an institution trying to carry out its original, though somewhat outdated, mandate to hold the global capitalist market together through the pursuit of orthodox short-term international financial policies. Its primary goal is the maintenance of an "orderly" international exchange system designed to promote monetary cooperation, expand international trade, control inflation, encourage exchange-rate stability, and, most important, help countries deal with *short-run* balance of payments problems through the provision of scarce foreign-exchange resources. Unfortunately, in a highly unequal trading world, the balance of payments problems of many Third World nations may be structural and *long-term* in nature, with the result that short-term stabilization policies may easily lead to long-run development crises.[10] For example, between 1982 and 1988, the IMF strategy was tested in 28 of the 32 nations of Latin America and the Caribbean. It was clearly not working. During that period, Latin America financed $145 billion in debt payments but at a cost of economic stagnation, rising unemployment, and a decline in per capita income of 7%.[11] These countries "adjusted" but did not grow. By 1988, only two were barely able to make their payments. The same situation prevailed in much of Africa.[12]

In the absence of a major restructuring of both the domestic LDC economy (with perhaps the help of the World Bank's **structural adjustment loans**,[13] to be discussed in detail in a later chapter) and the international economic order, the adoption of orthodox economic policies in pursuit of orthodox balance of payments objectives may in fact jeopardize the very system that the IMF seeks to preserve. Though its motives are probably not the sinister ones ascribed to it by Payer and other dependence theorists, the IMF's 1980s policies of severe financial austerity of debtor countries tended to inflict a harsh and often unnecessary economic burden on nations that in many cases could ill afford it. Fortunately, by early 1990s, the IMF had begun to show a greater flexibility and a willingness to modify its prescribed medicine to fit the varied illnesses of its patients.[14] This is a more logical, humane, and, in the long run, more developomental course of action than the harsh prescriptions of the earlier stabilization packages.

Global Dimensions of the LDC Debt Problem

LDC debt has become a worldwide problem with serious economic implications for both developed and less developed countries. In fact, the debt crisis of the 1980s, which was initiated by Mexico's declared *moratorium* on debt payments in 1982 (and came close to being repeated by Mexico again in 1995) called into question the stability and very viability of the international financial system. Fears were voiced that if one or two of the major debtor countries (Brazil, Mexico, or Argentina) were to default, if a group of debtor nations were jointly to repudiate their debts by forming a **debtors' cartel**, or if more countries followed Peru's early initiative to link debt servicing to export earnings, the economies of Western nations might be seriously affected. Following the onset of the debt crisis, most developing countries were cut off from the international capital market. Emergency meetings between international bankers and government officials of developed nations and LDC debtors were convened in the financial capitals of the world. Rumors of imminent default led currency speculators to purchase dollars, driving up the dollar's market value in 1983–1984 to a level well beyond its shadow value and adding even further to the dollar-denominated debt burdens of developing nations.

Numerous proposals for relieving or restructuring the debt burdens of highly indebted nations have been put forward.[15] These have ranged from a new allocation of special drawing rights to **restructuring** (on better terms for debtor countries) of principal payments falling due during an agreed-on consolidation period. Most notable have been the Paris Club arrangements, offering highly concessional conditions, the so-called Toronto terms. These bilateral arrangements for public loans permit creditor governments to choose from among three alternative concessional options—partial cancellation of up to one-third of nonconcessional loans, reduced interest rates, or extended (25-year) maturity of payments—to generate cash-flow savings for debtor countries. For commercial banks, the so-called 1989 **Brady Plan** links partial debt forgiveness for selected borrowers to IMF or World Bank financial support guaranteeing the payment of the remaining loans as well as LDC commitments to adopt stringent IMF-type adjustment programs, promote free markets, welcome foreign investors, and repatriate overseas capital. In addition, there has been much discussion of **debt-for-equity swaps**. These are the sale at a discount (sometimes in excess of 50%) of questionable LDC commercial bank debts to private investors (mostly foreign corporations) in secondary trading markets. These corporations then trade a debtor's IOU for a local state-owned asset, such as a steel mill or a telephone company. Commercial banks are now more willing to engage in such transactions because new interpretations and regulations for U.S. banks permit them to take a loss on the loan swap while not reducing the book value of other loans to that country. For the LDCs' part, they are able through debt-for-equity swaps to encourage private investments in local-currency assets from both foreign and resident investors as well as to reduce their overall debt obligations. Much of the privatization that has occurred in Latin American debtor countries has been financed through these swap arrangements. The flip side of these benefits, however, is the fact that foreign investors are buying up the state-owned real assets of developing nations, such as steel mills and telephone companies, at major discounts.

Observers who worry about developed-country penetration into LDC economies or the exacerbation of domestic dualistic tendencies are naturally troubled by these debt-for-equity swaps. Between 1985 and 1992, they accounted for over 36% of all debt conversions.

A more appealing, but much less significant, swap arrangement is the **debt-for-nature swap**, intended to win LDC government commitments to environmental preservation of such assets as the rain forests in Ecuador or a national park in Costa Rica (see Chapter 10). Most debt-for-nature swaps are carved out by nongovernmental organizations such as the World Wildlife Fund or the Nature Conservancy. They purchase the debtor nation's IOU at a discount from a local bank and then restructure it into local-currency payments, which are then used, say, to preserve an endangered natural resource. Unfortunately, such mutually beneficial debt-for-nature swaps accounted for only 2% of debt conversion between 1985 and 1992.

The problem with most proposals for debt alleviation, including debt-for-equity swaps, is that they require private international banks to initiate or endorse the policies. Most are unwilling to take any steps that would harm their short-run balance sheets. More significant, in the absence of unilateral **debt repudiation** by LDCs (a policy that surely would hurt both borrowers and lenders in both the short and the long term), most proposals (except debt-for-nature swaps) do not solve the debt problem but merely postpone the day when debts become once again due and another crisis erupts.

All in all, the debt crisis underlined the tremendous interdependence and political fragility of the international economic and financial system. It also demonstrated that not only were Third World economies terribly vulnerable to 1 or 2 percentage point increases in U.S. interest rates but, perhaps more significant, that developed countries could indeed be harmed by the economic failures or public policies of key developing nations.

Although many developing countries can be held at least partly responsible for the massive accumulation of debt, the adverse economic conditions they face are often beyond their control. In fact, this adverse economic climate was in part precipitated by the industrialized countries' own economic stabilization policies, which led to soaring interest rates, worldwide economic recession, and the resulting decrease in demand for developing-country exports. William R. Cline has estimated, for example, that almost 85% ($401 billion) of the total increase ($480 billion) in the external debt of the non-oil LDCs between 1973 and 1982 can be attributed to four factors outside of their control: OPEC oil price increases, the rise in dollar interest rates in 1981–1982, the decline in Third World export volume as a result of the worldwide recession, and the dramatic fall in commodity prices and the consequent worsening of their terms of trade.[16]

Has the Debt Problem Disappeared? Winners and Losers

Whereas the Third World debt problem was often referred to as the most significant international financial crisis of the 1980s, in the 1990s LDC debt seems to have all but disappeared from the pages of developed-country newspapers and magazines. This is because almost 80% of the outstanding debt owed to commercial banks by the most heavily indebted LDCs (Mexico, Argentina, Brazil, and Venezuala, among others), as well as a much smaller proportion owed to governments and multilaterial institutions, has now been restructured. Commercial bankers and financiers in the industrialized countries have declared that the debt crisis is over and that with the signing of a Brady-type restructuring accord with Argentina in April 1992 and with Brazil in July 1992, the banking industry could close its books on Third World debt. But the data contained in Tables 14.6 and 14.7 reveal that for many countries, especially those in Africa, the problem is as serious as ever—perhaps even more so. Most poor countries have seen little, if any, debt relief. Their debt-service payments still comprise anywhere from 15% to 20% of their export revenues—much higher than the 10% to 12% ratios of the precrisis period. The situation is particularly acute in sub-Saharan Africa, where the region's total debt has grown steadily. It now stands at over $180 billion, three times as large as the 1980 total and more than 10% higher than its collective GNP! Debt-service payments approach $10 billion annually, which is almost four times Africa's annual expenditure on health and education combined.[17] This represents a monstrous drain on the region's already depleted development finance (see Chapter 18).

Because of the large burden of repayment and the requirement that severely indebted LDCs swallow a heavy dose of IMF restrictive medicine, economic growth for many developing countries has turned negative, per capita consumption has steadily declined, and the investment necessary to generate the growth required to pay off debts and raise levels of living has all but disappeared. The crisis may by over for the developed-country commercial banks, whose outstanding Third World loans dropped from $67 billion in 1987 to $19 billion in 1992. For them, the IMF clearly did a good job. But for all the low- and middle-income citizens of the developing world whose economic welfare has been and continues to be sacrificed in order to prevent their indebted governments from sinking even further into insolvency, not only has the medicine been bitter, but the patient is clearly not recovering.[18] John Cavanagh, an expert on developing countries, put it this way:

> The IMF in many ways is like a medieval doctor where no matter what the ailment, you apply leeches and bleed the patient. My experience is that they [IMF quick fixes] are very successful in steering countries' resources toward paying debts to commercial banks, but they are disastrous in terms of the long-term economic health of these countries.[19]

Far from dead, the debt crisis is, at best, only sleeping. This was vividly revealed in late 1994 and early 1995 when one of the great "success stories" of debt rescheduling, Mexico, was forced to devalue its currency and seek special standby loans to pay off its short-term debt obligations. Almost half of the private portfolio investment capital that had flowed into Mexico (and other Latin American debtor nations, including Brazil, Argentina, and Venezuela) in the early 1990s was summarily withdrawn. Mexico was then forced to declare a new austerity program, further weakening the already deteriorating condition of its shrinking middle class and its working poor. As in 1982, the large commercial banks and Wall Street investors were once again surprised by Mexico's move. The "hot money" flows that had been universally hailed as a boon to the Mexican economic reform program now added to its burden of retrenchment as most investors withdrew their funds in the time that it took them to hit their computer keys.[20]

Many severely indebted LDCs, particularly those in Africa, have thus been caught in a vicious cycle in which the repayment of debt creates a drag on economic growth, yet accelerated growth is the only viable basis for escaping the confines of the debt trap. Perhaps more serious, their prolonged economic decline means that it will take at least a generation for them even to reestablish the low levels of living that they were experiencing in the late 1970s.

Conclusions

The burden of the global debt crisis must ultimately be shared by all. Many developing countries may have to undergo a period of difficult adjustment. At the same time, industrialized countries will have to relax restrictive monetary policies and encourage imports from the developing world. Since research shows that, along with political stability, the main determinant of LDC ability to repay debts and attract private investor capital is the level of global and domestic interest rates,[21] it is critical for creditor-country monetary authorities to keep this fact in mind as they pursue their macroeconomic strategies. Some additional debt relief (e.g., making interest payments in local currencies or putting a cap on real interest rates) will also be necessary. Commercial banks can no longer be permitted to pass on their losses to developed-country taxpayers. International organizations, primarily the IMF and the World Bank, will have to provide sufficient financial liquidity and policy flexibility so that the poorest developing countries can make the necessary adjustments without further sacrificing growth and equity. And perhaps most important of all from a long-run perspective is the need gradually to restructure the entire international trading and financial system. We will look at this last issue when we examine the future of the international economic order in Chapter 18.

CASE STUDY

The Economy of Venezuela

GEOGRAPHIC, SOCIAL, AND ECONOMIC INDICATORS

Capital Caracas

Area 912,050 km²

Population 21.8 million (1995)

Population (average annual growth rate) 2.5% (1985–1994)

GNP per capita U.S. $2,760 (1994)

GNP per capita (average annual growth rate) 0.6% (1985–1994)

Agriculture as share of GDP 2% (1994)

Exports as share of GDP 29% (1994)

Infant mortality rate (per 1,000 live births) 20.2 (1995)

Child malnutrition (underweight) 6% (1993)

Females as share of labor force 28% (1994)

Illiteracy rate (age 15+) 8% (1990)

Human Development Index 0.82 (high) (1992)

Venezuela spans the major sea and air routes linking the northern and southern parts of the Western Hemisphere. Its coastline is 2,816 kilometers on the Caribbean Sea and Atlantic Ocean. Most Venezuelans are of European, Amerindian, or African descent. The most recent influx of European immigration dates to the early 1950s, when large numbers of Spanish, Italian, and Portuguese immigrants arrived. The 1981 census showed that 94% of the people are native-born; of the foreign-born, most came from Spain, Italy, Portugal, Africa, and Colombia.

Venezuela is one of the Western Hemisphere's least densely populated countries, even though its annual population increase since 1950 has been over 3%. The population is rapidly changing from rural to urban. In 1936, only 35% of the population lived in cities and towns of more than 1,000 inhabitants; today about 80% does. One out of every five Venezuelans lives in Caracas.

Venezuela's wealth is distributed unevenly, and a significant percentage of the population has inadequate nutrition, housing, clothing, and education. These problems are complicated by the tremendous pressures created by rapid population growth. Venezuela doubles its population about every 29 years; 40% of its people are under 15 years of age, and 70% are under 30.

Until recently, Venezuela's major employment problem was a shortage of skilled workers and managers to operate what has been a burgeoning and increasingly technological economy. To fill the gap, Venezuela recruited many skilled foreign technicians, expanded its technical education facilities, and sent Venezuelans abroad for training. With the economic decline of the past decade, however, rising unemployment has become the primary labor concern, though the lack of technically qualified personnel remains a significant factor.

Venezuela is a major producer and exporter of oil. A founding member of the Organization of Petroleum Exporting Countries (OPEC), it plays a key role in the world oil market. Mexico and Venezuela have begun granting loans to Central America and Caribbean Basin nations on the basis of oil purchased from both countries.

521

In 1994, oil accounted for about 90% of Venezuela's total merchandise export income, 60% of the government's revenues, and some 22% of the gross domestic product. The government nationalized the industry on January 1, 1976. Since then, employment has doubled, income has quadrupled, and production of crude oil has declined.

Crude oil production peaked in 1970 at 3.7 million barrels per day. Production was 1.8 million in 1990. The initial decline was due to government conservation policies and low investment in exploration and development. In the latter half of the 1980s, however, it was attributable to the weak world oil market.

Because of the petroleum-based nature of the economy, Venezuela is especially vulnerable to shocks in the economies of the developed oil-consuming countries. Since the early 1980s, the Venezuelan economy has been damaged by depressed oil prices. The United States' battle against inflation, as well as its efforts to economize on petroleum use, adversely affected Venezuela and other OPEC members. Depressed petroleum prices also meant that Venezuela's terms of trade decreased, unemployment increased, and the country ran into major current account trade deficits that had to be financed by both foreign nations and the IMF. As a result, Venezuela's large external debt totaled $37.2 billion in 1993, the fifth largest in the developing world, including Poland.

The core issues that Venezuela must address in the late 1990s are related to the balance of public- and private-sector involvement in the economy and the need to solve the debt problem. In 1986, Venezuela negotiated a 6 billion SDR loan with the IMF (see Table 14.8). In return, it undertook IMF-induced draconian stabilization and austerity measures, including severe budget cuts to control inflation, wage controls, sale of public corporations, devaluation of the currency, and promotion of exports (especially tourism), to curtail current account deficits. However, the continuing decline in per capita income, which fell 4.4% per year between 1988 and 1990, combined with increases in poverty, inequality, and unemployment, led to popular discontent, urban riots directed at the IMF, and an attempted coup in 1992. Former President Carlos Andres Perez thereafter announced major political reforms and abandoned many IMF-induced austerity measures. Although growth turned positive once again and inflation fell to below 45% in 1993 (compared with 84% in 1989), prospects for alleviating the plight of the poor remain clouded.

Concepts for Review

Amortization	Debt repudiation
Balance of payments	Debt service
Basic transfer	Deficit
Brady Plan	External debt
Capital account	Hard currency
Capital flight	International reserve account
Cash account	International reserves
Conditionality*	Macroeconomic instability
Current account	Restructuring
Debt-for-equity swaps	Special drawing rights (SDRs)
Debt-for-nature swaps	Stabilization policies
Debtors' cartel	Structural adjustment loans
	Surplus

*Introduced in Appendix 14.1.

Questions for Discussion

1. Draw up a balance of payments table similar in format to Table 14.3 using the most recent data from any Third World country (consult the IMF's monthly publication *International Financial Statistics* for the most recent data). Explain the significance of the various entries in the current and capital accounts. What is the status of the country's international reserves, and how do they compare with those of one year ago?

2. Describe the basic transfer mechanism. Using the list of credits and debits from Table 14.2, identify which ones would fit into the basic transfer equation. How does the basic transfer help us analyze Third World debt problems?

3. Trace the evolution of the Third World debt problem during the 1970s and 1980s. What were the key ingredients? Explain.

4. Why was the problem of capital flight so serious in some highly indebted countries? What causes capital flight, and what do you think can be done about it?

5. Who should bear most of the burden of responsibility for the debt crisis, LDCs or MDCs?

6. What is petrodollar recycling, and how did it contribute to the debt crisis? Why were LDCs so eager to borrow money from international banks? Explain.

7. What is the significance of the debt-service ratio? Can indebted countries do anything to lower this ratio? Explain.

8. Describe the typical IMF stabilization package for SICs. What are the objectives of these policies, and why are international banks so eager for IMF negotiations to precede their discussions with SICs? What are the economic and social costs of these programs? Explain.

9. Is the debt crisis over? If so, what are the long-term implications for both lenders and borrowers? If not, what still needs to be done?

Notes

1. See, for example, John Williamson and Donald R. Lessard, *Capital Flight: The Problem and Policy Responses* (Washington, D.C.: Institute for International Economics, 1987), for an excellent review of data and issues.

2. *Ibid.*, p. 56.

3. The following discussion is based on Frances Stewart, "The international debt situation and North-South relations," *World Development* 13 (February 1985): 141–204.

4. John Charles Pool and Stephen C. Stamos, *The ABCs of International Finance* (Lexington, Mass.: Lexington Books, 1987), pp. 55–57.

5. *Ibid.*, p. 55.

6. For review and discussion of Third World stabilization programs from a developed-country perspective, see Rudiger Dornbusch, "Policies to move from stabilization to growth," and W. Max Corden, "Macroeconomic policy and growth: Some lessons of

experience," in *Proceedings of the World Bank Annual Conference on Development Economics, 1990* (Washington D.C.: World Bank, 1991).

7. However, for a lengthy economic critique of the IMF stabilization package and its effects on both the balance of payments and the overall economy, see Paul P. Streeten, "Stabilization and adjustment," *Labour and Society* 13 (January 1988): 1–18.

8. See, for example, James L. Dietz, "Debt and development: The future of Latin America," *Journal of Economic Issues* 20 (December 1986): 1029–1051, and Paul P. Streeten, *Strategies for Human Development* (Copenhagen: Handelshøjskolens Forlag, 1994), Part 2.

9. Cheryl Payer, *The Debt Trap: The IMF and the Third World* (New York: Monthly Review Press, 1974), pp. 1–49.

10. For an analysis of how IMF stabilization programs are typically imposed on Third World debtors and how such policies can be counterproductive in a climate of macroeconomic instability, see Dani Rodrik, "The limits of trade policy reform in developing countries," *Journal of Economic Perspectives* 6 (Winter 1992): 87–105.

11. Part of the explanation for this decline in per capita income, according to researchers like Jeffrey Sachs, Paul Krugman, and Andreas Savvides, relates to the *debt overhang hypothesis*. The argument is that the external debt burden provided a disincentive to domestic investment in LDCs and thus slowed economic growth because any additional foreign-exchange earnings would have to be turned over to foreign creditors. For a brief discussion and empirical test of this hypothesis, see Andreas Savvides, "Investment slowdown in developing countries during the 1980s: Debt overhang or foreign capital inflows?" *Kyklos* 45 (1992): 363–378.

12. See Howard Stein, "Deindustrialization, adjustment, the World Bank and the IMF in Africa," *World Development* 20 (January 1992): 83–95, and especially, Frances Stewart, "The many faces of adjustment," *World Development* 19 (December 1991): 1847–1864.

13. Unlike IMF stabilization policies, which are short-run in nature, the World Bank engages in what it calls long-run *structural adjustment* lending. The focus is on improving the macroeconomic policy environment with an emphasis on (a) mobilizing domestic savings through fiscal and financial policies, (b) improving public-sector efficiency by stressing price-determined allocation of public investments and improving the efficiency of public enterprises, (c) improving the productivity of public-sector investments by liberalizing trade and domestic economic policies, and (d) reforming institutional arrangements to support the adjustment process. For a description of the role of the bank in structural adjustment lending, see the World Bank's 1986 and 1987 *World Development Reports* and the appendix to this chapter.

14. Stewart, "Many faces of adjustment," 1857–1859. See also Jeffrey Sachs, "Beyond Bretton Woods: A new blueprint," *Economist*, October 1, 1994, pp. 23–27.

15. For a review and a description of debt-relief proposals, see World Bank, *World Debt Tables, 1991–1992* (Washington, D.C.: World Bank, 1992), chaps. 2–4.

16. William R. Cline, *International Debt and the Stability of the World Economy* (Washington, D.C.: Institute for International Economics, 1983).

17. Gary Gardner, "Third World debt is still growing," *World Watch*, January-February 1995, p. 37. See also Wayne Nafziger, *The Debt Crisis in Africa* (Baltimore: Johns Hopkins University Press, 1993).

18. LDC nationals are not the only losers in the debt game. Taxpayers in the developed countries are increasingly absorbing the former debts of commercial banks through government loan guarantees generated by the Brady Plan. For an excellent discussion, see

Benjamin J. Cohen, "What ever happed to the LDC debt crisis?" *Challenge*, May-June 1991, pp. 47–51.

19. Quoted in *New York Times*, April 26, 1992, sec. 3, p. 1.

20. For an interesting analysis of what determines private capital flows (basically, the level of international interest rates) and why the debt crisis is far from dead, see Michael P. Dooley, Eduardo Fernandez-Arias, and Kenneth M. Kletzer, *Recent Private Capital Inflows to Developing Countries: Is the Debt Crisis History?* National Bureau for Economic Research Working Paper No. 4792 (Washington, D.C.: National Bureau for Economic Research, 1994). For a review of the Mexican devaluation see Report of an Independent Task Force, *Lessons of the Mexican Peso Crisis* (New York: Council on Foreign Relations, 1995).

21. *Ibid.*, pp. 25–26.

Further Reading

The best overall source of empirical information on the debt crisis can be found in the World Bank's annual edition of *World Debt Tables*. Two excellent books are Harold Lever and Christopher Huhne, *Debt and Danger: The World Financial Crisis* (New York: Atlantic Monthly Press, 1985), and John Charles Pool and Stephen C. Stamos, *The ABCs of International Finance* (Lexington, Mass.: Lexington Books, 1987). In addition to the numerous citations in the notes to this chapter, the following articles are recommended: Anne O. Kreuger, "Debt, capital flows and LDC growth," *American Economic Review* 77 (May 1987); Manuel Pastor, Jr., "The effects of IMF programs in the Third World," *World Development* 15 (February 1987); Alejandro Foxley, "Latin American development after the debt crisis," *Journal of Development Economics* 27 (October 1987); the entire issue of the *Journal of Development Planning* 16 (1985), titled "The Debt Problem: Acute and Chronic Aspects," especially the articles by Carlos Massad, William R. Cline, and Albert Fishlow; Hans W. Singer, "Beyond the debt crisis," *Development* (January 1992): 35–38; and Wayne Nafziger, *The Debt Crisis in Africa* (Baltimore: Johns Hopkins University Press, 1993).

For a look at debt reduction efforts in Mexico, see Stephen C. Smith, *Case Studies*, Chapter 19.

APPENDIX 14.1

A Brief History and Analysis of the International Monetary Fund and the World Bank

In July 1944, as World War II began to turn strongly in favor of the Allied forces, representatives from 45 countries convened in Bretton Woods, New Hampshire, to plan the terms of postwar international economic cooperation. The economic devastation of the Great Depression in the 1930s followed by the ravages of the Second World War had led to the collapse of international financial markets and precipitous declines in the volume of international trade. The International Monetary Fund (IMF) and World Bank were created to rebuild international goods and capital markets, as well as the war-torn economies of Western Europe.

The designated roles of the IMF and the World Bank were quite different, though to some extent they were intended to complement each other. It was the prevailing wisdom at the time of the Bretton Woods conference that the stabilization of international capital markets was essential to the resumption of lively international trade and investment. This concern led to the establishment of the IMF, which became responsible for monitoring and stabilizing the international financial system through the short-term financing of balance of payments deficits. The World Bank's complementary role involved financing the reconstruction and development of member nations, primarily through the construction of national infrastructures. An attempt was also made to establish an international organization to encourage the liberalization of trade between countries, eventually leading to the creation of the General Agreement on Tariffs and Trade (GATT). It is widely recognized that the institutional structure provided by these organizations has facilitated the international flow of goods and capital, though there remains considerable dispute over the extent of their effectiveness.

Though the policies of the IMF and the World Bank have changed considerably since their inception, the institutional framework laid out at Bretton Woods remains intact and continues to exert tremendous influence over the global economy. This applies especially to the countries of the Third World, whose ability to attract foreign capital is largely determined by the stance of the IMF and World Bank. Furthermore, the increasing interdependence between developed and developing countries has served to intensify the interaction between these international financial institutions and the Third World. Consequently, the IMF and the World Bank now play critical and evolving roles in the development process.

International Monetary Fund

The participants at the Bretton Woods conference established a system of fixed exchange rates in which each country was required to peg the value of its currency relative to the U.S. dollar, which remained directly convertible into gold at $35 per ounce. Initially, it was the responsibility of the IMF to finance temporary balance of payments deficits arising as a consequence of these pegged exchange rates. Any country experiencing a "fundamental disequilibrium" in trade as a result of an overvalued exchange rate was required to obtain approval from the IMF before devaluing its currency (see Chapter 13). In its capacity as overseer of exchange-rate policy and the financial conduct of member countries, the IMF was to stabilize international financial markets by ensuring convertibility between currencies. In addition, by financing trade imbalances the IMF fulfilled the role of international lender of last resort, averting financial crises in countries experiencing acute foreign-exchange shortages. These activities were designed to maintain the viability of the international financial system created at Bretton Woods.

Progress toward international cooperation and compliance with the articles of agreement laid out at Bretton Woods continued until the mid-1960s, when a number of economic factors led many members to abandon their fixed exchange rates. Persistent declines in its gold reserves and chronic balance of payments deficits, in part resulting from overvaluation of the dollar, led the United States to abandon the convertibility of dollars into gold in August 1971. The ensuing collapse of the Bretton Woods system of exchange rates raised questions about the role of the IMF in international finance. The majority of the fund's resources had previously been used to maintain the value of several of the strongest currencies. The shift to a variety of floating-rate systems in the industrialized countries had obviated a principal IMF responsibility.

At the same time, however, the growing volume of international trade made it clear that a mechanism for expanding international liquidity was required. Therefore, in 1969 the IMF became responsible for the creation and allocation of a new international currency called special drawing rights (SDRs). The primary function of this new medium of exchange was to facilitate trade where shortages of international reserves of gold and dollars had imposed financial restrictions. In addition, the 1970s brought a new set of financial crises that helped reshape the role of the IMF in international markets. A combination of factors, including a world recession, rocketing OPEC fuel prices, and falling LDC exports, had led to large balance of payments deficits in many LDCs. This was a contributing factor in the decision by the IMF to more than double its total quota of SDRs. A substantial portion of the new funds were loaned through an agency, the Trust Fund, which provides concessional (low-interest) loans to finance trade deficits in the poorest developing countries.

Financing from the IMF is provisional in the sense that recipient countries must meet a set of requirements based on the purpose of the loan. During the IMF's first quarter century, the stipulations accompanying IMF funds were limited to exchange-rate behavior. However, following the demise of the system of fixed exchange rates and as the size and number of loans used for adjustment purposes increased, the restrictions placed on the economic policies of receiving countries also expanded and became known collectively as **conditionality**. These conditions are intended to increase the effectiveness of IMF resources by encouraging expedient behavior on the part of debtor governments facing chronic balance of payments troubles. Because the terms of conditionality are frequently draconian, imposing the greatest hardship on the poorest households in debtor countries, they have remained tremendously controversial.

The use of conditionality and the direct "surveillance" of Third World macroeconomic policy by the IMF marked its increasing involvement in the development process. Two other areas in which the fund began to expand its activities were in the provision of information services to the public and technical assistance to developing-country governments. These efforts were generally targeted toward achieving internal adjustments prescribed by the IMF to eliminate macroeconomic imbalances leading to payments deficits. Thus the direction of the IMF changed dramatically during the 1970s. According to a fund historian, "The use of resources was no longer undertaken in defense of a par value system but to promote effective and durable adjustment and restoration of the conditions for balanced and sustained economic growth."[1] Whether or not these policies were consistent with the development objectives of Third World countries, they have at times helped avert financial crises arising in international capital markets.

By 1982, the external debt of non-oil-exporting developing countries stood at roughly $600 billion, and more than half that figure was owed on commercial terms. Imminent default in a number of heavily indebted Third World countries experiencing high inflation, weak export markets, falling terms of trade, and large government deficits threatened to destabilize international financial markets. As the severity of crises in developing countries intensified, private sources of funding shrank rapidly, reducing the liquidity necessary to service debt. To avert widespread default and thus the threat of systemic failure in international capital markets, the IMF undertook exceptional measures to effect successful adjustment. Its role has been instrumental in the restructuring and financing of Third World debt during the debt crisis of the 1980s.

Perhaps the IMF's greatest influence has been exerted through its organization and negotiation of "financing packages." A financing package of stabilization policies is an agreement among the IMF, the debtor country, and private commercial banks designed to prevent default through the restructuring of macroeconomic policy and the garnering of new capital. In the negotiation and refinancing of loans, the IMF obtains prior commitment from private commercial banks to provide a portion of any new financing. Under this system, "debtor countries could obtain new loan commitments, especially from private creditors, only as part of 'financing packages.' "[2] Because each dollar provided by the IMF is matched with commercial money, the IMF essentially controls a much greater range of resources than those within its own budget. For this reason, the influence of the IMF among developing countries has increased dramatically over the past two decades.

World Bank

The structure of the World Bank is similar in a number of ways to that of the IMF. Each is jointly owned by more than 140 member governments, and the voting power of each country depends on its annual contribution, which is in turn proportional to the size of its economy. In addition, both institutions are primarily lending facilities. But they also serve as catalysts for outside investment and provide advice and expertise. Despite these similarities, the objectives of World Bank and IMF operations are quite different. Whereas the IMF was assigned a supervisory role over the external financial transactions of members of the international community created at Bretton Woods, internal reconstruction and development became the responsibility of the World Bank. The primary purpose of World Bank activity is to promote economic growth and prosperity by providing funds for investment in projects that help raise productivity and output. To push developing countries toward self-sustaining economic growth, the World Bank provides financial and technical assistance for the expansion of markets, construction of infrastructure, and creation of growth-oriented institutional frameworks.

Over the years, the institutional framework of the World Bank itself has changed considerably. Initially, all bank lending was channeled through the International Bank for Reconstruction and Development (IBRD), the branch of the World Bank established following Bretton Woods. At the time, its principal concern was rebuilding economies shattered during World War II. The structure of IBRD lending has been consistent since the 1940s, though the types of projects it supports have evolved. Loans are offered on commercial terms to borrowing governments or to private enterprises that have obtained government guarantees.

Largely due to the stunning success of the Marshal Plan, the reconstruction of Europe had become a fait accompli by the late 1950s, at which time the World Bank turned its primary focus toward investment in the poorer economies. The establishment in 1960 of the International Development Association (IDA), which provides additional support to the poorest countries, reflects this rising concern with the pace of economic development in the Third World. Though its responsibilities are much the same as those of the IBRD, the IDA differs in that the funds it lends, called *credits*, are offered on concessional terms to countries whose per capita incomes are below a critical level. These favorable terms involve repayment periods several times longer than those on IBRD loans and are interest-free. The preferred terms are an outgrowth of recognition that countries at the earliest stages of development are unable to borrow at commercial rates because they are more economically vulnerable and the financial returns to investment are slower to be realized.

Together the IBRD and IDA comprise what is known as the World Bank. A close affiliate of the World Bank is the International Finance Corporation (IFC), which shares the same staff but remains a separate entity both legally and financially. Established in 1956, the IFC was designed to complement the efforts of the World Bank by engaging in a range of economic activities from which the bank itself is restricted but which serve to further the interests of development. In contrast to the bank, the IFC lends directly to private enterprise in the absence of government guarantees. In addition, through a variety of activities such as underwriting or holding equity, it is capable of taking direct financial interests in the loan recipients. By spurring the development of new business activities among entrepreneurs who benefit directly from World Bank projects, the IFC helps magnify the economic rewards of World Bank investments.[3]

Changing Role

As previously mentioned, the original focus of the World Bank was on reviving economies destroyed during the Second World War. Though it was clearly expected that World Bank investments would lead to macroeconomic growth (and thus positive spillovers to international trade), the policies of the World Bank remained microeconomic in nature until the 1970s. For the first two decades following the war, the vast bulk of World Bank lending was used to finance the construction of infrastructure related to energy and transportation. This should not be surprising, as much of Europe's infrastructure had been destroyed. Rising pressure to increase the flow of funds to poorer nations, following the economic recovery of Europe, led to a similar pattern of investment in developing countries.

It was discovered, however, that infrastructural investments in the Third World failed to produce the same returns as those in Europe (see Chapter 4), due largely to the lack of institutional framework and skilled labor. It became clear that a reordering of investment priorities specific to the needs of developing regions was necessary for successful development. This led to the diversification of investments and a general recognition that smaller-scale projects that target the livelihoods of the poorest populations are necessary to generate lasting economic prosperity.

Expansion of World Bank lending has been most rapid in the agricultural sector, especially in the production of cash crops for export. The bank's rationale for promoting cash crops is multifaceted: In addition to expanding the inflow of foreign currencies, the production of export crops is believed to enhance the incomes of the poor while improving food security. Recognition that the primary beneficiaries of past agricultural programs have been large farmers with the greatest access to credit and resources has led to increased interest in small-scale agriculture. A few of the other areas that have received additional resources are education, water supply and sewage, health care, and small-scale enterprise. Though recently these programs have received ample attention, funding by the World Bank lags behind its vocalized support.

The range of other services offered by the World Bank has also expanded. These include technical support, research, public provision of information and statistics, cofinancing of enterprise, and cooperative ventures with other nonprofit institutions. Since the late 1970s, there has been a dramatic increase in the transfer of funds and technical assistance for purposes of structural adjustment. These resources are designed to promote a fundamental restructuring of the economies of countries plagued by chronic trade and budget deficits. Critics of structural adjustment programs point to the fact that they frequently lead to increased hardships for the very poor and on occasion have substantially reversed the benefits of earlier economic progress. Though the World Bank has recently attempted to assist publics directly harmed by adjustment programs, the compensation measures remain ad hoc and are often severely limited in scope. Evidence suggests that adjustment tends to worsen income inequalities and can intensify poverty, even in countries experiencing economic recovery.

Cooperation between the IMF and the World Bank

Prior to the 1970s, the IMF policy prescription for a balance of payments deficit was a temporary infusion of foreign capital to meet currency shortfalls or currency devaluation where deficits had become chronic. Because the Bretton Woods conference had assigned the task of supervising foreign-exchange flows exclusively to the IMF, there was little overlap between fund and bank activities. Thus the IMF remained responsible for the balancing of external accounts through macroeconomic adjustments, while the World Bank influenced domestic production through microeconomic policy. Events during the past quarter century, however, have reduced the mutual exclusivity of these roles. Oil price shocks, falling exports, declining terms of trade, and capital flight experienced by developing countries in the 1970s and 1980s made it clear that Third World trade imbalances had become structural in nature.

To improve the status of developing countries vis-à-vis their First World trading partners, the IMF deemed it necessary that Third World countries adopt stabilization policies to lower inflation, improve the efficiency of internal markets and institutions, lower domestic government spending, and review public investments, in addition to reforming their exchange-rate regimes. By becoming involved in these related negotiations, the IMF extended its activities into areas that had traditionally been within the sphere of influence of the World Bank. Similarly, the bank came to recognize that promoting domestic GNP growth would require consideration of external factors. Consequently, the structural adjustment programs of the World Bank began to include provisions for enhancing the international competitiveness of domestic products through the reform of trade policy and exchange-rates regimes. Thus in an analogous manner, the World Bank has intruded into the domain of the IMF.

Since maintaining equilibrium on external accounts is not conducive to long-term economic growth, fund and bank policies have not always been consistent with each other. The remarkable similarity between current IMF conditionality and World Bank structural adjustment policy is the result of a convergence in approaches that occurred during the 1970s and 1980s. There is a growing recognition that the successful resolution of both external and internal problems requires the simultaneous coordination of macroeconomic and microeconomic policies. This has led to greater cooperation between the World Bank and the IMF and a blurring of the distinctions in their roles.

The Dissenting Views of Other Institutions

Although the 1970s and 1980s led to greater congruence between World Bank and IMF policies, not all international development agencies have favored the reforms. Both structural adjustment and stabilization policies have been found to contribute to rising hardships among the poorest groups in developing countries. This is generally due to cuts in government services, rising unemployment, falling real wages, and the elimination of food subsidies. As a result, numerous countries, including some experiencing economic recovery, have witnessed rising infant mortality rates and malnutrition and declining school enrollment rates. Critics point out that the terms of conditionality associated with adjustment loans are antidevelopmental where they reverse or slow improvements in living conditions among the very poor.[4]

Many development agencies place greater emphasis on reducing or eradicating poverty and stress that it is misleading to include countries with rising rates of poverty and malnutrition among the adjustment success stories. In its 1990 *Human Development Report*, the United Nations Development Program introduced the Human Development Index, which it suggests should be used as an alternative measure of economic progress (see Appendix 2.1). Indicators of national income, life expectancy, and educational attainment are combined to provide a clearer picture of national economic well-being and may be used to determine the true benefits of adjustment. A study by UNICEF, *Adjustment with a Human Face*, finds that children are frequently the group most vulnerable to the harsh consequences imposed by the restrictive macroeconomic policies of adjustment. Though they affirm that structural changes are indeed necessary for economic recovery, it is argued that programs carefully designed to protect the lower income groups are needed to ensure that economic reforms are not achieved at the expense of the poor.[5]

Despite extensive criticism by the international community (especially by nongovernmental aid organizations) on humanitarian grounds,[6] the World Bank and the IMF have by and large failed significantly to restructure adjustment policies that hurt the poor. Though there is growing recognition of the importance of the problem within these institutions, compensatory programs have been ad hoc at best, and little or no effort has been made to restructure policies fundamentally.[7] For example, at a meeting of leaders of the seven major industrialized countries (the "Group of Seven") held in Canada in June 1995, several proposals designed to enhance the role of the IMF and the World Bank in monitoring and responding to member-country (especially LDC) economic problems were put forward. These proposals initiated a longer-term review of both institutions to make them more responsive to the changing global economy of the twenty-first century. But the critical question, whether such institutional changes will actually reduce or promote poverty in the Third World rather than simply reinforce past policies that emphasized growth and fiscal austerity at the expense of lower-income groups, was not addressed. Until this issue is dealt with directly, the IMF and World Bank will continue to be perceived by some observers as agents of the wealthy world with only limited interest in the plight of the poor.

Notes to Appendix 14.1

1. M. Garritsen de Vries, *The IMF in a Changing World, 1945–85* (Washington, D.C.: International Monetary Fund, 1986), p. 120. This work provides a valuable presentation of the origins and evolution of the IMF.

2. *Ibid.*, p. 188.

3. For a concise breakdown of the separate roles of the IBRD, IDA, and IFC, see World Bank, *The World Bank and the International Finance Corporation* (Washington, D.C.: World Bank, 1983). A brief review is provided in Michael Gavin and Dani Rodrik, "The World Bank in historical perspective," *American Economic Review* 85 (May 1995): 329–334.

4. For poverty-oriented discussions of recent development efforts, see Frances Stewart, "The many faces of adjustment," *World Development* 19 (1991): 1847–1864; Giovanni A. Cornia, Richard Jolly, and Frances Stewart, *Adjustment with a Human Face* (Oxford: Clarendon Press, 1987); and United Nations Development Program, *Human Development Report, 1995*. (New York: Oxford University Press, 1995).

5. Cornia *et al.*, *Adjustment with a Human Face*.

6. See, for example, Hillary F. French, "The World Bank: Now fifty but how fit?" *World Watch*, July-August 1994, pp. 10–18; *Hunger and the World Bank*, an NGO statement presented to the World Bank Hunger Conference, November 30, 1993; Jeffrey Sachs, "Beyond Bretton Woods: A new blueprint," *Economist*, October 1, 1994, pp. 23–27; and Bruce Rich, *Mortgaging the Earth: The World Bank, Environmental Impoverishment, and the Crisis of Development* (Boston: Beacon Press, 1994).

7. Stewart, "Many faces of adjustment."

CHAPTER 15

Foreign Finance, Investment, and Aid: Controversies and Opportunities

What the Third World must ask of the international order is . . . a genuine transfer of real resources, not the present "aid" charade.
— *Santiago Resolution of Third World Social Scientists,* April 1973

Foreign assistance must be linked to commonly agreed policy objectives— particularly to poverty reduction strategies.
—United Nations Development Program, *Human Development Report, 1994*

It is to perpetuate difficulties of the South for the North to relate to us as hapless victims to dictate to regarding loans and the employment of aid.
—Nelson Mandela, United Nations Social Summit, March 1995

The International Flow of Financial Resources

In Chapter 14, we learned that a country's international financial situation as reflected in its balance of payments and its level of monetary reserves depends not only on its current account balance (its commodity trade) but also on its balance on capital account (its net inflow or outflow of private and public financial resources). Because almost all non-oil-exporting developing nations incur deficits on their current account balance, a continuous net inflow of foreign financial resources represents an important ingredient in their long-run development strategies.

The international flow of financial resources takes two main forms: (1) *private foreign direct and portfolio investment,* consisting of (a) foreign "direct" investment by large multinational (or transnational) corporations with headquarters in the developed nations and (b) foreign "portfolio" investment (e.g., stocks, bonds and notes) in LDC "emerging" credit and equity markets by private institutions (banks, mutual funds, corporations) and individuals, and (2) *public and private development assistance (foreign aid),* from (a) individual national governments and multinational donor agencies and, increasingly, (b) private *nongovernmental organizations (NGOs),* most working directly with Third World nations at the local level. In this chapter, we examine the nature, significance, and controversy regarding private direct and portfolio investment and foreign aid in the context of the changing world economy. As in earlier chapters, our focus will be on ways in which private investment and foreign aid can contribute to Third World development and on ways in which they may be harmful. We then ask how foreign investment and aid might best serve development aspirations as we enter the new century.

Private Foreign Direct Investment and the Multinational Corporation

Few developments have played as critical a role in the extraordinary growth of international trade and capital flows during the past few decades as the rise of the **multinational corporation (MNC)**. An MNC is most simply defined as a corporation or enterprise that conducts and controls productive activities in more than one country. These huge firms, mostly from North America, Europe, and Japan (but also increasingly from newly industrializing countries like South Korea, Taiwan, and Brazil) present a unique opportunity and a host of serious problems for the many developing countries in which they operate.

The growth of private **foreign direct investment** (FDI) in the Third World was extremely rapid during the past decades. It rose from an annual rate of $2.4 billion in 1962 to $17 billion in 1980 and $31 billion in 1990 before surging to over $80 billion in 1993. Almost 60% of this total goes to Asia. Table 15.1 shows both the rapid recent growth of FDI and its concentration among 10 recipient nations that together account for 94% of all investment flows. Africa received less than 5% of the total, and the least developed countries got under 2%. This is not surprising given the

TABLE 15.1 Foreign Direct Investment (FDI) in Developing Countries, 1970–1993, and Major Recipients, 1988–1992 (billions of dollars)

Year	Net FDI	Ten Major Recipients of FDI	FDI Received, 1988–1992
1970	3.1	China	25.6
1980	10.9	Singapore	21.7
1990	31.0	Mexico	18.4
1991	38.7	Malaysia	13.2
1992	42.5	Argentina	10.6
1993	80.0	Thailand	9.5
		Hong Kong	7.9
		Brazil	7.6
		Taiwan	6.0
		Indonesia	5.6

SOURCES: United Nations Development Program, *Human Development Report, 1994* (New York: Oxford University Press, 1994), fig. 4.1; *Economist*, October 1, 1994, p. 23.

fact that private capital gravitates toward countries and regions with the highest financial returns and the greatest perceived safety. Where debt problems are severe, governments are unstable, and economic reforms are only beginning, the risks of capital loss can be high. We must recognize that multinational corporations are not in the development business; their objective is to maximize their return on capital. This is why over 90% of global FDI goes to other industrial countries and the fastest growing Third World nations. MNCs seek out the best profit opportunities and are largely unconcerned with issues such as poverty, inequality, and unemployment alleviation. We will examine the ramifications of this reality in due course.

MNCs employ a relatively small though rapidly growing number of people in LDCs. The jobs tend to be concentrated in the high-wage, modern urban sector. Despite their insignificance in terms of the overall national employment picture, these corporations often exert a disproportionate influence on urban salary scales and migrant worker perceptions.

But foreign direct investment involves much more than the simple transfer of capital or the establishment of a local factory in a developing nation. Multinationals carry with them technologies of production, tastes and styles of living, managerial services, and diverse business practices including cooperative arrangements, marketing restrictions, advertising, and the phenomenon of "transfer pricing" (to be discussed shortly). They engage in a range of activities, many of which have little to do with the development aspirations of the countries in which they operate. But before analyzing some of the arguments for and against private foreign investment in general and multinational corporations in particular, let us examine the character of these enterprises.

Multinational Corporations: Size, Patterns, and Trends

Two central characteristics of multinational corporations are their large size and the fact that their worldwide operations and activities tend to be centrally controlled by parent companies. They are the major force in the rapid globalization of world trade. MNCs control more than 70% of that trade and dominate the production, distribution, and sale of many goods from developing countries (e.g., tobacco, cereals). Almost one-fourth of international exchange involves intrafirm MNC sales of intermediate products or equipment from one nation's subsidiary to another. They have become in effect **global factories** searching for opportunities anywhere in the world. Many MNCs have annual sales volumes in excess of the GDP of the developing nations in which they operate. Table 15.2 shows, for example, that the largest MNC in 1993, General Motors, had sales revenues in excess of the GDP of Thailand. In fact, its gross sales exceeded the GDP of all but seven developing countries (China, India, Brazil, Indonesia, Mexico, Argentina, and South Korea). The five largest MNCs had combined revenues in excess of the GDP of many developed countries including Switzerland, Australia, Spain, Sweden, Canada, and Belgium. Were we to examine the 150 largest economic entities (both companies and countries), we would find that more than half (86) were MNCs. In fact, when

TABLE 15.2 Comparison of the Ten Largest Multinational Corporations (MNCs) and Selected Countries According to Size of Annual Sales and Gross Domestic Product (GDP), 1993

MNC Rank	Country or Company (Headquarters)	1993 GDP or Gross Sales (billions of dollars)
1	**General Motors** (United States)	133.6
	Thailand	124.8
2	**Ford Motor** (United States)	108.5
	Norway	103.4
3	**Exxon** (United States)	97.8
4	**Royal Dutch/Shell** (United Kingdom/Netherlands)	95.1
	Portugal	85.6
5	**Toyota Motor** (Japan)	85.3
	Finland	74.1
6	**Hitachi** (Japan)	68.6
	Malaysia	64.4
	Greece	63.2
7	**IBM** (United States)	62.7
8	**Matsushita Electric** (Japan)	61.4
9	**General Electric** (United States)	60.8
	Venezuela	59.9
10	**Daimler Benz** (Germany)	59.1
	Colombia	54.1
	Philippines	54.0
	Pakistan	46.3
	Nigeria	31.3
	Bangladesh	23.9
	Kenya	4.7
	Malawi	1.8

SOURCES: *Fortune*, August 7, 1995, p. 133; World Bank, *World Development Report, 1995*, (New York: Oxford University Press, 1995), tab. 3.

we reached the bottom of the list to locate the 150th ranking entity, we would find the Union Carbide Corporation, with sales well in excess of the median GDP for all U.N. member states!

In seeking a measure of the economic power of the largest companies versus countries, it is worth noting that the interests of these companies in their dealings with countries may frequently collide. Thus it is worthwhile to seek a measure of the collective economic power of these concerns. In 1985, the combined sales of the 500 largest U.S. industrial concerns came to $1.8 trillion. That was larger than the GNP of the USSR or Japan at that time and about 45% of U.S. GNP. If we add on the combined sales of the 500 largest non-U.S. industrial companies, we reach a level of over $3.7 trillion for these 1,000 companies, slightly less than the $4 trillion U.S. GNP of 1985. Though care should be taken in interpretating these figures, they strongly suggest that the economic power of the major industrial companies is very important even when compared to the largest developed countries.

The figures for 1993 also reveal a very high concentration of the largest industrial companies in a few countries. The United States is overwhelmingly the most important home country, with 44 of the 100 largest corporations. Japan is second with 18. Other important home countries are Germany, seven; Britain, six; France, five; and South Korea, four. Italy and Canada each have three, the Netherlands has two, and 10 other countries have one each.

In 1993, there were 184 industrial corporations with gross sales of over $5 billion. By comparison, that same year, World Bank figures show that 45 of 108 developing countries had a GDP under $5 billion. In Latin America, of 18 countries listed, 5 fell below this mark; in Africa, 24 of the 37 countries listed were below the $5 billion level. Finally, note that about 70 smaller countries were not included in the World Bank survey, which means that the figures just given underestimate the number of countries that fall under the $5 billion benchmark.

Such enormous size confers great economic (and sometimes political) power on MNCs vis-à-vis the countries in which they operate. This power is greatly strengthened by their predominantly oligopolistic market positions, that is, by the fact that they tend to operate in worldwide product markets dominated by a few sellers. This situation gives them the ability to manipulate prices and profits, to collude with other firms in determining areas of control, and generally to restrict the entry of potential competition by dominating new technologies, special skills, and, through product differentiation and advertising, consumer tastes.

The largest MNCs have many foreign branches and overseas affiliates. Nearly 200 have subsidiaries in 20 or more countries. Of the 10 largest MNCs, five are based in the United States, and U.S. firms exercise control over about 30% of all foreign affiliates. Japanese, British, German, French, and U.S. firms together control over 75% of all MNC affiliates. Latest estimates put the book value of total MNC foreign investment in excess of $910 billion, with over 80% of that total owned by firms in these five countries. Of this total, approximately one-third is located in developing countries. But given their small size, the LDCs feel the presence of multinational corporations more acutely than the developed countries do.

Historically, multinational corporations, especially those operating in developing nations, focused on extractive and primary industries, mainly petroleum, nonfuel minerals, and plantation activities where a few "agribusiness" MNCs became involved in export-oriented agriculture and local food processing. Recently, however, manufacturing operations and services (banks, hotels, etc.) have occupied an increasing share of MNC production activities. At present, manufacturing and services account for almost 50% of the estimated stock of foreign direct investment in LDCs, whereas petroleum and mining represent 33% and 7%, respectively.

Private Foreign Investment: Some Pros and Cons for Development

Few areas in the economics of development arouse so much controversy and are subject to such varying interpretations as the issue of the benefits and costs of private foreign investment. If, however, we look closely at this controversy, we will find that the disagreement is not so much about the influence of MNCs on traditional economic aggregates such as GDP, investment, savings, and manufacturing growth rates (though these disagreements do indeed exist) as about the fundamental economic and social meaning of development as it relates to the diverse activities of MNCs. In other words, the controversy over the role and impact of foreign private investment often has as its basis a fundamental disagreement about the nature, style, and character of a desirable development process. The basic arguments for and against the developmental impact of private foreign investment in the context of the type of development it tends to foster can be summarized as follows.[1]

Traditional Economic Arguments in Support of Private Investment: Filling Savings, Foreign-Exchange, Revenue, and Management Gaps

The pro-foreign-investment arguments grow largely out of the traditional neoclassical and new growth theory analysis of the determinants of economic growth. Foreign private investment (as well as foreign aid) is typically seen as a way of filling in gaps between the domestically available supplies of savings, foreign exchange, government revenue, and human capital skills and the desired level of these resources necessary to achieve growth and development targets. For a simple example of the "savings-investment gap" analysis, recall that the basic Harrod-Domar growth model postulates a direct relationship between a country's rate of savings, s, and its rate of output growth, g, via the equation $g = s/k$ where k is the national capital-output ratio. If the desired rate of national output growth, g, is targeted at 7% annually and the capital-output ratio is 3, the needed rate of annual saving is 21% (because $s = gk$). If the saving that can be domestically mobilized amounts to only, say, 16% of GDP, a "savings gap" equal to 5% can be said to exist. If the nation can fill this gap with foreign financial resources (either private or public), it will be better able to achieve its target rate of growth.

Therefore, the first and most often cited contribution of private foreign investment to national development (i.e., when this development is defined in terms of GDP growth rates—an important implicit conceptual assumption) is its role in filling the resource gap between targeted or desired investment and locally mobilized savings.

A second contribution, analogous to the first, is its contribution to filling the gap between targeted foreign-exchange requirements and those derived from net export earnings plus net public foreign aid. This is the so-called foreign-exchange or trade gap. ("Two-gap" models are discussed more fully later in the chapter.) An inflow of private foreign capital can not only alleviate part or all of the deficit on the balance of payments current account but can also function to remove that deficit over time *if* the foreign-owned enterprise can generate a net positive flow of export earnings. Unfortunately, as we discovered in the case of import substitution, the overall effect of permitting MNCs to establish subsidiaries behind protective tariff and quota walls is often a net *worsening* of both the current and capital account balances. Such deficits usually result both from the importation of capital equipment and intermediate products (normally from an overseas affiliate and often at inflated prices) and the outflow of foreign exchange in the form of repatriated profits, management fees, royalty payments, and interest on private loans.

The third gap said to be filled by foreign investment is the gap between targeted governmental tax revenues and locally raised taxes. By taxing MNC profits and participating financially in their local operations, LDC governments are thought to be better able to mobilize public financial resources for development projects.

Fourth, there is a gap in management, entrepreneurship, technology, and skill presumed to be partly or wholly filled by the local operations of private foreign firms. Not only do multinationals provide financial resources and new factories to poor countries, but they also supply a "package" of needed resources including management experience, entrepreneurial abilities, and technological skills that can then be transferred to their local counterparts by means of training programs and the process of learning by doing. Moreover, according to this argument, MNCs can educate local managers about how to establish contact with overseas banks, locate alternative sources of supply, diversify market outlets, and become better acquainted with international marketing practices. Finally, MNCs bring with them the most sophisticated technological knowledge about production processes while transferring modern machinery and equipment to capital-poor Third World countries. Such transfers of knowledge, skills, and technology are assumed to be both desirable and productive for the recipient nations.[2]

Arguments against Private Foreign Investment: Widening Gaps

There are two basic arguments against private foreign investment in general and the activities of MNCs in particular—the strictly economic and the more philosophical or ideological.

On the economic side, the four gap-filling pro-foreign-investment positions just outlined are countered by the following arguments:

1. Although MNCs provide capital, they may lower domestic savings and investment rates by stifling competition through exclusive production agreements with host governments, failing to reinvest much of their profits, generating domestic incomes for groups with lower savings propensities, inhibiting the expansion of indigenous firms that might supply them with intermediate products by instead importing these goods from overseas affiliates, and imposing high interest costs on capital borrowed by host governments.

2. Although the initial impact of MNC investment is to improve the foreign-exchange position of the recipient nation, its long-run impact may be to reduce foreign-exchange earnings on both current and capital accounts. The current account may deteriorate as a result of substantial importation of intermediate products and capital goods, and the capital account may worsen because of the overseas repatriation of profits, interest, royalties, management fees, and other funds.

3. Although MNCs do contribute to public revenue in the form of corporate taxes, their contribution is considerably less than it should be as a result of liberal tax concessions, the practice of transfer pricing, excessive investment allowances, disguised public subsidies, and tariff protection provided by the host government.

4. The management, entrepreneurial skills, ideas, technology, and overseas contacts provided by MNCs may have little impact on developing local sources of these scarce skills and resources and may in fact inhibit their development by stifling the growth of indigenous entrepreneurship as a result of the MNCs' dominance of local markets.

The truly significant criticism of MNCs is usually conducted on more fundamental levels. In particular, Third World countries have commonly raised a number of objections. First, the impact of MNCs on development is very uneven, and in many situations MNC activities reinforce dualistic economic structures and exacerbate income inequalities. They tend to promote the interests of a small number of local factory managers and relatively well paid modern-sector workers against the interests of the rest by widening wage differentials. They divert resources away from needed food production to the manufacture of sophisticated products catering primarily to the demands of local elites and foreign consumers. And they tend to worsen the imbalance between rural and urban economic opportunities by locating primarily in urban export enclaves and contributing to the flow of rural-urban migration.[3]

Second, multinationals typically produce inappropriate products (those demanded by a small, rich minority of the local population), stimulate inappropriate consumption patterns through advertising and their monopolistic market power, and do this all with inappropriate (capital-intensive) technologies of production. This is perhaps the major criticism of MNCs in light of the growing employment problems of developing nations.

Third, as a result of the first two points, local resources tend to be allocated for socially undesirable projects. This in turn tends to aggravate the already sizable inequality between rich and poor and the serious imbalance between urban and rural economic opportunities.

Fourth, multinationals use their economic power to influence government policies in directions unfavorable to development. They are able to extract sizable economic and political concessions from competing LDC governments in the form of excessive protection, tax rebates, investment allowances, and the cheap provision of factory sites and essential social services. As a result, the private profits of MNCs may exceed social benefits. In some cases, these social returns to host countries may even be negative! Alternatively, a MNC can avoid much local taxation in high-tax countries and shift profits to affiliates in low-tax countries by artificially inflating the price it pays for intermediate products purchased from overseas affiliates so as to lower its stated local profits. This phenomenon, known as **transfer pricing**, is a common practice of MNCs and one over which host governments can exert little control as long as corporate tax rates differ from one country to the next.

Fifth, MNCs may damage host economies by suppressing domestic entrepreneurship and using their superior knowledge, worldwide contacts, advertising skills, and range of essential support services to drive out local competitors and inhibit the emergence of small-scale local enterprises. In the context of recent LDC market reforms, the widespread privatization of public corporations, and the use of debt-for-equity swaps to reduce debt burdens, MNCs are today in a unique position to acquire some of the best and potentially most lucrative local businesses. They thereby can "crowd out" local investors and appropriate the profits themselves. For example, in a recent quantitative study of 11 developing countries outside the Pacific Basin, higher foreign direct investment was accompanied by lower domestic investment, lower national saving, larger current account deficits, and lower economic growth rates.[4]

Finally, at the political level, the fear is often expressed that powerful multinational corporations can gain control over local assets and jobs and can then exert considerable influence on political decisions at all levels. In extreme cases, they may even, either directly by payoffs to corrupt public officials at the highest levels or indirectly by contributions to "friendly" political parties, subvert the very political process of host nations (as occurred with International Telephone and Telegraph in the 1970s in Chile).

Table 15.3 attempts to summarize the debate about multinationals in terms of seven key issues and a range of questions that surrounds each of them: international capital movements (including income flows and balance of payments effects), displacement of indigenous production, extent of technology transfer, appropriateness of technology transfer, patterns of consumption, social structure and stratification, and income distribution and dualistic development.[5]

Reconciling the Pros and Cons

Although the foregoing discussion and the seven issues listed in Table 15.3 provide a range of conflicting arguments, the real debate ultimately centers on different ideological and value judgments about the nature and meaning of economic development and the principal sources from which it springs. The advocates of private foreign investment tend to be free-market, private-enterprise, laissez-faire proponents who firmly believe in the efficacy and beneficence of the free-market mechanism, where this is usually defined as a hands-off policy on the part of host governments. As we have seen, however, the actual operations of MNCs tend to be monopolistic and oligopolistic. Price setting is achieved more as a result of international bargaining and collusion than as a natural outgrowth of free-market supply and demand.

Theorists who argue against the activities of MNCs are often motivated more by a sense of the importance of national control over domestic economic activities and the minimization of dominance-dependence relationships between powerful MNCs and Third World governments. They see these giant corporations not as needed agents of economic change but more as vehicles of antidevelopment. Multinationals, they argue, reinforce dualistic economic structures and exacerbate domestic inequalities with wrong products and inappropriate technologies. Many analysts advocate a more stringent regulation of foreign investments, a tougher bargaining stance on the part of host governments, a willingness on the part of LDCs to "shop around" for better deals, the adoption of performance standards and requirements, increased domestic ownership and control, and a greater coordination of LDC strategies with respect to terms and conditions of foreign investment. One example of such coordinated strategies was a decision in the 1980s by the Andean Group in Latin America to require foreign investors to reduce their ownership in local

TABLE 15.3 Seven Key Disputed Issues about the Role and Impact of Multinational Corporations in Developing Countries

Key Issue	Sources of Dispute
1. International capital movements (income flows and balance of payments)	a. Do they bring in much capital (savings)? b. Do they improve the balance of payments? c. Do they remit "excessive" profits? d. Do they employ transfer pricing and disguise capital outflows? e. Do they establish few linkages to the local economy? f. Do they generate significant tax revenues?
2. Displacement of indigenous production	a. Do they buy out existing import-competing industries? b. Do they use their competitive advantages to drive local competitors out of business?
3. Extent of technology transfer	a. Do they keep all R&D in home countries? b. Do they retain monopoly power over their technology?
4. Appropriateness of technology transfer	a. Do they use only capital-intensive technologies? b. Do they adapt technology to local factor endowments or leave it unchanged?
5. Patterns of consumption	a. Do they encourage inappropriate patterns of consumption through elite orientation, advertising, and superior marketing techniques? b. Do they increase consumption of their products at the expense of other (perhaps more needed) goods?
6. Social structure and stratification	a. Do they develop allied local groups through higher wage payments, hiring (displacing) the best of the local entrepreneurs, and fostering elite loyalty and socialization through pressures for conformity? b. Do they foster alien values, images, and life-styles incompatible with local customs and beliefs?
7. Income distribution and dualistic development	a. Do they contribute to the widening gap between rich and poor? b. Do they exacerbate urban bias and widen urban-rural differentials?

SOURCE: Based on Thomas Biersteker, *Distortion or Development: Contending Perspectives on the Multinational Corporation* (Cambridge, Mass.: MIT Press, 1978), chap. 3.

enterprises to minority shares over a 15-year period. Tanzania adopted a similar policy of securing a controlling share of foreign enterprises, in line with its Arusha Declaration of 1967 on socialism and self-reliance. Not surprisingly, the annual flow of private foreign investment declined in both Andean nations and Tanzania.

The arguments both for and against private foreign investment are still far from being settled empirically and may never be as they ultimately reflect important differences in value judgments and political perceptions about desirable development strategies. Clearly, any real assessment of MNCs in development requires case studies of a given MNC in a specific country.[6] Perhaps the only valid general conclusion is that private foreign investment can be an important stimulus to economic and social development as long as the interests of MNCs and host-country governments coincide (assuming, of course, that they don't coincide along the lines of dualistic development and widening inequalities). As long as MNCs see their role in terms of global output or profit maximization with little interest in the long-run domestic impact of their activities, the accusations of the anti-private-investment school of thought will gain increasing Third World acceptance. Maybe there can never be a real congruence of interest between the profit-maximizing objectives of MNCs and the development priorities of LDC governments. However, a strengthening of the relative bargaining powers of host-country governments through their coordinated activities, while probably reducing the overall magnitude and growth of private foreign investment, might make that investment better fit the long-run development needs and priorities of poor nations while still providing profitable opportunities for foreign investors. Alternatively, it might be useful to explore some form of domestic and international guarantees of minimal rates of MNC return, financed, for example, by donor agency and local government contributions. Such guarantees against, say, asset expropriation or political upheaval would provide the necessary risk reduction to induce MNCs to adopt a longer-run perspective with particular emphasis on adapting their existing technologies of production to the resource needs of host nations.

The late 1990s should prove an interesting time to reassess the quantitative and qualitative impact of MNC investments in developing countries. As a result of the widespread adoption of market reforms, open economies, and privatization of state-owned enterprises, MNCs are likely to intensify their global factory strategy, particularly in Asia and Latin America. They will add to national output, create some jobs, pay some taxes, and generally contribute to a more modern economy. But they will also gravitate toward the most profitable investment opportunities, engage in transfer pricing, and repatriate profits. Whether the net outcome is more positive for Third World development than in the past remains to be assessed. It is to be hoped that ways can be found in which MNC profits and broad-based national development can be simultaneously served.

Private Portfolio Investment: Boon or Bane for LDCs?

In addition to foreign direct investment, the most significant and fastest-growing component of private capital flows between 1985 and 1994 was in the area of **portfolio investment**.[7] With the increased liberalization of LDC domestic financial markets and the opening up of these markets to foreign investors, private portfolio investment now accounts for one-third of overall net resource flows to developing countries. Basically, portfolio investment consists of foreign purchases of the stocks (equity), bonds, certificates of deposit, and commercial paper of LDCs. Between 1989 and 1993, total portfolio flows increased by more than 700% to $55.8 billion (see Table 15.4). Equity flows jumped by 400% between 1990 and 1993—mostly through newly formed "country" mutual funds subscribed to by individual developed-country investors and by large DC-based pension funds seeking to diversify their investments. Mexico was a principal beneficiary (and later a conspicuous victim) of these equity flows, having received almost 25% of its entire external 1991–1992 financing in this form.

As in the case of the FDIs of multinational corporations, the benefits and costs of private portfolio investment flows to both the DC investor and the LDC recipient have been subject to vigorous debate.[8] From the investor's point of view, investing in the stock markets of "emerging" countries (as some LDCs are called in the financial community) permits them to increase their returns while diversifying their risks. Early in the 1990s, annual returns on **emerging-country stock markets** were very high (e.g., 39% in Latin America between 1988 and 1993), but so was volatility. Many small investors in U.S.-based mutual funds were lured into the LDC stock markets to partake of these high rewards, only to be caught in a huge downdraft in December 1994 and January and February 1995 when the Mexican stock market collapsed after the 35% peso devaluation. Some investors lost as much as 60% of their money in dollar terms in a matter of weeks as both the Mexican Bolsa (stock market) plummeted and the peso continued to depreciate. Not surprisingly, in 1995, much of the money invested in emerging markets in the early 1990s was rapidly repatriated. The experience of these dramatic losses was reflected in the sharp downturn in total portfolio investment flows in 1995.

From the perspective of the recipient LDC, private portfolio flows in local stock markets are a potentially welcome vehicle for raising capital for domestic firms.

TABLE 15.4 Portfolio Flows to Developing Countries, 1989–1993

Type of Flow	1989	1990	1991	1992	1993[a]	Total 1989–1993[a]
Bonds, commercial paper, and certificates of deposit	4.0	5.5	12.7	23.7	42.6	88.5
Equity	3.5	3.8	7.6	13.0	13.2	41.1
New country funds	2.2	2.9	1.2	1.3	2.7	10.3
American and global deposit receipts	0.0	0.1	4.9	5.9	7.3	18.2
Direct equity	1.3	0.8	1.5	5.8	3.2	12.6
Total	7.5	9.3	20.3	36.7	55.8	129.6

SOURCE: Stijn Claessens, "The emergence of equity investment in developing countries: Overview," *World Bank Economic Review* 9 (January 1995): tab. 1.

[a] Estimated.

Well-functioning local stock markets also help domestic investors diversify their assets (an option usually open only to the wealthy) and can act to improve the efficiency of the whole financial sector by serving as a screening and monitoring device for allocating funds to industries and firms with the highest potential returns.

But from the policy perspective of developing-country governments, the key issue is whether large and volatile private portfolio flows into both local stock and short-term bond markets can be a destabilizing force for both the financial market and the overall economy. While some academic economists were arguing that these flows were not inherently unstable,[9] along came the Mexico crisis, and billions of dollars of these "hot money" flows disappeared from Mexico and much of the rest of Latin America in a matter of days—some say minutes! The lesson of the Mexican debacle was very clear: Third World countries that rely too heavily on private foreign portfolio investments to camouflage basic structural weakness in the economy (in Mexico's case, a grossly overvalued foreign-exchange rate leading to high current account deficits and dwindling foreign reserves) are more than likely to suffer serious long-term consequences. Like multinational corporations, portfolio investors are not in the development business. If developed-country interest rates rise or perceived Third World profit rates decline, foreign speculators will withdraw their "investments" as quickly as they brought them in. What LDCs need is true long-run economic investment (plants, equipment, physical and social infrastructure, etc.) and not speculative equity capital.

In summary, although private portfolio financial flows increased dramatically in the early 1990s, they were based largely on a mythical belief that free markets and a sound currency would *automatically* guarantee rapid economic growth. However, their inherent volatility and the fact that they respond primarily to global interest-rate diffentials, as well as to investor perceptions of political and economic stability, make them a very tenuous foundation on which to base medium- or long-term development strategies.[10]

Foreign Aid: The Development Assistance Debate

Conceptual and Measurement Problems

In addition to export earnings and private foreign direct and portfolio investment, the final two major sources of Third World foreign exchange are public (official) bilateral and multilateral development assistance and private (unofficial) assistance provided by nongovernmental organizations (NGOs). Both of these activities are forms of **foreign aid**, although only public aid is usually measured in official statistics.

In principle, all real resource transfers from one country to another should be included in the definition of foreign aid. Even this simple definition, however, raises a number of problems.[11] For one thing, many resource transfers can take disguised forms, such as the granting of preferential tariffs by developed countries to Third World exports of manufactured goods. This permits LDCs to sell their industrial products in developed-country markets at higher prices than would otherwise be possible. There is consequently a net gain for LDCs and a net loss for developed countries, which amounts to a real resource transfer to the LDCs. Such implicit capital transfers, or disguised flows, should be counted in qualifying foreign aid flows. Normally, however, they are not.

However, we should not include *all* transfers of capital to LDCs, particularly the capital flows of private foreign investors. For a number of years, aid was calculated as the sum of official and private capital flows, although now these two items are listed separately. Private flows represent normal commercial transactions, are prompted by commercial considerations of profits and rates of return, and therefore should not be viewed as aid to the LDCs. Commercial flows of private capital are *not* a form of foreign assistance, even though they may benefit the developing country in which they take place.

Economists have defined foreign aid, therefore, as any flow of capital to LDCs that meets two criteria: (1) Its objective should be noncommercial from the point of view of the donor, and (2) it should be characterized by **concessional terms**; that is, the interest rate and repayment period for borrowed capital should be softer (less stringent) than commercial terms.[12] Even this definition can be inappropriate, for it could include military aid, which is both noncommercial and concessional. Normally, however, military aid is excluded from international economic measurements of foreign aid flows. The concept of foreign aid that is now widely used and accepted, therefore, is one that encompasses all official grants and concessional loans, in currency or in kind, that are broadly aimed at transferring resources from developed to less developed nations on development or income distribution grounds. Unfortunately, there often is a thin line separating purely developmental grants and loans from sources ultimately motivated by security or commercial interests.

Just as there are conceptual problems associated with the definition of foreign aid, so too there are measurement and conceptual problems in the calculation of actual development assistance flows. In particular, three major problems arise in measuring aid. First, we cannot simply add together the dollar values of grants and loans; each has a different significance to both donor and recipient countries. Loans must be repaid and therefore cost the donor and benefit the recipient less than the nominal value of the loan itself. Conceptually, we should deflate or discount the dollar value of interest-bearing loans before adding them to the value of outright grants. Second, aid can be tied either by *source* (loans or grants have to be spent on the purchase of donor-country goods and services) or by *project* (funds can only be used for a specific project, such as a road or a steel mill). In either case, the real value of the aid is reduced because the specified source is likely to be an expensive supplier or the project is not of the highest priority (otherwise, there would be no need to tie the aid). Furthermore, aid may be tied to the importation of capital-intensive equipment, which may impose an additional real resource cost, in the form of higher unemployment, on the recipient nation. Or the project itself may require purchase of new machinery and equipment from monopolistic suppliers while existing productive equipment in the same industry is being operated at very low levels of capacity. Finally, we always need to distinguish between the nominal and real value of foreign assistance, especially during periods of rapid inflation. Aid flows are usually calculated at nominal levels and tend to show a steady rise over time. However, when deflated for rising prices, the actual real volume of aid from most donor countries has declined substantially during the past decade. For example, during the period 1960–1990, the nominal outflow of foreign aid from the United States increased by 130%, but the real value actually declined by nearly 30%.

Amounts and Allocations: Public Aid

The money volume of **official development assistance** (ODA), which includes bilateral grants, loans, and technical assistance as well as multilateral flows, has grown from an annual rate of $4.6 billion in 1960 to $58 billion in 1992. However, in terms of the percentage of developed-country GNP allocated to official development assistance, there has been a steady decline from 0.51% in 1960 to 0.32% in 1992.[13] Table 15.5 shows the disbursement of ODA by principal donors both in total amount and as a percentage of GNP in 1985 and 1992. Although the United States remains the largest donor in absolute terms, relative to others, it provides the lowest percentage of GNP—0.18% in 1992, compared to an average of 0.32% for all industrial countries and well below the internationally agreed United Nations target of 0.7%. Only the Scandinavian countries are currently providing ODA in excess of this target, with Sweden and Denmark contributing 1.03% and 1.02% of their 1992 GNPs, respectively. Not only is the United States' ODA-to-GNP ratio the lowest among industrial countries, but it has also declined sharply from its level of 0.31% in 1970 and is heading even lower.

More interesting than the total amount of aid is the way in which it is distributed. ODA is allocated in some strange and arbitrary ways.[14] In terms of regional

TABLE 15.5 Official Development Assistance Disbursements from Major Donor Countries, 1985 and 1992

	1985		1992	
Donor Country	Billions of Dollars	Percentage of GNP	Billions of Dollars	Percentage of GNP
Canada	1.6	0.49	2.5	0.46
Denmark	N.A	N.A	1.4	1.02
France	4.0	0.78	7.8	0.59
Germany	2.9	0.47	6.9	0.36
Italy	1.1	0.26	4.1	0.34
Japan	3.8	0.29	11.1	0.30
Netherlands	1.1	0.91	2.7	0.86
Sweden	N.A	N.A	2.5	1.03
United Kingdom	1.5	0.33	3.1	0.30
United States	9.4	0.24	10.8	0.18
Total (15 countries)	29.4	0.35	57.6	0.32

SOURCES: World Bank, *World Debt Tables, 1991–1992;* (Washington, D.C.: World Bank, 1992), vol. 1, tab. 2.1, and United Nations Development Program, *Human Development Report, 1994* (New York: Oxford University Press, 1994), tab. 4.4.

N.A. = not available.

TABLE 15.6 Official Development Assistance (ODA) by Region, 1990

Region	ODA per Capita (dollars)	GNP per Capita (dollars)	ODA per Capita as Percentage of GNP per Capita
Arab states	43	1,887	2.3
Sub-Saharan Africa	32	475	6.7
Latin America and the Caribbean	10	1962	0.5
East and Southeast Asia	5	625	0.8
South Asia	5	458	1.1

SOURCE: United Nations Development Program, *Human Development Report, 1992* (New York: Oxford University Press, 1992), tab. 3.9.

TABLE 15.7 Top Twenty LDC Recipients of Official Development Assistance (ODA), 1990

Developing Country	Total ODA (millions of dollars)	ODA as a Percentage of GNP
Egypt	5,584	17.2
Bangladesh	2,081	10.5
China	2,064	0.5
Indonesia	1,717	2.0
India	1,550	0.5
Philippines	1,266	3.0
Turkey	1,259	1.7
Tanzania	1,155	37.5
Pakistan	1,108	2.8
Kenya	989	11.3
Morocco	965	4.4
Mozambique	923	77.4
Jordan	884	16.7
Ethiopia	871	14.6
Zaire	816	9.2
Thailand	787	1.2
Sudan	768	9.5
Senegal	724	15.4
Ivory Coast	674	7.2
Sri Lanka	659	9.1
Subtotal (61% of total ODA)	26,844	2.4

SOURCE: United Nations Development Program, *Human Development Report, 1992* (New York: Oxford University Press, 1992), tab. 3.10.

NOTE: The top recipient of ODA has been and continues to be Israel, but it is not classified as a developing country.

TABLE 15.8 Foreign Aid Allocations and the Poor, 1992				
Ten Developing Countries with Greatest Number of Poor People	Number of Poor (millions)	Poor as a Percentage of Total World Poor	Official Development Assistance (ODA) per Poor Person (dollars)	ODA as a Percentage of Total ODA
India	350.0	26.9	7	5.2
China	105.0	8.1	28	6.5
Bangladesh	93.2	7.2	19	3.8
Brazil	72.4	5.6	3	0.5
Indonesia	47.8	3.7	44	4.6
Nigeria	46.4	3.6	7	0.5
Vietnam	37.6	2.9	16	1.3
Philippines	35.2	2.7	49	3.8
Pakistan	35.0	2.7	49	3.8
Ethiopia	31.9	2.5	41	2.9
Total	854.5	65.9	17	31.7

SOURCE: United Nations Development Program, *Human Development Report, 1994* (New York: Oxford University Press, 1994), tab. 4.2.

distribution, South Asia, where nearly 50% of the world's poorest people live, receives $5 per person in aid. The Middle East, with three times South Asia's per capita income, receives 11 times the per capita aid, $55. Table 15.6 shows the regional distribution of ODA in 1990. If we now look at the country distribution and calculate aid as a proportion of GNP, the results vary dramatically and inexplicably—0.5% for India, for example, 17% for Egypt, 38% for Tanzania, and 77% for Mozambique (see Table 15.7). If we next look at the relationship between aid allocation and poverty, we find even stranger results. For example, only 31% of aid goes to the 10 LDCs with 66% of the world's poorest people (Table 15.8). Moreover, the richest 40% of the Third World's people receives more than twice as much per capita aid as the poorest 40%. And this ratio has risen substantially since 1970. Finally, if we compare ODA allocation to LDCs with large and small military expenditures, we find that countries that spend more on their military (greater than 4% of GNP) receive twice as much aid per capita as countries that spend much less.

It is clear from the foregoing analysis that the allocation of foreign aid is rarely determined by the relative needs of developing countries. Most bilateral aid (with the exception of Scandinavian ODA) seems unrelated to development priorities, being based largely on political and military considerations and the unpredictable whims and ad hoc judgments of donor decision makers. Multilateral aid (e.g., from the World Bank and various U.N. agencies) is somewhat more economically rational, although here too the rich seem to attract more resources than the poor.

Because foreign aid is seen differently by donor and recipient countries, we must analyze the giving and receiving process from these two often contradictory viewpoints. One of the major criticisms of the literature on foreign aid is that it has concentrated almost exclusively on the motives and objectives of donor countries while devoting little attention to why LDCs accept aid and what they believe it will accomplish. After examining the aid question from both perspectives, we can summarize the conflicting views of the effects of traditional aid relationships over the past two decades.

Why Donors Give Aid

Donor countries give aid primarily because it is in their political, strategic, or economic self-interest to do so. Some development assistance may be motivated by moral and humanitarian desires to assist the less fortunate (e.g., emergency food relief programs), but there is no historical evidence to suggest that over longer periods of time, donor nations assist others without expecting some corresponding benefits (political, economic, military, etc.) in return. We can therefore characterize the foreign aid motivations of donor nations into two broad, but often interrelated, categories: political and economic.

Political Motivations

Political motivations have been by far the more important for aid-granting nations, especially for the major donor country, the United States. The United States has viewed foreign aid from its beginnings in the late 1940s under the Marshall Plan, which aimed at reconstructing the war-torn economies of Western Europe, as a means of containing the international spread of communism. When the balance of cold-war interests shifted from Europe to the Third World in the mid-1950s, the policy of containment embodied in the U.S. aid program dictated a shift in emphasis toward political, economic, and military support for "friendly" less developed nations, especially those considered geographically strategic. Most aid programs to developing countries were therefore oriented more toward purchasing their security and propping up their sometimes shaky regimes than promoting long-term social and economic development. The successive shifts in emphasis from South Asia to Southeast Asia to Latin America to the Middle East and back to Southeast Asia during the 1950s and 1960s and then toward Africa and the Persian Gulf in the late 1970s and the Caribbean and Central America in the 1980s reflect changes in U.S. strategic and political interests more than changing evaluations of economic need. A glance at Table 15.9 underlines this point even for the 1990s.

Even the Alliance for Progress, inaugurated in the early 1960s with great fanfare and noble rhetoric about promoting Latin American economic development, was in reality formulated primarily as a direct response to the rise of Fidel Castro in Cuba and the perceived threat of communist takeovers in other Latin American countries. As soon as the security issue lost its urgency and other more pressing problems came to the fore (the war in Vietnam, the growing dollar crisis, the rise in U.S. violence, etc.), the Alliance for Progress stagnated and began to fizzle out. Our point is simply that where aid is seen primarily as a means of furthering donor-country interests, the flow of funds tends to vary in accordance with the donor's political assessment of changing international situations and not the relative need of potential recipients.

The experience of other major Western donor countries like Great Britain and France has been similar to that of the United States. Although exceptions can be

TABLE 15.9 United States Official Development Assistance to Selected Strategic Allies and Poor Nations (dollars)

Country	GNP per Capita, 1991	U.S. Aid per Poor Person, 1990–1991
Strategic allies		
Israel	12,110	176.00
El Salvador	1,090	28.00
Bolivia	650	26.00
Egypt	610	63.00
Poor countries		
Bangladesh	220	1.70
Madagascar	210	15.00
Tanzania	120	2.70
Mozambique	80	3.60

SOURCE: United Nations Development Program, *Human Development Report, 1994* (New York: Oxford University Press, 1994), tab. 4.7.

cited (Sweden, Norway, perhaps Canada), by and large these Western donor countries have used foreign aid as a political lever to prop up or underpin friendly political regimes in Third World countries, regimes whose continued existence they perceived as being in their national security interests. Most socialist aid, especially that of the former Soviet Union, grew out of essentially the same political and strategic motivations, although its form and content may have been somewhat different.

With the end of the cold war and the demise of the Soviet Union (and, indeed, the whole Second World), we might ask whether these political motivations are likely to disappear. The answer is probably no. For example, the Persian Gulf War of 1991 saw aid flows directed to friendly allied governments like Egypt and Turkey. Moreover, in the 1990s, both bilateral and multilateral aid are being conditioned on a recipient country's willingness to promote free markets, open its economy, and structure itself in accordance with the donor's capitalist and democratic principles.

Economic Motivations: Two–Gap Models and Other Criteria

Within the broad context of political and strategic priorities, foreign aid programs of the developed nations have had a strong economic rationale. In fact, even though the political motivation may have been of paramount importance, the economic rationale was at least given lip service as the overriding motivation for assistance.

Let us examine the principal economic arguments advanced in support of foreign aid.

Foreign-Exchange Constraints External finance (both loans and grants) can play a critical role in supplementing domestic resources in order to relieve savings or foreign-exchange bottlenecks. This is the so-called two-gap analysis of foreign assistance.[15] The basic argument of the **two-gap model** is that most developing countries face either a shortage of domestic savings to match investment opportunities or a shortage of foreign exchange to finance needed imports of capital and intermediate goods. Most two-gap models assume that the **savings gap** (domestic real resources) and the **foreign-exchange gap** are unequal in magnitude and that they are independent, that is, that there is no substitutability between savings and foreign exchange. (This assumption is obviously unreal, but it greatly facilitates the mathematical analysis.)

The implication that follows is that one of the two gaps will be "binding" or "dominant" for any LDC at a given point in time. If, for example, the savings gap is dominant, this would indicate that the country is operating at full employment and is not using all of its foreign-exchange earnings. It may have enough foreign exchange to purchase additional capital goods from abroad, but there is not enough excess domestic labor or other productive resources to carry out additional investment projects. The importation of such capital goods would only redirect domestic resources from other activities and probably lead to inflation. As a result, "excess" foreign exchange, including foreign aid, might be spent on the importation of luxury consumption goods. Such a country is said to have a shortage of **productive resources**, which, from a different viewpoint, can be regarded as a shortage in savings. An outstanding example of savings-gap nations would be the Arab oil states during the 1970s. Note, however, that the savings gap analysis overlooks the possibility that excess foreign exchange *can* be used to purchase productive resources—for example, Saudi Arabia and Kuwait used their surplus petrodollars to pay for hired labor from non-oil-exporting countries in the region and overseas. Savings-gap countries therefore do not need foreign aid.

Most developing countries, however, are assumed to fall into the second category, where the foreign-exchange gap is binding. These countries have excess productive resources (mostly labor), and all available foreign exchange is being used for imports. The existence of complementary domestic resources would permit them to undertake new investment projects if they had the external finance to import new capital goods and associated technical assistance. Foreign aid can therefore play a critical role in overcoming the foreign-exchange constraint and raising the real rate of economic growth.

Algebraically, the simple two-gap model can be formulated as follows:

1. *The savings constraint or gap.* Starting with the identity that capital inflows (the difference between imports and exports) add to investible resources (domestic savings), the savings-investment restriction can be written as

$$I < F + sY \qquad (15.1)$$

where F is the amount of capital inflows. If capital inflows (F) plus domestic saving (sY) exceeds domestic investment (I) and the economy is at full capacity, a savings gap is said to exist.

2. *The foreign-exchange constraint or gap.* If LDC investment has a marginal import share m_1 (typically ranging from 30% to 60% in most LDCs) and the marginal propensity to import out of a unit of GNP (usually around 10% to 15%)

is given by the parameter m_2, the foreign-exchange constraint or gap can be written as

$$(m_1 - m_2)I + m_2Y - E \leq F \tag{15.2}$$

where E is the exogeneous level of exports.

The term F enters both inequality constraints and becomes the critical factor in the analysis. If F, E, and Y are initially assigned an exogenous current value, only one of the two inequalities will prove binding; that is, investment (and therefore the output growth rate) will be constrained to a lower level by one of the inequalities. Countries can therefore be classified according to whether the savings or foreign-exchange constraint is binding. More important from the viewpoint of foreign aid analysis is the observation that the impact of increased capital inflows will be greater where the foreign-exchange gap (Equation 15.2) rather than the savings gap (Equation 15.1) is binding. But this does not imply that savings-gap countries do not need foreign aid. Two-gap models simply provide a crude methodology for determining the relative need and ability of different LDCs to use foreign aid effectively.

The problem is that such gap forecasts are very mechanistic and are themselves constrained by the necessity of fixing import parameters and assigning exogenous values to exports and net capital inflows. In the case of exports, this is particularly constricting because a liberalization of trade relations between the developed and the developing world would contribute more toward relieving foreign-exchange gaps than foreign aid. Although E and F are substitutable in Equation 15.2, they can have quite different indirect effects, especially in the case where F represents interest-bearing loans that need to be repaid. Thus the alteration of import and export parameters through both LDC and MDC government policy can in reality determine whether the savings or foreign-exchange constraint is restricting the further growth of national output (or, in fact, whether neither is binding).

Growth and Savings External assistance also is assumed to facilitate and accelerate the process of development by generating additional domestic savings as a result of the higher growth rates that it is presumed to induce. Eventually, it is hoped, the need for concessional aid will disappear as local resources become sufficient to make development self-sustaining.

Technical Assistance Financial assistance needs to be supplemented by **technical assistance** in the form of high-level worker transfers to ensure that aid funds are used most efficiently to generate economic growth. This labor-gap-filling process is thus analogous to the financial-gap-filling process mentioned earlier.

Absorptive Capacity Finally, the amount of aid should be determined by the recipient country's **absorptive capacity**, a euphemism for its ability to use aid funds wisely and productively (often meaning as donors want them to be used). Typically, the donor countries decide which LDCs are to receive aid, how much, in what form (loans or grants, financial or technical assistance), for what purpose, and under what conditions on the basis of their donor countries' assessment of LDC absorptive capacities. But the total amount of aid rarely has anything to do with Third

World absorptive capacities; typically, foreign aid is a residual and low-priority element in donor-country expenditure. In most instances, the recipient countries have little say in the matter.

Economic Motivations and Self-Interest

The arguments on behalf of foreign aid as a crucial ingredient for LDC development should not mask the fact that even at the strictly economic level, definite benefits accrue to donor countries as a result of their aid programs. The increasing tendency toward providing loans instead of outright grants (interest-bearing loans now constitute over 80% of all aid, compared to less than 40% in earlier periods) and toward tying aid to the exports of donor countries has saddled many LDCs with substantial debt repayment burdens. It has also increased their import costs by as much as 40%. These extra import costs arise because aid tied to donor-country exports limits the receiving nation's freedom to shop around for low-cost and suitable capital and intermediate goods. **Tied aid** in this sense is clearly a second-best option to untied aid (and perhaps also to freer trade through a reduction of developed-country import barriers). As one former U.S. aid official candidly put it:

> The biggest single misconception about the foreign aid program is that we send money abroad. We don't. Foreign aid consists of American equipment, raw materials, expert services, and food—all provided for specific development projects which we ourselves review and approve. . . . Ninety-three percent of AID [Agency for International Development] funds are spent directly in the United States to pay for these things. Just last year [1967] some 4,000 American firms in 50 states received $1.3 billion in AID funds for products supplied as part of the foreign aid program.[16]

Similarly, a former British minister of overseas development once noted that "about two-thirds of our aid is spent on goods and services from Britain. . . . Trade follows aid. We equip a factory overseas and later on we get orders for spare parts and replacements. . . . [Aid] is in our long-term interest."[17]

Why LDC Recipients Accept Aid

The reasons why developing nations, at least until recently, have been eager to accept aid, even in its most stringent and restrictive forms, have been given much less attention than the reasons why donors provide aid. This omission is puzzling in view of the many instances where both parties may have conflicting rather than congruent motives and interests. Basically, we can identify three reasons—one major and two minor—why LDCs have sought foreign aid.

The major reason is clearly economic. Third World countries have often tended to accept uncritically the proposition—typically advanced by developed-country economists, taught in all university development courses, and supported by reference to success cases like Taiwan, Israel, and South Korea to the exclusion of many more failures—that aid is a crucial and essential ingredient in the development process. It supplements scarce domestic resources, it helps transform the economy structurally, and it contributes to the achievement of LDC takeoffs into self-sustaining economic growth. Thus the economic rationale for aid in LDCs is based largely on their acceptance of the donor's perceptions of what the poor countries require to promote their economic development.

Conflicts generally arise, therefore, not out of any disagreement about the role of aid but over its amount and conditions. Naturally, LDCs would like to have more aid in the form of outright grants or long-term low-cost loans with a minimum of strings attached. This means not tying aid to donor exports and granting greater latitude to recipient countries to decide for themselves what is in their best long-run development interests. Unfortunately, a good deal of aid that comes in this form has either been wasted in showcase but unproductive projects (e.g., monuments to the ruling family, an elaborate parliamentary building, an oversized airport) or actually been plundered by corrupt government officials and their local cronies. Much of the criticism of foreign aid—that it wastes resources, that it bolsters corrupt regimes, that it is appropriated by the rich at the expense of the poor—is justified. Some LDC recipients in the past have accepted aid simply because it was there and they were not held accountable. But they are the minority.

The two minor though still important motivations for LDCs to seek aid are political and moral. In some countries, aid is seen by both donor and recipient as providing greater political leverage to the existing leadership to suppress opposition and maintain itself in power. In such instances, assistance takes the form not only of financial resource transfers but of military and internal security reinforcement as well. South Vietnam provided the most dramatic illustration of this aid phenomenon in the 1960s, as perhaps Iran did in the 1970s and Central America in the 1980s; many other Third World nations have a similar political motivation. The problem is that once aid is accepted, the ability of recipient governments to extricate themselves from implied political or economic obligations to donors and prevent donor governments from interfering in their internal affairs can be greatly diminished.

Finally, we come to the moral motivation. Whether on grounds of basic humanitarian responsibilities of the rich toward the welfare of the poor or because of a belief that the rich nations owe the poor nations conscience money for past exploitation, many proponents of foreign aid in both developed and developing countries believe that rich nations have an obligation to support the economic and social development of the Third World. They then go on to link this moral obligation with the need for greater LDC autonomy with respect to the allocation and use of aid funds. The most recent example of this phenomenon was at the 1992 Earth Summit (UNCED) held in Rio Janeiro. Here developing nations pressed for substantial increases in foreign aid to permit them to pursue environmentally sustainable development programs. Implicit was the notion that industrialized countries were the major polluters of the world and they had no business telling LDCs to slow their growth to save the planet.

The Growing Role of Nongovernmental Organizations (NGOs)

While there is much debate about the pros and cons of multinational corporate investment and public foreign aid in Third World countries, few people doubt the value of one of the fastest-growing and most significant forces in the field of development assistance, private **nongovernmental organizations (NGOs)**. NGOs are voluntary organizations that work with and on behalf of mostly local grassroots people's organizations in developing countries. They also represent specific local and international interest groups with concerns as diverse as providing emergency relief, protecting child health, promoting women's rights, alleviating poverty, protecting the environment, increasing food production, and providing rural credit to small farmers and local businesses. NGOs build roads, houses, hospitals, and schools. They work in family-planning clinics and refugee camps. They teach in schools and universities and conduct research on increasing farm yields.

NGOs include religious groups, private foundations and charities, research organizations, and federations of dedicated doctors, nurses, engineers, agricultural scientists, and even economists. Many work directly on grassroots rural development projects; others focus on relief efforts for starving or displaced peoples. Some familiar NGOs include Save the Children, CARE, Oxfam, Planned Parenthood, World Vision, the World Wildlife Fund, Habitat for Humanity, the Ford Foundation, Christian Aid, and Anmesty International. Between 1970 and 1990, funding devoted to developed-country NGO projects and programs in LDCs grew from just under $1 billion to over $5 billion. Almost half of that total came from the United States, even though the highest per capita contributions to NGOs came from Sweden, Switzerland, Norway, and Germany.[18]

The great value of NGOs is twofold. First, being less constrained by political imperatives and motivated largely by humanitarian ideals, most NGOs are able to work much more effectively at local levels with the very people that they are trying to assist than massive bilateral and multilateral aid programs could. Second, by working directly with local people's organizations, many NGOs are able to avoid the suspicion and cynicism on the part of the mostly poor people that they serve that their help is less than sincere or likely to be short-lived. It is estimated that NGOs in developing countries are affecting the lives of some 250 million people; the fact that their voices are increasingly being listened to in the halls of developed-country governments and at international conferences on development, such as the 1992 Rio environmental summit, the 1994 Cairo Population Conference, and the 1995 Copenhagen Social Summit and Beijing women's conferences, makes it clear that the nature and focus of foreign aid are changing rapidly. A striking illustration of this changing environment was the pledge by the U.S. government at the 1995 Copenhagen Social Summit that within five years it would channel nearly half of its foreign aid to private NGOs (both in developed and developing countries) rather than directly to LDC governments.

The Effects of Aid

The issue of the economic effects of aid, especially public aid, like that of the effects of private foreign investment, is fraught with disagreement.[19] On one side are the economic traditionalists, who argue that aid has indeed promoted growth and structural transformation in many LDCs.[20] On the other side are critics who argue that aid does not promote faster growth but may in fact retard it by substituting for, rather than supplementing, domestic savings and investment and by exacerbating

LDC balance of payments deficits as a result of rising debt repayment obligations and the linking of aid to donor-country exports.

Official aid is further criticized for focusing on and stimulating the growth of the modern sector, thereby increasing the gap in living standards between the rich and the poor in developing countries. Some critics on the left would even assert that foreign aid has been a positive force for antidevelopment in the sense that it both retards growth through reduced savings and worsens income inequalities.[21] Rather than relieving economic bottlenecks and filling gaps, aid—and for that matter private foreign investment—not only widens existing savings and foreign-exchange resource gaps but may even create new ones (e.g., urban-rural or modern-sector–traditional-sector gaps). Critics on the right charge that foreign aid has been a failure because it has been largely appropriated by corrupt bureaucrats, has stifled initiative, and has generally engendered a welfare mentality on the part of recipient nations.[22]

Quite apart from these criticisms, donor countries over the past two decades have grown increasingly disenchanted with official foreign aid as domestic issues such as unemployment, government deficits, and balance of payments problems gained priority over international politics. The mood was one of **aid weariness**. Taxpayers wanted to focus on domestic economic problems, especially as they came to realize that their tax dollars allocated to foreign aid were often benefiting small elite groups in LDCs who in many cases were richer than themselves.

Conclusions: Toward a New View of Foreign Aid

The combination of aid disillusionment on the part of many Third World recipients and aid weariness among some traditional developed-country donors does not augur well for the continuation of past relationships. But it can be argued that this is desirable rather than disheartening. Dissatisfaction on both sides creates the possibility for new arrangements characterized by greater congruence of interests and motivation on the part of donor and recipient. A lower total volume of aid from the developed nations that is geared more to the real development needs of recipients and permits them greater flexibility and autonomy in meeting their development priorities would represent a positive step. The rising proportion of development assistance funds now being channeled through multilateral assistance agencies like the World Bank, whose political motives are presumably less narrowly defined compared with those of individual donor countries, and especially through a growing number of private NGOs in both developed and developing countries is also a welcome change. It tends to minimize one of the major criticisms of past foreign aid practices, the linking of economic aid to political conditions.

In the future, aid is more likely to be linked to market reforms and the building of institutional capacities and more effective forms of governance as preconditions for structural adjustment. It is also being linked once again to poverty alleviation as well as growth and to rising concerns about environmental consequences. However, a deep concern among Third World nations, particularly the least developed countries of Africa and Asia, relates to the aid implications of the **economic**

transition from socialism to capitalism in the former USSR and Eastern Europe. Fears are expressed that the enormous capital requirements of these nations will divert essential bilateral and multilateral aid (and investment) away from the LDCs and thereby further retard their economic recovery (we will examine this more fully in Chapter 18).

More aid is better than less aid for some of the reasons outlined earlier. But from the viewpoint of LDC recipients, whatever the source and volume of aid, the more it takes the form of outright grants and concessional loans, the less it is tied to donor exports, the more autonomy is permitted in its allocation, and the more it is supplemented by the reduction of donor-country tariff and nontariff trade barriers against Third World exports, the greater will be its development impact.[23] In fact, many observers argue that better opportunities for profitable trade with the industrial nations are much more vital to Third World economic growth than quantitative increases in official development assistance. Although it once seemed like wishful thinking to imagine that rich countries would move in the direction of such real development-oriented trade and aid policies, the recent successful conclusion of the Uruguay Round agreement and the decision by the United States to channel half of its future aid through NGOs shows that this hope was not so farfetched after all.

As the realities of global interdependence slowly penetrate the political perceptions of developed-nation governments, and perhaps eventually their populaces as well, it may lead to the realization that their real long-run economic and political interests in fact lie with the achievement of broad-based development in Third World nations. Eliminating poverty, minimizing inequality, promoting environmentally sustainable development, and raising levels of living for the masses of LDC peoples may turn out to be in the most fundamental self-interest of developed nations. This is not because of any humanitarian ideals (though we know that these are present in the works of most NGOs) but simply because in the long run, there can be no dual futures for humankind, one for the very rich and another for the very poor, without the proliferation of global or regional conflict. Enlightened self-interest may therefore be the only peg on which to hang the hope for a "new international economic order" in which both foreign assistance and private investment can begin to make a real and lasting contribution to Third World development.

CASE STUDY

The Economy of Uganda

GEOGRAPHIC, SOCIAL, AND ECONOMIC INDICATORS

Capital Kampala

Area 235,885 km^2

Population 21.3 million (1995)

Population (average annual growth rate) 2.5% (1985–1994)

GNP per capita U.S. $200 (1994)

GNP per capita (average annual growth rate) 3.0% (1985–1994)

Agriculture as share of GDP 49% (1994)

Exports as share of GDP 8% (1994)

Infant mortality rate (per 1,000 live births) 115 (1995)

Child malnutrition (underweight) 23% (1993)

Females as share of labor force 40% (1994)

Illiteracy rate (age 15+) 52% (1990)

Human Development Index 0.27 (low) (1992)

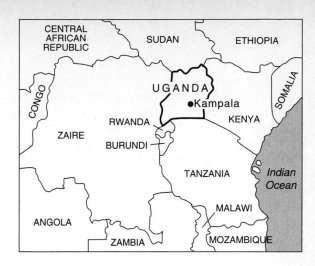

Uganda lies astride the equator in the center of Africa, bounded on the east by Kenya, on the south by Tanzania and Rwanda, on the west by Zaire, and on the north by Sudan. Uganda's population is predominantly rural, and its density is highest in the southern regions. Africans of three ethnic groups—Bantu, Nilotic, and Nilo-Hamitic—make up most of the population. Of these groups, the Bantu is the largest and includes the Baganda, which has more than 1 million members living on the most fertile land.

Until 1972, Asians constituted the largest nonindigenous ethnic group in Uganda. In that year, the regime of Idi Amin expelled 50,000 Asians, who had been engaged in trade, industry, and various professions. In the years since Amin's overthrow in 1979, Asians have slowly returned. Small numbers of Asians and about 3,000 Arabs of various national origins currently live in Uganda.

Uganda's economy has great potential. Endowed with significant natural resources, including ample fertile land, regular rainfall, and mineral deposits, it appeared poised for rapid economic growth and development at independence from Britain in 1962. Yet chronic political instability and erratic economic management have combined to produce a persistent economic decline that has left Uganda among the world's poorest and least developed countries.

After the turmoil of the Amin era, the country by 1981 had begun a program of economic recovery that was supported by considerable external assistance. From mid-1984 on, however, overly expansionist fiscal and monetary policies and the renewed outbreak of civil strife led to a setback in economic performance.

Since assumption of power in early 1986, the government of President Museveni has taken important first steps toward economic rehabilitation. With much of the country's infrastructure—notably its transportation and communication facilities—damaged or destroyed, progress to date has been limited but encouraging. For example, recognizing the need for increased external support, Uganda negotiated in 1987 a policy framework paper with the IMF and the World

559

Bank and subsequently adopted most of the proposals in a wide-ranging attempt at economic reform. The IMF document serves as a basis for Uganda's program of economic recovery, which aims to restore price stability and a sustainable balance of payments, improve capacity utilization, rehabilitate infrastructure, restore producer incentives through proper price policies, and improve resource mobilization and allocation in the public sector. The Ugandan government has also worked with Western countries offering assistance to reschedule the country's foreign debts in order to qualify for further foreign aid.

Agricultural products supply nearly all of Uganda's foreign-exchange earnings, with coffee alone accounting for 97% of the country's exports. Cotton, tea, and tobacco are other principal export crops.

Most industry is related to agriculture—processing of agricultural products or manufacturing of agricultural necessities, such as hoes and fertilizers. The industrial sector also is being rehabilitated to resume production of building and construction materials, such as cement, iron bars, corrugated roofing sheets, and paint.

Uganda has about 32,000 kilometers of roads; some 6,400 kilometres are paved. Most radiate from Kampala, the capital and largest city. The country also has about 1,280 kilometers of rail line. A railway originating at Mombasa, Kenya, on the Indian Ocean connects with Kampala. Uganda's important road and rail links to Mombasa serve its transport needs and also those of its neighbors, Rwanda, Burundi, and parts of Zaire and Sudan. An international airport is at Entebbe on the shore of Lake Victoria, some 32 kilometers south of Kampala. This was once a modest facility, but a new terminal built with Yugoslavian assistance has enabled it to become an important airport for handling high-value imports and exports for Uganda and the region.

Uganda has suffered many years of political turmoil and economic decline. Its real per capita income levels have fallen dramatically over the past two decades. Poverty and malnutrition are widespread, and major public-health problems associated with the spread of AIDS drain both human and financial resources. A reversal of these trends began in 1991 and its continuation will require a judicious combination of domestic economic and political reform. It will also require substantial foreign economic assistance.

Concepts for Review

Absorptive capacity	Nongovernmental organizations (NGOs)
Aid weariness	Official development assistance (ODA)
Concessional terms	Portfolio investment
Economic transition	Productive resources
Foreign aid	Savings gap
Emerging-country stock markets	Technical assistance
Foreign direct investment (FDI)	Tied aid
Foreign-exchange gap	Transfer pricing
Global factories	Two-gap model
Multinational corporation (MNC)	

Questions for Discussion

1. The emergence of giant multinational corporations over the past few decades is said to have altered the very nature of international economic activity. In what ways do these MNCs affect the structure and pattern of trading relationships between the developed world and the underdeveloped world?

2. Summarize the arguments for and against the role and impact of private foreign investment in less developed countries. What strategies might LDCs adopt to make private foreign investment fit their development aspirations better without destroying all incentives for foreign investors?

3. What are private portfolio flows? What factors do you believe are most important in determining the amount and direction of such flows?

4. To what extent do private portfolio investments in LDCs benefit the recipient countries? What are the potential costs and risks to both investors and recipients? Explain.

5. How important is foreign aid for the economies of the Third World in relation to their other sources of foreign-exchange receipts? Explain the various forms that official development assistance can take, and distinguish between bilateral and multilateral assistance. Which do you think is more desirable, and why?

6. What is meant by tied aid? Most nations have increasingly shifted from grants to loans and from untied to tied loans and grants. What are the major disadvantages of tied aid, especially when this aid comes in the form of interest-bearing loans?

7. Under what conditions and terms do you think LDCs should seek and accept foreign aid in the future? If aid cannot be obtained on such terms, do you think LDCs should accept whatever they can get? Explain your answer.

8. What are the differences between official development assistance (public foreign aid) and private development assistance from nongovernmental organizations (NGOs)? Which type of aid is more desirable from the perspective of recipient countries? Explain.

Notes

1. An excellent summary of the various issues pro and con surrounding MNCs can be found in Thomas Biersteker, *Distortion or Development: Contending Perspectives on the Multinational Corporation* (Cambridge, Mass.: MIT Press, 1978), chaps. 1–3; Theodore H. Moran, "Multinational corporations and the developing countries: An analytical overview," in Theodore H. Moran (ed.), *Multinational Corporations* (Lexington, Mass.: Heath, 1985), pp. 3–24; and Mark Cassen and Robert D. Pearce, "Multinational enterprises in LDCs," in Norman Gemmell (ed.), *Surveys in Development Economics* (Oxford: Blackwell, 1987), pp. 90–132.

2. Recall from Chapters 3 and 4 the critical role that human capital plays in the endogenous growth theories and the importance of concepts such as Romer's idea gap and

Homer-Dixon's ingenuity gap in explaining the differential growth performance between developed and less developed countries.

3. Michael Lind, "To have and have not: Notes on the progress of the American class war," *Harper's*, June 1995, p. 39.

4. Maxwell J. Fry, "Foreign direct investment, financing and growth," in Bernhard Fischer (ed.) *Investment and Financing in Developing Countries* (Baden-Baden, Germany: Nomos Verlagsgesellschaft, 1994), and *Foreign Direct Investment in Southeast Asia: Differential Impacts* (Singapore: Institute of Southeast Asian Studies, 1993).

5. Based on Biersteker, *Distortion or Development*, chap. 3.

6. For an interesting discussion of the bargaining power of LDCs with MNCs, see Stephen C. Smith, "Multinational corporations in the Third World: Bargaining power and development," *Towson State Journal of International Affairs* 19 (Fall 1984).

7. For an excellent quantitative and analytic review of portfolio flows to LDCs, see Stijn Claessens, "The emergence of equity investment in developing countries: An overview," *World Bank Economic Review* 9 (January 1995): 1–17, and Robert Feldman and Manmohan Kumar, "Emerging equity markets: Growth, benefits and policy concerns," *World Bank Research Observer* 10 (August 1995): 181–200.

8. Claessens, "Emergence of equity investment," 11–14.

9. See, for example, Stijn Claessens, Michael Dooley, and Andrew Warner, "Portfolio flows: Hot or cold?" *World Bank Economic Review* 9 (January 1995): 153–174.

10. For a provocative account of how free-market policies and private investment flows in the early 1990s constitututed a "speculative bubble," see Paul Krugman, "Dutch tulips and emerging markets," *Foreign Affairs* 74 (July–August 1995): 28–44.

11. Jagdish N. Bhagwati, "Amount and sharing of aid," in *Assisting Countries: Problems of Debt, Burden-sharing, Jobs, and Trade* (New York: Praeger, 1972), pp. 72–73.

12. *Ibid.*, p. 73.

13. Even these figures can be misleading and exaggerate the actual concessional aid component of developmental assistance. For a harsh critique of how official development assistance statistics can be misleading or even false, see Gunnar Myrdal, *The Challenge of World Poverty* (New York: Pantheon, 1970), p. 10.

14. United Nations Development Program, *Human Development Report, 1992* (New York: Oxford University Press, 1992), pp. 44–45.

15. See Hollis B. Chenery and Alan M. Strout, "Foreign assistance and economic development," *American Economic Review* 56 (September 1966): 680–733.

16. William S. Gaud, "Foreign aid: What it is, how it works, why we provide it," *Department of State Bulletin* 59 (1968). It is important to note that the economic self-interests of foreign aid are often linked to the activities of MNCs in recipient countries. One interesting example of both the bargaining context of MNC-LDC negotiations and the link between foreign investment and foreign aid concerns the selection of an automobile MNC joint venture by the government of Egypt in the mid-1980s. Egypt was seeking a joint venture with one of the major automobile MNCs to develop a local plant for the production of cars. For many years, Fiat, the Italian multinational, had operated an assembly-only plant and was the sole auto firm in Egypt. General Motors, Nissan, Saab, Fiat, and several other auto MNCs submitted proposals to the Egyptian government. The central bargaining issues included tax breaks, profit remittances, the proportion of foreign versus Egyptian ownership, and most important, the proportion of compo-

nent parts that would be manufactured by Egyptian firms. Egypt viewed this last issue as critical to its effort to promote domestic industrial growth. While the various proposals were being submitted, the United States Agency for International Development (USAID) announced that it had approved an aid package in support of the proposed GM project, in effect subsidizing the GM bid. With what it considered three equivalent bids, Egypt decided to award the contract to General Motors on the basis of the USAID subsidy. The decision in favor of GM was no doubt also influenced by the fact that U.S. military and economic aid to Egypt (the recipient of the largest annual aid package after Israel) was at that time still "pending" in the U.S. Congress. Thus foreign aid can be and often is used by developed-country governments as a leverage factor in support of their own domestic MNC investments. I am indebted to Professor Bruce Brunton for this illustration.

17. Earl Grinstead, *Overseas Development* (November 1968): 9. In a similar vein, one of the staunchest defenders of the role of foreign aid in the development process, economist Hollis B. Chenery, admitted that "in the most general sense, the main objective of foreign assistance, as of many other tools of foreign policy, is to produce the kind of political and economic environment in the world in which the United States can best pursue its own social goals." Quoted in "Objectives and criteria of foreign assistance," in Gustav Ranis (ed.), *The U.S. and the Developing Economies* (New York: Norton, 1964), p. 88.

18. For a thorough review of NGOs in developing nations, see United Nations Development Program, *Human Development Report, 1993* (New York: Oxford University Press, 1993), pp. 84–99. A more comprehensive analysis is provided in Mark Robinson and Roger Riddell, *Nongovernmental Organizations and Rural Poverty Alleviation* (New York: Oxford University Press, 1995).

19. For an excellent review of the aid experience and the economic effects on recipient nations, see Robert H. Cassen *et al., Does Aid Work?* (New York: Oxford University Press, 1986); Roger C. Riddell, "The contribution of foreign aid to development and the role of the private sector," *Development* 1 (1992): 7–15; and Tony Killick, *The Developmental Effectiveness of Aid to Africa*, World Bank Working Paper No. 646 (Washington, D.C.: World Bank, 1991).

20. See, for example, Hollis B. Chenery and Nicholas G. Carter, "Foreign assistance and development performance," *American Economic Review* 63 (1973): 459–468.

21. See, for example, Keith Griffin and John L. Enos, "Foreign assistance: Objectives and consequences," *Economic Development and Cultural Change* 18 (April 1970): 313–327.

22. See, for example, Peter T. Bauer, "Foreign aid: What is at stake?" *Public Interest*, Summer 1982, and "Foreign aid: Rewarding impoverishment?" *Swiss Review of World Affairs*, October 1985.

23. However, donors need greater safeguards against misappropriation of aid funds and evidence that the funds are reaching the intended beneficiaries, especially the rural poor.

Further Reading

For an economic analysis of private foreign investment and the role and influence of multinational corporations, see Sanjaya Lall, "Less developed countries and private foreign direct investment: A review article," *World Development* 2 (April–May 1974); Paul P. Streeten, "The multinational enterprise and the theory of development policy," *World Development* 1

(October 1973); United Nations Center on Transnational Corporations, *Transnational Corporations in World Development: Third Survey* (New York: United Nations, 1983); and especially, Thomas Biersteker, *Distortion or Development: Contending Perspectives on the Multinational Corporation* (Cambridge, Mass.: MIT Press, 1978), and Mark Cassen and Robert D. Pearce, "Multinational enterprises in LDCs," in Norman Gemmell (ed.), *Surveys in Development Economics* (Oxford: Blackwell, 1987), pp. 90–132.

For an account of the power and inside workings of MNCs, whose decisions shape the lives of all peoples and often transcend national and international laws, see Richard J. Barnet and Ronald E. Muller, *Global Reach: The Power of Multinational Corporations* (New York: Simon & Schuster, 1975). A strong defense of the economic benefits of MNCs for development can be found in Raymond Vernon, *Storm over the Multinationals* (London: Macmillan, 1977). Two useful surveys of the role and limitations of private portfolio investments and emerging stock markets in LDCS can be found in the entire issue of the *World Bank Economic Review* 9 (January 1995) and in the section "Latin America: The morning after," in *Foreign Affairs* 74 (July–August 1995): 28–75.

On the question of the benefits and costs of foreign aid, see Gunnar Myrdal, *The Challenge of World Poverty* (New York: Pantheon, 1970), chaps. 10 and 11; Jagdish N. Bhagwati and Richard S. Eckaus (eds.), *Foreign Aid* (Harmondsworth, England: Penguin, 1970); George C. Abbot, "Two concepts of foreign aid," *World Development* 1 (September 1973); Brandt Commission, *North-South: A Program for Survival* (Cambridge, Mass.: MIT Press, 1980); Anne O. Krueger, "Aid in the development process," *World Bank Research Observer* 1 (January 1986): 57–78; Roger C. Riddell, *Foreign Aid Reconsidered* (Baltimore: Johns Hopkins University Press, 1987); Robert H. Cassen *et al., Does Aid Work?* (New York: Oxford University Press, 1986); and Roger C. Riddell, "The contribution of foreign aid to development and the role of the private sector," *Development* 1 (1992): 7–15.

For a provocative and lively critique of foreign aid and its impact on the Third World from the perspective of a leading neoclassical counterrevolutionary, see Peter T. Bauer, "Foreign aid: What is at stake?" *Public Interest*, Summer 1982; "Foreign aid: Rewarding impoverishment?" *Swiss Review of World Affairs*, October 1985; and Peter T. Bauer and B. Jamey, "The political economy of foreign aid," *Lloyds Bank Review*, October 1981. Finally, a penetrating analysis of the role of the World Bank and other major aid organizations in promoting market reforms as conditions of assistance in the 1980s can be found in Paul Mosley, Jane Harrington, and John Toye, *Aid and Power: The World Bank and Policy-based Lending* (London: Routledge, 1991).

A review and analysis of politics toward MNCs in Argentina and South Korea can be found in Stephen C. Smith, *Case Studies*, Chapter 20.

THAILAND AND THE PHILIPPINES

Trade Strategy

Contributed by Stephen C. Smith

Discussions of trade strategy usually focus on high-profile countries like the four East Asian Tigers, Brazil, and Chile. To take a fresher look, we turn to two countries in Southeast Asia.

Thailand and the Philippines are reasonably well matched for a comparison of trade strategy: Both are lower-middle-income countries of about 65 million population and members of ASEAN, the free-trade area of the Association of Southeast Asian Nations. More exactly, the population of the Philippines is 68 million, with a 1994 GNP per capita of $960; Thailand has 61 million people but more than double the per capita GNP at $2,210. Thailand has grown much more quickly in the past quarter century, with an annual per capita GNP growth rate of 4.4%, enabling it to overtake the Philippines, which has had a per capita GNP growth rate of only 1.3% annually over the same period.

By now it is generally appreciated that the export success of South Korea and Taiwan was accomplished through active trade and industrial policies, not laissez-faire. But are these unique experiences that cannot be replicated? Thailand and the Philippines offer an interesting laboratory. They are in the same part of the world and in many ways face similar external conditions. But Thailand's debt by the end of the 1980s was only $13 billion, compared with $23 billion in the much smaller and more sluggish Philippine economy, and Thailand's debt was used for productive investment, whereas money borrowed by the Philippines was largely wasted. *Relatively* more efficient and less corrupt selection of policies and the political will to carry them out were part of the reason.

Thailand

Thailand is turning a current boom in manufactures exports into an industrial takeoff in the way that Taiwan and South Korea did in the 1970s. Thailand has an industrial policy that is somewhat less active than that of South Korea and Taiwan, but its "anything goes" free-market image is misleading. Despite its casino stock market and widespread corruption, Thailand's trade and industrial policy incentives have had significant positive effects on its industrial development.

Thailand's industrialization began in the 1960s, under the highly protectionist import substitution strategy of the First and Second Economic Plans (1961–1971). Under this regime, average annual growth rates of value added in manufacturing reached 11% in the 1960s, while the share of primary-process manufacturing declined from 60% to 40%. Consumer goods, petroleum products, and some producer goods industries were established. The Third Plan (1972–1976) inaugurated an active phase of export promotion interventions. As a result, the growth of manufacturing continued at 10% per annum throughout the 1970s. Clothing and electrical machinery gained in importance, as did producer goods in chemicals, transport equipment, and textiles. In the economically turbulent first half of the 1980s, the economy experienced an uneven economic performance. But since 1986, an explosive growth in exports and investments have renewed the speculation of the late 1970s that Thailand would become the fifth East Asian Tiger. Thailand has led the world in real GNP per capita growth, with over 8% annual increases in the 10-year period from 1985 to 1994.

A strategy of growth through the export of manufactured goods was at the core of this success. In 1965, just 4% of Thailand's exports were manufactured goods, but by 1992, this figure had reached 77% and a substantial diversification of manufactures exports had taken place. Since 1986, the annual growth rate of merchandise exports has reached 25%.

Movements up the ladder of comparative advantage, in which technological progress is key, are always complex. Undoubtedly, there were pull factors at work, as the first four East Asian Tigers were climbing to higher rungs and establishing high-value-added manufacturing. There was also a push from lower rungs by new manufactures exporters such as China and Indonesia. But these favorable external conditions are not enough to guarantee sustained rapid growth. Judging from the well-documented evidence on South Korea, Taiwan, and Singapore, we might expect that increasingly selective interventionist industrial policies are playing an important role in this transformation.

Many Thai departments and institutions are actively engaged in formulating and implementing industrial and trade policies, including the Board of Investment (BOI), the Ministry of Industry, the Ministry of Finance, the Ministry of Commerce, the Fiscal Policy Office (FPO), the Bank of Thailand, and the Department of Customs (DOC). Among these policies are the following seven.

1. *Domestic-content regulations.* Automobiles and motorcycles, among other sectors, are subject to stringent domestic-content regulations. Locally manufactured engines have been required since mid-1989 on all domestically assembled autos and motorcycles, in addition to previously established domestic-content minimums of 45% for autos and 70% for motorcycles.

2. *Export promotion.* The Thai BOI offers a series of arrangements to promote exports, including three- to five-year exemptions from corporate income taxes, reductions or exemptions from business taxes and import duties on imported raw materials and machinery, and additional tax reductions in so-called investment promotion zones. These breaks are increasingly targeted toward specific sectors, following the South Korean example, with an eye toward moving into higher-value-added, more technologically sophisticated exports. The BOI, DOC, and FPO also offer various extensive duty drawback and exemption systems for exports and special export credit facilities.

3. *Foreign investment.* Very favorable tax and other inducements are used to attract direct foreign investment. Thailand's export boom has been largely fueled by a massive inflow of direct foreign investment from Japan and the four Asian Tigers. These investors are believed to be responding to their own movement up the technological ladder of comparative advantage as well as to these incentives.

4. *Selective protection.* Tariffs on consumer and light intermediate goods rose dramatically in the 1970s (Thailand's pre-takeoff period), generally to about 35% to 60%. These goods continue to be relatively highly protected, despite reductions of nominal tariffs after industries had become established. The objective of recent reductions appears to be more a desire to reduce the incentive to smuggle in such products than liberalization per se. This suggests that these tariffs have been near their maximum level. At least as late as 1992, televisions were protected with 40% nominal tariffs, and many other consumer electronics, including VCRs and stereo equipment, were still at 30%. Average effective rates of protection of manufacturing appears to continue to be over 60%, and the World Bank found Thailand to be one of the most protectionist countries in East Asia. This pattern of strongly protecting the same goods it is pushing as exports is similar to the earlier patterns of Taiwan and South Korea. Thailand publicly describes its motive as raising revenue rather than protectionism. But its recent experience

argues against the universal ineffectiveness of import substitution. Instead, Thailand's experience is more consistent with an alternative interpretation that well-designed import substitution is the first stage in moving up a ladder of export promotion, not only as a country average over two successive periods but also on a continual basis at the sectoral level.

5. *Currency undervaluation.* The Thai baht was depreciated in 1981 and 1984; since then, it has been pegged to the U.S. dollar, which has depreciated steadily since 1985.

6. *Import bans and restrictions on about 40% of imports and exports.* These include 20 published import bans (down from 43 in 1985). A question worthy of further study is whether there is also a referral mechanism of import control, of the type found in Taiwan, in which companies wishing to import must show that they cannot get a similar price, quality, and lead time from a domestic producer.

7. *Export culture.* Following the example of South Korea, Thailand is working hard to establish an export culture in government and industry. The Export Promotion Committee, an influential advisory body with private and public representatives, is chaired by the deputy prime minister. The similar Joint Consultative Committee is chaired by the prime minister. Export awards and prizes on the South Korean model are being adopted.

One difference from South Korea is that Thailand has been very open to an active role for multinational corporations; it has placed much less emphasis on promoting indigenous firms and regulating multinationals. The problems mentioned in Chapter 15 cast doubt on the long-term viability of this strategy. Thailand will bear watching closely in the coming years.

For now, Thailand is not developing a large external surplus, though it has closed its deficit. Imports have been keeping pace with exports due to a surging demand for capital goods that is part of the investment boom.

The same pattern was seen in Taiwan and South Korea in the 1970s. Those countries developed their large surpluses only after they had completed the establishment of a domestic capital-goods industry. There is no fundamental reason to suppose that Thailand would develop differently given that it is now following a broadly similar strategy through similar policies and experiencing similar external conditions—though policies toward multinationals are different and global trade growth is slower.

The most fervent followers of the neoclassical counterrevolution school would (and do) suggest that Thailand remove such impediments to the freely functioning market. Some 20 years ago, it would have been suggested that Thailand focus on commodity exports in which it had a natural comparative advantage. Today some observers would argue that its exports and growth would be even higher in the absence of industrial policy. But if Thais were to speculate that some of their success to this stage is attributable to such industrial policies, it would be difficult to argue with them. There is much room for policy improvement in Thailand, where rent seeking is costly and pervasive and dedicated civil servants are much rarer than in South Korea. But Thailand's policies have nonetheless resembled the successes of Taiwan, South Korea, and Singapore more than the failures of countries actually implementing pure market neutrality.

A more consistently neoclassical view would recognize the value of selective government involvement in projects in which technological progress (product, process, or organizational) is a central concern. Such policies in the East Asian NICs can be traced from early attempts at achieving technology transfer in relatively basic industries to the current efforts of the four Asian Tigers to develop original innovative capacity in high-technology sectors. The interpretation that seems most favored by the evidence is that the East Asian industrial policy mix has served to overcome market failures involved in the process of technological progress. That such market failures are endemic to original technological progress is one of the best-known propositions in economics. But there may have been a massive underestimation of the importance and extent of such market failures in the transfer of product, process, and organizational innovations to developing countries.

Two factors working together help us see why policy in this case may accomplish what the market does not. On the one hand, there are market failures in skill upgrading and technological progress. On the other hand, firms cannot easily fool the government about the quality and quantity of output because exports can be "counted on the dock" and firms must successfully compete on world markets to receive incentives.

Of course, growth does not always equal true development. Thailand has serious problems, including choking urban pollution, one of the Third World's most menacing AIDS epidemics, and horrendous conditions for impoverished women, including teenage girls who are often sold as prostitutes into virtual slavery. The country has suffered politically under harsh authoritarian rule. Corruption is far more rampant than in South Korea, and economic policies seem to have more frequently reflected rent seeking. With prosperity has come civil strife. A military junta headed by General Sunthorn Kongsompong took over Thailand in early 1991. But the botched bloody suppression of a peaceful middle-class uprising in May 1992 led to parliamentary elections in September 1992 and a narrow victory for prodemocracy forces, despite massive vote buying and corruption in rural areas. As in the case of the original East Asian Tigers, rising living standards have also inspired demands for intangible human development goods, like freedom and democracy. In re-

sponse to the North American Free Trade Agreement and the European Union, the policy of the new government is to lead the way toward making ASEAN the first true free-trade area in the developing world.

In sum, Thailand has had an active, export-oriented industrial policy that seems by and large to have approximated a response to market failures in technology and skill upgrading. Its record on poverty, women, distribution, the environment, and inequality is not the best in its region, but Thailand's democratic revolt is bringing demands for action on these problems as well.

The Philippines

If industrial and trade polices of the NICs can lead to a first-best outcome, something close to laissez-faire is second best. The collection of haphazard, mutually inconsistent and corrupt policies pursued by most developing countries is a third-best policy. If they cannot implement first-best policy through lack of policy competence or political will to resist rent seekers, they might be better off with a laissez-faire policy, provided that environmental controls can be enforced and the government can at least muster targeted assistance for the poor. In many cases, though, corruption is so ingrained that even after a popular revolt, it will be all but impossible even to move from third-best to second-best. The Philippines is a case in point.

Despite the much-vaunted "people power" revolt in the Philippines that led to the 1986 ouster of the Marcos dictatorship and the installation of President Corazon Aquino, less has changed in the Philippines than many observers expected. Startling inequality, malnutrition, corruption, the thwarting of land reform, and a devastating rate of deforestation and natural resource degradation continue unabated.

The Philippines has a legacy of problems to contend with, from colonialism to Latin

American–style inequality. But a more recent source of its problems is the debt it accumulated in the 1970s under the Marcos dictatorship.

To understand the causes and effects of an accumulated debt that was used in a way that made hardly any contribution toward its eventual repayment, we must understand the culture of corruption that nurtured it. Marcos decreed that a nuclear power plant would be built in Bataan province. The contract was awarded to Westinghouse, an American nuclear power plant builder, under conditions of blatant corruption and probable bribery. Huge cost overruns brought the construction cost to $2.2 billion, financed by loans. The plant is located just 8 kilometers from a volcano, and known earthquake faults lie within 40 kilometers in three directions; consequently, the plant could not be brought on line. It is revealing to note the winners and losers in this fiasco. Any bribe money is long spent. The multinational corporation that built the plant has been paid. The banks that lent the money are being paid. Philippine taxpayers are footing the bill. The Aquino government eventually sued Westinghouse for bribery, and in spring 1992 the suit was settled in a complex and controversial deal that proponents say will offset at least part of the damage. Westinghouse will pay the Philippine government $100 million in cash and credits and will within 15 years compensate the Philippines for $400 million in new loans it needs to pay to have the plant brought up to higher but still controversial safety standards—work to be carried out by none other than Westinghouse, which will operate the plant.

One consequence of large debt-service burdens is accelerated natural resource exploitation and scaling back efforts to diversify manufacturing activities. The Philippines has been forced by its debt crisis to expand exports in the quickest and easiest ways possible; this has often meant commodity exporting, often at high environmental cost as well as longer-run economic cost as primary prices decline.

Government policy has been to promote exports of primary commodities, the nation's ostensible comparative advantage (though much progress in manufacturing has been made over the past two decades). Exports of wood products, fish, prawns, minerals, and pesticide-intensive crops have been promoted to earn foreign exchange so that the debt burden can be serviced, and the development repercussions have at times been serious.

On its most fertile land, on the island of Negros in particular, production was switched from local foods to sugar. This involved concentrating land into plantations. After sugar prices dropped below costs (falling from 22 cents per pound in 1981 to 5 cents per pound in 1986), child malnutrition became rampant in an area of very productive farmland. Here we have failure on the basis of all the development economics criteria, including poverty, inequality, employment, and sustainability, as well as growth. After a 5.9% annual GDP growth in the 1965–1980 period, negative annual growth of –0.5% was recorded for the 1980s, even before adjusting for annual population growth of 2.5% in this period. As debt payments have consumed an enormous part of the Philippine government's budget, social services such as prenatal care and immunization have had to be cut back. This has contributed to infant mortality; almost 150,000 Filipino children under the age of 5 die each year.

Environmental degradation on a cataclysmic scale has been one effect of the dash for natural resource exports. The tropical rain forests on Palawan Island are being destroyed by unregulated, irresponsible logging companies; as species are lost in the forests in violation of law, the island's watersheds are drying up, drinking and irrigation water for lowland farmers is threatened, and silt is smothering coral reefs and destroying fish resources. Prawn farming for export on Negros is lowering the water table; fisheries production fell by half in the 1980s as a result of dynamite and cyanide fishing techniques, siltation, and mangrove destruction. As elsewhere, significant degradation is contributed to by practices of the poor; severe poverty causes a short time horizon dictated by survival. One hopeful sign is that an environmental movement has arisen that is bringing together diverse segments of Philippine society, from lawyers to poor farmers and fishermen.

Countries considering expanding commodity exports, following small-country assumptions, usually take prices as given in their export analysis. This is convenient because economic analysis is far more difficult in a scenario in which monopoly or monopsony power or strategic interaction between producers and purchasers comes into play. But other developing countries around the world, often acting on development agency advice, are also expanding such commodity exports as coffee, cacao, palm and other tropical oils, sugarcane, rubber, and ores. When individual commodity expansion decisions are added up, it should be no surprise that there are terms of trade deteriorations in these commodities.

Summary

In sum, neither the Philippines nor Thailand has a pristine development record. Thailand has paid an environmental price for its growth, policy successes have often come in spite of corruption, and terrible social injustices persist. But the Philippines has had all of Thailand's ills and worse, without the compensation of dynamic growth and development. These experiences illustrate the idea that it is not just any exports, but increasingly sophisticated manufacturing or service exports, that matter for long-term growth. Government policy can make a large difference—either for good, as is more often the case in Thailand, or for ill, as has been more often the case in the Philippines.

Sources: Stephen C. Smith, *Industrial Policy in Developing Countries* (Washington, D.C.: Economic Policy Institute, 1991, from which Dr. Smith acknowledges financial support); World Bank, *Trade and Industrial Policies in the Developing Countries of East Asia*, Report No. 6952 (Washington, D.C.: World Bank, 1987), and various country studies and other documents; "Philippines settles bribery suit against Westinghouse," *Washington Post*, March 5, 1992; Robin Broad, *Unequal Alliance: The World Bank, the IMF, and the Philippines* (Berkeley: University of California Press, 1988); Robin Broad and John Cavanagh, "Marcos's ghost," *Amicus Journal*, Fall 1980; "Repaying debt kills a Filipino child per hour," *Philippine Daily Inquirer*, March 30, 1989; and lectures by Philippines expert John Cavanagh.

PART FOUR

POSSIBILITIES AND PROSPECTS

CHAPTER 16

Planning, Markets, and the Role of the State

If we could first know where we are, and whither we are tending, we could better judge what to do, and how to do it.

—Abraham Lincoln

The role of the state in the economic life of developing countries needs to be reappraised . . . not by strong ideological overtures, but by pragmatic considerations of feasible alternatives.

—Manmohan Singh, Secretary General of the South Commission, 1989

It is not a question of state or market: Each has a large and irreplaceable role.

—World Bank, *World Development Report, 1991*

The Planning Mystique

In the initial decades after the Second World War, the pursuit of economic development was reflected in the almost universal acceptance of development planning as the surest and most direct route to economic progress. Until recently, few people in the Third World would have questioned the advisability or desirability of formulating and implementing a national development plan. Planning had become a way of life in government ministries, and every five years or so the latest development plan was paraded out with great fanfare.

But why, until recently, has there been such an aura of mystique about development planning and such universal faith in its utility? Basically, because centralized national planning was widely believed to offer the essential and perhaps the only institutional and organizational mechanism for overcoming the major obstacles to development and for ensuring a sustained high rate of economic growth. In some cases, central economic planning even became regarded as a kind of "open sesame" that would allow Third World nations to pass rapidly through the barrier dividing their pitiably low standard of living from the prosperity of their former rulers. But to catch up, poor nations were persuaded that they required a comprehensive national plan. The planning record, unfortunately, has not lived up to its advance billing, and disillusionment with the planning mystique is now widespread.

In this chapter, we examine the role and limitations of planning as practiced in Third World nations, consider the problems of economic transition to competitive free-market economies, and ask the fundamental questions, What is the role of the state, and how can public and private economic activity best be made mutually supporting? We start with a brief review of the nature of development planning and a summary of general planning issues. After examining the main arguments for and against the role of planning in underdeveloped societies and briefly reviewing different models of planning and project appraisal, we examine the requirements of economic transition to market economies and evaluate the arguments for and against the role of the state in contemporary developing nations. In Chapter 17, we will look more closely at government macroeconomic policy, specifically, financial and fiscal policies for stabilization and adjustment.

The Nature of Development Planning

Basic Concepts

Economic planning may be described as a deliberate governmental attempt to coordinate economic decision making over the long run and to influence, direct, and in some cases even control the level and growth of a nation's principal economic variables (income, consumption, employment, investment, saving, exports, imports, etc.) to achieve a predetermined set of development objectives.[1] An **economic plan** is simply a specific set of quantitative economic targets to be reached in a given period of time. Economic plans may be either comprehensive or partial. A **comprehensive plan** sets its targets to cover all major aspects of the national economy. A **partial plan** covers only a part of the national economy—industry, agriculture, the public sector, the foreign sector, and so forth. Finally, the **planning process** itself can be described as an exercise in which a government first chooses social objectives, then sets various targets, and finally organizes a framework for implementing, coordinating, and monitoring a development plan.

In 1951, in one of its first publications dealing with developing countries, the United Nations' Department of Economic Affairs distinguished four types of planning, each of which has been used in one form or another by most LDCs:

> First, . . . [planning] refers only to the making of a program of public expenditure, extending over from one to say ten years. Second, it refers sometimes to the setting of production targets, whether for private or for public enterprises, in terms of the input of manpower, of capital, or of other scarce resources, or use in terms of output. Thirdly, the word may be used to describe a statement which sets targets for the economy as a whole, purporting to allocate all scarce resources among the various branches of the economy. And fourthly, the word is sometimes used to describe the means which the government uses to try to enforce upon private enterprise the targets which have been previously determined.[2]

Proponents of economic planning for developing countries argued that the uncontrolled market economy can, and often does, subject these nations to economic dualism, fluctuating prices, unstable markets, and low levels of employment. In particular, they claimed that the market economy is not geared to the principal operational task of poor countries: mobilizing limited resources in a way that will bring about the structural change necessary to stimulate a sustained and balanced growth of the entire economy. Planning came to be accepted, therefore, as an essential and pivotal means of guiding and accelerating economic growth in almost all Third World countries.

Planning in Mixed Developing Economies

Most development plans have been formulated and carried out within the framework of the mixed economies of the Third World. These economies are characterized by the existence of an institutional setting in which some of the productive resources are privately owned and operated and some are controlled by the public sector. The actual proportionate division of public and private ownership varies from country to country, and neither the private nor the public sector can really be considered in isolation from the other. However, unlike market economies where only a small degree of public ownership usually exists, LDC mixed economies are distinguished by a substantial amount of government ownership and control. The private sector typically comprises four distinct forms of individual ownership:

1. The traditional subsistence sector, consisting of small-scale private farms and handicraft shops selling a part of their products to local markets
2. Small-scale individual or family-owned commercial business and service activities in both the formal and informal urban sector
3. Medium-sized commercial enterprises in agriculture, industry, trade, and transport owned and operated by local entrepreneurs
4. Large jointly owned or completely foreign-owned manufacturing enterprises, mining companies, and plantations, catering primarily to foreign markets but sometimes with substantial local sales (The capital for such enterprises usually comes from abroad, and a good proportion of the profits tends to be transferred overseas.)

In the context of such an institutional setting, we can identify two principal components of development planning in mixed economies:

1. The government's deliberate use of domestic saving and foreign finance to carry out public investment projects and to mobilize and channel scarce resources into areas that can be expected to make the greatest contribution toward the realization of long-term economic objectives (e.g., the construction of railways, schools, hydroelectric projects, and other components of **economic infrastructure**, as well as the creation of import-substituting industries)
2. Governmental economic policy (e.g., taxation, industrial licensing, the setting of tariffs, and the manipulation of quotas, wages, interest rates, and prices) to

stimulate, direct, and in some cases even control private economic activity so as to ensure a harmonious relationship between the desires of private business operators and the social objectives of the central government.

The compromise nature of this situation between the extremes of market inducement and central control is readily evident from our simplified characterization of planning in mixed-market economies.

The Rationale for Planning in Developing Economies

The early widespread acceptance of planning as a development tool rested on a number of fundamental economic and institutional arguments. Of these we can single out four as the most often put forward.

Market Failure

Markets in LDCs are permeated by imperfections of structure and operation. Commodity and factor markets are often badly organized, and the existence of distorted prices often means that producers and consumers are responding to economic signals and incentives that are a poor reflection of the real cost to society of these goods, services, and resources. It is therefore argued that governments have an important role to play in integrating markets and modifying prices. Moreover, the failure of the market to price factors of production correctly is further assumed to lead to gross disparities between social and private valuations of alternative investment projects. In the absence of governmental interference, therefore, the market is said to lead to a misallocation of present and future resources or, at least, to an allocation that may not be in the best long-run social interests. This **market failure** argument is perhaps the most often quoted reason for the expanded role of government in less developed countries.

A clear statement of this viewpoint was presented in a 1965 report of a U.N. conference on planning, which asserted:

> It is an integral task of planning to achieve the best possible use of scarce resources for economic development. . . . The need for using appropriate criteria for selecting projects arose because of the failure of the market mechanism to provide a proper guideline. In less-developed economies, market prices of such factors of production as labor, capital and foreign exchange deviated substantially from their social opportunity costs and were not, therefore, a correct measure of the relative scarcity of abundance of the factor in question.[3]

A 1970 publication of the United Nations Industrial Development Organization (UNIDO) provided the following explicit market failure rationale for planning in LDCs:

> Governments cannot, and should not, take a merely passive role in the process of industrial expansion. Planning has become an essential and integral part of industrial development programmes, for market forces, by

themselves, cannot overcome the deep-seated structural rigidities in the economies of developing countries. . . . Today the need for some degree of economic planning is universally recognised. It is, of course, an integral part of the economy of the Soviet Union and the other centrally planned countries. . . . In developing countries, planning is more feasible and more desirable than in developed market economies. The greater feasibility is a result of the smaller number of variables that must be taken into consideration, and the greater desirability stems from the fact that the automatic mechanisms for coordination of individual actions function less satisfactorily in developing than in developed economies. Planning in developing countries is made necessary by, inter alia, the inadequacies of the market as a mechanism to ensure that individual decisions will optimize economic performance in terms of society's preferences and economic goals. . . . The inadequacy of the market mechanism as a means of allocating resources for industrial development sometimes results from government policy itself or because the theoretical assumptions (particularly with respect to the mobility of the factors of production) do not apply to the actual economic situation. Even more importantly, the market mechanism cannot properly allow for the external effects of investment.[4]

Resource Mobilization and Allocation

Third World economies cannot afford to waste their very limited financial and skilled human resources on unproductive ventures. Investment projects must be chosen not solely on the basis of partial productivity analysis dictated by individual industrial capital-output ratios but also in the context of an overall development program that takes account of external economies, indirect repercussions, and long-term objectives. Skilled workers must be employed where their contribution will be most widely felt. Economic planning is assumed to help modify the restraining influence of limited resources by recognizing the existence of particular constraints and by choosing and coordinating investment projects so as to channel these scarce factors into their most productive outlets. In contrast, it is argued, competitive markets will tend to generate less investment, to direct that investment into areas of low social priority (e.g., consumption goods for the rich), and to disregard the extra benefits to be derived from a planned and coordinated long-term investment program.

Attitudinal or Psychological Impact

It is often assumed that a detailed statement of national economic and social objectives in the form of a specific development plan can have an important attitudinal or psychological impact on a diverse and often fragmented population. It may succeed in rallying the people behind the government in a national campaign to eliminate poverty, ignorance, and disease. By mobilizing popular support and cutting across class, caste, racial, religious, or tribal factions with the plea to all citizens to work together toward building the nation, it is argued that an enlightened central government, through its economic plan, can best provide the needed incentives to overcome the inhibiting and often divisive forces of sectionalism and traditionalism in a common quest for widespread material and social progress.

Foreign Aid

The formulation of detailed development plans with specific sectoral output targets and carefully designed investment projects has often been a necessary condition for the receipt of bilateral and multilateral foreign aid. In fact, some cynics would argue that the real reason why LDCs construct development plans is to secure more foreign aid. With a shopping list of projects, Third World governments are better equipped to solicit foreign assistance and persuade donors that their money will be used as an essential ingredient in a well-conceived and internally consistent plan of action. To a certain extent, this process is a charade, motivated by developed-country desires for sophisticated and detailed project descriptions within the framework of a comprehensive development plan.

The Planning Process: Some Basic Models

Characteristics of the Planning Process

Despite a great diversity of development plans and planning techniques, certain basic characteristics of comprehensive planning have been common to most developing countries. Tony Killick has listed the following six characteristics as representative:

1. Starting from the political views and goals of the government, planning attempts to define policy objectives, especially as they relate to the future development of the economy.

2. A development plan sets out a strategy by means of which it is intended to achieve these objectives, which are normally translated into specific targets.

3. The plan attempts to present a centrally coordinated, internally consistent set of principles and policies, chosen as the optimal means of implementing the strategy and achieving the targets and intended to be used as a framework to guide subsequent day-to-day decisions.

4. It comprehends the whole economy (hence it is "comprehensive," in contrast to "colonial" or "public sector" planning).

5. To secure optimality and consistency, the comprehensive plan employs a more or less formalized macroeconomic model (often unpublished) to project the intended future performance of the economy.

6. A development plan typically covers a period of, say, five years and finds physical expression as a medium-term plan document, which may, however, incorporate a longer-term perspective plan and be supplemented by annual plans.[5]

Although the formulation of a comprehensive plan is the goal of most poor countries, it is sometimes necessary to base such plans on a more partial sectoral analysis. In very poor countries with limited data and minimal industrial diversification, partial plans may be the most that can be accomplished. In general, however, the ideal planning process can be broadly conceived as consisting of three basic stages, each of which is associated with a particular type of planning model.

Planning in Stages: Three Basic Models

Most development plans have traditionally been based initially on some more or less formalized macroeconomic model. Such economywide planning models can conveniently be divided into two basic categories: (1) aggregate growth models, involving macroeconomic estimates of planned or required changes in principal economic variables, and (2) multisector input-output models, which ascertain (among other things) the production, resource, employment, and foreign-exchange implications of a given set of final demand targets within an internally consistent framework of interindustry product flows. Finally, probably the most important component of plan formulation is the detailed selection of specific investment projects within each sector through the technique of project appraisal and social cost-benefit analysis. These three "stages" of planning—aggregate, sectoral, and project—provided the main intellectual tools of the planning authority.

Aggregate Growth Models: Projecting Macro Variables

The first and most elementary planning model used in almost every developing country is the **aggregate growth model**. It deals with the entire economy in terms of a limited set of macroeconomic variables deemed most critical to the determination of levels and growth rates of national output: savings, investment, capital stocks, exports, imports, foreign assistance, and so on. Aggregate growth models provide a convenient method for forecasting output (and perhaps also employment) growth over a three- to five-year period. Almost all such models represent some variant of the basic Harrod-Domar model described in Chapter 3.

Recall that the Harrod-Domar model views limited savings as the major constraint on aggregate economic growth. Given targeted GNP growth rates and a national capital-output ratio, the Harrod-Domar model can be used to specify the amount of domestic saving necessary to generate such growth. In most cases, this necessary amount of domestic saving is not likely to be realized on the basis of existing savings functions, and so the basic policy problem of how to generate additional domestic savings or foreign assistance comes into play. For planning purposes, the Harrod-Domar model is usually formulated as follows.[6]

We start with the assumption that the ratio of total output to reproducible capital is constant so that

$$K(t) = kY(t) \tag{16.1}$$

where $K(t)$ is capital stock at time t, $Y(t)$ is total output (GNP) at time t, and k is the average (equal to the marginal) capital-output ratio. We assume next that a constant share (s) of output (Y) is always saved (S), so that

$$I(t) = K(t + 1) - K(t) \; \delta K(t) = sY = S(t) \tag{16.2}$$

where $I(t)$ is gross investment at the time t and δ is the fraction of the capital stock depreciated in each period. Now if g is the targeted rate of growth of output such that

$$g = \frac{Y(t+1) - Y(t)}{Y(t)} = \frac{\Delta Y(t)}{Y(t)}, \tag{16.3}$$

then capital must be growing at the same rate because from Equation 16.1 we know that

$$\frac{\Delta K}{K} = \frac{k \Delta Y}{K} = \frac{k \Delta Y / Y}{K / Y} = \frac{\Delta Y}{Y}. \tag{16.4}$$

Using Equation 16.2, we therefore arrive once again at the basic Harrod-Domar growth formula (though this time with a capital depreciation parameter):

$$g = \frac{sY - \delta K}{K} = \frac{s}{k} - \delta. \tag{16.5}$$

Finally, because output growth can also be expressed as the sum of labor force growth (n) and the rate of growth of labor productivity (p), Equation 16.5 can be rewritten for planning purposes as

$$n + p = \frac{s}{k} - \delta. \tag{16.6}$$

Given an expected rate of labor force and productivity growth (labor force growth can be calculated from readily available demographic information, and productivity growth estimates are usually based either on extrapolations of past trends or on an assumed constant rate of increase), Equation 16.6 can then be used to estimate whether domestic savings will be sufficient to provide an adequate number of new employment opportunities to a growing labor force. One way of doing this is to disaggregate the overall savings function ($S = sY$) into at least two component sources of saving, normally, the propensity to save out of wage income, W, and profit income, π. Thus we define

$$W + \pi = Y \tag{16.7}$$

and

$$s_\pi \pi + s_W W = I \tag{16.8}$$

where s_π and s_W are the savings propensities from π and W, respectively. By manipulating Equation 16.5 and substituting Equations 16.7 and 16.8 into it, we arrive at a modified Harrod-Domar growth equation:

$$k(g + \delta) = (s_\pi - s_W)\left(\frac{\pi}{Y}\right) + s_W, \tag{16.9}$$

which can then serve as a formula for ascertaining the adequacy of current saving out of profit and wage income. For example, if a 4% growth rate is desired and if $\delta = 0.03$, $k = 3.0$, and $\pi / Y = 0.5$, Equation 16.9 reduces to $0.42 = s_\pi + s_W$.[7] If savings out of capital income amount to 25%, wage earners must save at a 17% rate to achieve the targeted rate of growth. In the absence of such a savings rate out of labor income, the government could pursue a variety of policies to raise domestic saving or seek foreign assistance.

In countries where inadequate foreign-exchange reserves are believed to be the principal constraint on economic growth, the aggregate growth model typically employed is some variant of the two-gap model described in Chapter 15. (Two-gap models are simply Harrod-Domar models generalized to take foreign-trade problems into account). In either case, aggregate growth models can provide only a rough first approximation of the general directions an economy might take. As such, they rarely constitute the operational development plan. Perhaps more important, the simplicity and relatively low cost in terms of data collection of using aggregate growth models can often blind us to their very real limitations, especially when application is carried out in a much too mechanical fashion. Average capital-output ratios are notoriously difficult to estimate and may bear little relation to marginal capital-output ratios, and savings rates can be highly unstable. The operational plan requires a more disaggregated multisector model of economic activity like the well-known input-output approach.

Input–Output Models and Sectoral Projections: Basic Idea

A much more sophisticated approach to development planning is to use some variant of the **interindustry** or **input-output model**, in which the activities of the major industrial sectors of the economy are interrelated by means of a set of simultaneous algebraic equations expressing the specific production processes or technologies of each industry. All industries are viewed both as producers of outputs and users of inputs from other industries. For example, the agricultural sector is both a producer of output (e.g., wheat) and a user of inputs from, say, the manufacturing sector (e.g., machinery, fertilizer). Thus direct and indirect repercussions of planned changes in the demand for the products of any one industry on output, employment, and imports of all other industries can be traced throughout the entire economy in an intricate web of economic interdependence. Given the planned output targets for each sector of the economy, the interindustry model can be used to determine intermediate material, import, labor, and capital requirements with the result that a comprehensive economic plan with mutually consistent production levels and resource requirements can, in theory, be constructed.

Interindustry models range from simple input-output models, usually consisting of 10 to 30 sectors in the developing economies and 30 to 400 sectors in advanced economies, to more complicated linear programming or activity analysis models where checks of feasibility (what is possible given certain resource constraints) and optimality (what is best among different alternatives) are also built into the model. But the distinguishing characteristic of the interindustry or input-output approach is the attempt to formulate an internally consistent, comprehensive development plan for the entire economy.[8]

Project Appraisal and Social Cost–Benefit Analysis

Although most planning agencies in developing countries employed a variant of the basic Harrod-Domar growth model and some worked with simplified input-output sectoral models, the vast majority of day-to-day operational decisions with regard to the allocation of limited public investment funds were based on a microeconomic technique of analysis known as **project appraisal**. The intellectual as well as the operational linkage among these three major planning techniques, however, should not be overlooked. Macro growth models set the broad strategy, input-output analysis ensures an internally consistent set of sectoral targets, and project appraisal is designed to ensure the efficient planning of individual projects within each sector. The degree to which these three stages of planning interact will determine to a large extent the success of the planning exercise.

Basic Concepts and Methodology The methodology of project appraisal rests on the theory and practice of social **cost-benefit analysis**.[9] The basic idea of cost-benefit analysis is simple: To decide on the worth of projects involving public expenditure (or, indeed, in which public policy can play a crucial role), it is necessary to weigh up the advantages (benefits) and the disadvantages (costs) to society as a whole. The need for social cost-benefit analysis arises because the normal yardstick of commercial profitability that guides the investment decisions of private investors may not be an appropriate guide for public investment decisions. Private investors are interested in maximizing private profits and therefore normally take into account only the variables that affect net profit: receipts and expenditures. Both receipts and expenditures are valued at prevailing market prices for inputs and outputs.

The point of departure for social cost-benefit analysis is that it does not accept that actual receipts are a true measure of social benefits or that actual expenditures a true measure of social costs. Not only will actual market prices often diverge from their true value, but private investors do not take into account the external effects of their decisions. These externalities can be sizable and pervasive.[10] In other words, where social costs and benefits diverge from private costs and benefits, investment decisions based entirely on the criterion of commercial profitability may lead to a set of wrong decisions from the point of view of social welfare, which should be the government's primary concern. Although social valuations may differ significantly from private valuations, the practice of cost-benefit analysis is based on the assumption that these divergences can be adjusted for by public policy so that the difference between social benefit and cost will properly reflect social profitability just as the difference between actual receipts and expenditures measures the private profitability of an investment.

Thus we can define **social profit** in any period as the difference between social benefits and social costs where these are measured both directly (the real costs of inputs and the real value of outputs) and indirectly (e.g., employment effects, distributional effects). The calculation of the social profitability of an investment then involves a three-step process.[11]

1. We must first specify the objective function to be maximized—ordinarily, net social benefit—with some measure of how different benefits (e.g., per capita consumption, income distribution) are to be calculated and what the trade-off between them might be.

2. To arrive at calculations of net social benefit, we need social measures of the unit values of all project inputs and outputs. Such social measures are often called **accounting prices** or **shadow prices** of inputs and outputs to distinguish them from actual **market prices**.[12] In general, the greater the divergence between shadow and market prices, the greater the need for social cost-benefit analysis in arriving at public investment decision rules.

3. Finally, we need some decision criterion to reduce the stream of projected social benefit and cost flows to an index, the value of which can then be used to select or reject a project or to rank it relative to alternative projects.

Let us briefly examine each of these steps of project appraisal.

Setting Objectives   The social worth of a project must be evaluated in light of national economic and social objectives. As we have seen, the setting of such objectives is the first and most important stage in the formulation of a development plan. Although all plans are designed to maximize social welfare in one form or another, it is essential that the main measures of social welfare be specified and quantified as carefully as possible. Given the difficulty of attaching numerical values to such objectives as national cohesion, self-reliance, political stability, modernization, and quality of life, economic planners typically measure the social worth of a project in terms of the degree to which it contributes to the net flow of future goods and services in the economy, that is, by its impact on future levels of consumption.

Recently, a second major criterion, the project's impact on income distribution, has also received increased attention. Rather than focusing on the simple quantitative increase in consumption generated by a particular investment, planners are now also asking how the particular project will benefit different income groups, particularly the low-income classes. If preference is to be given to raising the consumption standards of low-income groups, the social worth of a project must be calculated as a weighted sum of the distribution of its benefits, where additional consumption by low-income groups may receive a disproportionately high weight in the social welfare objective function. (This procedure is analogous to that of constructing a poverty-weighted index of economic growth, discussed in Chapter 5.) Beginning in 1991, project analysis at the World Bank also included an environmental impact evaluation as a third criterion.

Computing Shadow Prices and Social Discount Rates   The core of social cost-benefit analysis is the calculation or estimation of the prices to be used in determining the true value of benefits and the real magnitude of costs. There are many reasons for believing that in developing countries, market prices of outputs and inputs do not give a true reflection of social benefits and costs. Five such reasons, in particular, are often cited.

1. *Inflation and currency overvaluation.* Many developing countries are beset by rampant inflation, with a resulting proliferation of price controls. Controlled prices do not typically reflect the real opportunity cost to society of producing these goods and services. Moreover, in almost all countries, the government manages the price of foreign exchange. With inflation and unaltered foreign-exchange rates, the domestic currency becomes overvalued (see Chapter 13), so that

import prices underestimate the real cost to the country of purchasing foreign products and export prices (in local currency) understate the real benefit accruing to the country from a given volume of exports. In short, the official price of foreign exchange in most LDCs does not provide a true reflection of the social costs and benefits of importing and exporting. As a result, public investment decisions based on this price will tend to be biased against export industries and in favor of import substitutions.

2. *Wage rates, capital costs, and unemployment.* Almost all developing countries exhibit factor-price distortions resulting in wage rates exceeding the social opportunity cost (or shadow price) of labor and interest rates understating the social opportunity cost of capital. This leads, as we discovered in Chapter 7, to the widespread phenomenon of unemployment and underemployment and the excessive capital intensity of industrial production technologies. If governments were to use unadjusted market prices for labor and capital in calculating the costs of alternative public investment projects, they would grossly underestimate the real costs of capital-intensive projects and tend to promote these at the expense of the socially less costly labor-intensive projects. Moreover, if the social welfare objective function places a premium on improved income distribution, the choice of capital-intensive projects would not only underestimate costs but would also contribute marginally less to improved social welfare than the alternative labor-intensive project.

3. *Tariffs, quotas, and import substitution.* As we saw in Chapter 13, the existence of high levels of nominal and effective tariff protection in combination with import quotas and overvalued exchange rates discriminates against the agricultural export sector and in favor of the import-substituting manufacturing sector. In addition to reflecting incorrectly the real terms of trade between agriculture and industry, such distorted domestic product prices tend once again to favor upper-income groups (urban manufacturers and modern-sector workers) disproportionately in relation to society's lower-income groups (rural farmers and the urban and rural self-employed). It also encourages socially wasteful **rent seeking** on the part of competing exporters and importers. They vie with each other (often through bribes and threats as well as direct lobbying efforts) to capture the extra profits that can accrue to traders with import licenses, export subsidies, tariff protection, and industrial preferences.

4. *Savings deficiency.* Given the substantial pressures for providing higher immediate consumption levels to the masses of poor people, the level and rate of domestic savings in most developing countries is often thought to be suboptimal. Although the public understandably places a high premium on present compared with future consumption and thus does little saving, it is up to the government to adopt a longer-term perspective and consider the value of higher levels of present saving on accelerating future income and consumption. According to this argument, governments should use a discount rate that is *lower* than the market rate of interest in order to promote projects that have a longer payoff period and generate a higher stream of investible surpluses in the future. In short, governments should place a premium on projects that generate

savings (by placing a higher shadow price on saving) as opposed to those that merely generate consumption[13] in order to maximize consumption at some future, unspecified period.[14]

5. *The social rate of discount.* In our discussion of the shadow price of savings, we mentioned the need for governments to choose appropriate discount rates in calculating the worth of project benefits and costs that occur over time. The **social rate of discount** (also sometimes referred to as *social time preference*) is essentially a price of time—the rate that planners use to calculate the **net present value** of a time stream of project benefits and costs, where the net present value (NPV) is calculated as

$$\text{NPV} = \sum_t \frac{B_t - C_t}{(1+r)^t} \qquad (16.10)$$

where B_t is the expected benefit of the project at time t, C_t is the expected cost (both evaluated using shadow prices), and r is the government's social rate of discount. Social discount rates may differ from market rates of interest (normally used by private investors to calculate the profitability of investments), depending on the subjective evaluation that planners place on future net benefits: The higher the future benefits and costs are valued in the government's planning scheme, the lower will be the social rate of discount.

In view of these five forces leading to considerable product, factor, and money price distortions, as well as considerations of external economies and diseconomies of production and consumption (by definition, factors not taken into account in private investment decisions), it has been widely argued and generally agreed that a strong case can be made for concluding that a project's actual anticipated receipts and expenditures often do *not* provide an accurate measure of its social worth. It is primarily for this reason that the tools of social cost-benefit analysis for project appraisal are now considered essential to an efficient process of project selection in developing countries.

Choosing Projects: Some Decision Criteria Having computed relevant shadow prices, projected a time stream of expected benefits and costs (including indirect or external effects), and selected an appropriate social discount rate, planners are in a position to choose from a set of alternative investment projects those thought to be most desirable. They therefore need to adopt a decision criterion to be followed. Normally, economists advocate using the net present value (NPV) rule in choosing investment projects; that is, projects should be accepted or rejected according to whether their net present value is positive or negative. (Note the similarity between this project appraisal decision rule and our theory of rural-urban migration of Chapter 8.) As we have seen, however, NPV calculations are very sensitive to the choice of a social discount rate. An alternative approach is to calculate the discount rate that gives the project an NPV of zero, compare this **internal rate of return** with either a predetermined social discount rate or the market rate of interest, and choose projects whose internal rates exceed the predetermined or market rate. This approach is widely used in evaluating educational investments.

Because most developing countries face substantial capital constraints, the choice of investment projects will normally also involve a ranking of all projects that meet the NPV rule. Projects are ranked by descending net present value (more precisely, by their benefit-cost ratios, which are arrived at by dividing NPV by the constraint on total capital cost, K—that is, an NPV/K ratio, is calculated for each project). The project or set of projects (some investments should be considered as a package of projects) with the highest NPV/K ratio is chosen first, then the next highest, and so on down the line until all available capital investment funds have been exhausted.

Conclusions: Planning Models and Plan Consistency

The process of formulating a comprehensive, detailed development plan is obviously a more complicated process than that described by our three-stage approach. It involves a constant dialogue and feedback mechanism between national leaders who set priorities and planners, statisticians, research workers, and departmental or ministry officials. Internal rivalries and conflicting objectives (not to mention political pressure from powerful vested-interest groups) are always to be reckoned with. Nevertheless, our presentation should at least serve to provide a feel for the mechanics of planning and to demonstrate the ways in which aggregate, input-output, and project planning models can be interrelated and used to formulate an internally consistent and comprehensive development plan.

The Crisis in Planning: Problems of Implementation and Plan Failures

After more than three decades, the results of development planning in Third World countries have been generally disappointing. In an exhaustive study of the early development-planning experience in 55 countries, Albert Waterston concluded:

> An examination of postwar planning history reveals that there have been many more failures than successes in the implementation of development plans. By far the great majority of countries have failed to realize even modest income and output targets in their plans except for short periods. What is even more disturbing, the situation seems to be worsening instead of improving as countries continue to plan.[15]

In a similar vein, Derek T. Healey, in a review article on development policy over the postwar decades, concluded that the results of planned development have been "sadly disillusioning for those who believed that planning was the only way."[16] The widespread rejection of central planning based on poor performance has had a number of practical outcomes, the most important of which is the adoption in a growing number of LDCs of a more free-market-oriented economic system and a precipitous decline in development planning.

What went wrong? Why has the early euphoria about planning gradually been transformed into disillusionment and dejection? We can identify two interrelated sets of answers, one dealing with the gap between the theoretical economic benefits and the practical results of development planning and the other associated with more fundamental defects in the planning process, especially as it relates to administrative capacities, political will, and plan implementation.

Theory versus Practice

The principal economic arguments for planning briefly outlined earlier in this chapter—market failure, divergences between private and social valuations, resource mobilization, investment coordination, and the like—have often turned out to be weakly supported by the actual planning experience. Commenting on this planning failure, Killick has noted that

> it is doubtful whether plans have generated more useful signals for the future than would otherwise have been forthcoming; governments have rarely, in practice, reconciled private and social valuations except in a piecemeal manner; because they have seldom become operational documents, plans have probably had only limited impact in mobilizing resources and in coordinating economic policies.[17]

To take the specific case of the market failure argument and the presumed role of governments in reconciling the divergence between private and social valuations of benefits and costs, the experience of government policy in many LDCs has been one of often *exacerbating* rather than reconciling these divergences— **government failure** rather than market failure. We touched on these issues in several of the problem focused chapters, but to illustrate the point, let us look again at four crucial areas where private and social valuations tend to diverge and where the impact of government policy has often tended to increase rather than reduce these divergences.

Factor Prices, Choice of Technique, and Employment Creation

A presumed conflict between two major planning objectives—rapid industrial growth and expanded employment opportunities—has typically resulted in the neglect of employment creation in the interest of industrial growth. As we saw in Chapter 7, there need be no such conflict if government policies were more geared to adjusting factor-price signals to the real resource scarcities of developing societies. But in fact these private price signals have increasingly diverged from their implicit social valuations partly as a result of public policies that have raised the level of wages above labor's shadow price or scarcity value by various devices such as minimum-wage legislation, tying wages to educational attainment, and structuring rates of remuneration at higher levels on the basis of international salary scales. Similarly, we have seen that investment depreciation and tax allowances, overvalued exchange rates, low effective rates of protection, quotas, and credit rationing at low interest rates all serve to lower the private cost of capital far below its scarcity or social cost.

The net effect of these factor-price distortions has been to encourage private and public enterprises to adopt more capital-intensive production methods than would exist if public policy attempted to correct the prices. In short, private valuations of benefits and costs often dictate more capital-intensive methods of production when true social valuations would point to more labor-intensive technologies. This divergence between private and social valuation is one of the major reasons for the slow growth of employment opportunities. Within the mystique of development planning, the more powerful mystique of forced industrialization remained a high priority for many years. Contrary to the expectations of its most vocal advocates, planning has had a far from salutary effect on efficient resource allocation in most developing countries.[18] Planning advocates would probably claim that their arguments still hold. The problem has been bad planning, not the mere fact of planning.

Rural–Urban Imbalances and Migration

A second major area of divergence between private and social valuations where, until recently, LDC economic policy appears to have been counterproductive to social concerns relates to the widespread phenomenon of rural-urban migration. As we discovered in Chapter 8, government policies that are strongly biased in favor of urban development, as revealed by the existence of sizable urban-rural income differentials and disparities in locational economic opportunities, have stimulated an excessive outflow of rural migrants in search of limited but highly paid urban jobs. With growing urban unemployment and stagnating agriculture, the continued heavy influx of rural migrants represents a net social loss to society in the context both of lost agricultural output and higher social costs of their urban accommodation.

Demand for Education and the Employment Problem

In Chapter 11, we discovered that economic signals and incentives in many LDCs have served to exaggerate the private valuations of the returns to education to a point where the private demand for ever more years of schooling is greatly in excess of the social payoff. The tendency to ration scarce high-paying employment opportunities by level of completed education and the policy of most LDC governments to subsidize the private costs of education, especially at the higher levels, have together led to a situation in which the social returns to investment in further quantitative educational expansion seem hardly justified in comparison with alternative investment opportunities (e.g., the creation of productive employment). But as long as private benefit-cost valuations show high returns and in the absence of effective policies like those suggested in Chapter 11 to alter these signals to accord with social valuations, LDC governments will continue to face extraordinary public pressure to expand school places at all levels.

Structure of the Economy

As a final example of the way in which planning and government policy have often contributed to the maintenance or exaggeration of socially incorrect signals and incentives, consider the emphasis on import substitution. We saw in Chapter 13 that a wide range of external and internal pricing policies—including special tax concessions to foreign investors, overvalued foreign exchange, higher effective tariff rates designed to lower the cost of capital- and intermediate-goods imports, quotas, subsidized interest rates, credit rationing to new industries, and a whole array of bureaucratic industrial licensing procedures—have served to provide an artificial stimulus to import-substituting industrial expansion. But we also learned that for the most part, the experience of import substitution, especially in Latin America, has failed to meet planned expectations in terms of the eventual realization of low-cost efficient production by local industries. Moreover, the heavy emphasis on urban industrial growth and the concomitant attempt through an economic policy of distorted signals and incentives to reward private industrial activity have greatly contributed to the stagnation of the agricultural sector.

Reasons for Plan Failures

In view of the foregoing examples, we may conclude that the gap between the theoretical economic benefits of planning and its practical results in most Third World countries has been quite large. The gap between public rhetoric and economic reality has been even greater. While supposedly concerned with eliminating poverty, reducing inequality, and lowering unemployment, many LDC planning policies have in fact unwittingly contributed to their perpetuation. Some of the major explanations for this have to do with failures of the planning process itself; these failures in turn arise out of certain specific problems.[19]

Deficiencies in Plans and Their Implementation

Plans are often overambitious. They try to accomplish too many objectives at once without consideration that some of the objectives are competing or even conflicting. They are often grandiose in design but vague on specific policies for achieving stated objectives. Finally, the gap between plan formulation and implementation is often enormous (many plans, for reasons to be discussed, are never implemented).

Insufficient and Unreliable Data

The economic value of a development plan depends to a great extent on the quality and reliability of the statistical data on which it is based. When these data are weak, unreliable, or simply nonexistent, as in many poor countries, the accuracy and internal consistency of economywide quantitative plans are greatly diminished. And when these unreliable data are compounded by an inadequate supply of qualified economists, statisticians, and other planning personnel (as is also the situation in most poor nations), the attempt to formulate and carry out a comprehensive and detailed development plan is likely to be frustrated at all levels. In such situations, it can be both foolish and wasteful of scarce high-level human resources to engage in an extensive planning exercise.

Unanticipated Economic Disturbances, External and Internal

Because most LDCs are open economies dependent on the vicissitudes of international trade, aid, and private foreign investment, it becomes exceedingly difficult for them to engage in even short-term forecasting, let alone long-range planning.

The oil price increases of 1974 and 1979 obviously caused havoc in most LDC development plans. But the energy crisis was only an extreme case of a general tendency for economic factors over which most LDC governments have little control to determine the success or failure of their developmental policies.

Institutional Weaknesses

Much has been written about the institutional weaknesses of the planning processes of most developing countries. These include the separation of the planning agency from the day-to-day decision-making machinery of government; the failure of planners, administrators, and political leaders to engage in a continuous dialogue and internal communication about goals and strategies; and the international transfer of institutional planning practices and organizational arrangements that may be inappropriate to local conditions.

In addition, there has been much concern about incompetent and unqualified civil servants; cumbersome bureaucratic procedures; excessive caution and resistance to innovation and change; interministerial personal and departmental rivalries (e.g., finance ministries and planning agencies are often conflicting rather than cooperative forces in LDC governments); lack of commitment to national goals as opposed to regional, departmental, or simply private objectives on the part of political leaders and government bureaucrats; and in accordance with this lack of national as opposed to personal interest, the political and bureaucratic corruption that is pervasive in many governments.[20]

Though it is beyond the scope of this chapter to deal further with these substantial institutional weaknesses, do not underestimate their importance in holding back the structural and institutional reforms needed to accelerate economic and social development. They are critical factors, in addition to the three previously mentioned, in explaining the widespread failures of development planning.

Lack of Political Will

Poor plan performance and the wide gap between plan formulation and plan implementation are also attributable to a lack of commitment and **political will** on the part of many Third World leaders and high-level decision makers. Waterston summarizes his analysis of the development planning experience thus:

> The available evidence makes it clear that in countries with development plans, lack of adequate government support for the plans is the prime reason why most are never carried out. Conversely, the cardinal lesson that emerges from the planning experience of developing countries is that the sustained commitment of a politically stable government is the *sine qua non* for development. Where a country's political leadership makes development a central concern, the people can also be interested through a judicious use of economic incentives. And, although it is never easy to reform administrative and institutional inefficiency, commitment by political leaders is a necessary condition for reform; without it, reform is impossible.[21]

We might add, parenthetically, that such a political will to develop on the part of national leaders (a commitment toward eliminating poverty, inequality, and unemployment and promoting aggregate per capita GNP growth) will require an unusual ability to take a long-term view and to elevate national social interests above factional class, ethnic, or tribal interest. It will also necessitate the cooperation of the economic elites, who may correctly see their privileged positions challenged by such a development posture. Thus a political will to develop entails much more than high-minded purposes and noble rhetoric. It requires an unusual ability and a great deal of political courage to challenge powerful elites and vested-interest groups and to persuade them that such development is in the long-run interests of *all* citizens even though some of them may suffer short-term losses. In the absence of their support, be it freely offered or coerced, a will to develop on the part of politicans is likely to meet with staunch resistance, frustration, and growing internal conflict.

Government Failure and the Resurgent Preference for Markets over Planning

Problems of State Intervention and the Rise of Market Preferences

As a result of the disenchantment with central planning and the perceived failure of government intervention, a growing number of (mostly Western) economists, some finance ministers in developing countries, and the heads of the major international development organizations have begun in recent years to advocate the increased use of the market mechanism as a key instrument for promoting greater efficiency and more rapid economic growth. U.S. President Ronald Reagan became famous for his reference to the "magic of the marketplace" in a 1981 speech at Cancun, Mexico. Several Third World countries had already instituted major economic reforms in the direction of the free market in the hope that the "invisible foot" would provide a more powerful kick toward economic growth and development than the "visible hand" of central planning. If the decade of the 1970s could be described as a period of increased public-sector activity in the pursuit of more equitable development, the 1980s and 1990s witnessed the reemergence of free-market economics as part of the ever-changing development orthodoxy.

Among the early converts were some of the Latin American countries, including Chile (1973), Uruguay (1974), and Argentina (1976), although presumably their right-wing governments needed little "enlightenment." More recently, others have jumped on the free-market bandwagon, ranging from traditionally more market-oriented countries such as Kenya, Peru, the Philippines, and the Ivory Coast to formerly socialist-inclined countries such as India, Sri Lanka, Tanzania, Jamaica, and Turkey. As part of their domestic market liberalization programs, these countries have sought to reduce the role of the public sector, encourage greater private-sector activity, and eliminate distortions in interest rates, wages, and the prices of consumer goods. The intent of such changes is to lubricate the wheels of the market mechanism. In addition, these countries have sought to improve their comparative advantage in the international economy by lowering exchange rates, promoting exports, and eliminating protection. Moreover, the spread of market mania is not limited to LDCs. Almost every former Second World country from the USSR republics to Eastern Europe is now in the painful process of transition to a market economy (see Chapter 18).

Among the international organizations preaching the virtues of the free market are the IMF and the World Bank. The IMF is requiring substantial market liberalization programs and policies to improve comparative advantage and promote macroeconomic stabilization as conditions for access to its higher credit windows. The World Bank is carefully scrutinizing its project lending to ensure that the projects proposed could not otherwise be undertaken by the private sector. Furthermore, it is emphasizing joint ventures between governments and private enterprise as part of its structural adjustment lending.

What are the reasons behind all of this sudden "market madness"? In part, it has been fostered by the East Asian success stories, notably South Korea and Taiwan, which relied extensively on private enterprise, particularly in the later stages of development. However, for the most part it has arisen from the growing dissatisfaction with government intervention in general and central planning in particular. Many observers attribute the poor rates of growth, massive inflation, high debt, and growing balance of payments deficits during the 1970s and 1980s to the rising burden of public spending, excessive price distortions, and inward-looking trade policies.

In most developing countries, the public sector has grown dramatically over the past three decades, now accounting for 15% to 25% of GDP and some 50% to 60% of total investment. However, this growth has been accompanied by considerable inefficiency and waste. The returns to public investment, in terms of GDP growth, declined nearly 25% between 1960 and 1980. Much of this diminishing return has resulted from poor investment decisions, delays in construction, low capacity utilization, and insufficient maintenance of public projects. Given these problems, many of the "free marketeers" assert that a greater role for private enterprise in undertaking projects could lead to more efficient utilization of resources.

With regard to price distortions, the World Bank has argued that these distortions slowed GDP growth in many developing countries. It has estimated that countries with highly distorted prices experienced growth rates 2% lower than the average for developing countries. Moreover, it found that credit allocations and subsidized interest rates resulted in a bias toward capital-intensive industries; minimum-wage requirements reduced the demand for labor; and subsidized prices for consumer goods, especially for food, frequently discouraged producers and thereby created widespread shortages. As a result, many people are calling for the elimination of government-induced distortions in interest rates, wages, and the prices of consumer goods, in the hope that the market mechanism will operate more smoothly and produce a more efficient allocation of resources.

Table 16.1 provides a listing of some of the problems attributed to state intervention in developing countries. But just as market failure does not always justify public intervention (because governments, as we have seen, can often make things worse), so too government failure is not necessarily an argument for private markets. For example, in South Korea, the Pohange Steel Company is publicly operated and highly efficient, whereas the Steel Authority in India, also publicly owned and operated, is a model of inefficiency. Subsidized interest rates exist in both East Asia, where growth has accelerated, and in Latin America, where it has stagnated. Unproductive rent-seeking activities can just as easily be found in poorly functioning private markets as in inefficient state operations. Simple judgments about the relative merits of public versus private economic activities cannot therefore be made outside the context of specific countries and concrete situations. But for LDCs intent on pursuing market reforms, either because of their dissatisfaction with the performance of their public sectors or because of IMF or World Bank pressures, a number of sociocultural preconditions and economic practices must be met.

TABLE 16.1 Some Problems of Government Intervention in Developing Countries

1. Individuals may know more about their own preferences and circumstances than the government.
2. Government planning may increase risk by pointing everyone in the same direction—governments may make bigger mistakes than markets.
3. Government planning may be more rigid and inflexible than private decision making because complex decision-making machinery may be involved in government.
4. Governments may be incapable of administering detailed plans.
5. Government controls may block private-sector individual initiative if there are many bureaucratic obstacles.
6. Organizations and individuals require incentives to work, innovate, control costs, and allocate efficiently, and the discipline and rewards of the market cannot easily be replicated within public enterprises and organizations. Public enterprises are often inefficient and wasteful.
7. Different levels and parts of government may be poorly coordinated in the absence of the equilibrating signals provided by the market, particularly where groups or regions with different interests are involved.
8. Markets place constraints on what can be achieved by government; for example, resale of commodities on black markets and activities in the informal sector can disrupt rationing or other nonlinear pricing or taxation schemes. This is the general problem of "incentive compatibility."
9. Controls create resource-using activities to influence those controls through lobbying and corruption—often called rent seeking or directly unproductive activities.
10. Planning may be manipulated by privileged and powerful groups that act in their own interests, and planning creates groups with a vested interest in planning, for example, bureaucrats or industrialists who obtain protected positions.
11. Governments may be dominated by narrow interest groups interested in their own welfare and sometimes actively hostile to large sections of the population. Planning may intensify their power.

SOURCE: Adapted from Nicholas Stern, "The economics of development: A survey," *Economic Journal* 99 (September 1989), tab. 4.

Sociocultural Preconditions and Economic Requirements for a Market Economy

The problems of economic conversion to private markets are serious and often intractable. Although some economists may blithely assume an easy transition to full-fledged market economies, the fact remains that a well-functioning market system requires special social, institutional, legal, and cultural preconditions often absent in Third World nations. Fraud, corruption, and monopoly do not disappear with the wave of a magic neoclassical wand. Nathan Keyfitz and Robert Dorfman, for example, have listed the following 14 institutional and cultural requirements for the operation of effective private markets:[22]

1. Trust (in banks, insurance companies, suppliers, etc.)
2. Law and order (enforcement of contracts)
3. Security of persons and of property
4. Balancing competition with cooperation (for a safe workplace and a cleaner environment)
5. Division of responsibility and diffusion of power (an independent judiciary)
6. Community altruism (a social "safety net" for the impaired, chronically unemployed, the elderly, etc.)
7. Social mobility, legitimation of ambition, and toleration of competitiveness
8. Materialistic values as a stimulus to greater production
9. Deferring gratification to generate private saving
10. Rationality unconstrained by tradition
11. Honesty in government
12. Efficient forms of competition, as opposed to monopolistic control
13. Freedom of information (along with protection of privacy)
14. Flows of information without restrictions or favoritism

Given the existence of these institutional and cultural preconditions, a well-functioning market system requires at least the following 11 market-facilitating legal and economic practices:[23]

1. Property rights clearly established and demarcated; procedures for establishing property rights and transferring them
2. Commercial law and courts to enforce it, especially contract and bankruptcy laws
3. Freedom to establish businesses in all sectors except those with significant externalities, without excessive licensing requirements: analogous freedom to enter trades and professions and to attain government offices (equal economic opportunity)
4. A stable currency and a reliable and efficient system for making transfers (a banking system)

5. Public supervision or operation of natural monopolies (industries with increasing returns to scale) as occurs in industries where technological efficiency requires that a firm be large enough to supply 10% to 15% of the national market

6. Provision of adequate information in every market about the characteristics of the products offered and the state of supply and demand, to both buyers and sellers

7. Autonomous tastes—protection of consumers' preferences from influence by producers and purveyors

8. Public management of externalities (both harmful and beneficial) and provision of public goods

9. Instruments for executing stabilizing monetary and fiscal policies (see Chapter 17)

10. Safety nets—provisions for maintaining adequate consumption for individuals affected by certain economic misfortunes, especially involuntary unemployment, industrial injuries, and work disabilities

11. Encouragements to innovations, in particular, issuance and enforcement of patents and copyrights

So we see that market reforms involve much more than eliminating price distortions, privatizing public enterprises, and declaring markets free. The initial setbacks to market reforms in Eastern Europe and Russia (see Table 18.3) as well as in many LDCs is in no small measure attributable to the absence of some (or many) of the institutional preconditions and market practices.

Role and Limitations of the Market in LDCs

It is too early to come to any conclusions about the impact of market reforms on long-term economic growth and development. In light of the foregoing discussion, the question that naturally arises is the extent to which Third World countries can rely on the market mechanism, as opposed to central planning and widespread public intervention, to foster their development. Obviously, the answer will depend on the particular circumstances in individual countries. However, in many developing nations, a number of factors in addition to those mentioned may limit the extent to which heavy reliance on market forces is possible. In general, countries will not be able to rely on the market mechanism to the extent that the industrial countries did during their early stages of development. There are several reasons for this conclusion, some of which were mentioned at the beginning of this chapter.

Perhaps the most important reason is that in most developing countries, markets are in reality characterized by widespread imperfections.[24] One such imperfection not mentioned earlier is the lack of information and the presence of uncertainty that most individual producers and consumers face.[25] Thus in many developing countries, producers are often unsure about the size of local markets, the presence of other producers, and the availability of inputs, both domestic and imported. Consumers may be unsure about the quality and availability of products and their substitutes. Moreover, in contrast to their counterparts in developed countries, Third World producers and consumers usually lack the tools to ferret out this information because little is done by way of marketing. Under such circumstances, profit- and utility-maximizing behavior may be based on the wrong information and hence not lead to an efficient allocation of resources. The government may attempt to provide this information, but this is obviously too costly on a large scale, or it may decide to intervene in the market by guiding producers and consumers.

A second imperfection in the market is the lack of effective competition. In most developing countries, the existence of imperfect competition is widespread, particularly in the industrial sector, where heavy concentrations of monopoly power are usually found. This situation results from the economies of scale that often characterize modern industries coupled with the relatively small market for manufactured goods that limits the number of firms that can compete. The result is an inefficient allocation of resources, with output lower and prices higher than under perfect competition and a subsequent transfer of wealth from the consumer to the producer. The government must therefore often intervene to limit monopoly power by regulating the size of firms or controlling prices.

A third major imperfection in Third World markets is the presence of substantial externalities. Many goods may have a high social value that is not reflected in their market price. Because such goods, such as education and health services, must be provided at a price below their cost or even free, the private sector has no incentive to produce them. Thus the government must often be responsible for providing these goods in order to ensure a minimum of welfare. In view of the population growth and poverty that characterize many developing countries, it is likely that public-sector activity —what the World Bank calls "market-friendly" policies— in this area will continue to expand.

Even if the market operated relatively efficiently in allocating current resources, however, governments still have to contend with allocating resources over time. Capital formation is a fundamental requirement for economic development. Private savings are very low in the early stages of development, and hence through their fiscal and monetary policies, governments must usually play a major role in accumulating capital (see Chapter 17). Investment in infrastructure, particularly during the early stages of development, is of crucial importance as it sets the framework for subsequent investment by both the private and public sectors.[26] Furthermore, even in the later stages of development, the private sector may not be able to generate the massive funding required to establish certain industries, despite their long-run profitability. The government may also need to create certain linkages that will permit the private sector to flourish in the future. Lastly, the government must often assist in the creation of human capital through educating and training the labor force so that labor productivity will increase.

Another major concern in the debate over markets versus planning relates to income distribution. Although the market mechanism may result in a more efficient allocation of resources, it can also produce a distribution of income that is highly unequal. Most developing countries, as we have seen, have a very skewed pattern of income distribution. Excessive reliance on the market mechanism will not improve that distribution. In fact, it may tend to exacerbate the problem, for wealthy individuals with their monopoly of "dollar votes" determine the allocation of resources and hence income. This provides a strong social welfare case for government intervention.

Finally, it is important to remember that economic development is a process of structural change. The market may be efficient in allocating resources at the margin, allowing certain industries to emerge and others to fail, but may be ineffective in producing large discontinuous changes in the economic structure, changes that may be crucial to the country's long-term development. The government may therefore have to intervene in sectors crucial to the country's development to ensure that they change over time and flourish.

These above arguments have shown that the market mechanism can fail in the presence of the widespread imperfections and special concerns that characterize many developing countries. This does not mean that countries should not rely more on the market to allocate their products and resources. No Third World central-planning agency is capable of regulating the vast array of different goods and services. Rather, it means greater and more effective *cooperation* between the public and private sectors. It also means that governments must seek to determine in which areas the market can most efficiently operate and in which areas the government itself can achieve the best results given its own limited human resources. This public-sector–private-sector cooperation through a proactive government industrial policy, and not the triumph of free markets and laissez-faire economics, is the real lesson of the success stories of South Korea, Taiwan, and Singapore.[27]

In summary, there are degrees to which different developing countries will be able to rely on the market mechanism to foster economic development. It would appear that low-income countries in the early stages of development will have to continue to rely more on planning because the institutional and cultural preconditions for a market economy are in short supply and they face major structural changes in the future. Middle-income countries are likely gradually to become more market-oriented, although they will still remain mixed economies with a broad range of government participation. Countries in later stages of development, such as the NICs of East Asia and Latin America, already have conditions that allow a greater reliance on private markets and competitive prices. But they too must always remain wary of the pitfalls of relying solely on the private sector to allocate resources and distribute income in pursuit of both the economic and social objectives of long-term development. Commenting specifically on the Latin American experience of the 1980s, noted Chilean economist Alejandro Foxley made the following astute observation:

> Critical evaluations of past free market experiments are currently underway in Latin America. It is generally accepted now that a naive and radical hands-off attitude on the part of the governments leads to serious distortion in resource allocation: low investment, high capital flight, etc. This was often due to poor performance in specific markets, such as domestic capital markets that in some countries produced real interest rates in the range of 20%–50% for several years; to persistent goods and

labor market disequilibrium, to unchecked speculative behavior by economic agents that led to capital flight, to imperfect world markets for key export products, etc. Thus it seems that an active regulatory role for the government is needed, as well as government intervention for the protection of the poorer sectors through vigorous development of social programs.

The difference between this sort of active government presence and old-fashioned statism lies in the fact that what is stressed now is a decentralized, smaller government that opens channels for the private sector and organized labor to participate in the decision-making process. Discussions in Latin America today focus more on decentralized development, social pacts, and concerted action and less on an omnipresent state role or the advocacy of unrestricted free markets.[28]

Development Planning and the State: Concluding Observations

In view of the record of the past three decades, most development economists would now probably agree that their early and almost mystical belief in the efficacy and benefits of central planning and extensive public intervention has not been validated by Third World experience. Moreover, as mentioned earlier, economic policies have more often than not tended to be ad hoc responses to recurring and often unexpected crises rather than the playing out of a grand economic design for development. We should never forget that political leaders and decision makers are human beings like the rest of us, with all the usual human idiosyncrasies, foibles, and weaknesses. Except in very unusual cases, they will tend to take a parochial (class, caste, tribal, religious, ethnic, regional, etc.) rather than national point of view. In democracies, politicians will respond first to their political constituencies and the vested-interest groups within their home areas. In more autocratic forms of government, be it military dictatorship or strict one-party rule, political leaders will still have a natural tendency to respond to the groups to whom they owe their power or on whom their continued power depends. We must always bear in mind that economic policies are ultimately made not by economists or planners but by politicians, who may well be more interested in "muddling through" each emerging crisis and staying in power than in instituting major social and economic reforms. But this situation may change, if only because, as many experts now believe, the coming years will see a development crisis that may prove impossible to resolve without widespread economic and social reform.

We must therefore be pragmatic about the role and limitations of economic policies in developing nations. On the one hand, we should avoid the tendency to assume that political leaders and decision makers place the national interest above their own private interests or base their policies on some notion of social welfare as opposed to the private welfare of the groups to whom they are primarily indebted. On the other hand, we should equally avoid the cynical view that the social interest, especially the interest of the poor, the weak, and the inarticulate, will never be considered short of revolution. Social and political revolutions are notorious vehicles by which one elite replaces another while the welfare of the poor remains largely unaffected (China and possibly Cuba being the most notable exceptions). It appears more reasonable, therefore, to base our discussion of the role and limitations of the state on the proposition that most Third World governments are beset by conflicting forces, some elitist, others egalitarian, and that their economic policies will be largely a reflection of the relative strength of these competing forces. Although narrow elitist interests have tended to prevail in the past, the groundswell for a more egalitarian development process has now reached the point where politicians and planners can no longer ignore it or camouflage it behind noble but empty rhetoric.

Regardless of ideological preconceptions about the proper role of government versus the private sector, there can be no denying that over the past few decades, governments in developing countries have claimed major responsibility for the management and direction of their economies. It has been said that in many countries, especially in Africa, if the government does not induce development, it will not happen at all. This is probably an exaggeration. If nothing else, however, governments in these countries are the most important users of trained workers. How they deploy these limited human resources thus becomes a crucial issue for the success or failure of the development effort. In short, government structure and management of development have been vitally important and will continue to be so in the future.

In classical economies, the role of government was conceived simply in terms of maintaining law and order, collecting taxes, and providing a minimum of social services. With the Keynesian revolution, the economic role of government was greatly expanded. Governments were assigned prime responsibility within a market economy for stabilizing overall economic activity by means of countercyclical monetary and fiscal policies with the objective of maintaining full employment without inflation. At the same time that the Keynesian revolution in Western economic thought was occuring, the Soviet Union was demonstrating to the world the power of central planning to mobilize resources and accelerate industrial growth.

As indigenous leadership replaced colonial leadership in Third World nations, these two models of the role of the state were at hand. Impressed by the Soviet planning performance but inheriting a free-enterprise structure and philosophy from colonial days, most LDCs adopted the system of a mixed market combined with central planning, with, as we have seen, a relatively heavy emphasis on central coordination and public-sector participation in all aspects of economic activity. Given the rising concern with questions of poverty and inequality, however, the role of the state today has increased to an even greater extent despite the consensus that planning has not worked the magic that some theorists believed it would and that many public corporations are inefficient users of valuable financial and human resources.[29]

Thus there seems to be general agreement today among economists that LDC governments should not necessarily do less but should do what they are capable of doing better than in the past. Most observers would agree that the machinery of many Third World governments has become too cumbersome. There are too many ministries, often with competing interests, too many inefficient public corporations, and too many boards of one kind or another. Governments are criticized for being too centralized and too urban-oriented in both staff and outlook. Civil servants and other trained personnel are often poorly utilized, badly motivated, and less productive than they should be. There is too much corruption and too little innovation. Bureaucratic red tape and ossified procedures and processes sap originality and flexibility. In short, contemporary LDC governments are criticized for being not very different from almost any other government or international agency around the world!

But whether we like it or not, Third World governments must inevitably assume an active responsibility for the future well-being of their countries. As their primary tasks of nation building (in the newly independent countries) and generating rapid economic growth (in all LDCs) are gradually supplemented by preoccupations with problems of debts and deficits as well as poverty, population, unemployment, the environment, and inequality, Third World governments are forging a new role, one that will require innovation and change on a scale that has rarely occurred in the past. Central to this new role will be institutional and structural reform in the fields of land tenure, taxation, asset ownership and distribution, educational and health delivery systems, credit allocation, labor relations, pricing policies, the organization and orientation of technological research and experimentation, the operation or privatization of public-sector enterprises, and the machinery of government and planning itself.[30]

Whether or not such a transition from a purely growth-oriented development strategy to one also emphasizing the elimination of poverty and the reduction of inequality will require major political transformations, as some theorists have suggested, or whether the existing leadership can respond to the new environment of development by initiating and carrying out fundamental institutional and market reforms remains to be seen. But whatever the nature of the response, we can certainly predict that the public sector, whether centralized or decentralized, whether jointly with private enterprise or on its own, will in the coming decades continue to claim major responsibility for the commanding heights of most Third World economies. It is hoped, therefore, that LDC governments have learned much from their experiences of the past three decades and that future successes will more than compensate for past inadequacies.

CASE STUDY

The Economy of the Philippines

GEOGRAPHIC, SOCIAL, AND ECONOMIC INDICATORS

Capital Manila

Area 300,000 km^2

Population 68.4 million (1995)

Population (average annual growth rate) 2.1% (1985–1994)

GNP per capita U.S. $960 (1994)

GNP per capita (average annual growth rate) 1.8% (1985–1994)

Agriculture as share of GDP 22% (1994)

Exports as share of GDP 35% (1994)

Infant mortality rate (per 1,000 live births) 49 (1995)

Child malnutrition (underweight) 33% (1993)

Females as share of labor force 31% (1994)

Illiteracy rate (age 15+) 10% (1990)

Human Development Index 0.62 (medium) (1992)

The Republic of the Philippines consists of 7,107 islands located in the South China Sea northeast of Malaysia. The majority of Philippine people are of Malay stock, descendants of Indonesians and Malays who migrated to the islands thousands of years ago. The most significant ethnic minority group is the Chinese, who have played an important role in commerce since the ninth century, when they first came to the islands to trade. As a result of intermarriage, many Filipinos have some Chinese and Spanish ancestry. Americans and Spaniards, a legacy of the colonial era, constitute the next largest alien minorities in the country.

The Philippines' overall population density is about 195.7 per square kilometer, but it is greater in central Luzon. Manila, the capital and largest city, has a metropolitan population of about 7.5 million.

The annual population growth rate, about 3% in the 1960s, fell by the end of the 1970s to about 2.4%, where it has remained for two decades.

The Philippine economy grew rapidly after World War II. The pace slowed in the 1950s and early 1960s, with real gross national product rising only about 5.3% annually from 1955 to 1965. Expansionary monetary and fiscal policies in the late 1960s spurred renewed real GNP growth, which, despite erratic fluctuations, reached 10% in 1973. The Philippines experienced a severe economic recession in 1984–1985, during which the economy contracted by more than 10%. Since 1986, the Philippine economy has grown modestly. However, there remain major problems that must be dealt with. These include high levels of poverty, widespread unemployment, a large government deficit, low levels of savings and investment, and a massive external debt of $29 billion in 1993.

The country is well endowed with mineral and non-oil energy resources. Philippine

601

chromite, nickel, and copper deposits are among the largest in the world. Other important minerals are iron, silver, manganese, coal, gypsum, sulfur, mercury, and gold. Among nonmetallic minerals, clay, limestone, dolomite, feldspar, marble, silica, and phosphate are prevalent. Currently, only a small land area has been surveyed adequately and exploited for mineral resources.

Industrial production is centered on processing and assembly operations for food, beverages, tobacco, and rubber products; textiles, clothing, and footwear; pharmaceuticals; paints; plywood and veneer; paper and paper products; small appliances; and electronics. Heavier industries are dominated by the production of cement, glass, industrial chemicals, fertilizers, iron and steel, and refined petroleum products.

The industrial sector is concentrated in the urban areas, especially in the Manila region, and has only weak links to the rural economy. Inadequate infrastructure, transportation, communication, and especially electrical power inhibit faster industrial growth.

The government is seeking to revitalize the economy by encouraging both foreign and domestic investment and by restoring free-market forces.

Foreign trade is of great importance to the Philippine economy. The United States has traditionally been the Philippines' largest trading partner, taking about 35% of Philippine exports and providing about 1% of imports. Total trade with the United States in 1990 totaled more than $4 billion.

Major Philippine imports include petroleum, material for electronic equipment manufacture, transport equipment, iron and steel, chemicals, textiles, and grains. Major exports include semiconductors, garments, coconut products, sugar, bananas, coffee, minerals, and forestry products.

The Philippines faces severe economic challenges. It must attempt to raise incomes for the approximately 52% of its population who suffer from debilitating poverty. It must try to create jobs for a rapidly expanding labor force (increasing at an annual rate of 4.5%) where unemployment and underemployment already exceeds 30%. Finally, it must try to reverse the ecological deterioration of its heavily populated rural sector while paying off its burdensome foreign debt.

Concepts for Review

Accounting prices	Market failure ·
Aggregate growth model	Market prices
Comprehensive plan	Net present value
Cost-benefit analysis	Partial plan
Economic infrastructure	Planning process
Economic plan	Political will
Economic planning	Project appraisal
Government failure ·	Rent seeking
Input-output model	Shadow prices
Interindustry model	Social profit
Internal rate of return	Social rate of discount

Questions for Discussion

1. Why do you think so many Third World countries were convinced of the necessity of development planning? Were the reasons strictly economic? Comment.

2. Explain and comment on some of the major arguments or rationales, both economic and noneconomic, for planning in Third World economies.

3. Planning is said to be more than just the formulation of quantitative economic targets. It is often described as a process. What is meant by the planning process, and what are some of its basic characteristics?

4. Compare and contrast three basic types of planning models: aggregate growth models, input-output analysis, and project appraisal. What do you think are some of the strengths and weaknesses of these models from the standpoint of planning in developing nations?

5. There is much talk today about the demise of Third World planning. Many observers assert that development planning has been a failure. List and explain some of the major reasons for plan failures. Which reasons do you think are the most important? Explain.

6. Distinguish between market failure and government failure. Does rent-seeking behavior occur only as a result of government failure? Explain.

7. What are some of the difficulties associated with the establishment of market economies in LDCs? In what type of country is the market more likely to succeed? Why?

8. What do you think should be the role of government in contemporary LDCs? Is the choice between markets and government an either-or choice? Explain.

Notes

1. For a more detailed discussion of planning and planning models, see Michael P. Todaro, *Development Planning: Models and Methods* (Nairobi: Oxford University Press, 1971).

2. United Nations Department of Economic Affairs, *Measures for the Economic Development of Underdeveloped Countries* (New York: United Nations Department of Economic Affairs, 1951), p. 63.

3. United Nations, *Planning the External Sector: Techniques, Problems and Policies* (New York: United Nations, 1965), p. 12.

4. R. Helfgoth and S. Schiavo-Campo, "An introduction to development planning," *UNIDO Industrialization and Productivity Bulletin* 16 (1970): 11. A more sophisticated version of the market failure argument as applied to contemporary LDCs can also be found in H. W. Arndt, "Market failure and underdevelopment," *World Development* 16 (February 1988): 219–229.

5. Tony Killick, "The possibilities of development planning," *Oxford Economic Papers* 41 (July 1976): 163–164.

6. Lance Taylor, "Theoretical foundations and technical implications," in Charles R. Blitzer, Paul B. Clark, and Lance Taylor (eds.), *Economy-wide Models and Development Planning* (London: Oxford University Press, 1975), pp. 37–42.

7. *Ibid.*, p. 39.

8. For an introductory discussion of the nature and use of input-output models, see Todaro, *Development Planning*, chap. 5.

9. For a good introduction to cost-benefit analysis stressing links with economic theory, see Ajit K. Dasgupta and David W. Pearce, *Cost-Benefit Analysis: Theory and Practice* (London: Macmillan, 1972).

10. For an excellent assessment of the magnitude and policy significance of externalities in developing countries, see Frances Stewart and Ejaz Ghani, "How significant are externalities for development?" *World Development* 19 (June 1991): 569–591.

11. An excellent survey of various techniques of project appraisal can be found in Ivy Papps, "Techniques of project appraisal," in Norman Gemmell (ed.), *Surveys in Development Economics* (Oxford: Blackwell, 1987), pp. 307–338. For a look at contemporary issues in project appraisal, see Ian Little and James Mirrlees, "Project appraisal and planning twenty years on," *Proceedings of the World Bank Annual Conference on Development Economics, 1990* (Washington, D.C.: World Bank, 1991), pp. 351–382.

12. If you are familiar with the techniques of linear programming, you will recognize that shadow prices are merely the solution values of the dual to a linear-programming output or profit maximization problem; see Todaro, *Development Planning*, chap. 5.

13. Note the implicit change in the objective function from consumption maximization to savings maximization.

14. This approach is advocated by Ian Little and James Mirrlees in their highly regarded book, *Project Appraisal and Planning in Developing Countries* (New York: Basic Books, 1974).

15. Albert Waterston, *Development Planning: Lessons of Experience* (Baltimore: Johns Hopkins University Press, 1965), p. 293.

16. Derek T. Healey, "Development policy: New thinking about an interpretation," *Journal of Economic Literature* 10 (1973): 761.

17. Killick, "Possibilities of development planning," 3–4.

18. For an extensive analysis of how public policy and the proliferation of controls tended to exacerbate development problems in seven major developing countries, see Ian Little, Tibor Scitovsky, and Maurice Scott, *Industry and Trade in Some Developing Countries: A Comparative Study* (London: Oxford University Press, 1970).

19. Killick, "Possibilities of development planning," 4.

20. For an analysis of the effects of corruption, see M. S. Alam, "Some economic costs of corruption in LDCs," *Journal of Development Studies* 27 (October 1990): 89–97, and Michael Beenstock, "Corruption and development," *World Development* 7 (January 1979): 15–24.

21. Waterston, *Development Planning*, p. 367.

22. Nathan Keyfitz and Robert A. Dorfman, *The Market Economy Is the Best but Not the Easiest* (mimeograph, 1991), pp. 7–13. See also Robert Klitgaard, *Adjusting to Reality: Beyond "State versus Market" in Economic Development* (San Francisco: ICS Press, 1991), pp. 5–6.

23. Keyfitz and Dorfman, *Market Economy*, p. 14.

24. Arndt, "Market failure and underdevelopment," 219–229.

25. See, for example, Bruce C. Greenwald and Joseph E. Stiglitz, "Externalities in economies with imperfect information and incomplete markets," *Quarterly Journal of Economics* 101 (May 1986): 229–264.

26. For an in-depth analysis of the role of infrastructure in development, see World Bank, *World Development Report, 1994: Infrastructure for Development* (New York: Oxford University Press, 1994).

27. An interesting commentary on this issue was provided by Alice Amsden, who noted that when the operations evaluation division of the World Bank reported that South Korea and Taiwan used extensive government intervention to industrialize, the bank refused to publish this analysis. See the *op. ed.* essay by Alice H. Amsden, "From P.C. to E.C.," *New York Times*, January 12, 1993, as well as Richard Grabowski, "The successful development state: Where does it come from?" *World Development* 22 (March 1994): 413–422; Ajit Singh, "Openness and market-friendly approach to development: Learning the right lessons from development experience," *World Development* 22 (December 1994): 1811–1823; and Jene Kwon, "The East Asia challenge to neoclassical orthodoxy," *World Development* 22 (April 1994): 635–644.

28. Alejandro Foxley, "Latin American development after the debt crisis," *Journal of Development Economics* 27 (October 1987): 211–212.

29. An interesting issue beyond the scope of this book is the question whether in LDCs, authoritarian regimes are more likely than democracies to promote economic growth. Casual evidence indicates that this could well be the case, especially in view of the outstanding growth performances of authoritarian-ruled countries like China, South Korea, Singapore, Taiwan, and Chile. The empirical evidence is less clear, although it does seem to support the authoritarian hypothesis over short periods of time. It should be remembered, however, that *development* consists of more than economic growth and, in our definition, includes freedom of choice. For some empirical evidence on the growth differentials between authoritarian and democratic states, see Alberto Alesina and Roberto Perotti, "The political economy of growth: A critical survey of the recent literature," *World Bank Economic Review* 8 (September 1994): 352–355.

30. It is ironic that the principal actor in the transition to more market-oriented economies will have to be the LDC government itself and that successful liberalization may require more intervention, at least during a transitional period. See Paul P. Streeten, "Markets and states: Against minimalism," *World Development* 21 (August 1993): 1281–1298; and Ha-Joon Chang and Robert Rowthorn (eds.), *The Role of the State in Economic Change* (New York: Oxford University Press, 1995).

Further Reading

On the nature and role of development planning, see Jan Tinbergen, *Development Planning* (London: Weidenfeld & Nicolson, 1967); Michael P. Todaro, *Development Planning: Models and Methods* (Nairobi: Oxford University Press, 1971); Hollis B. Chenery (ed.), *Studies in Development Planning* (Cambridge, Mass.: Harvard University Press, 1971); Pradip K. Ghosh (ed.), *Development Policy and Planning: A Third World Perspective* (Westport, Conn.: Greenwood Press, 1984); and Francisco R. Sagesti, "National development planning in turbulent times: New approaches and criteria for institutional design," *World Development* 16 (April 1988): 431–448.

For a more advanced treatment of the use of mathematical models in development planning, see Charles R. Blitzer, Paul B. Clark, and Lance Taylor (eds.), *Economy-wide Models and Development Planning* (London: Oxford University Press, 1975).

An informative and thoughtful study of the methodology and use of cost-benefit analysis for project appraisal in developing countries can be found in Ian Little and James Mirrlees, *Project Appraisal and Planning for Developing Countries* (New York: Basic Books, 1974), and Ivy Papps, "Techniques of project appraisal," in Norman Gemmell (ed.), *Surveys in Development Economics* (Oxford: Blackwell, 1987), chap. 9. See also Arnold C. Harberger, "Reflections on social project evaluation," in Gerald M. Meier (ed.), *Pioneers in Development: Second Series* (New York: Oxford University Press, 1987), pp. 159–189.

For a review of the planning experience of Third World countries during the past decades as well as a critique of the "planning mystique," see Albert Waterston, *Development Planning: Lessons of Experience* (Baltimore: Johns Hopkins University Press, 1965); Mike Faber and Dudley Seers (eds.), *The Crisis in Planning* (London: Chatto & Windus, 1972), especially the article by Seers, "The prevalence of pseudo-planning"; and Tony Killick, "The possibilities of development planning," *Oxford Economic Papers* 41 (July 1976): 161–184.

Among the best references on the critical issue of markets versus planning, see Tony Killick, *A Reaction Too Far: Economic Theory and the Role of the State in Developing Countries* (London: Overseas Development Institute, 1989); "Development strategies: The role of the state and the private sector—a roundtable discussion," *Proceedings of the World Bank Annual Conference on Development Economics, 1990* (New York: Oxford University Press, 1991), pp. 421–435; World Bank, *World Development Report, 1991* (New York: Oxford University Press, 1991), chap. 7; Robert Klitgaard, *Adjusting to Reality: Beyond "State versus Market" in Economic Development* (San Francisco: ICS Press, 1991); Paul P. Streeten, *Strategies for Human Development* (Copenhagen: Handelshøjskolens Forlag, 1994), pt. 2; and Ha-Joon Chang and Robert Rowthorn (eds.), *The Role of the State in Economic Change* (New York: Oxford University Press, 1995).

See also Stephen C. Smith, *Case Studies*, Chapters 21 and 22 on the role of the state versus the market in Chile and Sri Lanka.

CHAPTER 17

Financial Reform
and Fiscal Policy

*There are extremely powerful structural factors in Latin America which lead to
inflation and against which traditional monetary policy is powerless.*

—Raul Prebish, Former Director General
of the Latin American Institute of Economic
and Social Planning

*The taxation potential in underdeveloped countries is rarely fully exploited. . . .
No more than one-fifth or possibly one-tenth of what is due [is collected].*

—Nicholas Kaldor, Cambridge University

Public finance shapes the course of development.

—World Bank, *World Development Report, 1988*

The Painful Road to Macroeconomic Stability

During the past decade, a combination of large foreign debts, growing fiscal
deficits, high inflation, and chronic balance of payments problems forced many
Third World governments to undertake painful measures to stabilize their
economies. **Macroeconomic stabilization** has three objectives: (1) getting inflation
under control; (2) restoring fiscal balance through reduced government expenditures, raising personal and business taxes, and reforming the financial system; and
(3) eliminating the current-account deficit through control over the exchange rate
(devaluation) and promotion of exports. As we learned in Chapter 13, the two
principal catalysts for these stabilization and adjustment policies are the IMF,
which holds the key to international private lending with its conditionality requirements, and the World Bank, which predicates the bulk of its multilateral development assistance on acceptance of its structural adjustment provisions. But all
too often the requirements of fiscal austerity, competitive real exchange rates,
sound financial markets, and the deregulation or privatization of industry in
pursuit of macroeconomic stability and structural adjustment have meant a slowdown in economic growth and a worsening of domestic poverty and inequality.
Fiscal austerity typically involves severe cutbacks in government expenditures

607

on social, educational, and health programs; massive layoffs of public-sector workers; disproprotionate declines in real wages; and the elimination of critical economic safety nets for the poor and the disadvantaged. These actions may have helped highly indebted LDCs pay off part of their loans and thus resolve the debt crisis for developed-country private banks, but they invariably reduced levels of living for the rural and urban poor.[1]

In this chapter, we first look behind the scenes of LDC government attempts to stabilize their economies by focusing on the unique nature and structure of their financial and fiscal systems. We will discover why it is so difficult for most Third World governments to pursue traditional monetary and financial policies, how some financial policies have led to low domestic savings and widespread inefficiencies within the commercial banking system, and how current tax structures often work against attempts to restore fiscal balance through revenue increases. We conclude with a brief look at problems of public administration (a critical constraint in many developing countries), examine the debate over the privatization of state-owned enterprises, and consider the role of large military expenditures in promoting or retarding economic development.

Financial Systems and Monetary Policy

Differences between MDC and LDC Financial Systems

In developed nations, monetary and financial policy plays a major direct and indirect role in governmental efforts designed to expand economic activity in times of unemployment and surplus capacity and to contract that activity in times of excess demand and inflation.[2] Basically, **monetary policy** works on two principal economic variables: the aggregate supply of money in circulation and the level of interest rates. The **money supply** (currency plus commercial bank demand deposits) is thought to be directly related to the level of economic activity in the sense that a greater money supply induces expanded economic activity by enabling people to purchase more goods and services. This in essence is the *monetarist theory* of economic activity. Its advocates argue that by controlling the growth of the money supply, governments of developed countries can regulate their nations' economic activity and control inflation.

On the other side of the monetary issue are the *Keynesian economists*, who argue that an expanded supply of money in circulation increases the availability of loanable funds. A supply of loanable funds in excess of demand leads to lower interest rates. Because private investment is assumed to be inversely related to prevailing interest rates, business people will expand their investments as interest rates fall and credit becomes more available. More investment in turn raises aggregate demand, leading to a higher level of economic activity (more employment and a higher GNP). Similarly, in times of excess aggregate demand and inflation, governments pursue restrictive monetary policies designed to curtail the expansion of aggregate demand by reducing the growth of the national money supply, lowering the supply of loanable funds, raising interest rates, and thereby inducing a lower level of investment and, it is hoped, less inflation.

Although this description of monetary policy in developed countries grossly simplifies a complex process, it does point out two important aspects that developing countries lack. First, the ability of developed-country governments to expand and contract their money supply and to raise and lower the costs of borrowing in the private sector (through direct and indirect manipulation of interest rates) is made possible by the existence of highly organized, economically interdependent, and efficiently functioning money and credit markets. Financial resources are continuously flowing in and out of savings banks, commercial banks, and other nationally regulated public and private "financial intermediaries" with a minimum of interference. Moreover, interest rates are regulated both by administrative credit controls and by market forces of supply and demand, so there tends to be consistency and a relative uniformity of rates in different sectors of the economy and in all regions of the country. Financial intermediaries are thus able to mobilize private savings and efficiently allocate them to their most productive uses. This is a critical ingredient in the promotion of long-term economic growth.

By contrast, markets and financial institutions in many developing countries are highly unorganized, often externally dependent, and spatially fragmented.[3] Many LDC commercial banks are merely overseas branches of major private banking institutions in developed countries. Their orientation therefore, like that of multinational corporations, may be more toward external and less toward internal monetary situations. The ability of Third World governments to regulate the national supply of money is further constrained by the openness of their economies and by the fact that the accumulation of foreign-currency earnings is a significant but highly variable source of their domestic financial resources. Even the money supply itself may be difficult to measure and more difficult to control when there exist, as in many LDCs, problems of **currency substitution**, whereby foreign currencies serve as an alternative store of value to the domestic currency (e.g., U.S. dollars in northern Mexico).[4] Most important, because of limited information and incomplete credit markets, the commercial banking system of many LDCs restricts its activities almost exclusively to rationing scarce loanable funds to "creditworthy" medium- and large-scale enterprises in the modern manufacturing sector. Small farmers and indigenous small-scale entrepreneurs and traders in both the formal and informal manufacturing and service sectors must normally seek finance elsewhere—sometimes from family members and relatives, but more typically from local moneylenders and loan sharks who charge exorbitant rates of interest.

Thus most developing countries have operated under a dual monetary system: a small and often externally controlled or influenced **organized money market** with severely binding legal restrictions on nominal interest rate ceilings, catering to the financial requirements of a special group of middle- and upper-class local and foreign businesses in the modern industrial sector, and a large but amorphous **unorganized money market**, uncontrolled, illegal, and often usurious, to which most low-income individuals are obliged to turn in times of financial need. This is just another manifestation of the dual structure of many LDC economies and their tendency, intentional or not, to serve the needs of wealthy elites while neglecting the requirements of the relatively poor. One possible step in the direction of removing the basis for the coexistence of organized and unorganized money markets as well as the elimination of a major factor-price distortion would be the removal of artificially low nominal interest rate ceilings in the organized market as well as other related steps toward **financial liberalization** (e.g., liberalization of the foreign-exchange rate). Higher interest rates should generate more domestic savings, whereas more market-oriented real interest rates should better allocate loanable funds to the most productive projects. However, such coordinated liberalization of domestic financial and foreign-exchange markets is unlikely to solve the problem of channeling credit to small investors and entrepreneurs.[5] That will require more direct new initiatives. We will discuss both financial market reform and measures to improve finance for the informal economy later in the chapter.

The second major limitation of standard (Western) monetary theory and policy is the assumption of a direct link among lower interest rates, higher investment, and expanded output. In Third World nations, investment decisions are often not very sensitive to interest rate movements. Moreover, as we will shortly discover, a number of larger and more industrially advanced countries in Latin America (e.g., Brazil and Argentina) have in the past followed a policy of inflation-financed industrial growth, in which expansionary monetary policy in conjunction with large budgetary deficits resulted in negative real interest rates (inflation rates exceeding nominal interest levels). The basic idea was that artificially low rates would encourage investment, finance the fiscal deficit, and promote industrial output growth. But as we discussed in Chapter 8, there may be severe structural supply constraints (low elasticities of supply) inhibiting the expansion of output even when the demand for it increases. These constraints include poor management, the absence of essential (usually imported) intermediate products, bureaucratic rigidities, licensing restrictions, and an overall lack of industrial-sector interdependence. Whatever the reasons, structural supply rigidities mean that any increase in the demand for goods and services generated by rapid money creation will not be matched by increases in supply. Instead, the excess demand (in this case, for investment goods) will merely bid up prices and cause inflation. In some Latin American nations, such "structural" inflation has been a chronic problem made even worse on the cost side by the upward spiral of wages as workers attempt to protect their real income levels by indexing wage increases to price rises. The long-standing debate between Latin American structuralists and monetarists about the causes of chronic inflation remains heated to this day.

Despite some of these limitations, however, Third World financial systems remain an integral component of the general economic system. For example, in the context of severe macroeconomic instability of the Latin American variety (high inflation accompanied by large budget and trade deficits), they represent a key element in any overall stabilization effort. Moreover, financial systems provide a variety of needed services, including savings mobilization, credit allocation, risk limitations, insurance protection, and foreign-exchange facilitation. Let's therefore begin our examination of the structure of LDC financial systems with a look at the central bank.

The Role of Central Banks

Role in Developed Nations

In developed nations, **central banks** conduct a wide range of banking, regulatory, and supervisory functions. They have substantial public responsibilities and a broad array of executive powers. Their major activities can be grouped into five general functions:[6]

1. Issuer of currency and manager of foreign reserves. Central banks print money, distribute notes and coins, intervene in foreign-exchange markets to regulate the national currency's rate of exchange with other currencies, and manage foreign-asset reserves to maintain the external value of the national currency.

2. Banker to the government. Central banks provide bank deposit and borrowing facilities to the government while simultaneously acting as the government's fiscal agent and underwriter.

3. Banker to domestic commercial banks. Central banks also provide bank deposit and borrowing facilities to commercial banks and act as a lender of last resort to financially troubled commercial banks.

4. Regulator of domestic financial institutions. Central banks ensure that commercial banks and other financial institutions conduct their business prudently and in accordance with relevant laws and regulations. They also monitor reserve ratio requirements and supervise the conduct of local and regional banks.

5. Operator of monetary and credit policy. Central banks attempt to manipulate monetary and credit policy instruments (the domestic money supply, the discount rate, the foreign-exchange rate, commercial bank reserve ratio requirements, etc.) to achieve major macroeconomic objectives such as controlling inflation, promoting investment, or regulating international currency movements.

Role in Developing Nations

Central banks are capable of effectively carrying out their wide range of administrative and regulatory functions in developed nations primarily because these countries have a highly integrated, complex economy; a sophisticated and mature financial system; and a highly educated, well-trained, and well-informed population. In developing countries, the situation is quite different. As we have seen in previous chapters, Third World economies may be dominated by a narrow range of exports accompanied by a much larger diversity of imports, the relative prices (the terms of trade) of which are likely to be beyond local control. Their financial systems tend to be rudimentary and characterized by (1) foreign-owned commercial banks that mostly finance domestic and export industries, (2) an informal and often exploitive credit network serving the bulk of the rural and informal urban economy, (3) a central banking institution that may have been inherited from colonial rulers and operates either as a **currency board** issuing domestic currency for foreign exchange at fixed rates[7] or simply to finance budget deficits, (4) a money supply that is difficult to measure (because of currency substitution) and more difficult to regulate, (5) an unskilled and inexperienced work force unfamiliar with the many complexities of domestic and international finance, and (6) a degree of political influence and control by the central government (over interest rates, foreign-exchange rates, import licenses, etc.) not usually found in more developed nations.

Under such circumstances, the principal task of a central bank is to instill a sense of confidence among local citizens and foreign trading partners in the credibility of the local currency as a viable and stable unit of account and in the prudence and responsibility of the domestic financial system. Unfortunately, many Third World central banks have limited control over the credibility of their currencies because fiscal policy—and large fiscal deficits—call the tune and must be financed either by printing money or through foreign or domestic borrowing. In either case, prolonged deficits inevitably lead to inflation and a loss of confidence in the currency.

Given the substantial differences in economic structure and financial sophistication between rich and poor nations, central banks in most of the least developed Third World countries simply do not possess the flexibility and the independence to undertake the range of monetary macroeconomic and regulatory functions performed by their developed-country counterparts. What, then, can they do? And are there alternatives to a full-fledged central bank for the many small, export-oriented developing countries?

Alternatives to Central Banks

Charles Collyns has suggested four alternatives to the standard central bank.[8] First, a *transitional central banking institution* can be formed as an intermediate step between a currency board and a central bank, with the government exerting a strong influence on its financial activities. The range of such activities, however, is checked by statutory limitations on the monetary authority's discretionary powers. British colonies and protectorates such as Fiji, Belize, Maldives, and Bhutan provide the most common examples of transitional central banks. Second, a *supranational central bank* may be created to undertake central banking activities for a group of smaller countries participating in a monetary union, perhaps also as part of a customs union (see Chapter 13). Examples of such monetary unions with regional central banks are the West African Monetary Union (franc zone), the Central African Monetary Area (also franc-related), and the East Caribbean Currency Authority. Third, a *currency enclave* might be established between an LDC central banking institution and a monetary authority of a larger trading partner, usually but not necessarily the former colonial power. Such an arrangement provides a certain degree of stability to the LDC currency, but the dominating influence of the partner with its own economic priorities renders the enclave almost as dependent as a colony. Examples include Liberia and Panama, which are tied to the U.S. dollar, although there is no formal support agreement with the U.S. government. Finally, in an *open-economy central banking institution*, where both commodity and international capital flows represent significant components of national economic activity, the monetary environment is likely to be subject to the dominating influence of world commodity and financial markets. As a result, the central banking institution will be engaged primarily in the regulation and promotion of a stable and respected financial system. Examples of such institutions are Singapore, Hong Kong, Kuwait, Saudi

Arabia, and the United Arab Emirates. Table 17.1 summarizes the major features of these four categories of central bank alternatives in comparison with the currency board and the central bank.

In the final analysis, however, it is not so much the organizational structure of the central banking institution or even its degree of political autonomy that matters. Rather, it is the extent to which such an institution is capable of financing and promoting domestic economic development, through its commercial and development banking system, in an international economic and financial environment characterized by various degrees of dominance and dependence. Commercial banks in Third World countries must take a much more active role in promoting new industries and financing existing ones than is usual for banks in developed nations. They have to be sources of venture capital as well as repositories of the commercial knowledge and business skills that are typically in short supply domestically. It is because of their failure to do this that new financial institutions, known as *development banks*, have emerged over the past few decades in a wide variety of Third World countries.

The Emergence of Development Banking

Development banks are specialized public and private financial institutions that supply medium- and long-term funds for the creation or expansion of industrial enterprises. They have arisen in many developing nations because the existing banks usually focus on either short-term lending for commercial purposes (commercial and savings banks) or, in the case of central banks, the control and regulation of the aggregate supply of money. Moreover, existing commercial banks set loan conditions that often are inappropriate for establishing new enterprises or for financing large-scale projects. Their funds are more often allocated to "safe" borrowers (established industries, many of which are foreign-owned or run by well-known local families). True venture capital for new industries rarely obtains approval.

To facilitate industrial growth in economies characterized by a scarcity of financial capital, development banks have sought to raise capital, initially focusing on two major sources: (1) bilateral and multilateral loans from national aid agencies like the U.S. Agency for International Development (USAID) and from international donor agencies like the World Bank and (2) loans from their own governments. However, in addition to raising capital, development banks have had to develop specialized skills in the field of industrial project appraisal. In many cases, their activities go far beyond the traditional banker's role of lending money to creditworthy customers. The activities of development banks often encompass direct entrepreneurial, managerial, and promotional involvement in the enterprises they finance, including government-owned and -operated industrial corporations. Development banks are thus playing an increasingly important role in the industrialization process of many LDCs.

Although development banks are a relatively new phenomenon in the Third World, their growth and spread have been substantial. In the mid-1940s, there were no more than 10 or 12 such institutions; by the end of the 1980s, their num-

TABLE 17.1 Central Banking Institutions

Institution	Function					
	Issuer of Currency	Banker to Government	Banker to Commercial Banks	Regulator of Financial Institutions	Operator of Monetary Policy	Promoter of Financial Development
Full-fledged central bank	3	3	3	3	3G	1
Supranational central bank	3E	2E	2	2	2E	2
Open-economy central banking institution	3C	2C	2	3	1	3
Transitional central banking institution	3CG	2C	2	1	2G	3
Currency enclave central banking institution	1,2CE	2CE	2	1	1	3
Currency board	3C	1	1	1	1	3

SOURCE: Charles Collyns, *Alternatives to the Central Bank in the Developing World*, International Monetary Fund Occasional Paper No. 20 (Washington, D.C.: International Monetary Fund, 1983), p. 22.

KEY: 1 = limited involvement; 2 = substantial involvement; 3 = full involvement; C = considerable constitutional restrictions; E = considerable external influence; G = considerable government influence.

bers had increased into the hundreds, and their financial resources had ballooned to billions of dollars. Moreover, although the initial sources of capital were agencies like the World Bank, bilateral aid agencies, and local governments (e.g., the Industrial Credit and Investment Corporation of India was established in 1954 with a 30-year interest-free advance of 75 million rupees from the Indian government), the growth of development bank finance has increasingly been facilitated by capital from private investors, institutional and individual, foreign and local. Almost 20% of the share capital of these banks was foreign-owned in 1980, with the remaining 80% derived from local investors.

In spite of their impressive growth and their increasing importance for Third World industrial expansion, development banks have come under mounting criticism for their excessive concentration on large-scale loans. Some privately owned finance companies (also categorized as development banks) refuse to consider loans of less than $20,000 to $50,000. They argue that smaller loans do not justify the time and effort involved in their appraisal. As a result, these finance companies almost totally remove themselves from the area of aid to small enterprises, even though such aid is of major importance to the achievement of broadly based economic development and often may constitute the bulk of assistance needed in the private sector. Small-scale entrepreneurs, often lacking technical, purchasing, marketing, organizational, and accounting skills, as well as access to bank credit, are thus forced to seek funds in the exploitive unorganized money markets. We may conclude, therefore, that in spite of the growth of development banks, there remains a need to channel more financial resources to small entrepreneurs, both on the farm and in the marginal or informal sector of urban areas, who often are excluded from access to credit at reasonable rates of interest.[9] In an attempt to respond to these needs of small-scale borrowers, Third World financial systems have spawned a whole array of unique, informal credit arrangements. Let's look briefly at some of them.

The Role of Informal Finance for Small-Scale Enterprise

Much economic activity in developing nations comes from small-scale producers and enterprises. Recent studies indicate that they employ anywhere from 40% to 70% of the labor force and account for about one-third of domestic recorded output. Most are noncorporate, unlicensed, unregistered enterprises including small farmers, producers, artisans, tradespeople, and independent traders operating in the informal urban and rural sectors of the economy. Their demands for financial services are unique and outside the purview of traditional commercial bank lending. For example, street vendors need short-term finance to buy stock, small farmers require buffer loans to tide them over uncertain seasonal income fluctuations, and small-scale manufacturers need minor loans to purchase simple equipment or hire nonfamily workers. In such situations, traditional commercial banks are both ill equipped and reluctant to meet the needs of these small borrowers. Because the sums involved are small (usually less than $500) but administration and carrying costs are almost as high as for a large loans, and because few informal borrowers have the necessary collateral to secure formal-sector loans, commercial banks simply are not interested. Most don't even have branch offices in rural villages, small towns, or on the periphery of cities where many of the informal activities take place. Thus most noncorporate borrowers have to turn to family or friends as a first line of finance and then warily to local professional moneylenders, pawnbrokers, and tradespeople as a backup. These latter sources of finance are extremely costly—moneylenders, for example, can charge up to 20% a *day* in interest for short-term loans to traders and vendors. In the case of small farmers requiring seasonal loans, the only collateral that they have to offer the moneylender or pawnbroker is their land or oxen. If these must be surrendered in the event of a default, peasant farmers become rapidly transformed into landless laborers, while moneylenders accumulate sizable tracts of land, either for themselves or to sell to large local landholders.

Fortunately, in recent years new, more reasonable and reliable forms of **informal finance** have emerged to replace the moneylender and pawnbroker in some instances.[10] These include local rotating savings and credit associations and group lending schemes. In the case of **rotating savings and credit associations**, which can be found in such diverse countries as Mexico, Bolivia, Egypt, Nigeria, Ghana, the Philippines, Sri Lanka, India, China, and South Korea, a group of 40 to 50 individuals selects a leader who collects a fixed amount of savings from each member. This fund is then allocated on a rotating basis to each member as an interest-free loan. Studies have revealed that many low-income people prefer to save and borrow this way, repayment rates are extremely high, and participation is very active.

In the case of **group lending schemes**, a group of potential borrowers forms an association to borrow funds from a commercial bank, a government development bank, or a private institution. The group then allocates the funds to individual members whose responsibility is to repay the group. The group itself guarantees the loan to the outside lender; it is responsible for repayment. The idea is simple: By joining together, a group of small borrowers can reduce the costs of borrowing and, because the loan is large, can gain access to formal commercial credit. Group members have a vested interest in the success of the enterprise and therefore exert strong moral pressure on borrowing members to repay on time. Again, the evidence shows that repayment rates compare favorably with formal-sector borrowers.

An outstanding example of a group lending program is the Grameen Rural Bank in Bangladesh. It was started in 1976 with government funds as a way to help the rural landless obtain credit. The bank's customers are organized into five-person groups of the very poor. Each group must demonstrate a weekly pattern of saving before seeking a loan. Loans are first allocated to two members, who must make regular weekly payments before any other members become eligible for loans. The funds are typically used to finance trading or purchase livestock. The program has been a great success. The Grameen Bank now operates more than 300 branches in over 5,400 villages catering to 250,000 people in Bangladesh, 75% of whom are women. Loans are small (less than $100), and the repayment rate is much better than that of the regular Bangladeshi commercial banking system. Records show, for example, that 97% of all Grameen loans are repaid within one year and 99% within two years.

Although these few examples of successful informal finance programs are impressive, the fact remains that throughout the Third World, the vast majority of rural and urban poor have little or no access to credit. Until legal reforms are enacted making it easier for small enterprises to gain access to the formal credit system or more government-supported credit programs are established to serve the needs of the noncorporate sector, the financial systems of most developing countries will remain unresponsive to the fundamental requirements of participatory national development.

Reforming Third World Financial Systems

Financial Liberalization, Real Interest Rates, Savings, and Investment

The restriction of loans to a few large borrowers, together with the widespread existence of high inflation, growing budget deficits, and negative real interest rates, led to a serious LDC "credit crunch" during the 1980s. The global recessions of 1981–1982 and 1987 exposed the frailty of many development bank loans so that by the end of the decade almost half of them were reporting at least 25% of their loans in arrears while another quarter had delinquency rates in excess of 50%. With real interest rates on savings deposits in the negative and expectations of continued inflation and exchange-rate devaluation contributing to substantial capital flight, it is not surprising that few individuals were willing to save.

In addition, commercial banks and other financial intermediaries were subject to numerous lending restrictions and faced mandatory interest rate ceilings on loanable funds at levels well below market-clearing rates.[11] These artificial interest rate ceilings were often set by LDC governments seeking to finance their budget deficits through the sale of low interest bonds to private commercial banks. These banks in turn had to resort to **rationing** the available credit. Figure 17.1 shows the impact of binding nominal interest rate ceilings at below market-clearing levels. With the interest rate ceiling at $\bar{r}$, which is below the market-clearing equilibrium rate r_E, the demand for loanable funds, L_2, greatly exceeds the available supply, L_1. This excess demand leads to a need to ration the limited supply—a phenomenon known as **financial repression** because investment is limited or "repressed" by a shortage of savings, which in turn results from administered real interest rates at below market-clearing levels. In the absence of outright corruption in the allocation of L_1 loanable funds, most commercial banks choose to allocate the available credit to a few large borrowers so as to minimize the administrative overhead costs as a proportion of the total costs of lending. Thus the net effect of government controls over lending rates is that even fewer loans will be allocated to small investors. Banks can cover the additional administrative costs and the added risks of smaller loans only by charging higher interest rates. Hence small farmers and urban entrepreneurs have no recourse but to seek finance from the unorganized money market, where, as we see from Figure 17.1, they are willing to pay above market-clearing rates of r_U.

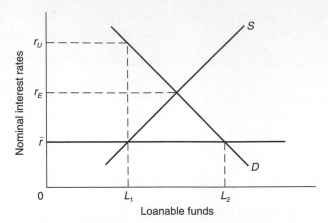

FIGURE 17.1 The Effects of Interest Rate Ceilings on Credit Allocation.

One suggested solution to the problem is to liberalize the financial sector by allowing nominal interest rates to rise to market-clearing levels. This would cause real interest rates to rise to positive levels and thus remove the explicit interest rate subsidy accorded to preferred borrowers (rent seekers) who are powerful enough to gain access to the rationed credit. Higher real rates should also generate more domestic savings and investment and permit some borrowers to shift from the unorganized to the organized credit market.[12] The World Bank cites evidence from a number of countries such as Thailand, Turkey, and Kenya, where the liberalization of interest rates generated more savings and investment.[13] However, evidence of the effects of financial reform in Chile during the 1970s revealed many shortcomings of the process. These included the acquisition of numerous banks by large conglomerates, or *grupos*, who used their new financial resources to buy recently privatized firms or to expand their own companies. When many of their firms faced financial losses, these *grupos* had to resort to additional funding to avoid bankruptcy. Hence the Chilean financial system was very vulnerable when the debt crisis struck in the 1980s.

Reform and liberalization of the organized money sector is therefore no panacea for the financial systems of developing nations. The success of South Korea and Taiwan (and, earlier, Japan) with financial systems that exhibited many of the attributes of repression demonstrates that judicious and selective government intervention can be a stimulus to industrial development. Although there is evidence that the elimination of interest rate distortions can promote greater saving and more rapid economic growth, financial reform must always be accompanied by other more direct measures to make sure that small farmers and investors have access to needed credit. Additionally, as shown in the next section, there needs to be careful governmental supervision of the banking and financial sectors to prevent undue concentration by local elites. As we have pointed out throughout Parts Two and Three (with regard to land reform, access to higher education, employment creation, and multinational corporate investment), "getting prices right" is only one step, albeit an important one, in making development serve the needs of the forgotten majority.

Financial Policy and the Role of the State

Does financial liberalization mean that LDC governments have no role to play in the financial sector? In an effort to identify how these governments can work effectively within the context of liberalized financial markets, Joseph Stiglitz has recently isolated seven major market failures that imply a potential role for state intervention.[14] His basic argument is "that [LDC] financial markets are markedly different from other markets; that market failures are likely to be more pervasive in these markets"; and that "much of the rationale for liberalizing financial markets is based neither on a sound economic understanding of how these markets work nor on the potential scope for government intervention."[15] The seven market failures Stiglitz identified are the following:

1. *The "public-good" nature of monitoring financial institutions.* Investors need information about the solvency and management of financial institutions. Like other forms of information, monitoring is a public good—everyone who places savings in a particular financial institution would benefit from knowing that the institution was prospering or close to insolvency. But like other public goods in free-market economies, there is an undersupply of monitoring information, and, consequently, risk-averse savers withhold their funds. The net result is fewer resources allocated through these institutions.

2. *Externalities of monitoring, selection, and lending.* Benefits are often incurred by lenders who learn about the viability of potential projects from the monitoring, selection, and lending decisions of other lenders. Investors can also benefit from information generated by other investors on the quality of different financial institutions. Like other positive (or negative) externalities, the market provides too little information and resources are underallocated (overallocated).

3. *Externalities of financial disruption.* In the absence of government insurance (whether or not an explicit policy has been issued), the failure of one major financial institution can cause a run on the entire banking system and lead to long-term disruptions of the overall financial system.

4. *Missing and incomplete markets.* In most developing countries, markets for insurance against a variety of financial (bank failure) or physical (e.g., crop failure) risks are missing. The basic problem is that information is imperfect and costly to obtain, so an LDC government has an important role in reducing these risks. It can, for example, force membership in insurance programs or require financial institutions as well as borrowers to disclose information about their assets, liabilities, and creditworthiness.

5. *Imperfect competition.* Competition in the banking sector of most Third World countries is extremely limited, meaning that potential borrowers usually face only a small number of suppliers of loanable funds, many of which are unwilling or unable to accommodate new and unknown customers. This is particularly true of small borrowers in the informal urban and rural sectors.

6. *Inefficiency of competitive markets in the financial sector.* Theoretically, for perfectly competitive markets to function efficiently, financial markets must be complete (no uninsured risks) and information must be exogenous (freely available

to all and not influenced by any one participant's action in the market). Clearly, there are special advantages to individuals or entities with privileged information in LDC financial markets, and risk insurance is difficult, if not impossible, to obtain. As a result, unfettered financial markets may not allocate capital to its most profitable uses, and there can be substantial deviations between social and private returns to alternative investment projects. In such cases, direct government intervention—for example, by restricting certain kinds of loans and encouraging others—may partly or completely offset these imbalances.

7. *Uninformed investors.* Contrary to the doctrine of consumer sovereignty, with its assumption of perfect knowledge, many investors in LDCs lack both the information and the appropriate means to acquire it in order to make rational investment decisions. Here again, governments can impose financial disclosure requirements on firms listed on local stock exchanges or require banks, for example, to inform customers of the differences between simple and compound interest rates or of the nature of penalties for early withdrawals of savings.

In each of these seven instances, Stiglitz argues, LDC governments have a proper role to play in regulating financial institutions, creating new institutions to fill gaps in the kinds of credit provided by private institutions (e.g., micro loans to small farmers and tradespeople), providing consumer protection, ensuring bank solvency, encouraging fair competition, and ultimately improving the allocation of financial resources and promoting macroeconomic stability.

Like other areas of economic development, the critical issue for financial policy is not about free markets versus government intervention. Rather it is about how both can work together to meet the urgent needs of Third World people.

Fiscal Policy for Development

Whereas financial policy deals with money, interest, and credit allocation, fiscal policy focuses on government taxation and expenditure. Together they represent the bulk of public-sector activities. Most stabilization attempts have concentrated on cutting government expenditures to achieve budgetary balance. But the burden of resource mobilization to finance essential public developmental efforts must come from the revenue side. Public domestic and foreign borrowing can fill some savings gaps. In the long run, it is the efficient and equitable collection of taxes on which governments must base their development aspirations.[16] In the absence of well-organized and locally controlled money markets, most developing countries have had to rely primarily on fiscal measures to stabilize the economy and to mobilize domestic resources.

Taxation: Direct and Indirect

Typically, **direct taxes**—those levied on private individuals, corporations, and property—make up 20% to 30% of total tax revenue for most LDCs and range from 12% to 20% of their GNP. **Indirect taxes**, such as import and export duties and excise taxes (purchase, sales, and turnover taxes), comprise the major source of fiscal revenue. Table 17.2 shows the tax structure and revenue sources of 22 selected LDCs, and Table 17.3 provides a more detailed structural breakdown by LDC income groupings. Table 17.4 shows how the tax burden is distributed among different groups in a sample of 12 LDCs. Note that the tax systems (both direct and indirect taxes combined) of many Third World countries are far from strongly progressive. In some, such as Mexico, they can be highly regressive (meaning that lower income groups pay a higher proportion of their income in taxes than higher income groups).

Taxation in developing countries has traditionally had two purposes. First, tax concessions and similar fiscal incentives have been thought of as a means of stimulating private enterprise. Such concessions and incentives have typically been

TABLE 17.2   Tax Structure and Revenue Sources of Selected Developing Nations (percentage of total taxes)

Country	Direct Taxes			Indirect Taxes			
	Personal and Corporate	Property	Total Direct	Foreign (Import and Export Duties)	Domestic (Excise Taxes)	Total Indirect	Other[a]
Ethiopia	24.9	2.1	27.0	42.0	28.5	70.0	3.0
India	15.3	1.3	16.6	17.7	62.9	80.4	3.0
Somalia	8.6	2.1	10.7	45.4	26.9	72.3	17.0
Indonesia	81.2	1.5	82.7	6.0	10.7	16.7	0.6
Congo	63.8	0.1	63.9	17.0	10.0	27.0	9.1
Kenya	32.7	2.2	34.9	22.7	41.0	63.7	1.4
Pakistan	18.6	0.3	18.9	40.5	40.6	81.1	0
South Korea	26.6	1.1	27.7	16.4	51.5	67.9	4.4
Sri Lanka	13.9	0.5	14.4	52.9	29.6	82.5	3.1
Thailand	20.7	1.3	22.0	23.0	49.0	72.0	6.0
Egypt	27.9	1.9	29.4	27.6	17.6	45.2	35.4
Philippines	22.7	4.2	26.9	24.8	46.4	71.2	1.9
Morocco	21.3	2.5	23.8	24.7	39.1	63.8	2.4
Tunisia	19.3	2.8	22.1	32.4	29.5	59.9	18.0
Paraguay	14.9	6.6	21.5	27.7	20.0	47.7	30.8
Ecuador	29.2	3.5	32.7	33.7	18.2	51.9	5.4
Brazil	13.1	1.8	14.9	29.6	48.3	77.9	7.8
Honduras	28.1	0.9	29.0	43.1	26.8	69.0	1.1
Ghana	26.8	n.a.	26.8	37.1	36.0	73.1	0.1
Guatemala	12.6	1.0	13.6	23.4	32.2	55.6	29.8
Costa Rica	15.5	2.4	17.9	20.4	32.1	52.5	29.6
Chile	20.5	2.3	22.8	3.3	53.0	56.3	10.1

SOURCE: Vito Tanzi, "Quantitative characteristics of the tax systems of developing countries." Excerpted from *The Theory of Taxation for Developing Countries*, edited by David Newbery and Nicholas Stern. Copyright © 1987 by the World Bank. Reprinted by permission of Oxford University Press, Inc.

[a]Other taxes can include poll (head) taxes, stamp taxes, social security taxes (see Table 17.3), and income taxes that cannot be clearly allocated to individuals or corporations.

TABLE 17.3 Tax Revenue, by Type of Tax and by Country Group (percentage of total taxes)

Per Capita Income (dollars)		Income Taxes				Domestic Taxes on Goods and Services			
Range	Average	Total	Individual	Corporate	Other	Total	General Sales, Turnover, VAT[a]	Excises	Other
0–349	241	19.68	8.71	10.73	0.97	32.28	14.98	12.86	4.44
350–849	548	29.55	12.25	15.47	1.22	26.19	8.63	15.73	3.46
850–1,699	1,195	30.29	11.05	17.50	3.77	25.76	10.11	10.54	5.14
1,700 or more	3,392	35.63	9.09	23.09	3.89	27.40	12.57	9.95	6.43
All countries	1,330	28.70	10.25	16.53	2.43	27.93	11.66	12.23	4.88

SOURCE: Vito Tanzi, "Quantitative characteristics of the tax systems of developing countries." Excerpted from *The Theory of Taxation for Developing Countries*, edited by David Newbery and Nicholas Stern. Copyright © 1987 by the World Bank. Reprinted by permission of Oxford University Press, Inc.

[a]VAT is value-added tax, which taxes items at each stage of production—whenever there is value added.

offered to foreign private investors to induce them to locate their enterprises in the less developed country. Such tax incentives may indeed increase the inflow of private foreign resources, but as we discovered in Chapter 15, the overall benefits of such special treatment of foreign firms is by no means self-evident.

The second purpose of taxation, the mobilization of resources to finance public expenditures, is by far the more important. Whatever the prevailing political or economic ideology of the less developed country, its economic and social progress depends largely on its government's ability to generate sufficient revenues to finance an expanding program of essential, non-revenue-yielding public services—health, education, transport, communications, and other components of the economic and social infrastructure. In addition, most Third World governments are directly involved in the economic activities of their nations through their ownership and control of public corporations and state trading agencies. Direct and indirect tax levies enable the government to finance the capital and recurrent expenditures of these public enterprises, many of which often operate at a loss.

In recent years, many LDCs faced problems of rising fiscal deficits—public expenditures greatly in excess of public revenues—resulting from a combination of ambitious development programs and unexpected negative external shocks. With rising debt burdens, falling commodity prices, growing trade imbalances, and declining foreign private and public investment inflows, Third World governments had little choice (given mounting IMF pressures) but to undergo severe fiscal retrenchment. This meant cutting government expenditures (mostly on social services) and raising revenues through increased or more efficient tax collections. In general, the taxation potential of a country depends on five factors:

1. The level of per capita real income
2. The degree of inequality in the distribution of that income

TABLE 17.3 (*continued*)

Foreign Trade

Total	Import Duties	Export Duties	Other	Social Security	Wealth and Property	Other
39.25	30.14	8.37	0.73	3.23	2.05	3.51
38.06	32.87	4.19	0.99	2.02	1.76	2.49
29.47	23.72	4.85	0.89	6.74	3.04	4.66
15.40	13.01	2.08	0.31	15.64	3.05	2.88
30.63	24.98	4.91	0.73	6.86	2.48	3.40

3. The industrial structure of the economy and the importance of different types of economic activity (e.g., the importance of foreign trade, the significance of the modern sector, the extent of foreign participation in private enterprises, the degree to which the agricultural sector is commercialized as opposed to subsistence-oriented)

4. The social, political, and institutional setting and the relative power of different groups (e.g., landlords as opposed to manufacturers, trade unions, village or district community organizations)

5. The administrative competence, honesty, and integrity of the tax-gathering branches of government

TABLE 17.4 Incidence of Taxation by Income Group in Selected Countries (direct and indirect taxes)

Country	Percentage of Income Paid in Taxes		
	Lowest Income	Middle Income	Highest Income
Argentina	17.2	19.8	21.4
Brazil	5.2	14.3	14.8
Chile	18.5	16.2	26.7
Colombia	17.1	13.1	29.9
Kenya	11.5	8.8	12.7
Lebanon	8.4	20.2	20.3
Malaysia	17.7	16.5	42.1
Mexico	40.2	22.7	14.9
Pakistan	15.0	9.6	25.3
Peru	4.8	17.4	26.6
Philippines	23.0	16.9	33.5
South Korea	16.4	15.7	21.6

SOURCE: Emmanuel Jiminez, "The public subsidization of education and health in developing countries," *World Bank Research Observer* 1 (January 1986), tab. 5.

We now examine the principal sources of direct and indirect public tax revenues. We can then consider how the tax system might be used to promote a more equitable and sustainable pattern of economic growth.

Personal Income and Property Taxes

Personal income taxes yield much less revenue as a proportion of GNP in the less developed countries than in the more developed nations. In the latter, the income tax structure is said to be progressive: People with higher incomes theoretically pay a larger percentage of that income in taxes. In practice, however, the average level of taxation in countries like the United States does not vary much between middle- and upper-income groups. Table 17.4 shows that a similar situation prevails in many developing countries. This is because of the many tax loopholes available to wealthy individuals. In developing countries, a combination of more exemptions, lower rates on smaller incomes, and a general administrative weakness in collecting income taxes means that less than 3% of Third World populations actually pay income tax. This figure compares with 60% to 80% of the populations of developed nations.

It would be administratively too costly and economically regressive to attempt to collect substantial income taxes from the poor. But the fact remains that most LDC governments have not been persistent enough in collecting taxes owed by the very wealthy. Because the highest-income groups offer the greatest potential yield to the tax collector, the large income inequalities prevailing in most Third World countries mean that there is great scope for expanding income tax revenues. Moreover, in countries where the ownership of property is heavily concentrated and therefore represents the major determinant of unequal incomes (e.g., most of Asia and Latin America), property taxes can be an efficient and administratively simple mechanism both for generating public revenues and for correcting gross inequalities in income distribution. But as can be seen from Table 17.2, in only one of the 22 countries listed does the property tax constitute more than 4.2% of total public revenues. Moreover, in spite of much public rhetoric about reducing income inequalities, the share of property taxes as well as overall direct taxation has remained roughly the same for the majority of developing countries over the past two decades. Clearly, this phenomenon cannot be attributed to government tax-collecting inefficiencies as much as to the political and economic power and influence of the large landowning and other dominant classes in many Asian and Latin American countries. The political will to carry out development plans must therefore include the will to extract public revenue from the most accessible sources to finance development projects. Where the former is absent, so too will be the latter.

Corporate Income Taxes

Taxes on corporate profits, of both domestically and foreign-owned companies, amount to less than 3% of GDP in most developing countries, compared with more than 6% in developed nations. The main reasons that these taxes generate such limited revenue in Third World countries is that there is relatively less corporate activity in the overall economy. Perhaps more important, LDC governments tend to offer all sorts of tax incentives and concessions to manufacturing and commercial enterprises. Typically, new enterprises are offered long periods (sometimes up to 15 years) of tax exemption and thereafter take advantage of generous investment depreciation allowances, special tax write-offs, and other measures to lessen their tax burden.

In the case of multinational foreign enterprises, the ability of LDC governments to collect substantial taxes is often frustrated. These locally run enterprises are able to shift profits to partner companies in countries offering the lowest levels of taxation through transfer pricing (discussed in Chapter 15). When local subsidiaries of multinational corporations buy from or sell to partner companies in other countries, the prices in such transactions are merely internal accounting prices of the overall corporation; it makes no difference to the calculation of total corporate profits what price one subsidiary charges another because the cost of one will be offset by the income of the other. For example, in high-tax countries, MNC exports to branches in low-tax countries can be invoiced at artificially low prices. This practice reduces corporate profits in the high-tax country and raises them in the low-tax one. The latter is often referred to as a *tax haven*. Thus by means of transfer pricing, multinational corporations are able to shift their profits from one place to another in order to lower their overall tax assessment while leaving their total profits unchanged. As long as such tax havens exist, this profit-sharing practice greatly limits the ability of individual LDCs to increase public revenues by raising taxes on foreign corporations.

Indirect Taxes on Commodities

The largest single source of public revenue in developing countries is the taxation of commodities in the form of import, export, and excise duties (see Tables 17.2 and 17.3). These taxes, which individuals and corporations pay indirectly through their purchase of commodities, are relatively easy to assess and collect. This is especially true in the case of foreign-traded commodities, which must pass through a limited number of frontier ports and are usually handled by a few wholesalers. The ease of collecting such taxes is one reason why countries with extensive foreign trade typically collect a greater proportion of public revenues in the form of import and export duties than countries with limited external trade. For example, in open economies with up to 40% of GNP derived from foreign trade, an average import duty of 25% will yield a tax revenue equivalent of 10% of GNP. By contrast, in countries like India and Brazil with only about 7% of GNP derived from exports, the same tariff rate would yield only 2% of GNP in equivalent tax revenues.

Although we discussed import and export duties in the context of LDC trade policies in Chapter 13, one further point about these taxes, often overlooked, must be mentioned. Import and export duties, in addition to representing the major sources of public revenue in many LDCs, can also be an efficient substitute for the corporate income tax. To the extent that importers are unable to pass on to local consumers the full costs of the tax, an import duty can serve as a proxy tax on the profits of the importer (often a foreign company) and only partly a tax on the local consumer. Similarly, an export duty can be an effective way of taxing the profits of producing companies, including locally based multinational firms that practice transfer pricing. But export duties designed to generate revenue should not be raised to the point of discouraging local producers from expanding their export production.

In selecting commodities to be taxed, whether in the form of duties on imports and exports or excise taxes on local commodities, certain general economic and administrative principles must be followed to minimize the cost of securing maximum revenue. First, the commodity should be imported or produced by a relatively small number of licensed firms so that evasion can be controlled. Second, the price elasticity of demand for the commodity should be low so that total demand is not choked by the rise in consumer prices that results from the tax. Third, the commodity should have a high income elasticity of demand so that as incomes rise, more tax revenue will be collected. Fourth, for equity purposes, it is best to tax commodities like cars, refrigerators, imported fancy foods, and household appliances, which are consumed largely by the upper income groups, while forgoing taxation on items of mass consumption like basic foods, simple clothing, and household utensils even though these may satisfy the first three criteria.

Problems of Tax Administration

In the final analysis, a developing nation's ability to collect taxes for public expenditure programs and to use the tax system as a basis for modifying the distribution of personal incomes will depend not only on the enactment of appropriate tax legislation but, more important, on the efficiency and integrity of the tax authorities who must implement these laws. As Nicholas Kaldor noted more than three decades ago:

> In many underdeveloped countries the low revenue yield of taxation can only be attributed to the fact that the tax provisions are not properly enforced, either on account of the inability of the administration to cope with them, or on account of straightforward corruption. No system of tax laws, however carefully conceived, is proof against collusion between the tax administrators and the taxpayers: an efficient administration consisting of persons of high integrity is usually the most important requirement for obtaining maximum revenue, and exploiting fully the taxation potential of a country.[17]

Thus the ability of Third World governments to expand their tax nets to cover the higher income groups and minimize tax evasion by local and foreign individuals and corporations will largely determine the efficiency of the tax system in achieving its dual function of generating sufficient public revenues to finance expanding development programs and transferring income from upper to lower income groups in order to reduce poverty and income inequality. Much will depend, once again, on the political will to enact and enforce such progressive tax programs.

Public Administration: The Scarcest Resource

In all our policy discussions, we have tended to gloss over one of the most critical shortages in the development process: the often binding constraint on economic progress caused by the shortage of public (and private) administrative capability.

Many observers would argue that the lack of such managerial and administrative capability is the single scarcest public resource in the developing world. The problem is not only a lack of training or experience. It also arises out of the political instability of numerous Third World nations. When power is constantly changing hands, considerations of efficiency and public welfare are likely to be subordinated to political loyalty. Moreover, the larger the group of officials affected by a change of power, the more difficult it will be to maintain continuity in the formulation and execution of policy.

Public administration is unlikely to function efficiently when the rule of law is in question, when there is public disorder, or when there is little consensus on fundamental issues. Acute conditions of class, tribal, or religious conflict within a society will usually be reflected in the management and operation of government departments and public agencies. In a highly traditional society, where kinship ties are strong and such concepts as statehood and public service have not yet taken firm root, there is little place for a merit system. Similarly, where the dominant values are religious or transcendental, traditional incentives to perform in the wider public interest may not have much appeal.

Many LDC governments may also have civil service goals other than performance: to break up traditional elites, to nationalize the civil service, to conform to ideological correctness, to reflect or favor an ethnic ratio, to include or exclude minorities. Most governments also are organized in the traditional hierarchical form. But some have experimented with negative hierarchy (from bottom to top), ad hocracy (temporary arrangements), and polyarchy (cooperation with outside organizations), this last being attempted particularly when some special form of expertise is involved.

Many LDC bureaucracies are hopelessly overstaffed at the bottom and hopelessly understaffed at the top. There is a chronic and desperate shortage of skilled competent managers capable of independent decision making. The greater the number of parastatal organizations set up—the more state-owned enterprises and nationalized industries, quasi-governmental bodies, development corporations, and training institutions—the thinner this layer of managers is spread.

In the case of nationalized industries, most experiments have been economically disastrous and have resulted in all kinds of strains within the central civil service. Personnel systems within the public service are usually not adequate for the increased management complexities of an industrial enterprise. So parallel personnel systems have been set up, multiplying the public service systems, draining skills, leading to disparities in terms and conditions of service, and resulting in manpower shortages and morale problems. Political considerations often affect the ability to recruit competent managers with special technical skills. In short, nationalization in many instances has often added to the financial burden of the government budget.

But whatever the organizational and political problems of public administration, the sheer difficulty of efficiently managing complex modern economic systems is often cited when referring to critical public policy issues in the Third World. A striking example of the administration problem is provided by the case of the Tazara railroad through Tanzania and Zambia.

The Tazara railway, giving Zambia access to the sea at Dar es Salaam, the capital of Tanzania, was built in less than five years by the Chinese and was formally opened in July 1976. In October 1978, President Kaunda of Zambia announced that effective immediately and despite U.N. sanctions, OAU pressures, and the civil war in Zimbabwe, he was reopening Zambia's border with Zimbabwe and resuming the interrupted rail link with the south. The reason was that massive administrative breakdowns had so impaired the functioning of the railway that it was threatening to strangle the entire Zambian economy.

In early 1978, the European Community had granted Zambia $8 million for fertilizer desperately needed by its ailing agricultural sector. The first consignments from the United States were unloaded at Dar es Salaam, where the railway was unable to handle them, and they were left in the open to rot. As the pileup increased, Tanzania was reported to have increased storage and demurrage charges by 1,000%. Zambia then ordered the fertilizer rerouted through Beira, Mozambique, whence it went by rail to the town of Moatize and then by road through Malawi and Zambia. After 60,000 tons had been transported, it became clear that Mozambique's railways and Zambia's transporters, already short of fuel and spare parts, could not cope. Shippers refused to take the remaining 90,000 tons to Dar es Salaam because of the congestion there. Zambia then suggested it go to Maputo, Mozambique, from which it could be carried by South African Railways through South Africa via Pretoria and Mafeking to Francistown, where an armada of small Zambian truckers would carry it across the Kazungulu ferry. By the end of September, Zambia had spent an extra $25,000 in transport costs, Maputo and Francistown were drowning in fertilizer, only 2,000 tons had arrived in Zambia, and the plowing season had begun. In addition, some 100,000 tons of Zambian copper was either awaiting transportation or trapped somewhere on the line. Further stockpiles at the mines reached 70,000 tons by early October, causing cash shortages to the copper companies, which do not get paid until the copper is on the high seas. Production was hampered by shortages of spare parts and lubricating oil, which were held up elsewhere.

In four years' time, Tanzania and Zambia would have to start repaying their $400 million debt to China. About 100 Chinese specialists were brought back to try to restore the line to working order; they saw little chance of its paying its way unless its administration was completely overhauled. More than half the locomotives were under repair. A quarter of the 2,100 freight cars were off the line at any one time. The accounting department wasn't getting the bills out, and the railway was owed millions of dollars. Without huge spending on new equipment and training programs, there was little possibility of Tazara handling a fraction of its capacity; even massive spending would not necessarily guarantee results.

This is a dramatic example of an administrative shortfall in one sector, unanticipated in any feasibility study or economic blueprint, the effects of which were felt not only in other sectors of the Zambian economy but also in neighboring states. It serves to illustrate the crucial importance of the administrative component in economic development planning—not only in relation to the particular project under consideration but also in relation to the functioning of the entire public and private economic system.

State–owned Enterprises: Improving Some, Privatizing Others

Associated with the problems of public administration in developing countries have been the widespread activities of **state-owned enterprises (SOEs)**, public corporations owned and operated by the government. During the past three or four decades, there has been a rapid growth in the number and size of these enterprises in developing countries. In addition to their traditionally dominant presence in utilities (gas, water, and electricity), transportation (railroads, airlines, and buses), and communications (telephone, telegraph, and postal services), SOEs have become active in such key sectors as large-scale manufacturing, construction, finance, services, natural resources, and agriculture. Sometimes they may dominate these sectors, particularly in the areas of natural resources and manufacturing. For example, in Senegal, Tanzania, Bangladesh, Myanmar, India, Mexico, and Nicaragua, SOEs produced more than 75% of the annual output in natural resources. In Syria, Tunisia, Egypt, and Ethiopia, SOEs accounted for 60% of the value added in manufacturing.[18]

Overall, it is clear that SOEs have played a major role in the economies of developing nations, contributing an average 7% to 15% of their GDP. In some cases, their contribution is considerably higher; for example, they produce 20% to 30% of the domestic output in Senegal, Guinea, Tunisia, and Venezuela and almost 40% of the output in Ghana and Zambia. In addition, SOEs account for a substantial amount of investment in developing countries, yielding at least a quarter of the total capital formation and in a few cases considerably more.

While contributing to domestic output and capital formation, SOEs are also absorbing substantial amounts of resources and, in many cases, are imposing a heavy fiscal burden on governments. For example, a study of 27 developing countries revealed that the net budgetary payments to nonfinancial SOEs averaged more than 3% of GDP. Current spending alone represented 1.4% of GDP. And SOEs were found to be major borrowers of foreign exchange, accounting for 28% of all Third World eurocurrency borrowing in 1980. They also absorb a large part of domestic credit, particularly in small countries; in Benin, Guinea, Mali, and Senegal, for example, over 40% of domestic credit was absorbed by SOEs.

Given the strategic importance of state-owned enterprises in the economies of developing countries and their increasing demands on scarce resources, it is important to understand the reasons for their creation, the causes underlying their increasing demands on resources, and the measures that might be undertaken to improve their efficiency and to help them meet their economic and social objectives.

Some of the reasons for the creation of SOEs were suggested in Chapter 16. One is the persistence of monopoly power in many Third World countries. Direct government control may be required to ensure that prices are not set above the marginal costs of producing the output. Moreover, as was also mentioned, certain goods that have a high social benefit are usually provided at a price below their costs or even free; hence the private sector has no incentive to produce such goods, and the government must be responsible for their provision.

The second rationale for the creation of SOEs is capital formation, which, as already suggested, is particularly strong at the early stages of development, when private savings are very low. Investment in infrastructure at this point is crucial to lay the groundwork for further investment. And SOEs remain important at later stages in industries that require massive funds.

The lack of private incentive to engage in promising economic activities because of factors such as uncertainty about the size of local markets, unreliable sources of supply, and the absence of technology and skilled labor is a third major motivation for creating public enterprises. Third World governments may also seek to expand employment and facilitate training of their labor force by engaging in public production. They may desire to increase export earnings by creating export industries, particularly those that might otherwise be unable to compete. For reasons of income distribution, the government may seek to locate enterprises in certain sectors, particularly in backward economic areas where there is no private incentive for creating such economic activity.

Other reasons for the creation of SOEs include the desire of some Third World governments to gain national control over strategic sectors of the economy such as defense, over foreign-owned enterprises (MNCs) whose interests may not coincide with those of the country, or over key sectors for planning purposes. Government involvement may also come about as a result of recent independence or of bankruptcy in a major private industry. Finally, ideological motivations may be a factor in the creation of state-owned enterprises.

Despite these many valid reasons for their existence, SOEs have come under increasing attack for wasting resources. As already mentioned, SOEs make significant demands on government finance, as well as on domestic and foreign credit. In many cases, the level of these demands is related to low profitability and inefficiency. Although it is difficult to generalize across countries, data from the World Bank for state-owned enterprises in 24 developing countries revealed only a small operating surplus.[19] And once factors such as interest payments, subsidized input prices, and taxes and accumulated arrears were taken into account, SOEs in many of these countries showed a large deficit. Turkish enterprises averaged net losses equivalent to 3% of GDP. Mexican SOEs showed a net loss of 1.2% of GDP. A study of SOEs in four African countries (Ghana, Senegal, Tanzania, and Zambia) also revealed generally poor performance. Most SOEs in these countries failed to show a profit. Operating at a deficit, they proved to be a massive drain on government resources. There was also evidence that labor and capital productivity were generally lower than in the private sector. These African SOEs were also found to be less successful in generating employment as a result of their bias toward capital intensiveness.[20]

Several factors contribute to the overall poor performance of SOEs in terms of profitability and efficiency. Perhaps the most important is that SOEs differ from private firms in that they are expected to pursue both commercial and social goals. Providing goods at prices below costs in an effort to subsidize the public or hiring extra workers to meet national employment objectives inevitably reduces profitability. Another factor adversely affecting the profitability and efficiency of SOEs is the overcentralization of their decision making, which allows little flexibility for managers in the everyday operation of the firm. An additional problem is the bureaucratization of management; many decision makers are not accountable for their performance, and little incentive is provided for improved decision making. Finally, despite the abundant labor supply and the employment mandate, access to capital at subsidized interest rates has often encouraged unnecessary capital intensiveness, as in the cases of the four African nations cited.

For the most part, however, the problems that have plagued many Third World public corporations are not beyond solution. Two alternative options typically mentioned are reorganization with a greater bottom-line focus for the SOE and the transfer of ownership and control from the public to the private sector, a process known as **privatization**. In the former option, decentralizing decision making to allow for more flexibility and providing better incentives for managers could increase production efficiency. Providing capital at its market rate may eliminate the bias toward capital intensiveness. The Chinese government took important steps in this direction in the 1980s when it gave greater autonomy to and increased competition among its numerous urban SOEs. In short, public corporations can still play an important role in economic development as long as the political will is there to minimize abuse of power and the economic will is there to correct socially unnecessary price and market distortions.

Privatization: Theory and Experience

The second option, the privatization of state-owned enterprises in the production and financial sectors, hinges on the neoclassical hypothesis that private ownership brings greater efficiency and more rapid growth. During the 1980s, privatization was actively promoted by major international bilateral (USAID) and multilateral agencies (World Bank, IMF). Many LDCs followed this advice, although the extent of their philosophical agreement, as opposed to the financial pressures exerted by these funding agencies, remains unclear. In addition to the belief that privatization improves efficiency, increases output, and lowers costs, proponents argue that it curbs the growth of government expenditure, raises cash to reduce public internal and external debt, and promotes individual initiative while rewarding entrepreneurship. Finally, supporters of privatization see it as a way to broaden the base of ownership and participation in the economy, thereby encouraging individuals to feel that they have a direct stake in the system.[21] Between 1980 and 1992, more than 15,000 enterprises were privatized throughout the world, more than 11,000 of them in the former East Germany. In the developing nations, the number of privatized companies amounted to 450 in Africa, 900 in Latin America, and approximately 180 in Asia. Mexico, Chile, and Argentina have led the movement in Latin America. Among low-income countries, the speed of privatization has been much more cautious, with the majority of transfers coming in small, low-value firms. Table 17.5 provides a list of the most significant high-value (more than $100 million) privatizations between 1988 and 1992. As can be seen, almost all of these transactions occurred in Latin America, particularly Mexico.

Most studies to date indicate that privatization appears to be successful in promoting greater efficiency and higher output, especially in high- and middle-income countries.[22] In poorer LDCs, the results are less clear-cut, though some positive results have been obtained. However, even though detailed data are yet to be compiled, the effects of privatization on income distribution are likely to be to increase

632 POSSIBILITIES AND PROSPECTS

	TABLE 17.5 Privatization Transactions Valued at $100 Million or More, 1988–1992			

Economy	Enterprise	Date of Sale	Gross Transaction Value (millions of U.S. dollars)	Sector
Mexico	Bancomer	10/91	2,550	Banking
Mexico	Bancamex	9/91	2,300	Banking
South Korea	Korea Electric Power	6/89	2,100	Power
Venezuela	CANTV	11/90	1,885	Telecommunications
Mexico	TELMEX	12/90	1,760	Telecommunications
Brazil	Usiminas	12/91	1,430	Steel
Mexico	Mexicana de Cobre	10/88	1,360	Mining
Argentina	ENTEL	11/90	1,244	Telecommunications
Mexico	Banca Serfin	1/92	909	Banking
Mexico	Multibanco Comermex	2/92	872	Banking
Malaysia	Telekom Malaysia	10/90	861	Telecommunications
Brazil	Copesul	5/92	839	Petrochemical
Mexico	Cananea	9/90	475	Mining
Argentina	Somisa	10/92	404	Steel
Philippines	Philippines Airlines	1/92	368	Airline
Mexico	Aerovias de México	11/88	339	Airline
Philippines	Nonoc	10/90	325	Mining
Taiwan	China Steel	4/89	285	Steel
Argentina	Aerolinas Argentinas	4/90	285	Airline
Mexico	Banca Cremi	6/91	248	Banking
Mexico	Multibanco de Mercantil	6/91	204	Banking
Mexico	Banpais	6/91	182	Banking
Mexico	Sicartsa 1	11/91	170	Steel
Chile	Compañía de Teléfonos	1/88	170	Telecommunications
Mexico	Sidermex North	11/91	145	Steel
Venezuela	VIASA	9/91	145	Airline
Mexico	Mexicana de Aviacíon	6/89	140	Airline
Brazil	Aracruz	5/88	130	Pulp and paper
Turkey	Petkim	6/90	125	Petrochemical
Peru	Hierro Peru	12/92	120	Mining
Poland	Kwidzyn	8/92	120	Pulp and paper
Hungary	Tungsram	5/89	110	Electric equipment
Mexico	Nikko Hotel	10/88	110	Hotel
Mexico	Terefaltos Mexicanos	1/88	106	Chemical
Colombia	Papelcol	8/90	100	Pulp and paper

SOURCE: Sunita Kikeri, John Nellis, and Mary Shirley, "Privatization: Lessons from market economies," *World Bank Research Observer* 9 (July 1994), tab. 1.

the gap between rich and poor. This is due to the simple fact that privatized assets are being concentrated in the hands of small groups of local and international elites. For example, many sales of former state-owned enterprises in Latin America were conducted without competitive bidding, often at predetermined concessionary ("fire sale") prices. Small groups of well-connected investors, both domestic and foreign, were enriched by the process. And some privatization merely replaced public monopolies with private monopolies, thereby allowing a few individuals to reap the monopoly profits that formerly accrued to the state.

Privatization therefore raises many complex issues. There are questions of feasibility, appropriate financing, the structure of legal and property rights, the role of competing elites and interest groups (e.g., public officials and bureaucrats versus domestic and foreign private business interests), and whether or not widespread privatization promotes or ultimately weakens existing dualistic economic, social, and political structures. It is not sufficient to claim, as many neoclassical counter-revolutionaries do, that privatization can lead to higher profits, greater output, or even lower costs. The key issue is whether such privatization better serves the long-run development interests of a nation by promoting a more sustainable and equitable pattern of economic and social progress. Despite all of the ideological trumpeting by free marketers on this issue, the evidence so far is less than compelling.[23] Nevertheless, there is great momentum toward privatization throughout the contemporary developing world. (For a detailed analysis of the experiences of privatization in Poland and Chile, see the Comparative Case Study that follows Chapter 18.)

Military Expenditures and Economic Development

Significance and Economic Impact

One important area of fiscal expenditures not often discussed in the development literature is that of mounting military outlays. Since the early 1970s, military expenditures by developing countries have been rising very rapidly despite a world recession, declining growth in export earnings, and skyrocketing foreign debts. Military spending in the Third World tripled during the 1970s, with countries in the Middle East and North Africa averaging annual increases of 22%. In 1994, total military expenditures by developing countries amounted to $118 billion, accounting for 15.4% of world military expenditures. Although this represented a decline from peak military outlays of $155 billion in 1984 (see Table 17.6), the decline had more to do with LDC budgetary constraints than progress toward a more peaceful world. Table 17.7 compares military expenditures between less developed and industrialized nations in relation to GDP and health and education outlays. Table 17.8 shows the ten highest and lowest ratios between military and social spending among Third World countries. It is clear from these tables that although developing countries spend approximately the same proportion of GDP on the military, the ratio of their military to their health and education outlays is six times higher than in developed countries. And within the Third World, this ratio can vary enormously, from 5.11 to 1 in Iraq to 1 to 25 in Costa Rica (Table 17.8).

Not only has military spending risen, but there has also been a shift in its composition, away from paying armies and toward the procurement of sophisticated weaponry. Imports of weapons by developing countries rose dramatically during the 1970s, increasing from $5.6 billion in 1970 to $16.1 billion in 1979, and the rate

TABLE 17.6 Trends in Global Military Spending, 1960–1994 (billions of dollars)

Year	Developing Countries	Industrial Countries	World	Developing Countries' Percentage of World Expenditures
1960	35	385	420	8.3
1970	75	545	620	12.1
1980	137	618	755	18.1
1984	155	750	905	17.1
1987	132	838	970	13.6
1990	123	762	885	13.9
1994	118	649	767	15.4

SOURCES: United Nations Development Program, *Human Development Report, 1992* and *1994* (New York: Oxford University Press, 1992, 1994), p. 85 and p. 48.

of growth of arms imports accelerated further in the 1980s. Developing countries are now importing 75% of the world's arms, with countries in the Middle East and North Africa emerging as leading arms importers. A few developing countries have emerged as arms exporters, including Brazil (now the world's sixth largest arms exporter), India, China, Argentina, Pakistan, and South Korea, although 80% of all arms exports are still supplied by the industrialized world.

Apart from its political implications, the recent military expansion in the Third World has stirred debate over the economic impact of military expenditures on developing countries, where resources are scarce and the opportunity costs of military spending may therefore be high. Arguments and empirical evidence have been presented in support of a positive net effect on economic growth and development; most recent studies, however, indicate that military spending has had more of an adverse effect.

TABLE 17.7 Military and Social Expenditures in Developing and Industrial Countries

	Military Expenditures (% of GDP)	Military Expenditures as a Percentage of Combined Education and Health Expenditures
All developing countries	4.4	169
Least developed countries	4.1	146
Sub-Saharan Africa	3.2	108
Industrialized countries	4.9	28
World	4.8	42

SOURCE: United Nations Development Program, *Human Development Report, 1992* (New York: Oxford University Press, 1992), tab. 20.

TABLE 17.8 Military Spending as a Percentage of Social Spending in Developing Countries: Highest and Lowest Ratios

Highest		Lowest	
1. Iraq	511	1. Costa Rica	4
2. Somalia	500	2. Mauritius	5
3. Nicaragua	318	3. Mexico	8
4. Oman	268	4. Jamaica	9
5. Ethiopia	239	5. Fiji	9
6. Pakistan	239	6. Sierra Leone	11
7. Syria	204	7. Ghana	13
8. Saudi Arabia	177	8. Ivory Coast	14
9. United Arab Emirates	174	9. Botswana	16
10. Bolivia	144	10. Algeria	18

SOURCE: United Nations Development Program, *Human Development Report, 1992* (New York: Oxford University Press, 1992), tab. 5.3.

Supporters of military spending argue that such expenditures have a positive impact on economic growth as a result of the relatively large benefits of increased aggregate demand generated by military spending, the creation of employment and training opportunities, and the construction of basic infrastructure. It is argued that the opportunity costs of military spending are relatively smaller because the resources devoted to military consumption might otherwise go to private consumption or social investment, such as housing, medical care, or education, which contribute little to current economic growth. Furthermore, it is argued that military spending has a relatively smaller opportunity cost because the resources used for military purposes might not otherwise be available for public use, considering that such resources are often available only through foreign military aid and loans.

The major empirical work in support of this view was a study conducted by Emile Benoit, which found a positive correlation between military expenditure and economic growth for 44 developing countries over the period 1950–1965.[24] The study concluded that countries with a heavy defense burden had the most rapid rates of growth, whereas those with the lowest defense burdens tended to have the lowest growth rates.

Critics dispute the purported large benefits of military expenditures. First, it is unlikely that military spending will significantly increase domestic demand because of its high import content. Instead, much of the military demand, which takes the form of demand for military equipment, will be diverted to suppliers abroad. In some of the poorer nations, even military demand for civilian-type goods such as uniforms, boots, and simple construction materials must be met with imported supplies. The remaining demand generated by workers in the defense sector with relatively higher incomes may divert resources from industries producing wage goods to those producing imported luxury items. Second, the benefits of employment creation and training may be considerably smaller than was thought. With the trend toward procurement of weapons rather than paying armies, employment creation for a given military outlay is rapidly diminishing. Furthermore, if increased military spending is compensated for by a reduction in public or private investment, overall employment is likely to fall. In addition, it is debatable that the military sector provides training for the labor force. With its increasingly technical and sophisticated activities, it generates a demand for workers who are already skilled and may in fact divert scarce technicians, engineers, and other skilled workers from local industry. Furthermore, it is not clear that the training of military personnel makes valuable additions to the labor force because skills acquired in the military are not easily transferable to the civilian sector. As to the last supposed benefit, the creation of a basic infrastructure to meet the needs of the military is less justifiable, on the grounds of long-term economic growth and employment generation, than the creation of an infrastructure to meet public- and private-sector needs.

Critics are equally skeptical of the purported relatively lower opportunity costs of military spending. First, it is not convincing that the opportunity costs of diverting revenues that could otherwise be spent on health, education, or generally improving people's lives are low because such expenditures contribute little to future economic growth. The argument ignores the effects of investment in human capital, which provides a foundation for long-term economic growth. Furthermore, it implicitly assumes that investment in the military sector provides a basis for generating future growth through increasing productive capacity. This has not been substantiated empirically. Second, the argument that resources used in the military sector have a low opportunity cost because they would not otherwise be available is no longer valid, given the decline in foreign aid in recent years and its concentration in a few select countries. Most developing countries must now rely on indigenous resources to support the military. With output constrained by scarce resources, increases in military spending can occur only at the high opportunity cost of lower capital formation or reduced civilian consumption. Magnifying the costs of reduced investment and private consumption is the recent trend toward arms imports, which require substantial amounts of scarce foreign exchange. When such imports are financed by export earnings, they compete with investment that might be used to increase a country's capacity to earn foreign exchange in the future. With most countries facing deteriorating terms of trade, the use of foreign exchange for arms will have a high opportunity cost. When financed by external loans, arms imports also add to the rising burden of external debt, which may force countries eventually to pursue fiscal and monetary policies that reduce private consumption and investment and hence diminish economic growth.

In summary, the purported benefits of military spending seem considerably smaller and, in fact, may become very costly in cases where military demand is diverted to foreign supplies or results in a shift away from the production of wage goods; where an increase in military expenditure is compensated by a decrease in public spending, causing a reduction of employment; where military demand diverts scarce skilled workers from other industries; or where it fails to create appropriate infrastructure. The costs of military spending are likely to be high in terms of reduced levels of human capital formation and private investment and hence lower long-term economic growth.

Empirical work supports this view that military spending has had a negative effect on economic growth. For example, David Lim examined the relationship between defense spending and economic growth for 54 developing countries over a more recent period than the earlier Benoit study (1965–1973) and reached the opposite conclusion, namely, that there is a negative correlation between military spending and economic growth rates in developing countries.[25] Similar results were obtained by Riccardo Faine, Patricia Annez, and Lance Taylor in a study of 69 countries.[26] A more definitive empirical study of 83 developing countries by Alfred Maizels and Machiko Nissanke clearly demonstrated that the impact of military spending on economic growth in developing countries has been unambiguously negative.[27] It has been suggested that the earlier Benoit study's findings that military spending and economic growth have a positive correlation could be spurious because high military spending was correlated with high foreign aid during the period examined. With the decline in foreign aid since the 1970s, it is argued, the relationship between military expenditure and economic growth has been reversed. Whatever the reasons, it is now clear that high military expenditures are draining Third World economies of scarce resources needed to finance long-term development efforts.

The End of the Cold War: Disarmament, Conflict Resolution, and Human Development

It is as yet unclear what impact the end of the cold war will have on Third World military expenditures. Some tensions are likely to ease considerably between countries formerly aligned with the United States and the former USSR. Together the superpowers provided over 80% of LDC arms imports. However, if arms transfers continue to reflect the strategic interests of these two world powers, the relative prominence of developing countries in their shifting global strategies will largely determine future patterns of military expenditure. Though the collapse of the Soviet Union has essentially halted its intervention in the Third World, the current policies of the U.S. Pentagon are likely to lead to a significant increase in the military involvement of the United States in developing countries of key strategic and economic interest. Past intervention in El Salvador has for some U.S. policymakers become a model for cooperative effort in the resolution of Third World conflicts.[28] For example, a report outlining U.S. strategic policy in the post-cold-war world, titled *Defense Planning Guidance*, clearly indicated an increasing focus of the U.S. military on the Third World.[29] To remain on friendly terms, LDC governments that seek to maintain continued development assistance are likely to pursue military spending patterns consistent with U.S. strategic and economic interests. Such policies suggest severe limitations for Third World disarmament.

The actual pace of disarmament in developing countries will ultimately depend, however, on the commitment of all governments to pursue peaceful methods of conflict resolution. There is a growing belief that a portion of the so-called peace dividend should be spread throughout the developing world to encourage the conversion of wasteful military expenditures into productive social and economic outlays. Policies to promote progress in this direction include the imposition of defense conditionality on development assistance to ensure that economic aid is not diverted to military uses, stricter arms export policies in supplier countries, increased economic aid to the Third World to promote economic prosperity and thus internal political stability, and the reallocation of resources in developing countries away from the military and toward human investment.[30] The United Nations Development Program put a concise and appropriate perspective on the issue when it stated, "If a government chooses to spend more on its army than on its people, it cannot be regarded as committed to human development."[31]

CASE STUDY

The Economy of Taiwan

GEOGRAPHIC, SOCIAL, AND ECONOMIC INDICATORS

Capital Taipei

Area 35,981 km^2

Population 21.5 million (1995)

Population(average annual growth rate) 0.9% (1994)

GNP per capita U.S. $10,600 (1993)

GNP per capita (average annual growth rate) 6% (1990–1994)

Agriculture as share of GDP 4% (1990)

Exports as share of GDP 38% (1993)

Infant mortality rate (per 1,000 live births) 5.6 (1995)

Child malnutrition (underweight) (not available)

Females as share of labor force (not available)

Illiteracy rate (age 15+) 9.3% (1985)

Human Development Index (not available)

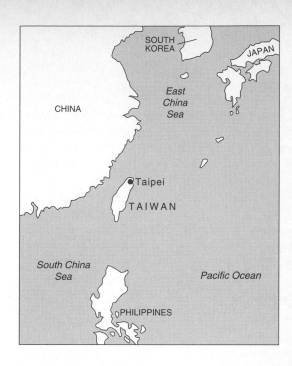

Taiwan—formally known as the Republic of China—is an island in the western Pacific Ocean between the East China Sea and the South China Sea. It is almost 36,000 square kilometers in size, with a population of 21.5 million. The island of Taiwan is separated by less than 100 miles of water from Mainland China. Taiwan has been seen as a prototype for other developing nations because of its great success in generating rapid economic growth with relatively low income inequalities. Along with other successful Pacific Rim nations (South Korea, Singapore, and Hong Kong), Taiwan is today viewed as a newly industrializing country (NIC).

Taiwan has come a long way from the very poor economic conditions that prevailed at the time the Nationalist Chinese administration took over from Japanese rule in 1945. Over the past half century, Taiwan has changed from an agricultural to an industri-alized economy. Foreign investment, mostly from overseas Chinese, the United States, Japan, and Western Europe, helped introduce modern, labor-intensive technology to the island in the 1960s, but the emphasis has changed from production of light-industry consumer goods for export to more sophisticated heavy industry and technology-intensive products.

In the decade 1973–1982, the gross domestic product rose at an annual average of 9.5% in real terms. During the recession following the 1973 oil embargo, Taiwan managed to overcome the slump in demand for its industrial exports by adopting a successful economic stabilization program. Ten major infrastructure projects were launched to stimulate economic activity. Taiwan's economic planners hoped that the sharp increase in investment for these major projects, coupled with revived demand for the island's exports, would establish a basis for continued prosperity. The authorities also encouraged foreign investment as a way to help finance the island's efforts to move away from light, labor-intensive export-oriented industry to more capital-intensive production for export and for import substitution.

Taiwan's continued success in the 1980s was based on a shift in industrial structure toward one that is more capital-intensive and more energy-efficient. Its economic policymakers wanted their export industries to account for 80% of GDP by 1990. Among the major new sectors developed by the Taiwan industrial effort, the most important were electronics and information processing, precision instruments and machinery, high-technology material sciences, energy sciences, aeronautical engineering, and genetic engineering.

Foreign trade has been a major factor in Taiwan's rapid growth. The value of trade roughly tripled in each five-year period since 1955 and increased nearly sixfold between 1975 and 1990. Taiwan's exports have changed from predominantly agricultural commodities to 90% industrial goods. Imports are dominated by raw materials and capital goods, which account for more than 90% of all imports. Taiwan, however, must rely on imports to meet more than 75% of its energy needs.

The success story of Taiwan's economic development can be traced to a number of factors. These include an early land reform program with emphasis on raising agricultural productivity so that Taiwan became self-sufficient in rice production, effective utilization of its educated and hardworking labor force through the initial adoption of labor-intensive light manufacturing for export markets, a judicious balance and cooperation between the public and private sectors, a sound financial system in which credit was carefully allocated to leading export industries despite the existence of financial repression, and most important, a realization that rapid economic growth and greater economic equality were congruent and not conflicting objectives.

Concepts for Review

Central bank	Informal finance
Currency board	Macroeconomic stabilization
Currency substitution	Monetary policy
Development banks	Money supply
Direct taxes	Organized money markets
Financial liberalization	Privatization
Financial repression	Rationing
Group lending schemes	Rotating savings and credit associations
Indirect taxes	State-owned enterprises (SOEs)
	Unorganized money markets

Questions for Discussion

1. Explain the distinction between organized and unorganized money markets. In the context of development priorities, what are the relative roles of central banks, commercial banks, development banks, and informal sources of credit such as the Grameen Rural Bank of Bangladesh?

2. What is meant by financial repression, financial liberalization, currency substitution, and unorganized money markets, and how do they relate to financial policy in developing countries?

3. List and briefly discuss the seven market failures that, according to Stiglitz, justify a strong government role in LDC financial sectors. Do you agree or disagree with this assessment? Explain.

4. What is meant by the terms *inflation* and *recession*? Is it possible for an economy to experience inflation and recession simultaneously? If so, can you explain how this could come about and give some recent examples? If not, explain why.

5. What are the principal sources of government revenues in LDCs? Why are many taxes so difficult to collect? Discuss.

6. In what ways do you think LDC taxation and expenditure systems could be improved? Be specific.

7. If the scarcity of administrative capabilities is a serious constraint on development policy implementation, what can LDCs do to relieve this constraint? What are the options? Discuss.

8. Summarize the arguments for and against the establishment of state-owned enterprises (SOEs) in developing nations. Do you think that SOEs should be encouraged or discouraged? What are the arguments for and against privatization of the public sector in developing countries? Explain.

9. Is military expenditure a positive or negative force in economic development? Do you think that international financial and technical assistance should be accorded to LDCs that spend more on their military than on social and educational services? Explain.

Notes

1. For an excellent account of how stabilization and adjustment measures adversely affected the poor and vulnerable during the 1980s, see Frances Stewart, "The many faces of adjustment," *World Development* 19 (December 1991): 1847–1864.

2. Space limitations prevent us from analyzing the possible relevance for LDCs of some of the more recent macroeconomic models of developed countries, including rational expectations and supply-side economics. However, given their widespread criticism as developed-country theories, their applicability to LDCs is very remote indeed. For an attempt, however, see W. Max Corden, "The relevance for developing countries of recent developments in macroeconomic theory," *World Bank Research Observer* 2 (July 1987): 171–188.

3. For a comprehensive text on money and financial development in the Third World, see Maxwell F. Fry, *Money, Interest, and Banking in Economic Development* (Baltimore: Johns Hopkins University Press, 1988), and World Bank, *World Development Report, 1991* (New York: Oxford University Press, 1991). One of the earliest and best descriptions of the unorganized and fragmented nature of money markets in developing countries can be found in U Tun Wai, "Interest rates outside the organized money markets," *IMF Staff Papers* 6 (November 1957): 80–125.

4. For a discussion of the phenomenon of currency substitution and the impact of unorganized money markets on the Third World, see Steven L. Green, "Monetary policies in developing countries and the new monetary economics," *Journal of Economic*

Development 11 (December 1986), and G. Ortiz, "Currency substitution in Mexico: The dollarization problem," *Journal of Money, Credit, and Banking* 15 (May 1983): 174–185.

5. For a discussion of privatization and the liberalization of financial markets in LDCs, see Laurence H. White, "Privatization of financial sectors," in Steven H. Hanke (ed.), *Privatization and Development* (San Francisco: Institute for Contemporary Studies, 1987), pp. 149–160.

6. Charles Collyns, *Alternatives to the Central Bank in the Developing World*, International Monetary Fund Occasional Paper No. 20 (Washington, D.C.: International Monetary Fund, 1983), p. 2. Much of the discussion that follows is based on this informative report.

7. Currency boards were common in the British colonial nations of Africa and Asia prior to independence. They typically issued domestic currency for foreign exchange and offered limited banking facilities to commercial banks. They could not create new money, conduct monetary policy, give policy advice, or supervise the banking system. They simply acted as agents for the colonial banks and were charged with the responsibility of maintaining a fixed parity with the colonial power's currency.

8. Collyns, *Alternatives to the Central Bank*, p. 21.

9. For one suggested approach to the problem, see C. Loganathan, "A new deal in development banking," *Development Digest*, October 1972, pp. 25–36. A more extensive discussion of how to improve the monetary control system and mobilize and better allocate domestic savings in LDCs can be found in Delano Villanueva, "Issues in financial sector reform," *Finance and Development* 25 (March 1988): 14–17.

10. For a review of the growth of informal finance in developing countries in the context of "consumption-smoothing" strategies, see Timothy Besley, "Nonmarket institutions for credit and risk sharing in low-income countries," *Journal of Economic Perspectives* 9 (Summer 1995): 115–127.

11. In addition to interest rate ceilings, developing country governments have often intervened in their financial markets in a variety of ways. These have included directed credit programs, high bank reserve requirements that effectively tax the financial system, and forced lending to the government to finance high budget deficits, for example by requiring banks to hold low yielding government bonds. These and other policies are linked to interest rate ceilings. In the presence of high and variable inflation and negative real interest rates, they lead not only to lower savings and growth, but also can cause the entire banking system to contract. I am grateful to Professor Valerie Bencivenga for these observations.

12. The classic writings on financial repression and the positive impact of financial liberalization on saving and investment are Ronald I. McKinnon, *Money and Capital in Economic Development* (Washington, D.C.: Brookings Institution, 1973), and Edward S. Shaw, *Financial Deepening in Economic Development* (New York: Oxford University Press, 1973). For a classic critique of this approach, see Carlos Diaz-Alexandro, "Good-bye financial repression, hello financial crash," *Journal of Development Economics* 19 (1985): 1–24.

13. World Bank, *World Development Report, 1987* (New York: Oxford University Press, 1987), pp. 117–122. However, for transnational evidence that interest rate levels have little or no effect on savings and investment, see Deena R. Khatkhata, "Assessing the impact of interest rates in less developed countries," *World Development* 16 (May 1988): 577–588; Gerado M. Gonzales Arrieta, "Interest rates, savings and growth in LDCs: An assessment of recent empirical research," *World Development* 16 (May 1988): 589–606; and Rudiger Dornbusch, "Policies to move from stabilization to growth," *Proceedings of the*

World Bank Annual Conference on Development Economics, 1990 (Washington, D.C.: World Bank, 1990), pp. 36–41.

14. Joseph E. Stiglitz, "The role of the state in financial markets," *Proceedings of the World Bank Annual Conference on Development Economics, 1993* (Washington, D.C.: World Bank, 1994), pp. 7–52.

15. *Ibid.*, p. 20.

16. For an excellent collection of articles and essays related to taxation and development, see Donald Newbery and Nicholas Stern (eds.), *The Theory of Taxation for Developing Countries* (New York: Oxford University Press, 1987). See also World Bank, *World Development Report, 1988* (New York: Oxford University Press, 1988), pt. 2; "Symposium on tax policy in developing countries," *World Bank Economic Review* 5 (September 1991): 459–574; and Robin Burgess and Nicholas Stern, "Taxation and development," *Journal of Economic Literature* 31 (June 1993): 762–830.

17. Nicholas Kaldor, "Taxation for economic development," *Journal of Modern African Studies* 1 (March 1963).

18. See World Bank, *World Development Report, 1983* (New York: Oxford University Press, 1983), figs. 5.4 and 5.5.

19. *Ibid.*, chap. 8. See also the discussion of SOEs in *World Development Report, 1988*, chap. 8.

20. Tony Killick, "The role of the public sector in the industrialization of African developing countries," *Industry and Development* 7 (1983): 57–88.

21. For a recent review of the successes of privatization in LDCs, see Sunita Kikeri, John Nellis, and Mary Shirley, "Privatization: Lessons from market economies," *World Bank Research Observer* 9 (July 1994): 241–272.

22. *Ibid.*, 249–253.

23. See, for example, Tony Killick, *A Reaction Too Far: Economic Theory and the Role of the State in Developing Countries* (London: Overseas Development Institute, 1989); a review of the Killick book by Paul P. Streeten in *Economic Development and Cultural Change* 39 (January 1991): 421–439; Robert Klitgaard, *Adjusting to Reality: Beyond "State vs. Market" in Economic Development* (San Francisco: Institute for Contemporary Studies, 1991); and United Nations Development Program, *Human Development Report, 1993* (New York: Oxford University Press, 1993), pp. 49–51.

24. Emile Benoit, "Growth and defense in developing countries," *Economic Development and Cultural Change* 25 (January 1978).

25. David Lim, "Another look at growth and defense in less developed countries," *Economic Development and Cultural Change* 31 (January 1983): 377–384.

26. Riccardo Faine, Patricia Annez, and Lance Taylor, "Defense spending, economic structure, and growth: Evidence among countries and over time," *Economic Development and Cultural Change* 32 (April 1984): 487–498.

27. Alfred Maizels and Machiko Nissanke, "The determinants of military expenditures in developing countries," *World Development* 14 (September 1986): 1125–1140.

28. Commission on Integrated Long-Term Strategy, *Discriminate Deterrence* (Washington, D.C.: U.S. Department of Defense, 1987).

29. Patrick E. Tyler, "Pentagon imagines new enemies to fight in post–Cold War era," *Washington Post*, February 17, 1992, p. A1.

30. Robert McNamara, "The Post–Cold War world: Implications for military expenditure in the developing countries," *Proceedings of the World Bank Annual Conference on*

Development Economics, 1991 (Washington, D.C.: World Bank, 1992): 95–125. See also Tamin Bayoumi, Daniel Hewitt, and Steven Symansky, "The impact of worldwide military spending cuts on developing countries," *International Monetary Fund Working Paper 93/86* (Washington D.C.: International Monetary Fund, 1994).

31. United Nations Development Program, *Human Development Report, 1991* (New York: Oxford University Press, 1991), p. 83.

Further Reading

On monetary and taxation issues as they relate to developing countries, consult some or all of the following books and articles: Maxwell J. Fry, *Money, Interest, and Banking in Economic Development* (Baltimore: Johns Hopkins University Press, 1988); W. Max Corden, "The relevance for developing countries of recent developments in macroeconomic theory," *World Bank Research Observer* 2 (July 1987); Steven L. Green, "Monetary policy in developing countries and the new monetary economics," *Journal of Economic Development* 11 (December 1986); Ronald I. McKinnon, *Money and Capital in Economic Development* (Washington, D.C.: Brookings Institution, 1973); Delano Villaneuva, "Issues in financial sector reform," *Finance and Development* 25 (March 1988); Gerado M. Gonzales Arrieta, "Interest rates, savings and growth in LDCs: An assessment of recent empirical research" *World Development* 16 (May 1988): 589–606; Rudiger Dornbusch and Alejandro Reynoso, "Financial factors in economic development," *American Economic Review,* 79 (May 1989): 204–209; Nouriel Roubini and Xavier Sala-i-Martin, "Financial repression and economic growth," *Journal of Development Economics* 39 (March 1992): 5–30; Valerie R. Bencivenga and Bruce D. Smith, "Deficits, inflation, and the banking system in developing countries: The optimal degree of financial repression," *Oxford Economic Papers 44* (1992): 767–790; Robert G. King and Ross Levine, "Finance, entrepreneurship, and growth," *Journal of Monetary Economics,* 32 (1993); 717–737; Donald Newbery and Nicholas Stern (eds.), *The Theory of Taxation for Developing Countries* (New York: Oxford University Press, 1987); Norman Gemmell, "Taxation and development," in Norman Gemmell (ed.), *Surveys in Development Economics* (London: Blackwell, 1987), chap. 8; Richard M. Bird, "A new look at indirect taxation in developing countries," *World Development* 15 (September 1987); and World Bank, *World Development Report, 1989* (New York: Oxford University Press, 1989).

An excellent introduction to the economics and politics of public policy in developing nations can be found in Tony Killick, *Policy Economics: A Text for Developing Countries* (London: Heinemann, 1981). For a review and a critique of the role of the state in development activities, see World Bank, *World Development Report, 1983* (New York: Oxford University Press, 1983), pp. 41–127; T. N. Srinivasin, "Neoclassical political economy, the state and economic development," *Asian Development Review* 3 (June 1985); Mahmood A. Ayub and Sven O. Hegstad, "Management of public industrial enterprises," *World Bank Research Observer* 2 (January 1987); and Stanislaw Wellisz and Ronald Findlay, "The state and the invisible hand," *World Bank Research Observer* 3 (January 1988).

In addition to the article on privatization cited in note 20, consult R. Hemming and A. M. Manson, *Privatization and Public Enterprises,* IMF Occasional Paper No. 56 (Washington, D.C.: International Monetary Fund, 1988); George Yarrow, "Privatization in theory and practice," *Economic Policy* (April 1986): 323–377; and Jonas Prager, "Is privatization a panacea for LDCs? Market failure versus public sector failure," *Journal of Developing Areas* 26 (April 1992): 301–322.

Readings on defense and development include Emile Benoit, *Defense and Economic Growth in Developing Countries* (Boston: Heath, 1973); Shaja Nawaz, "Economic impact of defense,"

Finance and Development 20 (March 1983); Pradip K. Ghosh (ed.), *Disarmament and Development: A Global Perspective* (Westport, Conn.: Greenwood Press, 1984); Riccardo Faine, Patricia Annez, and Lance Taylor, "Defense spending, economic structure, and growth: Evidence among countries and over time," *Economic Development and Cultural Change* 32 (April 1984): 487–498; Alfred Maizels and Machiko Nissanke, "The determinants of military expenditures in developing countries," *World Development* 14 (September 1986); United Nations Development Program, *Human Development Report, 1994* (New York: Oxford University Press, 1994), pp. 47–60 and Tamin Bayoumi, Daniel Hewitt, and Steven Symansky, "The impact of worldwide military spending cuts on developing countries," *International Monetary Fund Working Paper 93/86* (Washington D.C.: International Monetary Fund, 1994).

See also Stephen C. Smith, *Case Studies*, Chapter 23 for an analysis of tax reform in Bolivia, and Chapter 24 and 25 for a discussion of property rights reforms in China and civil service reforms in Mali and Mexico, respectively.

CHAPTER 18

Critical Issues for the Twenty-first Century

Globalization, the Environment, Economic Transition, Africa, and International Economic Reform

The most important challenges for the 1990s . . . have to be addressed in the context of the increasing interdependence and integration of the world economy.
—United Nations, *Declaration on International Economic Cooperation*, May 1990

For the first time in human history, the world is close to creating a single, unified global system.
—United Nations Development Program, *Human Development Report, 1992*

Absent major changes in North-South relations, the wretched should inherit the earth by about 2025.
—Matthew Connelly and Paul Kennedy, *Must It Be the Rest against the West?*

To understand the events of the next fifty years one must understand environmental scarcity, cultural and racial clash, geographic destiny, and the transformation of war.
—Robert Kaplan, *The Coming Anarchy*

Global Interdependence and the Growth of Third World Markets

We live in an increasingly interdependent world, and perhaps some day we will live in a "world without borders," to borrow from the title of a provocative book of the 1970s.[1] For Third World countries, dependence on rich nations is and has always been a stark fact of economic life. It is the principal reason for their heightened interest in promoting greater individual and collective self-reliance. At the same time, the developed world, which once prided itself on its apparent economic self-sufficiency, has come to realize that in an age of increasingly scarce natural and mineral resources, global environmental threats, accelerated international illegal migration, and burgeoning world trade, it too is becoming ever more economically dependent on the developing world. In the case of the United States, for example, developing nations supply 80% of its fuel imports, 26% of its imports of industrial supplies, 25% of its imports of capital goods, and 53% of its imports of consumer goods.

However, rich-nation dependence does not center solely on the need for energy and raw material supplies or on the ability of key nations like Brazil, India, and China to control their environmental damage. It is also manifested in the importance of Third World nations as markets for developed-country exports. As shown by Table 18.1, more than 40% of U.S. exports go to LDCs. Western Europe exports almost half of its total to the Third World, and 48% of Japan's exports are purchased by developing countries or former republics of the USSR.[2] The United States exports more to LDCs than to either Western Europe or Japan. Between 1990 and 1993, U.S. exports to Third World nations grew by an annual average rate of 12% while those to other industrialized countries expanded at a meager 2% pace. For Western Europe, exports to LDCs now account for twice as much revenue as exports to North America and Japan combined. Developing countries are expected to absorb almost 70% of the growth in world imports over the next 25 years. As their weight in the world economy grows and as they become more closely connected with today's developed countries through trade, capital, and labor flows, the Third World can be expected to exert increasing influence on the economic performance of rich nations. Some theorists even claim that early in the twenty-first century, the Third World will become the engine for growth in the First World. Others worry that a shift in manufacturing production to low wage developing countries will result in massive layoffs and stagnant wages for workers in developed nations.[3]

When Third World economies stagnate, however, industrial economies also feel the effects in terms of diminished exports and lost jobs. For example, during the 1981–1982 recession, sales to non-oil-exporting developing nations fell by over $24 billion. In the United States, the Commerce Department has estimated that each $1 billion in exports sustains approximately 25,200 American jobs. By that yardstick,

TABLE 18.1 Rich-Country Exports to Developing Countries, 1993 (percentage of total exports and GDP)

Country	Percentage of Total Exports	Percentage of GDP
Japan	48	4.1
United States	42	3.1
Italy	27	4.3
France	25	3.8
Germany	25	4.9
United Kingdom	23	4.0
Canada	8	2.0

SOURCE: Pam Woodall, "The global economy: War of the worlds," *Economist*, October 1, 1994, tab. 6.

declining U.S. exports to Latin America alone accounted for a loss of nearly 400,000 American jobs in 1982 and 1983, with an additional loss of almost 500,000 jobs by the late 1980s. By contrast, in 1991, when the share of U.S. exports going to LDCs rose once again above 40%, the Commerce Department calculated that without these exports there would have been 430,000 fewer American jobs and the U.S. GNP growth rate would have decreased by 50% from the previous year. For the first time in recent history, therefore, the economic progress of developing countries has both a direct and an indirect impact on the economic performance of industrialized nations. Research suggests that this "reverse economic dependence" will continue to grow over the coming decades.[4]

In this, the concluding chapter of the text, we examine some of the major manifestations of global interdependence by focusing on four key issues that are likely to dominate international economic prospects in the near future: the global environmental threat, the economic crisis in sub-Saharan Africa, the economic transition in Eastern Europe and the former USSR, and the globalization of international trade and finance. We close with a few observations on the outlook for the world economy in this age of increasing interdependence.

The Global Environmental Threat: Greenhouse Gases and Ozone Depletion

As the twentieth century draws to a close, rapidly rising global concentrations of atmospheric pollutants threaten to cause severe damage to the ozone layer as well as dramatic climatic changes such as global warming. To reduce the severity of these environmental threats, global emissions must be sharply curtailed. Responsibility for reducing emissions must be divided across the members of a tremendously diverse international community that may be remarkably different in terms of stage of industrial development, income, social structure, and political orientation. As a consequence, there is great controversy over the extent to which each government is obliged to control the emissions produced by its domestic population. The dispute is intensified by the fact that there is as yet no consensus concerning the environmental outcome of increased concentrations of **greenhouse gases**. However, it is becoming increasingly clear that given the potentially devastating effects of **global warming**, it is of paramount importance that steps be taken to limit harmful emissions.

Pollutants and Their Consequences for the Global Environment

The rapid rise in the production of pollutants has led to dramatic increases in the levels of concentration of a number of greenhouse and ozone-depleting gases. For example, global concentrations of carbon dioxide (CO_2) have increased by 26% since the start of the industrial revolution, and more than half of this increase has occurred since 1960. Total gaseous chlorides, usually ozone-depleting chlorofluorocarbons (CFCs), increased in concentration by 114% in the mere 16 years between

1975 and 1990. The level of concentration of another important greenhouse gas, methane, has increased by 143% since the start of the industrial revolution, and almost 30% of this increase has occurred since 1970. Due to rising incomes and rapid population growth, buildup of these chemicals will accelerate in the future unless sweeping international reforms are implemented.

A study jointly sponsored by the World Meteorological Organization and the United Nations Environment Program predicts that if current emission trends continue, mean global temperatures are likely to rise 0.3°C per decade, or 3°C (5.4°F) by the end of the twenty-first century. Due to the delayed impact of current emissions, the study found that to stabilize CO_2 and CFC concentrations at current levels, immediate reductions in emissions from human activities of over 60% would be required. According to the World Resources Institute:

> The 1980s was the warmest decade recorded since careful weather records began being kept. Six of the 10 hottest years on record have occurred since 1980—1989, 1988, 1987, 1983, 1981 and 1980 itself. Hotter still was 1990—the warmest year yet, according to the British Meteorological Office. . . . But scientists cannot yet say whether this warm weather is a trend, resulting from rising concentrations of greenhouse gases, or whether it is merely a natural fluctuation.[5]

It is not clear yet whether or not this constitutes a statistically significant pattern of warming. For example, some researchers note that current warming trends appear to be less significant than those predicted by computer simulations using past emission levels.[6] Scientists are aware that some pollutants may actually slow warming by deflecting ultraviolet light back into space, so it is a matter of controversy whether we are experiencing a permanent change or a temporary phenomenon that masks the long-term implications of rising concentrations of greenhouse gases and increased **ozone depletion**. Though statistically there is little proof that what appears to be warming is a significant trend, the potentially catastrophic consequences of climate changes have spurred widespread cries for preventive policy.

MDC and LDC Contributions to Greenhouse Gases

The burning of fossil fuels by automobiles and industry are obvious sources of greenhouse gases; less obvious sources include deforestation, animal husbandry, wet rice cultivation, decomposition of waste, and coal mining. A number of gases, including CFCs, carbon dioxide, methane, sulfur dioxide, and nitrous oxides, contribute significantly to the stock of greenhouse gases. However, CO_2 has the greatest impact, due to its relatively long lifetime in the atmosphere and the massive quantities produced globally. Sources of CO_2 emissions may be decomposed into two broad categories, industrial production (77% of emissions) and all others. Developing countries, with roughly three-quarters of the world's population, produce less than one-third of industrial CO_2—about one-fifth if we exclude China. Because incomes and consumption are higher in the wealthiest countries, per capita emissions are also much higher. For example, the level of per capita emissions in the United States is more than twice that of the average European's, 19 times higher than the average African's, and 25 times higher than the average Indian's. Figure 18.1 shows how energy consumption varies among 16 developed and developing countries.

Though Third World countries account for a relatively small proportion of industrial CO_2, they produce virtually all of the CO_2 in the second category, generally resulting from the burning of vegetation to clear new land. These emissions from "land use change" are calculated under the assumption that all the CO_2 in vegetation is released into the atmosphere upon its removal. It is estimated that deforestation accounts for roughly 25% of all CO_2 emissions worldwide. Of potentially equal or greater significance is the fact that deforestation leads to the destruction of a vital source of atmospheric oxygen. Because trees consume carbon dioxide and release oxygen during the process of photosynthesis, the tropical rain forests represent an important mechanism through which the ecosystem regenerates itself. Clearing the rain forests will reduce the **absorptive capacity** of the environment for CO_2. Thus it is through changes in patterns of land use that the developing countries currently make their largest contribution to global concentrations of greenhouse gases. This fact has served to intensify pressures on Third World governments to limit the destruction of rain forests. Although preserving forests might be in everyone's long-term interests, in the short term a number of international and domestic economic factors make it difficult to do so.

One factor is falling commodity prices and the need for foreign exchange. The bulk of the remaining rain forests are coincidentally located in a number of the most heavily indebted countries, whose export earnings have suffered greatly as a result

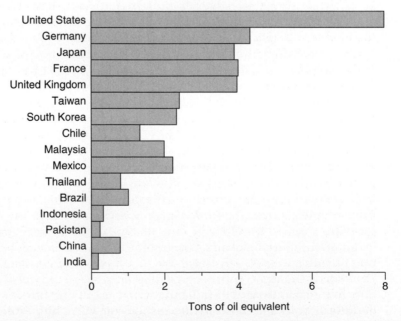

FIGURE 18.1 Energy Consumption Per Capita, 1992. *Source:* Pam Woodall, "The global economy: War of the worlds," *Economist*, October 1, 1994, tab. 15.

of low commodity prices. To raise sufficient foreign exchange to meet debt-service requirements, these countries must increase commodity exports at a time when demand is slack and market values are low. Because the price elasticity of demand for Third World commodities is also generally quite low, attempts to expand international sales further depress commodity prices, confounding efforts to raise sufficient foreign exchange. Because timber exports are an important source of revenue for a number of highly indebted countries, falling terms of trade may actually increase the rate of extraction and force prices far below the true social value of standing forests.

Falling commodity prices threaten the profitability of many export industries. As a result, Third World governments desperate for foreign exchange have frequently subsidized the production of exports. Occasionally these schemes have done tremendous damage to the environment while generating large losses for domestic governments, as is the case for many publicly subsidized cattle farms and timber concessions.

A second complicating factor was economic stagnation during the 1980s. The slowdown experienced in the industrialized countries during the 1980s was magnified in many LDCs. In the heavily indebted tropical countries with rain forests, labor force growth outpaced economic growth for the first time in 40 years. This fact, coupled with a worsening of disparities in the distribution of land, led to falling urban wages, slowing rural-urban migration, and rising numbers of landless rural workers. In Brazil, the agricultural labor force grew by 4% between 1981 and 1984, compared to 0.6% between 1971 and 1976. Rural wages fell by almost 40% in real terms between 1981 and 1985. Even though rain forest soils have only marginal cultivability, they represent the sole form of livelihood for many of the rural poor. Thus efforts to prohibit the clearing of rain forest land for agricultural use are likely to fail unless governments demonstrate a commitment to bring about extensive land reform and create alternative rural economic opportunities.

By providing additional, albeit marginal and only temporarily cultivable land, the rain forests may stave off political confrontations leading to reforms. A number of Third World governments have encouraged the cultivation of tropical forests through the transfer of land titles to the people clearing the property or by actively moving households from impoverished rural and urban areas through resettlement or transmigration programs. These policies may provide a cheap alternative to pursuing costly but more fundamental development reforms. Though the latter are more desirable from a long-term perspective, officials experiencing acute revenue shortages and pressures to reduce government spending may be unwilling or unable to implement development-oriented programs. Resettlement is also politically easier because any successful long-term solution to the problems of landlessness and poverty generally requires some type of land reform. Governments that prevent the settlement of rain forests but fail to provide effective rural development programs are likely to encounter rising political instability.

A third impediment to saving the forests is the Third World's dependence on traditional fuels. The vast majority of wood cut in the Third World is used for home heating and cooking. Timber accounts for 89% of all fuel in Africa, 70% in South America, and 74% in Asia. For the poorer, non-oil-exporting LDCs, traditional fuels are the predominant source of energy. Banning the use of timber for firewood would require increasing expensive foreign imports of fossil fuels. The transition away from traditional fuels would increase foreign-exchange outflows and necessitate that low-priced alternative fuels be made readily available to small family farmers who depend on the forests for their daily energy needs.

Rain Forest Preservation as a Public Good: Who Should Pay?

Each of these problems must be addressed in order to halt permanent destruction of rain forests. Long-term solutions will involve increasing the accessibility of cheap alternative fuels, managing sustainable timber schemes, and providing economic opportunities for the masses of impoverished peoples forced to clear large tracts of fragile rain forest land. Each program will require careful planning, technical expertise, and sustained management. Like most investments designed to yield enduring rewards, initial outlays are likely to exceed short-term gains. Thus preservation of the remaining rain forests will, at least temporarily, intensify existing hardships in highly indebted countries, unless revenue shortfalls are met with external funds.

In our discussion of public goods in Chapter 10, we found that in the absence of government intervention, the free market is likely to provide a suboptimal level of resource preservation (see Figure 10.4). We can thus conclude that when foreign countries are allowed a free ride—that is, allowed to benefit from rain forest preservation without contributing to it—deforestation will continue at an undesirable pace. To reduce the resulting inefficiencies, the model would suggest lowering the relative price per unit of protected forest for the LDC and increasing it for the outside beneficiaries. For the latter, this would simply entail the contribution of fees earmarked for the preservation of rain forests. For LDCs, there are a number of ways in which the price of forest conservation can be lowered.

One would be improved efficiency of existing rain forest use. Much of the timber that is now burned to open land for cultivation could be harvested for financial gain. For example, it is estimated that Brazil loses $2.5 billion annually in the burning of precious rain forest timber, while the cumulative figure for the Ivory Coast to date is $5 billion. Sustainable timber production for fuel or export can be achieved through the selective cutting of older growth, the restriction of cutting cycles to 30-year intervals, and the careful maintenance of new growth. It is generally impossible to regenerate a rain forest that has been clear-cut, so proper maintenance and supervision of logging are necessary. More careful oversight of timber concessions by LDC governments can prevent clear-cutting, reduce careless destruction of uncut trees, and increase the efficiency of revenue collection from concessions that are usually owned by domestic elites or large multinationals. A number of management projects of this sort, supported by multilateral development banks, are already under way. However, as yet less than 0.1% of tropical forests are sustainably managed.

Another boon to forest conservation would be development of markets for alternative rain forest products. Some of the costs of rain forest preservation can be offset by developing markets for sustainable forest products. Recent studies have indicated that the sale of products such as meats, nuts, fruits, oils, sweeteners, resins, tannins, fibers, construction materials, and medicinal compounds may provide a more lucrative and sustainable stream of income from tropical forests. Because their extraction is labor-intensive, more jobs are created for local populations, in turn creating alternatives to slash-and-burn cultivation of rain forest land. In addition, there is a broader distribution of the benefits from natural resources. However, for such schemes to succeed, First World markets must be made accessible to Third World producers. By opening their own markets to nontimber LDC exports and alternative rain forest products, developed countries can reduce the dependence of timber-rich, capital-poor countries on the destruction of their forests for quick earnings of foreign exchange.

Debt relief would also help. Because the shortage of foreign exchange is greatly exacerbated by external debt burdens, some form of debt relief will be necessary to reduce dependence on the exploitation of remaining forests. Debt-for-nature swaps effectively convert foreign-denominated debt held by a foreign public or private agency into domestic debt that is used to finance the management of natural resources. This debt may be tied to the preservation of forests, and interest payments may be used to provide salaries and maintenance costs for conservation efforts. Though debt-for-nature swaps offer a promising approach to reducing rain forest destruction, there are many obstacles to their widespread use (see Chapter 10). Consequently, the area of land now protected by the schemes is still very small.

Finally, forests could be saved through appropriate aid packages. First World aid for the support of programs to alleviate landlessness and poverty can help eliminate the socioeconomic causes of tropical deforestation. At the same time, it would be useful to halt unilateral and multilateral (mostly World Bank) subsidization of the environmentally destructive cattle ranching and timber industries.

Searching for Solutions: The 1992 Earth Summit

In June 1992, the second United Nations Conference on Environment and Development (UNCED)—the so-called **Earth Summit**—was held in Rio de Janeiro. The first meeting had been held in Stockholm in 1972. The Rio meeting brought together the leaders of 118 industrial and Third World nations along with hundreds of nongovernment environmental organizations and tens of thousands of concerned individuals. The task was to find ways to cope with the increasing dangers of permanent environmental damage resulting from the buildup of greenhouse gases (especially CO_2) leading to fears of global warming, the inexorable loss of **biodiversity** (diverse plants and species) resulting in part from the destruction of tropical rain forests, and the concerns over the environmental consequences of rapid population and industrial growth in the developing world.

Although the vast majority of global environmental damage represents the cumulative and contemporary impact of Western industrialization (see Table 6.5), the focus of much of the conference was on the Third World. With almost 100 million new births every year and major rural-to-urban population shifts under way, the developing world has the potential not only to add to current environmental degradation but ultimately to tip the balance against human survival. The principal concern of the developed world (often unexpressed) was that successful economic growth in the heavily populated developing world could bring with it such negative environmental externalities to the **global commons** that everyone would ultimately suffer—rich and poor alike. For their part, representatives of Third World nations feared that once again they would be coerced into bearing the major burdens of adjustment, that in some way the South's continued poverty was necessary for maintaining the North's prosperity. However, unlike the 1980s debt crisis, when LDCs had to bear almost all of the pain of IMF and World Bank stabilization and adjustment programs, in the case of the environment, developed-country lifestyles could be directly affected by Third World policy decisions. Such environmental interdependence allowed LDCs successfully to press their demands for more international financial and technical assistance to enable them to pursue environmentally sustainable development objectives. Although the major donor nation, the United States, made no specific additional aid commitments at the Rio conference, the 12 European Community (EC) countries indicated a willingness to offer $3 billion to $5 billion in environmental aid between 1993 and 1997, and Japan planned to increase its environmental aid to developing countries from $800 million per year in 1992 to $1.4 billion annually between 1993 and 1997. In addition, a developed-country donor group (including the United States) decided to create a new fund for the World Bank's International Development Agency (IDA) that would provide low-interest environmental loans to the world's least developed nations. Finally, the North agreed to double, and perhaps eventually triple, the $1.3 billion World Bank's Global Environment Facility (GEF) established in 1989 to finance Third World environmental projects.

The Rio summit also produced **Agenda 21**, a nonbinding 800-page blueprint to clean up the global environment and encourage environmentally sound development in the twenty-first century. Adopted by consensus, Agenda 21 emphasizes the following six areas of international activity.[7]

1. Allocating development assistance to programs focusing on poverty alleviation and environmental health such as providing sanitation and clean water, reducing indoor air pollution resulting from the burning of firewood, and meeting basic needs

2. Investing in research and extension services to reduce soil erosion and permit more environmentally sensitive agricultural practices

3. Allocating more resources to family planning and to expanding educational and job opportunities for women so that population growth can be reduced

4. Supporting LDC governments in their attempts to curtail or modify projects that harm the environment

5. Providing funds to protect natural habitats and biodiversity

6. Investing in research and development on noncarbon energy alternatives to respond to climate changes and reduce greenhouse gases

Analysts predict that global environmental concerns will continue to increase well into the next century. With the focus shifting from simple economic growth (GDP) to sustainable development and with worries mounting that the pattern and style of Third World development could lead to serious problems for the industrialized world, a new and more permanent form of global interdependence has emerged, one in which LDC leverage on international economic and political decisions is greater than at any time since the OPEC oil price increases of the 1970s. It is hoped that the common interest of all nations in a cleaner and more livable world will generate a new spirit of cooperation between rich and poor countries. Developing countries must be allowed to pursue their primary objective of raising the levels of living of their rural and urban poor, while both rich and poor nations alike must make every effort to reduce the damage that each causes to the earth's common heritage of land, sea, and air.

The Economic Crisis in Sub-Saharan Africa

Although the 1980s and 1990s have been a time of stagnating incomes, declining employment, and worsening poverty for many Third World countries, nowhere has the situation been more severe than in sub-Saharan Africa. At the heart of the African dilemma is an inexorable economic decline, a drop in per capita incomes, rapid increases in population, the loss of export revenues, the curtailment of foreign investment, the destruction of fragile ecosystems, and the inability of many countries even to feed their people and meet other basic human needs. A joint report by the International Institute for Environment and Development and the World Resources Institute expressed it well:

> Sub-Saharan Africa poses the greatest challenge to world development efforts to the end of the century and beyond. Recurrent famine there is only the symptom of much deeper ills. Africa is the only major region where per capita income, food production, and industrial production have declined over an extended period: the only developing region where development appears to be moving in reverse. . . . In recent years, Africa's farmers and herders, its soils and forests, have been chasing each other down a vicious spiral of environmental degradation and deepening poverty. Conventional development efforts by donors and governments have largely failed to halt the spiral, indeed in some cases have aggravated it.[8]

The specific quantitative dimensions of the economic predicament in sub-Saharan Africa are vividly portrayed in Tables 18.2 and 18.3. Between 1980 and 1990, per capita output fell by 42.5%, per capita consumption (a more significant measure of human well-being) fell by 40%, domestic investment declined by 29.7%, exports fell by 34.5%, per capita food production dropped by 12.2%, and the total external debt *rose* by 162% to a level as large as the region's total GNP! Debt service in 1990 was equal to 19% of total export earnings. Africa's poverty rate rose during the 1980s to 62%, or 325 million people; over the same period, real wages declined by over 30% (in some countries, the drop was in excess of 70%). Employment also suffered, with open unemployment growing at an annual rate of 10% in the second half of the 1980s. By 1994, open unemployment affected over 32 million Africans, and severe underemployment grew by another 33 million to a total of 95 million people.

TABLE 18.2 Economic Decline in Sub-Saharan Africa, 1980–1990

Economic Indicator	1980	1990	Change (%)
Per capita output ($)	582	335	−42.5
Per capita consumption ($)	465	279	−40.0
Investment (% of GDP)	20.2	14.2	−29.7
Exports of goods ($ billions)	48.7	31.9	−34.5
Per capita food production ($)	107	94	−12.2
Total external debt ($ billions)	56.2	147	+162
Poverty (% below poverty line)	N.A.	62	—

SOURCES: United Nations Development Program and World Bank, *African Development Indicators* (New York and Washington, D.C.: United Nations Development Program and World Bank, 1992); poverty data from Figure 2.3 of this text.

NOTE: Amounts are expressed in U.S. dollars at 1980 prices. N.A. = not available.

From a global perspective, Africa has fallen steadily behind the rest of the world. Its share of global GNP dropped from 1.9% in 1960 to 1.2% in 1993 (even though it has 10.3% of the world's population). In the ten years between 1985 and 1994, its real GDP growth rate consistently lagged behind Asia and Latin America (see Table 18.3). Its share of global trade fell from 3.8% in 1970 to less than 1% in 1994, primarily as a result of steep drops in commodity prices, which cost the continent more than $80 billion in lost export earnings in 1985–1994. Its share of Third World private investment dropped from 25% in 1970 to 15% in 1992. In 1993, Latin America attracted $190 a head in foreign-capital flows, while Africa received just $8 a head.

It is in the social and human realms, however, where the toll of Africa's current crisis is most acutely felt. Severe cuts in health and educational expenditures—in part due to IMF and World Bank lending preconditions—have resulted in sharp

TABLE 18.3 Rates of Growth of Real GDP by Region, 1985–1994

Year	Latin America	South and East Asia	Sub-Saharan Africa
1985	3.6	3.6	1.9
1986	4.2	6.2	2.6
1987	3.0	6.9	0.6
1988	0.7	8.5	2.9
1989	1.1	6.1	1.6
1990	−0.1	6.4	1.2
1991	2.8	5.3	0.4
1992	2.1	5.2	0.3
1993	3.3	5.4	1.8
1994[a]	2.8	6.3	2.3

SOURCE: United Nations, *World Economic and Social Survey, 1994* (New York: United Nations, 1994), p. 261.

[a]Estimates.

declines in school enrollment and disturbing increases in malnutrition and maternal and child mortality. For example, by 1989 there were 150 million severely malnourished people in Africa—70 million more than in 1975. In 1990, 27% of African children were underweight, 53% were stunted, and 10% were wasting. The under-5 mortality rate in 1990 was the highest in the world at 182 per 1,000. But the saddest and most disturbing health phenomenon to hit Africa in the 1980s and 1990s was the enormous impact of the spread of the **human immunodeficiency virus (HIV)**, which causes **AIDS**. The rapid spread of the AIDS virus now threatens to wreak havoc with Africa's people. The World Health Organization (WHO) has estimated that in excess of 7 million Africans were infected with HIV in 1994 (half the world's total). About 3.5 million women are infected, and the rate of increase continues to grow. During the remainder of the 1990s, several million children are expected to be born with the AIDS virus, many of whom will become "AIDS orphans" without home or family. The ultimate impact of this tragedy on the quality of Africa's human resources is likely to be substantial and to last for generations.

The causes of the African dilemma are many and varied. Some were beyond its control (drought, depressed commodity prices, foreign capital withdrawal, diminished foreign aid); others can be ascribed to poor government policies (neglect of agriculture, inefficient state-owned enterprises, lack of concern with promoting export growth). Surely rapid population growth, the highest in the world, must be also considered. Whatever the causes, if the disasters of recent decades are not to be repeated, coordinated efforts by African governments and international assistance agencies will be required to reverse the decline. More emphasis must be placed on agricultural and rural development, with enhanced price and investment incentives for small farmers being accompanied by institutional and structural reforms designed to improve the marketing and distribution of agricultural produce. Concern with preventing further environmental deterioration and desertification must be increased. Inefficient SOEs and ossified public-sector bureaucratic procedures must be addressed, and managers must be made more accountable for resource allocation and investment decisions. Privatization possibilities should be pursued where financially feasible and socially acceptable (e.g., with due regard to issues of income distribution and dualistic development).[9] The draconian cuts in health and educational expenditures during the 1980s and early 1990s must be reversed, and financial resources (both public and private) must once again flow back to African nations. Finally, major debt relief and population stabilization programs must be put in place, the former taking the form of significant debt cancellation (most is publicly owned) and the latter focusing on a combination of demand reduction through poverty alleviation and the promotion of women's economic progress along with supply improvements through more accessible and effective family-planning programs.

A difficult period lies ahead for sub-Saharan Africa. If development is going to succeed, Africa will be its severest test case. If it doesn't succeed, then not only will the 550 million Africans south of the Sahara be its victims, but directly and indirectly, the wealthy nations of the industrialized world will have to bear a major responsibility for this failure.

Economic Transition in Eastern Europe and the Former Soviet Republics: Implications for Third World Development Assistance

The **economic transition** from socialism to capitalism that has been initiated in Eastern Europe and the former USSR is unprecedented in scope, magnitude, and eventual impact on Third World economies. The initial stages of economic reform were traumatic, with economic contraction much greater than anticipated. The drop in real GDP in the two regions between 1990 and 1994 was estimated at 40%, with losses in some countries exceeding 50% (see Table 18.4). In addition, inflation accelerated to an annual rate in excess of 400% in Eastern Europe in 1993 and over 1,000% in Russia. Open unemployment rates also increased dramatically in both regions. At the same time, fiscal and current-account deficits widened, and intraregional trade contracted sharply. Although debt-restructuring agreements for Poland helped reduce Eastern Europe's external debt, Russia's debts reached 32% of its GDP in 1994, and debt-service payments are likely to put a further drag on many of these economies in coming years. Clearly, the prolonged economic contraction is testing the resolve of both the policymakers and the people of the former Second World and is slowing the overall pace of reform.

The eventual outcome of this dramatic experiment in economic transformation will continue to take shape over the next few years. However, even if these newly market-oriented nations survive the intitial trauma of radical structural change, it will take at least a generation for them to achieve self-sustaining growth. In the meantime, they will require huge amounts of international financial capital (estimated at $100 billion per year), funds that many people in the Third World (especially those in sub-Saharan Africa) fear will be diverted from their use for needed development projects. The specific concern of the least developed countries is that they will be crowded out of world capital markets as a result of the combined factors of the socialist economic transition, the substitution of speculative private portfolio investments based on short-term profits for long-term public financial aid, and the contraction in the total amount of available global long-term capital due to any slowdowns in the economic growth of such countries as Japan, the United States, and Germany. Reinforcing this **crowding-out phenomenon** will be the persistence of high real interest rates as these growing demands for investment capital are not met by a requisite increase in private savings. This could further compromise the ability of the poorest LDCs to repay their debts without further debt relief.

A critical issue for the remainder of the 1990s, therefore, will be the ability of global financial markets to meet the extraordinary capital needs of Eastern Europe and the republics of the former USSR without negating the equally vital credit and capital requirements of struggling Third World nations. Success in meeting these objectives will require a combination of steady economic growth and a restructuring of international development assistance away from the past political determinants of allocation and more toward genuine economic development needs and opportunities.

TABLE 18.4 Economic Transition in Selected Countries in Central and Eastern Europe and in Russia, 1990–1994

Country	Real GDP (annual percent change)					Consumer Prices (annual percent change)					Open Unemployment (percent)				
	1990	1991	1992	1993	1994	1990	1991	1992	1993	1994	1990	1991	1992	1993	1994
Central and Eastern Europe	—	–11.5	–11.7	–5.7	–5.4	—	103	370	442	217					
Albania	–10.0	–27.7	–9.7	11.0	7.4	—	110	185	138	88	—	12	29	22	19
Bulgaria	–9.1	–11.7	–5.7	–4.2	–2.0	24	334	82	73	81	1	11	15	16	13
Croatia	—	—	—	–3.2	1.8	—	—	—	1,516	98	9	18	18	16	17
Hungary	–3.5	–9.9	–5.1	–2.3	2.6	29	34	23	22	19	2	8	12	12	11
Poland	–11.6	–7.6	2.6	3.8	6.0	586	70	43	35	30	6	12	14	16	17
Romania	–7.4	–15.1	–13.5	—	—	5	161	210	256	156	1	3	6	9	11
Slovenia	—	—	—	1.3	5.0	—	—	—	32	18	5	8	13	16	14
Russia	—	–13.0	–19.0	–12.0	–12.0	—	93	1,353	915	336	—	—	5	5	6

SOURCE: International Monetary Fund, *World Economic Outlook, October 1994* and *May 1995* (Washington, D.C.: International Monetary Fund, 1994, 1995), tabs. 11 and 13 and tab. 10.

Globalization and International Financial Reform

During the past three decades, a remarkable **globalization** of the world economy has taken place.[10] The increasing integration of national economies into global markets promises to alter dramatically the volume and character of international resource flows. Because the expansion of global trade is essentially constrained by the domestic and international (IMF and World Bank) banking sector, which provides financing for international transactions, the increasing size, competitiveness, and diffusion of international financial markets has the potential to draw low-income economies into the economic mainstream. For Third World countries experiencing severe liquidity problems that constrain investment, limit the importation of inputs and replacement parts, and raise the level of risk associated with trade contracts, increased integration into expanding international financial markets could greatly improve prospects for economic flexibility and growth.

However, it is unclear whether or not low- and middle-income LDCs will in fact benefit from the globalization of international markets. For a variety of reasons, the full participation of many poor nations in the global economy is yet to be realized. At a time when national markets are opening up, it is ironic that some global financial markets remain restricted. In fact, prior to the 1994 GATT agreement, protectionism against Third World products had greatly increased, and the real rate of interest paid by developing countries on borrowed capital was on occasion more than 400% greater than that paid by their industrialized counterparts. The globalization of international financial markets thus reduces the transaction costs of trade for participants with access to international credit while increasing the relative disadvantage of those excluded from the benefits of financial globalization.

But even in cases where Third World countries are directly involved in the physical, technological, and financial globalization process, the implications for long-term development are ambiguous. Money and information can now be instantly transmitted from one corner of the earth to another. Multinational corporations are creating **global factories** with both horizontal and vertical integration spread over many countries. And a small group of newly industrializing countries in East Asia has captured the lion's share of Third World international flows of goods and services.

The effects of such globalization are threefold. First, the power and influence of individual nation-states, particularly many of those in the Third World, is weakened. LDCs that are not linked in some way to the new dollar-, yen-, or mark-dominated regional trading blocs in North America, the Pacific Rim, or Europe, respectively, face particularly difficult times ahead. Second, there are increased risks of financial market instability, access to global markets may become more difficult for low-technology producers, and the effects of economic growth in the North may no longer automatically benefit the poorest nations of the South. Indeed, the nature of past North-South relationships may have hindered the performance of many LDCs in the international arena. Third, a striking manifestation of the growing inequality of nations in an era of rapid global transmission of information via satellite is the tremendous increase in international *illegal* migration from the poor South to the industrialized North. Just as capital has become more internationally mobile, so too has labor. But unlike the movement of capital, the movement of unskilled Southern labor across Northern borders is not always a welcomed occurrence. In fact, some citizens of the industrialized world view this phenomenon as a threat to their economy, not to mention their culture and "way of life."[11]

If the dawn of the twenty-first century is to hold greater promise for the many LDCs that have been unable to share in the fruits of global progress, effective management of new global challenges—in money and finance, in environmental matters, and in resource, labor, and technology flows—will require reforms to the international system. Among the changes often mentioned are the following:[12]

1. A reduction in the debt-service burdens of the LDCs least able to afford continued austerity measures, expecially in sub-Saharan Africa

2. The creation of new LDC funding sources such as a tax on international currency transactions—the so-called Tobin tax[13]—or a per-gallon tax on developed-country oil consumption to discourage waste

3. The creation of new international institutions, such as a world central bank, to help stabilize global economic activity, promote global financial stability, and assist the economic development of poorer nations; such an entity could act as a lender of last resort to financial institutions and create new forms of liquidity

4. Reform of the two major existing institutions for global economic growth and stability, the IMF and the World Bank

Regarding this last point, the IMF must function more as a development institution and less as an international policeman for the developed world and its international banks. It should exhibit greater flexibility in its conditionality requirements and focus more on reviving growth in debt-laden countries and less on imposing a fixed menu of stabilization measures. Third World countries need a greater voice in its voting structure and policymaking bodies and greater access to expanded quantities of special drawing rights.

The World Bank, like the IMF, adopted an inflexible program of structural adjustment loans in the 1980s that on balance may have done more harm than good to many poor countries. The bank, which was established to borrow the savings of rich nations and lend them to poor countries to finance many of those projects (physical infrastructure, health and education facilities, etc.) that private investors would not undertake, has in recent years actually *withdrawn* resources (in excess of $500 million in the early 1990s) from poor nations.

The World Bank has two lending facilities. The International Bank for Reconstruction and Development (IBRD), the larger of the two, now offers only floating-rate loans linked to global interest rates. This is a departure from the original intention of the IBRD, which was to cushion LDCs against interest rate fluctuations and partially subsidize their loans with its own financial strength and the backing of its industrial-country contributors. The second lending facility, the International Development Association (IDA), does provide concessional loans (interest-free for 40 or 50 years) to countries with a per capita GNP below $805 in 1994. However, the IDA's share of total World Bank lending is only 20% to 25%.

After a decade of an almost messianic mission of preaching market-oriented stabilization and structural adjustment reforms, both the IMF and especially the World Bank have once again begun to focus on poverty alleviation by adopting greater flexibility in their programmatic activities. The challenge for the future is to increase their flow of resources from North to South and to adapt their lending to the real development needs of recipient nations. These reforms would help ensure that the Third World becomes integrated into global markets and that it benefits from expanding world trade.[14]

Summary and Concluding Remarks

Our discussion in this final chapter has touched on many of the economic and noneconomic manifestations of the growing globalization of trade and finance and the increasing interdependence of nations. We have seen that whereas three decades ago this interdependence was perceived primarily in terms of the dependence of poor nations on rich ones, today the situation is different. Third World nations are now the fastest-growing export markets for developed countries. With rising concerns about unpredictable energy prices and ever-greater mineral scarcities, as well as fears of global environmental damage, ethnic conflicts, and floods of illegal immigrants pouring across their borders, developed countries now understand that their future welfare depends increasingly on the economic performance and social achievements of the developing countries. Let there be no misunderstanding, however. Poor nations are now and will remain considerably more vulnerable to the economic events and policies of rich nations than vice versa. The special and tragic plight of sub-Saharan Africa bears witness to the particular dependence and vulnerability of the least developed countries.

The crucial question for the late 1990s and the start of the new century is whether this globalization of the international economy and the new economic interdependence among all nations will lead to greater cooperation or more conflict. Some experts view the period ahead as one of great promise; others are less confident. Some even foresee major problems and disruptions with potentially tragic consequences.[15]

As a result of the oil and resource scarcities of the 1970s, the debt crisis of the 1980s, and the environmental concerns and new international trade and finance patterns of the 1990s, industrialized countries must understand that the economic futures of *both* groups of nations are intimately linked. No longer can rich nations totally dominate the established international order without provoking harmful repercussions. Cooperation becomes essential. In the final anaylsis, therefore, the only feasible outcome of the movement toward globalization and international interdependence is one in which *everyone* wins or loses. In the interdependent world of the twenty-first century, global development can never again be a zero-sum game.

With each passing year, therefore, rich and poor nations alike share an increasingly common destiny. The world community must finally realize that a more equitable international economic order is not only possible but even essential. Such a new order should be based on the fundamental principle that each nation's and each individual's development is intimately bound to the development of every other nation and every other individual. The future of all humankind is linked more closely today than ever before. All indications are that it will become even more so in the coming century. Let us hope, therefore, that reason and good sense will prevail so that the First and Third Worlds can truly become part of One World—forged together by a common economic destiny and guided by the humane principles of peace, friendship, and mutual respect.

CASE STUDY

The Economy of Saudi Arabia

GEOGRAPHIC, SOCIAL, AND ECONOMIC INDICATORS

Capital Riyadh

Area 2,330,000 km^2

Population 18.5 million (1995)

Population (average annual growth rate) 3.6% (1985–1994)

GNP per capita U.S. $7,240 (1994)

GNP per capita (average annual growth rate) –1.2% (1985–1994)

Agriculture as share of GDP 6% (1994)

Exports as share of GDP 40% (1994)

Infant mortality rate (per 1,000 live births) 24 (1995)

Child malnutrition (underweight) (not available)

Females as share of labor force 8% (1994)

Illiteracy rate (age 15+) 38% (1990)

Human Development Index 0.74 (medium) (1992)

Saudi Arabia occupies about four-fifths of the Arabian peninsula. Recent estimates show Saudi Arabia's population at about 18.5 million, including about 4 million resident foreigners. Until the 1960s, most of the population was nomadic or seminomadic; however, under the impact of rapid economic growth, urbanization has advanced rapidly, and about 95% of the people are now settled. Some cities and oases have densities of 770 people per square kilometer.

Following the sharp rise in petroleum revenues in 1974, Saudi Arabia became one of the fastest-growing nations in the world. It enjoyed a substantial surplus in its overall trade with other countries, imports increased rapidly, and ample government revenues were available for development, defense, and aid to other Arab and Islamic countries. Saudi Arabian foreign assets grew from about $4.3 billion in 1973 to nearly $150 billion in 1982.

The world oil glut in 1982, however, introduced an element of planning uncertainty for the first time in a decade. Saudi Arabian oil production, which had increased to almost 10 million barrels per day in 1980–1981, dropped to about 2 million barrels a day in August 1985. Budgetary deficits emerged, and the government drew down its foreign assets, which have now fallen by more than $65 billion since 1982. Responding to these financial pressures, Saudi Arabia gave up its role as the dominant independent producer within OPEC in the summer of 1985 and accepted a production quota of its own. Since then, Saudi oil policy has been guided by a desire to maintain its market and quota shares.

Through five-year development plans, the government has sought to allocate its petroleum income to transform its relatively undeveloped oil-based economy into that of a modern industrial state while maintaining the kingdom's traditional Islamic values and customs. Although economic planners have not achieved all their goals, the economy has progressed rapidly, and the standard of living of most Saudis has improved significantly. Dependence on petroleum revenue continues, but industry and agriculture now account for a larger share of total economic activity. A shortage of Saudi skilled workers at all levels remains the principal obstacle to economic diversification and development. Some 4 million non-Saudis are employed in the economy.

Saudi Arabia's first two development plans, covering the 1970s, emphasized infrastructure—telecommunications, roads, ports, electricity, and water. The results were impressive: The total length of paved highways tripled, power generation increased by a multiple of 28, and the capacity of the seaports grew tenfold.

For the third plan (1980–1985), the emphasis changed. The share of infrastructure in development spending declined substantially, and spending on education, health, and social services rose markedly. The share allocated to expanding and diversifying the productive sectors of the economy (primarily industry) did not rise as planned, but Jubail and Yanbu, two new industrial cities built around the use of indigenous oil and gas as sources of energy and as feedstocks to produce steel, petrochemicals, fertilizer, and refined oil products, were largely completed.

The fourth plan, covering 1985–1990, continued these priorities. The country's basic infrastructure is largely complete, but education and training remain areas of concern. Private enterprise is encouraged, and foreign investment in the form of joint ventures with Saudi public and private companies is welcomed. The private sector has become an increasingly important element in the economy, expanding its share of non-oil GDP to about 80% by 1993. Though still concentrated in trade and commerce, private investment has increased in industry, agriculture, banks, and construction companies in recent years. These private investments have been supported by generous government financing and incentive programs. The government intends that all sectors of the economy except petroleum extraction will eventually be privately owned.

The fifth plan (1990–1995) placed emphasis on consolidation of the country's defenses, efficiency in the government sector, creation of greater private-sector employment opportunities for Saudis, reduction in the number of foreign workers, and regional development. Although the 1991 Persian Gulf War with Iraq imposed heavy financial burdens on the economy, Saudi Arabia today remains physically intact and economically strong.

Concepts for Review

Absorptive capacity	Global commons
Agenda 21	Global factories
AIDS	Globalization
Biodiversity	Global warming
Crowding-out phenomenon	Greenhouse gases
Earth Summit	Human immunodeficiency virus (HIV)
Economic transition	Ozone depletion

Questions for Discussion

1. The 1970s ushered in an era in which for the first time, developed nations began to recognize their growing dependence on and vulnerability to the policies of certain Third World groups of nations. What was the source of this developed-country dependence, and what happened to it in the 1980s and 1990s?

2. List the principal sources of greenhouse gases and causes of ozone depletion. Explain how Third World rain forest destruction contributes to global climate problems. What economic model can be used to justify First World contributions to tropical forest preservation? Explain.

3. In what ways was the Rio de Janeiro Earth Summit of 1992 a watershed in North-South relations? If the well-being of people in rich nations were not so directly involved, do you think similiar progress would have been achieved? Explain.

4. "The crisis in sub-Saharan Africa arose out of the unique circumstances and special conditions in Africa that negated traditional development strategies." Do you agree or disagree with this statement? Explain your answer, being sure to identify the nature of the economic crisis in sub-Saharan Africa.

5. What kinds of policies, both domestic and international, are required to reverse the African decline? Explain.

6. What impact will the success or failure of economic transition in Eastern Europe and the former USSR have on Third World development prospects? What can LDCs learn from the transition experiment? Explain.

7. How has globalization affected the world economy in general and North-South relations in particular? What might be the long-term results? Explain.

8. Can the objective of greater collective self-reliance in developing nations be reconciled with the tendency toward increased global economic and noneconomic interdependence? Explain.

Notes

1. Lester Brown, *World without Borders* (New York: Random House, 1972). For a more recent analysis of global interdependence, see Paul Kennedy, *Preparing for the Twenty-first Century* (New York: Random House, 1993).

2. Pam Woodall, "The global economy: War of the worlds," *Economist*, October 1, 1994, p. 12.

3. A provocative book by Adrian Wood, *North-South Trade, Employment, and Inequality* (New York: Oxford University Press, 1995) asserts that trade with LDCs has already led to a 20% decline in demand for unskilled developed country workers since 1970. For a counter argument, see Richard B. Freeman, "Are your wages set in Beijing?" *Journal of Economic Perspectives* 9 (Summer 1995): 15–32 and Woodall, p. 14–19.

4. Woodall, pp. 3–38. See also John W. Sewell, "Can the North prosper without growth and progress in the South?" in Martin McLaughlin (ed.), *The United States and World Development: Agenda 1979* (New York: Praeger, 1979), chap. 2.

5. World Resources Institute, *World Resources, 1992–1993* (New York: Oxford University Press, 1992), p. 205.

6. William D. Nordhaus, "Climates and economic development: Climates past and climate change future," *Proceedings of the World Bank Conference on Development Economics, 1993* (Washington, D.C.: World Bank, 1994), pp. 355–376.

7. World Bank, *World Development Report, 1992: Development and the Environment* (New York: Oxford University Press, 1992), box 9.5. For the full report plus analysis, see

United Nations, *The Global Partnership for Environment and Development: A Guide to Agenda 21* (New York: United Nations, 1992), and *World Resources, 1994–1995*, chap. 13.

8. International Institute for Environment and Development and the World Resources Institute, *World Resources, 1987* (New York: Basic Books, 1987), p. 221. See also Paul Collier, "The marginalization of Africa," *International Labor Review* 134 (December 1995): 541–558; Robert Berg and Jennifer Seymour Whitaker (eds.), *Strategies for African Development* (Berkeley: University of California Press, 1985); Paul Harrison, *The Greening of Africa* (New York: Penguin, 1987); Jennifer Seymour Whitaker, *How Can Africa Survive?* (New York: Harper & Row, 1988); World Bank, *Adjustment in Africa: Reforms, Results and the Road Ahead* (New York: Oxford University Press, 1994); and Paul Mosley, Turan Sabasat and John Weeks, "Assessing adjustment in Africa," *World Development* 23 (September 1995).

9. For an analysis of some of the problems of economic reform and privatization efforts in Africa from an institutional perspective, see Howard Stein, "Theories of institutions and economic reform in Africa," *World Development* 22 (December 1994): 1833–1849.

10. For an excellent survey of issues related to globalization, see Üner Kirdar (ed.), *Change: Threat or Opportunity? Vol. 3: Globalization of Markets* (New York: United Nations, 1992).

11. A somber and striking scenario of millions of impoverished Third World immigrants flooding across the borders of North America and Europe in the twenty-first century is portrayed by Matthew Connelly and Paul Kennedy in "Must it be the rest against the West?" *Atlantic*, December 1994, pp. 61–91. See also Hal Kane, "What's driving migration?" *World Watch*, January-February 1995, pp. 23–33.

12. See, for example, Manmohan Singh, "In a changing world: Challenges to the South," in Üner Kirdar (ed.), *Change: Threat or Opportunity? Vol. 2: Economic Change* (New York. United Nations, 1992), chap. 11, and United Nations Development Program, *Human Development Report, 1994* (New York: Oxford University Press, 1994), pp. 80–89.

13. Named after Nobel laureate James Tobin, who first proposed such a tax. See UNDP, *Human Development Report, 1994*, p. 70.

14. For a variety of innovative proposals designed to increase the impact of World Bank and IMF lending programs, see Jeffrey Sachs, "Beyond Bretton Woods: A new blueprint," *Economist*, October 1, 1994, pp. 23–27.

15. For a particularly provocative analysis of the threat of global anarchy rather than global harmony, see Robert D. Kaplan, "The coming anarchy: How scarcity, overpopulation, tribalism, and disease are rapidly destroying the social fabric of our planet," *Atlantic*, February 1994, pp. 44–76.

Further Reading

Two of the principal sources of information on the global environment and development mentioned in Chapter 10 are World Bank, *World Development Report, 1992: Development and the Environment* (New York: Oxford University Press, 1992), and World Resources Institute, *World Resources, 1994–1995* (New York: Oxford University Press, 1994). A provocative look at environmental issues for the twenty-first century can be found in Üner Kirdar (ed.), *Change: Threat or Opportunity? Vol. 1: Ecological Change* (New York: United Nations, 1992). See also United Nations, *The Global Partnership for Environment and Development: A Guide to Agenda 21* (New York: United Nations, 1992).

Works on the economic crises in Africa are abundant; three good ones are Paul Harrison, *The Greening of Africa* (New York: Penguin, 1987); Robert Berg and Jennifer Seymour Whitaker (eds.), *Strategies for African Development* (Berkeley: University of California Press, 1985); and World Bank, *Adjustment in Africa: Reforms, Results and the Road Ahead* (New York: Oxford University Press, 1994). See also Stephen Smith, *Case Studies*, Chapter 26.

The literature on economic transition in Eastern Europe and the former USSR is constantly changing. However, a good introduction can be found in Vaclav Klaus, "A perspective on economic transition in Czechoslovakia and Eastern Europe," *Proceedings of the World Bank Annual Conference on Development Economics, 1990* (Washington, D.C.: World Bank, 1991), pp. 13–18, and David Kennett and Marc Lieberman, *The Road to Capitalism: Economic Transformation in Eastern Europe and the Former Soviet Union* (New York: Dryden Press, 1992). For the latest data and current trends, see the International Monetary Fund's latest *World Economic Outlook* and its journal, *Economics of Transition*.

A useful collection of readings, most of which deal with the phenomenon of globalization, can be found in Üner Kirdar (ed.), *Change: Threat or Opportunity? Vol. 2: Economic Change* (New York: United Nations, 1992). See also World Bank, *World Development Report, 1995* (New York: Oxford University Press, 1995), Part Two; Pam Woodall, "The global economy: War of the worlds," *Economist*, October 1, 1994, pp. 3–38; Ajit Singh, "Global economic changes, skills and international competitiveness," *International Labor Review* 133 (June 1994): 167–183; and "Special Issue: Employment policy in the global economy," *International Labor Review* 134 (December 1995): 441–624.

Privatization: What, When, and to Whom?

Contributed by Stephen C. Smith

There is widespread agreement that there has been an imbalance in favor of too much public ownership in developing countries. The private sector does many things better, and even where this is not the case, government competence is limited and should be concentrated on the things it must do, not squandered on things it merely can do. The need for privatization poses some difficult questions: Who should be able to purchase state-owned enterprises (SOEs)? Whatever party has the most ready cash? Or should market imperfections in who is able to raise immediate capital be taken into account? Does it matter if the purchaser is a domestic citizen or a multinational corporation? Managers and workers in the company or citizens at large? Are some modes of privatization politically easier to carry out than others? Can creative approaches to arranging and financing ownership transfer agreements widen the possibilities? Can privatization be carried out in isolation from other programs, or does it have to be conceived as part of an integrated development strategy? Does privatization simply mean a long-overdue diminution of the government ownership role, or is it optimally implemented as part of a reorganized and renewed nonownership public role in development?

Domestic entrepreneurs and foreign investors will continue to be the purchasers of the largest part of shares sold. In postcommunist countries, and a number of developing countries as well, a voucher scheme will be used, which will entitle citizens to bid on shares of companies that they believe will be successful. These vouchers will be distributed to citizens at no charge to them. But countries are also beginning to take very seriously the prospect of privatizing a significant part of the company's shares to its employees. In this, enterprises in developing countries are following trends of firms in developed countries in involving employees in stock ownership, decision making, and gain sharing. Part of this new trend reflects direct market forces in a changing world economy, part reflects public policy decisions in the face of identified market failures, and part reflects a quest for political consensus, especially for privatization. This legislation is very recent; almost all of it has been introduced since 1989. Moreover, this is not a region-specific phenomenon. Legislation was pioneered in Asia and Latin America before the recent widespread adoption in postcommunist economies, and interest is growing rapidly in Africa.

By 1992, there were laws or regulations in more than 30 developing economies providing incentives, as well as some limitations, for employee ownership (EO), often, but not exclusively, in privatization initiatives. These EO provisions are varied in nature and extent. They range from seeking to restrain employee ownership to within modest levels, such as 10%, to encouraging employee ownership participation to as much as 100% of certain companies. Purchase price provisions range from no discount or subsidy for employee purchase of stock to modest discounts of 10% to 15%, paralleling internal discounts of by now a majority of private publicly traded U.S. and Japanese companies, to discounts of up to 70%. About half of the countries offer a subsidy of between 10% and 30%, the remaining half in excess of 30%. More than half limit the number of shares on which employees can get this special treatment to 20% or less of the total.

We will explore the questions and issues of privatization by examining the experiences of Chile and Poland, countries that are remarkably different in many respects. But their per capita income rankings are similar (the 1995 World Bank *World Development Report* ranked Poland 52nd in per capita income among countries with at least 1 million population, and Chile 38th). Much more important, these countries have had perhaps the two most sweeping privatization experiences to date and serve to represent the two types of privatization experiences we may expect to see implemented in postcommunist and noncommunist developing countries. The experiences of Chile and Poland also serve to illustrate the complexity of the privatization process and the development issues it raises.

Chile

For historically complex reasons, Chile, which pioneered the privatization movement, is well positioned economically and socially for successful long-term growth. It has a strongly market-based economy, in which government competently plays an active but targeted role in the areas in which it is most needed.

The privatization program in Chile has been the most far-reaching in the Third World. It is an integral part of a major socioeconomic and political transformation that began with the 1973 military coup that brought the Pinochet dictatorship to power. Chile has changed from an economy with pervasive government intervention in the early 1970s to become one of the most open and most market-oriented economies of Latin America. Every market (except the labor market) was largely freed from government control. Over an 18-year period, some 550 firms employing 5% of the country's workforce were privatized.

Even under Pinochet, Chile was never purely laissez-faire. Some hidden subsidies and inducements remained, including a mas-

sive government rescue of the financial sector, amounting to 4.6% of GDP from 1982 to 1986. Many banks that had been privatized in the preceding years had to be renationalized in the 1982 financial crash. In privatization itself, subsidies were offered to the private sector through the sale of assets at little more than half their real value. Fishing companies were privatized in the 1970s, but an extensive government role remained, including export-market development, technical assistance, and ecosystem regulation. Agriculture is the sector in which the lion's share of new nontraditional exports have been realized, especially in fruits. There the government has played an active role in targeting potential export sectors, providing infrastructure, developing markets, supporting research, and providing extension services to help realize higher productivity.

This has represented a modest but successful sector policy and has played an important part in the favorable growth performance of the late 1980s. But it remains unclear if policies for exports of fruit and other specialty farm and forest products centering around larger farms (*latifundios* and agribusiness) provide a sufficient development strategy in the longer term. Most farms are very small, and most seem to have benefited little, though it is interesting that in the sugarbeet sector, agribusinesses have found it in their interest to provide small farmers with a secure market and a source of credit and technical assistance.

Chile's new democratic government is continuing a broad commitment to market-oriented reforms but is also responding to the apparent need to expand the supporting government role. Thus privatization has an important role to play in most developing countries but must be understood in context and does not succeed by simply banishing government from the economic scene.

Privatization in Chile proceeded over several overlapping stages. In 1974 and 1975, some 360 firms that had been nationalized in the early 1970s were returned to their previous owners; most of the rest of these were reprivatized by 1978. This was far easier to carry out than the privatizations of long-term SOEs carried out in subsequent years (which are more the type that Eastern Europe faces in such daunting numbers). Of the 110 enterprises divested in 1975–1983, a large share were SOEs founded under the early-1970s Allende regime. Many others were existing private companies in which that government had bought shares. From 1978 to 1981, privatization of social services took place; the government officially continued to provide social services only for the poorest groups and focused on subsidizing demand rather than supply. By 1981, public enterprises represented 24% of GDP, down from 39% in 1973.

Chile experienced rapid growth in the 1976–1981 period, following three years of severe recession. But this expansion had the earmarks of a speculative bubble, including wild stock speculation. After the bubble burst in 1982, stocks crashed (falling 36% in 1982 and an additional 33% in 1983); there was a huge wave of bankruptcies, including one-fifth of all manufacturing companies employing 50 workers or more; and unemployment reached 24%.

In 1983–1986, many enterprises "rescued" (nationalized) by Pinochet in the 1982–1983 financial crash were reprivatized. Eight of the 15 largest corporations in Chile were privatized in the 1980s.

The renewed growth of the late 1980s had a qualitatively different character, owing to more judicious regulation of the financial system and macroeconomic management. Since 1986, at least 27 large industrial enterprises that had been in state hands for a longer time were privatized.

But the country has experienced an apparently permanent drop in the share of manufacturing in GDP, especially in sectors not intensive in their use of local natural resources. This makes its experience to date different from the long-run top-performing countries such as South Korea and Taiwan and may pose a challenge if opportunities for productivity gains are concentrated in manufacturing sectors; however, in Chile, manufacturing companies were often "infant" import substitution industries, which were, to say the least, not growing up very fast.

Privatization from the mid-1980s on was achieved through public auction, negotiation, sales to pension funds, "popular capitalism" (to small investors), and "labor capitalism" (to employees). Sales of the latter two types represented about 20% of privatization. Even SOEs not slated for privatization were subject to major internal reorganization, with the result that efficiency and profitability increased.

Popular capitalism was intended to spread ownership among many small individual investors, in part to increase popularity and acceptance of privatization. To become eligible for generous discounts, participants had to be taxpayers with no back taxes owed. Two major banks, Banco de Chile and Banco de Santiago, were privatized under this plan.

Under labor capitalism, workers could acquire a percentage of shares in their own companies, up to the value of 50% of a worker's pension fund that could be received in advance for this purpose. Retirement funds could be used as collateral for below-market government loans to buy additional shares. At retirement, workers could elect to trade these shares back for the value of their pension fund, so this provided the workers an essentially riskless investment. About 21,000 workers, 35% of those eligible, took part; other shares were purchased by groups of workers organized as investment societies. Between 1985 and 1990, a total of 15 SOEs were sold using some employee ownership, including three that became 100% employee-owned. Three others became 44%, 33%, and 31% employee owned, respectively, and the remaining nine had an average of about 12% employee ownership. These privatizations have been remarkably successful; not only have productivity and share values risen substantially, but employment too has risen. It remains to be seen whether significant employee ownership will continue in these firms into the future or if workers will resell their shares and ownership will become more concentrated among outsider investors. But for now the evidence is that employees are working more conscientiously (e.g., taking better care of company equipment), and in some cases firms are allowing workers to use greater judgment on the job.

An example is the National Computer and Information Corporation, which had long been performing poorly as an SOE and in which no investors except its employees showed any interest in buying. The privatization agency helped the employees arrange special financing. The surprising early results are that the company is turning around financially despite competition from the major multinational computer corporations.

To date, the conventional wisdom that EO may decrease attractiveness to foreign investors has not been borne out. An example is the National Sugar Industry in Chile, privatized in 1986, in which workers hold 45% of the shares. Despite this, several foreign investors purchased good-sized minority shares, and it is a highly regarded investment. Many firms are familiar with employee stock ownership plans (ESOPs) and similar programs in their own countries and may have introduced ESOPs themselves or seen firms with which they are familiar do so, precisely to improve labor relations and efficiency. In cases where foreign investors worry that the existing labor force has uncertain attitudes and loyalties or that the labor force views change with some apprehension, partial EO may be an ideal vehicle for the transition. Perhaps most important, employee stock purchases represent a positive market signal to other potential investors from a group possessing unique insider information. A public

policy encouraging some privatization to employees and providing accepted structures and conventions for this to occur may provide a valuable incentive for foreign investment.

Employee ownership may accomplish much to ensure the political viability of privatization; certainly it is viewed as reducing resistance to privatization by employees, and broadened share ownership among the public, which includes employees, is often a basic political goal of regimes engaged in privatization and marketization. Privatization to employees may jump-start stock markets by providing broad-based share ownership. Employee-owners may in many cases wish at some future time to diversify, a source of demand for transaction services. Ultimately, reduced politicization of the ever-difficult question of the role of government in the economy also improves capacity for effective sector policy.

Employee ownership in privatization may also help countries reduce the drastic increases in inequality that often accompany liberalization. In a quarter century of almost constant "structural adjustment" in Chile, the top 10% of the population has gained, but the bottom 90% remains worse off. Overall, poverty increased, but resources targeted to the poorest of the poor played a role in mitigating absolute poverty. In the late 1980s, high growth rates were finally reached, only to be followed by a slowdown at the start of the 1990s as the overheated economy cooled. Poverty and inequality are major concerns of the new democratic government. The finance minister, Alejandro Foxley, was one of the most able critics of the excesses of the ultra-orthodox economic policies under Pinochet.

Indicators are conflicting, and Chile's wild swings of expansion and contraction make an accurate assessment of long-term trends difficult. But it would appear that Chile today is in an excellent position to move toward maturity. The country first placed a strong emphasis on education and human development in the 1920s; superior conditions of basic education and health survived the dictatorship period, and Chile is enjoying the fruits of this long-term program today. Despite some errors of excess, for which a price was paid in the form of the financial crash, the modern market institutions that are the foundation of a developed economy were successfully created under the Pinochet regime. It is hoped that other countries can follow the constructive features of its example within the democratic process. The new democratic government is wisely giving greater attention to concerns for equity, reversing the cutbacks in social spending of the Pinochet regime by expanding programs in education, basic health care, nutrition, housing, water, and sewage. Tax reform passed in the first year of President Aylwin's government raised $1 billion for social projects and increased pay for schoolteachers. The government is also expanding public investment in other vital infrastructure such as roads, ports, and irrigation systems. And it is beginning to diversify the scope of its moderate industrial and export policies to assist development of manufacturing sectors. A first in Latin America, Chile seems to have permanently tamed inflation. It was only 12.3% in 1993. The country has traveled a rocky road to get there, but today the outlook for Chile's extensively privatized economy, supported where needed by a constructive government role, is very bright indeed.

Poland

Despite serious socioeconomic problems, Chile began privatization with well-established legal and accounting frameworks; fully functioning labor, capital, and product markets; and many formal and informal socioeconomic institutions that are taken for granted in market economies. But in Eastern Europe, these background institutions had been systematically suppressed under communism.

To get a market economy under way, in early 1990 the Polish government launched a five-part radical stabilization plan composed of price deregulation, introduction of a convertible currency, wage controls, increased interest rates, and budget-balancing measures. This was followed in the second half of 1990 by intensive legislative and administrative efforts to prepare for across-the-board privatization. GDP in Poland fell drastically in the early transition to a market economy, 11.6% in 1990; and unemployment reached high levels. The World Bank found that a significant part of the declines was attributable to collapse of Soviet–Eastern European trade agreements; while reorganizing its internal economy, Poland has had to reorder its external trading economy as well. But by the end of 1992, there were signs that the economic freefall had come to an end.

The Polish privatization plan was adopted in the summer of 1990. The first step in privatizing state enterprises, "commercialization," often requires the approval of the relevant ministry, management and employees to set up a joint-stock company that can be sold. The stock is valuated independently, and workers are then allowed to purchase up to 20% of the stock at half price. In capital-intensive companies, a subsidy limit based on the prior year's wages in the company may be set, making somewhat less than 20% of the stock eligible. This is done to avoid overly concentrating these subsidies among a few lucky employees.

An alternative strategy that circumvented administrative procedures, applying mainly to smaller firms, is "privatization through liquidation." This procedure permitted leveraged buyouts that could include substantial employee and management ownership. The process is initiated when the firm's managing director and the employees' council (an elected representative body) commissions a "preprivatization financial analysis." If financial conditions appear favorable, the firm petitions the government ministry that had control over the company under the central-planning system, which offers an opinion on the merits of the analysis and suggests a strategy for privatization. The employees' council or the assembly of all employees in the firm may then vote to modify the agreement. The old SOE is abolished, and the new firm buys some assets but normally leases others back from the state. The value of these leased assets is determined at the time of reorganization and does not change over the life of the contract (even to adjust for inflation). This constitutes a substantial subsidy to the new owners.

But of some 250 companies representing some 10% of employment commercialized by mid-1992, only about 10% were fully privatized. And only about 175 firms had self-privatized by mid-1992, by which time the government was considering a large-scale privatization plan that would organize several hundred companies representing about 10% of industrial employment into a kind of closed-end mutual fund.

Percentages in other Eastern European post-communist countries are similar. Hungary has probably had the most extensive experience, owing to its "spontaneous privatization" activity, in which managers or employee representatives sell the firm at a price and to a bidder of their own choosing. This has enabled privatization to proceed rapidly but has been viewed as unfair and perhaps damaging to the national interest. Some managers have sold firms to multinational corporations under what have since been characterized as sweetheart deals, in which the foreign firms sometimes appeared to have effectively offered the selling managers lifetime sinecures as a reward. But to speed privatization, Hungary has again allowed self-privatizations, and by mid-1992, some 300 small and medium-sized enterprises had privatized "spontaneously."

Much time, effort, and money has been spent trying to devise some optimally efficient and equitable privatization scheme. But the task of privatization in Eastern Europe by any means is daunting, and the countries have few resources to spare. The Polish privatization ministry has only 200 employees. This compares with 3,500 in the Treuhandanstalt, in charge of privatization in the former East Germany. Any form of privatization is likely to be perceived as unfair or inequitable by at least some members of society.

In Poland, Deputy Prime Minister and Minister of Finance Leszek Balcerowicz had opposed employee ownership as a vehicle of privatization. But he then stated that if he had it to do over again, he would have just given all the companies to their managers and workers, either to run the firms or to sell them; in that way, privatization would have occurred with maximum speed, and market incentives would have taken over. In effect, the previous policy encouraged anything but extensive employee ownership through means such as liquidation sales and citizen vouchers. Reasons for this antipathy are varied but include a fear of strikes and an imagined association of employee ownership with the type of workers' councils set up in factories in the waning years of communist rule, in a last-ditch attempt to retain power.

A smokescreen for party control until the mid-1980s, the workers' councils finally gained some real property rights in Poland and in several other post-communist countries in the 1980s. A privatization strategy based on the free-market-oriented, conservative property rights school of thought as advocated, for example, by Nobel laureate James Buchanan would be to recognize de facto property rights, legalize them, and then let markets spring up around these rights. Voucher strategies instead cancel de facto property rights and return ownership to the government, which is in turn expected to give these rights to citizens. Yet in many cases, the government is largely comprised of the old guard, who would prefer to slow this process and retain control. Privatizing to employees as a whole would also prevent the property rights from being usurped solely by the top Communist Party officials or *nomenklatura* who ran the firm under communism. Although this approach would succeed in creating property rights, it would probably backfire politically.

Summary

Despite the limitations on devising an optimal plan for privatization and market development, the case studies strongly suggest that privatization is best not implemented as an isolated part of a development strategy but rather as part of a general program for market development. The benefits of privatization will not occur automatically. The role of the state in the economy becomes significantly modified but is certainly not eliminated. The supporting institutions of the market will have to grow and develop. The proper balance will not be easy to find.

Some lessons are already clear. It makes a difference under what conditions state ownership came into being. Privatization is easiest when state ownership resulted from a historical accident rather than as a systematic policy or as a result of specific selections of a few "commanding heights" industries intended to play a specific role in the development process. A good example is Bangladesh, the subject of one of the poverty case studies at the end of Part Two, in which the large state-owned sector resulted from the abandonment of factories by Pakistanis fleeing during the civil war or shortly thereafter; Bangladesh has had one of the largest-scale privatization programs. Another example is Mexico, which incidentally acquired many bank-owned companies when banks were nationalized in the financial crisis of 1982. This has provided part of the basis for that country's systematic privatization program. Privatization is also easier when SOEs started as nationalizations, especially recent ones, as in the case of Chile's reprivatizations of the 1970s; when markets are already well developed; when there is a strong political will for privatization; and when ordinary employees and citizens perceive themselves to have a positive stake in privatization. All of these factors apply to a large extent to Chile. Recent privatizations in South Korea, also involving an employee ownership role, provide another good case in point. Privatization is most difficult in post-communist countries such as Poland, where none of these facilitating characteristics seem to be present.

Sources: World Bank, *Techniques of Privatization of State-owned Enterprises*, World Bank Technical Paper No. 90 (Washington, D.C.: World Bank, 1988); Zejlko Bogetic and Michael Conte, "Privatizing East European economies: A critique," unpublished manuscript; Stephen C. Smith, "Employee ownership in privatization in developing countries," unpublished manuscript; Alejandro Foxley, *Latin American Experiments in Neoconservative Economics* (Berkeley: University of California, 1983); Inter-American Development Bank, Chile, *Socioeconomic Report, August 1991*; James Buchanan, lecture papers; *Financial Times*, November 10, 1992; seminar presentation by Leszek Balcerowicz, Harvard University, March 25, 1992; and various World Bank documents.

Glossary

This glossary is designed to cover most of the major concepts and organizations discussed in the text. It includes all end of chapter "Concepts for Review" as well as general economic terms and concepts relevant to studying development economics. This should be especially helpful to non-economics students. Words that appear in *italics* in any definition are themselves defined elsewhere in the glossary.

Abatement technologies   Technologies designed to reduce pollution emissions, such as industrial scrubbers or catalytic converters.

Absolute advantage   If country A can produce more of a commodity with the same amount of real resources than country B (i.e., at a lower absolute *unit cost*), country A is said to have absolute advantage over country B. See also *comparative advantage*.

Absolute poverty   A situation where a population or section of a population is able to meet only its bare *subsistence* essentials of food, clothing, and shelter to maintain minimum *levels of living*. See also *international poverty line* and *subsistence economy*.

Absorptive capacity   The ability of a country to absorb foreign private or public financial assistance (to use the funds in a productive manner); also, the capacity of an ecosystem to assimilate potential pollutants—for example, the forests of the earth have a limited capacity to absorb additional CO_2 produced as a by-product of the burning of fossil fuels.

Accounting price   See *shadow price*.

Adjustment assistance   Public financial assistance provided to workers and industries hurt by imports of lower-priced foreign goods. Such assistance allows them to "adjust" to a new occupation during a transitional period.

Advanced capitalism   An *economic system* characterized by private ownership but with a major role played by the *public sector*. Most developed *market economies* like those in North America, Western Europe, Japan, and Australia are examples of advanced capitalism.

African Development Bank   A regional bank, established in 1966, to assist independent African countries through the provision of *loans* and *technical assistance*.

Agenda 21   The primary document discussed at the United Nations Conference on Environment and Development in June 1992, which outlines the areas for international cooperation in promoting environmentally sustainable growth and development.

Age structure of the population   The age composition of a given population. For example, in *LDCs*, the age structure of the population is typified by a large portion of population under 15 years old, a slightly smaller proportion aged between 15 and 45 years, and a very small proportion above 45 years old.

Aggregate demand   A measure of the real purchasing power of the community. Commonly referred to as the total effective demand or total expenditure, it normally comprises private consumption (*C*), private and public investment (*I*), government expenditure (*G*), plus net exports (*X − M*).

Aggregate growth model Formal economic model describing growth of the economy on one or at most a few sectors and variables. Examples include *Harrod-Domar* and *Solow* models.

Agrarian system The pattern of land distribution, ownership, and management, also the social and *institutional* structure of the agrarian economy. Many Latin American and Asian agrarian systems are characterized by concentrations of large tracts of land owned by a few powerful landlords. *Rural development* in many LDCs may require extensive reforms of the existing agrarian system.

Agricultural extension services Services offered to farmers, usually by the government, in the form of transmitting information, new ideas, methods, and advice about, for instance, the use of fertilizers, control of pests and weeds, appropriate machinery, soil conservation methods, and simple accounting, in a bid to stimulate high *farm yields*.

Agricultural labor productivity The level of agricultural output per unit of labor input, usually measured as output per worker-hour or worker-year. It is very low in LDCs compared to developed countries. See also *labor productivity* and *farm yields*.

Agricultural mechanization The extensive use of machinery in farm production activities, thereby reducing the amount of labor input necessary to produce a given level of output. See also *laborsaving technological progress*.

Agricultural sector The portion of the economy comprising agriculture, forestry, hunting, and fishing.

AID See *United States Agency for International Development* and *foreign aid*.

AIDS (Autoimmune Deficiency Syndrome) A deadly virus that is spreading throughout the developing world and transmitted predominantly through unprotected sexual contact. It is especially prevalent in Africa. See also *HIV*.

Aid weariness *Attitude* among some donor-country politicians and populations that foreign aid has been unsuccessful and that they are tired of giving it.

Allocative efficiency Producing the maximum output possible, given quantities of *inputs* and using cost-minimizing techniques of production.

Amortization Gradual payoff of a *loan* principal.

Andean Group A *customs union* formed in 1969 by Bolivia, Colombia, Ecuador, Peru, and Venezuela in an effort to promote *economic integration*, coordinate industrial development, regulate foreign investment, and maintain a common *external tariff* among the member countries.

Appropriate technology Technology that is appropriate for existing factor endowments. For example, a technology employing a higher proportion of labor relative to other factors in a labor-abundant economy is usually more appropriate than one that uses smaller labor proportions relative to other factors. See also *factor-price distortions, principle of economy*, and *neoclassical price-incentive model*.

Arab Bank for Economic Development in Africa   A development bank established in 1975 by Arab countries to assist non-Arab African countries through the provisions of *loans* and *technical assistance*.

Asian Development Bank (ADB)   A regional development bank founded in 1964 whose major objective is to assist the development of Asian nations through the provision of *loans* and *technical assistance*.

Asset ownership   The ownership of land, *physical capital* (factories, buildings, machinery, etc.), *human capital*, and financial resources that generate income for owners. The distribution of asset ownership is a major determinant of the distribution of personal income in any nonsocialist society. See also *income distribution*.

Attitude   A state of mind or feeling of an individual, group, or society regarding issues such as material gain, hardwork, saving for the future, sharing wealth, etc. See also *values*.

Autarchy   A *closed economy* that attempts to be completely self-reliant.

Average product   Total output or product divided by total factor input (e.g., the average product of labor is equal to total output divided by the total amount of labor used to produce that output). See *agricultural labor productivity* and *marginal product*.

Balanced trade   A situation in which the value of a country's exports and the value of its imports are equal.

Balance of payments   A summary statement of a nation's financial transactions with the outside world. See also *current account, capital account*, and *cash account*.

Barter transactions   The trading of goods directly for other goods in economies not fully monetized.

Basic education   The attainment of literacy, arithmetic competence, and elementary vocational skills.

Basic needs   A term used by the *International Labor Organization* to describe the basic goods and services (food, shelter, clothing, sanitation, education, etc.) necessary for a minimum standard of living.

Basic science and technological innovation   Basic science refers to a systematic scientific and objective investigation aimed at bringing into existence new knowledge or tools; technological innovation has to do with the application of *inventions* of basic science (such as the new tools or knowledge) to perform tasks in a more efficient way.

Basic transfer   Net foreign-exchange inflow or outflow related to a country's international borrowing. The quantitative difference between the net capital inflow (gross inflow minus amortization on past debt) and interest payments on existing accumulated debt.

"Big push" theory of development   Theory stating that all that LDCs require to take off into a period of self-sustaining *economic growth* is a massive investment program designed to promote rapid *industrialization* and the building up of *economic infrastructure*.

Bilateral assistance   See *foreign aid.*

Biodiversity   The variety of life forms within an ecosystem.

Biomass fuels   Any combustible organic matter that may be used as fuel, such as firewood, dung, or agricultural residues.

Birthrate   See *crude birthrate.*

Black market   A situation in which there is illegal selling of goods at prices above a legal maximum set by the government. It occurs due to relative *scarcity* of the goods concerned and the existence of an excess demand for them at the established price. See also *rationing* and *exchange control.*

Bottlenecks   Sectors in the economy where the development process leads to a more rapid expansion of demand than supply in the goods or factor markets.

Brady Plan   A program, launched in March 1989, designed to reduce the size of outstanding LDC commercial debt through private debt forgiveness procured in exchange for IMF and World Bank debt guarantees and greater LDC adherence to the terms of *conditionality.* Named after former U.S. Treasury Secretary Nicholas Brady.

Brain drain   The emigration of highly educated and skilled professional and technical manpower from the developing to the developed countries.

Buffer stocks   Stocks of commodities held by countries or international organizations to moderate the commodities' price fluctuations.

Calorie requirement   The calories needed to sustain the population at normal levels of activity and health, taking account of its age and sex distributions, average body weights, and physical environment.

Calorie supply per capita   The calorie equivalent of the available food supplies in a country divided by its total population.

Capital   See *physical capital* and *human capital.*

Capital account   The portion of a country's *balance of payments* that shows the volume of *private foreign investment* and public *grants* and *loans* that flow into and out of a country over a given period, usually one year. See also *current account* and *cash account.*

Capital accumulation   Increasing a country's stock of real *capital* (net investment in fixed assets). To increase the production of capital goods necessitates a reduction in the production of consumer goods. Economic development depends to a large extent on the rate of capital accumulation.

Capital-augmenting technological progress   *Technological progress* that raises the productivity of capital by *innovation* and *inventions.*

Capital flight   Transfer of funds to a foreign country by a local citizen or business.

Capital-intensive technique   A process of production that uses a higher proportion of capital relative to other *factors of production* such as labor or land per unit output.

Capitalism   See *pure market capitalism* and *advanced capitalism.*

Capital-labor ratio   The number of units of *capital* per unit of labor. In *traditional neoclassical growth theory*, lower capital-labor ratios in LDCs should mean higher returns to new investment and greater flows of capital from MDCs to LDCs. But see *new growth theory*.

Capital-output ratio   A ratio that shows the units of *capital* required to produce a unit of output over a given period of time. See *Harrod-Domar growth model*.

Capital-saving technological progress   *Technological progress* that results from some *invention* or *innovation* that facilitates the achievement of higher output levels using the same quantity of capital inputs.

Capital stock   The total amount of physical goods existing at a particular time that have been produced for use in the production of other goods (including services).

Cartel   An organization of producers agreeing to limit the output of their product in an effort to raise prices and profits.

Cash account   The balancing portion of a country's *balance of payments*, showing how cash balances (*foreign reserves*) and short-term financial claims have changed in response to *current account* and *capital account* transactions.

Cash crops   Crops produced entirely for the market (e.g., coffee, tea, cacao, cotton, rubber, pyrethrum, jute, wheat).

Casual employment   Employment on an ad hoc basis without regular hours or a wage contract; most often found in the *informal sector*.

Center   In *dependence* theory, the economic developed world.

Central American Common Market (CACM)   An economic union formed in 1960 and disbanded in the 1970s. It consisted of five Central American nations: Costa Rica, El Salvador, Guatemala, Honduras, and Nicaragua.

Central bank   Major financial institution responsible for issuing currency, managing foreign reserves, implementing monetary policy, and providing banking services to the government and *commercial banks*.

Centralized planning   The determination by the state of what shall be produced and how *factors of production* shall be allocated among different uses. Central planning is done by the central government and then dictated to various sections in the economy.

Ceteris paribus   A Latin expression widely used in economics, meaning "all else being equal," that is, all other variables are held constant.

Character of economic growth   The distributive implications of the process of *economic growth*; for example, participation in the growth process or asset ownership. In other words, how that *economic growth* is achieved and who benefits.

Child death rate   The number of deaths among children 1 to 4 years of age per 1,000 children of that age in a given year.

Clean technologies   Technologies that by design produce less waste and use resources more efficiently.

Closed economy   An economy in which there are no foreign trade transactions or any other form of economic contacts with the rest of the world. See also *autarchy* and *inward-looking development policies*.

Cognitive skills   The ability to perceive and understand abstract concepts and think logically, to have knowledge or be aware of a range of relevant information.

Collective self-reliance   See *self-reliance*.

Collectivism   An *economic system* in which the means of production are owned by collective agencies, such as the government or community, and not by private individuals or business firms.

Collusion   An agreement among sellers of a commodity (or commodities) to set a common price or share their commodity market.

Command socialism   An *economic system* where all *resources* are state-owned and their allocation and degree of utilization are determined by the centralized decisions of planning authorities rather than by a *price system*. The USSR was the most outstanding example of a command socialist economy.

Commercial bank   A financial institution that provides a wide range of services, including accepting deposits and making *loans* for commercial purposes.

Commercial policy   Policy encompassing instruments of trade protection employed by countries to foster industrial promotion, export diversification, employment creation, and other desired development-oriented strategies. They include *tariffs*, *quotas*, and *subsidies*.

Commodity terms of trade   See *terms of trade*.

Common external tariff   A tariff imposed by members of a *customs union, common market*, or *economic community* on imports from nonmembers.

Common market   A form of *economic integration* in which there is free internal trade, a common *tariff*, and the free movement of labor and capital among partner states. The *European Union* is an example. See also *customs union* and *free-trade area*.

Common property resource   A resource that is publicly owned and allocated under a system of unrestricted access.

Commonwealth of Independent States (CIS)   A coalition of 11 former Soviet republics, including Russia, that are technically independent but maintain a degree of economic and political integration.

Commune   A cooperative farm or other collectively organized unit.

Comparative advantage   A country has a comparative advantage over another if in producing a commodity it can do so at a relatively lower *opportunity cost* in terms of the forgone alternative commodities that could be produced. Taking two countries, A and B, each producing two commodities, X and Y, country A is also said to have comparative advantage in the production of X if its *absolute advantage* margin is greater or its absolute disadvantage is less in X than in Y.

Complementary investments   Investments that complement and facilitate other productive factors—for example, capital with labor, education and training of unskilled workers, pesticides and fertilizer on farmland.

Complementary resources   *Factors of production* that are necessarily used along with others to produce a given output or to accomplish a specific task; for example, worker-hours of farm labor are complementary to a hectare of land in the production of maize; machinery and equipment are complementary to labor in the construction of a road.

Comprador   A local labor recruiter or purchasing agent employed by a foreign firm.

Comprador **groups**   In *dependence* theory, local elites who act as fronts for foreign investors.

Comprehensive plan   An *economic plan* that sets targets to cover all the major sectors of the national economy.

Concessional terms   Terms for the extension of credit that are more favorable to the borrower than those available on the money markets.

Conditionality   The requirement imposed by the *International Monetary Fund* that a borrowing country undertake fiscal, monetary, and international commercial reforms as a condition to receiving a *loan* for *balance of payments* difficulties.

Consumer sovereignty   The notion central to neoclassical economic theory that consumers determine what and how much shall be produced in an economy. The free play of the *price system* and the *market mechanism* is then assumed to equilibrate consumer demand with producer supply of that commodity.

Consumer surplus   Excess utility over price derived by consumers because of negative sloping demand curve; measured as triangular area under demand curve above price line.

Consumption diseconomies   Problems (costs) that occur to individuals or a society as a whole as a result of the unpopular consumption habits of another individual. Examples include alcoholism, poor individual hygiene, and drug addiction.

Consumption economies   Advantages (benefits) that accrue to individuals or a society as a whole as a result of increases in the consumption of certain types of goods or services by other individuals (e.g., education, health care).

Consumption possibility line   In international *free-trade* theory, a locus of points showing the highest possible consumption combinations that can be attained as a result of trade. Graphically, the consumption possibility line is represented by the international price line at its tangency to the domestic *production possibility curve* of a country.

Cost-benefit analysis   A basic tool of economic analysis in which the actual and potential *private* and *social costs* of various economic decisions are weighed against actual and potential *private* and *social benefits*. Decisions or projects that yield the highest ratio of benefit to cost are usually thought to be most desirable. See also *project appraisal*.

Cost-push inflation *Inflation* that results primarily from the upward pressure of production costs, usually because of rising raw material prices (e.g., oil) or excessive wage increases resulting from trade union pressures. See also *demand-pull inflation* and *structural inflation*.

Creditor nation A nation with a *balance of payments* surplus.

Crowding-out phenomenon LDC fears that the foreign aid needs of former Soviet and Eastern European nations will divert funds away from them.

Crude birthrate The number of children born alive each year per 1,000 population (a crude birthrate of 20 per 1,000 is the same as a 2% increase). See also *fertility rate* and *death rate*.

Curative medicine Medical care that focuses on curing rather than preventing disease; requires extensive availability of hospitals and clinics. See also *preventive medicine*.

Currency board Form of *central bank* that issues domestic currency for foreign exchange at fixed rates.

Currency substitution The use of foreign currency (e.g., U.S. dollars) as a medium of exchange in place of or along with the local currency (e.g., Mexican pesos).

Current account The portion of a *balance of payments* that portrays the market value of a country's "visible" (e.g., commodity trade) and "invisible" (e.g., shipping services) exports and imports with the rest of the world. See also *capital account* and *cash account*.

Current account balance The difference between (1) exports of goods and services plus inflows of unrequited official and private transfers and (2) imports of goods and services plus unrequited transfers to the rest of the world. Included in this figure are all interest payments on external public and publicly guaranteed debt.

Customs union A form of *economic integration* in which two or more nations agree to free all internal trade while levying a *common external tariff* on all nonmember countries. See also *common market* and *free-trade area*.

Death rate The yearly number of deaths per 1,000 population—an annual crude death rate of 15 per 1,000 would involve 1.5% of the population. See also *crude birthrate* and *infant mortality rate*.

Debt-for-equity swap A mechanism used by indebted LDCs to reduce the real value of external debt by exchanging equity in domestic companies (stocks) or fixed-interest obligations of the government (bonds) for private foreign debt at large discounts—for example, replacing $100 million of debt obligations with $50 million of equity claims against domestic real assets.

Debt-for-nature swap The exchange of foreign debt held by an organization for a larger quantity of domestic debt that is used to finance the preservation of a natural resource or environment in the debtor country.

Debtor nation A nation with a *balance of payments* deficit.

Debtors' cartel   Group of LDC debtors who join together to bargain as a group with creditors.

Debt outstanding   The amount of public and publicly guaranteed *loans* that has been disbursed, net of canceled loan commitments and repayments of principal.

Debt renegotiation   Changing the terms of existing *loans*, usually by extending repayment dates without increases in nominal interest rates.

Debt repudiation   1980s MDC fear that LDCs would decide not to pay debt obligations.

Debt service   The sum of interest payments and repayments of principal on external public and publicly guaranteed debt.

Debt-service ratio   The ratio of interest and principal payments due in a year to export receipts for that year.

Decentralized planning   Regionalized or sectoral planning as opposed to planning at the center. See *centralized planning*.

Decile   A 10% portion of any numerical quantity; a population divided into deciles would be divided into 10 equal numeric groups. See also *quintile*.

Decreasing costs   If *increasing returns* exist, a given proportionate change in output will require a smaller proportionate change in quantities of factor inputs, thus implying a fall in cost per unit of output. In short, a fall in average costs of production as output expands.

Deficit   Excess of expenditures over receipts. See *trade deficit*.

Deficit expenditure   Amount by which government expenditure exceeds realized tax revenues. Deficit expenditure is normally financed by borrowed funds, and its major objective is to stimulate economic activity by increasing *aggregate demand*.

Deforestation   The clearing of forested land. Deforestation is generally divided into two broad categories, tropical deforestation, which involves the clearing of dense rain forests in regions with high levels of precipitation, usually for agricultural purposes, and dry forest clearing, which occurs in areas with less precipitation, where most trees are cut for firewood.

Demand curve   A graphical representation of the quantities of a commodity or resource that would be bought over a range of prices at a particular time, when all other prices and incomes are held constant. When demand curves of all consumers in the market are aggregated, a market demand curve is derived, showing the total amount of goods that consumers are willing to purchase at each price.

Demand-pull inflation   *Inflation* that arises because of the existence of excess Keynesian *aggregate demand*, when total effective demand exceeds the productive capacity (aggregate supply) of the economy.

Demographic transition   The phasing-out process of population growth rates from a virtually stagnant growth stage characterized by high *birthrates* and *death rates*, through a rapid-growth stage with high birthrates and low death rates, to a stable, low-growth stage in which both birth and death rates are low.

Demonstration effects   The effects of transfers of foreign ways of life on nationals of a country. Such effects are mainly cultural and attitudinal, including consumption habits, modes of dressing, and approaches to education, leisure, and recreation.

Dependence   A corollary of *dominance*; a situation in which the LDCs have to rely on developed-country domestic and international economic policy to stimulate their own *economic growth*. Dependence can also mean that the LDCs adopt developed-country education systems, technology, economic and political systems, attitudes, consumption patterns, dress, etc.

Dependency burden   The proportion of the total population aged 0 to 15 and 65+, which is considered economically unproductive and therefore not counted in the labor force. In many LDCs, the population under the age of 15 accounts for almost half of the total population, thus posing a burden to the generally small productive labor force and to the government, which has to allocate *resources* on such things as education, public health, and housing for the consumption of people who don't contribute to production.

Depreciation   The gradual decline over time in the value or price of one currency in terms of another as a result of market forces of supply and demand. See *devaluation and exchange rate*.

Derived demand   In education, demand for schooling derived from the ultimate demand for modern-sector jobs requiring a school certificate.

Desertification   The transformation of a region into dry barren land with little or no capacity to sustain life without an artificial source of water. Desertification frequently involves the loss of topsoil, which leads to the permanent loss of cultivability.

Devaluation   A lowering of the official *exchange rate* between one country's currency and all other currencies. See *depreciation*.

Development   The process of improving the quality of all human lives. Three equally important aspects of development are (1) raising people's living levels—their incomes and consumption levels of food, medical services, education, etc., through relevant *economic growth* processes; (2) creating conditions conducive to the growth of people's *self-esteem* through the establishment of social, political, and *economic systems* and *institutions* that promote human dignity and respect; and (3) increasing people's *freedom* by enlarging the range of their choice variables, as by increasing varieties of consumer goods and services.

Development banks   Specialized public and private *financial intermediaries* providing medium- and long-term credit for development projects.

Development economics   The study of how economies are transformed from stagnation to *growth* and from low-income to high-income status. See *development*.

Development plan   The documentation by a government planning agency of the current national economic conditions, proposed public expenditures, likely developments in the *private sector*, a macroeconomic projection of the economy, and a review of government policies. Many LDC's publish five-year development plans to announce their economic objectives to their citizens and others.

Diminishing returns   The principle that if one *factor of production* is fixed and constant additions of other factors are combined with it, the marginal productivity of variable factors will eventually decline.

Direct taxes   Taxes levied directly on individuals or businesses—for example, income tax. See *indirect taxes*.

Discouraged workers   Individuals who would like to work but have abandoned the search for employment following fruitless attempts to find jobs.

Disguised underemployment   A situation in which available work tasks are split among *resources* (typically labor) such that all seem fully employed, but in reality much of their time is spent in unproductive activities.

Disposable income   The income that is available to households for spending and saving after personal income taxes have been deducted.

Distributive share index   See *GNP growth rate index*.

Diversified farming   See *mixed farming*.

Division of labor   Allocation of tasks among workers such that each one engages in tasks that he or she performs most efficiently. Division of labor promotes worker specialization and thereby raises overall *labor productivity*. It has its historical origins in Adam Smith's *Wealth of Nations*.

Dominance   In international affairs, a situation in which the developed countries have much greater power than the less developed countries in decisions affecting important international economic issues, such as the prices of agricultural commodities and raw materials in world markets. See also *dependence*.

Doubling time   Period that a given population takes to increase by its present size. Doubling time is approximated by dividing the numerical growth rate into 72—a population growing at 2% per year will double in size approximately every 36 years.

Dropout rate   Proportion of school-aged children who do not complete a particular school cycle.

Dual exchange rate   Foreign exchange rate system with a highly *overvalued* and legally fixed rate applied to capital and intermediate good imports and a second, illegal (or freely floating) rate for imported consumption goods.

Dualism   The coexistence in one place of two situations or phenomena (one desirable and the other one not) that are mutually exclusive to different groups of society—for example, extreme poverty and affluence, modern and traditional economic sectors, growth and stagnation, university education among a few and mass illiteracy.

Dual price system   A government-operated pricing mechanism whereby producers of, say, a staple crop are paid a different price from the one that consumers (mostly urban consumers) are charged. In short, any system that features one price for sellers and another for buyers.

Earth Summit See *United Nations Conference on Environment and Development (UNCED)*.

East African Community (EAC) An integrated economic grouping of three East African countries—Kenya, Uganda, and Tanzania—established by the Treaty of East African Cooperation of 1967 but eventually dismantled in the mid-1970s. Cooperation took the form of joint administration of a number of common public services (railways, airways, ocean and lake transport, research) and a *customs union* that involved internal *free trade* and a *common external tariff* on imports.

Economic Commission for Africa (ECA) A regional branch of the *United Nations* system located in Addis Ababa, Ethiopia, devoted to the analysis of economic developments and trends in African nations. It publishes statistical bulletins and technical analyses of economic trends in individual countries and groups of countries in various regions of Africa.

Economic Commission for Asia and the Far East (ECAFE) A regional branch of the *United Nations* system located in Bangkok, Thailand, devoted to the technical and statistical analysis of economic developments and trends in the diverse countries of Asia and the Far East.

Economic Commission for Latin America (ECLA) A regional branch of the *United Nations* system located in Santiago, Chile, devoted to the regular publication of technical and statistical analyses of economic trends in Latin America as a whole and in individual Latin American nations.

Economic community *Economic union* of countries seeking to coordinate fiscal and monetary policies as a step toward a common currency. This takes place in addition to maintaining a *common external tariff* and similar commercial policies and to removing restrictions on trade within the community.

Economic Community of West African States (ECOWAS) An economic community, formed in 1975, of 15 West African countries—nine formerly French, five formerly British, and one formerly Portuguese—with a total population of over 195 million and a land area of 6.5 million square miles. It is the largest example of *economic integration* in Africa and includes such countries as Nigeria, Ghana, Burkina Faso, Senegal, Niger, and Chad.

Economic constraint A barrier to the attainment of a set target (e.g., *economic growth*) in a particular period of time. For example, *physical capital* has long been thought of as the major constraint on *economic growth* in LDCs.

Economic disincentives for fertility reduction Economic disadvantages (costs) and risks of having small families, such as parents' insecurity during their old age (no children or too few children to care for them) or shortages of parents' farm labor supply.

Economic efficiency In production, utilizing factors of production in the least-cost combinations; in consumption, allocating expenditures to maximize consumer satisfaction (utility).

Economic good   Any commodity or service that yields utility to an individual or community and must be paid for in money terms in a monetary economy or in kind in a nonmonetary economy.

Economic growth   The steady process by which the productive capacity of the economy is increased over time to bring about rising levels of national output and income.

Economic incentives for fertility reduction   Economic motivations aimed at encouraging parents to limit their families to a specified size. Such economic incentives include free or subsidized education for children of families within the specified family size, free or subsidized medical treatment for small families, and high wages for mothers with few children.

Economic infrastructure   The underlying amount of physical and financial capital embodied in roads, railways, waterways, airways, and other forms of transportation and communication plus water supplies, financial institutions, electricity, and public services such as health and education. The level of infrastructural development in a country is a crucial factor determining the pace and diversity of economic *development*.

Economic integration   The merging to various degrees of the economies and economic policies of two or more countries in a given region. See also *common market, customs union, free-trade area, trade creation*, and *trade diversion*.

Economic plan   A written document containing government policy decisions on how *resources* shall be allocated among various uses so as to attain a targeted rate of *economic growth* over a certain period of time. See *economic planning, centralized planning, planning model*, and *plan implementation*.

Economic planning   A deliberate and conscious attempt by the state to formulate decisions on how the *factors of production* shall be allocated among different uses or industries, thereby determining how much of total *goods* and *services* shall be produced in one or more ensuing periods. See also *economic plan* and *centralized planning*.

Economic policy   A statement of objectives and the methods of achieving these objectives (policy instruments) by government, political party, business concern, etc. Some examples of government economic objectives are maintaining *full employment*, achieving a high rate of *economic growth*, reducing *income inequalities* and regional development inequalities, and maintaining price stability. Policy instruments include fiscal policy, monetary and financial policy, and legislative controls (e.g., price and wage control, rent control).

Economic principles   Basic concepts of economic theory that provide the tools of economic analysis. Examples of economic principles are the principle of substitution, the *principle of economy*, the principle of *diminishing returns*, and the concept of *scarcity*.

Economic system   The organizational and institutional structure of an economy, including the nature of *resource* ownership and control (private versus public). Major economic systems include a *subsistence economy, pure market capitalism,* *advanced capitalism, market socialism, command socialism,* and the *mixed economic systems* that characterize most LDCs.

Economic transition   In Eastern Europe, the structural transformation of highly nationalized socialist economies to privatized capitalist markets.

Economic union   The full integration of two or more economics into a single economic entity. See *economic integration.*

Economic variable   A measure of economic activity such as income, consumption, or price that can take on different quantitative values. Variables are classified either as dependent or independent in accordance with the economic model being used. See *increasing returns* and *returns to scale.*

Economies of scale   Economies of growth resulting from expansion of the scale of productive capacity of a firm or industry, leading to increases in its output and decreases in its cost of production per unit of output.

Economizing spirit   The act of minimizing the real resource costs of producing any level of output. In general, allocating scarce *resources* with great care. See also *optimization principle.*

Economy   See *principle of economy.*

Educational certification   The phenomenon by which particular jobs require specified levels of education. Applicants must produce certificates of completed schooling in the *formal educational system.*

Educational gender gap   Male-female differences in school access and completion.

Effective rate of protection   Degree of protection on *value added* as opposed to final f.o.b. price of imported product—usually higher than *nominal rate of protection.*

Efficiency   See *allocative efficiency, economic efficiency,* and *technical efficiency.*

Efficiency wage   The notion that modern-sector urban employers pay a higher wage than the *equilibrium wage rate* in order to attract a higher-quality workforce or to obtain higher productivity on the job.

Elasticity of demand   See *price elasticity of demand* and *income elasticity of demand.*

Elasticity of factor substitution   A measure of the degree of substitutability between *factors of production* in any given production process when relative factor prices change.

Emerging-country stock markets   Equity markets used to finance private corporations in newly industrializing countries (NICs) such as Mexico, Malaysia, and South Korea.

Empowerment of women   The idea that giving women power over their economic, social, and *reproductive choices* will raise their status, promote development, and reduce population growth.

Enclave economies   LDC economies in which there are small pockets of economically developed regions (often due to the presence of colonial or foreign firms engaged in plantation and mining activities) with the rest of the larger outlying areas experiencing very little progress. See also *dualism.*

Endogenous growth   *Economic growth* generated by factors within the production process (e.g., *economies of scale, increasing returns,* induced technological change) as opposed to outside (exogenous) factors such as increases in population. See *new growth theory.*

Energy consumption per dollar of GDP   The ratio of total energy consumption of GDP in constant dollars. This indicator shows the intensity of energy use in the economy.

Enrollment ratios   Proportion of school-aged children actually enrolled in school.

Environmental accounting   The incorporation of environmental benefits and costs into the quantitative analysis of economic activities.

Environmental capital   The portion of a country's overall capital assets that directly relate to the environment—forests, soil quality, and rangeland.

Equalization (economic and social)   The promotion of more equality in opportunities, status, income, wealth, and general level of living. See also *modernization ideals.*

Equal-weights index   Welfare index in which each income group in a *size distribution of income* is given equal weight.

Equilibrium price   The price at which the quantity demanded of a good is exactly equal to the quantity supplied. It is often referred to as the price at which the market clears itself. See also *price system.*

Equilibrium wage rate   The wage rate that equates the demand for and supply of labor, that is, the wage at which all the people who want to work at that wage are able to find jobs and also at which employers are able to find all the workers they desire to employ. In other words, it is the wage rate that clears the labor market.

Eurodollars   Dollar deposits of European banks in American ones, or dollar deposits in European banks, which the European banks may use as reserves for dollar loans.

European Union (EU)   An economic federation (*common market*) established under the Treaty of Rome in 1957. In January 1993, all restrictions on the free movement of goods, services, capital, and labor were abolished. The 15 current members are Germany, Luxembourg, Great Britain, Italy, Denmark, Ireland, Belgium, Portugal, France, the Netherlands, Greece, Austria, Finland, Spain, and Sweden.

Exchange control   A governmental policy designed to restrict the outflow of domestic currency and prevent a worsened *balance of payments* position by controlling the amount of *foreign exchange* that can be obtained or held by domestic citizens. Often results from *overvalued exchange rates.*

Exchange rate   The rate at which *central banks* will exchange one country's currency for another (i.e., the official rate). See also *overvalued exchange rate* and *devaluation.*

Expected income   In the *Todaro migration model,* the product of the urban wage rate and the probability of finding an urban job.

Export dependence   A situation in which a country relies heavily on exports as the major source of finance needed for carrying out *development* activities. This is the situation of many LDCs, which must export *primary products* to earn valuable *foreign exchange*.

Export earnings instability   Wide and unpredictable fluctuations in LDC commodity export earnings resulting from low *price* and *income elasticities of demand* leading to erratic movements in export prices.

Export incentives   Public *subsidies*, tax rebates, and other kinds of financial and nonfinancial measures designed to promote a greater level of economic activity in export industries.

Export promotion   Governmental efforts to expand the volume of a country's exports through *export incentives* and other means in order to generate more *foreign exchange* and improve the *current account* of its *balance of payments*.

Exports   The value of all goods and nonfactor services sold to the rest of the world; they include merchandise, freight, insurance, travel, and other nonfactor services. The value of factor services (such as investment receipts and workers' remittances from abroad) is excluded from this measure. See also *merchandise exports and imports*.

External debt   Total private and public foreign debt owed by a country.

Externality   Any benefit or cost borne by an individual that is a direct consequence of another's behavior and for which there is no compensation. Externalities are internalized when adjustments are made such that each individual bears all the costs and benefits of his or her actions.

Factor endowment trade theory   The neoclassical model of *free trade*, which postulates that countries will tend to specialize in the production of the commodities that make use of their abundant *factors of production* (land, labor, capital, etc.). They can then export the surplus in return for imports of the products produced by factors with which they are relatively less endowed. The basis for trade arises because of differences in relative factor prices and thus domestic price ratios as a result of differences in factor supplies. See also *comparative advantage*.

Factor mobility   The unrestricted transference or free voluntary movement of *factors of production* among different uses and geographic locations.

Factor-price distortions   Situations in which *factors of production* are paid prices that do not reflect their true *scarcity* values (i.e., their competitive market prices) because of institutional arrangements that tamper with the free working of market forces of supply and demand. In many LDCs, the prices paid for *capital* and *intermediate producer goods* are artificially low because of special capital depreciation allowances, tax rebates, investment *subsidies*, etc., while labor is paid a wage above its competitive market value partly because of trade union and political pressures. Factor-price distortions can lead to the use of inappropriate techniques of production. See also *neoclassical price-incentive model* and *appropriate technology*.

Factor-price equalization In the *factor endowment trade theory*, the proposition that because countries trade at a common international price ratio, factor prices among trading partners will tend to be equalized given the assumption of identical technological possibilities for all commodities across countries. The prices of the more abundantly utilized *resources* will tend to rise, while those of the relatively scarce *factors of production* fall. Over time, international factor payments will tend toward equality; for example, real wages rates for labor will ultimately be the same in Britain and Botswana.

Factor share distribution of income See *functional distribution of income*.

Factors of production *Resources* or *inputs* required to produce a *good* or a *service*. Basic categories of factors of production are land, labor, and *capital*.

False-paradigm model The proposition that *Third World* countries have failed to develop because their *development* strategies (usually given to them by Western economists) have been based on an incorrect model of *development*, one that, for example, overstressed *capital accumulation* without giving due consideration to needed social and institutional change.

Family farms Mostly small farm plots owned and operated by a single household.

Family-planning programs Public programs designed to help parents plan and regulate their family size in accordance with their ability to support a family. The program usually includes supplying contraceptives to the adult population, education on the use of birth control devices, mass-media propaganda on benefits derived from smaller families, and pre- and postnatal health care for mothers.

Farmer cooperatives Associations of farmers mainly engaged in cash crop production to enable them to reap the benefits of *economies of scale*. Large tracts of farmland are jointly owned and operated by the cooperative, with profits being shared in accordance with a prearranged pattern of distribution (not necessarily equal for all farm families).

Farm yield A quantitative measure of the productivity of a given unit of farmland in producing a particular commodity—usually measured in terms of output per hectare.

Fertility rate The yearly number of children born alive per 1,000 women within the childbearing age bracket (normally between the ages of 15 and 49 years). See also *crude birthrate*. The *total fertility rate* (TFR) is the number of children that would be born to a woman if she were to live to the end of her childbearing years and bear children at each age in accordance with the prevailing age-specific fertility rates.

Final goods Commodities that are consumed to satisfy wants rather than passed on to further stages of production. Whenever a final good is not consumed but is used as an *input* instead, it becomes an *intermediate producer good*.

Financial intermediary Any financial institution, public or private, that serves to channel loanable funds from savers to borrowers. Examples include *commercial banks*, savings banks, *development banks*, and finance companies.

Financial liberalization   Eliminating various forms of government intervention in financial markets, thereby allowing supply and demand to determine the level of interest rates, for example.

Financial repression   The constraints on investment caused by the rationing of credit, usually to a few large borrowers, in financial markets where interest rates and hence the supply of savings are below market-clearing levels.

First World   The now economically advanced *capitalist* countries of Western Europe, North America, Australia, New Zealand, and Japan. These were the first countries to experience sustained long-term *economic growth*.

Fixed exchange rate   The exchange value of a national currency fixed in relation to another (usually the U.S. dollar), not free to fluctuate on the international money market.

Fixed input coefficients   A phenomenon in the economics of production in which any level of output requires a fixed ratio of factor *inputs*—for example, 3 units of labor are always required to produce 10 units of output, so to produce 50 units of output, 15 units of labor will be required. The labor (*input*) coefficient (L/Q) in this case would be 0.3 (= 3/10).

Fixed inputs   *Inputs* that do not vary as output varies. For example, a hectare of land is a fixed input on a small family farm because it can be used to produce different quantities of, say, maize output without its size changing. See also *variable inputs*.

Flexible exchange rate   The exchange value of a national currency that is free to move up and down in response to shifts in demand and supply arising from international trade and finance.

Flexible institutions   *Institutions* that are self-responsive or can be made to respond to changing development requirements—for example, a system of land tenure that can adjust itself or be adjusted to allow for a more equitable redistribution of land. See also *rigid institutions*.

Flexible wages   Wages that adjust upward or downward depending on the direction of the forces of demand for and supply of labor—for example, if the demand for labor increases (decreases) or its supply decreases (increases), *ceteris paribus*, wages will increase (decrease).

Food and Agricultural Organization (FAO)   A department of the *United Nations* based in Rome, Italy, whose major concern is to expand world food production in order to meet food intake requirements of the growing world population. The FAO conducts research into modern methods of increasing *farm yields* and educates farmers on their use. It also works in collaboration with such bodies as the World Food Council and the Overseas Food Organization.

Foreign aid   The international transfer of public funds in the form of *loans* or *grants* either directly from one government to another (*bilateral assistance*) or indirectly through the vehicle of a multilateral assistance agency like the *World Bank*. See also *tied aid*, *private foreign investment*, and *nongovernmental organization*.

Foreign direct investment (FDI) Overseas investments by private multinational corporations.

Foreign exchange Claims on a country by another held in the form of currency of that country. The foreign-exchange system enables one currency to be exchanged for (converted into) another, thus facilitating trade between countries. See also *exchange rate* and *foreign reserves*.

Foreign-exchange gap Exists when merchandise *trade deficit* exceeds the value of capital inflows thus causing output growth to be limited by inadequate *foreign exchange*. See *savings gap*.

Foreign reserves The total value (usually expressed in dollars) of all gold, currency, and *special drawing rights* held by a country as both a reserve and a fund from which international payments can be made.

Formal educational system The organized and accredited school system, with licensed teachers, standard curricula, regular academic years, and recognized certification. Encompasses primary, secondary, and tertiary educational institutions. See also *nonformal education*.

Freedom A situation in which a society has at its disposal a variety of alternatives from which to satisfy its wants. See also *development*.

Free market See *pure market capitalism, price system*, and *market mechanism*.

Free-market classical model Traditional model of price determination by supply and demand in a free-market economy.

Free-market exchange rate Rate determined solely by international supply and demand for domestic currency expressed in terms of, say, U.S. dollars.

Free-rider problem Situation in which people secure benefits that someone else pays for.

Free trade Trade in which goods can be imported and exported without any barriers in the forms of *tariffs, quotas*, or other restrictions. Free trade has often been described as an engine of growth because it encourages countries to specialize in activities in which they have *comparative advantages*, thereby increasing their respective production efficiencies and hence their total output of *goods* and *services*.

Free-trade area A form of *economic integration* in which there exists free internal trade among member countries but each member is free to levy different external tariffs against nonmember nations. See also *customs union* and *common market*.

Full employment A situation in which everyone who wants to work at the prevailing wage rate is able to get a job or, alternatively, a situation in which some job seekers cannot get employment at the going wage rate but *open unemployment* has been reduced to a desired level (such as 5%).

Functional distribution of income The distribution of income to *factors of production* without regard to the ownership of the factors.

Gains from trade The increase in output and consumption resulting from specialization in production and *free trade* with other economic units including persons, regions, or countries.

Gender gap   Any statistical gap between the measured characteristics of men and women in areas such as educational attainment, wage rates, or labor force participation.

General Agreement on Tariffs and Trade (GATT)   An international body set up in 1947 to probe into the ways and means of reducing tariffs on internationally traded goods and services. Between 1947 and 1962, GATT held seven conferences but met with only moderate success. Its major success was achieved in 1967 during the so-called Kennedy Round of talks when tariffs on primary commodities were drastically slashed and then in 1994 with the signing of the *Uruguay Round Agreement*. Replaced in 1995 by *World Trade Organization (WTO)*.

Gini coefficient   An aggregate numerical measure of *income inequality* ranging from 0 (perfect equality) to 1 (perfect inequality). It is measured graphically by dividing the area between the perfect equality line and the *Lorenz curve* by the total area lying to the right of the equality line in a Lorenz diagram. The higher the value of the coefficient, the higher the inequality of income distribution; the lower it is, the more equitable the distribution of income. See also *skewed distribution of income*.

Global commons   International resources shared by all countries such as oceans and air.

Global Environmental Facility (GEF)   An organization jointly administered by the *World Bank*, the *United Nations Development Program*, and the United Nations Environment Program that provides *grants* used to finance environmental programs in *Third World* countries.

Global factory   A production facility whose various operations are distributed across a number of countries in order to take advantage of existing price differentials.

Globalization   The increasing integration of national economies into expanding international markets.

Global warming   Theory that world climate is slowly warming as a result of both MDC and LDC industrial and agricultural activities.

GNP growth rate index   Welfare index measuring the GNP growth rate based on the existing *size distribution of income*. See *equal-weights index*.

Goods   See *economic good* and *final goods*.

Government failure   Situation in which government intervention in an economy worsens outcomes.

Grant   An outright *transfer payment*, usually from one government to another (*foreign aid*); a gift of money or *technical assistance* that does not have to be repaid. See also *loan* and *tied aid*.

Greenhouse gases   Gases that trap heat within the earth's atmosphere and can thus contribute to *global warming*. See also *ozone depletion*.

Green Revolution   The boost in grain production associated with the scientific discovery of new *hybrid seed* varieties of wheat, rice, and corn that have resulted in high *farm yields* in many LDCs.

Gross domestic investment The outlays for additions to fixed assets of both the private and public sectors plus the net value of inventory changes. See also *investment*.

Gross domestic product (GDP) The total final output of *goods* and *services* produced by the country's economy, within the country's territory, by residents and nonresidents, regardless of its allocation between domestic and foreign claims. See also *gross national product (GNP)*.

Gross domestic savings The amount of *gross domestic investment* financed from domestic output. It is calculated as the difference between *gross domestic investment* and the deficit on *current account* of *goods* and nonfactor *services* (excluding net current transfers). It comprises both public and private savings. See also *savings*.

Gross national product (GNP) The total domestic and foreign output claimed by residents of a country. It comprises *gross domestic product (GDP)* plus factor incomes accruing to residents from abroad, less the income earned in the domestic economy accruing to persons abroad. See also *national income* and *national expenditure*.

Group lending schemes A formal arrangement among a group of potential borrowers to borrow money from commercial or government banks as a single entity and then allocate funds and repay loans as a group, thereby lowering borrowing costs. See also *rotating savings and credit associations*.

Group of 7 The seven leading industrialized *First World* nations (the United States, Canada, Great Britain, France, Germany, Japan, and Italy), who meet annually to discuss global economic issues.

Group of 77 A loose coalition of over 100 developing countries originally formed by 77 countries at the *United Nations Conference on Trade and Development (UNCTAD)* in 1964, to express and further their collective interests in the world economic system.

Growth poles Regions that are more economically and socially advanced than others around them, such as urban centers versus rural areas in LDCs. Large-scale economic activity tends to cluster around growth poles due to economies of agglomeration and the lower costs of locating an industry in an area where *economic infrastructure* has been built up.

Hard currency The currency of a major industrial country, such as the U.S. dollar, the German mark, or the Japanese yen, that is freely convertible into other "soft" currencies.

Harrod-Domar growth model A functional economic relationship in which the growth rate of *gross domestic product* (g) depends directly on the national *savings* rate (s) and inversely on the national *capital-output ratio* (k), that is, $g = s/k$. The model takes its name from a synthesis of analyses of the growth process by two economists, Sir Roy Harrod of Britain and E. V. Domar of the United States.

Hidden momentum of population growth A dynamic latent process of population increase that continues even after a fall in *birthrates* because of a large youthful population that widens the population's parent base. Fewer children per couple in the succeeding few generations will not mean a smaller or stable population size because at the same time there will be a much larger number of childbearing couples. Hence a given population will not stabilize until after two or three generations.

Hidden unemployment A situation in which labor is fully employed but is unproductive because the workers are incapacitated, sick, uneducated, hungry, unmotivated, or using unsuitable tools in their tasks. See also *underemployment* and *disguised unemployment*.

Human capital Productive *investments* embodied in human persons. These include skills, abilities, ideals, and health resulting from expenditures on education, on-the-job training programs, and medical care. See also *physical capital*.

Human Development Index (HDI) An index measuring national socioeconomic development, based on measures of life expectancy at birth, educational attainment, and adjusted real per capita income.

Human immunodeficiency virus (HIV) The virus that causes *AIDS*.

Human resources The quantity and quality of a nation's labor force.

Hybrid seeds Seeds produced by cross-breeding plants or crops of different species through scientific research. See also *Green Revolution*.

Idea gap Notion that one explanation for *underdevelopment* is that LDCs lack knowledge, information, skills, and other attributes of modern production methods in comparison to more developed countries. See *ingenuity gap* and *object gap*.

Imperfect competition A market situation or structure in which producers have some degree of control over the price of their product. Examples include *monopoly* and *oligopoly*. See also *perfect competition*.

Imperfect market A market where the theoretical assumptions of *perfect competition* are violated by the existence of, for example, a small number of buyers and sellers, barriers to entry, nonhomogeneity of products, and *incomplete information*. The three imperfect markets commonly analyzed in economic theory are *monopoly, oligopoly*, and monopolistic competition.

Import substitution A deliberate effort to replace major consumer imports by promoting the emergence and expansion of domestic industries such as textiles, shoes, and household appliances. Import substitution requires the imposition of protective *tariffs* and *quotas* to get the new industry started. See also *infant industry*.

Income distribution See *functional distribution of income* and *size distribution of income*.

Income effect The implicit change in *real income* resulting from the effects of a change in a commodity's price on the quantity demanded.

Income elasticity of demand The responsiveness of the quantity demanded of a commodity to changes in the consumer's income, measured by the proportionate change in quantity divided by the proportionate change in income.

Income gap   The gap between the incomes accruing to the bottom (poor) and the top (rich) sectors of a population. The wider the gap, the greater the inequality in the *income distribution*. Also, the gap between *income per capita* levels in rich and poor nations. See *Gini coefficient*.

Income inequality   The existence of disproportionate distribution of total *national income* among households whereby the share going to rich persons in a country is far greater than that going to poorer persons (a situation common to most LDCs). This is largely due to differences in the amount of income derived from ownership of property and to a lesser extent the result of differences in earned income. Inequality of personal incomes can be reduced by *progressive income taxes* and wealth taxes. See also *Gini coefficient* and *Lorenz curve*.

Income in kind   A household's or firm's income in the form of *goods* or *services* instead of in the form of money. Payments in *barter transactions* and in *subsistence economies* are mainly made in kind.

Income per capita   Total *gross national product* of a country divided by total population. Per capita income is often used as an economic indicator of *level of living* and *development*. It can, however, be a biased index because it takes no account of *income distribution* and the ownership of the assets that are employed to generate part of that income.

Income terms of trade   A measure of the relative purchasing power of a country's exports arrived at by abstracting from relative export price movements. See *terms of trade*.

Incomplete information   Notion that LDC markets do not function well because producers and consumers do not possess the requisite information to make efficient decisions. See *imperfect market*.

Increasing returns   A disproportionate increase in output that results from a change in the scale of production. Some industries (e.g., utilities, transportation) are characterized by increasing returns over a wide range of output. This leads to *monopoly* situations. See also *economies of scale* and *returns to scale*.

Incremental capital-output ratio (ICOR)   The amount of *capital* needed to raise output by one unit.

Indirect taxes   Taxes levied on *goods* purchased by the consumer (and exported by the producer) for which the taxpayer's liability varies in proportion to the quantity of *goods* purchased or sold. Examples of indirect taxes are customs duties (*tariffs*), excise duties, sales taxes, and export duties. They are a major source of tax revenue for most LDCs as they are easier to administer and collect than *direct taxes* (e.g., income and property taxes).

Induced migration   Process in which the creation of urban jobs raises *expected incomes* and induces more people to migrate from rural areas. See *Todaro migration model*.

Industrialization   The process of building up a country's capacity to process raw materials and to manufacture *goods* for consumption or further production.

Industrial policy   Deliberate effort by governments to guide the market by coordinating and planning industrial activities.

Infant industry   A newly established industry, usually set up behind the protection of a *tariff* barrier as a part of a policy of *import substitution*. Once the industry is no longer an infant, the protective *tariffs* are supposed to disappear, but often they do not.

Infant mortality rate   Deaths among children between birth and 1 year of age per 1,000 live births.

Inferior good   A *good* whose demand falls as consumer incomes rise. The *income elasticity of demand* of an inferior good is thus negative.

Inflation   A period of above-normal general price increases as reflected, for example, in the consumer and wholesale price indexes. More generally, the phenomenon of rising prices. See also *cost-push inflation, demand-pull inflation*, and *structural inflation*.

Informal finance   *Loans* not passed through formal banking system—for example, family loans.

Informal sector   The part of the urban economy of LDCs characterized by small competitive individual or family firms, petty retail trade and services, labor-intensive methods, free entry, and market-determined factor and product prices. It often provides a major source of urban employment and economic activity.

Infrastructure   See *economic infrastructure*.

Ingenuity gap   LDC deficiency compared with MDCs in the capacity to invent and innovate with new or existing technology. See also *idea gap* and *object gap*.

Innovation   The application of *inventions* of new production processes and methods to production activities as well as the introduction of new products. Innovations may also include the introduction of new social and institutional methods of organization and management commensurate with modern ways of conducting economic activities. See *invention* and *modernization ideals*.

Input-output model   Formal planning model dividing the economy into sectors and tracing the flow of interindustry purchases (inputs) and sales (outputs).

Inputs   *Goods* and *services*, such as raw materials and hours of labor, used in the process of production. See also *factors of production, physical resources*, and *human resources*.

Institutions   Norms, rules of conduct, and generally accepted ways of doing things. Social institutions are well-defined, formal organizations of society that govern the way that society operates—for example, the class system, private versus communal ownership, or the educational system. Political institutions are the systems that govern the operations of the government of a particular society—formal power structures, political parties, and mechanisms for obtaining power.

Integrated rural development   The broad spectrum of rural development activities, including small-farmer agricultural progress; the provision of physical and social *infrastructure*; the development of rural nonfarm industries; and the capacity of the rural sector to sustain and accelerate the pace of these improvements over time.

Inter-American Development Bank   A regional *development bank*, established in 1959 by the Organization of American States, offering *loans* for project development and export financing in Latin America.

Interdependence   Interrelationship between *economic* and *noneconomic variables*. Also, in international affairs, the situation in which one nation's welfare depends to varying degrees on the decisions and policies of another nation, and vice versa. See also *dependence* and *dominance*.

Interest   The payment (or price) for the use of borrowed funds. See also *interest rate* and *social rate of discount*.

Interest rate   The annual amount that a borrower must pay a lender over and above the total amount borrowed, expressed as a percentage of the total amount of funds borrowed—for example, if a person borrowed 100 rupees for one year, at the end of which he or she had to repay 110 rupees, the interest rate would be 10% per annum.

Interindustry model   See *input-output model*.

Interlocking factor markets   Factor markets whose supply functions are interdependent, frequently because different *inputs* are provided by the same suppliers who exercise monopolistic or oligopolistic control over resources.

Intermediate producer goods   Goods that are used as *inputs* into further levels of production, such as leather in shoe manufacture or iron ore in steel production. See also *final goods*.

Intermediate technology   A technology that is halfway between the capital-intensive technologies of the developed countries and the primitive, indigenous techniques of many developing countries, usually relying on the use of local materials and skills. See *appropriate technology*.

Internalization   Process whereby external environmental costs are borne by the producers or consumers who generate them, usually through the imposition of pollution or consumption taxes. See also *externality*.

Internal rate of return   Discount rate that causes a project to have a net present value of zero. Used to rank projects in comparison with market rates of interest.

International Bank for Reconstruction and Development (IBRD)   See *World Bank*.

International commodity agreement   Formal agreement by sellers of a common internationally traded commodity (coffee, sugar) to coordinate supply to maintain price stability.

International Development Association (IDA)   An international body set up in 1960 to assist the *World Bank* in its efforts to promote the economic *development* of the underdeveloped countries by providing additional *capital* on a low-*interest* basis, especially to the poorest of the poor developing countries.

International Finance Corporation (IFC)   An international financial institution set up in 1956 to supplement the efforts of the *World Bank* in providing development *capital* to private enterprises (mainly industrial) of the underdeveloped countries.

International Labor Organization (ILO)   One of the functional organizations of the *United Nations*, based in Geneva, Switzerland, whose central task is to look into problems of world labor supply, its training, utilization, domestic and international distribution, etc. Its aim in this endeavor is to increase world output through maximum utilization of available *human resources* and thus improve *levels of living*.

International Monetary Fund (IMF)   An autonomous international financial institution that originated in the Bretton Woods Conference of 1944. Its main purpose is to regulate the international monetary exchange system, which also stems from that conference but has since been modified. In particular, one of the central tasks of the IMF is to control fluctuations in *exchange rates* of world currencies in a bid to alleviate severe *balance of payments* problems.

International poverty line   An arbitrary international *real income* measure, usually expressed in constant dollars (e.g., $270), used as a basis for estimating the proportion of the world's population that exists at bare levels of *subsistence*.

International reserve account   See *cash account*.

International reserves   A country's balance of gold, *hard currencies*, and *special drawing rights* used to settle international transactions.

Invention   The discovery of something new, for example, a new product (e.g., hybrid corn) or a new production process (a cheaper and more efficient way of producing synthetic rubber). See also *innovation*.

Investment   The part of *national income* or *national expenditure* devoted to the production of *capital goods* over a given period of time. Gross investment is the total expenditure on new *capital goods*, and net investment is the additional *capital goods* produced in excess of those that wear out and need to be replaced.

Investment in children   The process by which parents raise the quality and hence the earning capacity of children by providing them with an education in expectation of future returns. In this sense, children in poor societies are viewed as *capital goods* and a source of old-age security. See also *human resources*.

Invisible hand   A concept originating in Adam Smith's famous book *The Wealth of Nations*, published in 1776, that holds that the unbridled pursuit of individual self-interest automatically contributes to the maximization of the social interest. See also *laissez-faire, perfect competition,* and *pure market capitalism*.

Inward-looking development policies   Policies that stress economic *self-reliance* on the part of LDCs, including the development of indigenous *appropriate technology*, the imposition of substantial protective *tariffs* and *nontariff trade barriers* to promote *import substitution*, and the general discouragement of *private foreign investment*. See also *autarchy* and *outward-looking development policies*.

Jobless growth Widespread phenomenon in LDCs where the rate of *economic growth* greatly exceeds the rate of job creation, leading to higher levels of unemployment.

Keynesian model Model developed by Lord John Maynard Keynes in the early 1930s to explain the cause of economic depression and hence the unemployment of that period. The model states that unemployment is caused by insufficient *aggregate demand* and can be eliminated by, say, government expenditure that would raise *aggregate demand* and activate idle or underutilized resources and thus create jobs.

Kuznets curve A relationship between a country's *income per capita* and its equality of *income distribution* such that as per capita incomes increase, the distribution of income at first worsens and later improves from very low levels. Named after Nobel laureate Simon Kuznets, who first statistically identified this relationship for developed countries.

Labor-augmenting technological progress *Technological progress* that raises the productivity of an existing quantity of labor by general education, on-the-job training programs, etc. See also *laborsaving technological progress*.

Labor force All economically active persons, including the armed forces and the unemployed, but excluding housewives, students, and economically inactive groups.

Labor-intensive technique Method of production that uses proportionately more labor relative to other *factors of production*. See also *capital-intensive technique*.

Labor productivity The level of output per unit of labor *input*, usually measured as output per worker-hour or worker-year.

Laborsaving technological progress The achievement of higher output using an unchanged quantity of labor *inputs* as a result of some *invention* (e.g., the computer) or *innovation* (such as assembly-line production).

Labor theory of value In classical international trade theory, the proposition that relative commodity prices depend on the relative amounts of labor used to produce the commodities. Much of Marxist economics is based on the labor theory of value.

Labor turnover model Theory that the urban-rural wage gap is partly explained by fact that urban modern-sector employers pay higher wages to reduce labor turnover rates and retain skilled workers. See *efficiency wage*.

Laissez-faire Free-enterprise market capitalism. See *perfect competition* and *pure market capitalism*.

Landlord The proprietor of a freehold interest in land with rights to lease out to tenants in return for some form of payment for the use of the land.

Land reform A deliberate attempt to reorganize and transform existing *agrarian systems* with the intention of improving the distribution of agricultural incomes and thus fostering *rural development*. Among its many forms, land reform may entail provision of secured tenure rights to the individual farmer, transfer of land ownership away from small classes of powerful landowners to tenants who actually till the land, appropriation of land estates for establishing small new settlement farms, or instituting land improvements and irrigation schemes.

Latifundio   A very large landholding in the Latin American *agrarian system*, capable of providing employment for over 12 people, owned by a small number of *landlords*, and comprising a large proportion of total agricultural land. See also *minifundio*.

Law   A universal truth that holds in all situations and the validity of which is independent of the social and political context in which it is observed (e.g., in the physical sciences, the law of gravity holds whether an experiment is conducted in North America, China, Botswana, or Brazil). Compare *tendency*.

Least developed countries (LLDCs)   The poorest LDCs, those with a per capita income of under $695 in 1993 according to *World Bank* measures.

Less developed countries (LDCs)   See *Third World*.

Levels of living   The extent to which a person, family, or group of people can satisfy their material and spiritual wants. If they are able to afford only a minimum quantity of food, shelter, and clothing, their levels of living are said to be very low. If they enjoy a great variety of food, shelter, clothing, and other things, such as good health, education, and leisure, they are enjoying relatively high levels of living. See *development*.

Lewis two-sector model   Theory of development in which *surplus labor* from traditional agricultural sector is transferred to the modern industrial sector whose growth over time absorbs the surplus labor, promotes industrialization and stimulates sustained development.

Life expectancy at birth   The number of years newborn children would live if subject to the *mortality* risks prevailing for the cross section of population at the time of their birth. See also *crude birthrate*.

Literacy   The ability to read and write.

Literacy rate   The percentage of the population age 15 and over able to read and write. Literacy rates are often used as one of the many social and economic indicators of the state of development of a country.

Loan   A transfer of funds from one economic entity to another (government to government, individual to individual, bank to individual) that must be repaid with *interest* over a prescribed period of time. Hard loans are given at market rates of *interest*, soft loans are given at concessional or low rates of *interest*. See also *grant*.

Lorenz curve   A graph depicting the variance of the *size distribution of income* from perfect equality. See also *Gini coefficient*.

Low-income countries (LICs)   See *least developed countries*.

Macroeconomic instability   Situation in which country has high *inflation* accompanied by rising budget and trade deficits and a rapidly expanding *money supply*.

Macroeconomics   The branch of economics that considers the relationships among broad economic aggregates such as *national income,* total volumes of *saving, investment,* consumption expenditure, employment, and *money supply.* It is also concerned with determinants of the magnitudes of these aggregates and their rates of change over time. See also *Keynesian economics.*

Macroeconomic stabilization   Policies designed to eliminate *macroeconomic instability.*

Macro population-development relationship   A general cause-and-effect relationship between the *development* process and population growth. Development causes population growth rates to slow and stabilize by providing *economic incentives* that motivate people to have smaller families. Population growth (in the absence of a population problem) in turn affects *development* in many ways; it increases *aggregate demand,* which stimulates increases in national output, and it provides more people for national defense.

Malnutrition   A state of ill health resulting from an inadequate or improper diet, usually measured in terms of average daily protein consumption.

Malthusian population trap   An inevitable population level envisaged by Thomas Malthus (1766–1834) at which population increase was bound to stop because after that level, life-sustaining resources, which increase at an arithmetic rate, would be insufficient to support human population, which increases at a geometric rate. Consequently, people would die of starvation, disease, wars, etc. The Malthusian population trap therefore represents the maximum population size that can be supported by the available resources.

Marginal cost   The addition to total cost incurred by the producer as a result of varying output by one more unit.

Marginal net benefit   The benefit derived from the last unit of a *good* minus its cost.

Marginal product   The increase in total output resulting from the use of one additional unit of a variable *factor of production.* In the *Lewis two-sector model, surplus labor* is defined as workers whose marginal product is zero. See also *average product.*

Marginal utility   The satisfaction derived by consuming one additional unit of a *good.* In neoclassical theory, a consumer's marginal utility is said to be maximized if his or her marginal utility per last unit of expenditure on that *good* is equal to the marginal utilities of all other *goods* consumed, divided by their respective prices.

Market economy   A free private-enterprise economy governed by *consumer sovereignty,* a *price system,* and the forces of supply and demand.

Market failure   A phenomenon that results from the existence of market imperfections (e.g., *monopoly* power, lack of *factor mobility,* significant *externalities,* lack of knowledge) that weaken the functioning of a free-market economy—it fails to realize its theoretical beneficial results. Market failure often provides the justification for government interference with the working of the *free market.*

Market-friendly approach   *World Bank* notion that successful *development* policy requires governments to create an environment in which markets can operate efficiently and to intervene selectively in the economy in areas where the market is inefficient (e.g., social and economic *infrastructure, investment* coordination, economic "safety net").

Market mechanism   The system whereby prices of commodities or services freely rise or fall when the buyer's demand for them rises or falls or the seller's supply of them decreases or increases. See *price system*.

Market prices   Prices established by demand and supply in a free-market economy.

Market socialism   *Economic system* in which all resources are owned by the state but their allocation is done primarily by a *market price* system. See also *command socialism*.

Mass production   Large-scale production of *goods* or *services* achieved primarily through automation, *specialization*, and the *division of labor*.

Medium-sized farm   Multi-family farms in Latin America employing four to twelve workers. See also *minifundio* and *latifundio*.

Merchandise exports and imports   All international changes in ownership of merchandise passing across the customs borders of the raging countries. Exports are valued f.o.b. (free on board). Imports are valued c.i.f. (cost, insurance, and freight).

Merchandise trade balance   Balance on commodity exports and imports.

Microeconomics   The branch of economics concerned with individual decision units—firms and households—and the way in which their decisions interact to determine relative prices of *goods* and *factors of production* and how much of these will be bought and sold. The market is the central concept in microeconomics. See also *price system* and *traditional economics*.

Microeconomic theory of fertility   An extension of the theory of consumer behavior of individual couples. The central proposition of this theory is that family formation has costs and benefits and hence the size of families formed will depend on these costs and benefits. If the costs of family formation are high relative to its benefits, the rates at which couples will decide to bring forth children will decline, and vice versa. See also *opportunity cost of a woman's time, fertility rate,* and *crude birthrate*.

Middle-income countries (MICs)   LDCs with per capita income above $696 and below $8,626 in 1993 according to *World Bank* measures.

Minifundio   A landholding in the Latin American *agrarian system* considered too small to provide adequate employment for a single family. A *minifundio* is too small to provide the workers with *levels of living* much above the bare survival minimum. Holders of *minifundios* are often required to provide unpaid seasonal labor to *latifundios* and to seek outside low-paid employment to supplement their meager incomes. See also *latifundio*.

Mixed economic systems   *Economic systems* that are a mixture of both *capitalist* and *socialist* economies. Most developing countries have mixed systems. Their essential feature is the coexistence of substantial private and public activity within a single economy. See also *market socialism* and *advanced capitalism*.

Mixed farming The first step in the transition from *subsistence* to *specialized farming*. This evolutionary stage is characterized by the production of both staple crops and cash crops and, in addition, simple animal husbandry.

Model An analytic framework used to portray functional relationships among economic factors.

Modernization ideals Ideals often regarded as necessary for sustained *economic growth*. They include *rationality, economic planning*, social and economic equalization, and improved *institutions* and attitudes.

Monetary policy Activities of *central bank* designed to influence financial variables such as money supply and interest rates.

Money income The income accruing to a household or firm expressed in terms of some monetary unit, for example, 1,000 rupees or pesos per year.

Moneylender In Asia, a person who lends money at higher than market rates of *interest* to peasant farmers to meet their needs for seeds, fertilizers, and other *inputs*. Activities of moneylenders are often unscrupulous and can accentuate landlessness among the rural poor.

Money supply Sum total of currency in circulation plus *commercial bank* demand deposits and sometimes savings bank time deposits.

Monopolistic market control A situation in which the output of an industry is controlled by a single producer (or seller) or by a group of producers who make joint decisions.

Monopoly A market situation in which a product that does not have close substitutes is being produced and sold by a single seller. See also *perfect competition* and *oligopoly*.

More developed countries (MDCs) See *First World*.

Mortality See *death rate*.

Multi-fiber arrangement Non-tariff bilateral *quotas* established by developed countries on imports of cotton, wool, and synthetic textiles and clothing from individual LDCs.

Multilateral assistance agency See *foreign aid*.

Multinational corporation (MNC) An international or transnational corporation with headquarters in one country but branch offices in a wide range of both developed and developing countries. Examples include General Motors, Coca-Cola, Firestone, Philips, Volkswagen, British Petroleum, Exxon, and ITT.

National income Total monetary value of all *final goods* and services produced in an economy over some period of time, usually a year. See also *gross national product (GNP)* and *national expenditure*.

Natural increase See *population increase*.

Necessary condition A condition that must be present, although it need not be in itself sufficient, for an event to occur. For example, *capital* formation is a necessary condition for sustained *economic growth* (before growth in output can occur, there must be tools to produce it). But for this growth to continue, social, institutional, and attitudinal changes may have to occur.

Necessity goods Life-sustaining items (food, shelter, protection, medical care).

Neoclassical counterrevolution The 1980s resurgence of neoclassical free-market orientation toward *development* problems and policies; counter to the interventionist *dependence* revolution of the 1970s.

Neoclassical economics See *traditional economics*.

Neoclassical price-incentive model A model whose main proposition is that if *market prices* are to influence economic activities in the right direction, they must be adjusted to remove *factor-price distortions* by means of *subsidies*, taxes, or the like so that factor prices may reflect the true *opportunity cost* of the *resources* being used. See also *appropriate technology*.

Neocolonial dependence model A model whose main proposition is that *underdevelopment* exists in *Third World* countries because of continuing exploitative economic, political, and cultural policies of former colonial rulers toward *less developed countries*.

Net international migration Excess of persons migrating into a country over those who emigrate from that country. See *brain drain*.

Net present value Value of a future stream of net benefits discounted to the present by means of a competitive discount (interest) rate.

Net reproduction rate (NRR) The number of daughters that a newborn girl will bear during her lifetime, assuming fixed age-specific *fertility rates* and a fixed set of *mortality* rates. An NRR of 1 indicates that fertility is at replacement level.

Neutral technological progress Higher output levels achieved with same quantity or combination of all factor inputs.

New growth theory Also known as *endogenous growth* theory, an extension and modification of the *traditional growth theory* designed to explain why long-run equilibrium growth can be positive and divergent among countries and why *capital* tends to flow from poor to rich countries despite the former's low *capital-labor ratios*. See *traditional (old) growth theory* and *endogenous growth*.

New institutionalism Recent revival of the notion that *institutions* matter significantly in economic *development*.

Newly industrializing countries (NICs) A small group of countries at a relatively advanced level of economic *development* with a substantial and dynamic industrial sector and with close links to the international trade, finance, and investment system (Argentina, Brazil, Greece, Hong Kong, Mexico, Portugal, Singapore, South Korea, Spain, and Taiwan).

New political economy approach See *public-choice theory*.

New protectionism   Wide range of non-tariff trade barriers erected by developed countries against the manufactured exports of developing nations; typically as quotas or "voluntary" export restrain by LDCs. See *Multi-fiber arrangement*.

Nominal rate of protection   Ad valorem percentage *tariff* levied on imports. See *effective rate of protection*.

Noneconomic variables   Elements of interest to economists in their work but not given a monetary value or expressed numerically because of their intangible nature. Sometimes noneconomic variables such as educational, health, cultural, political, and institutional factors are more important than the quantifiable economic variables in promoting *development*.

Nonformal education   Any non-school-based program that provides basic skills and training to individuals. Examples include adult education, on-the-job training programs, and agricultural and other extension services. Compare *formal education system*.

Nongovernmental organizations (NGOs)   Privately owned and operated organizations involved in providing financial and *technical assistance* to LDCs. See *foreign aid*.

Nonrenewable resources   Natural *resources* whose quantity is fixed and cannot be replaced. Examples include petroleum, iron ore, and coal. Compare *renewable resources*.

Nontariff trade barrier   A barrier to *free trade* that takes a form other than a *tariff*, such as *quotas* or sanitary requirements for imported meats and dairy products.

Normal and superior goods   *Goods* whose purchased quantities increase as the incomes of consumers increase. Such *goods* have a positive *income elasticity of demand*. Compare *inferior goods*.

Normative economics   The notion that economics must concern itself with what "ought to be." Thus it is argued that economics and economic analysis always involve *value* judgments, whether explicit or implicit, on the part of the analyst or observer. See *positive economics*.

North-South trade models   Trade and development models that focus on the unequal exchange between the North (MDCs) and the South (LDCs) and attempt to show theoretically why the South gains less from trade than the North.

Object gap   Notion that LDCs suffer from a lack of material items including roads, buildings, machinery, etc., in comparison with developed countries. See *idea gap*.

Official development assistance (ODA)   Net disbursements of *loans* or *grants* made on *concessional terms* by official agencies of member countries of the *Organization for Economic Cooperation and Development (OECD)*.

Official exchange rate   Rate at which the *central bank* will buy and sell the domestic currency in terms of a foreign currency such as the US dollar.

Oligopolistic market control   A situation in which a small number of rival but not necessarily competing firms dominate an industry. All recognize the fact that they are interdependent and can maximize their individual advantages through explicit (*cartel*) or implicit (*collusion*) joint actions.

Oligopoly   A market situation in which there are a few sellers and many buyers of similar but differentiated products. The *Organization of Petroleum Exporting Countries (OPEC)* is a good example of international oligopoly. See also *imperfect competition*.

Open economy   An economy that encourages foreign trade and has extensive financial and nonfinancial contacts with the rest of the world in areas such as education, culture, and technology. See also *closed economy* and *outward-looking development policies*.

Open unemployment   Voluntary and involuntary unemployment. Voluntarily unemployed persons are those unwilling to accept jobs for which they could qualify, probably because they have means of support other than employment. Involuntary unemployment is a situation in which job seekers are willing to work but there are no jobs available for them. Open unemployment is most conspicuous in the cities of *less developed countries*. See also *underemployment*, *surplus labor*, and *disguised underemployment*.

Opportunity cost   In production, the real value of *resources* used in the most desirable alternative—for example, the opportunity cost of producing an extra unit of a manufactured *good* is the output of, say, food that must be forgone as a result of transferring resources from agricultural to manufacturing activities. In consumption, the amount of one commodity that must be forgone in order to consume more of another.

Opportunity cost of a woman's time   Real or monetary wages or *profits* that a woman sacrifices by deciding to stay home and raise children instead of working for a wage or engaging in profit-making self-employment activities. The higher the opportunity cost of a woman's time involved in rearing children, the more unwilling she will be to have more children, at least in terms of the *microeconomic theory of fertility*.

Opportunity cost of education   Lost income from paid employment during the time when an individual attends school.

Optimization principle   A principle that states that to minimize costs in production or maximize satisfaction in consumption, scarce *resources* should be used in the economically most efficient manner and *goods* and *services* should be consumed so that the last unit of expenditure yields the same *marginal utility* for all individuals. See also *principle of economy, appropriate technology*, and *economic efficiency*.

Organization for Economic Cooperation and Development (OECD)   An organization of 20 countries from the Western world including all of those in Europe and North America. Its major objective is to assist the *economic growth* of its member nations by promoting cooperation and technical analysis of national and international economic trends.

Organization of Petroleum Exporting Countries (OPEC)   An organization consisting of 13 major oil-exporting countries of the *Third World* that acts as a *cartel* or *oligopoly* to promote their joint national interests. Members are Algeria, Ecuador, Gabon, Indonesia, Iran, Iraq, Kuwait, Libya, Nigeria, Qatar, Saudi Arabia, United Arab Emirates, and Venezuela.

Organized money market   The formal banking system in which loanable funds are channeled through recognized and licensed *financial intermediaries*. See also *unorganized money market*.

Output-employment lag   The phenomenon whereby employment growth lags substantially behind output growth—normally, when output grows at a rate three to four times that of employment, as it has in most modern sectors of developing nations.

Output-employment macro model   Model focused on relationship between capital accumulation and aggregate output and employment growth.

Outward-looking development policies   Policies that encourage *free trade*; the free movement of *capital*, workers, enterprises, and students; a welcome to *multinational corporations*; and an open system of communications. See also *open economy*.

Overeducation   In countries with high unemployment, a situation in which many workers have more years of schooling than necessary to perform their jobs satisfactorily.

Overvalued exchange rate   An *official exchange rate* set at a level higher than its real or shadow value—for example, 7 Kenyan shillings per dollar instead of, say, 10 shillings per dollar. Overvalued rates cheapen the real cost of imports while raising the real cost of exports. They often lead to a need for *exchange control*.

Ozone   A highly reactive gas, O_3, that absorbs harmful ultraviolet rays in the upper atmosphere but is an important contributor to smog in the lower atmosphere.

Ozone depletion   The loss of *ozone* resulting from atmospheric pollution especially from carbon monoxide pollution. See also *greenhouse gases*.

Package of policies   A set of multidimensional economic and social policies aimed, for example, at removing inequalities and improving living standards for the masses. In short, a set of different but mutually reinforcing policies designed to achieve a single or multiple objective.

Paradigm   Implicit assumptions from which theories evolve; a *model* or framework of analysis.

Parallel exchange rate   See *dual exchange rate*.

Paris Club   A group formed by representatives from industrialized creditor nations with substantial outstanding debt owed them by the *Third World*. Their mandate was to restructure the bilateral debt of highly indebted countries.

Partial plan   A plan that covers only a part of the national economy (e.g., agriculture, industry, tourism).

Patrón   In Latin America, a landlord to whom sharecroppers and other workers owe an economic and often political and social allegiance.

Patterns-of-development analysis   See *structural-change theory*.

Per capita agricultural production   Total agricultural output, both food and fiber, divided by total population.

Per capita food production   Total food production divided by total population.

Per capita food production index   The average annual quantity of food produced per capita as a percentage of the average annual amount produced.

Per capita GNP   See *income per capita*.

Perfect competition   A market situation characterized by the existence of very many buyers and sellers of homogeneous *goods* or *services* with perfect knowledge and free entry so that no single buyer or seller can influence the price of the *good* or *service*. See also *price system, laissez-faire, traditional economics*, and *pure market capitalism*.

Periphery   In *dependence* theory, the *Third World*. Compare *center*.

Personal distribution of income   See *size distribution of income*.

Physical capital   Tangible *investment* goods (e.g., plant and equipment, machinery, buildings). See also *human capital*.

Physical Quality of Life Index (PQLI)   A composite social indicator reflecting the average of three indexes: *life expectancy at birth, literacy rate*, and *infant mortality rate*.

Physical resources   The nonhuman *factors of production* (land and capital) used to produce *goods* and *services* to satisfy wants.

Plan   See *economic plan* and *development plan*.

Plan implementation   The practical carrying out of the objectives set forth in the *development plan*. Some of the difficulties encountered in attempting to attain plan targets result from insufficient availability of economic *resources* (physical and financial capital, skilled labor, etc.), insufficient *foreign aid*, the effects of *inflation*, and most important, lack of *political will*.

Planning model   A mathematical model (e.g., an input-output *model* or macro planning model) designed to simulate quantitatively the major features of the economic structure of a particular country. Planning models provide the analytic and quantitative basis for most national and regional *development plans*. See also *economic plan* and *plan implementation*.

Planning process   Procedure for drawing up and carrying out a formal economic plan.

Policy instruments   See *economic policy*.

Political economy   The attempt to merge economic analysis with practical politics—to view economic activity in its political context. Much of classical economics was political economy, and today political economy is increasingly being recognized as necessary for any realistic examination of *development* problems.

Political will   A determined effort by persons in political authority to achieve certain economic objectives, such as elimination of inequality, poverty, and unemployment through various reforms of social, economic, and institutional structures. Lack of political will is often said to be one of the main obstacles to *development* and one of the main reasons for the failure of many *development plans.* See *plan implementation.*

Pollution tax   Tax levied on quantity of pollutants released into the physical environment.

Population density   The number of inhabitants per unit area of land (e.g., per square kilometer).

Population increase   The rate at which a population grows over a period of time, say, one year. The part of this rate that results entirely from increases in the number of births over deaths is called the rate of *natural increase* to distinguish it from the increase resulting from immigration.

Population-poverty cycle   Theory to explain how poverty and high population growth become reinforcing.

Portfolio investment   Financial investments by private individuals, corporations, pension funds, and mutual funds in stocks, bonds, certificates of deposit, and notes issued by private companies and the public agencies of LDCs. See also *private foreign investment.*

Positive checks   In Malthusian theory, the effects of war, disease, and famine in controlling excess population growth.

Positive economics   The notion that economics should be concerned with what is, was, or will be, with answers to economic questions based on facts or empirical observation. See also *normative economics.*

Potential output   The aggregate capacity output of a nation; the maximum quantity of *goods* and *services* that can be produced with available *resources* and a given state of technology.

Poverty   See *absolute poverty.*

Poverty gap   The sum of the difference between the *poverty line* and actual income levels of all people living below that line.

Poverty line   See *international poverty line.*

Poverty-weighted index   Welfare index in which income gains for lower income groups are given greater weight than gains for upper income groups. See *equal-weights index.*

Prebisch-Singer thesis   The argument that the primary-product export orientation of LDCs results in a decline in their *terms of trade* and a loss of income.

Premature retirement   Workers forced to leave their jobs before reaching their retirement age.

Present value   The discounted value at the present time of a sum of money to be received in the future.

Preventive checks   In Malthusian theory, the effects of delayed marriage, sexual abstinence, and birth control in controlling excess population growth.

Preventive medicine   Medical care that focuses on the prevention of sickness and disease through immunology and health education. See also *curative medicine.*

Price The monetary or real value of a *resource*, commodity, or *service*. The role of prices in a *market economy* is to ration or allocate *resources* in accordance with supply and demand; relative prices should reflect the relative *scarcity* of different *resources, goods*, or *services*. See *price system*.

Price bands A fixed range in which prices are free to fluctuate, but not allowed to exceed.

Price controls The setting of maximum or minimum prices by the government.

Price elasticity of demand The responsiveness of the quantity of a commodity demanded to a change in its price, expressed as the percentage change in quantity demanded divided by the percentage change in price.

Price elasticity of supply The responsiveness of the quantity of a commodity supplied to a change in its price, expressed as the percentage change in quantity supplied divided by the percentage change in price.

Price-incentive micro model See *neoclassical price-incentive model*.

Price system The mechanism whereby scarce *resources, goods*, and *services* are allocated by the free upward or downward movements of *prices* in accordance with the dictates of supply and demand in a *market economy*. See also *perfect competition* and *pure market capitalism*.

Primary industrial sector The part of the economy that specializes in the production of agricultural products and the extraction of raw materials. Major industries in this sector include mining, agriculture, forestry, and fishing.

Primary products Products derived from all extractive occupations—farming, lumbering, fishing, mining, and quarrying; foodstuffs and raw materials.

Principle of economy The proposition in *perfect competition* that for a given level of *resources* (*inputs*), producers will tend to minimize costs for a given level of output or maximize output for a given cost. The need to economize arises because *resources* are scarce and hence not cost-free.

Private benefits Gains that accrue to a single individual, such as profits received by an individual farm. See also *social benefits*.

Private benefits of education Benefits that accrue directly to a student and his or her family.

Private consumption The market value of all *goods* and *services* purchased or received as *income in kind* by households and nonprofit *institutions*; includes imputed rent for owner-occupied dwellings.

Private costs The direct monetary outlays or costs of an individual economic unit; the private costs of a firm are the direct outlays on *fixed* and *variable inputs* of production.

Private costs of education Direct and *opportunity costs* borne by a student and his or her family.

Private foreign investment The investment of private foreign funds in the economy of a developing nation, usually in the form of import-substituting industries by *multinational corporations (MNCs)*. See also *foreign aid* and *portfolio investment*.

Private sector   The part of an economy whose activities are under the control and direction of nongovernmental economic units such as households or firms. Each economic unit owns its own *resources* and uses them mainly to maximize its own well-being.

Privatization   Selling public assets (corporations) to individuals or private business interests. See *state-owned enterprises (SOEs)*.

Producer surplus   Excess of total revenue over total costs (*profits*); also referred to as *scarcity rent*.

Product cycle   In international trade, the progressive replacement of MDCs by LDCs in the production of manufactures of increasing complexity. For example, South Korea and Taiwan first exported textiles, then machinery, and now VCRs and computers.

Product differentiation   Attempt by producers to distinguish their product from similar ones by advertising or minor design changes.

Production function   A technological or engineering relationship between the quantity of a *good* produced and the quantity of *inputs* required to produce it.

Production possibility curve   A curve on a graph indicating alternative combinations of two commodities or categories of commodities (e.g., agricultural and manufactured goods) that can be produced when all the available *factors of production* are efficiently employed. Given available *resources* and technology, the curve sets the boundary between the attainable and the unobtainable. See also *opportunity cost* and *production function*.

Production technique   Method of combining *inputs* to produce the required output. A production technique is said to be appropriate ("best") if it produces a given output with the least cost (thus being economically efficient) or with the least possible quantity of real *resources* (technically efficient). A technique may be labor-intensive or capital-intensive.

Productive resources   See *physical resource* and *human resources*.

Productivity gap   The difference between per capita product of, say, the agricultural population (i.e., *agricultural labor productivity*) in LDCs versus developed countries. It has tended to be wide because of differences in the application of technological and biological improvements.

Profit   The difference between the market value of output and the market value of *inputs* employed to produce the output. Also, the difference between total revenue and total cost.

Profit maximization   Making the profits of a firm or a farm as large as possible. Producers often want to find the level of output that results in maximum profits, at least according to a fundamental assumption of *traditional economics*.

Progressive income tax   A tax whose rate increases with increasing personal incomes, such that the proportion of personal income paid in taxes by a rich person is higher than that paid by a poorer person. A progressive tax structure therefore tends to improve *income distribution*. Compare *regressive tax*.

Project appraisal   The quantitative analysis of the relative desirability (profitability) of investing a given sum of public or private funds in alternative projects—for example, building either a steel mill or a textile factory. *Cost-benefit analysis* is the main analytic tool of project appraisal.

Property rights   Legal titles given to landowners enabling them freely to buy and sell their plots.

Public bad   An entity that imposes costs on individuals. Compare *public good*.

Public-choice theory   Theory that self-interest guides all individual behavior and that governments are inefficient and corrupt because people use government to pursue their own agendas. *Free markets* are perceived as more efficient and more just.

Public consumption   All current expenditures for purchases of *goods* and *services* by all levels of government; includes capital expenditures on national defense and security.

Public development assistance   See *foreign aid*.

Public good   An entity that provides benefits to all individuals simultaneously and whose enjoyment by one person is in no way diminished by that of another. Compare *public bad*.

Public sector   The portion of an economy whose activities (economic and noneconomic) are under the control and direction of the state. See also *private sector*.

Purchasing power equivalent   The real buying power of a given monetary income.

Purchasing power parity (PPP)   The purchasing power of a country's currency: the number of units of that currency required to purchase the same basket of goods and services that a U.S. dollar would buy in the United States.

Pure market capitalism   *Economic system* in which all *resources* are privately owned and their allocation is done exclusively by a *price system*. See also *perfect competition, market economy, invisible hand,* and *laissez-faire*.

Quintile   A 20% proportion of any numeric quantity. A population divided into quintiles would be divided into five equal numeric groups. See also *decile*.

Quota   A physical limitation on the quantity of any item that can be imported into a country, such as so many automobiles per year. Also a method for allocating limited school places by noncompetitive means—for example, by income or ethnicity.

Rate of population increase   See *population increase*.

Rationality   One of the behavioral foundations of the theory of *traditional economics*, holding that an economically rational person will always attempt to maximize satisfaction or *profits* or minimize *costs*. The notion of rationality as one of the *modernization ideals* means the replacement of age-old traditional practices by modern methods of objective thinking and logical reasoning in production, distribution, and consumption. See also *principle of economy, optimization principle,* and *profit maximization*.

Rationing A system of distribution employed to restrict the quantities of *goods* and *services* that consumers or producers can purchase or be allocated freely. It arises because of excess demand and inflexible *prices*. Rationing can be done by coupons, points, or simply administrative decisions with regard to commodities, by academic credentialing with regard to job allocation, by industrial licenses with regard to capital good imports, etc. See also *black market*.

Real income The income that a household or firm receives in terms of the real *goods* and *services* it can purchase. Also *money income* adjusted by some price deflator.

Recession A period of slack general economic activity as reflected in rising unemployment and excess productive capacity in a broad spectrum of industries.

Redistribution policies Policies geared to reducing *income inequality* and expanding economic opportunities in order to promote *development*. Examples include *progressive income tax* policies, provision of services financed out of such taxation to benefit persons in the lower-income groups, *rural development* policies giving emphasis to raising *levels of living* for the rural poor through *land reform*, and other forms of asset and wealth redistribution.

Regional trading bloc An economic coalition among countries within a geographic region, usually characterized by liberalized internal trade and uniform restrictions on external trade, designed to promote regional economic integration and growth.

Regressive tax A tax structure in which the ratio of taxes to income tends to decrease as income increases. Relatively poor people will pay a larger proportion of their income in taxes than relatively rich people. A regressive tax therefore tends to worsen *income distribution*. See also *progressive tax*.

Renewable resources Natural *resources* that can be replaced so that the total supply is not fixed for all time. Examples include timber and other forest products. See also *nonrenewable resources*.

Rent In macroeconomics, the share of *national income* going to the owners of the productive *resource*, land (i.e., *landlords*). In everyday usage, the *price* paid for the use of property (e.g., buildings, housing). In microeconomics, economic rent is the payment to a *factor of production* over and above its highest *opportunity cost*.

Rent seeking Efforts by individuals and businesses in an LDC society to capture the economic *rent* arising from price distortions and physical controls caused by excessive government intervention, such as licenses, *quotas*, interest rate ceilings, and *exchange control*.

Replacement fertility The level of *fertility* at which childbearing women have just enough daughters to replace themselves in the population. This keeps the existing population size constant through an infinite number of succeeding generations. See also *fertility rate* and *crude birthrate*.

Reproductive choice Argument that women should be able to determine on an equal status with their husbands and for themselves how many children they want and what methods to use to achieve their desired family size. See *empowerment of women.*

Research and development (R&D)   Scientific investigation with a view toward improving the existing quality of human life, products, *profits, factors of production,* or knowledge. There are two categories of R&D: basic R&D (without a specific commercial objective) and applied R&D (with a commercial objective).

Reserves   The sum of a country's holdings of gold, *special drawing rights (SDRs),* the reserve position of *International Monetary Fund* members in the IMF, and holdings of *foreign exchange* under the control of monetary authorities. Also known as *gross international reserves.*

Resource balance   The difference between exports and imports of *goods* and nonfactor *services.*

Resource endowment   A nation's supply of *factors of production.* Normally such endowments are supplied by nature (e.g., mineral deposits, raw materials, timber forests, labor). See also *factor endowment trade theory.*

Resources   See *physical resources* and *human resources.* See also *fixed inputs* and *variable inputs.*

Restructuring   Alteration of the terms and conditions of LDC debt repayment, usually by lowering interest rates or extending the repayment period.

Returns to scale   How much output expands when all *inputs* are proportionately increased. See *economies of scale* and *increasing returns.*

Rigid institutions   *Institutions* designed in such a way that they cannot be adjusted or adjust themselves to accommodate *development* requirements. An example would be a social system—such as a religious unit—that has conservative *values* that render it resistant to *modernization ideals.*

Risk   A situation in which the probability of obtaining some outcome of an event is not precisely known; that is, known probabilities cannot be precisely assigned to these outcomes, but their general level can be inferred. In everyday usage, a risky situation is one in which one of the outcomes involves some loss to the decision maker (e.g., changes of demand, weather, or tastes). See also *uncertainty.*

Rotating savings and credit associations   A formal agreement among 40 to 50 individuals to pool their savings and allocate interest-free loans on a rotating basis to each member. See also *group lending schemes.*

Rural development   See *integrated rural development.*

Rural support systems   Systems designed to stimulate the productivity of both small- and large-scale agricultural farms. These include improving the efficiency of the rural *institutions* directly connected with production, such as banks, *moneylenders,* public credit agencies, and seed and fertilizer disbributors, and providing services such as technical and educational extension services, storage and marketing facilities, rural transport and feeder roads, and water.

Rural-urban migration   The movement of people from rural villages, towns, and farms to urban centers (cities) in search of jobs. See *Todaro migration model.*

Rural-urban migration models   See *Todaro migration model.*

Salinization The contamination of fresh water with salts. The process of salinization renders water supplies unfit for human consumption or use in irrigation.

Savings The portion of *disposable income* not spent on consumption by households plus *profits* retained by firms. Savings are normally assumed to be positively related to the level of income (personal or national).

Savings gap Exists where capital inflows plus domestic saving exceeds domestic investment and the economy is at full capacity. See also *foreign exchange gap*.

Savings ratio Savings expressed as a proportion of *disposable income* over some period of time. It shows the fraction of *national income* saved over any period. *Savings ratio* is sometimes used synonymously with average propensity to save. See also *Harrod-Domar growth model*.

Scale-neutral Unaffected by size; applied to *technological progress* that can lead to the achievement of higher output levels irrespective of the size (scale) of a firm or farm, making it equally applicable to small- and large-scale production processes. An often-cited example is the *hybrid seeds* of the *Green Revolution*, which can theoretically increase yields on both small and large farms (if *complementary resources* such as fertilizer, irrigation, and pesticides are available).

Scarcity In economics, a situation that arises when there is less of something (e.g., an *economic good, service,* or *resource*) than people would like to have if it were free. The quantity of goods and services are scarce relative to people's desire for them because the economy's resources used in their production are themselves scarce. Scarcity therefore gives rise to *price* and the need for efficient allocation of resources among alternative competing uses through, for example, the *free market* in capitalist economies or through a centralized *command system* in planned economies.

Scarcity rent The premium or additional *rent* charged for the use of a *resource* or *good* that is in fixed or limited supply. See *rent seeking*.

Scatter diagram A two-dimensional graph on which numeric values of statistically observed variables are plotted in pairs, one measured on the horizontal axis and the other on the vertical axis.

Secondary industrial sector The manufacturing portion of the economy, which uses raw materials and *intermediate products* to produce *final goods* or other intermediate products. Industries such as motor assembly, textiles, and building and construction are part of this sector.

Self-esteem The feeling of worthiness that a society enjoys when its *social, political,* and *economic systems* and *institutions* promote human respect, dignity, integrity, self-determination, etc. See *development*.

Self-reliance Reliance on one's own capabilities, judgment, resources, and skills in a bid to enhance political, economic, social, cultural, attitudinal, and moral independence. Countries may also desire self-reliance in particular aspects such as food production, labor, and skills. Increasingly, the concept of *collective self-reliance* is being used in *Third World* forums.

Self-sustaining growth   Economic growth that continues over the long run based on saving, investment, and complementary private and public activities.

Services   Economic activities other than industry and primary-goods production. Examples include banking, shipping, and tourism and legal, insurance, and financial activities. See also *tertiary industrial sector*.

Shadow price   A price that reflects the true *opportunity cost* of a *resource*.

Sharecropper   In the *agrarian systems* of LDCs, the tenant peasant farmer whose crop has to be shared with the *landlord*, who usually appropriates a large portion of total crop production.

Shifting cultivation   A peasant agricultural practice in Africa in which land is tilled by a family or community for cropping until such time as it has been exhausted of fertility. Thereafter, the family or community moves to a new parcel of land, leaving the former one to regain fertility until eventually it can be cultivated again.

Size distribution of income   The distribution of income according to size class of persons—for example, the share of total income accruing to, say, the poorest 40% of a population or the richest 10%, without regard to the sources of that income (whether it comes from wages, *interest, rent*, or *profits*). See also *functional distribution of income, Lorenz curve*, and *Gini coefficient*.

Skewed distribution of income   A distribution of income diverging from perfect equality. Skewness is a lack of symmetry in a frequency distribution. If income is perfectly distributed, such a distribution is said to be symmetrical. Highly skewed distributions of income occur in situations where the rich, say, the top 20% of the total population, receive more than half of the total *national income*. See also *Lorenz curve* and *Gini coefficient*.

Small farmer   A farmer owning a small family-based plot of land on which he grows subsistence crops and perhaps one or two cash crops, relying almost exclusively on family labor.

Small-scale industry   An industry whose firms or farms operate with small-sized plants, low employment, and hence small output capacity. *Economies of scale* do not normally exist for such firms or farms, but they often tend to utilize their limited *physical, human*, and financial *capital* more efficiently than many large firms or farms.

Social benefits   Gains or benefits that accrue or are available to the society as a whole rather than solely to a private individual, such as the protection and security provided by the police or the armed forces, the external economies afforded by an effective health delivery system, and the widespread benefits of a literate population. See *private benefits*.

Social benefits of education   Benefits of the schooling of individuals that accrue to the entire society, such as better government financing, improved teacher training and a more literate workforce and citizenry.

Social cost   The cost of an economic decision, whether private or public, to society as a whole. Where there exist external diseconomies of production (e.g., pollution) or consumption (alcoholism), social costs will normally exceed *private costs*, and decisions based solely on private calculations will lead to misallocation of *resources*.

Social costs of education   Costs borne by society from private education decisions, such as high educated unemployment.

Social indicators   Noneconomic measures of *development*, such as *life expectancy at birth, infant mortality rate, literacy rate*, and physicians per 100,000 population.

Socialism   See *command socialism* and *market socialism*.

Social profit   Difference between *social benefits* and *social costs*, both direct and indirect.

Social rate of discount   The rate at which a society discounts potential future *social benefits* to find out whether such benefits are worth their present *social cost*. The rate used in this discounting procedure is usually the social *opportunity cost* of the funds committed.

Social safety net   A set of government programs such as food stamps, welfare payments, free health clinics, and unemployment insurance designed to provide the absolute poor with a minimal *level of living* below which they should not fall.

Social science   The branch of study that concerns itself with human society, behavior, activities, and growth (e.g., anthropology, sociology, political science, and economics).

Social system   The organizational and institutional structure of a society, including its *value premises*, attitudes, power structure, and traditions. Major social systems include political processes, religions, and ethnic divisions.

Soil erosion   Loss of valuable topsoils resulting from deforestation and consequent flooding of productive farm lands.

Solow neoclassical growth model   Growth model in which there are *diminishing returns* to each *factor of production* but constant *returns to scale*. Exogenous technological change generates most long-term *economic growth*.

Solow residual   The proportion of long-term *economic growth* not explained by growth in labor or *capital* and therefore assigned primarily to exogenous technological change.

Special drawing rights (SDRs)   A form of international financial asset, often referred to as "paper gold," created by the *International Monetary Fund* in 1970 and designed to supplement gold and dollars in settling international *balance of payments* accounts.

Specialization   A situation in which *resources* are concentrated in the production of relatively few commodities. See also *comparative advantage* and *division of labor*.

Specialized farming   The final and most advanced stage of the evolution of agricultural production in which farm output is produced wholly for the market.

It is most prevalent in advanced industrial countries. High farm yields are ensured by a high degree of *capital formation, technological progress,* and scientific *research and development.* See also *subsistence farming* and *commercial farming.*

Stabilization policies   A coordinated set of mostly restrictive fiscal and monetary policies aimed at reducing *inflation,* cutting budget deficits, and improving the *balance of payments.* See *conditionality* and *Internal Monetary Fund (IMF).*

Stages-of-growth model of development   A theory of *development* associated with the American economic historian Walt W. Rostow. According to Rostow, in achieving *development,* a country inevitably passes through five stages: (1) the traditional and stagnant low per capita stage, (2) the transitional stage (in which the preconditions for growth are laid down), (3) the takeoff stage (beginning of the *economic growth* process), (4) the drive-to-maturity stage, and (5) the industrialized, mass production and consumption stage (*development* stage).

Staple food   A leading or main food consumed by a large portion of a country's population (e.g., maize meal in Kenya, Zambia, and Tanzania; rice in Southeast Asian countries; yams in West Africa; manioc in Brazil).

State-owned enterprises (SOEs)   Public corporations and parastatal agencies (e.g., agricultural marketing boards) owned and operated by the government.

Statism   The notion that the government has a major role to play in the direction of the economy both directly through the operation of *state-owned enterprises* and indirectly through management of the overall economy.

Structural adjustment loans   *Loans* by the *World Bank* designed to foster structural adjustment in the LDCs by supporting measures to remove excessive governmental controls, getting factor and product *prices* to reflect *scarcity* values, and promoting market competition. See *World Bank* and *International Development Agency (IDA).*

Structural-change theory   The hypothesis that *underdevelopment* in *Third World* countries is due to underutilization of *resources* arising from structural or institutional factors that have their origins in both domestic and international dualistic situations. *Development* therefore requires more than just accelerated *capital formation* as espoused in the *stages-of-growth* and *false-paradigm models of development.*

Structural inflation   *Inflation* that arises as a result of supply inelasticities and structural rigidities (e.g., inefficient marketing and distribution systems) in the industrial sectors of the economy. It is a form of *demand-pull inflation* that can exist with considerable excess capacity and unemployment.

Structural transformation   The process of transforming the basic industrial structure of an economy so that the contribution to *national income* by the manufacturing sector increasingly becomes higher than that by the agricultural sector. More generally, an alteration in the industrial composition of any economy. See *primary, secondary,* and *tertiary industrial sectors.*

Subsidy   A payment by the government to producers or distributors in an industry to prevent the decline of that industry (e.g., as a result of continuous unprofitable operations) or an increase in the *prices* of its products or simply to encourage it to hire more labor (as in the case of a *wage subsidy*). Examples are export subsidies to encourage the sale of exports; subsidies on some food-stuffs to keep down the cost of living, especially in urban areas; and farm sub-sidies to encourage expansion of farm production and achieve *self-reliance* in food production.

Subsistence economy An economy in which production is mainly for personal consumption and the standard of living yields no more than the basic necessi-ties of life—food, shelter, and clothing. See also *subsistence farming*.

Subsistence farming Farming in which crop production, stock rearing, and other activities are conducted mainly for personal consumption, characterized by low productivity, *risk*, and *uncertainty*. See also *subsistence economy*.

Sufficient condition A condition that when present causes an event to occur—for example, being a low-income university student may be a sufficient condi-tion to get a *loan* under a university education loan scheme. See also *necessary condition*.

Supply curve A positively sloped curve relating the quantity of a commodity sup-plied to its *price*.

Surplus An excess of revenues over expenditures. See *trade surplus*.

Surplus labor The excess supply of labor over and above the quantity demanded at the going free-market wage rate. In W. Arthur Lewis's two-sector model of economic development, surplus labor refers to the portion of the rural labor force whose *marginal productivity* is zero or negative. See also *underemployment*.

Sustainable development Pattern of *development* that permits future generations to live at least as well as the current generation.

Sustainable national income An *environmental accounting* measure of the total annual income that can be consumed without diminishing the overall *capital* assets of a nation (including *environmental capital*).

Sustenance The basic *goods* and *services*, such as food, clothing, and shelter, that are necessary to sustain an average human being at the bare minimum *level of living*.

Synthetic substitutes Commodities that are artificially produced but of like na-ture with and substitutes for the natural commodities (e.g., those involving rub-ber, cotton, wool, camphor, pyrethrum). Producers of raw materials, mainly LDCs, are becoming more and more vulnerable to competition from synthet-ics from industrialized countries as a result of the latter's more advanced state of scientific and technical progress.

Tariff A fixed percentage tax on the value of an imported commodity levied at the point of entry into the importing country.

Technical assistance *Foreign aid* (either bilateral or multilateral) that takes the form of the transfer of expert personnel, technicians, scientists, educators, eco-nomic advisers, and consultants rather than a simple transfer of funds.

Technical efficiency Producing the maximum output possible, given quantities of *inputs* and existing technology, without regard to effective market demand.

Technological progress Increased application of new scientific knowledge in form of *inventions* and *innovations* with regard to both *physical* and *human capital*. Such progress has been a major factor in stimulating the long-term *economic growth* of contemporary developed countries. See also *scale-neutral, labor-augmenting, laborsaving,* and *capital-augmenting technological progress.*

Tenant farmer One who farms on land held by a *landlord* and therefore lacks secure ownership rights and has to pay for the use of that land, for example, by surrendering part of his output to the owner. Examples are found in the Latin American and Asian *agrarian systems.* See also *sharecropper.*

Tendency A behavior or phenomenon that may occur under similar conditions but is not true in all social contexts. Compare *law.*

Terms of trade The ratio of a country's average export *price* to its average import *price*; also known as the *commodity terms of trade.* A country's terms of trade are said to improve when this ratio increases and to worsen when it decreases, that is, when import *prices* rise at a relatively faster rate than export *prices* (the experience of most LDCs in recent decades). See *income terms of trade.*

Tertiary industrial sector The services and commerce portion of an economy. Examples of *services* include repair and maintenance of *capital goods*, haircuts, public administration, medical care, transport and communications, finance, and teaching. See also *primary* and *secondary industrial sectors and services.*

Third World The present 145 developing countries of Asia, Africa, the Middle East, and Latin America, mainly characterized by low *levels of living*, high rates of *population growth*, low *income per capita*, and general economic and technological *dependence* on *First World* economies.

Tied aid *Foreign aid* in the form of bilateral *loans* or *grants* that require the recipient country to use the funds to purchase *goods* or *services* from the donor country.

Todaro migration model A theory that explains *rural-urban migration* as an economically rational process despite high urban unemployment. Migrants calculate urban *expected income* and move if this exceeds average rural income. See *induced migration.*

Toronto Terms The restructuring of LDC bilateral debt laid out by the terms for the *Paris Club* in Toronto in 1988.

Total factor productivity (TFP) Total monetary value of all units of output per unit of each and every *factor of production* in an economy. It is a measure of the average productivity of all factors employed in an economy.

Total fertility rate (TFR) See *fertility rate.*

Total net benefit Sum of net benefits to all consumers and/or producers resulting from environmental policy interventions. In general, total benefits minus total costs.

Trade creation   A situation in the theory of *customs unions* that occurs when, following the formation of the union, there is a shift in the geographic location of production from higher-cost to lower-cost member states. See also *trade diversion*.

Trade deficit   An excess of import expenditures over export receipts measured on the *current account*; also known as merchandise trade deficit. See also *balance of payments* and *trade surplus*.

Trade diversion   Shift, upon formation of a *customs union*, of the locus of production of formerly imported goods from a lower-cost nonmember state to a higher-cost member nation. See also *trade creation*.

Trade liberalization   Removal of obstacles to free trade, such as *quotas, nominal* and *effective rates of protection*, and *exchange controls*.

Trade-off   The necessity of sacrificing (trading off) something in order to get more of something else—for example, sacrificing consumption now for consumption later by devoting some present *resources* to *investment*. See also *opportunity cost*.

Trade optimists   Theorists who believe in the benefits of *free trade, open economies*, and *outward-looking development policies*.

Trade pessimists   Theorists who argue that without tariff protection or quantitative restrictions on trade, LDCs inevitably gain little or nothing from an export-oriented, open-economy posture. See also *import substitution, Prebisch-Singer thesis*, and *infant industry*.

Trade surplus   An excess of export receipts over import payments. See also *trade deficit*.

Traditional economics   The economics of capitalist *market economies* characterized by *consumer sovereignty, profit maximization, private enterprise*, and *perfect competition*. The major focus is on the efficient allocation of scarce *resources* (see *economic efficiency*) through the *price system* and the forces of supply and demand. See also *microeconomics, macroeconomics, laissez-faire, invisible hand*, and *market economy*.

Traditional (old) neoclassical growth theory   Growth models associated with Robert Solow and others in which long-run equilibrium growth is zero and *income per capita* tends to converge among different countries. Based on the theory of *perfect competition* with constant *returns to scale*. Compare *new growth theory*.

Transaction costs   Costs of doing business related to gathering information, establishing reliable suppliers, formulating contracts, obtaining credit, etc.

Transfer payment   Any payment from one economic entity to another that takes the form of a gift, that is, any payment not for a service rendered that need not be repaid. Examples include unemployment insurance, food stamps, welfare payments, *subsidies*, and *grants*.

Transfer pricing   An accounting procedure usually designed to lower total taxes paid by *multinational corporations* in which intracorporate sales and purchases of *goods* and *services* are artificially invoiced so that profits accrue to the branch offices located in low-tax countries (tax havens) while offices in high-tax countries show little or no taxable profits.

Trickle-down theory of development   The notion that *development* is purely an economic phenomenon in which rapid gains from the overall growth of *gross national product* and *income per capita* would automatically bring benefits (trickle down) to the masses in the form of jobs and other economic opportunities. The main preoccupation is therefore to get the growth job done while problems of *poverty*, unemployment, and *income distribution* are perceived to be of secondary importance.

Two-gap model   Theoretical *foreign aid* model comparing *savings* and *foreign exchange* gaps to determine which is the binding constraint on *economic growth*.

Uncertainty   A situation in which the probability of obtaining a given outcome of an event is not known. There are thus a number of possible outcomes to which no objective probability can be attached. See also *risk*.

Underdevelopment   An economic situation in which there are persistent low *levels of living* in conjunction with *absolute poverty*, low *income per capita*, low rates of *economic growth*, low consumption levels, poor health services, high *death rates*, high *birthrates*, *dependence* on foreign economies, and limited *freedom* to choose among activities that satisfy human wants. See also *development*.

Underemployment   A situation in which persons are working less than they would like to work, either daily, weekly, monthly, or seasonally. See also *disguised underemployment, open unemployment*, and *surplus labor*.

Underutilization of labor   The operation of the labor force at levels below capacity or potential output. See also *open unemployment, underemployment*, and *disguised underemployment*.

Unit cost   The average cost per unit of output of any *economic good* or *service*.

United Nations (U.N.)   A global organization set up at the end of World War II with the basic aim of cultivating international cooperation and hence ensuring that any conflicts or misunderstanding between or among countries would be resolved by peaceful means. At present, the United Nations has a membership of more than 170 countries drawn from both the developed and less developed nations.

United Nations Conference on Environment and Development (UNCED)   A conference held in Rio de Janeiro in June 1992, whose purpose was to enhance international cooperation in promoting sustainable environmental policy. Also known as the *Earth Summit*.

United Nations Conference on Trade and Development (UNCTAD)   A body of the *United Nations* whose primary objective is to promote *international trade* and commerce with a principal focus on trade and *balance of payments* problems of developing nations. Its first secretary general was Raul Prebisch.

United Nations Development Program (UNDP)   A body of the *United Nations* whose major function is to promote *development* in *Third World* countries. Major development-oriented projects financed and carried out by the UNDP include the initiation of nutrition, health, and education programs and the building up of agricultural, industrial, and transport *infrastructure*.

United Nations Educational, Scientific and Cultural Organization (UNESCO) A major agency of the *United Nations* charged with promoting international understanding by spreading ideas of knowledge through the educational process, encouraging multiracial coexistence through reconciliation of cultural values of different societies, and sponsoring educational, cultural, and scientific exchange programs that make it possible for educators, artists, writers, and scientists from a wide variety of countries and cultures to meet and exchange ideas and knowledge.

United States Agency for International Development (USAID) A *bilateral assistance* agency of the U.S. government whose primary objective is to assist *Third World* countries in their *development* efforts as part of U.S. foreign policy. The economic assistance given by USAID normally takes the form of educational *grants*, special-interest *loans*, and *technical assistance*. However, much of USAID's activity consists of noneconomic (mostly military) assistance to friendly LDC governments.

Unlimited supplies of labor Infinite elasticity of labor at a given wage as postulated in the Lewis two-sector model.

Unorganized money market The informal and often usurious credit system that exists in most developing countries (especially in rural areas) where low-income farms and firms with little collateral are forced to borrow from *moneylenders* and loan sharks at exorbitant rates of *interest*. Compare *organized money market*.

Urban bias The notion that most LDC governments favor the urban sector in their *development* policies, thereby creating a widening gap between the urban and rural economies. See *rural-urban migration*.

Urbanization The economic and demographic growth process of the urban centers.

Uruguay Round Agreement The latest of the *GATT* negotiations, started in Uruguay in 1986 and designed to promote international *free trade*. Signed in April 1994 and effective in 1995. See *World Trade Organization*.

Value added Amount of product's final value added at each stage of production.

Value premises See *values*.

Values Principles, standards, or qualities considered worthwhile or desirable. A value judgment reflects personal or class beliefs. See also *normative economics*.

Variable inputs *Inputs* or *resources* whose required use in a *production function* will vary with changes in the level of output. For example, in the production of shoes, labor is usually a variable *input* because as more shoes are produced, more labor must be used. See also *fixed inputs*.

Vent-for-surplus theory of international trade A theory that states that the opening up of world markets to developing countries through international trade provides them with the opportunity to take advantage of formerly underutilized land and labor *resources* to produce larger *primary-product* outputs, the surplus of which can be exported to foreign markets. Such economies will usually be operating at a point somewhere inside their production possibility frontiers so that trade permits an outward shift of this production point.

Vested-interest groups Groups of persons that have acquired rights or powers in any sphere of activities within a nation or in international affairs that they struggle to guard and maintain. Examples of powerful vested-interest groups in developing countries include *landlords*, political elites, the military, and wealthy private local and foreign investors.

Vicious cycle A self-reinforcing situation in which factors tend to perpetuate a certain undesirable phenomenon—for example, low incomes in poor countries lead to low consumption, which then leads to poor health and low *labor productivity* and eventually to the persistence of *poverty*.

Voluntary unemployment Unemployment by worker choice.

Wage-price spiral *Vicious cycle* in which higher consumer prices (e.g. as a result of *devaluation*) cause workers to demand higher wages which in turn cause producers to raise prices and worsen inflationary forces.

Wage subsidy A government financial incentive to private employers to hire more workers, as through tax deductions for new job creation.

World Bank An international financial institution owned by its 171 member countries and based in Washington, D.C. Its main objective is to provide *development* funds to the *Third World* nations in the form of *interest*-bearing *loans* and *technical assistance*. The World Bank operates with borrowed funds. See *International Development Association (IDA)*.

World Trade Organization (WTO) Geneva-based watch dog and enforcer of 1995 *Uruguay Round Agreement*. Replaces *GATT*.

Youth dependency ratio The proportion of young people under age 15 to the working population aged 16–64 in a country. See also *dependency burden*.

Name Index

Abbott, George C., 564
Adelman, Irma, 63, 64, 68, 149, 150, 184, 188
Ahlburg, Dennis A., 232, 233
Ahluwalia, Montek S., 170, 185
Ahmed, Habid, xiv
Ahmed, Manzoor, 400, 402
Akhavi-Pour, Hassein, xiv
Alam, M. S., 604
Alesina, Alberto, 127, 186, 261, 410, 605
Alfonsin, Raul, 458
Allen, R. L., 497
Amin, Samir, 103, 232
Amsden, Alice, 605
Anand, S., 185
Annez, Patricia, 637, 643
Antle, J. M., 376
Arndt, H. W., 101, 455, 603
Arrow, Kenneth, J., 455
Atkinson, Anthony B., 186, 187
Ayub, Mahmood A., 644

Bairoch, Paul, 262, 276
Balassa, Bela, 86, 262, 497
Balogh, Thomas, 456
Baran, Paul, 100
Barbier, Edward, 376
Bardhan, Pranab K., 103, 187, 336
Barnet, Richard J., 564
Barnum, Henry N., 279, 293, 410
Barraclough, Solan, 338
Barrett, Scott, 377, 564
Barro, Robert, 102
Bastor, Nancy, 25, 68
Bauer, Peter, 86, 101, 563, 564
Bayoumi, Tamin, 644, 645
Becker, Charles M., 292, 294
Beenstock, Michael, 604
Behrman, Jere, 103, 262, 409
Bencivenga, Valerie, xiv, 642, 644
Benoit, Emile, 635, 637, 643
Berelson, Bernard, 231
Berg, Alan, 60
Berg, Robert, 61, 667
Berghall, Pii Elina, 265, 294
Bernstam, Mikail S., 377
Berry, R. Albert, 262, 336
Besley, Timothy, 336, 642
Bhagwati, Jagdish, 86, 186, 187, 410, 456, 562
Biersteker, Thomas, 542, 561, 564
Bigsten, Arne, 185, 186, 187
Bilsborrow, Richard, 377
Binswanger, Hans, 337, 338
Bird, Richard, 644
Birdsall, Nancy, 186, 207, 231, 233, 409
Blackwood, D. L., 184
Blanchard, Francis, 295
Blanchard, Oliver J., 102
Blaug, Marc, 410, 411
Blitzer, Charles R., 604, 605
Bloom, David, 260
Bogetic, Zejlko, 675
Bohnung, W. R., 127
Bongaarts, John, 199, 231, 233, 376
Boserup, Ester, 314, 337

Boutros-Ghali, Boutros, 340
Boyce, James, xiv
Bradford, Colin I., 481, 494
Brinkman, Richard, 24
Broad, Robin, 570
Brown, Lester R., 232, 666
Bruce, Judith, 185, 188
Bruno, Michael, 233
Brunton, Bruce, 563
Bruton, Henry, 186, 261, 262, 497
Buchanan, James M., 101, 674, 675
Burgess, Robin, 643
Buvinic, Mayra, 184, 188
Byerlee, Derek, 281, 294

Cain, Mead, 311, 337
Call, David L., 60
Cardoso, Eliana, 153, 187, 261
Cardoso, F. H., 103
Carter, Nicholas G., 185, 563
Cassen, Mark, 561, 564
Cassen, Robert H., 219, 232, 563
Castro, Fidel, 97
Cavanaugh, John, 519, 570
Chang, Ha-Joon, 605
Chatterjee, Meera, 188
Chen, Lincoln, 234
Chen, Shoahua, 184
Chenery, Hollis, 75, 81, 100, 170, 185, 562, 563
Chichilnisky, Graciella, 449, 455, 456
Claessens, Stijn, 544, 562
Clark, Colin, 232
Clark, Paul B., 604, 605
Clarke, George R. G., 186
Clausen, A. W., 189
Cline, William R., 187, 336, 495, 518, 524, 525
Coase, Ronald, 101
Cobbe, James, xiv
Cochrane, Susan, 234
Cohen, Benjamin, 100, 525
Colclough, Christopher, 409
Cole, John P., 25, 60
Cole, William, xiv
Collier, Paul, 667
Collyns, Charles, 612, 614, 642
Compton, James, xiv
Connelly, Matthew, 127, 646, 667
Conroy, Michael, xiv
Conte, Michael, 675
Coombs, Philip H., 400, 402
Cooper, Charles, 497
Corden, W. Max, 293, 523, 641
Cornia, Giovanni, A., 336, 531
Crane, Barbara, 232
Cropper, Maureen L., 376
Curtis, Fred, xiv

Darity, William, xiv
Dasgupta, Ajit K., 604
Dasgupta, Partha, 186, 187, 232, 233
Datt, Gaurav, 184
Daugherty, Helen, 233
Davies, John, xiii
Davis, Kingsley, 377

Davison, Jean, 416
Deaton, Angus, 188
de Janvry, Alain, 336, 337, 338
De Kant, Emmanuel, 188
Deere, C. D., 337
Dellalfar, William, 411
Denison, Edward, 410
Desai, Padma, 26
Dias-Alexandro, Carlos, 642
Dietz, James L., 524
Domar, Evesey, 100, 696
Dooley, Michael, 525, 562
Dore, Ronald, 411
Dorfman, Robert, 103, 594, 604
Dornbush, Rudiger, 494, 495, 523, 642
Dorner, Peter, 338
Dos Santos, Theotonio, 83, 100
Drazen, A., 338
Drakakis-Smith, David, 61
Draper, William H., 458
Dreze, Jean, 232
Dube, Smile, xiv
Duloy, John, 170
Dutt, Amitova K., 101, 455
Dwyer, Daisy, 185, 188

Easterlin, Richard A., 233
Eatwell, John, 337
Eberstadt, Nicholas, 232
Eckaus, Richard S., 261, 564
Eckholm, Erik P., 339
Eckstein, Z., 338
Edwards, Edgar O., 186, 244, 260, 263, 409
Edwards, Sabastian, 494
Ehrlich, Anne H., 232
Ehrlich, Paul R., 232
Eicher, Carl, 339
Elson, Diane, 185
Emmerij, Louis, 261, 262
Enos, John L., 563
Esfahani, Hadi S., xiv
Esman, Milton J., 338

Faber, Michael, 606
Faine, Ricardo, 637, 643
Falcon, Walter, 339
Fei, John C. H., 76, 100
Feldman, Robert, 562
Fernandez-Arias, Eduardo, 525
Fields, Gary, 142–143, 184, 185, 187, 293, 495
Findlay, Ronald, 293, 644
Findlay, Sally, 294
Finkle, Jason, 232
Fischer, Stanley, 102
Fishlow, Albert, 186, 187, 525
Foland, Francis M., 304, 336
Folbre, Nancy, 233
Fong, Monica, 339
Fosu, Joseph, xiv
Foxley, Alejandro, 525, 597, 605, 672, 675
Freebairn, Donald K., 338
Freeman, Richard, 260, 666
Freire, Paulo, 25

728

Subject Index